D0855332

TEACHER'S WRAPAROUND EDITION

MULTIMEDIA EDITION

GLENCOE

WORLD GEOGRAPHY

Richard G. Boehm, Ph.D.

GLENCOE

McGraw-Hill

New York, New York Columbus, Ohio Mission Hills, California Peoria, Illinois

About the Authors

National Geographic Society

The National Geographic Society, founded in 1888 for the increase and diffusion of geographic knowledge, is the world's largest nonprofit scientific and educational organization. Since its earliest days, the Society has used sophisticated communication technologies, from color photography to holography, to convey geographic knowledge to a worldwide membership. The Educational Media Division supports the Society's mission by developing innovative educational programs—ranging from traditional print materials to multimedia programs including CD-ROMs, videodiscs, and software.

Richard G. Boehm

Richard G. Boehm, Ph.D., was one of seven authors of *Geography for Life,* national standards in geography, prepared under Goals 2000: Educate America Act. He was also one of the authors of the *Guidelines for Geographic Education,* in which the five themes of geography were first articulated. In 1990 Dr. Boehm was designated "Distinguished Geography Educator" by the National Geographic Society. In 1991 he received the George J. Miller award from the National Council for Geographic Education (NCGE) for distinguished service to geographic education. He was President of the NCGE and has twice won the *Journal of Geography* award for best article. He has received the NCGE's "Distinguished Teaching Achievement" award and is presently Professor of Geography at Southwest Texas State University in San Marcos, Texas.

Contributing Writers

Sarah W. Bednarz, Ph.D.
Visiting Assistant Professor of Geography
Department of Geography
Texas A&M University
College Station, Texas

Robert S. Bednarz, Ph.D.
Associate Professor of Geography
Department of Geography
Texas A&M University
College Station, Texas

James L. Swanson
Teacher and Chairperson,
History Department
Marin Country Day School
Corte Madera, California

Glencoe/McGraw-Hill
A Division of The ***McGraw-Hill*** *Companies*

Send all inquiries to:
Glencoe/McGraw-Hill, 936 Eastwind Drive, Westerville, Ohio 43081

ISBN 0-02-821713-6 (Student Edition)
ISBN 0-02-821714-4 (Teacher's Wraparound Edition)

Printed in the United States of America

2 3 4 5 6 7 8 9 10 071/043 01 00 99 98 97

Consultants

General Content Consultant
Theodore M. Black, Sr.
Chancellor Emeritus
New York State Board of Regents

Geography Consultant
Sarah W. Bednarz, Ph.D.
Visiting Assistant Professor of Geography
Department of Geography
Texas A&M University
College Station, Texas

Multicultural Consultant
Ricardo L. García, Ed.D.
Professor
University of Wisconsin
Stevens Point, Wisconsin

Religion Consultants
John L. Esposito, Ph.D.
Professor of Religion and International Affairs Director
Georgetown University
Washington, D.C.

Sayyid M. Syeed, Ph.D.
Secretary General
Islamic Society of North America
Plainfield, Indiana

Introduction to Geography
Burrell E. Montz, Ph.D.
Associate Professor of Geography and Environmental Studies
Binghamton University
Binghamton, New York

United States and Canada
David A. Lanegran, Ph.D.
Professor of Geography
Macalester College
St. Paul, Minnesota

Latin America
Gerald T. Hanson, Ph.D.
Professor of Geography
University of Arkansas
Little Rock, Arkansas

Europe
Gail L. Hobbs, Ph.D.
Associate Professor of Geography
Pierce College
Woodland Hills, California

Russia and the Eurasian Republics
Susan W. Hardwick, Ph.D.
Professor of Geography
California State University
Chico, California

Pavel Pankin
Principal
School No. 1741
Western District
Moscow, Russia

North Africa and Southwest Asia
Theodore H. Schmudde, Ph.D.
Professor of Geography
University of Tennessee
Knoxville, Tennessee

Jerrold D. Green, Ph.D.
Director
Middle East Studies Center
University of Arizona
Tucson, Arizona

Africa South of the Sahara
William R. Brown, Ph.D.
Assistant Professor Geography and Departmental Head
Prairie View A&M University
Prairie View, Texas

South Asia
Gary J. Hausladen, Ph.D.
Associate Professor of Geography
University of Nevada
Reno, Nevada

East Asia
Kenji Kenneth Oshiro, Ph.D.
Professor of Geography and Departmental Chair
Wright State University
Dayton, Ohio

Southeast Asia
Julie A. Tuason, Ph.D.
Rutgers University
New Brunswick, New Jersey

Australia, Oceania, and Antarctica
Laurie Molina, Ph.D.
Program Director
Geography Education and Technology Program
Florida State University
Tallahassee, Florida

Teacher Reviewers

Rosemary M. Brewer
Secondary Social Studies Teacher
Hall High School
Little Rock, Arkansas

Joseph Bryan
World Geography Teacher
John Jay High School
Northside Independent School District
San Antonio, Texas

Russell Parker Bush
Social Studies Department Chairperson
Buckhannon-Upshur Middle School
Buckhannon, West Virginia

Rebecca A. Corley
Social Studies Teacher
Evans Junior High School
Lubbock, Texas

Mary Real D'Angelo
Social Studies Teacher and Department Chair
Boys Town High School
Boys Town, Nebraska

Kevin Davis
Social Studies Teacher
Jacksonville High School
Jacksonville, Arkansas

Robert E. Edison
History Instructor
Pearl C. Anderson Middle School
Dallas, Texas

Mounir A. Farah, Ph.D.
Associate Director
Middle East Studies Program
University of Arkansas
Fayetteville, Arkansas

Mary Jane Fraser, Ph.D.
Teacher and Social Studies Curriculum Project Leader
Seattle School District
Seattle, Washington

Sherry Kay Henderson
World Geography Teacher
Northbrook High School Houston, Texas

Fred H. Huddleston
Department Chairperson Social Studies
McCollum High School
Harlandale Independent School District
San Antonio, Texas

Marianne Kenney
Social Studies Specialist
Colorado Department of Education
Denver, Colorado

Wardell Richards
Social Studies Teacher and Departmental Chair
W.W. Sammuell High School
Dallas, Texas

Judith Rosenstock
Middle School Principal
Trinity Preparatory School
Winter Park, Florida

Ruth W. Stas
K–12 Social Studies Coordinator
Manheim Township School District
Lancaster, Pennsylvania

Dale Zellmer
K–12 Social Studies Consultant
Department of Curriculum
Anoka-Hennepin School District
Coon Rapids, Minnesota

CONTENTS
Teacher's Wraparound Edition

Map and Geography Skills

Review & Reteach

Evaluate

Enrich

Humanities

Spanish Resources

Classroom Management

Multimedia

NATIONAL GEOGRAPHIC SOCIETY

Videodiscs

Glencoe Videodiscs

CONTENTS
Student Edition

PICTURING THE WORLD

SKILLS

MAP AND GRAPH SKILLS

CRITICAL THINKING SKILLS

STUDY AND WRITING SKILLS

CASE STUDIES

GEOFACTS

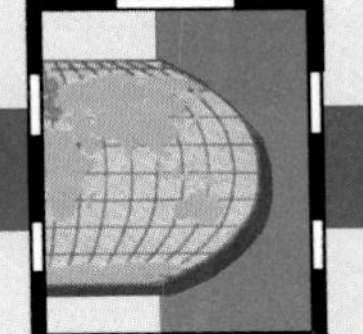

GEOGRAPHY AND HISTORY

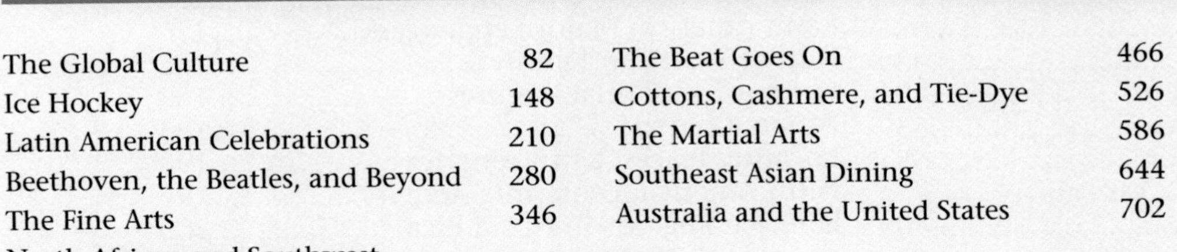

GEOGRAPHY CONNECTIONS

MAPS

Reference Atlas

Unit 1 Looking at the World

Unit 2 The United States and Canada

Unit 3 Latin America

Unit 4 Europe

Unit 5 Russia and the Eurasian Republics

Unit 6 North Africa and Southwest Asia

Unit 7 Africa South of the Sahara

Unit 8 South Asia

GRAPHS, TABLES, AND DIAGRAMS

NATIONAL STANDARDS IN GEOGRAPHY

Since 1994, states have been successfully implementing "standards" in a variety of school subjects, one of which is geography. The purpose of the geography standards is to provide guidance for teachers, parents, and school officials so that students can perform at internationally competitive levels as we approach the twenty-first century.

HISTORY National goals and standards in geography, published under the title *Geography for Life* (1994), were developed under *Goals 2000: Educate America Act* and were a response to evidence that students in the United States were not competitive internationally in the subject of geography. This same reality, almost a decade before, led to the preparation of the *Guidelines for Geographic Education* (1984) and the articulation of the five fundamental themes in geography: (1) location, (2) place, (3) human/environment interaction, (4) movement, and (5) region. These themes, the national standards, and current issues have become guideposts for the creative development of *Glencoe World Geography*. The five themes appear as chapter organizers throughout the book, providing an orderly progression through geographic concepts and information, both cultural and physical.

THE 18 STANDARDS There are 18 geography standards covering the basic content, skill, and concepts of the discipline. These standards provide a framework for the geographic knowledge students should have and the skills they should be able to execute. Students are expected to use maps, globes, and other graphic tools successfully to acquire and process geographic information. They are also expected to develop a spatial view of the world—including cultural and physical characteristics of places and regions. The standards identify, for example, critical physical and cultural processes that create patterns on the surface of the earth, such as climate, mountain-building forces, erosion, flooding, human migration, urbanization, transportation, and international trade. There is an emphasis on how people live on the earth (settlement patterns) and how people use the earth to satisfy basic needs (resources, economic development, and global interdependence). Issues-oriented geography is important in the arenas of human/environment interaction, multiculturalism, politics, and conflict and cooperation. The geography of everyday life is essential, and the well-educated student should be able to contrast how people live from one place or region to another. Finally, the standards require students to view critically the geography of past times in order to make logical decisions concerning the geography of the future.

GEOGRAPHIC LITERACY *Glencoe World Geography* is a program designed to assist students in the achievement of world-class standards in geography. The Student Edition, Teacher's Wraparound Edition, and resources have been prepared in an interesting, innovative, and realistic format that provides students with the geographic knowledge, skills, and practice they need to become informed and involved citizens in a world that is increasingly interdependent.

Physical and human phenomena are spatially distributed over the earth's surface. The outcome of *Geography for Life* is a geographically informed person (1) who sees meaning in the arrangement of things in space; (2) who sees relations between people, places, and environments; (3) who uses geographic skills; and (4) who applies spatial and ecological perspectives to life situations.

THE EIGHTEEN STANDARDS

THE WORLD IN SPATIAL TERMS *Geography studies the relationships between people, places, and environments by mapping information about them into a spatial context.*

The geographically informed person knows and understands:

1. How to use maps and other geographic representations, tools, and technologies to acquire, process, and report information from a spatial perspective
2. How to use mental maps to organize information about people, places, and environments in a spatial context
3. How to analyze the spatial organization of people, places, and environments on Earth's surface

PLACES AND REGIONS *The identities and lives of individuals and peoples are rooted in particular places and in those human constructs called regions.*

The geographically informed person knows and understands:

4. The physical and human characteristics of places
5. That people create regions to interpret Earth's complexity
6. How culture and experience influence people's perceptions of places and regions

PHYSICAL SYSTEMS *Physical processes shape Earth's surface and interact with plant and animal life to create, sustain, and modify ecosystems.*

The geographically informed person knows and understands:

7. The physical processes that shape the patterns on Earth's surface
8. The characteristics and spatial distribution of ecosystems on Earth's surface

HUMAN SYSTEMS *People are central to geography in that human activities help shape Earth's surface, human settlements and structures are part of Earth's surface, and humans compete for control of Earth's surface.*

The geographically informed person knows and understands:

9. The characteristics, distribution, and migration of human populations on Earth's surface
10. The characteristics, distribution, and complexity of Earth's cultural mosaics
11. The patterns and networks of economic interdependence on Earth's surface
12. The processes, patterns, and functions of human settlement
13. How the forces of cooperation and conflict among people influence the division and control of Earth's surface

ENVIRONMENT AND SOCIETY *The physical environment is modified by human activities, largely as a consequence of the ways in which human societies value and use Earth's natural resources, and human activities are also influenced by Earth's physical features and processes.*

The geographically informed person knows and understands:

14. How human actions modify the physical environment
15. How physical systems affect human systems
16. The changes that occur in the meaning, use, distribution, and importance of resources

THE USES OF GEOGRAPHY *Knowledge of geography enables people to develop an understanding of the relationships between people, places, and environments over time—that is, of Earth as it was, is, and might be.*

The geographically informed person knows and understands:

17. How to apply geography to interpret the past
18. How to apply geography to interpret the present and plan for the future

THE IMPORTANCE OF GEOGRAPHIC SKILLS

Geography for Life **emphasizes what students should know and understand about geography at grades 4, 8, and 12. These national standards also suggest that students be able to master five types of skills. These skills are discussed below.**

1. ASKING GEOGRAPHIC QUESTIONS

Successful geographic inquiry involves the ability and willingness to ask, speculate on, and answer questions about why things are where they are and how they got there. Students need to be able to pose questions about their surroundings: Where is something located? Why is it there? With what is it associated? What are the consequences of its location and associations? What is this place like?

2. ACQUIRING GEOGRAPHIC INFORMATION

Geographic information is information about locations, the physical and human characteristics of those locations, and the geographic activities and conditions of the people who live in those places. To answer geographic questions, students should start by gathering information from a variety of sources in a variety of ways.

3. ORGANIZING GEOGRAPHIC INFORMATION

Once collected, the geographic information should be organized and displayed in ways that help analysis and interpretation. Maps play a central role in geographic inquiry, but there are other ways to translate data into visual form, such as using different types of graphs, tables, spreadsheets, and time lines.

4. ANALYZING GEOGRAPHIC INFORMATION

Analyzing geographic information involves seeking patterns, relationships, and connections. Students can then synthesize their observations into a coherent explanation. Students should scrutinize maps to discover and compare spatial patterns and relationships; study tables and graphs to determine trends and relationships between and among items; and probe data through statistical methods to identify trends, sequences, correlations, and relationships.

5. ANSWERING GEOGRAPHIC QUESTIONS

Successful geographic inquiry culminates in the development of generalizations and conclusions based on the data collected, organized, and analyzed. Skills associated with answering geographic questions include the ability to make inferences based on information organized in graphic form (maps, tables, graphs) and in oral and written narratives.

—Adapted from *Geography for Life*, pp. 42–44.

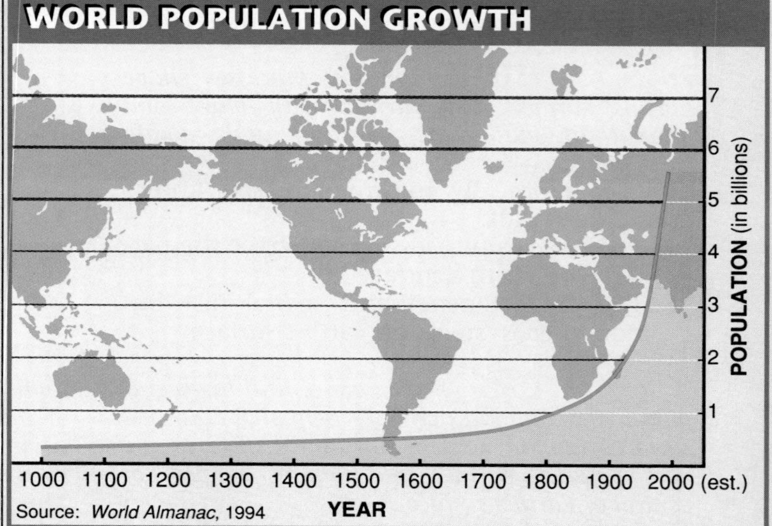

GRAPH STUDY

The earth's population began to grow dramatically after about 1800. ***What is the earth's estimated population in the year 2000?***

GEOGRAPHY THEMES

Geographers have identified five themes that can be used to study geography and the role it plays in our lives. Knowledge of the five fundamental themes of geography is essential to an understanding of geography itself. *Glencoe World Geography* introduces the five geographic themes in Chapter 1 and then continues to refer to them throughout the text. This constant usage enables students to learn to think like geographers.

LOCATION serves as a starting point by asking, "Where is it?" There are two types of location. *Absolute location* refers to the exact location on the earth's surface as measured by latitude and longitude. Every location on the earth can be found in this way. *Relative location* is less precise. It helps you orient yourself to a location that is relative to something else.

The idea of **PLACE** includes more than just where something is located. It includes those features and characteristics that give an area its own identity or personality. These can be *physical characteristics*—such as landforms, weather, plants, and animals—or *human characteristics*—language, religion, architecture, music, and politics.

HUMAN/ENVIRONMENT INTERACTION focuses on how people respond to and alter their environment. To live comfortably or even to survive in many parts of the world, people must make changes in the environment or adapt to conditions they cannot change, or both.

The **MOVEMENT** of people and things between places means that events in other places can have an impact on you personally. Transportation routes, communication systems, and trade connections link people and places throughout the world. Products, ideas, and information are sent around the globe, either slowly by ship or almost instantaneously by electronics. The movement of people is particularly important because it can spread ideas and cultural characteristics from one place to another.

A **REGION** is an area that is unified by some feature or a mixture of features. These features can be language, landscape, religion, location, occupation of people, or a legal definition such as "county." Because students cannot learn in detail the geography of every place, a region is used to generalize about parts of the earth's surface in either physical or human terms.

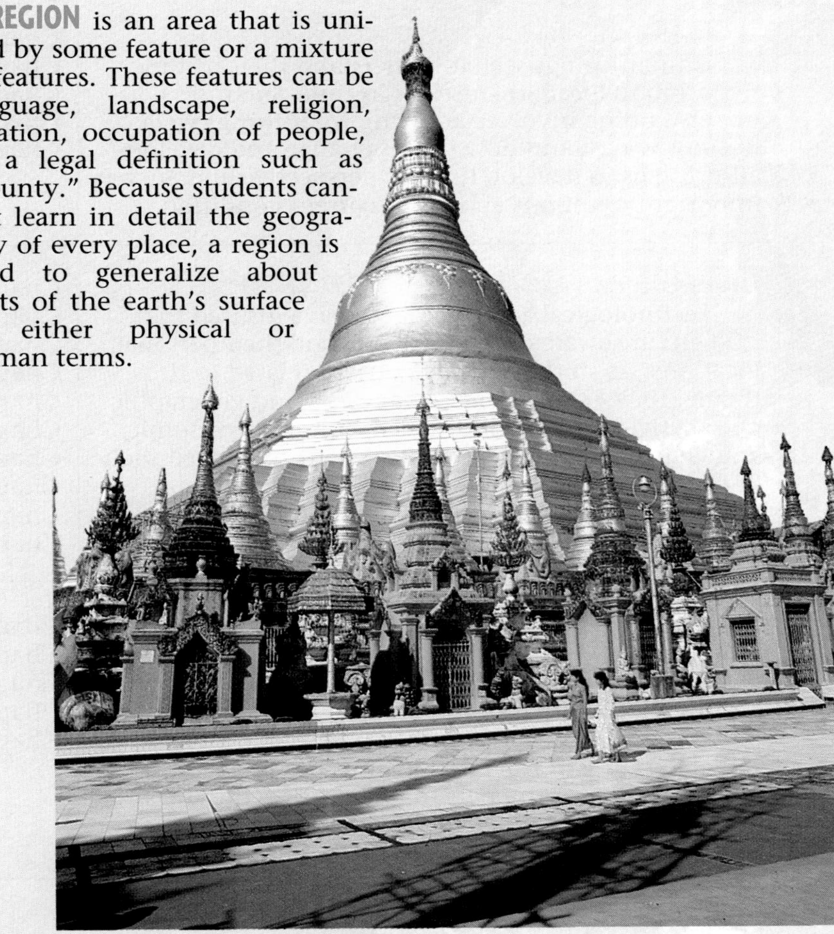

USING NCSS THEMATIC STRANDS IN WORLD GEOGRAPHY

In *Curriculum Standards for Social Studies: Expectations of Excellence,* the National Council for the Social Studies (NCSS) identified ten themes that serve as organizing strands for the social studies curriculum at every school level. These themes are interrelated and draw from all of the social science disciplines. Below is a correlation chart showing where the social studies themes are incorporated in *Glencoe World Geography*.

Social Studies Theme	Incorporated Within the Student Text	
I. CULTURE Human beings create, learn, and adapt culture. Human cultures are dynamic systems of beliefs, values, and traditions that exhibit both commonalities and differences. Understanding culture helps us understand ourselves and others.	Chapter 4 Chapter 7, Section 1 Chapter 10, Section 1 Chapter 13, Section 1 Chapter 16, Section 1 Chapter 19, Section 1	Chapter 22, Section 1 Chapter 25, Section 1 Chapter 28, Section 1 Chapter 31, Section 1 Chapter 34, Section 1
II. TIME, CONTINUITY, AND CHANGE Human beings seek to understand their historic roots and to locate themselves in time. Such understanding involves knowing what things were like in the past and how things change and develop—allowing us to develop historic perspective and answer important questions about our current condition.	Chapter 6, Section 2 Chapter 9, Section 2 Chapter 12, Section 2 Chapter 15, Section 2 Chapter 18, Section 2	Chapter 21, Section 2 Chapter 24, Section 2 Chapter 27, Section 2 Chapter 30, Section 2 Chapter 33, Section 2
III. PEOPLE, PLACES, AND ENVIRONMENT Technological advancements have insured that students are aware of the world beyond their personal locations. As students study content related to this theme, they create their spatial views and geographic perspectives of the world; social, cultural, economic, and civic demands mean that students will need such knowledge, skills, and understandings to make informed and critical decisions about the relationship between human beings and their environment.	Chapter 5, Sections 1, 2 Chapter 7, Section 2 Chapter 8, Sections 1, 2 Chapter 10, Section 2 Chapter 11, Sections 1, 2 Chapter 13, Section 2 Chapter 14, Sections 1, 2 Chapter 16, Section 2 Chapter 17, Sections 1, 2 Chapter 19, Section 2	Chapter 20, Sections 1, 2 Chapter 22, Section 2 Chapter 23, Sections 1, 2 Chapter 25, Section 2 Chapter 26, Sections 1, 2 Chapter 28, Section 2 Chapter 29, Sections 1, 2 Chapter 31, Section 2 Chapter 32, Sections 1, 2 Chapter 34, Section 2
IV. INDIVIDUAL DEVELOPMENT AND IDENTITY Personal identity is shaped by one's culture, by groups and by institutional influences. Examination of various forms of human behavior enhances understanding of the relationships between social norms and emerging personal identities, the social processes which influence identity formation, and the ethical principles underlying individual action.	Chapter 6, Section 3 Chapter 9, Section 3 Chapter 12, Section 3 Chapter 15, Section 3 Chapter 18, Section 3	Chapter 21, Section 3 Chapter 24, Section 3 Chapter 27, Section 3 Chapter 30, Section 3 Chapter 33, Section 3

Social Studies Theme	Incorporated Within the Student Text	
V. INDIVIDUALS, GROUPS, AND INSTITUTIONS Institutions exert enormous influence over us. Institutions are organizational embodiments to further the core social values of those who comprise them. It is important for students to know how institutions are formed, what controls and influences them, how they control and influence individuals and culture, and how institutions can be maintained or changed.	Chapter 6, Section 1 Chapter 9, Section 1 Chapter 12, Section 1 Chapter 15, Section 1 Chapter 18, Section 1	Chapter 21, Section 1 Chapter 24, Section 1 Chapter 27, Section 1 Chapter 30, Section 1 Chapter 33, Section 1
VI. POWER, AUTHORITY, AND GOVERNANCE Understanding of the historical development of structures of power, authority, and governance and their evolving functions in contemporary society is essential for the emergence of civic competence.	Chapter 6, Section 2 Chapter 9, Section 2 Chapter 12, Section 2 Chapter 15, Section 2 Chapter 18, Section 2	Chapter 21, Section 2 Chapter 24, Section 2 Chapter 27, Section 2 Chapter 30, Section 2 Chapter 33, Section 2
VII. PRODUCTION, DISTRIBUTION, AND CONSUMPTION Decisions about exchange, trade, and economic policy and well-being are global in scope and the role of government in policy making varies over time and from place to place. The systematic study of an interdependent world economy and the role of technology in economic decision making is essential.	Chapter 7, Section 1 Chapter 10, Section 1 Chapter 13, Section 1 Chapter 16, Section 1 Chapter 19, Section 1	Chapter 22, Section 1 Chapter 25, Section 1 Chapter 28, Section 1 Chapter 31, Section 1 Chapter 34, Section 1
VIII. SCIENCE, TECHNOLOGY, AND SOCIETY Technology is as old as the first crude tool invented by prehistoric humans, and modern life as we know it would be impossible without technology and the science which supports it. Today's technology forms the basis for some of our most difficult social choices.	Chapter 6, Section 3 Chapter 9, Section 3 Chapter 12, Section 3 Chapter 15, Section 3 Chapter 18, Section 3	Chapter 21, Section 3 Chapter 24, Section 3 Chapter 27, Section 3 Chapter 30, Section 3 Chapter 33, Section 3
IX. GLOBAL CONNECTIONS The realities of global interdependence require understanding of the increasingly important and diverse global connections among world societies before there can be analysis leading to the development of possible solutions to persisting and emerging global issues.	Chapter 7, Section 2 Chapter 10, Section 2 Chapter 13, Section 2 Chapter 16, Section 2 Chapter 19, Section 2	Chapter 22, Section 2 Chapter 25, Section 2 Chapter 28, Section 2 Chapter 31, Section 2 Chapter 34, Section 2
X. CIVIC IDEALS AND PRACTICES All people have a stake in examining civic ideals and practices across time, in diverse societies, as well as in determining how to close the gap between present practices and the ideals upon which our democratic republic is based. An understanding of civic ideals and practices of citizenship is critical to full participation in society.	Chapter 6, Section 1 Chapter 9, Section 1 Chapter 12, Section 1 Chapter 15, Section 1 Chapter 18, Section 1	Chapter 21, Section 1 Chapter 24, Section 1 Chapter 27, Section 1 Chapter 30, Section 1 Chapter 33, Section 1

BLOCK SCHEDULING

Class scheduling is an expression of the relationship between learning and time. Traditionally, schools schedule six or seven 40- to 55-minute classes per day. These classes usually meet for 180 school days per school year.

Block scheduling differs from traditional scheduling in that fewer class sessions are scheduled for larger blocks of time over fewer days. In block scheduling, for example, a course might meet for 90 minutes a day for 90 days, or half a school year. Does this type of scheduling have any advantage over more traditional scheduling methods? Those schools that have tried it believe that it does.

ADVANTAGES FOR SCHOOL SYSTEMS For the schools themselves, the greatest advantage of block scheduling is that there is a better use of resources. No additional teachers or classrooms may be needed, and more efficient use is made of those presently in school. The need for summer school is greatly reduced because the students that do not pass a course one term can take it the next term. These advantages are accompanied by an increase in the quality of teacher instruction and students' time on-task.

ADVANTAGES FOR TEACHERS There are many advantages for teachers who are in schools that use block scheduling. Teacher-student relationships are improved. With block scheduling, teachers have responsibility for a smaller number of students at a time, so students and teachers get to know each other better. Teachers are able to provide additional time and other resources for meeting the individual needs of students. Teachers can also be more focused on what they are teaching.

Block scheduling seems to result in changes in teaching approaches, classrooms that are more student centered, improved teacher morale, increased teacher effectiveness, and decreased burn-out. Teachers feel free to venture away from discussion and lecture to use more productive models of teaching.

Block scheduling cuts in half the time needed for introducing and closing classes. It also eliminates half of the time needed for class changes, which results in fewer discipline problems.

Flexibility is increased because less complex teaching schedules create more opportunities for cooperative teaching strategies such as team teaching and interdisciplinary studies. Block scheduling also increases the number of nontraditional, activity-based courses that can be offered.

ADVANTAGES FOR STUDENTS Student success rate is found to be greater than is found with traditional scheduling because students seem to learn more and retain it better. Problem-solving skills are better developed, grades are improved, and the failure rate is lower.

Improved student-teacher relationships and a more manageable work load help students also. Students feel better about what they are learning, outside interference is reduced, and students are better able to concentrate. Generally, students feel better organized and are more aware of their progress in the class.

Many curricular advantages are also present for students. At-risk students can be scheduled for required courses during the first term. If they do not pass the course, they can repeat it during the second term instead of taking an elective. Better students can move ahead more quickly and those students who develop a late interest in certain courses can take more of them. Block scheduling has been shown to increase the number of students who take upper-level classes and earn advanced studies diplomas.

MODIFIED BLOCK SCHEDULING Some schools use a modified form of block scheduling that combines two core classes. Under this system, students might study social studies for 90 minutes each day during the first semester and science during the second semester. Another modification has students take English and social studies blocks in one semester and science and mathematics blocks the second semester.

90-MINUTE BLOCK SCHEDULE PLANNING GUIDE The following is a suggested pacing chart for using *Glencoe World Geography* in 90-minute periods for a total of 90 days. It may be easily adjusted for alternative lengths of time or for varied course emphasis.

Unit/Chapter/Section	Days
Unit 1 Looking at the World	**8 1/2**
1 How Geographers Look at the World	
Section 1 Themes of Geography	1
Section 2 Geography Skills Handbook	1
Chapter Review and Test	1/2
2 Looking at the Earth	
Section 1 Planet Earth	1/2
Section 2 Earth's Features	1/2
Section 3 Earth's Resources	1/2
Chapter Review and Test	1/2
3 Climates of the Earth	
Section 1 Earth-Sun Relationships	1/2
Section 2 Factors Affecting Climate	1/2
Section 3 World Climate Patterns	1/2
Chapter Review and Test	1/2
4 Environments, Peoples, and Cultures	
Section 1 Limits and Opportunities	1/2
Section 2 Cultural Expressions	1/2
Section 3 World Culture Regions Today	1/2
Chapter Review and Test	1/2
Unit 2 The United States and Canada	**6**
5 The Physical Geography of the United States and Canada	
Section 1 The Land	1
Section 2 The Climate and Vegetation	1
Chapter Review and Test	1/2
6 The Cultural Geography of the United States and Canada	
Section 1 Population Patterns	1/2
Section 2 History and Government	1/2
Section 3 Cultures and Lifestyles	1/2
Chapter Review and Test	1/2
7 The United States and Canada Today	
Section 1 Living in the United States and Canada	1/2
Section 2 People and Their Environment	1/2
Chapter Review and Test	1/2
Unit 3 Latin America	**8 1/2**
8 The Physical Geography of Latin America	
Section 1 The Land	1
Section 2 The Climate and Vegetation	1
Chapter Review and Test	1/2
9 The Cultural Geography of Latin America	
Section 1 Population Patterns	1
Section 2 History and Government	1
Section 3 Cultures and Lifestyles	1
Chapter Review and Test	1/2
10 Latin America Today	
Section 1 Living in Latin America	1
Section 2 People and Their Environment	1
Chapter Review and Test	1/2

Unit/Chapter/Section	Days
Unit 4 Europe	**8 1/2**
11 The Physical Geography of Europe	
Section 1 The Land	1
Section 2 The Climate and Vegetation	1
Chapter Review and Test	1/2
12 The Cultural Geography of Europe	
Section 1 Population patterns	1
Section 2 History and Government	1
Section 3 Cultures and Lifestyles	1
Chapter Review and Test	1/2
13 Europe Today	
Section 1 Living in Europe	1
Section 2 People and Their Environment	1
Chapter Review and Test	1/2
Unit 5 Russia and the Eurasian Republics	**7 1/2**
14 The Physical Geography of Russia and the Eurasian Republics	
Section 1 The Land	1
Section 2 The Climate and Vegetation	1/2
Chapter Review and Test	1/2
15 The Cultural Geography of Russia and the Eurasian Republics	
Section 1 Population Patterns	1/2
Section 2 History and Government	1
Section 3 Cultures and Lifestyles	1
Chapter Review and Test	1/2
16 Russia and the Eurasian Republics Today	
Section 1 Living in Russia and the Eurasian Republics	1
Section 2 People and Their Environment	1
Chapter Review and Test	1/2
Unit 6 North Africa and Southwest Asia	**8 1/2**
17 The Physical Geography of North Africa and Southwest Asia	
Section 1 The Land	1
Section 2 The Climate and Vegetation	1
Chapter Review and Test	1/2
18 The Cultural Geography of North Africa and Southwest Asia	
Section 1 Population Patterns	1
Section 2 History and Government	1
Section 3 Cultures and Lifestyles	1
Chapter Review and Test	1/2
19 North Africa and Southwest Asia Today	
Section 1 Living in North Africa and Southwest Asia	1
Section 2 People and Their Environment	1
Chapter Review and Test	1/2

Unit/Chapter/Section	Days
Unit 7 Africa South of the Sahara	8 1/2
20 The Physical Geography of Africa South of the Sahara	
Section 1 The Land	1
Section 2 The Climate and Vegetation	1
Chapter Review and Test	1/2
21 The Cultural Geography of Africa South of the Sahara	
Section 1 Population Patterns	1
Section 2 History and Government	1
Section 3 Cultures and Lifestyles	1
Chapter Review and Test	1/2
22 Africa South of the Sahara Today	
Section 1 Living in Africa South of the Sahara	1
Section 2 People and Their Environment	1
Chapter Review and Test	1/2
Unit 8 South Asia	8 1/2
23 The Physical Geography of South Asia	
Section 1 The Land	1
Section 2 The Climate and Vegetation	1
Chapter Review and Test	1/2
24 The Cultural Geography of South Asia	
Section 1 Population Patterns	1
Section 2 History and Government	1
Section 3 Cultures and Lifestyles	1
Chapter Review and Test	1/2
25 South Asia Today	
Section 1 Living in South Asia	1
Section 2 People and Their Environment	1
Chapter Review and Test	1/2
Unit 9 East Asia	8 1/2
26 The Physical Geography of East Asia	
Section 1 The Land	1
Section 2 The Climate and Vegetation	1
Chapter Review and Test	1/2
27 The Cultural Geography of East Asia	
Section 1 Population Patterns	1
Section 2 History and Government	1
Section 3 Cultures and Lifestyles	1
Chapter Review and Test	1/2

Unit/Chapter/Section	Days
28 East Asia Today	
Section 1 Living in East Asia	1
Section 2 People and Their Environment	1
Chapter Review and Test	1/2
Unit 10 Southeast Asia	8 1/2
29 The Physical Geography of Southeast Asia	
Section 1 The Land	1
Section 2 The Climate and Vegetation	1
Chapter Review and Test	1/2
30 The Cultural Geography of Southeast Asia	
Section 1 Population Patterns	1
Section 2 History and Government	1
Section 3 Cultures and Lifestyles	1
Chapter Review and Test	1/2
31 Southeast Asia Today	
Section 1 Living in Southeast Asia	1
Section 2 People and Their Environment	1
Chapter Review and Test	1/2
Unit 11 Australia, Oceania, and Antarctica	8 1/2
32 The Physical Geography of Australia, Oceania, and Antarctica	
Section 1 The Land	1
Section 2 The Climate and Vegetation	1
Chapter Review and Test	1/2
33 The Cultural Geography of Australia, Oceania, and Antarctica	
Section 1 Population Patterns	1
Section 2 History and Government	1
Section 3 Cultures and Lifestyles	1
Chapter Review and Test	1/2
34 Australia, Oceania, and Antarctica Today	
Section 1 Living in Australia, Oceania, and Antarctica	1
Section 2 People and Their Environment	1
Chapter Review and Test	1/2

ALTERNATIVE COURSE OUTLINES

OUTLINE 1

Emphasizes physical geography (13 chapters)

Unit 1	Looking at the World Chapters 1, 2, 3
Unit 2	The United States and Canada Chapter 5
Unit 3	Latin America Chapter 8
Unit 4	Europe Chapter 11
Unit 5	Russia and the Eurasian Republics Chapter 14
Unit 6	North Africa and Southwest Asia Chapter 17
Unit 7	Africa South of the Sahara Chapter 20
Unit 8	South Asia Chapter 23
Unit 9	East Asia Chapter 26
Unit 10	Southeast Asia Chapter 29
Unit 11	Australia, Oceania, and Antarctica Chapter 32

OUTLINE 2

Emphasizes cultural geography (11 chapters)

Unit 1	Looking at the World Chapters 4
Unit 2	The United States and Canada Chapter 6
Unit 3	Latin America Chapter 9
Unit 4	Europe Chapter 12
Unit 5	Russia and the Eurasian Republics Chapter 15
Unit 6	North Africa and Southwest Asia Chapter 18
Unit 7	Africa South of the Sahara Chapter 21
Unit 8	South Asia Chapter 24
Unit 9	East Asia Chapter 27
Unit 10	Southeast Asia Chapter 30
Unit 11	Australia, Oceania, and Antarctica Chapter 33

OUTLINE 3

Emphasizes environmental geography (11 chapters)

Unit 1	Looking at the World Chapters 4
Unit 2	The United States and Canada Chapter 7
Unit 3	Latin America Chapter 10
Unit 4	Europe Chapter 13
Unit 5	Russia and the Eurasian Republics Chapter 16
Unit 6	North Africa and Southwest Asia Chapter 19
Unit 7	Africa South of the Sahara Chapter 22
Unit 8	South Asia Chapter 25
Unit 9	East Asia Chapter 28
Unit 10	Southeast Asia Chapter 31
Unit 11	Australia, Oceania, and Antarctica Chapter 34

OUTLINE 4

Emphasizes the Western Hemisphere (10 chapters)

Unit 1	Looking at the World Chapters 1, 2, 3, 4
Unit 2	The United States and Canada Chapter 5, 6, 7
Unit 3	Latin America Chapter 8, 9, 10

OUTLINE 5

Emphasizes the Eastern Hemisphere (28 chapters)

Unit 1	Looking at the World Chapters 1, 2, 3, 4
Unit 4	Europe Chapter 11, 12, 13
Unit 5	Russia and the Eurasian Republics Chapter 14, 15, 16
Unit 6	North Africa and Southwest Asia Chapter 17, 18, 19
Unit 7	Africa South of the Sahara Chapter 20, 21, 22
Unit 8	South Asia Chapter 23, 24, 25
Unit 9	East Asia Chapter 26, 27, 28
Unit 10	Southeast Asia Chapter 29, 30, 31
Unit 11	Australia, Oceania, and Antarctica Chapter 32, 33, 34

ADDRESSING DIFFERENT LEARNING STYLES

VISUAL LEARNERS Visual learners benefit the most when they can carefully look at the material to be studied. In general, visual learners retain more information if they are able to visualize what they are learning. The exercise of mental mapping used in this text is designed to heighten the learning of the visual student. These students also benefit from laserdisc presentations as well as from CD-ROMs. Visual learners benefit, too, from reading the text and studying the maps, charts, graphs, and other visuals.

AUDITORY LEARNERS Auditory learners retain the most information when they hear what they are to learn. Oral instructions from the teacher are ideal ways to introduce these learners to new concepts. Technology plays an essential role in helping these learners master the course content. Audiocassette transcripts of chapters or lessons provide these students with invaluable learning aids. These students also benefit from laserdisc presentations because the soundtracks help them comprehend the information with a higher retention rate. CD-ROMs also provide students with instant auditory directions and feedback.

KINESTHETIC LEARNERS Kinesthetic learners retain information more easily when they can actually perform basic tasks using the information. For these students, individual and group projects in which they construct models, charts, or graphs are ideal.

COOPERATIVE LEARNING

Although cooperative learning is a useful teaching strategy in many subjects, it occupies a special place in the social studies curriculum because of its success in imparting the abilities needed to work effectively in a group. Such social studies skills are beneficial for all citizens working in a democracy.

CHARACTERISTICS OF COOPERATIVE LEARNING Cooperative learning requires careful monitoring and structure by the teacher if it is to be more than a simple group activity. Characteristics of cooperative learning include the following:

- Students work face to face in heterogeneous groups.
- The activity promotes a sense of positive interdependence.
- Each member of a group has individual accountability.
- The group has a common product or goal.

THE ROLE OF THE TEACHER Although successful cooperative learning groups appear to work independently, this is due to the coaching of a good teacher. Students will need the teacher's help at key moments during the group's project—in agreeing upon goals, in establishing a structure of accountability, and so on.

AT-RISK STUDENTS

Most educators today agree that the nation's schools are facing an epidemic of students who are at risk of failure. It is difficult to define exactly what constitutes an at-risk student because being at risk is often linked to several environmental causes such as poverty, low self-esteem, substance abuse, or pregnancy. Current educational research has shown that certain teaching methods can help keep at-risk students from dropping out. One method is to maximize time-on-task to help students overcome distracting outside stimuli.

Another method is to establish high expectations and a school climate that supports learning. Many school activities involve parents in this process so that the expectations for success are not left inside the classroom after school is out. Many teachers give positive feedback at the end of each successfully completed assignment and include awards ceremonies for students who meet expectations.

Rather than emphasizing remedial techniques, many educators believe that at-risk students need to learn at a faster rate. Instruction emphasizes assets that at-risk students often bring to the classroom—interest in oral and artistic expression and kinesthetic learning abilities. For example, at-risk students may excel at dramatizations in which they also construct the sets.

MULTICULTURAL PERSPECTIVE

Glencoe World Geography furnishes a wealth of material that can help students learn to appreciate the cultural diversity of the world's peoples. By reading *Glencoe World Geography*, students receive a balanced, broad view of the interaction of people with their physical and cultural environments, both historically and present-day in today's global village. As the world shrinks in size because of high-speed communication and transportation, it becomes increasingly important for students to see peoples different from themselves as interesting neighbors who have different ideas, customs, and languages, but who also share many of the same values. Students will be given the opportunity to read about groups of people who have been misrepresented or omitted in the past. Inclusion of these groups will help all students develop more positive attitudes toward different cultural, racial, ethnic, religious, and gender groups.

The following four points have been identified as some of the major goals of multicultural education:

- Promoting the strength and value of cultural diversity
- Promoting human rights and respect for those who are different from oneself
- Promoting social justice and equal opportunity for all people
- Promoting equity in the distribution of power among groups

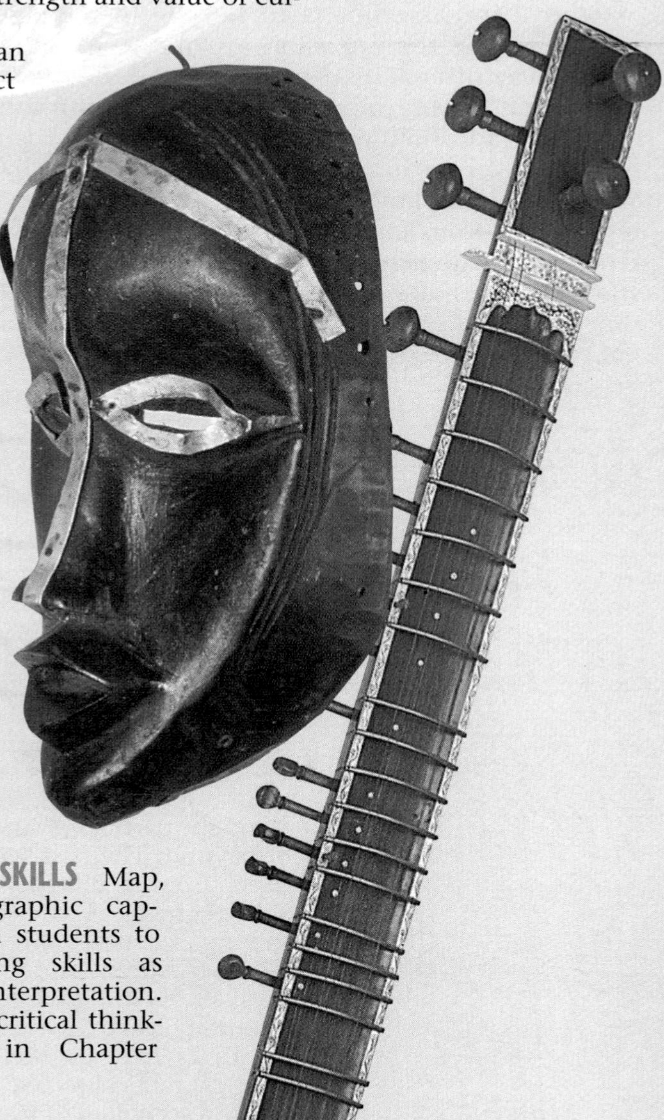

CRITICAL THINKING

To learn about physical and cultural geography in a way that prepares students to become thoughtful participants in this world, students must learn to think critically. They need to be able to evaluate and to question the meaning of what they see, read, and hear. The teacher plays a crucial role in this development by creating a classroom climate that actively encourages critical thinking. *Glencoe World Geography* teaches the skills used in critical thinking.

THE CLASSROOM CLIMATE The teacher can promote critical thinking in the classroom by verbalizing the inner thought processes that take place. Asking questions such as "What do I want to achieve?" and "What do I already know?" models for students the importance of setting goals and of assessing current knowledge. Asking "Have I understood what I have read?" establishes the importance of checking one's progress.

CRITICAL THINKING SKILLS Map, photograph, and graphic captions also call upon students to use critical thinking skills as applied to visual interpretation. Questions requiring critical thinking skills appear in Chapter Reviews.

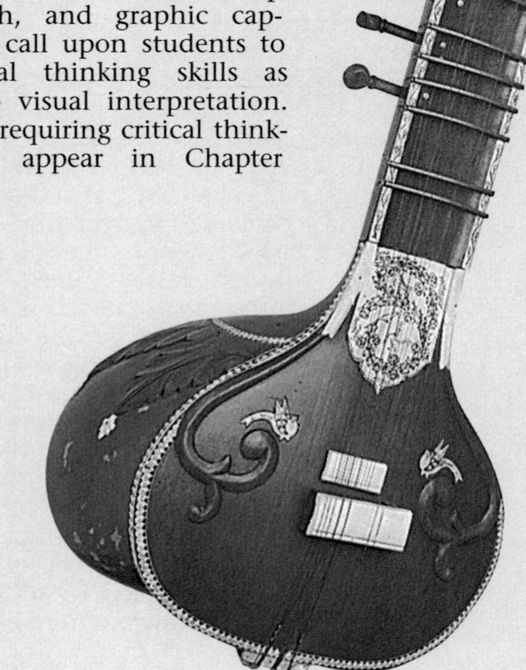

PERFORMANCE ASSESSMENT STRATEGIES

Assessment is a means of identifying the degree to which students have learned the objectives and goals for the unit or duration of study. For assessment to be considered valid, there must be a match among the expectations of the objectives, the instructional experiences offered by the teacher, and the type of assessment item.

Factual content and some forms of thinking skills may be measured by traditional methods of assessment. *Glencoe World Geography* provides you with such testing options as Chapter and Unit Tests, Section Quizzes, and Testmaker Software. Other, alternative means of testing are often known as "performance assessments" because they require an evidence of "knowing" through "doing" on the part of the student. Alternative assessments often require actions by the student that may be observed by the teacher or may result in a tangible product that may be submitted for assessment.

PERFORMANCE MEASURES The alternative measures most often utilized by classroom teachers are projects and investigations, teacher observation, performance-based essays, student interviews, and portfolios. Authentic assessment takes these means even further to place the student in a real or simulated scenario in order to find the extent to which he/she would use the expected competencies in "real life" and the degree to which progress has been made. These scenarios, particularly in the area of geography, might include roles in the world of work, roles involving use of leisure time, roles in problematical situations, or roles demonstrated through participation in one's community or beyond. The best types of tasks are formulated around a broad or complex thinking ability—such as decision making, problem solving, creative thinking, persuasion and argumentation, and predicting or forecasting—all of which will be required of students after they leave the classroom.

Tasks may be divided into three broad types: teacher-directed tasks, student-directed tasks, and collections over time. In teacher-directed tasks, students may be guided step-by-step through various phases of the task requiring differing abilities. It is often beneficial to begin with teacher-directed tasks. An example of this type of task would be one in which the teacher leads the class in brainstorming about ideas and formulating initial hypotheses, but when students realize that they do not have enough information in order to be successful, the teacher guides them to the "acquiring information" phase which takes the place of the typical lecture approach. The approach is student-centered rather than teacher-centered, with the teacher becoming the coach or facilitator. The benefits of the teacher-directed task are that the students themselves set a goal for their own learning and will actually use what they learned.

Student-directed tasks are typically used at the end of a unit of study in the place of or in concert with traditional tests. In these tasks, the teacher explains clearly what is expected of the students in process and product and makes known the criteria on which they will be graded or otherwise assessed.

Collections over time require longer periods to develop, but are helpful in allowing the student to discover a broader application for what is learned than can be accomplished in a one-time task. Collections often include news stories and articles, evidence found in products, literature, music, or other elements of culture, and samples of student applications which have been performed throughout the unit of study.

USING PERFORMANCE ASSESSMENT WITH THIS TEXT Throughout the Teacher's Wraparound Edition and in the Teacher's Classroom Resources, suggestions of performance tasks are supplied for each chapter. You will find that they exemplify the various formats for alternative assessment and the types of tasks described above.

ASSESSING PERFORMANCE TASKS Student performance can be measured by several different means. The most common forms of assessing performance tasks are by rubric or percent. By using percents, you are able to weight certain competencies over others. In this form, you build the total score by adding the percents gained by the student on each required quality.

If you desire to assign a range of numerical scores for the product as a whole, then a rubric is required. Most rubrics include three, four, or six points beyond zero. A score of zero is almost always indicative of a task which, for one reason or another, is non-scorable. The scorable points reflect the range of success for multiple qualities and skills required of the product and the student. A three-point rubric usually ranges from a Score Point One as unacceptable to Score Point Three as completely successful, with Score Point Two usually carrying terms such as some, general, average, or with errors.

In establishing a rubric, you should follow five simple steps:

1. Divide the task into its component parts.
2. Decide on characteristics required of the product.
3. Determine a range of abilities for each task. Use specific language.
4. Compile in list form all of the descriptors you developed for each score point.
5. Present and explain the rubric to the class before the task is begun. Be sure students are aware that a holistic impression always exists since no single task will usually exhibit all the descriptive qualities at a given score point.

JOURNALS The Journal approach to assessment is often used with performance-based assessment as part of an overall approach to authentic assessment. Journals contain samples of students' work collected over a period of time—often an entire grading period or even a semester.

The GeoJournal Activity, placed at the beginning of every unit of *Glencoe World Geography*, provides students an opportunity not only to find information but also to make sense of it and put that information in context. The journal activity is an excellent way to introduce students to the unit and can be a valuable tool for them during the course of the unit. The journal may be used in several ways—you may assign a percentage of the course grade to the journal writing activity listed in the Teacher's Wraparound Edition, you may use the journal activity as a basis for class discussion, or you may wish to give students other assignments to be completed in their journals. You may give students options in how they complete their journal assignments, or in the topics they choose. Journals may also be used for students' reflections about what they are learning and how it affects them. If you wish, the journal may be used as an ongoing dialogue between teacher and student. The GeoJournal Activity and the follow-up writing assignment found in every Chapter Review may be used in a portfolio approach.

EXAMPLE RUBRIC

Score Point 4

- Complete understanding of the concept of interdependence
- No major errors in content information
- Clear, specific oral communication of ideas
- Completely plausible predictions made
- Full understanding of the problem-solving process
- Highly effective participation in group discussions
- Evidence of extensive research

Score Point 3

- Minor misunderstandings of the concept of interdependence
- Minor errors in content information
- Generally clear communication
- Some steps in problem solving less developed than others
- Generally effective participation in group discussions but minor lapses may have occurred
- Enough research to support ideas

Score Point 2

- General understanding of the concept of interdependence
- Several errors in content information
- Oral communication sometimes unclear
- Some steps in problem solving omitted
- Occasional participation in group discussion
- Some relevant research

Score Point 1

- Little or no understanding of the concept
- Major errors in content information
- Unclear, brief, or vague oral communication
- Little or no understanding of the process of problem solving
- Little or no participation in group discussions
- Brief, general or irrelevant research

For the task accompanying the chapters in this text, possible rubric features are listed for each task.

CHAPTER 1
Have students keep a journal of their lives—their personal and family activities and the most important current events of the day during the chapter study. At the end of the chapter, have them reorganize their journals by the five themes of geography.

CHAPTER 2
Have students develop a list of questions to ask the earth about its features and its development. Have students act as different parts of the earth during a simulated interview.

CHAPTER 3
Have students collect names of movies with which they are familiar. Students should then try to determine all the possible locations for the production of each movie based on similar climate and vegetation.

CHAPTER 4
Have students compare a developing country with humans as they develop. They should find and write analogies or illustrate at least five similar problems or developments.

CHAPTER 5
Have students create a venn diagram of the commonalities and differences in physical features between the United States and Canada—countries in the same geographic region.

CHAPTER 6
Have students research cultural traditions of different locations in the region to find their origins from other countries or cultural groups. Students should make an appreciative statement about each.

CHAPTER 7
Have students act as college recruiters presenting their industry or career from a given area of the region to prospective graduates. They should include physical and cultural descriptions, and economic opportunities during their 4–5 minute session.

CHAPTER 8
Have students make videotapes as simulated travel programs. Each member of a group should take part in presenting information on the physical features of the region.

CHAPTER 9
Have students make a family tree for the region showing the diverse backgrounds and contributions of groups who comprise the ancestors of modern-day Latin Americans.

CHAPTER 10
Have students assume the roles of doctors, with the patient being the environment of Latin America. Have students complete an examination of the condition, diagnosis, prognosis, and plan for treatment.

CHAPTER 11
Have several students act as Europeans who have moved to the area from varying geographic locations in Europe. Have the rest of the class interview them about the differences, similarities, adaptations, and so on, that they had to make after the move.

CHAPTER 12
Have students create a European television game show for adults based on the elements of European culture. Students may add to text information through additional research. Game formats should be demonstrated for the class.

CHAPTER 13
Have students take the role of lawmakers in various areas of Europe. Have them investigate the economic and environmental problems, prioritize them according to need, and propose a law regarding one of the problems.

CHAPTER 14
Students should develop a lesson for a 4th–6th grade class on the physical characteristics of the region. Lessons should be kept to a given time limit and done on video, audio, or during a real class period.

CHAPTER 15
Have students take the part of a Russian student and keep a calendar of their events for one month. They should include celebrations, government activities, leisure, religious activities, visits to cities, and so on.

CHAPTER 16
Have students select a problem related to transportation or the environment in Russia and Eurasia. Have them prepare an open letter to the editor of a newspaper giving their opinion on the problem and how it should be solved.

CHAPTER 17
Have students create a nightly newscast, including the weather report for differing areas of the region. Elements involving physical features and their connection to events and natural resources should be included.

CHAPTER 18
Have students collect a portfolio on events related to religious conflict in the region of North Africa and Southwest Asia. Portfolios may come from any current source.

CHAPTER 19
Many American countries send workers to this region to assist with economic and environmental problems. Have students develop a Help Wanted section of the paper naming some of these companies, possible positions, and brief job descriptions.

CHAPTER 20
Have students develop a mural of illustrations or symbols for the physical features of South Africa. This may take the form of a graffiti wall, if preferred, on which all students present free-form information.

CHAPTER 21
Have students make a scrapbook of their lives during a hypothetical long-term stay in the region. Students should include artifacts or student-made replicas of the traditional types of things saved by high school students, but should reflect the culture of the region.

CHAPTER 22
Have students write a news story they might expect to see regarding a problem in the region. Publish all of these in a Sub-Saharan class newspaper.

CHAPTER 23
Have students create clues for a treasure hunt of resources in South Asia using characteristics of the physical geography and map skills in the clue set.

CHAPTER 24
Have students develop rules of etiquette based on religion and other cultural factors for tourists who travel to South Asia.

CHAPTER 25
Have students write a last will and testament for an endangered species or area of the region. Wills should clearly communicate the characteristics and current state of the subject.

CHAPTER 26
Have students design scenery for a play or movie set in East Asia. They should also describe the types of special effects that might be required to show the effect of the climate on the actors.

CHAPTER 27
Have individual students choose one country and give mock testimony to Congress regarding their opinions, supported by factual information, on what our official relationship with that government should be.

CHAPTER 28
Have students study the system of trade between the United States and East Asia. Students should research the current laws and data regarding trade imbalances and create an improvement of the system.

CHAPTER 29
Make a "big book" for younger students describing and illustrating the physical geography of Southeast Asia. Use the entire writing process through publication and share with libraries and classrooms in your district.

CHAPTER 30
Have students mind-map the information from the chapter using words, phrases, and illustrations. Students should synthesize and prioritize the information to write the five most interesting or critical attributes they determine about the cultural geography.

CHAPTER 31
Have students draw the names of countries in the region as their homes. Have them write and exchange several postcards with others in the class (or other classes) telling them about their lives and activities.

CHAPTER 32
Assign each student a physical feature of the area. Have each student write a myth that explains how that feature developed. Share myths in author groups and compile into a class book.

CHAPTER 33
Have students make a bulletin-board display of the cultural factors of one of the countries in the area. Their displays should include at least one graph and map, expository material, and illustrations.

CHAPTER 34
Have students make out a classified ad section for a newspaper. They should include products for sale, job openings, volunteer groups to join, and so on, in the South Pacific area.

ENRICHING CLASSROOM INSTRUCTION

Quality education in the field of geography demands teaching and learning that are both innovative and participatory. Because we are surrounded by geography in all its forms, active teaching and learning involve the use of all senses. In this way the enrichment process is heightened.

The National Standards in geography suggest not only what students should know, but also what they can do with their acquired knowledge. A variety of skills enable students to observe and map geographical phenomena, ask appropriate questions, and analyze and suggest answers to problems with geographic dimensions.

An effective model for enriched geographic education should include simulations, field experiences, and the use of resource persons. While these categories differ in focus, a general model can serve as a checklist for the appropriate implementation of each. Following are some suggestions for the use of classroom extensions for geographic learning:

SIMULATIONS Taking on different roles is often an effective means of learning by simulating a current event with spatial dimensions. For example, two- and three-student teams may represent heads of state and their staffs as they attend an international conference to discuss topics such as global warming, deforestation, or the pollution of the oceans. In another situation, students might represent a town's mayor, members of the planning and zoning commission, businesspersons, and citizens as they debate the importance of a new convention center and the resulting impact on the community. Finally, the class could assume the roles of neighborhood representatives and social workers as they debate the location of a youth services bureau.

FIELD EXPERIENCES Begin with a walk through the neighborhood, gathering data with which to create a map of the area. Use symbols to mark the location of businesses, residences, traffic movement, parks, and unusual places. A more extensive field trip may involve traveling to a sanitary landfill, a water purification plant, an electrical utility, a newspaper office, or a supermarket (to search for foods grown and processed in various countries). To collect data about interstate travel, commerce, or tourism, students may count state license plates on automobiles at a busy intersection and then plot the appropriate states on a map. For study at home, students could work with their parents or guardians in searching for items that were made in countries other than the United States. The students could then map the countries in which these items originated.

RESOURCE PERSONS As we become increasingly globally interdependent, more and more individuals are traveling to countries around the globe. Typically these world travelers are willing and eager to share comments about their experiences, along with pictures or slides of the areas they have seen. In addition to presenting material, these women and men may also interact with students, enhancing the experience for both.

Each of these three types of activities are valuable in and of themselves, and when implemented in conjunction with one another, provide for an integrated learning experience. As a means of enhancing this teaching and learning experience, preparation cannot be overlooked. The use of flow charts, accurately ordering the process from conception to debriefing and extension of the activity, is essential to the successful outcome of any activity.

TECHNOLOGY IN THE CLASSROOM

Advances in technology are continually being made, and these advances dramatically affect all aspects of the social studies. Social studies instruction should include an awareness of advances in technology. Glencoe has developed a number of programs designed for your use in the classroom.

SOFTWARE *Student Self-Test and Review Software* This highly motivational program allows students to check their comprehension by answering multiple-choice questions directly at the computer. If a student chooses a wrong answer, the computer explains why the choice is incorrect. The student then may try again. This process continues until the student chooses the correct answer. It is through this process that the student receives immediate feedback to reinforce correct responses. Chapter Summaries and a Glossary also are integrated in this software.

Testmaker The Testmaker that Glencoe has developed allows you to customize tests to fit the special needs of your students. These software programs are available in Macintosh and DOS formats. The designers of the software have constructed it so that you are free to edit the questions available, mix questions as you wish, and add questions to meet your particular needs.

Vocabulary PuzzleMaker Software Because vocabulary development and comprehension is such an important part of social studies instruction, Glencoe has developed a special program for vocabulary. The Vocabulary PuzzleMaker lets you create high-interest crossword puzzles and word searches covering the textbook's vocabulary program.

NATIONAL GEOGRAPHIC SOCIETY *ZipZapMap! World* and *ZipZapMap! USA* Students earn points by correctly placing the software's puzzle pieces as they tumble from the top of a computer screen.

NATIONAL GEOGRAPHIC SOCIETY *Picture Atlas of the World* CD-ROM This prize-winning resource contains more than 800 interactive maps, as well as more than 1,200 photographs. Fascinating audio and video clips demonstrate languages, music, and cultural traditions of nations around the globe.

Computer Training for Teachers

You must have a general knowledge of computer operation, but you do not have to have a knowledge of internal hardware elements or programming languages. Software hotlines are one of your best resources when using any type of software. **Glencoe's software HOTLINE is 1-800-437-3715.**

VIDEODISCS If your school has a basic system consisting of a videodisc player and a television receiver, the videodiscs provide an effective and interesting tool for classroom presentations. Students can see the connection between concepts and the real world. Students are also given opportunities to apply what they have learned.

NATIONAL GEOGRAPHIC SOCIETY videodiscs provide visual, in-depth study of regions and environmental systems of the world. Titles available include *Rain Forest, Solar System, Restless Earth,* and *Planetary Manager*. The World Geography series includes the following regions: *North America, Asia and Australia, Africa and Europe*, and *South America and Antarctica*.

MindJogger Videoquiz The MindJogger Videoquiz uses a game show format for review of key concepts. A bar code scanner allows you immediate access to specific chapters. The bar codes are placed on the Chapter opener and Chapter Review pages of the Teacher's Wraparound Edition. The MindJogger Videoquiz is also available in a VHS format.

Geography and the Environment: Infinite Voyage Video Program contains a series of videodiscs in which the earth and our relationship to it is examined.

Reuters Issues in Geography Video Program presents current environmental issues and challenges on a regional basis.

ABCNews InterActive™: *In the Holy Land* explores issues in this region of the world.

USING THE INTERNET

by Isobel Stevenson, Johnston High School, Austin, Texas

THE INTERNET The Internet (or the Net) is the collective name for the connections among computers throughout the world. The computers can communicate with one another because they follow a single standard called TCP/IP for passing information back and forth. The Internet has existed for about 25 years, originating as a military network and expanding through universities and into the commercial realm.

Think of the Internet as similar to using the telephone. If you know the name of the computer you want to contact, you look up its number, have your computer dial it, and talk to it. Sending messages from person to person is one of the Net's most popular uses. You can reach a specific person by using e-mail, or you can join a conference call by subscribing to bulletin boards and listservers. For example, you can join the listserver for people interested in geographic education by sending the message **subscribe geoged Your Name** to listserv@ukcc.uky.edu. The Internet, however, is used for much more than just getting and sending messages.

WORLD WIDE WEB Getting information through the Internet became much easier with the development of the World Wide Web. The Web is an exciting region of the Internet that contains pictures, sound, and video as well as text. You can scan the Web using "browsers"—programs such as Netscape and Mosaic. This software can navigate the Web for you, meaning that you no longer have to know the number of the computer you want. You don't even have to know where the information you want *is*.

Until recently, if you wanted to find information in a library, you had to know the name of the author. Now libraries have electronic catalogues that allow you to search not only by the name of the author, but also by the name of the book, topic, keyword, and so on. Similarly, there are several ways to find what you want on the Web. You can go directly to the information if you know its Uniform Reference Locator (URL), or address. Every photograph, map, diagram, and text file has one of these unique addresses, and your browser can keep track of these sources as "bookmarks."

Each site mentioned below is followed by its URL. You can also use the "search engines" that are incorporated into the program you use to access the Web. Or use another service such as Yahoo (http://www.yahoo.com/). These services work just like the electronic catalogue in a library, except that when you find the reference you want, you simply point and click and the information appears on your screen. Often, it is faster to use a search engine than to type in the URL, especially if the URL is particularly long.

The best part of the Web is that you can print and copy everything you find. If you or your school has a single computer connected to the Internet, you can print materials for your class or save files for later use. Access to a relatively inexpensive color ink jet printer allows you to print directly onto overhead transparencies.

School districts are establishing connections to the Internet at a rapid rate. One option is to join the Internet through a local university. Another option is to subscribe to a private provider such as CompuServe, America On-Line, or Microsoft Network. These private providers let you use the Web for a monthly fee or at an hourly rate.

SURFING THE GEOGRAPHY NET There is a wealth of on-line resources for geography teachers. Maps, images, data, and other information can be accessed from the following list. When you type the address, you will reach the organization's "homepage." This is the best place to start if you are browsing to find what is available.

- Library of Congress
  http://lcweb.loc.gov/homepage/lchp.html
- United States Geological Survey
  http://www.usgs.gov/
- Bureau of the Census
  http://www.census.gov/
- NASA
  http://www.nasa.gov/
- National Oceanic and Atmospheric Administration
  http://www.noaa.gov/

- Environmental Protection Agency
  http://www.epa.gov/
- CNN
  http://www.cnn.com/
- WorldPop is a counter showing the world's estimated population at any given moment and is updated constantly. Depending on the software, you can watch the counter tick at a brisk pace.
  http://sunsite.unc.edu/lunarbin/worldpop
- The CIA has the 1995 World Factbook on the Web, which is indexed by country and also contains reference maps.
  http://www.odci.gov/cia/publications/95fact/index.html
- You can get up-to-date information on earthquakes:
  http:www.civeng.carleton.ca/cgi-bin/quakes
- The Jason Project is an interactive, electronic field trip, complete with a teacher's guide.
  http:seawifs.gsfc.nasa.gov/scripts/JASON.html
- Weather images are available from several different sources. Try the Purdue University Weather Gopher
  gopher://thunder.atms.purdue.edu/
  or the University of Illinois Weather World
  http://www.atmos.uiuc.edu/wxworld/html/detailed.html
- The University of Texas has an on-line map collection with maps of just about everywhere.
  http://www.lib.utexas.edu/Libs/PCL/Map_collection/Map_collection.html

Increasingly, you no longer have to look up each address individually. Many sites will provide you with links to other sites, so you can travel the world by pointing and clicking. Or you can visit several sites that are clearinghouses for information:

- Armadillo from Rice University
  http://chico.rice.edu/armadillo/about.html
- ERIC Clearinghouse
  http://www.cua.edu/www/eric_ae/home.html
- Joint Education Initiative at Maryland
  http://jei.umd.edu/

interNET CONNECTIONS

Glencoe/McGraw-Hill's unique **Internet Connections** are a source for extended information related to Unit and Chapter content. The sites referenced in Glencoe's **Internet Connections** are not under the control of Glencoe and therefore Glencoe makes no representation concerning the content of these sites. We encourage teachers to preview these sites before students access them. Internet sites are sometimes under construction and may not always be available, sites may move, or sites may have been discontinued completely.

NATIONAL GEOGRAPHIC SOCIETY

The following 11 lesson plans have been developed by the National Geographic Society for use with their *Picture Atlas of the World* CD-ROM. Other corresponding activities can be found at the beginning of each unit in the student edition.

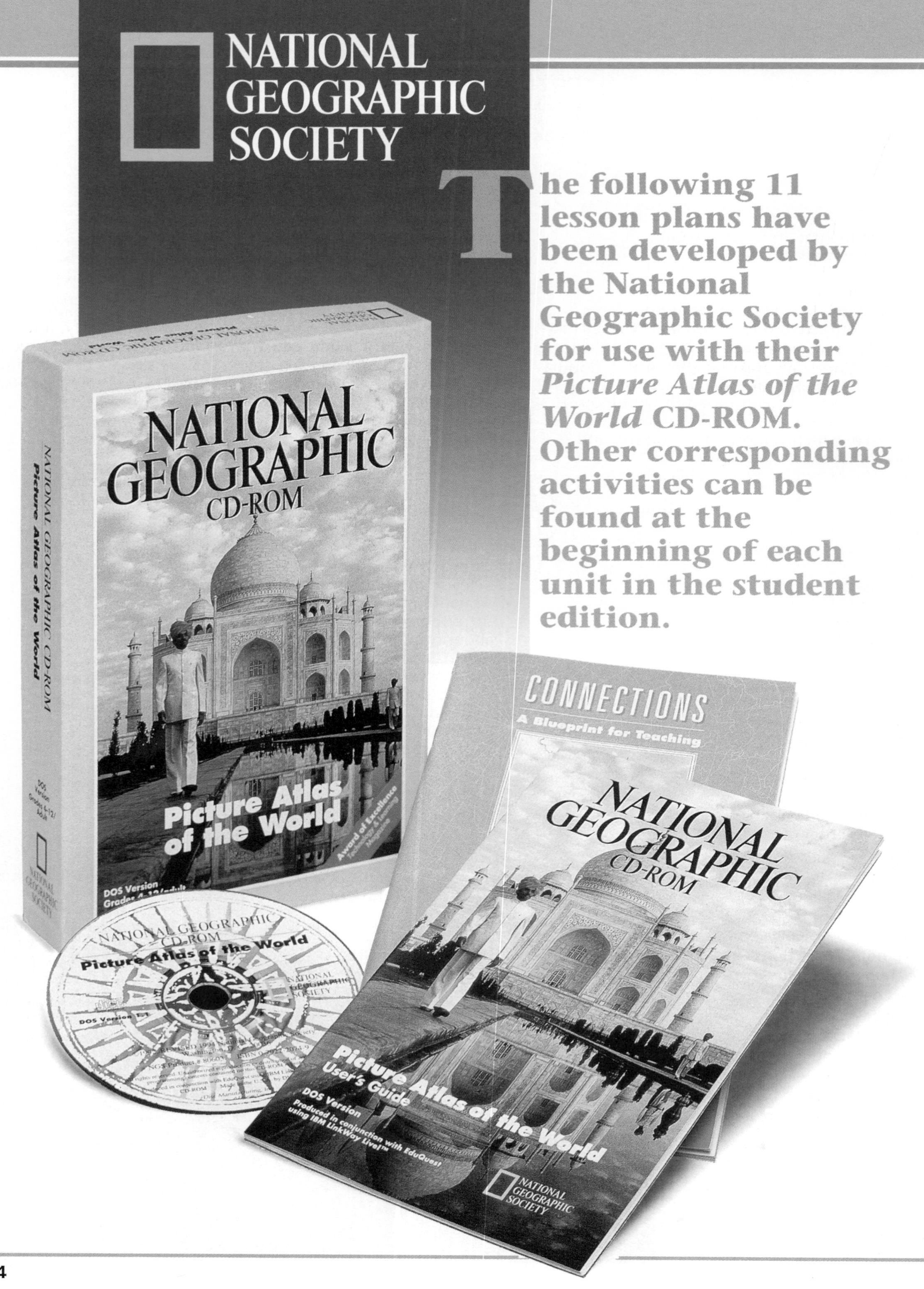

UNIT 1 POPULATION EXPLOSION

The world's population hit one billion in the early 19th century. By 1930, the figure had climbed to two billion. Since then, world population has more than doubled—reaching more than five billion in 1993. Currently, the global population is growing at the rate of more than ninety million a year. In this lesson, students examine some factors that affect population growth and the effects of increased population density on a location.

Objectives

- To identify factors that influence population density
- To calculate the population density of a location
- To speculate on the population density of a location by using statistical and map information

Materials

- *Picture Atlas of the World* CD-ROM
- World outline maps (with political boundaries)—one map per student
- Large pieces of newsprint

THE LESSON

1. Introduce students to the following terms: population, population growth rate, population doubling time, per capita income, literacy, life expectancy, fertility rate.

2. Distribute the world outline maps to the students. Then have students use *Picture Atlas* to identify the most populous country on each continent (excluding Antarctica) and shade in that country on the outline map. *Note: Except for Australia and Antarctica, this information can be found on each continent's Vital Statistics screen. To research total population and area for Australia, select Oceania and then select Australia.*

3. Write the term "population density" on the chalkboard and explain that it refers to the number of people per square mile (or kilometer). Have students go to the Country screen of the most populous country on each continent and calculate the population density for that country by dividing the country's total population by its area. Then have students discuss their findings.

4. Ask students to determine if the most populous country is also the most densely populated country. If it is not, have them determine the most densely populated country on each continent and discuss their findings. *Note: Students may want to refer to the Population Map—accessible from the World Map screen—to limit their searches. On most continents students will find several countries showing the highest density ranking (300 PPSM). Remind students to refer to each nation's Country screen or Vital Statistics screen to calculate the exact population density.*

5. List the following physical and cultural characteristics on the chalkboard: climate, access to water, relief features, life expectancy, literacy rate, fertility rate, per capita income, and population growth rate. Using these characteristics as a checklist, have the class speculate about why some countries develop denser populations than other countries. Record students' responses.

6. Organize the class into six groups and provide each group with a piece of newsprint.
   - Assign each group the most densely populated country on each of the six continents.
   - Have each group investigate, for its assigned country, the characteristics listed in step 5.

   Each group should record its findings on the newsprint.

7. Have the groups compare their findings with the original speculations. Ask students how each characteristic they investigated relates to, or may affect, the population density of a country. (For example, does a high literary rate have an effect on the fertility rate and therefore on a nation's population density?)

8. To assess students' understandings, display photos and statistical information for another country—without revealing the name of the country. Ask students to speculate on the country's population density and give reasons for their responses. Then disclose the name of the country and have students compare the country's actual population density with their guestimates.

UNIT 2 A LOOK AT THE LAND

North America exports more food than any other continent on the earth. Its farmers produce nearly 60 percent of the world's soybeans and 50 percent of the world's corn. On the interior plains of southern Canada and the American Midwest, fertile land and temperate climate combine to produce bumper crops of wheat and corn. Vast tracts of flat land allow farmers to use large machines to plant and harvest enormous quantities of one crop.

In Mexico and Central America, about half of the population farms. However, large landowners hold the vast majority of arable land. Campesinos struggle to feed their families on tiny parcels of land while large commercial plantations reap handsome profits. Land ownership has been a serious issue for many years—serious enough to lead to revolutions and civil war. In this lesson, students investigate the widely divergent agricultural methods practiced throughout North America.

Objectives

- To develop or enhance observation skills
- To gather and analyze data
- To identify and compare agricultural methods practiced across North America
- To introduce several types of agriculture: intensive, extensive, commercial, and subsistence

Materials

- *Picture Atlas of the World* CD-ROM
- Classroom atlases (optional)
- Blank political maps—one map per student (optional)

THE LESSON

1. Have students review and discuss the following terms: intensive, extensive, subsistence, and commercial agriculture. A few key concepts should emerge from the discussion:
    - Intensive agriculture is generally practiced where land is scarce and a great deal of labor is necessary—that is, the land is used intensively to produce as much as possible.
    - Extensive agriculture is practiced where land is abundant but not especially fertile, or where there is limited rainfall—for example, on large sheep ranches.
    - Commercial agriculture produces crops or animals to be sold.
    - Subsistence agriculture produces food for the farmer's own family.
2. Have students analyze agriculture in North America by investigating photos in various Photo Albums: Canada 10; Costa Rica 3, 5; Cuba 5; El Salvador 1, 4; Haiti 2; Mexico 11, 14; Nicaragua 1; United States 8, 11; St. Vincent and the Grenadines 3. Then ask students to determine or consider:
    - physical characteristics of the location
    - human modifications to the environment indicating agricultural activity
    - size of farm (if possible)
    - agricultural methods used (animals, machinery, or both?)
    - products and whether they are likely to be consumed locally or exported
    - type of agriculture (intensive or extensive, commercial or subsistence?)
    - impact of type of farming on the environment
3. Have students report their findings to the class. *Note: A chart or table could be created with either Country or Type of Agriculture as the column heading.*
4. Ask students to investigate landforms and climate characteristics of the sites researched, using the Major Sites Map and Vital Statistics screens. Have students find the appropriate photo on the map and then explore the sites to learn about relief features, transportation networks, and other data. Ask students to consider:
    - relationships between size and type of farm and terrain
    - effects of climate on agriculture
    - products produced and for what purposes
    - modifications to land to make it suitable for agriculture (how extensive?)
    - types of transportation used to ship products to market

    Note: You might also want your students to use atlases or encyclopedias to gather additional information about the physical characteristics of a place and the requirements for agriculture in that location.
5. Have students report their conclusions. *Note: You might want to focus the discussion on human/environment interactions and the movement of products from farm to market.*

UNIT 3 TOUR—UP THE AMAZON

A special tour has been organized to travel up the Amazon River. Playing the role of freelance writer/photographers for NATIONAL GEOGRAPHIC magazine, your students will cover the tour. As part of their assignment, they are to keep a daily journal, complete with photos, of their experiences.

Objectives

- To analyze pictures, captions, essays, and charts in order to gather information about the Amazon River Basin
- To demonstrate knowledge of climate, terrain, flora and fauna, economic activity, and important sites in the Amazon Basin
- To develop or enhance skills in using clip-and-copy functions of *Picture Atlas*

Materials

- *Picture Atlas of the World* CD-ROM
- Formatted diskettes
- Travel guides (optional)
- Encyclopedias (optional)

THE LESSON

1. Explain the journal assignments to the class.
2. Have students use *Picture Atlas* to explore Brazil. Students should gather information from photos and captions on the Major Sites Map along the Amazon River. They should also investigate the Country Essay, Music and Language clips, and the Climate box on the Vital Statistics screen.
3. Ask students to clip and copy to a diskette their favorite pictures of life along the Amazon and to keep a journal of their imaginary trip in the boxes provided for notes and captions. In their journals, students should record their impressions of the following features:
   - the river
   - the land
   - the flora and fauna of the river and adjacent land
   - the weather
   - the people in rural areas
   - the cities they visit and important city sights
   - the people in urban areas
   - the language
   - the music
   - examples of environmental pressures
   - examples of multiple-use resources that create conflicts

Note: You may want to make available additional resources, such as travel guides, encyclopedias, and magazines, to supplement students' research materials.

4. Have students present their electronic journals. Using the research guide in step 3 as a checklist, discuss students' impressions.

UNIT 4 TOUR—ROMANCING THE EMPIRE

The ancient Roman Empire reached far beyond southern Europe. It extended to the British Isles in the north and to African and Asian lands to the south and east. Although the empire included many different peoples who spoke many different languages, the Romans introduced Latin throughout the empire, and Roman law and government ruled throughout. We still see the influence of the Roman Empire today in Spanish, French, Italian, and other Romance languages derived from Latin and in the Roman-law-based legal systems of many Western nations. Assuming the role of modern-day historians, students will trace and map the spread of the Roman Empire and the diffusion of Roman culture.

Objectives

- To identify present-day countries and regions influenced by Roman culture
- To gather and organize information to support a point of view
- To develop or enhance skills in using clip-and-copy functions of *Picture Atlas*

Materials

- *Picture Atlas of the World* CD-ROM
- Blank outline maps that include Europe, western Asia, and northern Africa—one map per student
- Formatted diskettes
- Several compasses and rulers
- Transparency of the outline map
- Overhead projector and markers
- Historical atlases (optional)
- Encyclopedias (optional)

THE LESSON

1. Display this statement to the class: "The effects of cultural influence diminish with distance." Tell students the idea will come up in the lesson.
2. Assign students the role of modern-day historians tracing and mapping the diffusion of Roman culture around the world. Explain to students that they will research countries in Europe, Asia, and Africa to study two phenomena: (1) areas directly influenced by Roman culture, where Romance languages are spoken; (2) areas directly influenced by Roman culture, where Romance languages are not spoken. *Note: It may be necessary to explain the relationship between a Romance language and its parent language, Latin, and to discuss examples of cultural diffusion.*
3. Distribute the blank outline maps. Have each student use a compass to draw arcs or circles on the maps at intervals of 500, 1,000, 1,500, and 2,000 miles (or kilometers) from Rome.
4. Display the following list of countries that have been directly influenced by Roman culture: Italy, United Kingdom, France, Spain, Algeria, Libya, Lebanon, Syria, Croatia, Germany, Israel, Luxembourg, Tunisia, Greece, Yugoslavia, Romania, Macedonia, Slovenia.
5. Organize students into groups and assign each group four or five countries.
6. Have students use *Picture Atlas* to "tour" assigned countries in order to gather evidence of Roman influences and of Romance languages spoken in each country. Ask students to research Photo Albums, Videos, and written information to compile electronic essays and to include their own written captions in their essays. *Note: You may wish to suggest to students the following photos and captions in various Photo Albums: Italy 4, 8; United Kingdom, 10, also Text caption for Hadrian's Wall; France 9; Spain 6; Algeria 6; Tunisia 2, 6; Libya 1; Lebanon 6; Syria 6; Croatia 11; Germany 10. Other Photo Album captions that contain at least a mention of the Romans include Greece 2; Slovenia 3; Macedonia 1, 4; Israel 2; Yugoslavia 3; Tunisia 4, 5.*
7. Have each student indicate results of his or her research on the outline map. Ask students to shade outline maps to show countries where Roman influences have survived and to add diagonal lines across countries that speak a Romance language.
8. Display the outline map transparency. *Note: The transparency constructed by the teacher—with distance circles indicated—should be on display as presentations begin. The teacher or a group leader should transfer the groups' map findings to the transparency as groups present their research.*
9. Return to the statement in step 1 and ask students to apply their findings to either prove or disprove the statement. To focus the discussion on relevant concepts—such as physical barriers, cultural differences, cultural assimilation, and political/economic/military factors—you might introduce the following questions:
   - What distribution patterns did you find in the countries researched?
   - What could account for these patterns?
   - How can water or landforms affect cultural diffusion?
   - Does climate have an effect on cultural diffusion?
   - How can religion affect cultural diffusion?
   - How can technology affect cultural diffusion?
   - Why aren't Romance languages spoken in all countries influenced by Roman culture?

UNIT 5 WHAT'S DEVELOPING?

Definitions of "developed" and "developing" vary and are not precise. In general, developed countries are identified as those having a significant industrial base. Some social scientists consider a country to be developed if less than a fifth of the population is engaged in farming, mining, and forestry. At any rate, the majority of the world's population lives in developing countries where people struggle to make a living from the land. They rely on themselves and a few animals to grow their crops because either they lack money to buy machines or the terrain does not allow the use of machinery. In this lesson, students examine the concepts of developed and developing countries and research a few countries to determine their level of development.

Objectives

- To gather data about a country
- To identify criteria used to determine whether a country is developed or developing
- To analyze data to determine a country's level of development

Materials

- *Picture Atlas of the World* CD-ROM
- *The Statesman's Year-Book* (optional)
- *World Almanac* (optional)
- *CIA World Fact Book* (optional)
- Other atlases or encyclopedias (optional)

THE LESSON

1. Show students a series of pictures contrasting developed and developing countries. Ask them to observe what makes the places different and similar. *Note: Start with a scene clearly illustrating a developed nation—for example, a modern urban area such as Dublin (Photo Album, Ireland 5). Contrast that scene with a clear example in a developing nation—for example, a rural scene with a farmer using a plow or his own manual labor (Photo Album, Albania 3). After two or three clear examples, make distinctions less clear. You might show an urban scene from a developing nation (with many people but few cars) and a rural scene from a developed nation (where people farm with modern equipment).*

2. Discuss what people mean when they talk about developed and developing countries. Ask students to consider the following:
   - characteristics of a developed and a developing country
   - data that helps determine whether a country is developed or developing
   - physical characteristics that affect a country's level of development

3. Organize the class into research groups of five students or less and have each group select a country to research. Have students use *Picture Atlas* and other atlases, encyclopedias, and reference works along with the following criteria to determine whether a nation is developing or developed:

   Developed countries:
   —population generally employed in manufacturing or in service industries
   —vast communication and transportation networks
   —annual per capita income above $7,620
   —adequate food and housing
   —many schools
   —high literacy rate
   —low infant mortality rate
   —long life expectancy
   —population growth rate below 3 percent

   Developing countries:
   —population generally employed in farming, mining, or forestry
   —few natural resources for industrial development
   —few industries or small industries employing few people
   —few transportation or communication networks
   —low literacy rate
   —food and housing inadequate or poor
   —few schools
   —high infant mortality rate
   —short life expectancy
   —population growth rate above 3 percent

4. Ask students to determine whether there are any physical characteristics that impede development or may contribute significantly to future development in a selected country.

5. Have each group present its findings to the class and support its conclusions. After presentations have been made, ask students to discuss the patterns they identified.

UNIT 6 PETROLEUM—GLOBAL EXCHANGE

Today much of the world's population depends upon petroleum to help fulfill its daily energy needs. We use petroleum to heat our homes and to fuel our machines. As population soars and industrialization advances throughout the world, energy needs skyrocket. But our oil supply is limited—and may run out one day. In this lesson, students will gather data about the world's petroleum production and consumption in order to link personal use with a global perspective.

Objectives

- To define selected terms associated with energy use
- To identify examples of petroleum use in our daily life
- To identify and compare characteristics of major petroleum-producing and petroleum-consuming countries
- To identify factors that affect the transportation of petroleum
- To identify alternative energy resources

Materials

- *Picture Atlas of the World* CD-ROM
- Two colors of sticky dots
- Wall-size world political map
- Newsprint—one sheet per group
- Petroleum production and consumption graphs (Handout 3 in the *Picture Atlas*)

THE LESSON

1. Have students review the following terms: resource, natural resource, renewable resource, nonrenewable resource.
2. Organize the class into five groups and display the following questions:
   - What is a resource?
   - What are various categories of resources?
   - What resources do you use daily that you could not do without?
3. Have each group discuss, develop, and record the answers to these questions. Then display and discuss the groups' answers.
4. Focus the discussion on petroleum and whether it is considered a natural, renewable, or nonrenewable resource.
5. Display the questions listed below and have groups discuss and record on sheets of newsprint answers to the questions, based on students' general knowledge:
   - What activities in your daily life are directly or indirectly related to the use of petroleum?
   - Is our country one of the world's top 15 consumers of petroleum? Explain.
   - Does our country produce enough petroleum to meet its consumption needs?
   - What other countries might have a similar profile of petroleum consumption?
   - What countries are major producers of petroleum?
6. Display and discuss the groups' speculations, exploring reasons for their answers.
7. Distribute copies of the top producer and consumer graphs (Handout 3) to each of the five groups. Note the countries' locations on a wall map, using color-coded sticky dots to indicate petroleum-producing and petroleum-consuming countries. Have students compare the list of countries that are major producers with the list of countries that are major consumers. Key factors to consider might include:
   - What similarities and differences exist? (For example, the United States is a top producer and consumer while many Middle Eastern nations are top producers but are not among the top 15 consumers.)
   - What distribution patterns can be found? (For example, are top producers or top consumers located in particular cultural or geographic regions?)
8. Review the groups' original speculations regarding top producers and consumers and compare the speculations with more recent findings.
9. Develop a checklist as a guide for investigating petroleum-producing and petroleum-consuming countries. The checklist should include:
   - per capita income
   - literacy
   - level of industrial development
   - life expectancy
   - transportation networks
   - population density
10. Have each group use *Picture Atlas* to investigate a paired set of one of the top petroleum-producing countries and a top petroleum-consuming country. Students should browse through Photo Albums; investigate the information on Vital Statistics screens and in Essays, Maps, and Videos for their assigned producer-and-consumer pair; and record their findings. *Note: Group A will investigate the number one producer and number one consumer countries; Group B will investigate the number two producer and number two consumer countries, and so on.*
11. Have the students in each group present a report by describing the country-pair profiles developed. Ask them to support their conclusions.

UNIT 7 TOUR—ON SAFARI

The National Geographic Society has sent a research team, including photographers, to explore animal populations in various vegetation regions in Africa. Assuming the role of photographers, students "on assignment" for *NATIONAL GEOGRAPHIC* in Africa will gather information about wildlife habitats and vegetation regions.

OBJECTIVES

- To analyze maps, graphs, statistics, pictures, and essays in order to gather selected information about wildlife habitats and vegetation regions
- To examine possible relationships between climate/vegetation patterns and the distribution of wildlife species
- To develop or enhance skills in using clip-and-copy functions of *Picture Atlas*

MATERIALS

- *Picture Atlas of the World* CD-ROM
- Blank outline maps of Africa (with political boundaries); or outline maps with vegetation regions—one map per student
- Blank white paper—one sheet per student
- Formatted diskettes
- Map transparency (optional)
- Overhead projector (optional)

THE LESSON

1. Distribute the blank outline maps. Ask students to consult a map to locate vegetation regions, color in those regions on their own outline maps, and create a color-coded legend. *Note: If time is limited, you might prefer to hand out a prepared outline map showing vegetation regions. A handout could be created by printing out an Africa outline map and tracing in the regions.*
2. Have students browse through Photo Albums and Videos in *Picture Atlas* in the following countries: Namibia, Kenya, Nigeria, Tanzania, Botswana, South Africa, Rwanda, Swaziland, Equatorial Guinea, Madagascar, Mozambique, Seychelles, Zambia, Zimbabwe. Ask students to "photograph" six animals by copying the photos to a diskette. *Note: If your school does not have enough CD-ROMs to allow each student an opportunity to create his or her own diskette, ask students to sketch or describe animals in their photographers' notebooks.*
3. For each picture, students should write a caption that identifies the animal, notes where it was photographed, and describes its habitat.
4. Ask students to mark the location of each animal's habitat on the outline maps.
5. Have students investigate habitats by exploring the Climate box on Vital Statistics screens, the World Climate Map, Photo Albums, and Country Essays. *Note: You may want students to research animals in an encyclopedia or other reference works such as* Mammals: A Multimedia Encyclopedia *CD-ROM.*
6. Have students examine the distribution of wildlife in relation to the climate/vegetation regions and record their findings on separate sheets of paper. (For example, lions and gazelles inhabit the savanna, and gorillas inhabit the rain forest.)
7. Have students present their electronic photo journals and explain their findings. Have the class discuss possible reasons for the relationships discovered. (For example, gorillas live in Rwanda because they need the lush vegetation and precipitation of the rain forest.) *Note: You might want to prepare a map transparency that shows the habitat of each species. Display the map transparency on an overhead projector as students present their reports.*

UNIT 8 WHERE IN THE WORLD?

This activity is designed to familiarize your students with *Picture Atlas of the World* and to introduce them to Asia. After completing the Tutorial in *Picture Atlas*, students will track down introductory information by answering questions (listed here). Select a timekeeper to time students. The student or group that finds all the answers in the shortest time wins.

Objectives

- To gain a basic introduction to Asia
- To analyze maps, graphs, statistics, pictures, and essays in order to gather information
- To develop or enhance skills in using *Picture Atlas of the World*

Materials

- *Picture Atlas of the World* CD-ROM
- Handout with the Asia questions

THE LESSON

1. Have students complete the Tutorial in *Picture Atlas*.
2. Discuss *Picture Atlas* features and the types of information they provide.
3. Duplicate and distribute copies of the questions. Have students access Asia and research the questions. *Note: Answers are provided here.*
4. The student or group that finds all of the correct answers in the shortest time wins.

ASIA QUESTIONS

A. Pakistan and Israel were established primarily for religious reasons. Name the official religion of each country. *(Pakistan/Islam; Israel/Judaism)*

B. If you were on the road to Mandalay, what country would you be in? *(Myanmar)*

C. In India, many Hindus celebrate the New Year and other important occasions by bathing away their sins in a river they consider holy. Name the river. *(Ganges)*

D. The deepest freshwater lake on the earth is found in Russia. Name it. *(Lake Baikal)*

E. Who is fighting over Nagorno-Karabakh? Why? *(Armenia and Azerbaijan are engaged in an ethnic/religious fight over land.)*

F. What natural disaster occurs frequently in Bangladesh? *(flooding)*

G. Angkor Wat was built by people of an ancient Asian kingdom. Name the kingdom. *(Khmer)*

H. What Chinese river is known as the River of Sorrows? Why? *(Yellow River or Huang He; because it floods and changes course unpredictably, creating much human misery)*

I. What is the lowest point in Asia? *(Dead Sea)*

J. Name a once-divided Southeast Asian country that was unified by a decades-long war ending in the mid-1970s. *(Vietnam)*

K. Name seven of the eight Asian countries created by the breakup of the Soviet Union. *(Georgia, Armenia, Azerbaijan, Uzbekistan, Kazakhstan, Turkmenistan, Kyrgyzstan, Tajikistan)*

L. What is the name for a round tent that is a traditional form of shelter in Mongolia? *(yurt)*

UNIT 9 TOUR—A DIVINE TRIP

A tour of important religious sites in Asia tops the list of popular trips offered by a national travel agency. Company executives want to create a presentation that promotes a special upcoming tour. An itinerary for the sites on the tour must accompany the presentation. Assuming the role of travel-company executives, students will research major religions of Asia as they put together a five-star trip.

Objectives

- To gather information about major religions of Asia
- To enhance map skills
- To develop and enhance skills in using clip-and-copy functions of *Picture Atlas*

Materials

- *Picture Atlas of the World* CD-ROM
- Blank outline maps of Asia (with political boundaries)
- Formatted diskettes
- Colored pencils
- *Exploring Your World*, National Geographic Society (optional)
- Encyclopedias (optional)
- Atlases (optional)
- Almanacs (optional)
- Resources on major religions (optional)

THE LESSON

1. Distribute outline maps of Asia to the class. Then ask students to use *Picture Atlas* to shade in the maps and create color-coded legends showing the distribution of major religions of Asia. *Note: In most countries, several religions are practiced. In* Picture Atlas, *the most widely practiced faith appears first in the Religions entry on the Vital Statistics screen. Younger students might want to create a map showing only the predominant religions in each country, while older students may want to create color-coded patterns to indicate that several religions are practiced. A decision should be made to have students indicate all religions or only the predominant religion for each country.*
2. Have students display and discuss their maps and the distribution patterns they discovered.
3. Explain the travel executive role-playing activity to the class and then organize the class into five groups. Each group might include a president (to lead the group); several researchers (to operate the computer); a cartographer (to figure distances and stops); several recorders (to compile information); and a presenter (to make the promotional presentation to the class). *Note: It may be fun to have students create a company name, logo, and slogan.*
4. Distribute additional blank outline maps to each group. *Note: Groups will use maps to plot a trip and display information (listed in step 6).*
5. Assign each group a religion to research and have groups use the clip-and-copy function of *Picture Atlas* to develop reports. *Note: If students lack adequate background knowledge, make optional resources available.* Have students consult the following photos and captions in various Photo Albums to research and illustrate their presentations:
   - Islam—Saudi Arabia 5; Iraq 2, 5; Indonesia 1; Israel 1; Turkey 2, 7; Lebanon 4, 5; Iran 5; Pakistan 4; Brunei 1; Uzbekistan 1.
   - Buddhism—Myanmar 1, 5; Laos 4; Sri Lanka 2; Indonesia 8; Thailand 6; China 14; Mongolia 4; Nepal 1; Bhutan 1.
   - Hinduism—India 6, 9; Cambodia 5, 6; Indonesia 2; also India, Banaras Video.
   - Judaism—Israel 1, 2, 6; Turkey 6.
   - Christianity—Philippines 7; Turkey 2, 6, 7; Cyprus 2; Armenia 1, 7; Georgia 1, 5; also Text for Bethlehem on Israel Major Sites Map.
6. As student groups develop their presentations, display the following list of factors to include:
   —locations to be visited
   —sights to be seen
   —distances to be traveled between stops
   —climates and physical features to be encountered (for clothing considerations)
   —types of transportation needed
   —languages spoken (for translator purposes)
   —approximate length of tour
   —characteristics of the religion, based on the following questions:
      a. Is the religion built on the life or teachings of a specific person?
      b. If so, what qualities attracted followers to this spiritual leader?
      c. Do followers rely on a specific set of Scriptures?
      d. Do practitioners believe in one deity or many?
      e. Are rituals important? If so, what are they?
7. Have groups make their presentations. For an extra bit of realism, the students might make a promotional poster or pamphlet for their tour.

UNIT 10 RAIN FOREST AT RISK

Tropical rain forests are the most biologically diverse ecosystems on the earth. Located between the Tropics of Cancer and Capricorn, tropical rain forests once blanketed 12 percent of the earth's land. Now they cover about 5 percent. This decline in the earth's tropical rain forests poses a global concern. In this lesson, students explore characteristics of tropical rain forests and some of the causes and effects of deforestation.

Objectives

- To identify physical characteristics associated with tropical rain forests
- To define selected terms associated with tropical rain forests
- To identify possible human uses of tropical rain forests
- To analyze information to determine possible causes, consequences, and controversies associated with tropical rain forest destruction

Materials

- *Picture Atlas of the World* CD-ROM
- Unlabeled world outline maps (8 1/2" X 11" with political boundaries)—one map per student
- Chalkboard and chalk
- Overhead projector and screen
- Transparency sheet and markers (optional)

THE LESSON

1. Select a student to act as a recorder.
2. Display the term "tropical rain forest" on the chalkboard or overhead screen. Ask students to explore their ideas about tropical rain forests. In the brainstorming session, have the recorder list and display student responses in two categories: physical characteristics and human uses of the rain forest.
3. Taking care not to evaluate individual responses, have students review and discuss their ideas.
4. Distribute world outline maps. Instruct students to shade in countries they will investigate. (See list in steps 5 and 7.) Then introduce the following terms: ecosystem, emergent layer, canopy, understory, and floor.
5. Have students use *Picture Atlas* and other sources to research physical characteristics of the rain forest. Have them look at Vital Statistics, Maps, and the following photos and captions in various Photo Albums: Malaysia 1, 3, 6; Brazil 15; Guyana 2, 6; Suriname 1; Peru 9; Venezuela 1, 9; Madagascar 6, 8; Zaire 2, 3, 7. As students research, ask them to come up with a list, developed from their observations, of physical characteristics of a tropical rain forest. The list should include:
   - precipitation—a minimum of 4 inches (10 cm) per month, but generally at least 80 inches (203 cm) per year
   - elevation—usually low, below 4,300 feet (1,312 m)
   - temperature—a mean annual monthly temperature exceeding 75° F (24° C), with an absence of frost

   Note: The list might also include latitude position; soil composition; and the types, diversity, and density of flora and fauna.
6. Compare students' new findings with their original responses (discussed in step 2) noting misconceptions as well as valid ideas.
7. Have students develop a second list researching human uses of the rain forest, using Vital Statistics, Maps, Essays, and the following photos and captions in Photo Albums: Malaysia 2, 4, 6, 7; Myanmar 4; Thailand 7; Guatemala 2; Honduras 1, 4; Brazil 4, 5, 12, 16; Suriname 4, 6; Zaire 2, 3, 7; Madagascar 5, 7; Côte d'Ivoire 2. Again, students should come up with a list, developed from their observations, of human uses of the rain forest and possible consequences that may result from these uses. The list should include:
   - housing
   - agriculture (ranching)
   - construction of roads and towns
   - logging
   - mining
   - hunting
   - medicine
   - rubber tapping
8. Compare students' new findings with their original responses (discussed in step 2), noting misconceptions as well as valid ideas.
9. Discuss students' ideas about possible consequences of human interaction with the tropical rain forest environment. Direct the discussion to include human needs and resource use, focusing on cause-and-effect relationships associated with human uses of rain forests. Conclude the discussion with students' thoughts on controversial issues and on possible outcomes.

UNIT 11 TOUR—VOLCANOES, REEFS, AND ROCK

This tour adventure casts students in the role of the travel manager for a contemporary rock group. The music group wants to schedule several concerts throughout Oceania during a two-week period. They would like to stay near a beautiful beach, go snorkeling near a coral reef, and visit some interesting historic or cultural sites. Assuming the travel manager's role, students will prepare for the music group a report that demonstrates good business sense and provides an interesting vacation.

OBJECTIVES

- To analyze maps, graphs, statistics, pictures, and essays
- To develop or enhance skills in using clip-and-copy functions of *Picture Atlas*

MATERIALS

- *Picture Atlas of the World* CD-ROM
- Encyclopedias (optional)
- Travel brochures (optional)
- Formatted diskettes (optional)
- Overhead transparencies and markers (optional)
- Overhead projector and screen (optional)
- Tapes or CDs that fit students' musical tastes (optional)

THE LESSON

1. Introduce the tour and the role students are to play. Remind them that the concerts need to draw many fans—and thus should be held either in large cities or in an area easily accessible to many people. *Note: To set the mood, you might play music that suits students' tastes.*

2. Have students use *Picture Atlas* to calculate the distance from the West Coast of the United States to Australia or New Zealand. This can be done by placing the edge of a piece of paper on the computer screen or on a printed map and applying the distance to the linear scale. *Note: It may be necessary to help students develop a sense of how long it takes to fly from the West Coast of the U.S. to Australia. To help them understand the travel time and distance, you might provide local or regional time-and-distance comparisons.*

3. Have students prepare an itinerary by researching Maps, Vital Statistics, Photo Albums, and Videos. *Note: You may want to provide additional resources (encyclopedias and travel brochures) for students to use in their research.* Students should use the clip-and-copy function of *Picture Atlas* or overhead transparencies and markers to prepare their reports, which should include:
   - sites for performances (In what cities will they be held?)
   - modes of transportation (If they fly, locate the nearest airport by finding the airplane on the Transportation Map for each country.)
   - accommodations (In what cities or towns will they stay?)
   - clothing tips (What will the weather be like in each site they visit?)
   - currencies (What type of money will they need?)
   - languages spoken (Will they need phrase books?)
   - major sights or activities (What places should they visit? Will they need special clothing or equipment?)

4. Have students present their reports to the class, giving reasons for their decisions and discussing considerations that must be made when traveling great distances in an island region.

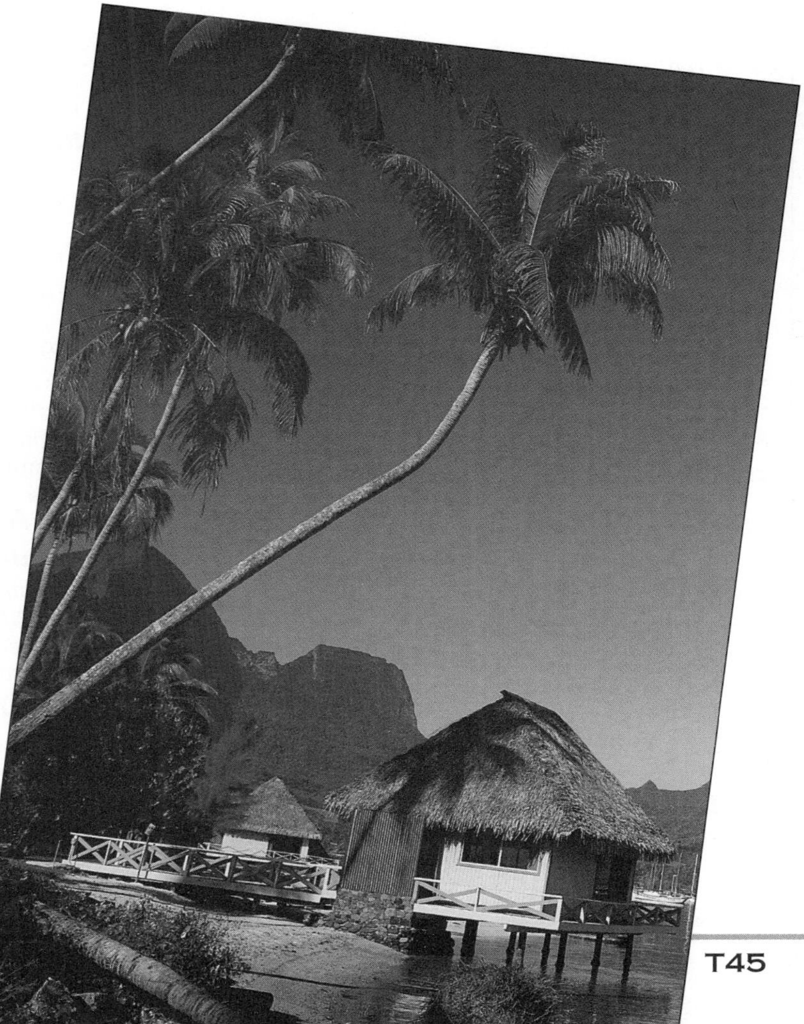

CHAPTER RESOURCES

CHAPTER 1

Readings for the Student

Geography Encyclopedia. London: Usborne, 1992.

McKinney, Kevin. *Everyday Geography.* Garden City: Guild American, 1993.

Readings for the Teacher

Davis, Kenneth C. *Don't Know Much About Geography.* New York: Morrow, 1992.

Grillet, Donnat. *Where On Earth?* New York: Prentice-Hall, 1991.

Multimedia

Smith, David. *Mapping the World By Heart.* Watertown: Tom Snyder Productions, 1992. VHS videocassette, reproducible handouts, 9 regional maps.

The Geography Tutor. Charleston: Cambridge Social Studies, 1991. VHS videocassettes, 18 min. Map and globe terms, types of maps and map projections, map skills.

CHAPTER 2

Readings for the Student

Cross, Wilbur. *Who, What, When, Where, Why—In the World of Geography.* Hauppauge: Barron's, 1991.

McKinney, Kevin. *Everyday Geography.* Garden City: Guild American, 1993.

Readings for the Teacher

Global Geography: Activities for Teaching the Five Themes of Geography. Boulder: Social Sciences Education Consortium, 1990.

Grillet, Donnat. *Where On Earth?* New York: Prentice-Hall, 1991.

Multimedia

CNN World Beat: Exploring Geography. Atlanta: CNN, 1990. VHS videocassette.

The Geography Tutor: Earth's Physical Features. Charleston: Cambridge Social Studies, 1991. VHS videocassette, 18 min.

CHAPTER 3

Readings for the Student

Geography on File: 1994 Edition. New York: Facts On File, 1994.

The World Almanac and Book of Facts 1994. Mahwah: Pharos: Funk and Wagnalls, 1994.

Readings for the Teacher

Cross, Wilbur. *Who, What, When, Where, Why—In the World of Geography.* Hauppage: Barron's, 1991.

Davis, Kenneth C. *Don't Know Much About Geography.* New York: Morrow, 1992.

Multimedia

CNN World Beat: Exploring Geography. Atlanta: CNN, 1990. Four VHS videocassettes, color; 60 min. each.

The Geography Tutor: Weather and Climate. Charleston: Cambridge Social Studies, 1991. VHS videocassette, 18 min.

CHAPTER 4

Readings for the Student

Axtell, Roger E., ed. *Do's and Taboos Around the World.* New York: John Wiley & Sons, 1993.

The Universal Almanac: 1994. Kansas City: Andrews and McMeel, 1993.

Readings for the Teacher

Demko, George J., Agel, Jerome, and Boe, Eugene. *Why in the World: Adventures in Geography.* New York: Anchor/Doubleday, 1992.

Meadows, Donella. *The Global Citizen.* Washington, D.C.: Island Press, 1991.

Multimedia

Geography Search. Watertown: Tom Snyder Productions, 1993. Computer classroom kit, Macintosh.

The Geography Tutor: Global Problems. Charleston: Cambridge Social Studies, 1991. VHS videocassette, 18 min.

CHAPTER 5

Readings for the Student

Canada: The Land. New York: Crabtree, 1993.

Burley, Tony and Latimer, Jim. *Geographic Themes and Challenges.* Edmonton: Arnold Publishing, Ltd., 1990.

Readings for the Teacher

North America. Chicago: Rand McNally, 1990. Map activity program.

Exploring Regions of the United States. Indianapolis: Cram, 1992. Maps, activity sheets.

Multimedia

Discovering Canada. San Ramon: Video Visits, 1992. VHS videocassette, color, 73 min.

Geography of the United States. Highland City: Rainbow, 1992. VHS videocassette, 18 min.

Understanding U.S. Geography Series. Charleston: Cambridge, 1992. VHS videocassettes, 30 minutes.

CHAPTER 6

Readings for the Student

Canada: The People and the Culture. New York: Crabtree, 1993.

The Land and People of Canada. Philadelphia: Lippincott, 1991.

Readings for the Teacher

Discovering America's Past: Customs, Legends, History, and Lore of Our Great Nation. Pleasantville: Reader's Digest, 1993.

Marchant, Garry. *Canada.* Oakland: Compass American Guides, 1991.

Multimedia

Great Cities of the World: Montreal. Princeton: Films for the Humanities and Sciences, Inc., 1992. VHS videocassette, 40 min.

PC USA: Version 2.0 Novato: PC Globe, Inc., 1990. Atlas, database.

CHAPTER 7

Readings for the Student

Canada: Celebrates Multiculturalism. New York: Crabtree, 1993.

Gay, Kathlyn. *Global Garbage: Exporting Trash and Toxic Waste.* New York: Watts, 1992.

Readings for the Teacher

Oh, Garbage! Decisions About Waste Disposal. Boulder: Social Science Education Consortium, 1990. Activity book with reproducible pages.

Meadows, Donella. *The Global Citizen.* Washington, D.C.: Island Press, 1991.

Multimedia

Anglo-America: The United States and Canada. Huntsville: Educational Audio Visual, 1990. Five sound filmstrips, 16-18 min. each.

The United States Today: An Atlas of Reproducible Pages. Wellesley: World Eagle, 1992. Book with reproducible pages.

CHAPTER 8

Readings for the Student

A Survey of World Cultures: Latin America. Culver City: Media Materials: Social Studies School Service, 1991.

Caribbean Connections: Overview of Regional History. Washington, D.C.: EPICA/NECA, 1991.

Readings for the Teacher

Dingle, James and Esler, Jon. *Geography Culture, History, Politics of Latin America.* Denver: CTIR, 1991. Reproducible activity book.

Latin America Today: An Atlas of Reproducible Pages. Wellesley: World Eagle, 1992. Reproducible maps, tables, graphs.

Multimedia

Global Studies with Country Databases. Program 2: Latin America. Hicksville: WorldView Software, 1993. Guide; Apple 5.25" disks or IBM 3.5" disk.

Toward a Better World, Kit 4: Tackling Poverty in Rural Mexico. Washington, D.C.: World Bank, 1992. Student books, pamphlets, sound filmstrip, guide.

CHAPTER 9

Readings for the Student

Latin America: Global Studies. Guilford: Duskin, 1992.

Portraits of the Nations: The Land and the People Series. Argentina; Bolivia; Venezuela. Philadelphia: Lippincott, 1992.

Reading for the Teacher

The Cambridge Encyclopedia of Latin America and the Caribbean. Charleston: Cambridge University Press, 1992.

Multimedia

Global Studies with Country Databases. Program 2: Latin America. Hicksville: WorldView Software, 1993. Guide; Apple 5.25" disk, or IBM 3.5" disk.

Toward a Better World, Kit 4: Tackling Poverty in Rural Mexico. Washington, D.C.: World Bank, 1992. Student books, pamphlets, sound filmstrip, guide.

CHAPTER 10

Readings for the Student

Bender, David L. and Leone, Bruno, eds. *Opposing Viewpoints: Central America.* San Diego: Greenhaven, 1990.

The Rainforests. Charleston: Cambridge Research Group, Ltd., 1991.

Readings for the Teacher

Exploring the Developing World: Life in Africa and Latin America. Denver: CTIR, 1993. Reproducible activities.

Our Only Earth Series: The Future of our Tropical Rainforests. Tucson: Zephyr Press, 1990. Eight reproducible lessons.

Multimedia

Amazon: Paradise Lost? Boston: Christian Science Monitor, 1991. VHS videocassette, 60 min.

Exploring Issues: Deforestation. General Learning Media, 1991. VHS videocassette, 13 min.

CHAPTER 11

Readings for the Student

CIS and Eastern Europe on File. New York: Facts on File, 1993. Binder with maps, charts.

Williams, Brian. *The Kingfisher Reference Atlas: An A-Z Guide to Countries of the World.* New York: Kingfisher, 1993.

Readings for the Teacher

Europe Today: An Atlas of Reproducible Pages. Wellesley: World Eagle, 1993.

Mapping Europe: A Curriculum Unit for Grades 6-10. Stanford: SPICE, 1992. Spiralbound lesson plans with reproducible pages.

Multimedia

Europe on the Brink. Atlanta: CNN, 1991. VHS videocassette, color, 106 min.

CHAPTER 12

Readings for the Student

Kronenwetter, Michael. *The New Eastern Europe.* New York: Watts, 1991.

Riccuiti, Edward. *War in Yugoslavia: The Breakup of a Nation.* Brookfield: Millbrook, 1993.

Readings for the Teacher

Eastern Europe. Stanford: SPICE, 1992. Reproducible activity books.

When Iron Crumbles: Berlin and the Wall. Stanford: SPICE, 1991. Reproducible units.

Multimedia

Eastern Europe. Stanford: SPICE, 1992. Three VHS videocassettes, color.

When Iron Crumbles: Berlin and the Wall. Stanford: SPICE, 1991. VHS videocassette, color.

CHAPTER 13

Readings for the Student

Dunnan, Nancy. *One Europe: Headliner Series.* Brookfield: Millbrook, 1992.

Roberts, Elizabeth. *The New Europe—Maastricht and Beyond: Hotspots.* New York: Gloucester Press, 1993.

Readings for the Teacher

Cipkowski, Peter. *Revolution in Eastern Europe.* Somerset: Wiley, 1991.

Walker, Tim. *War in Yugoslavia: The Return of Nationalism.* Alexandria: Close Up, 1993. Guide and booklet.

Multimedia

Cooperation and Community: The European Community—A Community of Nations. Stanford: SPICE, 1993. CD-ROM, reproducible teaching unit.

Decision Making and the European Communities. Stanford: SPICE, 1992. Activity book with reproducible pages.

CHAPTER 14

Reading for the Student

Diller, Daniel C., ed. *Russia and the Independent States.* Washington, D.C.: Congressional Quarterly, 1993.

Readings for the Teacher

CIS and Eastern Europe on File. New York: Facts On File, 1993. Reproducible maps and charts in binder.

Russia and Neighboring Countries: Political Wall Map. Maplewood: Hammond, 1992. Map distinguishing independent republics, new nations, new city names of former USSR.

The Soviet Union. Carthage: Good Apple, 1993. Activity book with reproducible pages, update of 15 constituent republics of former Soviet Union.

Multimedia

The Volga. Princeton: Films For the Humanities and Sciences, VHS color videocassette, 45 min.

CHAPTER 15

Readings for the Student

Goldman, Minton F., ed. *The Commonwealth of Independent States and Central Eastern Europe: Global Studies.* Guilford: Duskin, 1992.

Opposing Viewpoints: The Breakup of the Soviet Union. San Diego: Greenhaven Press, 1994. Student booklets, teacher's guide.

Readings for the Teacher

A Survey of World Cultures: Russia and the Former Soviet Republics. Culver City: Media Materials: Social Studies School Service, 1991. Six student paperbacks, teacher's manual, photocopy masters.

Hayman, Neil. *Russian History: McGraw Hill's College Core Books.* New York: McGraw Hill, 1993.

Multimedia

The New Russian Revolution. Atlanta: CNN, 1991. VHS videocassette, 47 min.

The Rise and Fall of the Soviet Union. Santa Monica: Xenon Entertainment, 1992. VHS videocassette, color and black and white; 124 min.

CHAPTER 16

Readings for the Student

Great Decisions 1994. New York: Foreign Policy Association, 1994.

Then and Now. Minneapolis: Lerner, 1992. Series includes: Armenia, Azerbaijan, Belarus, Georgia, Kazakhstan, Kyrgystan, Moldova, Russia, Tajikistan, Turkmenistan, Ukraine, Uzbekistan.

Readings for the Teacher

Boyd, Andrew. *An Atlas of World Affairs.* New York: Methuen, 1992.

Great Decisions 1994. New York: Foreign Policy Association, 1994. Activity book with reproducible pages.

Smith, Hedrick. *The New Russians.* New York: Avon, 1991.

Multimedia

The New Russian Revolution. Atlanta: CNN, 1991. VHS videocassette, 47 min.

The Rise and Fall of the Soviet Union. Tapeworm, 1992. VHS videocassette, color and black and white; 124 min.

CHAPTER 17

Readings for the Student

Pimiott, John. *Middle East: A Background to the Conflicts.* New York: Gloucester Press, 1991.

Russell, Malcolm B. *The Middle East and South Asia 1990 (World Today Series).* Washington, D.C.: Stryker-Post, 1990.

Readings for the Teacher

The Middle East Today: An Atlas of Reproducible Pages. Wellesley: World Eagle, 1993.

Steins, Richard. *The Mideast after the Gulf War.* Brookfield: Millbrook, 1992.

Multimedia

The Middle East: A Closer Look. Chicago: SVE, 1991. VHS color videocassette, 17 min.

CHAPTER 18

Readings for the Student

The Middle East. Washington, D.C.: Congressional Quarterly, 1991.

Pearson, Robert P. and Leon F. Clark, eds. *Through Middle Eastern Eyes.* New York: CITE (Center for International Training and Education), 1993.

Spencer, William, ed. *The Middle East: Global Studies.* Guilford: Dushkin, 1992.

Readings for the Teacher

A Survey of World Cultures: Asia and the Middle East. Culver City: Media Materials: Social Studies School Service, 1991. Six student paperbacks, teacher's manual, photocopy masters.

The World's Religions: Understanding the Living Faiths. Pleasantville: Reader's Digest, 1993.

Multimedia

Islam: The Faith and the People. Niles: United Learning, 1991. VHS color videocassette, 60 min., four reproducible worksheets.

The Shifting Sands: A History of the Middle East. New York: NBC News, 1991. VHS videocassette, color and black and white, 48 min.

CHAPTER 19

Readings for the Student

Opposing Viewpoints: Israel. San Diego: Greenhaven Press, 1994. Student booklets, teacher's guide.

Opposing Viewpoints: The Middle East. San Diego: Greenhaven Press, 1994. Student booklets, teacher's guide.

Reading for the Teacher

Yergin, Daniel. *The Prize: The Epic Quest for Oil, Money, and Power.* New York: Simon and Schuster, 1990.

Multimedia

Homeland: A Simulation of Conflict Resolution. Global Awareness Strategies, 1992. Simulation booklet.

World & Eastern Hemisphere. Indianapolis: George F. Cram Company, 1990. 30 desk maps, 30 markers, activity binder, 1 disk, Apple.

CHAPTER 20

Reading for the Student

Bechky, Allen. *Adventuring in East Africa: The Sierra Club Travel Guide to the Great Safaris of Kenya, Tanzania, Rwanda, Eastern Zaire & Uganda.* San Francisco: Sierra Club, 1990.

Readings for the Teacher

Africa Today: An Atlas of Reproducible Pages. Wellesley: World Eagle, 1990.

Grove, A. T. *The Changing Geography of Africa.* New York: Oxford University Press, 1990.

Multimedia

Africa: Continent of Contrasts. Huntsville: Educational Video Network, 1994. VHS color videocassette, 34 min.

Global Studies with Country Databases: Africa. Hicksville: WorldView Software, 1993. Software, Apple, IBM; disks, guide.

CHAPTER 21

Readings for the Student

Chu, Daniel and Skinner, Elliot P. *Roots of Time: A Portrait of African Life and Culture.* Trenton: Africa World Press, 1990.

Spencer, William, ed. *Africa: Global Studies.* Guilford: Dushkin, 1993.

Readings for the Teacher

African History on File. New York: Facts on File, 1993. Binder, 256 pages; reproducible maps and charts.

MacKay, Judith. *The State of Health Atlas.* New York: Touchstone, 1993.

A Survey of World Cultures: Africa. Culver City: Media Materials: Social Studies School Service, 1991. Six student paperbacks, teacher's manual, photocopy masters.

Multimedia

Literacy. New York: United Nations, 1990. VHS color videocassette, 18 min.

Meeting the Third World through Women's Perspectives: Contemporary Women in South Asia, Africa, and Latin America. St. Paul: Glenhurst, 1990. Lesson plans, handouts, VHS video, teacher's guide.

CHAPTER 22

Readings for the Student

Our Divided World: Poverty, Hunger, and Overpopulation. Culver City: Zephyr Press: Social Studies School Service, 1990. Six texts, reproducible pages.

Ricciuti, Edward. *Somalia: A Crisis of Famine and War.* Brookfield: Millbrook, 1993.

Readings for the Teacher

Exploring the Developing World: Life in Africa and Latin America. Denver: CTIR, 1993. Reproducible activities.

Opposing Viewpoints: Africa. San Diego: Greenhaven Press, 1992. Twenty student booklets, teacher's guide.

War: The Global Battlefield. Culver City: Zephyr Press: Social Studies School Service, 1990. Six texts, reproducible pages.

Multimedia

Jazz: A Multimedia History. Chicago: Compton's NewsMedia, 1993. CD-ROM. Multimedia PC standards.

Teaching about Africa: A Continent of Complexities. Denver: Center for Teaching International Relations, 1994. Activity book with reproducible handouts.

CHAPTER 23

Readings for the Student

India Emerges. Emeryville: Diablo, 1992.

India: The Land. New York: Crabtree, 1990.

Readings for the Teacher

Asia Today: An Atlas of Reproducible Pages. Wellesley: World Eagle, 1991. Reproducible masters.

India Emerges. Emeryville: Diablo, 1992. Teacher's guide.

Multimedia

Exploring the Himalayas, Nepal and Kashmir. Chicago: Questar, 1990. VHS color videocassette, 60 min.

India. Victoria, B.C.: VIDEA, 1990. VHS videocassette, 20 min.; spiralbound resource book.

CHAPTER 24

Readings for the Student

India: The People. New York: Crabtree, 1990.

Norton, James K., ed. *India and South Asia: Global Studies*. Guilford: Dushkin, 1993.

Readings for the Teacher

A Survey of World Cultures: Asia and the Middle East. Culver City: Media Materials: Social Studies School Service, 1991. Six student paperbacks, teacher's manual, photocopy masters.

The World's Religions: Understanding the Living Faiths. Pleasantville: Reader's Digest, 1993.

Multimedia

Hinduism: An Ancient Path in a Modern World. Niles: United Learning, 1992. VHS color videocassette, 20 min.

CHAPTER 25

Reading for the Student

India: The Culture. New York: Crabtree, 1990.

Readings for the Teacher

Asia Today: An Atlas of Reproducible Pages. Wellesley: World Eagle, 1991. Reproducible masters.

Our Divided World: Poverty, Hunger, and Overpopulation. Culver City: Zephyr Press: Social Studies School Service, 1990. Six texts, reproducible pages.

War: The Global Battlefield. Culver City: Zephyr Press: Social Studies School Service, 1990. Six texts, reproducible pages.

Multimedia

Rivers of Life: Bangladesh. Washington, D.C.: World Bank, 1990. VHS, 10 min.

World & Eastern Hemisphere. Indianapolis: George F. Cram Company, 1990. 30 desk maps, 30 markers, activity binder, 1 disk, Apple.

CHAPTER 26

Readings for the Student

Atlas of China. Chicago: Rand-McNally, 1990.

Hinton, Harold C. *East Asia and the Western Pacific 1990 (World Today Series)*. Washington, D.C.: Stryker-Post, D.C., 1990.

Readings for the Teacher

Asia Today: An Atlas of Reproducible Pages. Wellesley: World Eagle, 1991. Reproducible masters.

China: A Teaching Workbook. New York: East Asian Curriculum Project: Columbia University, 1991.

CHAPTER 27

Readings for the Student

Japan Emerges. Emeryville: Diablo, 1993.

Ogden, Suzanne ed. *China: Global Studies*. Guilford: Dushkin, 1993.

Readings for the Teacher

A Survey of World Cultures: Asia and the Middle East. Culver City: Media Materials: Social Studies School Service, 1991. Six student paperbacks, teacher's manual, photocopy masters.

Japan Emerges. Emeryville: Diablo, 1993. Teacher's guide.

The World's Religions: Understanding the Living Faiths. Pleasantville: Reader's Digest, 1993.

Multimedia

Exotic Japan. Irvington: Voyager, 1991. CD-ROM interactive program on language, people, and culture of Japan.

CHAPTER 28

Reading for the Student

Lands and Peoples: Asia, Australia, New Zealand, and Oceania. Danbury: Grolier, 1991.

Readings for the Teacher

Asia Today: An Atlas of Reproducible Pages. Wellesley: World Eagle, 1991. Reproducible masters.

U.S.-Japan Relations: The View from Both Sides of the Pacific. Stanford: SPICE, 1993. Fifteen slides, reproducible activity book.

Multimedia

World & Eastern Hemisphere. Indianapolis: George F. Cram Company, 1990. 30 desk maps, 30 markers, activity binder, 1 disk, Apple.

CHAPTER 29

Reading for the Student

Lands and Peoples: Asia, Australia, New Zealand, and Oceania. Danbury: Grolier, 1991. Parks, Carl. *Southeast Asia Handbook*. Chicago: Moon Publishing, 1990.

Readings for the Teacher

Fodor's Southeast Asia. New York: Fodor's Travel Publications, 1991.

Asia Today: An Atlas of Reproducible Pages. Wellesley: World Eagle, 1991. Reproducible masters.

Multimedia

Assignment: Southeast Asia—Vietnam and Cambodia. Boston: Christian Science Monitor, 1993. VHS videocassette color and black and white, 60 min.

CHAPTER 30

Readings for the Student

Lands and Peoples: Asia, Australia, New Zealand, and Oceania. Danbury: Grolier, 1991.

Parks, Carl. *Southeast Asia Handbook.* Chicago: Moon Publishing, 1990.

Readings for the Teacher

A Survey of World Cultures: Asia and the Middle East. Culver City: Media Materials: Social Studies School Service, 1991. Six student paperbacks, teacher's manual, photocopy masters.

The World's Religions: Understanding the Living Faiths. Pleasantvillle: Reader's Digest, 1993.

CHAPTER 31

Readings for the Student

Macmillan, Bill and Fell, Gordon. *Atlas of Economic Issues.* New York: Facts on File, 1992.

Taylor, Robert H., ed. *Asia and the Pacific.* (Handbooks to the Modern World Series). New York: Facts on File, 1990.

Readings for the Teacher

Our Divided World: Poverty, Hunger, and Overpopulation. Culver City: Zephyr Press: Social Studies School Service, 1990. Six texts, reproducible pages.

War: The Global Battlefield. Culver City: Zephyr Press: Social Studies School Service, 1990. Six texts, reproducible pages.

Multimedia

World & Eastern Hemisphere. Indianapolis: George F. Cram Company, 1990. 30 desk maps, 30 markers, activity binder, 1 disk, Apple.

World Resources 1994-95. Oxford: Oxford University Press/World Resources Institute, 1994. CD-ROM. Paperback, teacher's guide, IBM 5.25", 3.5" disk.

CHAPTER 32

Readings for the Student

Kurian, George T. *Facts on File National Profiles: Australia and New Zealand.* New York: Facts on File, 1990.

Lands and Peoples: Asia, Australia, New Zealand, and Oceania. Danbury: Grolier, 1991.

Readings for the Teacher

Dennis, Anthony. *Ticket to Ride: A Rail Journey around Australia.* New York: Prentice-Hall, 1990.

Morrison, Reg. *Australia: The Four-Billion Year Journey of a Continent.* New York: Facts on File, 1990.

Naveen, Ron. *Wild Ice: Antarctic Journey.* Washington, D.C.: Smithsonian Institution Press, 1990.

Multimedia

Regions of the World, Part 2: A Unit of Study. Niles: United Learning, 1990. Two VHS videos, photocopy masters, guide.

CHAPTER 33

Readings for the Student

Collongwood, Dean, ed. *Japan and the Pacific Rim: Global Studies.* Guilford: Duskin, 1993.

Lands and Peoples: Asia, Australia, New Zealand, and Oceania. Danbury: Grolier, 1991.

Macmillan, Bill and Fell, Gordon. *Atlas of Economic Issues.* New York: Facts on File, 1992.

Readings for the Teacher

Dennis, Anthony. *Ticket to Ride: A Rail Journey around Australia.* New York: Prentice-Hall, 1990.

Stansfield, Charles A. *Building Geographic Literacy.* New York: Macmillan, 1992.

CHAPTER 34

Readings for the Student

Besher, Alexander. *The Pacific Rim Almanac.* New York: Harper, 1991.

Lands and Peoples: Asia, Australia, New Zealand, and Oceania. Danbury: Grolier, 1991.

Stewart, John. *Antarctica: An Encyclopedia.* Jefferson: McFarland & Co., 1990.

Readings for the Teacher

Laws, Richard. *Antarctica: The Last Frontier.* New York: State Mutual Books, 1990.

Stansfield, Charles A. *Building Geographic Literacy.* New York: Macmillan, 1991.

Classroom Resources

Meet Your Needs

GEOLAB ACTIVITIES offer hands-on geography-based activities that give students participation in experiential events in geography.

Name ______________________ Date __________ Class ______________

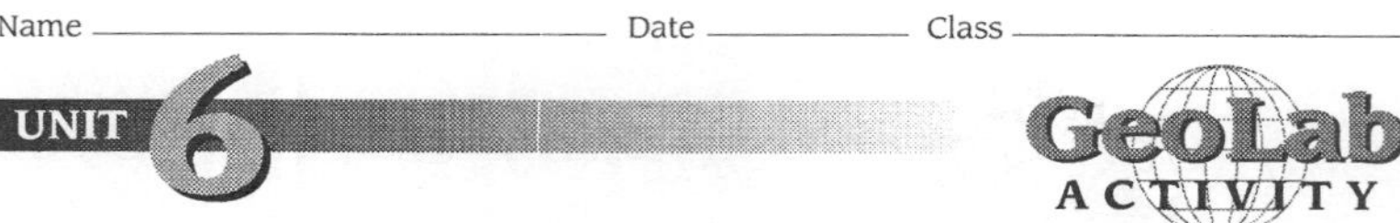

Recycling Paper

Overview

Ancient Egyptians built a civilization along the Nile River. The Egyptians' cultural achievements included building pyramids as tombs for their rulers and developing a calendar with a 365-day year. They also learned how to make paper from papyrus. The papyrus reed—today almost extinct—grew thickly along the banks of the Nile River. Egyptians picked the long papyrus reed and cut it into strips. These strips were then flattened and pressed together. The result was a very coarse paper also called papyrus. After writing on their sheets of papyrus, the Egyptians often rolled them into scrolls. Try making paper like the Egyptians did by recycling some newsprint you have around the house.

Objectives

After completing this activity, you will be able to:

1. make recycled paper.
2. appreciate the technology of ancient Egyptians.

Materials

- 2 full pages of newspaper torn into small pieces
- 2 to 3 cups of water
- a blender (a kitchen mixer or similar hand tool will also work)
- dishpan
- 1 woman's nylon stocking
- wire clothes hanger
- 2 tablespoons of school glue

Procedures

A. Untwist the clothes hanger and form it into a 6-inch square.

B. Carefully slip the nylon stocking around the wire square. Pull the nylon tight so it fits snugly. Tie a knot on both sides to keep it in place.

C. Put some torn newspaper into the blender. Close the lid and turn the blender on *high.* Slowly add the rest of the paper and small amounts of water until the paper disappears and the mixture turns into a large ball of pulp.

D. Put 4 inches of water into the dishpan. Add the glue and pulp mixture and stir.

E. While stirring the mixture, quickly slip the wire frame under the pulp and rest it on the bottom of the dishpan. Then lift the frame slowly as you count to 20. Your wire frame should be covered with pulp mixture.

F. Place the wire frame on paper towels or other flat surface to dry completely. When the paper is completely dry, gently peel it off the frame. Your paper is ready to use!

Actual size is 8 1/2" x 11".

GEOGRAPHY SIMULATIONS bring geography concepts to life by furnishing students with simulations of realistic ventures or events. Students are provided with problems that they must solve as active decision-makers.

NAME ______________________ DATE ______________ CLASS __________

Geography Simulation 7

Colonial Official: Redrawing the Map

Use with Unit 7

Imagine that you live in nineteenth-century Europe. The countries of Europe dominate the globe, and many have vast colonial empires. Yours is such a country. And, as an official of the government, you have a keen interest in your country's colonies. They serve as sources of raw materials and, in turn, markets for finished goods made in your country. Your government believes that expansion of its colonial empire will bring it increased wealth and power.

Your country has recently colonized a new region, mapped below. Managing the region would be simpler if the region were divided into smaller areas or nations. You have been assigned the task of dividing the region into as many smaller nations as you see fit.

Study the map, and think about a logical way to divide the region into nations. Ask yourself these and similar questions: What divisions will make the region easiest to govern and develop? Are there natural regions within the larger region? Are there natural boundaries? When you have decided how to divide the region, use the symbol for international boundary lines shown in the map key to indicate your divisions. Number each nation (1,2,3, and so on). Then answer the questions that follow.

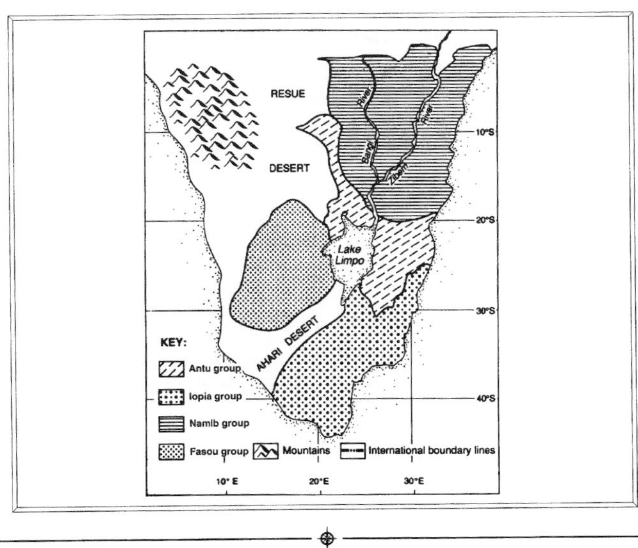

Actual size is 8 1/2" x 11".

UNIT ATLAS STRATEGIES AND ACTIVITIES offer additional physical and cultural geography activities utilizing the Unit Atlases found in the Student Edition.

NAME ______________________ DATE ____________ CLASS ____________

unit 5

Unit Atlas Activity 5-D

For use with Unit 5 — Cultural Geography Activity

Use the Unit Atlas on pages 284–289 of *Glencoe World Geography* to complete the following

1. Compare the communication statistics in the box below. What is the most common means of getting information in Russia? What form of media is least likely to be in a Russian home? How would you describe the difference in the availability of news and information in Russia compared to in the United States? ______________________

	Russia	United States
Population	150 mil.	257 mil.
Television sets	1/3.2 persons	1/1.3 persons
Radios	1/1.5 persons	1/0.5 persons
Telephones	1/6.7 persons	1/1.9 persons
Daily newspaper circulation	112/1,000 persons	255/1,000 persons

Source: *The World Almanac 1994*

2. Which Eurasian republics have no direct access to a large body of water?

3. What major Russian and Eurasian cities are also port cities? On what bodies of water do they lie?

4. What population densities are found above the Arctic Circle? Why do you think the population densities are so low in this area?

5. Compare the number and size of cities in the region east of the Ural Mountains and west of the Ural Mountains. How do you account for any differences?

Actual size is 8 1/2" x 11".

GEOGRAPHY SKILLS ACTIVITIES help students develop and reinforce a wide range of skills involving maps, charts, diagrams, and graphs.

NAME ____________ DATE ____________ CLASS ____________

Geography Skills Activity 5

Using a Grid

Use with Chapter 1.

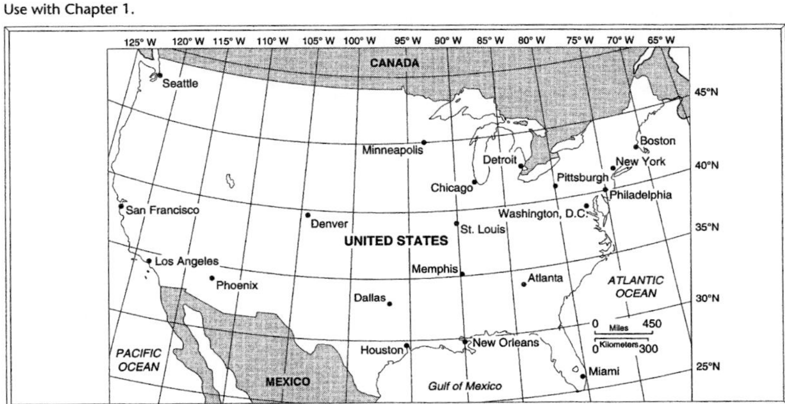

Use the map of the United States above to answer the following questions.

1. In what direction do lines of latitude run? ____________
2. In what direction do lines of longitude run? ____________
3. What city is located along 45° N latitude? ____________
4. What three cities are located closest to 90° W longitude? ____________
5. If you were at 30° N latitude and 75° W longitude, you would be in the ____________
6. What city is located at about 30° N latitude and 95° W longitude? ____________
7. What city is located at about 38° N latitude and 122° W longitude? ____________
8. What city is located at about 47° N latitude and 122° W longitude? ____________
9. What city is located at about 42° N latitude and 71° W longitude? ____________
10. What body of water is located at 25° N latitude and 90° W longitude? ____________
11. Atlanta is located at about ____________ N latitude and ____________ W longitude.
12. Phoenix is located at about ____________ N latitude and ____________ W longitude.

Actual size is 8 1/2" x 11".

BUILDING SKILLS IN GEOGRAPHY is a text-workbook based upon the five geographic themes. A Teacher's Annotated Edition is also available.

Lesson 14 Making Your Own Map

OBJECTIVE

Demonstrate mastery of map and graph skills

This lesson will challenge you to use the skills you have studied in units 1 and 2. If you are not sure how to complete any of the tasks, look back at the lesson or lessons which deal with the skill you need.

Using Your Skills

A Follow the instructions below to complete Map 2–13.

1. Read all the instructions before beginning work. What you do in one step may affect a later step, so you need to be aware of all parts of the project before you begin. Draw *lightly* in pencil in case you need to change something later on.
2. Draw in a coastline with Metro City on the west side of a bay. The coastline has been started for you at the top and bottom of the map. Be sure to draw the bay so that Metro City will be on the shore. Name your bay, and label it on the map.
3. Put a small town on the coast 225 miles southeast of Metro City. Put another small town 150 miles northwest of the center of the first town. Use the correct symbol to show the towns. Name the towns and label them.
4. Draw a small lake in cell F-3 and a swamp in cell E-12. Use the correct symbols for each.
5. Draw a river across the land that empties into the bay. Draw at least two tributaries that feed into the river. Draw rivers that lead into both the lake in cell F-3 and the swamp in E-12.
6. Place the symbol for a gold mine 100 miles southwest of the center of Metro City.
7. Locate the capital city in the exact center of the map with the correct symbol. Name the city and label it.
8. The land in cells C-9, C-10, and D-9 is used for farming. Outline this area with a heavy line. Choose a good color to represent farms, and color the area. Place the same color in the correct place in the legend.
9. Use the correct symbol to locate a small town near the center of the farming area. Name the town and label it.
10. Draw highways to connect the farming town, the capital city, and Metro City. Use the map scale to determine the distances between the towns. Measure from the center of one town to the center of the other town. Write the distances in miles between cities along the highways.
11. Connect the gold mine to the nearest city with a railroad. Then connect this city to Metro City with a railroad. Use the map scale to measure the distances between these places, and write the distances along the railroad.
12. Choose a resource that might be found in the northern part of your country, and a resource that might be found in the southern part of your country. Design a symbol for each resource. Draw the symbols on the map. Then draw the symbols in the blank boxes in the legend. Label the symbols in the legend.

Teacher's note: All student maps will not be identical. The shapes and exact locations of many of the required landforms and resource symbols will vary from student to student and must be looked at individually. Before grading this assignment, you should completely familiarize yourself with the student directions found on this page. The annotated map on the following page is provided for example use only.

86

87

Map 2-

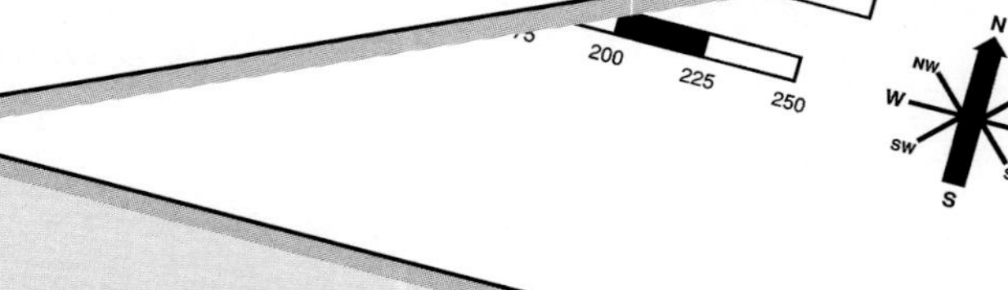

Actual size is 8 1/2" x 11".

GLENCOE WORLD GEOGRAPHY WORKBOOK gives students an opportunity to expand and apply their base of knowledge through reinforcing activities. A Teacher's Annotated Edition is also available.

NAME ____________ DATE ____________ CLASS ____________

Workbook Activity

Europe Today: Living in Europe

Use with Chapter 13, Section 1

The nations of Europe hope to share a common currency by the year 1999. Today each nation has its own currency unit. When the nations' businesspeople buy and sell goods among themselves, they must convert the value of the goods in their currency into the value of another currency. The rate of exchange, however, changes from day to day; the supply of and demand for the currencies determine the changes.

The table below gives a recent rate of exchange between the United States dollar and the currencies of several European nations. Study the table and answer the questions that follow.

Exchange Rates

Country	Currency unit	How many U.S. dollars to buy each unit	How many foreign units for U.S. $1
Austria	schilling	$ .11	9.38
France	franc	$ .22	4.55
Germany	Deutsche mark	$ .74	1.34
Great Britain	pound	$1.82	.55
Greece	drachma	$ .006	172.44
Hungary	forint	$ .02	64.57
Ireland	punt	$1.95	.51
Italy	lira	$ .0008	1,259.45
Netherlands	guilder	$ .66	1.51
Norway	krone	$ .18	5.55
Portugal	escudo	$ .009	116.56
Spain	peseta	$ .01	95.61
Switzerland	Swiss franc	$ .85	1.17

1. According to the table, how many dollars did a sweater that sells for 20 pounds cost? Later, the rate of exchange rose to $1.95 per pound. How many dollars did the sweater cost then?

   $36.40; $39

2. What will happen if the rate of exchange for Irish punts is low compared to other European currencies when much of Europe converts to a common currency? How will it affect workers and consumers in Ireland? The Irish will lose when they exchange their punts for the common currency. Irish workers may have to renegotiate for higher salaries in the new currency, and consumers will have comparatively less cash to buy goods than other Europeans whose rate of exchange was high at the time.

Actual size is 8 1/2" x 11".

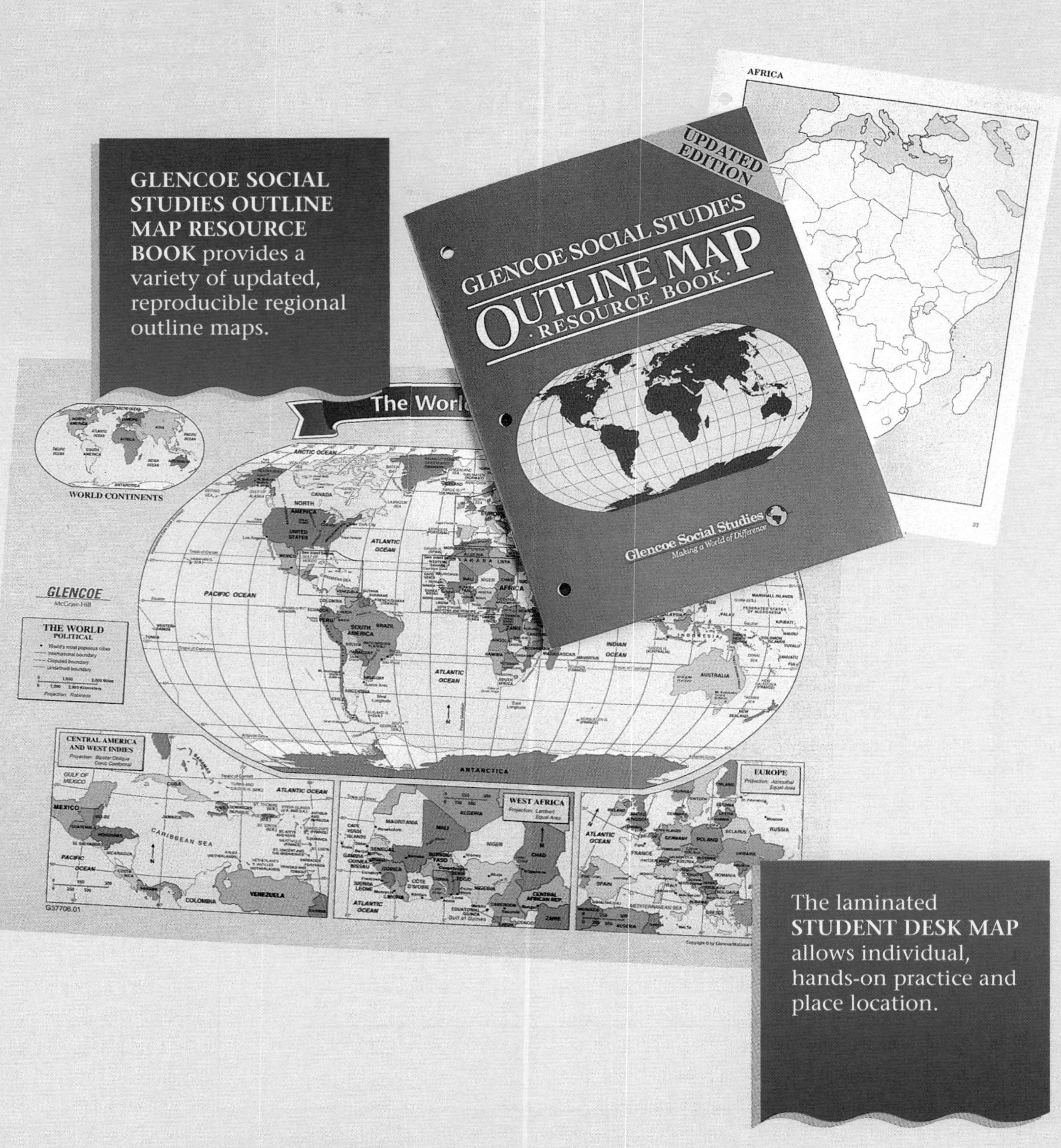

GLENCOE SOCIAL STUDIES OUTLINE MAP RESOURCE BOOK provides a variety of updated, reproducible regional outline maps.

The laminated **STUDENT DESK MAP** allows individual, hands-on practice and place location.

MAPS ON FILE I, MAPS ON FILE II, and **GEOGRAPHY ON FILE** offer excellent teaching and resource materials that include a wide selection of both regional and individual country maps, as well as special purpose maps and statistical information. Now you can have daily access to these comprehensive resources from **Facts On File**.

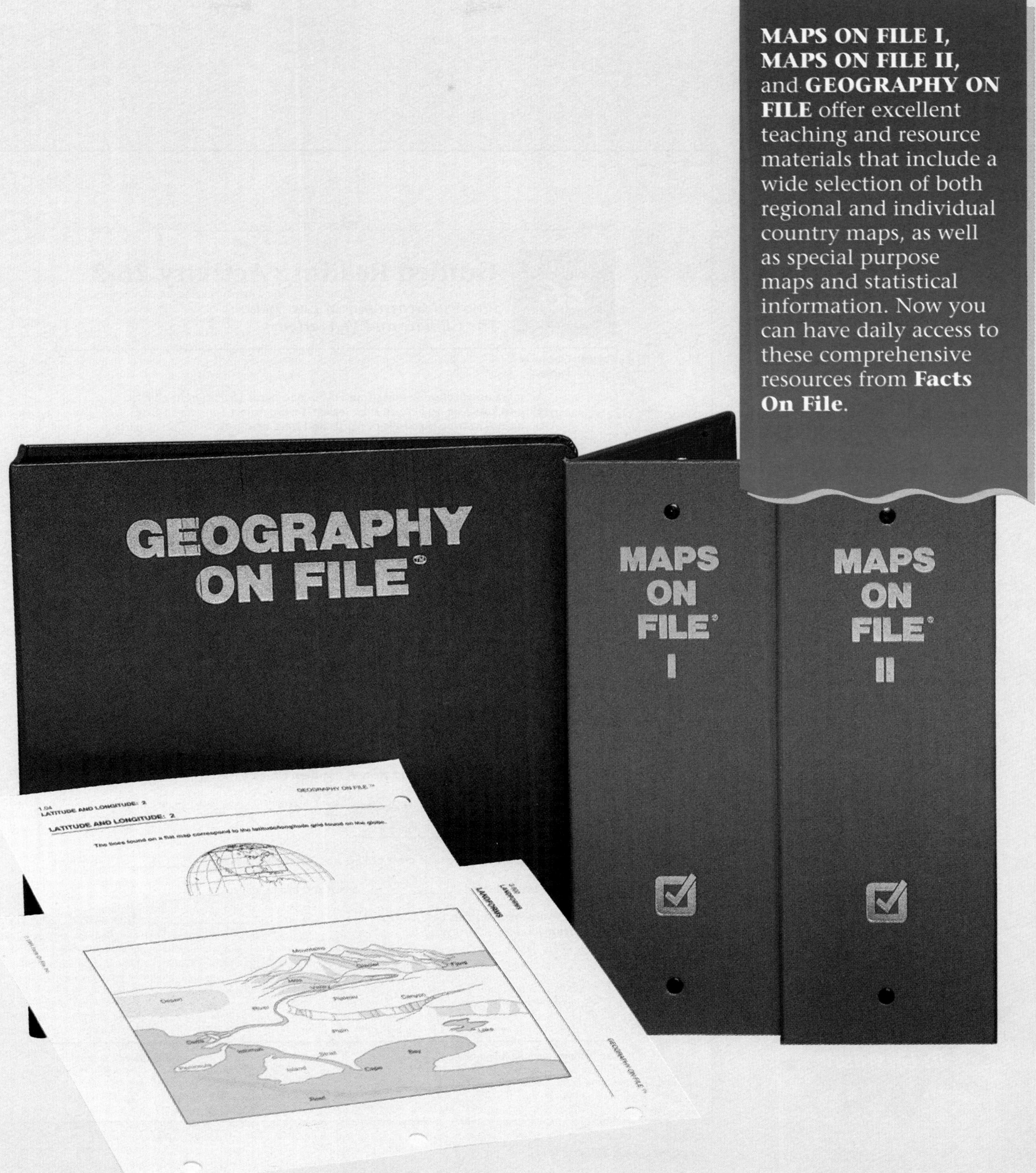

GUIDED READING ACTIVITIES for each section of every chapter help students master lesson concepts as they read the text. These activities are particularly useful for students who have difficulty with reading comprehension.

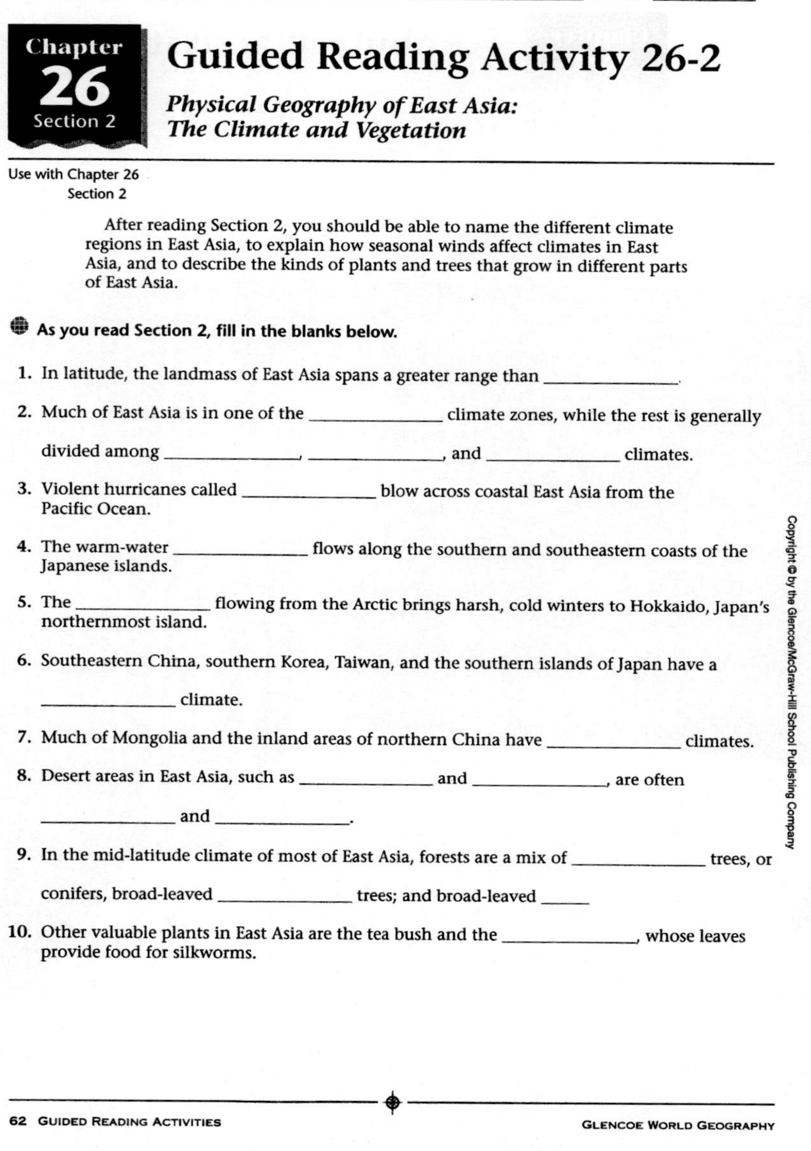
NAME ______________ DATE ______________ CLASS ______________

Chapter 26 Section 2

Guided Reading Activity 26-2

Physical Geography of East Asia: The Climate and Vegetation

Use with Chapter 26
Section 2

After reading Section 2, you should be able to name the different climate regions in East Asia, to explain how seasonal winds affect climates in East Asia, and to describe the kinds of plants and trees that grow in different parts of East Asia.

As you read Section 2, fill in the blanks below.

1. In latitude, the landmass of East Asia spans a greater range than ______________.
2. Much of East Asia is in one of the ______________ climate zones, while the rest is generally divided among ______________, ______________, and ______________ climates.
3. Violent hurricanes called ______________ blow across coastal East Asia from the Pacific Ocean.
4. The warm-water ______________ flows along the southern and southeastern coasts of the Japanese islands.
5. The ______________ flowing from the Arctic brings harsh, cold winters to Hokkaido, Japan's northernmost island.
6. Southeastern China, southern Korea, Taiwan, and the southern islands of Japan have a ______________ climate.
7. Much of Mongolia and the inland areas of northern China have ______________ climates.
8. Desert areas in East Asia, such as ______________ and ______________, are often ______________ and ______________.
9. In the mid-latitude climate of most of East Asia, forests are a mix of ______________ trees, or conifers, broad-leaved ______________ trees; and broad-leaved _____
10. Other valuable plants in East Asia are the tea bush and the ______________, whose leaves provide food for silkworms.

62 GUIDED READING ACTIVITIES GLENCOE WORLD GEOGRAPHY

Actual size is 8 1/2" x 11".

VOCABULARY ACTIVITIES encourage and assist students in learning the unique vocabulary of geography. Each activity reinforces the key geography vocabulary that appears in boldfaced type in the corresponding chapter of the student edition.

NAME ______________________ DATE ______________ CLASS __________

Chapter 21

Vocabulary Activity 21

The Cultural Geography of Africa South of the Sahara

Complete the following statements. Then use the missing words to fill in the answer blanks in the puzzle. After you have completed the puzzle, read down the column of boxed letters to find the mystery word.

1. The average annual income earnings of a nation's population is called ________________ .
2. ________________ is the movement of people from rural to urban areas.
3. People with similar histories and cultures are known as an ________________ .
4. Millions of Africans died during the ________________ .
5. When a large number of people can read and write, a nation is said to have a high ________________ .
6. The principle of equal voting rights is called ________________ .
7. ________________ refers to popular culture promoted by the media.
8. ________________ involves the passing down of legends.
9. ________________ are large groups of people related to each other.

What government policy in South Africa slowly ended as a result of the steps taken toward greater racial equality in the country?

7. _ [_] _ _ _ _ _ _ _ _ _
1. [_] _ _ _ _ _ _ _ _ _ _ _ _ _
9. _ _ [_] _
2. _ [_] _ _ _ _ _ _ _ _ _
5. _ _ [_] _ _ _ _ _ _ _ _
8. _ _ _ _ [_] _ _ _ _ _ _
3. [_] _ _ _ _ _ _ _ _ _ _
6. _ _ [_] _ _ _ _ _ _ _ _ _ _ _
4. _ _ [_] _ _ _ _ _ _ _ _ _

GLENCOE WORLD GEOGRAPHY — VOCABULARY ACTIVITY 21

Also Available in Spanish

Actual size is 8 1/2" x 11".

RETEACHING ACTIVITIES help students focus on the main ideas and themes presented in each chapter. These activities are particularly useful for students who have not yet mastered the basic ideas of the chapter.

NAME ______________ DATE ______________ CLASS ______________

Chapter 19

Reteaching Activity 19

North Africa and Southwest Asia Today

Use with Chapter 19

Using the information in Chapter 19, fill in each of the "Information Organizer" boxes. There are clues in each box to help you complete this activity.

INFORMATION ORGANIZERS

1. Impact of Oil
- A. increased industrial growth in the region
- B. ______________
- C. thousands of jobs created
- D. ______________

2. Causes of Highway Development
- A. ______________
- B. need to link major cities with oil fields and seaports

3. Reasons for Increased Air Traffic
- A. location of North Africa and Southwest Asia at the crossroads of three continents
- B. ______________
- C. ______________

4. Impact of the Formation of OPEC
- A. members gain greater control over production and price of oil
- B. ______________

5. Reasons for the Aswan High Dam
- A. ______________
- B. improve irrigation
- C. ______________
- D. create an artifical lake for Egypt's fishing industry

6. Effects of Aswan High Dame
- A. millions of acres of land open to irrigation
- B. ______________
- C. fertile alluvial soil trapped above dam and lost to farming
- D. ______________
- E. ______________

GLENCOE WORLD GEOGRAPHY RETEACHING ACTIVITIES 19

Actual size is 8 1/2" x 11".

PERFORMANCE ASSESSMENT STRATEGIES AND ACTIVITIES provide opportunities to implement alternative assessment strategies both in your classroom and field settings. The booklet also contains rubrics and classroom assessment lists that give teachers the flexibility of monitoring student progress or allowing students to evaluate themselves.

NAME ______________________ DATE ______________ CLASS __________

Performance Assessment

FOLKTALES

Use with Chapter 15

BACKGROUND

Did you know that you can learn about the geography, history, beliefs, values, customs, heritage, and ethnic background of a people through reading its folktales? As people tell stories about themselves, they often select the things that they feel are most important about their culture to weave into the stories. "Folktale detectives" study this form of literature to learn about a culture.

TASK

Your task is to write an "authentic" folktale based on information you have learned about a culture.

AUDIENCE

Students like you are the audience for your folktale.

PURPOSE

The purpose of your folktale is to both entertain the reader and to inform the reader about the important characteristics of the culture in which the folktale is based.

PROCEDURE

1. Refer to the Performance Task Assessment Lists for a Folktale, an Idea Web/Organizer, and Drawing/Illustration to help you plan your project.
2. Choose a nationality and a time period for your folktale.
3. Gather information on heritage, customs, beliefs, language, history, government, technology, and geography and organize it into an idea/graphic organizer.
4. Write a draft of your folktale. Keep in mind that the people of the culture about which this folktale is written should like what they read about themselves.
5. Share the draft with a friend and get his or her opinion.

ASSESSMENT

1. Use the Performance Task Assessment Lists mentioned above to check your work.
2. Add missing elements, or improve elements.
3. Make illustrations to include with your folktale.
4. Do a final self-assessment before you give your folktale to your teacher.

Actual size is 8 1/2" x 11".

NAME ______ DATE ______ CLASS ______

Unit 7

Unit 7 Test

NAME ______ DATE ______ CLASS ______

Chapter 31

Chapter 31, Test B

CHAPTER AND UNIT TESTS (Forms A and B) provide for evaluation of student understanding of the main facts, themes, and ideas at regular points throughout the text.

NAME ______ DATE ______ CLASS ______

Chapter 31

Chapter 31, Test A

Southeast Asia Today

I MATCHING

Match each item in Column A with the items in Column B. Write the correct letters in the blanks. (4 points each)

_____ **1.** sharp, curved knives

_____ **2.** a place where goods can be unloaded, stored, and reshipped without the payment of import duties

_____ **3.** 10,308-foot (3,142 m) volcano on Bali

_____ **4.** Philippine volcano

_____ **5.** an area of low atmospheric pressure surrounded by circulating winds

_____ **6.** capital of Thailand

_____ **7.** organization that helps to finance agricultural, transportation, and industrial-development projects throughout Southeast Asia

_____ **8.** country that has become rich from the oil industry

_____ **9.** one of the leading tin producers of Southeast Asia

_____ **10.** country whose economic growth has been slowed for many years due to a policy of isolationism

A. Indonesia
B. interdependent
C. Myanmar
D. Brunei
E. Bangkok
F. Mount Pinatubo
G. free port
H. shipbuilding
I. Ring of Fire
J. forestry
K. Malaysia
L. ADB
M. cyclone
N. Gunung Agung
O. sickles

II MULTIPLE CHOICE

In the blank at the left, write the letter of the choice that best completes the statement or answers the question. (5 points each)

_____ **11.** Malaysia is
a. one of the most economically successful countries in Southeast Asia.
b. one of the most economically disadvantaged countries in Southeast Asia.
c. a country in which there is very little opportunity for advancement.
d. a country that relies heavily on industry.

GLENCOE WORLD GEOGRAPHY CHAPTER TESTS 121

Actual size is 8 1/2" x 11".

SECTION QUIZZES offers section-by-section evaluation, providing you with a quick, effective way to monitor the daily progress of your students.

NAME ______________ DATE ____________ CLASS __________

Chapter 1 Section 2

Section Quiz

How Geographers Look at the World: Geography Skills Handbook

2 S

NAME ______________ DATE ____________ CLASS __________

Chapter 1 Section 1

Section Quiz

How Geographers Look at the World: Themes of Geography

I MATCHING

Match each item in Column A with the items in Column B. Write the correct letters in the blanks.

_____ 1. a description of the earth
_____ 2. two halves
_____ 3. a way of life
_____ 4. interdependent
_____ 5. pattern that makes it possible to find places on the earth's surface

A. relying on each other
B. geography
C. hemispheres
D. culture
E. grid system

II MULTIPLE CHOICE

In the blank at the left, write the letter of the choice that best completes the statement or answers the question.

_____ 6. Location is an important geographic theme because
A. not every place on the earth can be described in absolute terms.
B. places on the earth can only be located by using vertical lines on maps.
C. places on the earth can only be described in absolute terms.
D. every place on the earth can be described in both absolute and relative terms.

_____ 7. Movement is an important geographic theme because
A. throughout history there have been movements of large groups of people from one place to another.
B. groups of people move only for better land.
C. there have been movements of people throughout history.
D. movements of people only occurred in ancient times.

_____ 8. Regions are important in the study of geography because they
A. are based only on the physical features of the earth.
B. make the study of geography more manageable.
C. are based on certain human characteristics.
D. help people understand the earth only in terms of its similarities.

_____ 9. Geographers use history to help them understand
A. how people in different places are governed.
B. the culture of people in different places.
C. the way that places looked in the past.
D. the interdependence of people's economic activities.

_____ 10. Geographers use economics to help them understand
A. how and where services are provided.
B. the relationships between the physical environment and the social structure of different societies.
C. the way people governed themselves in the past.
D. societies in different places throughout the world.

GLENCOE WORLD GEOGRAPHY — SECTION QUIZZES 1

Also Available in Spanish

Actual size is 8 1/2" x 11".

ENVIRONMENTAL ISSUES HANDBOOK requires students to look at current environmental issues in a realistic, problem-solving way.

NAME DATE CLASS

Environmental Issues

Unit 2

SHOULD THE UNITED STATES CONTINUE TO USE LANDFILLS TO DISPOSE OF SOLID WASTE?

The United States is one of the world's richest nations and its standard of living is among the highest in the world. But with wealth comes certain problems. One such problem is dealing with the massive amounts of solid waste produced by an affluent society.

In the past, landfills and dumps were the accepted method of disposing of garbage. However, over the last 30 years questions have arisen about the wisdom of burying garbage in the ground. The contamination of groundwater by pollutants leaking from old landfills has made headlines. In communities throughout the country, voters vehemently oppose proposals to build landfills in their neighborhoods.

If we are no longer going to bury our garbage in landfills, how are we going to get rid of it? The most popular alternatives are recycling, "waste-to-energy" systems, in which trash is burned to produce electricity, and incineration, or high-temperature burning. Currently, about two-thirds of our garbage is buried in landfills (see accompanying chart).

Should the United States continue to depend on landfills as the primary method of solid waste disposal?

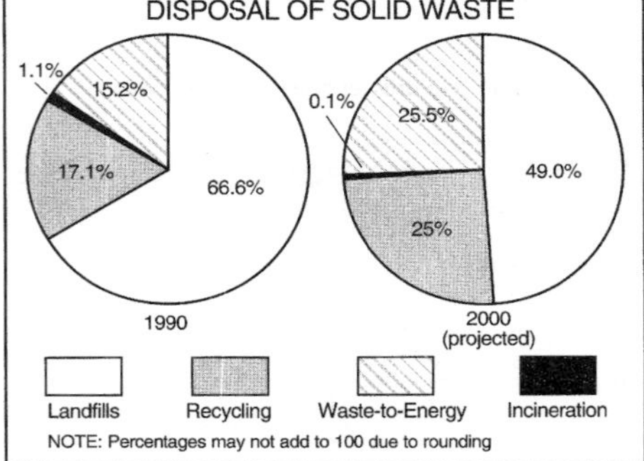

Read the pro and con arguments below. Then answer the questions under Examining the Issue. Use another sheet of paper for your answers if necessary.

PRO Opposition to landfills is based at least partly on ignorance, says Clark Wiseman, an economics professor from Spokane, Washington. Wiseman claims that modern landfills are much safer and less offensive than those from even 10 years ago. He also believes that the size of our waste-disposal problem has been exaggerated. And, according to Wiseman, the rush toward recycling and other alternatives to landfills is misguided.

At the current rate, if all the nation's solid waste for the next 500 years were piled or buried in a single landfill to a depth of 100 yards, this "national landfill" would require a square site less than 20 miles on a side. . . . The amount of solid waste generated nationally has grown at only a 2 percent average rate over the past 30 years, considerably less than the growth of GNP. This means that our "throwaway society" is actually throwing out a progressively smaller share of its output.

The solid waste problem is not one of space, economy, or even cost. The problem is a political one—that of siting new landfills. . . . The choking off of a viable alternative like low cost and environmentally sound landfills is wasteful of society's resources.

Clark Wiseman, *CQ Quarterly*, March 20, 1992 (excerpted from *The Wall Street Journal*, July 18, 1991)

Actual size is 8 1/2" x 11".

ENRICHMENT ACTIVITIES extend and expand each lesson through motivating activities that engage students in meaningful analyses and interpretations of geography. They encourage creativity and stimulate thinking.

NAME _______________ DATE _______________ CLASS _______________

Chapter 12

Enrichment Activity 12

The State of Vatican City

Use with Chapter 12.

The State of Vatican City is the official name for the independent state located within Rome, Italy. Vatican City is about 109 acres (44 hectares) in size and has a population of about 1,000. Vatican City is the headquarters of the Roman Catholic Church.

The government of Vatican City is led by the Pope, the head of the Roman Catholic Church. Like other governments in Europe, Vatican City has its own constitution, money system, postal system, seal, and flag. Citizenship is granted to those people living in Vatican City because of their special duties to the Pope.

Some people visit Vatican City on church business and government business. In addition, each year thousands of tourists visit Vatican City to see the historical architecture and some of the richest art treasures in the world.

Use the map and the reading to answer the following questions.

1. Where is the State of Vatican City located? _______________
2. What is the function of Vatican City? _______________
3. What is the size of Vatican City? _______________
4. In what general direction is the audience hall from Government Palace? _______________
5. How far is it from the helicopter pad to the Vatican Gardens? _______________

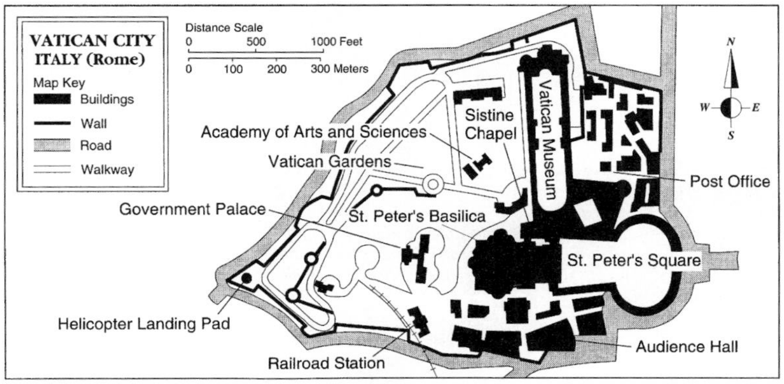

Actual size is 8 1/2" x 11".

AFRICAN HISTORY ON FILE from **Facts on File** includes more than 300 reproducible maps, charts, and drawings to help you present Africa's rich history.

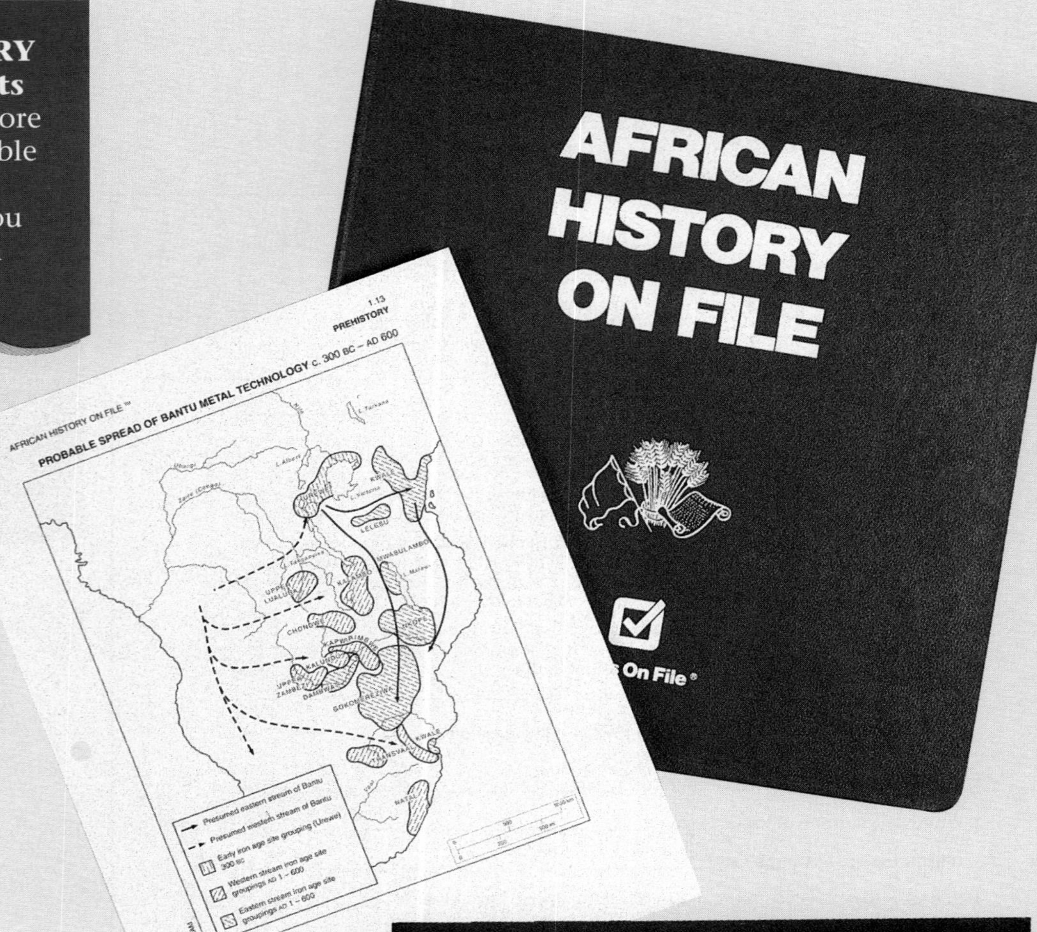

CURRENT EVENTS UPDATE booklets provide supplemental activities and define significant current political, social, and economic events on a biannual basis.

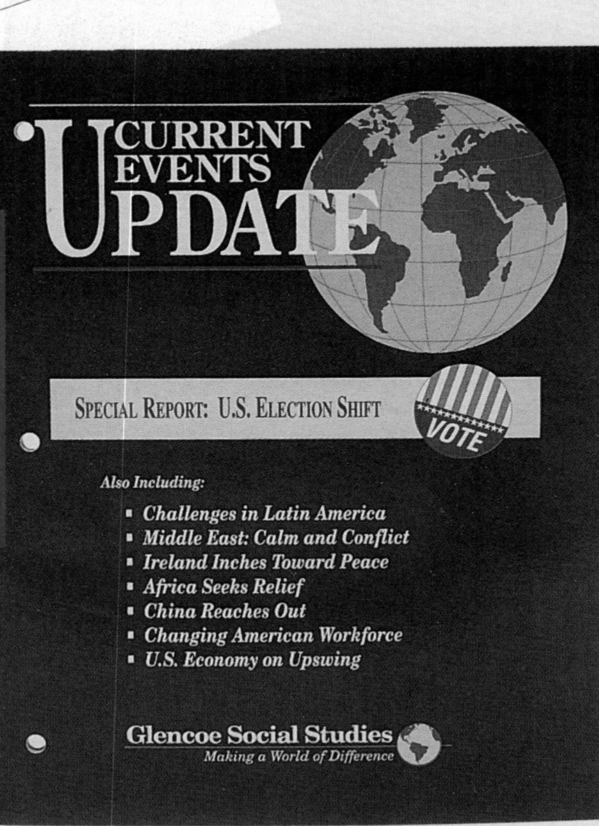

WORLD LITERATURE: 20TH CENTURY SELECTIONS is a collection of works designed to enable students to become familiar with the literary work of people in different regions of the world. These selections have been taken from a variety of sources and represent the creative talents of major writers of the 20th century.

NAME ______________ DATE ______________ CLASS ______________

don't know," I said, finally.

The English children in the front of the class—there were about eight or ten of them—giggled and twisted around in their chairs to look at me. I sat down quickly and opened my eyes very wide, hoping in that way to dry them off. The little girl with the braids put out her hand and very lightly touched my arm. She still didn't

me; only "apple" was new and incomprehensible.

When it was time for the lunch recess, I followed the girl with braids out onto the veranda. There the children from the other classes were assembled. I saw Premila at once and ran over to her, as she had charge of our lunchbox. The children were all opening packages and sitting down to eat

NAME ______________ DATE ______________ CLASS ______________

World Literature: 20th Century Selections

Use with Unit 8

About the Author

Santha Rama Rau was born in Madras, India, the daughter of a civil servant in the British-controlled administration. Rau has incorporated her diverse experiences into a body of work that includes travel writing, fiction, and autobiographical stories. The following excerpt describes a situation in which a young girl is forced to change her Indian name for a name that is more "British" and more easily pronounced.

GUIDED READING

As you read this passage from *By Any Other Name,* think how you would feel if you were asked to give up something very personal because it was not pleasing to someone else.

By Any Other Name

–Santha Rama Rau

The head mistress . . . smiled at her [own] helpless inability to cope with Indian names. . . . "Suppose we give you pretty English names. Wouldn't that be more jolly? . . ."

That first day at school is still, when I think of it, a remarkable one. At that age, if one's name is changed, one develops a curious form of dual personality. I remember having a certain detached and disbelieving concern in the actions of "Cynthia," but certainly no responsibility. Accordingly, I followed the thin, erect back of the headmistress down the veranda to my classroom feeling, at most, a passing interest in what was going to happen to me in this strange, new atmosphere of school. . . .

I suppose there were about a dozen Indian children in the school—which contained perhaps forty children in all—and four of them were in my class. They were all sitting at the back of the room, and I went to join them. I sat next to a small, solemn girl who didn't smile at me. She had long, glossy-black braids and wore a cotton dress, but she still kept on her Indian jewelry—a gold chain around her neck, thin gold bracelets, and tiny ruby studs in her ears. Like most Indian children, she had a rim of black kohl[1] around her eyes. The cotton dress should have looked strange, but all I could think of was that I should ask my mother if I couldn't wear a dress to school, too, instead of my Indian clothes.

I can't remember too much about the proceedings in class that day, except for the beginning. The teacher pointed to me and asked me to stand up. "Now, dear, tell the class your name."

I said nothing.

"Come along," she said, frowning slightly. "What's your name, dear?" "I

Actual size is 8 1/2" x 11".

FOODS AROUND THE WORLD gives students a glimpse of different cultures by looking at foods from various regions of the world. Included are suggestions for planning and organizing with students a Multicultural Food Fair.

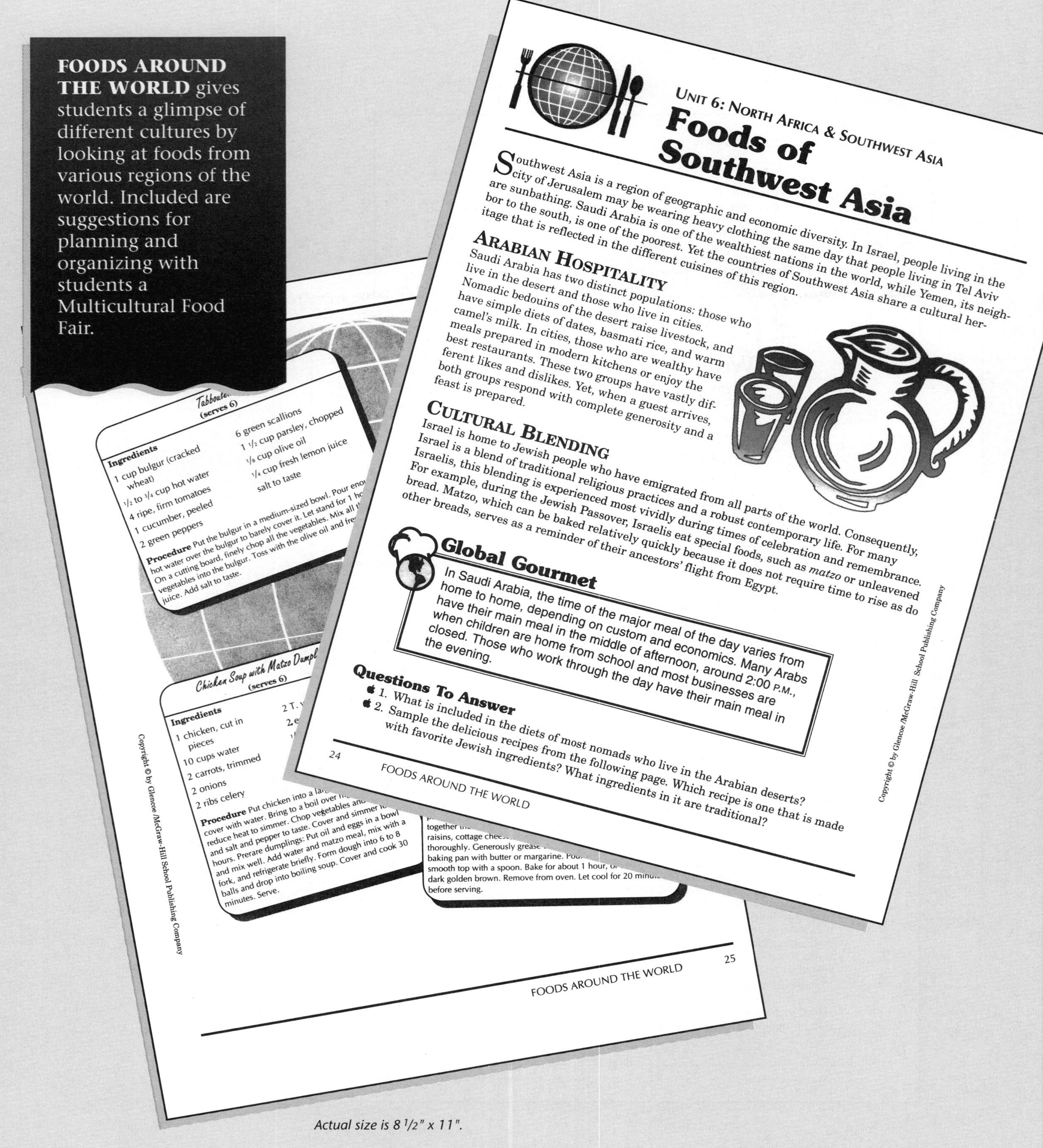

Unit 6: North Africa & Southwest Asia

Foods of Southwest Asia

Southwest Asia is a region of geographic and economic diversity. In Israel, people living in the city of Jerusalem may be wearing heavy clothing the same day that people living in Tel Aviv are sunbathing. Saudi Arabia is one of the wealthiest nations in the world, while Yemen, its neighbor to the south, is one of the poorest. Yet the countries of Southwest Asia share a cultural heritage that is reflected in the different cuisines of this region.

Arabian Hospitality

Saudi Arabia has two distinct populations: those who live in the desert and those who live in cities. Nomadic bedouins of the desert raise livestock, and have simple diets of dates, basmati rice, and warm camel's milk. In cities, those who are wealthy have meals prepared in modern kitchens or enjoy the best restaurants. These two groups have vastly different likes and dislikes. Yet, when a guest arrives, both groups respond with complete generosity and a feast is prepared.

Cultural Blending

Israel is home to Jewish people who have emigrated from all parts of the world. Consequently, Israel is a blend of traditional religious practices and a robust contemporary life. For many Israelis, this blending is experienced most vividly during times of celebration and remembrance. For example, during the Jewish Passover, Israelis eat special foods, such as *matzo* or unleavened bread. Matzo, which can be baked relatively quickly because it does not require time to rise as do other breads, serves as a reminder of their ancestors' flight from Egypt.

Global Gourmet

In Saudi Arabia, the time of the major meal of the day varies from home to home, depending on custom and economics. Many Arabs have their main meal in the middle of afternoon, around 2:00 P.M., when children are home from school and most businesses are closed. Those who work through the day have their main meal in the evening.

Questions To Answer

1. What is included in the diets of most nomads who live in the Arabian deserts?
2. Sample the delicious recipes from the following page. Which recipe is one that is made with favorite Jewish ingredients? What ingredients in it are traditional?

24 FOODS AROUND THE WORLD

Copyright © by Glencoe/McGraw-Hill School Publishing Company

Tabboule...
(serves 6)

Ingredients
1 cup bulgur (cracked wheat)
1/2 to 3/4 cup hot water
4 ripe, firm tomatoes
1 cucumber, peeled
2 green peppers
6 green scallions
1 1/2 cup parsley, chopped
1/8 cup olive oil
1/4 cup fresh lemon juice
salt to taste

Procedure Put the bulgur in a medium-sized bowl. Pour eno... hot water over the bulgur to barely cover it. Let stand for 1 ho... On a cutting board, finely chop all the vegetables. Mix all th... vegetables into the bulgur. Toss with the olive oil and fre... juice. Add salt to taste.

Chicken Soup with Matzo Dumpl...
(serves 6)

Ingredients
1 chicken, cut in pieces
10 cups water
2 carrots, trimmed
2 onions
2 ribs celery

Procedure Put chicken into a lar... cover with water. Bring to a boil over... reduce heat to simmer. Chop vegetables and... and salt and pepper to taste. Cover and simmer... hours. Prerare dumplings: Put oil and eggs in a bowl and mix well. Add water and matzo meal, mix with a fork, and refrigerate briefly. Form dough into 6 to 8 balls and drop into boiling soup. Cover and cook 30 minutes. Serve.

...together ... raisins, cottage chee... thoroughly. Generously grease ... baking pan with butter or margarine. Pou... smooth top with a spoon. Bake for about 1 hour, o... dark golden brown. Remove from oven. Let cool for 20 minu... before serving.

25 FOODS AROUND THE WORLD

Copyright © by Glencoe/McGraw-Hill School Publishing Company

Actual size is 8 1/2" x 11".

FOCUS ON WORLD ART PRINTS are poster-size prints that enhance student appreciation of fine arts and cultural expressions. The 25 posters are accompanied by a teacher's guide.

Kitagawa Utamaro
Reflected Beauty from the series *Seven Women Seen in a Mirror*
c. 1790. Color woodblock print. 36.3 x 24.1 cm (14⅓ x 9½").
Honolulu Academy of Arts, Honolulu, Hawaii. The James A. Michener Collection.

WORLD HISTORY AND ART TRANSPARENCIES give students an understanding of how art acts as a tool when learning about history and geography. Each transparency is accompanied by a teaching strategy and a student activity.

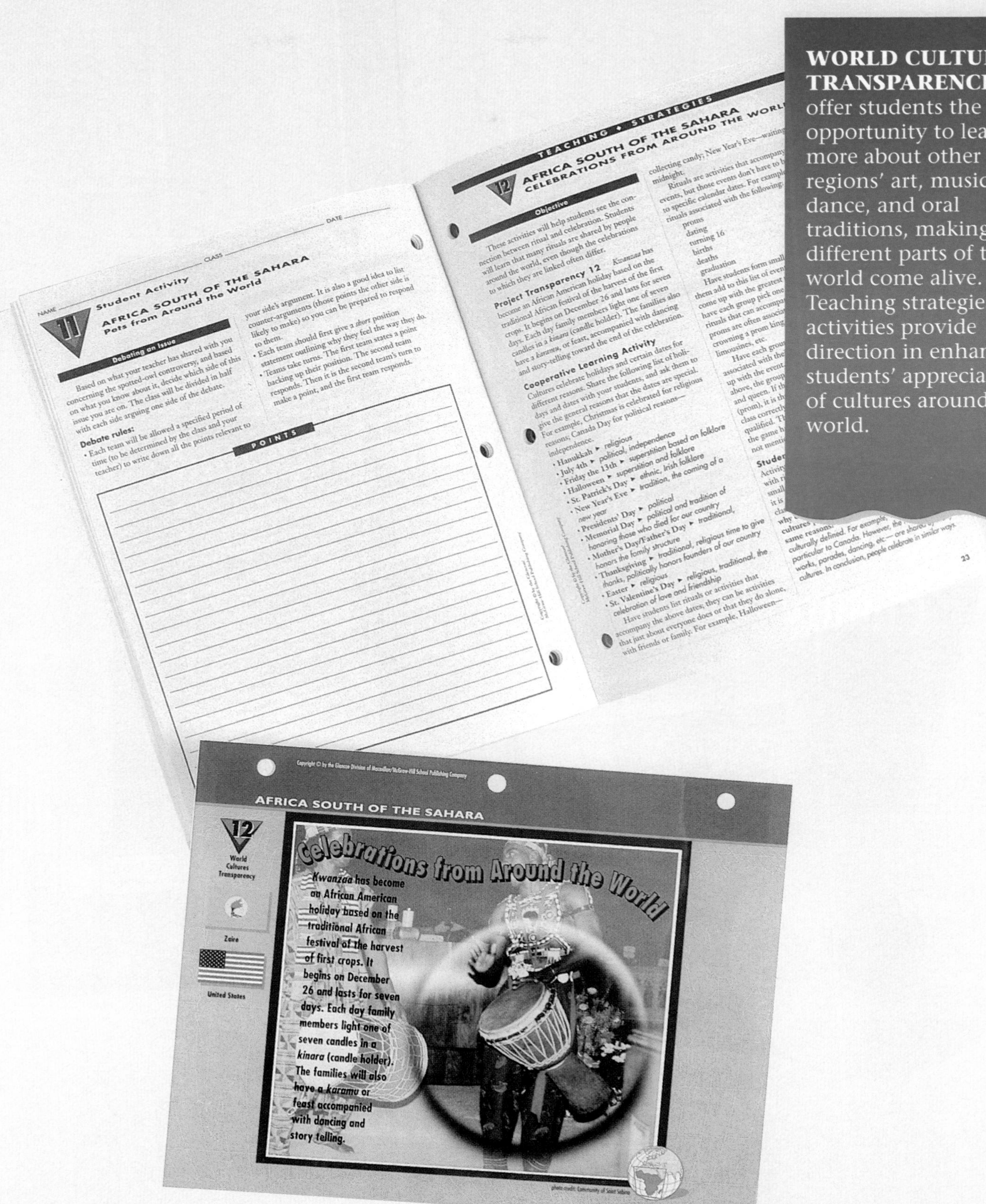

WORLD CULTURES TRANSPARENCIES offer students the opportunity to learn more about other regions' art, music, dance, and oral traditions, making different parts of the world come alive. Teaching strategies and activities provide direction in enhancing students' appreciation of cultures around the world.

WORLD MUSIC: CULTURAL TRADITIONS brings students into contact with music representing many cultures and regions of the world.

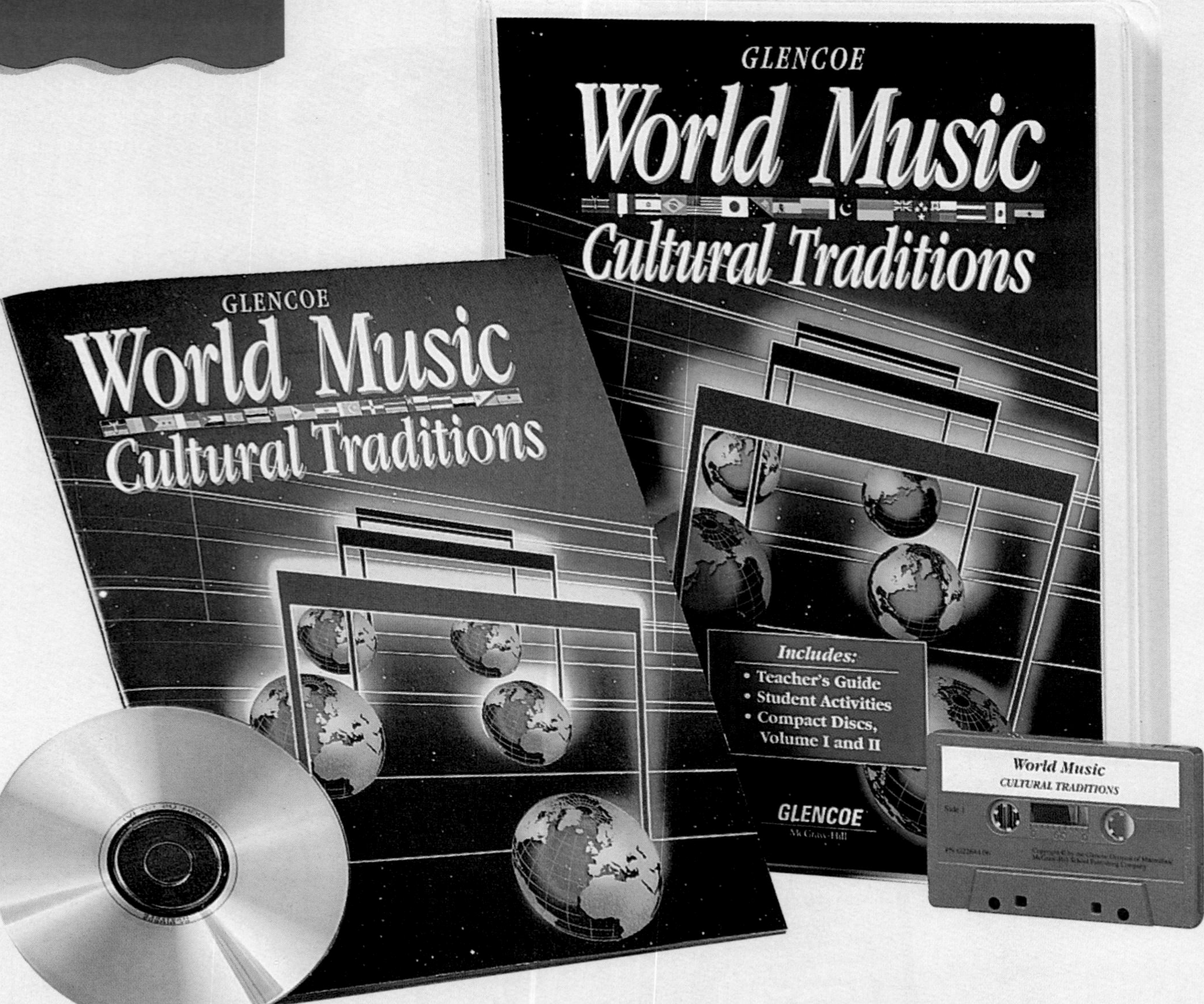

SPANISH RESOURCES include *Spanish Vocabulary Activities, Spanish Reteaching Activities, Spanish Section Quizzes,* and *Spanish Guided Reading Activities.* Spanish Chapter Digests Audiocassettes: Activities and Tests are also available.

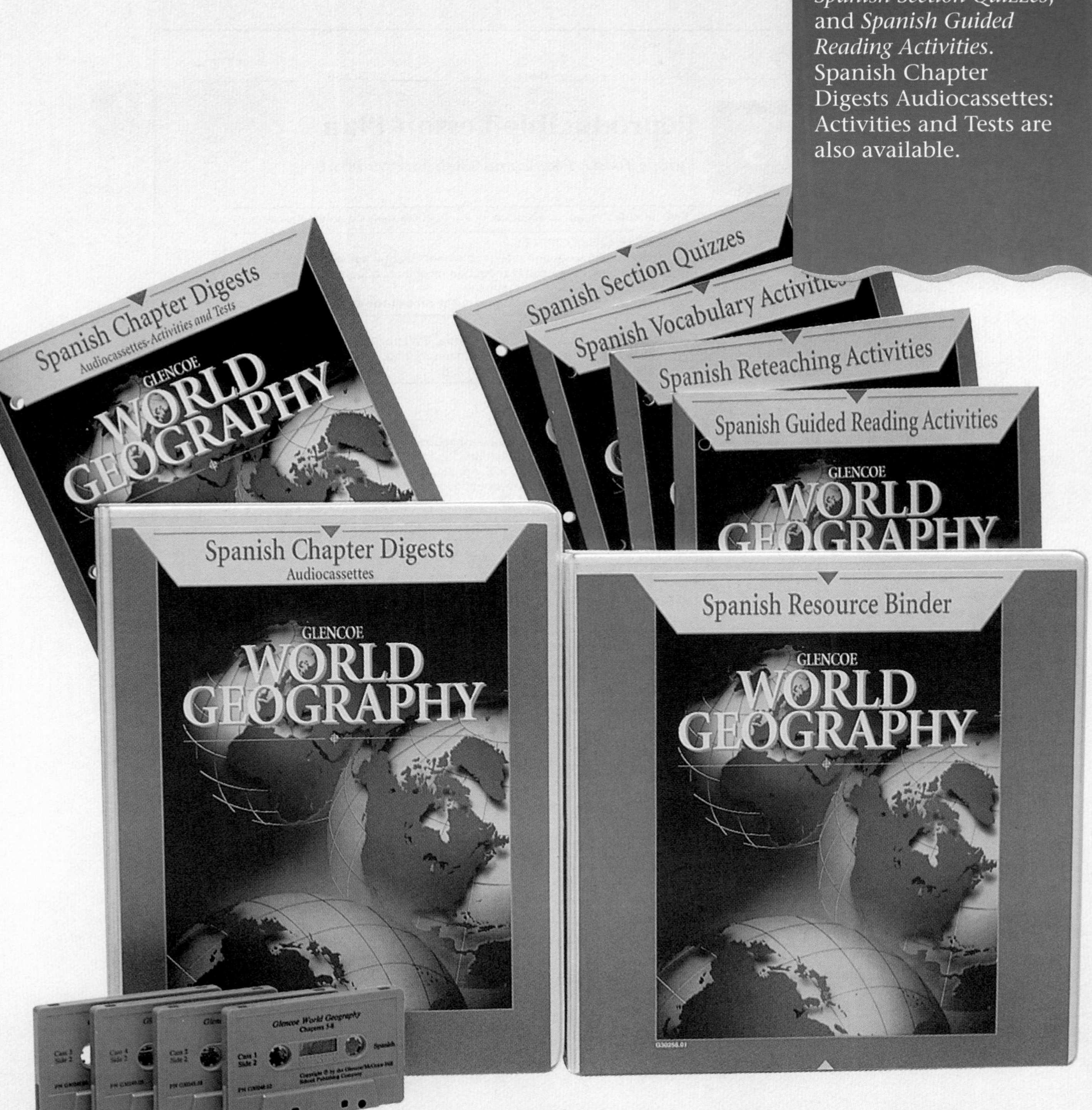

REPRODUCIBLE LESSON PLANS help you organize your instruction and shorten your preparation time. Their convenient format allows you to see, at a glance, all the strategies and supplementary materials available for a given lesson, giving you many options to fit your teaching style.

...E ____________ DATE ____________ CLASS ____________

...hapter 13 ...ection 2

Reproducible Lesson Plan

Europe Today: People and Their Environment

TWE: Teacher's Wraparound Edition   TCR: Teacher's Classroom Resources

LESSON OBJECTIVES
- __ Analyze the causes and effects of environmental pollution in Europe.
- __ Explain why cleanup and reduction of pollution requires cooperation among European governments.
- __ Identify steps Europeans are taking to protect the environment.

FOCUS
- __ Bellringer and Motivational Activities, TWE, p. 270
- __ *Section Focus Transparencies,* Transparency 13-2, TCR
- __ Preteaching Vocabulary, TWE, p. 270

TEACH

Guided Practice
- __ Activities, TWE, pp. 271-272
- __ *Political Map Transparencies,* Transparency 4, TCR
- __ *Geography Skills Activities,* Activity 13, TCR
- __ Geography Connection, TWE, pp. 280-281
- __ Geography and the Environment Video Program
- __ GTV: Planetary Manager
- __ STV: Atmosphere

Independent Practice
- __ Activities, TWE, p. 273
- __ *Guided Reading Activities,* Activity 13-2, TCR
- __ *Spanish Guided Reading Activities,* Activity 13-2, TCR

ASSESS
- __ Check for Understanding, TWE, p. 274
- __ Meeting Lesson Objectives, TWE, p. 274
- __ *Section Quizzes,* 13-2, TCR
- __ Chapter Highlights, TWE, p. 277
- __ Vocabulary PuzzleMaker Software, Chapter 13
- __ Audiocassettes (English and Spanish), Chapter 13
- __ *Audiocassette Activities and Tests* (English and Spanish), Chapter 13
- __ Mindjogger Videoquiz, Chapter 13
- __ *Chapter and Unit Tests,* Chapter 13 Form A and Form B, TCR
- __ Testmaker

RETEACHING
- __ *Reteaching Activities* (English and Spanish), Activity 13, TCR
- __ Student Self-Test and Review Software

ENRICHMENT
- __ *Enrichment Activities,* Activity 13, TCR

CLOSE
- __ Close, TWE, p. 275

32 REPRODUCIBLE LESSON PLANS   GLENCOE WORLD GEOGRAPHY

Actual size is 8 1/2" x 11".

The **BLOCK SCHEDULING IMPLEMENTATION GUIDE** outlines the benefits of block scheduling and how to use it in your classroom.

IMPLEMENTING BLOCK SCHEDULING IN YOUR CLASSROOM

Glencoe World Geography includes components that will facilitate your use of block scheduling and make possible a more in-depth study of important social studies concepts. A wealth of blackline masters allows students to work individually to reinforce their understanding of previously taught material. Because students are in the classroom for extended periods, they may use many of these materials during class sessions. Teachers can then immediately identify students who are having difficulty with major concepts and plan remediation activities—either individually or in peer groups.

Blackline masters suited for such uses include:

- *Guided Reading Activities*
- *Geography Skills Activities*
- *Reteaching Activities*
- *Vocabulary Activities*
- *Enrichment Activities*
- *Unit Atlas Strategies and Activities*
- *Outline Map Resource Book*

In addition to the above components, *Glencoe World Geography* provides unique opportunities for individual and group projects, multimedia applications, and extension.

INDIVIDUAL AND GROUP PROJECTS

Each unit of the Student Edition begins with *Geography Journal* activity. The Teacher's Wraparound Edition offers suggestions to assist you as you guide your students in the completion of this activity and as you evaluate each student's work. The extended class periods of block scheduling allow students to work on these activities in class, thus providing for immediate peer and teacher feedback. Teachers can then assess which students might need extra help with certain concepts as well as those students who might need additional challenges. Teachers can then make appropriate assignments during the class and launch the students onto the projects under teacher supervision. In this way, teachers can make certain that they have assessed each student's specific needs accurately and given the proper follow-up assignments.

Assessment Tools

An assessment component ideally suited for block scheduling is *Performance Assessment Strategies and Activities.* Designed to be completed individually or in groups, these strategies allow you to assess student progress. One of the most useful aspects of this approach is that students monitor and reinforce each other's progress as they work in groups. The additional uninterrupted time that block scheduling provides helps students concentrate on the task at hand.

Vocabulary PuzzleMaker allows students to work individually to challenge and reinforce vocabulary proficiency through the use of crossword puzzles and word searches that you create.

Actual size is 8 1/2" x 11".

The **BAR CODE CORRELATION** provides numerous frame number and bar code references that will enable you to incorporate a wide range of full motion videodiscs in your classroom. *Glencoe World Geography* is correlated to NATIONAL GEOGRAPHIC SOCIETY videodiscs, as well as ABCNews InterActive™, Reuters, and Glencoe videodiscs.

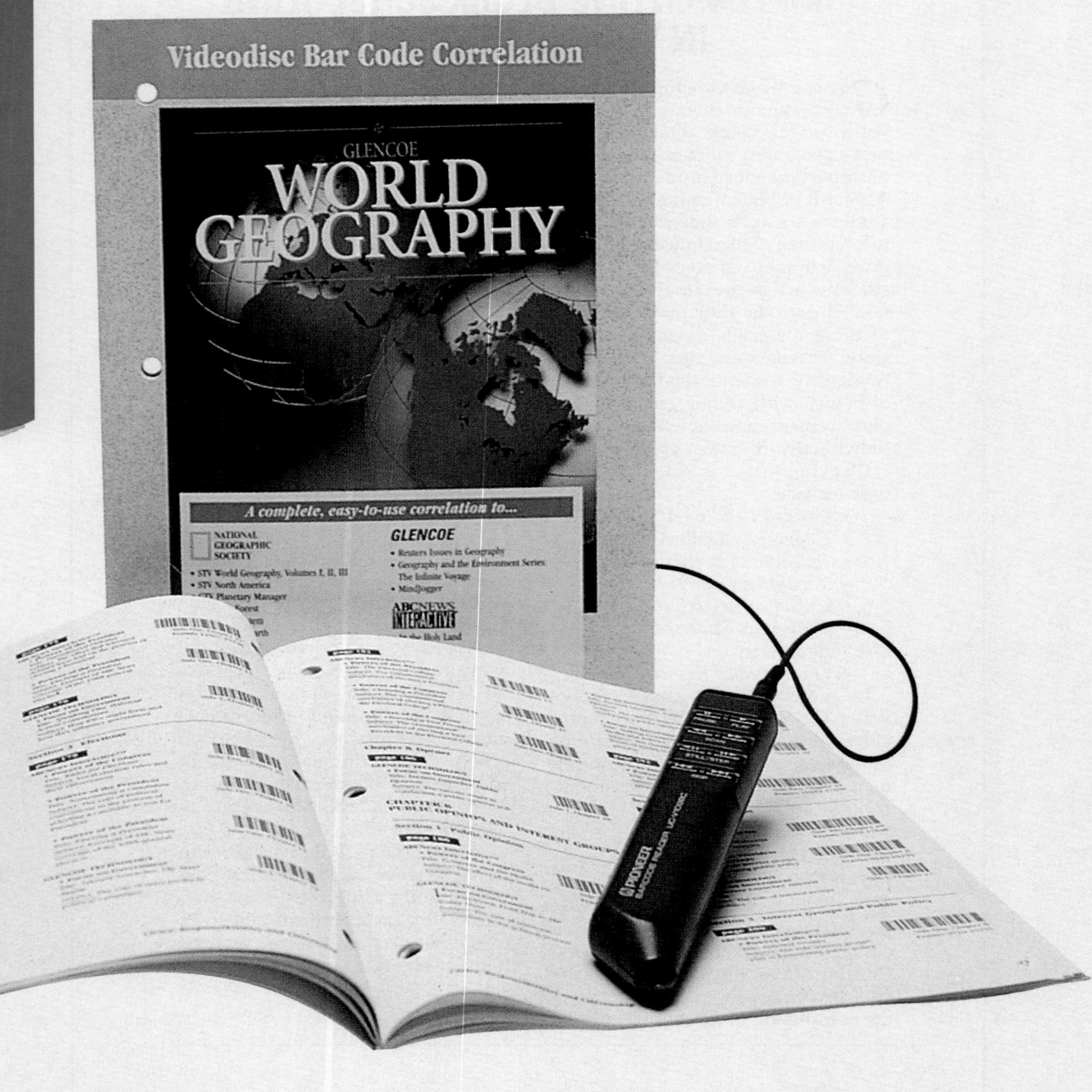

CHAPTER DIGEST AUDIOCASSETTES provide summaries of chapter content for review, reteaching, or for use when you do not have time to teach a particular chapter. Each summary is accompanied by a chapter activity and test based on the content of the audiocassettes.

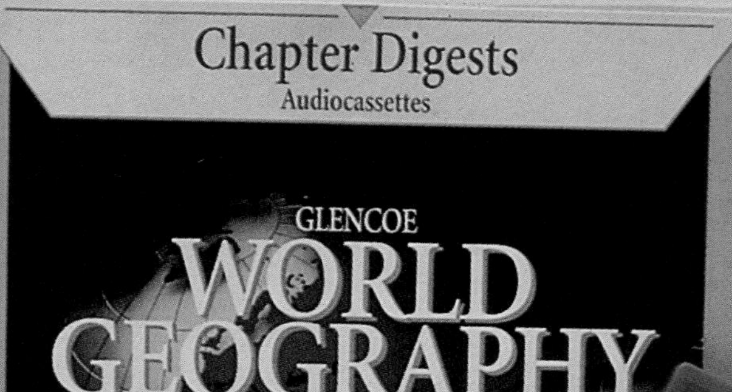

Spanish Chapter Digest Audiocassettes are also available

The following multiple-use **TEACHING TRANSPARENCIES** are included in this binder:

- Unit Map Overlay Transparencies
- Political Map Transparencies
- World Cultures Transparencies

SECTION FOCUS TRANSPARENCIES highlight a major point of emphasis for each of the 81 sections of the student text. Designed to be used as a bellringer activity, each transparency presents a challenge for the student in the form of a graph, cartoon, or other graphic.

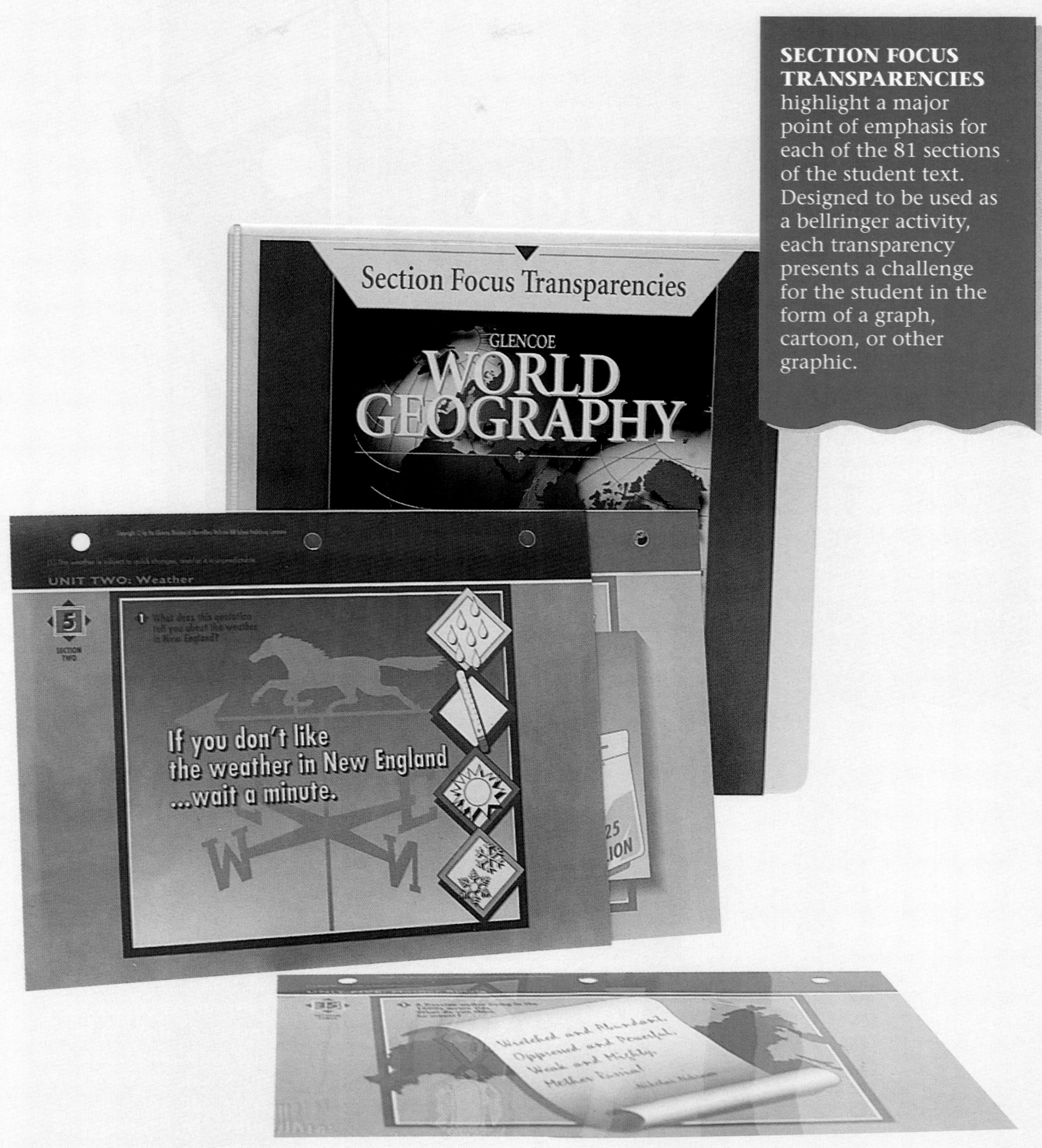

VOCABULARY PUZZLEMAKER SOFTWARE allows you to create crossword puzzles and word search puzzles to reinforce the geographic terms used in each chapter.

The **TESTMAKER** software lets you customize section, chapter, and unit tests. Use the existing database to create tests covering one or more sections, chapters, or units. In addition, you can edit the thousands of database questions or add your own. The software is available in Macintosh or DOS formats.

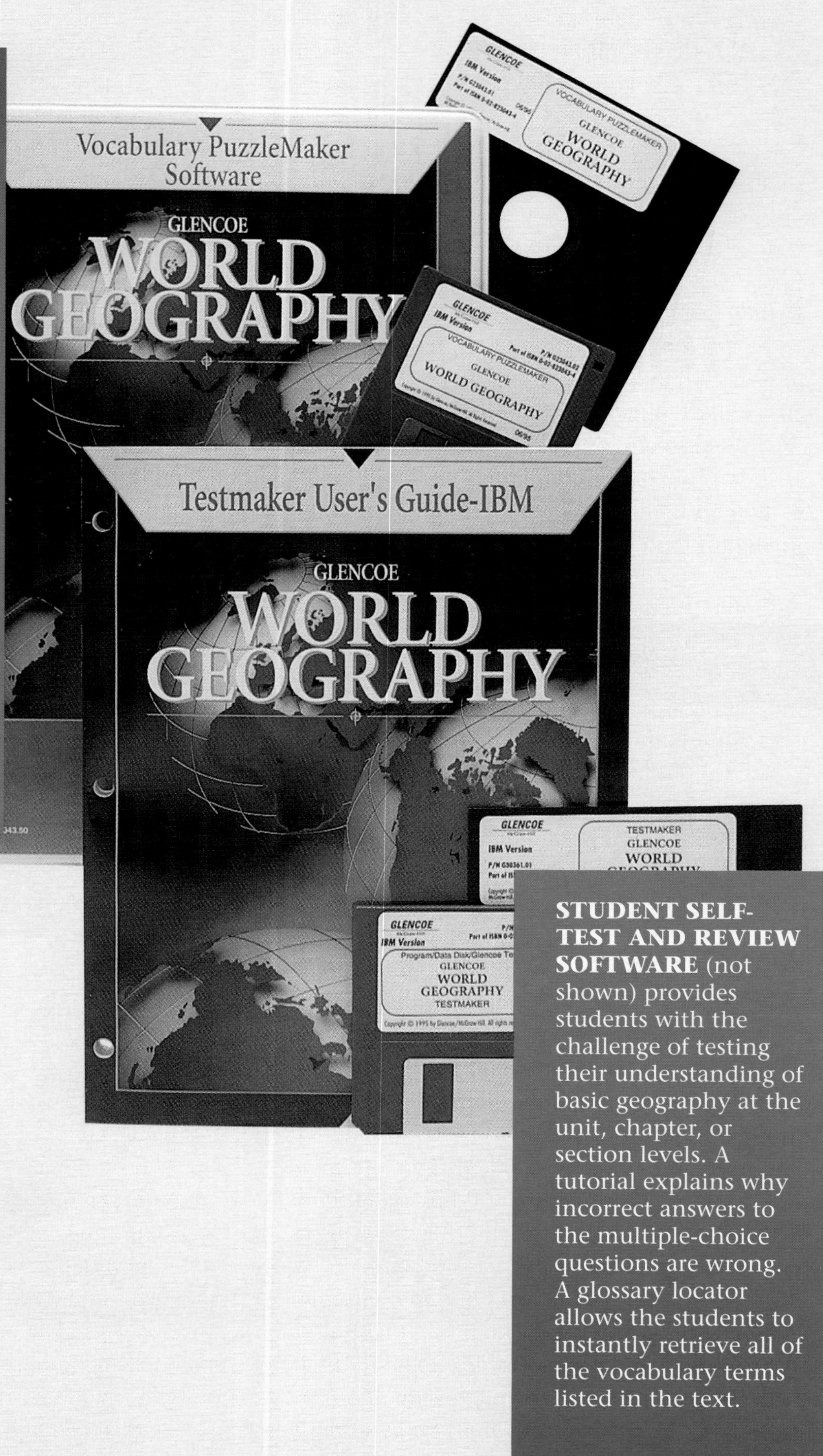

STUDENT SELF-TEST AND REVIEW SOFTWARE (not shown) provides students with the challenge of testing their understanding of basic geography at the unit, chapter, or section levels. A tutorial explains why incorrect answers to the multiple-choice questions are wrong. A glossary locator allows the students to instantly retrieve all of the vocabulary terms listed in the text.

NATIONAL
GEOGRAPHIC
SOCIETY

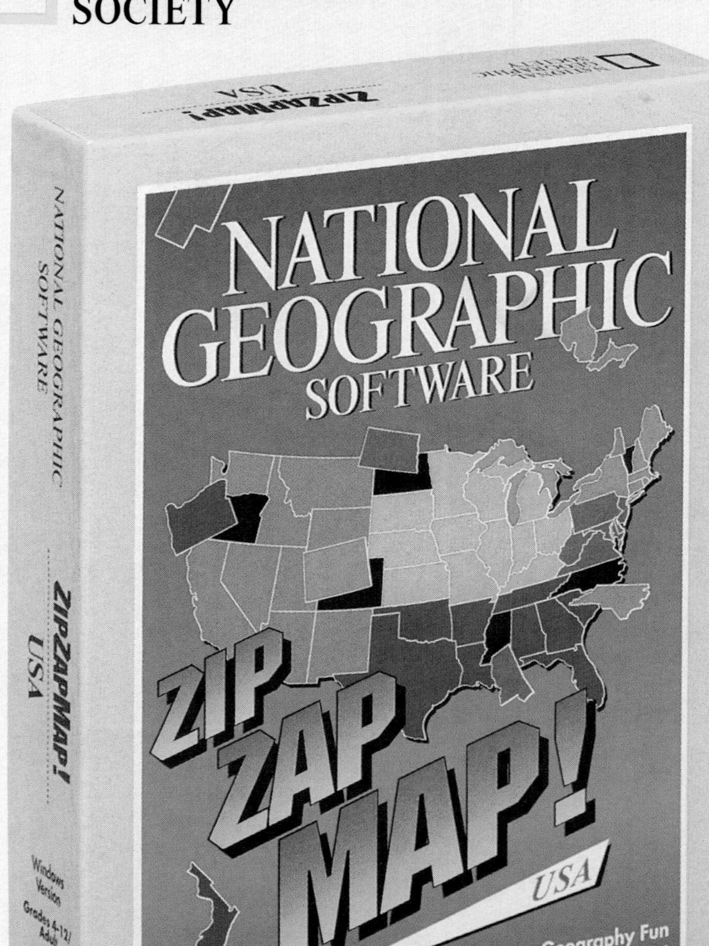

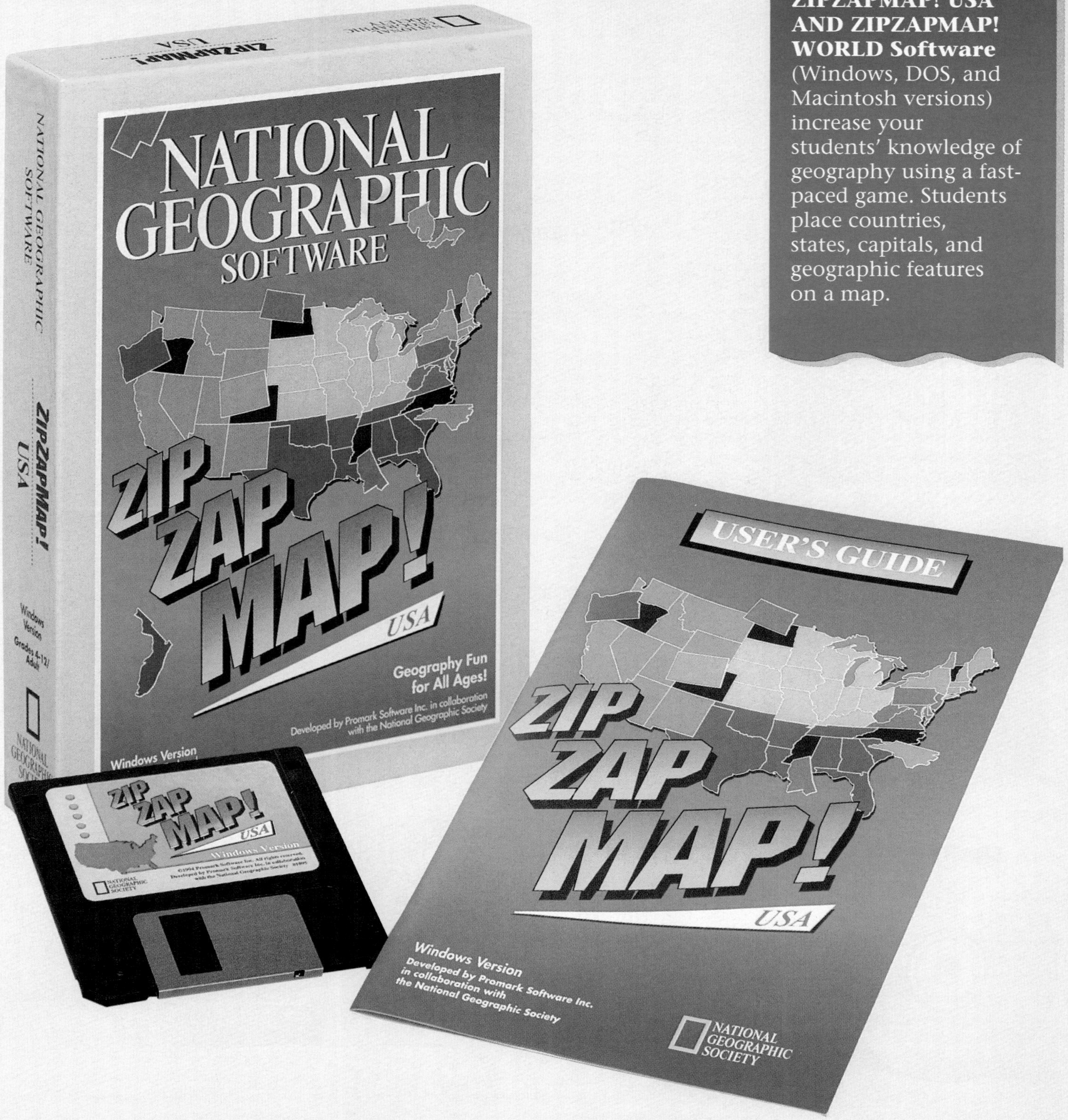

ZIPZAPMAP! USA AND ZIPZAPMAP! WORLD Software (Windows, DOS, and Macintosh versions) increase your students' knowledge of geography using a fast-paced game. Students place countries, states, capitals, and geographic features on a map.

PICTURE ATLAS OF THE WORLD CD-ROM provides more than 800 interactive maps plus fascinating audio and video clips that demonstrate the language, music, and cultural traditions of nations around the globe.

NGS PictureShow™: EARTH'S ENDANGERED ENVIRONMENTS CD-ROM helps students understand the challenges to the ecosystems of rain forests and wetlands.

NGS PictureShow™: GEOLOGY CD-ROM shows more than 100 images explaining rocks and minerals, weathering, and erosion.

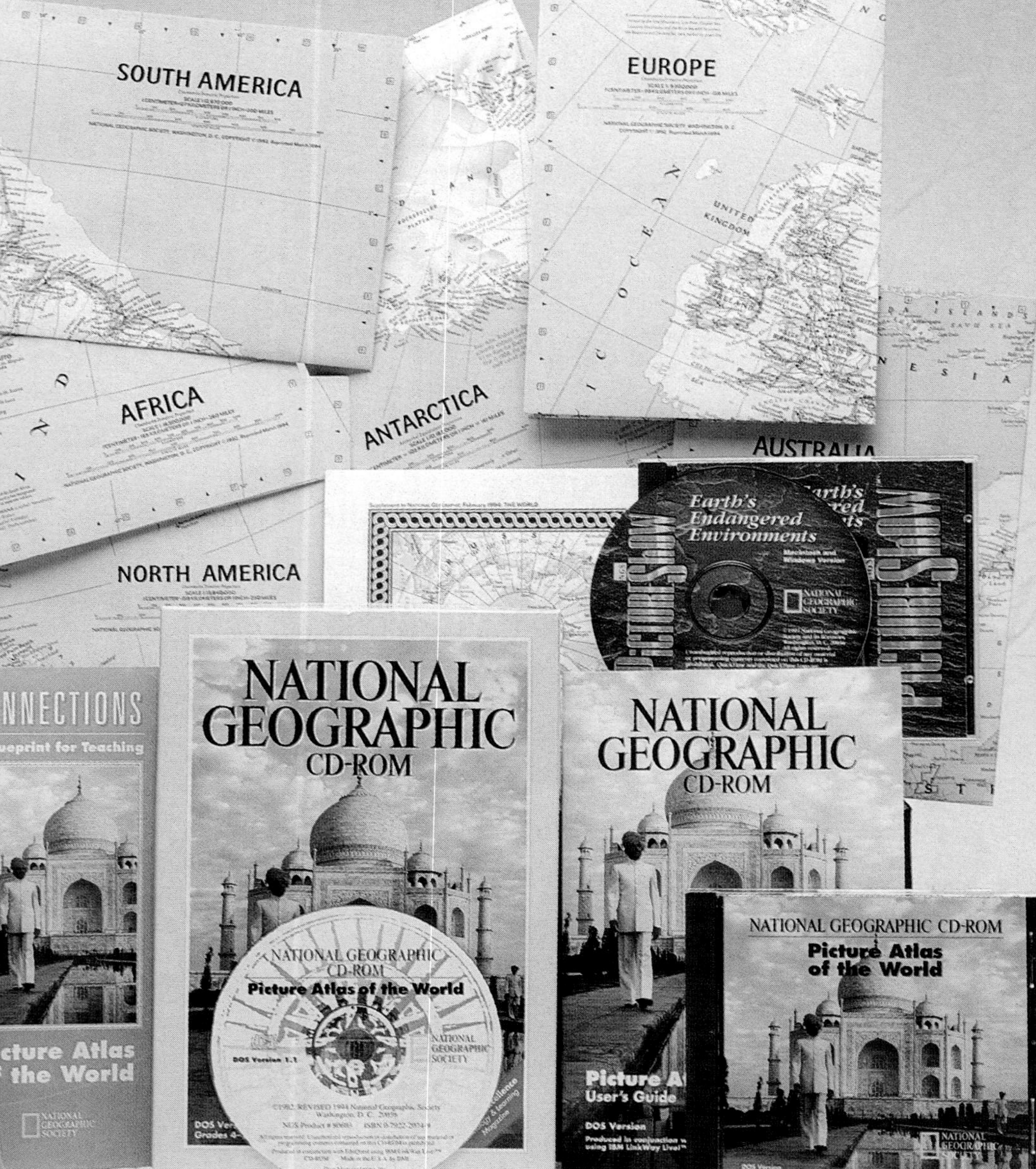

NATIONAL GEOGRAPHIC SOCIETY

EYE ON THE ENVIRONMENT posters highlight the challenges and solutions to some of the world's most pressing environmental dangers.

IMAGES OF THE WORLD posters show the human and physical features of each general region discussed in the student edition.

NATIONAL GEOGRAPHIC SOCIETY

PICTURE ATLAS OF OUR WORLD is an excellent resource for the geography classroom.

PICTURE ATLAS OF OUR 50 STATES is a colorful tool to aid students in learning about the United States.

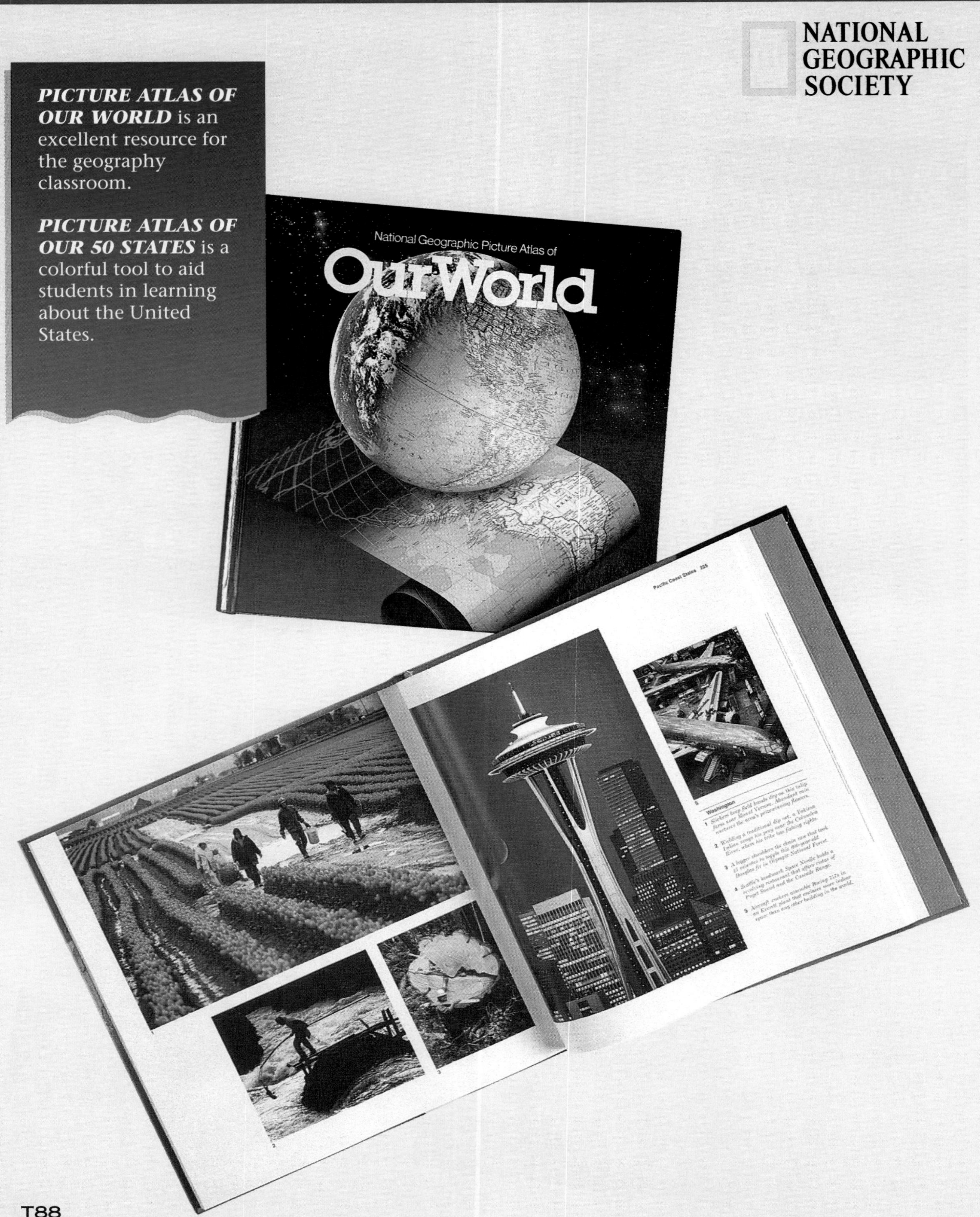

NATIONAL GEOGRAPHIC SOCIETY

PICTUREPACK TRANSPARENCIES are colorful additions to include in your lesson plans. Photographs from the NATIONAL GEOGRAPHIC have been developed into 80 transparencies showing the physical geography of the world.

Water

NGS PicturePack

12. Glacial lakes in Canada

George F. Mobley © Copyright 1994 National Geographic Society

NATIONAL GEOGRAPHIC SOCIETY

In the **STV WORLD GEOGRAPHY SERIES**, your students see the world and the unique landscapes, climates, plants, and animals of all the continents.

- **Volume 1: Asia and Australia**
- **Volume 2: Africa and Europe**
- **Volume 3: South America and Antarctica**

The **STV NORTH AMERICA** videodisc program gives your students a close-up view of the country's physical geography, including the East, the Northlands, the Central Lowlands, the Rocky Mountains, the Pacific Edge, and the Western Dry Lands.

Other NATIONAL GEOGRAPHIC videodisc programs include:

- STV: Solar System
- STV: Restless Earth
- STV: Rain Forest
- STV: Biodiversity
- STV: Water
- STV: Atmosphere
- GTV: Planetary Manager

ABCNews InterActive™: IN THE HOLY LAND videodisc reviews the roots of the conflict between the Israelis and the Palestinians. Religious, political, historical, and geographic issues are highlighted with more than 700 maps, charts, slides, and original documents.

ABCNEWS
INTERACTIVE™
In the Holy Land
The history of turmoil and conflict in the Middle East
with Ted Koppel
Includes:
2-sided CAV videodisc
HyperCard program
Curriculum guide
User manual
Disc directory
DISTRIBUTED BY
GLENCOE
Side 1
In the Holy Land
ABCNEWS
INTERACTIVE™

REUTERS ISSUES IN GEOGRAPHY contains primary source footage and interviews that demonstrate the impact of geography on people and places. (VHS and Videodisc)

GEOGRAPHY AND THE ENVIRONMENT: THE INFINITE VOYAGE, a three-disc program, allows your students to explore timely environmental issues and to learn how people around the world are confronting environmental challenges.

MINDJOGGER VIDEOQUIZ offers preview, review, and reinforcement of chapter content in a game-show format. Available in videodisc and VHS formats.

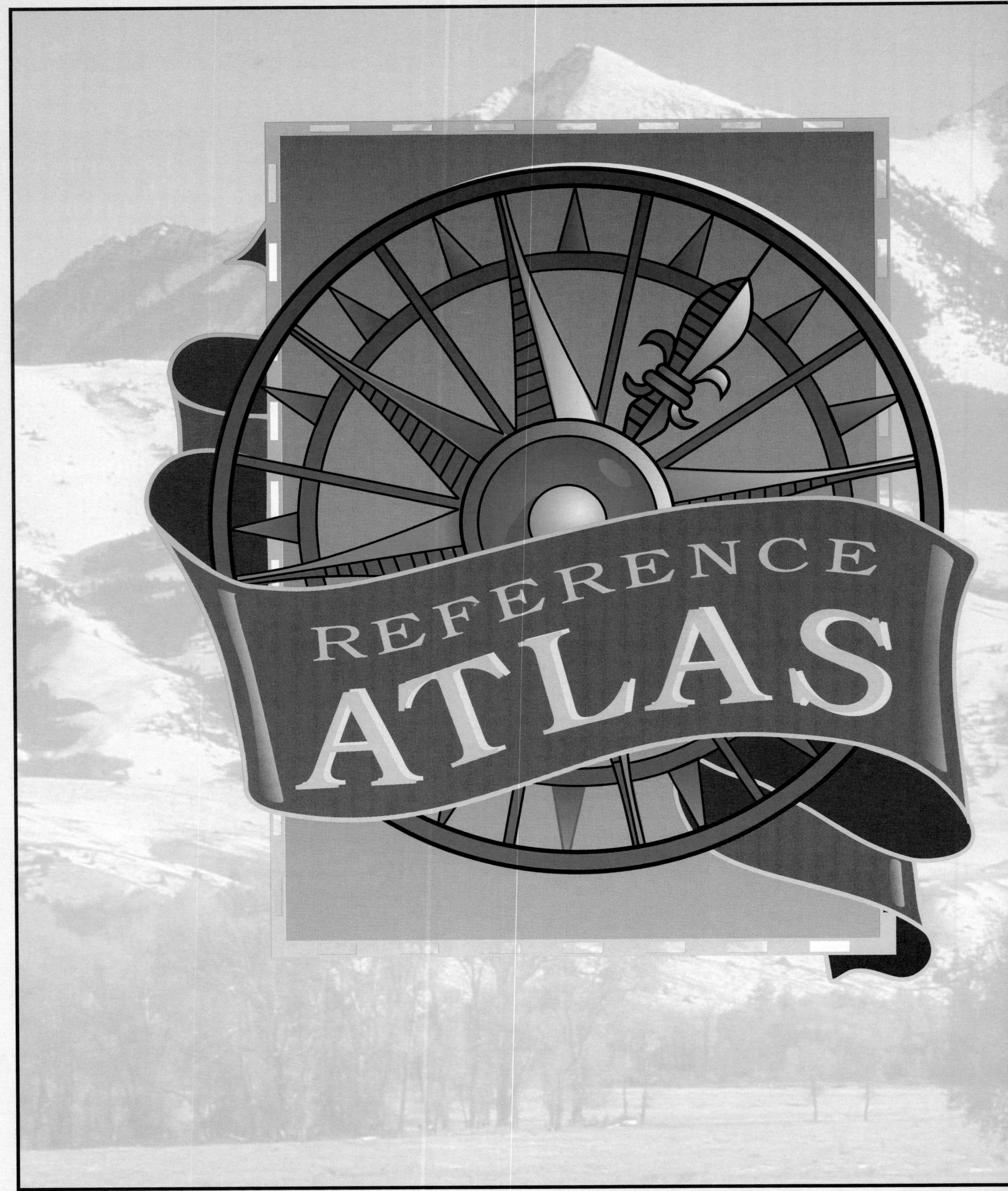
REFERENCE
ATLAS

Contents

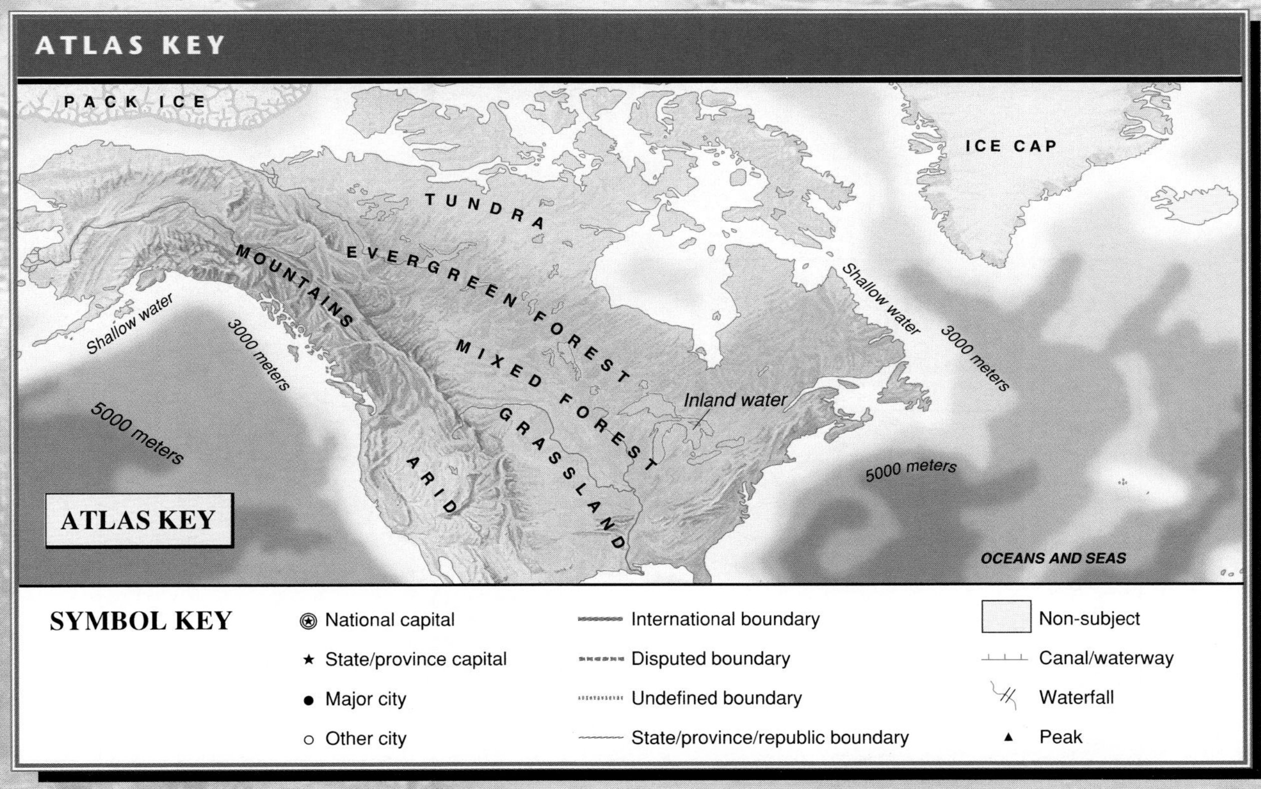

ATLAS KEY
PACK ICE
ICE CAP
TUNDRA
EVERGREEN FOREST
MOUNTAINS
MIXED FOREST
GRASSLAND
ARID
Shallow water
3000 meters
5000 meters
Inland water
OCEANS AND SEAS
ATLAS KEY
SYMBOL KEY
National capital
State/province capital
Major city
Other city
International boundary
Disputed boundary
Undefined boundary
State/province/republic boundary
Non-subject
Canal/waterway
Waterfall
Peak

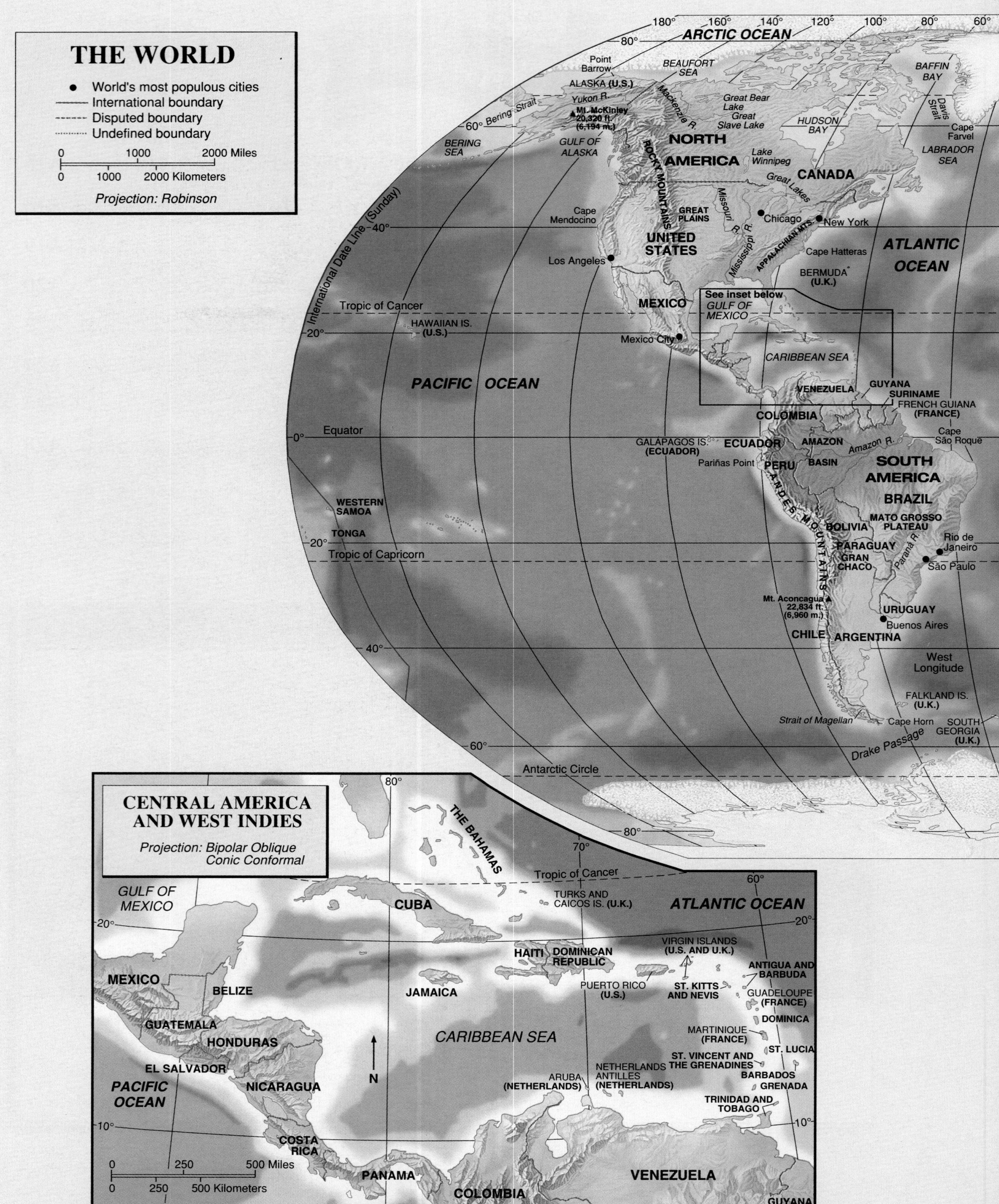
THE WORLD
World's most populous cities
International boundary
Disputed boundary
Undefined boundary
0 1000 2000 Miles
0 1000 2000 Kilometers
Projection: Robinson
ARCTIC OCEAN
BEAUFORT SEA
Point Barrow
ALASKA (U.S.)
Yukon R.
Bering Strait
Mt. McKinley 20,320 ft. (6,194 m.)
BERING SEA
GULF OF ALASKA
Mackenzie R.
Great Bear Lake
Great Slave Lake
HUDSON BAY
BAFFIN BAY
Davis Strait
Cape Farvel
LABRADOR SEA
NORTH AMERICA
ROCKY MOUNTAINS
Lake Winnipeg
CANADA
Great Lakes
Cape Mendocino
GREAT PLAINS
Missouri R.
Chicago
New York
UNITED STATES
Mississippi R.
APPALACHIAN MTS.
Cape Hatteras
ATLANTIC OCEAN
Los Angeles
BERMUDA (U.K.)
International Date Line (Sunday)
Tropic of Cancer
MEXICO
See inset below
GULF OF MEXICO
HAWAIIAN IS. (U.S.)
Mexico City
CARIBBEAN SEA
PACIFIC OCEAN
VENEZUELA
GUYANA
SURINAME
FRENCH GUIANA (FRANCE)
COLOMBIA
Equator
GALÁPAGOS IS. (ECUADOR)
ECUADOR
AMAZON BASIN
Amazon R.
Cape São Roque
Pariñas Point
PERU
SOUTH AMERICA
BRAZIL
ANDES MOUNTAINS
WESTERN SAMOA
MATO GROSSO PLATEAU
TONGA
BOLIVIA
Rio de Janeiro
Tropic of Capricorn
PARAGUAY
GRAN CHACO
Paraná R.
São Paulo
Mt. Aconcagua 22,834 ft. (6,960 m.)
URUGUAY
Buenos Aires
CHILE
ARGENTINA
West Longitude
FALKLAND IS. (U.K.)
Strait of Magellan
Cape Horn
SOUTH GEORGIA (U.K.)
Drake Passage
Antarctic Circle
CENTRAL AMERICA AND WEST INDIES
Projection: Bipolar Oblique Conic Conformal
THE BAHAMAS
GULF OF MEXICO
Tropic of Cancer
TURKS AND CAICOS IS. (U.K.)
ATLANTIC OCEAN
CUBA
HAITI
DOMINICAN REPUBLIC
VIRGIN ISLANDS (U.S. AND U.K.)
ANTIGUA AND BARBUDA
MEXICO
BELIZE
JAMAICA
PUERTO RICO (U.S.)
ST. KITTS AND NEVIS
GUADELOUPE (FRANCE)
DOMINICA
GUATEMALA
MARTINIQUE (FRANCE)
HONDURAS
CARIBBEAN SEA
ST. LUCIA
ST. VINCENT AND THE GRENADINES
EL SALVADOR
NETHERLANDS ANTILLES (NETHERLANDS)
BARBADOS
PACIFIC OCEAN
NICARAGUA
N
ARUBA (NETHERLANDS)
GRENADA
TRINIDAD AND TOBAGO
COSTA RICA
0 250 500 Miles
0 250 500 Kilometers
PANAMA
VENEZUELA
COLOMBIA
GUYANA

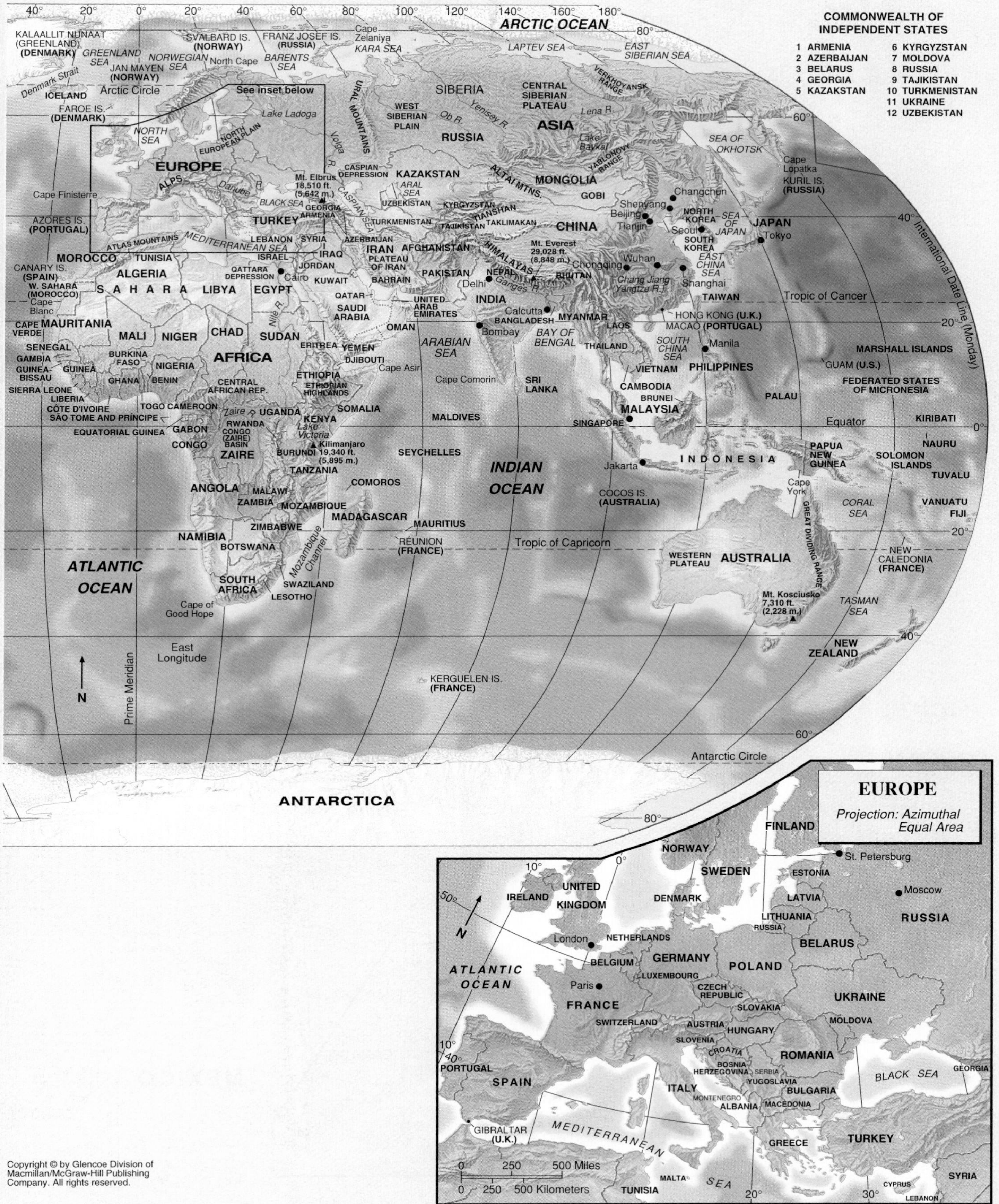

ARCTIC OCEAN
COMMONWEALTH OF INDEPENDENT STATES
1 ARMENIA
2 AZERBAIJAN
3 BELARUS
4 GEORGIA
5 KAZAKSTAN
6 KYRGYZSTAN
7 MOLDOVA
8 RUSSIA
9 TAJIKISTAN
10 TURKMENISTAN
11 UKRAINE
12 UZBEKISTAN
KALAALLIT NUNAAT (GREENLAND) (DENMARK)
GREENLAND SEA
SVALBARD IS. (NORWAY)
FRANZ JOSEF IS. (RUSSIA)
Cape Zelaniya
KARA SEA
LAPTEV SEA
EAST SIBERIAN SEA
NORWEGIAN SEA
JAN MAYEN (NORWAY)
North Cape
BARENTS SEA
Denmark Strait
Arctic Circle
ICELAND
See inset below
FAROE IS. (DENMARK)
Lake Ladoga
URAL MOUNTAINS
SIBERIA
WEST SIBERIAN PLAIN
CENTRAL SIBERIAN PLATEAU
VERKHOYANSK RANGE
Ob R.
Yenisey R.
Lena R.
ASIA
RUSSIA
NORTH SEA
NORTH EUROPEAN PLAIN
Volga R.
EUROPE
ALPS
Danube R.
Mt. Elbrus 18,510 ft. (5,642 m.)
CASPIAN DEPRESSION
KAZAKSTAN
ARAL SEA
Lake Baykal
YABLONOVY RANGE
SEA OF OKHOTSK
Cape Lopatka
KURIL IS. (RUSSIA)
MONGOLIA
ALTAI MTNS.
GOBI
Changchun
Shenyang
Beijing
Tianjin
NORTH KOREA
SEA OF JAPAN
JAPAN
Tokyo
Seoul
SOUTH KOREA
Cape Finisterre
BLACK SEA
GEORGIA
ARMENIA
UZBEKISTAN
KYRGYZSTAN
TIANSHAN
TAKLIMAKAN
CHINA
AZORES IS. (PORTUGAL)
TURKEY
CASPIAN SEA
TURKMENISTAN
TAJIKISTAN
ATLAS MOUNTAINS
MEDITERRANEAN SEA
LEBANON
SYRIA
AZERBAIJAN
Mt. Everest 29,028 ft. (8,848 m.)
HIMALAYAS
ISRAEL
IRAQ
IRAN
PLATEAU OF IRAN
AFGHANISTAN
Wuhan
Chongqing
EAST CHINA SEA
MOROCCO
TUNISIA
JORDAN
CANARY IS. (SPAIN)
ALGERIA
QATTARA DEPRESSION
Cairo
KUWAIT
BAHRAIN
PAKISTAN
NEPAL
BHUTAN
Chang Jiang (Yangtze R.)
Shanghai
W. SAHARA (MOROCCO)
SAHARA
LIBYA
EGYPT
Delhi
Ganges R.
QATAR
INDIA
TAIWAN
Tropic of Cancer
Cape Blanc
Nile R.
SAUDI ARABIA
UNITED ARAB EMIRATES
Calcutta
BANGLADESH
MYANMAR
HONG KONG (U.K.)
MACAO (PORTUGAL)
CAPE VERDE
MAURITANIA
MALI
NIGER
CHAD
SUDAN
OMAN
Bombay
BAY OF BENGAL
LAOS
ARABIAN SEA
SOUTH CHINA SEA
Manila
SENEGAL
GAMBIA
BURKINA FASO
AFRICA
ERITREA
YEMEN
DJIBOUTI
THAILAND
MARSHALL ISLANDS
GUINEA-BISSAU
GUINEA
NIGERIA
Cape Asir
VIETNAM
PHILIPPINES
GUAM (U.S.)
GHANA
BENIN
CENTRAL AFRICAN REP.
ETHIOPIA
ETHIOPIAN HIGHLANDS
Cape Comorin
SRI LANKA
CAMBODIA
FEDERATED STATES OF MICRONESIA
SIERRA LEONE
LIBERIA
CÔTE D'IVOIRE
TOGO
CAMEROON
Zaire R.
UGANDA
SOMALIA
BRUNEI
MALAYSIA
PALAU
SÃO TOME AND PRÍNCIPE
KENYA
MALDIVES
Equator
KIRIBATI
EQUATORIAL GUINEA
GABON
RWANDA
CONGO (ZAIRE) BASIN
Lake Victoria
SINGAPORE
NAURU
CONGO
BURUNDI
ZAIRE
Kilimanjaro 19,340 ft. (5,895 m.)
SEYCHELLES
PAPUA NEW GUINEA
SOLOMON ISLANDS
TANZANIA
INDIAN OCEAN
Jakarta
INDONESIA
TUVALU
ANGOLA
MALAWI
COMOROS
Cape York
ZAMBIA
MOZAMBIQUE
COCOS IS. (AUSTRALIA)
CORAL SEA
VANUATU
FIJI
MADAGASCAR
GREAT DIVIDING RANGE
ZIMBABWE
MAURITIUS
NAMIBIA
Mozambique Channel
RÉUNION (FRANCE)
Tropic of Capricorn
BOTSWANA
NEW CALEDONIA (FRANCE)
ATLANTIC OCEAN
WESTERN PLATEAU
AUSTRALIA
SOUTH AFRICA
SWAZILAND
LESOTHO
Mt. Kosciusko 7,310 ft. (2,228 m.)
TASMAN SEA
Cape of Good Hope
NEW ZEALAND
East Longitude
Prime Meridian
N
KERGUELEN IS. (FRANCE)
Antarctic Circle
ANTARCTICA
International Date Line (Monday)
40° 20° 0° 20° 40° 60° 80° 100° 120° 140° 160° 180°
80° 60° 40° 20° 0° 20° 40° 60° 80°
EUROPE
Projection: Azimuthal Equal Area
FINLAND
NORWAY
St. Petersburg
SWEDEN
ESTONIA
Moscow
IRELAND
UNITED KINGDOM
DENMARK
LATVIA
LITHUANIA
RUSSIA
N
London
NETHERLANDS
BELARUS
BELGIUM
GERMANY
POLAND
ATLANTIC OCEAN
LUXEMBOURG
Paris
CZECH REPUBLIC
UKRAINE
FRANCE
SLOVAKIA
SWITZERLAND
AUSTRIA
MOLDOVA
HUNGARY
SLOVENIA
CROATIA
ROMANIA
BOSNIA HERZEGOVINA
SERBIA
YUGOSLAVIA
BLACK SEA
GEORGIA
PORTUGAL
SPAIN
ITALY
MONTENEGRO
BULGARIA
ALBANIA
MACEDONIA
GIBRALTAR (U.K.)
MEDITERRANEAN SEA
GREECE
TURKEY
0 250 500 Miles
0 250 500 Kilometers
MALTA
TUNISIA
CYPRUS
SYRIA
LEBANON
10° 0° 50° 10° 40° 20° 30°

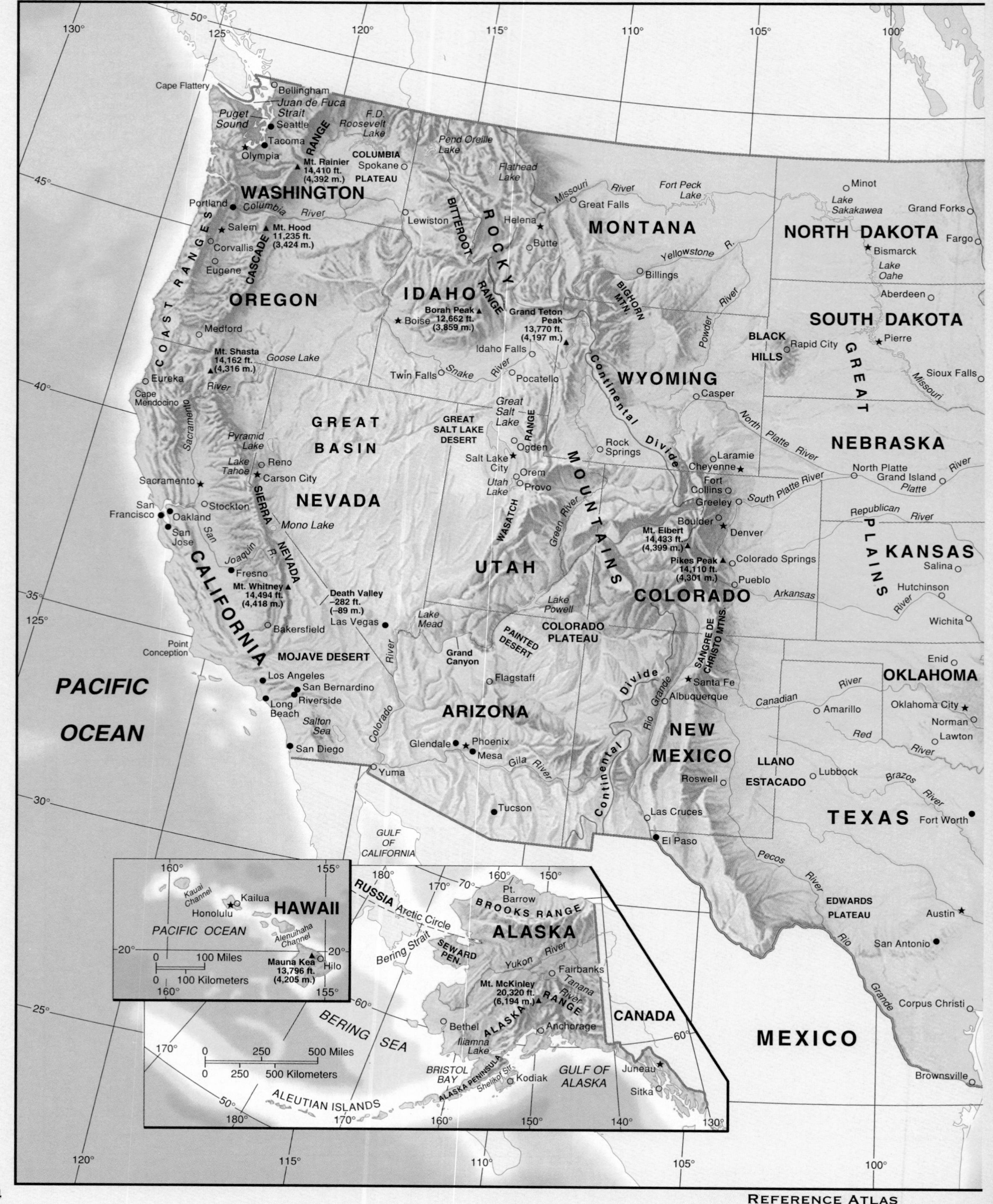

PACIFIC OCEAN
WASHINGTON
OREGON
IDAHO
MONTANA
WYOMING
NORTH DAKOTA
SOUTH DAKOTA
NEBRASKA
KANSAS
OKLAHOMA
TEXAS
NEW MEXICO
COLORADO
UTAH
ARIZONA
NEVADA
CALIFORNIA
MEXICO
GREAT BASIN
GREAT PLAINS
ROCKY MOUNTAINS
COAST RANGES
CASCADE RANGE
SIERRA NEVADA
COLUMBIA PLATEAU
COLORADO PLATEAU
MOJAVE DESERT
GREAT SALT LAKE DESERT
PAINTED DESERT
LLANO ESTACADO
EDWARDS PLATEAU
BLACK HILLS
Continental Divide
Mt. Rainier 14,410 ft. (4,392 m.)
Mt. Hood 11,235 ft. (3,424 m.)
Mt. Shasta 14,162 ft. (4,316 m.)
Borah Peak 12,662 ft. (3,859 m.)
Grand Teton Peak 13,770 ft. (4,197 m.)
Mt. Whitney 14,494 ft. (4,418 m.)
Death Valley −282 ft. (−89 m.)
Mt. Elbert 14,433 ft. (4,399 m.)
Pikes Peak 14,110 ft. (4,301 m.)
Seattle
Tacoma
Olympia
Portland
Salem
Spokane
Boise
Helena
Denver
Salt Lake City
Phoenix
Santa Fe
Sacramento
Carson City
Cheyenne
Bismarck
Pierre
Oklahoma City
Austin
Los Angeles
San Francisco
San Diego
Las Vegas
El Paso
HAWAII
Honolulu
Kailua
Hilo
Mauna Kea 13,796 ft. (4,205 m.)
PACIFIC OCEAN
ALASKA
BROOKS RANGE
ALASKA RANGE
Mt. McKinley 20,320 ft. (6,194 m.)
Fairbanks
Anchorage
Juneau
Sitka
Kodiak
Bethel
RUSSIA
CANADA
BERING SEA
GULF OF ALASKA
ALEUTIAN ISLANDS
GULF OF CALIFORNIA

CANADA
UNITED STATES
National capital
State capital
Major city
International boundary
State boundary
0 150 300 Miles
0 150 300 Kilometers
Projection: Albers Equal Area
ATLANTIC OCEAN
GULF OF MEXICO
THE BAHAMAS
CUBA
Straits of Florida
MAINE
N.H.
VT.
MASS.
R.I.
CONN.
NEW YORK
N.J.
PENNSYLVANIA
MD.
DEL.
D.C.
WEST VIRGINIA
VIRGINIA
NORTH CAROLINA
SOUTH CAROLINA
GEORGIA
FLORIDA
ALABAMA
MISSISSIPPI
LOUISIANA
ARKANSAS
TENNESSEE
KENTUCKY
OHIO
INDIANA
ILLINOIS
MICHIGAN
WISCONSIN
MINNESOTA
IOWA
MISSOURI
CENTRAL LOWLAND
APPALACHIAN MOUNTAINS
COASTAL PLAIN
OZARK PLATEAU
CUMBERLAND PLATEAU
ADIRONDACK MTNS.
Mt. Washington 6,288 ft. (1,905 m.)
Mt. Mitchell 6,684 ft. (2,037 m.)
Lake Superior
Lake Michigan
Lake Huron
Lake Erie
Lake Ontario
Lake of the Woods
Red Lake
Moosehead Lake
Lake Champlain
St. Lawrence River
Hudson R.
Susquehanna River
Mississippi River
Ohio River
Wabash R.
Cumberland River
Tennessee R.
Chattahoochee R.
Alabama R.
Roanoke River
DELAWARE BAY
CHESAPEAKE BAY
Cape Cod
Cape Hatteras
Cape Canaveral
Cape Sable
Lake Okeechobee
Lake Pontchartrain
Harry S. Truman Res.
R.S. Kerr Res.
Lake Eufaula
Lake Texoma
Toledo Bend Res.
Sam Rayburn Reservoir
Niagara Falls
Duluth
Minneapolis
St. Paul
Rochester
Green Bay
Appleton
Milwaukee
Madison
Racine
Rockford
Dubuque
Cedar Rapids
Davenport
Des Moines
Sioux City
Omaha
Council Bluffs
Lincoln
Chicago
Aurora
Joliet
Gary
Hammond
South Bend
Peoria
Springfield
Decatur
Grand Rapids
Lansing
Flint
Detroit
Ann Arbor
Toledo
Fort Wayne
Muncie
Indianapolis
Cleveland
Akron
Canton
Youngstown
Columbus
Dayton
Cincinnati
Parkersburg
Wheeling
Pittsburgh
Erie
Buffalo
Rochester
Syracuse
Utica
Albany
Binghamton
Burlington
Montpelier
Concord
Manchester
Bangor
Augusta
Lewiston
Portland
Boston
Worcester
Springfield
Providence
Hartford
New Haven
Yonkers
New York
Newark
Trenton
Allentown
Harrisburg
Philadelphia
Camden
Wilmington
Dover
Baltimore
Annapolis
Washington
Arlington
Charleston
Huntington
Richmond
Newport News
Norfolk
Roanoke
Durham
Raleigh
Greensboro
Winston-Salem
Charlotte
Spartanburg
Greenville
Columbia
Charleston
Augusta
Atlanta
Macon
Savannah
Columbus
Albany
Jacksonville
Tallahassee
Orlando
Tampa
St. Petersburg
Palm Beach
Miami Beach
Miami
Key West
Frankfort
Lexington
Louisville
Evansville
Owensboro
Nashville
Knoxville
Chattanooga
Memphis
Huntsville
Birmingham
Tuscaloosa
Montgomery
Mobile
Pensacola
Biloxi
Meridian
Jackson
Hattiesburg
Greenville
Baton Rouge
Lafayette
New Orleans
Lake Charles
Shreveport
Houston
Dallas
Tulsa
Fort Smith
North Little Rock
Little Rock
Hot Springs
Pine Bluff
Kansas City
Independence
Topeka
Lawrence
Jefferson City
St. Louis
East St. Louis

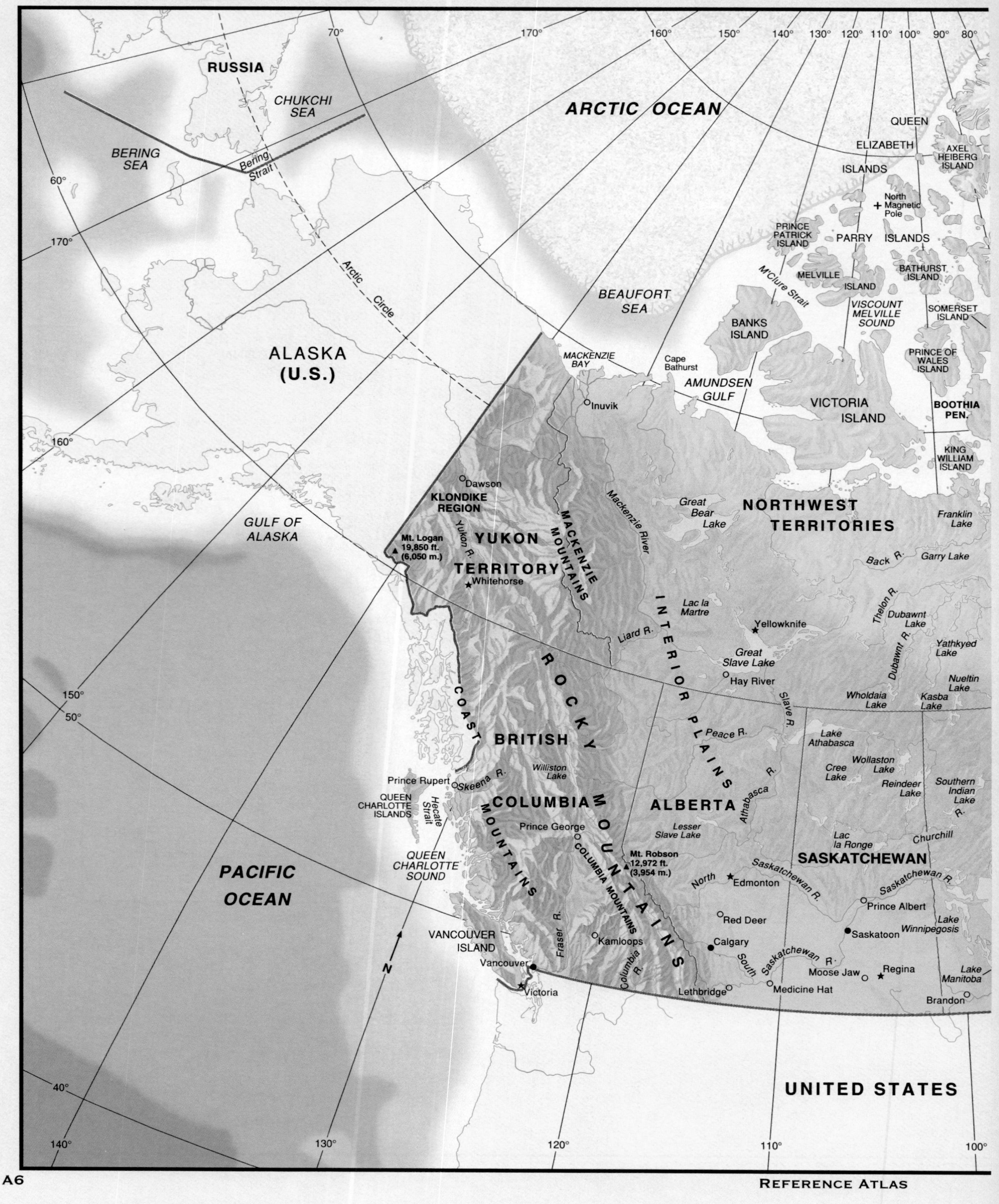
RUSSIA
CHUKCHI SEA
BERING SEA
Bering Strait
ARCTIC OCEAN
QUEEN ELIZABETH ISLANDS
AXEL HEIBERG ISLAND
North Magnetic Pole
PRINCE PATRICK ISLAND
PARRY ISLANDS
MELVILLE ISLAND
BATHURST ISLAND
M'Clure Strait
VISCOUNT MELVILLE SOUND
SOMERSET ISLAND
BEAUFORT SEA
BANKS ISLAND
PRINCE OF WALES ISLAND
Arctic Circle
ALASKA (U.S.)
MACKENZIE BAY
Cape Bathurst
AMUNDSEN GULF
VICTORIA ISLAND
BOOTHIA PEN.
Inuvik
KING WILLIAM ISLAND
Dawson
KLONDIKE REGION
Mackenzie River
Great Bear Lake
NORTHWEST TERRITORIES
Franklin Lake
GULF OF ALASKA
Mt. Logan 19,850 ft. (6,050 m.)
Yukon R.
YUKON TERRITORY
MACKENZIE MOUNTAINS
Whitehorse
Back R.
Garry Lake
INTERIOR PLAINS
Lac la Martre
Thelon R.
Dubawnt Lake
Liard R.
Yellowknife
Dubawnt R.
Yathkyed Lake
ROCKY MOUNTAINS
Great Slave Lake
Hay River
Nueltin Lake
COAST
Slave R.
Wholdaia Lake
Kasba Lake
BRITISH COLUMBIA
Peace R.
Lake Athabasca
Williston Lake
Wollaston Lake
Cree Lake
Prince Rupert
Skeena R.
Reindeer Lake
Southern Indian Lake
QUEEN CHARLOTTE ISLANDS
Hecate Strait
MOUNTAINS
ALBERTA
Athabasca R.
Prince George
Lesser Slave Lake
Lac la Ronge
Churchill R.
COLUMBIA MOUNTAINS
Mt. Robson 12,972 ft. (3,954 m.)
SASKATCHEWAN
QUEEN CHARLOTTE SOUND
PACIFIC OCEAN
North Saskatchewan R.
Edmonton
Saskatchewan R.
Prince Albert
Red Deer
Lake Winnipegosis
VANCOUVER ISLAND
Fraser R.
Kamloops
Saskatoon
Calgary
Vancouver
Columbia R.
South Saskatchewan R.
Moose Jaw
Regina
Lake Manitoba
Victoria
Lethbridge
Medicine Hat
Brandon
N
UNITED STATES
70°
170°
160°
150°
140°
130°
120°
110°
100°
90°
80°
60°
50°
40°

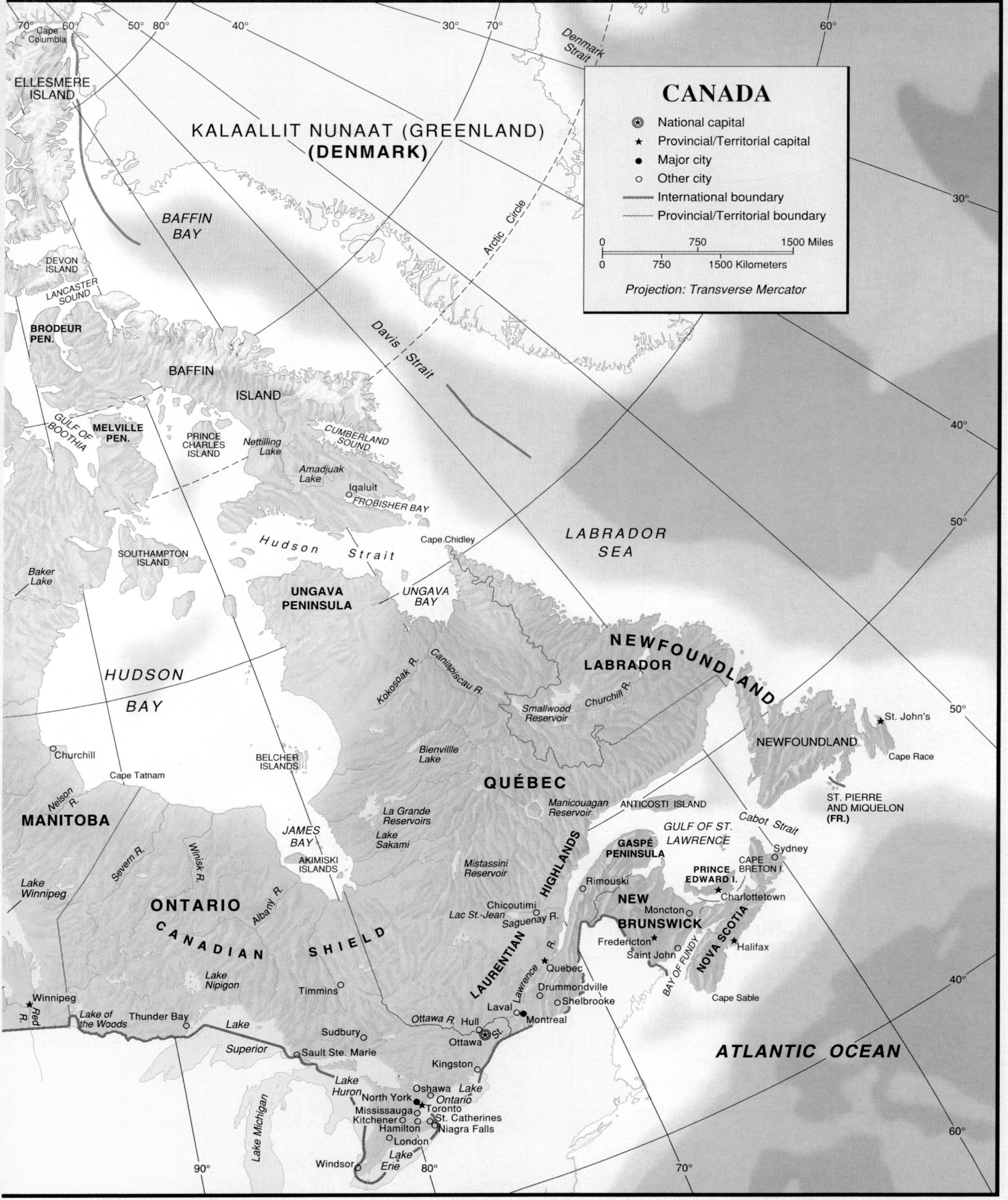
CANADA
National capital
Provincial/Territorial capital
Major city
Other city
International boundary
Provincial/Territorial boundary
0 750 1500 Miles
0 750 1500 Kilometers
Projection: Transverse Mercator
KALAALLIT NUNAAT (GREENLAND)
(DENMARK)
ELLESMERE ISLAND
Cape Columbia
BAFFIN BAY
DEVON ISLAND
LANCASTER SOUND
BRODEUR PEN.
BAFFIN ISLAND
GULF OF BOOTHIA
MELVILLE PEN.
PRINCE CHARLES ISLAND
Nettilling Lake
Amadjuak Lake
CUMBERLAND SOUND
Iqaluit
FROBISHER BAY
Davis Strait
Denmark Strait
Arctic Circle
Hudson Strait
Cape Chidley
LABRADOR SEA
SOUTHAMPTON ISLAND
Baker Lake
UNGAVA PENINSULA
UNGAVA BAY
HUDSON BAY
NEWFOUNDLAND
LABRADOR
Kokosoak R.
Caniapiscau R.
Smallwood Reservoir
Churchill R.
St. John's
NEWFOUNDLAND
Cape Race
Churchill
Cape Tatnam
BELCHER ISLANDS
Bienville Lake
QUÉBEC
Manicouagan Reservoir
ANTICOSTI ISLAND
ST. PIERRE AND MIQUELON (FR.)
Cabot Strait
GULF OF ST. LAWRENCE
Nelson R.
MANITOBA
La Grande Reservoirs
Lake Sakami
JAMES BAY
AKIMISKI ISLANDS
Mistassini Reservoir
HIGHLANDS
GASPÉ PENINSULA
Sydney
CAPE BRETON I.
PRINCE EDWARD I.
Charlottetown
Severn R.
Winisk R.
Lake Winnipeg
ONTARIO
Albany R.
Rimouski
NEW BRUNSWICK
Moncton
Chicoutimi
Lac St.-Jean
Saguenay R.
CANADIAN SHIELD
LAURENTIAN
Fredericton
Saint John
NOVA SCOTIA
Halifax
BAY OF FUNDY
Quebec
St. Lawrence R.
Lake Nipigon
Timmins
Drummondville
Shelbrooke
Cape Sable
Winnipeg
Red R.
Lake of the Woods
Thunder Bay
Lake Superior
Laval
Montreal
Sudbury
Ottawa R.
Hull
Ottawa
ATLANTIC OCEAN
Sault Ste. Marie
Kingston
Lake Huron
Oshawa
Lake Ontario
North York
Toronto
Mississauga
Kitchener
St. Catherines
Hamilton
Niagra Falls
London
Lake Michigan
Lake Erie
Windsor
70° 60° 50° 80° 40° 30° 70° 60° 30° 40° 50° 50° 40° 60° 90° 80° 70°

MEXICO, the CARIBBEAN, and CENTRAL AMERICA
National capital
Major city
International boundary
0
250
500 Miles
0
250
500 Kilometers
Projection: Azimuthal Equal Area
115°
110°
105°
100°
95°
90°
35°
30°
25°
20°
15°
10°
5°
BAJA CALIFORNIA PENINSULA
GULF OF CALIFORNIA
SIERRA MADRE OCCIDENTAL
SIERRA MADRE ORIENTAL
MEXICAN PLATEAU
MEXICO
Ciudad Juárez
Chihuahua
Rio Grande
Monterrey
San Pedro River
Tampico
León
Guadalajara
Mexico City
Puebla
Veracruz
Balsas River
SIERRA MADRE DEL SUR
GULF OF MEXICO
Tropic of Cancer
CAMPECHE BAY
Mérida
YUCATÁN PENINSULA
Belize City
Belmopan
BELIZE
Dolores
GULF OF HONDURAS
GUATEMALA
El Progreso
Quezaltenango
Guatemala
Tegucigalpa
Santa Ana
San Salvador
EL SALVADOR
PACIFIC OCEAN
N

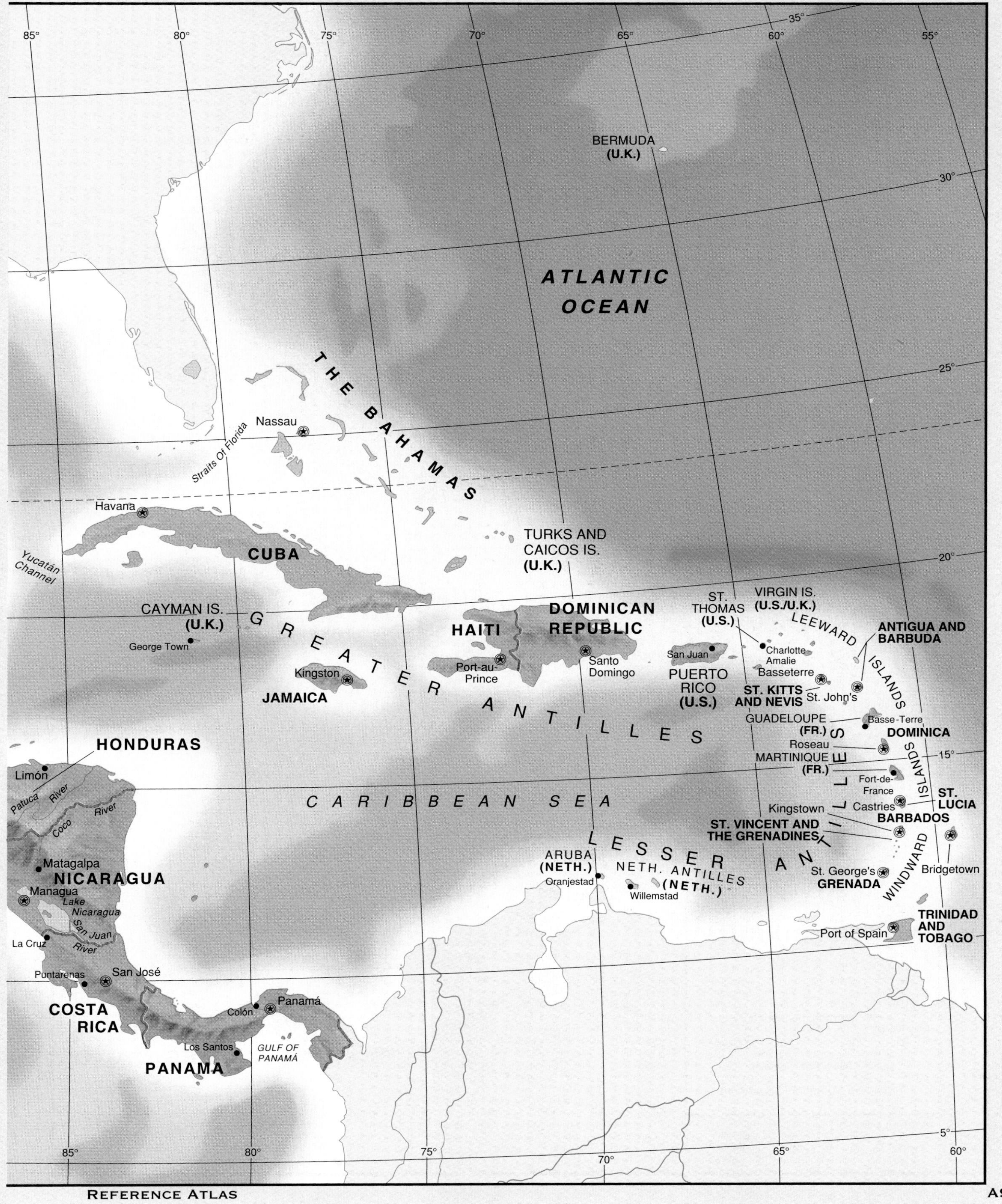

BERMUDA
(U.K.)
ATLANTIC
OCEAN
THE BAHAMAS
Nassau
Straits Of Florida
Havana
CUBA
Yucatán Channel
TURKS AND
CAICOS IS.
(U.K.)
CAYMAN IS.
(U.K.)
George Town
GREATER ANTILLES
HAITI
DOMINICAN
REPUBLIC
Port-au-
Prince
Santo
Domingo
Kingston
JAMAICA
ST.
THOMAS
(U.S.)
VIRGIN IS.
(U.S./U.K.)
Charlotte
Amalie
San Juan
PUERTO
RICO
(U.S.)
LEEWARD ISLANDS
ANTIGUA AND
BARBUDA
Basseterre
ST. KITTS
AND NEVIS
St. John's
GUADELOUPE
(FR.)
Basse-Terre
DOMINICA
Roseau
MARTINIQUE
(FR.)
Fort-de-
France
Castries
ST.
LUCIA
Kingstown
BARBADOS
ST. VINCENT AND
THE GRENADINES
WINDWARD ISLANDS
Bridgetown
St. George's
GRENADA
TRINIDAD
AND
TOBAGO
Port of Spain
LESSER ANTILLES
ARUBA
(NETH.)
Oranjestad
NETH. ANTILLES
(NETH.)
Willemstad
CARIBBEAN SEA
HONDURAS
Limón
Patuca River
Coco River
Matagalpa
NICARAGUA
Managua
Lake Nicaragua
San Juan River
La Cruz
Puntarenas
San José
COSTA
RICA
Colón
Panamá
Los Santos
GULF OF
PANAMÁ
PANAMA
85°
80°
75°
70°
65°
60°
55°
35°
30°
25°
20°
15°
5°

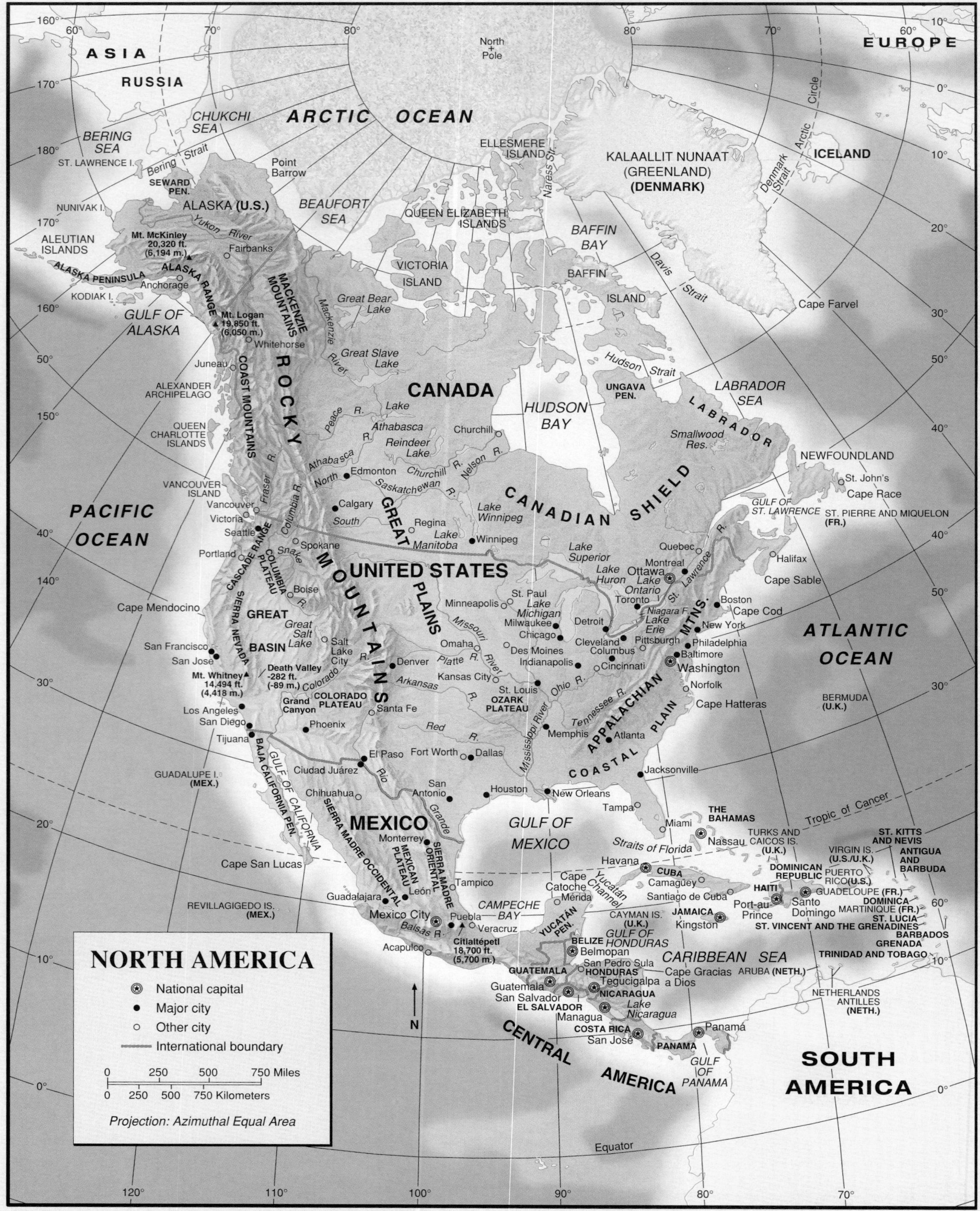
NORTH AMERICA
National capital
Major city
Other city
International boundary
0 250 500 750 Miles
0 250 500 750 Kilometers
Projection: Azimuthal Equal Area
ARCTIC OCEAN
PACIFIC OCEAN
ATLANTIC OCEAN
CANADA
UNITED STATES
MEXICO
CENTRAL AMERICA
SOUTH AMERICA
ASIA
RUSSIA
EUROPE
KALAALLIT NUNAAT (GREENLAND) (DENMARK)
ICELAND
HUDSON BAY
GULF OF MEXICO
CARIBBEAN SEA
ROCKY MOUNTAINS
GREAT PLAINS
CANADIAN SHIELD
APPALACHIAN MTNS.
COASTAL PLAIN
Tropic of Cancer
Equator

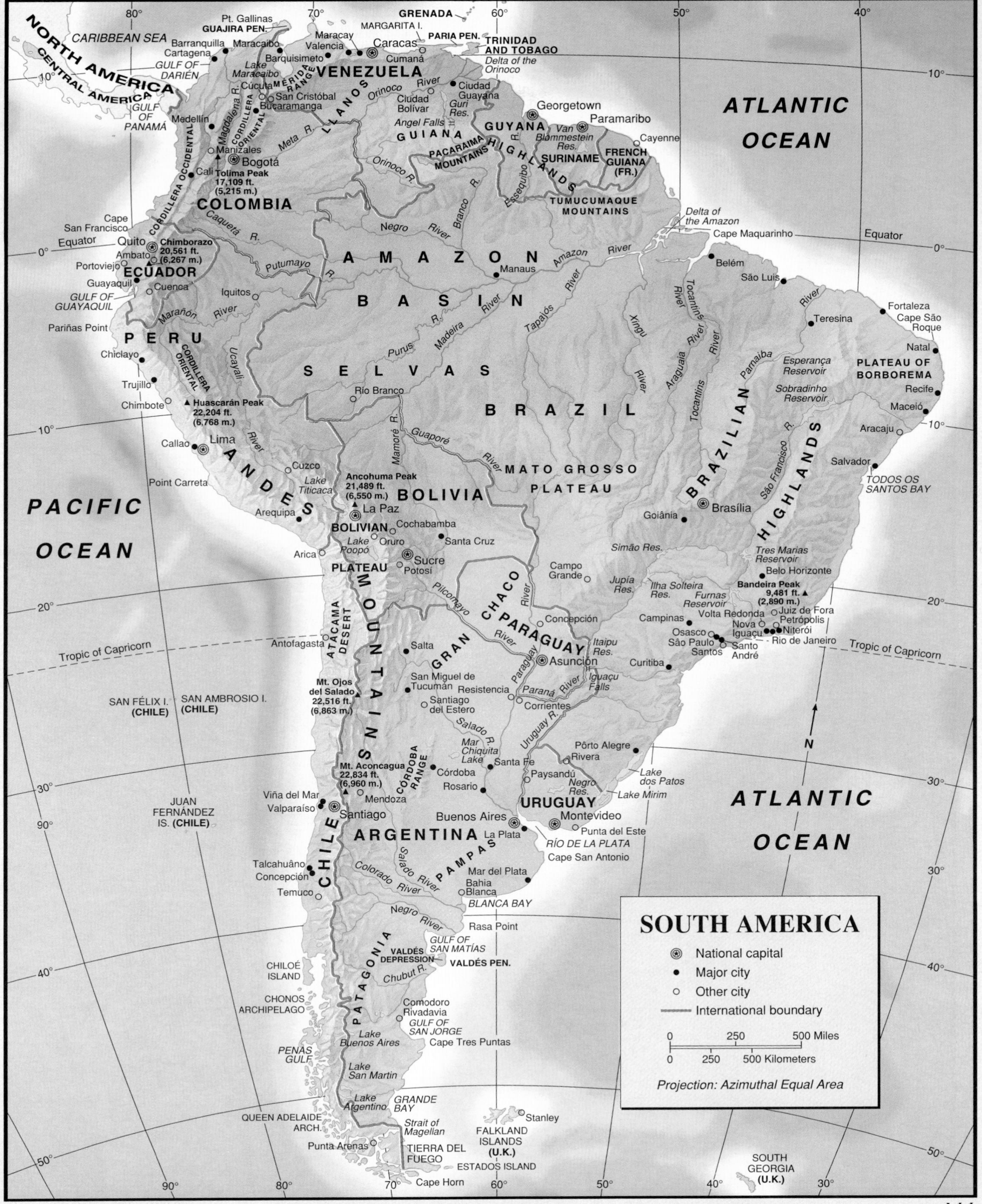

SOUTH AMERICA
National capital
Major city
Other city
International boundary
0 250 500 Miles
0 250 500 Kilometers
Projection: Azimuthal Equal Area
ATLANTIC OCEAN
PACIFIC OCEAN
CARIBBEAN SEA
NORTH AMERICA
CENTRAL AMERICA
COLOMBIA
VENEZUELA
GUYANA
SURINAME
FRENCH GUIANA (FR.)
ECUADOR
PERU
BRAZIL
BOLIVIA
PARAGUAY
URUGUAY
ARGENTINA
CHILE
TRINIDAD AND TOBAGO
GRENADA
AMAZON BASIN
SELVAS
ANDES
GUIANA HIGHLANDS
BRAZILIAN HIGHLANDS
MATO GROSSO PLATEAU
BOLIVIAN PLATEAU
GRAN CHACO
PAMPAS
PATAGONIA
ANDES MOUNTAINS
ATACAMA DESERT
PLATEAU OF BORBOREMA
TUMUCUMAQUE MOUNTAINS
PACARAIMA MOUNTAINS
LLANOS
CÓRDOBA RANGE
FALKLAND ISLANDS (U.K.)
SOUTH GEORGIA (U.K.)
TIERRA DEL FUEGO
Chimborazo 20,561 ft. (6,267 m.)
Tolima Peak 17,109 ft. (5,215 m.)
Huascarán Peak 22,204 ft. (6,768 m.)
Ancohuma Peak 21,489 ft. (6,550 m.)
Mt. Ojos del Salado 22,516 ft. (6,863 m.)
Mt. Aconcagua 22,834 ft. (6,960 m.)
Bandeira Peak 9,481 ft. (2,890 m.)
Equator
Tropic of Capricorn

EUROPE
National capital
Major city
Other city
International boundary
Republic boundary
Canal
0 100 200 300 Miles
0 100 200 300 Kilometers
Projection: Azimuthal Equal Area
ICELAND
Reykjavik
Arctic Circle
NORWEGIAN SEA
Prime Meridian
FAROE IS. (DEN.)
SHETLAND IS. (U.K.)
ORKNEY ISLANDS
OUTER HEBRIDES IS.
Cape Wrath
NORWAY
Trondheim
Bergen
Oslo
Goldhöpiggen 8,097 ft. (2,468 m.)
SCANDINAVIAN HIGHLANDS
SWEDEN
GULF OF BOTHNIA
Uppsala
Stockholm
Lake Vänern
Lake Vättern
Göteborg
ÅLAND I.
HIIUMAA I.
SAAREMAA I.
GOTLAND I.
ÖLAND I.
Skagerrak
Kattegat
JUTLAND
DENMARK
Copenhagen
Odense
Malmö
BORNHOLM I.
BALTIC SEA
NORTH SEA
SCOTLAND
NORTHERN IRELAND (U.K.)
Glasgow
Edinburgh
Belfast
PENNINE RANGE
UNITED KINGDOM
IRELAND
Dublin
Cork
Cape Clear
IRISH SEA
ISLE OF MAN
Manchester
Liverpool
Leeds
Sheffield
St. George's Channel
WALES
ENGLAND
Birmingham
Cardiff
Bristol
London
English Channel
Strait of Dover
GUERNSEY I. (U.K.)
JERSEY I. (U.K.)
ATLANTIC OCEAN
NETHERLANDS
Amsterdam
The Hague
Rotterdam
Hamburg
Bremen
Kiel Canal
Elbe R.
Mittelland Canal
Rostock
Gdańsk
RUSSIA
Szczecin
NORTH
POLAND
Berlin
Hannover
Poznań
Vistula R.
Warsaw
Łódź
Antwerp
BELGIUM
Brussels
Essen
Dortmund
Magdeburg
Cologne
Bonn
GERMANY
Leipzig
Dresden
Wroclaw
Liège
LUXEMBOURG
Luxembourg
Frankfurt
Chemnitz
Prague
Katowice
CZECH REPUBLIC
Ostrava
Krakow
Le Havre
Seine River
Paris
Marne R.
Marne-Rhine Canal
Rhine R.
BRETON PEN.
Nantes
Loire River
Strasbourg
Stuttgart
Danube River
Brno
SLOVAKIA
Bratislava
FRANCE
Munich
Bodensee
LIECHTENSTEIN
Vienna
Linz
Salzburg
Zürich
Bern
Vaduz
Innsbruck
AUSTRIA
Miskolc
Lausanne
Geneva
SWITZERLAND
L. Geneva
Budapest
Graz
HUNGARY
L. Balaton
Cape Finisterre
BAY OF BISCAY
Bordeaux
Lyon
Mt. Blanc 15,771 ft. (4,807 m.)
Mt. Rosa 15,203 ft. (4,634 m.)
ALPS
Garonne R.
CENTRAL MASSIF
Milan
PO VALLEY
Turin
Po R.
Venice
Ljubljana
SLOVENIA
Zagreb
Pécs
Tisza
CROATIA
Sava R.
Novi Sad
CANTABRIAN MTNS.
Bilbao
PYRENEES
Toulouse
Midi Canal
Rhône R.
Genoa
Porto
Valladolid
Ebro River
Montpellier
Nice
Monaco
MONACO
Bologna
SAN MARINO
San Marino
DINARIC ALPS
BOSNIA-HERZEGOVINA
Belgrade
Sarajevo
PORTUGAL
Duero River
IBERIAN
Zaragoza
Aneto Peak 11,168 ft. (3,404 m.)
ANDORRA
Andorra la Vella
Marseille
GULF OF LION
Florence
APENNINES
Split
ADRIATIC SEA
Lisbon
Tagus River
Madrid
Setúbal
PENINSULA
Barcelona
CORSICA (FR.)
VATICAN CITY
Rome
MONTENEGRO
Guadiana River
Valencia
ITALY
MACEDONIA
Cape St. Vincent
SIERRA MORENA
SPAIN
Seville
Palma
BALEARIC IS. (SP.)
SARDINIA (IT.)
TYRRHENIAN SEA
Naples
Bari
Tiranë
ALBANIA
Murcia
Granada
Málaga
Cagliari
G. OF TARANTO
Strait of Gibraltar
GIBRALTAR (U.K.)
MEDITERRANEAN
Strait of Sicily
Palermo
SICILY
Catania
IONIAN SEA
KEFALLINIA I.
PANTELLERIA (IT.)
MALTA
Valletta
AFRICA
SEA

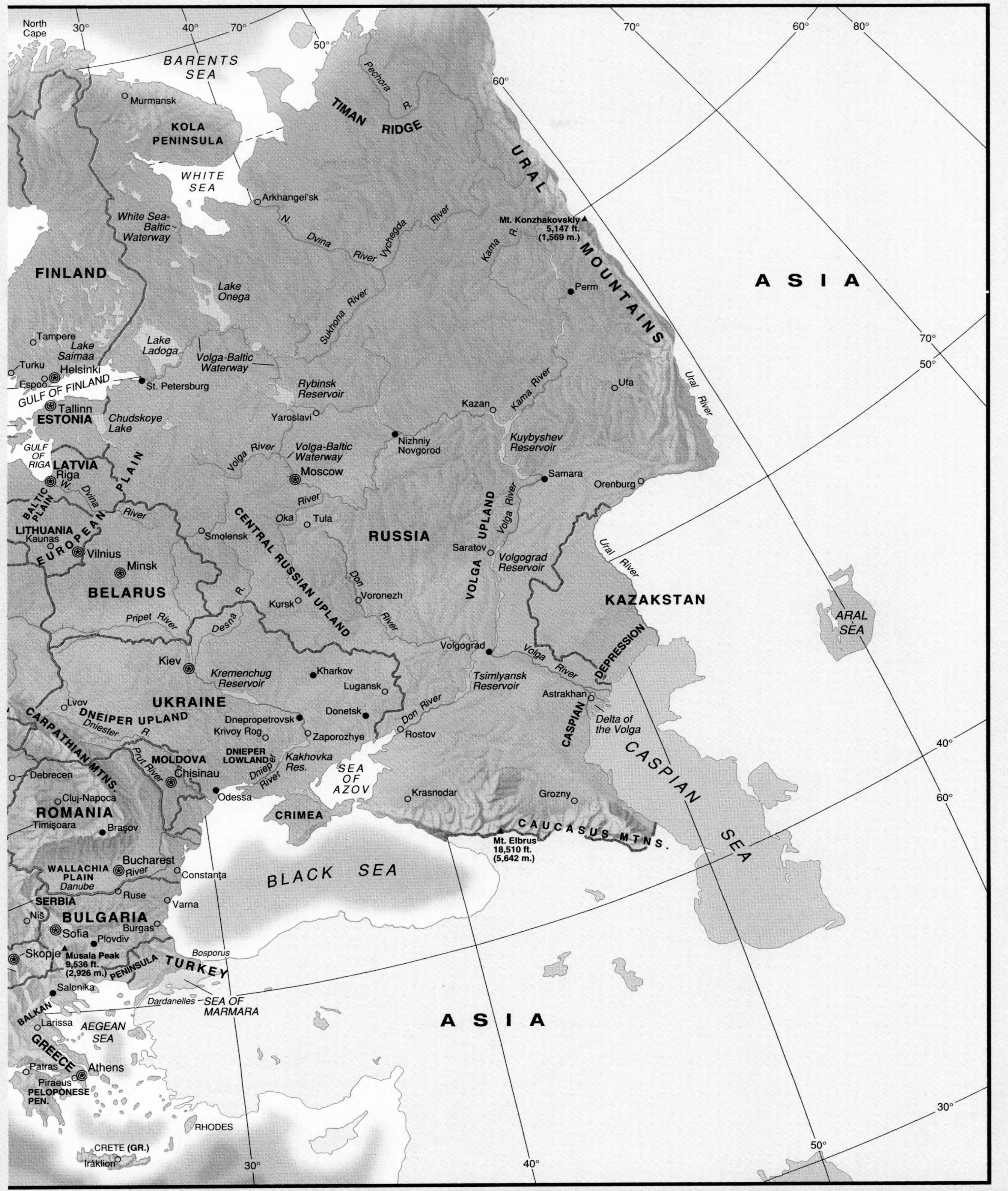

BARENTS SEA
Murmansk
KOLA PENINSULA
WHITE SEA
Arkhangel'sk
TIMAN RIDGE
URAL MOUNTAINS
Mt. Konzhakovskiy 5,147 ft. (1,569 m.)
Perm
FINLAND
Lake Onega
Lake Ladoga
Tampere
Lake Saimaa
Turku
Helsinki
Espoo
GULF OF FINLAND
St. Petersburg
Tallinn
ESTONIA
Chudskoye Lake
Volga-Baltic Waterway
White Sea-Baltic Waterway
Rybinsk Reservoir
Yaroslavl
Nizhniy Novgorod
Kazan
Ufa
Kuybyshev Reservoir
Samara
Orenburg
GULF OF RIGA
LATVIA
Riga
Moscow
LITHUANIA
Kaunas
Vilnius
Minsk
BELARUS
EUROPEAN PLAIN
BALTIC PLAIN
Smolensk
Tula
CENTRAL RUSSIAN UPLAND
RUSSIA
VOLGA UPLAND
Saratov
Volgograd Reservoir
Voronezh
Kursk
KAZAKSTAN
ARAL SEA
ASIA
Volgograd
CASPIAN DEPRESSION
Astrakhan
Delta of the Volga
CASPIAN SEA
Kiev
Kremenchug Reservoir
Kharkov
Lugansk
Donetsk
UKRAINE
Lvov
DNEIPER UPLAND
CARPATHIAN MTNS.
Dnepropetrovsk
Krivoy Rog
Zaporozhye
Rostov
Tsimlyansk Reservoir
MOLDOVA
Chisinau
DNIEPER LOWLAND
Kakhovka Res.
SEA OF AZOV
Odessa
CRIMEA
Krasnodar
Grozny
CAUCASUS MTNS.
Mt. Elbrus 18,510 ft. (5,642 m.)
Debrecen
Cluj-Napoca
ROMANIA
Timişoara
Braşov
Bucharest
WALLACHIA PLAIN
Constanţa
BLACK SEA
Ruse
Varna
SERBIA
Niš
BULGARIA
Sofia
Plovdiv
Burgas
Skopje
Musala Peak 9,536 ft. (2,926 m.)
BALKAN PENINSULA
Bosporus
TURKEY
Salonika
Dardanelles
SEA OF MARMARA
Larissa
AEGEAN SEA
GREECE
Patras
Athens
Piraeus
PELOPONESE PEN.
RHODES
CRETE (GR.)
Iráklion

ARCTIC OCEAN
FRANZ JOSEF ISLANDS
BARENTS SEA
Cape Zelaniya
NOVAYA ZEMLYA
KARA SEA
Kara Strait
EUROPE
BALTIC SEA
GULF OF FINLAND
(RUSSIA)
Arctic Circle
Murmansk
KOLA PENINSULA
WHITE SEA
Arkhangel'sk
Lake Ladoga
Baltic-White Sea Canal
St. Petersburg
Lake Onega
Volga-Baltic Waterway
VALDAI HILLS
TIMAN RIDGE
YAMAL PEN.
GYDAN PENINSULA
Yenisey River
Minsk
BELARUS
Dnieper R.
Lvov
DNIEPER UPLAND
Rybinsk Res.
Vologda
Sukhona R.
N. Dvina R.
Vychegda R.
Pechora River
Yaroslavl
Moscow
Ivanovo
NORTHERN HILLS
Volga
Kiev
UKRAINE
DNIEPER LOWLAND
Tula
Ryazan'
Nizhniy Novgorod
URAL MOUNTAINS
Ob River
WEST SIBERIAN PLAIN
Urengoy
MOLDOVA
Chisinau
Kamsk Res.
Mt. Konzhakovskiy 5,147 ft. (1,569 m.)
Odessa
Nikolayev
Krivoy Rog
Kharkov
Don River
Voronezh
Dnepropetrovsk
Zaporozh'ye
Kuybyshev Res.
Ul'yanovsk
Kazan
Izhevsk
Perm
Kama R.
Ob
Vakh R.
Penza
Donetsk
Lugansk
VOLGA UPLAND
Saratov
Tol'yatti
Samara
Ufa
Yekaterinburg
Irtysh River
SEA OF AZOV
Mariupol
Rostov
Volgograd Reservoir
Chelyabinsk
Tobol R.
BLACK SEA
Volgograd
Tsimlyansk Res.
Ural R.
Orenburg
Ishim R.
Krasnodar
Omsk
L. Chany
Tomsk
Novosibirsk
Kemerovo
CAUCASUS MTS.
Mt. Elbrus 18,510 ft. (5,642 m.)
CASPIAN DEPRESSION
Astrakhan
KYRGYZ STEPPE
TURGAY PLATEAU
Novosibirsk Res.
Novokuznetsk
Barnaul
GEORGIA
Tbilisi
KAZAKSTAN
KAZAKH UPLAND
Karaganda
Semipalatinsk
Mt. Belukha 14,783 ft. (4,506 m.)
ARMENIA
Yerevan
AZERBAIJAN
CASPIAN SEA
ARAL SEA
Syr Darya
L. Zaysan
Baku
USTYURT PLATEAU
BETPAK-DALA DESERT
Kzyl-Orda
Lake Balkhash
PLAINS OF TURAN
KARA BOGAZ GOL GULF
TURKMENISTAN
UZBEKISTAN
Ili R.
L. Alakol
ASIA
KARAKUM DESERT
Ashkhabad
Amu Darya
Bishkek
Almaty
Tashkent
KYRGYZSTAN
L. Issyk-Kul
Samarkand
ALAY MOUNTAINS
Dushanbe
TAJIKISTAN
Communism Pk. 24,590 ft. (7,495 m.)
60°
70°
80°
50°
40°
30°
20°
10°
0°

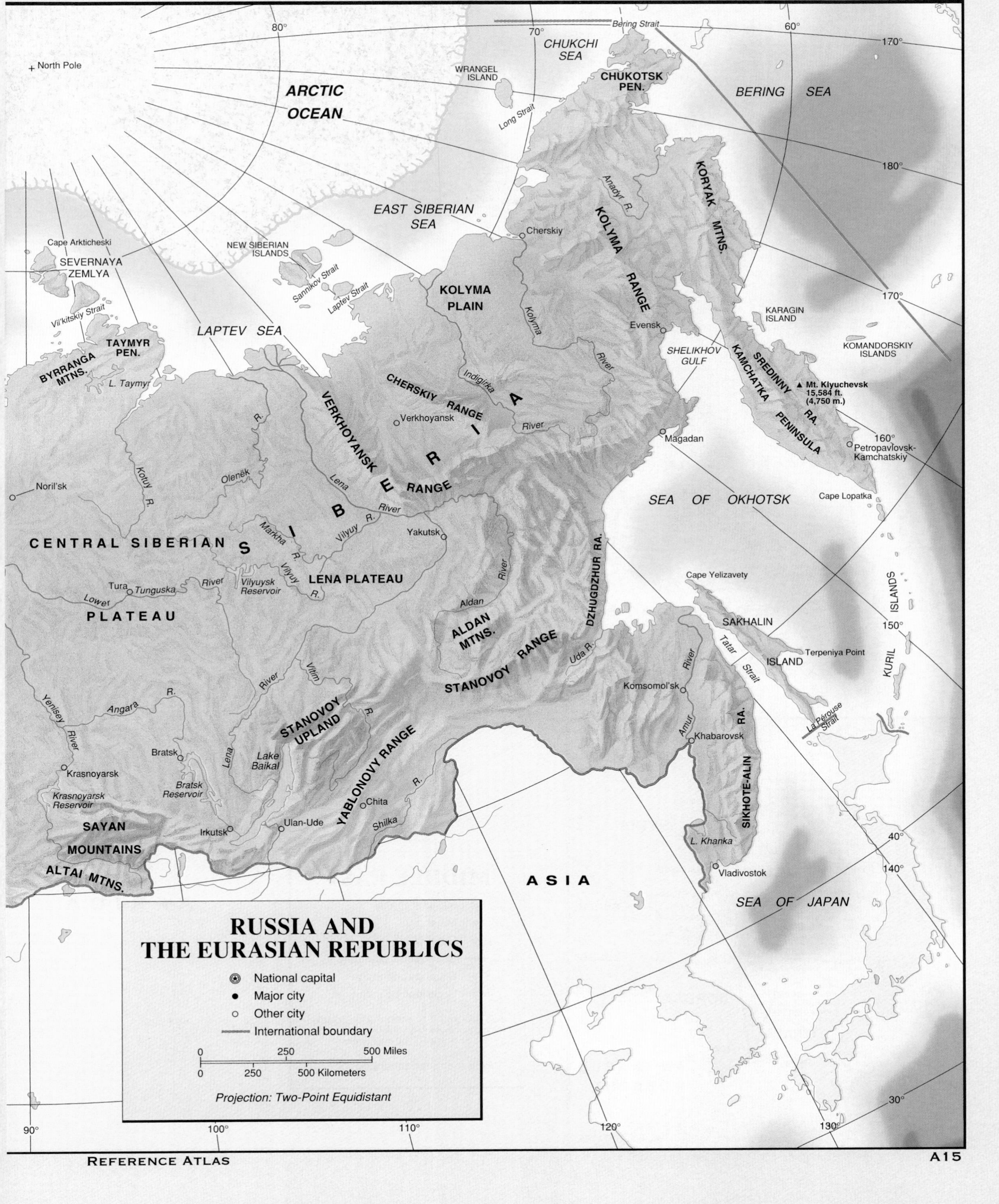

RUSSIA AND THE EURASIAN REPUBLICS
National capital
Major city
Other city
International boundary
0 250 500 Miles
0 250 500 Kilometers
Projection: Two-Point Equidistant
ARCTIC OCEAN
North Pole
CHUKCHI SEA
BERING SEA
EAST SIBERIAN SEA
LAPTEV SEA
SEA OF OKHOTSK
SEA OF JAPAN
ASIA
SIBERIA
CENTRAL SIBERIAN PLATEAU
LENA PLATEAU
KOLYMA PLAIN
VERKHOYANSK RANGE
CHERSKIY RANGE
KOLYMA RANGE
KORYAK MTNS.
SREDINNY RA.
KAMCHATKA PENINSULA
Mt. Klyuchevsk 15,584 ft. (4,750 m.)
DZHUGDZHUR RA.
ALDAN MTNS.
STANOVOY RANGE
STANOVOY UPLAND
YABLONOVY RANGE
SIKHOTE-ALIN RA.
SAYAN MOUNTAINS
ALTAI MTNS.
BYRRANGA MTNS.
TAYMYR PEN.
CHUKOTSK PEN.
SEVERNAYA ZEMLYA
Cape Arkticheski
NEW SIBERIAN ISLANDS
WRANGEL ISLAND
KARAGIN ISLAND
KOMANDORSKIY ISLANDS
KURIL ISLANDS
SAKHALIN ISLAND
SHELIKHOV GULF
Bering Strait
Long Strait
Sannikov Strait
Laptev Strait
Vil'kitskiy Strait
Tatar Strait
La Pérouse Strait
Cape Lopatka
Cape Yelizavety
Terpeniya Point
L. Taymyr
L. Khanka
Lake Baikal
Bratsk Reservoir
Krasnoyarsk Reservoir
Vilyuysk Reservoir
Lena River
Kolyma River
Indigirka River
Anadyr R.
Olenëk R.
Kotuy R.
Markha R.
Vilyuy R.
Lower Tunguska River
Aldan River
Uda R.
Amur River
Vitim River
Angara R.
Yenisey River
Shilka R.
Cherskiy
Verkhoyansk
Evensk
Magadan
Petropavlovsk-Kamchatskiy
Yakutsk
Noril'sk
Tura
Komsomol'sk
Khabarovsk
Vladivostok
Bratsk
Krasnoyarsk
Irkutsk
Ulan-Ude
Chita
80°
70°
60°
50°
40°
30°
170°
180°
160°
150°
140°
130°
120°
110°
100°
90°

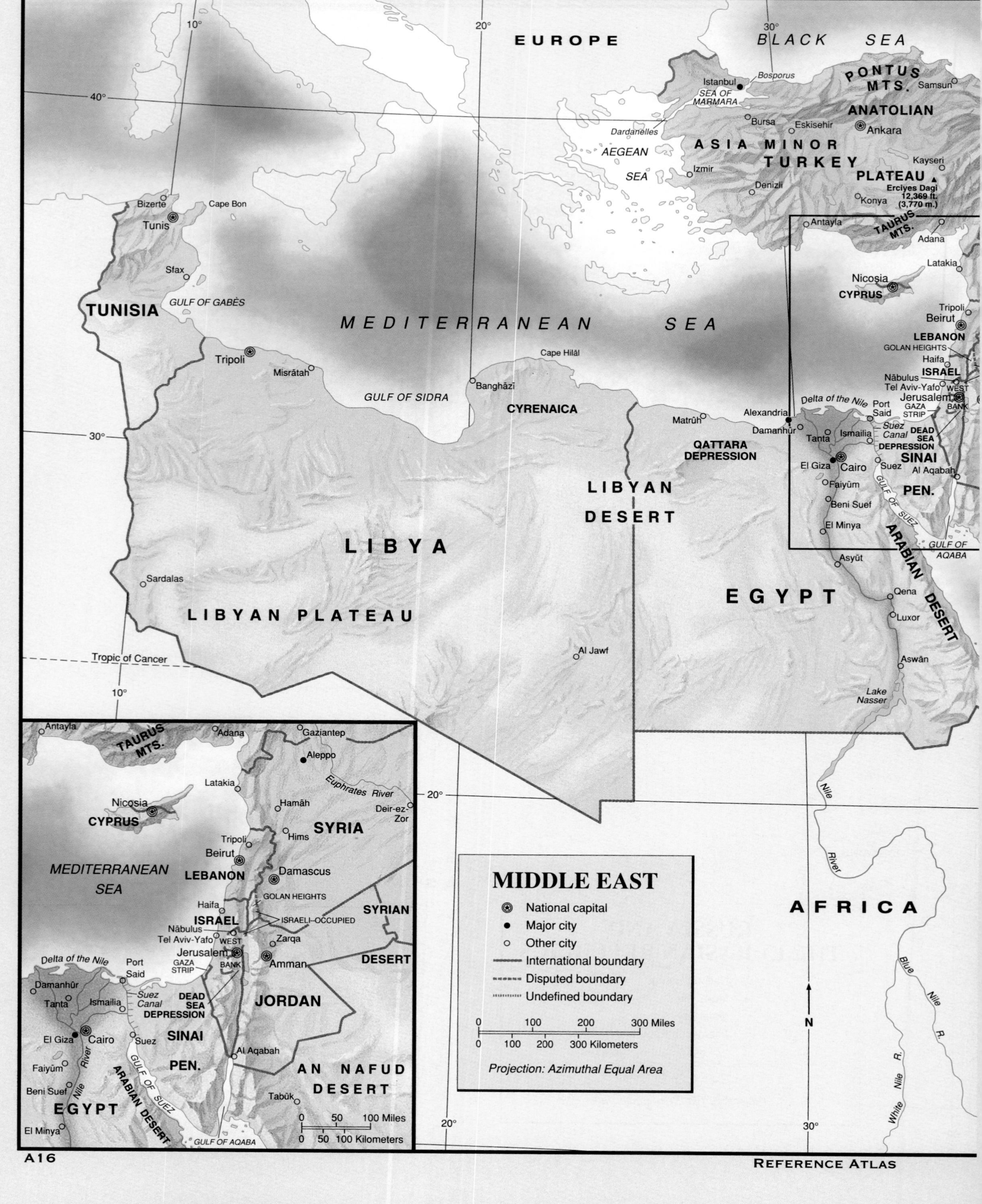
EUROPE
BLACK SEA
Istanbul
Bosporus
SEA OF MARMARA
PONTUS MTS.
Samsun
ANATOLIAN
Ankara
Bursa
Eskisehir
Dardanelles
AEGEAN SEA
ASIA MINOR
TURKEY
Izmir
Denizli
Kayseri
PLATEAU
Erciyes Dagi 12,369 ft. (3,770 m.)
Konya
Antayla
TAURUS MTS.
Adana
Latakia
Nicosia
CYPRUS
Tripoli
Beirut
LEBANON
GOLAN HEIGHTS
Haifa
ISRAEL
Nābulus
Tel Aviv-Yafo
WEST BANK
Jerusalem
GAZA STRIP
Delta of the Nile
Port Said
Suez Canal
Ismailia
DEAD SEA DEPRESSION
SINAI PEN.
Al Aqabah
Suez
Tanta
Damanhûr
Alexandria
El Giza
Cairo
Faiyûm
Beni Suef
El Minya
GULF OF SUEZ
GULF OF AQABA
ARABIAN DESERT
Asyût
Qena
Luxor
Aswân
Lake Nasser
Bizerte
Tunis
Cape Bon
Sfax
TUNISIA
GULF OF GABÈS
MEDITERRANEAN SEA
Tripoli
Misrātah
Cape Hilāl
Banghāzī
GULF OF SIDRA
CYRENAICA
Matrûh
QATTARA DEPRESSION
LIBYAN DESERT
LIBYA
EGYPT
Sardalas
LIBYAN PLATEAU
Al Jawf
Tropic of Cancer
Nile River
Blue Nile R.
White Nile R.
AFRICA
10°
20°
30°
40°
N
Gaziantep
Aleppo
Euphrates River
Hamāh
Deir-ez-Zor
Hims
SYRIA
Damascus
SYRIAN DESERT
ISRAELI-OCCUPIED
Zarqa
Amman
JORDAN
AN NAFUD DESERT
Tabūk
0 50 100 Miles
0 50 100 Kilometers
MIDDLE EAST
National capital
Major city
Other city
International boundary
Disputed boundary
Undefined boundary
0 100 200 300 Miles
0 100 200 300 Kilometers
Projection: Azimuthal Equal Area

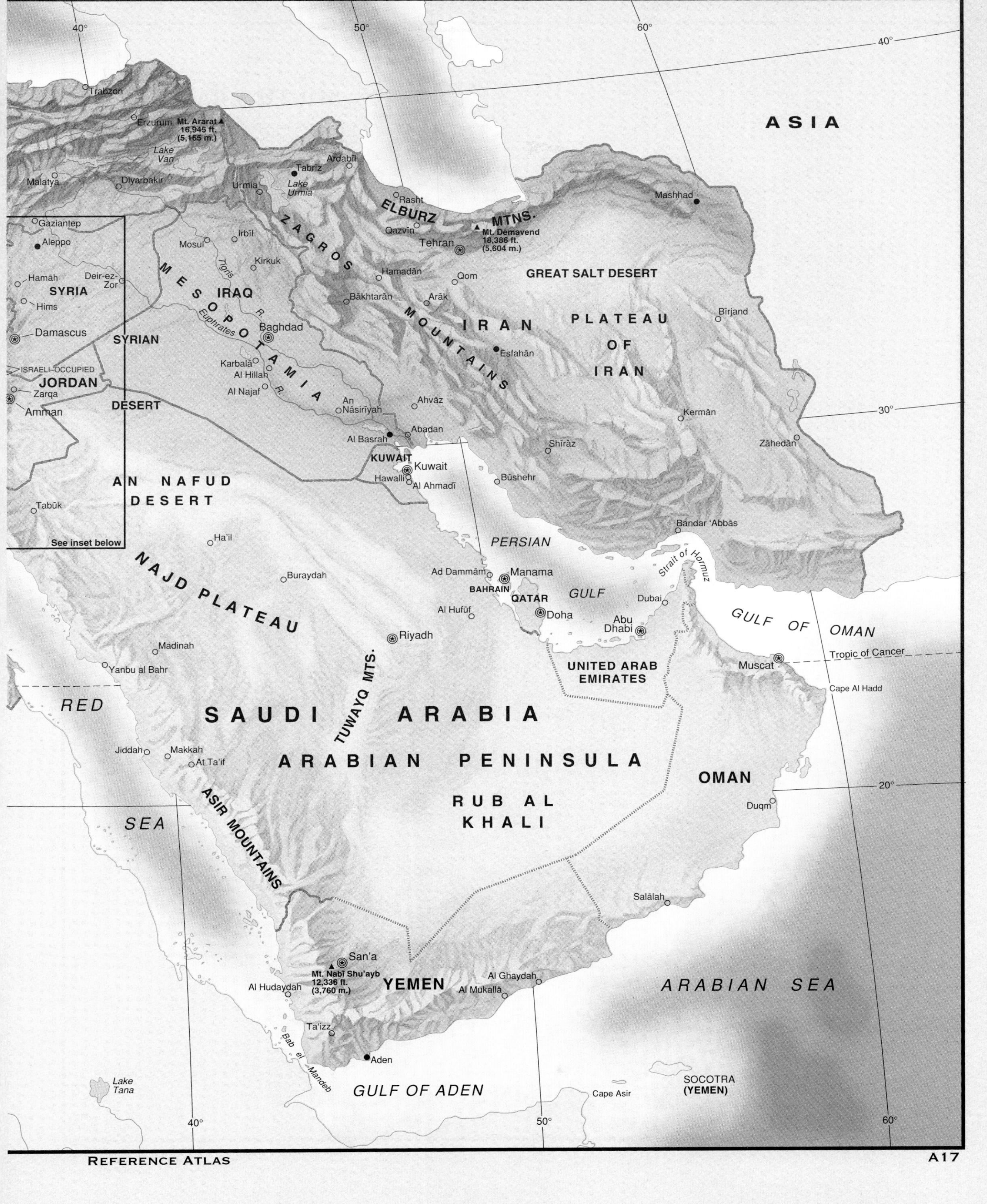
ASIA
Trabzon
Erzurum
Mt. Ararat
16,945 ft.
(5,165 m.)
Lake Van
Malatya
Diyarbakir
Tabriz
Ardabil
Urmia
Lake Urmia
Rasht
ELBURZ MTNS.
Mt. Demavend
18,386 ft.
(5,604 m.)
Mashhad
Qazvin
Tehran
Gaziantep
Aleppo
Mosul
Irbil
Kirkuk
ZAGROS MOUNTAINS
Hamadan
Qom
GREAT SALT DESERT
Hamah
Deir-ez-Zor
SYRIA
Hims
MESOPOTAMIA
IRAQ
Tigris R.
Euphrates R.
Bakhtaran
Arak
Birjand
Damascus
Baghdad
IRAN
PLATEAU OF IRAN
SYRIAN DESERT
Esfahan
ISRAELI-OCCUPIED
JORDAN
Karbala
Al Hillah
Zarqa
Amman
Al Najaf
An Nasiriyah
Ahvaz
Kerman
Al Basrah
Abadan
Zahedan
Shiraz
KUWAIT
Kuwait
Hawalli
Al Ahmadi
Bushehr
AN NAFUD DESERT
Tabuk
See inset below
Bandar 'Abbas
Ha'il
PERSIAN GULF
Strait of Hormuz
NAJD PLATEAU
Buraydah
Ad Dammam
Manama
BAHRAIN
QATAR
Doha
Dubai
Al Hufuf
Abu Dhabi
GULF OF OMAN
Riyadh
Madinah
Muscat
Tropic of Cancer
Yanbu al Bahr
TUWAYQ MTS.
UNITED ARAB EMIRATES
Cape Al Hadd
RED SEA
SAUDI ARABIA
Jiddah
Makkah
At Ta'if
ARABIAN PENINSULA
OMAN
ASIR MOUNTAINS
RUB AL KHALI
Duqm
Salalah
San'a
Mt. Nabi Shu'ayb
12,336 ft.
(3,760 m.)
Al Hudaydah
YEMEN
Al Ghaydah
Al Mukalla
ARABIAN SEA
Ta'izz
Bab el Mandeb
Aden
Lake Tana
GULF OF ADEN
Cape Asir
SOCOTRA
(YEMEN)
40°
50°
60°
30°
20°

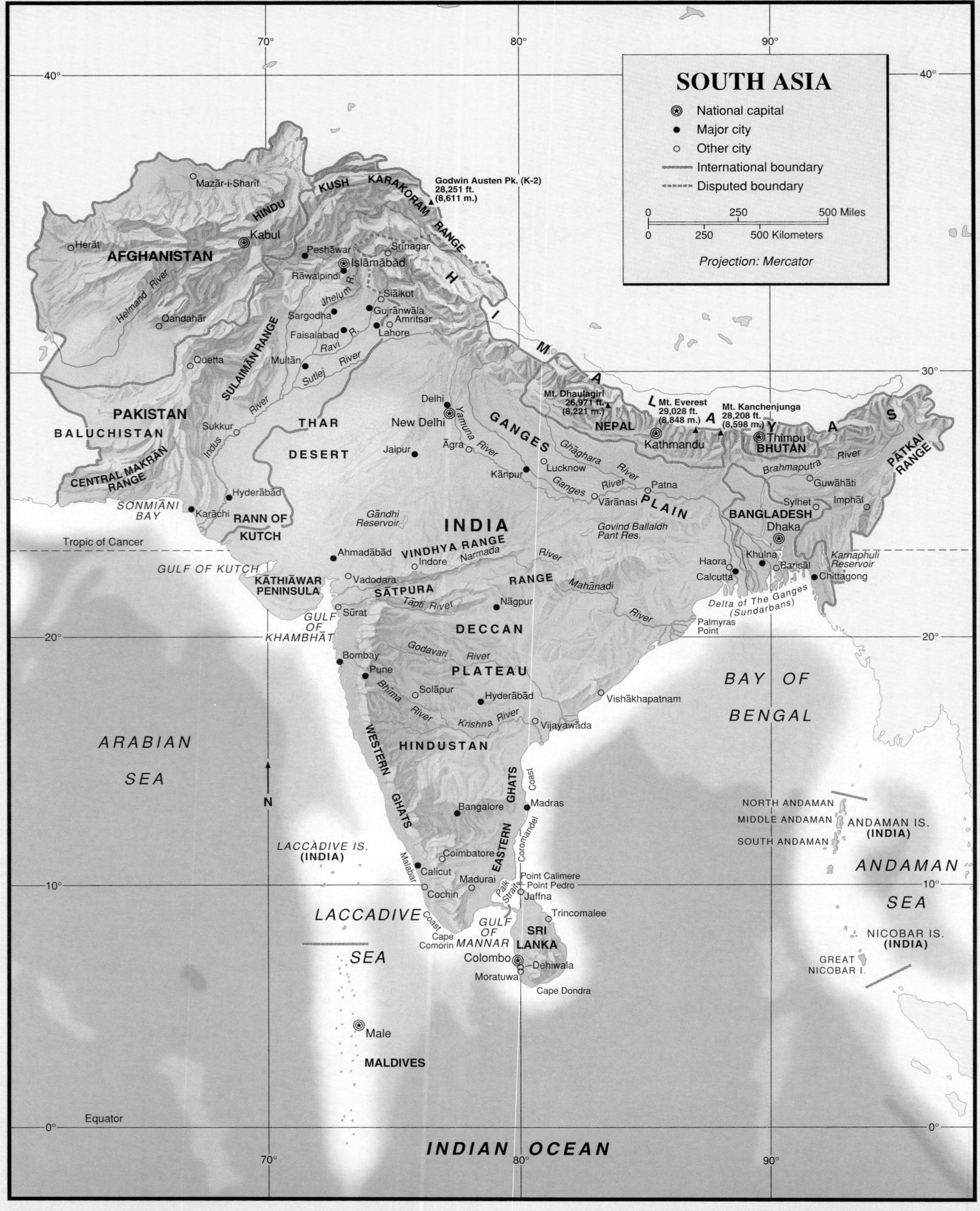

SOUTH ASIA
National capital
Major city
Other city
International boundary
Disputed boundary
0 250 500 Miles
0 250 500 Kilometers
Projection: Mercator
AFGHANISTAN
PAKISTAN
INDIA
NEPAL
BHUTAN
BANGLADESH
SRI LANKA
MALDIVES
Kabul
Islāmābād
New Delhi
Kathmandu
Thimpu
Dhaka
Colombo
Male
Mazār-i-Sharīf
Herāt
Qandahār
Quetta
Peshāwar
Rāwalpindi
Srinagar
Siālkot
Gujrānwāla
Amritsar
Sargodha
Faisalabad
Lahore
Multān
Sukkur
Hyderābād
Karāchi
Delhi
Jaipur
Āgra
Kānpur
Lucknow
Vārānasi
Patna
Guwāhāti
Imphāl
Sylhet
Haora
Calcutta
Khulna
Barisāl
Chittagong
Ahmadābād
Indore
Vadodara
Sūrat
Nāgpur
Bombay
Pune
Solāpur
Hyderābād
Vishākhapatnam
Vijayawāda
Bangalore
Madras
Coimbatore
Calicut
Madurai
Cochin
Jaffna
Trincomalee
Dehiwala
Moratuwa
Cape Dondra
Cape Comorin
Point Calimere
Point Pedro
Palmyras Point
Godwin Austen Pk. (K-2) 28,251 ft. (8,611 m.)
Mt. Dhaulagiri 26,971 ft. (8,221 m.)
Mt. Everest 29,028 ft. (8,848 m.)
Mt. Kanchenjunga 28,208 ft. (8,598 m.)
HINDU KUSH
KARAKORAM RANGE
H I M A L A Y A S
SULAIMAN RANGE
CENTRAL MAKRAN RANGE
BALUCHISTAN
THAR DESERT
RANN OF KUTCH
GANGES PLAIN
VINDHYA RANGE
SATPURA RANGE
DECCAN PLATEAU
HINDUSTAN
WESTERN GHATS
EASTERN GHATS
PĀTKAI RANGE
KATHIĀWAR PENINSULA
Helmand River
Jhelum R.
Ravi R.
Sutlej River
Indus River
Yamuna River
Ganges River
Ghāghara River
Brahmaputra River
Narmada River
Tāpti River
Mahānadi River
Godavari River
Bhima River
Krishna River
Gāndhi Reservoir
Govind Ballaldh Pant Res.
Karnaphuli Reservoir
Delta of The Ganges (Sundarbans)
Malabar Coast
Coromandel Coast
Palk Strait
GULF OF MANNAR
SONMIĀNI BAY
GULF OF KUTCH
GULF OF KHAMBHĀT
Tropic of Cancer
Equator
ARABIAN SEA
LACCADIVE IS. (INDIA)
LACCADIVE SEA
BAY OF BENGAL
ANDAMAN IS. (INDIA)
NORTH ANDAMAN
MIDDLE ANDAMAN
SOUTH ANDAMAN
ANDAMAN SEA
NICOBAR IS. (INDIA)
GREAT NICOBAR I.
INDIAN OCEAN
N
70°
80°
90°
40°
30°
20°
10°
0°

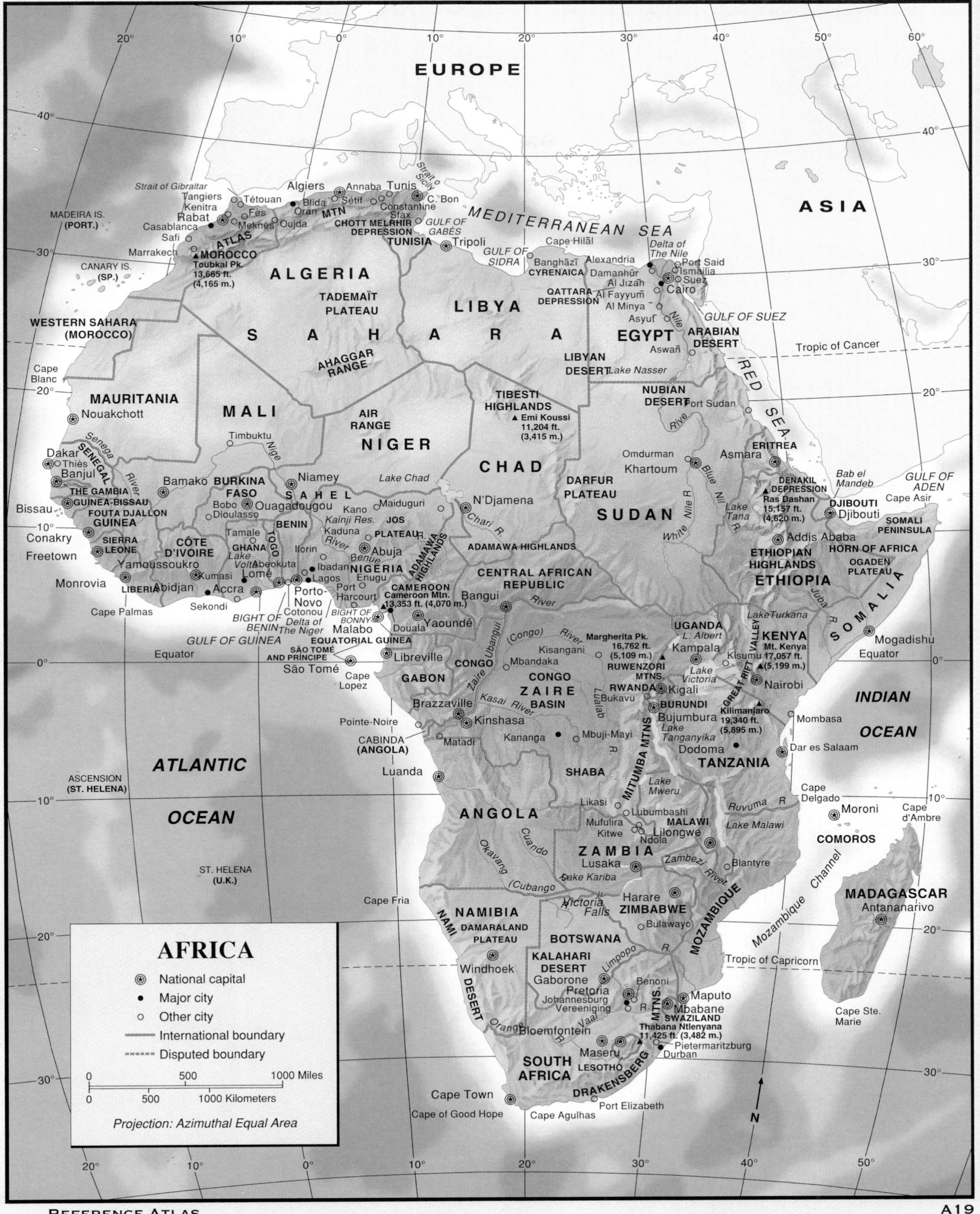
AFRICA
National capital
Major city
Other city
International boundary
Disputed boundary
0 500 1000 Miles
0 500 1000 Kilometers
Projection: Azimuthal Equal Area
EUROPE
ASIA
MEDITERRANEAN SEA
ATLANTIC OCEAN
INDIAN OCEAN
ALGERIA
LIBYA
EGYPT
MOROCCO
TUNISIA
WESTERN SAHARA (MOROCCO)
MAURITANIA
MALI
NIGER
CHAD
SUDAN
ERITREA
DJIBOUTI
ETHIOPIA
SOMALIA
KENYA
UGANDA
RWANDA
BURUNDI
TANZANIA
SENEGAL
THE GAMBIA
GUINEA-BISSAU
GUINEA
SIERRA LEONE
LIBERIA
CÔTE D'IVOIRE
BURKINA FASO
GHANA
TOGO
BENIN
NIGERIA
CAMEROON
CENTRAL AFRICAN REPUBLIC
EQUATORIAL GUINEA
SÃO TOMÉ AND PRÍNCIPE
GABON
CONGO
ZAIRE
ANGOLA
CABINDA (ANGOLA)
ZAMBIA
MALAWI
MOZAMBIQUE
ZIMBABWE
NAMIBIA
BOTSWANA
SOUTH AFRICA
LESOTHO
SWAZILAND
MADAGASCAR
COMOROS
MADEIRA IS. (PORT.)
CANARY IS. (SP.)
ASCENSION (ST. HELENA)
ST. HELENA (U.K.)
S A H A R A
SAHEL
Toubkal Pk. 13,665 ft. (4,165 m.)
Emi Koussi 11,204 ft. (3,415 m.)
Ras Dashan 15,157 ft. (4,620 m.)
Margherita Pk. 16,762 ft. (5,109 m.)
Mt. Kenya 17,057 ft. (5,199 m.)
Kilimanjaro 19,340 ft. (5,895 m.)
Cameroon Mtn. 13,353 ft. (4,070 m.)
Thabana Ntlenyana 11,425 ft. (3,482 m.)
Tropic of Cancer
Tropic of Capricorn
Equator
Cairo
Tripoli
Tunis
Algiers
Rabat
Khartoum
Addis Ababa
Nairobi
Kinshasa
Lusaka
Harare
Pretoria
Cape Town
Dakar
Lagos
Mogadishu
Antananarivo
REFERENCE ATLAS
A19

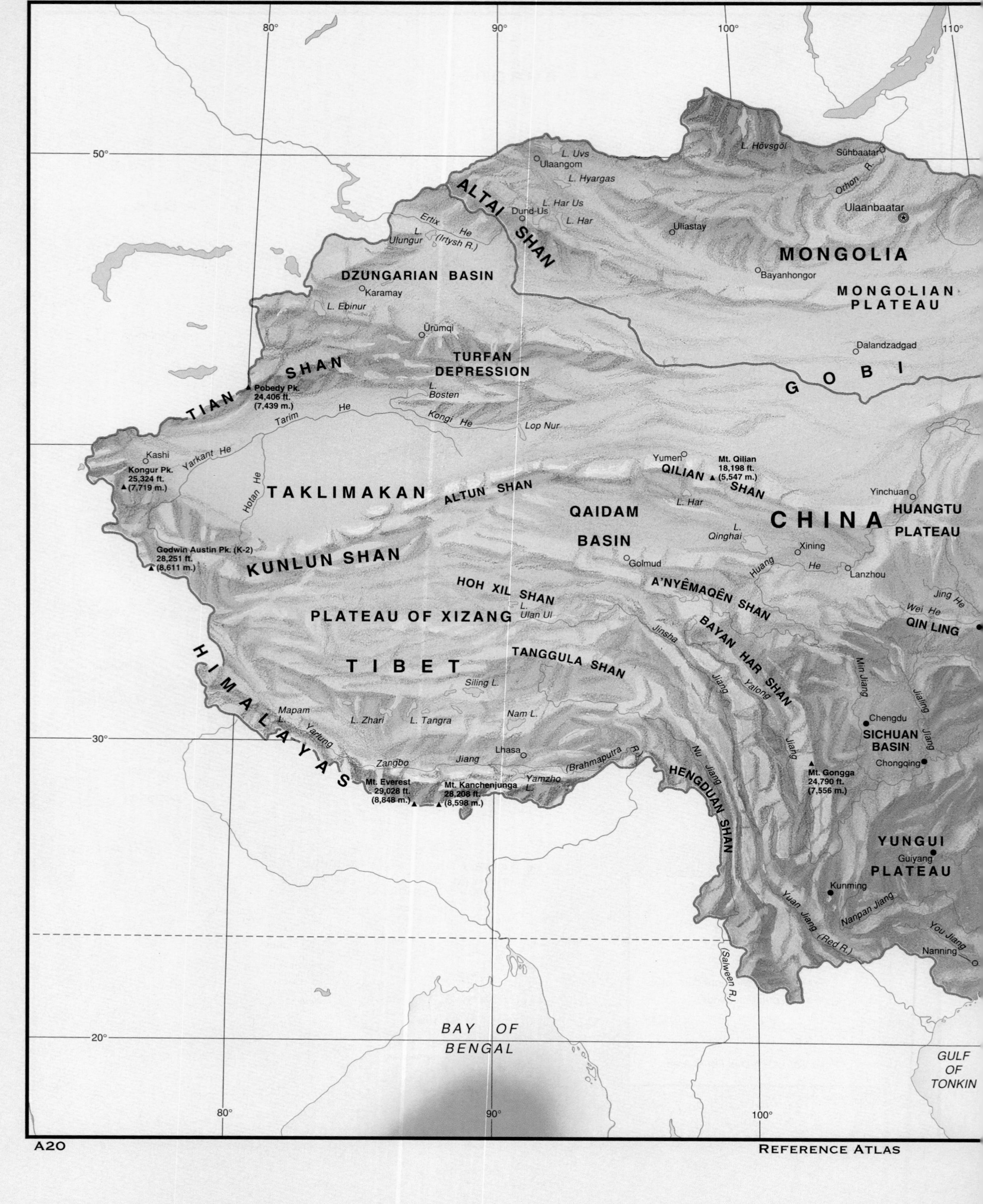

MONGOLIA
MONGOLIAN PLATEAU
GOBI
CHINA
ALTAI SHAN
DZUNGARIAN BASIN
TIAN SHAN
TURFAN DEPRESSION
TAKLIMAKAN
ALTUN SHAN
QILIAN SHAN
QAIDAM BASIN
HUANGTU PLATEAU
KUNLUN SHAN
HOH XIL SHAN
A'NYÊMAQÊN SHAN
PLATEAU OF XIZANG
TIBET
TANGGULA SHAN
BAYAN HAR SHAN
QIN LING
HIMALAYAS
HENGDUAN SHAN
SICHUAN BASIN
YUNGUI PLATEAU
BAY OF BENGAL
GULF OF TONKIN
Pobedy Pk. 24,406 ft. (7,439 m.)
Kongur Pk. 25,324 ft. (7,719 m.)
Godwin Austin Pk. (K-2) 28,251 ft. (8,611 m.)
Mt. Qilian 18,198 ft. (5,547 m.)
Mt. Everest 29,028 ft. (8,848 m.)
Mt. Kanchenjunga 28,208 ft. (8,598 m.)
Mt. Gongga 24,790 ft. (7,556 m.)
Ulaanbaatar
Sühbaatar
Ulaangom
Dund-Us
Uliastay
Bayanhongor
Dalandzadgad
Karamay
Ürümqi
Kashi
Yumen
Golmud
Xining
Lanzhou
Yinchuan
Lhasa
Chengdu
Chongqing
Guiyang
Kunming
Nanning
L. Hövsgöl
L. Uvs
L. Hyargas
L. Har Us
L. Har
L. Ulungur
Ertix He (Irtysh R.)
Orhon R.
L. Ebinur
L. Bosten
Tarim He
Kongi He
Lop Nur
Yarkant He
Hotan He
L. Har
L. Qinghai
Huang He
Jing He
Wei He
L. Ulan Ul
Jinsha Jiang
Yalong Jiang
Min Jiang
Jialing Jiang
Siling L.
Nam L.
Mapam L.
L. Zhari
L. Tangra
Yarlung Zangbo Jiang
(Brahmaputra R.)
Yamzho L.
Nu Jiang
(Salween R.)
Yuan Jiang (Red R.)
Nanpan Jiang
You Jiang
80°
90°
100°
110°
50°
30°
20°

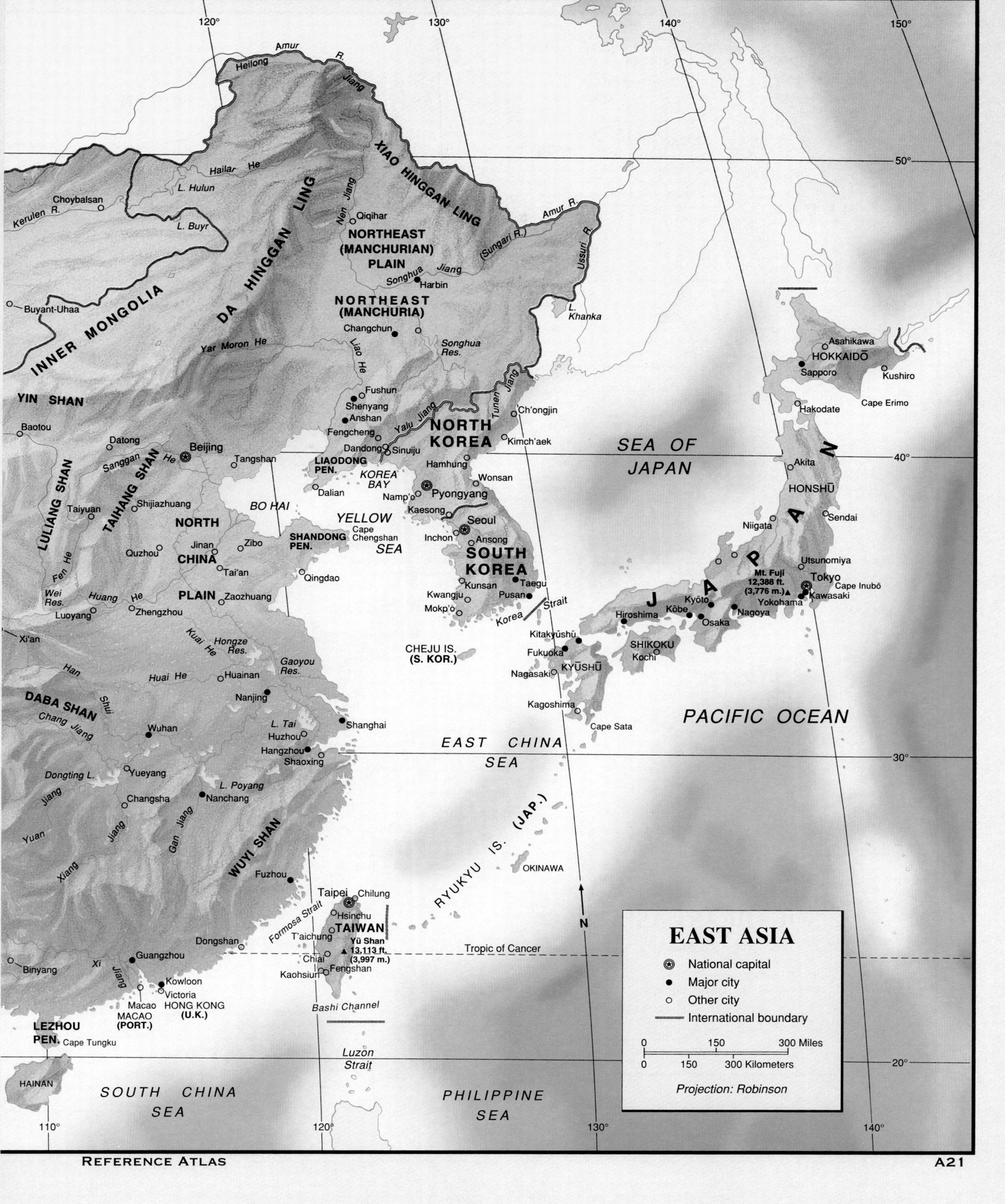
EAST ASIA
National capital
Major city
Other city
International boundary
0 150 300 Miles
0 150 300 Kilometers
Projection: Robinson
120°
130°
140°
150°
50°
40°
30°
20°
110°
Amur R.
Heilong Jiang
Hailar He
L. Hulun
Choybalsan
Kerulen R.
L. Buyr
DA HINGGAN LING
XIAO HINGGAN LING
Nen Jiang
Qiqihar
NORTHEAST (MANCHURIAN) PLAIN
Songhua Jiang
(Sungari R.)
Harbin
Ussuri R.
L. Khanka
NORTHEAST (MANCHURIA)
Changchun
Songhua Res.
Buyant-Uhaa
INNER MONGOLIA
Yar Moron He
Liao He
Fushun
Shenyang
Anshan
YIN SHAN
Baotou
Datong
Beijing
Sanggan He
Tangshan
TAIHANG SHAN
LULIANG SHAN
Taiyuan
Shijiazhuang
Fengcheng
Dandong
Sinuiju
Yalu Jiang
Tumen Jiang
Ch'ongjin
NORTH KOREA
Kimch'aek
Hamhung
LIAODONG PEN.
KOREA BAY
Dalian
Wonsan
Namp'o
Pyongyang
Kaesong
Seoul
Inchon
Ansong
BO HAI
NORTH CHINA PLAIN
Jinan
Zibo
Tai'an
Quzhou
SHANDONG PEN.
Cape Chengshan
YELLOW SEA
Qingdao
SOUTH KOREA
Kunsan
Taegu
Kwangju
Pusan
Mokp'o
Korea Strait
Fen He
Wei Res.
Huang He
Zhengzhou
Luoyang
Zaozhuang
Xi'an
Kuai He
Hongze Res.
Gaoyou Res.
Han Shui
Huai He
Huainan
Nanjing
DABA SHAN
Chang Jiang
Wuhan
L. Tai
Huzhou
Shanghai
Hangzhou
Shaoxing
Dongting L.
Yueyang
Changsha
L. Poyang
Nanchang
Xiang Jiang
Yuan Jiang
Gan Jiang
WUYI SHAN
Fuzhou
Taipei
Chilung
Hsinchu
TAIWAN
T'aichung
Yü Shan 13,113 ft. (3,997 m.)
Chiai
Fengshan
Kaohsiung
Formosa Strait
Dongshan
Guangzhou
Xi Jiang
Binyang
Kowloon
Victoria
Macao
MACAO (PORT.)
HONG KONG (U.K.)
LEZHOU PEN.
Cape Tungku
HAINAN
Bashi Channel
Luzon Strait
SOUTH CHINA SEA
PHILIPPINE SEA
Tropic of Cancer
CHEJU IS. (S. KOR.)
EAST CHINA SEA
RYUKYU IS. (JAP.)
OKINAWA
N
SEA OF JAPAN
PACIFIC OCEAN
JAPAN
HOKKAIDŌ
Asahikawa
Sapporo
Kushiro
Cape Erimo
Hakodate
Akita
HONSHŪ
Sendai
Niigata
Utsunomiya
Tokyo
Mt. Fuji 12,388 ft. (3,776 m.)
Cape Inubō
Yokohama
Kawasaki
Nagoya
Kyōto
Kōbe
Osaka
Hiroshima
SHIKOKU
Kochi
Kitakyūshū
Fukuoka
KYŪSHŪ
Nagasaki
Kagoshima
Cape Sata

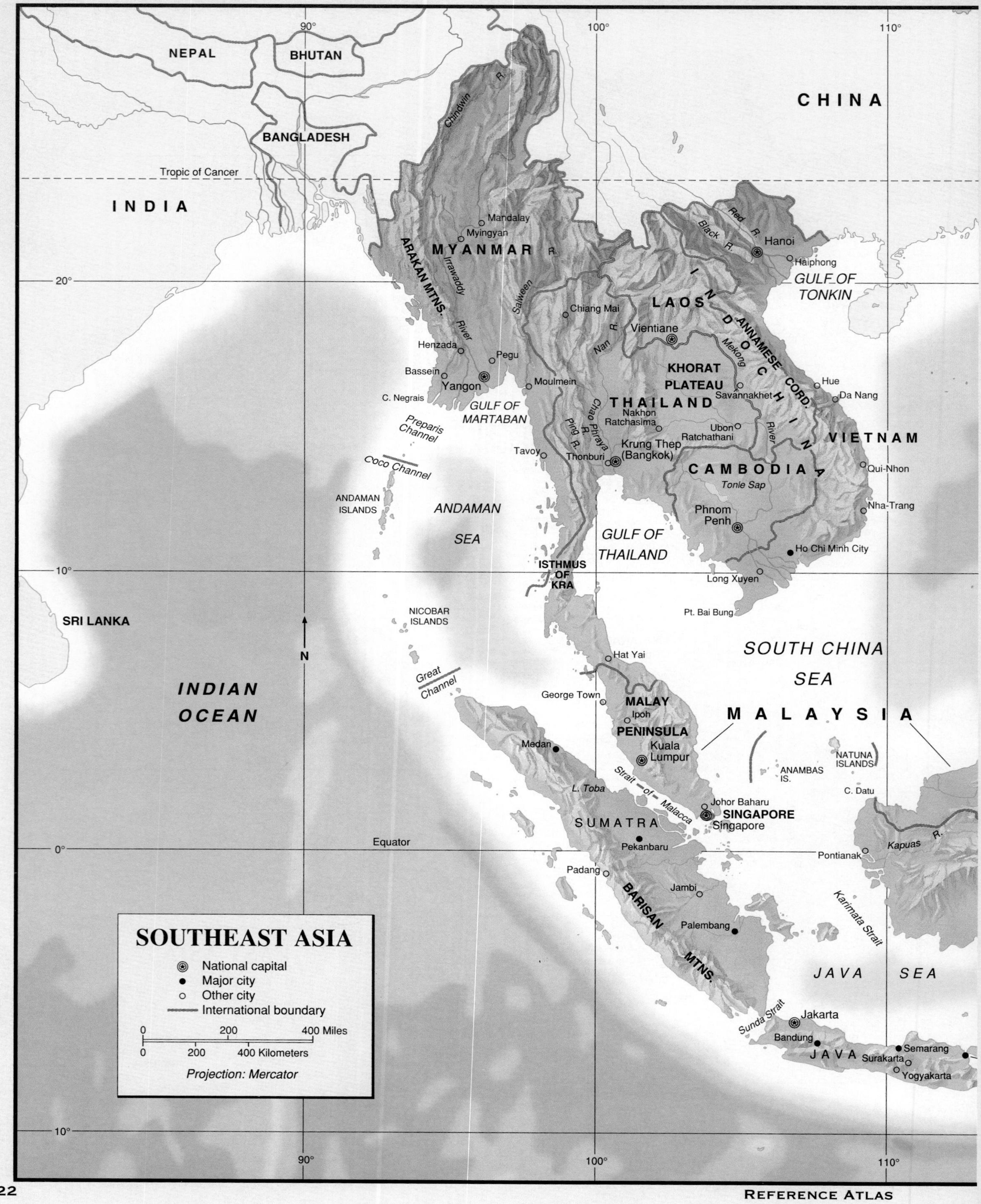
SOUTHEAST ASIA
National capital
Major city
Other city
International boundary
0 200 400 Miles
0 200 400 Kilometers
Projection: Mercator
NEPAL
BHUTAN
BANGLADESH
CHINA
INDIA
Tropic of Cancer
MYANMAR
ARAKAN MTNS.
Irrawaddy River
Chindwin R.
Salween R.
Mandalay
Myingyan
Henzada
Pegu
Bassein
Yangon
C. Negrais
GULF OF MARTABAN
Moulmein
Tavoy
Preparis Channel
Coco Channel
ANDAMAN ISLANDS
ANDAMAN SEA
LAOS
Vientiane
Chiang Mai
Nan R.
THAILAND
KHORAT PLATEAU
Nakhon Ratchasima
Chao Phraya R.
Ping R.
Thonburi
Krung Thep (Bangkok)
Ubon Ratchathani
Savannakhet
Mekong River
INDOCHINA
ANNAMESE CORD.
Red R.
Black R.
Hanoi
Haiphong
GULF OF TONKIN
Hue
Da Nang
VIETNAM
Qui-Nhon
Nha-Trang
Ho Chi Minh City
CAMBODIA
Tonle Sap
Phnom Penh
GULF OF THAILAND
Long Xuyen
Pt. Bai Bung
ISTHMUS OF KRA
NICOBAR ISLANDS
SRI LANKA
INDIAN OCEAN
N
Great Channel
SOUTH CHINA SEA
Hat Yai
George Town
MALAY PENINSULA
Ipoh
Kuala Lumpur
MALAYSIA
NATUNA ISLANDS
ANAMBAS IS.
C. Datu
Medan
L. Toba
Strait of Malacca
Johor Baharu
SINGAPORE
Singapore
SUMATRA
Pekanbaru
Equator
Pontianak
Kapuas R.
Padang
Jambi
BARISAN MTNS.
Palembang
Karimata Strait
JAVA SEA
Sunda Strait
Jakarta
Bandung
JAVA
Semarang
Surakarta
Yogyakarta
90°
100°
110°
20°
10°
0°
10°

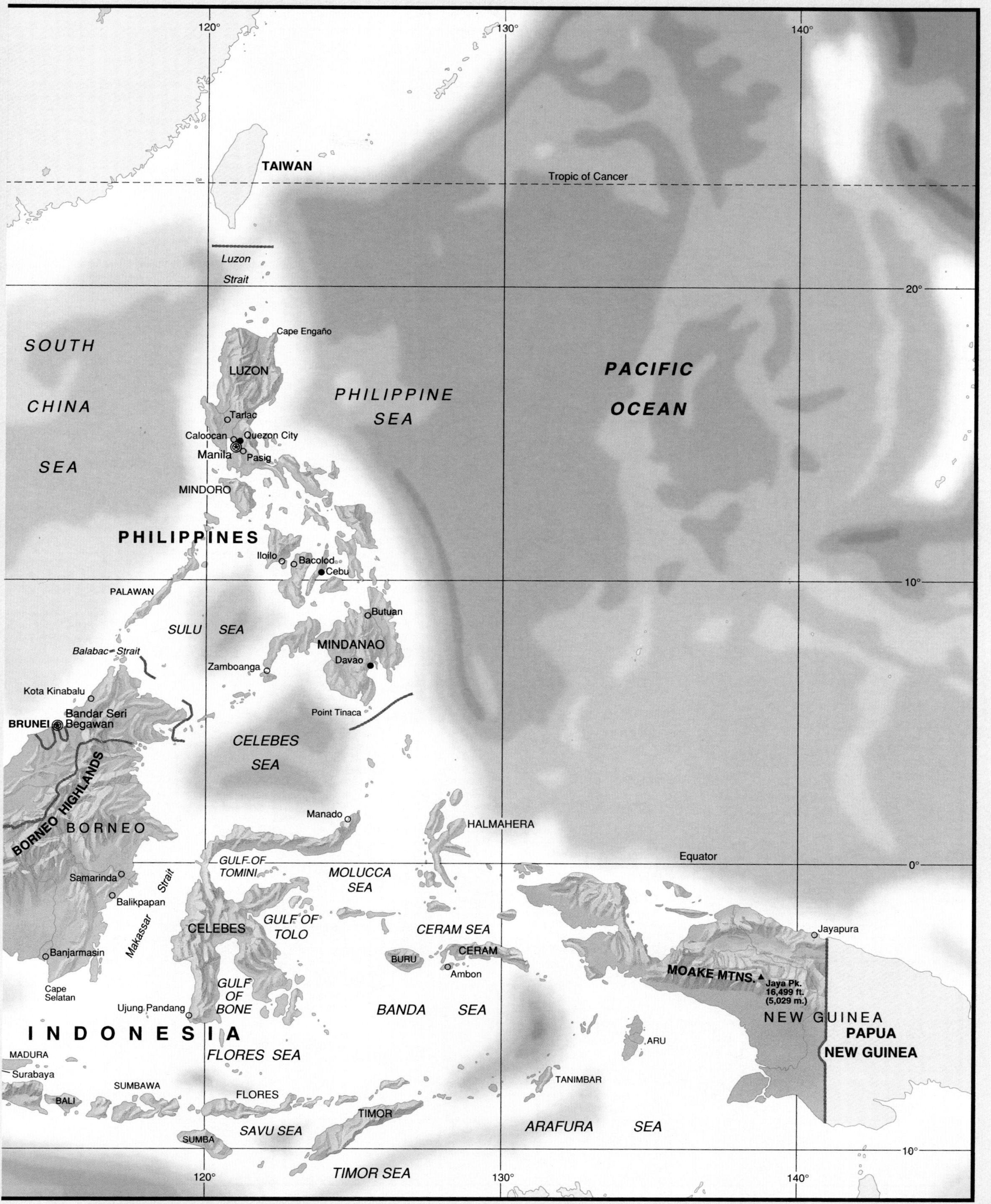
120°
130°
140°
TAIWAN
Tropic of Cancer
Luzon
Strait
20°
Cape Engaño
SOUTH
CHINA
SEA
LUZON
PHILIPPINE
SEA
PACIFIC
OCEAN
Tarlac
Caloocan
Quezon City
Manila
Pasig
MINDORO
PHILIPPINES
Iloilo
Bacolod
Cebu
10°
PALAWAN
Butuan
SULU SEA
MINDANAO
Balabac Strait
Zamboanga
Davao
Kota Kinabalu
Point Tinaca
BRUNEI
Bandar Seri Begawan
CELEBES
SEA
BORNEO HIGHLANDS
Manado
BORNEO
HALMAHERA
Equator
GULF OF
TOMINI
MOLUCCA
SEA
0°
Samarinda
Strait
Balikpapan
Makassar
CELEBES
GULF OF
TOLO
CERAM SEA
Jayapura
Banjarmasin
BURU
CERAM
Ambon
MOAKE MTNS.
Jaya Pk.
16,499 ft.
(5,029 m.)
Cape
Selatan
GULF
OF
BONE
Ujung Pandang
BANDA SEA
NEW GUINEA
INDONESIA
PAPUA
NEW GUINEA
ARU
MADURA
FLORES SEA
Surabaya
SUMBAWA
TANIMBAR
BALI
FLORES
TIMOR
ARAFURA SEA
SUMBA
SAVU SEA
10°
TIMOR SEA

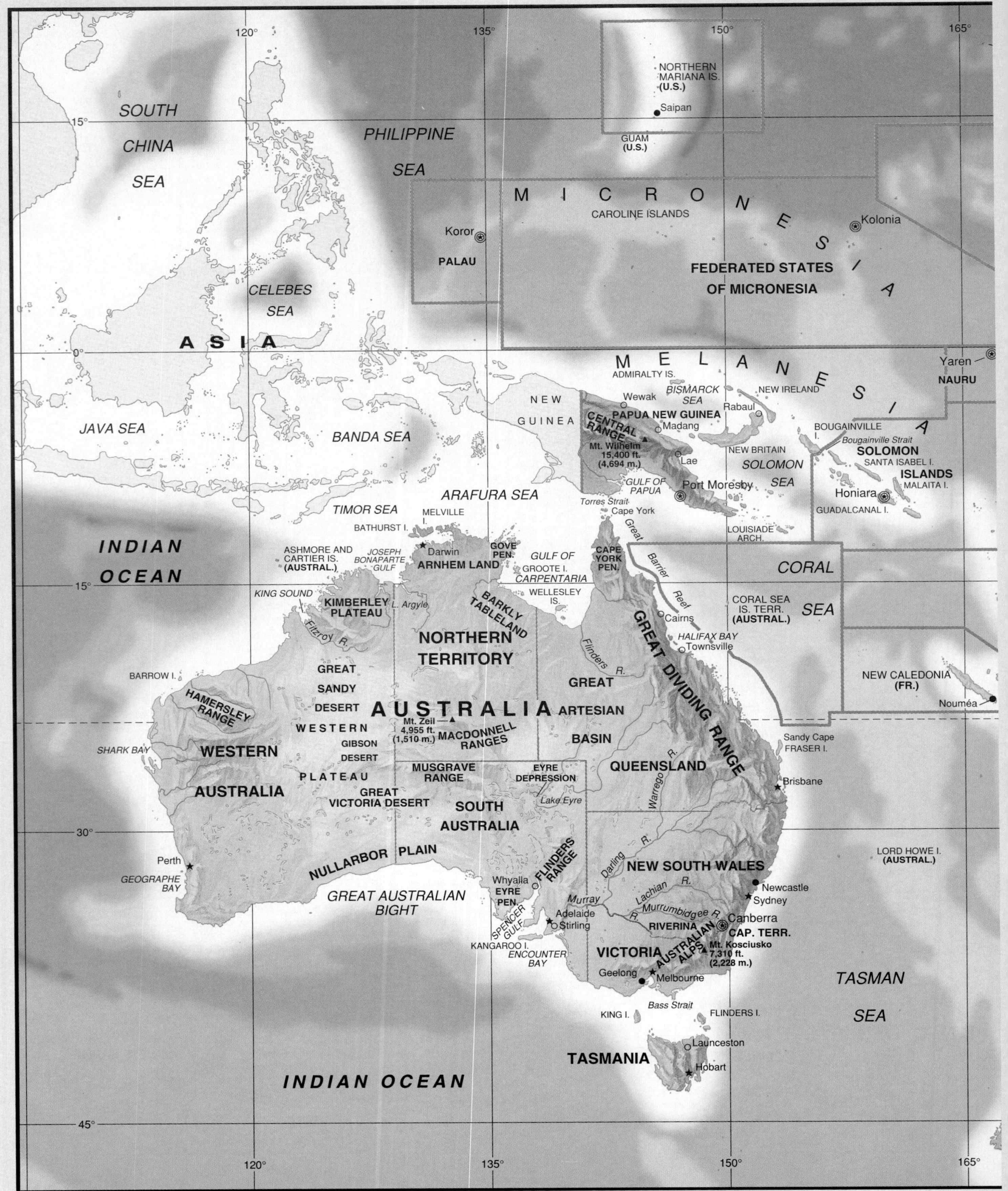
SOUTH CHINA SEA
PHILIPPINE SEA
NORTHERN MARIANA IS. (U.S.)
Saipan
GUAM (U.S.)
MICRONESIA
CAROLINE ISLANDS
Koror
PALAU
Kolonia
FEDERATED STATES OF MICRONESIA
CELEBES SEA
ASIA
MELANESIA
ADMIRALTY IS.
BISMARCK SEA
NEW IRELAND
Yaren
NAURU
Wewak
NEW GUINEA
PAPUA NEW GUINEA
Madang
Rabaul
CENTRAL RANGE
Mt. Wilhelm 15,400 ft. (4,694 m.)
Lae
NEW BRITAIN
BOUGAINVILLE I.
Bougainville Strait
SOLOMON ISLANDS
SANTA ISABEL I.
MALAITA I.
SOLOMON SEA
Honiara
GUADALCANAL I.
JAVA SEA
BANDA SEA
ARAFURA SEA
GULF OF PAPUA
Port Moresby
Torres Strait
Cape York
LOUISIADE ARCH.
TIMOR SEA
MELVILLE I.
BATHURST I.
Darwin
INDIAN OCEAN
ASHMORE AND CARTIER IS. (AUSTRAL.)
JOSEPH BONAPARTE GULF
ARNHEM LAND
GOVE PEN.
GULF OF CARPENTARIA
GROOTE I.
CAPE YORK PEN.
Great Barrier Reef
CORAL SEA
KING SOUND
KIMBERLEY PLATEAU
L. Argyle
BARKLY TABLELAND
WELLESLEY IS.
Cairns
CORAL SEA IS. TERR. (AUSTRAL.)
Fitzroy R.
NORTHERN TERRITORY
HALIFAX BAY
Townsville
GREAT DIVIDING RANGE
Flinders R.
BARROW I.
GREAT SANDY DESERT
GREAT ARTESIAN BASIN
NEW CALEDONIA (FR.)
Nouméa
HAMERSLEY RANGE
AUSTRALIA
Mt. Zeil 4,955 ft. (1,510 m.)
MACDONNELL RANGES
WESTERN PLATEAU
GIBSON DESERT
SHARK BAY
WESTERN AUSTRALIA
Sandy Cape
FRASER I.
MUSGRAVE RANGE
EYRE DEPRESSION
QUEENSLAND
Warrego R.
Brisbane
GREAT VICTORIA DESERT
SOUTH AUSTRALIA
Lake Eyre
LORD HOWE I. (AUSTRAL.)
Perth
GEOGRAPHE BAY
NULLARBOR PLAIN
FLINDERS RANGE
Darling R.
NEW SOUTH WALES
Whyalla
EYRE PEN.
Newcastle
GREAT AUSTRALIAN BIGHT
Murray R.
Lachlan R.
Sydney
Murrumbidgee R.
SPENCER GULF
Adelaide
Stirling
RIVERINA
Canberra
CAP. TERR.
KANGAROO I.
ENCOUNTER BAY
VICTORIA
AUSTRALIAN ALPS
Mt. Kosciusko 7,310 ft. (2,228 m.)
Geelong
Melbourne
TASMAN SEA
Bass Strait
KING I.
FLINDERS I.
Launceston
TASMANIA
Hobart
INDIAN OCEAN
120°
135°
150°
165°
15°
0°
15°
30°
45°

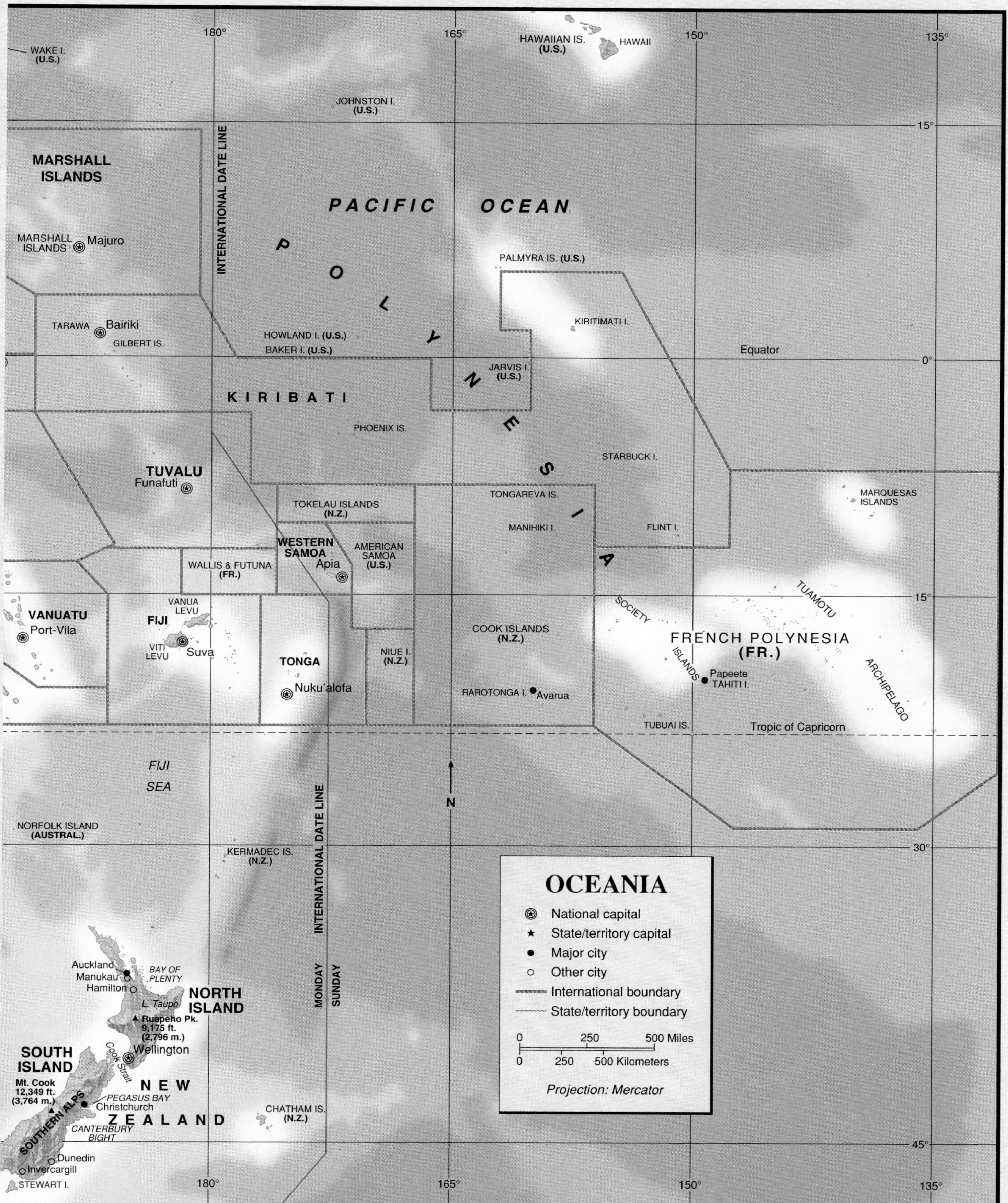
OCEANIA
National capital
State/territory capital
Major city
Other city
International boundary
State/territory boundary
0 250 500 Miles
0 250 500 Kilometers
Projection: Mercator
PACIFIC OCEAN
POLYNESIA
WAKE I. (U.S.)
HAWAIIAN IS. (U.S.)
HAWAII
JOHNSTON I. (U.S.)
MARSHALL ISLANDS
MARSHALL ISLANDS
Majuro
INTERNATIONAL DATE LINE
PALMYRA IS. (U.S.)
KIRITIMATI I.
TARAWA
Bairiki
GILBERT IS.
HOWLAND I. (U.S.)
BAKER I. (U.S.)
JARVIS I. (U.S.)
Equator
KIRIBATI
PHOENIX IS.
STARBUCK I.
TUVALU
Funafuti
TOKELAU ISLANDS (N.Z.)
TONGAREVA IS.
MARQUESAS ISLANDS
MANIHIKI I.
FLINT I.
WESTERN SAMOA
Apia
AMERICAN SAMOA (U.S.)
WALLIS & FUTUNA (FR.)
VANUATU
Port-Vila
VANUA LEVU
FIJI
VITI LEVU
Suva
TONGA
Nuku'alofa
NIUE I. (N.Z.)
COOK ISLANDS (N.Z.)
RAROTONGA I.
Avarua
SOCIETY ISLANDS
TUAMOTU ARCHIPELAGO
FRENCH POLYNESIA (FR.)
Papeete
TAHITI I.
TUBUAI IS.
Tropic of Capricorn
FIJI SEA
N
NORFOLK ISLAND (AUSTRAL.)
KERMADEC IS. (N.Z.)
INTERNATIONAL DATE LINE
MONDAY
SUNDAY
Auckland
Manukau
Hamilton
BAY OF PLENTY
NORTH ISLAND
L. Taupo
Ruapeho Pk. 9,175 ft. (2,796 m.)
Wellington
Cook Strait
SOUTH ISLAND
Mt. Cook 12,349 ft. (3,764 m.)
SOUTHERN ALPS
PEGASUS BAY
Christchurch
NEW ZEALAND
CANTERBURY BIGHT
CHATHAM IS. (N.Z.)
Dunedin
Invercargill
STEWART I.
180°
165°
150°
135°
15°
0°
15°
30°
45°

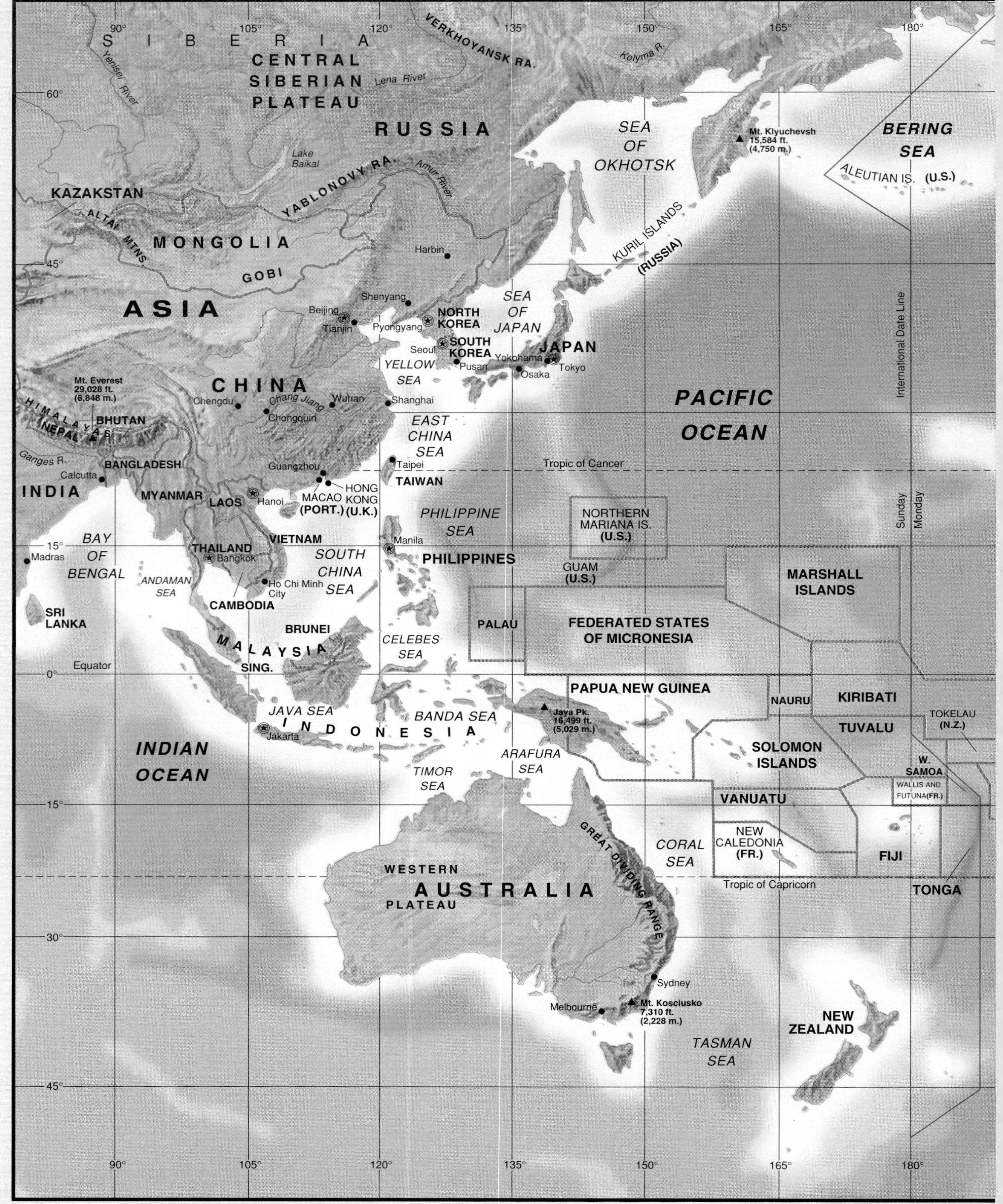

SIBERIA
CENTRAL SIBERIAN PLATEAU
Yenisei River
Lena River
VERKHOYANSK RA.
Kolyma R.
RUSSIA
SEA OF OKHOTSK
Mt. Klyuchevsh 15,584 ft. (4,750 m.)
BERING SEA
ALEUTIAN IS. (U.S.)
Lake Baikal
YABLONOVY RA.
Amur River
KAZAKSTAN
ALTAI MTNS.
MONGOLIA
GOBI
Harbin
KURIL ISLANDS (RUSSIA)
ASIA
Shenyang
Beijing
Tianjin
Pyongyang
NORTH KOREA
SEA OF JAPAN
Seoul
SOUTH KOREA
Pusan
JAPAN
Yokohama
Tokyo
Osaka
YELLOW SEA
International Date Line
Mt. Everest 29,028 ft. (8,848 m.)
CHINA
Chengdu
Chang Jiang
Wuhan
Shanghai
Chongquin
PACIFIC OCEAN
HIMALAYAS
BHUTAN
NEPAL
EAST CHINA SEA
Ganges R.
BANGLADESH
Guangzhou
Taipei
Tropic of Cancer
Calcutta
TAIWAN
INDIA
MYANMAR
LAOS
Hanoi
MACAO (PORT.)
HONG KONG (U.K.)
PHILIPPINE SEA
NORTHERN MARIANA IS. (U.S.)
Sunday
Monday
BAY OF BENGAL
Madras
THAILAND
Bangkok
VIETNAM
SOUTH CHINA SEA
Manila
PHILIPPINES
GUAM (U.S.)
MARSHALL ISLANDS
ANDAMAN SEA
Ho Chi Minh City
CAMBODIA
SRI LANKA
BRUNEI
PALAU
FEDERATED STATES OF MICRONESIA
MALAYSIA
CELEBES SEA
Equator
SING.
PAPUA NEW GUINEA
NAURU
KIRIBATI
JAVA SEA
INDONESIA
Jakarta
BANDA SEA
Jaya Pk. 16,499 ft. (5,029 m.)
TOKELAU (N.Z.)
TUVALU
SOLOMON ISLANDS
INDIAN OCEAN
ARAFURA SEA
TIMOR SEA
W. SAMOA
WALLIS AND FUTUNA(FR.)
VANUATU
GREAT DIVIDING RANGE
CORAL SEA
NEW CALEDONIA (FR.)
FIJI
WESTERN PLATEAU
AUSTRALIA
Tropic of Capricorn
TONGA
Sydney
Mt. Kosciusko 7,310 ft. (2,228 m.)
Melbourne
NEW ZEALAND
TASMAN SEA
60°
45°
15°
0°
15°
30°
45°
90°
105°
120°
135°
150°
165°
180°

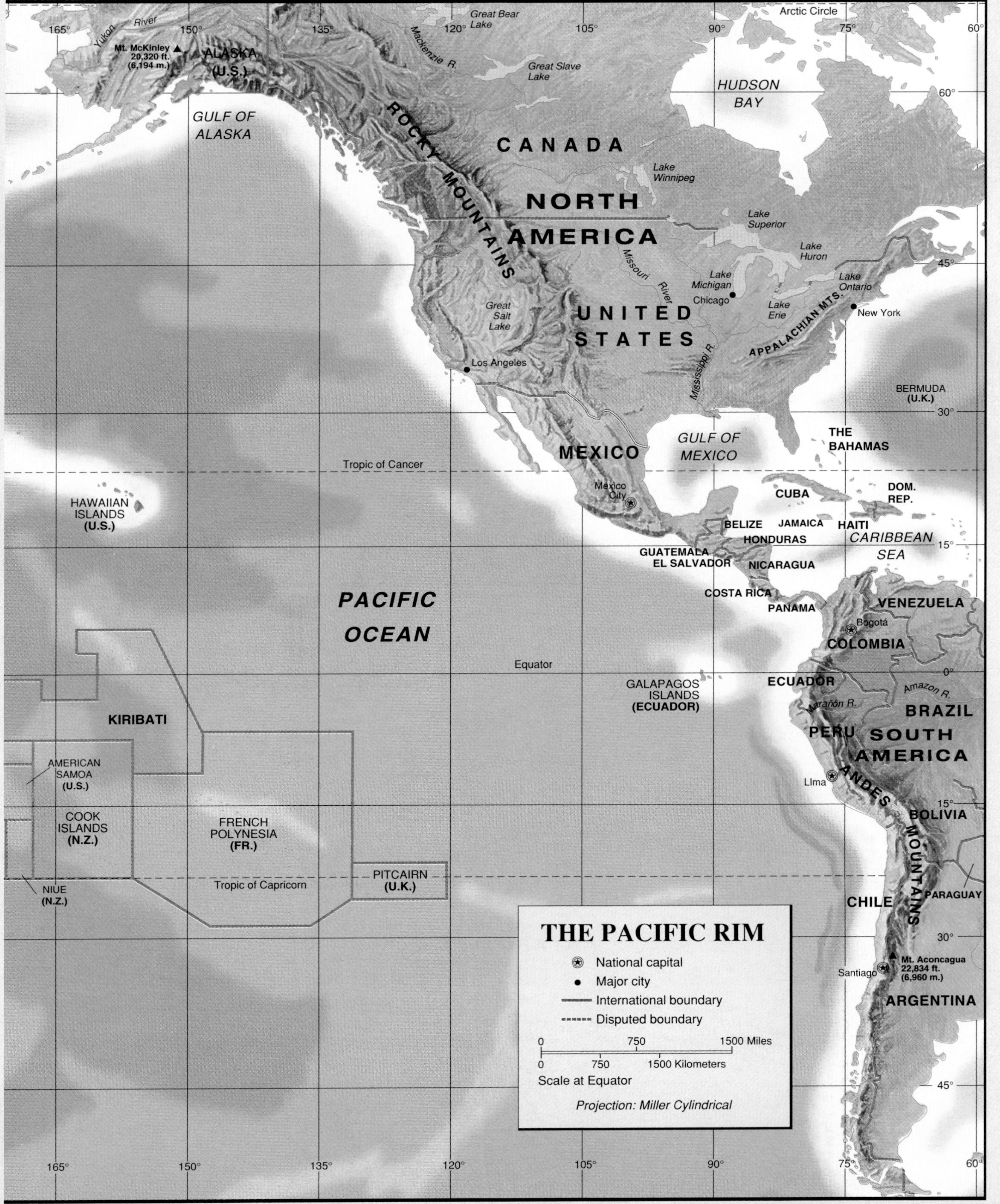
THE PACIFIC RIM
National capital
Major city
International boundary
Disputed boundary
0 750 1500 Miles
0 750 1500 Kilometers
Scale at Equator
Projection: Miller Cylindrical
NORTH AMERICA
CANADA
UNITED STATES
MEXICO
ALASKA (U.S.)
Mt. McKinley 20,320 ft. (6,194 m.)
Yukon River
Mackenzie R.
Great Bear Lake
Great Slave Lake
HUDSON BAY
Arctic Circle
GULF OF ALASKA
ROCKY MOUNTAINS
Lake Winnipeg
Lake Superior
Lake Huron
Lake Michigan
Lake Ontario
Lake Erie
Missouri River
Mississippi R.
APPALACHIAN MTS.
Great Salt Lake
Chicago
New York
Los Angeles
BERMUDA (U.K.)
GULF OF MEXICO
THE BAHAMAS
Tropic of Cancer
Mexico City
CUBA
DOM. REP.
HAITI
JAMAICA
BELIZE
HONDURAS
GUATEMALA
EL SALVADOR
NICARAGUA
COSTA RICA
PANAMA
CARIBBEAN SEA
HAWAIIAN ISLANDS (U.S.)
PACIFIC OCEAN
Equator
GALAPAGOS ISLANDS (ECUADOR)
VENEZUELA
Bogotá
COLOMBIA
ECUADOR
Amazon R.
Marañón R.
BRAZIL
PERU
SOUTH AMERICA
Lima
ANDES MOUNTAINS
BOLIVIA
PARAGUAY
CHILE
Mt. Aconcagua 22,834 ft. (6,960 m.)
Santiago
ARGENTINA
KIRIBATI
AMERICAN SAMOA (U.S.)
COOK ISLANDS (N.Z.)
FRENCH POLYNESIA (FR.)
PITCAIRN (U.K.)
NIUE (N.Z.)
Tropic of Capricorn
165° 150° 135° 120° 105° 90° 75° 60°
60° 45° 30° 15° 0° 15° 30° 45° 60°

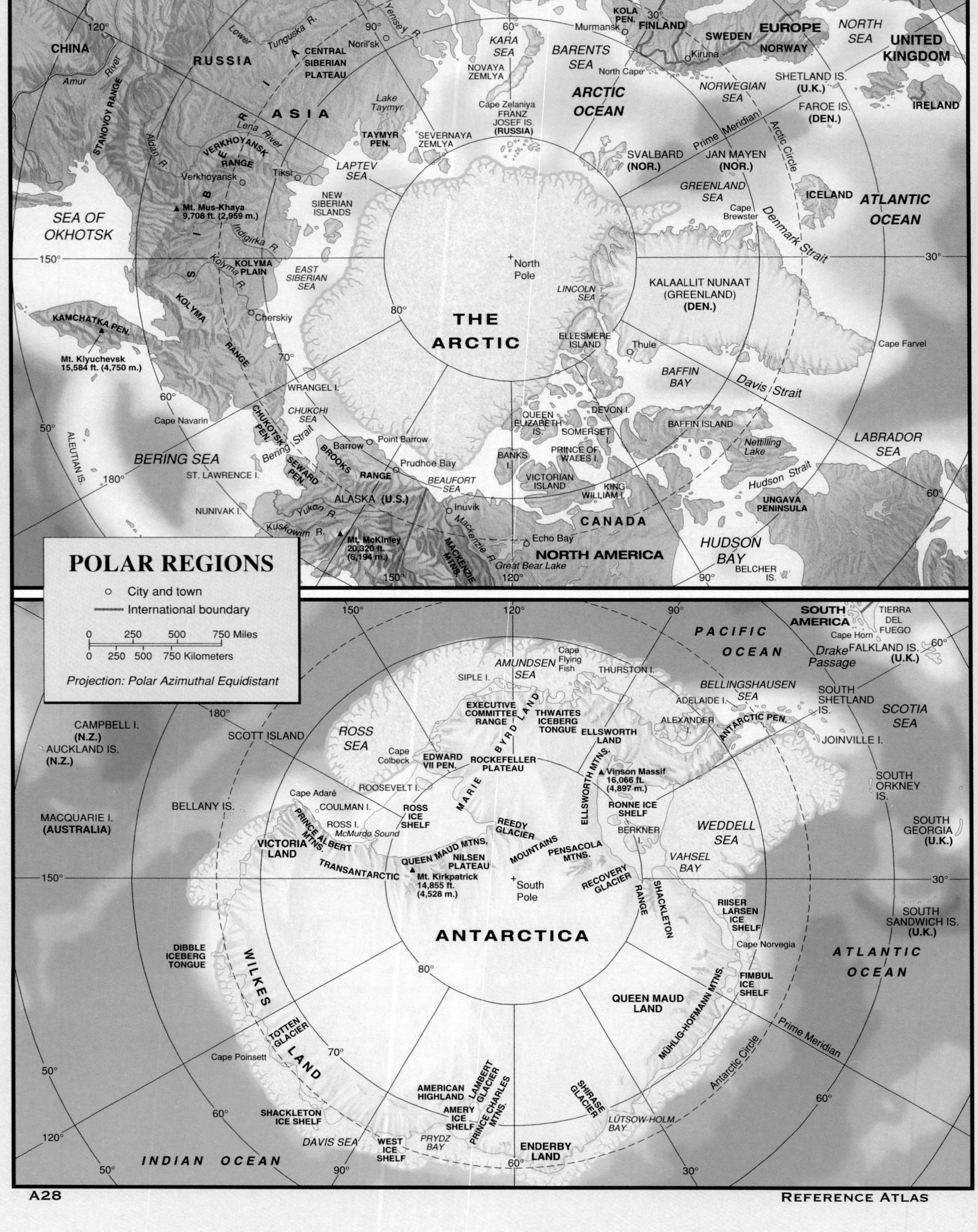
POLAR REGIONS
City and town
International boundary
0 250 500 750 Miles
0 250 500 750 Kilometers
Projection: Polar Azimuthal Equidistant
THE ARCTIC
North Pole
CHINA
RUSSIA
ASIA
SIBERIA
CENTRAL SIBERIAN PLATEAU
STANOVOY RANGE
VERKHOYANSK RANGE
Verkhoyansk
Mt. Mus-Khaya 9,708 ft. (2,959 m.)
SEA OF OKHOTSK
KOLYMA PLAIN
KOLYMA RANGE
KAMCHATKA PEN.
Mt. Klyuchevsk 15,584 ft. (4,750 m.)
Cherskiy
Tiksi
Noril'sk
Lake Taymyr
TAYMYR PEN.
SEVERNAYA ZEMLYA
LAPTEV SEA
NEW SIBERIAN ISLANDS
EAST SIBERIAN SEA
WRANGEL I.
CHUKCHI SEA
CHUKOTSK PEN.
Cape Navarin
BERING SEA
Bering Strait
ALEUTIAN IS.
ST. LAWRENCE I.
NUNIVAK I.
SEWARD PEN.
BROOKS RANGE
Barrow
Point Barrow
Prudhoe Bay
ALASKA (U.S.)
Mt. McKinley 20,320 ft. (6,194 m.)
BEAUFORT SEA
Inuvik
MACKENZIE MTNS.
Great Bear Lake
Echo Bay
CANADA
NORTH AMERICA
BANKS I.
VICTORIAN ISLAND
PRINCE OF WALES I.
KING WILLIAM I.
SOMERSET I.
QUEEN ELIZABETH IS.
DEVON I.
ELLESMERE ISLAND
BAFFIN ISLAND
Nettilling Lake
BAFFIN BAY
Davis Strait
Hudson Strait
HUDSON BAY
BELCHER IS.
UNGAVA PENINSULA
LABRADOR SEA
Thule
LINCOLN SEA
KALAALLIT NUNAAT (GREENLAND) (DEN.)
Cape Farvel
Cape Brewster
Denmark Strait
GREENLAND SEA
JAN MAYEN (NOR.)
SVALBARD (NOR.)
ICELAND
ATLANTIC OCEAN
FAROE IS. (DEN.)
SHETLAND IS. (U.K.)
NORWEGIAN SEA
North Cape
ARCTIC OCEAN
BARENTS SEA
KARA SEA
NOVAYA ZEMLYA
Cape Zelaniya
FRANZ JOSEF IS. (RUSSIA)
Murmansk
KOLA PEN.
FINLAND
SWEDEN
Kiruna
NORWAY
EUROPE
NORTH SEA
UNITED KINGDOM
IRELAND
Prime Meridian
Arctic Circle
Lena River
Aldan R.
Amur River
Lower Tunguska R.
Yenisey R.
Indigirka R.
Kolyma R.
Yukon R.
Kuskokwim R.
Mackenzie R.
ANTARCTICA
South Pole
PACIFIC OCEAN
SOUTH AMERICA
TIERRA DEL FUEGO
Cape Horn
Drake Passage
FALKLAND IS. (U.K.)
SOUTH SHETLAND IS.
SCOTIA SEA
JOINVILLE I.
SOUTH ORKNEY IS.
SOUTH GEORGIA (U.K.)
SOUTH SANDWICH IS. (U.K.)
ATLANTIC OCEAN
BELLINGSHAUSEN SEA
ADELAIDE I.
ALEXANDER I.
ANTARCTIC PEN.
AMUNDSEN SEA
Cape Flying Fish
THURSTON I.
SIPLE I.
EXECUTIVE COMMITTEE RANGE
MARIE BYRD LAND
THWAITES ICEBERG TONGUE
ELLSWORTH LAND
ELLSWORTH MTNS.
Vinson Massif 16,066 ft. (4,897 m.)
RONNE ICE SHELF
BERKNER I.
WEDDELL SEA
VAHSEL BAY
ROSS SEA
Cape Colbeck
EDWARD VII PEN.
ROCKEFELLER PLATEAU
ROOSEVELT I.
ROSS ICE SHELF
SCOTT ISLAND
CAMPBELL I. (N.Z.)
AUCKLAND IS. (N.Z.)
MACQUARIE I. (AUSTRALIA)
BELLANY IS.
Cape Adaré
COULMAN I.
ROSS I.
McMurdo Sound
PRINCE ALBERT MTNS.
VICTORIA LAND
TRANSANTARCTIC MOUNTAINS
QUEEN MAUD MTNS.
NILSEN PLATEAU
Mt. Kirkpatrick 14,855 ft. (4,528 m.)
REEDY GLACIER
PENSACOLA MTNS.
RECOVERY GLACIER
SHACKLETON RANGE
RIISER LARSEN ICE SHELF
Cape Norvegia
FIMBUL ICE SHELF
MÜHLIG-HOFMANN MTNS.
QUEEN MAUD LAND
SHIRASE GLACIER
LÜTSOW-HOLM BAY
ENDERBY LAND
AMERICAN HIGHLAND
LAMBERT GLACIER
PRINCE CHARLES MTNS.
AMERY ICE SHELF
PRYDZ BAY
WEST ICE SHELF
DAVIS SEA
SHACKLETON ICE SHELF
Cape Poinsett
TOTTEN GLACIER
WILKES LAND
DIBBLE ICEBERG TONGUE
INDIAN OCEAN
Antarctic Circle
Prime Meridian

World Facts

WHAT IS THE . . .	ANSWER	LOCATION	SIZE
largest continent?	Asia	Eastern Hemisphere	17,400,000 sq. miles
smallest continent?	Australia	South Pacific	2,941,290 sq. miles
largest nation?	Russia and the Russian Federation	Europe-Asia	6,592,800 sq. miles
smallest nation?	Vatican City	Europe	.17 sq. miles
largest ocean?	Pacific		64,186,300 sq. miles
longest river?	Nile	East Africa	4,160 miles long
largest lake?	Caspian Sea	Eurasia	143,244 sq. miles
deepest lake?	Baikal	Asia	5,315 feet deep
highest mountain?	Mt. Everest	Nepal-Tibet	29,028 feet high
highest waterfall?	Angel Falls	Venezuela	3,212 feet high
largest desert?	Sahara	North Africa	3,500,000 sq. miles
highest continental point?	Mt. Everest	Nepal-Tibet	29,028 feet high
lowest continental point?	Dead Sea	Israel-Jordan	1,312 feet below sea level

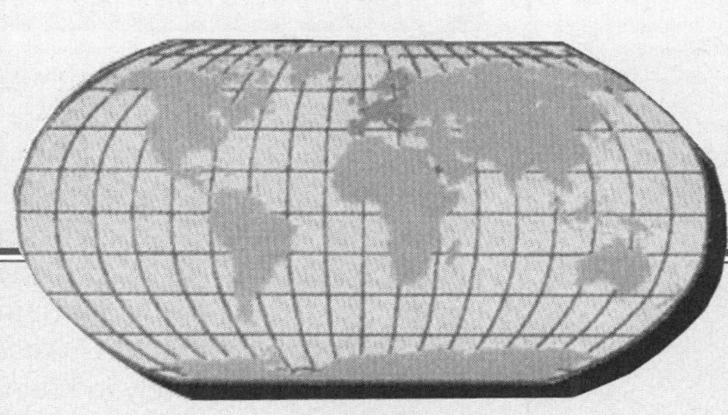

UNIT OVERVIEW

The four chapters that comprise this unit introduce students to the five geographic themes and the physical geography of the earth. Factors that influence ways of life—such as locale, climate, and population—are included.

GEOGRAPHY JOURNAL

Activity Students may wish to designate sections of their notebooks for each geographic theme. They may also work in teams—each student responsible for collecting data on a particular theme.

Students may gather information by listening to local radio and television programs and by reading local newspapers and magazines.

Students may use their journal notes to compose general statements about their community for each geographic theme.

- This journal activity provides the basis for the "Writing About Geography" exercise in the Chapter Review.

- The Geography Journal may be used as an integral part of Performance Assessment.

GLENCOE TECHNOLOGY

Videodisc

GEOGRAPHY AND THE ENVIRONMENT
THE INFINITE VOYAGE
To the Edge of the Earth

Chapter 1
Disc 1 Side B
Title: ***Great Explorers***
Subject: Explorers Club sponsors expeditions to all corners of the globe

UNIT 1

Looking at the World

GeoJournal Activity

While studying world geography, think like a geographer. Take note of where things occur. Observe and describe the human and physical characteristics of places where you go. See how people have affected the environment and how the environment affects people.

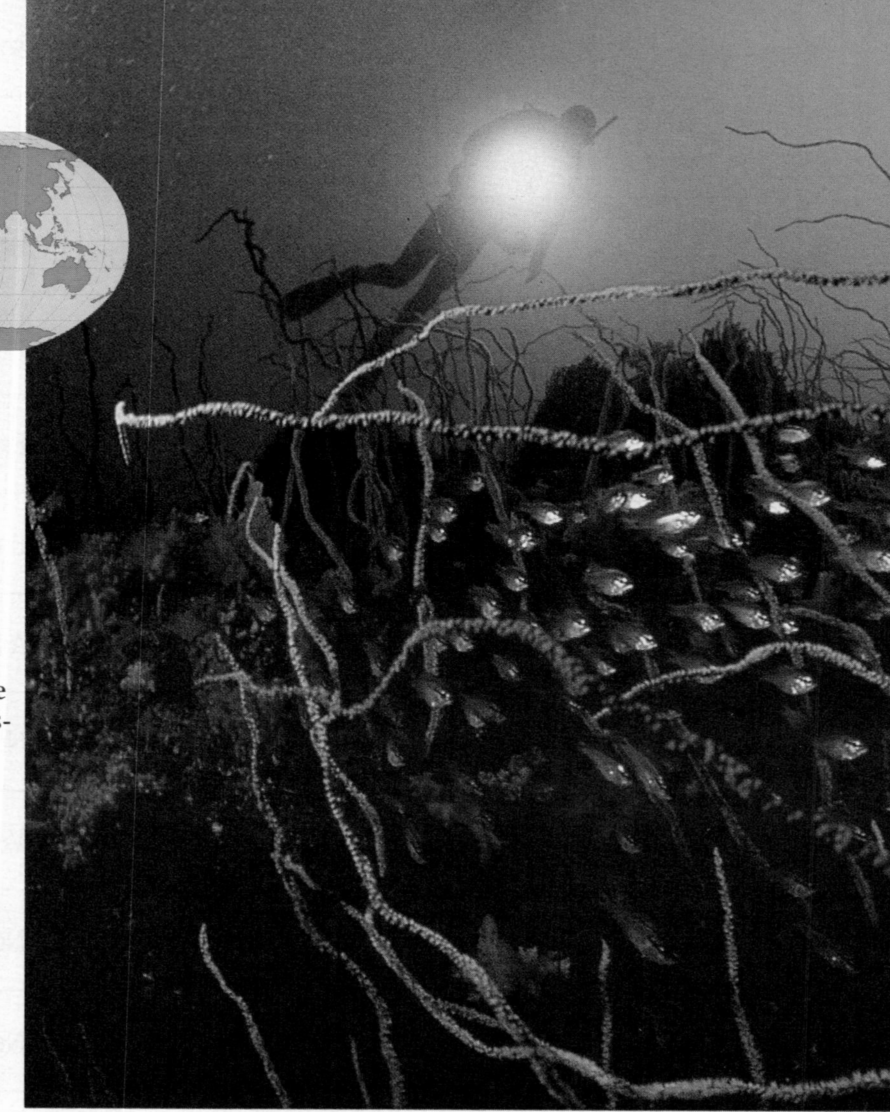

David Doubilet

2

Where in the World . . . .

Have students look at pages A2 and A3. Display Political Map Transparency 1 and ask the following questions. What are the world's oceans? *(Atlantic, Pacific, Arctic, Indian)* Continents? *(Africa, Antarctica, Asia, Australia, Europe, North America, South America)* What imaginary line divides the earth into Northern and Southern Hemispheres? *(Equator)* Which continents lie completely in the Northern Hemisphere? *(North America, Europe)* Completely in the Southern Hemisphere? *(Australia, Antarctica)* Which continents lie in both hemispheres? *(Asia, Africa, South America)*

What ocean do you cross when traveling from the United States to Europe? *(Atlantic)* Africa? *(Atlantic)* Australia? *(Pacific)* What continent do you cross when traveling east from the United States to Russia? *(Europe)*

Picturing the World

A diver inspects a school of cardinalfish swimming through a forest of wire coral off the coast of Japan. Seventy percent of our planet is covered by water and only three percent of that is freshwater. The salty oceans contain most of the earth's water. To date, we have explored less than one percent of the deep seafloor. Look at the map on pages A2-A3.

1. Name the four oceans of the world.
2. What is the largest sea in Europe?
3. Now look at the photograph on page 26. What is the name of the large sea in the center of the photograph?

Picture Atlas CD-ROM Enrichment Corner

Create a file of ocean information. (See the *Picture Atlas of the World* User's Guide on how to use the Collector but-ton.) Include the essays for all the oceans and the caption in the western Pacific Ocean off the coast of Ecuador. Then answer the following questions:

1. What is the largest and deepest ocean in the world?
2. What ocean current brings warmth and moisture to Europe?
3. What is the name of the mountains on the floor of the Atlantic Ocean?
4. Which ocean is ringed by North America, Europe, and Asia?
5. What is the name of the system of warm water currents sometimes occurring in the eastern Pacific off the coast of Ecuador?

3

interNET CONNECTIONS

Views of the Solar System are available at the following address:

World Wide Web:
http://www.c3.lanl.gov/~cjhamil/SolarSystem/homepage.html

CD-ROM

PICTURE ATLAS OF THE WORLD
See page T35 for an additional CD-ROM activity to enrich Unit 1, Looking at the World.

0:00 OUT OF TIME?

If time does not permit teaching the entire unit, you may use the Chapter Highlights and the Audiocassettes that include a 1-page activity and a 1-page test for each chapter.

ANSWERS TO PICTURING THE WORLD

1. Atlantic, Pacific, Arctic, Indian
2. Mediterranean
3. Arabian Sea

Enrichment Corner Answers

1. Pacific
2. North Atlantic Drift
3. Mid-Atlantic Ridge
4. Arctic
5. Peru Current

CHAPTER 1

PLANNING GUIDE

How Geographers Look at the World

CHAPTER ORGANIZER

Daily Lesson Objectives	Multimedia	Teacher Classroom Resources
SECTION 1 Themes of Geography 1. Appreciate what geography is. 2. Understand how geographers see the world. 3. Explain how geography relates to other disciplines and to you personally.	Section Focus Transparency 1-1 Chapter 1 Vocabulary PuzzleMaker Software Political Map Transparencies 1 and 12 Unit Map Overlay Transparency 1-9 Testmaker GTV: Planetary Manager Picture Atlas of the World	Reproducible Lesson Plan 1-1 Guided Reading Activity 1-1 Spanish Guided Reading Activity 1-1 Performance Assessment Activity 1 Workbook Activity 1-1 Section Quiz 1-1
Geography Skills Handbook 1. Understand parts of maps. 2. Describe locations with parallels and meridians. 3. Distinguish among types of maps. 4. Compare maps and globes. 5. Interpret graphs, charts, and diagrams.	Picture Atlas of the World	Reproducible Lesson Plan 1-2 Outline Map Resource Book, p. 6 Geography Skills Activities 4, 10, 11, 12
CHAPTER REVIEW AND EVALUATION	Chapter 1 English (or Spanish) Audiocassettes Political Map Transparency 12 MindJogger Videoquiz Testmaker Student Self-Test and Review Software	Reteaching Activity 1 Spanish Reteaching Activity 1 Chapter 1 Test Form A and Form B

0:00 *If time does not permit teaching the entire chapter, summarize using the Chapter 1 Highlights on page 23, and Chapter 1 English (or Spanish) Audiocassettes. Review students' knowledge using the Glencoe MindJogger Videoquiz.*

KEY TO ABILITY LEVELS

Teaching strategies have been coded for varying learning styles and abilities.

L1 **BASIC** activities for all students

L2 **AVERAGE** activities for average to above-average students

L3 **CHALLENGING** activities for above-average students

LEP **LIMITED ENGLISH PROFICIENCY** activities

Performance Assessment

Applying the Five Themes Have students assume the role of geographers. They should form groups and choose a country, state, or city to discover. Each group should web information from nonfiction sources based on the five themes of geography, classifying material accordingly. Students should pay particular attention to maps, adding information found in different types of maps. When the webbing is concluded, students should realign into new groups. Individuals in the new groups, using only their webs as sources, should tell other group members what they had previously found. Each group should add the new information to its web under each theme.

The teacher should then conduct a loop writing, asking students to first write about the five themes of geography in two minutes. Students should then loop five times—preparing one two-minute writing on each theme. After this task, students should be prepared to assume the role of a famous geographer who has been asked to write an informational article for a student or professional journal about the role of the themes in the lives of the earth's people.

POSSIBLE RUBRIC FEATURES: Content information, collaborative skills, written communication skills

For additional professional and classroom resources, see Chapter Resources, pages T46–T51.

TEACHER'S CORNER

NATIONAL GEOGRAPHIC SOCIETY

INDEX TO NATIONAL GEOGRAPHIC MAGAZINE

The following articles may be used for research relating to this chapter:

- "Blueprints for Victory," by John F. Shupe, May 1995.
- "Our Year in Review," by Gilbert M. Grosvenor, December 1989.
- "New Perspectives on the World," by John B. Garver, Jr., December 1988.
- "Humboldt's Way," by Loren McIntyre, September 1985.

NATIONAL GEOGRAPHIC SOCIETY PRODUCTS AVAILABLE FROM GLENCOE

To order the following products for use with this chapter, contact your local Glencoe sales representative or call Glencoe at 1-800-334-7344:

- *Picture Atlas of Our World* (Book)
- *Picture Atlas of the World* (CD-ROM)
- *GTV: Planetary Manager* (Videodisc)
- *GeoBee* (Software)

ADDITIONAL NATIONAL GEOGRAPHIC SOCIETY PRODUCTS

To order the following products for use with this chapter, call National Geographic Society at 1-800-368-2728:

- *More Than Maps: A Look at Geography*, "What is Geography?" "Geography and the World Around You," "Geography at Work." (Filmstrip)

Introducing
CHAPTER 1

PERFORMANCE ASSESSMENT

Refer to the Planning Guide on page 4B for a Performance Assessment Activity for this chapter. See the *Performance Assessment Activities* booklet for additional suggestions.

CHAPTER OBJECTIVES

1. **Understand** the five themes of geography.
2. **Use** geographic tools and methodologies in various forms.

GLENCOE TECHNOLOGY

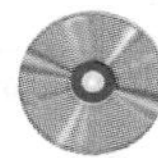

Videodisc

Use Chapter 1 MindJogger Videoquiz to preview chapter content.

MINDJOGGER VIDEOQUIZ

Chapter 1
Disc 1 Side A

The MindJogger Videoquiz is also available on videocassette.

chapter 1 How Geographers Look at the World

CHAPTER FOCUS

Geographic Setting

The surface of the earth varies from place to place in terms of its physical features, climate, and resources. The people who inhabit our world vary as well.

Geographic Themes

Geographers use five geographic themes to analyze the earth and its patterns:
LOCATION "Where is it?"
PLACE "What is it like there?"
HUMAN/ENVIRONMENT INTERACTION "What is the relationship between people and their environment?"
MOVEMENT "How are people and places connected?"
REGION "How is a place similar to and different from other places?"

▲ Photograph: *Golden Gate Bridge, San Francisco, California*

EXTRA CREDIT PROJECT

Creating Visual Aids Have interested students mount landscape pictures on paper, explain the locations on the backs, and slip the pictures into acetate protectors. Then ask them to make a cardboard spinner, divide it into five parts, and label the parts:

LOCATION "Where is it?"
PLACE "What is it like there?"
HUMAN/ENVIRONMENT INTERACTION "What is the relationship between people and their environment?"
MOVEMENT "How are people and places connected?"
REGION "How is this place similar to and different from other places?"

Have students choose a picture, use the spinner to select a geography theme, and answer the question.

1 SECTION
Themes of Geography

SETTING THE SCENE

Read to Discover . . .
- what geography is.
- how geographers see the world.
- how geography relates to other disciplines and to you personally.

Key Terms
- geography
- absolute location
- hemisphere
- latitude
- longitude
- grid system
- relative location
- interdependent
- culture

Identify and Locate
Equator, Tropic of Cancer, Tropic of Capricorn, Prime Meridian

The study of the earth and of the ways people live and work on it is called **geography.** The word "geography" comes from the Greek word *geographia*, which means "a description of the earth." Geographers are people who study the earth. They study the way places on the earth differ and the ways people organize themselves and use the earth's resources. Geography also deals with the location of these places and the complex relationships between people and their environments.

Five Geographic Themes

The study of geography can be organized around five themes: location, place, human/environment interaction, movement, and region. These five themes offer a structured way of thinking about the world and can be used to study all kinds of geographic issues at local, national, and global levels.

Location

The theme of location is concerned with the question "Where is it?" Geographers study the location and distribution of almost everything on the surface of the earth. The **absolute location** of a place—its precise position on the globe—is an important part of their study.

To determine absolute location, geographers use a network of imaginary lines around the earth. The Equator is an important line that circles the earth midway between the North Pole and the South Pole. It divides the earth into **hemispheres**, or two halves. The Northern Hemisphere includes all of the land and water between the Equator and the North Pole. The Southern Hemisphere includes all of the land and water between the Equator and the South Pole.

Latitude

Other imaginary lines called lines of **latitude**, or parallels, circle the earth parallel to the Equator and measure the distance north or south of the Equator in degrees. The Equator is measured at 0° latitude, while the Poles lie at latitudes 90° N (north) and 90° S (south).

Two lines of latitude are important indicators to geographers—the Tropic of Cancer located at 23½° N, and the Tropic of Capricorn at 23½° S. Because the earth is tilted 23½° in its revolutions around the sun, these two lines of

LESSON PLAN
Chapter 1, Section 1

FOCUS

SECTION OBJECTIVES

1. Appreciate what geography is.
2. Understand how geographers see the world.
3. Explain how geography relates to other disciplines and to you personally.

BELLRINGER MOTIVATIONAL ACTIVITY

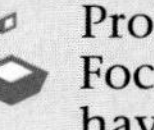
Project the Section 1 Focus Transparency and have students answer the questions.

PRETEACHING VOCABULARY

After students complete their reading, have them match Key Terms with geographic themes. Have volunteers list the Key Terms (except *geography* and *culture)* under the appropriate themes on the chalkboard. *(LOCATION: absolute location, hemisphere, latitude, longitude, grid system, relative location; MOVEMENT: interdependent)*

Use the Vocabulary PuzzleMaker Software to create a crossword or word search puzzle.

CD-ROM

PICTURE ATLAS OF THE WORLD
Have students view the Mapping Our World animation "Where in the World," which introduces the concepts of latitude and longitude.

Classroom Resources for Section 1

BLACKLINE MASTERS:
Reproducible Lesson Plan 1-1
Guided Reading Activity 1-1
Spanish Guided Reading Activity 1-1
Workbook Activity 1-1
Performance Assessment Activity 1
Section Quiz 1-1

Picture Atlas of the World

TRANSPARENCIES:
Section Focus Transparency 1-1
Political Map Transparencies 1, 12
Unit Map Overlay Transparency 1-9

MULTIMEDIA:

Vocabulary PuzzleMaker Software
Testmaker

GTV: Planetary Manager

TEACH

GUIDED PRACTICE

L1 Compare Project Political Map Transparency 12 and Unit Map Overlay Transparency 1-9. Tell students to compare the map grid with the diagrams on page 6. Ask how and why the lines of longitude on the map differ from the lines of longitude on a globe. *(The lines on the map are parallel and the lines on the globe meet at the poles because the map has a flat surface while a globe has a round surface.)*

L1 Describe Location Have students identify at least ten ways to describe the school's relative location. List them on the chalkboard.

USING MAPS

Answers:
1. The Tropic of Cancer is at 23°30'N and the Tropic of Capricorn is at 23°30'S; **2.** between 60° N and 80° N; **3.** the North Pole and the South Pole

Map Skills Practice
Reading a Diagram Is North America east or west of the Prime Meridian? *(west)*

Videodisc

GTV: PLANETARY MANAGER

Side 1, Chapter 4
Frames 15415-19710
Title: *The Human Factor*
Subject: The saga of human impact on the environment

THE GLOBAL GRID

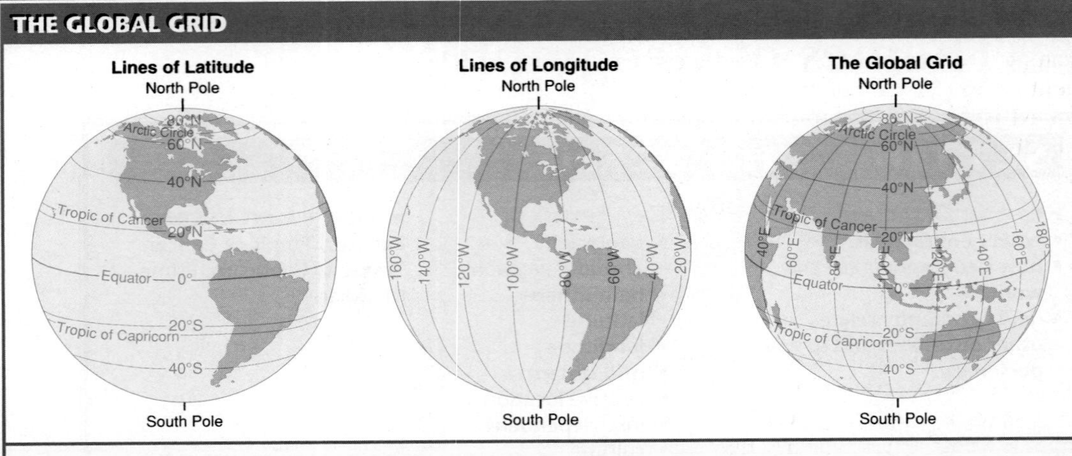

FOCUS ON GEOGRAPHIC THEMES

1. **Location: At what lines of latitude on the globe are the Tropic of Cancer and the Tropic of Capricorn located?**
2. **Location: Between which lines of latitude is the Arctic Circle located?**
3. **Place: What are the northern and southern extremities of the globe?**

latitude mark the limits of the areas—called tropics—on the earth that receive the most heat from the sun.

Longitude

A second set of imaginary lines is called lines of **longitude**, or meridians. These lines from Pole to Pole measure distances east or west of the starting line, which lies at 0° longitude and is called the Prime Meridian. By international agreement, the Prime Meridian is the line of longitude that runs through the Royal Observatory in Greenwich, England. Longitude is measured in degrees east and west of the Prime Meridian up to 180° in each direction.

Places east of the Prime Meridian up to 180° are known as east longitude. Places west of the Prime Meridian up to 180° are known as west longitude. It is important to indicate whether a location is east or west longitude. The distance between meridians is measured in degrees—the same as the distance between lines of latitude.

Absolute Location

The lines of latitude and longitude cross one another, forming a pattern called a **grid system.** This system makes it possible to find exact places on the earth's surface. Many places can be found along a line of latitude. Only one place, however, can be found at the point where a certain line of latitude crosses a certain line of longitude.

By using degrees and minutes, people can find the precise point where one line of latitude crosses one line of longitude. Thus, people can locate ships at sea, planes in the sky, and places on land. For example, a ship at sea might be located off the coast of Japan at latitude 36° N and longitude 144° E. Dallas, Texas, lies at latitude 32° N and longitude 96° W. Both of these examples pinpoint exact locations, or absolute locations, on the earth.

Relative Location

Absolute location is not the way people usually think about where a place is. Instead,

Cooperative Learning Activity

Give students practice in identifying characteristics that define *place.* First, have a student draw a large outline map of your state on poster board. Have another student research the state's plants, animals, and major products using an encyclopedia, and list the items on the chalkboard.

Then distribute magazines (gardening, wildlife, and local magazines would be most useful) and tell the students to find and cut out pictures of the items listed on the board. Finally, direct the students to paste the pictures on the outline map, creating a montage of distinctive characteristics of their state.

people tend to think of a place in relation to other places, or by its **relative location.** For example, New Orleans is located near the mouth of the Mississippi River, and St. Louis is located where the Missouri River flows into the Mississippi. Knowing the relative location of people, places, and things helps you to orient yourself in space and to develop an awareness of the geography of the world.

Place

Another important geographic theme is place. Place is concerned with "What is it like there?" Each place on earth has its own physical features. It can be described in terms of its land, water, weather, soil, and plant and animal life.

Each place on the earth also has its own human features. It can be described in terms of the number and kinds of people who live there. Each place can also be described by the activities that take place there. People's activities change the way a place looks. Thus, a place may look quite different depending on whether it is used for hunting and fishing, herding, farming, manufacturing, or shopping. People's religions, languages, and cultural backgrounds also provide distinctive characteristics for places.

Human/ Environment Interaction

An important theme in geography is human and environmental interaction. It answers the question "What is the relationship between people and their environment?" Geographers strive to understand the relationships of places on the earth to people and to other places. All places have some desirable and some undesirable features.

Places attract people for various reasons. People may be attracted to a place by an ocean, a river, or a lake. They may be attracted to a place by the amount of sunshine it receives. Different groups of people may use the features of a place in different ways. For example, some people are interested in warm, sunny places for growing crops. Other people are interested in the same places for recreational activities.

Geographers are interested in how people adapt to their environment. For example, people wear light clothing in hot places and warm clothing in cold places. Geographers are also

THE HEMISPHERES

North Pole
Northern Hemisphere
Equator
Southern Hemisphere
South Pole
Western Hemisphere
Prime Meridian
Eastern Hemisphere

FOCUS ON GEOGRAPHIC THEMES

1. **Location: What line of longitude divides the globe in half?**
2. **Location: In which three hemispheres is the South Pole located?**

Meeting Special Needs

Study Strategy Help students who do not seem to have a fluent study strategy by guiding their practice. Point out that Section 1 is long. Explain that by focusing their reading energies on the section objectives and main ideas (the five themes of geography), they can search for the most relevant information and save time. Stress that the purpose of this approach is to help them work efficiently and to focus their attention on the relevant parts of the text.

L2 Human/Environment Interaction Test students' understanding of how humans adapt. First, collect a bag of items such as mittens, sunglasses, a small spade, and a rain hood. Display a picture of an environment such as a farm field, a stormy coast, a tropical beach, or a snowy peak. Have a volunteer select an item from the bag and explain whether people could use it to adapt to the environment. Repeat with other students and other environments.

USING DIAGRAMS

Answers:
1. Prime Meridian; **2.** Southern Hemisphere, Eastern Hemisphere, and Western Hemisphere

Skills Practice

Interpreting a Diagram What line of latitude divides the globe into the Northern Hemisphere and the Southern Hemisphere? *(the Equator)* What hemispheres do you live in? *(The United States is in the Northern and Western Hemispheres.)*

CURRICULUM CONNECTION

CIVICS

Geographic knowledge and perspectives help people be responsible citizens, especially when making decisions that affect their community, region, country, and world.

INDEPENDENT PRACTICE

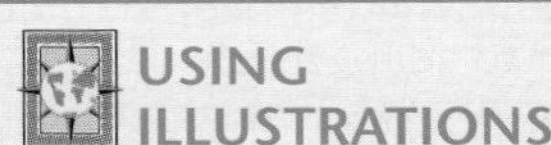

Guided Reading Have students complete Guided Reading Activity 1-1 in the TCR. **LEP**

L3 Make a Chart Ask an interested student to make a flow chart showing how people in a community are interdependent.

USING ILLUSTRATIONS

REGION The northeastern United States and Southeast Asia have similarities as well as differences. For example, the Northeast experiences hot, humid summers as do places in Southeast Asia.

Answer to Caption: *land type, plant and animal life, and human characteristics, such as the way people are governed or their language*

DID YOU KNOW?

Formal regions **are characterized by the presence of a common human property (e.g., language, religion, nationality, political identity) or common physical property (e.g., climate, landforms, vegetation cover).** *Functional regions* **are organized around a node or focal point with surrounding areas linked to that node through transportation or communication systems or economc associations.** *Perceptual regions* **reflect human feelings or attitudes and are defined by subjective images of the area (e.g., Dixie, Southern California, the upper Midwest).**

Geographic Themes

Region: Northeastern United States and Southeast Asia
The northeastern United States has cold winters, while Southeast Asia has a year-round tropical climate. *In addition to climate, what other characteristics define regions?*

interested in how people change their environment. For example, at one time deserts were considered by many people to be undesirable places to live. Today people use irrigation to change desert land into farmland.

Geographers are also concerned with how people have created problems with their environment. Among these problems are air pollution, water pollution, and waste material, much of which is hazardous to living things.

Movement

Another important geographic theme is movement. This theme relates to the question "How are people and places connected?" Throughout history, there have been movements of large groups of people from one place to another. Groups have moved for different reasons—better land, religious freedom, a chance to earn a better living. Movement has now become a daily part of our lives. People use automobiles, buses, subways, and commuter trains to move from one place to another.

Geographers are also interested in the movement of goods, information, and ideas. Nearly everywhere, people are **interdependent**, relying on each other for goods, services, and ideas near and far. Geographers help us to understand the importance of these movements as well.

Region

Yet another important theme in geography is region. Geographers often divide the world into regions, or areas, based on physical features, such as land type or plant and animal life. Geographers also divide the world into regions based on human characteristics, such as the way people are governed or the language they speak.

There are two basic types of regions. One is a uniform region, which has boundaries determined by the distribution of some uniform characteristic. A uniform region could be the corn-hog-cattle belt centering on Iowa and Illinois or the irrigated-cotton belt in the Central Valley of California. A second type of

Critical Thinking

Analyzing Information Read the following passage from *Death Comes to the Archbishop* by Willa Cather:

In New Mexico he always awoke a young man. . . . He had noticed that this peculiar quality in the air of new countries vanished after they were tamed by man and made to bear harvests . . . that lightness, that dry aromatic odor . . . one could breathe that only on the bright edges of the world, on the great grass plains or the sagebrush desert.

Ask students whether they have ever felt about a place the way the person in the passage feels about New Mexico. Have them write a description of a wild, unsettled area that they know or can imagine.

region is a functional region, an area that focuses on a central point with surrounding territory linked to that central point by arteries (roads, railroads) or by people's wants and needs (jobs, shopping, entertainment). The metropolitan area surrounding a city is a functional region. Regions make the study of geography more manageable.

Geography and Other Subjects

Geographers study both the physical and human features of the earth and analyze the patterns and relationships of each. In the process, these areas of geographic study are linked to other subjects, including science, history, economics, and sociology.

Science and Technology

Like all scientists, geographers observe, hypothesize, and collect data to prove or disprove their theories. Aiding them in their tasks are advanced technological tools such as satellites, remote sensors, and computers. Satellites orbiting the earth carry remote sensors, or high-tech cameras and/or radar, that collect information and photographs about such topics as the earth's environment, weather, human settlement patterns, and vegetation. This information is sent to computers on the earth. Computer programs known as Geographic Information Systems (GIS) process and organize the satellite images with other data collected through censuses, cartographers, and so on. The GIS technology is already invaluable to urban planners, engineers, and geographers, and it may some day help you plan your vacation!

History and Political Science

Geographers use history to help them understand the way places looked in the past. For example, geographers might want to know how Boston, Massachusetts, looked during colonial times. They might also wish to look at the changes that have occurred in Boston over the past two centuries.

RELATIVE LOCATION OF DALLAS, TX

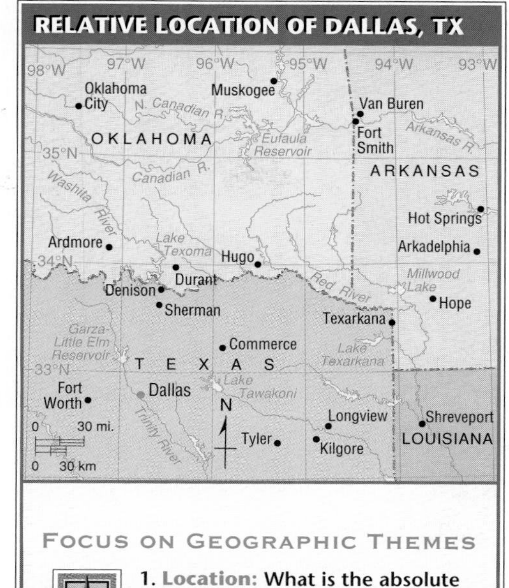

FOCUS ON GEOGRAPHIC THEMES

1. **Location: What is the absolute location of Dallas, Texas, in terms of latitude and longitude?**
2. **Place: What body of water lies northwest of Dallas? What river runs through Dallas?**

Geographic Themes

Place: Dallas, Texas

The city of Dallas lies on the rolling prairies of northeast Texas. Dallas is a major commercial and financial center. *How can a place like Dallas be described?*

ASSESS

CHECK FOR UNDERSTANDING

Assign Section 1 Review as homework or an in-class activity.

MEETING LESSON OBJECTIVES

Each objective below is tested by the questions that follow it in parentheses.

1. **Appreciate** what geography is. *(1)*
2. **Understand** how geographers see the world. *(3)*
3. **Explain** how geography relates to other disciplines and to you personally. *(4, 5)*

USING MAPS

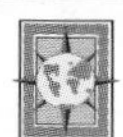

Answers:
1. 32° N and 96° W; **2.** Garza-Little Elm Reservoir, Trinity River

Map Skills Practice

Reading a Map Which city is due west of Shreveport, Louisiana? *(Longview, Texas)*

USING ILLUSTRATIONS

PLACE Skyscrapers have made the skyline an identifying feature of Dallas and other cities.

Answer to Caption: *by its physical and human characteristics*

EVALUATE

Assign the Section 1 Quiz in the TCR.

Use the Testmaker to create a customized quiz for Section 1.

Extending the Content

Human/Environment Interaction Geographers work for the federal government in the Defense Mapping Agency, United States Geologic Survey, Central Intelligence Agency, Army Corps of Engineers, National Science Foundation, Smithsonian Institution, and Office of the Geographer in the Department of State.

State environmental and transportation agencies hire geographers as analysts, planners, and cartographers. Some states even have an Office of the State Geographer. In the private sector, geographers work as professors, researchers, and cartographers for high-tech computer mapmakers. Businesses as varied as fast-food chains and ski resorts consult geographers about issues such as the optimal locations for new restaurants and the effects of pollution on the slopes.

RETEACH

Have each student read a subsection, write its title and key words on an index card, and present the facts orally, using the card as a memory aid.

ENRICH

Introduce the concept of a geography of smell by having students identify aromas they associate with certain places.

CLOSE

Ask students to draw a superhero and illustrate a geographic theme in the hero's costume. For example, Region Person's cape might show landforms and vegetation.

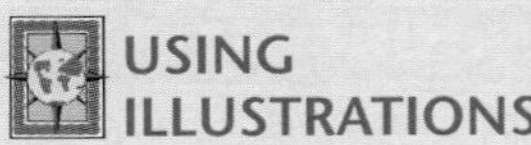

USING ILLUSTRATIONS

LOCATION The Soviets used to falsify maps of their country to foil foreign agents. Now satellite data enables other countries to make more accurate maps of the former Soviet Union than the Soviets made.

Answer to Caption: because they observe, hypothesize, and collect data to prove or disprove their theories

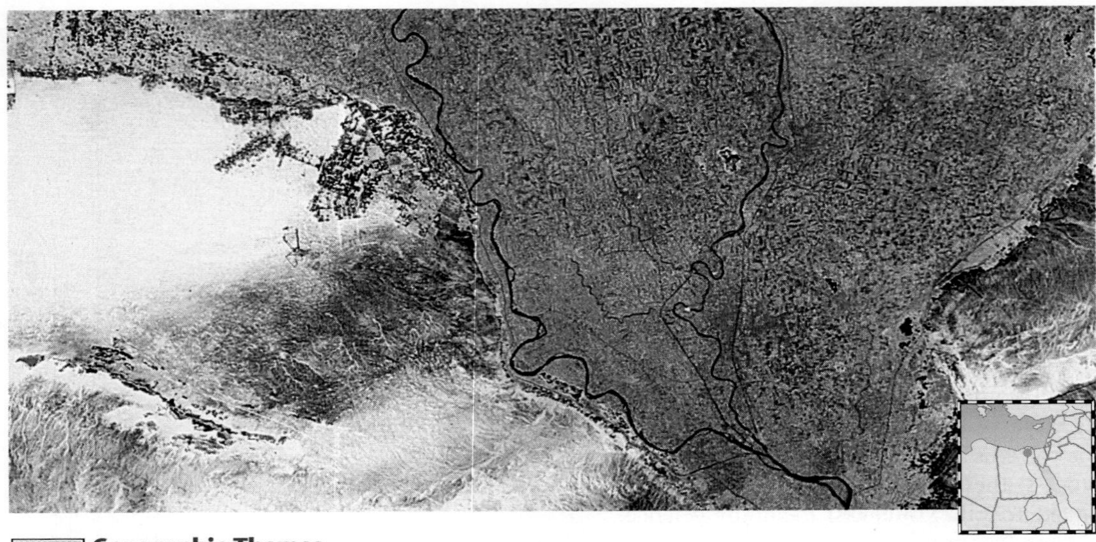

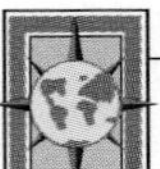

Geographic Themes

Location: Nile River valley, Egypt

This image of Egypt's Nile River valley comes from satellite data. It enables geographers to study population and vegetation patterns. *Why are geographers considered scientists?*

Geographers use political science to help them see how people in different places are governed. They look at how political boundaries have been formed and how they have been changed. Geographers are also interested in how the natural environment has influenced political decisions.

Sociology and Anthropology

Geographers use sociology to help them understand societies throughout the world. They study the relationships between the physical environment and social structure.

Geographers use anthropology to help them gain insights into the **culture,** or way of life, of people in different places. Geographers are interested in how the activities of people affect their physical environment.

Economics

Geographers use economics to help them understand how the location of resources affects the way people make, transport, and use goods. They are also concerned with how and where services are provided.

Geographers are interested in how locations are chosen for various economic activities, such as farming, mining, manufacturing, and selling. They are also interested in the interdependence of people's economic activities throughout the world.

Section 1 Review

Checking for Understanding

1. **Define** geography, absolute location, hemisphere, latitude, longitude, grid system, relative location, interdependent, culture.
2. **Locating Places** State the absolute location of Dallas.
3. What are the five themes of geography?
4. Why do geographers use other fields of study?

Critical Thinking

5. **Making Generalizations** What types of uniform regions do you live in?

ANSWERS TO SECTION 1 REVIEW

1. **geography:** the study of the earth and the people, plants, and animals that live on it; **absolute location:** a place's position on the globe; **hemisphere:** half of the earth; **latitude:** lines that measure the distance north and south of the Equator; **longitude:** lines that measure distance east and west of the Prime Meridian; **grid system:** network of lines used to find location; **relative location:** location of a place in relation to another place; **interdependent:** relying on one another; **culture:** a people's way of life
2. 32° N and 96° W
3. location, place, human/environment interaction, movement, region
4. to understand our world
5. Answers will vary.

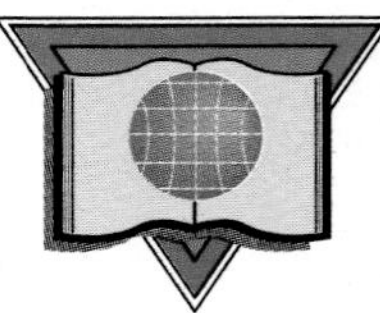

Geography Skills Handbook

KNOWING HOW to use maps and graphs is an important skill in the study of geography—and in daily life. Maps and graphs are used during the nightly news on television and appear in magazines and newspapers. Maps and graphs are invaluable sources of information that can help you understand the world around you. This Geography Skills Handbook introduces you to the basic kinds of maps and graphs and explains how to use them. It will help you to get the most out of your textbook and will provide you with skills that you can use every day for the rest of your life.

PARTS OF MAPS

Maps are important tools. They compare places and relate people's activities to the locations where they live. To read a map you must know the elements, or parts, of a map.

Road Map Symbols

Symbol	
Roads and Related Symbols:	
Free limited access highways	
Under construction	
Other four-lane divided highways	
Principal highways	
Other through highways	
Other roads	
Unpaved roads	
Scenic routes	
Interstate highways	85 675
U.S. highways	1
State and provincial highways	11 166 11
Cities and Towns:	
National capital; state/provincial capital	
Cities and towns; county seats; neighborhoods	
Parks, Recreation Areas, Points of Interest:	
Parks; recreation areas	
Campsites	
Points of interest	
Other Symbols:	
Airport	
Mountain peak; highest point in state	
Swamp	
Ferry	
Railroad	

Source: *Rand McNally Road Atlas*

Map Symbols Cartographers, or mapmakers, use symbols to present information on a map. In this way, maps can be read and understood by people throughout the world. Look at the chart of major map symbols on this page and the maps of Mexico City and France on pages 12 and 13. Note the different elements that are shown.

PRETEACHING VOCABULARY

Display a house key, a rose, and a bathroom scale beside examples of a map key, an elaborate compass rose, and a map scale. Have students hypothesize about what the two kinds of keys, roses, and scales have in common. After students complete the reading, ask if the facts and illustrations in the lesson support their hypotheses.

TEACH

PARTS OF MAPS

L1 Explain Ask students to leaf through the textbook, looking for map symbols not shown on page 11. Have them copy each symbol they find on the chalkboard, list the page it was on, and explain its meaning.

DID YOU KNOW?

The Chinese invented the compass and applied it to navigation about A.D. 1000.

Have students complete Geography Skills Activity 10 in the TCR.

Map Activity

Make a Map Copy and distribute page 6 from the Outline Map Resource Book. Have students color the state or states where they have lived one color and the states they have visited or driven through another color. Then give each student an adhesive label. Tell students to put their labels in the corner of their maps and use them to make a key that explains the meanings of the colors.

L2 Interpret On slips of paper, write the page number of a map from the textbook and a question that requires the use of the map key. Ask volunteers to select slips and answer the questions.

L3 Apply Show the students how to mark a distance scale on the edge of a sheet of paper. Then have them use the map scale on page 12 to measure the distance between the Palace of Fine Arts and the Basilica of Guadalupe *(about 3 miles or 5 km)* and between the Azteca Soccer Stadium and the Ibero-American University *(about 6 miles or 10 km).*

DID YOU KNOW?

Early Arab mapmakers placed north at the bottom rather than the top of maps. Marco Polo used one of these early Arab maps on his journey to the Far East.

Ways of the World

THE ARCTIC The early Inuit labeled distances on their maps with the time they took to travel rather than with miles. A map would show the distance between what is now Nome and Point Barrow as 10 days rather than 525 miles (845 km).

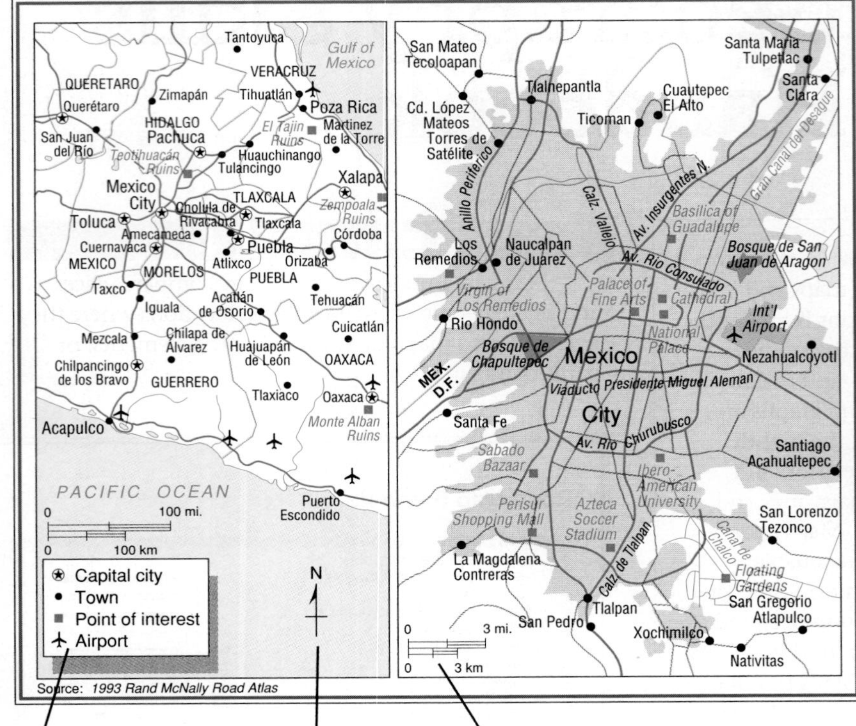

The Key explains the symbols used on a map. On this map, dots are used to indicate towns. A circle with a star means a capital city.

Scale A map can show a small area, such as a city block, or a large area, such as a continent. All maps are drawn to a certain scale. **Scale** means that a certain measurement on a map represents a certain measurement on the earth's surface. The scale bars found on maps give you this relationship. For example, on this map, the scale bar shows that ½ inch on the map represents 3 miles. The scale bar varies from map to map.

The Compass Rose is a direction marker that shows the cardinal directions—north, south, east, west. It may show the intermediate directions—northeast, northwest, southeast, and southwest. Sometimes, the compass rose may point in only one direction because the locations of the other directions can be determined in relation to the given direction. On the map above, north is given.

MAP SKILLS REVIEW

1. **What is the symbol for principal highways?**
2. **What is the symbol for an airport?**
3. **What is the purpose of a map key?**
4. **How far is Toluca from Mexico City?**

ANSWERS TO MAP SKILLS REVIEW

1. a wavy line
2. an airplane
3. It explains the symbols used on a map.
4. about 25 miles (40 km)

PARALLELS AND MERIDIANS

There are two sets of lines on a map. One set is called parallels, or lines of latitude. These east-west lines form circles that run in the same direction as the Equator. The other set is called meridians, or lines of longitude. These are north-south lines that form half circles from the North Pole to the South Pole.

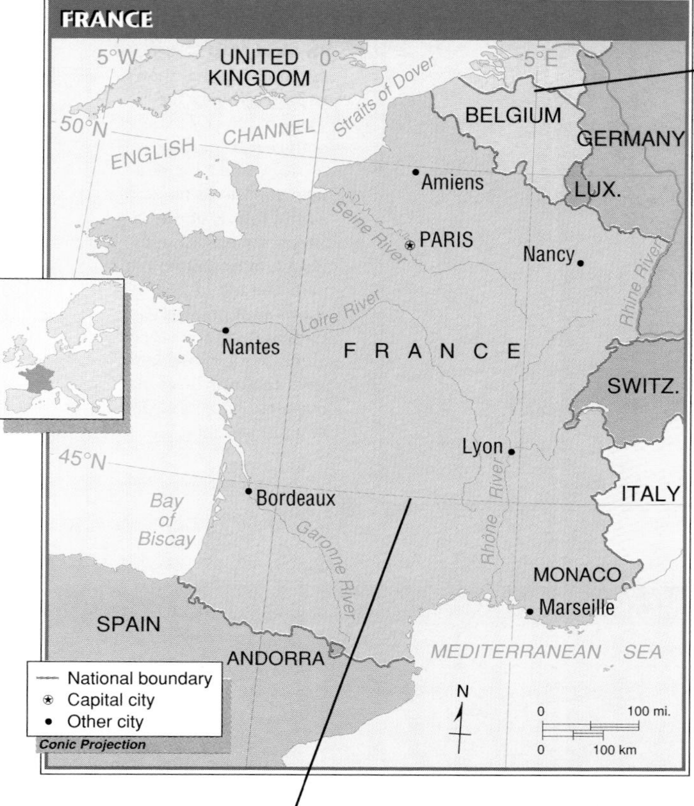

Longitude The vertical lines of longitude measure distances east and west of the Prime Meridian (0° longitude) that passes through Greenwich, England. Lines of longitude to the east of the Prime Meridian are called east longitude. Lines of longitude to the west are called west longitude. On this map, the Prime Meridian is shown along with west longitude line 5° W and east longitude line 5° E.

Latitude The horizontal lines of latitude are used to measure distances north and south of the Equator. Each line of latitude has a measurement in degrees. Lines of latitude north of the Equator (0° latitude) are called lines of north latitude. On this map, they are shown as latitude 45° N and 50° N.

MAP SKILLS REVIEW

1. What line of longitude passes close to Bordeaux?
2. On this map, what city is closest to 50° N?
3. In what body of water is the intersection of 50° N and the Prime Meridian?
4. On this map, what city is located east of 5° E and south of 45° N?

Skills Handbook

TEACH

PARALLELS AND MERIDIANS

L1 Identify List the following coordinates on the chalkboard and have students identify the city at each location.
49° N and 2° E *(Paris)*
45° N and 5° E *(Lyon)*
47° N and 1° W *(Nantes)*
45° N and .5° W *(Bordeaux)*

L2 List Have students list the coordinates for the cities in the political map on page 14. *(Monterrey: 25° N, 100° W; Guadalajara: 20° N, 103° W; Mexico City: 19° N, 99° W; Veracruz: 19° N, 96° W)*

DID YOU KNOW?

Until the 1700s, sailors seldom knew exactly where they were because they had only lines of latitude to guide them. John Harrison, an English instrument maker, created longitude by inventing a clock that could keep accurate time at sea. A navigator can determine the longitude by figuring the difference between Greenwich Mean Time (GMT), the exact time at the Prime Meridian, and the time where the ship is.

Have students complete Geography Skills Activity 4 in the TCR.

ANSWERS TO MAP SKILLS REVIEW

1. 0° W
2. Amiens
3. the English Channel
4. Marseille

PRETEACHING VOCABULARY

Have a student read aloud all the dictionary definitions for *relief.* Then ask the class to hypothesize which meaning of *relief* will be used in the lesson.

TEACH

TYPES OF MAPS

L1 Classify Have students classify the maps in their textbook according to type: physical, political, or special purpose.

DID YOU KNOW?

National boundaries run to the center of the earth and to the top of the atmosphere. Airplanes need a country's permission to fly into its air space. In 1986 French officials refused to let American bombers fly over France on their way to bomb Libya.

TYPES OF MAPS

GENERAL PURPOSE MAPS

Maps that show a wide range of general information about an area are called **general purpose maps.** Two of the most common are physical and political maps.

Physical maps show landforms and bodies of water, while political maps show national and regional boundaries and cities.

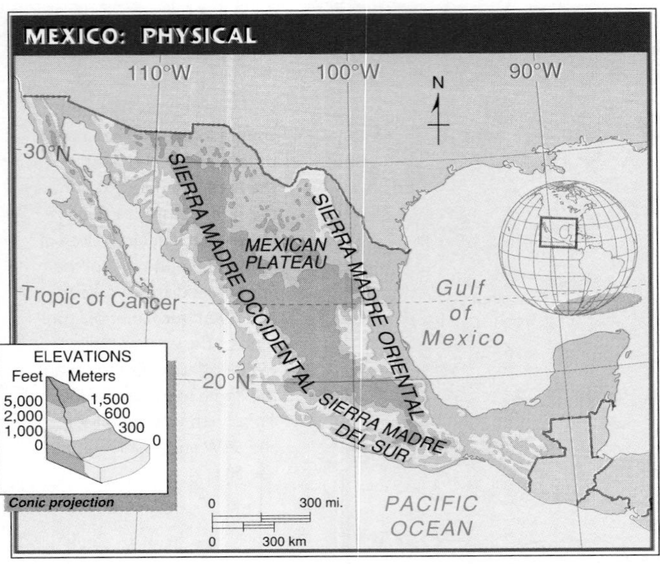

Physical Map A general purpose map that shows **topography,** or the shape of physical features of the earth's surface, is usually called a physical map. It presents the earth's **relief,** or the differences in elevation, or height, of landforms in a particular area. It also shows such physical features as rivers and valleys. Some physical maps also have **contour lines** that connect all points of land of equal elevation.

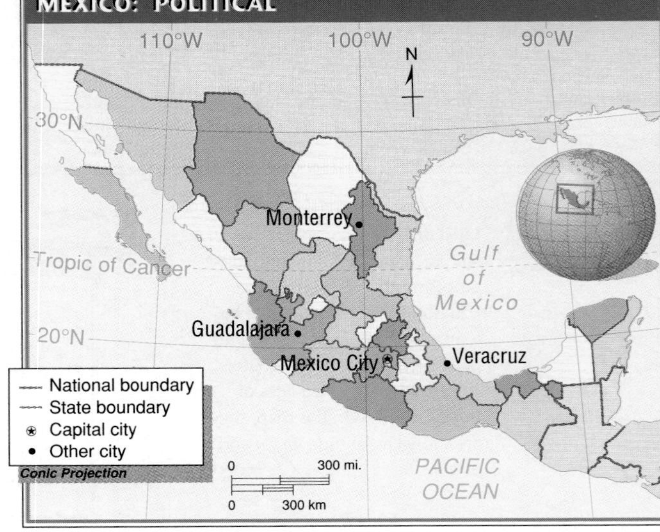

Political Map Another general purpose map is a political map. This map shows the boundaries between countries and often smaller divisions, such as states or counties. Capitals and cities are also frequently shown.

Map Activity

Region Organize the class into groups and assign each group a region of the world. Have the groups create bulletin-board displays of both general purpose and special purpose maps of their regions. They will locate, photocopy, and color maps that show their region's climate, land use, resources, products, time zones, wildlife, transportation, and so on.

Also have them write captions for the maps, identify the types, explain the keys, and tell who might use each map.

SPECIAL PURPOSE MAPS

Maps that emphasize a single idea about an area are called **special purpose maps.** There are many kinds of special purpose maps. There are road maps, natural resource maps, economic activity maps, and time zone maps, to name a few. Each map serves a different purpose. For example, a resource map provides the location of natural resources in a country or region, while an economic activity map focuses on different kinds of economic activities in which people participate and where these activities take place.

Special purpose maps often use different colors and symbols to show the location or distribution of a product or resource in a region or in the world. Colors also may indicate how much of a product or resource is grown or manufactured by certain areas.

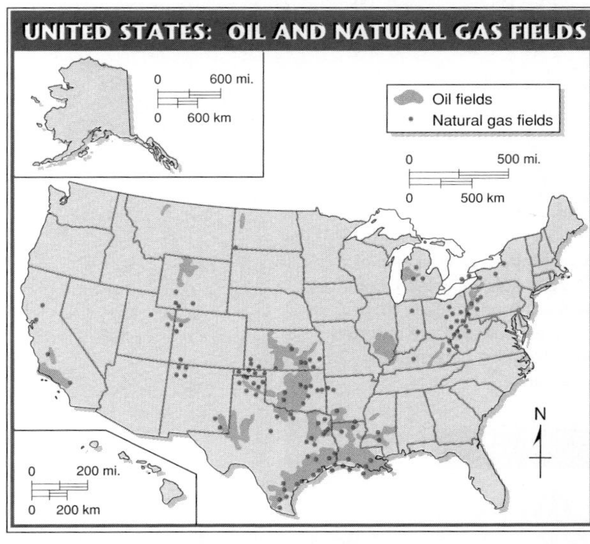

Natural Resource Map
One interesting kind of special purpose map is a natural resource map. The map to the left is a natural resource map that shows the distribution of oil and natural gas fields in the United States.

MAP SKILLS REVIEW

1. What areas of Mexico have the lowest elevation?
2. What do the thin lines in the key for the political map of Mexico represent?
3. Compare both physical and political maps. Of the four cities shown on the political map of Mexico, which has the highest elevation?
4. In what parts of the United States is oil a major industry?
5. How many states have both major oil and natural gas industries?

Skills Handbook

L2 Identify On the chalkboard, copy the following information:

MAPS: population map, time zone map, and historical landmark map

GROUPS: tourists, couriers, fast-food chain planners

Ask students to match each group with the map that would be most useful and to explain their answers. *(Tourists would use the historical landmark map to plan their tour, couriers would use the time zone map to deliver packages on time, and fast-food chain planners would use the population map to determine store locations.)*

CURRICULUM CONNECTION

LITERATURE

Anthony Trollope, Thomas Hardy, Sinclair Lewis, and Robert Louis Stevenson all drew maps to help readers picture characters in their literary landscapes.

DID YOU KNOW?

The creators of the television series "Twin Peaks" developed a map of the fictional town. They needed to know the location of the lumber mill and other key places before they could draw up a list of suspects in a crime.

ANSWERS TO MAP SKILLS REVIEW

1. coasts
2. state boundaries
3. Mexico City
4. the eastern part of the Midwest and the central southern states
5. eight

PRETEACHING VOCABULARY

On a globe, show the class two routes from Philadelphia to Beijing. With your finger, trace the first route west across the United States and the Pacific Ocean. Trace the second route along the nearest meridian. Explain that the second route is called a "great circle route." Tell students to read the lesson to find out which route is shorter.

TEACH

COMPARING MAPS AND GLOBES

L1 Explain Pair students whose English vocabulary is limited with students proficient in English. Have the pairs discuss the lesson together. Reassure students that they do not have to master the names of the projections. Rather, they should concentrate on understanding the problems that occur when cartographers draw maps. **LEP**

DID YOU KNOW?

Flemish mapmaker Gerardus Mercator created his well-known projection in 1569.

NATIONAL GEOGRAPHIC SOCIETY

CD-ROM

PICTURE ATLAS OF THE WORLD

You and your students can see the challenges and solutions involved in making maps by viewing the Mapping Our World animation "Round Earth on Flat Paper."

COMPARING MAPS AND GLOBES

A map is a symbolic representation of the earth or a part of the earth on a flat piece of paper. A globe shows the earth's continents and oceans, but it is round in shape. Because it is a scale model of the earth, a globe is a truer representation of the earth than a map is. A map, however, can be folded and easily stored or taken from place to place. A globe cannot be.

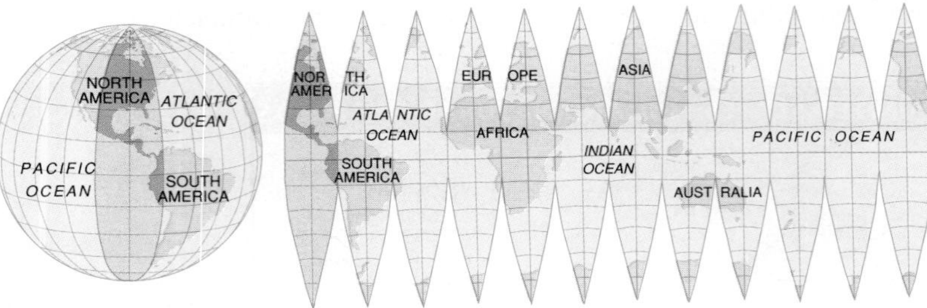

From Globes to Maps With the help of mathematics, mapmakers are able to represent the earth on a flat surface. Size, shape, distance, and/or area, however, are distorted when the curves of a globe become the straight lines of a map.

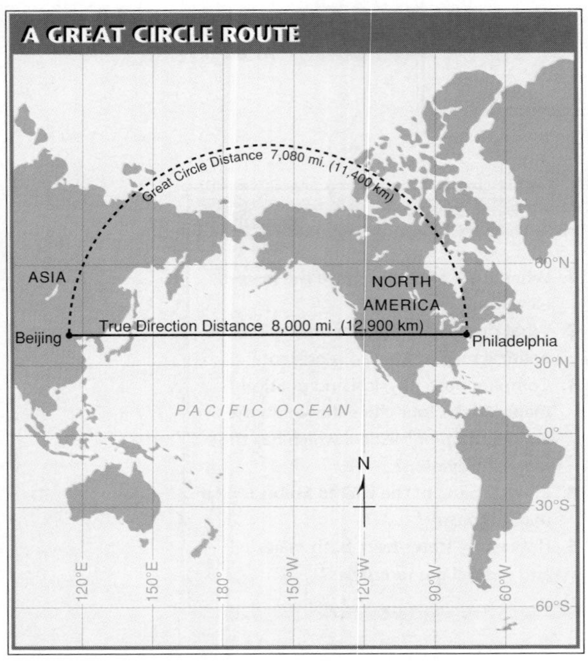

A Great Circle Route Because of their round shapes, globes can accurately show great circle routes. A **great circle** is the shortest possible distance between any two places on the earth's surface. Ships and airplanes often follow the curve of the great circle. By following great circle routes, ships and airplanes use less fuel, and passengers and cargo reach their destinations sooner.

Map Activity

Movement Have students use commercial and economic atlases as well as other reference books to locate great circle air routes between the Western and Eastern hemispheres and between North America and Europe. Ask students to compare distances and flight times between two points by polar and non-polar routes.

MAP PROJECTIONS

The curved surface of the earth cannot be shown accurately on a map because such a surface must be stretched and/or broken in some places as it is flattened. For this reason, mapmakers use map projections. A **map projection** is a way of representing the round earth on a flat surface. No map projection, however, can show the earth as accurately as a globe does. Each kind of projection—and there are several—has some distortion, or inaccuracy. Typical distortions involve distance, direction, shape, and/or area.

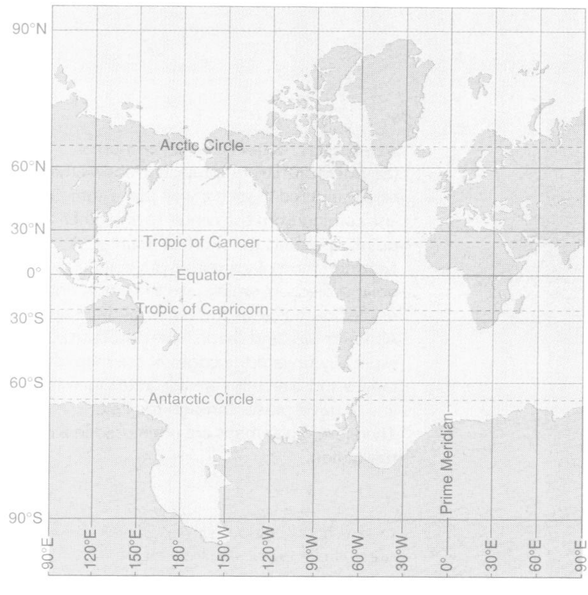

Mercator Projection A Mercator projection is based on the idea of wrapping a piece of paper around a globe to make a cylinder. Such a map shows shapes fairly accurately, but not size or distance. Areas in high latitudes away from the Equator are quite distorted. Thus, Greenland and Alaska appear much larger than they do on a globe. However, because true directions are shown, a Mercator map is very useful for sea travel.

Conic Projection A conic projection comes from the idea of placing a cone over part of a globe. This type of map is accurate for showing small east-west areas in the middle latitudes. Distances and directions on this kind of map are fairly accurate.

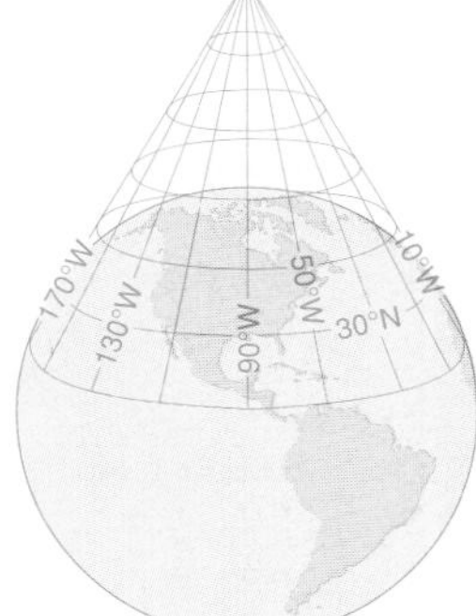

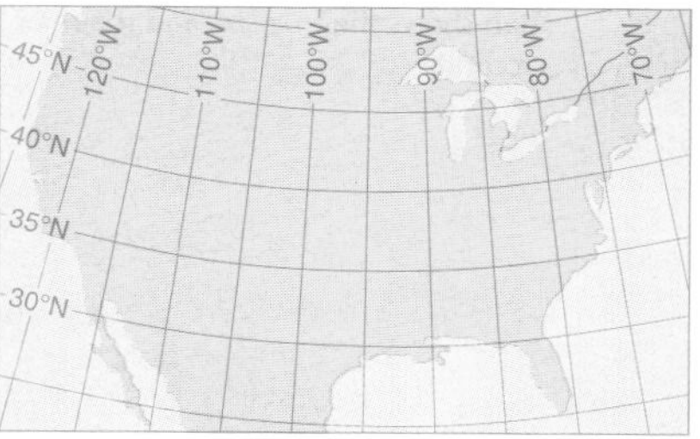

Skills Handbook

Have students complete Geography Skills Activities 11 and 12 in the TCR.

L2 Contrast Have a student trace the same continents from different projections on sheets of acetate, overlay the sheets on a projector, and project them for the class to compare. Then have students identify the projection of each outline and explain why the shapes and sizes differ.

L3 Research Ask interested students to research early and more recent instruments used in conjunction with maps for navigation at sea. Refer them to encyclopedias and books on inventions, such as Daniel J. Boorstin's *The Discoverers*. Have them explain to the class how some of these ancient and modern devices worked.

DID YOU KNOW?

The mapmaking industry earns $200 million a year. One American map company sold 4 million maps of the Middle East after the Gulf War broke out. A book of maps of New York City includes the locations of public restrooms.

Map Activity

Movement Help students locate early maps that include unknown areas. Then have them research the arrivals of explorers such as Balboa, Alexander Mackenzie, Lewis and Clark, John C. Fremont, Zebulon Pike, and other people who enabled cartographers to fill in unknown areas of the maps. Refer students to encyclopedias and books such as *The Discoverers* by Daniel Boorstin and *Why in the World: Adventures in Geography* by George J. Demko. Ask them to explain their findings in a report.

L1 Problem Solve Ask students to solve this riddle: Every direction I face is south. Where am I? Explain that a map on page 18 offers a clue to the answer. *(the North Pole)*

L2 Classify Draw a grid on the chalkboard. Across the top, write the headings "true size," "true shape," and "true distance." To the left of the grid, list the map projections in the lesson. Then ask students to place checks next to each projection under the headings that apply to that projection.

L3 Rank Ask interested students to draw a grid similar to that in the above activity, except across the top they will list the purposes for maps. Refer them to *Why in the World: Adventures in Geography* by George J. Demko for examples. The names of map projections will again be listed on the left. Under each purpose, have students rank that projection's usefulness, using a scale from 1 (not useful) to 4 (most useful).

Sinusoidal Projection In a sinusoidal (siy•nyuh•SOYD•uhl) projection, all parallels and the central meridian are straight lines, with the other meridians curved. Shapes are fairly accurate in the center but have increasing distortion toward the edges. This kind of map has no lines of true distance.

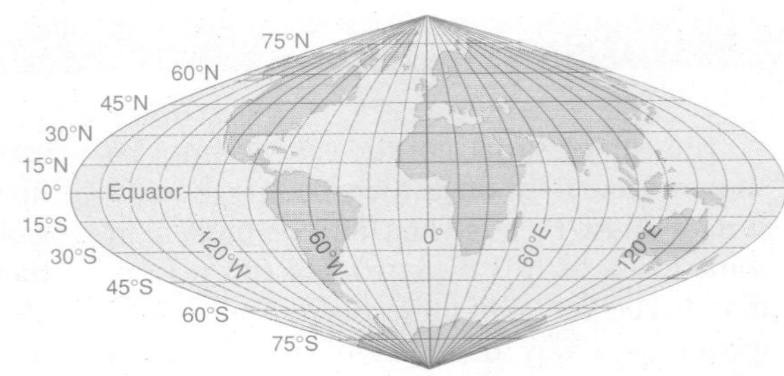

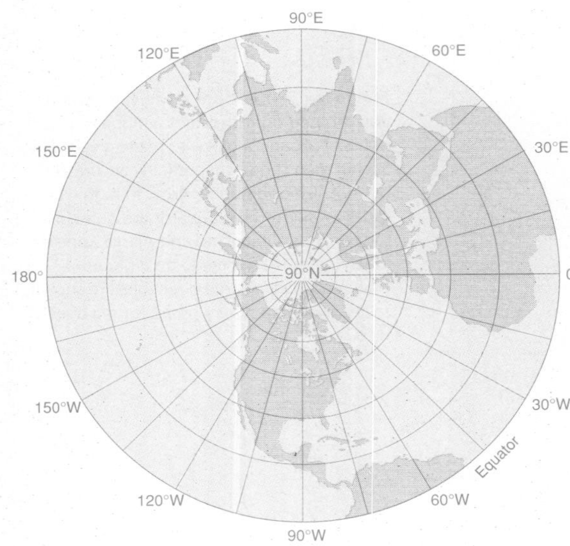

Azimuthal Projection An azimuthal (az•uh•MUHTH•uhl) projection shows the earth centered in such a way that a straight line coming from the center to any other point represents the shortest distance. A common form of azimuthal projection is a polar projection, which uses the North Pole or the South Pole as the center of the map. Although size and shape have distortion, especially toward the edges of the map, distances and directions are accurate when the line of travel passes through the Pole. Therefore, polar maps are often used in air navigation.

Goode's Interrupted Equal-Area Projection The Goode's Interrupted Equal Area projection shows the true size and shape of the earth's landmasses, but distances are generally not accurate.

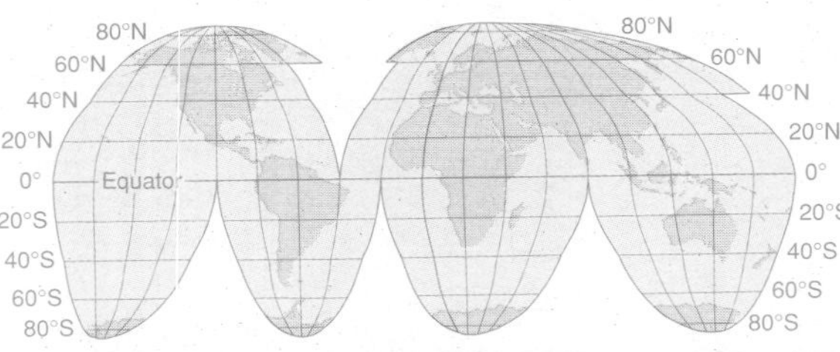

Map Activity

Making a Map Challenge students to make their own "map projections" by trying to depict a curved surface on a flat map. Have each student draw several imaginary countries on a balloon. Then tell students to measure the length and width of their countries and the distances between them on the balloon. Have them try to reproduce the same measurements on a flat sheet of paper. Afterward, ask them to analyze differences between the countries on the balloon and those on the map. *(The shapes of the countries on the flat map probably will be distorted.)*

Robinson Projection A Robinson projection has minor, but not major, distortions. The sizes and shapes near the eastern and western edges of the map are accurate, and the outlines of the continents appear much as they do on a globe. However, the shapes of areas near the poles appear somewhat flat.

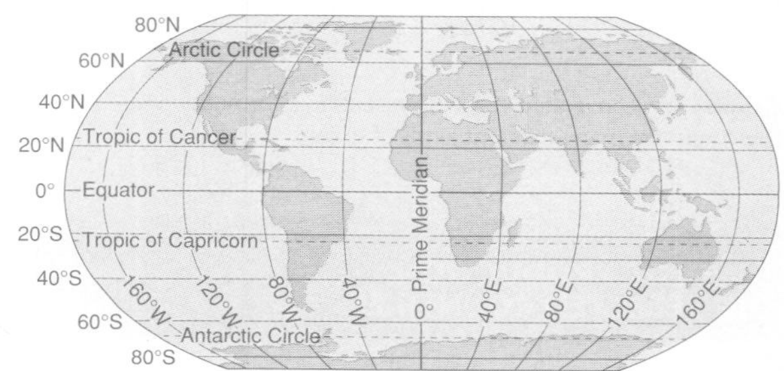

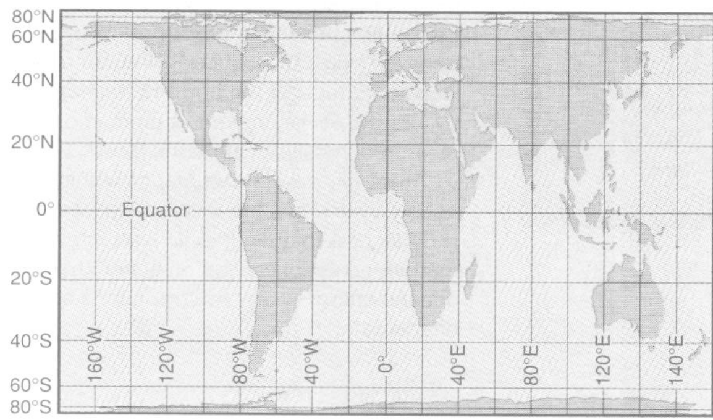

Gall-Peters Projection A Gall-Peters projection has standard parallels of 45 degrees. The sizes of landmasses are accurate. In particular, South America, Africa, and Southeast Asia are shown in their correct size relationship to Europe and North America. Their shapes, however, are greatly distorted. Distances also are inaccurate.

MAP SKILLS REVIEW

1. Why are there different map projections?
2. Why is the Mercator projection useful to navigators?
3. What map projection would best show Antarctica?
4. What projection has shapes that are fairly accurate in the center but have increasing distortion toward the edges?
5. What projection shows true size and shape of landmasses, but inaccurate distances?
6. How does the size of South America on the Gall-Peters projection map compare with its size on the Mercator projection map on page 17?

L2 Review After students read the lesson, ask them to write the name of each projection on one side of an index card and to sum up the advantages and disadvantages of that projection on the other side of the card. Then organize the class into pairs and have students review the main ideas of the lesson using their flash cards.

CURRICULUM CONNECTION

COMPUTER LITERACY
Computers have revolutionized cartography. They reduce distortions and calculate changes at incredible speeds. They gather, process, and store data about contour reliefs, ethnicities, economics, waterways, and much more. They even produce animated "flow maps," such as those that show storm movement.

ANSWERS TO MAP SKILLS REVIEW

1. Each has some distortion or inaccuracy.
2. It shows true direction.
3. Azimuthal
4. Sinusoidal
5. Goode's Interrupted Equal-Area Projection
6. The size on the Gall-Peters is more accurate than the size on the Mercator.

PRETEACHING VOCABULARY

Reduce the graphs, chart, and diagram in the lesson to fit in one column on a sheet of paper. In a second column, write *bar graph, line graph, circle graph, pictograph, chart* or *table*, and *diagram*. Make copies and have students match each term to a graphic. After they finish reading, have them change any incorrect matches.

TEACH

GRAPHS, CHARTS, AND DIAGRAMS

L1 Interpreting Graphs Ask students to study the line graph on page 20 and identify the ten-year period during which the population of the United States increased least rapidly. *(1930 to 1940)* Explain that the depression in the 1930s caused people to marry late and postpone having families.

DID YOU KNOW?

Most growth in the world population has been recent. Ninety percent of all the people who ever lived are alive today.

GRAPHS, CHARTS, AND DIAGRAMS

Graphs, charts, and diagrams are important tools for gaining and interpreting data related to geography. They provide geographers with much valuable information in ways that are well organized and easy to read.

Graphs are convenient ways of presenting information visually. There are many different kinds of graphs.

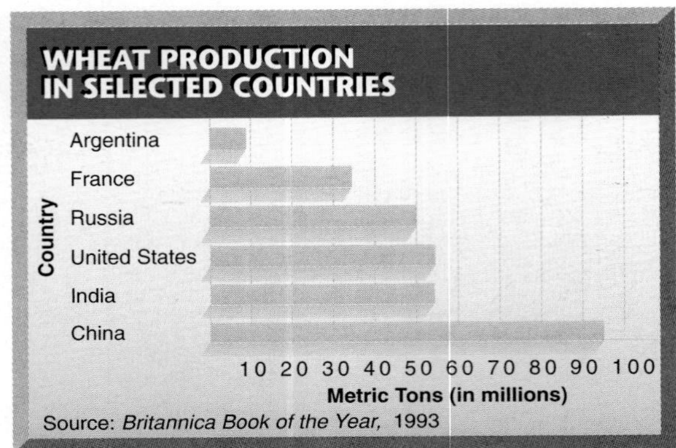

Bar Graphs show comparisons, making highs and lows stand out clearly.

The bar graph to the left shows wheat production in selected countries of the world. Like all bar graphs, it shows two sets of data, one displayed along the vertical axis and the other displayed along the horizontal axis.

Labels on these axes identify the data and units of measurement. In this case, the vertical axis lists the wheat-producing countries from the smallest producer at the top to the largest producer at the bottom; the horizontal axis shows the amount of production measured in millions of metric tons.

Analyzing data on bar graphs requires noting all changes and relationships, especially differences in quantities. Using such information, geographers and others can make generalizations and draw conclusions based on the data.

Line Graphs show changes in two variables, or changing sets of circumstances. They generally show changes over periods of time. The line graph to the right shows how the population of the United States has changed since 1900. The vertical axis lists population in millions, while the horizontal axis indicates the passage of time at ten-year intervals from 1900 to 1990.

Analyzing data on line graphs involves studying changes and trends and drawing conclusions based on the information.

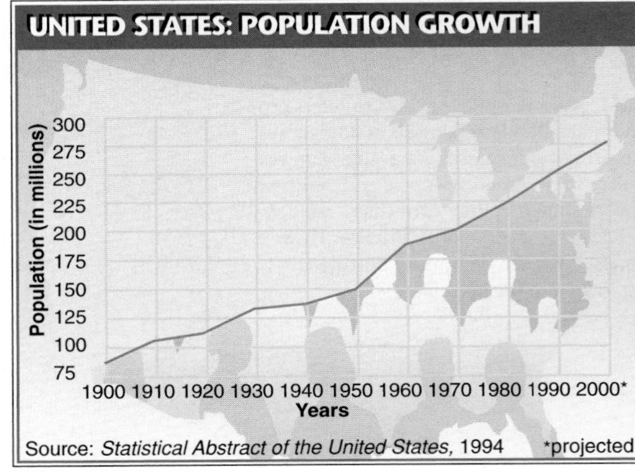

Graph Activity

Movement Have students research the United States 1990 census. Suggest that they look for answers to questions such as these:

How is the population distributed throughout the United States?

Where are particular ethnic groups concentrated?

Which states have lost population since 1980 and which states have gained population?

How do the census results affect the House of Representatives?

Have students report their answers to these questions in the form of bar graphs. For instance, a student might make a bar graph comparing the number of Congressional representatives from different states.

WORLD LAND AREAS

Africa 20.2%
Asia 29.5%
North America 16.2%
South America 11.8%
Europe 7.0%
Antarctica 9.5%
Australia 5.1%
Other 0.7%

Source: *Hammond Ambassador World Atlas*

Circle Graphs use percentages to show how the parts of the whole compare. Because of their shape, circle graphs sometimes are called pie graphs. The circle graph to the left shows the land areas of the world's continents and other landforms. The information indicates the relative sizes of the areas.

Studying data on circle graphs involves noting the relationships of areas to each other and to the whole.

Pictographs are special graphs using a picture of the subject to present important information. Like bar graphs, pictographs show comparisons. The pictograph to the right illustrates wheat production in selected countries of the world. The countries are arranged in order from the smallest producer to the largest producer. Each symbol is a bag of wheat and stands for 10 million metric tons.

As in the case of bar graphs, analyzing the data on pictographs requires analyzing differences in quantities.

Skills Handbook

L1 Demonstrate On the chalkboard, copy the population figures of Africa, Europe, North America, and South America from page 22. Have students cut out red paper figures and label them "10 million people" and blue paper figures and label them "100 million people." Ask students to create a row of figures to represent the population of each continent (rounded off to the nearer 10 million). Tell them to label each set with the continent's name. Then distribute large grids and ask students to create the same pictographs on the grids. Show them how to label the grids and title their pictographs.

L2 Statistics Point out to students that statistical information can often be shown in more than one way. Ask them to convert the circle graph and pictograph on page 21 into bar graphs. Suggest that they use the bar graph on page 20 as a model. Remind them to label the vertical and horizontal axes and to include a title.

Chart Activity

Place Point out that the numbers on the chart on page 22 can be used to produce other information. Demonstrate how to calculate population density by dividing the population by the square miles or square kilometers. Ask the students to determine which populated continent has the lowest population density *(Australia)* and which has the highest *(Asia).*

L3 Contrast Have students imagine that they are employers trying to decide which salesperson makes the best use of his or her time and resources. Ask which graphic aid would be more helpful—a chart logging the activities of each salesperson or a bar graph comparing the amount of sales by each person. *(the chart)* Have students explain their answers. *(Nonnumerical information can be shown in a chart; charts show comparisons in more than one category; charts can provide exact numbers.)*

DID YOU KNOW?

About 250,000 babies are born each day. At that rate, another China will be added to the world's population in ten years.

THE CONTINENTS OF THE WORLD

Continent	Population*	Land Area
Africa	700,000,000	11,707,000 sq. mi. 44,362,815 sq. km.
Antarctica	———	5,500,000 sq. mi. 14,245,000 sq. km.
Asia	3,392,000,000	17,128,500 sq. mi. 44,362,815 sq. km.
Australia	18,000,000	2,966,136 sq. mi. 7,682,300 sq. km.
Europe	728,000,000	4,057,000 sq. mi. 10,507,630 sq. km.
North America	290,000,000	9,363,000 sq. mi. 24,250,170 sq. km.
South America	470,000,000	6,875,000 sq. mi. 17,806,250 sq. km.

*Estimated to nearest million. Antarctica has no permanent population. Europe's population includes Russia, Belarus, Moldova, and Ukraine. South America includes Mexico, Central America, and the Carribean.
Source: 1994 World Population Data Sheet and *Hammond Ambassador World Atlas*

Charts and Tables are useful tools that show facts arranged in columns and rows. They present information in an organized way, providing easy access to data and making comparisons easier to see.

Diagrams are drawings that show what something is or how something is done. Often, diagrams have several parts that show the steps in a process. When you buy an unassembled bicycle, for example, the instructions usually include diagrams to make it easier to assemble the bike.

The diagram below shows how the moon appears to change shape. Note that as the moon revolves around the earth, it goes from the full moon phase—when it appears as a giant orb—to the new moon phase—when it is all but invisible.

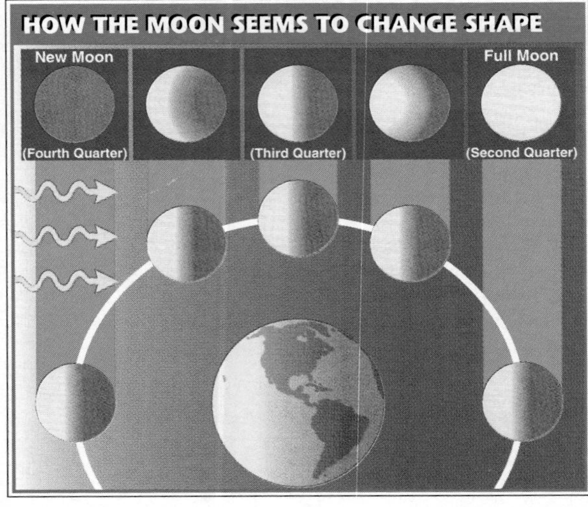

HOW THE MOON SEEMS TO CHANGE SHAPE

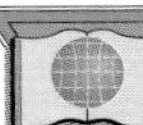

MAP SKILLS REVIEW

1. Study the chart above and name the continent that has the largest population.
2. Look at the pictograph on page 21 and the bar graph on page 20 and list the countries that have the largest and smallest wheat production.
3. Study the line graph on page 20. What was the population of the United States in 1900? In 1930?
4. Study the circle graph on page 21. What percentage of the earth's land area is occupied by Africa?
5. Study the diagram on this page. When is the moon not seen from the earth?

ANSWERS TO MAP SKILLS REVIEW

1. Asia
2. China and Argentina
3. 75 million, 125 million
4. 20.2 percent
5. the fourth quarter

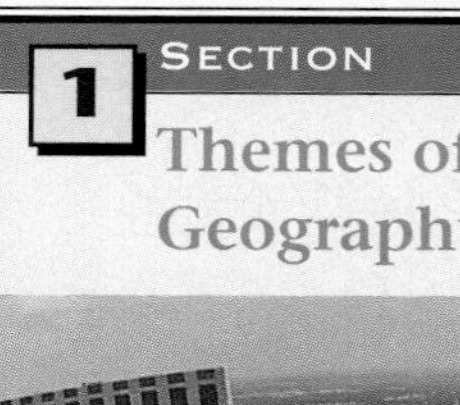

HIGHLIGHTS

1 SECTION	KEY TERMS	SUMMARY
Themes of Geography	**geography** (p. 5) **absolute location** (p. 5) **hemisphere** (p. 5) **latitude** (p. 5) **longitude** (p. 6) **grid system** (p. 6) **relative location** (p. 7) **interdependent** (p. 8) **culture** (p. 10)	• The five themes of location, place, human/environment interaction, movement, and region are important to the study of geography. • Geographers use themes to help them locate places and to understand relationships among places and between people and places. • Geographers also use information from the fields of history, political science, sociology, anthropology, and economics to help them understand the interactions of people with their environments.

Dallas, Texas

GEOGRAPHY SKILLS HANDBOOK	KEY TERMS	SUMMARY
	key (p. 12) **compass rose** (p. 12) **scale** (p. 12) **general purpose maps** (p. 14) **topography** (p. 14) **relief** (p. 14) **contour lines** (p. 14) **special purpose maps** (p. 15) **great circle** (p. 16) **map projection** (p. 17) **graph** (p. 20) **chart** (p. 22) **table** (p. 22) **diagram** (p. 22)	• Geographers use maps and graphs to gather, interpret, and analyze geographic information. Charts, graphs, and diagrams are also important tools of geographers. • Reading a map requires you to know the elements or parts of a map. Those parts include the key, the compass rose, the scale, and a global grid. • The curved surface of the earth is difficult to represent accurately on a flat map. Different projections show the round earth on flat maps with some distortion.

Robinson projection

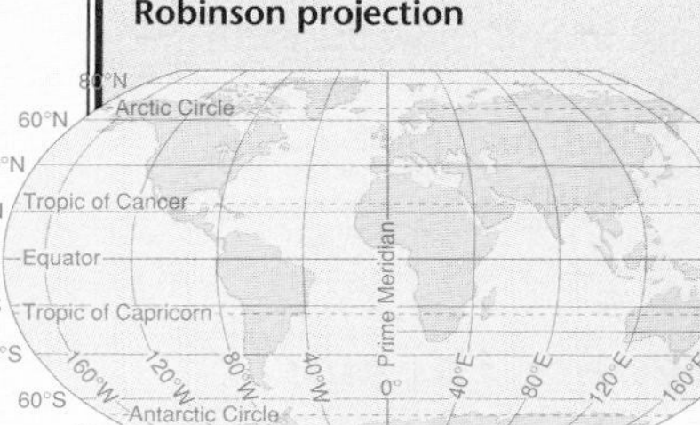

CHAPTER 1 HIGHLIGHTS

USING THE CHAPTER 1 HIGHLIGHTS

Use the Chapter 1 Highlights to preview, review, condense, or reteach the chapter.

PREVIEW/REVIEW

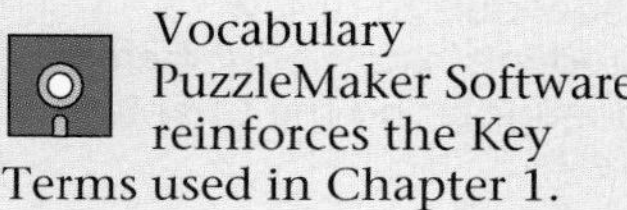

Vocabulary PuzzleMaker Software reinforces the Key Terms used in Chapter 1.

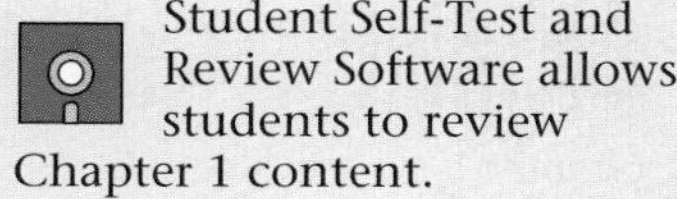

Student Self-Test and Review Software allows students to review Chapter 1 content.

CONDENSE

Have students read the Chapter 1 Highlights.

  Have students listen to the Chapter 1 Audiocassettes in the TCR. Spanish audiocassettes are also available.

Assign the Chapter 1 Audiocassette Activity and give the students the Chapter 1 Audiocassette Quiz.

  Have students complete Guided Reading Activities for Chapter 1 in the TCR. Spanish Guided Reading Activities are also available.

RETEACH

  Have students complete Reteaching Activity 1 in the TCR. Spanish Reteaching Activities are also available.

Map Activity

Identify and Locate Project Political Map Transparency 12 on the chalkboard and have students locate and label the continents and oceans.

GLENCOE TECHNOLOGY

Videodisc

Use Chapter 1 MindJogger Videoquiz to review students' knowledge before administering the Chapter 1 Test.

MINDJOGGER VIDEOQUIZ

Chapter 1
Disc 1 Side A

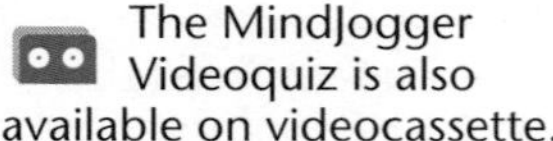

The MindJogger Videoquiz is also available on videocassette.

ANSWERS

Reviewing Key Terms

1. hemisphere
2. grid system
3 absolute location
4. geography
5. relative location
6. culture
7. interdependent
8. latitude
9. longitude
10. scale
11. map projection

chapter 1 REVIEW

Reviewing Key Terms

Choose the vocabulary term that best completes each of the sentences below. Write your answers on a separate sheet of paper.

geography (p. 5)
absolute location (p. 5)
hemisphere (p. 5)
latitude (p. 5)
longitude (p. 6)
grid system (p. 6)
relative location (p. 7)
interdependent (p. 8)
culture (p. 10)
scale (p. 12)
map projection (p. 17)

Section 1

1. A ____ is one of the two halves of the earth divided by the Equator.
2. A global network of horizontal and vertical lines is called a ____ .
3. ____ refers to a place's position on the globe.
4. ____ is the study of the earth and the ways people live and work on it.
5. Telling where a place is in relation to another place is describing its ____ .
6. ____ refers to a people's way of life.
7. Because of improved transportation and communications links, countries in today's world are ____ .
8. Lines of ____ are used to locate places north and south of the Equator.

Geography Skills Handbook

9. Lines of ____ are used to locate places east and west of the Prime Meridian.
10. A line or bar on a map that translates distance on the earth to distance on the map is called its ____ .
11. A ____ is a way of showing the round earth on flat paper.

Reviewing Facts

Section 1

12. Why are location and place important geographic themes?
13. Why is movement an important part of geography?
14. What are two ways that every place on the earth can be located?

Geography Skills Handbook

15. What kind of map would you use to study the boundaries between countries and distance between the capital cities of those countries?
16. What kind of graph would you use to best show the change in the volume of trade between the United States and Japan since 1945? Why would this kind of graph be better than the alternatives available?
17. Which of the map projections available shows the true size and shape of the earth's landmasses?

Critical Thinking

18. **Drawing Conclusions** Of what value to geographers are the five themes of geography?
19. **Expressing Problems Clearly** All map projections distort and show the earth inaccurately although some distort less than others. Which map projection is best for general purposes?

Geographic Themes

20. **Place** What are the physical and human characteristics of your community?
21. **Location** Which map projection would be best to plan a sea voyage around the world?

Reviewing Facts

12. Location is important because it answers the question "Where is it?" Geographers study the location and distribution of almost everything on earth. Place is important because each place on earth can be described in terms of physical features.

13. Geographers are interested in the movement of goods, people, and ideas. They help us understand how almost everyone on earth is interdependent.

14. absolute and relative location

15. political map

16. a line graph; A line graph shows changes over time better than a bar graph, pictograph, or circle graph.

17. Goode's Interrupted Equal-Area projection

Projects

Individual Activity

Collect a variety of maps used in newspapers and newsmagazines. Watch the television news and write descriptions of the maps used to illustrate some features. Organize these into a map scrapbook. Write a definition of a map based on your collection and summarize why maps are useful.

Cooperative Learning Activity

Working in a group of five, describe the geography of your community using the five themes. Each group member should take a theme. Use the following five skills to organize your description. Collect information, present it, analyze it, and draw conclusions to make generalizations.

Writing About Geography

Description

Using the material in your journal, write a two-page letter describing the geography of your community. You may base the organization of your letter on the five geographic themes. It should be so clear that someone who lives in another country would be able to know what it is like to live in your town. Describe where you are, how people in your community make a living, where they came from, how you get to school every day, and other items of interest.

Locating Places

THE WORLD: PHYSICAL GEOGRAPHY

Match the letters on the map with the places and physical features of the earth. Write your answers on a separate sheet of paper.

1. North America
2. South America
3. Africa
4. Asia
5. Europe
6. Australia
7. Antarctica
8. Indian Ocean
9. Atlantic Ocean
10. Pacific Ocean

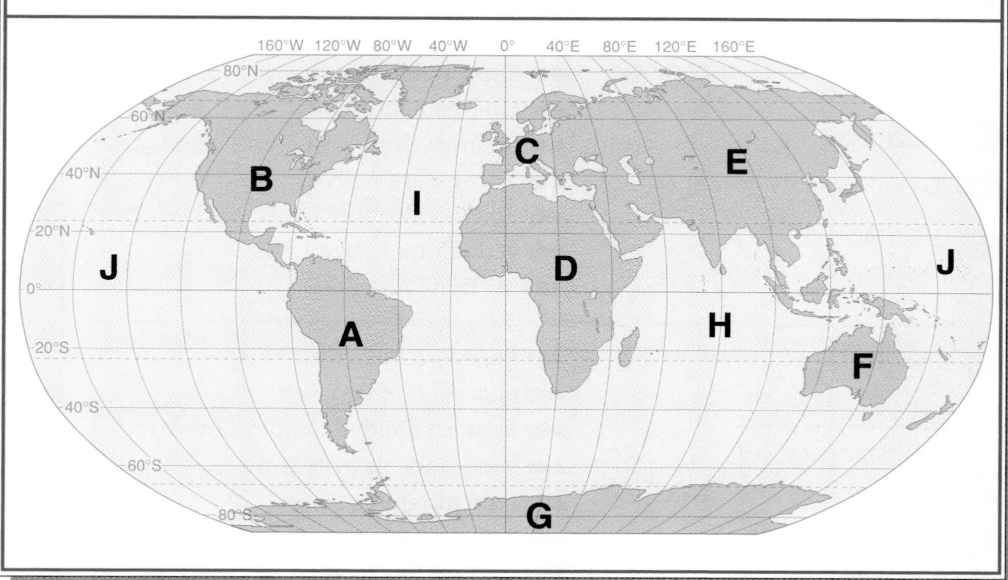

Chapter 1 Review

Critical Thinking

18. The five themes offer a structured way of thinking about the world and can be used to study all kinds of geographic issues.

19. a Robinson projection

Geographic Themes

20. Answers will vary, but students should include details on weather and climate, landforms, plants, animals, population size, ethnic groups, and popular recreation.

21. a Mercator projection

Locating Places

1. B
2. A
3. D
4. E
5. C
6. F
7. G
8. H
9. I
10. J

Chapter Bonus Test Question

This question may be used for extra credit on the chapter test. Choose the letter of the correct response.

Which of the following projections would be most useful in comparing the land area of the continents?

(1) Mercator projection
(2) Conic projection
(3) Azimuthal projection
(4) Goode's Interrupted Equal-Area projection

Answer: (4)

CHAPTER 2

PLANNING GUIDE

Looking at the Earth

CHAPTER ORGANIZER

Daily Lesson Objectives	Multimedia	Teacher Classroom Resources
SECTION 1 Planet Earth 1. Describe the nature and structure of the earth. 2. Explain the forces that affect the surface of the earth.	Section Focus Transparency 2-1 Chapter 2 Vocabulary PuzzleMaker Software Political Map Transparency 1 Geography and the Environment STV: Restless Earth STV: Solar System GTV: Planetary Manager STV: Atmosphere Geology PictureShow	Reproducible Lesson Plan 2-1 Guided Reading Activity 2-1 Spanish Guided Reading Activity 2-1 Performance Assessment Activity 2 Section Quiz 2-1
SECTION 2 Earth's Features 1. Appreciate the variety of the earth's landforms. 2. Name the features of the earth's oceans and seas. 3. Explain how the earth's water is recycled.	Section Focus Transparency 2-2 Testmaker GTV: Planetary Manager STV: Water	Reproducible Lesson Plan 2-2 Guided Reading Activity 2-2 Spanish Guided Reading Activity 2-2 Vocabulary Activity 2 Spanish Vocabulary Activity 2 Workbook Activity 2-2 Section Quiz 2-2
SECTION 3 Earth's Resources 1. Understand the importance of natural resources. 2. Identify the ways in which the distribution of resources affects people and countries.	Section Focus Transparency 2-3 Unit Map Overlay Transparency 1-8 Testmaker GTV: Planetary Manager Geography and the Environment	Reproducible Lesson Plan 2-3 Guided Reading Activity 2-3 Spanish Guided Reading Activity 2-3 Workbook Activity 2-3 Enrichment Activity 2 Skill Activity 2 Section Quiz 2-3
CHAPTER REVIEW AND EVALUATION	Chapter 2 English (or Spanish) Audiocassettes MindJogger Videoquiz Testmaker Student Self-Test and Review Software	Reteaching Activity 2 Spanish Reteaching Activity 2 Chapter 2 Test Form A and Form B

0:00 *If time does not permit teaching the entire chapter, summarize using the Chapter 2 Highlights on page 41, and the Chapter 2 English (or Spanish) Audiocassettes. Review students' knowledge using the Glencoe MindJogger Videoquiz.*

KEY TO ABILITY LEVELS

Teaching strategies have been coded for varying learning styles and abilities.

L1 **BASIC** activities for all students

L2 **AVERAGE** activities for average to above-average students

L3 **CHALLENGING** activities for above-average students

LEP **LIMITED ENGLISH PROFICIENCY** activities

Performance Assessment

Comparing Geographic Features Have individual students design hypothetical planets, showing different types of land and water features, the effects of internal and external forces on the features, and the location of renewable and nonrenewable natural resources. Students should then write brief histories of their planets in which they explain through logical reasoning how the geographic features were developed. Students should then present their creations and histories to the class or to smaller groups.

Once this task has been completed, each student should draw a class member's name and write an informative classificatory paper comparing the features of the class member's planet with that of the earth. Students should be guided to the text or to other sources of information.

POSSIBLE RUBRIC FEATURES: Content information, creativity, logical reasoning, written communication skills

For additional professional and classroom resources, see Chapter Resources, pages T46–T51.

TEACHER'S CORNER

NATIONAL GEOGRAPHIC SOCIETY

INDEX TO NATIONAL GEOGRAPHIC MAGAZINE

The following articles may be used for research relating to this chapter:

- "Living with California Faults," by Rick Gore, April 1995.
- *Water*, a National Geographic Special Edition, November 1993.
- "Ogallala Aquifer: Wellspring of the High Plains," by Erla Zwingle, March 1993.
- "Volcanoes: Crucibles of Creation," by Noel Grove, December 1992.
- "A Comeback for Nuclear Power? Our Electric Future," by Peter Miller, August 1991.
- "The Quest for Oil," by Fred Hapgood, August 1989.
- "Our Restless Planet Earth," by Rick Gore, August 1985.
- "New World of the Ocean," by Samuel W. Matthews, December 1981.
- *Energy*, a National Geographic Special Report, February 1981.
- "Solar Energy, the Ultimate Powerhouse," by John L. Wilhelm, March 1976.

NATIONAL GEOGRAPHIC SOCIETY PRODUCTS AVAILABLE FROM GLENCOE

To order the following products for use with this chapter, contact your local Glencoe sales representative or call Glencoe at 1-800-334-7344:

- *Picture Atlas of the World* (CD-ROM)
- *Geology PictureShow* (CD-ROM)
- *Earth's Endangered Environments PictureShow* (CD-ROM)
- *GeoBee* (Software)
- *STV: Solar System* (Videodisc)
- *STV: Restless Earth* (Videodisc)
- *STV: Water* (Videodisc)
- *GTV: Planetary Manager* (Videodisc)

ADDITIONAL NATIONAL GEOGRAPHIC SOCIETY PRODUCTS

To order the following products for use with this chapter, call National Geographic Society at 1-800-368-2728:

- *This World of Energy I*, "Energy in the Earth," "Using Energy," "Fossil Fuels." (Filmstrip)
- *This World of Energy II*, "Our Energy Problem," "Nuclear Energy," "Synthetic Fuels and Other Alternative Sources." (Filmstrip)
- *Atmosphere: On the Air* (Video)
- *Energy: The Fuels and Man* (Video)
- *The Living Earth* (Video)
- *Water: A Precious Resource* (Video)

Introducing CHAPTER 2

PERFORMANCE ASSESSMENT

Refer to the Planning Guide on page 26B for a Performance Assessment Activity for this chapter. See the *Performance Assessment Activities* booklet for additional suggestions.

CHAPTER OBJECTIVES

1. **Describe** how sections of the earth's crust move to shape the land surface.
2. **List** the earth's many different landforms.
3. **Understand** that people depend on the earth for the materials for basic survival.

GLENCOE TECHNOLOGY

Videodisc

Use Chapter 2 MindJogger Videoquiz to preview chapter content.

MINDJOGGER VIDEOQUIZ

Chapter 2
Disc 1 Side A

The MindJogger Videoquiz is also available on videocassette.

NATIONAL GEOGRAPHIC SOCIETY

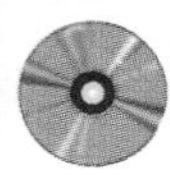

Videodisc

STV: SOLAR SYSTEM

Side 1, Chapter 1
Frames 00691-11815
Title: ***The Big Picture* (in its entirety)**
Subject: The work of astronomers and the solar system and how it operates

chapter 2 Looking at the Earth

CHAPTER FOCUS

Geographic Setting

Earth's distance from the sun, its daily rotation, slight tilt, and gaseous atmosphere all work together to make most of our world habitable.

Geographic Themes

Section 1 Planet Earth
MOVEMENT Sections of the earth's crust move to shape the land surface.

Section 2 Earth's Features
REGION The earth's land surface consists of many different landforms, such as mountains, hills, plateaus, and plains.

Section 3 Earth's Resources
HUMAN/ENVIRONMENT INTERACTION People depend on the earth for the materials necessary for basic survival.

▲Photograph: ***View of Earth from space***

EXTRA CREDIT PROJECT

Television News Show Tell students to research how the view of Earth from space affects astronauts' outlook on human/environmental interaction. A helpful source is Frank White's *The Overview Effect: Space Exploration and Human Evolution.* Then have students report on whether the astronauts' outlook from space has changed their lives, and if so, how.

SECTION 1
Planet Earth

SETTING THE SCENE

Read to Discover . . .
- the nature and structure of the earth.
- the forces that affect the surface of the earth, the setting for human life.

Key Terms
- atmosphere
- hydrosphere
- lithosphere
- biosphere
- mantle
- fold
- fault
- weathering
- erosion
- glacier

Identify and Locate
Mount Everest, Dead Sea, Mariana Trench, Grand Canyon of the Colorado River

The first astronaut to walk on the moon described the earth as looking "like a beautiful jewel in space." The earth's great beauty was seen as a contrast of water and land beneath huge swirls of white clouds. Together these features form the physical environment of the earth.

Earth Viewed From Outer Space

The earth is part of a system of objects that revolve around the sun. The earth's surface is made up of water and land and is surrounded by air. Great contrasts exist in the heights and depths of the earth's surface.

The Solar System

Earth is part of the solar system, which is made up of the sun and all the objects that revolve around it. The sun is a star and the center of the solar system. The sun's great mass—the amount of matter it contains—creates the gravitation that keeps the other objects revolving around it.

The planets are the largest objects that revolve around the sun. Planets are spheres. There are at least 9 planets in our solar system, each with its own orbit around the sun. Planets vary in their distance from the sun. Mercury, Venus, Earth, and Mars are nearest to the sun. Jupiter, Saturn, Uranus, Neptune, and Pluto are farthest away from the sun. The planets vary in size. Jupiter is the largest. Earth ranks fifth in size among the planets. All the planets except Mercury and Venus have moons. The number of moons a planet has also varies. Earth has 1 moon, while Saturn has perhaps as many as 22 moons.

There are thousands of smaller objects that revolve around the sun. Asteroids are planet-like objects. These small, irregularly shaped objects are found mainly between the orbits of Mars and Jupiter. Comets are bodies of dust and frozen gases. They resemble bright balls with long tails. Meteoroids are pieces of rock and iron. Many meteoroids fall into the earth's **atmosphere**—the air that surrounds the earth—but most are burned up by friction before they reach the surface of the earth.

Earth's Measurements

Earth is about 93 million miles (150 million km) from the sun. Earth is the third planet from the sun. Only Mercury and Venus are closer.

The diameter of Earth at the Equator is about 8,000 miles (12,700 km). The distance around Earth is shorter at the poles than at the Equator.

Water, Land, and Air

The surface of the earth is made up of water and land. About 70 percent of the

LESSON PLAN
Chapter 2, Section 1

FOCUS

SECTION OBJECTIVES

1. Describe the nature and structure of the earth.
2. Explain the forces that affect the surface of the earth.

BELLRINGER MOTIVATIONAL ACTIVITY

Project the Section 1 Focus Transparency and have students answer the questions.

PRETEACHING VOCABULARY

Translate the Greek roots of *atmosphere, hydrosphere, lithosphere,* and *biosphere.* Then write the words' meanings on the chalkboard and ask students to match each word with its correct meaning.

Use the Vocabulary PuzzleMaker Software to create a crossword or word search puzzle.

GLENCOE TECHNOLOGY

Videodisc

GEOGRAPHY AND THE ENVIRONMENT
THE INFINITE VOYAGE
Living With Disaster

Chapter 5
Disc 3 Side A
Title: ***Earthquakes: A Turbulence Beneath the Earth***
Subject: The nature and cause of earthquakes are explained through animation

Classroom Resources for Section 1

BLACKLINE MASTERS:
Reproducible Lesson Plan 2-1
Guided Reading Activity 2-1
Performance Assessment Activity 2
Section Quiz 2-1

TRANSPARENCIES:
Section Focus Transparency 2-1
Political Map Transparency 1

MULTIMEDIA:

Vocabulary PuzzleMaker Software
Testmaker

Geography and the Environment
STV: Solar System
GTV: Planetary Manager
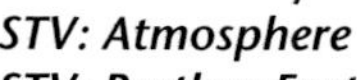
STV: Atmosphere
STV: Restless Earth

Geology PictureShow

TEACH

GUIDED PRACTICE

L1 Vocabulary Before students read the section, go over the pronunciations of the following terms: *silicon, oxygen, aluminum,* and *magnesium.* LEP

L2 Mobile Suggest students make a solar system mobile. Tell them to include the asteroid belt in addition to the sun and its planets.

USING CHARTS

Answers: Jupiter; Pluto

Skills Practice

Reading a Chart Which two planets have higher temperatures than Earth? *(Mercury and Venus)* Why? *(They are closer to the sun.)*

Global Gourmet

The bread of choice at the National Aeronautics and Space Administration (NASA) is tortillas. They do not crumble like other kinds of bread, leaving crumbs to float about in the weightless environment of a spacecraft.

NATIONAL GEOGRAPHIC SOCIETY

Videodisc

STV: ATMOSPHERE

Side 1, Chapter 1
Frames 00400-22294
Title: ***What is the Atmosphere?*** **(in its entirety)**
Subject: Introduces definition of and basic concepts of Earth's atmosphere

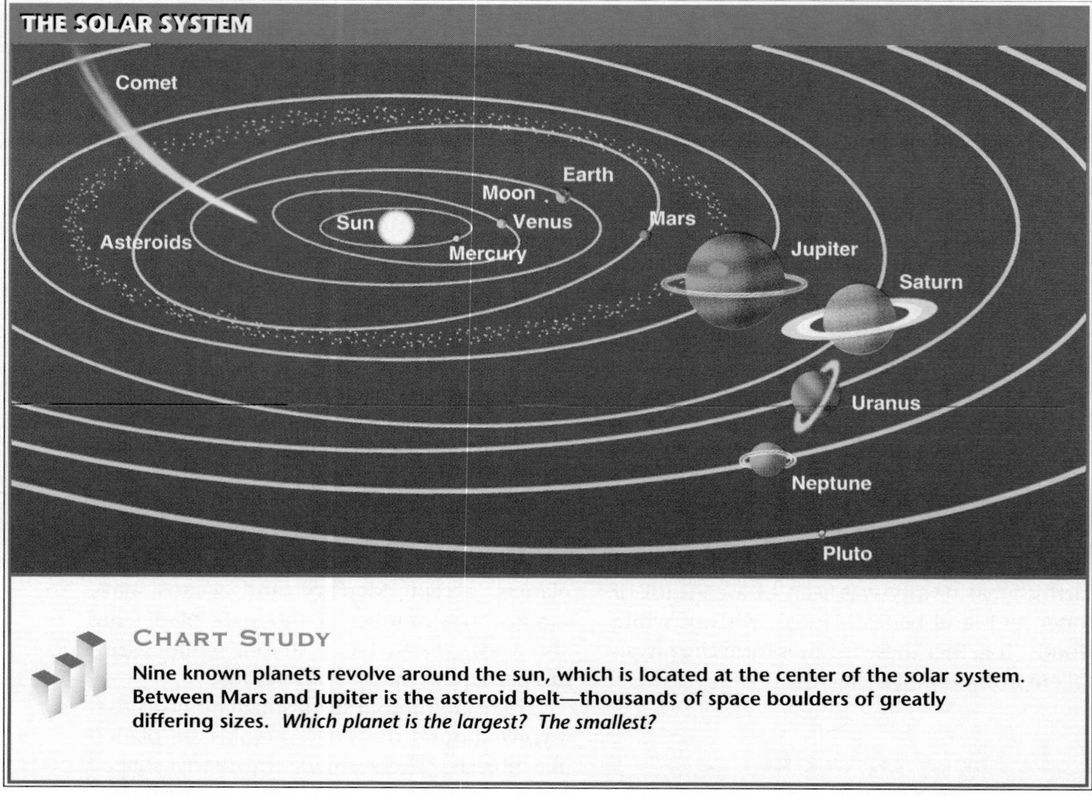

CHART STUDY

Nine known planets revolve around the sun, which is located at the center of the solar system. Between Mars and Jupiter is the asteroid belt—thousands of space boulders of greatly differing sizes. ***Which planet is the largest? The smallest?***

surface is water. Oceans, lakes, rivers, and other bodies of water make up a part of the earth called the **hydrosphere.**

About 30 percent of the earth's surface is land. Land makes up a part of the earth called the **lithosphere,** the earth's crust. The largest bodies of land, which are known as continents, and the ocean basins, which are the lands beneath the oceans, are part of the lithosphere.

The atmosphere of the earth extends about 1,000 miles (about 1,600 km) above the earth's surface. About 78 percent of the atmosphere is nitrogen and 21 percent, oxygen. The remaining 1 percent consists of argon and small amounts of other gases.

All people, animals, and plants live on the earth's surface, close to the earth's surface, or in the atmosphere. The part of the earth where life is found is called the **biosphere.**

Earth's Heights and Depths

The average height of the earth's land is about 2,800 feet (850 m) above sea level. The highest point on the earth is the top of Mount Everest in Asia, which is 29,028 feet (about 8,850 m) above sea level. The lowest point on the earth is the shore of the Dead Sea, which is 1,312 feet (400 m) below sea level.

The average depth of the earth's oceans is 12,450 feet (3,975 m). The deepest part of the ocean is the Mariana Trench, a long, narrow depression in the Pacific Ocean, southwest of Guam. The Mariana Trench is about 35,800 feet (10,900 m) deep.

Cooperative Learning Activity

Organize the class into three groups. Assign each group one of the following topics: earthquakes, volcanic eruptions, and tidal waves. Tell the groups to make bulletin-board displays showing how these natural disasters occur. Suggest that they make their displays three-dimensional by using pop-up art and papier-maché.

PLACE

Earth's Structure

The earth's surface is always changing. Internal forces bring about changes in the earth's surface over time. Surface forces, such as wind, flowing water, and ice also change the earth's surface.

Inside the Earth

The inside of the earth is composed of three layers—the core, the **mantle**, and the crust. The inner core makes up the center of the earth. It lies about 4,000 miles (6,400 km) below the surface of the earth. Scientists believe that the inner core is solid and consists of iron and nickel. The other part of the core, the outer core, begins about 1,800 miles (2,900 km) below the surface of the earth. It is made up of melted iron and nickel.

Next to the outer core is a thick layer of dense, hot rock called the mantle. The rock in the mantle consists of silicon, oxygen, aluminum, iron, and magnesium.

Next to the mantle is the earth's crust. This is a relatively thin layer, extending perhaps 3 to 30 miles (5 to 50 km) below the surface. The crust consists of huge platelike sections of rock that rest—or more accurately, float—on a partially melted layer in the upper mantle. The crust includes the continents and ocean basins.

Internal Forces

The surface of the earth has changed greatly over time. These changes have been largely the result of internal forces. These internal forces cause the plates of the earth's crust to move. Generally they move very slowly—only about 4 inches (10 cm) each year. When the plates spread apart, melted rock rises through the gaps and forms ridges. When the plates bump together, one may slide under another, forming a trench.

Shaking or sudden movements in the plates, called earthquakes, change the surface of the land and the floor of the ocean. Volcanoes are mountains formed when lava, or melted rock, rises through the earth's crust. If the lava is too thick, the flow is blocked and pressure builds. A sudden release may then occur, often with great force.

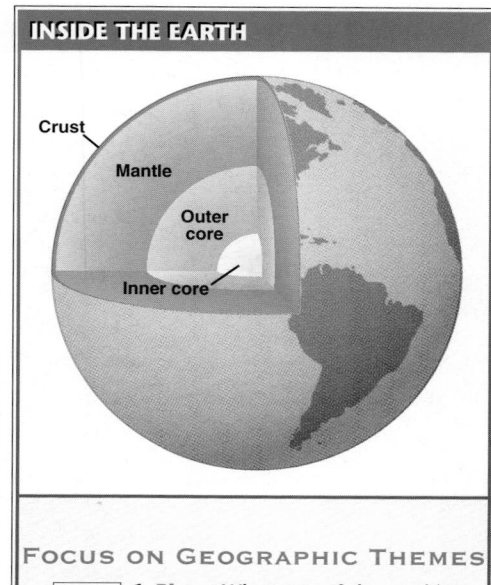

Internal forces can build or break down mountains in other ways, such as by **folds** or **faults.** Folds are bends in layers of rock. Such bends occur when the moving plates squeeze the earth's surface until it buckles.

Faults, or breaks in the earth's crust, occur when the folded land cannot be bent any further. Then the earth's crust cracks and breaks into huge blocks. Movement occurs along the faults and may be in any direction. Mountains formed by faults, or fault-block mountains, are generally steep on one side and gently sloping on the other.

Earthquakes and volcanoes under the ocean can cause as much damage as those on land. The release of these forces beneath the ocean often causes seismic sea waves, or tsunami. Such a wave may move through the water

INSIDE THE EARTH

Crust
Mantle
Outer core
Inner core

FOCUS ON GEOGRAPHIC THEMES

1. **Place:** What part of the earth's interior is solid and consists of iron and nickel?
2. **Place:** What part of the earth's interior consists of melted iron and nickel?

L1 Movement Have students demonstrate how folds occur in the earth's surface. Tell them to push together the top and bottom edges of a flat sheet of paper with the palms of their hands.

L1 Movement Explain to students that the shocks of an earthquake move like waves, traveling fast or in slow ripples. Have them demonstrate a fast wave by stretching a spring and then letting go. To demonstrate slower waves, have them snap a rope to make ripples.

INDEPENDENT PRACTICE

Guided Reading Have students complete Guided Reading Activity 2-1 in the TCR. **LEP**

L2 Demonstrate Suggest that students reproduce the effects of chemical weathering by dropping a seashell in lemon juice. Have them observe and report on the changes that occur.

USING DIAGRAMS

Answers:
1. the inner core;
2. the outer core

Skills Practice

Reading a Diagram
Which layer of the earth is closest to the surface? *(the crust)*

Videodisc

STV: RESTLESS EARTH

Side 1, Chapter 1
Frames 00001-14511
Title: *Introduction* **(in its entirety)**
Subject: Movement of the Earth's landmasses

Meeting Special Needs

Inefficient Organizers Skimming is a technique that is especially useful for students who have difficulty organizing information. Explain to students that skimming a section will help them formulate ideas about what will be covered in the section. Demonstrate skimming by saying: "First, I look at the section title, then I read the subsection headings. Next, I look at the pictures and other illustrations, and finally I read the words in bold type, the Setting the Scene, and the first and last paragraphs of the section."

Have students follow along and practice each step after you announce it.

USING MAPS

Answers:
1. west of South America; **2.** the Nazca Plate and the Caribbean Plate; **3.** the Indo-Australian Plate; **4.** the Eurasian Plate and the Pacific Plate

Map Skills Practice
Reading a Map Which plate is moving away from the western part of the American plate? *(the Pacific Plate)*

CURRICULUM CONNECTION

HISTORY
One of the most violent volcanic eruptions in history occurred in 1883 on the island of Krakatau in Indonesia. The volcano collapsed from a height of 2,640 feet (692 meters) to 1,000 feet (300 meters) below sea level. Its collapse triggered a tidal wave that killed 36,000 people in nearby Java and Sumatra.

GLENCOE TECHNOLOGY

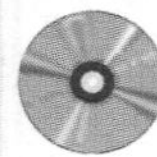

Videodisc

GEOGRAPHY AND THE ENVIRONMENT
THE INFINITE VOYAGE
Living With Disaster

Chapter 6
Disc 3 Side A
Title: ***Predicting Earthquakes: The Parkfield Experiment***
Subject: Lasers and computers join in a prediction experiment to determine if the land around the San Andreas fault has shifted

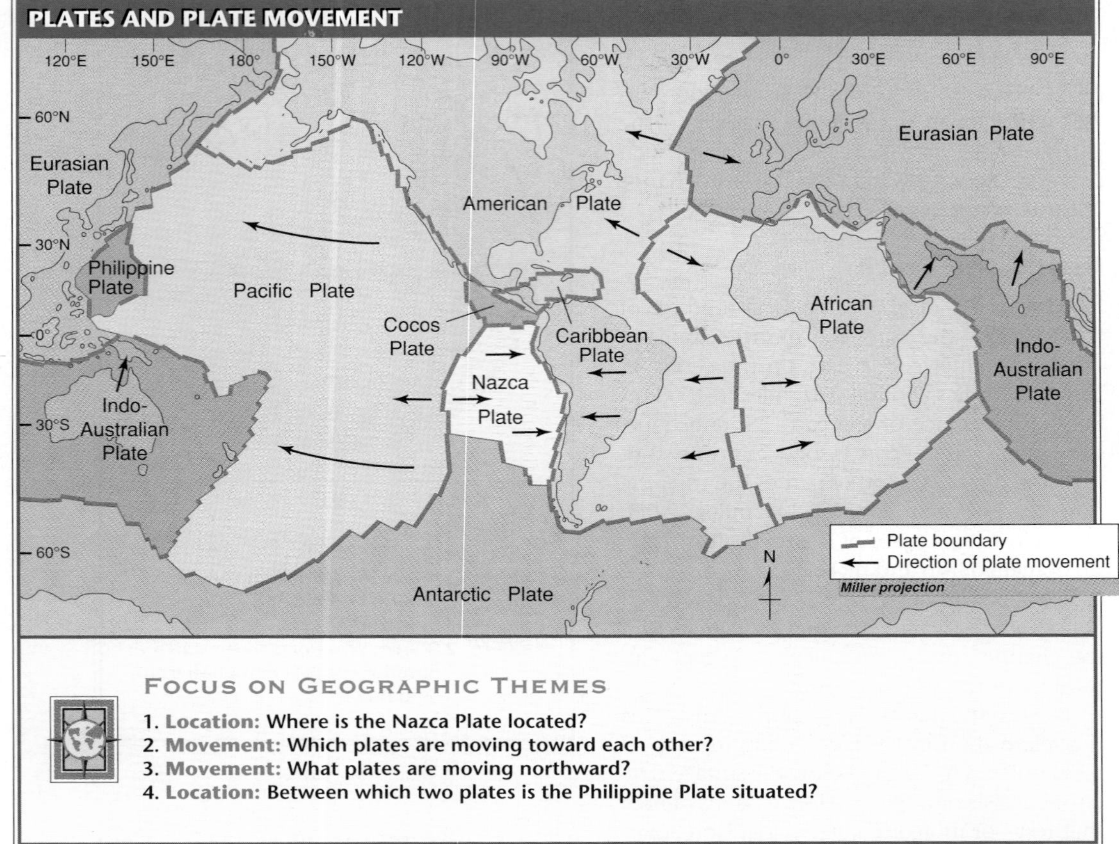

FOCUS ON GEOGRAPHIC THEMES

1. **Location:** Where is the Nazca Plate located?
2. **Movement:** Which plates are moving toward each other?
3. **Movement:** What plates are moving northward?
4. **Location:** Between which two plates is the Philippine Plate situated?

faster than 400 miles (644 km) per hour. Near the shore, tsunami can pile up and reach a height of more than 100 feet (30 m).

Earthquakes often occur where different plates meet one another. Many major earthquakes and volcanoes occur along the edges of the plates beneath the Pacific Ocean. Geologists call the area of earthquake and volcano activity that rims the Pacific Ocean the Ring of Fire. The Ring of Fire marks the boundary where the plates that cradle the Pacific meet the plates that hold the continents surrounding the Pacific.

Geologists believe that about 240 million years ago all the earth's landmasses were joined together. For example, Africa and South America were next to each other. Over time, the spreading of the ocean floor caused Africa and South America to be located as they are today, with the Atlantic Ocean between them. The idea that the continents were once joined and then slowly drifted apart is called continental drift.

External Forces

Other forces also change the surface of the earth. Rocks are always breaking into smaller pieces. The process that breaks down rocks is called **weathering.** There are two basic kinds of weathering—chemical weathering and physical weathering.

Chemical weathering results when water dissolves some of the chemicals in rocks, causing them to disintegrate or when parts of iron-bearing rocks rust—just as metal does—and break apart. Physical weathering, by contrast, breaks rocks into large pieces. For example,

Critical Thinking

Determining Cause and Effect Students have read about the causes of earthquakes and volcanic eruptions. Now ask them to determine the effects of these natural disasters on the environment and people's lives. Suggest that they research the eruption of Mount St. Helens in 1991 and the earthquake in Yucca Valley, California, in July 1992, or the January 17, 1994 California earthquake, using periodicals at the library. Then instruct them to make oral presentations explaining different effects of these disasters, such as weather changes as a result of ash in the air or new construction codes for houses and highways.

water seeps into the cracks in a rock and freezes, expanding and causing the rock to split. Physical weathering can also result when tree roots grow through cracks in a rock, forcing it apart.

Another force that changes the surface of the earth is **erosion**—the wearing away of the earth's surface. Erosion occurs by means of wind, flowing water, and glaciers.

Wind erosion involves the movement of dust, sand, and soil from one place to another. Plants help to protect the land from wind erosion; however, in dry places where people have cut down trees and plants, winds pick up large amounts of soil and blow it away. In deserts and on some beaches, windblown sands form hills called dunes. In general, vegetation grows on beach dunes and helps stop drastic erosion. The vegetation also helps protect the shoreline from erosion caused by pounding waves. As humans develop beachfront properties, however, they often destroy the protective dunes and hasten erosion.

Water erosion begins when rainwater flows off the land downhill in streams. As the water flows, it cuts into the land, wearing away the soil and rock. Over a period of time, the eroding action of water works to form first a gully and then a valley. Sometimes valleys are eroded even further to form valleys with high, steep walls called canyons. The Grand Canyon of the Colorado River is a good example of the eroding power of water. Over millions of years, the Colorado River has cut a canyon that is more than 1 mile (1.6 km) deep.

Erosion can also occur as **glaciers**, or large bodies of ice, move across the surface of the earth. As they move, glaciers change the land, destroying forests, carving out valleys, altering the course of rivers, and wearing down mountain tops. Scientists believe that in the last 2 million years glaciers have covered large areas of the earth's surface for long periods of time.

Collectively these periods are called the Ice Ages. The last part of the last one took place during the Pleistocene epoch—long before

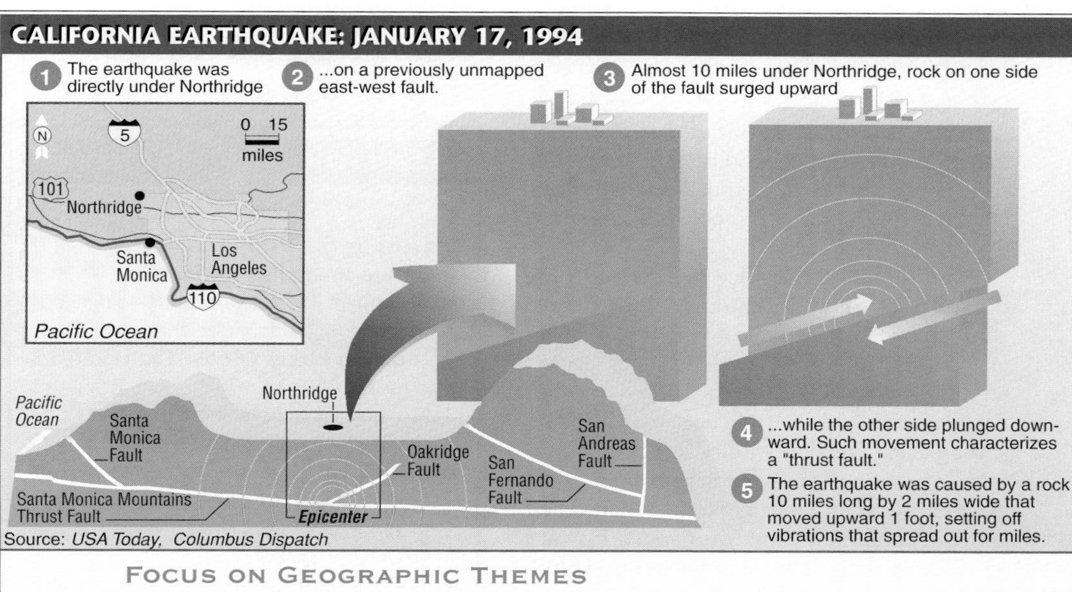

CALIFORNIA EARTHQUAKE: JANUARY 17, 1994
1 The earthquake was directly under Northridge
2 ...on a previously unmapped east-west fault.
3 Almost 10 miles under Northridge, rock on one side of the fault surged upward
N
5
0 15
miles
101
Northridge
Santa Monica
Los Angeles
110
Pacific Ocean
Pacific Ocean
Santa Monica Fault
Northridge
Oakridge Fault
San Fernando Fault
San Andreas Fault
Santa Monica Mountains Thrust Fault
Epicenter
4 ...while the other side plunged downward. Such movement characterizes a "thrust fault."
5 The earthquake was caused by a rock 10 miles long by 2 miles wide that moved upward 1 foot, setting off vibrations that spread out for miles.

Source: *USA Today, Columbus Dispatch*

FOCUS ON GEOGRAPHIC THEMES

Place: Los Angeles, California

The earthquake that struck the Los Angeles area on January 17, 1994, was caused by a "thrust fault" located about 10 miles (16 km) beneath the town of Northridge. ***What kind of underground activity occurs in a "thrust fault" earthquake?***

Extending the Content

Location Refer students to page A4 at the front of the book. Tell them to locate the Colorado River and the Grand Canyon. Then tell them to find Greenland on page A6 and Antarctica on page A28. Ask them to generalize about why glaciers still remain in Greenland and Antarctica. *(Answers will vary but should indicate that Greenland and Antarctica are always cold and glaciers there do not melt.)* Then ask students to predict where other glaciers might be found. Have them research the places they name to find out if their predictions are valid.

ASSESS

CHECK FOR UNDERSTANDING

Assign Section 1 Review as homework or an in-class activity.

MEETING LESSON OBJECTIVES

Each objective below is tested by the questions that follow it in parentheses.

1. Describe the nature and structure of the earth. *(2)*

2. Explain the forces that affect the surface of the earth. *(3, 4, 5)*

EVALUATE

Assign the Section 1 Quiz in the TCR.

Use the Testmaker to create a customized quiz for Section 1.

USING DIAGRAMS

Answer: Rock on one side of the fault moves upward while the other side moves downward.

Skills Practice

Interpreting a Diagram What two faults shown on the diagram are closest to the Epicenter? *(Oakridge Fault and Santa Monica Mountains Thrust Fault)*

NATIONAL GEOGRAPHIC SOCIETY

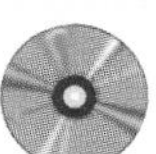

Videodisc

STV: RESTLESS EARTH

Side 2, Chapter 4
Frames 00001-10743
Title: ***Translation in California*** **(in its entirety)**
Subject: Describes translation—the act of one plate grinding against another—and how people in California live with the ever present danger of earthquakes

RETEACH

Have students complete Workbook Activity 2-1 found in the TCR.

ENRICH

Display and discuss different rocks that make up the earth's crust.

CLOSE

Point out to students that Jules Verne's *Journey to the Center of the Earth* was written before scientists knew much about the inside of the earth. Have students write synopses of a realistic journey to the center of the earth based on facts from the section.

USING ILLUSTRATIONS

PLACE Mount Everest rises 29,028 feet (8,850 meters) high. Death Valley lies 282 feet (86 meters) below sea level. What is the difference in elevation? *(29,310 feet or 8,936 meters)*

Answer to Caption: *the shore of the Dead Sea*

NATIONAL GEOGRAPHIC SOCIETY

Videodisc

GTV: PLANETARY MANAGER

Side 1, Chapter 1
Frames 2-5832
Title: ***S.O.S!***
Subject: "Spaceship Earth" (Earth as a system)

CD-ROM

GEOLOGY PICTURESHOW
Learn about "Weathering and Erosion" and "Rocks and Minerals." Classroom activities and a glossary also are available.

Geographic Themes

Place: High and Low Points
South Asia's Mount Everest is the world's highest mountain. California's Death Valley contains the lowest point in the Western Hemisphere. *Where is the world's lowest point?*

humans developed civilizations. It ended about 10,000 years ago. Some scientists theorize that as the earth's orbit around the sun changes, the planet will cool and glaciation will take place again.

Even though the last Ice Age ended in the distant past, some glaciation remains on the earth today. Glaciers are of two types—sheet glaciers and mountain glaciers. Sheet glaciers are sheets of ice that cover large areas. Most of Greenland and all of Antarctica are covered by sheet glaciers, generally called ice caps. Mountain glaciers are more common than sheet glaciers. Mountain glaciers form when fallen snow in mountains builds up and turns into ice. Gravity then pulls these glaciers downhill. As they move downward, mountain glaciers pick up rocks and soil in their paths and carve U-shaped valleys. When a glacier melts, it deposits its rock and soil.

SECTION 1 REVIEW

Checking for Understanding

1. **Define** atmosphere, hydrosphere, lithosphere, biosphere, mantle, fold, fault, weathering, erosion, glacier.
2. **Locating Places** Where is Earth located in relation to the sun?
3. **Movement** How have internal forces changed the surface of the earth?
4. **Movement** How does water erosion change the surface of the earth?

Critical Thinking

5. **Predicting Consequences** Imagine that the mantle of the earth ceased to circulate molten rock. What would be the consequences on land formation on the surface of the earth?

ANSWERS TO SECTION 1 REVIEW

1. **atmosphere:** earth's air; **hydrosphere:** earth's water; **lithosphere:** earth's land; **biosphere:** where life is found; **mantle:** thick rock layer around the earth's outer core; **fold:** bend in the earth's crust; **fault:** a break in the earth's crust; **weathering:** breaking down rock; **erosion:** wearing away of earth's surface; **glacier:** large moving body of ice
2. It is the third planet from the sun.
3. They have moved the earth's plates, causing melted rock to rise and to form ridges and causing plates to slide under other plates to form trenches.
4. Flowing rainwater wears away soil and rocks, later forming gullies, valleys, and canyons.
5. Earthquakes, volcanic eruptions, and mountain building would cease.

2 SECTION Earth's Features

SETTING THE SCENE

Read to Discover . . .
- the variety of the earth's landforms.
- the features of the earth's oceans and seas.
- how the earth's water is recycled.

Key Terms
- isthmus
- plateau
- archipelago
- continental shelf
- groundwater
- water cycle
- evaporation

Identify and Locate
The continents: North America, South America, Europe, Asia, Africa, Australia, Antarctica; Isthmus of Suez; Isthmus of Panama; The oceans: Atlantic, Pacific, Indian, Arctic

Photographs of the earth taken from space show that the surface of the earth is far from uniform. The first section of this chapter discussed the internal and external forces that act on the natural features of the earth. In this section, you will read about the planet's variety of land and water areas.

PLACE

Landforms

The natural features of the earth's land surfaces are called landforms. These features are classified by type in order to describe and define them. The names given to these features help people locate specific places.

Continents

Geographers divide most of the land surface of the earth into seven large landmasses called continents. North America and South America are the continents in the Western Hemisphere. Australia and Asia are in the Eastern Hemisphere. Most of Europe and Africa are in the Eastern Hemisphere, but a small part of their western coastal areas is in the Western Hemisphere. Antarctica, which includes the South Pole, is located in both the Western Hemisphere and the Eastern Hemisphere. Asia is the largest continent, and Australia is the smallest.

Some continents, like Australia and Antarctica, stand alone, while others are joined in some way. An **isthmus** is a narrow piece of land that connects two large landmasses and separates two bodies of water. The Isthmus of Panama joins North America and South America and separates the Atlantic and Pacific oceans.

Europe and Asia are actually parts of one huge landmass. Some people consider this landmass to be one continent and call it Eurasia. Most geographers, however, use natural or political boundaries to divide the area into two separate continents. The Ural Mountains serve as a natural boundary between Europe and Asia.

Major Landforms

The landforms of the earth vary greatly from place to place. The four major kinds of landforms are mountains, hills, plateaus, and plains. These landforms can be described in terms of their shapes and elevations.

Parts of the land that rise noticeably above the rest of the land are called either mountains or hills. Mountains have steep slopes and some kind of peak or summit. Mountains are

LESSON PLAN
Chapter 2, Section 2

FOCUS

SECTION OBJECTIVES

1. **Appreciate** the variety of the earth's landforms.
2. **Name** the features of the earth's oceans and seas.
3. **Explain** how the earth's water is recycled.

BELLRINGER MOTIVATIONAL ACTIVITY

Project the Section 2 Focus Transparency and have students answer the questions.

PRETEACHING VOCABULARY

Have students write each Key Term on one side of an index card and its definition on the other side. Tell them to master the terms by studying their flash cards.

MULTICULTURAL PERSPECTIVE

Community Resources
Invite an engineer from a water treatment facility to answer the class's questions about their water, such as: Where does it come from and how is it processed? Then have students research water treatment facilities in another country, such as Saudi Arabia, and compare the two.

Classroom Resources for Section 2

BLACKLINE MASTERS:
Reproducible Lesson Plan 2-2
Guided Reading Activity 2-2
Spanish Guided Reading Activity 2-2
Vocabulary Activity 2
Spanish Vocabulary Activity 2
Workbook Activity 2-2
Section Quiz 2-2

TRANSPARENCIES:
Section Focus Transparency 2-2

MULTIMEDIA:
Testmaker

GTV: Planetary Manager
STV: Water

TEACH

GUIDED PRACTICE

L2 Model Have students use clay to mold a model landscape with all the features mentioned on pages 33 and 34. Suggest that they paint the model after the clay dries to make it more realistic.

INDEPENDENT PRACTICE

L3 Write Direct students to research the ocean floor to learn more about its features. Then have them write science fiction adventures of underwater explorers who discover and name canyons and mountain peaks just as early explorers did in North America.

USING DIAGRAMS

Answers: **1.** isthmus; **2.** at the mouth of a river; **3.** a peninsula; **4.** a tributary

Skills Practice

Comparing and Contrasting What are the water body equivalents of an island and an isthmus? *(a lake and a strait)*

Videodisc

GTV: PLANETARY MANAGER

Side 2, Chapter 7
Frames 38779-41076
Title: ***Water, Water Everywhere***
Subject: Amount of available drinking water

LANDFORMS AND WATER BODIES

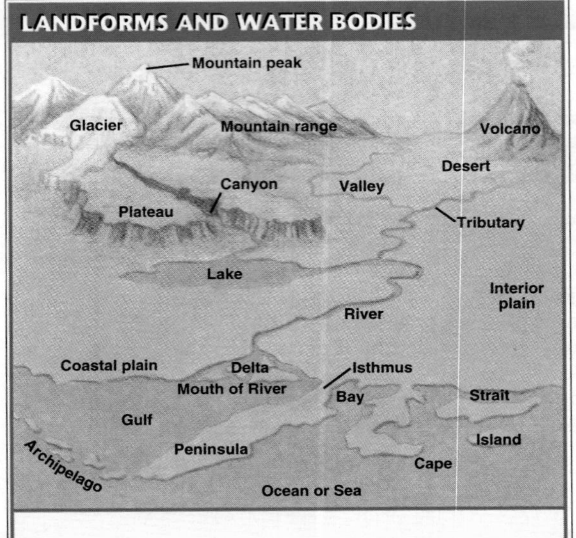

FOCUS ON GEOGRAPHIC THEMES

1. **Place: What landform connects two large landmasses?**
2. **Location: Where is a delta located?**
3. **Place: What landform is surrounded by water on three sides?**
4. **Place: What is a river branch called?**

also called highlands because they are the highest landforms and have the greatest relief. Hills are generally more rounded, lower, and have less relief.

Two large areas of flatland with very little relief are plateaus and plains. A **plateau** is higher than the surrounding land and usually has at least one steep side, called a cliff. A plateau is sometimes called a tableland. Mountains often surround high-altitude plateaus. Plains are flat or gently rolling lands. Plains along the coasts of continents generally have low elevations and are called coastal plains. Interior plains are those that are located away from the coasts of continents. They generally have higher elevations.

Other Landforms

A valley and a canyon are two other kinds of landforms. A piece of land that extends outward from a continent and that is surrounded by water on three sides is called a peninsula. An island is any body of land smaller than a continent that is completely surrounded by water. A group of closely scattered islands is called an **archipelago.**

The earth's oceans also have many kinds of landforms. There are as many different kinds of landforms on the bottoms of the oceans as there are on the continents. The underwater extension of a continent is known as a **continental shelf.** Continental shelves are narrow in some places and wide in others. They slope out from the land for up to 800 miles (about 1,290 km) and descend to a depth of about 600 feet (183 m) before dropping steeply to the ocean floor.

In some places the ocean floor is a flat plain. In other places there are high mountain ranges, great cliffs, valleys, deep trenches, and seamounts. Seamounts are underwater mountains with steep sides that rise above the ocean floor.

PLACE

Water Features

Water covers most of the earth's surface. Water makes up a portion of all living things, and all living things need water in order to live. The amount of water on the earth remains relatively constant as it moves from ocean to air to ground to ocean.

Oceans and Seas

About 70 percent of the earth's surface is water—almost all of it salt water. This large, continuous body of salt water is generally divided into four oceans. The oceans are named the Pacific, the Atlantic, the Indian, and the Arctic. The Pacific, the largest of the oceans, covers more area than all the earth's land combined. The Pacific Ocean is also deep enough in some places to cover the world's highest mountain with more than 1 mile (1.6 km) to spare.

Bodies of salt water that are smaller than oceans are called seas, gulfs, and bays. These

Cooperative Learning Activity

Organize the class into teams. Then refer them to pages A-2 and A-3. Challenge each team to find and list names of oceans, seas, gulfs, bays, lakes, and rivers that begin with the letters in *WATER FEATURES.* After a specified time, have the teams compare answers. The team with names for the most letters wins.

bodies of water are often partially enclosed by land. The Mediterranean Sea is one of the earth's largest seas. It is almost entirely encircled by the southern part of Europe, the northern part of Africa, and the southwestern part of Asia. The Gulf of Mexico is nearly encircled by the coasts of the United States and Mexico. The Bay of Bengal borders Southeast Asia and part of southern Asia.

Although 97 percent of the world's water is found in oceans, the water is too salty to be used for drinking, farming, or manufacturing. Today, only a small amount of freshwater can be obtained from the ocean by removing salt. Efficient and low-cost methods of changing seawater into freshwater will need to be developed in order to meet the world's increasing shortage of freshwater.

Lakes, Streams, and Rivers

Other water features of the earth include lakes, streams, and rivers. A lake is a body of water completely surrounded by land. The greatest number of lakes are found in areas where glacial movement has cut deep valleys, and glacial deposits have acted as dams as the ice melted. Northern North America contains thousands of these glacial lakes. Most lakes contain freshwater.

A stream is a body of water flowing through the land. Streams combine to form a river—a stream of water of considerable volume. Most rivers begin high in the mountains and hills. The river's source might be a melting glacier or an overflowing lake. As a river flows along, it picks up additional water from rainfall. Often rivers flow into one another, creating major waterways that flow for thousands of miles before emptying into a gulf, sea, or ocean.

The water in lakes and rivers makes up a small percentage of the earth's water supply. This water, however, is very important to people because it is freshwater. Unlike ocean water, freshwater can be used by people for drinking, farming, or manufacturing. These water sources are so important that most large urban areas began as settlements along the shores of lakes and rivers where people would have a constant supply of water.

Groundwater

Another source of freshwater is **groundwater,** which lies beneath the earth's surface and supplies wells and springs. The main source of groundwater is rain and melted snow that filter through the soil. Water that seeps into the ground from lakes and rivers also contributes to groundwater. People in many rural areas and in some cities depend on groundwater for their needs.

Of the earth's total water supply, only 3 percent is freshwater, and most of this is not available for human consumption. More than 2 percent is locked in glaciers and ice caps. The Antarctic ice cap, for example, contains more freshwater than the rest of the world's regions combined. Another 0.5 percent is groundwater. Rivers and lakes contain far less than 1 percent of the earth's water.

THE WATER CYCLE

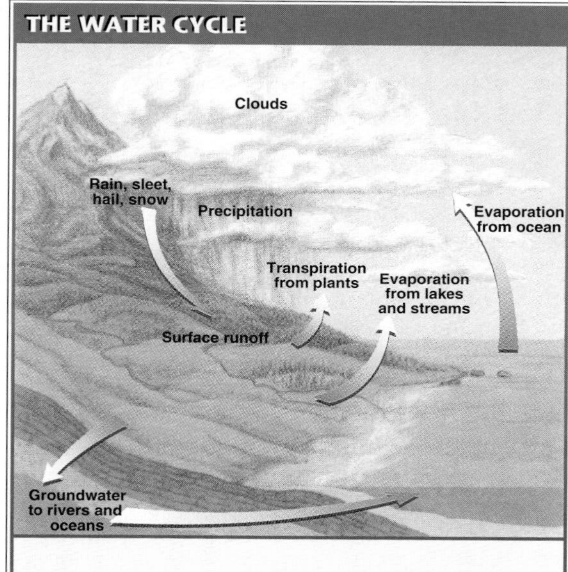

Focus on Geographic Themes

1. **Movement:** What process begins the water cycle?
2. **Place:** What source of water supplies wells and springs?
3. **Movement:** To where does all water return before the cycle repeats?

Chapter 2, Section 2

USING DIAGRAMS

Answers:
1. evaporation;
2. groundwater;
3. the ocean

Skills Practice

Interpretation Where does surface runoff come from? *(precipitation)*

ASSESS

CHECK FOR UNDERSTANDING

Assign Section 2 Review as homework or an in-class activity.

MEETING LESSON OBJECTIVES

Each objective below is tested by the questions that follow it in parentheses.
1. **Appreciate** the variety of the earth's landforms. *(2, 3)*
2. **Name** the features of the earth's oceans and seas. *(4, 5)*
3. **Explain** how the earth's water is recycled. *(1)*

EVALUATE

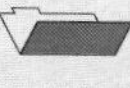

Assign the Section 2 Quiz in the TCR.

Use the Testmaker to create a customized quiz for Section 2.

RETEACH

Have students complete Workbook Activity 2-2 found in the TCR.

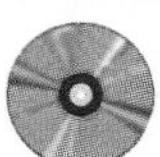

Videodisc

GTV: PLANETARY MANAGER

Side 1, Chapter 2
Frames 5834-10218
Title: *'Round and 'Round*
Subject: Natural cycles (water, oxygen-carbon dioxide) that repeat in the biosphere

Meeting Special Needs

Reading Disabilities Students with reading disabilities should find that the text is organized in such a way that it makes understanding the material easy. Because poor word attack skills impede reading comprehension, however, find out the level at which each student has mastered these skills. Present each student with a list of 20 words from Section 2 to read aloud. Judge responses by both their fluency (time) and power (correctness).

ENRICH

Have students bring in and display travel brochures with pictures of vacation spots near scenic landforms or water bodies.

CLOSE

Ask students to give examples of things they recycle. Then ask what and how nature recycles. *(The sun's heat changes water into vapor. Water vapor rises and is gathered by the air. The moist air cools and forms clouds. The clouds release the moisture as precipitation and it returns to the earth.)*

USING ILLUSTRATIONS

PLACE Tiny sea animals called coral make their home on volcanic islands or undersea mountains, die, and leave behind their skeletons. Other coral build on the old skeletons and eventually an atoll appears.

Answer to Caption: *The Pacific is the largest ocean.*

NATIONAL GEOGRAPHIC SOCIETY

Videodisc

STV: WATER

Side 1, Chapter 1
Frames 00392-17833
Title: ***Water Quality*** **(in its entirety)**
Subject: Describes the hydrologic cycle and why the quality of our freshwater is threatened; shows student experiments with water

STV: WATER

Side 1, Chapter 2
Frames 17877-33972
Title: ***Water Conservation*** **(in its entirety)**
Subject: Describes how farmers conserve water

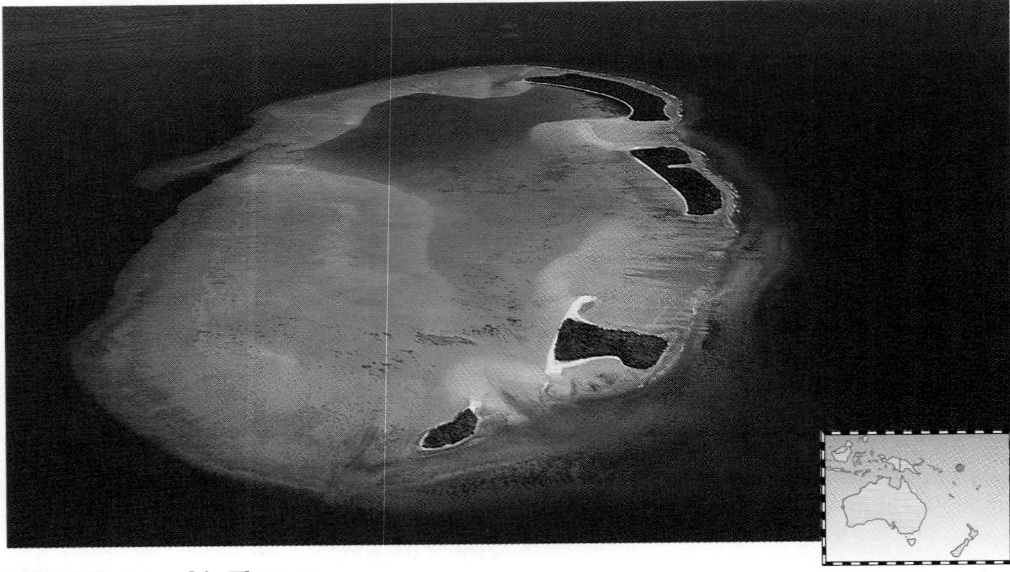

Geographic Themes

Place: Kayangel Atoll, South Pacific

This ring-shaped low island in the Pacific Ocean surrounds an inner lagoon. *How does the Pacific Ocean compare to the world's other oceans?*

The Water Cycle

The earth today has as much water as there was and as much as there ever will be. This is because all of the water that is used eventually comes back to the oceans. The regular movement of water from ocean to air to ground to ocean is called the **water cycle.**

The cycle begins with **evaporation**—the changing of liquid water into vapor, or gas. The sun's heat causes evaporation. Water vapor rising from the oceans, other bodies of water, and plants is gathered by the air. How much moisture can be carried by the air depends mainly on the temperature. Warmer air carries more moisture than cooler air.

When moisture-filled warm air rises, it cools and forms clouds. Certain clouds release moisture, which returns to the earth as precipitation. Because of gravity, returned water flows downhill toward the ocean. It forms streams, rivers, and lakes. It sinks into the ground and becomes groundwater. Sometimes it forms ice caps and glaciers. Eventually, however, the water returns to the ocean and the cycle repeats.

The amount of water that evaporates is approximately the same amount that falls back to the earth. This amount varies little from year to year. Thus, the total volume of water in the cycle is more or less constant.

SECTION 2 REVIEW

Checking for Understanding

1. **Define** isthmus, plateau, archipelago, continental shelf, groundwater, water cycle, evaporation.
2. **Locating Places** What continents are joined by the Isthmus of Panama?
3. **Region** What are the four basic types of landforms?
4. **Location** Where is freshwater found?

Critical Thinking

5. **Making Comparisons** How are the landforms of the ocean floor similar to the landforms of the continents?

ANSWERS TO SECTION 2 REVIEW

1. **isthmus:** narrow piece of land connecting two large landmasses; **plateau:** high flatland with little relief; **archipelago**: group of islands; **continental shelf:** shallow areas near coasts of continents; **groundwater:** water beneath the earth's surface; **water cycle:** regular movement of water from ocean to air to ground to ocean; **evaporation:** changing of water into a gas.
2. North America and South America
3. mountains, hills, plateaus, and plains
4. Freshwater is found frozen in polar ice caps and glaciers; in lakes, rivers, and streams; and in groundwater.
5. Landforms are as varied under the ocean as on the continents.

3 SECTION Earth's Resources

SETTING THE SCENE

Read to Discover . . .
- the importance of natural resources.
- the ways in which the distribution of resources affects people and countries.

Key Terms
- natural resource
- renewable resource
- nonrenewable resource
- imports
- exports

Identify and Locate
Southwest Asia, Japan

Elements from the earth that are not made by people but can be used by them are called **natural resources.** Even though a place might be rich in natural resources, people must develop them. For example, some places have fertile soil, but people must work that soil in order to produce crops and have large supplies of food.

HUMAN/ENVIRONMENT INTERACTION

Importance of Resources

The earth supports human life because it provides what is needed for survival. The basic elements include air, water, soil, plants, and animals. The air that is around the earth contains oxygen, which people and animals breathe. People, animals, and plants depend upon freshwater to live. The earth's soils support the growth of vegetation. Plants and animals form part of the food chain for humans.

Minerals and Fuels

People use the earth's resources to make their lives better. Minerals and fossil fuels are among these resources. Minerals are substances from the earth that are not living or made from living things. Fossil fuels are fuels—including coal, oil, and gas—that formed from the remains of plants and animals that lived millions of years ago.

Value of Resources

Use, supply, and changes over time help determine how important certain natural resources are. People living in separate parts of the world and at different times may not give the same value to the same resource. For example, a resource such as copper can serve as a raw material for making useful things, such as water pipes in houses. On the other hand, an artist may prize copper because of its worth in making works of art, such as wall decorations. Some people think resources such as gold and silver are valuable because of their use in making jewelry or as a form of money. Photographers might assign a different value to silver because of its importance in making and processing film.

Supply, often influenced by location, also affects value. When there is a small supply of something, it is generally given a greater value. For example, Native Americans who lived far from the oceans used shells as a form of money. Those groups who lived near the shore, where there were many shells, did not place as much value on them. Rubber is another example. People once thought of rubber trees as important natural resources because they provided all the world's rubber. Later synthetic, or artificial, rubber was developed. This made it possible for people to produce large amounts of

LESSON PLAN
Chapter 2, Section 3

FOCUS

SECTION OBJECTIVES

1. Understand the importance of natural resources.
2. Identify the ways in which the distribution of resources affects people and countries.

BELLRINGER MOTIVATIONAL ACTIVITY

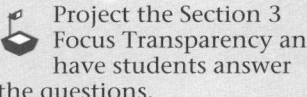

Project the Section 3 Focus Transparency and have students answer the questions.

PRETEACHING VOCABULARY

Write *renewable* and *nonrenewable* on the chalkboard. Ask students to define the terms by analyzing the prefixes and the root word.

TEACH

GUIDED PRACTICE

L1 Classify Display several items such as coins, gloves, boxes, and jewelry. Have students examine the items and determine what natural resources went into making them. Ask students to classify the resources as renewable or nonrenewable.

Classroom Resources for Section 3

BLACKLINE MASTERS:
Reproducible Lesson Plan 2-3
Guided Reading Activity 2-3
Spanish Guided Reading Activity 2-3
Workbook Activity 2-3
Section 2-3 Quiz
Reteaching Activity 2
Enrichment Activity 2
Skill Activity 2
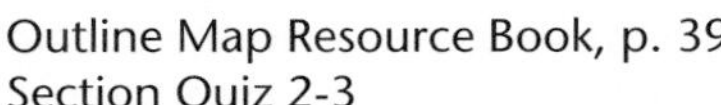
Outline Map Resource Book, p. 39
Section Quiz 2-3

TRANSPARENCIES:
Section Focus Transparency 2-3
Unit Map Overlay Transparency 1-8

MULTIMEDIA:

Testmaker

GTV: Planetary Manager
Geography and the Environment

INDEPENDENT PRACTICE

Guided Reading Have students complete Guided Reading Activity 2-3 in the TCR. **LEP**

USING ILLUSTRATIONS

PLACE After known oil reserves are depleted, the only major new deposits will be found under water.

Answer to Caption: *gas and coal*

ASSESS

CHECK FOR UNDERSTANDING

Assign Section 3 Review as homework or an in-class activity.

MEETING LESSON OBJECTIVES

Each objective below is tested by the questions that follow it in parentheses.

1. Understand the importance of natural resources. *(3, 4, 5)*

2. Identify the ways in which the distribution of resources affects people and countries. *(2)*

EVALUATE

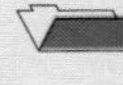

Assign the Section 3 Quiz in the TCR.

Videodisc

GTV: PLANETARY MANAGER

Side 2, Chapter 4
Frames 18754-25234
Title: ***Holy Smoke!***
Subject: The use and abuse of fossil fuels

Geographic Themes

Place: Arabian Peninsula

The Arabian Peninsula of Southwest Asia is rich in oil, a fossil fuel on which modern industrialized countries depend. *What are other examples of fossil fuels?*

a substance that could be used in place of natural rubber. The increased use of synthetic rubber lowered the value of natural rubber.

The value of a resource may change over time. The energy resource uranium is an example. Uranium is needed to split atoms to release nuclear energy. Before the development of nuclear energy, uranium had few uses. Therefore, people did not give it as much value as they do today.

HUMAN/ENVIRONMENT INTERACTION

Managing Resources

Resources are renewable if they replace themselves naturally or if people can grow or raise continuous supplies of them. Some **renewable resources** are forests and animal life.

People are important in determining how resources are used and renewed. For example, lumber companies can carefully choose which trees to cut and how many. They can also plant a harvested area with new trees to help renew forestland resources.

The earth's crust, however, has many **nonrenewable resources**—resources that can never be replaced. Such resources include most minerals and fossil fuels. People may recycle, or reuse, these resources, but natural growth or human skill cannot replace them.

People also affect the quality of the basic elements of air, water, and soil. These resources cannot be replaced but can be conserved, or protected, through proper management. Farmers, for example, can keep soil fertile by changing the crops that are grown on a plot of land from year to year.

Minerals form most of the earth's land resources and are often found naturally in the ores that people mine. Many of the earth's more than 2,000 different minerals help support or improve human life, and so people

Cooperative Learning Activity

Organize the class into pairs and assign each pair a different natural resource. Have each pair research locations throughout the world where their resource is found. Then tell pairs to decide on a symbol for their resource and to make a small paper symbol for each place they found in their research. Have them post their symbols on a large outline map of the world. Before students begin, project Unit Transparency 1-8 to help students visualize what their map should look like.

value them. Certain mineral resources provide important medicines and building materials. Factories often mix minerals to make different kinds of materials. For example, factories blend iron ore with alloys such as manganese to produce steel. Minerals in the form of fertilizers aid in producing greater amounts of food.

Fossil fuels are an especially valued resource today. Because these fuels were formed over thousands of lifetimes, they are considered nonrenewable. Such resources provide heat, light, and the energy necessary to run machines. They are also used in the manufacturing of plastics, fertilizers, and other goods.

Geographic Themes

Movement: Alaska

The trans-Alaska pipeline carries oil from northern Alaska to the port of Valdez. *Why is oil a nonrenewable resource?*

HUMAN/ENVIRONMENT INTERACTION

Distribution of Resources

The natural distribution of resources greatly influences how countries relate to one another. Most natural resources are not evenly distributed over the earth. Some places may have large amounts of a certain resource while others may have little or none.

The scarcity of certain resources and goods has led to trade among the world's countries. For example, in order to build jet aircraft, the United States must buy certain resources from other countries. Resources or goods brought into one country from another are known as **imports.** Resources or goods sent from one country to another are known as **exports.**

Because of the scarcity of resources, countries are interdependent, relying on each other for goods and services. Some southwestern Asian countries, for example, depend on the United States for wheat, other food products, and certain manufactured goods. The United States, in turn, depends on these countries for part of its oil supply. In another case, Japan sells steel, automobiles, and other manufactured goods throughout the world. Yet Japan, which is poor in natural resources, must get oil and raw materials from other countries to manufacture the items that it sells.

The uneven distribution of the earth's resources has effects other than promoting trade. At many times in the earth's history, it has led to conflict. Many wars have begun because rulers believed that their countries needed the resources or goods that another country possessed.

SECTION 3 REVIEW

Checking for Understanding

1. **Define** natural resource, renewable resource, nonrenewable resource, imports, exports.
2. **Locating Places** What region is a leading oil producer?
3. **Place** What determines the importance of natural resources?
4. **Human/Environment Interaction** How are renewable and nonrenewable resources different?

Critical Thinking

5. **Expressing Problems Clearly** Summarize the relationship between resource use and supply.

ANSWERS TO SECTION 3 REVIEW

1. **natural resource:** elements used by people but not made by them; **renewable resource:** resource that replaces itself; **nonrenewable resource:** resource that cannot be replaced; **imports:** resources or goods brought into one country from another; **exports:** resources or goods sent from one country to another
2. Southwest Asia
3. Use, supply, and changes over time
4. Resources are renewable if they can be replaced; nonrenewable resources cannot be replaced.
5. Resources are not always found where they are needed and used. This unequal match of supply and demand leads to trade. Because of the scarcity of resources, countries are interdependent on one another for goods.

Use the Testmaker to create a customized quiz for Section 3.

RETEACH

Have students complete Reteaching Activity 2 in TCR.

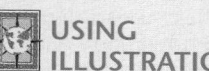

USING ILLUSTRATIONS

MOVEMENT Alaska's oil is shipped to other states by way of oil tankers and the Trans-Alaska Pipeline.

Answer to Caption: *It is a resource that can never be replaced.*

ENRICH

Have students complete Enrichment Activity 2 in the TCR.

CLOSE

On the chalkboard, have students list all the natural resources from the section. Then challenge them to add others that were not mentioned in their reading.

GLENCOE TECHNOLOGY

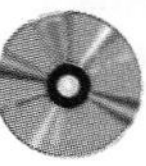

Videodisc

GEOGRAPHY AND THE ENVIRONMENT
THE INFINITE VOYAGE
Crisis in the Atmosphere

Chapter 11
Disc 2 Side A
Title: ***Worldwide Energy Conservation Solutions***
Subject: Areas of conservation concerns include increasing world population, deforestation, fossil fuel use; also explores need for energy in developing countries

TEACH

To give students a perspective regarding the length of the Mid-Ocean Ridge, tell them that the longest river in the world is the Nile, which is 4,160 miles long. The Trans-Siberian Railroad—the longest railroad in the world—is longer than 5,000 miles. Ask students to calculate how many Nile Rivers and Trans-Siberian Railroads would be needed to equal the length of the Mid-Ocean Ridge. *(11 Nile Rivers; 9 Trans-Siberian Railroads)*

CURRICULUM CONNECTION

GEOLOGY

As the plates meeting at the Mid-Atlantic Ridge move apart, the North American plate moves slowly to the west. Some geographers think Americans might be able to walk to Japan in about 50 million years!

DID YOU KNOW?

In the movie *The Hunt for Red October*, a Soviet typhoon-class submarine eludes its enemies—in this case, the Soviet Navy. Show students clips from the movie in which the *Red October* maneuvers through the Mid-Atlantic Ridge near Iceland.

NATIONAL GEOGRAPHIC GEOFACTS

Where is the world's largest mountain range?

The largest mountain range on the earth is not the Himalaya, the Andes, or the Rockies. It is larger than those three combined. Concealed from view at the bottom of the seas, the Mid-Ocean Ridge boasts higher mountains, deeper canyons, and longer escarpments than anywhere else on the surface of the continents.

Along the crest of the system, fissures mark the boundary between the great plates that form the earth's crust. These cracks are the birthplace of new seafloor. Hot lava erupts and welds to each side of the separating plates.

The Mid-Atlantic Ridge (drawing) is the most rugged section of the system. Here crustal plates carrying North America, Africa, and Europe separate at the rate of an inch (3 cm) a year.

MID-OCEAN RIDGE

The ridge winds around the globe for 46,000 miles (74,000 km).

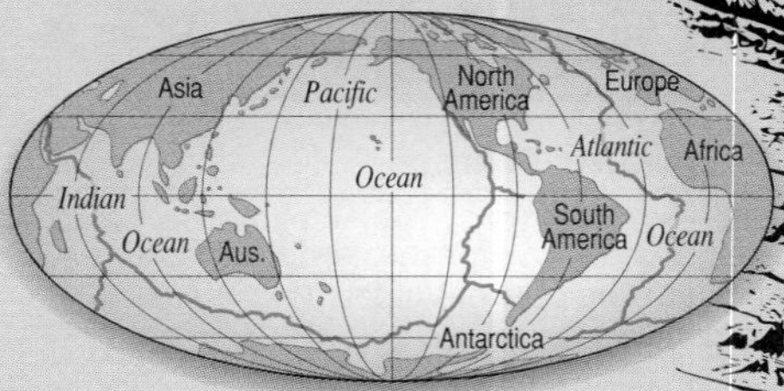

Fracture Zones

These zones cleave the Mid-Atlantic Ridge at right angles.

Rift Valley

A rift valley on the scale of the Grand Canyon runs the length of the Mid-Atlantic Ridge. In some places the valley stretches 20 miles (30 km) across and plunges 5,000 feet (1,524 m). The chart below compares the vertical scale of the ridge and valley with selected Atlantic features.

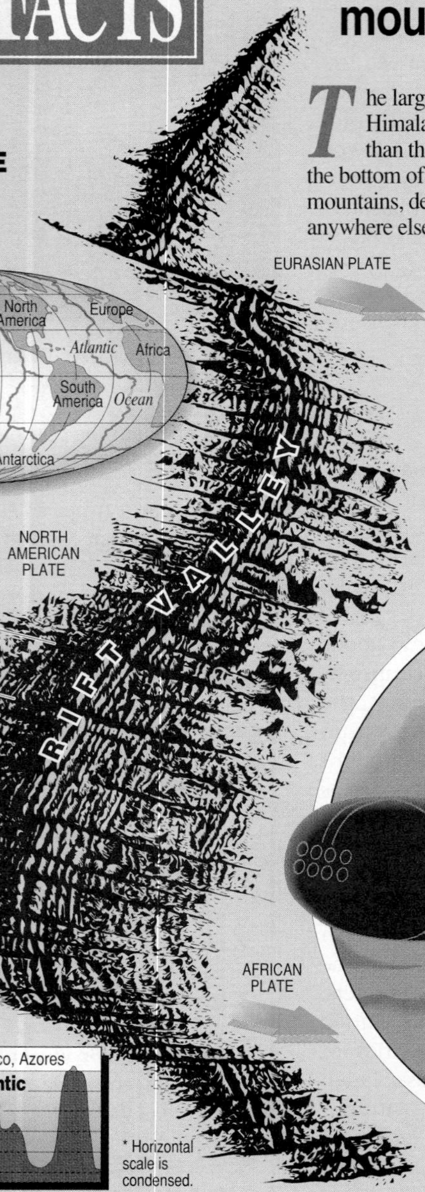

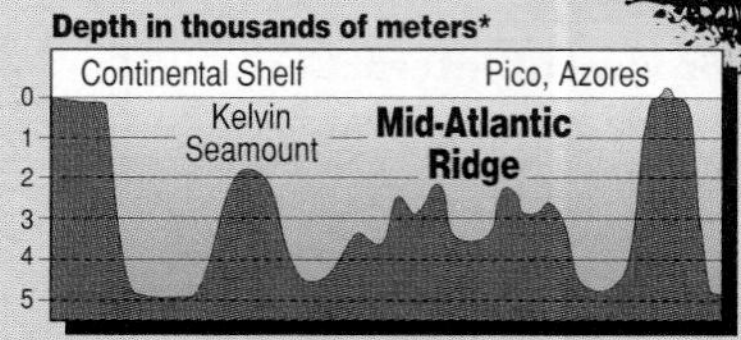

* Horizontal scale is condensed.

During the Cold War, Soviet missile-firing submarines used parts of the Mid-Atlantic Ridge to elude detection by U.S. subs in an elaborate game of high-tech hide-and-seek.

Ridge drawing by William Bond, NGS

Designed by BILL PITZER

chapter 2

HIGHLIGHTS

SECTION 1 Planet Earth

Mount Everest in the Himalaya range of South Asia

KEY TERMS

atmosphere (p. 27)
hydrosphere (p. 28)
lithosphere (p. 28)
biosphere (p. 28)
mantle (p. 29)
fold (p. 29)
fault (p. 29)
weathering (p. 30)
erosion (p. 31)
glacier (p. 31)

SUMMARY

- The earth is made up of water, land, and air. Water makes up the earth's hydrosphere. Land makes up part of the earth's lithosphere, while the air comprises earth's atmosphere.
- Sections of the earth's crust float and move on a mantle layer, causing some continents to move apart and some to move together.
- External forces, such as water, wind, and gravity, help to shape the earth's surface through erosion, movement, and new landforms.

SECTION 2 Earth's Features

KEY TERMS

isthmus (p. 33)
plateau (p. 34)
archipelago (p. 34)
continental shelf (p. 34)
groundwater (p. 35)
water cycle (p. 36)
evaporation (p. 36)

Kayangel Atoll in the South Pacific

SUMMARY

- Landforms are the physical features that make up the surface of the earth. Four major types are mountains, hills, plains, and plateaus.
- Water is both a physical feature and a resource. Oceans, rivers, lakes, and streams are water features.
- Water is a limited resource that is circulated and purified repeatedly through the water cycle.

SECTION 3 Earth's Resources

KEY TERMS

natural resource (p. 37)
renewable resource (p. 38)
nonrenewable resource (p. 38)
imports (p. 39)
exports (p. 39)

The Arabian Peninsula

SUMMARY

- The earth's many natural resources are not divided evenly among the countries of the world. Use, supply, and changes over time are factors in deciding how important natural resources are.
- Renewable resources replace themselves naturally or can be raised in continuous supply by people. Nonrenewable resources, such as fossil fuels, can never be replaced.

Map Activity

Identify and Locate Distribute page 39 from the Outline Map Resource Book. Then ask students to identify and label the four oceans on the map. *(the Pacific, the Atlantic, the Indian, and the Arctic)*

CHAPTER 2 HIGHLIGHTS

USING THE CHAPTER 2 HIGHLIGHTS

Use the Chapter 2 Highlights to preview, review, condense, or reteach the chapter.

PREVIEW/REVIEW

Vocabulary PuzzleMaker Software reinforces the Key Terms used in Chapter 2.

Student Self-Test and Review Software allows students to review Chapter 2 content.

CONDENSE

Have students read the Chapter 2 Highlights.

 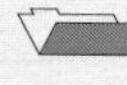
Have students listen to the Chapter 2 Audiocassettes in the TCR. Spanish Audiocassettes are also available.

Assign the Chapter 2 Audiocassette Activity and give students the Chapter 2 Audiocassette Quiz.

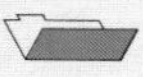 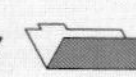
Have students complete Guided Reading Activities for Chapter 2 in the TCR. Spanish Guided Reading Activities are also available.

RETEACH

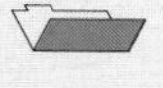
Have students complete Reteaching Activity 2 in the TCR. Spanish Reteaching Activities are also available.

GLENCOE TECHNOLOGY

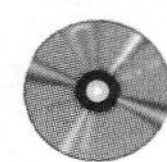

Videodisc

Use Chapter 2 MindJogger Videoquiz to review students' knowledge before administering the Chapter 2 Test.

MINDJOGGER VIDEOQUIZ

Chapter 2
Disc 1 Side A

The MindJogger Videoquiz is also available on videocassette.

ANSWERS

Reviewing Key Terms

1. folds
2. mantle
3. weathering
4. hydrosphere
5. lithosphere
6. glaciers
7. archipelago
8. water cycle
9. plateau
10. groundwater
11. natural resources
12. exports
13. imports

Reviewing Facts

14. bodies of dust and frozen gases; planetlike objects
15. Water dissolves chemicals in rocks, causing rocks to crumble.
16. continental shelves, plains, mountains, seamounts, cliffs, valleys, and deep trenches
17. where glaciers cut valleys
18. oil, gas, and coal
19. renewable resources

Critical Thinking

20. Answers will vary but should deal with internal forces (earthquakes, faults, mountain building) if they exist and external forces of erosion and weathering.
21. Supplies of freshwater are limited. World population is placing greater burdens on existing supplies and human action is affecting the quality of freshwater.
22. The demand for natural resources is increasing because the earth's population is increasing. Students might also include that improvements in technology and world trade make more people want more things, placing an even greater burden on resources.

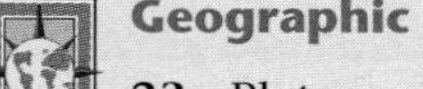

Geographic Themes

23. Plates collide and drift apart, producing mountain ranges, ocean basins, faults, earthquakes, and volcanoes. Once formed by internal forces, landforms are worn down by external forces such as wind and water erosion. Eroded materials move, carried by the wind, ice, and water, are deposited, and form new land features.

chapter 2 REVIEW

Reviewing Key Terms

Choose the vocabulary term that best completes each of the sentences below. Write your answers on a separate sheet of paper.

hydrosphere (p. 28)	lithosphere (p. 28)
mantle (p. 29)	folds (p. 29)
weathering (p. 30)	glaciers (p. 31)
plateau (p. 34)	archipelago (p. 34)
groundwater (p. 35)	water cycle (p. 36)
natural resources (p. 37)	imports (p. 39)
exports (p. 39)	

SECTION 1

1. ____ are bends in layers of rock formed by internal forces in the earth.
2. The mixture of solid and liquid rock around the earth's core is called the ____.
3. The process that breaks down rocks is called ____.
4. The earth's ____ consists of oceans, lakes, and other bodies of water.
5. Land makes up part of the earth called the ____.
6. ____ are large masses of ice that carve out U-shaped valleys.

SECTION 2

7. A group of islands is called a/an ____.
8. The ____ purifies water and keeps a global water balance.
9. A ____ is a large flatland with one steep side and little relief.
10. The main source of ____ is rain that filters through the soil.

SECTION 3

11. Earth elements used by humans but not made by them are called ____.
12. Resources sent from one country to another are called ____.
13. ____ are resources brought into one country from another.

Reviewing Facts

SECTION 1

14. What are comets and meteoroids?
15. How does chemical weathering occur on the earth?

SECTION 2

16. Oceans cover most of the earth's surface. What are some features of the ocean floor?
17. Where are the greatest number of lakes found?

SECTION 3

18. Many of the earth's resources are available in limited quantities and cannot replenish themselves. What fossil fuels are classified as nonrenewable resources?
19. What are the earth's resources that replace themselves naturally called?

Critical Thinking

20. **Determining Cause and Effect** What forces—both external and internal—shaped the landforms in your immediate region?
21. **Identifying Central Issues** What are the important factors facing the earth in regard to supplies of freshwater?
22. **Analyzing Information** Why is the demand for the earth's natural resources increasing?

Geographic Themes

23. **Movement** Explain how eroded soil and the movement of plates shape landforms.
24. **Place** Describe the physical features of your community.
25. **Place** Which of the earth's natural resources do you use on a daily, weekly, and periodic basis?

Projects

Individual Activity

Prepare a chart like the one below with six headings: mountains, hills, plateaus, plains, and two other landforms of your choice. Use an atlas to find at least seven of each feature, one from each continent. What conclusions can you draw about landforms?

Cooperative Learning Activity

Work in teams of three to create an advertising campaign about the wise use of resources in your part of the country. Posters, pamphlets, and informational skits are a few ways to draw attention to issues.

Writing About Geography

Narration

Choose two or three landforms in your community. Describe the relief, slope, and elevation of each and the processes that caused each landform. Then write a descriptive paragraph telling how these landforms have caused people to follow a certain way of life. Use your journal notes as reference.

	Mountains	Hills	Plateaus	Plains		
Africa						
Antarctica						
Asia						
Australia						
Europe						
North America						
South America						

Locating Places

THE WORLD: PHYSICAL GEOGRAPHY

Match the letters on the map with the places and physical features of the earth. Write your answers on a separate sheet of paper.

1. Arctic Ocean
2. Himalayas
3. Gulf of Mexico
4. Isthmus of Panama
5. Pacific Ocean
6. Bay of Bengal
7. Asia
8. Mediterranean Sea
9. Australia
10. Atlantic Ocean
11. North America
12. Africa
13. Indian Ocean
14. Antarctica
15. Ural Mountains

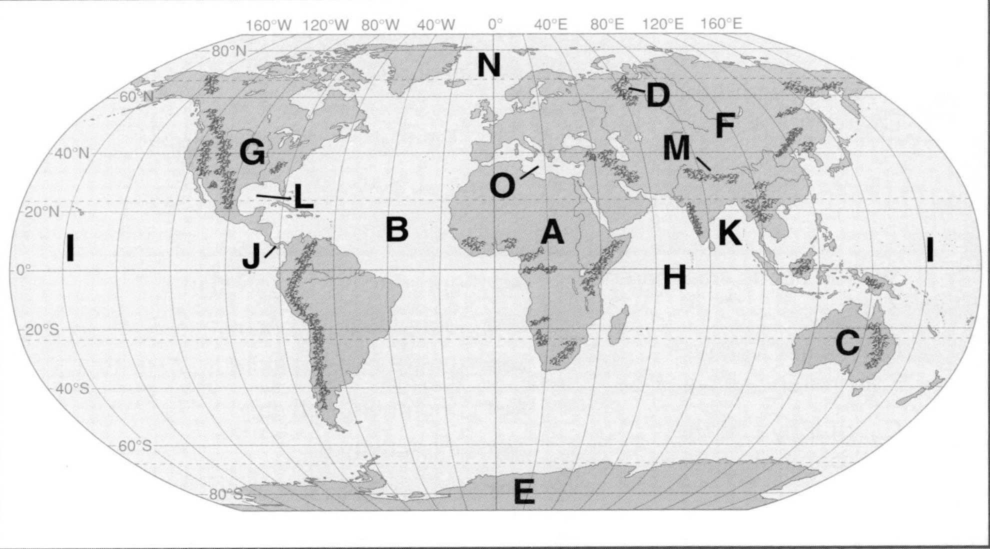

Chapter 2 Review

24. Answers will vary but should include a description of landforms and bodies of water as well as a list of natural resources.

25. Answers will vary but should include water, air, and food raised as crops or livestock.

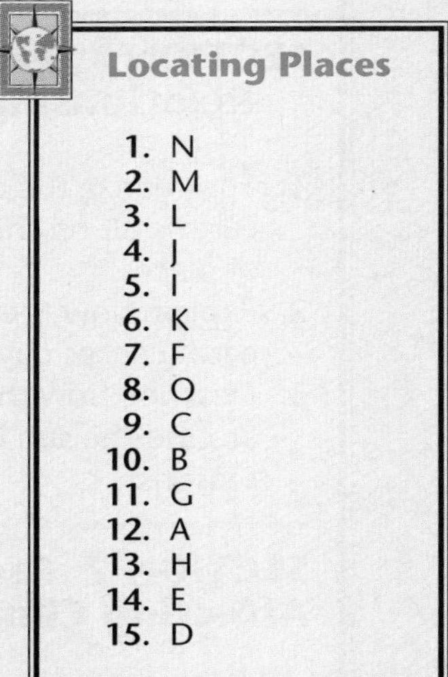

Locating Places

1. N
2. M
3. L
4. J
5. I
6. K
7. F
8. O
9. C
10. B
11. G
12. A
13. H
14. E
15. D

Chapter Bonus Test Question

This question may be used for extra credit on the chapter test.

How do you think glaciation during the Ice Age affected the migration of animals?

(Answers will vary but may point out that plant eaters probably migrated away from the glaciers because they destroyed their plant food and that meat eaters probably followed their food source, the plant eaters.)

CHAPTER 3

PLANNING GUIDE

Climates of the Earth

CHAPTER ORGANIZER

Daily Lesson Objectives	Multimedia	Teacher Classroom Resources
SECTION 1 Earth-Sun Relationships 1. Summarize the effect of the earth's tilt on the temperature of places. 2. Explain how the spinning of the earth causes day and night. 3. Describe how the earth's motion around the sun causes the seasons.	Section Focus Transparency 3-1 Chapter 3 Vocabulary PuzzleMaker Software Unit Map Overlay Transparency 1-1 Testmaker GTV: Planetary Manager	Reproducible Lesson Plan 3-1 Guided Reading Activity 3-1 Spanish Guided Reading Activity 3-1 Workbook Activity 3-1 Performance Assessment Activity 3 Section Quiz 3-1
SECTION 2 Factors Affecting Climate 1. Identify the patterns of winds and ocean currents. 2. Explain the role temperature and precipitation play in describing climates. 3. Examine factors that control the locations of climates around the world.	Section Focus Transparency 3-2 Unit Map Overlay Transparency 1-2 Testmaker Geography and the Environment	Reproducible Lesson Plan 3-2 Guided Reading Activity 3-2 Spanish Guided Reading Activity 3-2 Workbook Activity 3-2 Section Quiz 3-2
SECTION 3 World Climate Patterns 1. Enumerate the climate regions of the world. 2. Describe ways that climate affects humans and their environment. 3. Predict how climates change over time.	Section Focus Transparency 3-3 Unit Map Overlay Transparencies 1-4, 1-5 Geography and the Environment Testmaker	Reproducible Lesson Plan 3-3 Guided Reading Activity 3-3 Spanish Guided Reading Activity 3-3 Enrichment Activity 3 Skill Activity 3 Section Quiz 3-3
CHAPTER REVIEW AND EVALUATION	Chapter 3 English (or Spanish) Audiocassettes MindJogger Videoquiz Testmaker Student Self-Test and Review Software	Reteaching Activity 3 Spanish Reteaching Activity 3 Chapter 3 Test Form A and Form B

0:00 *If time does not permit teaching the entire chapter, summarize using the Chapter 3 Highlights on page 59, and the Chapter 3 English (or Spanish) Audiocassettes. Review students' knowledge using the Glencoe MindJogger Videoquiz.*

KEY TO ABILITY LEVELS

Teaching strategies have been coded for varying learning styles and abilities.

L1 **BASIC** activities for all students

L2 **AVERAGE** activities for average to above-average students

L3 **CHALLENGING** activities for above-average students

LEP **LIMITED ENGLISH PROFICIENCY** activities

Performance Assessment

Humans and Their Environment Have students simulate the roles of tour directors for a trip around the world. Students should spin the globe, pointing at random to ten different locations. Working in groups, they should use different types of maps—climate, vegetation, ocean currents, elevation, and so on—to predict what they will find when they travel to each place.

According to their predictions, designated "tour directors" in each group should then make packing lists that include clothing and other various special items needed for the climate and terrain. The lists should be specific, stating the type of clothing (light cotton sweater or heavy wool sweater) and the size of cases allowed. The tour directors' last task should involve giving explicit directions for departure, itinerary, and arrival. Teachers should make arrangements for the directors to share their ideas with the "tourists" who make up the rest of the class.

POSSIBLE RUBRIC FEATURES: Content information, collaboration skills, logical conclusions, oral communication skills, map reading skills

For additional professional and classroom resources, see Chapter Resources, pages T46–T51.

TEACHER'S CORNER

INDEX TO NATIONAL GEOGRAPHIC MAGAZINE

The following articles may be used for research relating to this chapter:

- "The American Prairie: Roots of the Sky," by Douglas H. Chadwick, October 1993.
- "Lightning: Nature's High-voltage Spectacle," by William R. Newcott, July 1993.
- "Siberia: In from the Cold," by Mike Edwards, March 1990.
- "Tornado!" by Peter Miller, June 1987.
- "Monsoons: Life Breath of Half the World," by Priit J. Vesilind, December 1984.
- "El Niño's Ill Wind," by Thomas Y. Canby, February 1984.
- "Rain Forests: Nature's Dwindling Treasures," by Peter T. White, January 1983.
- "Hurricane!" by Ben Funk, September 1980.
- "The Desert: An Age-old Challenge Grows," by Rick Gore, November 1979.

NATIONAL GEOGRAPHIC SOCIETY PRODUCTS AVAILABLE FROM GLENCOE

To order the following products for use with this chapter, contact your local Glencoe sales representative or call Glencoe at 1-800-334-7344:

- *Picture Atlas of the World* (CD-ROM)
- *GeoBee* (Software)
- *STV: Solar System* (Videodisc)
- *STV: Restless Earth* (Videodisc)
- *GTV: Planetary Manager* (Videodisc)

ADDITIONAL NATIONAL GEOGRAPHIC SOCIETY PRODUCTS

To order the following products for use with this chapter, call National Geographic Society at 1-800-368-2728:

- *Ancient Forests* (Video)
- *Old-Growth Forest: An Ecosystem* (Video)
- *A Swamp Ecosystem* (Video)
- *Weather: Come Rain, Come Shine* (Video)

Introducing CHAPTER 3

PERFORMANCE ASSESSMENT

Refer to the Planning Guide on page 44B for a Performance Assessment Activity for this chapter. See the *Performance Assessment Activities* booklet for additional suggestions.

CHAPTER OBJECTIVES

1. **Explain** how the relationship between the earth and the sun affects climates around the world.
2. **Describe** the many factors that affect world climate.
3. **Discuss** how temperature, precipitation, and types of vegetation can be used to define climate regions of the earth.

GLENCOE TECHNOLOGY

Videodisc

Use Chapter 3 MindJogger Videoquiz to preview chapter content.

MINDJOGGER VIDEOQUIZ

Chapter 3
Disc 1 Side A

The MindJogger Videoquiz is also available on videocassette.

chapter 3 Climates of the Earth

CHAPTER FOCUS

Geographic Setting

Climate is a significant factor in describing the geography of places on the earth. The climate of a place affects the way that people in an area live.

Geographic Themes

Section 1 Earth-Sun Relationships
LOCATION The relationship between the earth and the sun affects climates around the world.

▲ Photograph: *Brazilian research station, King George Island, Antarctica*

Section 2 Factors Affecting Climate
PLACE Many factors affect world climate.

Section 3 World Climate Patterns
REGION Temperature, precipitation, and types of vegetation can be used to define climate regions.

EXTRA CREDIT PROJECT

Log Have students keep a log of weather conditions in different places around the world, such as storms in Southeast Asia and cold snaps in Canada. Then have students determine if these conditions fit the typical climate patterns of the areas.

1 SECTION Earth-Sun Relationships

SETTING THE SCENE

Read to Discover . . .
- the effect of the earth's tilt on the temperature of places.
- how the spinning of the earth causes day and night.
- how the earth's motion around the sun causes the seasons.

Key Terms
- weather
- climate
- axis
- temperature
- revolution
- equinox
- solstice

Identify and Locate
Tropic of Cancer, Tropic of Capricorn

Weather is the condition of the atmosphere in one place during a short period of time. It can be described as cold or hot, windy or calm, wet or dry. **Climate**, on the other hand, is the term for weather patterns that an area typically experiences during a long period of time. Weather and climate are influenced by the amount of direct sunlight a place receives. They are also affected by ocean currents, winds, and the features of the earth's surface.

The relationship between the earth and the sun especially affects climates around the world. The sun provides the earth with heat and light. Different parts of the earth, however, receive different amounts of sunlight at different times.

The Greenhouse Effect

Only a small amount of the sun's radiation reaches the earth's atmosphere. Some of the radiation is reflected back into space by the atmosphere and by the earth's surface. Enough radiation, however, remains to warm the earth's land and water.

The atmosphere also keeps heat from escaping back into space too quickly. In this sense, the earth's atmosphere has been compared to a greenhouse, which traps the sun's warmth for growing plants. Without this greenhouse effect, the earth would be too cold for most living things.

Even inside the "greenhouse" of the atmosphere, not all places on earth get the same amount of heat and light from the sun. Day and night, seasonal change, and differing climates all depend somewhat on the relative positions of the sun and the earth.

Earth's Tilt and Rotation

The earth has an **axis**—an imaginary line that runs through its center between the North Pole and the South Pole. The earth's axis is tilted at a 23½° angle. The axis is always tilted in the same direction.

Because the earth's axis is tilted, not all places on earth receive the same amount of direct sunlight. Therefore, the earth's tilt affects the **temperature** of places. Temperature is a measure of how hot or cold something is. Temperature is generally measured in degrees on a set scale. Air temperature is usually measured in Fahrenheit (F) or Celsius (C).

The earth rotates, or spins, on its axis. The earth makes one complete rotation every 24

LESSON PLAN
Chapter 3, Section 1

FOCUS

SECTION OBJECTIVES

1. Summarize the effect of the earth's tilt on the temperature of places.
2. Explain how the spinning of the earth causes day and night.
3. Describe how the earth's motion around the sun causes the seasons.

BELLRINGER MOTIVATIONAL ACTIVITY

Project the Section 1 Focus Transparency and have students answer the questions.

PRETEACHING VOCABULARY

Explain that the Latin roots of *equinox* mean "equal night." Have students find the definition of *equinox* in the section and compare it to the Latin meaning.

Use the Vocabulary PuzzleMaker Software to create a crossword or word search puzzle.

TEACH

GUIDED PRACTICE

L1 Demonstrate Spin and stop a globe while shining a flashlight at it and have students identify places in "daylight" and in "dark."

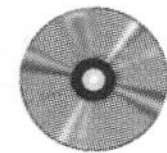
Videodisc

GTV: PLANETARY MANAGER

Side 2, Chapter 2
Frames 5931-12204
Title: ***Greenhouse of Eden***
Subject: The greenhouse effect and air pollution

Classroom Resources for Section 1

BLACKLINE MASTERS:
- Reproducible Lesson Plan 3-1
- Guided Reading Activity 3-1
- Spanish Guided Reading Activity 3-1
- Workbook Activity 3-1
- Performance Assessment Activity 3
- Section Quiz 3-1

TRANSPARENCIES:
- Section Focus Transparency 3-1
- Unit Map Overlay Transparency 1-1

MULTIMEDIA:
- Vocabulary PuzzleMaker Software
- Testmaker

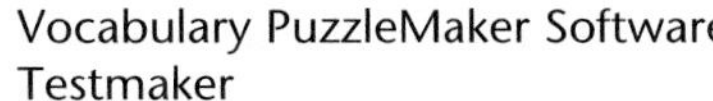

GTV: Planetary Manager

INDEPENDENT PRACTICE

 **Guided Reading** Have students complete Guided Reading Activity 3-1 in the TCR. **LEP**

USING DIAGRAMS

 ***Answers:*** **1.** when one hemisphere leans toward the sun the other leans away; **2.** the beginning of spring; **3.** the Tropic of Cancer

Skills Practice
Reading a Diagram When does the sun never set at the South Pole? *(between September 23 and March 21)*

ASSESS

CHECK FOR UNDERSTANDING

Assign Section 1 Review as homework or an in-class activity.

MEETING LESSON OBJECTIVES

Each objective below is tested by the questions that follow it in parentheses.
1. Summarize the effect of the earth's tilt on the temperature of places. *(4)*
2. Explain how the spinning of the earth causes day and night. *(1)*
3. Describe how the earth's motion around the sun causes the seasons. *(3, 5)*

hours, turning from west to east. The earth's rotation causes day and night.

The sun shines on the earth all the time. As the earth spins on its axis, the part of the earth that faces the sun has daylight. The part of the earth facing away from the sun has darkness.

Earth's Revolution

As it rotates on its axis, the earth also travels in an orbit, or path, around the sun. The earth's **revolution**, or trip around the sun, takes 1 year, or 365¼ days.

The earth's revolution and tilt cause the changing seasons. They also cause changes in the amount of daylight during the year.

On about March 21, the sun is directly over the equator and the days and nights are equal in length. This day is called an **equinox**. In the Northern Hemisphere, March 21 marks the beginning of spring. In the Southern Hemisphere, the seasons are reversed. The earth gradually moves so that the direct rays of the sun strike the latitude 23½° N, or the Tropic of Cancer, on about June 21. This is the northernmost point on the earth that receives the direct rays of the sun. This day is called a

THE SEASONS IN THE NORTHERN HEMISPHERE

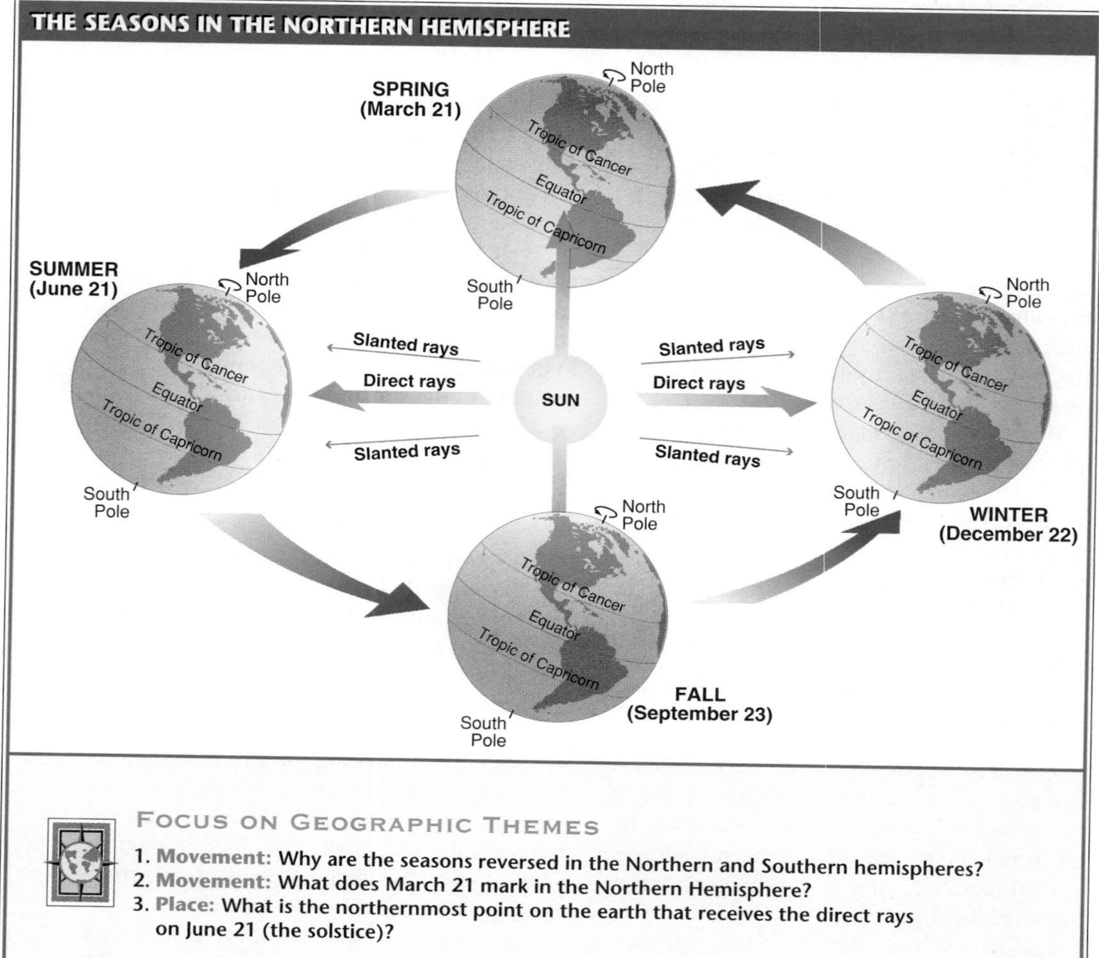

FOCUS ON GEOGRAPHIC THEMES

1. **Movement:** Why are the seasons reversed in the Northern and Southern hemispheres?
2. **Movement:** What does March 21 mark in the Northern Hemisphere?
3. **Place:** What is the northernmost point on the earth that receives the direct rays on June 21 (the solstice)?

Cooperative Learning Activity

Organize the class into groups and tell each group to make a mini-greenhouse. Allow the groups to choose their greenhouse materials, but give them suggestions such as egg cartons wrapped in plastic, clear plastic boxes, or wooden boxes with glass tops. Also, suggest that they find pictures of greenhouses to give them more ideas. After they assemble their greenhouses and fill them with soil, distribute lima beans to plant. Place the greenhouses in direct sunlight and have the students compare the progress of the beans. Encourage them to analyze why the beans in one greenhouse grow faster than those in another.

Geographic Themes

Place: Great Plains, United States

This meeting of two dissimilar air masses over part of the Great Plains is bringing dramatic changes in weather to the region. *What factor distinguishes weather from climate?*

solstice. In the Northern Hemisphere, June 21 marks the beginning of summer. It is the day of longest sunlight there.

The earth moves until on about September 23, the sun is again directly over the Equator. In the Northern Hemisphere, this equinox marks the beginning of fall. The earth gradually moves so that the direct rays of the sun strike 23½° S, or the Tropic of Capricorn, on about December 22. This is the southernmost point that receives the direct rays of the sun. In the Northern Hemisphere, this solstice marks the beginning of winter and is the shortest day of the year. Then the earth's movement causes the direct rays of the sun to move north, and the cycle repeats itself.

The amount of sunlight at the poles varies the most dramatically as the earth's revolution and tilt causes the changing seasons. At the North Pole, the sun never sets from about March 20 to September 23. At the South Pole, it never sets from about September 23 to March 20. The tilting of the earth's axis as it revolves around the sun causes this natural phenomenon, known as the midnight sun. For six months one Pole is slanted toward the sun and receives continuous sunlight, while the other Pole is slanted away from the sun and receives no sunlight at all.

Section 1 Review

Checking for Understanding

1. **Define** weather, climate, axis, temperature, revolution, equinox, solstice.
2. **Locating Places** What latitude is the Tropic of Cancer? Tropic of Capricorn?
3. **Movement** How does the revolution of the earth cause seasons?
4. **Movement** How are the temperatures of places affected by the earth's tilt?

Critical Thinking

5. **Analyzing Information** Why does March 21 generally mark the beginning of spring in the Northern Hemisphere?

EVALUATE

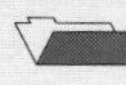

Assign the Section 1 Quiz in the TCR.

Use the Testmaker to create a customized quiz for Section 1.

RETEACH

On the chalkboard, write false statements such as *The earth rotates toward the west.* Refer students to the section for facts to correct the statements.

USING ILLUSTRATIONS

PLACE Texas, a Great Plains state, had 160 tornadoes in 1989.

Answer to Caption: *length of time*

ENRICH

Have students collect pictures such as those in *NATIONAL GEOGRAPHIC* of different seasons at different latitudes.

CLOSE

Ask students how their lives would be different if the earth did not spin on its axis.

ANSWERS TO SECTION 1 REVIEW

1. **weather:** condition of atmosphere over short period; **climate:** weather over long period; **axis:** imaginary line through the earth; **temperature:** measure of heat; **revolution:** earth's trip around the sun; **equinox:** when the sun is directly over the Equator; **solstice:** when the Tropic of Cancer gets direct rays of the sun
2. 23°N; 23°S
3. The part of earth tilted toward the sun has summer; the part tilted away has winter. When the sun is directly over the Equator, spring begins in the Northern Hemisphere and fall begins in the Southern Hemisphere.
4. Some places receive more sunlight than others and so have higher temperatures.
5. The sun is directly over the Equator.

LESSON PLAN
Chapter 3, Section 2

FOCUS

SECTION OBJECTIVES

1. Identify the patterns of winds and ocean currents.
2. Explain the role temperature and precipitation play in describing climates.
3. Examine factors that control the locations of climates around the world.

BELLRINGER MOTIVATIONAL ACTIVITY

Project the Section 2 Focus Transparency and have students answer the questions.

PRETEACHING VOCABULARY

Ask students what people mean when they say that someone is "in the doldrums." *(listless, bored)* Then tell students to find the meaning of doldrums in the section. Have them explain the connection between the phrase and the term. *(A person in the doldrums feels as sluggish as a person in a hot, windless place.)*

USING ILLUSTRATIONS

LOCATION Not only is Quito one of the highest cities in the Western Hemisphere, it is also one of the oldest.

Answer to Caption: *the lines between 23°N (the Tropic of Cancer) and 23°S (the Tropic of Capricorn)*

SECTION 2

Factors Affecting Climate

SETTING THE SCENE

Read to Discover . . .
- the patterns of wind and ocean currents.
- the role temperature and precipitation play in describing climates.
- the factors that control the locations of climates around the world.

Key Terms
- prevailing wind
- doldrums
- current
- precipitation
- windward
- leeward
- rain shadow

Identify and Locate
High, middle, and low latitudes; Arctic Circle, Antarctic Circle

All places on the earth are not heated or cooled equally. The kind of climate that a place has depends in part on latitude, elevation, wind and ocean currents, and landforms.

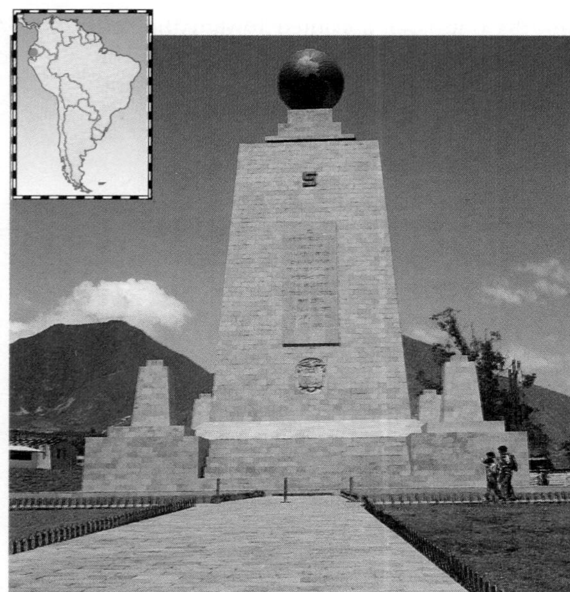

Geographic Themes
Location: Quito, Ecuador
This monument near Quito, Ecuador in South America marks the line of the Equator. *What major lines of latitude define the low latitudes?*

PLACE

Latitude

Bands of latitude can be used to describe climate in a general way according to certain climate zones. The zones indicate how the rays of the sun strike the places within the zones. During the earth's yearly revolution around the sun, the sun's direct rays fall on the earth in a regular pattern.

Low Latitudes

The latitudes between the Tropic of Cancer and the Tropic of Capricorn are known as the low latitudes. The low latitudes receive direct rays of the sun year-round. Places in these latitudes have a very warm to very hot climate and are often said to be in the tropics.

Polar Areas

When either the Northern Hemisphere or the Southern Hemisphere is tilted toward the sun, its polar area receives continuous sunlight. Starting on about June 21, the sun never sets above a line called the Arctic Circle (66½° N). In the Southern Hemisphere, the Antarctic Circle (66½° S) is a line that marks the boundary of endless daylight starting on about December 22. During the times when there is

Classroom Resources for Section 2

BLACKLINE MASTERS:
Reproducible Lesson Plan 3-2
Guided Reading Activity 3-2
Spanish Guided Reading Activity 3-2
Workbook Activity 3-2
Section Quiz 3-2

TRANSPARENCIES:
Section Focus Transparency 3-2
Unit Map Overlay Transparency 1-2

MULTIMEDIA:

Testmaker

Geography and the Environment

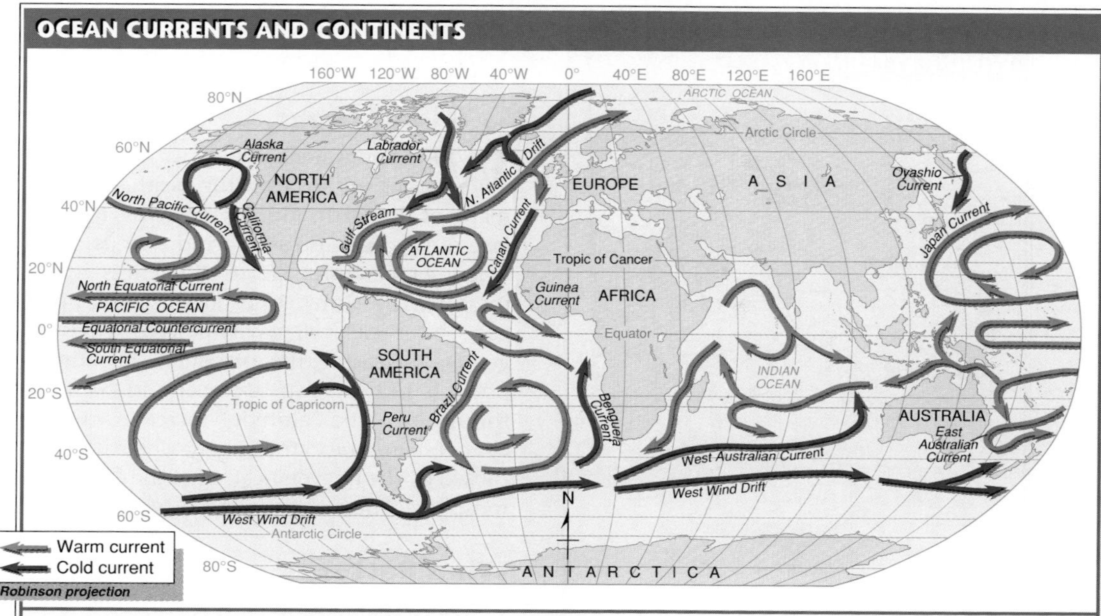

FOCUS ON GEOGRAPHIC THEMES

1. **Region:** What continent is affected by the North Atlantic Current?
2. **Movement:** What current moves along the northwestern coast of Africa?
3. **Movement:** What currents cross the Tropic of Cancer?
4. **Place:** What current brings cooler temperatures to Japan?

endless daylight at the poles, they actually receive very little heat from the sun. This is because the sun's rays that far from the Equator always hit the earth as slanted rays rather than as direct rays.

High and Middle Latitudes

The latitudes between the North Pole and the Arctic Circle and between the South Pole and the Antarctic Circle are known as the high latitudes. Places in the high latitudes receive slanted rays of the sun throughout the year and have a generally cold climate.

The latitudes between the Tropic of Cancer and the Arctic Circle in the Northern Hemisphere and between the Tropic of Capricorn and the Antarctic Circle in the Southern Hemisphere are known as the middle latitudes. The middle latitudes receive warm masses of air from the tropics during summer and cold masses of air from the high latitudes during winter. Thus, many places at these latitudes have a temperate climate—or one that ranges from fairly hot to fairly cold. The weather of most places in the middle latitudes changes dramatically with the seasons.

PLACE

Elevation

The temperature of a place depends on its elevation. The earth's atmosphere gets thinner as altitude increases, so air temperatures decrease with elevation. For every 1,000

Cooperative Learning Activity

Organize the class into four groups. Assign each group different latitudes. Tell the group members to plan a basic year-round wardrobe for a person living in their area. Give examples of possible wardrobe items, such as fur-lined boots for a person living in high latitudes. After all the groups have completed their plans, have them compare wardrobes and determine where people need the greatest variety of clothing.

TEACH

GUIDED PRACTICE

L1 Demonstrate Create a current in a sink by filling it with water and then pulling the plug. Point out how even this small current moves clockwise in the Northern Hemisphere. **LEP**

INDEPENDENT PRACTICE

L2 Write Ask students to solve the following conundrum: I live near the Equator and get plenty of sunlight, but my home is covered in ice and snow year-round. Where am I? *(on top of a high mountain)* Challenge students to write their own conundrums about somewhere or something in the section. Allow them time to read and figure out one another's conundrums.

USING MAPS

Answers:
1. Europe; **2.** the Canary Current; **3.** the North Pacific Current, the California Current, the Gulf Stream, the Canary Current, and the Japan Current; **4.** Oyashio Current

Map Skills Practice

Reading a Map Is the current along South America's Pacific coast warm or cold? *(cold)* How does the current along Northern Europe's coast affect climate there? *(warms temperatures)*

USING MAPS

Answers:
1. the Arctic and Antarctic circles;
2. the westerlies

Map Skills Practice

Reading a Map Which winds blow over your home? *(probably westerlies)*

ASSESS

CHECK FOR UNDERSTANDING

Assign Section 2 Review as homework or an in-class activity.

MEETING LESSON OBJECTIVES

Each objective below is tested by the questions that follow it in parentheses.

1. Identify the patterns of winds and ocean currents. *(2)*

2. Explain the role temperature and precipitation play in describing climates. *(3, 5)*

3. Examine factors that control the locations of climates around the world. *(3, 4, 5)*

EVALUATE

Assign the Section 2 Quiz in the TCR.

Use the Testmaker to create a customized quiz for Section 2.

RETEACH

Have students complete Workbook Activity 3-2 found in the TCR.

ZONES OF LATITUDE AND WIND PATTERNS

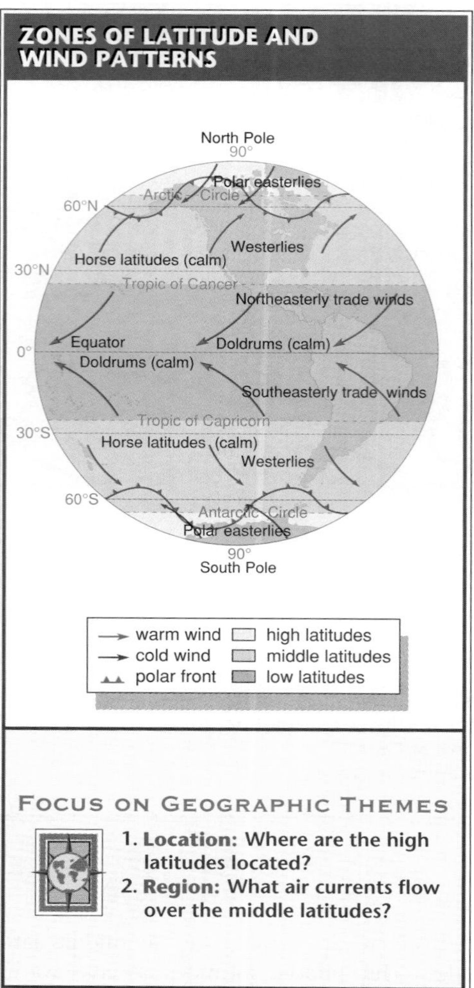

FOCUS ON GEOGRAPHIC THEMES

1. **Location:** Where are the high latitudes located?
2. **Region:** What air currents flow over the middle latitudes?

feet (305 m) gained, the temperature drops about 3.5°F (1.9°C). For example, Quito, the capital city of Ecuador, lies nearly on the Equator. Nevertheless, Quito's elevation of more than 9,000 feet (2,743 m) causes its average temperature to be about 25°F (14°C) cooler than that of the surrounding lowlands.

Sunlight is very bright on top of mountains because there is less atmosphere to filter out rays of the sun. High mountains, however, are generally cold places covered with ice and snow year-round, even if the mountains are located near the Equator.

MOVEMENT

Wind and Ocean Currents

Wind and water combine with the effects of the sun to create the weather and climates of the earth. Air moving across the surface of the earth is called wind. Winds occur when temperatures create differences in air pressure. The earth's atmosphere is made up of gases. Near sea level, gravity pulls the gases together, increasing the pressure. The atmosphere is heavier near sea level and becomes thinner as the altitude increases. Other changes in the atmospheric pressure are caused by the uneven heating of the earth's atmosphere. These changes create winds.

Wind Patterns

Winds that blow in fairly constant patterns are called **prevailing winds**. The prevailing winds are divided into belts of latitude. Trade winds are the prevailing winds in the low latitudes. They blow toward the Equator from about 30° N latitude and 30° S latitude. The prevailing winds in the belts between 30° N and 60° N latitude and between 30° S and 60° S latitude are called westerlies. These winds generally blow in a west to east direction. The belts of the polar easterlies lie between 60° N latitude and the North Pole and between 60° S latitude and the South Pole. These winds blow somewhat from east to west and push cold polar air toward the middle latitudes. At the Equator is a frequently windless area called the **doldrums**.

Ocean Currents

Cold and warm "rivers" of seawater, known as **currents**, flow in the oceans. Ocean currents generally flow in circular patterns, moving clockwise in the Northern Hemisphere and counterclockwise in the Southern Hemisphere.

Currents are caused by the rotation of the earth, moving air, and differences in water temperature in the ocean itself. Currents may be warm or cold.

Meeting Special Needs

Inefficient Organizers Have students combine words and graphics to visualize the information in this section. For example, have the students scan the paragraph under "Wind Patterns" to find the names of winds in different latitudes. Then direct them to find the names of these winds on the map on page 50. This method enables students to have a graphic reinforcement of the material.

Cold water from the polar areas moves slowly toward the Equator. The water warms as it nears the Equator. The warm water, in turn, moves away from the Equator. This water forms the warm ocean currents. As the warm water moves away from the Equator, it becomes colder and forms a cold current.

Ocean currents affect the climates of coastal lands that they flow along. Cold currents cool the lands they pass. Warm currents have a warming effect. For example, the warm water extension of the Gulf Stream current—called the North Atlantic Drift—flows near western Europe. This current gives western Europe a rather mild climate in spite of its northerly latitude.

Water and winds interact with temperature to cause **precipitation**—the falling of moisture to the earth. Precipitation falls in the forms of rain, sleet, hail, or snow.

RAIN SHADOW

Precipitation
Hot, dry air
Mountain range
Rain shadow
Windward side
Leeward side
Ocean

FOCUS ON GEOGRAPHIC THEMES

1. **Place: On what side of a mountain does precipitation fall?**
2. **Place: How do landforms cause the formation of a rain shadow?**

PLACE

Landforms

The earth's surface features can also affect climates. The climates of places located at the same latitude can be very different depending on whether large bodies of water are nearby. Water is slower to heat and to cool than land. Therefore, water temperatures are more constant and uniform than land temperatures. For the same reason, temperatures of land areas located near oceans do not change as much as temperatures of interior land areas.

Interior land temperatures can change dramatically. The middle of a landmass will generally have much hotter summers and much colder winters than land areas near the ocean, even though these locations may be on the same line of latitude.

Temperatures, precipitation, and surface features interact with wind to affect climate. Winds that blow over an ocean and then meet a mountain range on the **windward** side—the side facing toward the direction from which the wind is blowing—are pushed upward. As the winds rise and cool, they drop moisture gathered through evaporation. Thus the air that descends the other side of the mountains, the **leeward** side, is dry and becomes warmer as it falls. This hot, dry air results in a dry area called a **rain shadow.**

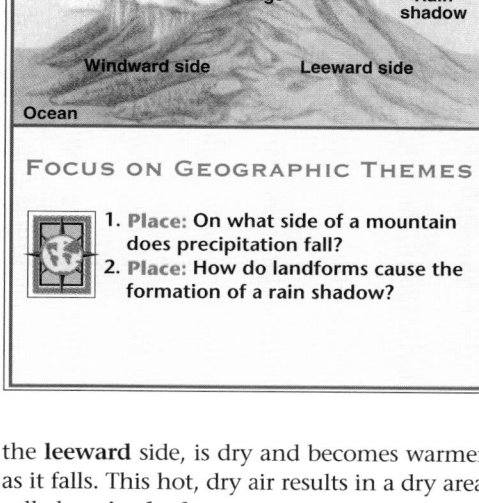

SECTION 2 REVIEW

Checking for Understanding

1. **Define** prevailing wind, doldrums, current, precipitation, windward, leeward, rain shadow.
2. **Locating Places** What and where are the trade winds, westerlies, and polar easterlies?
3. **Region** Why do the climates of the low latitudes, the high latitudes, and the middle latitudes differ?
4. **Movement** How do winds and ocean currents affect climate?

Critical Thinking

5. **Making Generalizations** What factors affect climate in your region?

ANSWERS TO SECTION 2 REVIEW

1. **prevailing wind:** wind blowing in fairly constant patterns; **doldrums:** often windless area; **current:** "river" of seawater; **precipitation:** falling moisture; **windward:** facing the wind; **leeward:** away from the wind; **rain shadow:** dry side of mountain
2. trade winds: blow in the low latitudes; westerlies: blow west-to-east in the middle latitudes; polar easterlies: blow east to west from the poles
3. Direct rays warm low latitudes while slanted rays cool high latitudes; tropical air warms middle latitudes in summer; polar air cools them in winter.
4. They affect temperature and precipitation.
5. Answers will vary but should mention latitude, elevation, currents, etc.

USING DIAGRAMS

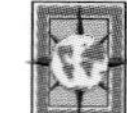

Answers: **1.** the windward side; **2.** Mountains force moist air to rise, cool, and drop its moisture. Thus the air that descends mountains is hot and dry, resulting in dry areas called rain shadows.

Skills Practice

Drawing Conclusions
Where did the wind in the diagram pick up its moisture? *(from the ocean)*

ENRICH

Have students find and read poems about wind, such as, Robert Frost's "Wind and Window Flower."

CLOSE

Have students describe their ideal vacation spots and identify the latitudes where the spots would most likely be found.

MULTICULTURAL PERSPECTIVE

Culturally Speaking
Russians call a strong northeasterly wind a *buran,* North Africans call a blinding sandstorm a *haboob,* and Alaskans call a sudden windstorm a *williwaw.*

GLENCOE TECHNOLOGY

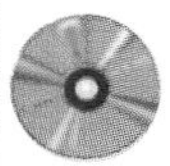

Videodisc

GEOGRAPHY AND THE ENVIRONMENT
THE INFINITE VOYAGE
Crisis in the Atmosphere

Chapter 3
Disc 2 Side A
Title: ***Our Future Climate***
Subject: Earth's present and possible future climate patterns depicted in a 3-D model

LESSON PLAN
Chapter 3, Section 3

FOCUS

SECTION OBJECTIVES

1. **Enumerate** the climate regions of the world.
2. **Describe** ways that climate affects humans and their environment.
3. **Predict** how climates change over time.

BELLRINGER MOTIVATIONAL ACTIVITY

Project the Section 3 Focus Transparency and have students answer the questions.

PRETEACHING VOCABULARY

Have students look up *chaparral* and *taiga* in the dictionary and tell the class from which language each term originated. (*Chaparral* comes from Spanish, and *taiga* is a Russian word.) Tell the students these are names of vegetation, and ask them to predict at least one country where each is found. *(Spain and Russia respectively)*

GLENCOE TECHNOLOGY

Videodisc

Use the following to enrich Chapter 3:

GEOGRAPHY AND THE ENVIRONMENT
THE INFINITE VOYAGE
Crisis in the Atmosphere

Chapter 3
Disc 2 Side A

Title: ***Our Future Climate***
Subject: Earth's present and possible future climate patterns depicted in a 3-D model

SECTION 3

World Climate Patterns

SETTING THE SCENE

Read to Discover . . .

- the climate regions of the world.
- ways that climate affects humans and their environment.
- how climates change over time.

Key Terms

- natural vegetation
- oasis
- deciduous
- mixed forest
- chaparral
- prairie
- permafrost
- taiga
- timberline
- hypothesis
- smog

Identify and Locate

Major global climate regions: tropical, dry, mid-latitude, high latitude, highland

Climate affects the soil and **natural vegetation.** Natural vegetation is the plant life that grows in an area if the natural environment has not been changed by people.

Geographers often divide the earth into five major climate regions—tropical, dry, mid-latitude, high latitude, and highland. Because climates vary within these broad regions, geographers further divide the major regions into smaller ones.

REGION

Tropical Climates

Tropical climate regions are found in or near the low latitudes—the tropics. The two kinds of tropical climate regions are tropical rain forest and tropical savanna.

Tropical Rain Forest Climate

Hot and wet throughout the year, tropical rain forest climate regions are found near the Equator. Direct rays of the sun keep the temperatures high, averaging around 80°F (27°C), year-round. The warm, humid air produces rain almost daily. Yearly rainfall averages about 80 inches (203 cm).

Tropical rain forest vegetation grows thick in layers formed at different heights. Tall teak or mahogany trees form a high canopy over shorter trees and bushes. Vines and shade-loving plants grow on the floor of the rain forest.

The Amazon River basin in South America contains the world's largest tropical rain forest. This same climate is found in other parts of South America, in the Caribbean area, and in parts of Africa and Asia.

Tropical Savanna Climate

Areas that have a dry season in winter and a wet season in summer are called tropical savanna climate regions. Although savannas are located farther from the Equator than tropical rain forest regions, temperatures are high.

In the dry season the tough ground is covered with clumps of coarse grass. Few trees dot the large savannas of Africa and South America.

Classroom Resources for Section 3

BLACKLINE MASTERS:
Reproducible Lesson Plan 3-3
Skill Activity 3
Enrichment Activity 3
Section Quiz 3-3

TRANSPARENCIES:
Section Focus Transparency 3-3
Unit Map Overlay Transparencies 1-4, 1-5

MULTIMEDIA:
Testmaker

Geography and the Environment

REGION

Dry Climates

Because of vegetation, dry climate regions are also divided into two types, desert and steppe.

Desert Climate

Dry areas with sparse plant life are called deserts. Scattered vegetation such as scrubs and cacti can survive with little rain. Flowering plants that lie dormant during the dry season bloom when the rains come.

Yearly rainfall in deserts seldom is more than 10 inches (about 25 cm). Underground springs, however, may support an **oasis**, an area of lush vegetation. Some deserts have fertile soil in which plants can grow if irrigated. Others have dunes or rocky surfaces.

Deserts can be extremely hot during the day and cold at night. The Gobi in central Asia has hot summers and harsh winters with temperatures as cold as –40°F (–40°C).

Desert climates cover about one-fifth of the earth's land surface. The Sahara extends over nearly the entire northern one-third of Africa.

Steppe Climate

Dry areas, often bordering deserts, are called steppes. Yearly rainfall in steppe zones averages 10 to 20 inches (25.4 to 50.8 cm).

Steppe vegetation consists of bushes and patches of short grasses without many trees. The world's largest steppe stretches across eastern Europe and western and central Asia. Steppes are also found in North America, South America, Africa, and Australia.

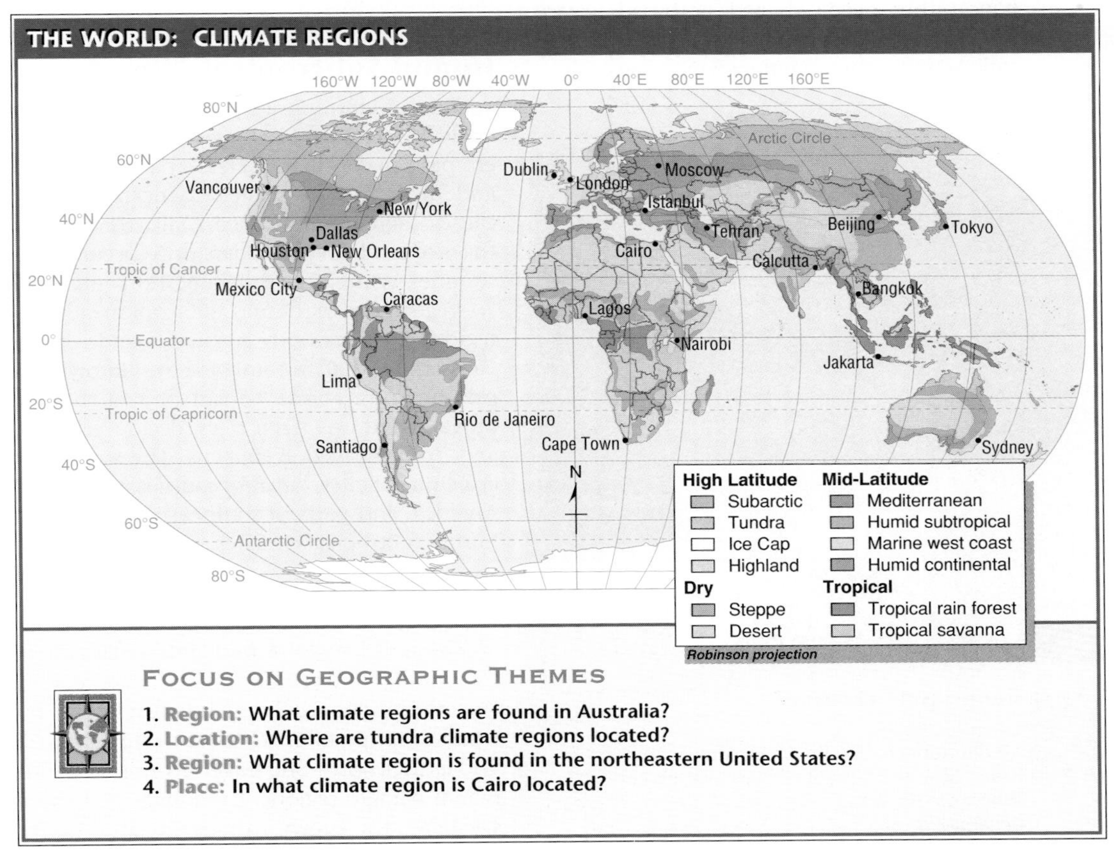

FOCUS ON GEOGRAPHIC THEMES

1. **Region: What climate regions are found in Australia?**
2. **Location: Where are tundra climate regions located?**
3. **Region: What climate region is found in the northeastern United States?**
4. **Place: In what climate region is Cairo located?**

Chapter 3, Section 3

TEACH

GUIDED PRACTICE

L1 Outline On the chalkboard write the names of the five major climate regions as main headings for an outline. Have students add the types of climates in each region as subheads, and their location and types of vegetation as details.

L2 Identify Label a bookshelf with the names of types of climates. Ask students to bring in books set in each climate. For example, Rudyard Kipling's *Jungle Book* might go under the label "tropical rain forest."

USING MAPS

Answers:

1. Mediterranean, humid subtropical, marine west coast, tropical savanna, steppe, and desert; **2.** within the Arctic Circle; **3.** humid continental; **4.** desert

Map Skills Practice

Reading a Map Which part of the United States has a humid subtropical climate? *(the Southeast)*

DID YOU KNOW?

Rain forests cover 7 percent of the earth's surface but are home to more than half of its plant and animal species.

Cooperative Learning Activity

Have students choose a climate region to recreate in the classroom. Suggest that they draw murals showing vegetation found in that climate. Have students bring appropriate plants from home, such as a cactus for a desert climate or a rubber tree for a tropical one. They might also add a humidifier to simulate a wet climate or a dehumidifier for a dry climate. After the classroom is "climatized," declare a climate day and ask students to dress appropriately for the climate in the classroom.

INDEPENDENT PRACTICE

Guided Reading Have students complete Guided Reading Activity 3-3 in the TCR. **LEP**

L1 Classify Ask students to group broad and needle-shaped leaves under the correct headings *evergreen* and *deciduous*. Tell them to help one another identify and label the leaves as elm, maple, and so on.

L2 Montage Have students create montages with pictures of vegetation, clothing, and housing from a certain type of climate. One montage, for example, might show the chaparral and Spanish villas in Mediterranean climates. Have the class identify the climates in the montages.

USING ILLUSTRATIONS

LOCATION Despite the wet winters, farmers in Israel have to adjust to an ever-decreasing supply of water by irrigating with treated wastewater from the cities.

Answer to Caption: *in coastal lands between latitudes 30° and 40° north and south*

Global Gourmet

Shoots of bamboo, a reed that grows in tropical regions, are used in many Chinese dishes. They must be cooked before eaten, however, because they are poisonous when raw.

REGION

Mid-latitude Climates

The world has four mid-latitude climate regions. They are marine west coast, Mediterranean, humid subtropical, and humid continental.

Marine West Coast Climate

Climate areas generally found along western coastlines between latitudes 30° and 60° north and south are called marine west coast climate regions. Ocean winds produce cool summers and mild but damp winters. Rainfall, quite heavy in places, supports both evergreen and **deciduous** trees.

Deciduous trees lose their leaves in autumn. Most deciduous trees, including oak, maple, and elm, have broad leaves. Evergreens have either needle-shaped or broad leaves. Needle-leaved pine and spruce trees are also called conifers because they have cones.

Geographic Themes

Location: Israel

Mediterranean climate areas, such as that in Israel, have the benefit of mild, wet winters. *Where are the world's Mediterranean climate areas generally located?*

Mixed forests are those with both evergreen and deciduous trees. Marine west coast climate regions cover much of western Europe as well as the Pacific coast of North America. South America, Africa, and Australia also have marine west coast climate regions.

Mediterranean Climate

Areas that have weather patterns and vegetation like those near the Mediterranean Sea are called Mediterranean climate regions. These regions are generally found in coastal lands between latitudes 30° and 40° north and south. They have mild rainy winters and hot, sunny summers.

Vegetation in Mediterranean climate regions includes woody bushes and short trees, such as olive and cork oak, which grow in dense forests. This type of vegetation is called **chaparral.** Southern California has a Mediterranean climate.

Humid Subtropical Climate

Humid subtropical climate regions are generally found at mid-latitudes in the southeastern parts of continents. Here a pattern of wind and high pressure related to nearby oceans causes high humidity. Rain falls throughout the year but heavy thunderstorms occur in the summer. Winters are generally short and mild.

Vegetation in humid subtropical climate regions includes both grasslands and forests. Grasslands that lie inland are known as **prairie** lands. Forests consist of a mixture of broad-leaved evergreen trees, deciduous trees, and needle-leaved evergreens. The southeastern United States, areas of southeastern South America, and parts of southeastern Asia have humid subtropical climates.

Humid Continental Climate

The fourth type of mid-latitude climate is the humid continental climate. These regions are more influenced by landmasses than by winds, precipitation, or ocean temperatures. The farther north one travels in humid continental climate regions, the longer and more severe are the snowy winters and the shorter

Meeting Special Needs

Reading Disability Students with reading problems are often helped when the teacher gives them a specific purpose for reading. Focused reading exercises help readers in two ways: (1) by giving them a limited goal, and (2) by making them more active learners. Ask students to find at least two ways to identify a Mediterranean climate region as they read "Mediterranean Climate."

THE WORLD: NATURAL VEGETATION

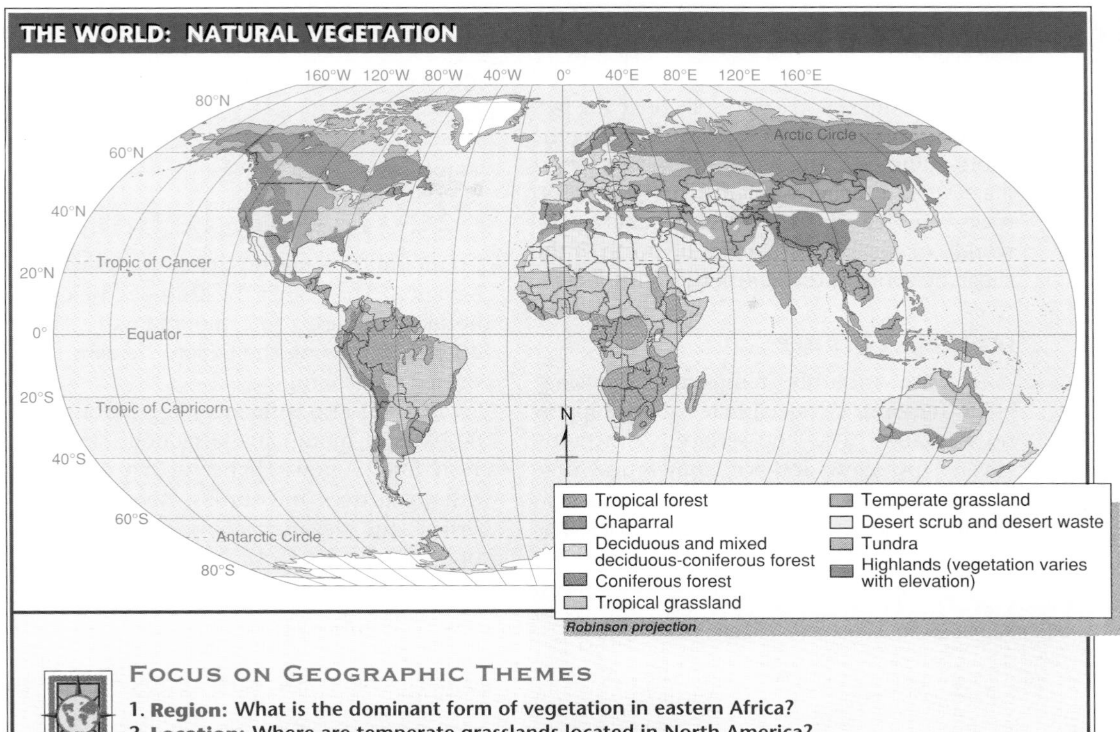

FOCUS ON GEOGRAPHIC THEMES

1. **Region:** What is the dominant form of vegetation in eastern Africa?
2. **Location:** Where are temperate grasslands located in North America?
3. **Location:** What continents have large tropical forests?

and cooler the summers. These regions are located only in the Northern Hemisphere.

REGION

High Latitude Climates

There are three types of high latitude climates—subarctic, tundra, and ice cap. Just south of the Arctic Circle lie the subarctic climate regions. Temperatures average below freezing for half the year. Winters are bitterly cold, and summers are short and cool. In some places only a thin layer of surface soil thaws. The frozen subsoil is known as **permafrost.** Relatively high temperatures may occur for a few brief summer days. Subarctic climates have the world's greatest range of temperature—as much as 120°F (65°C).

Subarctic Climate

The subarctic's severe conditions limit the variety of plant life. Vegetation consists mainly of needle-leaved evergreen trees. One vast subarctic forest stretches across northern Russia. Geographers often use **taiga**, the Russian word for this forest, to refer to subarctic climate regions in general. Another large subarctic region stretches across Canada.

Tundra Climate

Like the subarctic climate regions, the tundra climate regions have bitterly cold winters

USING MAPS

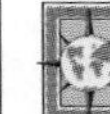

Answers:
1. tropical grassland; **2.** in the central part; **3.** South America, Africa, and Asia

Map Skills Practice

Reading a Map What kinds of vegetation grow where you live? *(Answers will vary; check them against the map.)*

L3 Write Have students write letters to the local newspaper urging people to drive less and thus cut down on smog. Direct them to the *Readers' Guide to Periodical Literature* to help them find articles with facts that they can use in their letters.

CURRICULUM CONNECTION

LITERATURE

Settings in adventure books such as Farley Mowat's **Never Cry Wolf** ***help readers imagine climate regions. Mowat described the Arctic this way: "For three days there had been a howling blizzard; then, during the third day, with visibility reduced to zero by blinding snow squalls, an aircraft came over the hotel at nought feet and with an expiring stutter flopped down on the ice of a nearby pond."***

Critical Thinking

Predicting Consequences Explain that billions of years ago, the atmospheres of Mars, Venus, and Earth resembled one another. But today the atmosphere on Mars is very thin and the temperatures are far below freezing. On Venus, the atmosphere is very thick and the temperatures get as high as 900°F (464°C). Then ask students: If volcanic activity drastically changed Earth's atmosphere, which would our planet most resemble—Mars or Venus? *(Mars)* If people increase their burning of fossil fuels, creating more and more carbon dioxide, which planet will Earth resemble then—Mars or Venus? *(Venus)*

ASSESS

CHECK FOR UNDERSTANDING

Assign Section 3 Review as homework or an in-class activity.

MEETING LESSON OBJECTIVES

Each objective below is tested by the questions that follow it in parentheses.
1. Enumerate the climate regions of the world. *(2)*
2. Describe ways that climate affects humans and their environment. *(4)*
3. Predict how climates change over time. *(5)*

EVALUATE

Assign the Section 3 Quiz in the TCR.

Use the Testmaker to create a customized quiz for Section 3.

RETEACH

Have students complete Reteaching Activity 3 in the TCR.

USING ILLUSTRATIONS

PLACE Alpine skiing has made tourism a major industry in Austria.
Answer to Caption: *elevation*

ENRICH

Have students complete Enrichment Activity 3 in the TCR.

with greatly reduced sunlight. In summer the sun's slanted rays bring constant light but little heat.

The tundra region's thin soil above the permafrost supports certain low plants during the short summers. Mosses, bushes, very short grasses, and lichens—plants that grow on rocks—survive on the treeless plain. The world's major tundra climates lie north of the subarctic zones in the Northern Hemisphere.

Ice Cap Climate

Because monthly temperatures average below freezing, ice cap climate regions support no vegetation. The land surface is constantly covered by snow and ice, sometimes more than 2 miles (3 km) thick. Only plants that can live on rocks grow in ice-cap regions. The earth's greatest polar ice cap spreads over almost all of Antarctica. The interior of Greenland also has an ice-cap climate.

Geographic Themes
Place: The Alps, Austria
This village in Austria is located in the Alps, a mountain chain that stretches across central Europe. *What geographic factor affects the type of highland climate found in mountainous areas?*

REGION

Highland Climates

In mountain areas the climate varies with elevation. The higher the altitude, the cooler the air becomes. Some mountains in South America that lie on the Equator remain snow covered year-round.

Elevation also influences vegetation. Near the bases of mountains, deciduous and evergreen forests grow. Higher up are meadows with small trees and shrubs. Above the **timberline**, the elevation above which it is too cold for trees to grow, are scattered tundra plants.

HUMAN/ENVIRONMENT INTERACTION

People, Climate, and Environment

Climate affects the kinds of clothing people wear and the kinds of houses they build. It can also affect methods of transportation they use. Changes that people make in the environment also affect climate.

Adaptations

People adapt to the climate. In cold regions they wear clothing made of warm material such as wool. People in warm regions wear light-colored linen and cotton clothing that reflects the sun's rays.

In cold regions people build well-insulated houses with furnaces or other means of heating. In some cold regions, the frozen ground melts in summer so that houses sink. Houses here are built on gravel pads or pilings—heavy poles driven into the permafrost.

Houses in deserts often have light-colored roofs to reflect the sun's heat. Often these houses are made of sun-dried bricks, because in hot weather they stay cool. In wet regions

Extending the Content

Human/Environment Interaction When people burn fossil fuels, sulfur dioxide and nitrogen compounds are released. These react with each other in sunlight to form sulfuric and nitric acids. Rain mixed with these acids is called acid rain. Normal rain has a pH of 5.6. The polluted rain that falls in most of New England and nearby Canada has a pH between 4.0 and 4.5, or about the same acidity as grapefruit juice. Rains that fall on mountaintops in New Hampshire have been measured at a pH of 2.1, about the same acidity as lemon juice. Acid rain with a pH below 5.1 kills fish, destroys aquatic ecosystems, weakens and kills trees, and stunts the growth of crops and other plants. Have students collect local rainfall and use litmus strips to measure its pH.

houses may have steep, pointed roofs so that rain or snow run off easily.

Climate affects transportation. For example, in some tropical rain forests, plants and trees grow so quickly that building and maintaining roads is very difficult. Rivers often substitute for roads in these regions. At the other extreme, people in cold, snowy regions may use snowmobiles.

Climatic Changes

Climates change gradually over time. During the last 1 to 2 million years, for example, the earth passed through four eras when large areas were covered with glaciers.

Geographers have developed several possible explanations for what caused glacial eras. One explanation is that variations in the sun's output of energy and in the earth's orbit may have caused our world to absorb less solar energy and cool off.

Another **hypothesis**, or scientific explanation, suggests that volcanic activity, which put massive amounts of dust in the atmosphere, might have had a cooling effect. Volcanic dust reflected sunlight into space, keeping it from warming the earth.

Geographers also believe that human activity causes changes in the world's climates. Particles in smoke from the burning of fossil fuels may stay in the air for years, scattering the sun's rays. This reduces the sunlight reaching the ground, lowering the temperature.

An opposite effect of burning fossil fuels is the release of carbon dioxide. This gas allows sunlight to reach the ground but prevents some surface heat from leaving the atmosphere. This causes temperatures near the earth's surface to rise—a greenhouse effect. Also, gases produced by burning fuels mix with water in the air, forming acids. These damaging acids fall in rain and snow.

The exhaust from automobiles helps create **smog**, a haze caused by the sun's ultraviolet radiation. Smog endangers people's health.

People also affect climate through water projects, such as dams and river diversions. Dams built for industrial water supplies or for irrigation sometimes cause new areas to become dry.

Geographic Themes

Human/Environment Interaction: South Asia

The monsoons, or seasonal winds, bring practically all the rain that falls on South Asia. Fields and villages can be swept away by flooding. *How do people in various parts of the world respond to climate?*

SECTION 3 REVIEW

Checking for Understanding

1. **Define** natural vegetation, oasis, deciduous, mixed forest, chaparral, prairie, permafrost, taiga, timberline, hypothesis, smog.
2. **Locating Places** What and where are the five main climate regions?
3. **Region** Why do tropical climates have high temperatures year-round?
4. **Human/Environment Interaction** How does climate affect human activities?

Critical Thinking

5. **Distinguishing Fact from Opinion** In what ways may the earth's climate change due to human and natural processes?

Chapter 3, Section 3

CLOSE

List the climate regions on the chalkboard. Have students look through the text (they are not limited to Chapter 3) and find a photo representative of each climate region.

USING ILLUSTRATIONS

HUMAN/ENVIRONMENT INTERACTION India suffers from heavy monsoon weather. One year, Cherapunji, India, recorded more than 1,000 inches (2,550 cm) of rain.

Answer to Caption: *they adapt*

GLENCOE TECHNOLOGY

Videodisc

GEOGRAPHY AND THE ENVIRONMENT
THE INFINITE VOYAGE
Crisis in the Atmosphere

Chapter 1
Disc 2 Side A
Title: ***Historical Aspects of the Greenhouse Effect and Fossil Air***
Subject: Analysis of frozen air samples from glaciers indicates the human-caused rise of carbon dioxide and methane in the atmosphere

Chapter 4
Disc 2 Side A
Title: ***The Greenhouse Effect: Future and Past***
Subject: Possible consequences of this effect (melting of polar ice caps, rising sea levels, increasing storm intensity and drought)

ANSWERS TO SECTION 3 REVIEW

1. **natural vegetation:** an area's plants; **oasis:** area of vegetation in a desert; **deciduous:** tree that loses leaves in autumn; **mixed forest:** deciduous and evergreen trees; **chaparral:** woody bushes and small trees; **prairie:** grasslands; **permafrost:** frozen soil; **taiga:** subarctic forest; **timberline:** elevation above which trees cannot grow; **hypothesis:** scientific explanation; **smog:** haze caused by sun's rays
2. tropical: low latitudes; dry: one-fifth of the earth's land surface; mid-latitude: middle latitudes; high-latitude: high latitudes; highland: varies
3. direct rays warm the tropics all year
4. clothing, housing, and transportation
5. less sunlight, lower temperatures, a greenhouse effect, acid rain, and more dry areas

TEACH

On the chalkboard, have students draw a map of the classroom including walls, windows, doors, and some objects. Then discuss whether the map accurately represents relative lengths and distances between objects. Then ask, "How could we draw this map more accurately?" *(Decide that a unit of measurement on the map will represent a particular length in the room.)* Explain that this process is called "drawing the map to scale." Have students determine a scale of distance and correct the map using this scale.

SKILLS PRACTICE

For additional practice, have students complete Skill Activity 2 in the TCR.

MAP & GRAPH SKILLS

Understanding Scale

Maps are a visual representation of the earth's surface. A map can show an area as small as a backyard or as large as the world. How can cartographers draw something as large as a continent on a piece of paper?

REVIEWING THE SKILL

Cartographers draw maps to **scale**. On each map, a measured distance will represent a fixed distance on the earth. For example, 1 inch on a map may represent 100 miles; however, on another map, 1 inch might represent 1,000 miles. This relationship, or **scale of distance**, often is shown as a **scale bar**—a line with numbers specifying the unit of measurement and the number of miles or kilometers this unit represents. On some maps, scale appears as a fraction.

To use the scale of distance on a map, apply the following steps:

- Find the scale bar or scale fraction, and identify the unit of measurement and the distance that unit represents.
- Using this unit of measurement, measure the distance between two points on the map.
- Multiply that number by the number of miles or kilometers represented by each unit.

PRACTICING THE SKILL

Use the maps below to answer the following questions about scale:

1. On each map, what unit measures scale?
2. On Map 1, what is the scale of distance?
3. How far is Orlando from Atlanta?
4. Suppose you are traveling through West Palm Beach on I-95. About how far is it from the intersection of Route 702 to the intersection of Route 98?

For additional practice in this skill, see Practicing Skills on page 60 of the Chapter 3 Review.

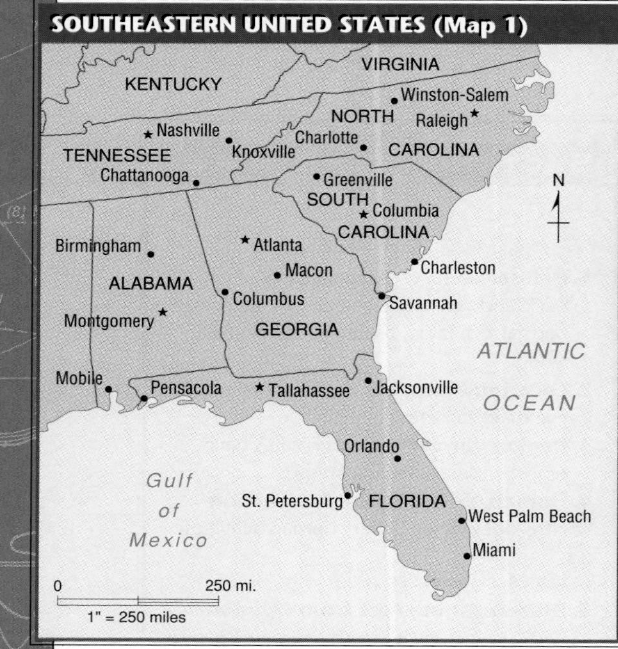

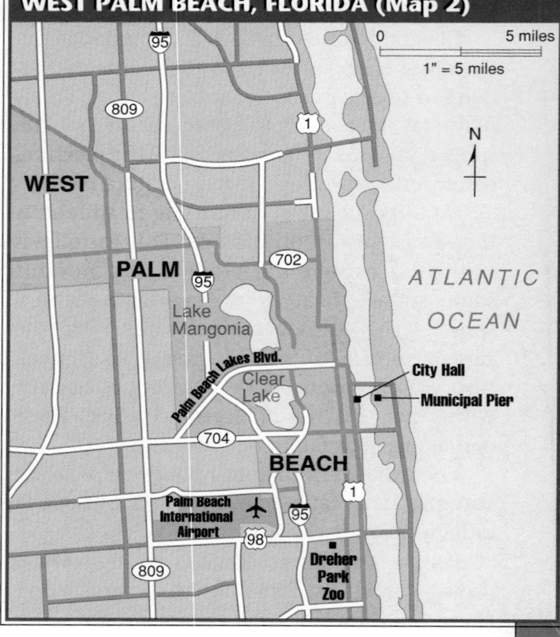

ANSWERS TO PRACTICING THE SKILL

1. inches
2. 1 inch = 250 miles, or 1/250
3. about 450 miles (725 km)
4. about 12 miles (20 km)

chapter 3

HIGHLIGHTS

1 Section: Earth-Sun Relationships

Weather system crossing the Great Plains

Key Terms

weather (p. 45)
climate (p. 45)
axis (p. 45)
temperature (p. 45)
revolution (p. 46)
equinox (p. 46)
solstice (p. 47)

Summary

- The relationship between the earth and the sun affects climates around the world.
- The sun provides the earth with heat and light. Different areas of the planet, however, receive different amounts of sunlight at different times.

2 Section: Factors Affecting Climate

Monument near Quito, Ecuador, marking the line of the Equator

Key Terms

prevailing wind (p. 50)
doldrums (p. 50)
current (p. 50)
precipitation (p. 51)
windward (p. 51)
leeward (p. 51)
rain shadow (p. 51)

Summary

- All places on earth are not heated or cooled equally by the sun.
- Latitude, elevation, wind and ocean currents, and landforms also affect climate.

3 Section: World Climate Patterns

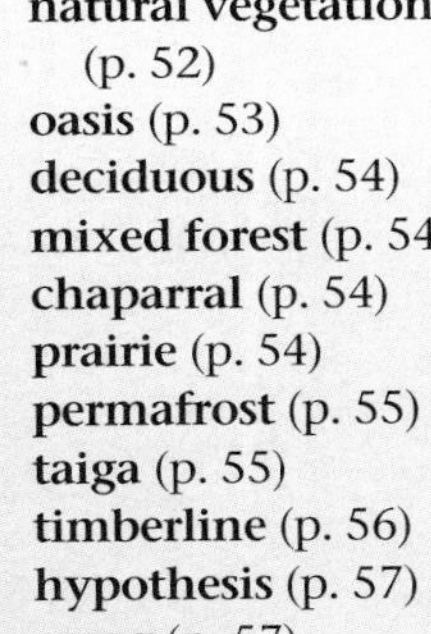

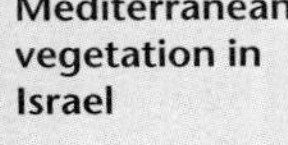

Mediterranean vegetation in Israel

Key Terms

natural vegetation (p. 52)
oasis (p. 53)
deciduous (p. 54)
mixed forest (p. 54)
chaparral (p. 54)
prairie (p. 54)
permafrost (p. 55)
taiga (p. 55)
timberline (p. 56)
hypothesis (p. 57)
smog (p. 57)

Summary

- Geographers often divide the earth into five major climate regions, generally on the basis of latitude.
- These regions are tropical, dry, mid-latitude, high latitude, and highland.
- Major climate regions are further divided into smaller regions based on such factors as plant life, location, landscape, and temperature.
- Climates change over time due to natural and human causes.

CHAPTER 3 HIGHLIGHTS

USING THE CHAPTER 3 HIGHLIGHTS

Use the Chapter 3 Highlights to preview, review, condense, or reteach the chapter.

PREVIEW/REVIEW

Vocabulary PuzzleMaker Software reinforces the Key Terms used in Chapter 3.

Student Self-Test and Review Software allows students to review Chapter 3 content.

CONDENSE

Have students read the Chapter 3 Highlights.

Have students listen to the Chapter 3 Audiocassettes in the TCR. Spanish Audiocassettes are also available.

Assign the Chapter 3 Audiocassette Activity and give students the Chapter 3 Audiocassette Quiz.

 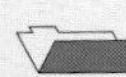

Have students complete Guided Reading Activities for Chapter 3 in the TCR. Spanish Guided Reading Activities are also available.

RETEACH

 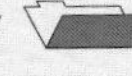

Have students complete Reteaching Activity 3 in the TCR. Spanish Reteaching Activities are also available.

Map Activity

Identify and Locate Copy and distribute page 39 of the Outline Map Resource Book. Using the Atlas map on pages A2 and A3 of the text, have students place and identify the following on their outline maps: the Equator, the Tropic of Cancer, the Tropic of Capricorn, the Arctic Circle, and the Antarctic Circle.

GLENCOE TECHNOLOGY

Videodisc

Use Chapter 3 MindJogger Videoquiz to review students' knowledge before administering the Chapter 3 Test.

MINDJOGGER VIDEOQUIZ

Chapter 3
Disc 1 Side A

The MindJogger Videoquiz is also available on videocassette.

ANSWERS

Reviewing Key Terms

1. equinox
2. revolution
3. solstice
4. prevailing winds
5. rain shadow
6. leeward
7. prevailing winds
8. taiga
9. prairie
10. permafrost
11. smog
12. mixed forest

Reviewing Facts

13. the earth's rotation on its axis
14. result of the earth's atmosphere keeping heat from escaping into space and warming the earth's surface
15. high latitudes
16. moving air, the rotation of the earth, and differences in water temperatures in the ocean itself
17. about one-fifth
18. In cold regions, people wear heavy clothing and live in well-insulated houses that have some form of heating. In warm regions, they wear clothing of lightweight materials and keep their houses cool. In deserts, houses often have light-colored roofs that reflect the sun's heat and are made of sun-dried bricks, because in hot weather they stay cool. In wet regions, people often build houses with steep, pointed roofs.

chapter 3 REVIEW

Reviewing Key Terms

Choose the vocabulary term that best completes each of the sentences below. Write your answers on a separate sheet of paper.

revolution (p. 46)
equinox (p. 46)
solstice (p. 47)
prevailing wind (p. 50)
leeward (p. 51)
rain shadow (p. 51)
mixed forest (p. 54)
prairie (p. 54)
permafrost (p. 55)
taiga (p. 55)
smog (p. 57)

SECTION 1

1. The day on which the sun is directly over the Equator and the days and nights are equal in length is called an _____.
2. _____ refers to the earth's trip around the sun.
3. The day on which the direct rays of the sun strike the Tropic of Cancer is called a _____.

SECTION 2

4. _____ are divided into belts of latitude.
5. A _____ is caused by hot, dry air.
6. _____ refers to the dry side of a mountain.
7. _____ blow in fairly constant patterns.

SECTION 3

8. _____ refers to forested subarctic climate regions.
9. Grasslands that lie inland are _____ areas.
10. Frozen subsoil is known as _____.
11. The exhaust from automobiles affects climate by causing _____.
12. Areas with both evergreen and deciduous trees are called _____.

Reviewing Facts

SECTION 1

13. What causes day and night on the earth?
14. What is the greenhouse effect?

SECTION 2

15. What are the latitudes between the North Pole and the Arctic Circle?
16. What causes ocean currents?

SECTION 3

17. How much of the earth's land surface is covered by desert areas?
18. How does climate affect the way people are clothed and housed?

Critical Thinking

19. **Expressing Problems Clearly** Why is March 21 usually the first day of spring in the Northern Hemisphere?
20. **Making Generalizations** Why do the middle latitudes have a temperate climate?
21. **Analyzing Information** Why do scrubs and cacti grow in desert climates?

Geographic Themes

22. **Movement** How does the earth's tilt affect the temperature of places?
23. **Place** How does the temperature of a place depend on its elevation?
24. **Human/Environment Interaction** Why do people who live in some desert areas wear loose, flowing clothing?

Practicing Skills

Understanding Scale

Refer to the maps on page 58. Suppose you want to travel to the Dreher Park Zoo from City Hall. The most direct route is Route 1. About how many miles would you travel to the zoo? About how many miles would you travel from West Palm Beach to Knoxville, Tennessee?

Critical Thinking

19. The sun is directly over the Equator and the days and nights are about equal in length.
20. Tropical air masses warm the middle latitudes in the summer and air masses from high latitudes cool them in the winter.
21. because these plants can survive long periods where there is no rainfall

Geographic Themes

22. Because the earth's axis is tilted, not all places receive the same amount of direct sunlight.
23. The earth's atmosphere thins and the air temperature decreases as altitude increases.
24. to protect themselves from the desert sun during the days and the desert cold at night

Projects

Individual Activity

Prepare a chart of climate regions. The first column should describe the climate, the second column should list locations where the climate is found, and the third column should rank the climate according to desirability. Use a world map and the climate map to describe climate in reference to temperature and precipitation. Note at least 4 places on the earth where certain climates occur. Which one would you like to live in? Mark your preference by placing 1 in the third column beside the climate in which you would most like to live, 2 beside your second choice, and so on.

Cooperative Learning Activity

Working in pairs, take climate data from different locations and create a climate graph that shows monthly precipitation and temperature averages. Exchange the climate graphs with other teams of students. Deduce the location of the climate graphs by observing elements such as seasons, precipitation, and temperatures. Let each team prepare clues if help is needed.

Writing About Geography

Cause and Effect

Sections of this chapter review the natural and human causes that may affect climate patterns. Using your journal for reference, write a story that takes place in a future in which the climate has changed in your community. Include details about how this change has affected vegetation, economic activities, and human and animal populations.

Locating Places

THE WORLD: PHYSICAL GEOGRAPHY

Match the letters on the map with the places and physical features of the earth. Write your answers on a separate sheet of paper.

1. Arctic Circle
2. Antarctic Circle
3. Cold Water, Pacific
4. Equator
5. Tropic of Cancer
6. Tropic of Capricorn
7. Warm Water, Atlantic

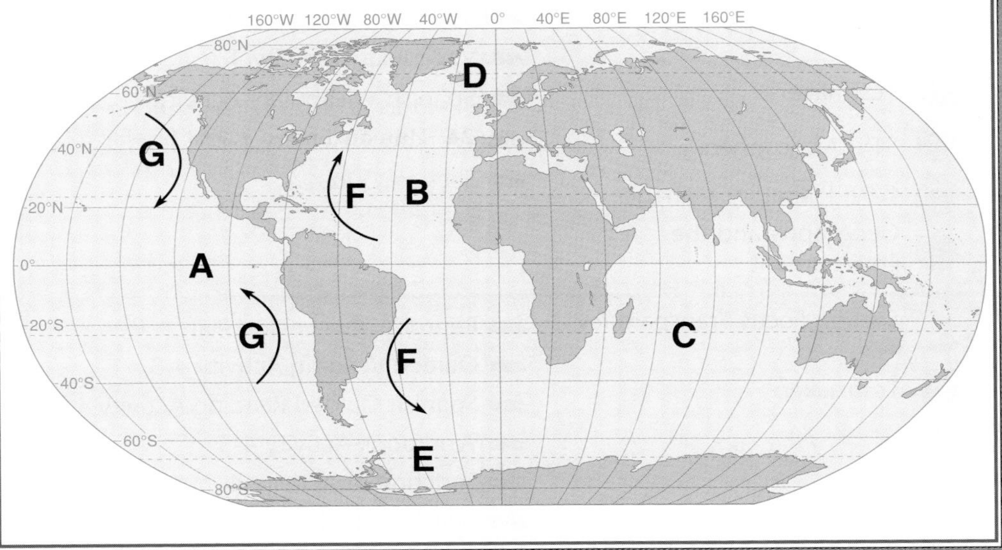

Chapter 3 Review

Practicing Skills

about 5 miles; about 700 miles

Locating Places

1. D
2. E
3. G
4. A
5. B
6. C
7. F

Chapter Bonus Test Question

This question may be used for extra credit on the chapter test. Choose the letter of the correct response.

If you were at the North Pole and your friend was at the South Pole on March 21, who would see the sun?

(1) you
(2) your friend
(3) neither of you
(4) both of you

Answer: (4)

CHAPTER 4

PLANNING GUIDE

Environments, Peoples, and Cultures

CHAPTER ORGANIZER

Daily Lesson Objectives	Multimedia	Teacher Classroom Resources
SECTION 1 Limits and Opportunities 1. Distinguish between developed countries and developing countries. 2. Appreciate the challenges that rapid population growth brings to the planet. 3. Examine the impact of environmental hazards on people's lives.	Section Focus Transparency 4-1 Chapter 4 Vocabulary PuzzleMaker Software Political Map Transparency 12 Unit Map Overlay Transparency 1-6 Geography and the Environment Testmaker GTV: Planetary Manager	Reproducible Lesson Plan 4-1 Guided Reading Activity 4-1 Spanish Guided Reading Activity 4-1 Section Quiz 4-1
SECTION 2 Cultural Expressions 1. Describe how the first civilizations developed. 2. Discuss the ways in which the movement of people, goods, and ideas has caused cultural change. 3. Identify the factors that have contributed to cultural contact and cultural barriers.	Section Focus Transparency 4-2 World History & Art Transparencies 1, 2, 3, 4, 5, 6 Testmaker STV: Atmosphere GTV: Planetary Manager Geography and the Environment	Reproducible Lesson Plan 4-2 Guided Reading Activity 4-2 Spanish Guided Reading Activity 4-2 Vocabulary Activity 4 Spanish Vocabulary Activity 4 Workbook Activity 4-2 Section Quiz 4-2
SECTION 3 World Culture Regions Today 1. Name the factors that determine the earth's culture regions. 2. Relate how other social sciences help geographers determine culture regions.	Section Focus Transparency 4-3 Testmaker	Reproducible Lesson Plan 4-1 Guided Reading Activity 4-3 Spanish Guided Reading Activity 4-3 Workbook Activity 4-3 Enrichment Activity 4 Skill Activity 4 Section Quiz 4-3
CHAPTER REVIEW AND EVALUATION	Chapter 4 English (or Spanish) Audiocassettes MindJogger Videoquiz Testmaker Student Self-Test and Review Software	Reteaching Activity 4 Spanish Reteaching Activity 4 Chapter 4 Test Form A and Form B

0:00 *If time does not permit teaching the entire chapter, summarize using the Chapter 4 Highlights on page 79, and the Chapter 4 English (or Spanish) Audiocassettes. Review students' knowledge using the Glencoe MindJogger Videoquiz.*

KEY TO ABILITY LEVELS

Teaching strategies have been coded for varying learning styles and abilities.

L1 **BASIC** activities for all students

L2 **AVERAGE** activities for average to above-average students

L3 **CHALLENGING** activities for above-average students

LEP **LIMITED ENGLISH PROFICIENCY** activities

Performance Assessment

Cultural Development Just as children are often measured on growth charts, a culture's development can also be measured. Have students make growth or development charts for hypothetical cultures. Organize the class into five groups, and give each group a written description of its hypothetical culture's physical environment. Then ask the groups to research the development of two or three actual cultures to give them a sense of the challenges that cultures have faced.

Based on this research, have each group create a development chart for their hypothetical culture, including the impact of such factors as physical environment and outside influences on beliefs, lifestyles, and economic and political organization. Each group's growth chart should be both verbal and visual, indicating milestones in the culture's development. The groups should present their completed growth charts to the class. After all presentations have been given, the class should make inferences about cultural development.

POSSIBLE RUBRIC FEATURES: Concept information, predictive and cause/effect skills, collaborative skills, abilities to see connections and make inferences

For additional professional and classroom resources, see Chapter Resources, pages T46–T51.

TEACHER'S CORNER

NATIONAL GEOGRAPHIC SOCIETY

INDEX TO NATIONAL GEOGRAPHIC MAGAZINE

The following articles may be used for research relating to this chapter:

- "Age of Pyramids: Egypt's Old Kingdom," by David Roberts, January 1995.
- "Recycling," by Noel Grove, July 1994.
- *Water*, a National Geographic Special Edition, November 1993.
- "Once and Future Landfills," by William L. Rathje, May 1991.
- "Iraq: Crucible of Civilization," by Merle Severy, May 1991.
- "Population, Plenty, and Poverty," by Paul L. Ehrlich and Anne H. Ehrlich, December 1988.
- "Hazardous Waste," by Allen A. Boraiko, March 1985.
- "The World's Urban Explosion," by Robert W. Fox, August 1984.
- "Acid Rain: How Great a Menace?" by Anne LaBastille, November 1981.

NATIONAL GEOGRAPHIC SOCIETY PRODUCTS AVAILABLE FROM GLENCOE

To order the following products for use with this chapter, contact your local Glencoe sales representative or call Glencoe at 1-800-334-7344:

- *Picture Atlas of the World* (CD-ROM)
- *Earth's Endangered Environments PictureShow* (CD-ROM)
- *GeoBee* (Software)
- *GTV: Planetary Manager* (Videodisc)

ADDITIONAL NATIONAL GEOGRAPHIC SOCIETY PRODUCTS

To order the following products for use with this chapter, call National Geographic Society at 1-800-368-2728:

- *Ancient Civilizations*, "Africa," "Mesopotamia and Egypt," "Greece," "Rome," "China." (Filmstrip)
- *Pollution: Problems and Prospects*, "The Land," "Air and Water." (Filmstrip)
- *Healing the Earth* (Video)
- *Ozone: Protecting the Invisible Shield* (Video)
- *Pollution: World at Risk* (Video)
- *Recycling: The Endless Circle* (Video)

chapter 4 Environments, Peoples, and Cultures

PERFORMANCE ASSESSMENT

Refer to the Planning Guide on page 62B for a Performance Assessment Activity for this chapter. See the *Performance Assessment Activities* booklet for additional suggestions.

CHAPTER OBJECTIVES

1. **Understand** that humans and the natural environment have an effect on each other.
2. **Recognize** that throughout history people have exchanged ideas and goods.
3. **Understand** that geographers divide the world into culture regions.

GLENCOE TECHNOLOGY

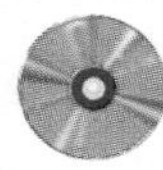

Videodisc

Use Chapter 4 MindJogger Videoquiz to preview chapter content.

MINDJOGGER VIDEOQUIZ

Chapter 4
Disc 1 Side A

The MindJogger Videoquiz is also available on videocassette.

CHAPTER FOCUS

Geographic Setting

More than 5.5 billion people live on the earth. Their ways of life make up a complex pattern of learned customs, beliefs, and actions.

▲ Photograph: *Rice field after a harvest, Japan*

Geographic Themes

Section 1 Limits and Opportunities
HUMAN/ENVIRONMENT INTERACTION Humans and the natural environment have an effect on each other.

Section 2 Cultural Expressions
MOVEMENT Throughout history peoples have exchanged ideas and goods.

Section 3 World Culture Regions Today
REGION Geographers divide the world into culture regions.

EXTRA CREDIT PROJECT

Public Opinion Survey Have students ask friends and family members the following questions: What are the essential elements of our civilization? What would you bring to a colony on Mars to preserve our civilization among the colonists? Tell students to record the answers on an audiotape or a videotape and to play the tape for the class.

SECTION 1

Limits and Opportunities

SETTING THE SCENE

Read to Discover . . .
- the differences between developed countries and developing countries.
- the challenges that rapid population growth brings to the planet.
- the impact of environmental hazards on people's lives.

Key Terms
- culture
- subsistence farming
- population distribution
- population density
- tornado
- hurricane
- tsunami
- pollution

Identify and Locate
Canada, Bangladesh, Tornado Alley, Armenia

Culture is the way of life of a group of people with common traditions, interests, and beliefs. A society's culture includes the way in which people meet their needs. The culture of a society also includes its history, government, language, religious beliefs, art, literature, and music.

HUMAN/ENVIRONMENT INTERACTION

Making a Living

Cultures are shaped by the various ways groups of people meet their economic needs. At least 10,000 years ago, agriculture, the earliest form of economic activity, began to develop. Eventually early farmers stopped moving from place to place and began to farm the same land from one season to the next. Successful farmers produced a surplus of food. Because everyone no longer had to raise their own food, some people started to specialize, or do one kind of work, such as weaving or milling grain. They traded their goods and services for the surplus food of farmers. The exchange of goods and services was easier when people gathered in one place. Therefore, villages, towns, and cities often began and grew where trade routes crossed.

Agriculture

Today about half of the world's people still make their living through agriculture. There are two ways to classify agriculture—traditional and commercial. Traditional agriculture, or **subsistence farming**, depends heavily on human labor, animal power, and basic farm

Geographic Themes

Place: Guatemala, Central America
Farmers gather to sell their produce in an outdoor market in the Central American country of Guatemala. *About how many people in the world make their living through agriculture?*

LESSON PLAN
Chapter 4, Section 1

FOCUS

SECTION OBJECTIVES

1. **Distinguish** between developed countries and developing countries.
2. **Appreciate** the challenges that rapid population growth brings to the planet.
3. **Examine** the impact of environmental hazards on people's lives.

BELLRINGER MOTIVATIONAL ACTIVITY

Project the Section 1 Focus Transparency and have students answer the questions.

PRETEACHING VOCABULARY

Explain that *subsistence farming* means "growing only enough food to live on." Then ask students to hypothesize about the meaning of commercial farming. *(growing food for sale)*

Use the Vocabulary PuzzleMaker Software to create a crossword or word search puzzle.

USING ILLUSTRATIONS

PLACE Guatemala is covered with rich volcanic soil, which is not surprising since the country has more than 30 volcanoes in an area about the size of Ohio.

Answer to Caption: *half*

Classroom Resources for Section 1

BLACKLINE MASTERS:
Reproducible Lesson Plan 4-1
Guided Reading Activity 4-1
Section Quiz 4-1

TRANSPARENCIES:
Section Focus Transparency 4-1
Political Map Transparency 12
Unit Map Overlay Transparency 1-6

MULTIMEDIA:

Vocabulary PuzzleMaker Software
Testmaker

Geography and the Environment GTV: Planetary Manager

TEACH

GUIDED PRACTICE

L2 Discuss Have students discuss the pros and cons of living in a developed country. After their discussion, ask them if living in a developing country has pros as well as cons. Have them explain their answers.

INDEPENDENT PRACTICE

Guided Reading Have students complete Guided Reading Activity 4-1 in the TCR. LEP

USING MAPS

Answers:
1. the United States and Europe;
2. subsistence farming;
3. northern Europe;
4. nomadic herding

Map Skills Practice

Drawing Conclusions
Which economic activities cover the most area in the United States? *(agriculture and livestock raising)*

GLENCOE TECHNOLOGY

Videodisc

Use the following to enrich Chapter 4:

GEOGRAPHY AND THE ENVIRONMENT
THE INFINITE VOYAGE
Living with Disaster

Chapter 7
Disc 3 Side A

Title: ***Documenting Tragedy—Developing a Cure; Soviet Armenia***

THE WORLD: ECONOMIC ACTIVITY

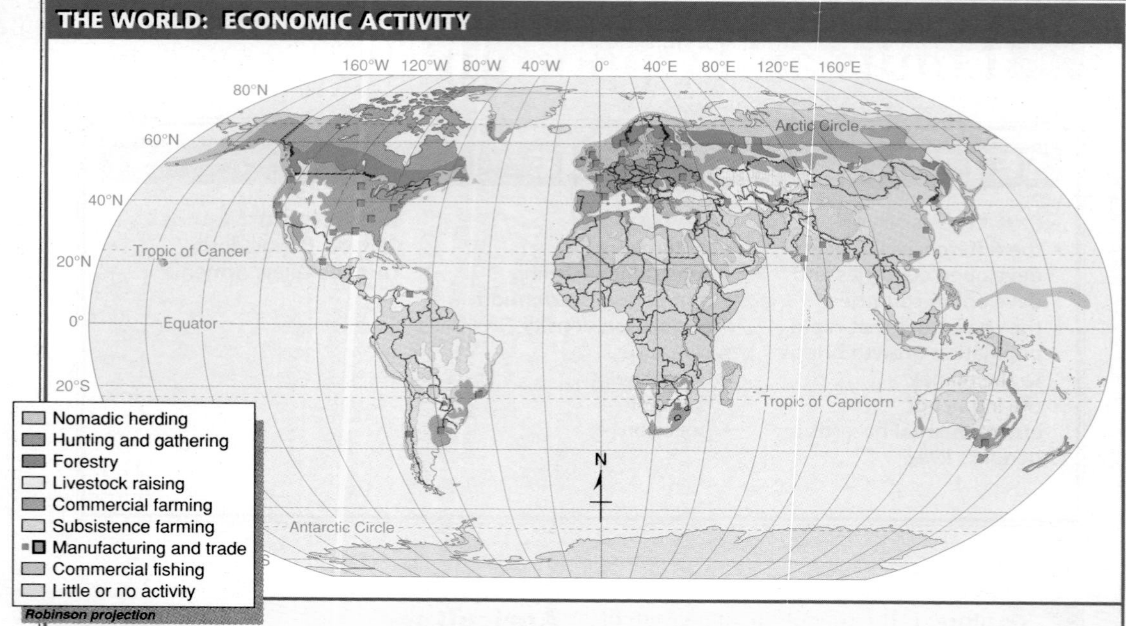

FOCUS ON GEOGRAPHIC THEMES

1. **Location: Where are the world's heavily industrialized areas located?**
2. **Region: What is the principal form of economic activity in Africa?**
3. **Region: What part of Europe is heavily forested?**
4. **Place: What is the principal form of economic activity in central Asia?**

tools. Traditional farmers usually grow just enough food for themselves. If they are fortunate enough to have a very good crop or have extra livestock, they may sell or trade it; however, most of their efforts involve growing food to eat, not to sell. Most farmers in the world are traditional farmers.

In commercial agriculture, food crops and animals are produced chiefly for sale. Modern fertilizers, pesticides—chemicals used to control pests—and machinery are used to produce crops. Commercial farmers can farm large areas of land using little human labor.

Industry

A business that produces goods or services is called an industry. The number and kinds of industries vary from country to country. Countries that produce great quantities of goods and services and employ many of their workers in industry are known as developed countries. People in these countries use science to improve their technology and to build well-developed economies. Developed countries generally have adequate food, clothing, and housing as well as good health care and education for their people.

People in many countries in the world meet their needs in much the same way their ancestors did. These countries, known as developing countries, often do not have modern technology and industries. Most lack the money, resources, and skilled workers needed for economic growth. Although populations in their cities have rapidly increased, developing countries are still mainly rural, and the majority of their workers are traditional farm-

Cooperative Learning Activity

Assign pairs of students the name of a different country. (Avoid countries such as India and China with population densities in the thousands.) Direct students to find their country's population density in an almanac or other source. Then give each pair a linoleum tile or cardboard about 12 inches square, and tell them that the square represents a square mile in their country. Next, pass out dried beans, saying that the beans represent people. Tell them to glue as many beans on their square as people in a square mile. Have students label the squares with the names of the countries and display them on a table in the classroom. Explain that these models are not to scale; even so, they show the countries' comparative densities.

ers. Developing countries often have a poor distribution of income, clothing, and housing. Few people get proper health care or attend school, and life expectancy is relatively short.

REGION

Population Growth and Distribution

The world's population is more than 5.5 billion and growing rapidly. Scientists estimate that by the year 2000 it will be more than 6.3 billion; and by 2025, more than 8.5 billion.

Growth Rates

The world's population, however, is not growing at the same rate in every country. A country's population growth rate is largely based on the relationship between its birthrate and its death rate. The birthrate is the number of births per year for every 1,000 people. The death rate is the number of deaths per year for every 1,000 people. The difference between those two rates is the natural growth rate.

When the two rates are more or less equal, a country has reached what is called zero population growth. This situation exists in some highly industrialized countries today. In less industrialized countries, however, birthrates are still high, while death rates have fallen because of improved health and living conditions. Population in these countries is growing rapidly compared with the overall world growth rate.

Rapid population growth presents many challenges. As the number of people grows, so does the difficulty of producing enough food to feed them. The birthrates of developing countries are higher than the birthrates of developed countries. Developing countries, however, already have shortages of food, clothing, and housing. Rapidly growing populations in these countries only heighten the problems. Another challenge that faces the world as a result of rapid population growth is the increasing rate at which nonrenewable resources are being used up.

Population Distribution

The **population distribution,** or the population pattern, of the world shows that the continents are not evenly populated. About a third of the earth's surface is land. Mountains, deserts, and climatic extremes, however, make about half of this land nearly uninhabitable. Therefore, almost everyone on earth lives on a relatively small percentage of the earth's surface. Most people live where the soil is fertile, water is available, and the climate is favorable for growing crops and raising animals.

Population Density

Population density—the average number of people in a square mile or square kilometer—varies widely from country to country. Some countries have a low population density; others have many people crowded into a relatively small area. For example, Canada has about 8 people per square mile (3 people per sq. km), while the country of Bangladesh has about 2,320 people per square mile (895 people per sq. km).

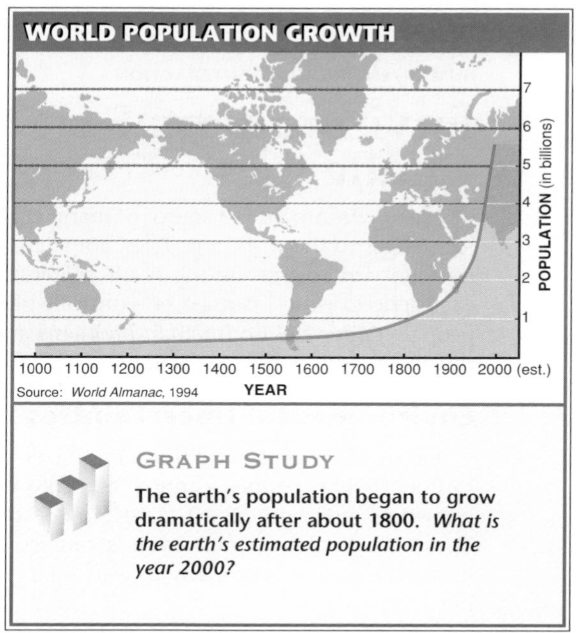

GRAPH STUDY

The earth's population began to grow dramatically after about 1800. ***What is the earth's estimated population in the year 2000?***

L1 Making Maps Ask students to clip news stories of natural disasters. Post the stories on a large outline map of the world made by tracing a projection of Political Map Transparency 12. Supply a different colored push pin for each kind of disaster: red for hurricanes, blue for tornadoes, etc., so students can see at a glance what happened where.

USING GRAPHS

Answer: more than 6.3 billion

Skills Practice

Reading a Graph How many times larger is the world population today than the world population in 1800? *(5.5 times larger)*

CURRICULUM CONNECTION

ECONOMICS

To many people in developing countries, large families mean economic security. More children help earn more wages to support the family and to take care of parents in their later years.

Meeting Special Needs

Language Deficient Students with language problems often have difficulty seeing differences among words with similar uses. For example, they are often called on to "identify," "discuss," and "explain." Point out that "identifying" usually involves listing by category, "discussing" requires giving pros and cons, and "explaining" requires giving reasons in complete form. Provide opportunities for identification, discussion, and explanation in the context of the lesson.

L3 Compare Refer students to the most recent *Information Please Environmental Almanac* to find the amount of toxic wastes their state and five others release each year. Then tell students to compare the states in the form of a bar graph.

USING MAPS

Answers:
1. most of Europe and southern and southeastern Asia; **2.** the central part and southern tip of South America, the southern part of Africa, and much of Australia; **3.** Tokyo, Osaka; **4.** Los Angeles, New York

Map Skills Practice
Reading a Map Which city in Africa has more than 5 million people? *(Cairo)*

DID YOU KNOW?

When a natural disaster hits, relief agencies need to know exactly where to send food, medicine, and blankets. Maps were indispensable in 1988 after an earthquake devastated Armenia and in 1989 after Hurricane Hugo whipped through South Carolina.

ASSESS

CHECK FOR UNDERSTANDING

Assign Section 1 Review as homework or an in-class activity.

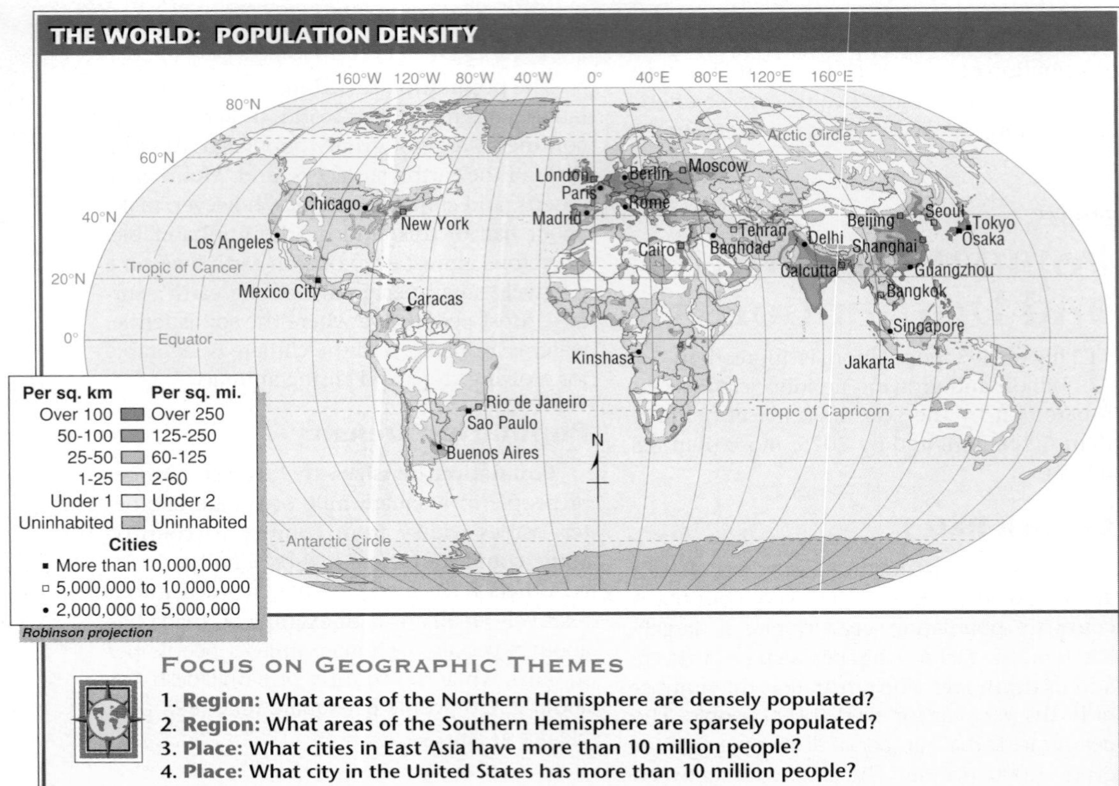

FOCUS ON GEOGRAPHIC THEMES

1. **Region:** What areas of the Northern Hemisphere are densely populated?
2. **Region:** What areas of the Southern Hemisphere are sparsely populated?
3. **Place:** What cities in East Asia have more than 10 million people?
4. **Place:** What city in the United States has more than 10 million people?

HUMAN/ENVIRONMENT INTERACTION

Environmental Challenges

The environment is a source of many challenges to the world's peoples. Some environmental problems are the result of natural occurrences, which cannot be controlled by people. Other environmental problems are the direct result of people's actions.

Environmental Uncertainties

Occurrences and conditions in the environment that people cannot control are known as environmental hazards, or sources of danger. Environmental hazards can result in damage or loss of property, as well as loss of life.

Weather is often the cause of environmental hazards. One type of weather-related hazard is a **tornado**, a powerful, whirling windstorm. The tornado is the most violent of all storms. It may last several hours or just a few minutes and can measure up to 1.5 miles (2.4 km) in diameter. The winds of a tornado, rotating at up to 300 miles (483 km) per hour, destroy almost everything in their path. Only the strongest buildings made of steel and concrete can escape great damage. In the United States, an area of land about 460 miles (740 km) long and 400 miles (644 km) wide extending from northern Texas through Oklahoma, Kansas, and Missouri is known as Tornado Alley. More tornadoes occur annually here than in any other place on the earth.

Another kind of weather-related hazard is a **hurricane**, a powerful, whirling storm that

Critical Thinking

Analyzing Information Copy the following statements on the chalkboard:
(1) Developing nations must limit their population to curb world pollution.
(2) Developed nations must cut back on their consumption of fuel and other goods to stop pollution.
(3) Both types of nations must change to save the air and water.

Have students analyze the information in the section to help them determine with which statement they agree. Then have them write a paragraph defending their position, using the statement that they choose from the chalkboard as the topic sentence, and facts from the section as supporting details.

forms over oceans. Unlike a tornado, a hurricane measures several hundred miles (or km) in diameter. The winds and rain of a hurricane combine with the forces of the sea to produce huge waves, called storm surges. The environmental importance of hurricanes lies in the extent of destruction that they can bring to islands and coastal areas.

Earthquakes are another kind of environmental hazard. Most earthquakes are mild and occur beneath the sea. Earthquakes that occur near large cities, however, can result in much damage and loss of life. A disastrous earthquake in Armenia in 1988 resulted in more than 50,000 deaths and 130,000 injuries. Earthquakes occurring primarily under the ocean can result in **tsunami**, or ocean waves. These waves can cause additional damage where they sweep up onto land.

Eruptions of volcanoes and lava flows are severe environmental hazards. Volcanic eruptions have resulted in loss of life and the destruction of towns and cities.

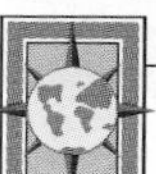

Geographic Themes

Human/Environment Interaction: Kansas, United States
A whirling tornado sweeps across Sumner County in the state of Kansas. Many tornadoes occur yearly in central parts of the United States. *What effect do tornadoes have on an area?*

Pollution

A serious environmental problem today is **pollution**—unclean or impure elements in the environment. Pollution affects the air, the water, and the land.

Most air pollution is caused by burning fossil fuels. Burning fuel gives off poisonous gases and tiny particles of solid or liquid matter. Homes, industries, and motor vehicles that burn such fuels are the major sources of air pollution. The burning of garbage and trash also contributes to air pollution.

The most harmful result of air pollution is its effect on people's health. The gases and particles in the air burn people's eyes and irritate their lungs. Air pollution can worsen some respiratory diseases, such as bronchitis and asthma, and cause other diseases, such as cancer. Air pollution can also destroy plants and animals and erode the surfaces of buildings.

There are several causes of water pollution. Tankers and offshore drilling accidents sometimes cause oil spills that pollute the water. Industries dump large amounts of waste products, which include chemicals, into bodies of water. Untreated sewage, which is made up of people's wastes and garbage, is another major source of water pollution.

Water pollution harms all living things. Plants and animals cannot live in polluted waters. Polluted water is also very harmful to people's health. Higher-level living organisms often store up pollutants obtained by eating lower-level organisms. The pollutants are passed upward in the food chain. Eventually the food eaten by humans may be poisoned to a dangerous level.

Soil pollution involves damage to the thin layer of fertile soil that covers a large portion of the earth's land. Fertilizers and pesticides are the main causes of soil pollution. Soil pollution can damage and contaminate fertile soils that are necessary for growing the world's food.

Extending the Content

Human/Environment Interaction Many people think, "The solution to pollution is dilution." So each year, factories and cities dump 8 trillion tons of industrial and sewage wastes into waterways that carry it to the ocean. Water runoff from farms adds fertilizers and pesticides to ocean water. Even nuclear wastes were dumped in the oceans before the 1980s. Pollution has closed beaches, destroyed aquatic ecosystems, contaminated fisheries, and eliminated species of sea life. Under the Ocean Dumping Act of 1972, the Environmental Protection Agency (EPA) has the power to regulate ocean pollution.

USING ILLUSTRATIONS

HUMAN/ENVIRONMENT INTERACTION In April 1991, seven Midwestern states experienced more than 70 tornadoes.

Answer to Caption: *They destroy almost everything in their path.*

MEETING LESSON OBJECTIVES

Each objective below is tested by the questions that follow it in parentheses.

1. Distinguish between developed countries and developing countries. *(3)*
2. Appreciate the challenges that rapid population growth brings to the planet. *(4)*
3. Examine the impact of environmental hazards on people's lives. *(4)*

EVALUATE

Assign the Section 1 Quiz in the TCR.

Use the Testmaker to create a customized quiz for Section 1.

RETEACH

Ask three questions for each subhead in the section. Have students find the answers in the material under the subheads.

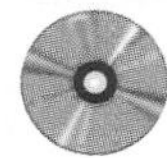

Videodisc

GTV: PLANETARY MANAGER

Side 2, Chapter 5
Frames 25236-31905
Title: *Tidy World*
Subject: Solid wastes and how we might clean up the Earth

ENRICH

Recommend that students read *Earth in the Balance: Ecology and the Human Spirit* by Albert Gore, Jr.

CLOSE

Ask students who garden to raise their hand. Have them explain how their lives would differ if they had to subsist on the food they raise, as do many families in developing countries.

USING ILLUSTRATIONS

PLACE Hawaii is not the only state with active volcanoes. Besides Washington (with Mount St. Helens), Alaska has at least 5 volcanoes that have erupted in the past 20 years.

Answer to Caption: *Volcanic eruptions can cause air pollution, the loss of life, and the destruction of towns and cities.*

NATIONAL GEOGRAPHIC SOCIETY

Videodisc

GTV: PLANETARY MANAGER

Side 1, Chapter 8
Frames 37896-41785
Title: ***Making a Difference***
Subject: People who have tried to make a difference in solving environmental problems

GTV: PLANETARY MANAGER

Side 1, Chapter 9
Frames 41787-47422
Title: ***Where You Gonna Go?***
Subject: Music that reinforces the message that if we continue to harm our environment, there will be no safe place to go

Geographic Themes
Place: Hawaiian Islands
Volcanoes formed the Hawaiian Islands. Hawaii, the largest Hawaiian island, has active volcanoes, including Mount Kilauea. *How do volcanoes, such as Mount Kilauea, pose an environmental hazard?*

Solid wastes are a major form of land pollution. People throw out billions of tons of solid wastes each year. Examples of solid wastes are used tires, cans, plastics, and scrap metal. Some of this waste ends up littering roadsides and floating in streams. Many solid wastes end up in open dumps. These dumps provide areas for disease-carrying animals, such as rats, to breed.

Many industrial processes create toxic or hazardous wastes. Nuclear power plants, for example, create radioactive wastes that must be stored properly if they are not to become a threat to society. Poisonous chemical wastes, all too often dumped in streams and ditches, have caused people to get sick and have led to birth defects. They also have contributed to the rise in cancer and other life-shortening diseases.

Attempts at Cleanup

People have developed different ways to control pollution. One way is to use fuels that cause less air pollution. Other ways include removing chemicals from the wastes dumped into water, and improving water treatment facilities. The use of organic farming instead of fertilizers and pesticides helps control soil pollution. Recycling is another step that has been taken to lessen pollution.

Attempts at Regulation

National and local governments in many countries have taken steps to control pollution. Laws have been passed that limit the harmful materials that automobiles and industries can put into the environment. Funds have been established to conduct research into ways of controlling pollution.

SECTION 1 REVIEW

Checking for Understanding

1. **Define** culture, subsistence farming, population distribution, population density, tornado, hurricane, tsunami, pollution.
2. **Locating Places** Where is Tornado Alley located?
3. **Region** Why is industry more important in developed countries than it is in developing countries?
4. **Human/Environment Interaction** What factors have contributed to the pollution of air and water?

Critical Thinking

5. **Making Comparisons** How does traditional agriculture compare with commercial farming?

ANSWERS TO SECTION 1 REVIEW

1. **culture:** way of life of a people; **subsistence farming:** farming with basic tools; **population distribution:** population pattern; **population density:** average number of people in a square mile; **tornado:** windstorm that forms over land; **hurricane:** windstorm that forms over an ocean; **tsunami:** tidal wave; **pollution:** impure elements in the environment
2. from northern Texas through Oklahoma, Kansas, and Missouri
3. Developed economies depend on industry.
4. the burning of fossil fuels, the spilling of oil, and the dumping of industrial wastes
5. Traditional agriculture employs basic tools, and the farmer consumes most of the crop; commercial agriculture uses machines and chemicals, and the crop is sold.

2 SECTION Cultural Expressions

SETTING THE SCENE

Read to Discover . . .
- how the first civilizations developed.
- the ways in which the movement of people, goods, and ideas has caused cultural change.
- the factors that have contributed to cultural contact and cultural barriers.

Key Terms
- civilization
- history
- prehistory
- culture hearth
- cultural diffusion

Identify and Locate
Egypt, Iraq, Pakistan, China, Greece

A society expresses its culture through such things as language, religion, and the arts. From the beginning of time, people developed different ways of expressing their cultures.

REGION

Cultural Origins

Over the centuries, many cultures have built cities, developed writing systems, and achieved varying kinds of development in the arts, sciences, government, and business. These cultures are often called **civilizations.**

Learning From the Past

Before the rise of civilizations, people focused their attention on meeting basic needs and did not leave many written records. Some of the records they did leave were written in a form that is not understood by people today. Studying the written information about a people's past to learn what, how, and why things happened is called **history.** The time in a people's past before written records were kept is known as **prehistory.**

Geographers have learned about the prehistory of different groups of people with the help of other scientists called archaeologists. Archaeologists study the sites where people once lived, looking for evidence left by these people. Such evidence includes things like buildings and ruins of buildings, bones, and artifacts. Artifacts are objects that were made or used by people, such as weapons, tools, and pottery. Sometimes only bits and pieces of artifacts are found. Archaeologists use artifacts to look for hints about the way people lived before written history. These hints show how cultures developed at certain locations and times.

Culture Hearths

Four ancient civilizations made special contributions to world cultures. These civilizations developed in areas of the world known today as Egypt, Iraq, Pakistan, and China. These areas are known as **culture hearths**, or places where civilizations began.

These culture hearths had certain common geographic features that were helpful for the beginning of early agriculture. Each location was characterized by a mild climate and fertile lands. Each civilization was near a major river. The people discovered ways to make use of these good conditions. For example, they dug canals and ditches in order to use the rivers to

LESSON PLAN
Chapter 4, Section 2

FOCUS

SECTION OBJECTIVES

1. **Describe** how the first civilizations developed.
2. **Discuss** the ways in which the movement of people, goods, and ideas has caused cultural change.
3. **Identify** the factors that have contributed to cultural contact and cultural barriers.

BELLRINGER MOTIVATIONAL ACTIVITY

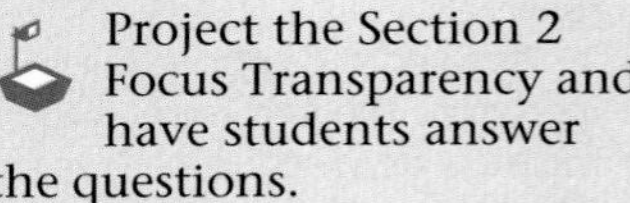
Project the Section 2 Focus Transparency and have students answer the questions.

PRETEACHING VOCABULARY

Tell students that sometimes *hearth* means "home." Then ask them to hypothesize about why *hearth* is used in culture hearth.

TEACH

GUIDED PRACTICE

L1 Study Strategy Have students close the book and write a summary of what they read after finishing each subhead.

MULTICULTURAL PERSPECTIVE

Cultural Diffusion
The oldest marbles ever found were artifacts from the 5000-year-old grave of an Egyptian child.

Classroom Resources for Section 2

BLACKLINE MASTERS:
Reproducible Lesson Plan 4-2
Guided Reading Activity 4-2
Spanish Guided Reading Activity 4-2
Vocabulary Activity 4
Spanish Vocabulary Activity 4
Workbook Activity 4-2
Section Quiz 4-2

TRANSPARENCIES:
Section Focus Transparency 4-2
World History & Art Transparencies 1, 2, 3, 4, 5, and 6

MULTIMEDIA:

Testmaker

GTV: Planetary Manager
STV: Atmosphere
Geography and the Environment

INDEPENDENT PRACTICE

Guided Reading Have students complete Guided Reading Activity 4-2 in the TCR. **LEP**

USING ILLUSTRATIONS

MOVEMENT Today the Chinese rely on their army—the largest in the world—rather than the Great Wall to keep out foreign invaders. Three million Chinese are under arms, and 5 million are in reserve.

Answer to Caption: *It increased the fear and mistrust between the Chinese and other peoples.*

ASSESS

CHECK FOR UNDERSTANDING

Assign Section 2 Review as homework or an in-class activity.

MEETING LESSON OBJECTIVES

Each objective below is tested by the questions that follow it in parentheses.

1. **Describe** how the first civilizations developed. *(2)*
2. **Discuss** the ways in which the movement of people, goods, and ideas has caused cultural change. *(4)*
3. **Identify** the factors that have contributed to cultural contact and cultural barriers. *(3, 5)*

irrigate the land. In this way, people were able to grow surplus crops.

MOVEMENT

Cultural Change

Cultures often are changed by both internal and outside influences. Within a specific culture, discoveries and inventions can promote change. Outside influences come through **cultural diffusion**, or the spread of people, ideas, practices, and goods from one culture to another.

Cultural Contacts

Travel and trade are two age-old activities that have encouraged cultural contacts among different groups of people. As a culture developed better ways of moving over land and water, its trade increased. Inventions like the magnetic compass improved navigation and led to the exploration of new lands. Consequently, contacts were made among many cultures.

Many times people migrated, or made a permanent move to live in another place. Throughout history, migrations have generally occurred as a reaction to natural or political conditions. The Ice Age, for example, caused people to move to warmer climates. People have also migrated to avoid harsh governments, wars, religious persecutions, and famines.

When people migrate, they carry their culture with them. In their new homelands their ideas and ways of doing things generally become mixed with the ideas and ways of the people already living there.

Cultural Barriers

While some factors have encouraged cultural contact, others have created barriers to it. Natural barriers, such as huge deserts, high mountains, dense rain forests, and unknown ocean waters, have sometimes restricted the movement of goods and ideas between cultures.

People have also created cultural barriers. Such barriers generally come about because of

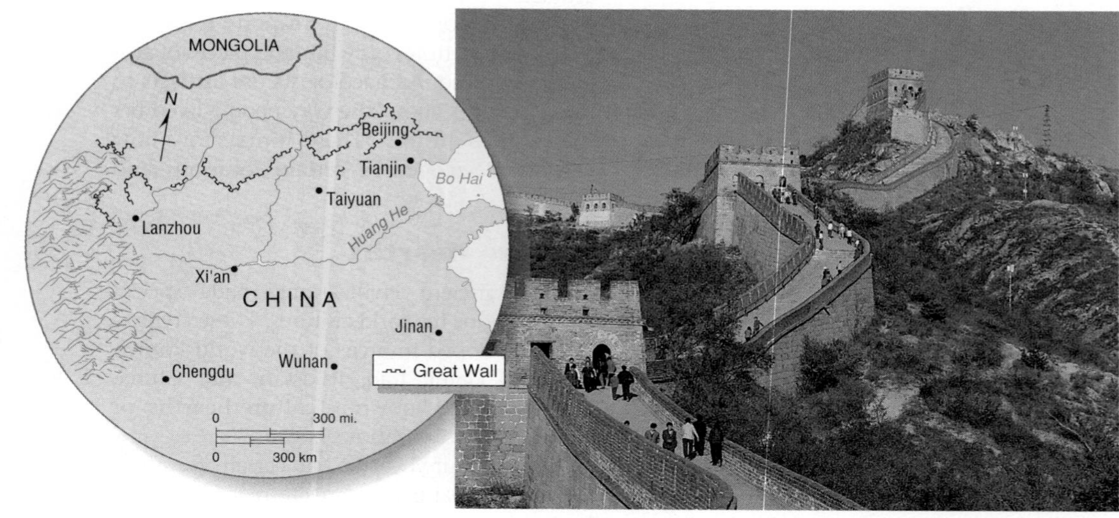

Geographic Themes

Movement: Northern China

The early Chinese built the Great Wall in the northern part of their country to keep out foreign invaders. *What impact did the Great Wall have on Chinese relations with the outside world?*

Cooperative Learning Activity

Organize the class into groups. Tell each group to imagine a civilization and to list its artistic and intellectual characteristics. Then have group members find or make artifacts, such as jewelry and books, that give clues to these characteristics and bury the artifacts in a box of sand. Direct the groups to exchange boxes, to dig up the artifacts, and to draw conclusions about the civilizations based on the clues. Allow time for the groups to discuss their conclusions with one another.

CULTURE HEARTHS

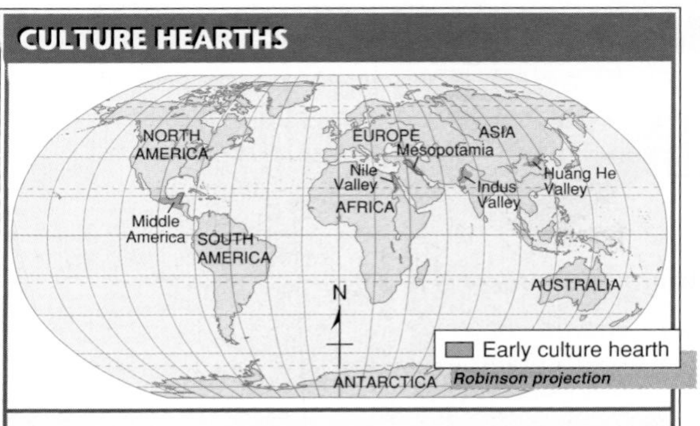

FOCUS ON GEOGRAPHIC THEMES

1. **Region:** What culture hearths emerged in Asia?
2. **Region:** On what continent did the Nile Valley culture hearth develop?

people's beliefs. One culture might not understand or accept another culture's activities or viewpoints. This lack of understanding leads to fear or mistrust. Such feelings encouraged the ancient Chinese to build their Great Wall to keep others from crossing their boundaries.

Today the barriers posed by distance and natural features are gradually disappearing. Technology enables people to speak to others almost anywhere in the world. Satellites broadcast television signals around the globe. As modern communications systems spread more information, cultural exchange will increase.

Far-reaching Changes

Peoples and their cultures change and evolve through time. Historians have labeled periods of time when change has taken place on a large scale and created a great impact. The time when European countries were exploring the world, for example, is called the Age of Discovery. The mobility of this period encouraged cultural diffusion.

The Industrial Revolution was another time of great change. Power-driven machinery and mass production were introduced at a rapid pace. This led to great changes in the economies of many countries, since goods could be produced quickly and cheaply. The Industrial Revolution also led to social changes. Many people moved to large cities in order to get jobs in factories.

Historians also have labeled periods when great ideas are stressed. One such period is known as the Age of Classical Greece. This period is known for its democratic ideas of government and for its great achievements in art. The Renaissance (REN•uh•SAHNTS), meaning rebirth, is the name given to a period that took place hundreds of years after the time of classical Greece. During the Renaissance, many ideas of early civilizations were reintroduced, and there was a great search for knowledge that led to many changes in the arts, the sciences, and education.

At certain times in history, ideas about government have been rethought. People often wanted more freedom from their rulers. Sometimes, the desire for freedom led to revolutions, or complete changes in government in short periods of time. An age of nationalism also developed. Nationalism involves loyalty and devotion to country. Before the development of nationalism, people generally expressed their loyalty to individual rulers. Nationalism includes a people's pride in their heritage, or those things handed on to people from their ancestors. A people's history and culture are a part of their heritage.

SECTION 2 REVIEW

Checking for Understanding

1. **Define** civilization, history, prehistory, culture hearth, cultural diffusion.
2. **Locating Places** Where did the earliest civilizations develop?
3. **Movement** What factors have affected contact between cultures?
4. **Movement** How have cultural changes had far-reaching effects?

Critical Thinking

5. **Identifying Central Issues** Why do people create cultural barriers?

EVALUATE

 Assign the Section 2 Quiz in the TCR.

 Use the Testmaker to create a customized quiz for Section 2.

RETEACH

Copy the subheads on the chalkboard and have students list details from the section under each subhead.

ENRICH

Display pictures of artifacts such as Egyptian hieroglyphs.

CLOSE

Ask students which era listed in the section they would most like to visit and why.

USING MAPS

Answers: **1.** Mesopotamia, Indus Valley, and Huang He; **2.** Africa

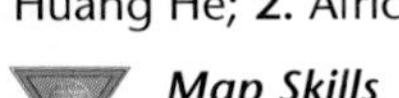

Map Skills Practice

Interpretation What water feature do the hearths have in common? *(rivers)*

ANSWERS TO SECTION 2 REVIEW

1. civilization: culture that has reached a high level of development; **history:** the study of written information about a people's past; **prehistory:** the time in a people's past before written records were kept; **culture hearth:** place where a civilization began; **cultural diffusion:** the spread of people, ideas, and goods from one culture to another

2. in what is today Egypt, Iraq, Pakistan, and China

3. travel, trade, and migration

4. They have influenced political geography, ideas about government, national economies, the development of technology, and shifting population patterns.

5. lack of understanding that leads to fear or mistrust

FOCUS

Share the following information with students before beginning to read:

Too much of the sun's ultraviolet radiation causes:

- skin cancer, including a kind that can be fatal;
- eye cataracts, which cloud the vision and can cause blindness;
- weakening of the human body's immune system.

TEACH

L1 Identify When students have completed reading, have them identify the ozone layer and explain its importance to Earth.

L2 Drawing Conclusions Share with students the information under Did You Know? Ask them to draw conclusions about the ultimate fate of plant and marine life should the ozone continue to be destroyed. *(end of life on Earth as we know it)* Require students to support their conclusions with data from the case study.

Videodisc

STV: ATMOSPHERE

Side 1, Chapter 2
Frames 29261-31674
Title: ***Atmosphere in Action***
Subject: Ozone

GTV: PLANETARY MANAGER

Side 2, Chapter 3
Frames 12206-18752
Title: ***Caution: Sunny Days Ahead***
Subject: The threat of ozone depletion and our response to it

CASE STUDY

OUT OF OZONE

Though the news keeps breaking, good and bad, the Montreal Protocol is a real achievement. For once, nations worked together to prevent an environmental catastrophe instead of trying haplessly to repair one that has already happened.

The Global Citizen, 1991

In March 1985, British scientists announced that they had recorded a steady loss of ozone in the upper atmosphere during the previous 10 years. NASA confirmed the British report. Later in the year, American scientists added alarming figures of their own: ozone above Antarctica was depleted 40 to 60 percent.

Discovery of the "ozone hole," as the media dubbed it, shocked the world. Scientific teams around the globe began a burst of research and environmental and diplomatic activities to push national governments into action.

In September of 1987, representatives from 46 countries met in Montreal, Canada, to consider the proposal. From this meeting came the Montreal Protocol, the first multinational treaty to curb a global air pollutant.

THE ISSUE

The Montreal Protocol called on the world's nations to cut in half their use of chemicals proven devastating to the ozone layer. Developed nations, accounting for 97 percent of such use, supported the treaty. Many had already begun to search for substitute chemicals.

Developing nations, however, protested the treaty. They pointed out that the chemicals in question were so widely used in their growing industries that to cut their use would stop economic progress in their countries. In addition, they said, their governments could not afford the costs of finding substitutes.

THE BACKGROUND

The ozone layer is a "buffer zone" of pale blue gas between 14 and 15 miles up in the atmosphere. It protects the earth from the sun's deadly ultraviolet rays.

The same studies that exposed the ozone hole also exposed the factor destroying it: *chlorofluorocarbons* (CFCs). CFCs are "wonder" gases that do not rust, explode, burn, or pose immediate dangers to users. They are found in refrigerators, air conditioners, fire extinguishers, plastic foams, aerosol sprays, and many other products. CFCs, however, are very hard to contain. Millions are produced every year, and most find their way to the upper atmosphere. There they devour highly unstable ozone molecules.

Most scientists agree, however, that ozone-damaging CFCs will remain in the atmosphere for 75 years.

THE POINTS OF VIEW

Developing nations, led by China, India, and Brazil, protested that cutting CFC use would considerably hurt their economic progress. In China, for example, refrigerator production is the fastest growing sector of their economy. Besides, developing nations used only a small percentage of CFCs: China, India, and Brazil—the 3 largest—account

Extending the Content

Human/Environment Interaction Using the material in the case study, as well as the additional information in **Did You Know?,** have students produce labeled illustrations showing the causes and effects of the loss of the ozone layer. Encourage students to use science almanacs or yearbooks to find additional information and figures to make their illustrations more graphically arresting.

HOW CFCs DESTROY OZONE

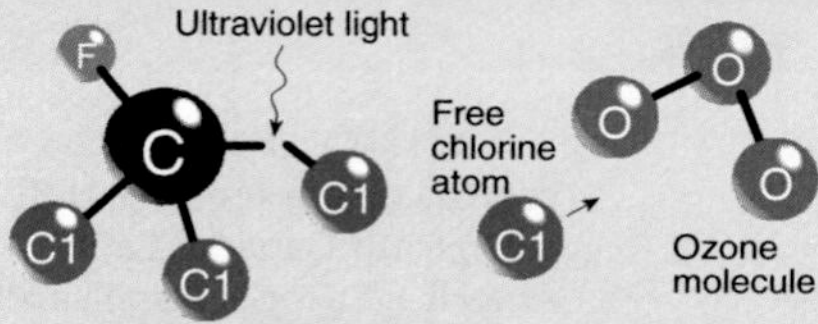

Free chlorine atom

Ozone molecule

Chlorine monoxide

Oxygen molecule

Chlorofluorocarbon molecule

Carbon, fluorine, and chlorine atoms make up CFC molecules. Ultraviolet rays break chlorine atoms free.

A free chlorine atom "steals" an oxygen atom from an ozone molecule.

Oxygen and the chlorine atoms then form a molecule of chlorine monoxide. The two remaining oxygen atoms form an oxygen molecule.

The chlorine monoxide molecule can break up again and again to "eat" more ozone molecules. A single atom of chlorine can devour 100,000 molecules of ozone!

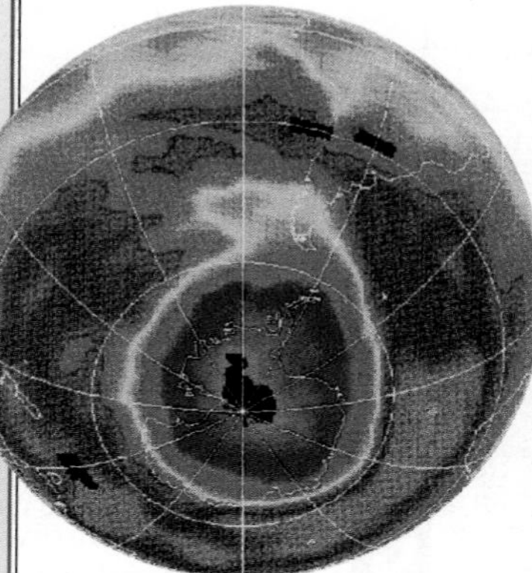

A computer-generated image shows the "hole" that has appeared in the ozone layer above Antarctica.

for 2 percent of the world's CFC use. A Chinese environmental official stated, "Developed countries are responsible for most of the damage to the ozone layer so they should do the most to clean up the problem."

Without that buffer, more of the sun's ultraviolet rays would reach the earth. Such rays cause skin cancer and eye cataracts, weaken the body's immune system, and harm plants, wildlife, and marine food chains.

THE ISSUE TODAY

By the end of 1989, continuing reports that the ozone layer was disappearing more rapidly than first thought caused another UN-sponsored meeting. In Helsinki, Finland, delegates from 80 nations revised the Montreal Protocol to completely ban CFC use in industrialized nations by the year 2000, and in developing nations by 2010. Developed countries agreed to establish a global fund to help developing nations find substitute chemicals.

In 1992 both the European Union and the United States announced that their industries would stop the use of CFCs by 1995. Most scientists agree, however, that ozone-damaging CFCs will remain in the atmosphere for 75 years. The ozone layer may not return to its full strength until at least 2100.

Reviewing the Case

1. **What was the final main provision of the Montreal Protocol?**
2. **Why did developing nations object to the treaty's demands?**
3. **Human/Environment**

Interaction What concerns does the Montreal Protocol address?

ANSWERS TO REVIEWING THE CASE

1. that the use of CFCs be halted by the year 2000
2. the businesses using CFCs were necessary for economic well-being; that they had no money to look for substitutes for CFCs; that they contributed very little to the ozone depletion problem
3. the destruction of Earth's ozone layer by CFCs (chlorofluorocarbons)

DID YOU KNOW?

Unchecked ultraviolet radiation interferes with photosynthesis—plants' ability to make their own food.

ASSESS

Have students answer the Reviewing the Case questions on page 73.

CLOSE

Have students share personal opinions about the points of view in the ozone debate. Following the discussion, have students vote for whose point of view they support.

GLENCOE TECHNOLOGY

Videodisc

To further student understanding of the ozone crisis, use the following:

GEOGRAPHY AND THE ENVIRONMENT
THE INFINITE VOYAGE
Crisis in the Atmosphere

Chapter 5
Disc 2 Side A
Title: ***Chlorofluorocarbons and Their Effect on the Ozone Layer***

NATIONAL GEOGRAPHIC SOCIETY

EYE ON THE ENVIRONMENT POSTER SERIES

Display the three posters describing ozone—*Overview*, *Focus Antarctica*, and *A Global Look*. Discussion questions and activities are presented on page 9 of the Poster Series Teacher's Guide.

LESSON PLAN
Chapter 4, Section 3

FOCUS

SECTION OBJECTIVES

1. **Name** the factors that determine the earth's culture regions.
2. **Relate** how other social sciences help geographers determine culture regions.

BELLRINGER MOTIVATIONAL ACTIVITY

Project the Section 3 Focus Transparency and have students answer the questions.

PRETEACHING VOCABULARY

Have students skim the section to find the definitions of the Key Terms. Direct them to use the terms and definitions to create crossword puzzles.

TEACH

GUIDED PRACTICE

L1 Interview Tell students to ask their family members from which culture region they or their ancestors came and to place a dot in that region on a large outline map of the world.

3 SECTION World Culture Regions Today

SETTING THE SCENE

Read to Discover . . .
- what factors are considered to determine the earth's culture regions.
- how other social sciences help geographers determine culture regions.

Key Terms
- culture region
- government
- standard of living
- economic system
- per capita income
- free enterprise
- capitalism
- socialism
- language family
- religion

Identify and Locate
World culture regions: United States and Canada; Latin America; Europe; Russia and the Eurasian Republics; North Africa and Southwest Asia; Africa South of the Sahara; South Asia; East Asia; Southeast Asia; Australia, Oceania, and Antarctica

Geographers often divide the planet into areas called **culture regions.** These culture regions may not have clear boundaries. For this reason geographers with varying viewpoints may use different ways to decide the number of culture regions and the countries included in each. The authors of this book have divided the world into the 10 culture regions shown on the map. Geographers, as well as political scientists, economists, sociologists, and anthropologists, might divide the world into different culture regions based on government, social groups, economic systems, languages, or religions.

REGION

Governments

People who study **governments,** or groups' political systems, are political scientists. The kind of government a society has reflects the values of a culture. Democracy—a form of government in which the people of a country vote for their leaders—shows that the people value individual freedom.

Among some cultures, the power of the government is more important than individual freedom. These governments are called authoritarian governments. A government in which one leader has full power over a country is a dictatorship. Iraq and North Korea are dictatorships.

Some countries combine elements. For example, some countries that have monarchs—kings or queens—also have elected a lawmaking group. This type of government is called a constitutional monarchy.

REGION

Social Groups

Those who study people's relationships to one another in groups are called sociologists. Sociologists study the structure of a society, people's social institutions, and the quality of life in a society.

Sociologists use certain measures to determine how well a society meets its needs. For example, the infant survival rate—the number of babies that live to be 1 year old out of the number of babies born—is often used. This figure and a group's life expectancy, or the average number of years a person can expect to live, show the level of health care. The number of people in a group who can read and write is the literacy rate. This figure shows how

Classroom Resources for Section 3

BLACKLINE MASTERS:
Reproducible Lesson Plan 4-3
Guided Reading Activity 4-3
Spanish Guided Reading Activity 4-3
Workbook Activity 4-3
Enrichment Activity 4
Skill Activity 4
Section Quiz 4-3

TRANSPARENCIES:
Section Focus Transparency 4-3

MULTIMEDIA:

Testmaker

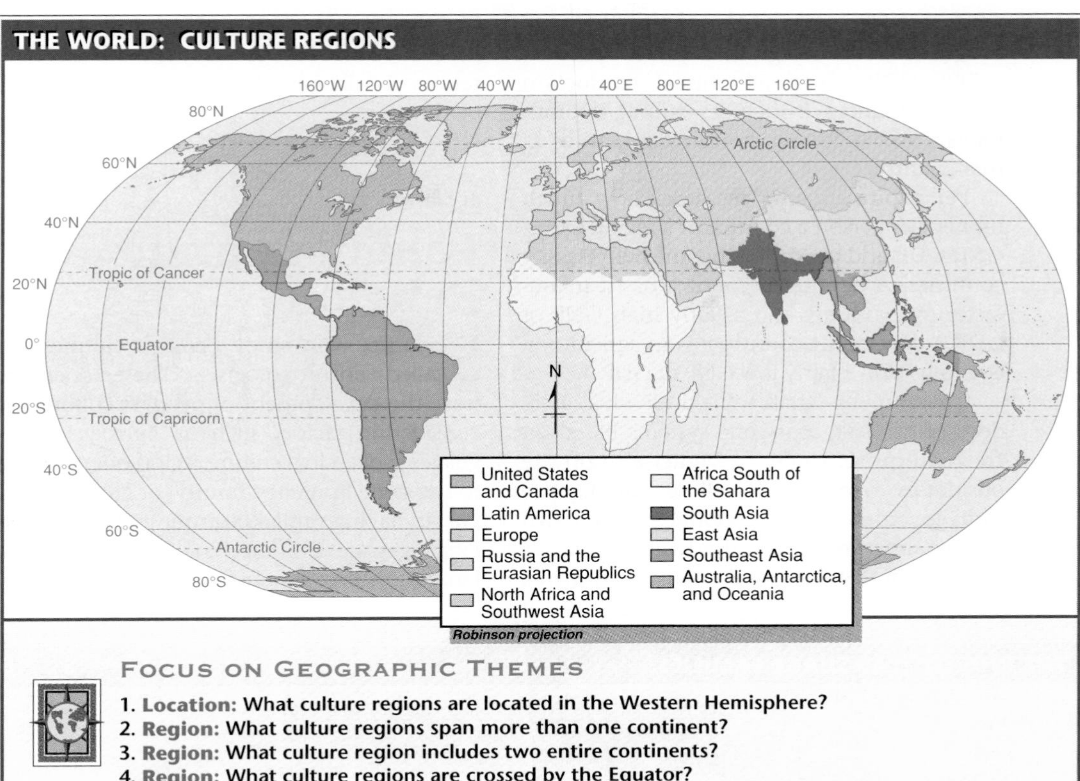

FOCUS ON GEOGRAPHIC THEMES

1. **Location:** What culture regions are located in the Western Hemisphere?
2. **Region:** What culture regions span more than one continent?
3. **Region:** What culture region includes two entire continents?
4. **Region:** What culture regions are crossed by the Equator?

widely people are educated. The **standard of living** measures the quality of life based on available material goods.

Sometimes quality of life is affected by urbanization—the growth of large cities. Rapid growth can be a problem if the city cannot provide such things as food and housing.

REGION

Economic Systems

A country's **economic system** is the way in which the people of the country produce, get, and use goods and services. Economists are people who study and describe how economic systems work.

The value of all goods and services produced annually by the citizens, working inside or outside the country, is the gross national

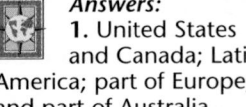

Geographic Themes

Place: Nairobi, Kenya
The African country of Kenya—along with its modern capital, Nairobi—has prospered under a free enterprise economy. *What is the relationship between government and business in a free enterprise economy?*

INDEPENDENT PRACTICE

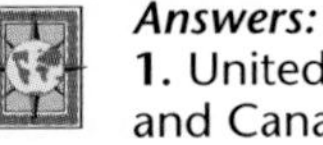

Guided Reading Have students complete Guided Reading Activity 4-3 in the TCR. **LEP**

USING MAPS

Answers:
1. United States and Canada; Latin America; part of Europe; and part of Australia, Antarctica, and Oceania; **2.** Latin America; Europe; North Africa and Southwest Asia; and Australia, Antarctica, and Oceania; **3.** Australia, Antarctica, and Oceania; **4.** Latin America, Africa South of the Sahara, and Southeast Asia

Map Skills Practice
Reading a Map What country shares a region with the United States? *(Canada)*

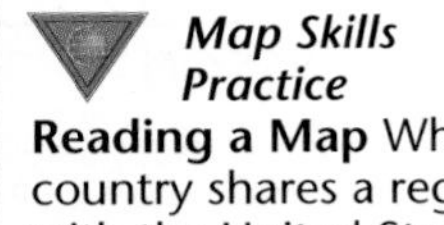

USING ILLUSTRATIONS

PLACE Despite economic progress, fighting in Kenya in 1992 left 50,000 homeless.

Answer to Caption: *Government interferes little with business.*

ASSESS

CHECK FOR UNDERSTANDING

Assign Section 3 Review as homework or an in-class activity.

Cooperative Learning Activity

Have students explore possible criteria for regions. Suggest that they tour the community with a large street map, placing a blue "X" at each address where the house is mostly frame, a red "B" where the house is mostly brick, a yellow "M" where the house is half brick and half frame, and a green "O" where the house is built of other materials. Display the completed map and have the class decide whether or not the community could be divided into regions based on types of houses.

USING MAPS

Answers:
1. eastern Asia; **2.** Dravidian; **3.** Indo-European; **4.** on islands in the Indian and Pacific Oceans

Map Skills Practice
Drawing Conclusions Do people in the same language family necessarily speak the same language? *(no)* Support your answer with facts from the map. *(Example: the Americans and the French are in the same language family but speak different languages.)*

MEETING LESSON OBJECTIVES

Each objective below is tested by the questions that follow it in parentheses.
1. Name the factors that determine the earth's culture regions. *(3)*
2. Relate how other social sciences help geographers determine culture regions. *(4)*

EVALUATE

Assign the Section 3 Quiz in the TCR.

Use the Testmaker to create a customized quiz for Section 3.

RETEACH

Have students complete Reteaching Activity 4 in the TCR.

product (GNP). Many nations prefer the more precise measure of gross domestic product (GDP). GDP covers all annual production *within* a country. It includes output by both foreign and domestic concerns operating in that country.

Per capita income measures how much money per person a country or a region earns. GNP, GDP, and per capita income help classify countries. A developed country has a manufacturing economy and a fairly high GNP or GDP. A developing country has an agricultural economy and a fairly low GNP or GDP.

Governments that value individual freedom often have economic systems based on **free enterprise.** Under free enterprise private businesses operate with little interference from government. An economic system based on free enterprise, as in the United States, is called **capitalism**. Authoritarian governments often use an economic system called **socialism**, in which the government decides how resources will be used and how businesses will be run.

REGION

Language and Religion

Scientists who study people's cultures are called anthropologists. These scientists trace the development of people's cultures by considering factors such as language. Languages spoken in a culture region often belong to the same **language family**, or group of languages having similar beginnings. Some major languages are Chinese, English, Hindi, Russian, Spanish, and Arabic.

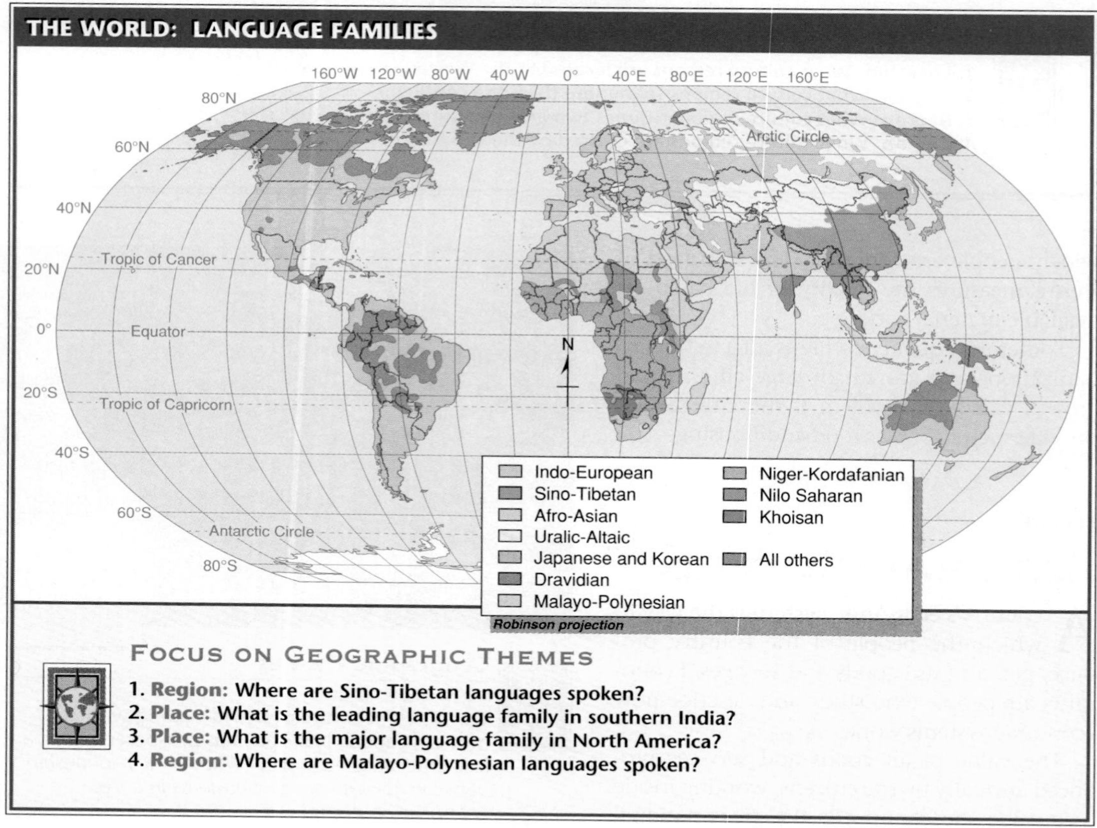

FOCUS ON GEOGRAPHIC THEMES

1. **Region:** Where are Sino-Tibetan languages spoken?
2. **Place:** What is the leading language family in southern India?
3. **Place:** What is the major language family in North America?
4. **Region:** Where are Malayo-Polynesian languages spoken?

Meeting Special Needs

Language Delayed To help students with language concept problems, discuss the meanings of "infant survival rate" and "life expectancy" in class. Read aloud the portion under "Social Groups" and ask why infant survival rate and life expectancy show the level of health care in a country. Have students define "standard of living" and tell how rapid growth of a city can result in a lower standard of living there.

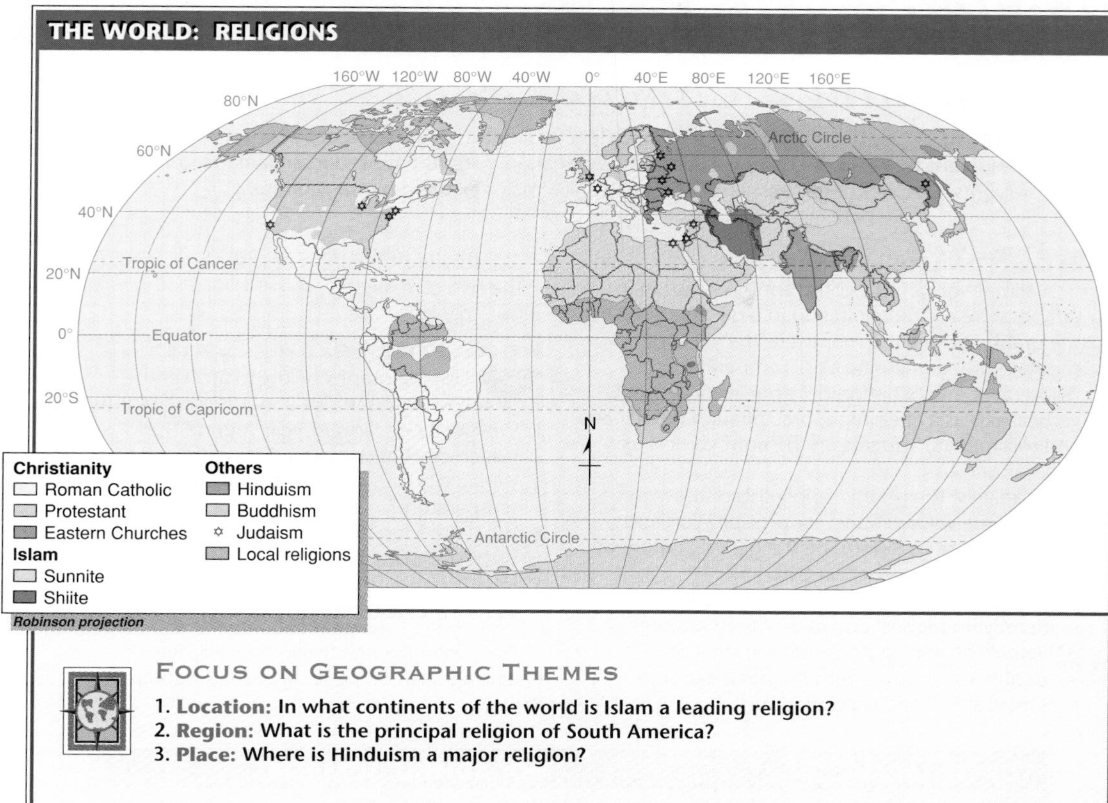

Focus on Geographic Themes

1. **Location:** In what continents of the world is Islam a leading religion?
2. **Region:** What is the principal religion of South America?
3. **Place:** Where is Hinduism a major religion?

Language is a powerful tool of communication. It offers a way for people to share information and experiences. Language also permits people to preserve their past and present experiences through history and literature. Through the written word, the people of one generation can pass their knowledge and skills to later generations.

Anthropologists also consider people's **religion** when studying their cultures. Religion is an organized way of worshiping a spiritual being or thinking about life. Anthropologists study which religions are practiced in different parts of the world. Some of the major religions in the world today are Judaism, Christianity, Buddhism, Islam, Hinduism, and Confucianism. Religion and language are part of a society's traditions, or the practices and beliefs passed on to people throughout the ages.

Section 3 Review

Checking for Understanding

1. **Define** culture region, government, standard of living, economic system, per capita income, free enterprise, capitalism, socialism, language family, religion.
2. **Locating Places** In what parts of the world do each of the world's major religions predominate?
3. **Region** What factors are considered when describing different culture regions?

Critical Thinking

4. **Analyzing Information** Why do scientists use such measures as GNP, GDP, and literacy rate in studying groups of people?

ENRICH

Have students complete Enrichment Activity 4 in the TCR.

CLOSE

Ask students to list different ways to divide the world. *(government, social groups, economic systems, and so on.)*

USING MAPS

Answers:
1. Africa and Asia; **2.** Roman Catholic; **3.** southern Asia

Map Skills Practice
Reading a Map What is the leading religion in the United States? *(Protestant)*

ANSWERS TO SECTION 3 REVIEW

1. **culture region:** area of the world; **government:** a political system; **standard of living:** quality of life; **economic system:** way to produce, get, and use goods and services; **per capita income:** money per person a country earns; **free enterprise:** businesses operate with little government interference; **capitalism:** system based on free enterprise; **socialism:** system in which the government decides how businesses run; **language family:** languages of similar origins; **religion:** organized worship
2. Judaism: Israel and major cities; Christianity: the Americas and Europe; Islam: Africa and Asia; Hinduism: Asia
3. governments, social groups, economic systems, languages, and religions
4. to show how well a society meets its needs

Teaching Skills

TEACH

Say: "Imagine that you are going to Japan. How can you determine which month will have the best weather for sightseeing?" *(ask a travel agent, consult a travel guide)* Point out that climate graphs are a good source for this information. Have students read the skill lesson on page 78. Then ask: "Which kinds of graphs are combined in a climate graph?" *(bar and line graphs)* "What climate information is shown on the graphs?" *(average monthly temperatures and precipitation)* "Which city has a tropical climate? Why?" *(Mogadishu; it has warm temperatures year-round)*

Skills Practice
For additional practice, have students complete Skill Activity 4 in the TCR.

MAP & GRAPH SKILLS

Interpreting a Climate Graph

Throughout history people have adapted to different climates. The discoveries of fire and clothing allowed humans to live in cold climates. Dams and irrigation systems have reduced damage from floods and droughts. Despite these discoveries, climate is still a major factor in human culture.

REVIEWING THE SKILL

A climate graph shows the annual variation in temperature and precipitation in a given region. In the graphs below, the months of the year are shown on the horizontal axis. Temperature (in °Fahrenheit and °Centigrade) appears on the left vertical axis as a line graph; precipitation (in inches and millimeters) appears on the right vertical axis as a bar graph.

To analyze the graphs, apply these steps:

- Study the values shown for precipitation and temperature to determine the general nature of the climate (hot/cool, wet/dry).
- Determine annual temperature variation by identifying highest and lowest temperatures.
- Determine annual precipitation variation.
- Identify the months with the most extreme temperatures and precipitation.
- Use this information to describe and compare the two climates.

PRACTICING THE SKILL

Use the graphs below to answer the following questions about climate graphs:

1. Which city is warmest year-round?
2. Which city has the wettest climate?
3. Which city has the greatest annual variation in temperature?
4. What are Mogadishu's driest months? Its wettest month?
5. In which months do both cities have about the same average temperature?

For additional practice in this skill, see Practicing Skills on page 80 of the Chapter 4 Review.

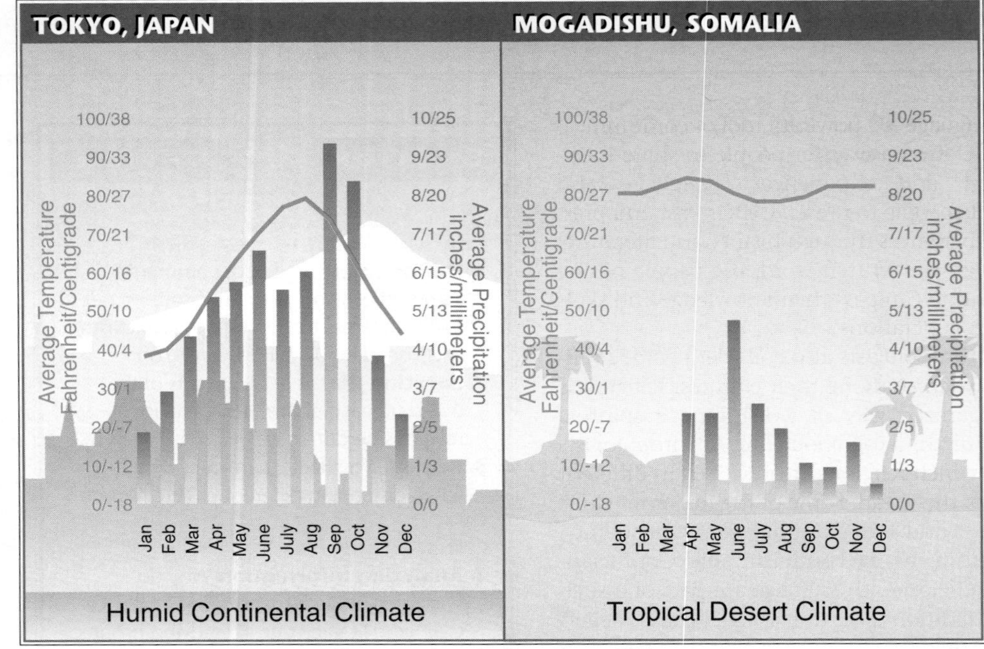

Source: *World Weather Guide*, 1990

*lines measure temperature/bars measure precipitation

ANSWERS TO PRACTICING THE SKILL

1. Mogadishu
2. Tokyo
3. Tokyo
4. January, February, March; June
5. July and August, about 80°F (26°C)

chapter 4

HIGHLIGHTS

1 Section: Limits and Opportunities

Market scene in Guatemala

Key Terms

- **culture** (p. 63)
- **subsistence farming** (p. 63)
- **population distribution** (p. 65)
- **population density** (p. 65)
- **tornado** (p. 66)
- **hurricane** (p. 66)
- **tsunami** (p. 67)
- **pollution** (p. 67)

Summary

- Nations can be classified as either developed or developing. Developed countries are highly industrialized, while developing countries are largely agricultural.
- The rapidly growing population of the world is creating many challenges, including meeting food needs and conserving resources.
- Environmental hazards include weather-related phenomena and pollution.

2 Section: Cultural Expressions

Archaeological dig

Key Terms

- **civilization** (p. 69)
- **history** (p. 69)
- **prehistory** (p. 69)
- **culture hearth** (p. 69)
- **cultural diffusion** (p. 70)

Summary

- Cultures express themselves in different ways. Some important cultural expressions are language, religion, and the arts.
- Early civilizations developed near major rivers in areas where the climate was mild and the lands were fertile.
- As cultures developed better modes of transportation, trade increased and cultural contacts were made.

3 Section: World Culture Regions Today

Nairobi, Kenya

Key Terms

- **culture region** (p. 74)
- **government** (p. 74)
- **standard of living** (p. 75)
- **economic system** (p. 75)
- **per capita income** (p. 76)
- **free enterprise** (p. 76)
- **capitalism** (p. 76)
- **socialism** (p. 76)
- **language family** (p. 76)
- **religion** (p. 77)

Summary

- To help them describe people and cultures, geographers divide the world into culture regions.
- Different factors are used to determine world culture regions. Among the factors considered are environment, history, language, religion, government, social structure, and economy.

CHAPTER 4 HIGHLIGHTS

Use the Chapter 4 Highlights to preview, review, condense, or reteach the chapter.

PREVIEW/REVIEW

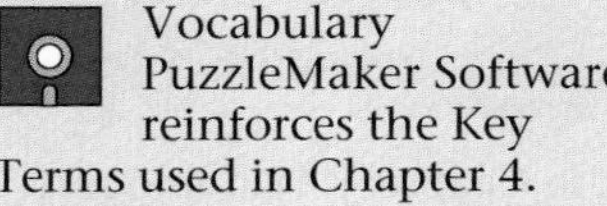
Vocabulary PuzzleMaker Software reinforces the Key Terms used in Chapter 4.

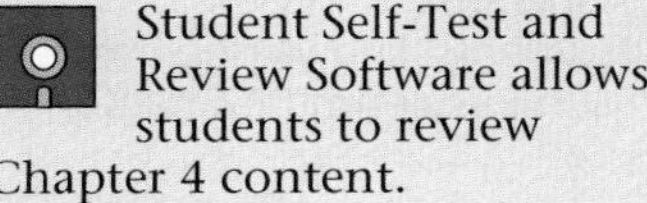
Student Self-Test and Review Software allows students to review Chapter 4 content.

CONDENSE

Have students read the Chapter 4 Highlights.

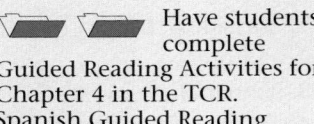

Have students listen to the Chapter 4 Audiocassettes in the TCR. Spanish Audiocassettes are also available.

Assign the Chapter 4 Audiocassette Activity and give students the Chapter 4 Audiocassette Quiz.

Have students complete Guided Reading Activities for Chapter 4 in the TCR. Spanish Guided Reading Activities are also available.

RETEACH

Have students complete Reteaching Activity 4 in the TCR. Spanish Reteaching Activities are also available.

Map Activity

Identify and Locate On the chalkboard, copy the following letters and place names:

A. Canada
B. Bangladesh
C. Egypt
D. Iraq
E. Pakistan
F. China
G. Greece
H. Australia
I. Antarctica

Distribute page 39 of the Outline Map Resource Book and tell students to locate each of the places listed on the chalkboard by writing its letter in the correct place on the map.

Chapter 4 Review

GLENCOE TECHNOLOGY

Videodisc

Use Chapter 4 MindJogger Videoquiz to review students' knowledge before administering the Chapter 4 Test.

MINDJOGGER VIDEOQUIZ

Chapter 4
Disc 1 Side A

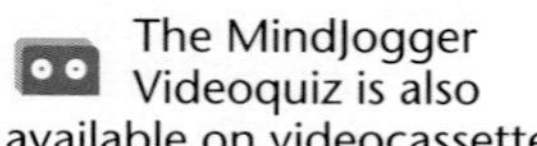

The MindJogger Videoquiz is also available on videocassette.

ANSWERS

Reviewing Key Terms

1. tornado
2. culture
3. tsunami
4. subsistence farming
5. cultural diffusion
6. civilization
7. capitalism
8. free enterprise
9. socialism

Reviewing Facts

10. producing enough food and housing for all of the world's people and maintaining an adequate level of nonrenewable resources

11. prehistory: time before written records; history: information gathered from written records about a people's past

12. Chinese, English, Hindi, Russian, Spanish, and Arabic

chapter 4 REVIEW

Reviewing Key Terms

Choose the vocabulary term that best completes each of the sentences below. Write your answers on a separate sheet of paper.

culture (p. 63)
subsistence farming (p. 63)
tornado (p. 66)
tsunami (p. 67)
civilization (p. 69)
cultural diffusion (p. 70)
capitalism (p. 76)
free enterprise (p. 76)
socialism (p. 76)

SECTION 1

1. A ____ is a powerful, whirling storm that ranks as the most violent of all storms.
2. ____ is the way of life of a group of people having common traditions, interests, and beliefs.
3. Earthquakes under the ocean can result in ____, or ocean waves.
4. Many people in developing countries engage in ____.

SECTION 2

5. The spread of ideas and practices from one part of the world to another is called ____.
6. A culture with a high level of development in the arts and sciences is called a ____.

SECTION 3

7. ____ is an economic system based on free enterprise.
8. The American economy is based on the principles of ____.
9. Under ____, a government decides how resources will be used and how businesses will be run.

Reviewing Facts

SECTION 1

10. What challenges does the world's rapidly growing population present?

SECTION 2

11. What is prehistory? History?

SECTION 3

12. What are some major languages of the world today?

Critical Thinking

13. **Making Comparisons** How do developed and developing countries differ?
14. **Identifying Central Issues** What steps have governments taken to solve environmental problems?
15. **Analyzing Information** Why are countries increasingly preferring gross domestic product (GDP) over gross national product (GNP) as a measure of economic well-being?

Geographic Themes

16. **Human/Environment Interaction** What is the most harmful result of air pollution?
17. **Region** What geographic features did culture hearths have in common?
18. **Movement** Why have cultures changed over the years?

Practicing Skills

Interpreting a Climate Graph

Refer to the climate graph on page 78.

19. Referring to the climate graph for Mogadishu, how would you describe a desert climate?
20. Referring to the climate graph for Tokyo, how would you describe a humid continental climate?
21. What is the total annual precipitation for each city?
22. What are the highest and lowest average monthly temperatures for each city?

Critical Thinking

13. Developed countries are highly productive and industrialized and have few shortages. Developing countries have much farming, little industry, and many shortages.

14. They have passed laws to limit pollution, funded research to find ways to control pollution, and established the EPA to set and enforce pollution standards.

15. The GDP is considered more precise because it includes all forms of production.

Geographic Themes

16. impairment of people's health

17. mild climate, fertile land, and location near a river

18. political and economic factors and cultural diffusion

Projects

Individual Activity

Make a list of objects that you own or use, such as clothes, radios, and sports gear. Note where each item was manufactured. Locate these places on a world map. What culture regions of the world have contributed most to your way of life?

Cooperative Learning Activity

Working with a partner, use a world almanac and other data sources to create an economic data chart of selected countries of the world. Pick 10 countries from different culture regions. For each country, find information that provides evidence of its level of economic development. Rank the countries by level of development. Compare your findings with those of other groups.

Writing About Geography

Narration

In this chapter, you have read about the characteristics of cultures, such as political systems, economic systems, religions, and languages. Pick a current international event that is significant and write a geographic analysis of the story. Apply the observations recorded in your journal as well as the ideas and concepts that you have learned in this chapter to discuss the event in geographic terms.

Locating Places

THE WORLD: CULTURE REGIONS

Match the letters on the map with the culture regions of the world. Write your answers on a separate sheet of paper.

1. The United States and Canada
2. Latin America
3. Europe
4. Russia and the Eurasian Republics
5. North Africa and Southwest Asia
6. Africa South of the Sahara
7. South Asia
8. East Asia
9. Southeast Asia
10. Australia, Oceania, and Antarctica

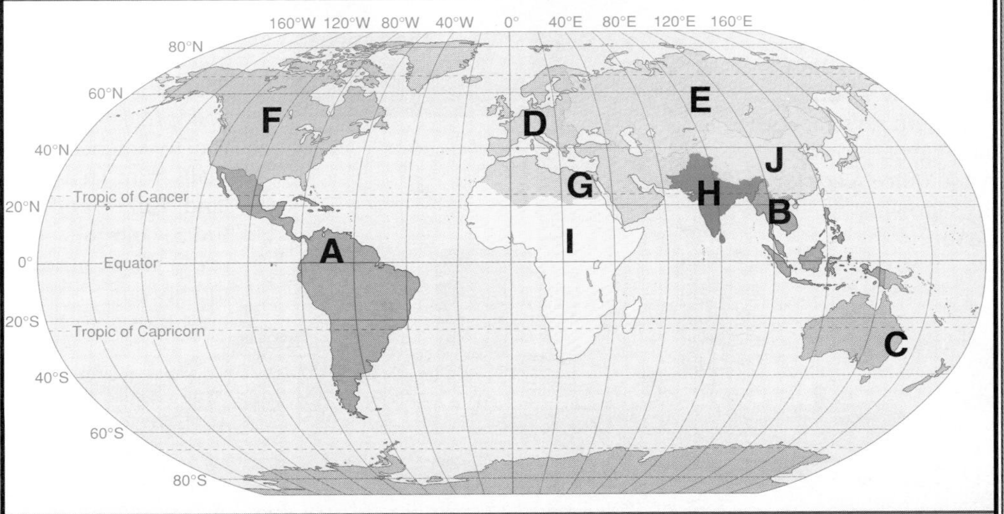

Chapter 4 Review

Practicing Skills

19. warm and dry
20. cool and dry in winter and warm and wet in the summer
21. Tokyo receives 63.5 inches (161.3 cm) of precipitation. Mogadishu gets 18 inches (45.7 cm) of precipitation.
22. In Tokyo, the highest average monthly temperature is 80°F (27°C), and the lowest monthly temperature is 40°F (4°C). In Mogadishu, the highest average monthly temperature is 85°F (30°C) and the lowest average monthly temperature is 75°F (24°C).

Locating Places

1. F
2. A
3. D
4. E
5. G
6. I
7. H
8. J
9. B
10. C

Chapter Bonus Test Question

This question may be used for extra credit on the chapter test.

What is the culture region, language family, and dominant religion of the area known as the Nile Valley culture hearth?

(Answer: North Africa and Southwest Asia, Afro-Asian, and Islam)

Geography Connection

FOCUS

Ask students to inventory their clothes, shoes, bookbags, purses, athletic equipment, and so on. List imported items on the board, as well as the country from which each item comes.

TEACH

L1 Define Prior to reading, have students define the term *global culture*. Ask them to name the categories of culture suggested by the photos. *(music, architecture, technology, cuisine, clothing).*

L2 Making Inferences After reading, have students name additional items that they feel are part of the global culture.

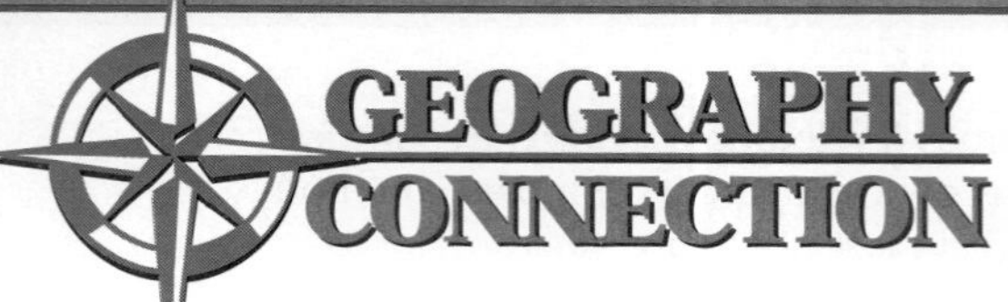

The World and the United States

THE GLOBAL CULTURE

Since the end of World War II, the fads and fashions of the United States have spread across the globe. American television, American businesses and industries, and American products have greatly influenced today's global culture.

ROCK AS WELL AS COUNTRY AND WESTERN MUSIC ▶ are popular from Mozambique to Japan. Rock began as rock 'n roll, getting its start in the 1950s with American musicians Chuck Berry and Elvis Presley. Country and western developed from early American folk tunes. During the mid-1980s, country music began to gain in worldwide popularity. This Japanese teenager is part of a rock band performing before an outdoor audience.

▼ SKYSCRAPERS are found in many countries of the world. These structures first reached skyward in Chicago and New York. Steel-and-concrete buildings now define skylines throughout the world. These modern skyscrapers in Cairo, Egypt, provide living and office space for the city's growing population.

◀ PRODUCTS FROM OTHER NATIONS, such as this German sports car, influence American culture. From Japanese assembly lines come automobiles and electronic products. Silk, batik, and bamboo goods make their way to American malls from Thailand, Turkey, and India. Colorful textiles from Africa modify our fashions.

Making the Connection

Encourage students to make a collage or world map with global culture as its theme. Suggest they look through magazines and newspapers for advertisements and/or announcements of products from other countries as well as articles (headlines) about foreign businesses in the United States. Students can contribute tags from their clothing, wrappers and containers of imported items from a local supermarket, and so on. If students prefer, they may also render items in an artistic medium of their choice.

Should students choose to do a world map, their items can form a frame around the map, with "leaders" between the product and the country from which it comes.

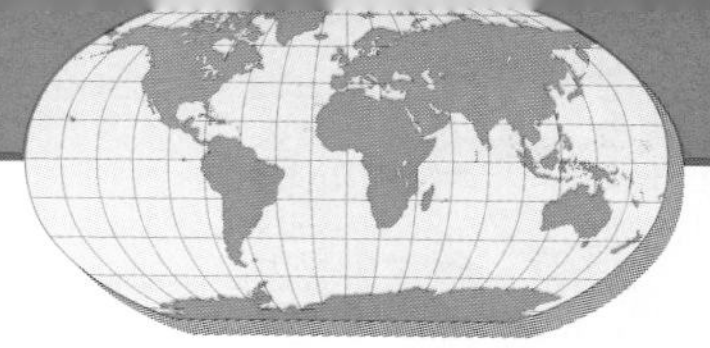

JEANS AND SNEAKERS, worn by these students in Latin America, are two of the most popular products from the United States ever to reach global markets. Developed in the 1860s by Levi Strauss, jeans took off globally in the 1950s, when jeans-wearing American movie stars Marlon Brando and James Dean roared onto movie screens. United States Rubber introduced rubber-soled Keds in 1917. As other brands of rubber-soled footwear appeared, they became known as sneakers because wearers could "sneak" around almost soundlessly on the rubber soles.

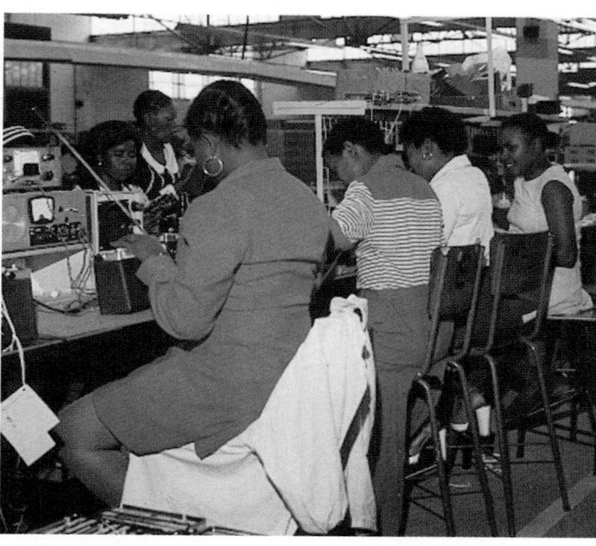

MASS PRODUCTION AND MOVING ASSEMBLY LINES characterize manufacturing in most of the world's nations. The American automobile industry developed assembly lines during the early 1900s. Mass production is now an indispensable part of manufacturing worldwide. These South African workers are assembling transistor radios.

AMERICAN FAST FOODS are as much a part of global culture as they are of American culture. Shoppers in Moscow and Milan enjoy Kentucky Fried Chicken. Coca-Cola fills glasses in Budapest, Beijing, and Bogotá. This customer is buying a McDonald's hamburger in Tokyo.

Checking for Understanding

1. What are the main features of the global culture?
2. **Movement** In what ways are you a global citizen?

Geography Connection

ASSESS

Have students answer the Checking for Understanding questions on page 83.

CLOSE

Ask students to tell why they think other cultures have adopted the facets of American life shown on pages 82–83. Ask them to also comment on how their lifestyles would be affected by the removal of any item shown.

DID YOU KNOW?

In 1993, tourism emerged as the world's biggest industry, contributing more to global economic development than either arms or oil.

ANSWERS TO CHECKING FOR UNDERSTANDING

1. similarities in urban architecture, clothing, foods, goods production, and music
2. Answers will vary, but should indicate an awareness of using products from other countries.

UNIT OVERVIEW

The three chapters that comprise this unit introduce students to the geography and the peoples of the United States and Canada. Various aspects of American and Canadian life—such as the economy, lifestyles, and human/environment interaction—are also presented.

GEOGRAPHY JOURNAL

Activity In addition to the sources listed in the Student Edition, students may also consult various travel books and tour guides, as well as interview people who have lived or traveled in various states or Canada.

Using information collected and recorded in their journals, have students compare and contrast areas of concern in the United States and Canada.

• This journal activity provides the basis for the "Writing About Geography" exercise in the Chapter Review.

• The Geography Journal should be used as an integral part of Performance Assessment.

GLENCOE TECHNOLOGY

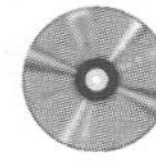

Videodisc

Use the following to introduce or enrich Unit 2:

REUTERS ISSUES IN GEOGRAPHY

Chapter 1
Disc 1 Side A

Title: ***The United States and Canada: The Water Supply***
Subject: Sources and uses of water in the United States and Canada

UNIT 2

The United States and Canada

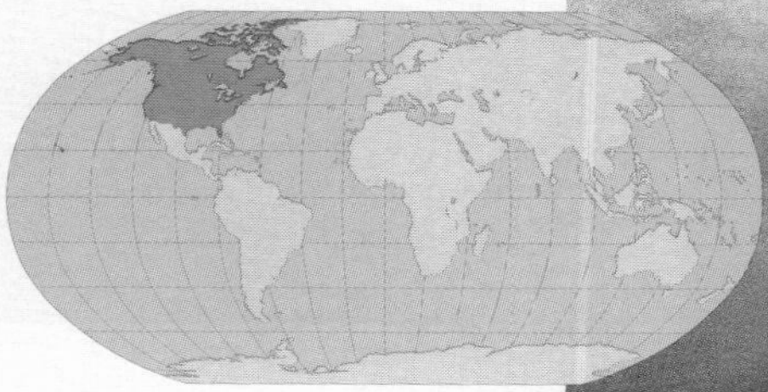

GeoJournal Activity

As you study this region of the world, look through newspapers and magazines for articles about the United States and Canada. Cut out any articles you find and place them in the following categories: Geography, Peoples and Cultures, and Economy and Environment.

84

© Annie Griffiths Belt

Where in the World . . . .

Have students look at the maps on pages A4 and A6 of their texts. Ask students the following questions. On what continent are Canada and the United States? *(North America)* What body of water separates the continent from Europe? *(Atlantic)* Asia? *(Pacific)* In what hemispheres do the two countries lie? *(northern, western)* What continent lies south of the United States? *(South America)* Where is the United States in relation to Canada? *(south)* What direction would you fly traveling from Canada to Africa? *(southeast)* What direction would you sail to get from the United States to Australia? *(southwest)*

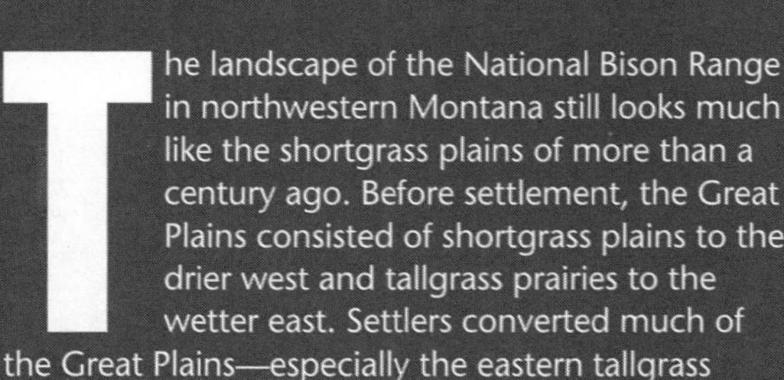

Picturing the World

The landscape of the National Bison Range in northwestern Montana still looks much like the shortgrass plains of more than a century ago. Before settlement, the Great Plains consisted of shortgrass plains to the drier west and tallgrass prairies to the wetter east. Settlers converted much of the Great Plains—especially the eastern tallgrass prairie—to fields of corn and wheat. Look at the map on page 88.

1. What large mountain system (visible in the photo) is located to the west of the Great Plains?
2. What is the elevation range of the western shortgrass plains?
3. Now look at the map on page 99. What is the climate of the western shortgrass plains?

Picture Atlas CD-ROM Enrichment Corner

Assemble a file of Great Plains information. (See the *Picture Atlas of the World* User's Guide for information on how to use the Collector button.) Include in your file the essays on the United States and Canada and the two photographs of the Great Plains. Then answer the following questions:

1. What percent of the world's corn does the United States produce?
2. The United States leads the world in the export of what grain?
3. What nickname describes the Great Plains?
4. Canada ranks second worldwide in the export of what crop?

85

interNET CONNECTIONS

For earthquake information and ideas for classroom activities, contact Geological Survey Education at the following address:

World Wide Web
http://info.er.usgs.gov/education/index.html

Weather maps and satellite images are available at:

World Wide Web
http://www.mit.edu:8001/usa.html

NATIONAL GEOGRAPHIC SOCIETY

CD-ROM

PICTURE ATLAS OF THE WORLD
See page T36 for an additional CD-ROM activity to enrich Unit 2, the United States and Canada.

0:00 OUT OF TIME?

If time does not permit teaching each chapter in this unit, you may use the Chapter Highlights and the Audiocassettes that include a 1-page activity and a 1-page test for each chapter.

ANSWERS TO PICTURING THE WORLD

1. Rocky Mountains
2. 2,000-5,000 ft.
3. steppe

Enrichment Corner Answers

1. 50 percent
2. wheat
3. the region's breadbasket
4. wheat

LESSON PLAN
Unit 2 Atlas

These features and activities may be used as an introduction to the unit or as teaching tools throughout the course of the unit.

FOCUS

Have students recall or list ways in which physical geography can influence where cities and towns develop. Have students use the maps on pages 87–88 to suggest examples of such geographical influence.

TEACH

Drawing Conclusions As students read the facts presented, have them draw and support conclusions about the effects of each fact on the corresponding region.

Implement Foods Around the World 1 as a class activity.

Have students complete World Cultures Transparencies Activities 1 and 2 in the TCR.

Have students complete World Literature Reading 1 in the TCR.

Have students complete Unit Atlas Activity 2B.

UNIT 2 ATLAS

THE UNITED STATES
Cultural Geography

EXPLORING CULTURAL DIVERSITY

1. *What areas of this region are the most populated? Least populated?*
2. *Which states of the United States have Spanish roots?*
3. *What countries border the United States?*

French Canadians make up a little more than one-fourth of Canada's population. Most French Canadians live in the province of Quebec.

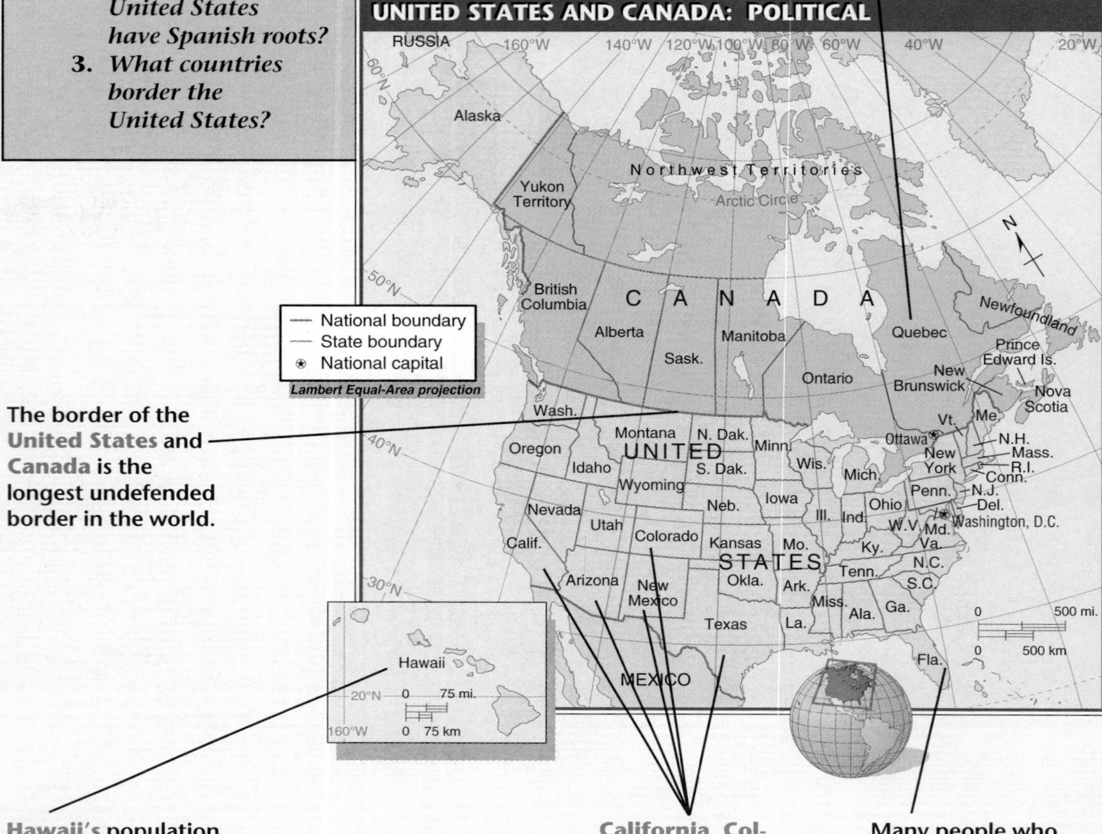

The border of the **United States** and **Canada** is the longest undefended border in the world.

Hawaii's population includes many citizens of Japanese, Filipino, Chinese, Korean, and Polynesian ancestry.

California, Colorado, Arizona, New Mexico, and **Texas** once belonged to Spain. The area's culture reflects its Spanish roots.

Many people who live in **Miami, Florida,** claim a Cuban heritage. During the 1970s, 1980s, and 1990s, many Cuban refugees risked death to sail to Florida.

Classroom Resources for Unit 2

BLACKLINE MASTERS:
Geography Simulation 2
Environmental Issue 2
Unit Atlas Activity 2B

TRANSPARENCIES:
Unit Map Overlay Transparency 2
World Cultures Transparencies 1, 2
Political Map Transparency 2

World History and Art Transparency 36

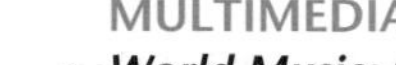
MULTIMEDIA:

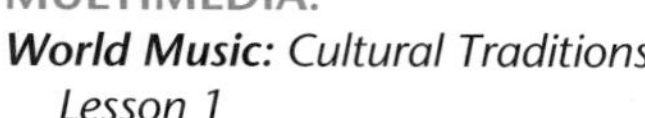
World Music: *Cultural Traditions, Lesson 1*

Reuters Issues in Geography

Testmaker

Images of the World Poster Set

Picture Atlas of the World

UNITED STATES AND CANADA: POPULATION DENSITY

Per sq. km	Per sq. mi.
Over 100	Over 250
50-100	125-250
25-50	60-125
1-25	2-60
Under 1	Under 2
Uninhabited	Uninhabited

Cities
- Over 5,000,000
- 2,000,000 – 5,000,000
- 1,000,000 – 2,000,000
- 250,000 – 1,000,000
- Under 250,000

Lambert Equal-Area projection

About 6 of every 10 Canadians live in Ontario or Quebec.

California is the most populous of the 50 American states.

During the 1980s, many Americans moved to the southern and western Sunbelt states to take advantage of growing business opportunities and the mild climate.

The deserts of Arizona and New Mexico are home to many Native Americans.

New York City is the largest urban center in the United States and one of the most famous cities in the world.

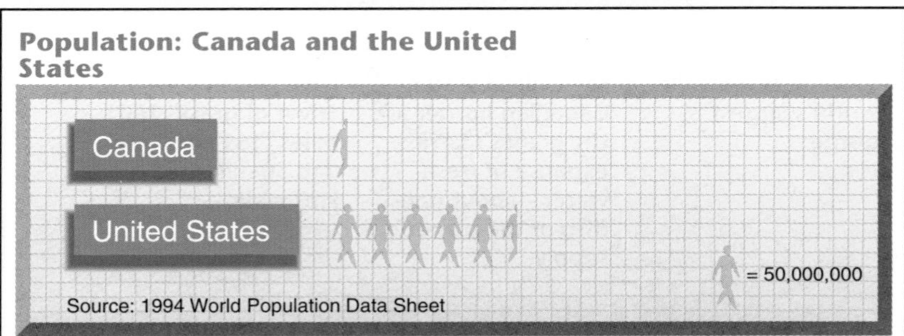

The population of the United States is almost 10 times that of Canada.

LESSON PLAN
Unit 2 Atlas

Play World Music: Cultural Traditions, Lesson 1, and have students complete the Lesson 1 activity.

DID YOU KNOW?

North America is a lightly populated continent, home to about 5 percent of the world's population.

ASSESS

Have students answer the Exploring Cultural Diversity questions on page 86.

EXPLORING CULTURAL DIVERSITY

This feature may be used to introduce students to the cultural geography of the United States and Canada. Use questions to stimulate class discussion and help students become familiar with the region. Accept reasonable answers based on the maps, graph, and captions.

DID YOU KNOW?

Life expectancy in North America is the world's highest: 74 years. The continent's infant death rate is the world's lowest: 14 per 1,000 births.

CLOSE

Ask students to decide what information given on pages 86–87 is most relevant to them, and why.

Map Activity

Place Assign small groups of students to briefly research the cultural contributions of the ethnic groups highlighted on the map on page 86: southwestern Spanish food and architecture, French-Canadian cuisine, and Cuban food. Have students note the origins of each contribution and its significance within the cultural groups, as well as any geographical characteristic that may have contributed to it. Have students also discuss how each cultural contribution enriches their own lives.

These features and activities may be used as an introduction to the unit or as teaching tools throughout the course of the unit.

FOCUS

To introduce students to the physical geography of the United States and Canada, have students complete Unit Map Overlay Transparency 2 Activity in the TCR.

TEACH

Human/Environment Interaction Ask students to recall how physical geography can affect peoples' lives and cultures. Have students volunteer ways in which the physical geography of the area in which they live affects their lives. Suggest that they consider their clothing and homes, leisure activities, and the area's businesses and industries.

Implement Geography Simulation 2 as a class activity.

NATIONAL GEOGRAPHIC SOCIETY

CD-ROM

PICTURE ATLAS OF THE WORLD

You and your students can learn about the physical features, music, economy, and population of the United States and Canada by selecting "North America" on the main menu.

UNIT 2 ATLAS

THE UNITED STATES

Physical Geography

CHARTING YOUR COURSE

1. *What ocean borders this region to the east? To the west?*
2. *Name two mountains located in this region.*
3. *What are four of this region's principal natural resources?*
4. *What major waterways are found in the United States and Canada?*

UNITED STATES AND CANADA: PHYSICAL FEATURES

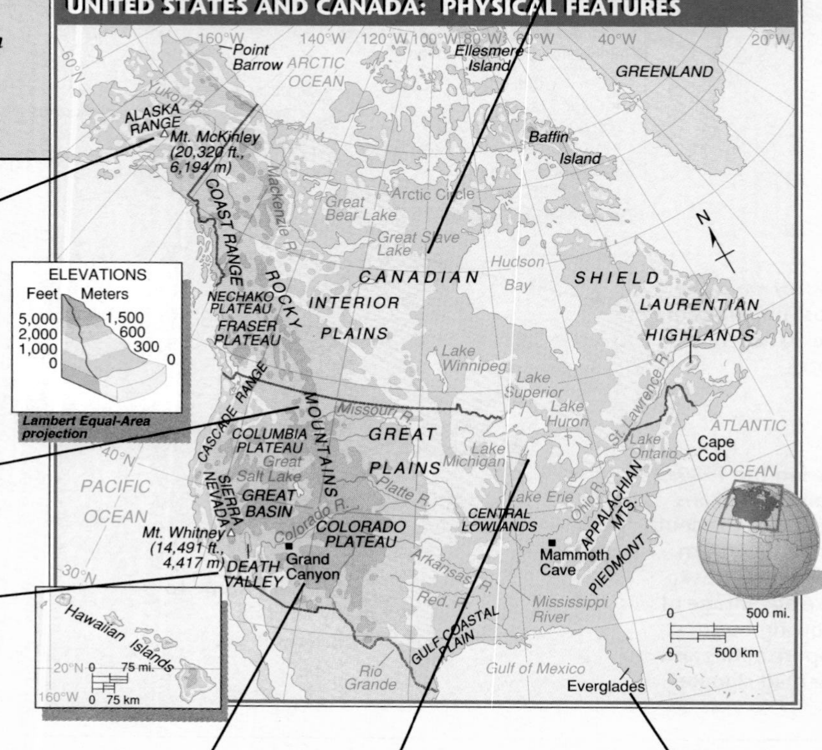

The **Canadian Shield,** which covers almost half of Canada, is a huge area of ancient rock.

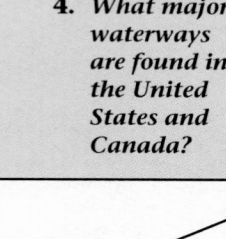

Mt. McKinley, rising 20,320 feet (6,194 m) in Alaska, is North America's highest mountain.

The Rockies, the region's largest mountain system, stretch more than 3,000 miles (4,827 km) from Alaska to New Mexico.

Death Valley in California, the continent's hottest spot, is the lowest place in the Western Hemisphere—282 feet (89 m) below sea level.

Arizona's **Grand Canyon** is the world's largest gorge.

The **Great Lakes** on the United States-Canadian border are the planet's largest expanse of freshwater—about one-fifth of the planet's supply.

Florida's **Everglades** have been called a "river of grass" 100 miles (161 km) long and 50 miles (81 km) wide.

88 UNIT 2

Map and Graph Activity

Location Allow students several moments to study the graphics on pages 88–89, looking for similarities and differences between the United States and Canada in physical geography and natural resources. Have students work together to create a class comparison/contrast chart. Physical characteristics/resources can be listed vertically, countries' names horizontally, and similarities may be shown with a check. When the chart is completed, have students formulate factual statements about the differences between the two countries. For example, students might note that, although the two countries share the Rocky Mountains and the Great Plains, only the United States has desert and semi-tropical areas, while only Canada has a huge area of rocky, ancient land.

UNITED STATES AND CANADA: NATURAL RESOURCES

Iron ore
Petroleum
Coal
Copper
Zinc
Gold
Silver

Lambert Equal-Area projection

Alaska
CANADA
UNITED STATES
Hawaii
Arctic Circle

The Canadian Shield holds rich stores of copper, nickel, zinc, and iron ore.

Forests cover almost half of Canada. The country is the world's leading exporter of lumber and producer of newsprint.

The fertile soil of the Midwest of the United States helps make the country the world's agricultural leader.

The fertile soil of the eastern Great Plains produces large quantities of soybeans and corn.

The region's greatest quantities of fish are caught in coastal waters off the Gulf of Mexico.

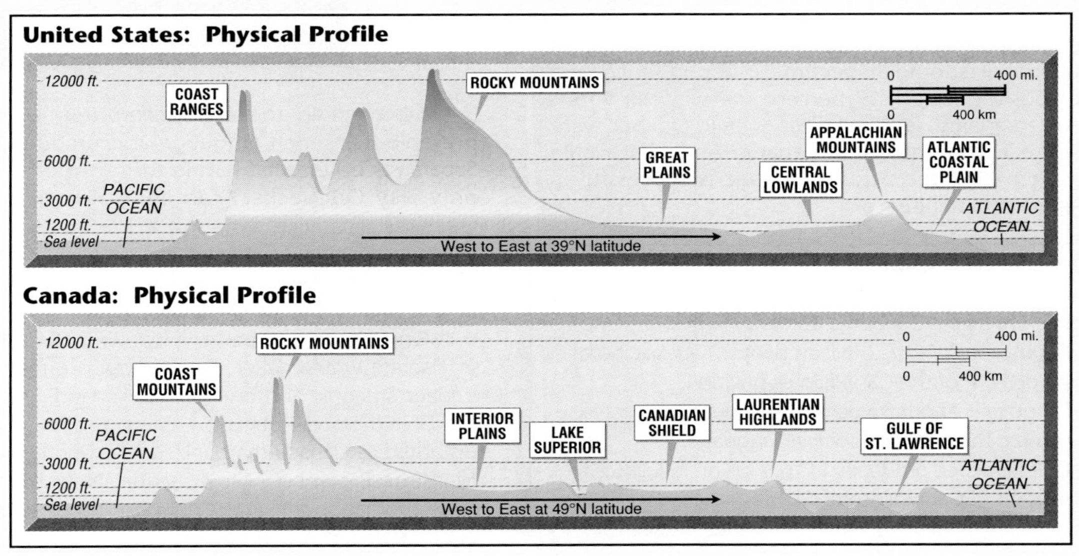

Map Activity

Region Organize the class into small groups, and assign each group a geographical region from the map on page 89 and/or the physical profile diagram above. Have students use atlases, almanacs, and other appropriate resources to research the contributions of each region to the national economies of both countries. Students should discover the leading resources of each area, what percentage of the national economy the area's resources represent, and what part geography plays in the region's economic standing. Students may present their findings in chart and/or graph form.

LESSON PLAN
Unit 2 Atlas

ASSESS

Have students answer the Charting Your Course questions on page 88.

CHARTING YOUR COURSE

This feature may be used to introduce students to the physical geography of the United States and Canada. Use questions to stimulate class discussion and help students become familiar with the region. Accept reasonable answers based on the maps, graph, and captions.

CLOSE

Have students recall the types of maps and diagrams they used to study the physical geography of Canada and the United States. Ask them which graphic, or combination of graphics, they found most useful in helping them to understand the physical geography of the two countries. Encourage them to analyze why the graphic(s) was of such help.

DID YOU KNOW?

Mammoth Caves, underneath the forests of Kentucky, is the most extensive cave system in the world.

IMAGES OF THE WORLD POSTER SET

Display the poster "The United States and Canada." Have students hypothesize about the climate zone and population density of each photo.

These features and activities may be used as teaching tools throughout the course of the unit.

Ways of the World

CANADA For the most part, Canadians are more conservative than U.S. citizens. Etiquette is important when visiting, and a wise visitor follows the lead of the host or hostess.

DID YOU KNOW?

The United States and Canada are often called *Anglo America,* because many of their settlers came from England, and the main language of the two countries is English.

Ways of the World

UNITED STATES Individualism is often cited as an American characteristic. Even when working as a team, Americans usually think of distinct individuals blending their efforts rather than a group working as a unit.

MULTICULTURAL PERSPECTIVE

Why is Quebec French? French explorers settled the region in the 16th and 17th centuries. The United Kingdom acquired Quebec in 1763 after defeating France in war, but soon granted French Canadians political and religious rights.

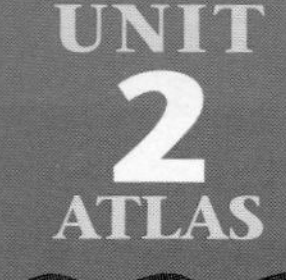

COUNTRY PROFILE

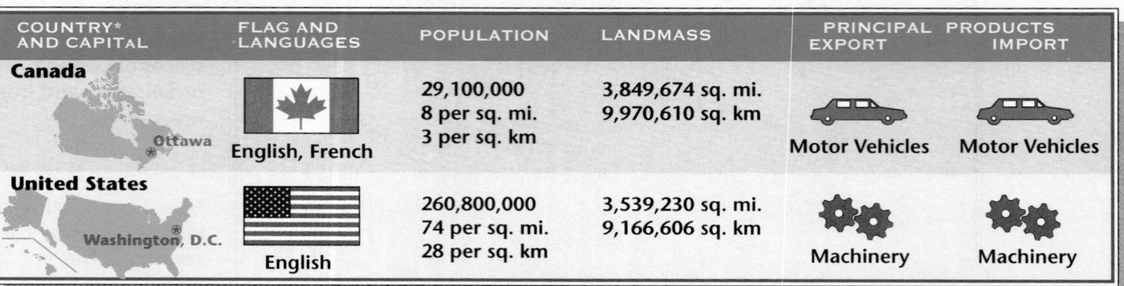

COUNTRY* AND CAPITAL	FLAG AND LANGUAGES	POPULATION	LANDMASS	PRINCIPAL PRODUCTS EXPORT	PRINCIPAL PRODUCTS IMPORT
Canada (Ottawa)	English, French	29,100,000 8 per sq. mi. 3 per sq. km	3,849,674 sq. mi. 9,970,610 sq. km	Motor Vehicles	Motor Vehicles
United States (Washington, D.C.)	English	260,800,000 74 per sq. mi. 28 per sq. km	3,539,230 sq. mi. 9,166,606 sq. km	Machinery	Machinery

*Country maps not drawn to scale.

The United States and Canada both are democracies. The United States Congress meets in the United States Capitol in Washington, D.C. (below). The Canadian Parliament assembles in the Parliament Building in Ottawa (left).

A NEW CANADA?

On October 30, 1995, voters in Quebec faced a decision: Should Quebec remain a province of Canada or should it become independent? By a perilously close 51-49 percent margin, the voters decided against secession. Why would Quebec want to secede from the rest of Canada? And what would happen if, in the future, Quebec is successful in gaining independence?

Quebec At a Glance

- Area: At 594,860 square miles—more than twice the size of Texas—Quebec is Canada's largest province.
- Population: With 7.2 million people, Quebec holds 25 percent of the Canadian population.
- Language: About 82 percent of Quebeckers speak French, the province's official language.
- GDP: Quebec produces $116.9 billion in GDP, 22 percent of Canada's total GDP.

Quebec's desire to secede springs from a desire to preserve its French language and unique culture. Separatists believe that having their own nation is the only way Quebeckers can control their destiny. Quebec's separatists, who lost a 1980 independence referendum by a 60-40 percent vote, narrowed the margin so dramatically in 1995 that another attempt at nationhood is sure to be launched.

If Quebec were to become its own nation, the rest of Canada would suffer. Quebec holds one-fourth of Canada's people and one-sixth of its land. Trade with the United States—about $1 billion a day—would be disrupted as Canada reorganized its economy. And the Maritime Provinces—Nova Scotia, New Brunswick, Newfoundland, and Prince Edward Island—would be cut off from the rest of Canada.

Country Profile Activity

Although Canada and the United States are democracies, significant differences exist between the two governments. Have students research such areas as the countries' leaders, methods of choosing leaders, branches of the governments, political parties, elections, powers of the national governments and powers of the states and the provinces.

Have students present their information during an informal discussion. Create a class comparison/contrast chart for the governments of the two countries.

THE ST. LAWRENCE SEAWAY

90°W 85°W 80°W 75°W 70°W 65°W
50°N 45°N 40°N
CANADA
UNITED STATES
Gulf of St. Lawrence
Thunder Bay
Duluth
Superior
Lake Superior
St. Mary's River
Soo Locks
Lake Michigan
Lake Huron
Mississippi River
St. Clair River
Detroit
Detroit River
Chicago
Illinois Drainage Canal
Toronto
Welland Canal
Lake Ontario
Buffalo
Lake Erie
Cleveland
New York State Barge Canal
New York
Quebec
St. Lawrence River
Montreal
St. Lambert Lock
Côte-Ste.-Catherine Lock
Melocheville Lock
Iroquois Lock
Beauharnois Lock
Snell Lock
Eisenhower Lock
ATLANTIC OCEAN
N
0 150 mi.
0 150 km

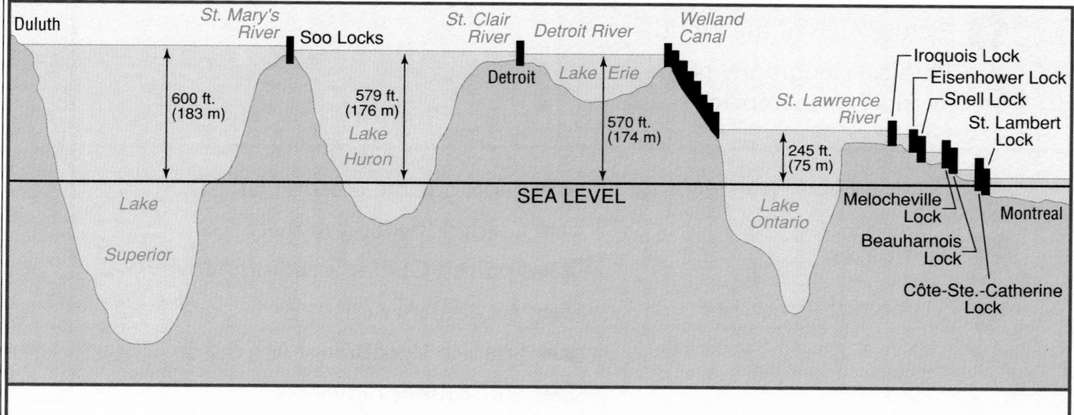

Focus on Geographic Themes

1. **Location: At about what line of longitude is the Iroquois Lock located?**
2. **Place: Which of the Great Lakes is the deepest?**
3. **Place: Which city is near the St. Lambert Lock?**
4. **Movement: What is the purpose of the St. Lawrence Seaway?**

Country Profile Activity

Organize students into small groups; have them work together to list as much information as they can from the two graphics on page 91. After five or ten minutes, have groups pool their information. Should groups' information disagree, require students to identify supporting evidence from the graphics.

Global Gourmet

Food connoisseurs consider Quebec cuisine, with its definite French flavor, to be one of North America's best. Most often associated with the food of Quebec are pea soup, French pastries and breads, and highly spiced meat pies.

USING MAPS

Answers:
1. 75° W; **2.** Lake Superior; **3.** Montreal; **4.** to connect the Great Lakes and the Atlantic Ocean

Map Skills Practice

Reading a Map Which Great Lake does not have a lock? (Lake Michigan)

Ways of the World

CANADA In Ontario and the Western Provinces, guests often remove their shoes when entering a home to avoid tracking in dirt.

Ways of the World

UNITED STATES A common greeting between friends is *How are you?* The response should be *Fine, thanks.* Americans do not really expect any further answer.

CHAPTER 5

PLANNING GUIDE

The Physical Geography of the United States and Canada

CHAPTER ORGANIZER

Daily Lesson Objectives	Multimedia	Teacher Classroom Resources
SECTION 1 The Land 1. Compare the landforms of the United States and Canada. 2. Describe the water resources that the environments of the United States and Canada offer. 3. List the kinds of natural resources found in the United States and Canada.	Section Focus Transparency 5-1 Chapter 5 Vocabulary PuzzleMaker Software Reuters Issues in Geography Geography and the Environment Testmaker STV: North America Picture Atlas of the World Physical Geography of the World Transparencies 1–10	Reproducible Lesson Plan 5-1 Guided Reading Activity 5-1 Spanish Guided Reading Activity 5-1 Workbook Activity 5-1 Performance Assessment Activity 5 Section Quiz 5-1
SECTION 2 The Climate and Vegetation 1. Describe the climate regions of the United States and Canada. 2. Identify the kinds of natural vegetation found in the United States and Canada.	 Section Focus Transparency 5-2 Testmaker STV: North America	Reproducible Lesson Plan 5-2 Guided Reading Activity 5-2 Spanish Guided Reading Activity 5-2 Vocabulary Activity 5 Spanish Vocabulary Activity 5 Enrichment Activity 5 Skill Activity 5 Section Quiz 5-2
CHAPTER REVIEW AND EVALUATION	Chapter 5 English (or Spanish) Audiocassettes MindJogger Videoquiz Testmaker Student Self-Test and Review Software	Reteaching Activity 5 Spanish Reteaching Activity 5 Chapter 5 Test Form A and Form B

0:00 *If time does not permit teaching the entire chapter, summarize using the Chapter 5 Highlights on page 103, and the Chapter 5 English (or Spanish) Audiocassettes. Review students' knowledge using the Glencoe MindJogger Videoquiz.*

KEY TO ABILITY LEVELS

Teaching strategies have been coded for varying learning styles and abilities.

L1 **BASIC** activities for all students

L2 **AVERAGE** activities for average to above-average students

L3 **CHALLENGING** activities for above-average students

LEP **LIMITED ENGLISH PROFICIENCY** activities

Performance Assessment

Appreciating Physical Features Have students gather and use information about the physical features of the United States and Canada. Groups of students should list four or five areas known for their distinctive physical features. They should web all they think they know about these areas' physical attractions. The groups should then write letters to tourist bureaus, chambers of commerce, acquaintances residing in the areas, or other informed sources to gather as much information as possible about the "sights" to see.

Once the information has arrived, the students should adjust their webs by reading the information and viewing the pictures that accompany the replies. They should then prioritize the areas in order of preference for a vacation or expedition. The task may be extended by giving students a budget for the trip and having them make inquiries about accommodations, tours, flights, and other travel expenses.

POSSIBLE RUBRIC FEATURES: Content information, collaborative skills, decision-making process skills, ability to integrate with other subjects

For additional professional and classroom resources, see Chapter Resources, pages T46–T51.

TEACHER'S CORNER

INDEX TO NATIONAL GEOGRAPHIC MAGAZINE

The following articles may be used for research relating to this chapter:

- "Our National Parks," by John G. Mitchell, October 1994.
- "The Saint Lawrence: River and Sea," by Thomas J. Abercrombie, October 1994.
- "Anything But Empty: The Sonoran Desert," by Priit J. Vesilind, September 1994.
- "The American Prairie: Roots of the Sky," by Douglas H. Chadwick, October 1993.
- "Ogallala Aquifer: Wellspring of the High Plains," by Erla Zwingle, March 1993.
- "Sagebrush Country: America's Outback," by Douglas H. Chadwick, January 1989.
- "The Untamed Fraser River," by David S. Boyer, July 1986.
- "Susquehanna: America's Small-Town River," by Peter Miller, March 1985.
- "Heart of the Canadian Rockies," by Elizabeth A. Moize, June 1980.

NATIONAL GEOGRAPHIC SOCIETY PRODUCTS AVAILABLE FROM GLENCOE

To order the following products for use with this chapter, contact your local Glencoe sales representative or call Glencoe at 1-800-334-7344:

- *Picture Atlas of the World* (CD-ROM)
- *STV: North America* (Videodisc)
- *ZipZapMap! USA* (Software)
- *GeoBee* (Software)
- *Images of the World* (Posters)
- *Eye on the Environment* (Posters)
- *Physical Geography of the World* (Transparencies)
- *Picture Atlas of Our 50 States* (Book)

ADDITIONAL NATIONAL GEOGRAPHIC SOCIETY PRODUCTS

To order the following products for use with this chapter, call National Geographic Society at 1-800-368-2728:

- *The Water's Edge: Life Along the Great Rivers,* "The Amazon," "The Mississippi," "The Nile." (Filmstrip)
- *Great Lakes, Fragile Seas* (Video)
- *National Parks: Playground or Paradise?* (Video)

Introducing
CHAPTER 5

PERFORMANCE ASSESSMENT

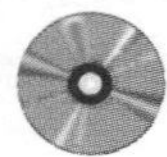

Refer to the Planning Guide on page 92B for a Performance Assessment Activity for this chapter. See the *Performance Assessment Activities* booklet for additional suggestions.

CHAPTER OBJECTIVES

1. **Describe** the physical characteristics of the United States and Canada.
2. **Explain** how the locations and landforms of the United States and Canada influence climate and vegetation.

GLENCOE TECHNOLOGY

Videodisc

Use Chapter 5 MindJogger Videoquiz to preview chapter content.

MINDJOGGER VIDEOQUIZ

Chapter 5
Disc 1 Side B

The MindJogger Videoquiz is also available on videocassette.

CD-ROM

PICTURE ATLAS OF THE WORLD

Have students click the "Photos" button and the "Essay" button to see and read about the physical geography of the United States and Canada.

chapter 5 The Physical Geography of the United States and Canada

CHAPTER FOCUS

Geographic Setting

The United States and Canada both are located on the continent of North America. Because they occupy the same landmass, they also share many of the same landforms and kinds of vegetation.

Geographic Themes

Section 1 The Land

PLACE The United States and Canada both have mountains framing eastern and western coasts and a large plains area in the center.

▲ Photograph: *Bass Head, Maine*

Section 2 The Climate and Vegetation

LOCATION The climates of the United States and Canada range from frigid tundra in northern Canada to subtropical areas in the southern United States. Hawaii is the only truly tropical area in the region.

EXTRA CREDIT PROJECT

Calendar Have students collect or draw pictures of 12 landscapes in the United States and Canada. Direct them to use the pictures to illustrate a calendar. Suggest that they choose an appropriate landscape for each month. Each picture should be accompanied by a caption that identifies its location.

1 SECTION

The Land

SETTING THE SCENE

Read to Discover . . .

- the landforms of the United States and Canada.
- the water sources that the environments of the United States and Canada offer.
- the natural resources found in the United States and Canada.

Key Terms

- plateau
- mesa
- continental divide
- headwaters
- tributary
- fishery

Identify and Locate

Pacific Ranges, Rocky Mountains, Great Basin, Great Plains, Canadian Shield, Appalachian Mountains, Mackenzie River, Mississippi River, Great Lakes

Ontario, Canada

Traveling across Canada — from the eastern Atlantic coastline to the western Rocky Mountains — I see many changes in the landscape. As a young Canadian, I feel that Canada's strength lies in its natural resources as the basis for its economic growth and legacy for future generations.

Jasmin Lalonde

Jasmin Lalonde, who comes from the Canadian province of Ontario, refers to her country's diverse landscape, a geographic characteristic shared by Canada's North American neighbor, the United States. Both nations are huge. Together, they cover more than 7 million square miles (18 million sq. km). Their continental land area extends from the Arctic Ocean in the north to the Gulf of Mexico and the Rio Grande in the south; and from the Pacific Ocean in the west to the Atlantic Ocean in the east.

PLACE

Landforms

The United States and Canada generally share the same landforms. Both nations have towering, snowcapped mountains in the west; fertile, rolling plains in the center; and low, smoothly formed mountains in the east.

Western Mountain Ranges

The Pacific Ocean forms the western border of both the United States and Canada. Paralleling the coastline are a series of mountain ranges that were formed by the collision of two tectonic plates millions of years ago. This mountain system includes the Alaska Range, the Coast Range, the Cascade Range, and the Sierra Nevada. Together, these mountains are called the Pacific Ranges.

Another western chain called the Rocky Mountains lies east of the Pacific Ranges. The massive, craggy Rocky Mountains stretch more than 3,000 miles (about 4,800 km) from northern Alaska to northern New Mexico.

Like the Pacific Ranges, the Rockies were formed by tectonic forces millions of years

LESSON PLAN
Chapter 5, Section 1

FOCUS

SECTION OBJECTIVES

1. **Compare** the landforms of the United States and Canada.
2. **Describe** the water sources that the environments of the United States and Canada offer.
3. **List** the kinds of natural resources found in the United States and Canada.

ABOUT THE POSTCARD

Jasmin is an eleventh-grade student and lives in Curran, Ontario. She likes geography and sports, especially skiing and cycling.

BELLRINGER MOTIVATIONAL ACTIVITY

Project the Section 1 Focus Transparency and have students answer the questions.

PRETEACHING VOCABULARY

Inform students that the word *plateau* comes from a French term meaning "flat." The word *mesa* comes from a Spanish word for "table." The two terms refer to raised landforms with flat surfaces.

Use the Vocabulary PuzzleMaker Software to create a crossword or word search puzzle.

Classroom Resources for Section 1

BLACKLINE MASTERS:
Reproducible Lesson Plan 5-1
Guided Reading Activity 5-1
Spanish Guided Reading Activity 5-1
Workbook Activity 5-1
Performance Assessment Activity 5
Section Quiz 5-1

TRANSPARENCIES:
Section Focus Transparency 5-1
Physical Geography of the World Transparencies 1-10

MULTIMEDIA:

Vocabulary PuzzleMaker Software
Testmaker

Picture Atlas of the World

Reuters Issues in Geography
Geography and the Environment
STV: North America

TEACH

GUIDED PRACTICE

L1 Creating a Chart Have students create a chart with the following headings: *Landforms, Water Systems,* and *Resources*. Under each heading, have students list features found in the United States and in Canada. Have them indicate with a star those features found in both nations.

MULTICULTURAL PERSPECTIVE

Cultural Heritage Place names reflect the multicultural heritage of the United States and Canada. For example, Mississippi is a Native American word for "Great Water;" Hudson Bay is named for the English sea captain who explored it; Sierra Nevada is Spanish for "Snow-clad range."

INDEPENDENT PRACTICE

Guided Reading Have students complete Guided Reading Activity 5-1 in the TCR. **LEP**

Videodisc

STV: NORTH AMERICA

Side 3, Chapter 4
Frames 0020-22832
Title: ***The Rocky Mountains* (in its entirety)**
Subject: Geological history, region, and climate of the Rocky Mountains

STV: NORTH AMERICA

Side 1, Chapter 1
Frames 00025-27602
Title: ***The East* (in its entirety)**
Subject: Physical characteristics of the eastern region of North America

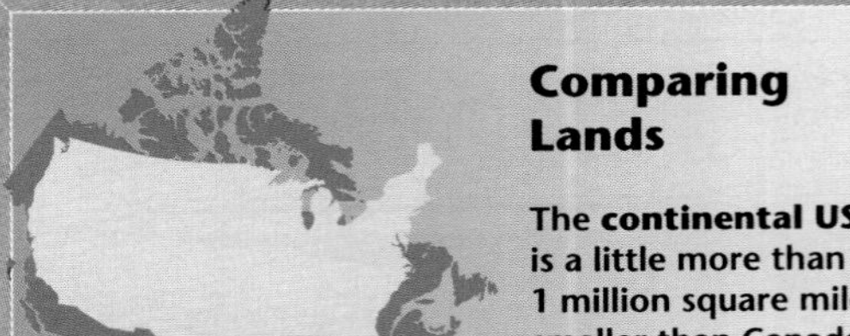

Comparing Lands

The **continental USA** is a little more than 1 million square miles smaller than Canada.

ago. Many peaks in the Rockies, especially those in the state of Colorado, rise more than 12,000 feet (3,658 m).

The area that lies between the Pacific Ranges and the Rocky Mountains is known as the intermontane basins and plateaus. The northern and southern parts of this dry expanse are **plateaus**, or high, level surfaces. The Columbia Plateau, in the north, was created by lava seeping out of cracks in the earth. The southern plateau, the Colorado Plateau, is heavily eroded. This natural activity has produced unusual landforms, such as the Grand Canyon and various flat-topped natural elevations called **mesas.**

Between the Columbia and Colorado plateaus lies the Great Basin. This broad, low bowl includes the hottest and lowest place in the United States—Death Valley.

Farther north, the distance between the Rockies and the Pacific Ranges narrows. As a result, Canada's Fraser Plateau and Nechako Plateau are smaller than the plateaus of the United States.

Plains Areas

The area east of the Rockies marks the beginning of the Great Plains. The Great Plains is a broad, flat upland extending for about 400 miles (about 644 km) from the Rocky Mountains through the central parts of Canada and the United States. In Canada and parts of the United States, the Great Plains is sometimes called the Interior Plains or High Plains, because of the area's high elevation. This elevation reaches up to 6,000 feet (1,829 m).

The Great Plains area is flat and has no significant change in landforms. Its elevation, however, descends gradually to the east at a rate of about 10 feet per mile (about 2 m per km). In the United States, this lower elevation signals the beginning of another plains area, the Central Lowlands. In Canada, the Interior Plains area continues to the Canadian Shield.

Eastern Mountains and Lowlands

The Appalachian Mountains lie to the east of the plains. This mountain system is North America's second-longest mountain range. Its 1,500-mile (2,400-km) length extends from the Canadian province of Quebec to Alabama in the United States. The Appalachians also are North America's oldest mountains, and erosion has worn them down and rounded their ancient peaks.

East and south of the Appalachians in the United States lie coastal lowlands. To the east, the Piedmont, a wide area of low, rolling hills, and the Atlantic Coastal Plain lead to the Atlantic Ocean. To the south, the Gulf Coastal Plain fans out and extends westward into Texas. In Canada, the Canadian Shield is bordered by lowlands around Hudson Bay.

MOVEMENT

Water Systems

The United States and Canada have an abundance of water systems. Large rivers and lakes supply freshwater for metropolitan and rural areas in both nations.

Because rivers flow downhill, the pattern of landforms determines the direction in which water systems flow. A **continental divide** is a line that separates rivers that flow toward opposite ends of a continent. In North America, a high ridge of the Rockies known as the Continental Divide, or the Great Divide, separates the waters flowing west to the Pacific Ocean from those flowing east toward the Mississippi River and Atlantic Ocean. In Canada, the Continental Divide joins another divide known as the Height of Land, which separates the waters flowing into the Arctic Ocean.

Cooperative Learning Activity

Organize students into three groups and assign one of the following topics to each group: western water systems, plains water systems, eastern water systems. Instruct members of each group to create a large poster map showing the major rivers and lakes that make up the water systems in their assigned region of the United States and Canada. Have students consult the text as well as other references. Tell students to label all water bodies and prepare an explanation of the importance of the water systems.

THE UNITED STATES AND CANADA: PHYSICAL-POLITICAL

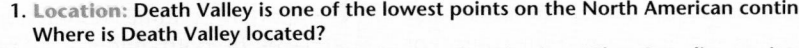

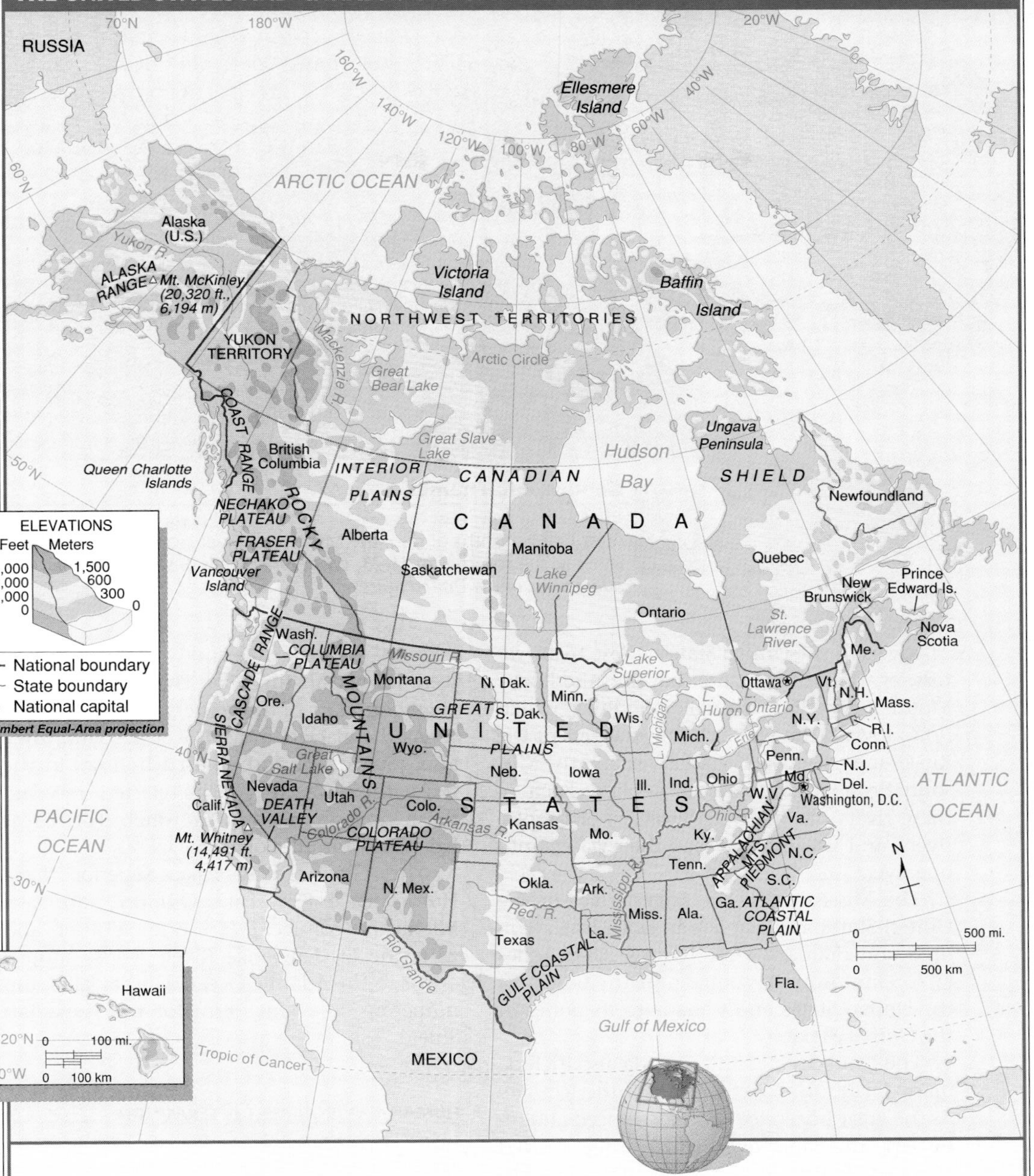

Focus on Geographic Themes

1. **Location:** **Death Valley is one of the lowest points on the North American continent. Where is Death Valley located?**
2. **Region:** **Canada is made up of provinces and territories. What Canadian territory borders the American state of Alaska?**

USING MAPS

Answers:
1. in east central California; **2.** Yukon Territory

Map Skills Practice

Reading a Map Have students use the map to find one example of each of the Key Terms from this section. **LEP**

ASSESS

CHECK FOR UNDERSTANDING

Assign Section 1 Review as homework or an in-class activity.

MEETING LESSON OBJECTIVES

Each objective below is tested by the questions that follow it in parentheses.

1. Compare the landforms of the United States and Canada. *(1, 2, 3)*

2. Describe the water resources that the environments of the United States and Canada offer. *(1, 5)*

3. List the kinds of natural resources found in the United States and Canada. *(4)*

Meeting Special Needs

Learning Disability Students with learning disabilities can benefit from creating a topographic model of the United States and Canada. Have students work together to create an outline map on heavy poster board. Then have them use clay or other media to form mountain ranges. Students might paint the model, using a key to indicate elevation. They may also add details, such as water bodies and deserts.

GLENCOE TECHNOLOGY

Videodisc

Use the following to introduce or enrich Unit 2:

REUTERS ISSUES IN GEOGRAPHY

Chapter 1
Disc 1 Side A

Title: ***The United States and Canada: The Water Supply***
Subject: Sources and uses of water in the United States and Canada

HUMAN/ENVIRONMENT INTERACTION As a result of the Great Flood of '93, Illinois, Iowa, Missouri, Wisconsin, and Minnesota were declared federal disaster areas.

Answer to Caption: *blizzards, tornadoes, hurricanes, typhoons*

CURRICULUM CONNECTION

GEOLOGY
The Canadian shield is a horseshoe-shaped expanse of rock that covers half of Canada and parts of the northeastern United States. Some of the rock formations in the Canadian Shield are 2 billion to 4 billion years old, making them some of the oldest formations in the world.

EVALUATE

Assign the Section 1 Quiz in the TCR.

Use the Testmaker to create a customized quiz for Section 1.

RETEACH

Have students work in pairs to make labels for major landforms, rivers, and lakes in the United States and Canada. Then have the partners take turns drawing a label from the pile and locating the feature on a map.

Geographic Themes
Human/Environment Interaction: The Great Flood of 1993
After eight months of rain, the Mississippi River reached record flood levels in the summer of 1993. *What other kinds of severe weather affect parts of the United States?*

Rivers in the United States whose **headwaters**, or water sources, are found in the Rocky Mountains include the Colorado River, which flows toward the west. The headwaters of the Rio Grande, the MacKenzie River, and the Missouri River are also in the Rockies. Each of these rivers has many **tributaries**, or brooks, rivers, and streams that feed their waters into one river.

The Mississippi is the largest river in the United States and Canada in both water volume and drainage area. It runs 2,340 miles (3,765 km) from its source near the border of the United States and Canada to its outlet in the Gulf of Mexico.

The United States and Canada also include many lakes formed as a result of the Ice Age. As the great frozen ice sheets advanced and retreated, the land over which they moved changed. As the ice moved relentlessly south, it formed dams on river systems and forced the waters to follow the glaciers' boundaries. It was this action that established the courses of the Missouri and Ohio rivers.

Some of this water blocked by glacial dams became lakes. In northern Canada, two major lakes—Great Bear Lake and Great Slave Lake—were formed in this way. They mark the ancient boundary of the glaciers.

As the glaciers moved over the land, they also gouged out and scoured hollows in the rocks they passed. As the glaciers receded, these hollows filled with water. The Great Lakes are examples of glacial lakes.

The Great Lakes—Lake Superior, Lake Huron, Lake Erie, Lake Ontario, and Lake Michigan—connect with one another and with the St. Lawrence River, whose mouth opens to the Atlantic Ocean. Glacial lakes, too numerous to count, also dot the Canadian Shield.

HUMAN/ENVIRONMENT INTERACTION

Resources

The United States and Canada have many important natural resources. The rivers and lakes of both nations supply plentiful amounts of freshwater. The waters of the shallow continental shelf along the Atlantic Ocean and the Gulf of Mexico teem with fish

Critical Thinking

Synthesizing Information Challenge students to use information about the landforms, water systems, and resources of the United States and Canada to answer the following question: Has physical geography aided or hindered the economic development of these two nations? Have students support their answers. *(Answers will vary but should indicate an understanding of the advantages of rich soil and water transportation in relation to economic development.)*

LEVEES AND DAMS

FOCUS ON GEOGRAPHIC THEMES

Human/Environment Interaction: How Levees Work

People build levees to prevent flooding and to use the natural floodplain. Levees prevent rivers from widening during heavy rains. Therefore, the water level rises, and the river flows faster. As the river's pressure increases, levees may break or the river may overflow the levee. *Why is flood damage from a broken levee more severe than damage from a river overflowing its natural banks?*

and shellfish as do the waters along the Pacific coastline. The major freshwater **fisheries** of the United States include the inland waters of the southern states and the Great Lakes. Fisheries are places for catching fish and other sea animals. The Great Lakes are the center of the freshwater fishing industry in Canada.

Mineral resources of the United States and Canada include gold, silver, nickel, iron, copper, uranium, and zinc. The Rocky Mountains contain a great wealth of gold, silver, and copper. Parts of the Canadian Shield have deposits of iron and nickel. Canadian officials estimate that the mostly unexplored northern areas of Canada may hold as much as 40 percent of the country's mineral riches. Important energy resources, such as oil, natural gas, and coal, are found throughout both nations. Rich coal deposits are found in the Appalachian Mountains and in the central and western parts of the United States and Canada.

Timber reserves include the huge forests that cover about one-third of each nation. More than 1,000 animal species thrive in these woodland areas.

Parts of the United States and Canada have excellent conditions for agriculture. The Great Plains and the Central Lowlands in the United States have some of the world's most fertile soil. Fertile farmlands also cover the vast Interior Plains of Canada.

SECTION 1 REVIEW

Checking for Understanding

1. **Define** plateau, mesa, continental divide, headwaters, tributary, fishery.
2. **Locating Places** What two mountain systems dominate the western portion of the United States and Canada?
3. **Region** What landform claims much of the land in the central portion of the United States and Canada?
4. **Region** What mineral resources can be found in the United States and Canada?

Critical Thinking

5. **Making Generalizations** How do the Rocky Mountains affect the rivers of this region?

ANSWERS TO SECTION 1 REVIEW

1. **plateau:** high, level surface; **mesa:** flat-topped natural elevation; **continental divide:** line that separates rivers that flow toward opposite ends of a continent; **headwaters:** water sources; **tributary:** brook, river, or stream that feeds its waters into one river; **fishery:** place for catching fish and other sea animals
2. Pacific Ranges and Rocky Mountains
3. plains
4. gold, silver, nickel, iron, copper, uranium, and zinc
5. They form a divide that separates waters flowing west toward the Pacific Ocean from those flowing east toward the Atlantic Ocean.

USING DIAGRAMS

Answer: Levees enclose a river so that water is high above the surrounding land. A breached levee results in a wall of water rushing across the countryside and smashing everything in its way.

Skills Practice

Reading a Diagram How do levees enable people to use natural floodplains? *(prevent rivers from overflowing banks during heavy rains)*

ENRICH

Have students research Niagara Falls. Suggest that students collect pictures or draw diagrams to illustrate a travelogue about this natural wonder.

CLOSE

Have students write a postcard to Jasmin describing a landscape found in the United States.

PHYSICAL GEOGRAPHY OF THE WORLD TRANSPARENCIES

Display and discuss the physical features of the following transparencies:

1. Oregon Coast, United States
2. Sonoran Desert, United States
3. Rocky Mountains, Canada
4. Grand Canyon, United States
5. Interior Plains, Canada
6. Mississippi River, United States
7. Lake Superior, United States
8. Baffin Island, Canada
9. Appalachian Mountains, United States
10. The Everglades, United States

LESSON PLAN
Chapter 5, Section 2

FOCUS

SECTION OBJECTIVES

1. **Describe** the climate regions of the United States and Canada.
2. **Identify** the kinds of natural vegetation found in the United States and Canada.

BELLRINGER MOTIVATIONAL ACTIVITY

Project the Section 2 Focus Transparency and have students answer the questions.

PRETEACHING VOCABULARY

Inform students that the words *blizzard, tornado, hurricane,* and *chinook* all refer to seasonal winds. Ask if they can identify the season in which these winds generally occur. *(Blizzard—winter, tornado—summer, hurricane—summer and autumn, chinook—winter and early spring)*

USING ILLUSTRATIONS

REGION Spring wheat is raised in the northern Great Plains states and in the Prairie Provinces. Winter wheat is grown in the southern Great Plains states.

Answer to Caption: *humid continental*

NATIONAL GEOGRAPHIC SOCIETY

Videodisc

STV: NORTH AMERICA

Side 1, Chapter 2
Frames 27647-53050
Title: ***The Northlands* (in its entirety)**
Subject: Characteristics of the Northlands, located mainly in Canada

SECTION 2

The Climate and Vegetation

SETTING THE SCENE

Read to Discover . . .
- the climate regions of the United States and Canada.
- the kinds of natural vegetation found in the United States and Canada.

Key Terms
- blizzard
- tornado
- hurricane
- typhoon
- chinook
- timberline

Identify and Locate
Climate regions: tropical rain forest, tropical savanna, marine west coast, Mediterranean, desert, humid continental, humid subtropical, highland, tundra, subarctic.

The locations and vast sizes of landforms in the United States and Canada influence the climate regions and vegetation in these nations. Many types of climate regions can be found in the United States and Canada.

REGION

Climates

In the United States and Canada, most of the earth's climate types are represented. Even a tropical rain forest climate can be found 2,400 miles (3,862 km) away from the United States mainland, on the islands of Hawaii.

Geographic Themes

Region: Great Plains

The Great Plains that stretch through the central part of the United States and Canada include vast wheat fields. *What kind of climate dominates the Great Plains region?*

Climate Regions

Winds, ocean currents, and protective mountains along the Pacific coast help create a marine west coast climate from northern California through British Columbia to the southern border of Alaska.

As they blow eastward, the Pacific winds encounter the Pacific Ranges. As the winds are forced over the mountains, the air cools and moisture is released. This means that the west coast enjoys tremendous rainfall, and some parts of the area receive more than 100 inches (254 cm) of rain each year.

The Pacific Ranges also create a rain shadow, which limits the amount of rainfall east of the mountains. This place of plateaus and basins, bordered in the east by the Rocky Mountains, is known for its hot, dry air. The only deserts in the northern part of North America are found here. These deserts include the Great Salt Lake Desert, the Blackrock Desert, and Death Valley.

The higher parts of the Rocky Mountains and Pacific Ranges have highland climates. Even in Hawaii, with its tropical rain forest climate, some mountains have snowy peaks.

Large parts of Canada and Alaska lie in a subarctic climate zone with very cold winters. Two-thirds of Canada has January tempera-

Classroom Resources for Section 2

BLACKLINE MASTERS:
Reproducible Lesson Plan 5-2
Guided Reading Activity 5-2
Spanish Guided Reading Activity 5-2
Vocabulary Activity 5
Spanish Vocabulary Activity 5
Skill Activity 5
Enrichment Activity 5
Section Quiz 5-2

TRANSPARENCIES:
Section Focus Transparency 5-2

MULTIMEDIA:

Testmaker

STV: North America

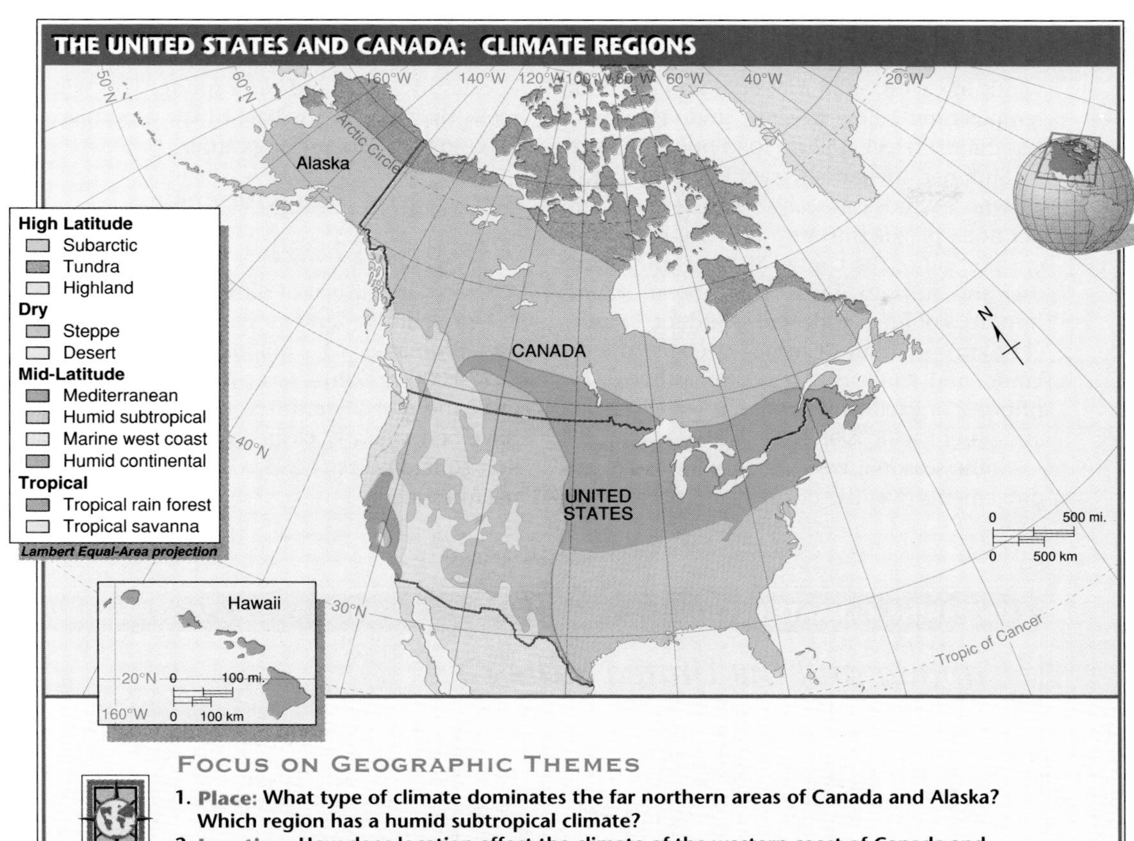

FOCUS ON GEOGRAPHIC THEMES

1. **Place:** **What type of climate dominates the far northern areas of Canada and Alaska? Which region has a humid subtropical climate?**
2. **Location:** **How does location affect the climate of the western coast of Canada and the northwestern United States?**

tures that average below 0°F (–18°C). Winter temperatures of –70°F (–57°C) have been recorded in some places. A persistent high pressure cell in this area spawns the cold winds that chill much of the central United States during the winter.

Farther north, lands across the Arctic coastlines lie in a tundra climate zone. These areas experience bitter winters and cool summers. This vast expanse of land is still a wilderness, inhabited by few people.

The Great Plains are far from oceans or other large bodies of water that moderate climate. Although western mountains block moisture-bearing Pacific winds, the Great Plains are not completely dry because moisture travels with winds that blow north along the Rockies from the Gulf of Mexico and south from the Arctic region. The region is classified as a humid continental climate region with bitter winters and hot summers.

The humid continental climate region continues east to the Atlantic. Most of the southern states, however, are in a humid subtropical climate region. Only the tip of Florida is far enough south to have a tropical savanna climate.

Seasonal Weather Conditions

Canada and the United States are affected by seasonal weather conditions. In winter,

TEACH

GUIDED PRACTICE

L2 Apply Have students list the many ways in which climate affects their life. Then ask them to categorize each effect as economic or social. *(Examples: varieties of crops, economic; outdoor activities, social)*

USING MAPS

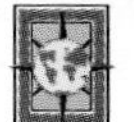

Answers:
1. tundra; southern United States
2. Winds, ocean currents, and protective mountains along the Pacific coast create a marine west coast climate.

Map Skills Practice
Reading a Map What climate region do you live in? What geographic factors influence the climate? *(Answers will vary; influences include location, landforms, winds, and bodies of water.)*

INDEPENDENT PRACTICE

Guided Reading Have students complete Guided Reading Activity 5-2 in the TCR. **LEP**

L2 Apply Have students make a graph comparing wind velocities of blizzards, tornadoes, and hurricanes.

Cooperative Learning Activity

Organize students into groups of three or four. Assign or allow groups to choose a major city in the United States or Canada. Make sure cities are scattered throughout different climate regions. Instruct members of each group to find information about the climate of their city, including average temperatures and precipitation. Students must also be prepared to explain what geographic features influence the climate of their city. Provide time for groups to share their information.

ASSESS

CHECK FOR UNDERSTANDING

Assign Section 2 Review as homework or an in-class activity.

MEETING LESSON OBJECTIVES

Each objective below is tested by the questions that follow it in parentheses.

1. Describe the climate regions of the United States and Canada. *(2, 3)*

2. Identify the kinds of natural vegetation found in the United States and Canada. *(3)*

USING GRAPHS

Answers: Quebec: 68°F (20°C), 4 in. (10 cm); Seattle: 62°F (17° C), 1 in. (2.5 cm)

Skills Practice

Interpreting a Graph

How much precipitation does each city receive in January? *(Quebec: almost 4 in. (10 cm); Seattle: 5 in. (12.5 cm)*

EVALUATE

Assign the Section 2 Quiz in the TCR.

Use the Testmaker to create a customized quiz for Section 2.

much of northern North America experiences blizzards. **Blizzards** are snowstorms with winds in excess of 35 miles (56 km) per hour, temperatures below freezing, and visibility of less than 500 feet (152 m) for 3 hours or more.

Summer **tornadoes,** swirling columns of air whose winds can reach 300 miles (483 km) per hour, plague the Great Plains and the eastern portion of the United States. During summer and autumn, **hurricanes**—ocean storms hundreds of miles wide with winds of 74 miles (119 km) per hour or more—threaten the Atlantic and Gulf of Mexico coastlines. **Typhoons,** or Pacific hurricanes, threaten Hawaii and other Pacific islands each year.

Some seasonal weather conditions are improvements over the normal patterns for a climate zone. For example, a warm wind called the **chinook** blows down the slopes of the Rockies in winter and early spring. This wind melts the snow at the base of the mountains, exposing grass for grazing cattle.

HUMAN/ENVIRONMENT INTERACTION

Vegetation

Before the arrival of settlers, almost half of present-day United States and Canada—an estimated 3 million square miles (7,770,000 sq. km)—was covered with forests. Over the past 2 centuries, humans, however, have permanently cleared over one-half million square miles (1,295,000 sq. km) of original forestland.

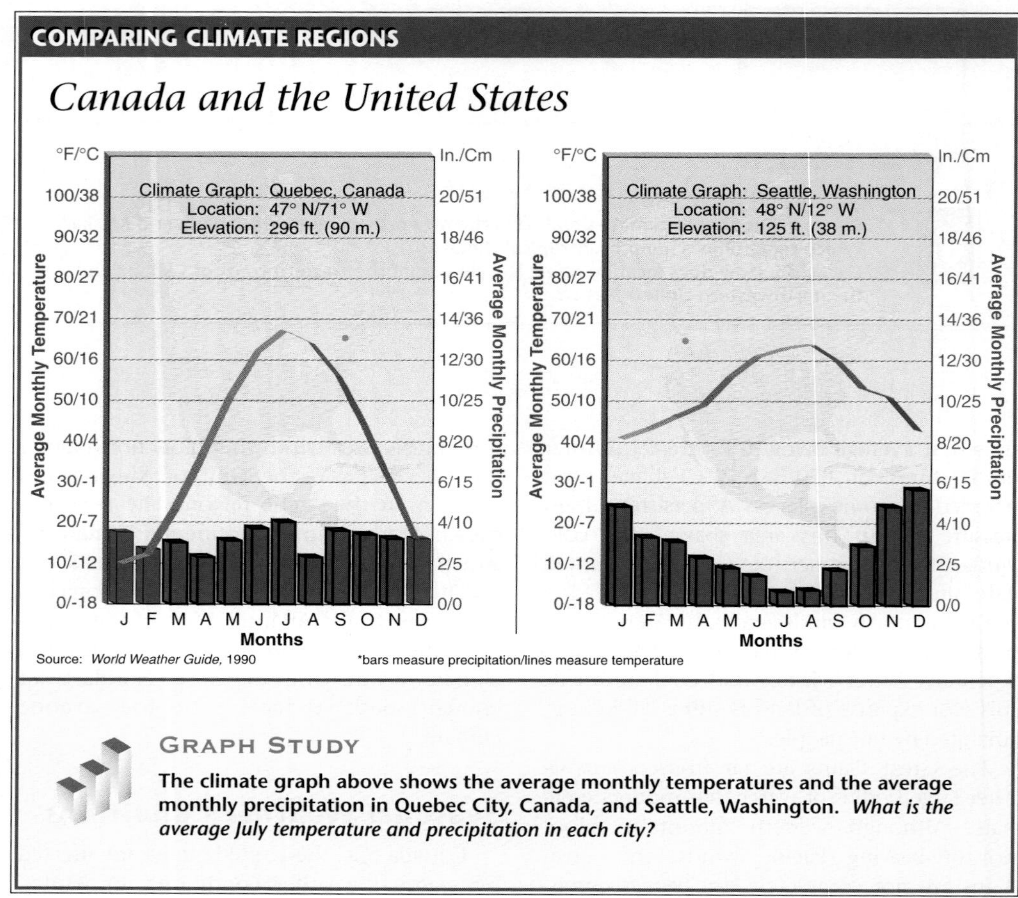

GRAPH STUDY

The climate graph above shows the average monthly temperatures and the average monthly precipitation in Quebec City, Canada, and Seattle, Washington. ***What is the average July temperature and precipitation in each city?***

Meeting Special Needs

Organizing Help students organize the material in this section by creating a chart listing the following climate regions: tundra, humid continental, highland, tropical rain forest, subarctic, humid subtropical, and tropical savanna. Have students skim the text to find and list information about each climate. Then have them list places in the United States and Canada that are in each region. Display the completed chart for reference.

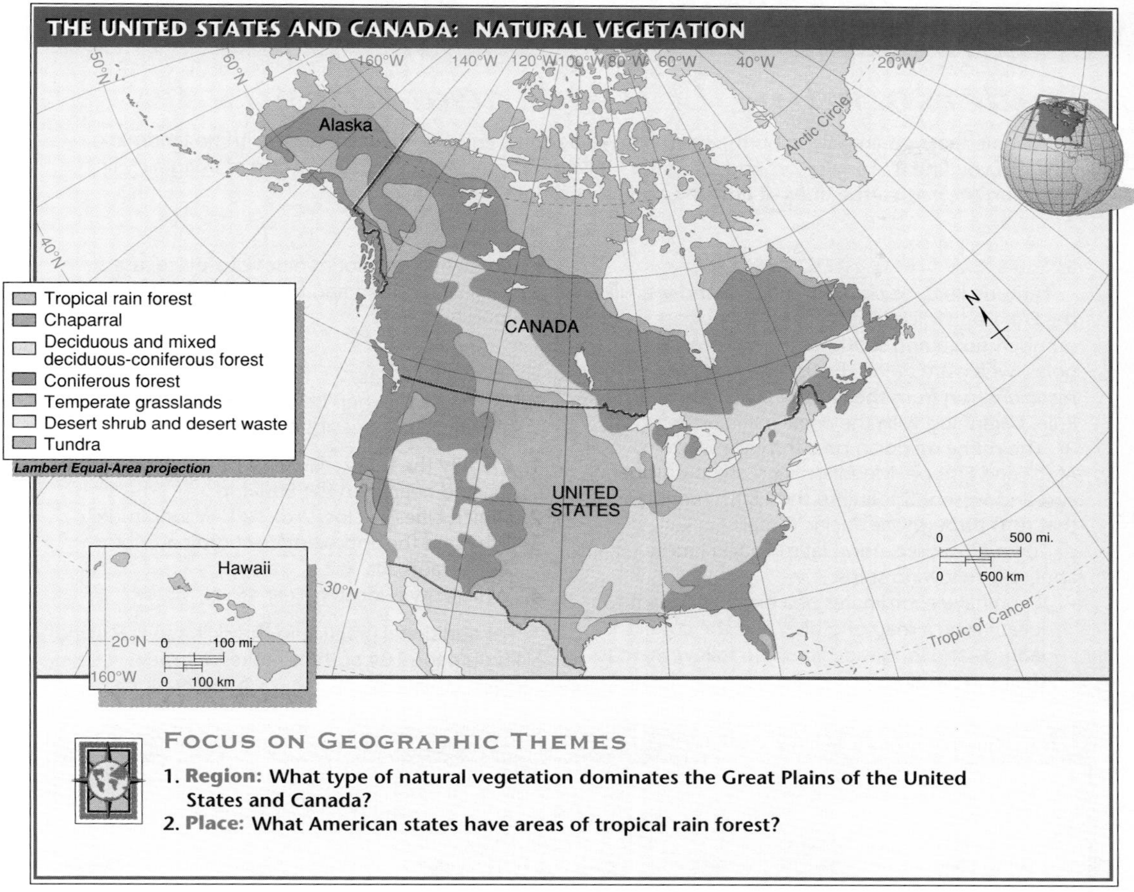

Focus on Geographic Themes

1. **Region:** **What type of natural vegetation dominates the Great Plains of the United States and Canada?**
2. **Place:** **What American states have areas of tropical rain forest?**

Despite human pressures on the land's resources, a vast forest area still spans subarctic Canada. Forests also cover the sides of the western mountain ranges until they reach the **timberline**, or the elevation above which trees cannot grow.

The Great Plains of the United States and Canada were once a prairie region, a treeless expanse of grasses whose tangled roots formed dense layers of vegetation called sod. Settlers, however, soon populated the plains, broke up the sod, and used it to build homes. These changes led to dust bowl conditions in the 1930s. Since then, scientific farming methods have improved conditions on the Great Plains, and the region now supplies most of North America's wheat.

Section 2 Review

Checking for Understanding

1. **Define** blizzard, tornado, hurricane, typhoon, chinook, timberline.
2. **Locating Places** What deserts lie in the rain shadow of the Pacific Ranges?
3. **Region** Through what two climate regions does the Mississippi River flow?
4. **Region** In what climate region can most of Canada's forest area be found?

Critical Thinking

5. **Making Comparisons** How do the Pacific winds and the Arctic winds differ in their impact on climate?

RETEACH

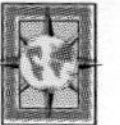

Have students complete Reteaching Activity 5 in the TCR.

ENRICH

Have students complete Enrichment Activity 5 in the TCR.

CLOSE

Ask students to compare and contrast the environments of the United States and Canada

USING MAPS

Answers: **1.** temperate grasslands **2.** Hawaii, Florida

Map Skills Practice

Comparing Maps Compare the maps on pages 99 and 101. What kind of climate produces chaparral in the western United States? *(highland)*

ANSWERS TO SECTION 2 REVIEW

1. blizzard: snowstorm with winds in excess of 35 miles (56 km) per hour, temperatures below freezing, and visibility of less than 500 feet (152 m) for 3 hours or more; **tornado:** swirling column of air whose rotating winds can reach 400 miles (644 km) per hour; **hurricane:** churning ocean storms hundreds of miles wide with winds of 74 miles (119 km) per hour or more; **typhoon:** Pacific hurricane; **chinook:** warm wind that blows down mountain slopes of the Rockies; **timberline:** elevation above which trees cannot grow

2. Great Salt Lake Desert, Blackrock Desert, Death Valley

3. humid continental and humid subtropical

4. subarctic

5. Pacific winds bring wet, mild weather to the coast year round. Arctic winds chill much of the central United States in winter.

TEACH

Say: "Suppose you have asked a friend to meet you at a restaurant, but you know only the street name, not the whole address. How can you describe its location?" *(by identifying the nearest intersecting street)* Explain: "In the same way, all points on the earth can be located by identifying the nearest intersecting lines of latitude and longitude."

Have students read the skill lesson on page 102. Then ask: "Why are latitude lines called *parallels?*" *(They run parallel to the Equator.)* Which lines intersect the North and South Poles? *(longitude lines)* Have students use the map on page 102 to give coordinates of cities.

Skills Practice
For additional practice, have students complete Skill Activity 5 in the TCR.

MAP & GRAPH SKILLS

Understanding Latitude and Longitude

Imagine that you are sailing on the open ocean and must find a particular island. With no landmarks, how can you find it? Early sailors and navigators solved this problem by creating a grid of imaginary lines encircling the earth—**the lines of latitude and longitude.**

Reviewing the Skill

Latitude lines, or *parallels,* run east and west like the Equator, which is at 0°. Parallels increase in number, north and south, as they approach the poles, which are at 90°. Longitude lines, or *meridians,* run from the North Pole to the South Pole, beginning with the *prime meridian,* which is 0°. The prime meridian runs through western Africa and Europe. Meridians increase in number east and west of this line to the 180th meridian that runs through the Pacific Ocean.

To find locations using latitude and longitude, apply the following steps:

- If you have coordinates of a place and want to locate it on a map or globe, find the correct latitude and longitude lines and follow them to their intersection.
- To identify the coordinates of a place, use a map or globe to find the nearest latitude and longitude lines.

Practicing the Skill

Use the map below to answer the following questions about latitude and longitude:

1. Identify the three mainland cities on this map located nearest to the Equator.
2. Which cities lie closest to 120° W longitude?
3. What are the approximate coordinates of Anchorage, Alaska?
4. Which city is located near 45° N, 90° W?

For additional practice in this skill, see Practicing Skills on page 104 of the Chapter 5 Review.

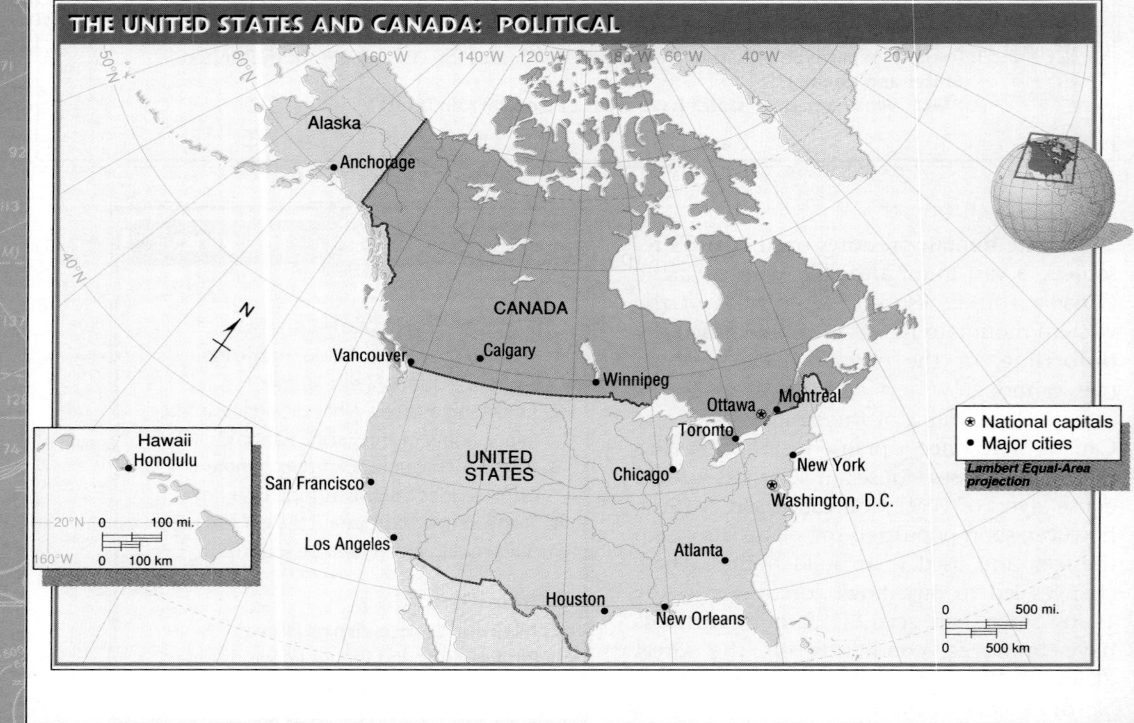

ANSWERS TO PRACTICING THE SKILL

1. Houston, New Orleans, Atlanta
2. Los Angeles, San Francisco, Vancouver
3. 60°N, 150°W
4. Chicago

chapter 5

HIGHLIGHTS

Section 1: The Land

Key Terms

plateau (p. 94)
mesa (p. 94)
continental divide (p. 94)
headwaters (p. 96)
tributary (p. 96)
fishery (p. 97)

The Mississippi River

Summary

- The nations of the United States and Canada form a region that makes up most of the North American continent.
- Two mountain ranges dominate the landforms to the west, with plateaus and basins lying between the ranges.
- Western mountain ranges, and another major range in the east, border the vast interior plains that mark the central portion of this region.
- Several major rivers help drain the land's water into the oceans that border the region.
- This region is rich in many renewable and nonrenewable natural resources.

Section 2: The Climate and Vegetation

Key Terms

blizzard (p. 100)
tornado (p. 100)
hurricane (p. 100)
typhoon (p. 100)
chinook (p. 100)
timberline (p. 101)

Summary

- Although Canada and the United States share some climate regions, others are particular to each nation.
- The winds from the Pacific Ocean, the Arctic Ocean, and the Gulf of Mexico exert tremendous influence on the region's climates.
- Most climate regions—from desert to tundra—are represented in this region.
- Humans have had an enormous impact on the natural vegetation of the region.

Harvesting grain in the Great Plains

Map Activity

Identify and Locate Copy and distribute page 23 of the Outline Map Resource Book. Have students number the location of each of the following places on their map: (1) Rocky Mountains, (2) Great Plains, (3) Canadian Shield, (4) Great Lakes, (5) Mississippi River. Then have them color the map to indicate the following climate regions: blue = tundra, green = subarctic, orange = humid continental, yellow = humid subtropical.

CHAPTER 5 HIGHLIGHTS

USING THE CHAPTER 5 HIGHLIGHTS

Use the Chapter 5 Highlights to preview, review, condense, or reteach the chapter.

PREVIEW/REVIEW

Vocabulary PuzzleMaker Software reinforces the Key Terms used in Chapter 5.

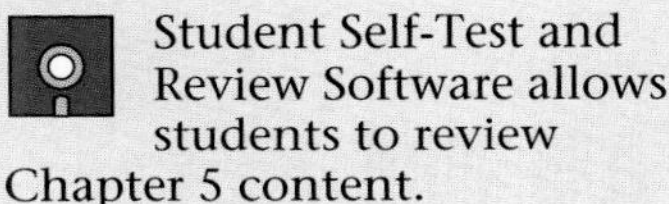
Student Self-Test and Review Software allows students to review Chapter 5 content.

CONDENSE

Have students read the Chapter 5 Highlights.

Have students listen to the Chapter 5 Audiocassettes in the TCR. Spanish Audiocassettes are also available.

Assign the Chapter 5 Audiocassette Activity and give students the Chapter 5 Audiocassette Quiz.

Have students complete Guided Reading Activities for Chapter 5 in the TCR. Spanish Guided Reading Activities are also available.

RETEACH

Have students complete Reteaching Activity 5 in the TCR. Spanish Reteaching Activities are also available.

GLENCOE TECHNOLOGY

Videodisc

Use Chapter 5 MindJogger Videoquiz to review students' knowledge before administering the Chapter 5 Test.

MINDJOGGER VIDEOQUIZ

Chapter 5
Disc 1 Side B

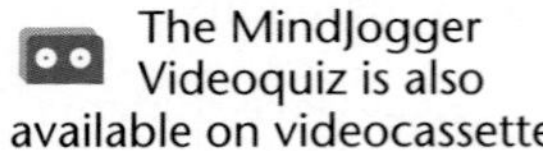

The MindJogger Videoquiz is also available on videocassette.

ANSWERS

Reviewing Key Terms

1. tributaries
2. mesa
3. continental divide
4. blizzard
5. typhoons
6. timberline
7. hurricanes

Reviewing Facts

8. coastal lowlands
9. Rocky Mountains
10. Rio Grande
11. tropical rain forest
12. Pacific Ranges and Rocky Mountains
13. humid subtropical

chapter 5 REVIEW

Reviewing Key Terms

Choose the vocabulary term that best completes each of the sentences below. Write your answers on a separate sheet of paper.

mesa (p. 94)	hurricanes (p. 100)
continental divide (p. 94)	blizzard (p. 100)
	typhoons (p. 100)
tributaries (p. 96)	timberline (p. 101)

SECTION 1

1. The brooks, rivers, and streams that feed a river are called its ____.
2. ____ is the name given flat-topped natural elevations of the southwest.
3. The Great Divide is a ____.

SECTION 2

4. During a ____, snow-filled, frigid winds buffet an area.
5. Hurricanes that occur in the Pacific Ocean are called ____.
6. In high mountains, the ____ indicates the point above which trees cannot grow.
7. ____ are swirling ocean storms with sustained high winds that plague the Atlantic and Gulf of Mexico coasts during summer and fall.

Reviewing Facts

SECTION 1

8. What landform includes the Piedmont, the Atlantic Coastal Plain, and the Gulf Coastal Plain?
9. In what mountain range is North America's Continental Divide located?
10. What river forms part of the border between the United States and Mexico?

SECTION 2

11. What kind of climate does Hawaii have?
12. What mountain systems are separated by desert areas?
13. The states of the southeast lie in what kind of climate region?

Critical Thinking

14. **Analyzing Information** Compare the map of oil and natural gas resources in the United States on page 15 of the Geography Skills Handbook with the physical features map of the United States and Canada on page 88. What kind of landform seems to support deposits of these resources?
15. **Determining Cause and Effect** How did settlers' farming techniques lead to the tremendous loss of soil in the Great Plains of the United States?

Geographic Themes

16. **Human/Environment Interaction** How did human settlement alter the forests of this region?
17. **Region** What kind of vegetation grew in the Great Plains before human settlement?

Practicing Skills

Understanding Latitude and Longitude

Using the map on page 102, find the cities located nearest to these coordinates:

18. 30° N, 95° W
19. 33° N, 84° W
20. 52° N, 96° W
21. 40° N, 75° W

Using the Unit Atlas

Refer to the physical geography section of the Unit Atlas on pages 88–89.

22. In what mountain range is Mt. McKinley located?
23. What part of Canada and the United States is a major grain-producing area?

Critical Thinking

14. plains
15. Settlers broke up the sod, which led to dust bowl conditions in the 1930s.

Geographic Themes

16. Over the past two centuries, humans have permanently cleared over one half million square miles (1,295,000 sq. km) of original forestland.
17. grasses

Projects

Individual Activity

In this chapter you have learned about the landforms that cross the United States and Canada. Choose one of these landforms. Create a collage illustrating the landform you have chosen. Use pictures from magazines, newspapers, or your own drawings. Present your collage to the class, explaining what each illustration represents.

Cooperative Learning Activity

In a group of six, assign each member one of the climate regions of Canada. Each member is to research and prepare a report on the animal life in the assigned climate zone. When the reports are finished, share the information with the group. Then determine whether some climate regions share species of animals, and report what you have learned to the class.

Writing About Geography

Description

Select a place described in your journal under the heading Geography. Write a letter in which you describe how this area differs from your home in landforms, water, climate, and vegetation. Use the information and photographs presented in the text as well as the information in the journal. You may wish to use an encyclopedia or other resource book to obtain additional details.

Locating Places

THE UNITED STATES AND CANADA: PHYSICAL GEOGRAPHY

Match the letters on the map with the physical features of the United States and Canada. Write your answers on a separate sheet of paper.

1. Pacific Ranges
2. Rocky Mountains
3. Appalachian Mountains
4. Mississippi River
5. Mackenzie River
6. Río Grande
7. Great Bear Lake
8. Great Slave Lake
9. Great Lakes
10. Hudson Bay
11. Great Plains
12. Canadian Shield

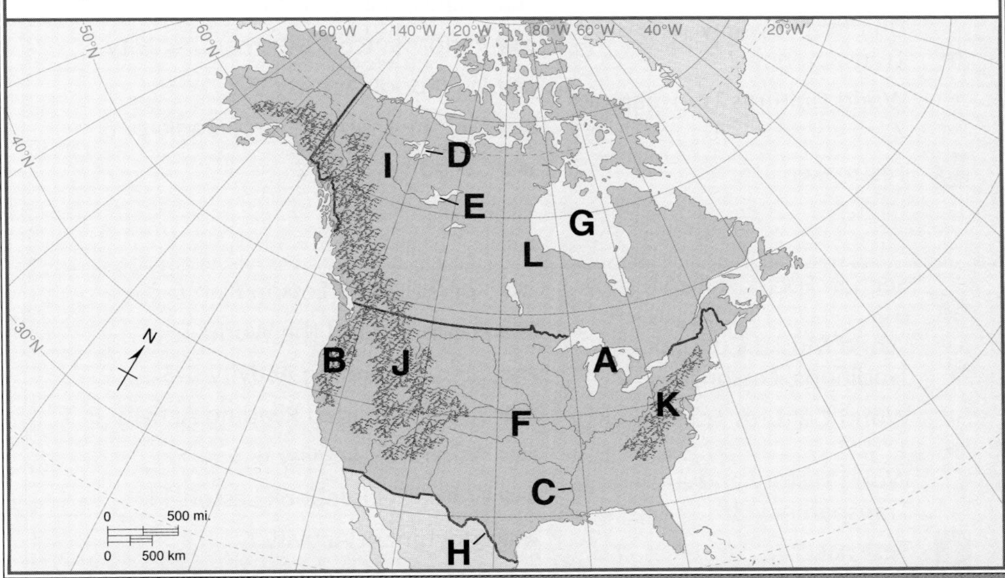

Practicing Skills

18. Houston, Texas
19. Atlanta, Georgia
20. Winnipeg, Manitoba
21. Washington, D.C.

Using the Unit Atlas

22. Alaska Range
23. Great Plains

Locating Places

1. B
2. J
3. K
4. C
5. I
6. H
7. D
8. E
9. A
10. G
11. F
12. L

Chapter Bonus Test Question

This question may be used for extra credit on the chapter test.

Why does the United States have more climate regions than does Canada?

(Answer: The United States extends from Alaska, which is partly in the subarctic climate zone, to Hawaii, which is in the tropics. Most of Canada lies north of 50° north latitude.)

CHAPTER 6

PLANNING GUIDE

The Cultural Geography of the United States and Canada

CHAPTER ORGANIZER

Daily Lesson Objectives	Multimedia	Teacher Classroom Resources
SECTION 1 Population Patterns 1. Describe the human characteristics of the United States and Canada. 2. Explain population distribution in the United States and Canada. 3. Discuss advances in transportation that led to the development of large cities.	Section Focus Transparency 6-1 Chapter 6 Vocabulary PuzzleMaker Software Testmaker Geography and the Environment Picture Atlas of the World	Reproducible Lesson Plan 6-1 World Literature Reading 1 Guided Reading Activity 6-1 Spanish Guided Reading Activity 6-1 Workbook Activity 6-1 Vocabulary Activity 6 Spanish Vocabulary Activity 6 Section Quiz 6-1
SECTION 2 History and Government 1. Describe how the United States and Canada were settled and became separate nations. 2. Explain how the United States and Canada expanded their territories and developed strong economies.	Section Focus Transparency 6-2 Political Map Transparency 2 Unit Map Overlay Transparency 2 World Cultures Transparency 2 Testmaker	Reproducible Lesson Plan 6-2 Guided Reading Activity 6-2 Spanish Guided Reading Activity 6-2 Performance Assessment Activity 6 Workbook Activity 6-2 Outline Map Resource Book, p. 6 Section Quiz 6-2
SECTION 3 Cultures and Lifestyles 1. Relate how the cultures of these countries developed. 2. Point out how the lifestyles of the United States and Canada compare with each other.	Section Focus Transparency 6-3 World Music: Cultural Traditions, Lesson 1 World Cultures Transparency 1 World History and Art Transparency 36 Testmaker Picture Atlas of the World	Reproducible Lesson Plan 6-3 Foods Around the World 1 Guided Reading Activity 6-3 Spanish Guided Reading Activity 6-3 Workbook Activity 6-3 Writer's Guidebook Lesson 11 Enrichment Activity 6 Section Quiz 6-3
CHAPTER REVIEW AND EVALUATION	Chapter 6 English (or Spanish) Audiocassettes MindJogger Videoquiz Testmaker Student Self-Test and Review Software	Reteaching Activity 6 Spanish Reteaching Activity 6 Chapter 6 Test Form A and Form B

0:00 *If time does not permit teaching the entire chapter, summarize using the Chapter 6 Highlights on page 125, and the Chapter 6 English (or Spanish) Audiocassettes. Review students' knowledge using the Glencoe MindJogger Videoquiz.*

KEY TO ABILITY LEVELS

Teaching strategies have been coded for varying learning styles and abilities.

- L1 **BASIC** activities for all students
- L2 **AVERAGE** activities for average to above-average students
- L3 **CHALLENGING** activities for above-average students
- LEP **LIMITED ENGLISH PROFICIENCY** activities

Performance Assessment

History and Culture Organize the class into groups, and ask the groups to write "revised" editions of Section 2 on the historical events that occurred in the United States and Canada. Students should take the eras of migration, exploration, and colonization and totally change the time frame, countries, locations, and so on, of the early settlement of the culture region. When students have rewritten the history, they should describe the modern-day cultures of the United States and Canada in terms of a different heritage. Their descriptions may be written or may be done on a series of maps showing cultural elements. Provision should be made for students to share their revised culture region with others in the class.

POSSIBLE RUBRIC FEATURES: Concept information, interdependence of history and culture, predictive and cause/effect skills, communication skills (written), graphic and map skills

For additional professional and classroom resources, see Chapter Resources, pages T46–T51.

TEACHER'S CORNER

INDEX TO NATIONAL GEOGRAPHIC MAGAZINE

The following articles may be used for research relating to this chapter:

- "Boston, Breaking New Ground," by William S. Ellis, July 1994.
- "In the Heart of Appalachia," by Jeannie Ralston, February 1993.
- "The Hard Ride of Route 93," by Michael Parfit, December 1992.
- "Vancouver: Good Luck City," by Andrew Ward, April 1992.
- "Montreal: Spirited Heart of French Canada," by Douglas B. Lee, March 1991.
- "The Cajuns: Still Loving Life," by Griffin Smith, Jr., October 1990.
- "Common Ground, Different Dreams," by Priit J. Vesilind, February 1990.
- "Discovering America," by Malgorzata Niezabitowska, January 1988.
- "The Plain People of Pennsylvania," by Douglas Lee, April 1984.
- "Calgary: Canada's Not-So-Wild West," by David S. Boyer, March 1984.

NATIONAL GEOGRAPHIC SOCIETY PRODUCTS AVAILABLE FROM GLENCOE

To order the following products for use with this chapter, contact your local Glencoe sales representative or call Glencoe at 1-800-334-7344:

- *Picture Atlas of the World* (CD-ROM)
- *STV: North America* (Videodisc)
- *ZipZapMap! USA* (Software)
- *GeoBee* (Software)
- *Images of the World* (Posters)
- *Eye on the Environment* (Posters)
- *Physical Geography of the World* (Transparencies)
- *Picture Atlas of Our 50 States* (Book)

ADDITIONAL NATIONAL GEOGRAPHIC SOCIETY PRODUCTS

To order the following products for use with this chapter, call National Geographic Society at 1-800-368-2728:

- *Canada*, "The Atlantic Provinces," "Quebec," "Ontario," "The Prairie Provinces and the Northwest Territories," "British Columbia and the Yukon Territory." (Filmstrip)
- *Government in the United States*, "Local and County Government," "State Government," "Federal Government: The Legislative Branch," "Federal Government: The Judicial Branch," "Federal Government: The Executive Branch." (Filmstrip)
- *The United States as a World Power: From the 1890s to the 1970s*, "Before 1921," "1921 to 1945," "After World War II." (Filmstrip)
- *Branches of Government: The Legislative Branch* (Video)
- *Branches of Government: The Executive Branch* (Video)
- *Branches of Government: The Judicial Branch* (Video)

Introducing
CHAPTER 6

chapter 6 The Cultural Geography of the United States and Canada

PERFORMANCE ASSESSMENT

Refer to the Planning Guide on page 106B for a Performance Assessment Activity for this chapter. See the *Performance Assessment Activities* booklet for additional suggestions.

CHAPTER OBJECTIVES

1. **Identify** the human characteristics of the United States and Canada.
2. **Describe** the historical development of the United States and Canada.
3. **Compare** the lifestyles of the United States and Canada.

GLENCOE TECHNOLOGY

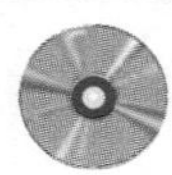

Videodisc

Use Chapter 6 MindJogger Videoquiz to preview chapter content.

MINDJOGGER VIDEOQUIZ

Chapter 6
Disc 1 Side B

The MindJogger Videoquiz is also available on videocassette.

CD-ROM

PICTURE ATLAS OF THE WORLD

You and your students can click the "Stats" button to find facts and figures about the population of the United States and Canada.

CHAPTER FOCUS

Geographic Setting

Most Americans and Canadians trace their ancestral roots to other parts of the world. Some came voluntarily; others were forced to come either as enslaved labor or as exiles.

▲ Photograph: *Street fair in New York City, New York*

Geographic Themes

Section 1 Population Patterns

REGION Canada's population is concentrated in relatively small areas near the United States-Canadian border. Population in the United States tends to be concentrated along the coasts or in the Great Lakes region.

Section 2 History and Government

PLACE The United States and Canada share a British political heritage.

Section 3 Cultures and Lifestyles

MOVEMENT The United States and Canada have culturally diverse societies.

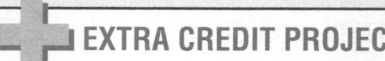

EXTRA CREDIT PROJECT

Brochure Challenge students to create a travel brochure for a state of the United States or a province of Canada. Brochures should include pictures and descriptions of historical sites and other places of interest to visit.

SECTION 1

Population Patterns

SETTING THE SCENE

Read to Discover . . .
- the human characteristics of the United States and Canada.
- how population is distributed across the United States and Canada.
- how advances in transportation led to the development of large cities.

Key Terms
- immigrant
- Sunbelt
- suburbs
- metropolitan area
- megalopolis

Identify and Locate
New York City, Chicago, Detroit, Pittsburgh, Boston, Philadelphia, Washington, D.C., St. Louis, Los Angeles, Atlanta, Denver, San Francisco, Houston, Dallas, New Orleans, Toronto, Montreal, Winnipeg, Calgary, Vancouver, Ottawa

Ontario, Canada

Traveling across Canada — from the eastern Atlantic coastline to the western Rocky Mountains — I see many changes in the landscape. As a young Canadian, I feel that Canada's strength lies in its natural resources as the basis for its economic growth and legacy for future generations.

Jasmin Lalonde

Jeffrey Lee belongs to the Ojibway nation, one of the many Native American peoples who were the first to settle the area that is today the United States and Canada. The region was later settled by people from other areas of the world. Today the region's culture comes from the Europeans, Africans, and Asians who arrived after A.D. 1500. This mixing of different peoples and cultures has given the United States and Canada unique identities.

PLACE

Human Characteristics

Both Canada and the United States are home to various groups of native peoples. These huge countries, however, are largely populated by many groups of **immigrants**—people who leave their home countries to settle permanently in others—and their descendants. A large number of these immigrants came from Europe. Many others came from various Asian, African, and Latin American countries.

MOVEMENT

Population Distribution and Density

More than 285 million people—about 5 percent of the world's population—live in the United States and Canada. Of these,

LESSON PLAN
Chapter 6, Section 1

FOCUS

SECTION OBJECTIVES
1. **Describe** the human characteristics of the United States and Canada.
2. **Explain** population distribution in the United States and Canada.
3. **Discuss** advances in transportation that led to the development of large cities.

ABOUT THE POSTCARD

Jeffrey is planning to enter a Native Studies program upon graduation.

BELLRINGER MOTIVATIONAL ACTIVITY

Project Section 1 Focus Transparency and have students answer the questions.

PRETEACHING VOCABULARY

Teach the following roots derived from Greek words: *polis* (city), *metro* (mother), and *mega* (great). Then guide students to understand the meanings of *metropolitan* (major city) and *megalopolis* (great urban area).

Use the Vocabulary PuzzleMaker Software to create a crossword or word search puzzle.

Classroom Resources for Section 1

BLACKLINE MASTERS:
- Reproducible Lesson Plan 6-1
- World Literature Reading 1
- Guided Reading Activity 6-1
- Spanish Guided Reading Activity 6-1
- Vocabulary Activity 6
- Spanish Vocabulary Activity 6
- Workbook Activity 6-1
- Section Quiz 6-1

TRANSPARENCIES:
- Section Focus Transparency 6-1

MULTIMEDIA:

Vocabulary PuzzleMaker Software
Testmaker

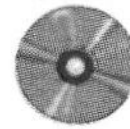
Geography and the Environment

Picture Atlas of the World

TEACH

GUIDED PRACTICE

L2 Comparing Create a Venn diagram to compare the populations of the United States and Canada. Draw two intersecting circles on the chalkboard. List facts about each country's population in one of the circles.

USING GRAPHS

Answer: 25.7%

Skills Practice

Reading a Graph: What percentage of Americans are of Hispanic origin? *(10.2%)*

INDEPENDENT PRACTICE

Guided Reading Have students complete Guided Reading Activity 6-1 in the TCR. **LEP**

ASSESS

CHECK FOR UNDERSTANDING

Assign Section 1 Review as homework or an in-class activity.

MEETING LESSON OBJECTIVES

Each objective below is tested by the questions that follow it in parentheses.

1. **Describe** the human characteristics of the United States and Canada. *(1, 3)*
2. **Explain** population distribution in the United States and Canada. *(2, 4)*
3. **Discuss** advances in transportation that led to the development of large cities. *(4, 5)*

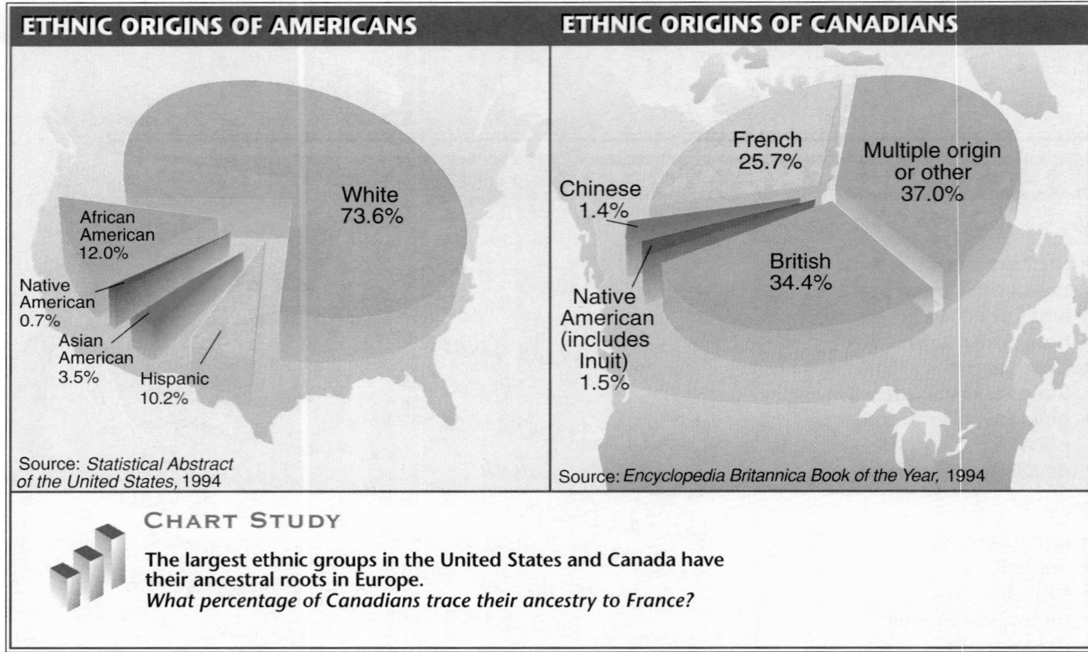

CHART STUDY

The largest ethnic groups in the United States and Canada have their ancestral roots in Europe.
What percentage of Canadians trace their ancestry to France?

about 261 million live in the United States. The average population density of the United States is about 74 people per square mile (28 people per sq. km). The United States population is growing slowly. The average yearly population growth rate in the United States is about 1 percent. Canada, with a population of about 29 million people, averages only 8 people per square mile (3 people per sq. km) of land. The Canadian population is increasing at a rate slightly less than 1 percent per year.

Canada and the United States differ noticeably in population distribution as well as in population size. The population of the United States is largely concentrated in certain areas. The northeastern part of the United States is the most densely populated part of the country. A large part of the American population is concentrated in the Great Lakes region. These two areas are located near transportation routes and manufacturing centers. Parts of the western coast of the United States are also heavily populated. An abundance of natural resources, available land, and economic opportunities have helped the western coast of the United States grow in population. Since the 1970s, the fastest-growing areas in the United States have been the South and the Southwest, including California. Industrial growth and an appealing climate have encouraged migration to the southern United States. Because of its mild climate, the southern United States is often called the **Sunbelt.**

Other areas of the United States are sparsely populated. Few people, for example, live in the subarctic climate of Alaska or in the dry climate of the Great Basin. In addition, thinly populated areas exist in parts of the interior plains.

Most Canadians live in the Great Lakes region and along the St. Lawrence River. These areas extend along the southern parts of Canada's two major industrial provinces: Quebec and Ontario. Pockets of population are also found in southern sections of the Prairie Provinces farther west, and along the Pacific coast of the province of British Columbia. All of these areas have relatively mild climates and are close to the United States, Canada's main trading partner. The remaining two-thirds of Canada, however, remains sparsely inhabited.

Cooperative Learning Activity

Organize students into groups of three. Assign, or allow each group to choose, one of the major cities in the United States or Canada. Instruct members of each group to prepare a one-minute commercial encouraging tourists to visit their city. Commercials should include interesting facts about the location, climate, economy, and physical and human characteristics of each city. Students may use sound effects, music, or visual aides. Provide time for each group to present its commercial to the class.

MOVEMENT

Urbanization

Both the United States and Canada have large urban populations. About three-fourths of the people live in or near cities and small towns.

Many of the urban areas in the United States and Canada consist of a central city, nearby neighborhoods, and outlying communities called **suburbs.** A central city and its surrounding suburbs are often called a **metropolitan area.** Because of the use of automobiles and mass-transit systems, more people live in suburbs than in central cities.

Coastal Cities

There are more than 70 urban areas in the United States and Canada with populations of more than 500,000 people. Several major cities lie along the northern Atlantic coast of the United States. The largest are Boston, New York, Philadelphia, Baltimore, and Washington, D.C. These cities are so close to one another that their surrounding areas overlap to form a single urban area. This type of urban pattern is called a **megalopolis.** The megalopolis formed by the cities between Boston and Washington, D.C., is sometimes called Boswash. Cities within Boswash have benefited from their coastal location. New York City, the culture region's largest city, is one of the world's leading centers for overseas trade.

Large port cities in the southern part of the United States include Miami, New Orleans, and Houston. Miami is on the Atlantic Ocean and is a major connection between the United States and the islands in the Caribbean Sea. New Orleans and Houston are busy transportation centers on the Gulf of Mexico.

Major port cities on the Pacific Ocean are Los Angeles, San Diego, San Francisco, Seattle, and Vancouver. In Los Angeles and Seattle, an important industry is the production of airplanes. An area near San Francisco called Silicon Valley is important for producing electronic equipment. Vancouver in the Canadian province of British Columbia is an important shipping center for western Canada.

Inland Cities

Many cities in the United States and Canada are located near inland waterways. In Canada Toronto, Montreal, Quebec City, and Ottawa are near the Great Lakes, the St. Lawrence River, or the Ottawa River.

In the United States, the cities of Chicago, Detroit, Milwaukee, and Cleveland are located on the Great Lakes. These cities grew partly because industries were able to use the Great Lakes to transport natural resources and manufactured goods. Pittsburgh's location on the Ohio River has been important for the shipment of goods related to western Pennsylvania's steel industry. St. Louis is situated near the confluence of the Missouri River and the Mississippi River. St. Louis's location made it a gateway to the settlements of the West during the 1800s.

Other major cities in the interior parts of the United States and Canada include Dallas, San Antonio, Atlanta, Memphis, Minneapolis, Kansas City, Denver, Salt Lake City, Winnipeg, Calgary, and Edmonton. These cities serve as transportation and business centers for their surrounding areas.

Section 1 Review

Checking for Understanding

1. **Define** immigrant, Sunbelt, suburbs, metropolitan area, megalopolis.
2. **Locating Places** Where is North America's biggest megalopolis located?
3. **Place** What major ethnic groups make up the population of the United States? The population of Canada?
4. **Location** Where in Canada do most people live?

Critical Thinking

5. **Making Comparisons** Compare population patterns of the United States and Canada.

ANSWERS TO SECTION 1 REVIEW

1. **immigrant:** person who leaves one country to settle permanently in another; **Sunbelt:** southern and southwestern regions of the United States, known for temperate climates; **suburbs:** outlying communities of a city; **metropolitan area:** central city and its surrounding suburbs; **megalopolis:** two or more metropolitan areas that meet
2. along the northern Atlantic coast from Boston to Washington, D.C.
3. White, African American, Hispanic; British, French
4. in the Great Lakes region and along the St. Lawrence River
5. About three-fourths of the people of the United States and Canada live in urban areas.

EVALUATE

Assign the Section 1 Quiz in the TCR.

Use the Testmaker to create a customized quiz for Section 1.

RETEACH

Have students make a list of similarities and differences between the populations of the United States and Canada.

ENRICH

Have students research and report on the building of the St. Lawrence Seaway. They should explain how the governments of the United States and Canada cooperated on this major transportation link and how the seaway benefits both countries.

CLOSE

Have students write a postcard to Jeffrey Lee, telling about a custom in their family or community.

GLENCOE TECHNOLOGY

Videodisc

GEOGRAPHY AND THE ENVIRONMENT
THE INFINITE VOYAGE
To the Edge of the Earth

Chapter 6
Disc 1 Side B
Title: ***Exploring Life in the Canadian Arctic***
Subject: Endangered, open-sea areas of the Canadian Arctic provide a source of food for large mammals and arctic birds

TEACH

Tell students that the forests in the Pacific Northwest hold some of the oldest plants on the continent. These forests are labeled as old-growth forests: where the trees generally are older than 150 years, where dead trees are left standing, and where trees have never been harvested. Old-growth ecosystems are places where plants and animals are dependent upon one another.

Ask how a dead tree can be vital to an ecosystem. *(When a tree dies, the trunk may remain standing, offering animals a place to live and a source of food. Insects help the wood decompose, which attracts more insects that are food for other animals. When the trunk falls to the ground, amphibians and fungi contribute to the rotting of the wood, which fertilizes the soil and enables young seedlings to grow.)*

DID YOU KNOW?

One of the trees in the Pacific Northwest is the Pacific yew. In the past, loggers viewed the yews as trash trees. Recently, however, a cancer-battling chemical known as taxol was discovered in the bark of this tree. Taxol may cause remissions in some patients whose cancers have not responded to other treatments.

Videodisc

STV: NORTH AMERICA

Side 3, Chapter 5
Frames 22880-53412
Title: ***The Pacific Edge*** **(in its entirety)**
Subject: The landscapes, climate, and region of the Pacifc Edge

---

NATIONAL GEOGRAPHIC GEOFACTS

What is the tallest living thing on earth?

Survivors of ice ages and chain saws, California's coast redwoods are the tallest living things on the earth. The largest of these giant trees towers 367.8 feet (112 m) —higher than the Statue of Liberty.

Sprouting from seeds no larger than the head of a pin, coast redwoods grow at a rate of 2 feet (more than 0.5 m) a year, finally maturing in 400 years. With few natural enemies, the redwoods can live for 2,000 years. Thick bark shields them from insects and fires. Even disease and floods don't often kill them.

But redwoods do need a lot of moisture, a fact that limits their range to rainy, foggy stretches of southern Oregon and northern California. Their durable wood is prized by loggers. Only about 10 percent of the virgin redwood forest remains. Today 260,000 acres (104,000 ha) of redwood forests are protected in state and in national parks.

Coast Redwood
Sequoia sempervirens

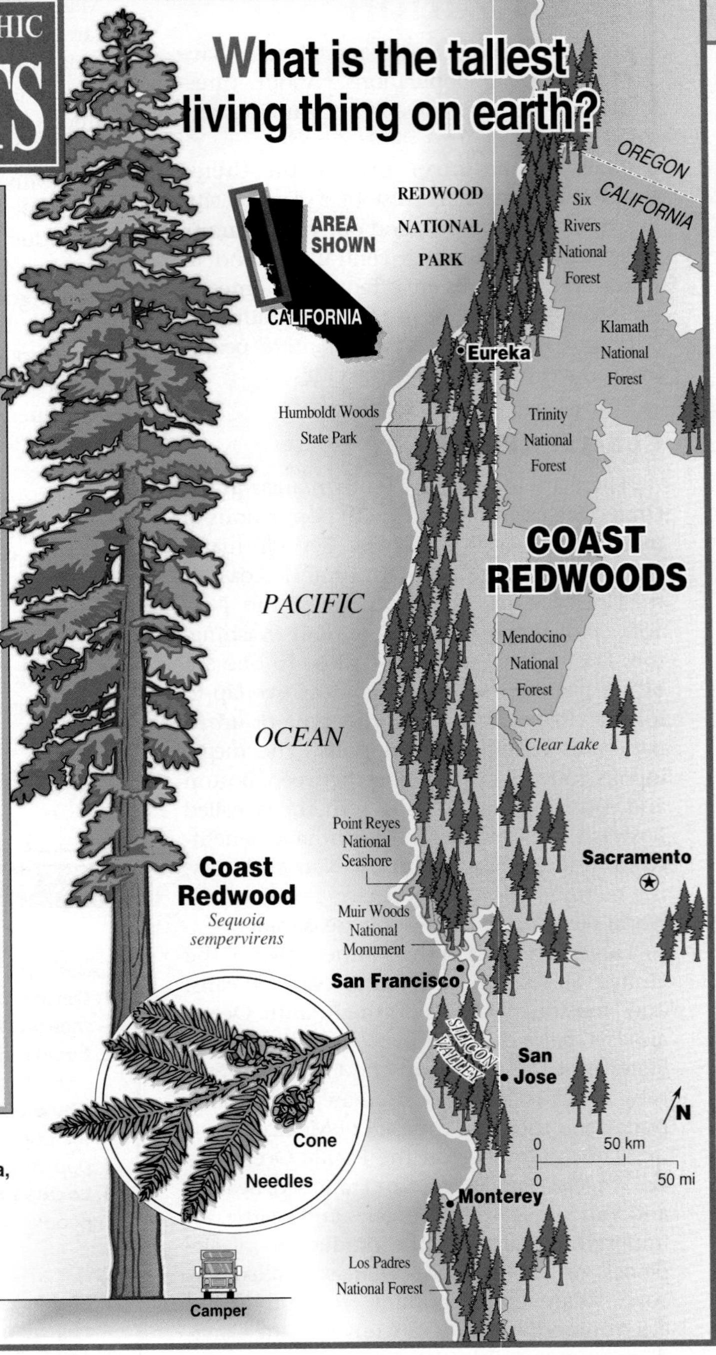

Another California redwood, the giant sequoia, is shorter and fatter than the coast redwood. With a 35-foot (10.7-m) diameter, the giant sequoia is wider than many city streets.

Designed by BILL PITZER

2 SECTION
History and Government

SETTING THE SCENE

Read to Discover . . .
- how the United States and Canada were settled and became separate nations.
- how the United States and Canada expanded their territories and developed strong economies.

Key Terms
- strait
- cash crop
- republic
- industrialization
- dry farming
- Constitution
- amendment
- cabinet

Identify and Locate
Florida, Louisiana Purchase, Newfoundland, Nova Scotia, New Brunswick, Quebec, Ontario, Manitoba, British Columbia, Prince Edward Island, Alberta, Saskatchewan

The first people to come to what is now the United States and Canada migrated from Asia. These people developed cultures that were influenced in part by the various environments in which they settled. After A.D. 1500 most of the region's settlers came from Europe. The Europeans used the land and its resources very differently from the region's first settlers.

MOVEMENT

History

The northwestern part of North America is separated from the northeastern part of Asia by a **strait**—a narrow passageway connecting two large bodies of water. The Bering Strait connects the Arctic Ocean and the Pacific Ocean. It is believed that during the last Ice Age the level of the water in the Pacific Ocean lowered, exposing a land bridge across the Bering Strait.

Many archaeologists believe that 25,000 or more years ago people from Asia used the land bridge to migrate to the nearby lands of North America. The cold northern climate encouraged many of these people to migrate throughout the continent in search of better living conditions. By 10,000 years ago, people were living in almost every part of the present-day United States and Canada. The early people became known as Native Americans. The kinds of cultures formed by these early groups of people varied and were influenced by their location.

Early Americans

The Inuit lived in the cold tundra lands of the Arctic. The harsh polar climate there made them rely upon such animals as caribou for fur and food because other resources were scarce and farming was impossible. The Native Americans of the Far North, who lived in the subarctic, also relied on the animals they hunted to help fill their needs for food and clothing.

The Native Americans along the Pacific Coast lived where the climate was mild and the natural resources, especially fish, were abundant. Large trees and a variety of plants covered the land. With stone and copper woodworking tools these Native Americans split cedar, fir, and redwood trees into planks to make elaborate houses and large canoes. They also developed ways to harvest salmon with fiber nets, spears, and wooden traps.

Native Americans who settled in the high desert regions of present-day Arizona, New Mexico, Colorado, and Utah had fewer resources than those who settled in other areas. Nevertheless, the Native Americans of the

LESSON PLAN
Chapter 6, Section 2

FOCUS

SECTION OBJECTIVES

1. **Describe** how the United States and Canada were settled and became separate nations.
2. **Explain** how the United States and Canada expanded their territories and developed strong economies.

BELLRINGER MOTIVATIONAL ACTIVITY

Project the Section 2 Focus Transparency and have students answer the questions.

PRETEACHING VOCABULARY

Have students categorize the Key Terms in the following ways: terms dealing with government *(republic, Constitution, amendment, cabinet);* terms dealing with technology *(industrialization, dry farming);* terms dealing with farming *(cash crop, dry farming).*

Classroom Resources for Section 2

BLACKLINE MASTERS:
- Reproducible Lesson Plan 6-2
- Guided Reading Activity 6-2
- Spanish Guided Reading Activity 6
- Performance Assessment Activity 6
- Workbook Activity 6-2
- Outline Map Resource Book, p. 6
- Section Quiz 6-2

TRANSPARENCIES:
- Section Focus Transparency 6-2
- Political Map Transparency 2
- Unit Map Overlay Transparency 2
- World Cultures Transparency 2

MULTIMEDIA:
- Testmaker

TEACH

GUIDED PRACTICE

Display Political Map Transparency 2. Have students locate the Bering Strait. Then ask them to explain how archaeologists believe early people migrated from Asia to North America. *(They crossed a land bridge formed during the Ice Age.)* Discuss how this migration creates a shared history between the United States and Canada. *(Early people, who became known as Native Americans, settled throughout the present-day United States and Canada.)* **LEP**

USING ILLUSTRATIONS

HUMAN/ENVIRONMENT INTERACTION The cliff dwellers of southwestern Colorado built their homes on protected ledges along overhanging walls. Some structures were four stories high and had several rooms.

Answer to Caption: *They invented techniques of irrigation to farm the land.*

Geographic Themes

Human/Environment Interaction: Mesa Verde National Park, Colorado

Mesa Verde is a huge plateau covered with pine forests where Native Americans built cliff dwellings hundreds of years ago. *How did Native Americans in other parts of the Southwest make use of their environment?*

Southwest adapted to their environment. For example, they invented techniques of irrigation to farm the land. One community in southern Arizona dug an irrigation canal 3 miles (4.8 km) long to draw the river's waters onto fields planted with corn, beans, and squash.

Native Americans living on the grasslands of the Great Plains found farming very difficult because the thick plains sod was hard to plow. Although some farming was done along streams, most Plains Native Americans depended on the great herds of buffalo that roamed the plains. From earliest times, they followed the herds from one grazing ground to another. They used every part of the buffalo for their food, clothing, shelter, and tools.

Native Americans of the woodlands east of the Mississippi River hunted a variety of animals. Deer, turkeys, geese, and squirrels were common in eastern forests. Like the Plains people, Woodlands Native Americans made use of every part of the animals they killed—eating deer meat, wearing deerskin clothing, and making tools out of animal bones and antlers. Because summers were warm, rainfall abundant, and soil fertile throughout most of the Eastern Woodlands, the people of this region lived in farming villages and grew crops such as corn, squash, beans, and tobacco.

European Colonization

European migration to the United States and Canada had begun by the late 1500s. Europeans came to the region in search of land to farm, valuable minerals, and political and religious freedom.

Most early European settlers came from Spain, France, and England. People from these nations established colonies in different parts of the present-day United States and Canada. By the 1700s, England had colonies or controlled land along much of the Atlantic Coast and around Hudson Bay.

The settlers in the northern English colonies were not able to farm very well because of the thin, rocky soil and the short

Cooperative Learning Activity

Organize students into five groups and assign one of the following Native American culture regions to each group: Far North, Pacific Coast, Southwest, Plains, and Woodlands. Instruct each group to create a diorama showing how Native American ways of life related to the environment. Each member of a group should contribute to the research and construction of the diorama. Students should prepare a written or oral explanation for the rest of the class.

growing season. The area, however, had excellent harbors, good timber, many types of fish, and cheap waterpower. As a result, the settlers generally made their living by fishing, shipbuilding, trade, and manufacturing.

The English colonies just south of the northern colonies had wide river valleys, level land, and rich soil. They also had mild winters; warm, long summers; and a long growing season. Many of the settlers were farmers who raised **cash crops**, or crops that are raised to be sold.

The English colonies farthest south produced surpluses for export because the mild climate, rich soils, and open land encouraged large-scale plantation agriculture. Most plantation owners used enslaved Africans to provide the labor such large-scale farming required.

The French came to North America primarily for economic reasons, especially the fur trade. French trappers, traveling such major rivers as the St. Lawrence and the Mississippi, settled at places along waterways where beaver pelts and other furs could be collected and shipped to Europe. Most did not plan to settle, wanting to make money and then return to France. Those who did settle lived primarily near the St. Lawrence River, where they founded Quebec. Other French settlements thrived along the Mississippi River and the Gulf of Mexico, especially the port city of New Orleans.

The Spanish ruled large areas of the present-day United States west of the Mississippi River. These lands were part of the vast Spanish Empire that included much of South America and all of Central America and Mexico. In 1565 Spain set up the first European settlement in the present-day United States at St. Augustine, Florida. Most Spanish settlements made during the colonial era, however, were in the Southwest—Texas, New Mexico, Arizona, and California. Many of these communities were founded as barriers to block

Geographic Themes

Movement: Quebec City, Canada

This street in Quebec City reveals the French character of the Canadian province of Quebec. *What other areas of North America were settled by the French?*

CURRICULUM CONNECTION

ARCHAEOLOGY

Folsom points—long, thin prehistoric spearheads—have been discovered in New Mexico, Colorado, and Texas. These weapons were mingled with the bones of an extinct species of bison. Archaeologists regard this as evidence that people had migrated to North America by about 8000 B.C.

Display Unit Map Overlay Transparency 2. Have students use markers to indicate areas of English, French, and Spanish settlement in North America. Discuss ways of describing the locations of these areas. *(relative to bodies of water, relative to one another, or relative to present-day boundaries)*

USING ILLUSTRATIONS

MOVEMENT Quebec, the only walled city in North America, is sometimes called the "Cradle of New France." It became the main base of early French explorers and missionaries on the continent.

Answer to Caption: *along the Mississippi River and the Gulf of Mexico; New Orleans*

Meeting Special Needs

Learning Disability Students with learning disabilities often have difficulty organizing information. Have students create a chart or other graphic organizer to compare French, English, and Spanish settlement in North America. Headings should include location of settlements, reasons for settlement, and major economic activities. Display the completed chart for reference.

 USING ILLUSTRATIONS

PLACE During Loyalist Days, held annually in July, New Brunswickers celebrate the landing of the Loyalists in St. John. A granite boulder marks the site where Loyalists landed in 1783.

Answer to Caption: *They were American colonists who remained loyal to the British monarch during the War for Independence.*

L3 Creating Time Lines Have students create parallel time lines for the United States and Canada from 1763 to 1900. Students should list major events in each country's history during that time period. Compare the similarities and differences between the nations.

 Have students complete World Cultures Transparency 2 Activity in the TCR.

Geographic Themes

Movement: Loyalist Historic Site, New Brunswick, Canada
Loyalists from the 13 American colonies also settled in Nova Scotia, New Brunswick, and Prince Edward Island. *How did the Loyalists receive their name?*

potential expansion by such colonial powers as France and Great Britain. They served two purposes—as military outposts and as missions, or religious settlements to convert Native Americans to Christianity. Although the population of the Spanish colonies remained small, Spanish settlers in time started farms and huge cattle ranches, based largely on practices brought from their European homelands.

Two Nations

In 1763 France was forced to give up a great part of its empire in North America to the British. Conflicts soon arose between the Native Americans and the settlers in the British colonies. The settlers' methods of cutting down forests and clearing fields in order to farm destroyed the Native Americans' hunting grounds. Conflict also affected the fur trade. Some Native Americans began to resent the number of traders entering their lands.

During the 1760s relations between the American colonies and Great Britain began to worsen. The British government gradually extended its control over the colonies by passing laws that taxed the colonists and limited their freedoms. The colonists had become accustomed to governing themselves, and had developed a sense of unity and independence. As a result they deeply resented what they viewed as British interference in their affairs.

Another development in the American colonies at this time was growing opposition to monarchy as a form of government. Along with independence, some colonists favored the creation of a **republic**, a form of government in which people elect their own officials, including their head of state. Beginning in 1775, 13 of the British colonies along the Atlantic coast fought a war to gain independence. As a result of the War for Independence, a new republic—the United States of America—was formed.

A number of colonists, however, did not want to sever ties with Great Britain. During the war, more than 40,000 American colonists who remained loyal to the British monarch

Critical Thinking

Drawing Conclusions Have students write a paragraph explaining why the English were more successful in colonizing North America than were the French or Spanish. Suggest that they consider the reasons each group had for coming to America and the kinds of settlements each group established. Provide time for students to share and discuss their paragraphs.

moved north to Canada, which had a large French population. Known as United Empire Loyalists, they settled mainly in sparsely inhabited areas of the present-day Canadian provinces of Quebec, Ontario, Nova Scotia, and New Brunswick.

Unlike its southern neighbor, Canada united slowly, and without the violence of war. The American War for Independence, however, did have a great impact on Canada. The arrival of the United Empire Loyalists meant that the French Canadians in Quebec no longer enjoyed a comfortable majority. Great Britain divided Quebec into Lower Canada and Upper Canada in an attempt to give representation to both the French Canadians and the Loyalist settlers. The colony of Lower Canada was situated along the eastern part of the St. Lawrence River, where mostly French Canadians lived. English-speaking Canadians occupied the colony of Upper Canada, which included the area above the Great Lakes and around the western part of the St. Lawrence River.

Upper and Lower Canada became united in 1841, and self-government was approved by Great Britain in 1849. In 1867 the Dominion of Canada was established and the four provinces of Quebec, Ontario, Nova Scotia, and New Brunswick were united. Between 1869 and 1873, Canada established the provinces of Manitoba, British Columbia, and Prince Edward Island. Saskatchewan, Alberta, and Newfoundland were added in the 1900s.

Industry and Expansion

The growth of industry changed the development of the United States and Canada. The northeastern United States has many waterfalls that could be harnessed to produce power to run machines. Partly for this reason, the first water-powered cotton mill was built in Rhode Island in 1793. Other factories soon sprang up where waterpower was available. **Industrialization**—the setting up of manufacturing that uses machinery—spread. Because waterpower was limited to a few places, people in industry searched for a new source of power. In the 1800s, steam became the dominant source of power. The large supplies of coal in Pennsylvania and Ohio, which were used to power steam engines, made steam power cheap and manufacturing very profitable. Soon the Midwest became a leading center of industry and business. The many rivers in the Midwest, improved by the building of canals, were used to transport goods from factories to port cities.

A growing demand for cotton by the textile industry in the Northeast made cotton production highly profitable. Cotton became the South's major cash crop. Swamps were drained and pine forests cleared for more cotton plantations. The labor of enslaved Africans became more important than ever before.

During this period of great economic development, the West became a source of raw materials for the markets of the East. In 1803 the United States bought nearly all the land between the Mississippi River and the Rocky Mountains from France. This agreement, known as the Louisiana Purchase, gave the United States control of the Mississippi River and access to the port of New Orleans. The purchase also nearly doubled the land size of the United States and gave the United States fertile farmland and access to the Far West.

The territories of the West were rich in natural resources. The discovery of gold and silver deposits encouraged settlement in parts of the Far West, the Southwest, and the Far North. Texas, a former Mexican territory that became an independent republic in 1836 and joined the United States in 1845, was valued for cotton production and cattle ranching. The land in parts of present-day California, Arizona, and New Mexico belonged to Mexico. The United States wanted to build a railroad through this land to the Pacific coast. In the 1840s, as a result of a war with Mexico, the Treaty of Guadalupe Hidalgo gave the United States all of the present-day states of California, Utah, and Nevada, and parts of Colorado, Wyoming, Arizona, and New Mexico. This agreement between the United States and Mexico also established the southern border of Texas at the Rio Grande.

The good climate and the rich soil for farming in the northwestern United States

INDEPENDENT PRACTICE

Guided Reading Have students complete Guided Reading Activity 6-2 in the TCR. **LEP**

Have students complete Performance Assessment Activity 6 in the TCR.

L2 Geography: Movement Have students use the map of the United States on page 6 of the Outline Map Resource Book to indicate territorial expansion. Ask them to list the date when each state was established. Then have them color code the maps to show expansion during specific time periods, such as 1775–1825, 1826–1875, 1876–1925, 1926–1975, 1976–present.

Extending the Content

Political Heritage The governments of the United States and Canada share a political heritage that includes the following characteristics: (1) a federal system in which the powers of government are shared between the central government and the state or provincial governments; (2) a bill of rights that guarantees certain basic rights and freedoms of individual citizens; and (3) an economy based on principles of free enterprise in which almost all industries and services are privately owned and operated.

L3 Write Ask students to write an advertisement that might have been used to attract settlers to the Great Plains in the late 1800s. Provide time for students to share their work.

USING ILLUSTRATIONS

MOVEMENT Donald Smith, shown driving the spike, was the chief promoter of the Canadian Pacific Railway (now CP Rail). The railroad extended from Montreal, Quebec, to Vancouver, B.C.

Answer to Caption: *made it possible to transport goods from the East to the West and to transport food products and beef cattle from the West to the East*

Have students complete Workbook Activity 6-2 in the TCR.

Geographic Themes

Movement: Craigallachie, British Columbia

The Canadian Pacific Railway was completed in 1885 with the nailing of the last spike. *What impact did transcontinental railroads have on the United States and Canada?*

and southwestern Canada began to attract settlers in the 1840s. This part of the region was known as the Oregon Country. Both the United States and Great Britain claimed the Oregon Country. In 1846 the two countries agreed to divide Oregon's territory between them, extending the United States-Canadian border along the 49th parallel from the Rocky Mountains to the Pacific Ocean.

During the late 1800s, settlement of the Great Plains was encouraged by both the United States and Canada. The governments wanted to ease the crowding in eastern cities, caused by people coming to these cities from Europe. They also wanted people to farm the region, thus providing more food for city populations. Thousands of people from the crowded lands in the eastern parts of the region, as well as European immigrants, started farms on the Great Plains of Canada and the United States.

In 1867 the United States bought Alaska from Russia. Alaska was rich in fur-bearing animals and in fish. Alaska later proved to be important for its deposits of gold, oil, and other valuable resources.

Technology and Growth

Settlers on the dry Great Plains used a special farming method, called **dry farming**, to ease the shortage of water there. Dry farming is a way of saving water in the soil by plowing land so that it holds rainwater.

Advances in farm machinery also helped the farmers. Steel plows replaced iron plows. Stronger than iron plows, steel plows were better able to cut through the prairie sod. During the late 1880s, steam tractors and planting and harvesting machines made it possible to farm large areas of land faster and easier.

Cooperative Learning Activity

Organize students into ten groups and assign each group one of the provinces of Canada. Tell students to find and reproduce the symbol for their assigned province. These symbols, which are cut into stone on the walls of the Canadian House of Commons at Ottawa, show the main industries of each province. Have each group display its symbol and relate the industry to a geographic feature of the province.

The completion of transcontinental railroads in the United States and Canada made it possible to transport goods from the East to the West and to transport food products and beef cattle from the West to the East. Chinese, Irish, Mexicans, and other groups of people were recruited to come to the region to help build the railroads.

By the early 1900s, the Industrial Revolution led to the development of new and better methods of mass production. These new industrial developments greatly changed the lives of many people in the United States and Canada. Now, more people lived in cities rather than in rural areas. The use of standard parts and assembly lines in automobile factories cut the time and cost needed to build an automobile. Because more people could afford automobiles, more roads had to be built. The automobile made it possible for great numbers of people to move out of the central cities by enabling them to commute to their jobs.

In the 1900s industries grew dramatically during the two world wars. The vast resources of the United States and Canada were used to supply the manufacture of military equipment needed for their armed forces and for their allies around the world. Agricultural products, such as cattle and grains, were also in great demand. Because the United States and Canada were separated from the war zones by the Atlantic and Pacific oceans, the countries' resources were vital to their European and Asian allies.

United States Government

In 1787 a group of leaders of the United States drafted a plan of government for the United States, called the **Constitution.** Over the years changes in the Constitution, called **amendments,** have been made to meet the changing needs of the people. The first 10 amendments to the Constitution are called the Bill of Rights. These amendments guarantee the basic rights of citizens, such as freedom of speech, freedom of religion, and freedom of the press.

The Constitution created a national government and gave it certain powers over

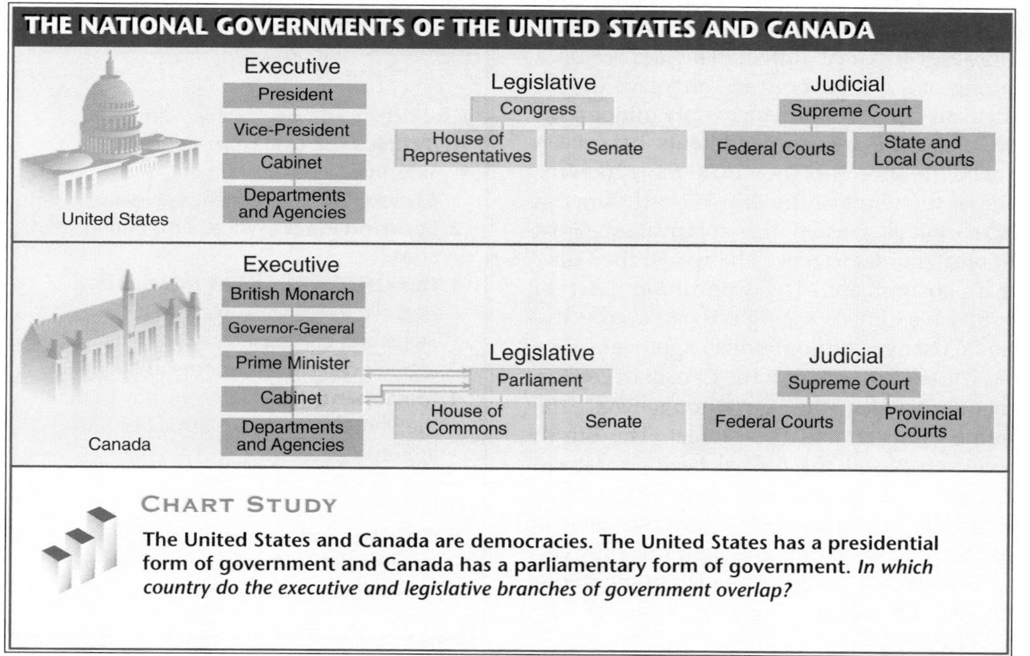

CHART STUDY

The United States and Canada are democracies. The United States has a presidential form of government and Canada has a parliamentary form of government. ***In which country do the executive and legislative branches of government overlap?***

USING DIAGRAMS

Answer: **Canada**

Skills Practice

Reading a Diagram: How are the judicial branches of each government alike? *(Both have a Supreme Court, federal courts, and lower courts.)*

ASSESS

CHECK FOR UNDERSTANDING

Assign Section 2 Review as homework or an in-class activity.

MEETING LESSON OBJECTIVES

Each objective below is tested by the questions that follow it in parentheses.

1. Describe how the United States and Canada were settled and became separate nations. *(2, 3, 5)*

2. Explain how the United States and Canada expanded their territories and developed strong economies. *(1, 3, 4)*

Critical Thinking

Determining Cause and Effect Have students create flow charts to illustrate the cause-and-effect relationships described under the headings "Industry and Expansion" and "Technology and Growth." Display the completed charts for reference.

EVALUATE

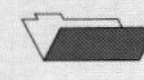 Assign the Section 2 Quiz in the TCR.

 Use the Testmaker to create a customized quiz for Section 2.

RETEACH

Have students work in study groups of four. Each member of a group is responsible for summarizing two pages of this section and quizzing other members on the material.

ENRICH

Have students do research to find present-day reminders of English, French, and/or Spanish influences in the United States and Canada. Examples include place names and historic sites.

CLOSE

Summarize the influences that helped shape a shared history for the United States and Canada.

things that affected the entire country, such as defense and foreign affairs. Each of the former colonies of Great Britain became a state, and was also given certain powers, such as control over education. The national government and the state governments, along with various forms of local government, share the governing of the country. The government of the United States is a representative democracy in which people elect those who govern them.

The national government of the United States has three branches: executive, legislative, and judicial. The executive branch includes the President, the Vice President, and the executive departments that administer various divisions of the national government. The heads of these departments are members of the President's **cabinet**—a group of special advisers. The legislative branch consists of Congress, made up of the Senate and the House of Representatives. The judicial branch of the United States government is made up of the Supreme Court and other courts throughout the country.

Canada's Government

The British North America Act of 1867 made Canada a self-governing nation with close ties to Great Britain. This act set up a strong national government and gave the individual Canadian provinces only minor powers. Over the years amendments have been added to give the provinces more powers. Under the terms of the British North America Act, Canada needed the approval of Great Britain in order to make changes in the Canadian government. The Constitution Act of 1982 gave Canada the right to make constitutional changes without British approval.

The executive part of the Canadian government includes the governor-general, the prime minister, and the cabinet. The British monarch is still the official head of state in Canada and appoints a governor-general to act in his or her place. The governor-general has little actual power and performs only certain ceremonial duties. Canada's prime minister is the actual working head of the government.

The national legislature of Canada is called the Parliament and is made up of the Senate and the House of Commons. The Supreme Court of Canada, which is the highest court in the country, has nine judges. There are also other lower courts.

States, Provinces, and Territories

The United States is made up of 50 states and several territories. United States territories include the Commonwealth of Puerto Rico and the Virgin Islands of the United States in the Caribbean Sea. American Samoa, Guam, and several other Pacific islands and island groups are also territories of the United States.

Canada is made up of 10 provinces and 2 territories. The territories, located in the extreme northern part of the country, are the Yukon Territory and the Northwest Territories. In 1999 a third territory—Nunavut—will be carved out of part of the Northwest Territories. Nunavut will have a largely Inuit population.

SECTION 2 REVIEW

Checking for Understanding

1. **Define** strait, cash crop, republic, industrialization, dry farming, Constitution, amendment, cabinet.
2. **Locating Places** Where is the Bering Strait?
3. **Human/Environment Interaction** How did the early peoples of the United States and Canada interact with the region's different environments?
4. **Movement** How has technology helped the United States and Canada become industrial leaders?

Critical Thinking

5. **Making Comparisons** How are the governments of Canada and the United States similar? How are they different?

ANSWERS TO SECTION 2 REVIEW

1. **strait:** narrow passageway connecting two large bodies of water; **cash crop:** crop raised to be sold; **republic:** government in which citizens elect their officials; **industrialization:** setting up of manufacturing that uses machinery; **dry farming:** plowing land so it holds rainwater; **Constitution:** plan of U.S. government; **amendment:** change made to U.S. Constitution; **cabinet:** group of advisers
2. between the Arctic and the Pacific oceans
3. Many relied on animals and plants to fill their needs. Others developed farming.
4. Methods of mass production and advances in transportation led to the growth of industry.
5. Both are democracies. The British monarch is the official head of state in Canada, whereas the United States has an elected president.

Geography and History

Canada's Two Languages

As you read, examine how Canada became a bilingual country.

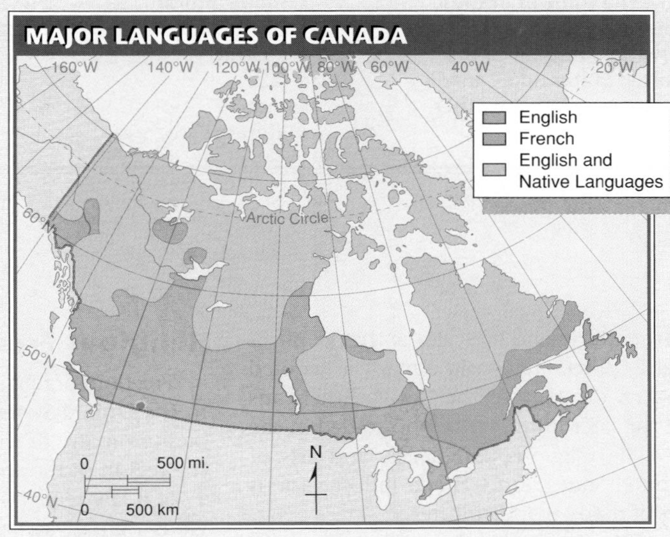

Loyalists Move to Canada

The Treaty of Paris opened to British settlement a huge area of land in the north. Known as Quebec, the British-ruled territory later provided a perfect refuge for residents of the 13 American colonies who opposed the American Revolution. Known as Loyalists, these immigrants left the unpleasant situation in the 13 colonies to resettle in Canada. With them, they brought the English language, as well as British law and customs.

French Culture Recognized

Quebec, however, was home to thousands of French Canadians. Although the British Parliament guaranteed them political and religious rights, the French Canadians felt at a disadvantage with their British rulers and the English-speaking Loyalists.

The British tried to solve the problem by dividing Quebec into two colonies in the Constitutional Act of 1791. Lower Canada, along the lower St. Lawrence River, remained largely French in population and law. Upper Canada, along the Great Lakes, was British in population and law.

Two Languages Recognized

When the modern nation of Canada was formed in 1867, both French and English were recognized as Canada's official languages. In many places, however, English continued to be used almost exclusively.

Finally, in 1969, the Canadian Parliament passed the Official Languages Act. This law guarantees all Canadians the right to communicate with the Canadian federal government in English or French.

In 1974 the Quebec legislature strengthened the position of the French language in the province by making French the sole official language for the provincial government. In 1977 it adopted the Charter of the French Language, making French the language of business and communications.

Checking for Understanding

1. **How did the relocation of the Loyalists lead to Canada's present-day system of two languages?**
2. **Location** **Study the map at the top of the page. Why was Canada "the perfect place" for British Loyalists?**

Geography and History

TEACH

Explain to students that France and the United Kingdom fought a series of wars from 1689 until 1763 in Europe as well as in North America. In 1763, the United Kingdom was victorious, gaining control of the French territory in Canada with the signing of the Paris Peace Treaty. By then, the political situation in the 13 American colonies was tense. Loyalists who supported the British Crown often found themselves victims of verbal and physical attacks.

Regions How is Quebec unique among the Canadian provinces? *(has retained French ties rather than British, has much different culture)*

Extending the Content

Language Less than one million people in Quebec speak English as their primary language. Most of the rest have French as their first language. Many people are bilingual, and French and English are sometimes mixed in daily conversation—especially in urban areas.

ANSWERS TO CHECKING FOR UNDERSTANDING

1. Quebec was originally a French colony. When British settlers moved in, they brought English laws and language with them.
2. Canada was the nearest place governed by British law; the Loyalists could easily reach it.

LESSON PLAN
Chapter 6, Section 3

FOCUS

SECTION OBJECTIVES

1. Relate how the cultures of these countries developed.
2. Point out how the lifestyles of the United States and Canada compare with each other.

BELLRINGER MOTIVATIONAL ACTIVITY

Project the Section 3 Focus Transparency and have students answer the questions.

PRETEACHING VOCABULARY

Teach the meanings of the prefixes *multi-* (many) and *bi-* (two). Explain that *lingua* is Latin for "tongue" or "language." Help students understand that *bilingual* refers to two languages and *multicultural* refers to many cultures.

CD-ROM

PICTURE ATLAS OF THE WORLD
Have students click the "Video," "Speech," and "Music" buttons to see and hear the sights and sounds of the United States and Canada.

SECTION 3

Cultures and Lifestyles

SETTING THE SCENE

Read to Discover . . .
- how the cultures of these countries developed.
- how the lifestyles of the United States and Canada compare with each other.

Key Terms
- multicultural
- bilingual
- abstract
- jazz
- mobile
- literacy rate

Identify and Locate
New Orleans, Quebec, New Mexico

The cultures and lifestyles of the people of the United States and Canada are rooted in the rich diversity of the Native Americans and of the later immigrants who settled in the region. The religions, languages, and arts of the United States and Canada reflect various aspects of many world cultures.

REGION

A Region's Cultures

Because of their diversity, the United States and Canada are considered **multicultural** societies—that is, societies having more than one culture. One Canadian refers to his country in the following way:

> *. . . Canadians believe . . . in a mosaic [an elaborate design] of separate pieces with each chunk becoming part of the whole physically but retaining its own separate color and identity.*

Whether described as a mosaic or some other term, these cultures offer a bounty of beliefs and traditions that help define the region of the United States and Canada.

Religious Freedom

Freedom of religion has always been valued in the United States and Canada. This is true because many of the people who migrated to the region did so to worship freely. As early as 1774 a law recognizing French Canadian religious rights was passed by the British Parliament. After the United States became an independent country, citizens were guaranteed religious freedom under the Constitution.

Most people who are members of an organized religion in the United States and Canada today are Christians. In the United States more than one-half of all religious people are Protestants, while another one-third are Roman Catholics. In Canada, Roman Catholics make up almost one-half of all religious people. Judaism, Islam, and Buddhism are among other religions in the United States and Canada. Religion and where people live today often reflect earlier settlement patterns.

Languages

Like religion, language in the United States and Canada also reflects the identities of early settlers. People from Great Britain brought English to the United States as the primary language. In some areas of the United States that were first colonized by Spain or France,

Classroom Resources for Section 3

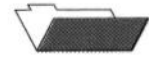

BLACKLINE MASTERS:
Reproducible Lesson Plan 6-3
Guided Reading Activity 6-3
Foods Around the World 1
Writer's Guidebook Lesson 11
Workbook Activity 6-3
Enrichment Activity 6
Section Quiz 6-3

TRANSPARENCIES:
Section Focus Transparency 6-3
World Cultures Transparency 1
World History and Art Transparency 36

MULTIMEDIA:

Testmaker

***World Music:** Cultural Traditions, Lesson 1*

Picture Atlas of the World

however, many people speak Spanish or French. Many Spanish-speaking people live in the Southwest and many French-speaking people live in southern Louisiana.

Many recent Spanish-speaking immigrants to the United States have come from Latin America. These immigrants have generally settled in the Southwest, in Florida, and in such major cities as New York and Chicago. Therefore, in many of these places, information in public places is often printed in English and Spanish. In New Mexico, which is officially a **bilingual** state, any communications with the state government or with local governments may be in Spanish or English. *Bilingual* means "having two languages." Canada is a bilingual nation, with English and French as the two official languages. In California the presence of Asian cultures is evident in the signs written in Korean, Japanese, and Chinese.

The Arts

Early people in the region used objects from their environment to make artwork. Native Americans who settled in the Ohio and Mississippi river valleys made detailed carvings of shell or stone. Native Americans living in the Southwest used clay from their area to make pottery, and wove baskets, sandals, and mats from native plants.

After European settlement, the arts of the region were greatly influenced by European styles. By the mid-1800s, however, the region's artists began to create art that showed the beauty of the land and life in their own countries.

In the early 1900s, a group of American artists painted scenes that reflected the reality of city life. This group of artists became known as the Ashcan school. Later in the 1900s, American and Canadian artists began to use the new European **abstract** style of art. In abstract art, the artist tries to show his or her own attitudes and emotions.

Like art, architecture in colonial times in the United States and Canada was greatly influenced by European styles. Later the region developed its own approach to architecture. The skyscraper, which can house many people or businesses over a small land area, was developed in the United States.

Literature in the United States and Canada at first dealt mainly with history and religion and reflected European themes. Later, writers such as James Fenimore Cooper, Thomas Chandler Haliburton, and Edgar Allan Poe wrote about life in North America. Since the late 1800s some American and Canadian authors have written about different regions of the country. Mark Twain wrote about life on the Mississippi River, Margaret Laurence focused on the prairies of Manitoba, and a later writer, Willa Cather, described life on the Great Plains. More recently, African American writers, such as Richard Wright, and Jewish writers, such as Isaac Bashevis Singer, have explored the experiences of their people.

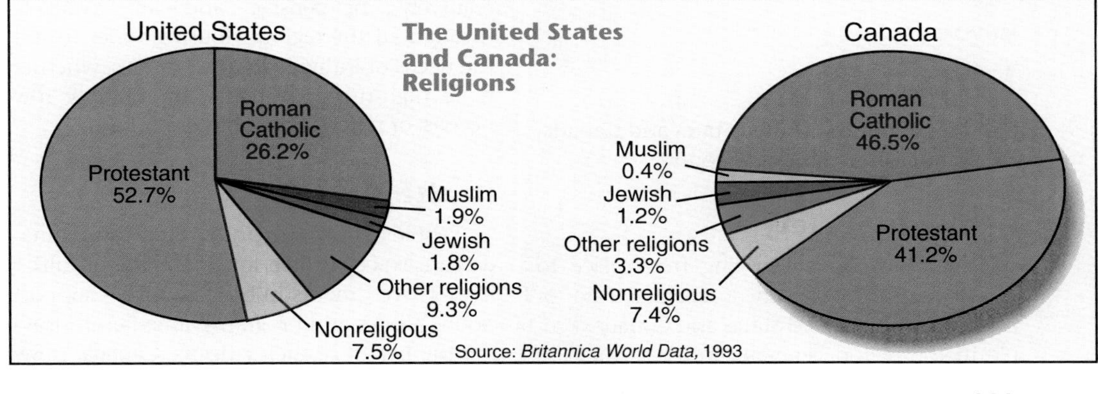

Cooperative Learning Activity

Organize students into three groups and assign one of the following topics to each group: art, literature, or music. Instruct members of each group to find out how the arts reflect the environments and cultures of the United States and Canada. Students should find examples of the works of artists and writers listed in the text. Students in the music group might find and play recordings of Native American music, jazz, and rock 'n' roll.

TEACH

GUIDED PRACTICE

L1 Interpret Ask students to differentiate between two terms sometimes used to describe a multicultural society—"melting pot" and "mosaic." *(Melting pot implies that cultures blend together to form one; mosaic implies that each culture retains its identity in the whole.)*

USING GRAPHS

Skills Practice

Interpreting a Graph: What are the largest religious groups in the United States and Canada? *(Protestants and Roman Catholics)*

MULTICULTURAL PERSPECTIVE

Culturally Speaking
Invite bilingual students or those studying a foreign language to teach the class a common phrase, such as "How are you?" or "What time is it?"

INDEPENDENT PRACTICE

Guided Reading Have students complete Guided Reading Activity 6-3 in the TCR. **LEP**

USING ILLUSTRATIONS

PLACE Animal bones, landscapes, and desert flowers appear in many of O'Keeffe's works.

Answer to Caption: *the ashcan school*

ASSESS

CHECKING FOR UNDERSTANDING

Assign Section 3 Review as homework or an in-class activity.

MEETING LESSON OBJECTIVES

Each objective below is tested by the questions that follow it in parentheses.

1. Relate how the cultures of these countries developed. *(5)*

2. Point out how the lifestyles of the United States and Canada compare with each other. *(3, 4)*

EVALUATE

Assign the Section 3 Quiz in the TCR.

Use the Testmaker to create a customized quiz for Section 3.

RETEACH

Have students complete Reteaching Activity 6 in the TCR.

ENRICH

Have students complete Enrichment Activity 6 in the TCR.

NATIONAL GEOGRAPHIC SOCIETY

CD-ROM

PICTURE ATLAS OF THE WORLD

You and your students can hear an example of jazz by clicking the "Music" button of the United States.

Geographic Themes

Region: The American Southwest

Georgia O'Keeffe's paintings reflect her interest in the landscape of the American Southwest. *What group of Americans painted urban life?*

Native Americans developed their own music, while Europeans brought European folk and religious music to the region. At the beginning of the 20th century, a distinctive form of music known as **jazz** developed in the United States. Jazz blends African rhythms with the harmony of European music. In the 1950s another unique form of music—rock 'n' roll—became an instant success.

MOVEMENT

Lifestyles

Throughout the United States and Canada, various lifestyles can be found.

A Mobile Society

Being **mobile**, or moving from place to place, has always been a characteristic of lifestyles in the United States and Canada. People in the region generally move to increase their business opportunities, to get better housing, or to get a better education. Widespread use of the automobile has given people a greater choice of where to work and live.

Standard of Living

The United States and Canada are among the richest countries in the world. Because the region has an agricultural surplus, foods are relatively inexpensive and are available throughout the region. Housing varies to suit the needs of individuals and families, whether it be high-rise apartments, multifamily row houses, or ranch-style suburban houses.

Health Care

People in both the United States and Canada can expect to live long, generally healthy lives. Governments in both countries support public clinics and programs aimed at improving the health of their citizens. Canada, how-

Meeting Special Needs

Inefficient Readers To help students organize the material under "Lifestyles," list the following three headings on the chalkboard: Canada, United States, Canada and the United States. Demonstrate how to scan the text for the words in the headings. Then list the information from the text under the appropriate heading on the chalkboard.

ever, spends more money ensuring the health of its citizens than does the United States.

Many people in the United States have health insurance, but the cost of this insurance, as well as of medical costs, is skyrocketing. Although the United States government does offer public insurance—Medicare and Medicaid—for older and disabled citizens, no national health insurance plan now exists. In the early 1990s, the government offered hotly debated proposals for a national health-care system.

Education

These nations have similar educational systems. Each has public and private schools. Both countries require a minimum number of years be spent in school. In the United States, school systems have 12 grades. In Canada, most provinces also have 12 grades. In addition, every province and every state has colleges and universities.

The literacy rates of the countries reflect this concern for education. The United States has a **literacy rate** of 97 percent. This means that 97 of every 100 residents can read and write. Canada's literacy rate is 96 percent.

Sports and Recreation

Citizens of both nations have plenty of leisure time. Many use this time to play and watch sports. In the United States, baseball, football, and basketball are very popular.

Ice hockey tops the list of popular Canadian sports. Other winter sports, such as skiing, snowshoeing, and ice skating, are popular as well.

The United States and Canada offer their citizens a grand series of national parks in which to play. Since the establishment of Yellowstone National Park in 1872, the United States has created 330 national parks that together offer 124,000 square miles (321,000 sq. km) of parkland.

In Canada, every province and territory boasts at least one national park. Some of these parks are huge. The Wood Buffalo Park, lying partly in Alberta and partly in the Northwest Territories, encompasses 17,296 square miles (44,807 sq. km).

Geographic Themes

Region: The Sunbelt

The Sunbelt region of the United States is a popular recreation area that draws tourists from other parts of the country. *What natural areas are popular recreation spots for Americans and Canadians?*

Celebrations

The United States and Canada share several holidays. For example, some religious holidays are observed in both countries. Other celebrations pay tribute to certain people or patriotic holidays, such as Independence Day in the United States and Canada Day in Canada.

SECTION 3 REVIEW

Checking for Understanding

1. **Define** multicultural, bilingual, abstract, jazz, mobile, literacy rate.
2. **Locating Places** What Canadian provinces lie west of Ontario?
3. **Region** Why has religious freedom been valued in the United States and Canada?
4. **Place** How do people in the United States and Canada spend their leisure time?

Critical Thinking

5. **Analyzing Information** Why did early art in the United States and Canada reflect a European influence?

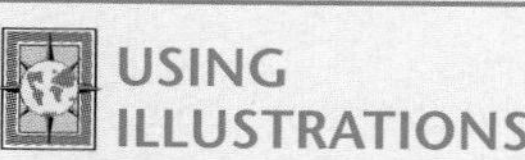

USING ILLUSTRATIONS

PLACE The Breakers in Palm Beach, Florida, is popular among golfers. How does geography influence the kinds of sports people play? *(Climate and physical features influence outdoor sports, such as skiing or swimming.)*

Answer to Caption: *national parks*

CLOSE

Ask students to imagine that a visitor from Canada is going to spend the day with them. Have them write a paragraph explaining what aspects of their way of life they would like to share with the visitor and why.

ANSWERS TO SECTION 3 REVIEW

1. **multicultural:** society having more than one culture; **bilingual:** having two languages; **abstract:** style in which artists express their feelings and attitudes; **jazz:** music style blending African rhythms and European harmony; **mobile:** moving from one place to another; **literacy rate:** the percent of people who can read and write
2. Manitoba, Saskatchewan, Alberta, British Columbia
3. Many immigrants professing a variety of religions came to the country to worship freely.
4. People enjoy sports and vacations.
5. Student answers should indicate that since so many of the early settlers were European, they brought their painting styles with them.

TEACH

Say: "Suppose you must write a report on problems students in this school face. How can you organize the information and ideas for this topic? First, restate the topic as a question." *(What problems do students in this school face?)* Have students suggest problems and write suggestions on the chalkboard in separate columns. Request more specific information about each problem, and write it in the appropriate columns. Point out that this is the beginning of an outline of this topic. Each problem is a main idea; the other information forms the subtopics and supporting facts of the outline.

Have students read the skill lesson on page 124 and rewrite the information on the chalkboard in outline form.

Skills Practice For additional practice, have students complete Lesson 11 in the Writer's Guidebook.

STUDY AND WRITING SKILLS

Outlining

In studying for exams or writing reports, two common problems arise: 1) identifying the most important information, and 2) keeping related information together. Outlining is an excellent tool for organizing information in a clear, logical order.

REVIEWING THE SKILL

In an outline, related ideas and facts are grouped together. Each group begins with a broad idea, followed by increasingly specific information. For example, an outline begins with two or more main ideas. Under each main idea two or more subtopics, or parts of main ideas, can be listed. Finally, supporting details follow each subtopic.

Letters and numbers identify and separate the different categories of information in an outline. Roman numerals usually identify main ideas. Capital letters mark subtopics, while Arabic numerals and lowercase letters identify supporting facts.

Outlines can be used in several ways. First, creating an outline is a good way to study textbook material for exams. Use the main headings in the chapter as main ideas in your outline. Then, read the material under each main heading and identify subtopics and supporting details. Second, when researching and writing essays or reports, use an outline to help clarify and organize your thoughts. Decide what main ideas to include and flesh out each main idea with subtopics and supporting details.

To use the technique of outlining, apply these steps:

- Identify the general topic of the outline and write the topic as a question.
- Write the main ideas that answer this question. Label these with Roman numerals.
- Write subtopics under each main idea. Label these with capital letters.
- Write supporting details for each subtopic. Label these with Arabic numerals and lowercase letters.

PRACTICING THE SKILL

Study the incomplete outline of Chapter 6. The main ideas in the outline correspond to the section headings in the chapter. On a separate sheet of paper, copy this outline and fill in the missing information for Section 1.

General topic: Cultural Geography of the United States and Canada

Topic as question: ______________________

I. Population Patterns
    A.
        1.
            a. Most are of European descent
            b.
        2. Ethnic composition of Canada
            a.
            b. Others—Asian, Inuit, or Native American descent
    B. Population Distribution and Density
        1. Population Size
            a. United States: 261 million, about 74 people/sq. mile (28 per sq. km)
            b.
        2. Low growth rate
        3. Population Spread
            a.
            b. Most Canadians live within 200 miles of the U.S. border
    C. Urbanization
        1.
            a.
            b. Southern port cities
            c.
        2. Inland cities
            a. Near inland waterways
            b.

II. History and Government
III. Culture and Lifestyles

For additional practice in this skill, see Practicing Skills on page 126 of the Chapter 6 Review.

ANSWERS TO PRACTICING THE SKILL

Topic as question: *What is the cultural geography of the United States and Canada?*

I. A. Human Characteristics
- **1.** Ethnic composition of the U.S.
    - **b.** Others—Hispanic, African, Asian, Native American
- **2. a.** 95% of European descent, mostly British and French

B. 1. b. Canada: 29 million, about 8 people/sq. mile (3 per sq. km.)
- **3. a.** United States most heavily populated in northeast, Great Lakes, southwest and south

C. 1. Coastal cities
- **a.** Northeast
- **c.** Pacific Coast
- **2. b.** Other major inland cities

chapter 6

HIGHLIGHTS

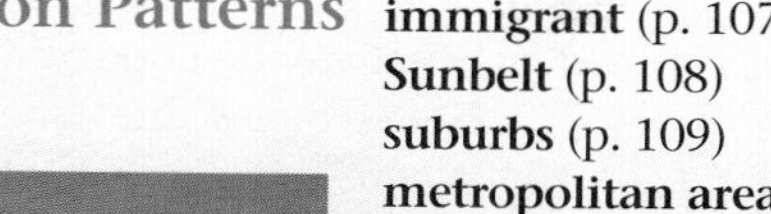

Section 1 Population Patterns

Key Terms

immigrant (p. 107)
Sunbelt (p. 108)
suburbs (p. 109)
metropolitan area (p. 109)
megalopolis (p. 109)

Summary

- Most immigrants to the United States and Canada were of European descent, with Great Britain supplying the greatest number.
- Other ethnic groups include French, African American, Hispanic, and those of Asian ancestry.
- Climate limits the population of Canada's northern two-thirds, and most people live along Canada's border with the United States.
- Most of the people of the region live in urban areas.

Skyline of Chicago

Section 2 History and Government

St. Louis Street in old Quebec City

Key Terms

strait (p. 111)
cash crop (p. 113)
republic (p. 114)
industrialization (p. 115)
dry farming (p. 116)
Constitution (p. 117)
amendment (p. 117)
cabinet (p. 118)

Summary

- Scientists believe that the first humans to settle in the region crossed a land bridge between Asia and North America.
- Colonists fought the War of Independence to free themselves from Great Britain.
- The British North America Act of 1867 made Canada a self-governing nation with ties to Great Britain.

Section 3 Cultures and Lifestyles

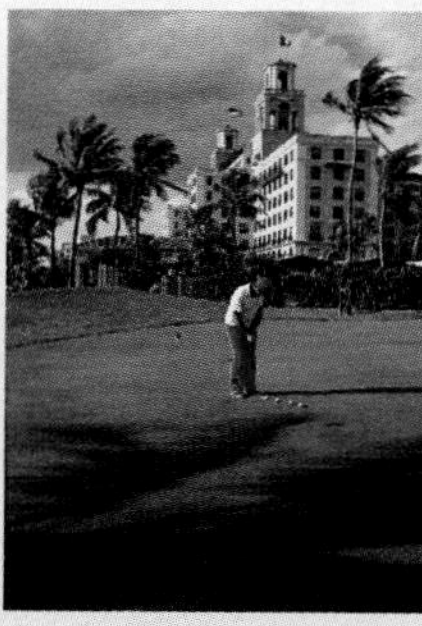

Golfers in southern Florida

Key Terms

multicultural (p. 120)
bilingual (p. 121)
abstract (p. 121)
jazz (p. 122)
mobile (p. 122)
literacy rate (p. 123)

Summary

- Freedom of religion has always been valued in the region.
- The United States has a largely English-speaking population, although many Americans speak Spanish and other languages. Canada recognizes both English and French as its official languages.
- Citizens of both countries enjoy a variety of cultures and a high standard of living.

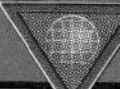

Map Activity

Identify and Locate Provide each student with an outline map of North America found on page 23 of the Outline Map Resource Book. Have students locate and label each of the places listed at the beginning of the sections in this chapter.

CHAPTER 6 HIGHLIGHTS

USING THE CHAPTER 6 HIGHLIGHTS

Use the Chapter 6 Highlights to preview, review, condense, or reteach the chapter.

PREVIEW/REVIEW

Vocabulary PuzzleMaker Software reinforces the Key Terms used in Chapter 6.

Student Self-Test and Review Software allows students to review Chapter 6 content.

CONDENSE

Have students read the Chapter 6 Highlights.

 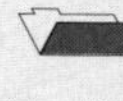

Have students listen to the Chapter 6 Audiocassettes in the TCR. Spanish Audiocassettes are also available.

Assign the Chapter 6 Audiocassette Activity and give students the Chapter 6 Audiocassette Quiz.

Have students complete the Guided Reading Activities for Chapter 6 in the TCR. Spanish Guided Reading Activities are also available.

RETEACH

Have students complete Reteaching Activity 6 in the TCR. Spanish Reteaching Activities are also available.

GLENCOE TECHNOLOGY

Videodisc

Use Chapter 6 MindJogger Videoquiz to review students' knowledge before administering the Chapter 6 Test.

MINDJOGGER VIDEOQUIZ

Chapter 6
Disc 1 Side B

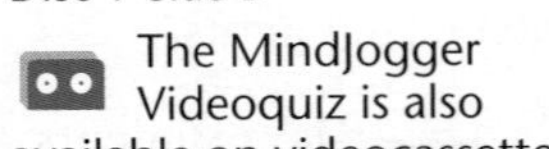

The MindJogger Videoquiz is also available on videocassette.

ANSWERS

Reviewing Key Terms

1. immigrants
2. Sunbelt
3. cash crops
4. strait
5. amendments
6. cabinet
7. republic
8. bilingual
9. abstract
10. mobile
11. jazz

Reviewing Facts

12. The average population density of the United States is about 74 people per square mile (28 people per sq. km). Canada averages only 8 people per square mile (3 people per sq. km).
13. the North
14. Europeans cleared forests for farms.
15. New Brunswick, Nova Scotia, Ontario, Quebec
16. People from the United Kingdom brought English as the primary language. In some parts of the United States first colonized by Spain or France, many people speak Spanish or French. Some recent Spanish-speaking immigrants live in bilingual areas. French is still spoken in Quebec; almost all Canadians west of Ontario speak English because the United Kingdom controlled the area during settlement.
17. health insurance for disabled, poor, and older United States citizens

Critical Thinking

18. Climates are milder than in the north.
19. Archaeologists believe that people migrated from Asia to North America by crossing a land bridge across the Bering Strait. The land bridge is believed to have been exposed 25,000 years ago, during the Ice Age.
20. All government documents, as well as anything submitted to the government, might have to be in two languages; all street signs would be in two languages; all federal employees might be required to speak both languages.

Geographic Themes

21. Pittsburgh's location on the Ohio River has been important for the shipment of goods related to western Pennsylvania's steel industry.

chapter 6 REVIEW

Reviewing Key Terms

Choose the vocabulary term that best completes each of the sentences below. Write your answers on a separate sheet of paper.

immigrants (p. 107)
Sunbelt (p. 108)
strait (p. 111)
cash crops (p. 113)
republic (p. 114)
amendments (p. 117)
cabinet (p. 118)
bilingual (p. 121)
abstract (p. 121)
jazz (p. 122)
mobile (p. 122)

SECTION 1

1. Those who leave their homes to settle in another country are ____.
2. The ____ includes southern and southwestern states with temperate climates.

SECTION 2

3. Middle Colonies produced ____ for sale.
4. A narrow body of water called a ____ often separates two larger seas.
5. The first 10 ____ to the United States Constitution are known as the Bill of Rights.
6. The heads of executive departments in the United States government are members of the President's ____.
7. A ____ is a form of government in which citizens elect their own officials.

SECTION 3

8. Because Canada has two official languages, it is considered ____.
9. In ____ art, the artist tries to show his or her own emotions and attitudes.
10. ____ means moving from place to place.
11. A musical blend of African rhythms and European harmony is called ____.

Reviewing Facts

SECTION 1

12. What are the population densities for the United States and Canada?
13. Where is Canada's least populated area?

SECTION 2

14. How was the land of the United States and Canada changed by European settlers?
15. What were the first four provinces to join the Dominion of Canada?

SECTION 3

16. How has immigration affected language in the United States and Canada?
17. What are Medicare and Medicaid?

Critical Thinking

18. **Analyzing Information** Why do most Canadians live near the United States?
19. **Determining Cause and Effect** How do archaeological finds suggest when people first came to North America?
20. **Predicting Consequences** How would things be different if the United States were officially bilingual?

Geographic Themes

21. **Human/Environment Interaction** Why was Pittsburgh's location favorable for the development of the steel industry?
22. **Human/Environment Interaction** How did early art reflect the environment?
23. **Movement** Why do most people in the United States and Canada generally move?

Practicing Skills

Outlining

Create a detailed outline of Chapter 6, Section 2, similar to the one you completed for Section 1 in the skill lesson on page 124.

Using the Unit Atlas

Refer to the cultural geography section of the Unit Atlas on pages 86–87.

24. What are the two most densely populated provinces of Canada?
25. What five states once belonged to Spain?

Projects

Individual Activity

Use an encyclopedia to help you select a United States territorial acquisition, such as the Louisiana Purchase. Write a report on the area's importance today.

Cooperative Learning Activity

Working in groups of four, imagine your class is immigrating to the region. Use your text's physical and climatic maps to select a location. Present a speech explaining your choice. After all speeches are heard, take a class vote on your future home.

Writing About Geography

Description

Using your journal as well as reference works in your library, find out what major group or groups of immigrants settled in your local area. Write an essay about the cultural influences these people have had.

Locating Places

THE UNITED STATES AND CANADA: PHYSICAL/POLITICAL

Match the letters on the map with the places and physical features of the United States and Canada. Write your answers on a separate sheet of paper.

1. Yukon Territory
2. Great Salt Lake
3. Nova Scotia
4. Quebec
5. Alberta
6. Saskatchewan
7. Prince Edward Island
8. Manitoba
9. Ontario
10. British Columbia

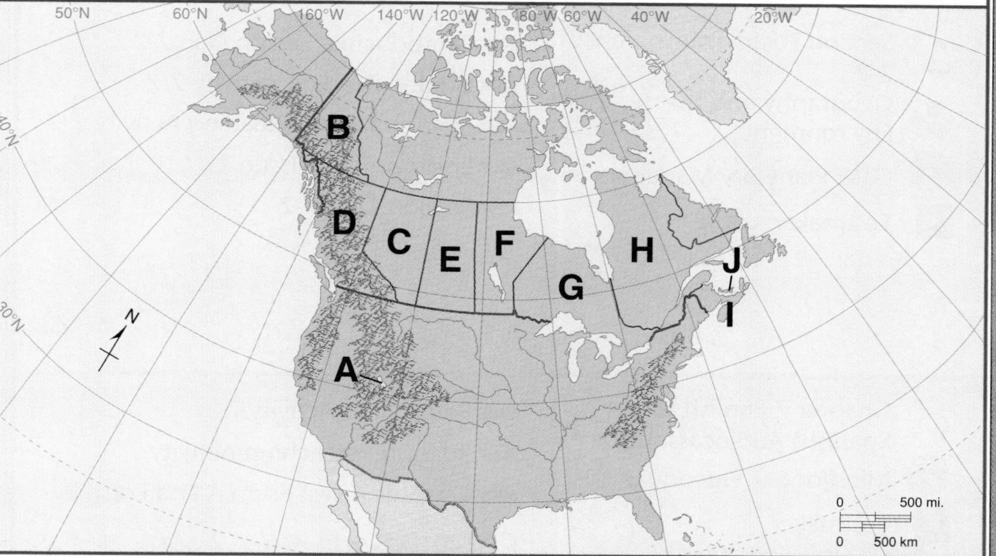

Chapter 6 Review

22. Early artists used objects from their environment to make artwork.
23. to increase their business opportunities, get better housing, or get a better education

Practicing Skills

Answers will relate to the material in Section 2 "History and Government" on pages 111–118.

Using the Unit Atlas

24. Ontario, Quebec
25. California, Colorado, Arizona, New Mexico, and Texas

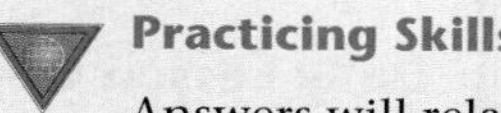

Locating Places

1. B
2. A
3. I
4. H
5. C
6. E
7. J
8. F
9. G
10. D

Chapter Bonus Test Question

This question may be used for extra credit on the chapter test.

What effect do you think physical regions have on the way of life of people in the United States and Canada?

(Answers will vary but should indicate that landscapes and climates influence housing, clothing, economic activities, and recreation. These factors may also influence human characteristics, such as friendliness or formality.)

CHAPTER 7

PLANNING GUIDE

The United States and Canada Today

CHAPTER ORGANIZER

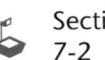

Daily Lesson Objectives	Multimedia	Teacher Classroom Resources
SECTION 1 Living in the United States and Canada 1. Discuss how agriculture and industry affect the economies of the United States and Canada. 2. Explain how a nation's surplus leads to trade. 3. Specify what methods of transportation and communication are most important to the United States and Canada.	Section Focus Transparency 7-1 Unit Map Overlay Transparencies 2-3, 2-6 World Cultures Transparency 2 Testmaker Picture Atlas of the World	Reproducible Lesson Plan 7-1 Guided Reading Activity 7-1 Spanish Guided Reading Activity 7-1 Workbook Activity 7-1 Performance Assessment Activity 7 Vocabulary Activity 7 Spanish Vocabulary Activity 7 Section Quiz 7-1
SECTION 2 People and Their Environment 1. Understand how pollution can cause international problems. 2. Examine how overuse of natural resources is affecting the economies of the region.	 Section Focus Transparency 7-2 Geography and the Environment GTV: Planetary Manager Testmaker	Reproducible Lesson Plan 7-2 Guided Reading Activity 7-2 Spanish Guided Reading Activity 7-2 Environmental Issue 2 Section Quiz 7-2
CHAPTER REVIEW AND EVALUATION	Chapter 7 English (or Spanish) Audiocassettes MindJogger Videoquiz Testmaker Student Self-Test and Review Software	Reteaching Activity 7 Spanish Reteaching Activity 7 Chapter 7 Test Form A and Form B

0:00 *If time does not permit teaching the entire chapter, summarize using the Chapter 7 Highlights on page 145, and the Chapter 7 English (or Spanish) Audiocassettes. Review students' knowledge using the Glencoe MindJogger Videoquiz.*

KEY TO ABILITY LEVELS

Teaching strategies have been coded for varying learning styles and abilities.

L1 **BASIC** activities for all students

L2 **AVERAGE** activities for average to above-average students

L3 **CHALLENGING** activities for above-average students

LEP **LIMITED ENGLISH PROFICIENCY** activities

Performance Assessment

Geography and Employment Have students carry out a decision-making performance task regarding employment in the United States and Canada. Ask them to study a variety of maps (physical features, natural resources, population density, climate, and political) and to make a list of possible job opportunities in different areas of the culture region. Then have students consult newspapers from different cities of both countries to find job opportunities and add them to the list. When students have a comprehensive picture of employment opportunities, they should choose cities in which to relocate and job opportunities to pursue. Each student should compose a hypothetical resume that explains in realistic terms the skills and experiences that might qualify him or her for a certain position. Students should be able to compare and contrast the environment and economy of their local area with that of other areas in which they might one day live.

POSSIBLE RUBRIC FEATURES: Content information, decision-making skills, map skills, compare and contrast skills, inference skills, communication and organization skills

For additional professional and classroom resources, see Chapter Resources, pages T46–T51.

TEACHER'S CORNER

NATIONAL GEOGRAPHIC SOCIETY

INDEX TO NATIONAL GEOGRAPHIC MAGAZINE

The following articles may be used for research relating to this chapter:

- "Dead or Alive: The Endangered Species Act," by Douglas H. Chadwick, March 1995.
- "Canada's Highway of Steel," by Michael Parfit, December 1994.
- "Recycling," by Noel Grove, July 1994.
- "Alaska Highway: Wilderness Escape Route," by Richard Olsenius, November 1991.
- "Once and Future Landfills," by William L. Rathje, May 1991.
- "The Great Lakes' Troubled Waters," by Charles E. Cobb, Jr., July 1987.
- "Hazardous Waste: Storing Up Trouble," by Allen A. Boraiko, March 1985.
- "Do We Treat Our Soil Like Dirt?" by Boyd Gibbons, September 1984.

NATIONAL GEOGRAPHIC SOCIETY PRODUCTS AVAILABLE FROM GLENCOE

To order the following products for use with this chapter, contact your local Glencoe sales representative or call Glencoe at 1-800-334-7344:

- *Picture Atlas of the World* (CD-ROM)
- *STV: North America* (Videodisc)
- *ZipZapMap! USA* (Software)
- *GeoBee* (Software)
- *Images of the World* (Posters)
- *Eye on the Environment* (Posters)
- *Physical Geography of the World* (Transparencies)
- *Picture Atlas of Our 50 States* (Book)

ADDITIONAL NATIONAL GEOGRAPHIC SOCIETY PRODUCTS

To order the following products for use with this chapter, call National Geographic Society at 1-800-368-2728:

- *Pollution: Problems and Prospects*, "The Land," "Air and Water." (Filmstrip)
- *Recycling: The Endless Circle* (Video)

Introducing CHAPTER 7

chapter 7 The United States and Canada Today

PERFORMANCE ASSESSMENT

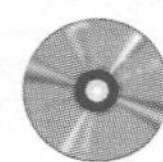

Refer to the Planning Guide on page 128B for a Performance Assessment Activity for this chapter. See the *Performance Assessment Activities* booklet for additional suggestions.

CHAPTER OBJECTIVES

1. **Compare** the economies of the United States and Canada.
2. **Investigate** the challenges of conserving resources in the United States and Canada.

GLENCOE TECHNOLOGY

Videodisc

Use Chapter 7 MindJogger Videoquiz to preview chapter content.

MINDJOGGER VIDEOQUIZ

Chapter 7
Disc 1 Side B

The MindJogger Videoquiz is also available on videocassette.

NATIONAL GEOGRAPHIC SOCIETY

CD-ROM

PICTURE ATLAS OF THE WORLD

Have students click the "Stats" button to find facts and figures about the economy of the United States and Canada.

CHAPTER FOCUS

Geographic Setting

The climate and landforms of the United States and Canada allow a variety of economic activities to flourish. As they use the area's resources, however, people drastically alter the region's environment.

Geographic Themes

Section 1 Living in the United States and Canada

PLACE The United States and Canada have highly developed economies based on agriculture, industry, and the provision of services.

▲ Photograph: *Skyline of Toronto, Ontario, Canada*

Section 2 People and Their Environment

HUMAN/ENVIRONMENT INTERACTION The people and governments of the United States and Canada face challenges in conserving the resources on which they depend.

EXTRA CREDIT PROJECT

Editorial Have students choose one of the issues from this chapter and write an editorial expressing their opinion about it. Then ask volunteers to use a computer to publish the editorials for a class newspaper.

1 SECTION

Living in the United States and Canada

SETTING THE SCENE

Read to Discover . . .
- how agriculture and industry affect the economies of the United States and Canada.
- how a nation's surplus leads to trade.
- what methods of transportation and communication are most important to the United States and Canada.

Key Terms
- free enterprise
- truck farm
- contour plowing
- crop rotation
- service industry
- interdependent
- North American Free Trade Agreement (NAFTA)

Identify and Locate
Midwest, Wheat Belt, Corn Belt, California, Utah, New York, Toronto, St. Lawrence River, Ohio River

Toronto, Ontario

39 CANADA

In my spare time I play baseball and softball. I usually attend a baseball game at the Skydome once a week. I also spend a lot of time at my computer, either playing games or running a Bulletin Board Service.

Colin Lee

Colin Lee, an outstanding mathematics student, is preparing for a career in Canada's diverse economy. The United States and Canada both have highly developed economies and are among the world's top 10 economic powers. Their economies are based on **free enterprise**, or capitalism, which allows individuals to own, operate, and profit from their own businesses. Canada, however, also has a number of government-owned corporations that carry out public services.

The many natural resources available combined with the use of advanced technology have boosted the economic growth of the United States and Canada. With its small population, Canada is a major exporter of mineral products, largely to the United States. The United States, a major producer, imports many goods for several reasons: because of the depletion of United States resources such as petroleum; because of improvements in foreign products; and because of the enormous demands of the United States economy.

HUMAN/ENVIRONMENT INTERACTION

Agriculture

Farmers in the United States and Canada produce a wide variety of agricultural goods. Different parts of the region support different products.

LESSON PLAN
Chapter 7, Section 1

FOCUS

SECTION OBJECTIVES

1. Discuss how agriculture and industry affect the economies of the United States and Canada.
2. Explain how a nation's surplus leads to trade.
3. Specify what methods of transportation and communication are most important to the United States and Canada.

ABOUT THE POSTCARD

Colin is also involved in the music department as a vocalist, and is the sound director for productions.

BELLRINGER MOTIVATIONAL ACTIVITY

Project the Section 1 Focus Transparency and have students answer the questions.

PRETEACHING VOCABULARY

Have students make pictionary clues for each of the Key Terms. Then have them work with a partner to identify the terms from the clues.

Use the Vocabulary PuzzleMaker Software to create a crossword or word search puzzle.

Classroom Resources for Section 1

BLACKLINE MASTERS:
Reproducible Lesson Plan 7-1
Guided Reading Activity 7-1
Vocabulary Activity 7
Spanish Vocabulary Activity 7
Workbook Activity 7-1
Performance Assessment Activity 7
Section Quiz 7-1

TRANSPARENCIES:
Section Focus Transparency 7-1
World Cultures Transparency 2
Unit Map Overlay Transparencies 2-3, 2-6

MULTIMEDIA:

Vocabulary PuzzleMaker Software
Testmaker

Picture Atlas of the World

TEACH

GUIDED PRACTICE

L1 Geography: Human/ Environment Interaction Based on the map on page 130, have students identify the economic activities of the state in which they live. Ask them to write one or more statements about their state's economy, using as many of the Key Terms as possible. **LEP**

USING MAPS

Answers:
1. in southeastern Canada near the U.S. border; **2.** commercial farming; **3.** southwest; **4.** hunting and gathering

Map Skills Practice

Interpreting a Map What geographic feature influences the location of manufacturing centers in both the U.S. and Canada? *(Great Lakes)*

Display Unit Map Overlay Transparencies 2-3 and 2-6. Have students determine how climate influences agricultural activities.

Native Americans in Mexico ate wild corn about 10,000 years ago. By the late 1400s, corn had spread as far south as Argentina and as far north as Canada. Christopher Columbus introduced corn to Europe when he returned from his first voyage to the Americas.

Many Climates, Many Products

One-fourth of the land in the United States is pastureland. Huge western ranches and ranches in the South and Midwest support 100 million head of cattle. Beef is one of the most important agricultural products in the United States.

Cattle also provide the most important agricultural products in Canada. Beef cattle ranches prosper in the drier, western parts of the Prairie Provinces—Alberta, Saskatchewan, and Manitoba. In addition, the north central part of the United States and the Canadian provinces of Quebec and Ontario support dairy farming and raise hogs and chickens.

The three most important grains in the world—wheat, corn, and rice—are grown in the United States and Canada. The region is a world leader in the production of both wheat and corn.

In the United States, the Great Plains has been called the Wheat Belt because so much wheat is grown there. The Prairie Provinces of Canada also are great wheat producers.

In the short growing season of the northern United States, spring wheat, which is planted in early spring and harvested in the fall, is grown. The southern parts of the Wheat Belt produce winter wheat. Winter wheat is planted in the fall so that the roots can grow before the soil freezes. The winter's snow

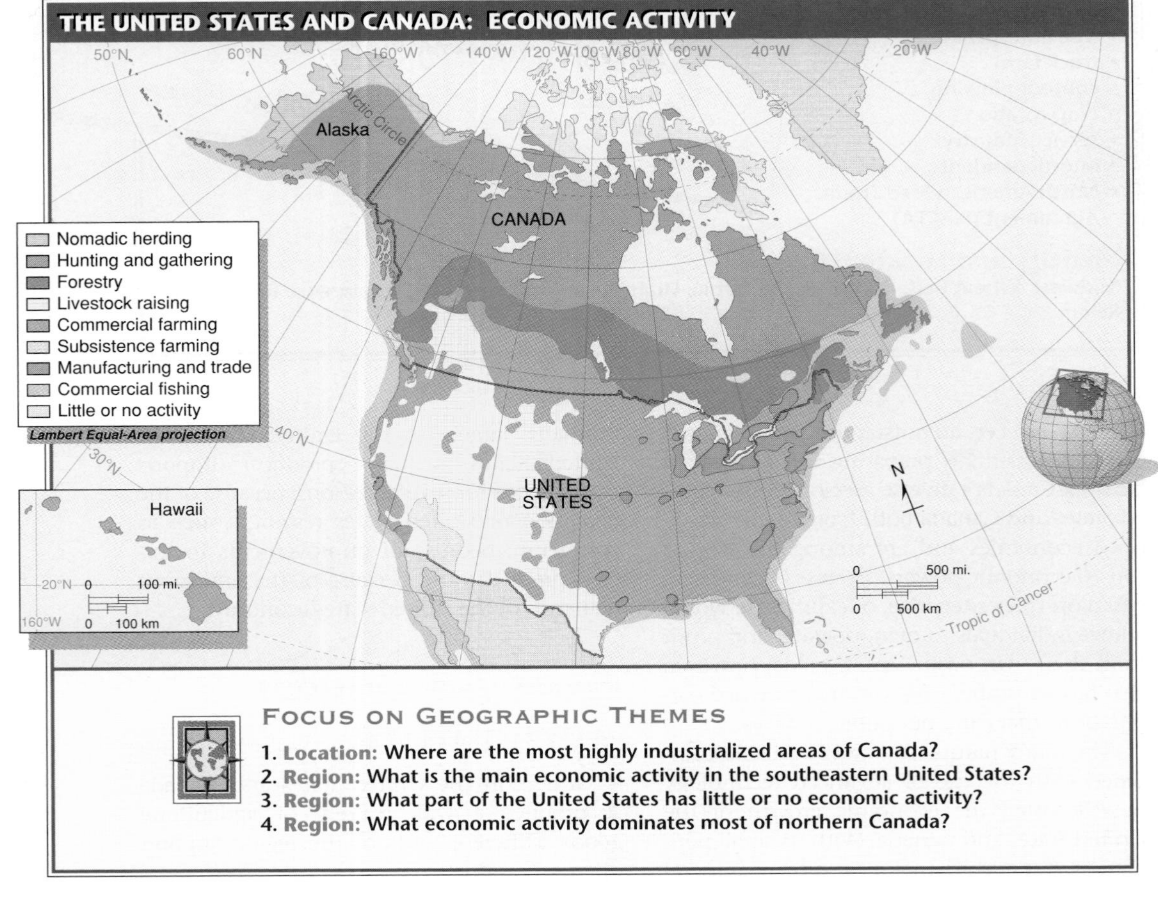

Focus on Geographic Themes

1. **Location:** Where are the most highly industrialized areas of Canada?
2. **Region:** What is the main economic activity in the southeastern United States?
3. **Region:** What part of the United States has little or no economic activity?
4. **Region:** What economic activity dominates most of northern Canada?

Cooperative Learning Activity

Organize students into three groups and assign one of the following grains to each group: wheat, corn, rice. Instruct members of each group to prepare a short, documentary-style presentation about the growth, processing, and uses of their grain crop. Students should use posters and other visual aides for their presentations.

covering protects the young plants and provides spring watering as it melts. Winter wheat is harvested during the summer.

Corn, grown by Native Americans long before the arrival of Europeans, also thrives in the United States and Canada. The United States alone grows more than 40 percent of the world's corn. The nation's Corn Belt extends through the northern Great Plains in a rough band from Ohio to Nebraska. The Canadian provinces of Ontario, Quebec, and Manitoba also count corn as a major crop. About 96 percent of the corn crop is used for animal feed; only about 4 percent is eaten by humans.

The United States and Canada also grow many other products. In the United States, soybeans, tobacco, and peanuts grow well in the South, while cotton thrives in the South and on irrigated land in the Southwest. Midwest farmers bring oats, sorghum, and barley to market. In Canada, barley, flaxseed, oats, and rye thrive in a belt north of Canada's wheat-growing areas. Southern Ontario's warm summers and relatively long growing season produce a variety of specialty crops, such as soybeans and tobacco.

The United States and Canada also grow vegetables. Potatoes are an important crop in the Canadian provinces of Prince Edward Island and New Brunswick. **Truck farms** in the northeastern United States produce vegetables such as tomatoes, cabbages, and string beans. Located near large cities, truck farms can ship vegetables quickly to market. In the southeastern United States, vegetables such as tomatoes, cabbages, and celery are grown to ship north during the winter. Parts of the Pacific Coast region also produce vegetables. California ranks first among the states in the production of tomatoes, lettuce, and dozens of specialty vegetables, such as peas, asparagus, okra, and avocados.

The United States and Canada also grow many kinds of fruit. Apples, peaches, and cherries flourish in the Great Lakes region. California produces a great diversity of fruits, especially grapes and strawberries. Citrus fruits are grown in central and southern Florida, in the lower Rio Grande Valley of Texas, and in southern California. In Canada, southeastern British Columbia, the St. Lawrence River valley, and areas of Quebec and Ontario are important fruit-growing areas.

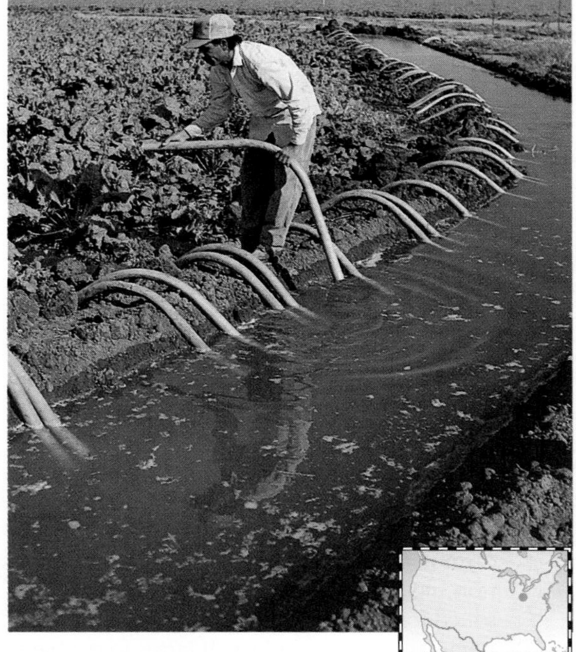

Geographic Themes

Human/Environment Interaction: American Midwest

Irrigation systems help crops survive during periods when there is too little rainfall. *What other techniques do American and Canadian farmers use?*

Agriculture and Technology

Technology boosts agricultural production in the United States and Canada. Modern methods of irrigation, for example, improve the harvest on more than 40 million acres (16 million ha) in both countries. Farmers also try to conserve precious soil by **contour plowing**, or plowing along the natural curves of the land to keep topsoil from washing away with rainwater runoff. **Crop rotation**, in which farmers grow different crops in succession on the same land, helps preserve the soil's nutrients. Farmers also allow some land to lie fallow—plowed but not seeded—during a growing season. In addition, farmers often ro-

USING ILLUSTRATIONS

HUMAN/ENVIRONMENT INTERACTION Four major methods of irrigation are surface irrigation (shown in picture); sprinkler irrigation; trickle irrigation, which furnishes water through plastic tubes with tiny openings; and subirrigation, which waters from underneath roots.

Answer to Caption: *contour plowing and crop rotation*

L3 Apply Ask the following questions to help students apply their understanding of the relationship between place characteristics and economic activity: During what season would wheat be harvested in the Prairie Provinces? Why? *(Fall, because only spring wheat can be raised in the short, northern growing season.)* Why would people in Boston be less likely to buy Florida tomatoes in summer than in winter? *(Local truck farms provide northeasterners with fresh vegetables in summer.)*

Meeting Special Needs

Language Disability Some students with language processing problems have difficulty interpreting the way word meanings change with context. The terms *Corn Belt* and *truck farm*, for example, may be confusing to them. Discuss the possible meanings of these terms. Then have students locate the terms in the text and determine their meanings in context.

INDEPENDENT PRACTICE

Guided Reading Have students complete Guided Reading Activity 7-1 in the TCR. LEP

CURRICULUM CONNECTION

AGRONOMY

The branch of agricultural science that deals with the study of crops and soils is called agronomy. Agronomists research methods of crop rotation, irrigation, plant breeding, and weed control. They work to improve soil and increase crop production.

L1 **Technology** Have students create a bulletin-board display illustrating the development of farm machinery over the years. Instruct students to draw or obtain pictures of farm equipment from the time of Native Americans and early settlers to the present. Students should write a brief caption for each picture, explaining how the tool or machine advanced farming techniques.

tate regular crops, such as soybeans which nourish the soil, with fallow fields.

Scientific developments aid the growth and productivity of farming. Advances in pesticides—substances that kill crop-eating pests—and chemical fertilizers—mixtures that make soil more fertile—increase crop yields. Scientific developments in the breeding of both plants and animals improve output. Hybrid seeds, or seeds from two different types of plants that are crossbred, has led to the production of stronger plants and higher yields.

Inventions of farm machinery such as the tractor, the reaper, the thresher, and eventually the combine—a combination of reaper and thresher—have made farmers more efficient. In the last 60 years, new farming methods have quadrupled the yield in the Midwest alone.

Owners of smaller farms, however, often cannot afford this new equipment. In addition, combines and other machines are best suited for very large farms. These factors make it harder for owners of small farms to compete with the owners of large farms.

As a result, the size of the region's farms has increased, while the number of farmers has decreased. In the last 70 years, the average farm in the United States has more than tripled in size from about 143 acres (58 ha) to about 462 acres (187 ha). Less than 2.5 percent of the United States population now works in farm occupations compared to more than 70 percent in the early 1800s. Only about 4.5 percent of all Canadians still make their living through farming.

New technologies have enabled farmers to grow surplus crops. Farmers export their surpluses to international markets. This enriches the economies of their nations.

HUMAN/ENVIRONMENT INTERACTION

Manufacturing and Service Industries

About one in five workers in the United States and Canada makes a living in manufacturing. The region is a world leader in manufactured goods largely because of technologies such as robotics and computerized automation.

Transportation equipment, which includes airplanes, cars, and their parts, ranks near the top of both nations' manufacturing industries. Transportation equipment and machinery is the United States' largest export. The United States manufactures about 18 percent of the world's motor vehicles and ranks second, after Japan, in production.

Food processing is big business in both the United States and Canada. Everything from canned fruits to soft drinks is manufactured in the region. Canada's manufacture of wood pulp, paper, and newsprint makes it a world leader in wood-related industries. Other goods manufactured in this region include clothing, iron, steel, and petroleum products.

Economies produce both goods and services. **Service industries** provide services rather than produce goods. Some services provided by service industries include financial help (banks and insurance), distribution and sale of goods (shipping companies and retail stores), credit cards, financial investment, education, health care, and tourism.

In the United States and Canada, service industries employ more people than any other kind of industry. More than two-thirds of all workers—including doctors, lawyers, teachers, secretaries, and government employees—offer services to others. Service industries account for most of the gross domestic product in both nations as well.

In contrast to manufacturing industries, service industries are growing at a fast rate. Some of the fastest-growing service occupations include computer technicians, analysts, operators, health care, insurance, advertising, and legal services.

MOVEMENT

Trade and Interdependence

In any modern economy, surpluses produced by agriculture and industry can be traded with others. Sometimes this trade takes place

Critical Thinking

Determining Cause and Effect Have students create flow charts to illustrate the multiple cause-and-effect relationships between agriculture and technology. Charts should include advances that have increased farm production. They should also show the effects of increased production on the size of farms and the number of farmers in the United States and Canada. Based on the charts, ask students to discuss reasons for the farm crisis.

inside a nation's boundaries. At other times trade occurs between two different countries.

Foreign Trade

Trade makes up an important part of the economies of the United States and Canada. Thousands of jobs are connected to exporting, sending goods to other countries, and importing, bringing goods into the country.

The United States leads the world in trade, supplying one-tenth of all goods exported worldwide and importing an even higher percentage. American farmers export more than one-fourth of their crops, including cotton, soybeans, tobacco, and wheat. Many manufactured goods, especially aircraft and spacecraft, computers, and electrical equipment, are exported as well.

The United States imports goods either that it cannot provide or that are cheaper from other countries. Important imports include large amounts of raw materials, such as copper, nickel, and petroleum.

Canada also depends on foreign trade to bolster its economy. The nation exports transportation equipment, wood and wood products, ores, petroleum, and grain. Three-fourths of the fish caught and processed by Canadians enter the export market as well. Among Canada's most important imports are cars and car parts, industrial machinery, computers, and textiles.

The United States and Canada are major trading partners. The United States trades more with the Canadian province of Ontario than with the entire nation of Japan, the United States's second-largest trading partner. In the early 1960s, President John F. Kennedy expressed American-Canadian trade ties when he told a Canadian audience:

> *Geography made us neighbors. History made us friends. And economics has made us partners.*

This trading partnership, however, is not equal. Imports from and exports to Canada account for about 20 percent of the United States's total trade. In contrast, trade with the United States accounts for 70 percent of Canada's exports and imports. These huge trade revenues—totaling billions of dollars for each nation—lead to an interdependence between nations.

Interdependence

The economies of the United States and Canada, and many other nations as well, have become increasingly **interdependent**, or reliant on each other, during the last few decades. For example, the United States and Saudi Arabia, a country in southwestern Asia, have become interdependent. The United States produces a surplus of food, but it cannot produce enough oil to meet its large energy needs. On the other hand, Saudi Arabia produces much more oil than it uses, but its farmers cannot feed all the Saudi people. The United States depends on Saudi Arabia for part of its oil imports, and Saudi Arabia depends on exports of food, machinery, and other finished

Geographic Themes

Movement: Los Angeles, California
An extensive freeway system links cities in the United States. *What freeway system links eastern and western Canada?*

L2 Transportation Have students consult road maps and plan a cross-country trip on a major highway system in Canada or in the United States. Provide students with outline maps from the Outline Map Resource Book. Ask them to indicate the route they would take and write a travel itinerary listing the places they would visit.

USING ILLUSTRATIONS

MOVEMENT Freeways are main highways, which vehicles can enter or leave only at certain locations called interchanges.
Answer to Caption: *Trans-Canada Highway*

Have students complete Workbook Activity 7-1 found in the TCR.

MULTICULTURAL PERSPECTIVE

Culturally Speaking Karel Capek, a Czech playwright, became famous for introducing the word *robot* into the modern vocabulary. The word comes from a Czech term meaning "drudgery."

Extending the Content

Technology Robotics—the use of mechanical devices to perform specific tasks—has revolutionized manufacturing. Robots are especially useful for doing jobs that are too boring, difficult, or dangerous for people. In the automobile industry, for example, robots efficiently carry out such routine tasks as welding, bolting, and painting.

L3 Interdependence Challenge students to illustrate the trading partnership between the United States and Canada. Some students might create a graph indicating the value of imports and exports between the two countries. Others might design a poster showing products that the two countries exchange.

DID YOU KNOW?

The Federal Interstate Highway System, begun in the 1950s during the Eisenhower administration, is expected to cost a total of $100 billion. Under this system, even-numbered highways run east and west; odd-numbered highways run north and south.

L3 Debate Divide students into two teams to debate the pros and cons of the North American Free Trade Agreement (NAFTA).

USING DIAGRAMS

Answer: *Canada*

Skills Practice

Reading a Diagram
Besides television ownership, in which other categories do Canadians lead Americans? *(car ownership, hours per week worked)*

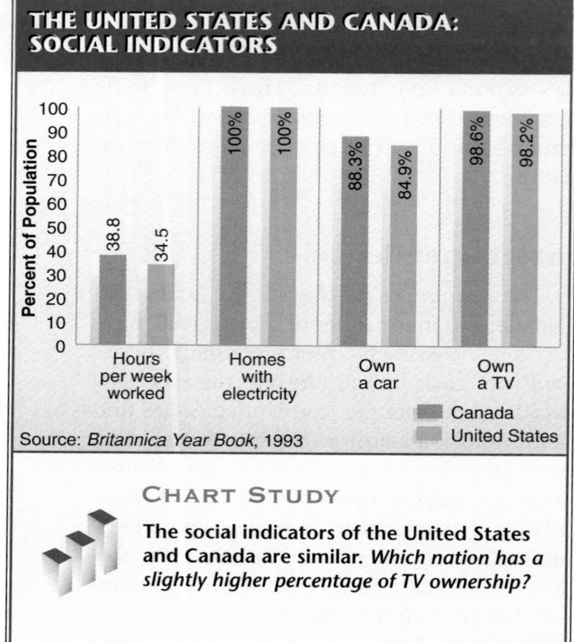

CHART STUDY

The social indicators of the United States and Canada are similar. ***Which nation has a slightly higher percentage of TV ownership?***

goods from the United States. Similarly, Japan depends on Canada's raw materials, while Canada depends on Japan's manufactured products.

Countries often worry about increased interdependence, especially when their imports exceed their exports. They sometimes restrict trade, hoping to become more self-reliant by supporting domestic production. At times Canada has passed legislation trying to restore balance to its trading relationship with the United States.

Recently, however, the United States and Canada have signed trade agreements that ensure their continued interdependence. The early 1990s saw significant steps taken toward the elimination of remaining trade barriers and the creation of a free trade pact called the **North American Free Trade Agreement (NAFTA).** The new trading area includes Canada, the United States, and Mexico. NAFTA has created one of the world's most productive economic blocs, rivaled only by the European Union and Japan.

MOVEMENT

Transportation and Communications

The United States and Canada lead the world in transportation and communications systems. The many methods of moving people and goods and of exchanging information are very efficient and depend on the latest technology.

An Economy on the Move

The United States and Canada have excellent roadway systems. In the United States, about 190 million motor vehicles travel the 4 million miles (6.4 million km) of streets, roads, and highways that crisscross the nation. Canada's smaller, more concentrated population relies on about 14.5 million motor vehicles and 550,000 miles (885,000 km) of roads. Most of the roadways in the region have paved surfaces.

The Federal Interstate Highway System in the United States is a 42,500-mile (68,383 km) network of freeways designed to link 90 percent of the country's cities that have populations greater than 50,000. The interstate system is scheduled to be finished during the 1990s. In Canada, the freeway system includes the Trans-Canada Highway. This two-lane highway, completed in 1962, extends almost 5,000 miles (8,045 km) across the nation, from British Columbia to Newfoundland.

All these roads are used by millions of cars and trucks each day. The trucking industry carries almost 25 percent of the total freight hauled in the United States. In Canada, the trucking industry transports a smaller share of the country's total freight—partly because Canada's severe winters can create poor conditions for shipping freight by road. Still, more than 110 million short tons (100 million t) of freight are transported over Canada's road system each year.

Automobiles account for more than four-fifths of the passenger traffic in the cities of the United States and Canada. Therefore,

Critical Thinking

Analyzing Information Have students analyze the trends identified under "Manufacturing and Service Industries." Then ask them to identify three jobs that have potential growth for the 1990s and beyond. Students should be prepared to support their choices with sound reasoning. They might consult a reference, such as the *Occupational Outlook Handbook,* for additional information.

automobile manufacturing and sales are important businesses in both countries. The automobile's great popularity and the development of freeway systems have also encouraged the rise of other businesses, including motels, shopping malls, and drive-in banks and restaurants.

The railroad changed the face of the region forever. The tracks created a link between East and West, ending the West's isolation and opening it for settlement. On May 10, 1869, two rail lines in the United States connected in Utah, creating the world's first transcontinental railroad. One observer for the *New York Times* described its effect on the country's unity:

The inhabitants of the Atlantic seaboard and the dwellers on the Pacific slopes are henceforth emphatically one people.

In 1885, Canada also opened its western lands when it pounded the last spike into its own transcontinental railroad.

Industry in the United States and Canada has always relied heavily on the railroads. United States railroad lines carry about 35 percent of the freight transported each year. About 30 percent of Canada's freight moves over that nation's rails.

Although passenger use has declined on the regular rail lines, commuter trains—trains that carry workers between the outlying communities and central cities such as New York, San Francisco, and Toronto—are important passenger carriers. One commuter train can carry as many commuters as 1,000 cars. Underground rail systems and elevated rail systems also transport people from one part of a city to another.

The natural waterways of the region were the most important means of transportation for early settlers. The French used the St. Lawrence River, the Great Lakes, and the Mississippi River as their routes to the interior of the continent. To the south, pioneers depended on the Ohio River to guide them westward.

Geographic Themes

Place: Niagara Falls, New York
Power plants harness the waterpower of the Niagara River to generate electricity. *What Great Lakes waterway is also important to the economies of the United States and Canada?*

Today, about 15 percent of all United States freight travels the nation's inland waterways—canals, rivers, and lakes that can be used by boats, mainly barges. Half of this amount is shipped on the Mississippi River, which together with the Ohio and its tributaries is the United States' busiest inland waterway.

Canada's most important waterways are the Great Lakes and the St. Lawrence Seaway. A joint project between the United States and Canada that was completed in 1959, the St. Lawrence Seaway is a system of canals and locks that opened a shipping lane from the Great Lakes to the Atlantic Ocean.

This new seaway made ocean ports out of inland cities like Montreal and Toronto. Although closed by ice from December to April, the St. Lawrence Seaway is used heavily during the rest of the year. Canadian barges carry most of the 50 million short tons (45 million t) of freight shipped each year on this inland waterway.

Pipelines are another important means of freight transportation in the United States and Canada. Pipelines carry such cargo as natural gas, oil, gasoline, and kerosene. About one-

USING ILLUSTRATIONS

HUMAN/ENVIRONMENT INTERACTION Major hydroelectric power plants stand on both sides of the Niagara River below Niagara Falls. These plants have attracted many industries to Ontario and New York.

Answer to Caption: *St. Lawrence Seaway*

ASSESS

CHECK FOR UNDERSTANDING

Assign Section 1 Review as homework or an in-class activity.

MEETING LESSON OBJECTIVES

Each objective below is tested by the questions that follow it in parentheses.

1. **Discuss** how agriculture and industry affect the economies of the United States and Canada. *(2, 5)*
2. **Explain** how a nation's surplus leads to trade. *(3)*
3. **Specify** what methods of transportation and communication are most important to the United States and Canada. *(4)*

Cooperative Learning Activity

Organize students into three groups and assign one of the following forms of transportation to each group: waterways, railroads, highways. Have each group prepare a short presentation describing the importance of its assigned form of transportation to the economies of the United States and Canada.

EVALUATE

 Assign the Section 1 Quiz in the TCR.

 Use the Testmaker to create a customized quiz for Section 1.

RETEACH

Have students use the headings in this section to outline the material. Then ask them to write one summary statement for each heading.

ENRICH

Have interested students obtain a Canadian newspaper, magazine, or television guide to compare with similar forms of communication in the United States. Ask them to share their findings with the class.

CLOSE

Have students write a postcard to Colin Lee in which they describe their leisure activities.

fourth of the total freight shipped within the United States is carried by pipeline. The Trans-Alaska Pipeline carries oil 800 miles (1,287 km) from the northern tundra lands of Alaska southward to the port of Valdez, where warmer waters make pickup by oil tankers possible. In Canada the 2,500-mile-long (4,022-km-long) Interprovincial Pipeline and the slightly shorter Trans-Canada Pipeline transport petroleum and natural gas from Alberta to Montreal.

Dependable Communications Networks

Advanced communications systems help provide this region with ways to share information and exchange ideas. One of the basic, government-supported communications systems found in both nations is the postal systems. The postal systems help people and businesses stay in communication with one another.

Telephones also provide networks for exchanging information. The United States and Canada have about 200 million telephones—more than 1 telephone for every 2 people. The United States alone uses about two-fifths of all the telephones in the world.

The use of computers and other advanced technologies, such as microwave relays and communications satellites, have advanced the telecommunications systems in this region. Telecommunications systems send and receive messages over long distances.

Some telecommunications systems not only cover long distances but also reach large audiences. Television and radio are examples of this kind of mass communication. In the United States, 98 percent of all households have at least 1 television, and most of the televisions are color. In both the United States and Canada, there is more than 1 television for every 2 people—as many televisions as there are telephones. Radios, however, are the most popular form of communication. In Canada the number of radios almost equals the number of people, and in the United States, there are 2 radios for every person.

In the United States, most telecommunications systems used for mass communication, like television and radio stations, are owned privately. The government, however, does regulate their use to some extent. The Federal Communications Commission (FCC) licenses stations, decides which broadcast channels should be used, and requires each station to offer public service programs. Canada's government exerts greater control over mass communications industries than does the United States'. For example, a government agency called the Canadian Radio-television and Telecommunications Commission regulates and licenses all electronic communications systems in Canada. It also requires that 30 percent of all musical radio programs and 60 percent of all television programs involve Canadian writers or performers.

Written materials are another vital form of mass communications in this region. In both countries, thousands of private publishers produce newspapers, books, and magazines. The United States has more than 1,500 daily newspapers. Canada has more than 100 daily newspapers printed in English and about 10 printed in French. In addition, the United States publishes about 45,000 book titles each year, while Canada publishes about 20,000. Several thousand magazine titles also are produced in this region.

SECTION 1 REVIEW

Checking for Understanding

1. **Define** free enterprise, truck farm, contour plowing, crop rotation, service industry, interdependent, North American Free Trade Agreement.
2. **Locating Places** Where is the United States Corn Belt?
3. **Movement** Why does the United States import goods?
4. **Place** What is the St. Lawrence Seaway?

Critical Thinking

5. **Determining Cause and Effect** How have advances in farm machinery affected the owners of small farms?

ANSWERS TO SECTION 1 REVIEW

1. **free enterprise:** economic system that allows individual ownership of businesses; **truck farm:** vegetable or fruit farm located near large city markets; **contour plowing:** plowing along the curves of the land; **crop rotation:** growing different crops in succession on the same land; **service industry:** industry that provides services; **interdependent:** reliant on each other; **NAFTA:** elimination of trade barriers among Canada, the United States, and Mexico
2. northern Great Plains, Ohio to Nebraska
3. It imports goods it cannot provide or that are cheaper from other countries.
4. a system of canals and locks that connect the Great Lakes and the Atlantic Ocean
5. They cannot afford new and bigger equipment; and they cannot compete with owners of large farms.

2 SECTION

People and Their Environment

THE ENVIRONMENT

SETTING THE SCENE

Read to Discover . . .
- how pollution can cause international problems.
- how the overuse of natural resources is affecting the economies of the region.

Key Terms
- acid rain
- smog
- eutrophication
- bycatch

Identify and Locate
Adirondack Mountains, Los Angeles, Cleveland, Pacific Northwest, Grand Banks

As the people of the United States and Canada look to the future, they confront many challenges. Over the past two centuries, the United States and Canada have created mighty economies. Sometimes, however, people have lost sight of the importance of preserving resources as well as utilizing them. As a result, they have harmed the land that gives them both life and livelihoods. Some of this harm comes in the form of human-made pollutants. At other times, overuse of natural resources is the problem.

HUMAN/ENVIRONMENT INTERACTION

Pollution

To thrive, plants and animals need clean air, uncontaminated water, and wholesome nutrients. Pollution, however, is threatening the natural environment. Pollution—the introduction of harmful materials into the environment—damages the quality of air, water, and land. Some of this pollution has natural causes. For example, active volcanoes toss millions of tons of ash into the atmosphere every year.

Now, however, human-made pollution is interfering with nature's ability to adjust. One ecologist expressed the change pollution has brought to each person in this way:

As the tide of chemicals born of the Industrial Age has arisen to engulf our environment, a drastic change has come about. . . . For the first time in the history of the world, every human being is now subject to contact with dangerous chemicals, from the moment of conception until death.

Acid Rain

One kind of pollution that affects plants and fish is **acid rain**—precipitation that carries abnormally high amounts of acidic material. This acidic material is created when the chemicals emitted by cars, factories, and power plants react with the water vapor in the air. For example, fumes belching out of industrial smokestacks may carry high amounts of sulfur dioxide—which becomes sulfuric acid—while car exhaust includes nitrogen oxide—which becomes nitric acid. Scientists estimate that about 60 percent of the nitrogen oxide in the whole region comes from cars and trucks.

Sulfuric acid and nitric acid are found in acid rain. As acid rain falls to the ground, it corrodes stone and metal buildings and bridges, damages crops, and pollutes the soil.

Acid rain also takes a terrible toll on the waters of the region. Fish and other marine life cannot live in waters with high acid levels.

LESSON PLAN
Chapter 7, Section 2

FOCUS

SECTION OBJECTIVES

1. **Understand** how pollution can cause international problems.
2. **Examine** how overuse of natural resources is affecting the economies of the region.

BELLRINGER MOTIVATIONAL ACTIVITY

Project the Section 2 Focus Transparency and have students answer the questions.

PRETEACHING VOCABULARY

Help students understand how the Key Terms are related to human/environment interaction. The term *smog*, for example, was first used to describe the combination of smoke and fog over industrial cities. Today, smog also refers to a condition caused by the action of sunlight on exhaust gases from automobiles and factories.

Videodisc

GTV: PLANETARY MANAGER

Side 2, Chapter 1
Frames 2-5929
Title: ***Up, Up, and Away?***
Subject: Consequences of air pollution

Classroom Resources for Section 2

BLACKLINE MASTERS:
Reproducible Lesson Plan 7-2
Guided Reading Activity 7-2
Environmental Issue 2
Section Quiz 7-2

TRANSPARENCIES:
Section Focus Transparency 7-2

MULTIMEDIA:

Testmaker

Geography and the Environment GTV: Planetary Manager

TEACH

GUIDED PRACTICE

L1 Geography: Human/ Environment Interaction Write each of the Key Terms from this section in the center of a web diagram on the chalkboard. Have students fill in the circles around each web with factors that add to the problem listed in the center. Discuss which of these problems affects the region in which students live. **LEP**

USING MAPS

Answers:
1. around lake Erie and in eastern Ohio and western Pennsylvania; **2.** over 35 kg per hectare; **3.** Toronto

Map Skills Practice
Reading a Map In which state of the southeastern United States are trees least likely to show effects of acid rain? *(Florida)*

INDEPENDENT PRACTICE

Guided Reading Have students complete Guided Reading Activity 7-2 in the TCR. **LEP**

GLENCOE TECHNOLOGY

Videodisc

GEOGRAPHY AND THE ENVIRONMENT
THE INFINITE VOYAGE
Crisis in the Atmosphere

Chapter 10
Disc 2 Side A
Title: ***Los Angeles Smog and Air Quality Control Plan***
Subject: 120 pollution-control measures are phased in to cut emissions 80 percent by the year 2007

ACID RAIN

CANADA
UNITED STATES
Sudbury, Montreal, Ottawa, Toronto, Detroit, Chicago, New York

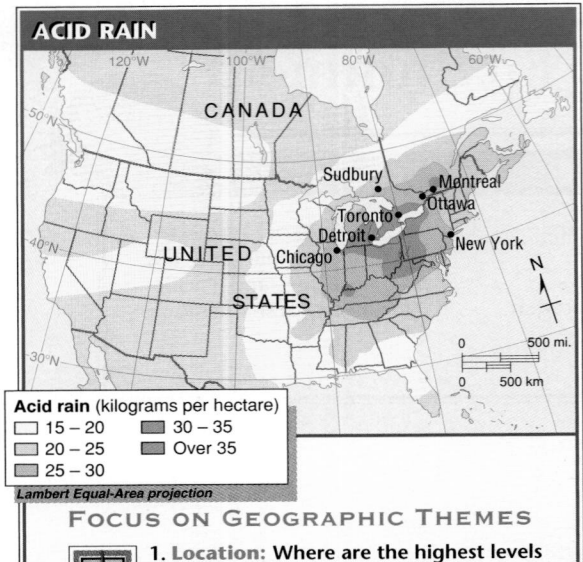

Acid rain (kilograms per hectare)
- 15 – 20
- 20 – 25
- 25 – 30
- 30 – 35
- Over 35

Lambert Equal-Area projection

FOCUS ON GEOGRAPHIC THEMES

1. **Location:** Where are the highest levels of acid rain concentrated?
2. **Place:** What level of acid rain is found in Detroit?
3. **Place:** What Canadian city has the highest level of acid rain?

Acid rain is held responsible for the deaths of at least 15,000 Canadian lakes, as well as 8 percent of the lakes found in New York's Adirondack Mountains. An additional 150,000 North American lakes have been damaged by this form of pollution.

Because the emissions that help create acid rain are carried by the wind, the source of these chemicals often is far from where the rain finally falls. This results in emissions from United States industries accounting for much of Canada's acid rain. Nearly one-half of the acid rain that falls on eastern Canada comes from emissions in the midwestern and northeastern sections of the United States.

As a result of acid rain crossing country borders, these 2 nations have spent the last 15 years working together to solve this problem. In the 1980s, they worked to identify causes of acid rain. Then, in 1991, the governments signed a pact to reduce by half the 1980 level of emissions that contribute to acid rain by the end of the century.

Smog

The nitrogen oxides that help create acid rain also are a major ingredient in **smog,** a haze caused by the sun's interaction with exhaust gases. Smog kills plants and also harms the human population, burning people's eyes and irritating their throats and lungs.

The California city of Los Angeles is plagued by smog. In Los Angeles, the 8 million cars and trucks on the road produce between 70 and 80 percent of all smog-causing emissions. Smog is measured daily in Los Angeles. On days when the smog's yellow haze is too thick, smog alerts are issued. During these alerts people with respiratory diseases are asked to stay inside, and everyone is told to drive only if necessary.

To deal with this problem of smog, many governments have passed laws regulating car emissions. California and several other states are requiring that, by 1998, 2 percent of all cars sold in the state create no emissions. By the year 2003, that figure jumps to 10 percent. In response, Chrysler recently introduced a "zero-emission" minivan that runs on electricity instead of nitrogen-producing gasoline. In addition a Massachusetts company has a solar-powered car on the drawing board. It is estimated that by the turn of the century 200,000 cars that run on alternate fuel sources will be on California's roads.

Pollution and the Great Lakes

Water systems in the United States and Canada are polluted not only by acid rain but also by sewage and industrial and agricultural wastes dumped by humans into the water supplies. The Great Lakes have been polluted in this way. Once considered an inexhaustible resource, these waters have been used as dumping sites. This problem grew as industries and cities began to spring up along the shores and dump their wastes into the lakes. In 1976, one writer described one of the sources of Lake Erie's pollution like this:

Cooperative Learning Activity

Organize students into four groups. Two of the groups represent loggers and forest conservationists. The other two groups represent commercial fishers and marine conservationists. Instruct members of each group to become experts on the issues they represent. Then have opposing sides debate the issues.

One can stand, for example, at the top of a Cleveland skyscraper and see the Cuyahoga River running out into Erie as a thick, chocolate-brown stream carrying the washings of a dozen steel works.

Surrounding industries also expose the Great Lakes to the effects of thermal pollution, caused by the release of heated industrial water into the cooler lake water. Runoff from farms using chemical fertilizers and pesticides also damages life in the lakes.

All this pollution has had a profound effect on the marine life of the Great Lakes. In recent years the amount of fish provided by Great Lake fisheries has decreased by millions of pounds. Pollution has had a particularly severe impact on some fish species such as the valuable lake herring.

Another result of all this pollution is the speedup of eutrophication (yu•TROH•fuh•KAY•shuhn). **Eutrophication** is the process in which a lake, or other body of water, becomes rich in dissolved nutrients. These nutrients nourish many small plants, especially algae. In extreme cases, these masses of plants—in their growing, dying, and decomposing—can use up all the oxygen in a body of water, leaving none for the fish. The algae also can choke the lake, eventually turning it first into a marsh, and finally into dry land. Normally, eutrophication takes thousands of years. The minerals spilled into the waters as humans pollute, however, speeds up this process. Scientists fear that this pollution is causing eutrophication to occur in sections of Lake Erie.

Today the governments of Canada and the United States have passed legislation designed to decrease the pollution in the Great Lakes region and other waters. In addition, the United States offers financial aid to state and local governments to encourage construction of sewage treatment and water treatment facilities. These facilities work to remove contaminated particles before the waste reaches water sources. As a result of the efforts of federal, state or provincial, and local governments, some progress has been made in bringing the waters of the Great Lakes and other bodies of water to their natural state.

Geographic Themes

Human/Environment Interaction: North Carolina
This forest near the Great Smoky Mountains of North Carolina was damaged by acid rain. *How have American and Canadian governments responded to the dangers of pollution?*

HUMAN/ENVIRONMENT INTERACTION

Overuse of Resources

As pioneers struggled to settle this region, they slashed, hacked, and burned their way through the forests that stood before them. At the same time, fishing fleets from many European nations discovered the wealth of marine life in the North American coastal waters and began filling their holds with fish. These activities, begun and often continued without regard to conservation, have seriously

L2 Apply Have students examine the causes of pollution discussed in this section. Then ask them to design a bumper sticker to promote public awareness of the issues. Display the completed bumper stickers and have students vote on the ones they think are most effective.

L3 Research Have students make a list of endangered species of animals and/or plants in the United States and Canada. Have them determine which of these species are endangered because of pollution or overuse of resources. Students might create a poster to illustrate their findings.

USING ILLUSTRATIONS

HUMAN/ENVIRONMENT INTERACTION Acid rain is one of the chief causes of deforestation in parts of eastern North America.

Answer to Caption: *They signed a pact to reduce by half, by the end of the century, the 1980 level of emissions that contribute to acid rain.*

ASSESS

CHECK FOR UNDERSTANDING

Assign Section 2 Review as homework or an in-class activity.

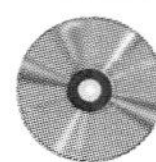

Videodisc

GTV: PLANETARY MANAGER

Side 2, Chapter 6
Frames 31907-38777
Title: *Dust in the Wind*
Subject: Time travel shows the consequences of overgrazing, excessive irrigation, and deforestation

Meeting Special Needs

Memory Disability Notetaking benefits all students but especially those with memory problems. Explain that notes help students focus on important information in the text, organize the information, and help review for tests. Have students take notes on "Pollution and the Great Lakes." Then discuss their notetaking procedures and suggest ways to improve, if necessary.

MEETING LESSON OBJECTIVES

Each objective below is tested by the questions that follow it in parentheses.

1. Understand how pollution can cause international problems. *(3, 5)*

2. Examine how the overuse of natural resources is affecting the economies of the region. *(2, 4, 5)*

USING ILLUSTRATIONS

PLACE Washington is one of the leading states in forest products. The Douglas fir pictured here is the chief timber tree in the Blue Mountains.

Answer to Caption: *clearcutting*

DID YOU KNOW?

Since the 1960s, spending to protect the environment has grown three times faster than the United States gross domestic product (GDP). In 1992 environmental protection spending reached $170 billion, or 2.8 percent of the nation's GDP.

EVALUATE

Assign the Section 2 Quiz in the TCR.

Use the Testmaker to create a customized quiz for Section 2.

depleted two resources on which the economies of the United States and Canada depend.

Logging

Wood and wood products are important economic contributors to this region. The United States leads all other nations, producing 15 percent of the world's wood. Canada, to which lumber represents an even more important export, supplies more than 5 percent. All this lumber production requires more than 1.5 million workers and 45,000 manufacturing facilities. These huge numbers indicate the importance of the lumber industry to employment in the region.

In the United States, logging companies are allowed to harvest logs from public lands. The United States Forest Service is charged with monitoring this harvesting. The Forest Service's job is to balance timber harvests with other uses of public forestland, including recreation and preservation of wildlife habitats. Some conservation leaders claim that the Forest Service is putting lumber profits above other concerns, because its budget is partly based on money earned from lumber sales.

Another concern is the Forest Service's approval of clearcutting. When a forest is clearcut, all trees are cut down. In addition, roads must be built into the forests so that the lumber can be brought out. The Forest Service has constructed 365,000 miles (587,000 km) of roads for logging companies—more than eight times the lengths of roads comprising the Federal Interstate Highway System. Conservationists argue that the combination of road-building and clearcutting destroys the natural ecosystem of the area.

Clearcutting also threatens the remaining old-growth forests of the Pacific Northwest. A common definition for old-growth forests is forests "containing at least 8 big trees per acre and exceeding 300 years in age or measuring more than 40 inches (102 cm) in diameter at breast height." Between 1986 and 1988, more than 100,000 acres (40,500 ha) of old-growth forest were cleared each year. If this rate continues, all old-growth forests will disappear from the Pacific Northwest by the end of the 20th century.

This clearcutting of old-growth trees also endangers the wildlife of a region. For example, the northern spotted owl, whose home is the old-growth forests of the Pacific Northwest, was placed on the endangered species list in 1990. Experts say that to save the bird from extinction, logging in this area will have to be cut back drastically. This has pitted the fate of a species against the jobs of a region. Clearcutting deprives humans of other benefits of old growth as well. For example, a potential treatment for cancer was discovered using the bark of the yew tree. Yew trees thrive in old-growth forests and were traditionally viewed by loggers as trash trees, burned during the clearcutting process. Some scientists worry about what valuable discoveries will be gone with the lost old-growth forests.

Geographic Themes

Region: Pacific Northwest

The United States Forest Service has sought to balance timber harvests with forest conservation. *What practice allowed by the Forest Service has been opposed by many conservationists?*

Critical Thinking

Predicting Consequences Have students write a short story based on the following question: What might life be like in the twenty-first century if present trends in pollution and overuse of resources continue? Call on volunteers to share their stories with the class.

One alternative to clearcutting is called sustainable forestry. When this method is used, certain trees in a forest are targeted for harvesting while other trees are left untouched. In addition, trees harvested in this way can be taken from the forest by mule or horse, which means extensive roads would not have to be built. Sustainable forestry would protect the area's natural ecosystem and preserve old growth.

The confrontation between the lumber industry and conservationists is far from over. In response to the concern about lost lumber jobs, one environmentalist said:

> *The question in the Pacific Northwest is not whether the logging of old growth should stop, but when. The supply of ancient trees is limited.*

Fishing

The abundance of fish in the oceans along the Atlantic Coast was in part responsible for original European settlement of this region. As early as 1497, explorer John Cabot reported bountiful fishing in the Grand Banks area. The Grand Banks consists of a 139,000-square-mile (360,010-sq.-km) area off the southeast coast of Newfoundland. Fishing fleets from England, France, and Spain came to reap the fishing site's economic benefits. Immigrants, mostly from Ireland, England, and France, settled the coasts of Newfoundland and became actively involved in catching and preparing fish for regional and foreign markets.

By the mid-1900s, fishing by ships from many nations had depleted the fish population. As a result, Canada imposed a fishery conservation zone covering a 200-nautical-mile (370-km) band around its coast. This zone, however, was not wide enough to include the Grand Banks. Fishing off the eastern coast, especially by foreign fleets, has continued even as the number of fish decline.

In 1992, the Canadian government, concerned about dwindling populations of cod in the waters, lowered cod-fishing quotas by 35 percent and announced the temporary closing of Newfoundland's east coast cod fishery. These actions caused the largest layoff in Canadian history, putting 20,000 people out of work. Newfoundlanders, so reliant on fishing, are still trying to recover from these economic blows.

A combination of pollution and overfishing also has damaged the fishing industry in the United States. In one recent seven-year period, the total United States catch declined by more than 25 percent.

Waste in the fishing industry also is partly responsible for the depletion of fish populations. High-tech trawlers sweep the oceans for fish, often catching unwanted fish species, marine mammals, and birds. This dead **bycatch**, as it is called, is simply tossed overboard. Scientists estimate that more than 10 percent of the fish caught worldwide are bycatch, thrown away by commercial fishers. It is believed this amount easily equals the amount of fish caught in all United States waters every year. Conservationists urge increased government funding to develop fishing gear that will cut down on the amount of bycatch netted by fishing ships.

Section 2 Review

Checking for Understanding

1. **Define** acid rain, smog, eutrophication, bycatch.
2. **Locating Places** Where are this region's old-growth forests located?
3. **Human/Environment Interaction** How has pollution affected the Great Lakes?
4. **Human/Environment Interaction** What caused the largest layoff in Canadian history?

Critical Thinking

5. **Drawing Conclusions** Why has acid rain made it necessary for the governments of the United States and Canada to work together?

RETEACH

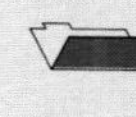 Have students complete Reteaching Activity 7 in the TCR.

ENRICH

Have students complete Enrichment Activity 7 in the TCR.

CLOSE

Have students evaluate solutions to the problems of pollution and overuse of resources in the United States and Canada. Ask them to rank the solutions in order of priority. Discuss students' responses.

 **Videodisc**

GTV: PLANETARY MANAGER

Side 2, Chapter 7
Frames 38779-41076
Title: ***Water, Water Everywhere***
Subject: Amount of available drinking water

GTV: PLANETARY MANAGER

Side 2, Chapter 8
Frames 41078-46201
Title: ***Shall We Gather at the River?***
Subject: Everyday sources of water pollution and how we can clean up our water

ANSWERS TO SECTION 2 REVIEW

1. **acid rain:** precipitation that carries abnormally high amounts of acidic material; **smog:** a haze caused by the sun's interaction with exhaust gases; **eutrophication:** a process by which a lake becomes rich in dissolved nutrients, which nourish small plants that then choke the lake, eventually turning it into dry land; **bycatch:** unwanted fish, marine mammals, and birds caught by fishing fleets
2. in the Pacific Northwest
3. killed millions of fish, led to speedup of eutrophication
4. the Canadian government's decision to lower fishing quotas and close Newfoundland's east coast cod fishery
5. The problem of acid rain crosses national borders, and much of Canada's acid rain comes from U.S. industries.

FOCUS

Have students quickly list items they throw away in the course of an average day. Allow time for sharing; have students guess how many pounds of trash the class as a whole generates daily.

TEACH

Implement Environmental Issue 2 as a class activity.

L1 Discuss Have students review the list they made prior to reading. Have them figure out those items they might recycle and those whose use they can reduce.

L2 Debate Have students debate which of the three solutions proposed by environmentalists to the landfill crisis is the most realistic. Suggest that students also discuss how well they think the public has responded to recycling efforts.

DID YOU KNOW?

By the year 2000, half of the landfills in America—about 3000—will be filled to capacity.

Videodisc

GTV: PLANETARY MANAGER

Side 2, Chapter 5
Frames 25236-31905
Title: *Tidy World*
Subject: Solid wastes and how we might clean up the Earth

CASE STUDY

NOT IN MY BACKYARD!

As the landfills close, America is finally admitting that there's no 'away' to throw things to. . . . But human beings are above all creative creatures, and ingenious solutions to waste problems are popping up all over. . . . If there was ever a solvable problem, this is it.

The Global Citizen, 1991

In 1987 the town of Islip, New York, ran out of room for its garbage. The city appealed to the state to expand its dump. The state, however, refused. An Alabama businessman offered to sail a load of garbage to North Carolina. The town loaded more than three thousand tons of stinking refuse onto a barge, and it set out.

North Carolina, however, refused to let the barge drop off its cargo. So began the barge's spring search along the coast of the southern United States and beyond. It stopped at Florida, Alabama, Mississippi, Louisiana, Texas, Mexico, Belize, and the Bahamas. There were no "trash takers."

Barge loaded with garbage from Islip, New York

THE ISSUE

In a very graphic way, the Islip garbage barge focused attention on America's growing problem of too much garbage and nowhere to take it.

The smelly boat did for the environmental cause what environmentalists had been trying to do for several decades: shock the American public into an awareness of the seriousness of the landfill situation.

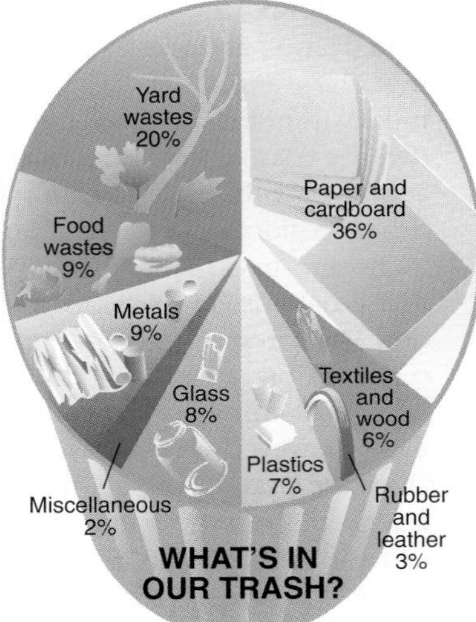

Extending the Content

Have students do some "hands on" research to discover more about packaging material and junk mail, two major kinds of trash. For one week, have students collect all packaging material—food bags, product cartons, padding/peanuts, and so on. Have them also collect throw-away catalogs, advertisements, mail solicitations, and so on. Set aside a class period for students to bring in their "savings" and sort and count it. Have them graph the results, then discuss the purpose of each kind of packaging and/or mail and how well each fills its purpose. Have students identify *overpackaging*—designed merely to make a product appear bigger. Have students discuss and carry out the best way to dispose of the trash.

THE BACKGROUND

In the mid-1950s, *Life* magazine reported on a popular trend called "throw-away living." The report pointed to an American buying binge of disposables: disposable plates, eating utensils, razors, ballpoint pens, diapers—anything that promised to cut down on the tedium of everyday tasks. Most disposable items were made of paper or plastic. Both were light, inexpensive, and, in the case of plastic, extremely durable.

"Suddenly," Goeller said, "there was this wonderfully awful symbol of the problem—a huge plate of garbage that no one wanted to take a bite out of."

When *Life* magazine published its report, very few Americans were concerned about the explosive growth of trash. By the early 1960s, environmentalists were sounding the alarm for eventual landfill overflow and calling for recycling programs.

During the next 30 years, environmental concerns grew as studies showed the reason that the dumps were filling so rapidly. Very little of the material was disintegrating. Dumps covered each day's garbage with dirt to keep out rats, flies, and other scavenging animals as well as minimize the odor. The dirt, however, also kept out the natural "ingredients" of decomposition: bacteria and sunlight. Garbage in landfills was being preserved, not decomposing.

When the Islip barge appeared, most states and communities were aware of the problems of overflow and pollution from which America's landfill system suffered.

THE POINTS OF VIEW

Transporting garbage to another place seemed reasonable to Islip. Angry North Carolina environmentalists, however, were having none of somebody else's garbage. Dave Goeller of Environmental Action, a Washington-based group, recalled that environmentalists had tried to spark interest in the landfill crisis for years, and no one cared. "Suddenly," Goeller said, "there was this wonderfully awful symbol of the problem—a huge plate of garbage that no one wanted to take a bite out of."

THE ISSUE TODAY

After 57 days at sea, the barge was allowed to return to Islip. The garbage was finally burned in Brooklyn.

Since that embarrassing spring, Islip has gotten rid of 75 percent of its landfill with a vigorous recycling program. It has also built a mass fill incinerator to handle 50 percent of its garbage intake.

Many communities around the country followed Islip's lead. Recycling programs are in place in many cities; plans for more than a thousand huge incinerators to be built during the 1990s are in the works.

Environmentalists, however, continue to be concerned. Each American generates about 4 pounds (1.8 kg) of trash and garbage a day, some of which, particularly the plastic, will never decompose. Landfills are closing, incinerators are highly controversial, and fewer communities want either in their backyards. So, to their call for recycling programs, environmentalists have added the need to reduce the use of throwaway items. They maintain that recycling is better than disposal, reuse is better than recycling, and reduction is best of all.

Reviewing the Case

1. **What is the landfill crisis?**
2. **How do environmentalists think the landfill problem can be solved?**
3. **Human/Environment Interaction What effects have landfills had on the environment?**

ANSWERS TO REVIEWING THE CASE

1. Landfills are reaching capacity because the garbage in them is not decomposing. In addition, people have not reduced the amount of garbage they generate, and the population is increasing.
2. People should reduce their use of throwaway items, reuse items when they can, and recycle as many items as they can.
3. They prohibit decomposition and biodegradation as well as more productive use of the land.

Case Study

ASSESS

Have students answer the Reviewing the Case questions on page 143.

CLOSE

Have students identify all the resources—recycling, incinerator, landfill, etc.—available in their community to reduce the amount of trash.

GLENCOE TECHNOLOGY

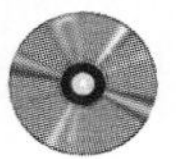

Videodisc

GEOGRAPHY AND THE ENVIRONMENT
THE INFINITE VOYAGE
Miracles by Design

Chapter 4
Disc 3 Side B
Title: ***Biodegradable Plastic: The Miracle Material?***

NATIONAL GEOGRAPHIC SOCIETY

Videodisc

GTV: PLANETARY MANAGER

Side 1, Chapter 9
Frames 41787-47422
Title: ***Where You Gonna Go?***
Subject: Music reinforces the message that if we continue to harm our environment, there will be no safe place to go

EYE ON THE ENVIRONMENT POSTER SERIES

Display the three posters that discuss trash—*Overview, Focus United States*, and *A Global Look*. Discussion questions and Activities are presented on page 13 of the Teacher's Guide.

TEACH

Have students compare the cartogram on page 144 with the world map on pages A2–A3 and observe differences. *(In the cartogram, countries appear as rectangular shapes, and relative sizes of countries differ.)* Explain: "In the cartogram on page 144, country size is **not** based on land area; instead, it represents some other value. What value determines country size in this cartogram?" *(population)* Ask: "Why are cartograms useful?" *(They illustrate comparisons between countries.)* Have students read the skill on page 144. Then ask: "Which two countries have the largest populations?" *(China, India)* "Why does Japan appear larger than Australia on this map?" *(Japan has more people than Australia.)*

Skills Practice
For additional practice, have students complete Skill Activity 7 in the TCR.

MAP AND GRAPH SKILLS

Reading a Cartogram

On most maps, land areas are drawn in proportion to the actual surface areas on the earth. In a **cartogram**, country size is based on some value *other* than land area, such as population, or gross national product.

REVIEWING THE SKILL

A cartogram provides clear visual comparisons of whatever value it measures.

To read a cartogram, apply the following steps:

- Read the map title and key to identify the kind of information presented on the cartogram.
- Look for relationships among the countries. Determine which countries are largest and smallest.
- Compare the cartogram with a conventional land-area map to determine the degree of distortion of particular countries.

PRACTICING THE SKILL

Use the cartogram below to answer the following questions:

1. What value determines the relative sizes of countries on this cartogram?
2. Compare the cartogram with the conventional land-area map on pages A2–A3. How has the relative size of Canada been changed on the cartogram? How would you explain this change?

For additional practice in this skill, see Practicing Skills on page 146 of the Chapter 7 Review.

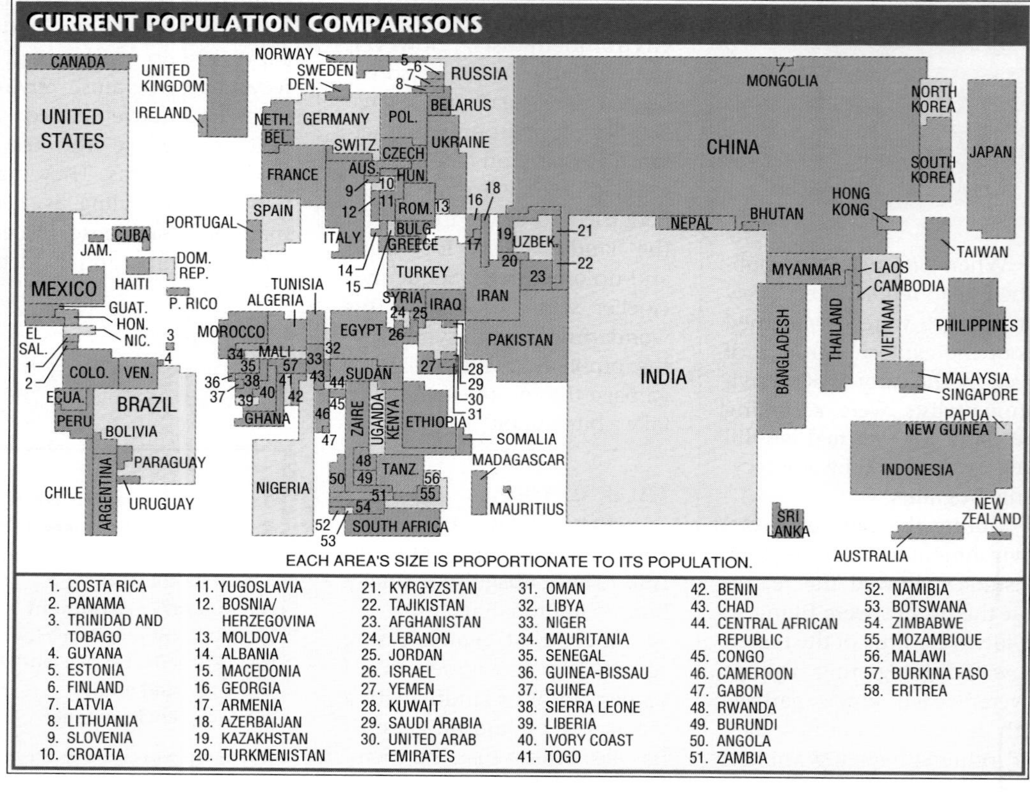

ANSWERS TO PRACTICING THE SKILL

1. population
2. much smaller; because it has a relatively small population

chapter 7 HIGHLIGHTS

Section	Key Terms	Summary
1 Living in the United States and Canada  Irrigation on a farm in the Midwest	**free enterprise** (p. 129) **truck farm** (p. 131) **contour plowing** (p. 131) **crop rotation** (p. 131) **service industry** (p. 132) **interdependent** (p. 133) **North American Free Trade Agreement** (p. 134)	• The rich soils, plentiful waters, and varied climates of farms in the United States and Canada encourage the production of a wide variety of meats, grains, vegetables, and fruits. • Advanced farming technologies have increased crop yield and farm size but decreased the number of farm workers. • The culture region of the United States and Canada is a world leader in the production of manufactured goods, but its service industries employ more people than its factories. • The many agricultural and manufactured products of the United States and Canada help the region lead the world in trade. • Complex networks for transportation and communications support the peoples and economies of the region.
2 People and Their Environment  Forest in North Carolina damaged by acid rain	**acid rain** (p. 137) **smog** (p. 138) **eutrophication** (p. 139) **bycatch** (p. 141)	• Pollutants include acid rain and smog, both caused by emissions from factories and cars. • The water supply in the United States and Canada is polluted by industry wastes, agricultural chemicals, and sewage. • Pollution of the waters severely impacts the fish population and also speeds up eutrophication. • Logging, especially of public lands, is endangering the old-growth forests of the Pacific Northwest. • Overfishing and waste in the fishing industry have seriously depleted the fish population, resulting in economic hardship for areas dependent on the sea.

Map Activity

Identify and Locate Provide an outline map of North America, found on page 23 of the Outline Map Resource Book. Have students color-code the map and create a key to indicate the following: areas of Canada and the United States affected by acid rain; logging areas; commercial fishing areas. Discuss how the maps illustrate the interdependence of the two nations.

CHAPTER 7 HIGHLIGHTS

USING THE CHAPTER 7 HIGHLIGHTS

Use the Chapter 7 Highlights to preview, review, condense, or reteach the chapter.

PREVIEW/REVIEW

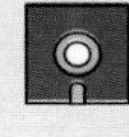

Vocabulary PuzzleMaker Software reinforces the Key Terms used in Chapter 7.

Student Self-Test and Review Software allows students to review Chapter 7 content.

CONDENSE

Have students read the Chapter 7 Highlights.

Have students listen to the Chapter 7 Audiocassettes in the TCR. Spanish Audiocassettes are also available.

Assign the Chapter 7 Audiocassette Activity and give students the Chapter 7 Audiocassette Quiz.

Have students complete the Guided Reading Activities for Chapter 7 in the TCR. Spanish Guided Reading Activities are also available.

RETEACH

Have students complete Reteaching Activity 7 in the TCR. Spanish Reteaching Activities are also available.

GLENCOE TECHNOLOGY

Videodisc

Use Chapter 7 MindJogger Videoquiz to review students' knowledge before administering the Chapter 7 Test.

MINDJOGGER VIDEOQUIZ

Chapter 7
Disc 1 Side B

The MindJogger Videoquiz is also available on videocassette.

ANSWERS

Reviewing Key Terms

1. truck farms
2. service industries
3. crop rotation
4. interdependent
5. contour plowing
6. free enterprise
7. North American Free Trade Association
8. acid rain, smog
9. bycatch
10. eutrophication

Reviewing Facts

11. in the West, South, and Midwest of the United States and in Canada's Prairie Provinces
12. transportation equipment and machinery
13. the United States
14. It has killed life in thousands of lakes and damaged thousands more.
15. It is the government agency charged with balancing timber harvest with other uses of public forestland, such as recreation and preservation of wildlife.
16. The Grand Banks is a 139,000 square mile (360,000 sq. km) area off the southeast coast of Newfoundland known for its plentiful fish.

chapter 7 REVIEW

Reviewing Key Terms

Choose the vocabulary term that best completes each of the sentences below. Write your answers on a separate sheet of paper.

free enterprise (p. 129)
truck farms (p. 131)
contour plowing (p. 131)
crop rotation (p. 131)
service industries (p. 132)
interdependent (p. 133)
North American Free Trade Agreement (p. 134)
acid rain (p. 137)
smog (p. 138)
eutrophication (p. 139)
bycatch (p. 141)

SECTION 1

1. _____ are located near large cities so that vegetables grown on them can be shipped to urban markets.
2. Education, health care, and tourism are examples of _____.
3. To preserve nutrients, farmers practice _____ by growing different crops in succession, or they let land lie fallow.
4. In recent decades, the economies of the United States and Canada have become increasingly _____.
5. _____ keeps topsoil from washing away.
6. _____ refers to an economic system that allows individuals to own, operate, and profit from their own businesses.
7. The _____ was developed to eliminate trade barriers.

SECTION 2

8. Pollution partly created by car emissions includes _____ and _____.
9. The _____ snared by trawlers' nets is thrown overboard.
10. _____ can eventually turn a body of water into dry land.

Reviewing Facts

SECTION 1

11. Where in the United States and Canada are most beef cattle raised?
12. What is the United States's leading export?
13. What country is Canada's chief trade partner?

SECTION 2

14. How has acid rain affected lakes in the United States and Canada?
15. What is the United States Forest Service and what are its responsibilities?
16. What is the Grand Banks?

Critical Thinking

17. **Analyzing Information** How has agricultural surplus added to the economies of the United States and Canada?
18. **Identifying Central Issues** How does NAFTA reflect interdependence between the United States and Canada?

Geographic Themes

19. **Movement** In what ways is the St. Lawrence Seaway important to the movement of freight in the United States and Canada?
20. **Human/Environment Interaction** Why do conservationists prefer sustainable forestry to clearcutting?

Practicing Skills

Reading a Cartogram

21. Refer to the cartogram on page 144. How have the relative sizes of Japan and Australia been changed on the cartogram? What do the sizes of these countries on the cartogram tell us about them?

Critical Thinking

17. It has allowed the United States and Canada to export one-fourth of their agricultural products, which positively affects these two countries.
18. NAFTA eliminates remaining trade barriers and furthers the linkage of the economies of the United States, Canada, and Mexico.

Geographic Themes

19. It opened the Great Lakes to the Atlantic Ocean, creating ocean ports out of several inland cities; this made transportation of goods easier.
20. Sustainable forestry protects forests because it does not require extensive road systems and leaves some trees untouched.

Using the Unit Atlas

Refer to the physical geography section of the Unit Atlas on pages 88–89.

22. What mineral resources are found in the Canadian Shield?

23. Where are the Everglades located?

Projects

Individual Activity

In this chapter, you learned about the many agricultural products grown in the United States and Canada. Research the agriculture of either country. Use your research, as well as the material in this chapter, to create an agricultural map of your chosen nation.

Cooperative Learning Activity

Divide your group of four into two. Have two students imagine they are loggers dependent on the harvesting of old-growth forests. The other two students are environmentalists concerned with preserving the old-growth forests. Prepare and present a debate on the use of old-growth forests on public lands.

Writing About Geography

Cause and Effect

Imagine you are a reporter researching environmental issues in the United States and Canada. Use your journal, the text, and other resources to decide which issues you will address. Write a newspaper story in which you discuss how you think these issues will continue to affect these nations.

Locating Places

THE UNITED STATES AND CANADA: PHYSICAL/POLITICAL

Match the letters on the map with the places and physical features of the United States and Canada. Write your answers on a separate sheet of paper.

1. Midwest
2. Prairie Provinces
3. California
4. New York
5. Toronto
6. St. Lawrence River
7. Ohio River
8. Alaska
9. Texas
10. Pacific Northwest

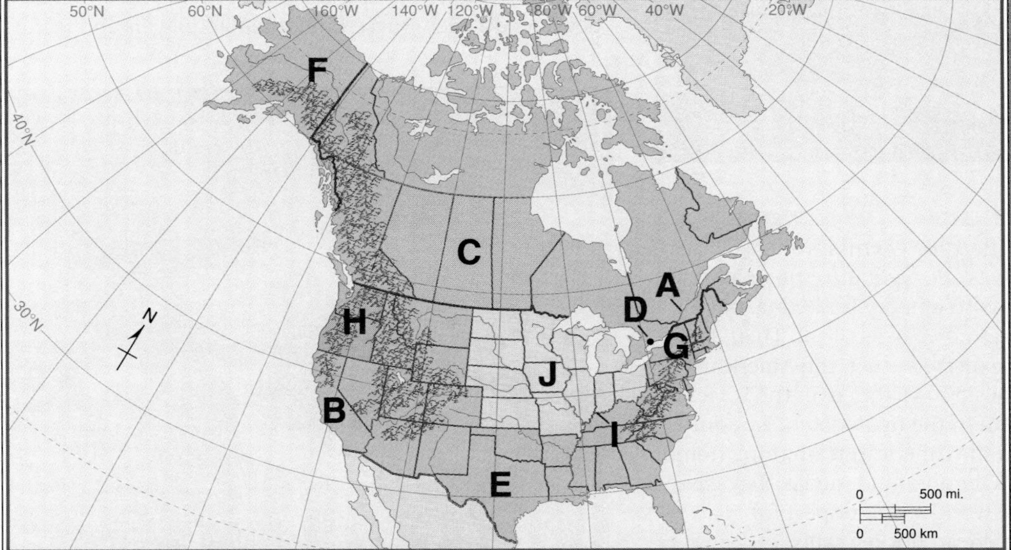

Chapter Bonus Test Question

This question may be used for extra credit on the chapter test.

Explain the relationship between environment and economy in the United States and Canada.

(Answer: Both nations have highly developed economies based on agriculture and industry. Natural resources support both economic activities. The overuse and/or abuse of natural resources impacts agricultural and industrial production and affects employment.)

Chapter 7 Review

Practicing Skills

21. Japan is larger and Australia is smaller than on the land-area map; Japan has a larger population.

Using the Unit Atlas

22. copper, nickel, zinc, and iron ore

23. Florida

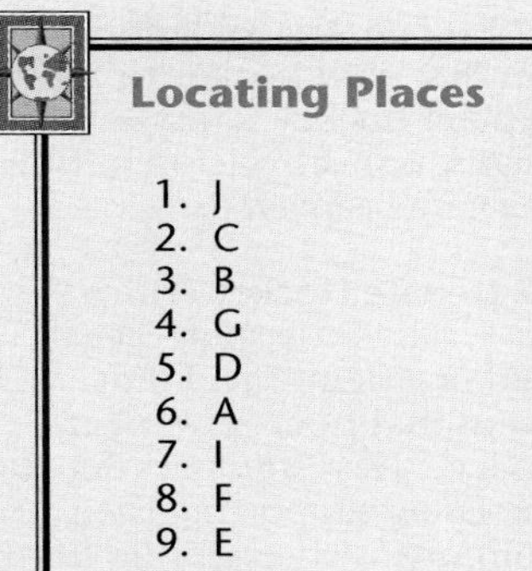

Locating Places

1. J
2. C
3. B
4. G
5. D
6. A
7. I
8. F
9. E
10. H

FOCUS

Have students recall ice hockey games they have seen or heard about. Allow a minute or two for students to volunteer adjectives and verbs that capture and explain the feelings they had during the game.

TEACH

L2 Explain Ask students familiar with hockey to explain hockey terms as well as give a short version of how the game is played.

L2 Debate Hockey critics have called the sport "legalized mayhem;" avid fans claim that hockey is "poetry on ice." Have students debate the issue, supporting their opinions with examples from games they have seen. At the end of the debate, have students compare hockey skills and violence to that in other sports—baseball, basketball, football, boxing, and so on.

Canada and the United States

Ice Hockey

One day in the mid-1860s, at the frozen harbor of Kingston, Ontario, a group of bored Canadian soldiers cleared the snow from the ice. Then they strapped on their skates, and using their field hockey sticks and balls, proceeded to "invent" Canadian ice hockey. By 1900 hockey had become Canada's national pastime. During the 20th century, millions of Americans have developed the same passionate interest in this fast, entertaining sport.

◀ **THE SPREAD OF HOCKEY** from Canada to the United States began in the 1880s and 1890s when Canadians sparked interest in the game among their American relatives, friends, or business contacts. By the end of the 1890s, Americans along the East Coast and in the Midwest had developed a keen interest in Canadian players and teams.

THE AMERICAN HOCKEY TEAM ▶ at the 1980 Olympics at Lake Placid, New York, went into the final playoffs a heavy underdog, having lost to the Soviets 11-3. Then, in an unexpected upset, the Americans plowed to victory over the Soviet team in the final match. Not only did the American team bring home an Olympic gold medal, they gave the world a new respect for American hockey skills.

148

Making the Connection

Research Organize students into teams of five or six. Allow each team to choose a facet of hockey to research: history, equipment, teams, heroes. Challenge teams to use books and magazine articles to "flesh out" the basic information they obtain from encyclopedias. Suggest to students that they present their research in as graphic and interesting a way as possible: time lines, captioned photographs or drawings, equipment displays, a Hockey Heroes Hall of Fame, or a hockey trivia booklet. When students have completed their research, have them work together to create a hockey exhibit. They can then present their information informally, as if they were guides at a museum.

Geography Connection

◀ **THE FIRST PRO HOCKEY CIRCUIT** was formed during the first decade of the 20th century. Dr. J. L. Gibson, a retired Canadian hockey player who later became a dentist, hired a team of Canadian hockey professionals. For three years Gibson's team played teams in the American Midwest.

▲ **ENTHUSIASTIC FANS** still are attracted to hockey in the 1990s. Hockey teams play in almost every American state. The Kid hockey system has divisions for boys and girls, men and women. Significantly, at the boys' "Bantam" level (13 and 14 years old), promising youngsters are scouted, and at the Junior level (17 to 19 years old) the most talented American players are prepared for the National Hockey League.

CANADIAN AND AMERICAN HOCKEY GREAT WAYNE GRETZKY▶ owned the ice in the 1980s. In 1989 he became the National Hockey League's all-time leading scorer with 1,851 points. Hockey stars packed crowds into arenas throughout North America beginning in the 1920s. The stars included Howie Morenz, dubbed Lightning Legs, for his grace and speed. Morenz and other players made hockey a major league attraction on both sides of the border.

Checking for Understanding

1. **How did ice hockey spread from Canada to the United States?**
2. **Place What role does ice hockey play in your community?**

ASSESS

Have students answer the Checking for Understanding questions on page 149.

CLOSE

Ask students: "How do enthusiastic sports fans help to expand a sport? How did fans aid the spread of ice hockey?"

DID YOU KNOW?

So powerful are the swings of hockey players that a puck, when struck, can travel across the ice at speeds faster than 100 miles per hour.

ANSWERS TO CHECKING FOR UNDERSTANDING

1. Canadians told American relatives, friends, and business contacts about the sport.
2. Answers will vary.

UNIT OVERVIEW

The three chapters that comprise this unit introduce students to the geography and peoples of Latin America. Various aspects of Latin American life—such as the economy, lifestyles, and human/environment interaction—are also presented.

GEOGRAPHY JOURNAL

Activity Remind students that the headline and first paragraph of a news story give the most important information: who, what, when, where. The remainder of the news article explains why and/or how. Students may find that highlighting headlines and opening paragraphs of news stories will help them summarize.

Using their journals, students can form generalizations about Latin America, providing supporting examples from collected articles.

- This journal activity provides the basis for the "Writing About Geography" exercise in the Chapter Review.

- The Geography Journal may be used as an integral part of Performance Assessment.

CD-ROM

PICTURE ATLAS OF THE WORLD

See page T37 for an additional CD-ROM activity to enrich Unit 3, Latin America.

UNIT 3

Latin America

GeoJournal Activity

While studying Latin America, keep a record of news stories on the region's physical geography, its cultures and lifestyles, its economies and environments. Write short summaries of each news story.

Where in the World . . . .

Display Political Map Transparency 3 and ask students the following questions: What continents form Latin America? *(South America and part of North America)* What part of North America is part of Latin America?*(southwesternmost region)* Why might this area also be called Middle or Central America? *(geographically in the middle or center between North and South America)* What other landforms are part of Latin America? *(islands)* In what part of Latin America are there groups of islands? *(Caribbean)* By what group names are these islands known? *(West Indies, Caribbean Islands, Antilles)* What body of water is west of the islands? *(Gulf of Mexico)* South? *(Caribbean Sea)* East? *(Atlantic Ocean)*

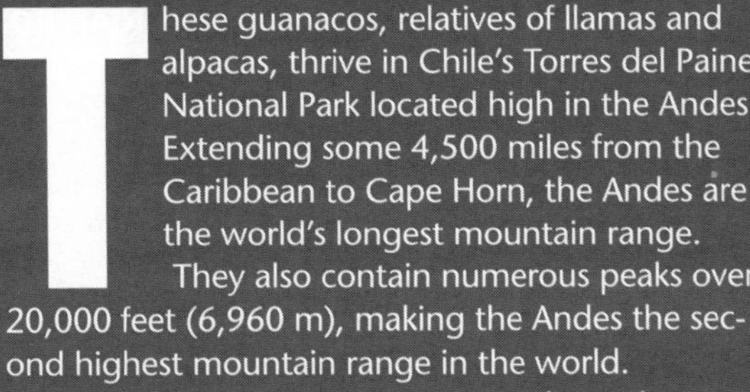

Picturing the World

These guanacos, relatives of llamas and alpacas, thrive in Chile's Torres del Paine National Park located high in the Andes. Extending some 4,500 miles from the Caribbean to Cape Horn, the Andes are the world's longest mountain range.

They also contain numerous peaks over 20,000 feet (6,960 m), making the Andes the second highest mountain range in the world.

1. Using the map on page A11, jot down the name and elevation of the highest peak in the Andes.
2. What country is it in?

Picture Atlas CD-ROM Enrichment Corner

Put together a cultural reference file on the Andes. (See the *Picture Atlas of the World* User's Guide on how to use the Collector button.) Collect the items on the CD-ROM for the following three countries: Ecuador—photographs of crafts and Canari peoples; Peru—photographs of Native Americans near Cuzco, boys kicking a ball, Native Americans in hats, video of Lake Titicaca, and Inca music; Bolivia—photographs of market day in Sucre, young Bolivians, and guitar music. Read the photo captions and answer the following questions:

1. Crafts of the Andes enjoy an international reputation. Name a popular product tourists often buy in the villages of the Andes.
2. Name a major textile product of Peru.
3. What instrument did the ancient Incas play?
4. What is a sampoña?

interNET CONNECTIONS

Learn about the history, geography, and culture of Honduras, Belize, Panama, Guatemala, Nicaragua, and El Salvador at the following address:

World Wide Web
http://www.greenarrow.com/welcome.htm

GLENCOE TECHNOLOGY

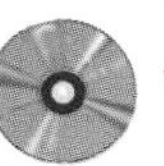

Videodisc

REUTERS ISSUES IN GEOGRAPHY

Chapter 2
Disc 1 Side A
Title: ***Latin America: The Disappearing Rain Forests***
Subject: The complex issues surrounding the rain forests of Latin America

GEOGRAPHY AND THE ENVIRONMENT
THE INFINITE VOYAGE
To the Edge of the Earth

Chapter 4
Disc 1 Side B
Title: ***Exploring the Galapagos Islands***
Subject: Animal life in the underwater caves of Galapagos Islands

ANSWERS TO PICTURING THE WORLD

1. Mt. Aconcagua (22,834 ft./6,960 m)
2. Argentina

Enrichment Corner Answers

1. colorful, tightly woven cloth
2. wool
3. flute
4. reed panpipe

0:00 OUT OF TIME?

If time does not permit teaching each chapter in this unit, you may use the Chapter Highlights and the Audiocassettes that include a 1-page activity and a 1-page test for each chapter.

These features and activities may be used as an introduction to the unit or as teaching tools throughout the course of the unit.

FOCUS

Remind students that Latin America has the greatest latitudinal span of any world region. Ask students to predict how the region's geographical location might affect settlement, clothing, housing, and leisure time activities. Students may wish to write predictions in their journals.

TEACH

Implement Foods Around the World 2 as a class activity.

Have students complete World Cultures Transparencies 3 and 4 in the TCR.

Have students complete Unit Atlas Activity 3B.

ASSESS

Have students answer the Exploring Cultural Diversity questions on page 152.

UNIT 3 ATLAS

LATIN AMERICA
Cultural Geography

EXPLORING CULTURAL DIVERSITY

1. *What areas of Latin America are the most heavily populated? Most sparsely populated?*
2. *What nations make up Latin America?*
3. *What cities in Latin America have more than 5 million people?*
4. *What countries border Brazil?*

Brazil is the only South American country in which Portuguese is the official language.

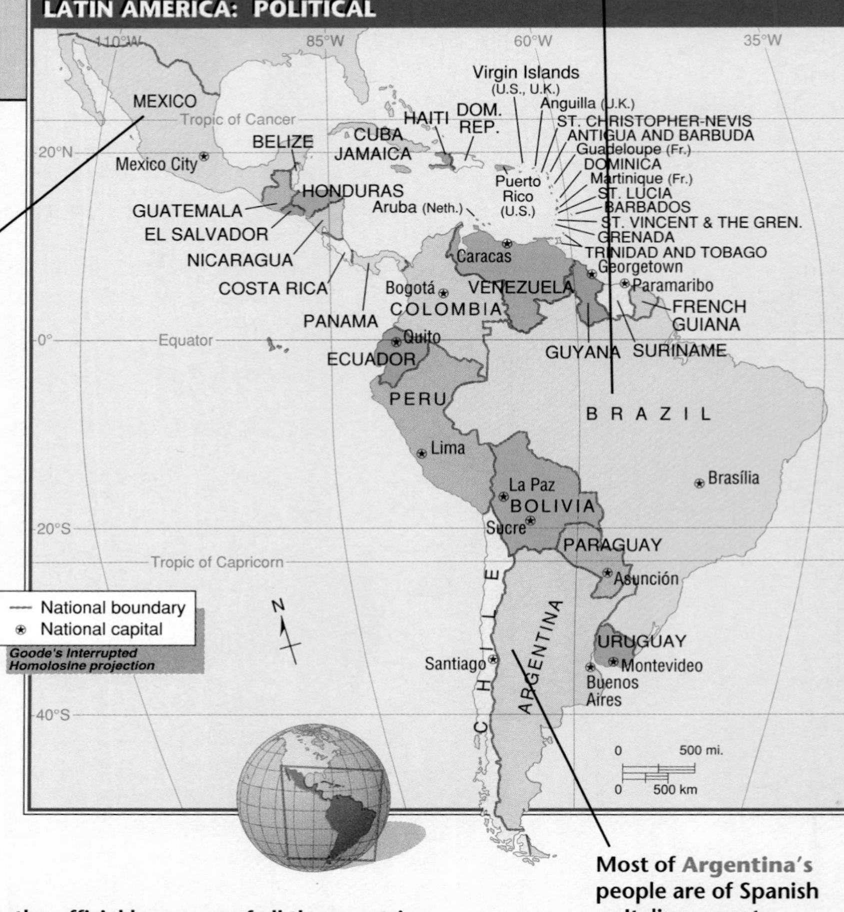

The great majority of Mexico's people are of mixed European and Native American ancestry.

Spanish is the official language of all the countries of Central America, except Belize. English is the official language of Belize.

Most of Argentina's people are of Spanish or Italian ancestry. Native Americans—the original inhabitants—make up only a small part of the country's population.

Classroom Resources for Unit 3

BLACKLINE MASTERS:
Geography Simulation 3
World Literature Reading 2
Foods Around the World 2
Unit Atlas Activity 3B

TRANSPARENCIES:
Political Map Transparency 3
Unit Map Overlay Transparency 3

MULTIMEDIA:

World Music: *Cultural Traditions, Lesson 2*

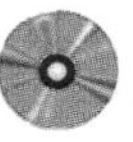

Geography and the Environment
Reuters Issues in Geography

Picture Atlas of the World

Images of the World Poster Set

Mexico City is Latin America's largest city. It has the world's second-largest population.

Caracas is Venezuela's capital and largest city. About four-fifths of Venezuela's population lives in cities and towns.

Brazil is one of the largest, most populated of the world's countries. About half of South America's population lives here.

The growing population of La Paz, in Bolivia, is nearly one-half Native American.

Argentina's capital, Buenos Aires, is home to one-third of Argentina's people.

LATIN AMERICA: POPULATION DENSITY

Per sq. km	Per sq. mi.
Over 100	Over 250
50-100	125-250
25-50	60-125
1-25	2-60
Under 1	Under 2
Uninhabited	Uninhabited

Cities
- Over 10,000,000
- 5,000,000 – 10,000,000
- 2,000,000 – 5,000,000
- 1,000,000 – 2,000,000
- 250,000 – 1,000,000

Goode's Interrupted Homolosine projection

Latin America has almost twice as many people as the United States.

Population: Latin America and the United States

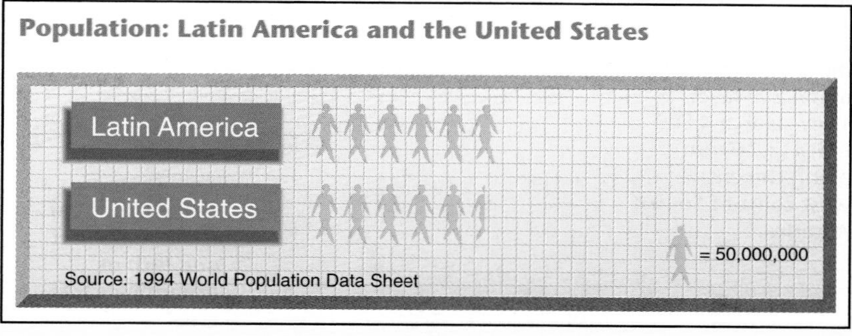

LESSON PLAN
Unit 3 Atlas

EXPLORING CULTURAL DIVERSITY

This feature may be used to introduce students to the cultural geography of Latin America. Use questions to stimulate class discussion and help students become familiar with the region. Accept reasonable answers based on the maps, graph, and captions.

CLOSE

Have students generalize about Latin America's population centers and the diversity of the Latin American people.

CD-ROM

PICTURE ATLAS OF THE WORLD

You and your students can learn about the physical features, music, economy, and population of Latin America by selecting "South America" on the main menu.

Map Activity

Place Assign a country or island group to pairs of students. Have students research how the geographical characteristics of each country determined the location of cities and towns. Students can note their findings on index cards, then use those notes to formulate clear, concise facts. Have students write their facts on strips of paper and share orally, or tack the strips to the appropriate place on the classroom map.

These features and activities may be used as an introduction to the unit or as teaching tools throughout the course of the unit.

FOCUS

Tell students that Latin America has the greatest latitudinal span of any world region; Mexico's northernmost part lies at about 33°N, Tierra del Fuego at 56°S. Have them speculate on how this span from the Equator almost to the South Pole might affect the continent's geography, climate, and weather.

TEACH

Movement Have students suppose they are touring Latin America. Ask them to consider how the geographical information they learn might affect them, as well as their travel.

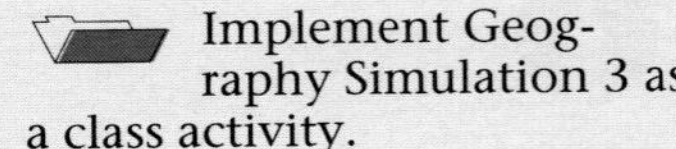

Implement Geography Simulation 3 as a class activity.

Have students complete Unit Atlas Activity 3A.

ASSESS

Have students answer the Charting Your Course questions on page 154.

NATIONAL GEOGRAPHIC SOCIETY

IMAGES OF THE WORLD POSTER SET

Display the poster "Latin America." Have students hypothesize about the climate zone and population density of each photo.

LATIN AMERICA
Physical Geography

CHARTING YOUR COURSE

1. *What large lake is found in the Andes?*
2. *Name two highland regions in South America.*
3. *What are three major natural resources of Latin America?*
4. *What islands are located in the West Indies?*

The Amazon is the second-longest river in the world. It winds about 4,000 miles (6,438 km) from its source in the Peruvian Andes to its mouth in Brazil.

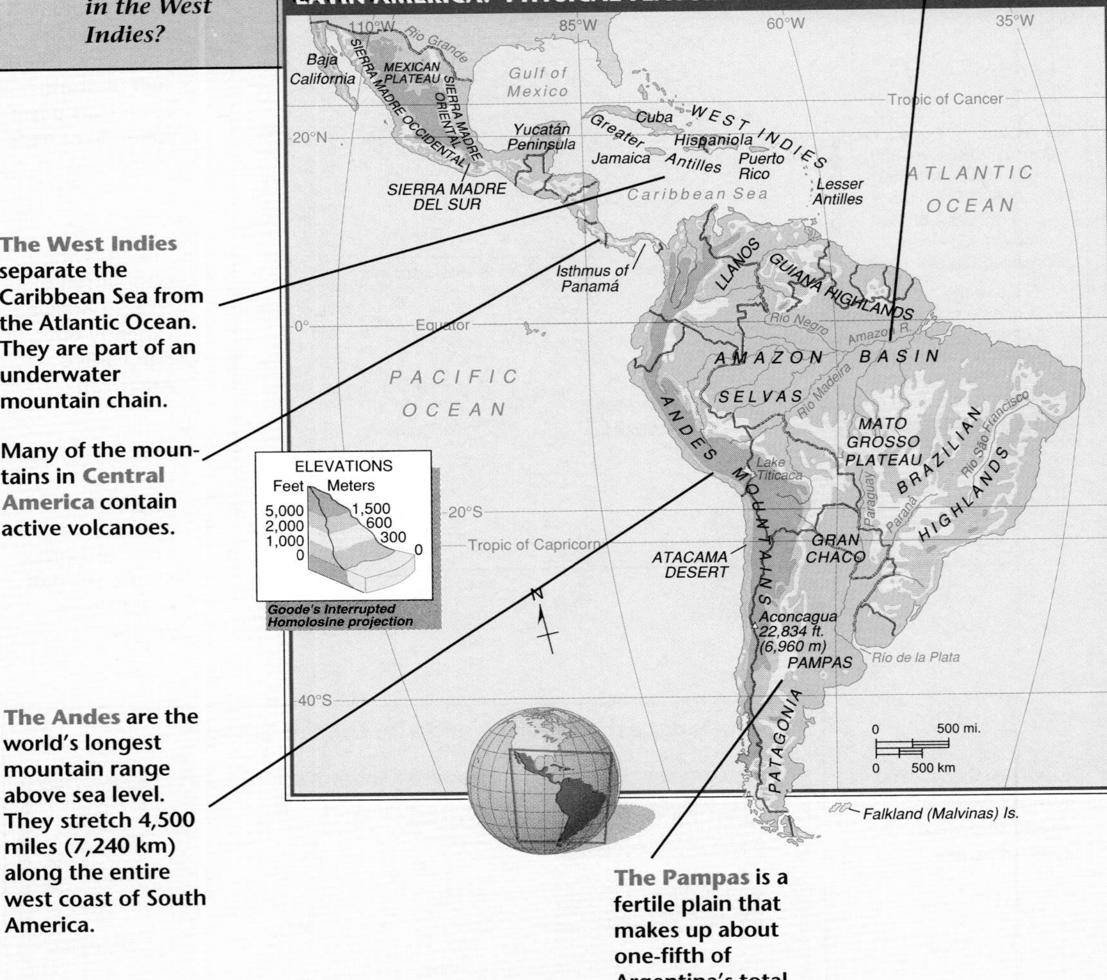

The West Indies separate the Caribbean Sea from the Atlantic Ocean. They are part of an underwater mountain chain.

Many of the mountains in Central America contain active volcanoes.

The Andes are the world's longest mountain range above sea level. They stretch 4,500 miles (7,240 km) along the entire west coast of South America.

The Pampas is a fertile plain that makes up about one-fifth of Argentina's total area.

Map Activity

Place Organize students into small groups. Allow them a specified amount of time to write several geographic place riddles whose answers can be determined from the graphics on pages 154–155. For example, "What country has coal mines along its southern Atlantic coast and is one of the two South American countries that does not border Brazil?" *(Chile)* Encourage students to be creative in composing their questions. Allow time for groups to challenge each other with their material, then vote on the best-worded question.

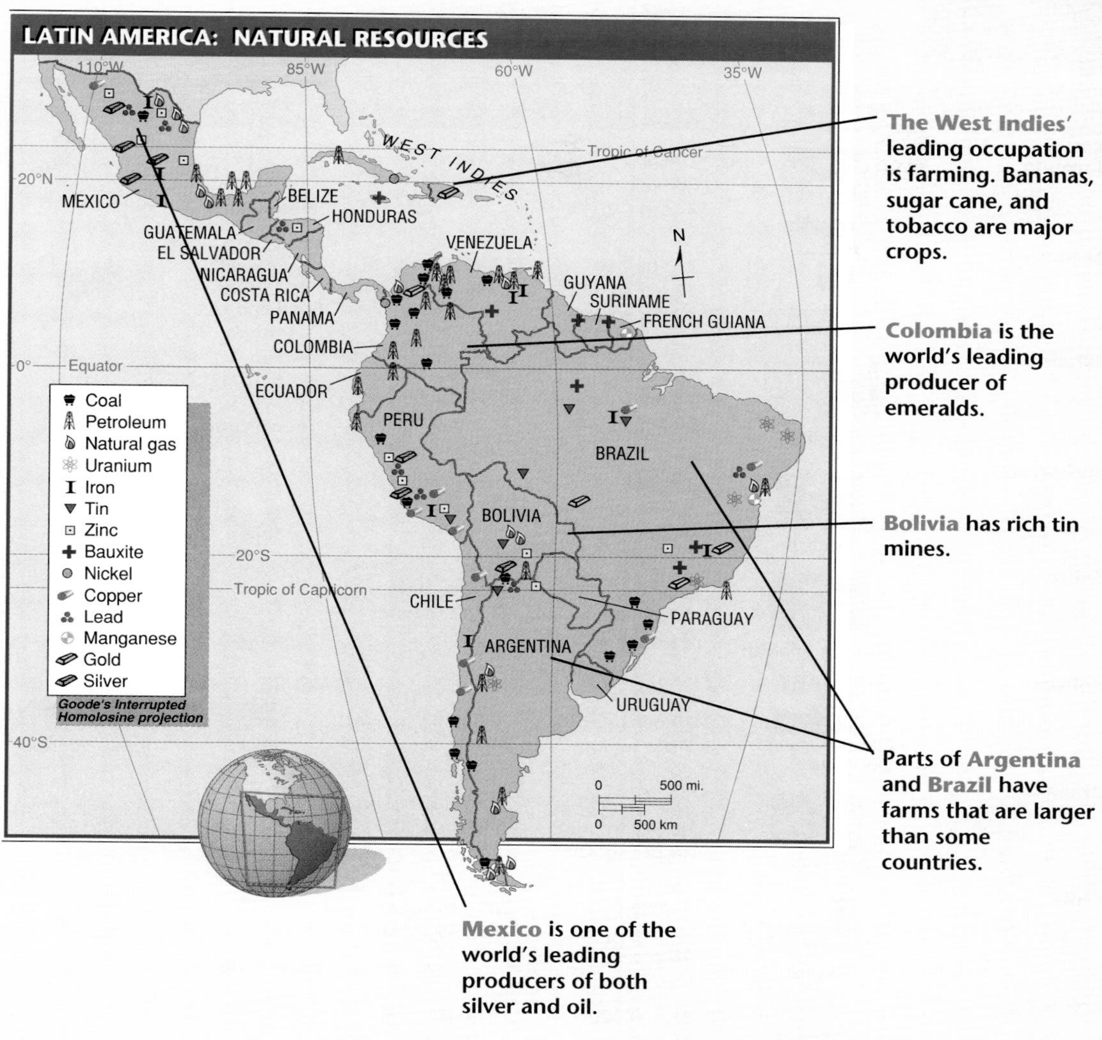

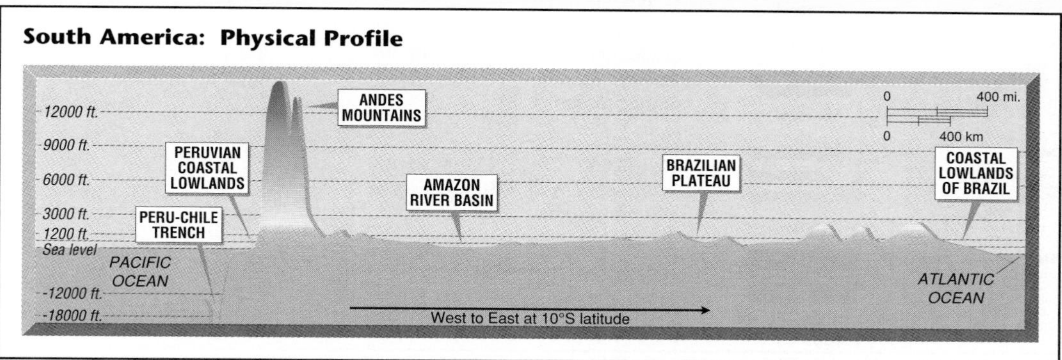

CHARTING YOUR COURSE

This feature may be used to introduce students to the physical geography of Latin America. Use questions to stimulate class discussion and help students become familiar with the region. Accept reasonable answers based on the maps, graph, and captions.

CLOSE

Remind students that they have been viewing the physical features and natural resources of Latin America as tourists. Which graphic most clearly helped them to see the terrain over which they traveled? Which Latin American region are they most interested in learning more about? Why?

DID YOU KNOW?

The west coasts of Mexico, Central America, and South America are part of a geologically-active rim called the Ring of Fire. Great plates of the earth's crust move against each other along Latin America's western coasts, causing earthquakes and volcanic eruptions.

Map and Graph Activity

Place Assign a country to every pair of students. Using current tour guides, travel articles, and encyclopedias, as well as the maps on pages 154–155, have students develop itineraries for trips in their assigned countries. When planning, students should take into account the geography of the region they will be touring, and decide upon appropriate methods of travel that will allow them the most extensive and greatest viewing pleasure. Students may plot their itineraries on maps, noting with a brief phrase at each stop the reason for visiting that particular location. Encourage students to illustrate or provide magazine photographs to accompany their itinerary. Provide an area in the classroom for students to display and discuss completed itineraries.

LESSON PLAN
Unit 3 Atlas

These features and activities may be used as teaching tools throughout the course of the unit.

Ways of the World

LATIN AMERICA
People and relationships are considered more important than schedules. Punctuality is not as important as in North America.

DID YOU KNOW?

At 12,001 ft. (more than 2.5 miles above sea level), Bolivia's capital of La Paz is the highest capital city in the world. The air there is 35 percent thinner than at sea level and people raised in or around the city develop unusually large lungs.

UNIT 3 ATLAS

COUNTRY PROFILE

COUNTRY* AND CAPITAL	FLAG AND LANGUAGES	POPULATION	LANDMASS	PRINCIPAL PRODUCTS EXPORT	PRINCIPAL PRODUCTS IMPORT
Antigua and Barbuda (St. Johns)	English	100,000 588 per sq. mi. 227 per sq. km	170 sq. mi. 440 sq. km	Petroleum	Food and Live Animals
Argentina (Buenos Aires)	Spanish	33,900,000 32 per sq. mi. 12 per sq. km	1,056,640 sq. mi. 2,736,698 sq. km	Food and Live Animals	Machinery
Bahamas (Nassau)	English	300,000 78 per sq. mi. 30 per sq. km	3,860 sq. mi. 9,997 sq. km	Petroleum	Crude Oil
Barbados (Bridgetown)	English	300,000 1,765 per sq. mi. 682 per sq. km	170 sq. mi. 440 sq. km	Sugar	Machinery
Belize (Belmopan)	English, Spanish	200,000 23 per sq. mi. 9 per sq. km	8,800 sq. mi. 22,792 sq. km	Sugar	Machinery
Bolivia (La Paz, Sucre)	Spanish, Aymara, Quechua	8,200,000 19 per sq. mi. 7 per sq. km	418,680 sq. mi. 1,084,381 sq. km	Zinc	Raw Materials
Brazil (Brasília)	Portuguese	155,300,000 48 per sq. mi. 18 per sq. km	3,265,060 sq. mi. 8,456,505 sq. km	Machinery	Petroleum
Chile (Santiago)	Spanish	14,000,000 47 per sq. mi. 18 per sq. km	289,110 sq. mi. 748,795 sq. km	Paper Products	Intermediate Goods
Colombia (Bogotá)	Spanish	35,600,000 89 per sq. mi. 34 per sq. km	401,040 sq. mi. 1,038,694 sq. km	Petroleum	Machinery
Costa Rica (San José)	Spanish	3,200,000 167 per sq. mi. 65 per sq. km	19,710 sq. mi. 51,049 sq. km	Garments	Petroleum
Cuba (Havana)	Spanish	11,100,000 259 per sq. mi. 100 per sq. km	42,400 sq. mi. 109,816 sq. km	Sugar	Crude Oil
Dominica (Roseau)	English, French, Creole	100,000 345 per sq. mi. 133 per sq. km	290 sq. mi. 751 sq. km	Bananas	Machinery

*Country maps not drawn to scale.

156 UNIT 3

Country Profile Activity

Economics Many Latin American countries are considered developing countries that have yet to meet their full economic potential.

Assign a country to each student. Have them use encyclopedias, world almanacs, and atlases to research the economic standing of their assigned countries. Have them find and jot down the GDP (gross domestic product), the economic activities of the country and their corresponding percentages of the GDP, per capita income, areas of concern and areas of strength. Have students present their economic profiles in table-and-graph form on charts titled *"(Country): Economics at a Glance."* When students have finished their research, provide a time for them to share their findings.

COUNTRY* AND CAPITAL	FLAG AND LANGUAGES	POPULATION	LANDMASS	PRINCIPAL PRODUCTS EXPORT	PRINCIPAL PRODUCTS IMPORT
Dominican Republic Santo Domingo	Spanish	7,800,000 407 per sq. mi. 157 per sq. km	18,680 sq. mi. 48,381 sq. km	Ferro nickel	Petroleum
Ecuador Quito	Spanish	10,600,000 96 per sq. mi. 37 per sq. km	106,890 sq. mi. 276,845 sq. km	Petroleum	Raw Materials
El Salvador San Salvador	Spanish	5,200,000 650 per sq. mi. 251 per sq. km	8,000 sq. mi. 20,720 sq. km	Coffee	Chemicals
French Guiana Territory of France Cayenne	French	127,505 4 per sq. mi. 1 per sq. km	35,126 sq. mi. 91,000 sq. km	Shrimp	Food
Grenada St. George's	English, French patois	100,000 769 per sq. mi. 297 per sq. km	130 sq. mi. 337 sq. km	Bananas	Machinery
Guatemala Guatemala City	Spanish, Mayan languages	10,300,000 239 per sq. mi. 92 per sq. km	41,860 sq. mi. 108,417 sq. km	Coffee	Petroleum
Guyana Georgetown	English, Amerindian dialects	800,000 11 per sq. mi. 4 per sq. km	76,000 sq. mi. 196,840 sq. km	Sugar	Fuels
Haiti Port-au-Prince	French, Haitian Creole	7,000,000 611 per sq. mi. 236 per sq. km	10,640 sq. mi. 27,558 sq. km	Textiles	Food
Honduras Tegucigalpa	Spanish	5,300,000 130 per sq. mi. 50 per sq. km	43,200 sq. mi. 111,888 sq. km	Bananas	Machinery
Jamaica Kingston	English, Creole	2,500,000 585 per sq. mi. 226 per sq. km	4,180 sq. mi. 10,826 sq. km	Alumina	Fuels
Mexico Mexico City	Spanish	91,800,000 125 per sq. mi. 48 per sq. km	736,950 sq. mi. 1,908,701 sq. km	Machinery	Machinery
Nicaragua Managua	Spanish	4,300,000 90 per sq. mi. 35 per sq. km	45,850 sq. mi. 118,752 sq. km	Coffee	Petroleum

*Country maps not drawn to scale.

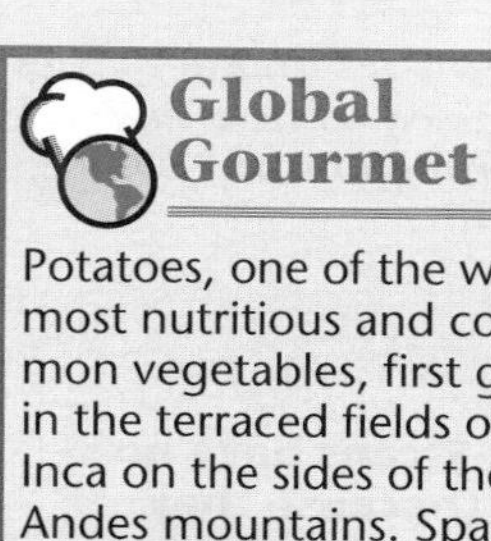

Global Gourmet

Potatoes, one of the world's most nutritious and common vegetables, first grew in the terraced fields of the Inca on the sides of the Andes mountains. Spanish explorers and conquistadors took the versatile vegetable back to Europe. For almost 200 years, however, Europeans refused to grow or eat many potatoes. Some medical experts predicted that potatoes would cause leprosy or other diseases because they were so ugly and misshapen. Many religious leaders thought eating potatoes would be sinful since they were not mentioned in the Bible. Some agriculturalists believed that growing potatoes would destroy the soil.

Ways of the World

COSTA RICA In return for a meal, a guest is expected to remain after the meal for at least an hour. Guests share their knowledge and participate in conversation as a way of giving of themselves.

Country Profile Activity

Identify Working as a class, have students identify the official languages spoken in Latin America, along with the number of countries that speak each language. Have students construct a bar graph showing the results of their search. Have them use the completed graph to help them compose and support a statement concerning languages spoken in Latin America. Encourage students to briefly research those countries whose main language is not Spanish or English, and learn the reason for the choice of that official language. (Students might prefer to assign a color to each language; then, on a map, shade each country the color that corresponds to the language that is spoken there.)

LESSON PLAN
Unit 3 Atlas

These features and activities may be used as teaching tools throughout the course of the unit.

DID YOU KNOW?

Costa Ricans have no army (because they despise militarism). In school, Costa Rican children learn that armies are created to oppress people.

Ways of the World

ECUADOR Young people will often "go Dutch" when eating out, and split the bill. However, they call it "doing as the Americans."

UNIT 3 ATLAS

COUNTRY PROFILE

COUNTRY* AND CAPITAL	FLAG AND LANGUAGES	POPULATION	LANDMASS	PRINCIPAL PRODUCTS EXPORT	PRINCIPAL PRODUCTS IMPORT
Panama (Panamá)	Spanish, English	2,500,000 86 per sq. mi. 33 per sq. km	29,340 sq. mi. 75,991 sq. km	Bananas	Fuels
Paraguay (Asunción)	Spanish, Guaraní	4,800,000 31 per sq. mi. 12 per sq. km	153,400 sq. mi. 397,306 sq. km	Cotton	Machinery
Peru (Lima)	Spanish, Quechua	22,900,000 46 per sq. mi. 18 per sq. km	494,210 sq. mi. 1,280,004 sq. km	Copper	Machinery
Puerto Rico (San Juan)	Spanish	3,600,000 1,047 per sq. mi. 404 per sq. km	3,420 sq. mi. 8,858 sq. km	Chemicals	Chemicals
Saint Kitts and Nevis (Basseterre)	English	40,000 286 per sq. mi. 110 per sq km	140 sq. mi. 363 sq. km	Sugar	Food
St. Lucia (Castries)	English, French patois	100,000 417 per sq. mi. 161 per sq. km	240 sq. mi. 622 sq. km	Bananas	Machinery
Saint Vincent & the Grenadines (Kingstown)	English	100,000 667 per sq. mi. 257 per sq. km	150 sq. mi. 389 sq. km	Bananas	Food
Suriname (Paramaribo)	Dutch, English	400,000 7 per sq. mi. 3 per sq. km	60,230 sq. mi. 155,996 sq. km	Alumina	Machinery
Trinidad & Tobago (Port of Spain)	English	1,300,000 657 per sq. mi. 257 per sq. km	1,980 sq. mi. 5,128 sq. km	Petroleum	Food
Uruguay (Montevideo)	Spanish	3,200,000 47 per sq. mi. 18 per sq. km	67,490 sq. mi. 174,799 sq. km	Textiles	Machinery
Venezuela (Caracas)	Spanish	21,300,000 63 per sq. mi. 24 per sq. km	340,560 sq. mi. 882,050 sq. km	Petroleum	Machinery
Virgin Islands (U.S.) (Charlotte Amalie)	English	101,809 771 per sq. mi. 298 per sq. km	132 sq. mi. 342 sq. km	Sugar	Food

*Country maps not drawn to scale.

158 UNIT 3

Country Profile Activity

Culture and History Latin America has some of the oldest Native American civilizations in the Western Hemisphere, as well as many of the earliest European sites.

Allow students to choose a country or island that interests them, and research its most historic and/or cultural sites. Students may use tour guides, travel magazines or videos, and interview people who have been to their chosen country.

Have students choose two or three historical and/or cultural sites or events that they would like to see. Allow students to share their choices in a very informal "round robin" discussion.

Native Americans form a large part of the population in the Andes region of South America.

Ruins of the Maya civilization are seen today in the steamy lowland forests of southern Mexico and Guatemala.

The Congress Building is one of many modern structures in Brasília, the capital of Brazil.

Religious festivals and processions are an important part of life for the largely Roman Catholic population of Latin America.

Global Gourmet

Mexican food enjoys widespread popularity in the United States. Tacos, guacamole, frijoles, enchiladas, quesadillas, and sopapillas have become as "American" as hot dogs and pizza.

Ways of the World

BRAZIL Soccer is Brazil's national sport. So passionate are they about it that they have closed businesses and schools during the Soccer World Cup or important national competitions.

Country Profile Activity

Location In their journals, have students list countries in groups according to principal exports. Have students then locate each group of countries on the map on pages A8–A9. Ask students to speculate about geographical characteristics the region has that produce a particular export, and note such speculations with the appropriate list in their journals. Students may either research briefly to discover if their speculations are correct, or they may save them to check as they read through the unit.

CHAPTER 8

PLANNING GUIDE

The Physical Geography of Latin America

CHAPTER ORGANIZER

Daily Lesson Objectives	Multimedia	Teacher Classroom Resources
SECTION 1 The Land 1. Identify the diverse landforms of Latin America. 2. Describe the abundant natural resources of Latin America.	Section Focus Transparency 8-1 Chapter 8 Vocabulary PuzzleMaker Software Unit Map Overlay Transparency 3-5 Geography and the Environment Testmaker STV: World Geography: Volume 3 Picture Atlas of the World Physical Geography of the World Transparencies 11–20	Reproducible Lesson Plan 8-1 Guided Reading Activity 8-1 Spanish Guided Reading Activity 8-1 Performance Assessment Activity 8 Section Quiz 8-1
SECTION 2 The Climate and Vegetation 1. Name the climate regions of Latin America. 2. Discuss the kinds of vegetation found in Latin America.	Section Focus Transparency 8-2 Testmaker STV: World Geography, Volume 3	Reproducible Lesson Plan 8-2 Guided Reading Activity 8-2 Spanish Guided Reading Activity 8-2 Workbook Activity 8-2 Enrichment Activity 8 Section Quiz 8-2 Skill Activity 8 Outline Map Resource Book, p. 25
CHAPTER REVIEW AND EVALUATION	Chapter 8 English (or Spanish) Audiocassettes MindJogger Videoquiz Testmaker Student Self-Test and Review Software	Reteaching Activity 8 Spanish Reteaching Activity 8 Chapter 8 Test Form A and Form B

0:00 *If time does not permit teaching the entire chapter, summarize using the Chapter 8 Highlights on page 171, and the Chapter 8 English (or Spanish) Audiocassettes. Review students' knowledge using the Glencoe MindJogger Videoquiz.*

KEY TO ABILITY LEVELS

Teaching strategies have been coded for varying learning styles and abilities.

L1 **BASIC** activities for all students

L2 **AVERAGE** activities for average to above-average students

L3 **CHALLENGING** activities for above-average students

LEP **LIMITED ENGLISH PROFICIENCY** activities

Performance Assessment

Environmental Relationships Understanding the physical geography of a region involves recognizing relationships among latitude, elevation, climate, and resources. Ask students to study the maps on pages 152, 153, and 167, as well as other maps and chapter material. Then have them construct a matrix of locations in Latin America, listing the latitude, elevation, climate type, and resources found at each location.

Upon completion of the matrix, students should write inference statements or generalizations through which they can make connections. After these are formulated, students should map in color or relief a hypothetical region, placing landforms and elevations at different latitudes. They should also complete climate and resource maps for the regions that logically convey probable climatic conditions and resources. The map sets should either be displayed in a classroom museum or compiled in a class atlas.

POSSIBLE RUBRIC FEATURES: Content information, concept attainment (interdependence of physical features), ability to recognize relationships, planning and product completion skills, inference skills, map skills

For additional professional and classroom resources, see Chapter Resources, pages T46–T51.

TEACHER'S CORNER

NATIONAL GEOGRAPHIC SOCIETY

INDEX TO NATIONAL GEOGRAPHIC MAGAZINE

The following articles may be used for research relating to this chapter:

- "Amazon: South America's River Road," by Jere Van Dyk, February 1995.
- "Anything But Empty: The Sonoran Desert," by Priit J. Vesilind, September 1994.
- "Chile's Uncharted Cordillera Sarmiento," by Jack Miller, April 1994.
- "Roaring Through Earth's Deepest Canyon," by Joe Kane, January 1993.
- "Sacred Peaks of the Andes," by John Reinhard, March 1992.
- "Mexico's Bajío—The Heartland," by Charles E. Cobb, Jr., December 1990.
- "The High Andes: South America's Islands in the Sky," by Loren McIntyre, April 1987.
- "Earthquake in Mexico," by Allen A. Boraiko, May 1986.
- "Eruption in Columbia," by Bart McDowell, May 1986.

NATIONAL GEOGRAPHIC SOCIETY PRODUCTS AVAILABLE FROM GLENCOE

To order the following products for use with this chapter, contact your local Glencoe sales representative or call Glencoe at 1-800-334-7344:

- *Picture Atlas of the World* (CD-ROM)
- *STV: North America* (Videodisc)
- *STV: World Geography, South America and Antarctica* (Videodisc)
- *STV: Rain Forest* (Videodisc)
- *ZipZapMap! World* (Software)
- *GeoBee* (Software)
- *Images of the World* (Posters)
- *Eye on the Environment* (Posters)
- *Physical Geography of the World* (Transparencies)
- *Picture Atlas of Our 50 States* (Book)

ADDITIONAL NATIONAL GEOGRAPHIC SOCIETY PRODUCTS

To order the following products for use with this chapter, call National Geographic Society at 1-800-368-2728:

- *Central America*, "Geography," "Everyday Life," "Cultural and Ethnic Heritage," "Conflict in the Region." (Filmstrip)
- *The Water's Edge: Life Along the Great Rivers*, "The Amazon," "The Mississippi," "The Nile." (Filmstrip)
- *Amazon: Land of the Flooded Forest* (Video)
- *Living on Our Changing Planet* (Video)
- *Our Dynamic Earth* (Video)

PERFORMANCE ASSESSMENT

Refer to the Planning Guide on page 160B for a Performance Assessment Activity for this chapter. See the *Performance Assessment Activities* booklet for additional suggestions.

CHAPTER OBJECTIVES

1. **Describe** the dominant landforms of Latin America.
2. **Explain** why the climate and vegetation of Latin America are diverse.

GLENCOE TECHNOLOGY

Videodisc

Use Chapter 8 MindJogger Videoquiz to preview chapter content.

MINDJOGGER VIDEOQUIZ

Chapter 8
Disc 1 Side B

The MindJogger Videoquiz is also available on videocassette.

CD-ROM

PICTURE ATLAS OF THE WORLD

You and your students can see and read about the physical geography of South America by clicking the "Photos" and "Essay" buttons of selected countries.

chapter 8 The Physical Geography of Latin America

CHAPTER FOCUS

Geographic Setting

Latin America is made up of Mexico, Central America, South America, and the island-countries in the Caribbean Sea.

Geographic Themes

Section 1 The Land

PLACE **Towering mountain ranges, broad plateaus, and rolling plains are the dominant landforms of Latin America.**

Section 2 The Climate and Vegetation

LOCATION **Latin America's vast territorial expanse—from 33°N latitude to 56°S latitude—makes its climate and vegetation diverse.**

▲ Photograph: *Iguaçu Falls, Brazil*

EXTRA CREDIT PROJECT

Rebus After the class reads about climate regions in the chapter, draw cake and ice cream (dessert) – S = on the chalkboard. Have the class guess the climate region to which the rebus refers. *(desert)* Then challenge interested students to create rebuses for the names of other climate regions in Latin America. Make copies of the best rebuses and distribute them to the class. Have students decode the rebuses and suggest that they use them as memory aids to recall the different kinds of climate regions.

SECTION 1

The Land

SETTING THE SCENE

Read to Discover . . .
- the diverse landforms of Latin America.
- the abundant natural resources of Latin America.

Key Terms
- escarpment
- *llanos*
- *Pampas*
- hydroelectric power

Identify and Locate
Middle America, Central America, South America, Sierra Madre Occidental, Sierra Madre Oriental, Sierra Madre del Sur, Andes, *Altiplano,* Amazon River basin, Río de la Plata, Amazon River, Rio Grande, Lake Maracaibo

VENEZUELA Bs 50

Margarita Island, Venezuela

¡Hola! ¿Cómo estás? From the time we landed, the white sand beaches, warm ocean air, and blue water of Margarita welcomed us. This island off the coast of Venezuela has many small fishing villages along its coastline. Palm trees are everywhere. From most any high spot, there is a wonderful view of the nearby islands of Coche and Cubagua. Wish you were here!
Carla Martinez

Carla Martinez describes the tropical beauty of the Caribbean coastline of Venezuela, one of the many countries of Latin America. Most of the region was settled by people from Spain or Portugal. To this day, Spanish and Portuguese are the official languages of most countries. Because these languages are based on Latin, the region became known as Latin America.

REGION

The Americas and the Caribbean

Geographers often divide Latin America into three areas—Middle America, the Caribbean, and South America. Middle America consists of Mexico and the seven countries of Central America. Central America is the narrow land link between North and South America. The islands of the Caribbean, also known as the West Indies, fall into three groups—the Bahamas, the Greater Antilles, and the Lesser Antilles.

The continent of South America is by far the largest land area of Latin America. Among South America's 13 countries, Brazil is the largest. More than half of all South American land and people are Brazilian.

PLACE

Mountains, Plateaus, and Hills

The physical geography of Latin America is diverse. Dominating all other physical features, however, are the vast rain forests of

LESSON PLAN
Chapter 8, Section 1

FOCUS

SECTION OBJECTIVES

1. **Identify** the diverse landforms of Latin America.
2. **Describe** the abundant natural resources of Latin America.

ABOUT THE POSTCARD

Carla enjoys travelling throughout her native Venezuela. She especially likes seeing different architectural styles.

BELLRINGER MOTIVATIONAL ACTIVITY

Project the Section 1 Focus Transparency and have students answer the questions.

PRETEACHING VOCABULARY

Direct students to page 164 to find the meanings of *llanos* and *pampas*. Ask them what areas of the United States are similar to these areas of South America. *(prairie land and plains)*

Use the Vocabulary PuzzleMaker Software to create a crossword or word search puzzle.

Videodisc

STV: WORLD GEOGRAPHY, VOLUME 3

Side 1, Chapter 1
Frames 00001-50061
Title: ***South America*** **(in its entirety)**
Subject: Visit South America, a land of diverse landscapes

Classroom Resources for Section 1

BLACKLINE MASTERS:
Reproducible Lesson Plan 8-1
Guided Reading Activity 8-1
Performance Assessment Activity 8
Section Quiz 8-1

TRANSPARENCIES:

Section Focus Transparency 8-1
Unit Map Overlay Transparency 3-5
Physical Geography of the World Transparencies 11–20

MULTIMEDIA:
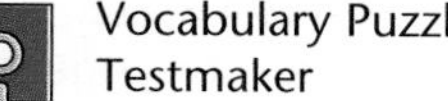
Vocabulary PuzzleMaker Software
Testmaker

Geography and the Environment
STV: World Geography, Volume 3

Picture Atlas of the World

TEACH

GUIDED PRACTICE

Project Unit Map Overlay Transparency 3-5 and have students locate the following: the Andes, Sierra Madre Occidental, Sierra Madre Oriental, Guiana Highlands, Brazilian Highlands, Anáhuac, the *Altiplano,* and Patagonia. Ask them how they might classify these regions. *(as highlands)*

USING ILLUSTRATIONS

REGION The mountains of Mexico include North America's third highest peak—Orizaba at 18,700 feet (6,090 m).

Answer to Caption: *Anáhuac, Altiplano, Mato Grasso, Guiana Highlands, Brazilian Highlands, and Patagonia*

GLENCOE TECHNOLOGY

Videodisc

GEOGRAPHY AND THE ENVIRONMENT
THE INFINITE VOYAGE
Living With Disaster

Chapter 8
Disc 3 Side A
Title: ***Nevado del Ruiz: A Volcanic Disaster***
Subject: This volcano was covered with a glacier that melted during its eruption in 1985, resulting in a mud slide that buried a town

Geographic Themes

Region: The Mexican Plateau
Mexico, the largest part of Middle America, consists of a large central plateau and surrounding mountains. *What plateaus are located in South America?*

the Amazon River basin and the towering mountain chain of the Andes.

Mountains

High mountain ranges cover much of Latin America. Many of the Caribbean islands are actually the exposed peaks of an underwater mountain range. In Central America, mountains thread through much of the interior. Two prominent mountain ranges in Mexico—the Sierra Madre Occidental and the Sierra Madre Oriental—meet near Mexico City to form the sharp-peaked Sierra Madre del Sur.

In South America mountains interrupt the Guiana Highlands—in the northeast—and the Brazilian Highlands of eastern Brazil. The eastern edge of the Brazilian Highlands drops sharply to the Atlantic Ocean, forming an **escarpment,** a slope or long cliff between a higher and lower surface.

None of Latin America's mountains, however, compare with the 4,500-mile (7,250-km) stretch of the Andes, the world's longest mountain chain. Some peaks in the Andes rise more than 20,000 feet (6,096 m) above sea level, making the Andes the second-highest range in the world. Only the Himalayas of South Asia are higher.

Many people have settled in valleys near the mountains of Latin America because these areas are rich in mineral and soil resources. Mountain ranges often block communications, however, thus isolating regions and peoples.

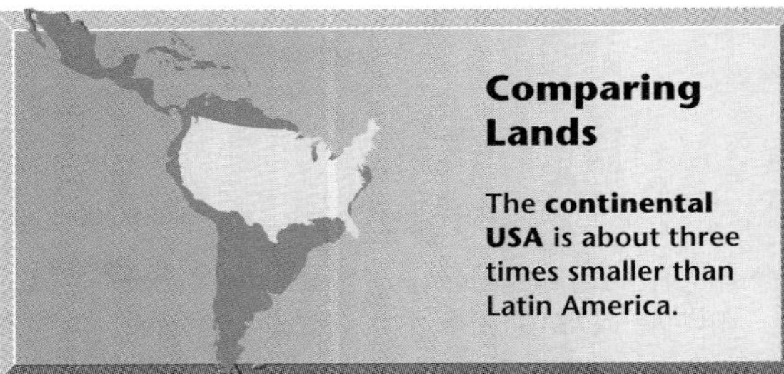

Comparing Lands

The **continental USA** is about three times smaller than Latin America.

Plateaus and Hills

Latin America is also a region of large plateaus, high flatlands often used for grazing and farming. For example, in Mexico, lodged between the Sierra Madre Oriental and Sierra Madre Occidental, is Anáhuac (uh•NAH•WAHK), the densely populated Mexican Plateau.

In Bolivia and Peru, nestled among the Andes, is the *Altiplano* (AHL•tih•PLAH•NOH)—

Cooperative Learning Activity

Direct students' attention to the last subhead in the section, "Mineral Resources," on page 165. Tell them to note that these include bauxite, copper, tin, and silver. Next, have them list things that are made with these minerals on the chalkboard. Then organize the class into groups, have each group copy the list from the chalkboard, and tell the groups to "scavenge" as many items on the list as they can find in or near the school. After a specified time, have the groups return to the classroom and compare their collections.

LATIN AMERICA: PHYSICAL-POLITICAL

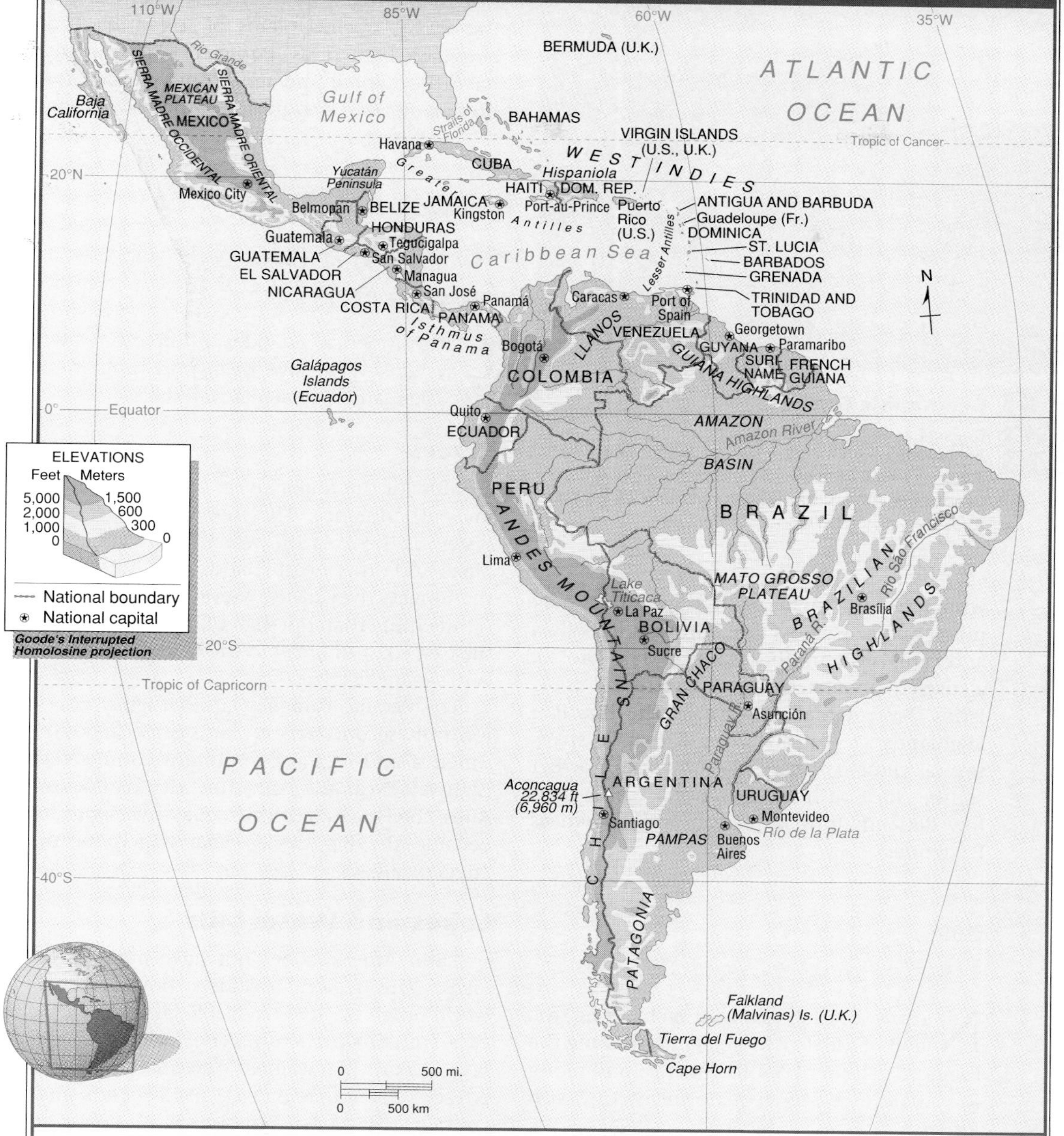

ELEVATIONS

Feet	Meters
5,000	1,500
2,000	600
1,000	300
0	0

National boundary
National capital

Goode's Interrupted Homolosine projection

0 500 mi.
0 500 km

Focus on Geographic Themes

1. **Region:** What landform connects Central America and northern South America?
2. **Place:** What is the capital of Chile?
3. **Location:** What country lies east of Colombia?
4. **Region:** In what kind of physical environment is Brasília, Brazil, located?

INDEPENDENT PRACTICE

Guided Reading Have students complete Guided Reading Activity 8-1 in the TCR. **LEP**

L2 Write Ask students to make brochures about places they would like to see in Latin America. Tell them to include reasons why tourists should visit.

USING MAPS

Answers:
1. the Isthmus of Panama; **2.** Santiago; **3.** Venezuela; **4.** highlands

Map Skills Practice

Reading a Map List five Latin American capitals that are at an elevation of 5,000 feet (1,500 meters) or more. *(Mexico City, Bogotá, Quito, Santiago, and Sucre)*

GLENCOE TECHNOLOGY

Videodisc

GEOGRAPHY AND THE ENVIRONMENT
THE INFINITE VOYAGE
Living With Disaster

Chapter 9
Disc 3 Side A
Title: ***The Nature of Volcanoes: Nevado del Ruiz***
Subject: Discusses different methods for determining force of previous eruptions and for predicting when future eruptions may occur

Meeting Special Needs

Study Strategies This textbook includes several features that will help students with special learning needs to understand the material. Ask students to look at the beginning of Section 1 and notice the "Setting the Scene" feature. Point out that this feature sums up the content of the section. Have students speculate on what the section will cover based on the information in "Setting the Scene."

PLACE Argentina is the only Latin American country that produces enough beef to export.
Answer to Caption: *the llanos*

ASSESS

CHECK FOR UNDERSTANDING

Assign Section 1 Review as homework or an in-class activity.

MEETING LESSON OBJECTIVES

Each objective below is tested by the questions that follow it in parentheses.
1. Identify the diverse landforms of Latin America. *(1, 2, 3)*
2. Describe the abundant natural resources of Latin America. *(4, 5)*

EVALUATE

Assign Section 1 Quiz in the TCR.

Use the Testmaker to create a customized quiz for Section 1.

RETEACH

Have students reread the section. Then tell them to include the following in a written summary of their reading: the objectives, Key Terms, and places included in Setting the Scene on page 161.

Geographic Themes
Place: The Pampas, Argentina
Argentine cowhands known as *gauchos* ride the Pampas herding livestock, the major agricultural product of Argentina. *What prominent plains area is located in northern South America?*

which means "high plain." Spreading over much of Brazil, across the southwest to Bolivia and Peru, is yet another plateau, Mato Grosso, a sparsely populated area of forests and grasslands. East of Mato Grosso lie the Brazilian Highlands, a plateau so vast that it spans several climate and vegetation zones. Farther south, in southern Argentina, hills and low flatlands form a plateau area known as Patagonia.

PLACE

Plains Areas

Narrow coastal plains stretch along the Gulf of Mexico. More plains lie along the Pacific coastline of South America and along the Atlantic coastline of northeastern South America.

People of Venezuela and Colombia have been raising cattle for hundreds of years on the large, fertile plains areas called ***llanos*** (LAH•nohz), which run along the Caribbean coast of South America. To the south of the llanos lies the Amazon River basin, the largest lowland area of South America. Just south of the Amazon River basin is the Gran Chaco, a heavily forested lowland. In direct contrast are the grassy, treeless plains of Argentina and Uruguay, known as ***Pampas.*** The Pampas have the rainfall and fertile soils needed for producing grain and grazing cattle and sheep.

MOVEMENT

Rivers, Lakes, and Waterfalls

Latin America includes numerous water systems—extensive rivers and tributaries, large lakes, and spectacular waterfalls.

Rivers

Most of the major rivers of the region are in South America. The most extensive river system is the Amazon, which drains much of Brazil and other nearby lands. The Amazon is the longest river in the Western Hemisphere. A little more than one-half of its length—from the east coast of Brazil to the city of Iquitos in Peru—is navigable.

The Paraná, Paraguay, and Uruguay rivers form the second-largest river system in South America and its most important commercial highway. Near the Argentine city of Buenos Aires, the Paraguay and Uruguay rivers join to become the Río de la Plata, which means "river of silver."

Lakes and Waterfalls

Latin America does not have many large lakes. The region includes, however, the world's highest large navigable lake, Lake Titicaca (TIHT•ih•KAHK•uh). The region's largest lake—Lake Maracaibo (MAR•uh•KY•BOH)—covers 5,217 square miles (13,512 sq. km) and contains the most important oil fields in Venezuela. The largest lake in Central America is Lake Nicaragua, which lies on the border between Nicaragua and Costa Rica.

Waterfalls grace the region, especially in South America. Angel Falls, in Venezuela, drops 3,212 feet (979 m), making it the world's highest uninterrupted waterfall.

Critical Thinking

Determining Cause and Effect Direct students' attention to the picture of Iguaçu Falls on the Chapter Opener page and show them where on the Brazil-Argentine border the Falls are located. Then list other falls and their locations in South America—Patos-Maribondo on the Grande River and Paulo Alfonso on the Sáo Francisco River in Brazil; Catarata de Candelas on the Cusiana River and Tequendama on the Bogatá River in Colombia; Agoyan on the Pastaza River in Ecuador; and Kaieteur on the Potaro River, and Marina on the Ipobe River in Guyana. Have students find the approximate locations of the falls on a map and note what the locations have in common. Then ask them what combination of physical features causes so many falls in South America. *(rivers and highlands)*

Geographic Themes

Place: Atacama Desert, Chile

Chile's Atacama Desert, formed by dry westerly winds, is one of the driest and most barren spots on the earth. *What mineral resource is found in the Atacama Desert?*

REGION

Natural Resources

Latin America has significant natural resources, some not yet utilized.

Energy Resources

Latin American countries are among the world's leading producers of oil and natural gas. The oil fields along the Gulf of Mexico, for example, have helped make Mexico the world's fifth-largest oil producer. Venezuela also produces large quantities of oil.

Natural gas is extracted in many of the same areas that produce oil. Coal is found in varying quantities in Colombia, Mexico, Brazil, Chile, Ecuador, and Honduras. Deposits of uranium are located in Brazil and Argentina. Rivers and waterfalls give many countries the capacity for **hydroelectric power**, the energy of water generating electricity.

Mineral Resources

In addition to energy resources, Latin America is rich in a number of mineral resources. Bauxite, used to make aluminum, is mined in Jamaica and Guyana. The Atacama Desert in Chile contains deposits of copper. Bolivia and Brazil have reserves of tin. Peru and Mexico are known for silver.

Section 1 Review

Checking for Understanding

1. **Define** escarpment, *llanos, Pampas,* hydroelectric power.
2. **Locating Places** What are the three geographic areas of Latin America?
3. **Region** What is the largest mountain range in Latin America?
4. **Region** What are two major river systems of Latin America?

Critical Thinking

5. **Drawing Conclusions** Why does much of Latin America have the potential to produce hydroelectric power?

ANSWERS TO SECTION 1 REVIEW

1. **escarpment:** a slope or long cliff; ***llanos:*** plains area of Colombia and Venezuela; ***Pampas:*** fertile plains of Argentina and Uruguay; **hydroelectric power:** using water energy to produce electricity
2. Middle America, the Caribbean, and South America
3. the Andes
4. the Amazon River and the Paraná, Paraguay, and Uruguay rivers
5. because they have rivers and waterfalls to generate the energy

ENRICH

Read aloud the passage from Chapter 1 of Gabriel Garcia Marquez's *One Hundred Years of Solitude* that begins "Jose Arcadio Buendia was completely ignorant of the geography of the region." Identify Marquez as a Colombian author.

CLOSE

Have students write Carla Martinez a postcard in which they describe a favorite vacation location to her.

USING ILLUSTRATIONS

PLACE Only Antarctica is drier than the Atacama Desert. In fact, rain has never fallen on the Atacama Desert town of Calama.

Answer to Caption: *copper*

PHYSICAL GEOGRAPHY OF THE WORLD TRANSPARENCIES

Display and discuss the physical geography of the following transparencies:

11. Popocatépetl, Mexico
12. Yucatán Peninsula, Mexico
13. Cloud Forest, Costa Rica
14. Sangay, Ecuador
15. Angel Falls, Venezuela
16. Martinique, in the West Indies
17. Atacama Desert, Chile
18. Tierra del Fuego, Chile
19. Pampas, Argentina
20. Amazon River, Brazil

LESSON PLAN
Chapter 8, Section 2

FOCUS

SECTION OBJECTIVES

1. **Name** the climate regions of Latin America.
2. **Discuss** the kinds of vegetation found in Latin America.

BELLRINGER MOTIVATIONAL ACTIVITY

Project the Section 2 Focus Transparency and have students answer the questions.

PRETEACHING VOCABULARY

Invite a Spanish-speaking student to pronounce and translate *tierra caliente, tierra templada,* and *tierra fría* for the rest of the class. If no one speaks Spanish, supply a student with a Spanish-English dictionary to look up the pronunciations and meanings for the class.

MULTICULTURAL PERSPECTIVE

Cultural Diffusion
Coffee is not indigenous to Latin America. Spanish missionaries brought coffee seeds from the Middle East to Colombia. Today, coffee is Colombia's leading export crop.

Videodisc

STV: WORLD GEOGRAPHY, VOLUME 3

Side 1, Chapter 1
Frames 19680-21955
Title: ***South America***
Subject: Western South America: The Atacama

SECTION 2

The Climate and Vegetation

SETTING THE SCENE

Read to Discover . . .
- the climate regions of Latin America.
- the kinds of vegetation found in Latin America.

Key Terms
- *tierra caliente*
- *tierra templada*
- *tierra fría*
- canopy

Identify and Locate
Atacama Desert, Climate regions: Mediterranean, marine west coast, tropical rain forest, tropical savanna, humid subtropical, desert, steppe, highland.

Latin America has a wide range of climates and vegetation, the two being closely linked. Traveling the region, a person can go from desert to tropical rain forest, from subtropical plain to grassy plateau to barren, cold steppe. Other smaller climate regions, such as in central Chile where the climate is Mediterranean, or on the lower slopes of the Chilean Andes, where a marine west coast climate brings constant rain and winds, exist throughout the region.

REGION

Climate Regions

Much of Latin America lies in the low latitudes—between the Tropic of Cancer and the Tropic of Capricorn. As a result, most of the region has some form of tropical climate.

Tropical Climates

Southern Mexico, eastern Central America, the eastern shores of some Caribbean Islands, and large parts of South America—especially the Amazon River basin—have a tropical rain forest climate. In these areas, hot temperatures and abundant rainfall occur year-round.

Most of Central America and the Caribbean Islands, however, have a tropical savanna climate. These areas are hot and very wet, but not all year round. During certain times of the year, they tend to be cooler and drier than the tropical rain forest regions. Parts of Colombia, Venezuela, Brazil, Bolivia, and Paraguay also have a tropical savanna climate.

Humid Subtropical Climate

A humid subtropical climate prevails in much of southeastern South America, stretching from the Brazilian city of Rio de Janeiro to the Pampas of northern Argentina. In these places winters are short and mild, and summers are long and humid. Sometimes the summer brings a short dry period, but at other times there is no dry period at all.

Desert Climate

Climatic conditions are almost the opposite in parts of northern Mexico and southern and northwestern Argentina. In these areas a hot and dry climate prevails most of the time. Here, as in Pacific coastal areas of Peru and Chile, a desert climate affects large areas. The Atacama Desert, which runs south from Chile's northern border with Peru, is one of the driest places in the world. In some parts of this desert area, no rainfall has ever been recorded.

Classroom Resources for Section 2

BLACKLINE MASTERS:
Reproducible Lesson Plan 8-2
Guided Reading Activity 8-2
Spanish Guided Reading Activity 8-2
Workbook Activity 8-2
Enrichment Activity 8
Section Quiz 8-2
Skill Activity 8
Outline Map Resource Book, p. 25

TRANSPARENCIES:
Section Focus Transparency 8-2

MULTIMEDIA:

Testmaker

STV: World Geography, Volume 3

Steppe Climate

Some parts of Latin America receive little rainfall but do not have a desert climate. Instead, they have a steppe climate—hot summers, cold winters, light rainfall. Areas with this kind of climate include northern Mexico, highland areas in South America near the Andes, and coastal areas of South America along the Caribbean Sea and the Pacific Ocean.

Highland Climates

In Mexico along the Sierra Mountains and along the Andes in Colombia, Ecuador, Peru, Bolivia, Argentina, and Chile, highland climates dominate. How warm, cool, or cold an area is depends on latitude and elevation. The farther from the Equator and the higher the elevation, the colder it is.

Highland climates are commonly arranged vertically by altitude into three major zones. Lands at the lowest altitudes—sea level to 3,000 feet (914 m) above sea level at or near the Equator—fall in the zone called ***tierra caliente,*** which means "hot country." Lands from 3,000 to 6,000 feet (914 to 1,829 m) above sea level are considered ***tierra templada,*** which means "temperate country." Lands at the highest altitudes—6,000 to 10,000 feet (1,829 to 3,048 m)—are said to be ***tierra fría,*** meaning "cold country." Although frost may occur in some areas of *tierra fría,* average temperatures usually do not fall much below 45° F (7.2° C), because most of the lands lie in the tropics.

LATIN AMERICA: CLIMATE REGIONS

110°W 85°W 60°W 35°W
20°N
Tropic of Cancer
N
0° Equator
20°S
Tropic of Capricorn
40°S
0 1000 mi.
0 1000 km

Tropical
- Tropical rain forest
- Tropical savanna

Dry
- Steppe
- Desert

Mid-Latitude
- Mediterranean
- Humid subtropical
- Marine west coast

- Highland

Goode's Interrupted Homolosine projection

FOCUS ON GEOGRAPHIC THEMES

1. **Region: What area of South America has a tropical wet climate?**
2. **Place: What are the dominant climate regions in Mexico?**
3. **Location: Where is Latin America's Mediterranean climate region located?**

REGION

Vegetation

The natural vegetation of Latin America mainly consists of rain forests and grasslands. Like the climate, the vegetation varies from one place to another throughout the region.

Tropical Rain Forests

A number of tropical rain forests are scattered across Latin America, mostly in the warm, humid regions near the Equator. The countries of Belize, Guatemala, Honduras, El Salvador, Nicaragua, Costa Rica, Panama, Puerto Rico, Colombia, Venezuela, Guyana, Suriname, French Guiana, Peru, and Brazil contain rain forests. The largest rain forest is in Brazil in the Amazon River basin. This rain forest covers about one-third of the South American continent.

In Latin America's tropical rain forests, broad-leaved and needle-leaved evergreen trees grow tall and lush. Their tops come together to form a dense **canopy,** or covering, that keeps the sun from reaching the forest floor. As a result not many small ground plants survive. More kinds of trees and more species of animals live in these forests than in

Cooperative Learning Activity

Organize the class into groups. Assign each group a climate region of Latin America, and have students research the animal and plant life of the region. Next, distribute a deck of cards. Have the students glue a blank piece of paper over each card front. Tell them to draw an animal or a plant from their region on the card and label the picture with the name of the region. Pin the cards picture side down on a bulletin board. Then have the groups play Concentration: A player turns over two cards, trying to choose an animal and an animal, a plant and a plant, or an animal and a plant from the same climate region. If the player succeeds, his or her team earns a point and the cards are returned face up. If the player fails, his or her team earns no points and the cards are returned face down.

TEACH

GUIDED PRACTICE

L1 Identify After reading the section, give a clue to help a student identify a climate or vegetation region, such as "the Amazon River basin" for "tropical climate." If the student guesses incorrectly, give a second clue to another student. Give three clues before revealing the answer.

INDEPENDENT PRACTICE

Guided Reading Have students complete Guided Reading Activity 8-2 in the TCR. **LEP**

USING MAPS

Answers: **1.** the north central part; **2.** desert, steppe, tropical rain forest, tropical savanna, and highland; **3.** Chile's southern coast

Map Skills Practice

Reading a Map What climate regions lie along the border between Mexico and the United States? *(desert and steppe)*

ASSESS

CHECK FOR UNDERSTANDING

Assign Section 2 Review as homework or an in-class activity.

Videodisc

STV: WORLD GEOGRAPHY, VOLUME 3

Side 1, Chapter 1
Frames 32121-43167
Title: ***South America***
Subject: Amazon Basin

MEETING LESSON OBJECTIVES

Each objective below is tested by the questions that follow it in parentheses.
1. Name the climate regions of Latin America. *(2, 3, 5)*
2. Discuss the kinds of vegetation found in Latin America. *(4)*

EVALUATE

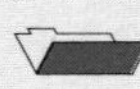
Assign Section 2 Quiz in the TCR.

Use the Testmaker to create a customized quiz for Section 2.

USING GRAPHS

Answers: Buenos Aires shows 55°F (13°C) and 3.5 inches (8.75 cm). Dallas shows 80°F (27°C) and 3 inches (7.5 cm).

Skills Practice
Comparing Which month is the warmest in Buenos Aires but the coolest in Dallas? *(January)*

USING ILLUSTRATIONS

PLACE The highest point in Puerto Rico is Cerro de Punta at 4,390 feet (1,338 meters).

Answer to Caption: *broad-leaved evergreen trees and crops such as coffee, sugar cane, fruits, and vegetables*

COMPARING CLIMATE REGIONS

Argentina and the United States

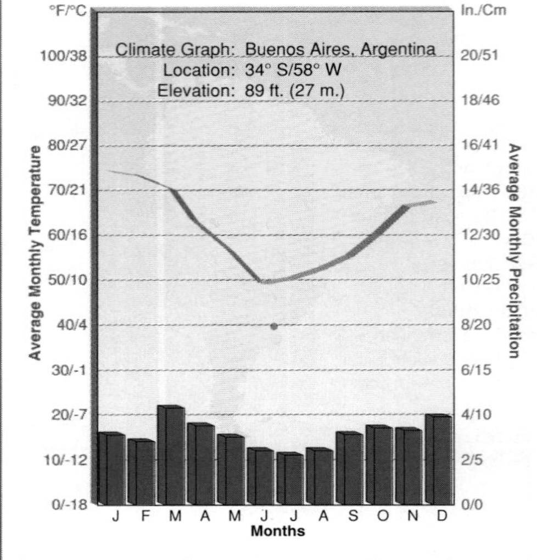

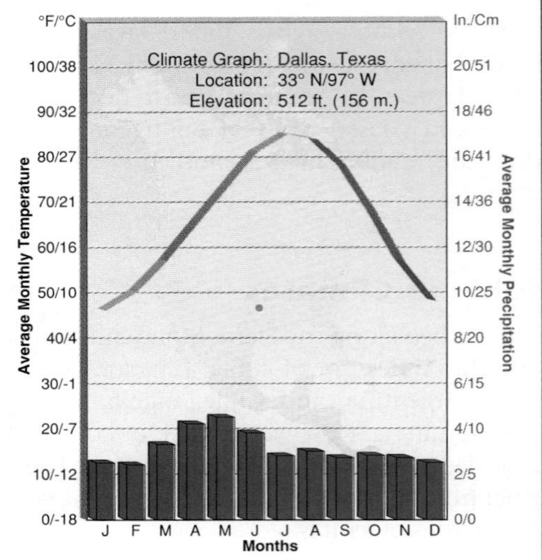

Source: *World Weather Guide*, 1990

*lines measure temperature/bars measure precipitation

GRAPH STUDY

The climate graphs above show the average monthly temperature and the average monthly precipitation in Buenos Aires, Argentina, and Dallas, Texas. ***What is the average September temperature and precipitation in each city?***

Geographic Themes

Place: Puerto Rico's Highlands
A tropical climate characterizes this village in the foothills of Puerto Rico's interior mountains. *What kind of vegetation thrives at this elevation?*

any other area of the world. A writer painted this picture of rain forest activity:

> *With imperious gaze, an endangered Guiana crested eagle searches for prey. A harpy eagle, also endangered, homes in for a landing. The [bird of prey's] perch wins in the incessant competition for sunlight. Poking above the dense canopy of its neighbors, the tree gets a boost in its propagation when winds scatter its seeds. Birds such as the lemon-throated barbet and the channel-billed toucan help other trees by dispersing seeds . . . as they fly.*

Meeting Special Needs

Writing Disability Help students with writing problems glean essential information from the text by making questions from each subhead. For example, "Where are tropical rain forests?" "What plants are found in a tropical rain forest?" and "Why does a rain forest have some kinds of plants and not other kinds?" can be derived from the subhead "Tropical Rain Forests." Ask students to read about tropical rain forests and to write brief responses for each question. Then have them answer the following question, using the information in their responses: "Where are Latin American rain forests and what do you find there?" After students answer the question, discuss where they could find more information to answer the question more completely.

Grasslands and Deserts

In areas with a humid subtropical climate, such as parts of Paraguay and Uruguay and parts of the Pampas of northern Argentina, prairie-like grasses grow. The grasses tend to be short and to grow in clumps that leave the soil between them exposed.

Because of their rainy seasons, some of these grassland areas, such as the llanos of northern South America, are covered with scattered trees. As a result, geographers often consider them as transition regions between grasslands and forests. In the Pampas of Argentina and the grasslands of Paraguay, the cooler climate enables only short grasses to thrive, depending on the amount of rainfall.

In desert areas such as those of northern Mexico, southern Chile, and the coasts of Peru, very few plants grow. The plant life that does thrive usually consists of prickly cacti and small bushes with thick leaves that store water. In some of the deserts, seeds lying within the soil may sprout and suddenly burst into bloom after a heavy rain, only to die and disappear quickly.

Vertical Climate Zones

In tropical highland and mountain areas, the vegetation, like the climate, varies with elevation. Because air cools as it rises in altitude, a variety of vegetation thrives on Latin America's mountainsides. Thus, the foot of a mountain may be dry and have scattered grasses, while farther up the mountain, abundant rainfall produces many different trees and plants. In the hot, wet *tierra caliente,* the lush vegetation of the tropical rain forest flourishes. Crops such as rice, sugar cane, and cacao (which has seeds used in making chocolate) are grown in this area. A little higher, in the *tierra templada,* where most people have chosen to settle, coffee is the chief crop. Sugar cane, fruits, and vegetables are also cultivated. The broad-leaved evergreen trees that grow at the lower levels of this zone, where it is moister and hotter, give way to needle-leaved cone-bearing evergreens as the elevation rises. Higher still, in the *tierra fría,* hardy crops such as potatoes and barley are grown.

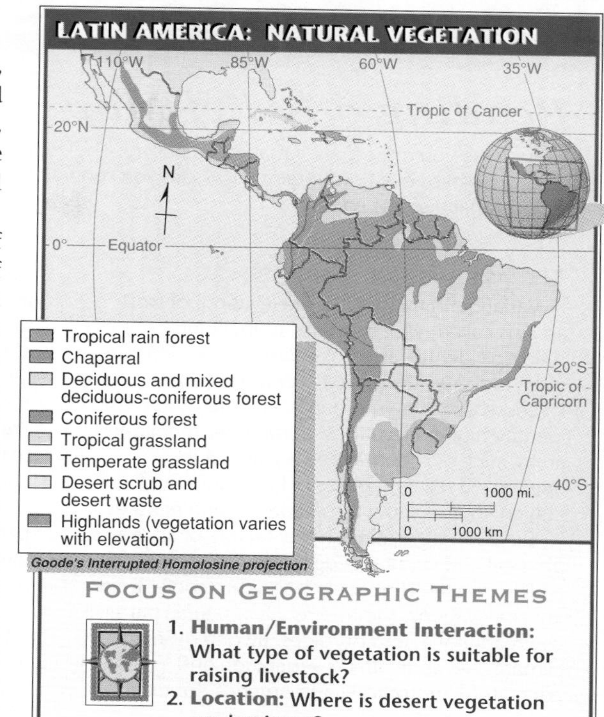

Focus on Geographic Themes

1. **Human/Environment Interaction:** What type of vegetation is suitable for raising livestock?
2. **Location:** Where is desert vegetation predominant?
3. **Place:** What type of vegetation is found in Cuba?

Section 2 Review

Checking for Understanding

1. **Define** *tierra caliente, tierra templada, tierra fría,* canopy.
2. **Locating Places** What kind of climate does Cuba have?
3. **Place** What areas in Latin America have a humid subtropical climate?
4. **Place** Why is it difficult for small ground plants to survive in Latin America's tropical rain forests?

Critical Thinking

5. **Determining Cause and Effect** How are climate and vegetation in Latin America affected by elevation above sea level?

Chapter 8, Section 2

RETEACH

Have students complete Reteaching Activity 8 in the TCR.

ENRICH

Have students complete Enrichment Activity 8 in the TCR.

CLOSE

Make a transparency of the physical profile of South America on page 153, but delete the labels. Challenge students to identify the features on the profile.

USING GRAPHS

Answers:
1. tropical and temperate grassland; 2. Mexico, west coast of Chile, central Argentina; 3. tropical rain forest and tropical grassland

Map Skills Practice
Reading a Map Where are coniferous forests found? *(central Mexico)*

Videodisc

STV: WORLD GEOGRAPHY, VOLUME 3

Side 1, Chapter 1
Frames 08105-9955
Title: ***South America***
Subject: Western South America: The Llanos

ANSWERS TO SECTION 2 REVIEW

1. ***tierra caliente:*** hot country; ***tierra templada:*** temperate country; ***tierra fría:*** cold country; **canopy:** the covering that the tree tops in a rain forest form by coming together
2. tropical savanna
3. some parts of northeastern Mexico and much of southeastern South America
4. because the dense canopy keeps the sunlight from reaching the forest floor
5. The kind of vegetation in an area depends on the climate, which in turn depends on the elevation and latitude of an area. Elevation and latitude affect how warm an area is. Areas grow cooler the farther their location from the Equator and the higher their elevation.

TEACH

Allow students five minutes to complete the following activity: "Compare life in flat and mountainous regions. Consider landscape, work and leisure activities, climate, and so on. Write as many differences as possible." Have students share their comparisons with the class, and have them draw conclusions about terrain and elevation. Have students read the skill on page 170. Then ask: "What do relief maps show?" *(variations in elevation)* "How do maps show relief?" *(Different colors or shadings represent different elevations.)*

Skills Practice
For additional practice, have students complete Skill Activity 8 in the TCR.

MAP & GRAPH SKILLS

Reading a Relief Map

Suppose you must draw a map of a country. The country you are mapping is not flat. It contains hills, valleys, perhaps even mountains. How can you show these three-dimensional features on a two-dimensional piece of paper?

REVIEWING THE SKILL

Variation in the height, or elevation, of land areas is called *relief.* In a relief map, colors or shadings identify areas of different elevation. Green often indicates the lowest elevations (closest to sea level), while yellows, oranges, browns, and reds identify higher elevations. Sometimes the highest areas, such as mountain peaks, are white. Specialized relief maps, called contour maps, use curved lines to show the shapes of land features.

Elevation determines many factors of an area's physical and cultural geography. Elevation directly affects climate. Higher elevations are cooler than lower elevations. Mountains affect rainfall patterns by creating wet and dry sides. By determining climate, elevation affects vegetation and agriculture. In tropical Latin America, for example, climates are arranged into zones by altitude. This arrangement results from the cooling of the air as it rises in elevation. Air temperature decreases with altitude at a rate of about 3.6°F (1.7°C) per 1,000 feet (304.8 m) of height. The three major vertical climatic zones found in the tropics of Latin America are the *tierra caliente* (hot country), the *tierra templada* (cool country), and the *tierra fría* (cold country).

Elevation also influences land use and settlement patterns. Both farming and transportation are easier in low-lying, relatively flat regions than in mountainous areas. Elevation also affects the cultural and political development of a region. Although mountains provide natural defenses against enemies, they may also hamper trade and communication.

Because elevation affects many aspects of geography, relief maps are an important source of geographic information. To read a relief map, apply the following steps:

- Read the map title to identify the land area shown on the map.
- Use the map key to determine what elevations are shown in the map.
- Identify the areas of highest and lowest elevation on the map.

PRACTICING THE SKILL

Use the relief map to answer the following questions:

1. What country is highlighted on the map?
2. What is the elevation of the green areas on the map?
3. What elevation on the map does the color orange represent?
4. What color is used to show the highest elevations on the map? How many feet high are these areas? How many meters?

For additional practice in this skill, see Practicing Skills on page 172 of the Chapter 8 Review.

ANSWERS TO PRACTICING THE SKILL

1. Peru
2. under 1,000 feet (300 meters)
3. 5,000–10,000 feet (1,500–3,000 meters)
4. white; over 10,000 feet (3,000 meters)

chapter 8

HIGHLIGHTS

Section	Key Terms	Summary
1 The Land	**escarpment** (p. 162) ***llanos*** (p. 164) ***Pampas*** (p. 164) **hydroelectric power** (p. 165)	• Latin America is made up of Mexico, Central America, South America, and the Caribbean Islands. • Huge mountain ranges, the largest of which is the Andes, dominate much of Latin America, often blocking communications. • Large plateaus, used for grazing and farming, dot the Latin American landscape. • Plains areas of Latin America have provided significant land areas for pastureland, farmland, and forestland. • Most of the major river systems of Latin America, including the Amazon and the Río de la Plata, are in South America.

Gaucho riding the Pampas of Argentina

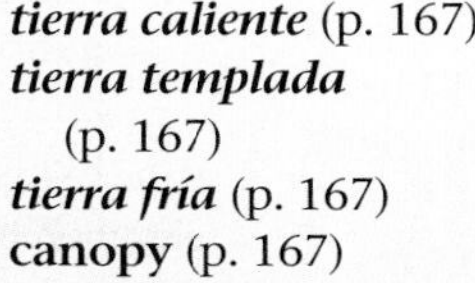

Section	Key Terms	Summary
2 The Climate and Vegetation	***tierra caliente*** (p. 167) ***tierra templada*** (p. 167) ***tierra fría*** (p. 167) **canopy** (p. 167)	• Tropical climates such as tropical rain forest and tropical savanna are the most common climates in Latin America. • While a subtropical climate brings mild winters, hot summers, and a short dry season to grassland areas, other areas have a desert climate or a steppe climate. • One of the most significant features of Latin America's climate and vegetation are three highland zones based on elevation. • The natural vegetation of Latin America varies according to climate and ranges from lush tropical rain forest evergreens to desert cacti. • Among the major natural resources of Latin America are oil, natural gas, bauxite, tin, copper, gold, silver, and valuable gems.

Village in the central highlands of Puerto Rico

CHAPTER 8 HIGHLIGHTS

USING THE CHAPTER 8 HIGHLIGHTS

Use the Chapter 8 Highlights to preview, review, condense, or reteach the chapter.

PREVIEW/REVIEW

Vocabulary PuzzleMaker Software reinforces the Key Terms used in Chapter 8.

Student Self-Test and Review Software allows students to review Chapter 8 content.

CONDENSE

Have students read the Chapter 8 Highlights.

Have students listen to the Chapter 8 Audiocassettes in the TCR. Spanish Audiocassettes are also available.

Assign the Chapter 8 Audiocassette Activity and give the students the Chapter 8 Audiocassette Quiz.

Have students complete the Guided Reading Activities for Chapter 8 in the TCR. Spanish Guided Reading Activities are also available.

RETEACH

Have students complete Reteaching Activity 8 in the TCR. Spanish Reteaching Activities are also available.

Map Activity

Identify and Locate Distribute the outline map of South America on page 25 of the Outline Map Resource Book and have students locate, draw, and color code the following features and regions:

A. Amazon River
B. Andes
C. Patagonia
D. the Brazilian Highlands
E. tropical rain forest climate regions
F. desert climate regions

Remind students to include a key to the colors on their map. Refer them to the maps in the chapter for help.

GLENCOE TECHNOLOGY

Videodisc

Use Chapter 8 MindJogger Videoquiz to review students' knowledge before administering the Chapter 8 Test.

MINDJOGGER VIDEOQUIZ

Chapter 8
Disc 1 Side B

The MindJogger Videoquiz is also available on videocassette.

ANSWERS

Reviewing Key Terms

1. *Pampas*
2. hydroelectric power
3. *llanos*
4. escarpment
5. *tierra templada*
6. *tierra caliente*
7. canopy
8. *tierra fría*

Reviewing Facts

9. the Bahamas, the Greater Antilles, and the Lesser Antilles
10. because the areas are rich in mineral and soil resources
11. the Amazon River basin
12. Mediterranean, marine west coast, tropical rain forest, tropical savanna, humid subtropical, desert, steppe, and highland
13. southern Mexico, eastern Central America, eastern shores of some Caribbean islands, and large parts of South America, especially the Amazon River basin
14. the lush vegetation of the tropical rain forest, rice, sugar cane, and cacao

chapter 8 REVIEW

Reviewing Key Terms

Choose the vocabulary term that best completes each of the sentences below. Write your answers on a separate sheet of paper.

escarpment (p. 162)
llanos (p. 164)
Pampas (p. 164)
hydroelectric power (p. 165)
tierra caliente (p. 167)
tierra templada (p. 167)
tierra fría (p. 167)
canopy (p. 167)

SECTION 1

1. The fertile plains in Argentina and Uruguay are called _____.
2. _____ results from the use of water to produce electricity.
3. The fertile plains in Colombia and Venezuela are called _____.
4. In the Brazilian Highlands, low mountain ranges drop sharply to the sea to form an _____.

SECTION 2

5. Lands from 3,000 to 6,000 feet (914 to 1,829 m) above sea level are in the zone called _____.
6. Lands at sea level to 3,000 feet (914 m) above sea level at or near the Equator fall in the zone called _____.
7. The tops of the trees in a rain forest form a _____.
8. Lands at 6,000 to 10,000 feet (1,829 to 3,048 m) above sea level are in the zone called _____.

Reviewing Facts

SECTION 1

9. Into what three groups is the West Indies divided?
10. Why are settlers attracted to the mountain areas of Latin America?
11. What is the largest lowland area of South America?

SECTION 2

12. What are the eight climate regions of Latin America?
13. Where are the rain forests of Latin America found?
14. What kind of vegetation and crops grow in the *tierra caliente*?

Critical Thinking

15. **Drawing Conclusions** Why is the Amazon River an important water system to Latin America?
16. **Making Generalizations** What generalization can be made about the types of climate and vegetation found in Latin America?

Geographic Themes

17. **Place** What two Latin American nations are leading producers of oil and natural gas?
18. **Region** Why is a tropical climate dominant in much of Latin America?

Practicing Skills

Reading a Relief Map

Refer to the relief map on page 170.

19. In what direction do Peru's mountains run?
20. How might Peru's elevation affect its trade patterns?

Using the Unit Atlas

Refer to the physical geography section of the Unit Atlas on pages 154–155.

21. What river makes up two-thirds of the boundary between Mexico and the United States?

Critical Thinking

15. Answers may vary but should include that the river system drains much of South America and more than half its length is navigable.
16. Answers will vary but may mention that latitude and elevation play important roles in the types of climate and vegetation found in Latin America.

Geographic Themes

17. Mexico and Venezuela
18. Much of Latin America lies in the low latitudes.

22. How can the landscape of the Pampas be described?

Projects

Individual Activity

You have learned about the different types of physical features in various parts of Latin America. Select one to research, such as the Andes or the Amazon River basin, and write a brief report explaining why the feature is significant to the region.

Cooperative Learning Activity

Work in a group of eight to learn more about the climates and vegetation of Latin America. Each group member will select a different type of climate and research it using encyclopedias, atlases, and other resources. Determine what causes the particular type of climate, in what areas of Latin America it is found, and what vegetation grows in each climate area. Relate vegetation and soils with animal life and human activity. As a group, prepare a written report, poster, or map that will illustrate the group's findings.

Writing About Geography

Description

Imagine that you are visiting the rain forest of the Amazon River basin. Use your journal, textbook, travel books and magazines, and videos to learn about the area's physical features, climate, and peoples. Then write a poem describing the forest environment and the lifestyles of its inhabitants.

Locating Places

LATIN AMERICA: PHYSICAL GEOGRAPHY

Match the letters on the map with the places and physical features of Latin America. Write your answers on a separate sheet of paper.

1. Gulf of Mexico
2. Pampas
3. Lake Maracaibo
4. Rio Grande
5. Mexican Plateau
6. Orinoco River
7. Lake Titicaca
8. Hispaniola
9. Caribbean Sea
10. Amazon River

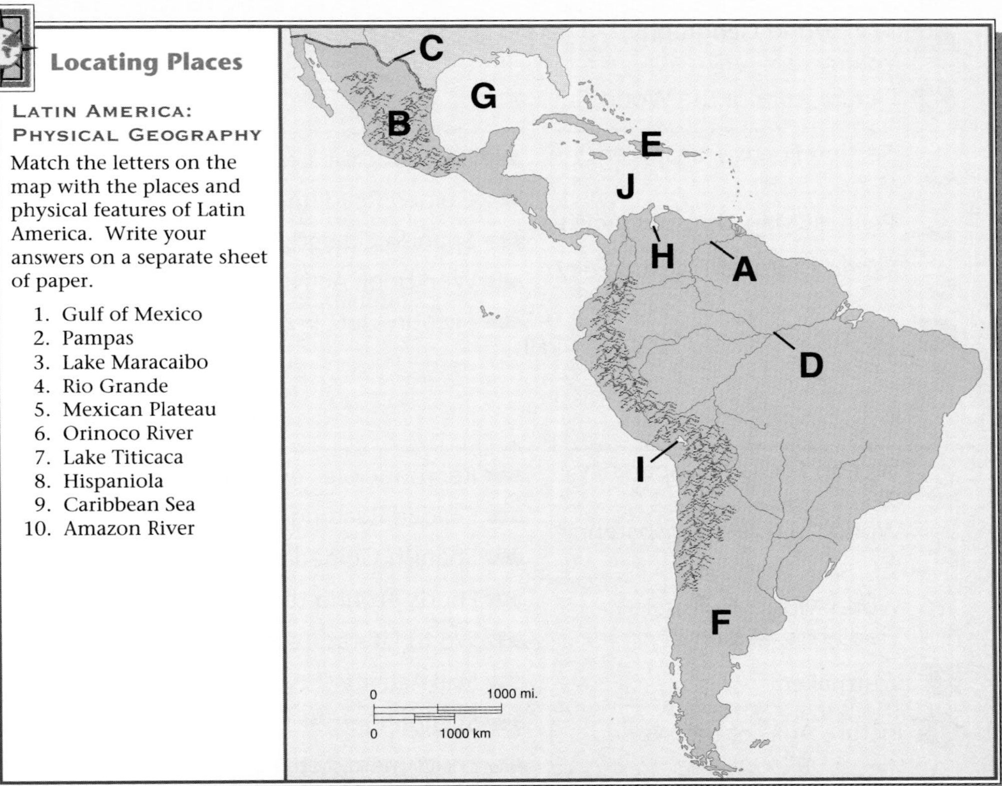

Chapter 8 Review

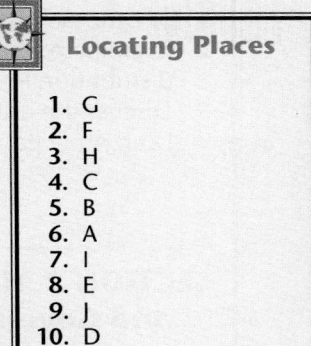

Practicing Skills

19. northwest to southeast
20. The mountains cutting through the country have probably hampered trade between the eastern and the western portions of the country.

Using the Unit Atlas

21. Rio Grande
22. low grasslands

Locating Places

1. G
2. F
3. H
4. C
5. B
6. A
7. I
8. E
9. J
10. D

Chapter Bonus Test Question

This question may be used for extra credit on the chapter test. Choose the letter of the correct response.

What are the dominant climate regions of Brazil?

(1) tropical rain forest, tropical savanna, and humid subtropical

(2) desert, steppe, and humid subtropical

(3) desert, highland, and tropical rain forest

(4) desert, highland, and Mediterranean

Answer: (1)

CHAPTER 9

PLANNING GUIDE

The Cultural Geography of Latin America

CHAPTER ORGANIZER

Daily Lesson Objectives	Multimedia	Teacher Classroom Resources
SECTION 1 Population Patterns 1. Appreciate the ethnic diversity of Latin America. 2. Examine population density and distribution in Latin America. 3. Discuss the urbanization of Latin America.	Section Focus Transparency 9-1 Chapter 9 Vocabulary PuzzleMaker Software Unit Map Overlay Transparencies 3-1 and 3-4 Testmaker STV: World Geography, Volume 3 Picture Atlas of the World	Reproducible Lesson Plan 9-1 Guided Reading Activity 9-1 Spanish Guided Reading Activity 9-1 Workbook Activity 9-1 Performance Assessment Activity 9 Section Quiz 9-1
SECTION 2 History and Government 1. Locate Native American civilizations of Latin America. 2. Describe European empires of Latin America. 3. Discuss modern government in Latin America.	Section Focus Transparency 9-2 Political Map Transparency 3 World Cultures Transparency 3 Testmaker	Reproducible Lesson Plan 9-2 Guided Reading Activity 9-2 Spanish Guided Reading Activity 9-2 Workbook Activity 9-2 Section Quiz 9-2
SECTION 3 Cultures and Lifestyles 1. Name the religions of Latin America. 2. Examine health care and education in Latin America. 3. Discuss the arts of Latin America. 4. Describe life and leisure in Latin America.	Section Focus Transparency 9-3 World Cultures Transparency 4 World Music: Cultural Traditions, Lesson 2 Testmaker Picture Atlas of the World	Reproducible Lesson Plan 9-3 Guided Reading Activity 9-3 Spanish Guided Reading Activity 9-3 Foods Around the World 2 World Literature Reading 2 Skill Activity 9 Section Quiz 9-3 Enrichment Activity 9
CHAPTER REVIEW AND EVALUATION	Chapter 9 English (or Spanish) Audiocassettes MindJogger Videoquiz Testmaker Student Self-Test and Review Software	Reteaching Activity 9 Spanish Reteaching Activity 9 Chapter 9 Test Form A and Form B

0:00 *If time does not permit teaching the entire chapter, summarize using the Chapter 9 Highlights on page 191, and Chapter 9 English (or Spanish) Audiocassettes. Review students' knowledge using the Glencoe MindJogger Videoquiz.*

KEY TO ABILITY LEVELS

Teaching strategies have been coded for varying learning styles and abilities.

L1 **BASIC** activities for all students

L2 **AVERAGE** activities for average to above-average students

L3 **CHALLENGING** activities for above-average students

LEP **LIMITED ENGLISH PROFICIENCY** activities

Performance Assessment

Migration One-way migration has created many challenges for Latin American urban areas and for American states, such as California and Texas. Have students work in groups to simulate a joint committee of the United States and Latin American countries that is addressing the issue. Have them work through the following problem-solving steps:

(1) What is the current situation?
(2) What would be the ideal situation?
(3) What are the barriers to obtaining the ideal?
(4) What are possible means of overcoming the barriers?
(5) What would be the benefit to both areas of addressing the issue?

Have the groups use their answers to questions 2–5 to write a mission statement, or set of beliefs, for their committee. This mission statement should be communicated through pamphlets, letters, speeches, or other political formats.

POSSIBLE RUBRIC FEATURES: Content information, concept attainment, goal setting, problem-solving process steps, inference, summarization and analysis skills, collaborative skills, communications skills

For additional professional and classroom resources, see Chapter Resources, pages T46–T51.

TEACHER'S CORNER

INDEX TO NATIONAL GEOGRAPHIC MAGAZINE

The following articles may be used for research relating to this chapter:

- "Maya Masterpiece Revealed at Bonampak," by Mark Miller, February 1995.
- "Simon Bolivar: El Libertador," by Bryan Hodgson, March 1994.
- "The Wild Mix of Trinidad and Tobago," by A. R. Williams, March 1994.
- "Pizarro: Conqueror of the Inca," by John Hemming, February 1992.
- "Brazil: Moment of Promise and Pain," by Priit J. Vesilind, March 1987.
- "Panama: Ever at the Crossroads," by Charles E. Cobb, Jr., April 1986.
- "Following Cortéz: Path to Conquest," by S. Jeffrey K. Wilkerson, October 1984.
- "The Two Souls of Peru," by Harvey Arden, March 1982.
- "The Aztecs," by Bart McDowell, December 1980.

NATIONAL GEOGRAPHIC SOCIETY PRODUCTS AVAILABLE FROM GLENCOE

To order the following products for use with this chapter, contact your local Glencoe sales representative or call Glencoe at 1-800-334-7344:

- *Picture Atlas of the World* (CD-ROM)
- *STV: North America* (Videodisc)
- *STV: World Geography, South America and Antarctica* (Videodisc)
- *STV: Rain Forest* (Videodisc)
- *ZipZapMap! World* (Software)
- *GeoBee* (Software)
- *Images of the World* (Posters)
- *Eye on the Environment* (Posters)
- *Physical Geography of the World* (Transparencies)
- *Picture Atlas of Our 50 States* (Book)

ADDITIONAL NATIONAL GEOGRAPHIC SOCIETY PRODUCTS

To order the following products for use with this chapter, call National Geographic Society at 1-800-368-2728:

- *Central America*, "Geography," "Everyday Life," "Cultural and Ethnic Heritage," "Conflict in the Region." (Filmstrip)
- *Nations of the World Series*, "Mexico," "Central America." (Video)
- *Lost Kingdoms of the Maya* (Video)

chapter 9

The Cultural Geography of Latin America

PERFORMANCE ASSESSMENT

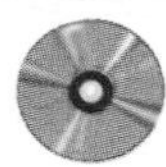

Refer to the Planning Guide on page 174B for a Performance Assessment Activity for this chapter. See the *Performance Assessment Activities* booklet for additional suggestions.

CHAPTER OBJECTIVES

1. **Understand** that the people of Latin America represent diverse ethnic groups.
2. **Recognize** that Latin American countries were once European colonies.
3. **Explain** how Roman Catholicism has influenced Latin American culture.

GLENCOE TECHNOLOGY

Videodisc

Use Chapter 9 MindJogger Videoquiz to preview chapter content.

MINDJOGGER VIDEOQUIZ

Chapter 9
Disc 2 Side A

The MindJogger Videoquiz is also available on videocassette.

CHAPTER FOCUS

Geographic Setting

More than 70 percent of the people of Latin America live in urban areas.

▲ Photograph: *Carnival, Rio de Janeiro, Brazil*

Geographic Themes

Section 1 Population Patterns
REGION The people of Latin America represent diverse ethnic groups, with more than one-half being of mixed ethnic heritage.

Section 2 History and Government
MOVEMENT Latin American countries were once European colonies.

Section 3 Cultures and Lifestyles
PLACE Roman Catholicism has influenced Latin American culture.

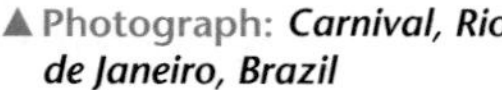

EXTRA CREDIT PROJECT

Display Suggest that students bring pictures of paintings, murals, architecture, mosaics, pottery, and weavings by Latin American artists, as well as samples of crafts such as jewelry, and piñatas to the classroom. Suggest that they also bring tapes of reggae, salsa, and other kinds of Latin American music. Display the items that students contribute according to country and play the tapes quietly in the background while students study the display.

SECTION 1

Population Patterns

SETTING THE SCENE

Read to Discover . . .

- the ethnic diversity of Latin America.
- the population density and distribution in Latin America.
- the urbanization of Latin America.

Key Terms

- *mestizos*
- mulatto
- dialect
- primate city

Identify and Locate

Mexico, Guatemala, Ecuador, Peru, Bolivia, Argentina, Brazil, Cuba, Honduras, El Salvador, Dominican Republic, Caracas, Santiago, Patagonia, Mexican Plateau, Barbados, Bahamas, Suriname, Mexico City, São Paulo, Rio de Janeiro, Buenos Aires, Montevideo

MEXICO EXPORTA $100 CORREOS FRESAS

Acapulco, Mexico

¡Hola! ¿Como están?

I am 15 years old and I live in Mexico City with my family, but every Christmas we drive to my uncle's house in Acapulco. The beaches are beautiful. On Christmas morning Santa brings toys for the younger children, but I look forward to January 5 when the Three Kings bring us clothes. For Christmas dinner, we usually eat Mexican specialties such as romeritos or red snapper a la Veracruzana. I hope you visit someday.

Lorena Lopez

Lorena Lopez comments on two of the many holiday celebrations enjoyed by people in Latin America. Each of these festivals reflects the diverse backgrounds of the region's population. In spite of this diversity, there are common threads binding the people into a single culture region.

MOVEMENT

Human Characteristics

About 470 million people live in Latin America—about 8 percent of the world's population. Latin Americans come from many different backgrounds and are members of various ethnic groups. There are Native Americans, Europeans, Africans, Asians, and mixtures of these groups.

Ethnic Diversity

Native Americans were the first to settle present-day Latin America. They built great civilizations long before the Europeans even knew of their region's existence. Chief among them were the Aztec of Mexico, the Maya of the Yucatán Peninsula and surrounding areas of Central America, and the Inca of the highlands of Peru. Over the centuries, the Native American cultures blended with the cultures of the other groups that later conquered and settled the region. Many Native American cultural characteristics, however, still remain. Today most Native Americans in Latin America live in Mexico, Central America, and the

Classroom Resources for Section 1

BLACKLINE MASTERS:
Reproducible Lesson Plan 9-1
Guided Reading Activity 9-1
Workbook Activity 9-1
Performance Assessment Activity 9
Section Quiz 9-1

TRANSPARENCIES:

Section Focus Transparency 9-1
Unit Map Overlay Transparencies 3-1, 3-4

MULTIMEDIA:

Vocabulary PuzzleMaker Software
Testmaker

STV: World Geography, Volume 3

Picture Atlas of the World

LESSON PLAN
Chapter 9, Section 1

FOCUS

SECTION OBJECTIVES

1. **Appreciate** the ethnic diversity of Latin America.
2. **Examine** population density and distribution in Latin America.
3. **Discuss** the urbanization of Latin America.

ABOUT THE POSTCARD

One of Lorena's favorite places is Acapulco. She goes to the beaches there as often as possible.

BELLRINGER MOTIVATIONAL ACTIVITY

Project the Section 1 Focus Transparency and have students answer the questions.

PRETEACHING VOCABULARY

On the chalkboard, write the Key Terms in one column and their meanings in random order in a second column. Have students match each term with a meaning. Then tell them to find out whether their matches are correct as they read the section.

Use the Vocabulary PuzzleMaker Software to create a crossword or word search puzzle.

NATIONAL GEOGRAPHIC SOCIETY

CD-ROM

PICTURE ATLAS OF THE WORLD
Have students click the "Stats" button of selected countries to find facts and figures about the population of South America.

TEACH

GUIDED PRACTICE

L2 Locate After the class reads "Population Distribution," project Unit Map Overlay Transparency 3-4. Ask volunteers to shade the populated areas of the South American rim. Then add Unit Map Overlay Transparency 3-1 to check their accuracy.

USING CHARTS

Answer: **Asians**

Skills Practice

Making Comparisons Which country has the largest percentage of Europeans in its population? *(Argentina)*

MULTICULTURAL PERSPECTIVE

Culturally Speaking
In Costa Rica, a country with a population of 3 million, the official language is Spanish, English is widely understood, African Americans speak Patua (a mix of French and English), and Native Americans speak Bribri.

NATIONAL GEOGRAPHIC SOCIETY

Videodisc

STV: WORLD GEOGRAPHY, VOLUME 3

Side 1, Chapter 1
Frames 00880-3425
Title: ***South America***
Subject: Overview

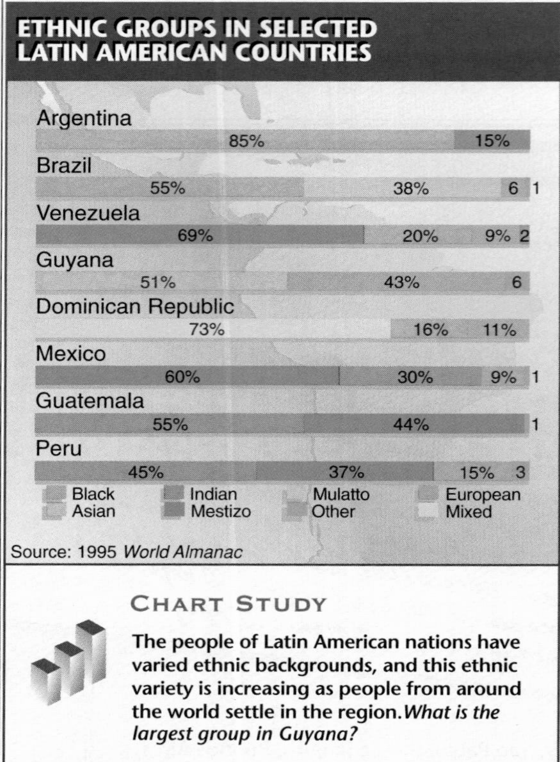

CHART STUDY

The people of Latin American nations have varied ethnic backgrounds, and this ethnic variety is increasing as people from around the world settle in the region. ***What is the largest group in Guyana?***

Andes area of Ecuador, Peru, and Bolivia. Many Native Americans live in isolated villages and continue to practice the traditional ways of their ancestors. In areas where they are a large part of the population, Native American peoples have worked to preserve their own cultures.

Europeans first arrived in present-day Latin America in the late 1400s. Since that time, millions of immigrants have come to the region. Most of the early European settlers were Spanish and Portuguese. Until the 1800s, about 2,000 Spaniards and Portuguese came each year. Over the years, however, many other groups came as well—Italians, British, French, and Germans. In modern times, so many Europeans settled in Argentina and Uruguay that these countries became known as immigrant nations. Descendants of the Europeans continue to follow many of the ways of life their ancestors brought with them.

Africans first came to Latin America in the 1500s. They arrived as enslaved people, forcibly brought by the Europeans to work the plantations in Brazil and the Caribbean Islands. Their labor helped build the economy, and their culture remains a vital part of the Latin American way of life.

Asians first settled Latin America during the 1800s. They, too, worked on plantations. Unlike the Africans, however, the Asians came voluntarily. Today the Caribbean Islands and some countries of South America have large Asian populations. In Guyana, about one-half of the population is of Asian descent. Many Chinese make their homes in Peru, Mexico, and Cuba, and many Japanese live in Brazil.

A Blending of Peoples

More than 50 years ago, a Latin American author, Germán Arciniegas, wrote these words about her fellow Latin Americans:

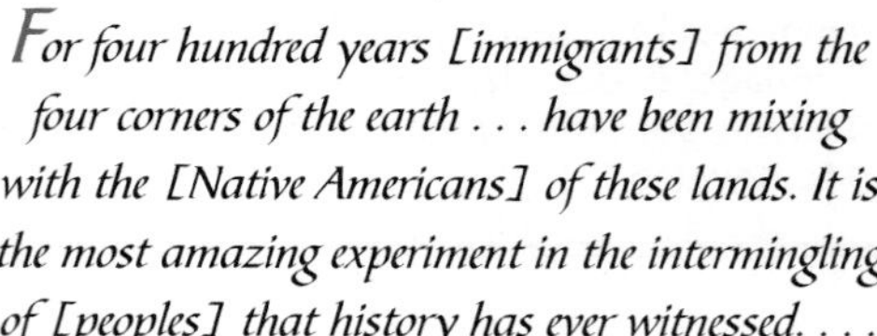

For four hundred years [immigrants] from the four corners of the earth . . . have been mixing with the [Native Americans] of these lands. It is the most amazing experiment in the intermingling of [peoples] that history has ever witnessed. . . .

The writer's words continue to ring true today. The blending of peoples can be seen throughout Latin America. In some countries, such as Mexico, Honduras, and El Salvador, ***mestizos***—people of mixed Native American and European descent—make up the biggest part of the population. In other countries, such as Cuba and the Dominican Republic, **mulattoes**—people of mixed African and European descent—form a large percentage of the population.

Language

Germán Arciniegas, who spoke about the blending of races and cultures in Latin America, also said this about the languages of the region:

Cooperative Learning Activity

Have students compile a picture dictionary of Latin American words. Tell them to start with words from the chapter, such as *tierra caliente, mestizo, fazenda,* and *chicle.* Then add English words derived from Spanish to their list: arroyo, bosque, bronco, corral, coyote, loco, palomino, pronto, and so on. Refer students to an English dictionary for the meanings of these words. Suggest that they interview community members from Latin American countries to gather more words and phrases. Also, refer them to books by Latin American authors; even English editions should include some words from the authors' native language. Assign students to edit, type, and illustrate the pages and to bind them into a dictionary. Suggest the class donate their dictionary to the school library.

. . . Ours has been a dual world, one part of which speaks Portuguese—Brazil—and the other . . . Spanish—Spanish America. But inland, in the heart of the [region], other accents are heard.

Most of the countries of Latin America adopted the languages of the countries that colonized them. The official language of Brazil, for example, became Portuguese; of Haiti and Martinique, French; and of Jamaica and Guyana, English.

Today Spanish is the official language of most of the countries of Latin America. In most cases, however, the Spanish spoken is no longer that of Spain. Over the years, it has been changed by the addition of certain Native American words. The word *chicle* (CHIK•uhl), for example, which means "chewing gum," comes from a Native American language. Each nation also has its own **dialects,** forms of a language peculiar to a particular place or group. Meanings of words and the words themselves often differ from one place to another.

Millions of Latin Americans speak Native American languages such as Quechua (KECH•wuh), Guaraní, and Mayan. Some Latin Americans speak only a Native American language. Many others speak both a Native American language and their country's official European language. Peru, for example, has two official languages—Spanish and Quechua.

LATIN AMERICA: MAJOR LANGUAGES

FOCUS ON GEOGRAPHIC THEMES

1. **Place:** What is the official language of Brazil?
2. **Location:** Where are Native American languages spoken?
3. **Place:** What is the most widely spoken language in Haiti?

REGION

Population Density and Distribution

About 470 million people live in Latin America. As in other regions of the world, they are not evenly distributed across the region. Some parts of the region are more populated than others. The same holds true in individual countries.

Population Distribution

Much of the land of Latin America is not densely populated. Most Latin Americans live on only about one-third of its land. A significant number of people are clustered in two general areas—around the coasts of South America or in a broad strip of land that reaches south from central Mexico into Central America.

More than 66 percent of Latin Americans—311 million—live in South America. Most of them live in or around cities on or near the coast in what one geographer calls "the populated rim of South America."

Geographers often divide this rim into two major parts. The larger of the two parts in size and number of people stretches along the eastern edge of South America—from the mouth of the Amazon River in Brazil to the grasslands around Buenos Aires, Argentina. The smaller

INDEPENDENT PRACTICE

Guided Reading Have students complete Guided Reading Activity 9-1 in the TCR. **LEP**

Have students complete Workbook Activity 9-1 found in the TCR.

USING MAPS

Answers:
1. Portuguese; **2.** parts of Middle America and much of central and western South America; **3.** Creole

Map Skills Practice
Reading a Map What is the dominant language in southern South America? *(Spanish)*

DID YOU KNOW?

The Maya of Mexico discovered chewing gum when they sampled the sapodilla tree's milky sap called "chicle." Their descendants collected chicle for commercial gum manufacturers for many years until most manufacturers replaced it with an artificial gum base.

ASSESS

CHECK FOR UNDERSTANDING

Assign Section 1 Review as homework or an in-class activity.

Meeting Special Needs

Visual Learning Disability Visual processing problems often impair a student's ability to recall words by sight, and this affects reading and comprehension. Confusion between similar words is common because of weaknesses in visual attention to detail or visual memory problems. In private sessions, have students read aloud the first two paragraphs under "Ethnic Diversity" and the last paragraph under "A Blending of Peoples." Note if they read "must" for "most," "from" for "form," and "were" for "where." Encourage students to reread and self-correct their mistakes.

USING ILLUSTRATIONS

REGION Although southern Patagonia has few people, it does have its own glacier—the Perito Moreno Glacier in the province of Santa Cruz.

Answer to Caption: *the eastern edge of South America from the mouth of the Amazon to the grasslands around Argentina; the broad strip of land from central Mexico south into Central America*

MEETING LESSON OBJECTIVES

Each objective below is tested by the questions that follow it in parentheses.

1. **Appreciate** the ethnic diversity of Latin America. *(1, 5)*
2. **Examine** population density and distribution in Latin America. *(2, 3, 4)*
3. **Discuss** the urbanization of Latin America. *(4)*

EVALUATE

Assign the Section 1 Quiz in the TCR.

Use the Testmaker to create a customized quiz for Section 1.

Geographic Themes

Region: Patagonia, South America

A shepherd tends his flock in the sparsely populated region of Patagonia in southern South America. *What two areas of Latin America are heavily populated?*

part includes land along the coast and in the Andes. It stretches along the western side of South America from Caracas, Venezuela, to Santiago, Chile.

The populated rim of South America is often interrupted. For example, the eastern coast between the mouth of the Amazon River and Caracas, an area that has hot and rainy weather most of the time, is sparsely populated. Another sparsely populated area is in the far south in the Andes and Patagonia, where the climate and the land are harsh.

The next largest number of Latin Americans—123 million—live in Middle America, most of them in the Mexican Plateau and along the Pacific coast of Central America, largely in the highlands. In these areas, the land is fertile and the climate is relatively mild.

Population Density

Population density varies greatly in Latin America. About 92 million people live in Mexico—more than 3 times as many as in all of Central America. Mexico is the most populated Spanish-speaking nation in the world. It is also the second most heavily populated country in Latin America after Brazil. The land area of Brazil, however, is more than 3 million square miles (7.8 million sq. km), while that of Mexico is about 700,000 square miles (1.8 million sq. km). Thus, population density is much greater in Mexico. In Mexico there are 125 people per square mile (48 per sq. km). In Brazil there are 48 people per square mile (18 per sq. km). In contrast, the most sparsely populated country is Suriname, with only 7 people per square mile (3 per sq. km).

Caribbean countries are small, and have areas not suitable for settlement or for farming. In addition, most Caribbean countries have a high birthrate. The combination of a small land area and a growing number of people creates high population density. Barbados, with 1,765 people per square mile (682 per sq. km), has the highest density in the area. The Bahamas, in contrast, contain only 78 people per square mile (30 per sq. km).

In South America, population densities are relatively low. Even Ecuador, with the highest population density of the continent, has only about 96 people per square mile (37 per sq. km). Suriname has the lowest density—7 people per square mile (fewer than 3 per sq. km).

In most Latin American countries, population density varies by region. Few people live where a harsh climate, poor soil, or the physical landscape make life difficult. About four-fifths of all Mexicans, for example, live in the southern half of the Mexican Plateau. Three-fourths of the people of Argentina live in Buenos Aires or the nearby Pampas. In most of the island countries of the Caribbean, however, people tend to be more evenly distributed.

MOVEMENT

Urbanization

In the past most Latin Americans lived in the countryside and worked the land. Now most live in urban areas.

Critical Thinking

Making Predictions Read aloud the following passage from a recent news story: ". . . In Petion-Ville, Port-au-Prince's hilltop suburb of contradiction, the elite live in luxury while the rest of the city starves. . . . 'Why do people think the rich are so bad? What did we do?' said a wealthy woman . . . .

"Others say the rich think only of themselves and need to start caring about the interests of others. They would like to see the rich pay taxes to fund social programs and improve the city's crumbling infrastructure. They would like to see them pay their maids and cooks, waiters and busboys more than subsistence wages." Ask students to predict what might happen if the conditions in Haiti do not change. *(Students probably will say that the poor will rebel.)*

One-Way Migration

Living conditions are poor in many rural areas of Latin America. As a result, each year thousands of Latin Americans migrate to the cities. There they hope to find a new life—a better education, higher-paying jobs, broader markets, and decent health care. Most people do not find what they seek, largely because they cannot read or write or do not have the skills needed to qualify for the available jobs. Nevertheless, they stay.

The resulting urban population explosion has brought problems. Latin American urban areas lack the resources to meet the needs of their people. Most migrants are now living under the very conditions they wanted to escape. They cannot get a decent job—if they can get any job at all. They have little or no money and are forced to live in slums and shantytowns, often without water or sanitary facilities.

Geographic Themes

Movement: Mexico City, Mexico

Like most Latin American cities, Mexico City has seen a tremendous population increase that has strained local resources. *From what area do most of Latin America's new city dwellers come?*

The Cities

As a result of people moving to the cities, today most Latin American nations are urbanized. More than 20 Latin American cities have populations of more than 1 million. Four cities rank among the 10 largest urban areas in the world—Mexico City, Mexico; São Paulo and Rio de Janeiro, Brazil; and Buenos Aires, Argentina.

Many Latin American cities have become what some geographic experts call **primate cities**, cities with a concentrated urban population that dominate the economy, culture, and government. Caracas, Venezuela; Montevideo, Uruguay; and Santiago, Chile, all are primate cities. So are Mexico City, Buenos Aires, and Havana.

Many of the cities of Latin America were founded in the 1500s and 1600s by the Spanish. Each city, large and small, is unique and offers benefits people could not find in the countryside. At the same time, however, the cities are crushed by rapid population growth.

Some of the fastest-growing cities in the world are in Latin America. For example, some experts predict that by 2000, Mexico City will have a population of 30 million. The city is the nation's capital and functions as Mexico's leading business, industrial, and cultural center. It has broad avenues, a skyline dominated by modern, high-rise office towers, and a fairly new and efficient subway system. Yet Mexico City also is one of the most polluted cities in the world. It, too, shares the other urban problems of most rapidly growing cities—poverty, slums, and crime.

Section 1 Review

Checking for Understanding

1. **Define** *mestizos,* mulatto, dialect, primate city.
2. **Locating Places** In what two general areas do most Latin Americans live?
3. **Place** What are the two most densely populated countries of Latin America?
4. **Place** What 4 Latin American cities are among the world's 10 largest urban areas?

Critical Thinking

5. **Analyzing Information** Latin America has been called the "melting pot of the Western Hemisphere." What reasons can you give for this?

RETEACH

Say words or phrases from the section and have volunteers come up with questions for which the words or phrases are the answers.

ENRICH

Display travel brochures with pictures of Caracas, Montevideo, Santiago, Mexico City, São Paulo, Rio de Janiero, and Buenos Aires. Ask each student to plan a day's itinerary in at least one city.

CLOSE

Have students write Lorena Lopez a postcard in which they describe their activities on a holiday of their choice.

Movement The United Nations predicts that the population of Mexico City will be over 30 million by the year 2025.

Answer to Caption: *rural areas*

ANSWERS TO SECTION 1 REVIEW

1. *mestizos:* people of mixed Native American and European descent; **mulatto:** people of mixed African and European descent; **dialect:** form of a language peculiar to a particular place or group; **primate city:** city in which a country's urban population is concentrated and which dominates the economy, culture, and government
2. in a broad strip of land that reaches south from central Mexico well into Central America and around the coasts of South America
3. Barbados and Puerto Rico
4. Mexico City, São Paulo, Rio de Janiero, and Buenos Aires
5. ethnic diversity and intermarriage

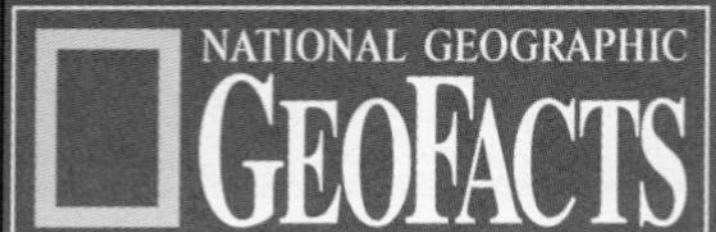

TEACH

Colca Canyon's remote location might be a blessing. After a protected area becomes a tourist attraction, the environment becomes threatened. In 1990 alone, almost 4 million tourists visited the Grand Canyon in Arizona. Ask students how ecotourism, or nature travel, can both benefit and harm a site. *(Benefits: tourists' dollars generate much revenue and provide incentive to protect an area and its species; Drawbacks: plant and animal species are stressed, animals may change their behavioral patterns, local cultures are disrupted, pollution and traffic increase)*

DID YOU KNOW?

Popular Destinations for U.S. Tourists

Trekking:
- Nepal
- Kenya
- Tanzania
- China

Bird watching:
- Kenya
- Mexico
- Costa Rica
- Tanzania

Photography:
- Kenya
- Tanzania

Wildlife Safaris:
- Kenya
- Tanzania

NATIONAL GEOGRAPHIC GEOFACTS

Where is the deepest canyon on earth?

Plummeting more than twice the depth of Arizona's Grand Canyon, a gorge through the Peruvian Andes is the deepest canyon on the surface of the earth.

From its lower rim, Colca Canyon, carved by the Colca River, descends 10,500 feet (3,200 m). The river cuts a trench through the high mountains as it makes its way down to the Pacific Ocean.

Accessible only by boat, the V-shaped gorge is one of the world's great natural challenges. The first recorded expedition of the roaring river canyon wasn't made until 1981. Rafters have to navigate churning white-water currents and breakneck plunges—the most precipitous one dropping 3,000 feet (914 m) over 50 miles (80 km).

Unlike the Grand Canyon—the largest on earth—visited by millions every year, the isolated heart of Colca Canyon has been seen by only a handful of people. Boulders thunder unheard down its barren walls. Floods, avalanches, and earthquakes are constantly changing its features.

Source of the Amazon
Cailloma
A N D E S
Señal Yajirhua
Colca
Maca
0 20 km
0 20 mi
Cerro Luceria
COLCA CANYON
PERU
Lima
SOUTH AMERICA
Amazon
Area shown
Camaná
Pacific Ocean

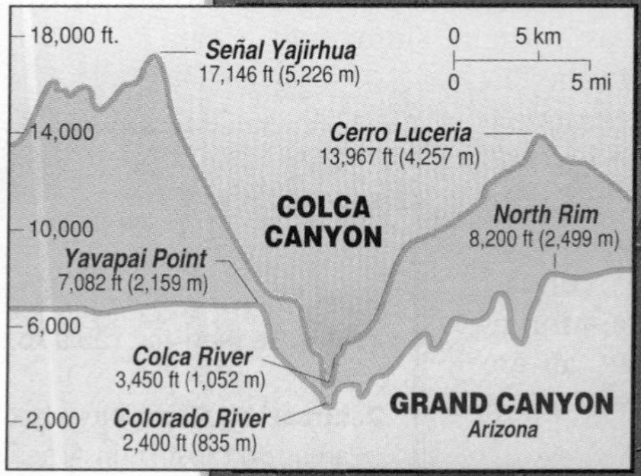

18,000 ft.
14,000
10,000
6,000
2,000
Señal Yajirhua 17,146 ft (5,226 m)
Cerro Luceria 13,967 ft (4,257 m)
COLCA CANYON
North Rim 8,200 ft (2,499 m)
Yavapai Point 7,082 ft (2,159 m)
Colca River 3,450 ft (1,052 m)
Colorado River 2,400 ft (835 m)
GRAND CANYON Arizona
0 5 km
0 5 mi

Designed by BILL PITZER

2 SECTION

History and Government

SETTING THE SCENE

Read to Discover . . .
- the Native American civilizations of Latin America.
- the European empires of Latin America.
- the status of modern government in Latin America.

Key Terms
- *chinampas*
- *quipu*
- *conquistador*
- viceroy
- *fazenda*
- *caudillo*

Identify and Locate
Yucatán Peninsula, Lake Texcoco, Tenochtitlán, Cuzco, Ecuador, Chile, Lima, Brazil, Haiti, Mexico, Cuba

Latin America has a long and often violent history. Its past includes Native American civilizations, European colonial empires, and struggles for independence.

REGION

Native American Empires

Native Americans came to the Western Hemisphere thousands of years ago, probably across the Bering Strait that now separates Alaska and Siberia. Years before Christopher Columbus arrived in the Americas in 1492, three Native American civilizations—the Maya, the Aztec, and the Inca—emerged.

The Maya

The Maya created an empire in Central America and southern Mexico. They built many cities, the greatest of which was Tikal, located in present-day Guatemala. Pyramid-shaped temples, terraces, and courts stood in these cities. Priests and nobles ruled the cities and surrounding areas. The Maya based their economy on trade and agriculture.

Skilled in mathematics, the Maya used a number system based on 20 and developed a symbol for the mathematical concept of zero. Basing their calculations on the orbit of the earth around the sun, they created a calendar of a little more than 365 days.

The Aztec

The Aztec were originally wanderers. In the 1300s they finally built a permanent capital city called Tenochtitlán on an island in the center of a large lake. Farmers grew crops of beans and maize on ***chinampas***, floating artificial islands. They made the islands by building large rafts and covering them with mud from the bottom of the lake.

The Aztec developed a complex political system headed by an emperor. They worshiped many gods and goddesses and held ceremonies to win the deities' favor and guarantee good harvests.

The Inca

At about the same time the Aztec were building their empire, the Inca were establishing a civilization. The Inca empire stretched along the Andes from Ecuador to Chile. The Inca built their capital, Cuzco, in Peru and ruled their lands through a central government headed by an emperor.

Incan farmers cut terraces into the slopes of the Andes to keep the soil from washing away, and built irrigation systems to bring water to desert areas along the coast. They also domesticated the alpaca and the llama, which they used both for food and for wool.

The Inca, known for their building skills, constructed stone temples and fortresses. Inca

LESSON PLAN
Chapter 9, Section 2

FOCUS

SECTION OBJECTIVES

1. Locate Native American civilizations of Latin America.
2. Describe European empires of Latin America.
3. Discuss modern government in Latin America.

BELLRINGER MOTIVATIONAL ACTIVITY

Project the Section 2 Focus Transparency and have students answer the questions.

PRETEACHING VOCABULARY

Tell students to identify a Key Term from a Native American language *(quipu)*, one from Spanish *(conquistador* or *caudillo)*, and one from Portuguese *(fazenda)* as they read the section.

TEACH

GUIDED PRACTICE

L1 Compare On the chalkboard, draw a chart with *Maya, Inca,* and *Aztec* across the top and *location, ruler(s),* and *accomplishments* along the side. Have students fill the chart with details from the section.

Classroom Resources for Section 2

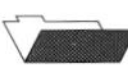
BLACKLINE MASTERS:
Reproducible Lesson Plan 9-2
Guided Reading Activity 9-2
Spanish Guided Reading Activity 9-2
Workbook Activity 9-2
Section Quiz 9-2

TRANSPARENCIES:
Section Focus Transparency 9-2
Political Map Transparency 3
World Cultures Transparency 3

MULTIMEDIA:

Testmaker

INDEPENDENT PRACTICE

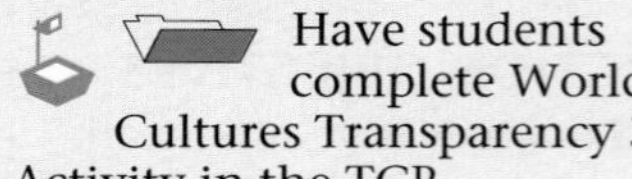

Have students complete World Cultures Transparency 3 Activity in the TCR.

L2 Essay Read excerpts from the writings of Bartolomé de las Casas in the first chapter of *A People's History of the United States* by Howard Zinn. Then ask interested students to write essays suggesting ways conquistadors might have obtained riches without mistreating Native Americans.

USING MAPS

Answers:
1. Inca;
2. Tenochtitlán;
3. to keep the soil from washing away

Map Skills Practice

Drawing Conclusions In what kind of climate region were the major Aztec and Inca cities located? *(highland)*

ASSESS

CHECK FOR UNDERSTANDING

Assign Section 2 Review as homework or an in-class activity.

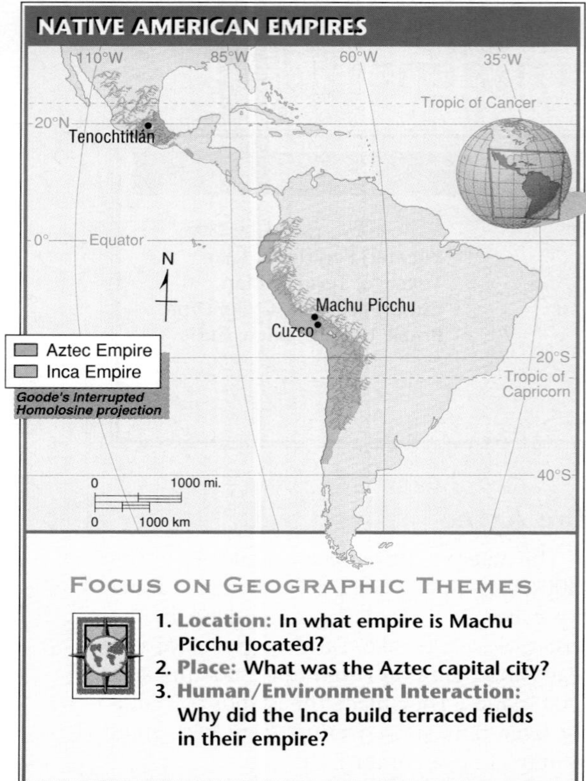

FOCUS ON GEOGRAPHIC THEMES

1. **Location: In what empire is Machu Picchu located?**
2. **Place: What was the Aztec capital city?**
3. **Human/Environment Interaction: Why did the Inca build terraced fields in their empire?**

buildings often were adorned with gold and silver. The Inca had no written language. They kept records and sent messages using a ***quipu*** (KEE•poo), a rope with knotted cords of various lengths and colors.

MOVEMENT

European Empires

In the late 1400s, European explorers set out to find new trade routes to Asia. In the process, the explorers reached the Americas. Spain and Portugal vied for land in the Americas. To avoid conflicts, the Pope drew an imaginary line—the Line of Demarcation—that ran from the North Pole to the South Pole. All lands east of the line were to belong to Portugal, all those to the west of the line to Spain. Thus, Portugal claimed present-day Brazil, and Spain claimed Central America and the rest of South America.

Spanish Conquests

The European search for trade routes eventually turned into a search for riches—and for opportunities to convert Native Americans to Christianity. Spanish ***conquistadors,*** or conquerors, overpowered the Aztec and Inca empires, seizing their wealth for Spain.

Spain soon established colonies from Mexico to Bolivia and set out to mine gold and silver in its new lands. To provide bases for exploration and for mining, the Spaniards built cities and towns, many of them on the sites of Native American cities.

In the tropics, the Spaniards set up plantations. In the highlands, where it was cooler, they established farms and huge cattle ranches. The Spaniards at first used Native Americans to work the plantations. When hundreds of thousands of Native Americans died from being forced to work in the hot tropical climate and from European diseases, the Spaniards brought in enslaved Africans to replace the Native Americans.

The Spanish monarch appointed **viceroys** from distant Spain to govern the colonies and make sure that Spanish law was enforced. A strict social structure emerged in the Spanish colonies. Europeans were at the top of society, and Native Americans and Africans were at the bottom.

The Portuguese and Brazil

The Portuguese, meanwhile, had claimed Brazil as early as 1500. Although the land seemed to contain no precious metals, it did have brazilwood, a tree from which red dyes could be made. The land also was good for raising livestock. On the coastal lowlands, which were well-suited for raising sugarcane, the Portuguese built sugar plantations called ***fazendas.*** Like the Spaniards, the Portuguese relied on enslaved peoples to work the plantations, first Native Americans and then Africans.

Cooperative Learning Activity

Read these words by Simón Bolívar to the class: "Let us give our republic a fourth power . . . to watch over the education of the children, to supervise national education, to purify whatever may be corrupt in the republic, to denounce ingratitude, coldness in the country's service, egotism, sloth, idleness, and to pass judgment upon the first signs of corruption . . . ." Then have each student choose a phrase from the quote and frame a law that would enforce the ideal that Bolívar expressed in the phrase. For example, "to denounce . . . sloth" a student might write "All government workers loafing on the job will be fined." Have volunteers write their laws on the chalkboard. Then ask if these laws would violate people's rights and have them explain why or why not.

Independence

Beginning in the late 1700s, many people in Latin America began to resent European rule. Upper-class Latin Americans born in the Americas resented the strict social structure, which limited their rights. Native Americans and Africans also wanted their freedom. Feelings of patriotism were strengthened by revolutions in the United States and France.

The first Latin American country to rid itself of European rule—Haiti—was ruled by the French. Unrest first erupted there in 1794 when enslaved Africans led by a former slave named Francois Toussaint L'Ouverture (TOO•SAN LOO•vuhr•TYUHR) revolted. In 1804, Haiti finally became independent.

Mexico was the first Spanish-ruled nation in Latin America to gain freedom. The struggle for independence went on for many years, and in 1824, Mexico became an independent republic.

Other countries of Latin America sought to gain independence. By the mid-1800s most of them had achieved their goal under such leaders as Simón Bolívar of Venezuela and José de San Martín of Argentina. Only one nation—Brazil—became independent without revolution. In 1822 it became the only independent South American country to choose monarchy—rule by a king or queen—as its form of government.

With the exception of Haiti, independence was longer in coming to the islands of the Caribbean. Cuba, for example, did not win its independence from Spain until 1898, and many of the other islands did not gain their independence until well into the 1900s.

EUROPEAN COLONIAL EMPIRES

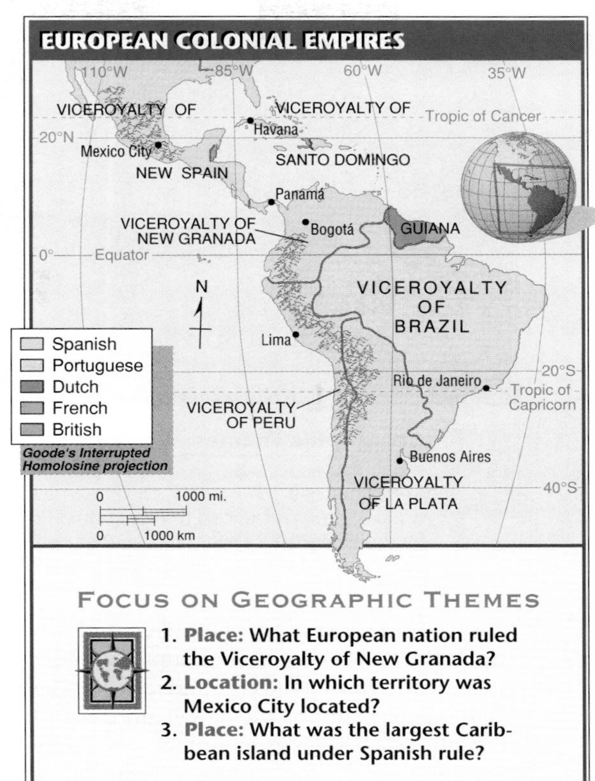

FOCUS ON GEOGRAPHIC THEMES

1. **Place: What European nation ruled the Viceroyalty of New Granada?**
2. **Location: In which territory was Mexico City located?**
3. **Place: What was the largest Caribbean island under Spanish rule?**

REGION

Dictatorships and Democracies

Wars of independence created political and economic confusion in the countries of Latin America. Leaders of the newly independent countries wanted to build stable governments and prosperous economies. In

Geographic Themes

Movement: Haiti

Toussaint L'Ouverture led an independence movement to bring colonial rule in Haiti to an end. *What foreign events inspired his efforts?*

USING MAPS

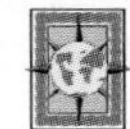

Answers:
1. Spain; **2.** Viceroyalty of New Spain; **3.** Cuba

Map Skills Practice

Determining Cause and Effect What long-lasting effects did colonization have on Latin America? *(Latin Americans still speak the languages brought over by the European colonists.)*

USING ILLUSTRATIONS

PLACE Miguel Hidalgo, a Catholic priest, began the struggle for Mexican independence in 1810.

Answer to Caption: revolutions in the United States and France

MEETING LESSON OBJECTIVES

Each objective below is tested by the questions that follow it in parentheses.
1. Locate Native American civilizations of Latin America. *(2, 3, 5)*
2. Describe European empires of Latin America. *(4)*
3. Discuss modern government in Latin America. *(5)*

EVALUATE

Assign the Section 2 Quiz in the TCR.

Use the Testmaker to create a customized quiz for Section 2.

Meeting Special Needs

Study Strategies As you present the information in this section, model the study strategy SQ3R (Survey, Question, Read, Recite, Review) for students with weak reading skills. First, skim the first page, reading the head and subheads. Second, rephrase these as questions, and have students read the paragraphs under a subhead to find the answer to the question about the subhead. Third, have a student recite what he or she remembers from the reading. Finally, tell students to review the material to find errors or omissions from the recitation.

RETEACH

Have students reread the section. Ask them to list at least five cause and effect relationships from their reading.

ENRICH

Have students assemble and display dioramas of Mayan cities, Chichen Itzá and Tulum, including temples, plazas, and marketplaces.

CLOSE

Tape each Key Term from the section on a different student's back so that everyone but the student can read it. Have students ask questions such as "Am I a person?" or "Am I a place?" until they have enough facts to guess their Key Term.

USING ILLUSTRATIONS

PLACE In an August 1993 poll conducted by the Panamanian newspaper *La Prensa*, 70 percent of the respondents wanted Americans to stay in Panama after the year 2000.

Answer to Caption: democratic reform

Geographic Themes

Place: Panama Canal

As a result of a 1977 treaty, the Panama Canal will pass from American to Panamanian control by the year 2000. *What has been the dominant political trend in Latin America since the 1970s?*

most countries, however, political control was still in the hands of a small group of wealthy landowners, army officers, and clergy. The huge size of many of the new countries and such physical barriers as mountains and dense rain forests made communications and trade difficult.

Power of the Strong

New leaders, known as ***caudillos***, or "strong men," promised to solve Latin America's problems. Almost all caudillos were military rulers supported by wealthy landowners eager to protect their interests.

In the later 1800s and early 1900s, caudillos ruled as dictators in many Latin American countries.

Desire for Change

Rapid industrialization between 1940 and 1970 brought social changes to Latin America. Much of the region's newfound wealth simply enriched the upper classes. The growing gap between rich and poor spread unrest among farmers and workers. Military governments resisted demands for reform and fought political unrest with terror. Nonetheless, democracy was a political goal in most nations, the greatest exception being the Communist rule of Fidel Castro in Cuba.

Military leaders were unable to solve the rising political and economic problems of the 1970s, and their tactics inspired calls for democratic reform. By the early 1990s, new democratic governments began to replace the old, harsh political systems.

SECTION 2 REVIEW

Checking for Understanding

1. **Define** *chinampas, quipu, conquistador,* viceroy, *fazenda, caudillo.*
2. **Locating Places** Where were the Maya, Aztec, and Inca civilizations located?
3. **Movement** How did the Line of Demarcation affect Spanish and Portuguese colonization in the Americas?
4. **Region** What changes took place in Latin America under Spanish and Portuguese rule?

Critical Thinking

5. **Determining Cause and Effect** Why did Latin Americans seek independence in the late 1700s and early 1800s?

ANSWERS TO SECTION 2 REVIEW

1. **chinampas:** floating artificial islands; ***quipu:*** knotted cords used for keeping records and sending messages; ***conquistador:*** Spanish conqueror; **viceroy:** Spanish colonial governor; ***fazenda:*** a sugar plantation in Brazil; ***caudillo:*** military dictator
2. Maya: Central America and southern Mexico; Aztec: central Mexico; Inca: along the Andes from Ecuador to Chile
3. The line divided newly discovered lands between Portugal and Spain.
4. Native American civilizations were destroyed; Native Americans were enslaved; Africans were introduced as slaves; cities, plantations, ranches, and a strict social structure were set up.
5. Latin Americans wanted freedom, resented Europeans, and felt inspired by the American and French revolutions.

Geography and History

Buenos Aires, Argentina's Gateway

As you read, examine how Buenos Aires became a leading Latin American metropolis.

The metropolitan area of Buenos Aires spreads over 1,421 square miles (3,680 sq. km). The city is a leading Latin American banking, business, and cultural center. Around the central business district, residential neighborhoods called barrios fan out to the northwest, west, and southern city limits. City residents number more than 11.5 million: More than one-third of all Argentinians are *porteños,* or "port dwellers."

Few skyscrapers dominate the skyline of Buenos Aires, but the city has broad avenues and many parks and plazas. As a result, Buenos Aires has a sense of openness and peace. The Avenida 9 de Julio, the widest street in the world, runs north and south through the city's central business district. It links the president's residence with the Congress Building, site of the national legislature.

Location

Buenos Aires is located at the mouth of Argentina's widest river, on the edge of Argentina's fertile Pampas. For nearly two centuries, however, Buenos Aires's broad harbor remained little more than a backwater smuggling port and slave market. As a Spanish colony, *la grand aldea,* "the big village," could not engage in trade with any country except Spain.

In the early 1800s, with the onset of independence movements in Latin America, Buenos Aires set up its own government. By mid-century, Argentina was an independent nation; Buenos Aires became its capital in 1880.

Between 1880 and 1940, Buenos Aires enjoyed a Golden Age. Beef, lamb, wool, and wheat were brought from the fertile Pampas to markets in Buenos Aires, and from there shipped to markets around the world. Ships docked in the harbor, and goods and produce were unloaded and routed to marketplaces in Argentina's interior. Building and construction changed *la grand aldea* into a gracious metropolis of broad avenues and European-like architecture. Immigrants swelled the city's population.

Contemporary Buenos Aires handles more than 80 percent of Argentina's trade. Meat packing, food processing, and textile, rubber, and electrical manufacturing employ hundreds of thousands of workers.

Like most huge urban areas, Buenos Aires struggles with overpopulation and poverty. Although immigration has dwindled, thousands of rural migrants come annually seeking work. Even though the city is prosperous, it is struggling to create jobs for its poor.

Checking for Understanding

1. **Why is Buenos Aires called Argentina's Gateway?**
2. **Location How did Buenos Aires's location help it to become a center of commerce?**

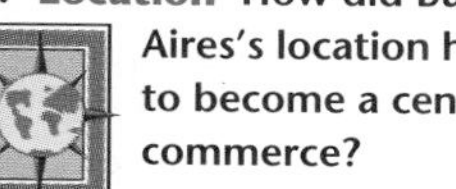

Geography and History

TEACH

Display Unit Map Overlay Transparency 3-5. Have students identify the location of Buenos Aires. Point out that the city's favorable location includes a broad, protected, funnel-shaped harbor. Early Spanish sailors named the city for Nuestra Señora Santa Maria del Buen Aire, the patron saint of fair winds.

Place Have students read the caption under the photograph, then compare the photo with that of the city on page 79. Do they agree that the absence of skyscrapers makes Buenos Aires seem more open? In what other ways do the two cities seem to differ?

Extending the Content

Architecture Buenos Aires has often been called "The Paris of South America" and likened to European cities. Many streets and much of the city's architecture were purposely fashioned to resemble famous European counterparts. The Avenida de Mayo was constructed to resemble the Gran Via in Madrid, the Colon Theater copies Milan's La Scala, and Carrio Norte (The North Neighborhood) resembles London's Right Bank.

ANSWERS TO CHECKING FOR UNDERSTANDING

1. It is the main entrance and exit for people and goods going to or coming from Argentina.
2. It is a harbor on the coast, it is at the mouth of Argentina's river system, and it is on the edge of the Pampas, Argentina's most productive agricultural area.

LESSON PLAN
Chapter 9, Section 3

FOCUS

SECTION OBJECTIVES

1. **Name** the religions of Latin America.
2. **Examine** health care and education in Latin America.
3. **Discuss** the arts of Latin America.
4. **Describe** life and leisure in Latin America.

BELLRINGER MOTIVATIONAL ACTIVITY

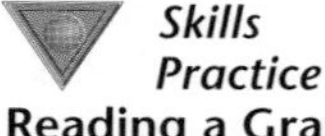

Project the Section 3 Focus Transparency and have students answer the questions.

PRETEACHING VOCABULARY

Ask students to hypothesize about what language the word *fùtbol* came from. *(English)* Then have Spanish-speaking students share Spanish words with altered spellings or pronunciations in English. *(Answers may include* tamal *and* rancho.*)*

USING GRAPHS

Skills Practice

Reading a Graph What percentage of Latin Americans are not Roman Catholic? *(13%)*

NATIONAL GEOGRAPHIC SOCIETY

CD-ROM

PICTURE ATLAS OF THE WORLD

Have students click the "Video," "Speech," and "Music" buttons of selected Latin American countries to see and hear the sights and sounds of the region.

SECTION 3

Cultures and Lifestyles

SETTING THE SCENE

Read to Discover . . .
- the religions of Latin America.
- the concerns of health care and education in Latin America.
- the arts of Latin America.
- what life and leisure in Latin America is like.

Key Terms
- malnutrition
- mosaic
- modernism
- extended family
- *fútbol*
- jai alai

Identify and Locate
Santo Domingo, Caracas, Rio de Janeiro, Brasília

The culture of Latin America is rooted in its history. Beginning with the Native Americans, each group that settled the region had an impact on cultural development. As the peoples intermingled, so did their cultures.

MOVEMENT

Religion

When the Spaniards and the Portuguese came to Latin America, they brought with them Roman Catholicism. Since then the Roman Catholic Church has had a strong influence in the region.

Roman Catholicism

During colonial times, Roman Catholicism was the official religion of the Spanish colonies and Brazil. Priests had come to the Americas with the conquistadors. Priests worked to convert Native Americans to Christianity, and when European settlers came, the priests saw to their spiritual needs as well.

Before long, church leaders were playing an important part in political affairs, and the Roman Catholic Church had become wealthy. When the fight for independence came, church leaders backed the European powers. This led some Latin Americans to question the

Latin America: Religions

Religion	Number
Roman Catholic	397,810,000
Protestant	16,930,000
Other Christian	12,676,000
Non-Christian	10,930,500
Nonreligious	19,990,000

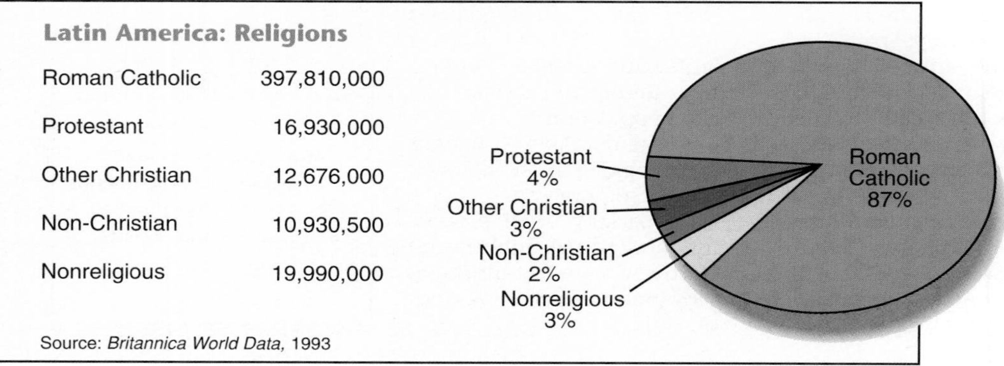

Source: *Britannica World Data,* 1993

Classroom Resources for Section 3

BLACKLINE MASTERS:
Reproducible Lesson Plan 9-3
Foods Around the World 2
World Literature Reading 2
Section Quiz 9-3

TRANSPARENCIES:
Section Focus Transparency 9-3
World Cultures Transparency 4

MULTIMEDIA:

Testmaker

***World Music:** Cultural Traditions, Lesson 2*

Picture Atlas of the World

Geographic Themes

Place: Guadalajara, Mexico

Nicknamed the "Pearl of the West," Guadalajara's modern buildings and colorful shops convey a sense of excitement and progress. *What are two areas of concern for the people of Latin America?*

Church's privileges and to work to reduce its power.

The Roman Catholic Church remains strong in Latin America today, but it does not have the influence it once did. Church leaders have shifted their support from the wealthy and powerful to the poor and oppressed. In recent years, the church has been active in movements for land reform and for improvements in education and health care.

Growth of Protestantism

Some of the Europeans who came to Latin America in the 1800s were Protestant. In time Protestant missionaries, primarily from the United States, came and built hospitals, schools, and colleges. After years of being a minority religion, in the 1960s Protestantism began to attract large numbers of Latin Americans. If Protestantism keeps growing at its current rate, many Latin Americans will be Protestants by the year 2000.

PLACE

Health Care and Education

Health care and education are two major areas of concern in Latin America. While advances have been made over the years, much remains to be done.

Health Care

Because of medical advances, better health care services, improved diets, and better sanitation, more Latin Americans are living longer. In addition more infants are surviving, and there are fewer epidemic diseases. Health care, however, is still poor in many rural and urban areas. In some places, **malnutrition**, poor nutrition because of badly balanced diet or not enough food, is a major problem. Many people do not have enough money to spend on the right kind of foods.

Cooperative Learning Activity

Describe Carnival, the five-day festival before Lent when Brazilians celebrate. Organize the class into groups and assign each group some aspect of Carnival. For example, have one group research the kinds of costumes worn during the festivities and have the members make masks to distribute. Have another group listen to *samba* music and learn some Latin American rhythms to play. Designate a part of a class period for Carnival and have the groups share what they have learned.

TEACH

GUIDED PRACTICE

Implement Foods Around the World 2 as a class activity.

INDEPENDENT PRACTICE

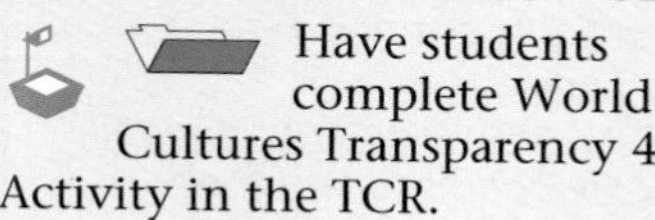

Have students complete World Cultures Transparency 4 Activity in the TCR.

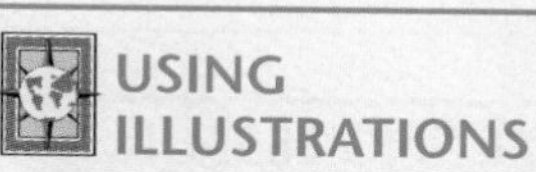

USING ILLUSTRATIONS

PLACE Guadalajara's most important industries include food processing, textiles, iron and steel, glass, and pottery.

Answer to Caption: *health care and education*

ASSESS

CHECK FOR UNDERSTANDING

Assign Section 3 Review as homework or an in-class activity.

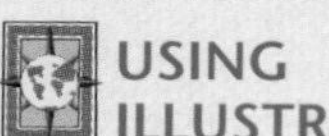

USING ILLUSTRATIONS

PLACE Isabel Allende, another Chilean author, wrote a Latin American version of *A Thousand and One Tales of the Arabian Nights* entitled *Eva Luna.*

Answer to Caption: *daily life and history of their countries*

MEETING LESSON OBJECTIVES

Each objective below is tested by the questions that follow it in parentheses.

1. **Name** the religions of Latin America. *(3)*
2. **Examine** health care and education in Latin America. *(4, 5)*
3. **Discuss** the arts of Latin America. *(1, 2)*
4. **Describe** life and leisure in Latin America. *(1)*

EVALUATE

Assign the Section 3 Quiz in the TCR.

Use the Testmaker to create a customized quiz for Section 3.

RETEACH

Have students complete Reteaching Activity 9 in the TCR.

ENRICH

Have students complete Enrichment Activity 9 in the TCR.

Educational Opportunities

Education in Latin America remains a challenge. The literacy rate is low in many countries, and there are too few schools and teachers. More than half the teachers, especially in rural areas, do not have teaching degrees. In addition, many children cannot go to school because their families need the money the children earn by working.

Latin American education, however, has improved in recent years. In the past, only the children of the wealthy went to school. Today all children can go for free for 12 years, and there are private schools for those who can afford them. Also, more children than ever before can read and write. In some countries the literacy rate has risen to more than 90 percent.

Students who pass special examinations can go on to colleges or universities. Institutions like the University of Santo Domingo and the Central University of Caracas provide higher education at little or no cost. Some students attend vocational and agricultural schools. Latin American leaders have encouraged students—as well as adults—to attend these schools.

Geographic Themes

Place: Mexico City, Mexico

Diego Rivera and other 20th-century Mexican artists painted murals that showed key events in Mexico's history. *What themes have been popular among modern Latin American artists and writers?*

PLACE

The Arts and Literature

For hundreds of years, the arts and literature of Latin America were dominated by European standards. Today's Latin American artists have developed unique styles, many of which reflect their diverse ethnic heritages.

Traditional Arts and Literature

Native Americans produced the earliest Latin American art forms. They left a legacy of weavings, wood carvings, pottery, and metalwork. They built temples decorated with colored murals and **mosaics**—pictures or designs made by setting small bits of colored stone, glass, or tile in mortar. Native Americans also created the region's earliest music and dance.

During colonial times, almost all arts were European-inspired. During this time, however, Africans brought to the region the rhythms, songs, and dances out of which calypso, reggae, and samba evolved.

Most colonial-era paintings had religious themes. Murals mixed the brightly colored abstract designs of the Native Americans with realistic European styles. Churches built in Spanish and Portuguese designs often were enlivened by the ethnic details added by Native American and African artists.

After independence, Latin American painters and composers began mixing European and Native American themes. In the late 1800s a literary movement known as **modernism** developed, in which writers and poets focused on artistic expression for its own sake.

Art and Literature

In the 1900s Mexican artists, such as Diego Rivera, began using art to educate. They created huge murals that combined modern forms with traditional Native American designs to present the daily life and history of their countries. Latin American writers also began to show more interest in social and political subjects.

During the last 50 years, Latin American artists and writers have become recognized in-

Meeting Special Needs

Reading Disability Even students with adequate decoding and sight skill development have reading comprehension problems. To assess students' ability to comprehend the section, do the following: Copy the last paragraph on page 187 but delete every sixth or seventh word that is not a Key Term. Distribute copies of the adjusted paragraph to the students and ask them to fill in the missing words. Those who provide the correct words, or synonyms, show good comprehension.

ternationally. The Brazilian architect Oscar Niemeyer, who designed many of the buildings in the Brazilian capital of Brasília, is known worldwide for his curved sculptures and his use of Native American designs in mosaics. Audiences in many countries have applauded the skillful footwork of dance companies like the Ballet Folklórico of Mexico, which performs traditional Native American and Spanish dances. Writers like Gabriela Mistral and Pablo Neruda of Chile, Octavio Paz of Mexico, Miguel Angel Asturias of Guatemala, and Gabriel García Márquez of Colombia have all won Nobel Prizes for Literature.

REGION

Life and Leisure

Latin Americans place great emphasis on social status and family life. They also cherish values, such as personal honor and individual freedom.

Way of Life

Latin Americans have a strong sense of family. Each person is part of an **extended family** that includes aunts, uncles, and other relatives besides parents and children. Life and most social events are often centered in the family and home. In Latin America a person's quality of life depends on his or her social class, nationality, and place of residence. A large gap exists between the lower class and the middle and upper classes, however.

Leisure Time and Celebrations

Latin Americans enjoy sports, especially ***fútbol,*** or soccer. In many South American countries, it is the national sport and a way of life. Latin Americans also appreciate baseball, basketball, and volleyball. A traditional favorite among many Mexicans and Cubans is **jai alai** (HY•LY), a fast-paced game much like handball that is played with a ball and a long curved basket that is strapped to a player's wrist.

Other Latin American pastimes are musical events, dances, the theater, movies, and parties. Most Latin Americans celebrate their independence days and religious holidays. The festival known as Carnival, for example, is celebrated just before the beginning of Lent, the Christian holy season that comes before Easter. The biggest Carnival is held each year in Rio de Janeiro, Brazil.

Geographic Themes

Place: Rio de Janeiro, Brazil

In Latin America, every village has some kind of soccer field, and the larger cities have stadiums. In Rio de Janeiro, the stadium can seat 220,000 fans. *What other competitive sports are popular in Latin America?*

SECTION 3 REVIEW

Checking for Understanding

1. **Define** malnutrition, mosaic, modernism, extended family, *fútbol*, jai alai.
2. **Locating Places** In what country did artists begin using art to educate?
3. **Region** What was the official religion of the Spanish colonies and Brazil?
4. **Place** Why is the literacy rate improving in some Latin American countries?

Critical Thinking

5. **Drawing Conclusions** How have medical advances affected population growth?

CLOSE

Challenge the class to write the name of a person, group, place, or sport from the section for each letter in the word *Latin America.*

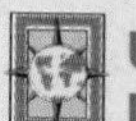

USING ILLUSTRATIONS

PLACE Latin American soccer teams have won 8 of the 15 World Cups.

Answer to Caption: *baseball, basketball, volleyball, and jai alai*

CURRICULUM CONNECTION

STATISTICS

College enrollment in Uruguay jumped from 9.9% in 1970 to 47.8% in the 1990s.

ANSWERS TO SECTION 3 REVIEW

1. **malnutrition:** poor nutrition; **mosaic:** picture or design made by setting bits of colored stone, glass, or tile into mortar; **modernism:** literary movement in which Latin American writers and poets called for art for art's sake; **extended family:** family that includes relatives in addition to parents and children; **fútbol:** soccer; **jai alai:** game played with a ball and a long curved basket
2. Mexico
3. Roman Catholicism
4. because free education is provided for all children
5. They have increased life expectancy and lowered infant mortality, resulting in a higher population growth rate.

Teaching Skills

TEACH

Have students follow these steps to create a population pyramid: 1) count the students in the class; 2) define several age groups, using six-month intervals if necessary; 3) count males and females in each age group; 4) calculate the percentage of each age and sex group; 5) convert the results into a population pyramid. Have students read the skill on page 190. Then ask: "What kinds of information do population pyramids reveal?" *(whether a population is increasing, decreasing, or remaining stable; whether there are mortality risks for certain age groups)*

Skills Practice For additional practice, have students complete Skill Activity 9 in the TCR.

MAP & GRAPH SKILLS

Interpreting a Population Pyramid

Demography is the study of population. Demographers measure population density (how many people live in a given area), distribution (where people live), and migration patterns (who is moving where). Demographers also illustrate age distribution by a **population pyramid.**

REVIEWING THE SKILL

A population pyramid is a bar graph that shows the percentages of males and females by age group. Its shape indicates whether the population is increasing or decreasing. If a population is growing, the pyramid is wider at the base because children will be more numerous than adults. If the graph appears almost rectangular, it indicates a stable population.

To interpret a population pyramid:

- Identify the age groups and percentages shown on the graph.
- Look for differences among males and females, and compare the various age groups.
- Use the data to draw conclusions about age distribution in the given countries.

PRACTICING THE SKILL

Use the graphs to answer the following questions:

1. What countries are shown in the graphs?
2. What percentage of Uruguay's male population is between the ages of 20–29?
3. What percentage of Cuba's total population is between the ages of 40–59?
4. Which country has a declining population?
5. In which country is there a greater percentage of older women than men?
6. Which country has the most even distribution of men and women?

For additional practice in this skill, see Practicing Skills on page 192 of the Chapter 9 Review.

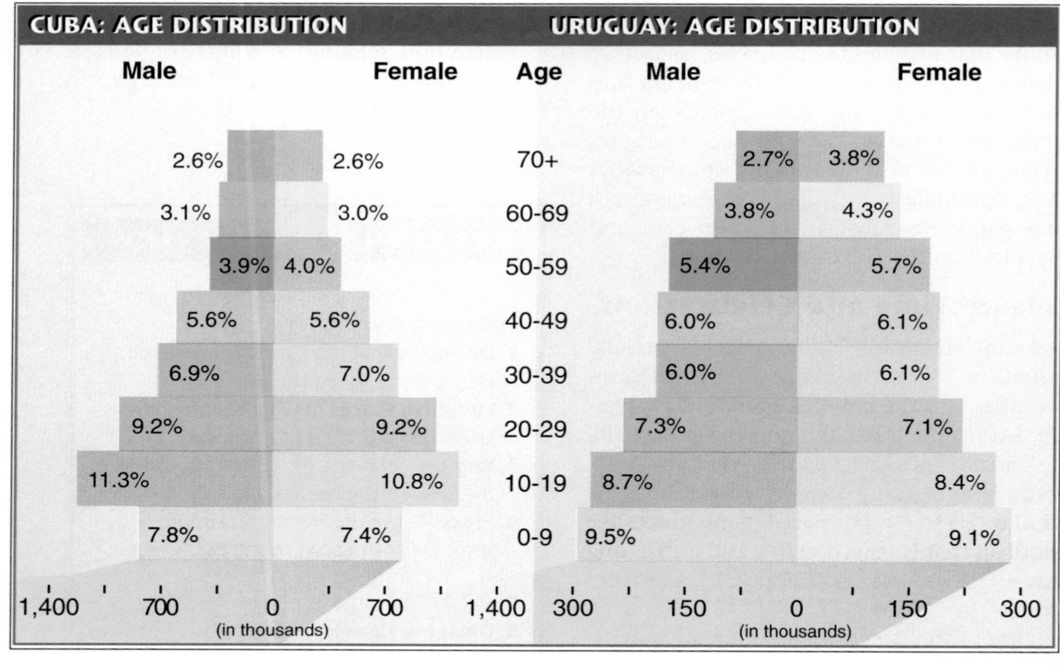

ANSWERS TO PRACTICING THE SKILL

1. Uruguay, Cuba
2. 7.3%
3. 19.1%
4. Cuba
5. Uruguay
6. Cuba

chapter 9

HIGHLIGHTS

SECTION 1 Population Patterns

Outdoor market in Mexico City

KEY TERMS

mestizos (p. 176)
mulatto (p. 176)
dialect (p. 177)
primate city (p. 179)

SUMMARY

- Latin America's ethnically diverse population includes Native Americans, Europeans, Africans, Asians, *mestizos,* and mulattoes.
- The Latin American population is not evenly distributed.
- Latin America's urban population has increased rapidly as people have moved from rural to urban areas.

SECTION 2 History and Government

Toussaint L'Ouverture, Latin American independence leader

KEY TERMS

chinampas (p. 181)
quipu (p. 182)
conquistador (p. 182)
viceroy (p. 182)
fazenda (p. 182)
caudillo (p. 184)

SUMMARY

- Maya, Aztec, and Inca built highly developed civilizations long before Europeans arrived in the Americas.
- Spain and Portugal controlled most of Latin America for more than 300 years.
- Most present-day leaders want a stable government and an improved quality of life for Latin Americans.

SECTION 3 Cultures and Lifestyles

Soccer fans in Rio de Janeiro's Marcana Stadium

KEY TERMS

malnutrition (p. 187)
mosaic (p. 188)
modernism (p. 188)
extended family (p. 189)
fútbol (p. 189)
jai alai (p. 189)

SUMMARY

- The major religion of Latin America, Roman Catholicism, was brought to the region by the Spaniards and the Portuguese.
- Many advances have been made in Latin America in health care and education.
- Arts and literature have become less European and more uniquely Latin American.
- Although social class, way of life, and leisure activities may differ, all Latin Americans have a strong sense of family.

CHAPTER 9 HIGHLIGHTS

USING THE CHAPTER 9 HIGHLIGHTS

Use the Chapter 9 Highlights to preview, review, condense, or reteach the chapter.

PREVIEW/REVIEW

Vocabulary PuzzleMaker Software reinforces the Key Terms used in Chapter 9.

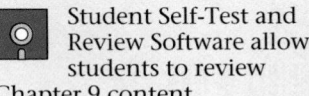

Student Self-Test and Review Software allows students to review Chapter 9 content.

CONDENSE

Have students read the Chapter 9 Highlights.

Have students listen to the Chapter 9 Audiocassettes in the TCR. Spanish Audiocassettes are also available.

Assign the Chapter 9 Audiocassette Activity and give students the Chapter 9 Audiocassette Quiz.

Have students complete the Guided Reading Activities for Chapter 9 in the TCR. Spanish Guided Reading Activities are also available.

RETEACH

Have students complete Reteaching Activity 9 in the TCR. Spanish Reteaching Activities are also available.

Map Activity

Identify and Locate On the chalkboard, copy the following names from the chapter. Do not include the country names in parentheses.

A. Francois Toussaint L'Ouverture *(Haiti)*
B. Simón Bolívar *(Venezuela)*
C. José de San Martín *(Argentina)*
D. Diego Rivera *(Mexico)*
E. Oscar Niemeyer *(Brazil)*
F. Gabriela Mistral *(Chile)*
G. Pablo Neruda *(Chile)*
H. Octavio Paz *(Mexico)*
I. Miguel Angel Asturias *(Guatemala)*
J. Gabriel García Márquez *(Colombia)*

On pages 23 and 25 of the Outline Map Resource Book, have students label the country connected with each name and write the letter of the name on the country. Refer students to the chapter for help.

GLENCOE TECHNOLOGY

Videodisc

Use Chapter 9 MindJogger Videoquiz to review students' knowledge before administering the Chapter 9 Test.

MINDJOGGER VIDEOQUIZ

Chapter 9
Disc 2 Side A

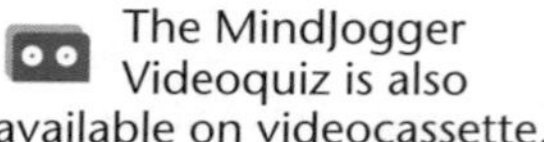

The MindJogger Videoquiz is also available on videocassette.

chapter 9 REVIEW

Reviewing Key Terms

Choose the vocabulary term that best completes each of the sentences below. Write your answers on a separate sheet of paper.

mestizos (p. 176)
mulattoes (p. 176)
primate city (p. 179)
quipu (p. 182)
conquistadors (p. 182)
caudillos (p. 184)
mosaics (p. 188)
extended family (p. 189)
jai alai (p. 189)

Section 1

1. People of mixed African and European ancestry are known as ____ .
2. A ____ dominates a country's economy, culture, and government.
3. People of mixed Native American and European ancestry are known as ____ .

Section 2

4. The Inca used a rope with knotted cords called a ____ .
5. The Aztec and Inca empires were conquered by Spanish ____ .
6. In the 1800s many Latin Americans were ruled by dictators called ____ .

Section 3

7. ____ is a game like handball enjoyed by Cubans and Mexicans.
8. An ____ includes relatives other than a husband, wife, and children.
9. Pictures made from small bits of colored glass set in mortar are called ____ .

Reviewing Facts

Section 1

10. What is the official language of more than one-half of Latin America?
11. Why are most Caribbean countries so densely populated?

Section 2

12. What was the Aztec capital?
13. What was the only independent South American country to choose monarchy?

Section 3

14. What are some problems associated with education in Latin America?
15. Who created the earliest dance and music of Latin America?

Critical Thinking

16. **Expressing Problems Clearly** What has been the effect of the migration to cities of large numbers of rural people?
17. **Determining Cause and Effect** What problems did the leaders of the newly independent Latin Americans encounter?
18. **Predicting Consequences** How might the Catholic Church in Latin America be affected if Protestantism continues to grow rapidly?

Geographic Themes

19. **Movement** From where did most of the early settlers of Latin America come?
20. **Region** What European nation controlled most of Latin America?
21. **Place** Where and when is the largest Carnival celebration of Latin America?

Practicing Skills

Interpreting a Population Pyramid

Refer to the population pyramids on page 190.

22. In Uruguay, at what age do women begin to outnumber men by at least 0.3 percent? What is the difference in percentage at age 70+?
23. In each country, what is the largest age group?

ANSWERS

Reviewing Key Terms

1. mulattoes
2. primate city
3. *mestizos*
4. *quipu*
5. *conquistadors*
6. *caudillos*
7. jai alai
8. extended family
9. mosaics

Reviewing Facts

10. Spanish
11. Caribbean islands are small, have areas unsuitable for living or farming, and have a high birthrate.
12. Tenochtitlán
13. Brazil
14. too few schools and teachers, teachers without teaching degrees, children who cannot attend school because they have to work to support their families
15. Native Americans

Critical Thinking

16. overcrowded cities that cannot supply services for all their people, high unemployment, and the breakup of extended families
17. political control in the hands of a wealthy few, army officers, and clergy; barriers to trade and communications, such as mountains and the huge size of countries
18. Answers will vary but should point out that Roman Catholicism will lose even more of its influence in Latin America

Geographic Themes

19. Spain and Portugal
20. Spain
21. Rio de Janeiro, Brazil, just before Lent

Using the Unit Atlas

Refer to the cultural geography section of the Unit Atlas on pages 152–153.

24. Where are the uninhabited areas of Latin America?

25. What is the official language of Brazil? Of Belize?

Projects

Individual Activity

Select a Latin American writer, painter, architect, or some other type of artist. Research several of his or her best known works. Write a two-paragraph overview of the most important features of his or her work.

Cooperative Learning Activity

Working in groups of three, research one of the major early civilizations of Latin America. Find information about the following: the area in which the civilization developed; how government and society were organized; and why the civilization declined. Working as a group, prepare a chart comparing the three civilizations.

Writing About Geography

Description

Select one Latin American city, and imagine that you are a member of a committee organized to attract tourists to that city. Be sure to check your journal for notes or comments about the city you select. Write a travel brochure or visitor's guide for the city that will accomplish the committee's goal.

Locating Places

LATIN AMERICA: POLITICAL GEOGRAPHY

Match the letters on the map with the places and physical features of Latin America. Write your answers on a separate sheet of paper.

1. Mexico City
2. Lima
3. Port-au-Prince
4. Montevideo
5. Havana
6. La Paz, Sucre
7. Quito
8. Brasília
9. Buenos Aires
10. Bogota
11. Santiago
12. Caracas

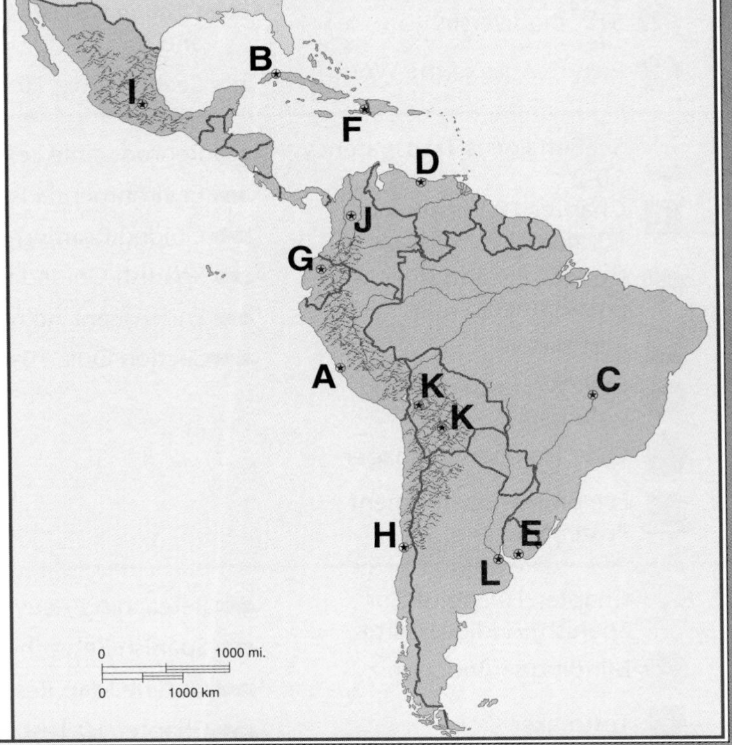

Chapter 9 Review

Practicing Skills

22. 50–59; at 70+ women outnumber men by 1.1 percent

23. Uruguay: 0–9 years; Cuba: 10–19 years

Using the Unit Atlas

24. southwestern corner of Bolivia, northwestern and southernmost corners of Argentina

25. Portuguese; English

Locating Places

1. I
2. A
3. F
4. E
5. B
6. K
7. G
8. C
9. L
10. J
11. H
12. D

Chapter Bonus Test Question

This question may be used for extra credit on the chapter test.

What measures would best prepare Latin American peasants for a move to a city?

(Answer: practicing a skill and learning to read and write)

CHAPTER 10

PLANNING GUIDE
Latin America Today

CHAPTER ORGANIZER

Daily Lesson Objectives	Multimedia	Teacher Classroom Resources
SECTION 1 Living in Latin America 1. Investigate agriculture and industry in Latin America. 2. Summarize the role of trade and interdependence in Latin America. 3. Describe the transportation and communications systems of Latin America.	Section Focus Transparency 10-1 Unit Map Overlay Transparencies 3-4, 3-5 Testmaker Reuters Issues in Geography STV: Rain Forest STV: Biodiversity Picture Atlas of the World	Reproducible Lesson Plan 10-1 Guided Reading Activity 10-1 Spanish Guided Reading Activity 10-1 Performance Assessment 10 Chapter 10 Vocabulary Activity Spanish Chapter 10 Vocabulary Activity Outline Map Resource Book, pp. 23 and 25 Section Quiz 10-1
SECTION 2 People and Their Environment 1. Explain how human development of the Amazon River basin has impacted the environment. 2. Recognize the major challenges that have accompanied rapid urban growth in Latin America and possible solutions for them.	Section Focus Transparency 10-2 Chapter 10 Vocabulary PuzzleMaker Software Geography and the Environment Testmaker STV: World Geography, Volume 3 GTV: Planetary Manager Eye on the Environment Poster Series	Reproducible Lesson Plan 10-2 Environmental Issue 3 Guided Reading Activity 10-2 Spanish Guided Reading Activity 10-2 Enrichment Activity 10 Section Quiz 10-2
CHAPTER REVIEW AND EVALUATION	Chapter 10 English (or Spanish) Audiocassettes MindJogger Videoquiz Testmaker Student Self-Test and Review Software	Reteaching Activity 10 Spanish Reteaching Activity 10 Outline Map Resource Book, p. 25 Chapter 10 Test Form A and Form B

0:00 *If time does not permit teaching the entire chapter, summarize using the Chapter 10 Highlights on page 207, and Chapter 10 English (or Spanish) Audiocassettes. Review students' knowledge using the Glencoe MindJogger Videoquiz.*

KEY TO ABILITY LEVELS

Teaching strategies have been coded for varying learning styles and abilities.

L1 **BASIC** activities for all students

L2 **AVERAGE** activities for average to above-average students

L3 **CHALLENGING** activities for above-average students

LEP **LIMITED ENGLISH PROFICIENCY** activities

Performance Assessment

Conflict over the Environment Economic developers and environmentalists take opposing sides over the issue of deforestation in Latin America. Organize the class into two groups, and hold a debate in which one group represents the developers and the other group the environmentalists. Each group should present the most current information on the position of the side it represents. To organize the material, portfolios can be created that include newspaper articles, letters from advocates or opponents, magazine or library sources, laser disc or CD-ROM material, or other appropriate documentation. Each side may choose spokespersons, but all students must have roles in preparing for the debate. When the debate has concluded, all students should write on each of the following topics:

(1) What were the most convincing arguments for both your side and your opponent?
(2) What is your position regarding this power struggle?

POSSIBLE RUBRIC FEATURES: Content information, concept attainment, persuasive skills, research skills, communication skills, organizational and collaborative skills

For additional professional and classroom resources, see Chapter Resources, pages T46–T51.

TEACHER'S CORNER

INDEX TO NATIONAL GEOGRAPHIC MAGAZINE

The following articles may be used for research relating to this chapter:

- "Rain Forest Canopy: The High Frontier," by Edward O. Wilson, December 1991.
- "Coca: An Ancient Indian Herb Turns Deadly," by Peter T. White, January 1989.
- "Last Days of Eden: Rondônia's Urveu-Wau-Wau Indians," by Loren McIntyre, December 1988.
- "Rondônia's Settlers Invade Brazil's Imperiled Rain Forest," by William S. Ellis, December 1988.
- "Rain Forests: Nature's Dwindling Treasures," by Peter T. White, January 1983.
- "The Incredible Potato," by Robert E. Rhoades, May 1982.

NATIONAL GEOGRAPHIC SOCIETY PRODUCTS AVAILABLE FROM GLENCOE

To order the following products for use with this chapter, contact your local Glencoe sales representative or call Glencoe at 1-800-334-7344:

- *Picture Atlas of the World* (CD-ROM)
- *STV: North America* (Videodisc)
- *STV: World Geography, South America and Antarctica* (Videodisc)
- *STV: Rain Forest* (Videodisc)
- *ZipZapMap! World* (Software)
- *GeoBee* (Software)
- *Images of the World* (Posters)
- *Eye on the Environment* (Posters)
- *Physical Geography of the World* (Transparencies)
- *Picture Atlas of Our 50 States* (Book)

ADDITIONAL NATIONAL GEOGRAPHIC SOCIETY PRODUCTS

To order the following products for use with this chapter, call National Geographic Society at 1-800-368-2728:

- *Rain Forest* (Video)

Introducing CHAPTER 10

PERFORMANCE ASSESSMENT

Refer to the Planning Guide on page 194B for a Performance Assessment Activity for this chapter. See the *Performance Assessment Activities* booklet for additional suggestions.

CHAPTER OBJECTIVES

1. **Understand** that most nations of Latin America are increasing their efforts to modernize and industrialize.
2. **Specify** ways that the development of resources in the Amazon River basin has seriously affected the environment of the area.

GLENCOE TECHNOLOGY

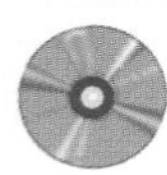

Videodisc

Use Chapter 10 MindJogger Videoquiz to preview chapter content.

MINDJOGGER VIDEOQUIZ

Chapter 10
Disc 2 Side A

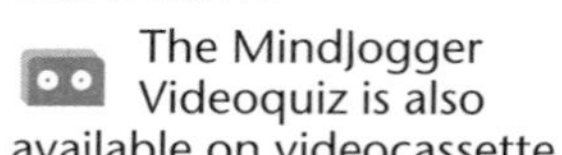

The MindJogger Videoquiz is also available on videocassette.

NATIONAL GEOGRAPHIC SOCIETY

CD-ROM

PICTURE ATLAS OF THE WORLD

You and your students can learn about the economies of Latin American countries by clicking the "Stats" button of selected countries.

chapter 10 Latin America Today

CHAPTER FOCUS

Geographic Setting

In many areas of Latin America, vegetation and landforms, such as tropical rain forests and steep mountains, create natural barriers to the movement of people and goods.

Geographic Themes

Section 1 Living in Latin America

REGION Most nations of Latin America are increasing their efforts to modernize and industrialize.

Section 2 People and Their Environment

HUMAN/ENVIRONMENT INTERACTION The development of resources in the Amazon River basin has seriously affected the environment of the area.

▲ Photograph: *Skyline of Caracus, Venezuela*

EXTRA CREDIT PROJECT

Environmental Issues Have volunteers assess where on the school grounds trees are needed, and then have them ask school authorities for permission to plant some. Encourage the class to raise funds to buy saplings. After the students have raised enough money, you might take them to a nursery to select the trees. Have nursery workers plant the trees, but allow the class to plan and attend a "ground breaking" ceremony.

SECTION 1 Living in Latin America

SETTING THE SCENE

Read to Discover . . .

- the status of agriculture and industry in Latin America.
- the role of trade and interdependence in Latin America.
- the transportation and communications systems of Latin America.

Key Terms

- developing country
- export
- cash crop
- *campesinos*
- *latifundia*
- *minifundia*
- service industry
- *maquiladoras*

Identify and Locate

Brazil, Mexico, Costa Rica, Argentina, Chile, Ciudad Juárez, Rio Grande, Manaus, Isthmus of Panama, Bogotá, Lima, Santiago

Kingston, Jamaica

I live in Jamaica, where tourism plays a big part in the economy. The Jamaican dollar is very weak against the American dollar. While this is good for tourists, it isn't so good for people who live here.

Christine Bennett

JAMAICA $5 Strombus gallus Rooster Tail Conch

Christine Bennett from the Caribbean island of Jamaica describes one of the many problems of economic development. Latin America consists largely of **developing countries,** countries in the process of becoming industrialized. Most Latin American countries, however, are moving slowly toward this goal.

HUMAN/ENVIRONMENT INTERACTION

Agriculture

The economies of many Latin American countries are based on agriculture. Most of what Latin Americans **export,** or send to other countries for sale or trade, comes from the land.

Cash Crops and Livestock

Coffee is an example of a **cash crop,** a crop produced to sell or trade. Brazil, Colombia, Mexico, and El Salvador rank among the world's leading coffee producers. This is largely because they have the fertile volcanic slopes and warm moist climate in which coffee trees thrive.

Because tropical coastal areas are well-suited for growing bananas, Central America, along with Cuba, Jamaica, Brazil, and Ecuador, produce much of the world's bananas. Cuba and Brazil also are among the world's leaders in the production of sugarcane, the most

LESSON PLAN
Chapter 10, Section 1

FOCUS

SECTION OBJECTIVES

1. **Investigate** the status of agriculture and industry in Latin America.
2. **Summarize** the role of trade and interdependence in Latin America.
3. **Describe** the transportation and communications systems of Latin America.

ABOUT THE POSTCARD

Christine tells us that there are many ways to travel in her country—by car, bus, or the most popular method—minibus.

BELLRINGER MOTIVATIONAL ACTIVITY

Project the Section 1 Focus Transparency and have students answer the questions.

PRETEACHING VOCABULARY

Explain that *export* comes from the Latin word for "to carry out" and have students hypothesize about what kinds of goods exports are. *(those shipped out of the country)*

Use the Vocabulary PuzzleMaker Software to create a crossword or word search puzzle.

Classroom Resources for Section 1

BLACKLINE MASTERS:
Reproducible Lesson Plan 10-1
Guided Reading Activity 10-1
Performance Assessment Activity 10
Outline Map Resource Book, pp. 23 and 25
Section Quiz 10-1

TRANSPARENCIES:
Section Focus Transparency 10-1
Political Map Transparency 3
Unit Map Overlay Transparencies 3-4 and 3-5

MULTIMEDIA:
Vocabulary PuzzleMaker Software
Testmaker

STV: Rainforest
STV: Biodiversity
Reuters Issues in Geography

Picture Atlas of the World

TEACH

GUIDED PRACTICE

L1 Making Maps Have a student read aloud the material under "Roads and Railroads" and "Inland Waterways" as other students draw the general routes of highways and waterways described in the reading on Unit Map Overlay Transparency 3-4. After students finish, place Unit Map Overlay Transparency 3-5 atop the first transparency to show the physical barriers that the routes go through or circumvent.

USING ILLUSTRATIONS

HUMAN/ENVIRONMENT INTERACTION In addition to coffee, bananas and cut flowers also earn export dollars for Colombia.

Answer to Caption: *Coffee thrives on the fertile volcanic slopes and in the warm moist climate.*

MULTICULTURAL PERSPECTIVE

Cultural Heritage
During the late 1800s, profits from Brazil's booming international rubber trade helped build the city of Manaus in the Amazon rain forest. Today, the city's opera house and other historic buildings are national architectural treasures.

Geographic Themes
Human/Environment Interaction: Andes, Colombia
Many farmers in the foothills of the Andes of western Colombia grow coffee, Colombia's major crop. *Why is coffee a major crop in countries such as Colombia, Brazil, Mexico, and El Salvador?*

important agricultural product in the Caribbean.

Some Latin American countries have based their entire economy on a single crop. Honduras, for example, relies on bananas. Cuba depends largely on sugarcane. Specializing in one crop often puts the national economy at risk. For example, if drought or disease seriously damages the crop, the country's entire economy can be severely affected. In addition, if a country uses most of its farmland to grow just one cash crop, little land is left to grow the food crops needed to feed the population.

Some Latin American countries have much grazing land on which to raise livestock. Argentina, Mexico, and Brazil are among the world's leaders in cattle production. Beef is also a major export of Costa Rica, Paraguay, and Uruguay.

Latifundia and Minifundia

In the past many Latin Americans lived and worked in the countryside. Now only about one-third of the people are ***campesinos,*** people who live and work in rural areas.

The farms on which these people work often are divided into two classes. One is ***latifundia,*** large estates owned by families or corporations. The other class of farm is ***minifundia,*** small farms that produce food chiefly for family use and the local market.

Whether campesinos own or work small plots of land or labor on the large landholdings of the wealthy, almost all are poor. Among the poorest are the Native Americans who live in places like the *Altiplano* where the soil is poor and the climate unfavorable. Their crops generally are staples like beans, corn, potatoes, and cassavas, plants whose large root supplies the starch used to make tapioca.

HUMAN/ENVIRONMENT INTERACTION

Industry

Most Latin American countries recognize the need to modernize and industrialize. Some, however, are moving faster than others. In many countries, **service industries,** enterprises such as banking that provide services rather than goods, have grown sharply in the last 25 years.

Industrial Progress

One Latin American country that has made great progress in recent years is Mexico. Among the goods produced in Mexico are motor vehicles, electrical goods, and processed foods. Over the last 50 years, American and other foreign firms have set up manufacturing plants in Mexican cities close to the Mexican-American border to take advantage of low-cost labor.

One such city is Ciudad Juárez, which lies across the Rio Grande from El Paso, Texas. To-

Cooperative Learning Activity

Have a group of students create a board game about Latin American industry, trade, transportation, and communications. Tell them that the players are international business people and that the board represents the path to profits with windfalls and pitfalls along the way. For example, one square might read: *You buy copper in Peru for a song but lose time transporting it across unpaved roads. Miss a turn.* Another space might read: *The North Dakota sugar beet crop fails, and the profits at your Caribbean sugar refinery go sky high. Collect $200.* Tell the students to get their facts from Section 1 and other sources about Latin America. Have artistic students design "funny money" for the game, and make enough copies to supply four players.

gether these cities' factories, known as ***maquiladoras,*** employ a large number of Mexicans. Unlike many other Latin American countries, Mexico has a large workforce, well-developed power sources and transportation networks, and abundant natural resources. These advantages, combined with a stable government, an involved business community, and foreign investors, have made industrial expansion possible.

Brazil, like Mexico, has increased its industrial production in recent years. It is a major producer of iron and steel, automobiles, textiles, cement, paper, machinery, chemicals, airplanes, processed food, and electrical goods. Also like Mexico, Brazil has profited from plentiful natural resources, a large workforce, well-developed power sources, and a government that has worked to promote industrial growth.

Both Mexico and Brazil produce handicrafts—jewelry, baskets, rugs. Other leading manufacturers of such items are Venezuela and Argentina. Argentina processes and packages meat and other foods and produces textiles, electrical equipment, automobiles, and railroad cars. Chile, Costa Rica, Nicaragua, and Bolivia all produce foods and textiles. Bolivia also mines and refines tin. For most Caribbean nations, sugar refining is a leading industry.

LATIN AMERICA: ECONOMIC ACTIVITY

110°W 85°W 60°W 35°W
Tropic of Cancer
20°N
N
0° Equator
20°S Tropic of Capricorn
40°S
0 1000 mi.
0 1000 km

- Forestry
- Livestock raising
- Commercial farming
- Subsistence farming
- Manufacturing and trade
- Commercial fishing
- Little or no activity

Goode's Interrupted Homolosine projection

FOCUS ON GEOGRAPHIC THEMES

1. **Place:** What are the leading economic activities in Mexico?
2. **Human/Environment Interaction:** What natural resource promotes manufacturing in Venezuela?
3. **Region:** What areas have little or no economic activity?

Industrial Development

Latin American countries have not been able to industrialize more rapidly for a variety of reasons. Factories and machinery cost money—money that many Latin American countries do not have. Some countries, like Mexico, have been able to attract foreign investment. Foreign investors, however, are reluctant to provide funds to a country whose government appears unstable or that has political problems. Investors are afraid that if something happens to the government, they will lose their investment.

Industry requires skilled workers—engineers, scientists, technicians. Industry also requires certain kinds of raw materials and natural resources, including energy resources. Many countries of Latin America do not have the necessary trained workers, materials, or resources.

MOVEMENT

Trade and Interdependence

Few Latin American countries manufacture enough goods or grow enough food to satisfy all the needs of their people. As a result, they must trade with other countries—many of which are outside of the region.

Much of the interdependence that exists between Latin American countries and nations outside the region is a result of Latin America's desire to industrialize. Industrialization has made much of the region dependent on imported goods, raw materials, technology,

INDEPENDENT PRACTICE

Guided Reading Have students complete Guided Reading Activity 10-1 in the TCR. **LEP**

Have students complete Performance Assessment Activity 10 in the TCR.

L2 Creating a Newspaper Ask students to sum up news stories about Latin American economies and to compile the rewritten stories in a "newspaper."

USING MAPS

Answers: **1.** livestock raising and subsistence farming; **2.** oil; **3.** northern and southern Chile, southwestern Bolivia, and west central Paraguay

Map Skills Practice

Reading a Map What characteristics of developing countries are evident in many Latin American nations? *(little manufacturing and much subsistence farming)*

CURRICULUM CONNECTION

MATH

In November 1993, United States tourists in South America figured out what they could afford by multiplying each Argentine peso times $1.04 in United States dollars, each Bolivian quetzal times $.18, and each Venezuelan bolivar times $.01.

Meeting Special Needs

Inefficient Readers Students often profit by using a form of rapid reading called scanning to locate specific information. Tell the students to use scanning to find all the products of Latin America named in Section 1. Take your finger and model the scanning procedure by sliding your finger down the middle of the column rapidly. Demonstrate finding the names of Latin American products under "Industrial Progress": iron and steel, chemicals, motor vehicles, electrical goods, textiles, processed foods, automobiles, cement, paper, jewelry, airplanes, baskets, rugs, processed and packaged meat, railroad cars, tin, and refined sugar.

USING ILLUSTRATIONS

MOVEMENT The Andes make Peruvian highways and railways very scenic.

Answer to Caption: *Pan-American Highway*

ASSESS

CHECK FOR UNDERSTANDING

Assign Section 1 Review as homework or an in-class activity.

MEETING LESSON OBJECTIVES

Each objective below is tested by the questions that follow it in parentheses.

1. Investigate the status of agriculture and industry in Latin America. *(1, 2, 3, 5)*

2. Summarize the role of trade and interdependence in Latin America. *(3)*

3. Describe the transportation and communications systems of Latin America. *(4)*

EVALUATE

Assign the Section 1 Quiz in the TCR.

Use the Testmaker to create a customized quiz for Section 1.

Geographic Themes

Movement: Trans-Andean Highway, Peru

The Trans-Andean Highway connects Lima, the capital of Peru, to Chile through the Andes. *What major highway in Latin America extends from Mexico to Chile?*

and foreign capital. This dependence has created large foreign debts.

MOVEMENT

Transportation and Communications

Transportation and communications systems in Latin America are not highly developed outside of urban areas. This is largely because of cost and physical barriers—rugged terrain, dense vegetation, and mountains.

Roads and Railroads

In Latin America the building of good roads and railroads has been difficult and slow. In South America, for example, the Andes are a formidable barrier. In Central America, because of dense vegetation near the Caribbean coast and highland areas in the interior, very few roads run east and west.

Some nations have networks of modern highways. Argentina, for example, has one of the better-developed highway systems in South America. Mexico also has a large number of modern highways known as *autopistas*. Most other countries, however, do not have roads like these. In Brazil, for example, less than 10 percent of the roads are paved. A new series of roads known as the Trans-Amazonian Highway, however, is under construction in Brazil. One of the main purposes of the project is to stimulate the development of the Amazon River basin.

The major road system of Latin America is the Pan-American Highway. This network of roadways stretches from northern Mexico to southern Chile, linking the capitals of 17 Latin American nations.

In some Latin American countries, excellent railway networks compensate in part for poor roads. Mexico, Guatemala, Argentina, Panama, and Brazil have well-developed railroad networks. In most of the Caribbean countries, however, railway systems are inadequate for the needs of local economies and populations.

Inland Waterways

In some parts of Latin America, inland waterways provide the only means of transportation. The Plata river system formed by the Paraná, Paraguay, and Uruguay rivers, for example, helps link Buenos Aires and northeastern Argentina with Paraguay, Uruguay, and Brazil.

A major natural waterway exists in the Amazon River basin. Thick vegetation and swamps in the basin often make overland travel difficult. The Amazon River and its tributaries, however, provide a natural waterway on which people and goods can be transported.

The Panama Canal is another important waterway, but it is not a natural one. Built in the early 1900s, it crosses the Isthmus of Panama, making it possible for ships to travel between the Atlantic Ocean and Pacific Ocean without having to go around the southern tip of South America.

Air Travel

In recent years, airplanes and air travel have become increasingly important in Latin America. Airplanes can go where roads and railroads often cannot. Airplanes provide a fast and efficient means of travel over rough ter-

Critical Thinking

Making Comparisons On the chalkboard, copy the following profile of United States transportation and communications: 173,903 miles of railroads; 187 million motor vehicles; 834 airports with scheduled flights; one television per 1.3 persons; two radios per one person; one telephone per 1.9 persons; 255 newspapers per 1,000 people. Have volunteers read aloud similar statistics for Latin American countries from a world almanac. Then ask students to compare these figures with those for the United States and to hypothesize about how the differences in transportation and communications cause differences in the economies of the United States and Latin America.

rain, dense vegetation, and mountains that cover many areas of the region.

Brazil, Argentina, and Mexico are among the world's leading countries in numbers of airports. Bogotá, Lima, Santiago, Buenos Aires, São Paulo, and Rio de Janeiro all have major airports that serve both domestic and international airlines. The busiest airport in the entire region, however, is Mexico City's International Airport. More than 10 million passengers pass through it each year.

Communications

The same dense vegetation and rough terrain that have made it so difficult to build roads and railroads in much of Latin America have also slowed the development of communications networks.

Millions of people in Latin America use telephones to communicate with others. Yet many countries in the region do not have the funds to buy the equipment needed to build modern telephone systems. Even in wealthier countries like Brazil, Mexico, Argentina, and Venezuela, many people do not own telephones. In fact, for every 100 people, there are only about 5 to 10 telephones. In some poorer nations, such as Haiti, there may be only one telephone for every 79 persons.

Many countries are trying to improve their communications systems by building more and better radio and television stations and making greater use of international telecommunications satellites. Every country in Latin America has at least one radio station. However, not every nation has its own television station. And not every household or family owns a television set. Currently, there is approximately 1 television for every 10 people in Latin America.

Newspapers are a major means of communication. About one-seventh of the world's daily newspapers are published in Latin America. Most of these are printed in Brazil, Mexico, and Argentina. Latin America also publishes about 5 percent of the world's books each year, mostly in the Spanish or Portuguese language.

Geographic Themes

Movement: Bermuda
Millions of tourists visit Bermuda and the Caribbean countries each year to enjoy the pleasant climate and the beautiful beaches. *How has transportation aided tourism?*

Section 1 Review

Checking for Understanding

1. **Define** developing country, export, cash crop, *campesinos, latifundia, minifundia,* service industry, *maquiladoras.*
2. **Locating Places** What Latin American countries rank among the world's leading coffee producers?
3. **Human/Environment Interaction** What factors have made industrial expansion possible in Mexico?
4. **Movement** What is the major road system of Latin America? Where is it located?

Critical Thinking

5. **Making Comparisons** What do *latifundia* and *minifundia* have in common?

RETEACH

Have students find each place name under "Identify and Locate" in Section 1, locate it on pages 23 and 25 of the Outline Map Resource Book, and sum up why that place is significant.

ENRICH

Display a large picture of an area of rain forest. Then have students isolate and try to identify plant and animal species in the picture.

CLOSE

Have students write Christine Bennett a postcard describing tourism in their country.

USING ILLUSTRATIONS

MOVEMENT Another Caribbean country that depends on tourism is the Bahamas.

Answer to Caption: *International airlines bring tourists to Latin America.*

DID YOU KNOW?

Many Hondurans communicate by placing messages on the radio. Only major cities in Honduras have telephones while most towns have one public telephone and a telegraph office.

ANSWERS TO SECTION 1 REVIEW

1. **developing country:** country being industrialized; **export:** goods sent to other countries; **cash crop:** crop for sale or trade; ***campesinos:*** rural workers; ***latifundia:*** large estates; ***minifundia:*** small farms; **service industry:** a business that provides services; ***maquiladoras:*** foreign-owned factories in Mexico near the U.S. border
2. Brazil, Colombia, Mexico, El Salvador
3. A large workforce, developed power sources and transportation, abundant resources, stable government, an involved business community, and foreign investors
4. Pan-American Highway; from Mexico to Chile
5. Both are farms. ***Latifundia*** produce food for profit; ***munifundia*** produce only enough food for a family or local market.

FOCUS

Write the following question on the chalkboard: What does the loss of the world's rain forests mean to you? Have students jot down their thoughts in their journals. Allow volunteers to share their answers.

TEACH

L1 Location Use Unit Map Overlay Transparency 3-2 to familiarize students with the location of the Costa Rican rain forests.

L2 Debate Show the videos about the rain forest. Ask students to debate which video best presents the case for the rain forests.

GLENCOE TECHNOLOGY

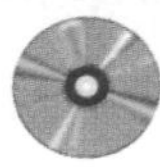

Videodisc

REUTERS ISSUES IN GEOGRAPHY

Chapter 2
Disc 1 Side A

Title: ***Latin America: The Disappearing Rain Forests***
Subject: The complex issues surrounding the rain forests of Latin America

NATIONAL GEOGRAPHIC SOCIETY

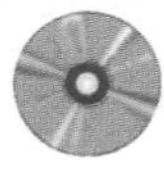

Videodisc

STV: RAIN FOREST

Side 1, Chapter 1
Frames 00002-08879
Title: ***Introduction*** **(in its entirety)**
Subject: Introduction to climatic conditions and animals of the rain forest

RAIN FORESTS FOR FARMLANDS

I think the whole planet is caught in this problem. If we want to make it to the 21st century, we need to find the other frontier—efficiency and sustainable development.

Alvaro Ugalde, former head of the Costa Rican Park Service

In the late 1970s, the tiny Latin American country of Costa Rica suddenly found itself faced with disaster. Studies showed that the country's three major industries—cattle ranching, lumbering, and farming—had depleted the nation's rain forests by almost half.

THE ISSUE

To feed its people, create industries, and raise money to repay foreign debts, Costa Rica sold parcels of land to cattle ranchers and farmers. The ranchers and farmers cleared thousands of acres of land, selling the felled trees for lumber.

"Clearing the land" in Costa Rica, however, meant chopping down the lush evergreens that are the mainstay of the country's rain forests.

THE BACKGROUND

In 1940, evergreen rain forests covered between 65 and 80 percent of Costa Rica. In the early 1960s, however, a growing population began cutting into the forests to clear land for cattle ranches. Also in the late 1960s, the Costa Rican government began to sell small lots of rain forest land. People who wanted to farm could buy the lots at low prices. For the most part, the country's forestry laws allowed the new land owners to cut down any tree on their property.

The logging industry also expanded, buying and towing the felled trees to sawmills. They sold the cut lumber to builders and exported it.

By the early 1980s, Costa Rica had lost almost half of its rain forests and was rapidly losing its soil.

Without the trees' root systems to hold the soil in place, or the trees' canopy overhead, the soil was eroding or being baked hard by the sun.

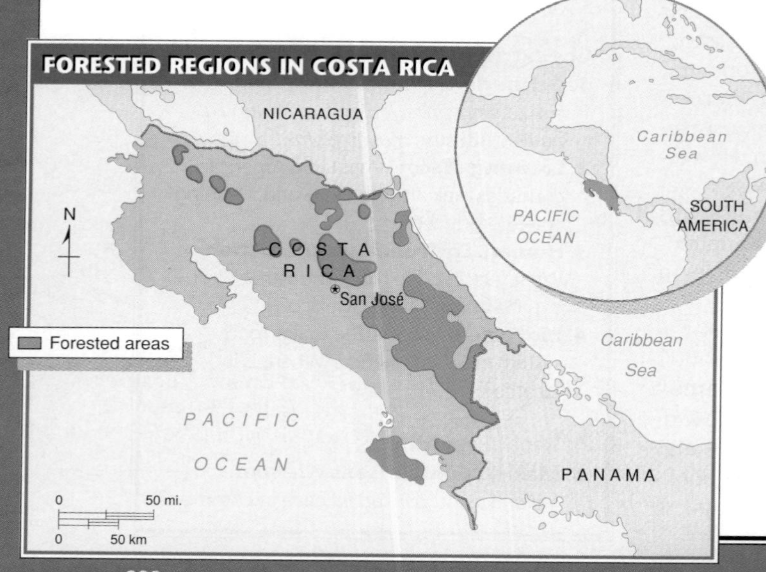

THE POINTS OF VIEW

Conservationists demanded that the remaining forests receive government protection as parks and preserves. They pointed out that more than 600 tons of soil per acre (about

Extending the Content

Interdependence In the early 1960s, American fast food chains needed a cheap source of beef. Demand for the lean, grass-fed Costa Rican cattle boomed. Many Costa Rican cattle ranchers quickly cleared land to create pasture for the cattle. Using Costa Rican beef reduced the cost of a hamburger by five cents, and provided jobs for Costa Ricans.

Share the preceding information with students. Have students give their opinions concerning the fast food chains' point of view.

300 tons per ha) was being lost every year. Just as serious, they maintained, was the loss of plant and animal species that lived in the rain forest. Such species are essential for making improved foods, new environmentally safe pesticides, and more effective medicines.

By the early 1980s, Costa Rica had lost almost half of its rain forests and was rapidly losing its soil.

The lumber industry claimed that *deforestation*, or the removal of large areas of forest, was due mostly to the way the farmers and ranchers cleared the land. Said one trucker, "We only haul trees 12 to 15 inches (30 cm to 38 cm) across or bigger. The owners of the farms cut everything down because it's easier to plant that way."

Cattle ranchers and farmers spoke of their need to make a living. In the words of one farmer, who had been a day laborer, "I had nothing, no future, no life." His neighbor added proudly, "I used to have to work for a *patron* (landowner), but now the patron is me."

THE ISSUES TODAY

In the late 1970s, the Costa Rican government began conservation efforts. Parks and forest preserves now protect almost all of what is left of Costa Rica's rain forests—about 20 percent of the country's territory. The government tightened forestry laws and established a permit system. The Forestry Department provides ranchers and farmers with fast-growing, debranched laurel trees. Planted as "living fences," the trees slow the wind and hold the thinning topsoil in place. Some communities have started tourist businesses built around the rich plant and animal life of the rain forest. Conservationists warn that much still needs to be done. Almost 30,000 acres (about 57,000 ha) of rain forest are still lost annually.

Land also must be provided for Costa Rica's ever-increasing population. Costa Rica has a rising birthrate, and the country has received thousands of people fleeing civil wars in El Salvador and Nicaragua.

Conservationists feel that the government must maintain an ongoing educational program. Such a program is the only way to convince the people that it is in their long-term interest to preserve their environments. These environments themselves can provide the nation with future economic prosperity.

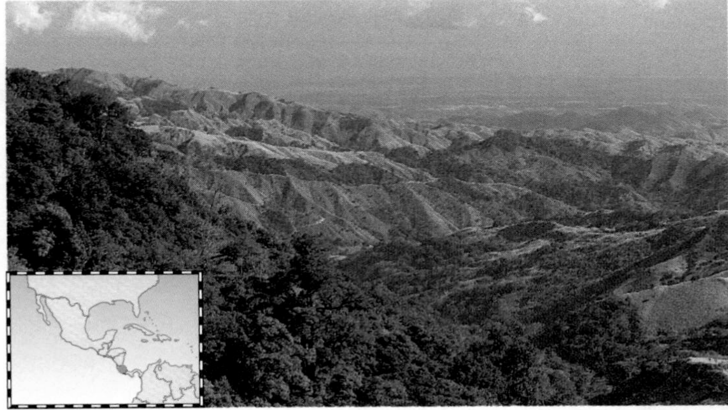

After deforestation had eliminated about 80 percent of Costa Rica's forests, the government established parks and conservation areas to protect the forests that remained.

Reviewing the Case

1. What groups are involved with Costa Rica's rain forests?
2. What problems does Costa Rica face?
3. **Human/Environment Interaction** What problems occur when the rain forest is cleared away?

ASSESS

Have students answer the Reviewing the Case Questions on page 201.

CLOSE

Have students agree or disagree with the statements they wrote at the lesson's beginning. Encourage them to use material from the Case Study as support.

DID YOU KNOW?

Costa Rica has a rich biodiversity, even though some species are threatened or endangered. The country recently licensed a major drug company to explore its plant and animal life for pharmaceutical purposes. The precedent-setting agreement calls for part of the license fees and any future royalties to be used to help preserve Costa Rican biodiversity.

NATIONAL GEOGRAPHIC SOCIETY

Videodisc

STV: BIODIVERSITY

Side 1, Chapter 1
Frames 00386-22598
Title: ***Destroying Diversity* (in its entirety)**
Subject: Examines how human action is threatening the balance of life

STV: BIODIVERSITY

Side 1, Chapter 2
Frames 22598-44538
Title: ***Preserving Diversity* (in its entirety)**
Subject: Examines some attempts by zoos and botanical gardens to protect plants and animals in artificial environments

ANSWERS TO REVIEWING THE CASE

1. the Costa Rican government, farmers, ranchers, loggers, conservationists
2. creating living areas and jobs for its population, paying back money borrowed from other countries, protecting its rain forests
3. The soil erodes or bakes hard and many plant and animal species are lost.

LESSON PLAN
Chapter 10, Section 2

FOCUS

SECTION OBJECTIVES

1. **Explain** how human development of the Amazon River basin has impacted the environment.
2. **Recognize** the major challenges that have accompanied rapid urban growth in Latin America and possible solutions for them.

BELLRINGER MOTIVATIONAL ACTIVITY

Project the Section 2 Focus Transparency and have students answer the questions.

PRETEACHING VOCABULARY

On the chalkboard, write the words *deform, deface, redo,* and *reopen.* Discuss the meanings of these words with the students and have them define the prefixes *de-* and *re-* based on the words' meanings. Then have students hypothesize about the meanings of *deforestation* and *reforestation* and compare their hypotheses with the meanings of the terms in the section.

NATIONAL GEOGRAPHIC SOCIETY

Videodisc

STV: WORLD GEOGRAPHY, VOLUME 3

Side 1, Chapter 1
Frames 32121-43167
Title: ***South America***
Subject: Amazon Basin

GTV: PLANETARY MANAGER

Side 2, Chapter 6
Frames 31907-38777
Title: ***Dust in the Wind***
Subject: Time travel shows the consequences of overgrazing, excessive irrigation, and deforestation

SECTION 2

People and Their Environment

THE ENVIRONMENT

SETTING THE SCENE

Read to Discover . . .

- how human development of the Amazon River basin has affected the environment.
- the major challenges that have accompanied rapid urban growth in Latin America and possible solutions for them.

Key Terms

- ecosystem
- deforestation
- slash-and-burn farming
- reforestation

Identify and Locate

Amazon River basin, Brazil, Mexico City, São Paulo

An **ecosystem** is a complex variety of life in a delicately balanced environment. Humans acting within an ecosystem probably upset the balance more than any other organism. In Latin America, environmental disruption has been occurring in several different places, including the tropical rain forest of the Amazon River basin and many urban areas across the region.

HUMAN/ENVIRONMENT INTERACTION

The Amazon River Basin

The Amazon River basin covers about 2.7 million square miles (7 million sq. km), an area about the size of the United States east of the Rocky Mountains. The basin contains the world's largest tropical rain forest. About two-thirds of this forest is in Brazil. The rest covers parts of Bolivia, Peru, Ecuador, Colombia, Venezuela, Guyana, Suriname, and French Guiana.

Deforestation

In recent years many people have become concerned about the **deforestation**—the cutting down and clearing away of trees in the rain forest. According to recent estimates, about 10 percent of Amazon rain forest has already been destroyed.

Several activities have contributed to the deforestation. One is construction of the Trans-Amazonian Highway and of access roads into the forest. A great deal of forest land, especially in the Brazilian Amazon rain forest, had to be cleared to make way for these roads.

Another of the most widespread activities is the clearing of forest land along new access routes so that migrant families might permanently farm the land. Traditionally migrant farmers use what is often called **slash-and-burn farming.** They cut down all the plants and strip any trees of bark. After the plants and trees have dried out, they are set on fire. The ash from the fire puts nutrients into the soil. Within two or three years, however, the soil begins to lose its fertility and crop yields decline. When this happens, the farmers move on to a new piece of land and start the same process over again. The cycle is repeated, and each time more forest is destroyed.

Attempts to develop commercial cattle ranches have also caused much deforestation. Cattle need a large amount of pastureland for grazing. To support large-scale ranching, huge amounts of forest land must be cleared, and

Classroom Resources for Section 2

BLACKLINE MASTERS:
Reproducible Lesson Plan 10-2
Guided Reading Activity 10-2
Environmental Issue 3
Section Quiz 10-2

TRANSPARENCIES:
Section Focus Transparency 10-2

MULTIMEDIA:

Vocabulary PuzzleMaker Software
Testmaker

Geography and the Environment
STV: World Geography, Volume 3
GTV: Planetary Manager

Eye on the Environment Poster Series

Geographic Themes

Human/Environment Interaction: Amazon River Basin

The Amazon River basin contains more than 50,000 species of plants—about 20 percent of all plant species on the earth. *How is human activity threatening the basin's vegetation?*

slash-and-burn techniques are used. Grasses at first grow well in the charred soil. After four or five years, however, fewer grasses grow, and the land cannot support as many cattle as it once did. In time, the growth of weeds takes over the production of grasses, and the cattle ranches are abandoned.

Still another activity that has contributed to deforestation is the commercial exploitation of trees for lumber and other products. Profits are made from the export of these products. In the view of some scientists, however, deforestation may have serious long-term negative effects that may be difficult or even impossible to overcome. These scientists point out that some of the damage could be corrected if lumber companies would practice **reforestation,** the planting of young trees or the seeds of trees, on the lands they have stripped.

Yet in many cases, replanting has not happened. The environmental impact of logging has been growing steadily, partly because of an increasing demand to develop the resources of the Amazon River basin.

Major Concerns

Scientists and other experts do not always agree on the nature, significance, or possible harmful effects of deforestation. Several years ago, it was thought that widespread deforestation would upset the oxygen balance of the entire world. This occurrence is no longer thought to be likely. Now the concern is that deforestation may upset the world's heat balance, causing a dangerous warming effect. Some scientists also believe that major deforestation might produce an imbalance in the world's water cycle, affecting rainfall in certain areas.

Another concern is that deforestation eventually will cause many plants and animals to become extinct. Certain species of plants have extracts that are valuable to humans as medicine and for commercial and industrial

TEACH

GUIDED PRACTICE

L1 Graph Give students the following data:

CITIES	APPROXIMATE POPULATIONS *(in thousands)*
Mexico City	20,899
São Paulo	18,701
Buenos Aires	11,657
Lima	6,815
Bogotá	5,913
Santiago	5,378

Then tell students to make bar graphs comparing the cities' populations.

Implement Environmental Issue 3 as a class activity.

INDEPENDENT PRACTICE

Guided Reading Have students complete Guided Reading Activity 10-2 in the TCR. **LEP**

Have students complete Vocabulary Activity 10 in the TCR. **LEP**

USING ILLUSTRATIONS

HUMAN/ENVIRONMENT INTERACTION Between 1981 and 1990, 20.5 million acres were deforested annually in Latin America.

Answer to Caption: *Highway construction, slash-and-burn farming, and ranch development have caused deforestation.*

GLENCOE TECHNOLOGY

Videodisc

GEOGRAPHY AND THE ENVIRONMENT
THE INFINITE VOYAGE
To the Edge of the Earth

Chapter 4
Disc 1 Side B

Title: ***Exploring the Galapagos Islands***

Cooperative Learning Activity

Have the class compile an atlas featuring special purpose maps of places in Latin America. Assign each student a country and direct him or her to find land use, resource, and vegetation maps of that country as well as street maps of the country's major cities. Refer them to travel agencies, foreign embassies, back issues of NATIONAL GEOGRAPHIC, and travel books at the library as sources for maps. Students may make black and white copies of maps in books or magazines, but tell them to recolor the maps like the originals. Remind them to recolor the map key as well. Take apart a scrapbook and give pages to each student for pasting on and labeling maps. After the students have finished, reassemble the scrapbook. Suggest the class donate its atlas to the school library.

USING ILLUSTRATIONS

HUMAN/ENVIRONMENT INTERACTION Every year, 27,000 species of rain forest plants and animals are destroyed

Answer to Caption: *Some believe deforestation may warm the planet, imbalance the water cycle, and destroy species.*

ASSESS

CHECK FOR UNDERSTANDING

Assign Section 2 Review as homework or an in-class activity.

MEETING LESSON OBJECTIVES

Each objective below is tested by the questions that follow it in parentheses.

1. **Explain** how human development of the Amazon River basin has impacted the environment. *(3)*
2. **Recognize** the major challenges that have accompanied rapid urban growth in Latin America and possible solutions for them. *(4, 5)*

EVALUATE

Assign the Section 2 Quiz in the TCR.

Use the Testmaker to create a customized quiz for Section 2.

uses. The value of other species found in the rain forest has not yet been determined. Scientists fear that these species might become extinct before their value can be known.

Many people believe that the huge Amazon rain forest can regenerate itself over time. Others, however, point out that such a secondary forest is almost always less healthy and less productive than the original one.

Toward the Future

No one knows how extensive the consequences of deforestation will become. Many Latin Americans, as well as others around the world, are hopeful that better methods of utilizing the resources in the Amazon River basin can be developed.

Many people believe that the Amazon River basin is important to the world as an abundant supply of natural resources and that controlled fishing, mining, and logging can be done without doing serious harm to the environment. Many also think that the Amazon basin holds the promise for a better future for thousands of people. Many people agree that new and more flexible methods must be found to settle families in the area engaged in small-scale farming so that they do not move from one part of the forest to another.

Most experts see a need for stronger governmental regulation and more national parks and Native American reserves throughout the area for the groups who will have to move from their traditional land. To keep migrant families and commercial developers from misusing parks and reserves, tough measures and strict enforcement are needed.

Geographic Themes

Human/Environment Interaction: Amazon Basin
This brilliant tree frog is one of about 4,000 species of frogs living in the rain forests whose habitats are threatened. *What do the world's scientists believe about the effects of deforestation?*

PLACE

Population Growth

Latin American cities have experienced tremendous population growth in recent years. Mexico City, for example, has become home to about one-fourth of the people of Mexico and has the second-greatest population of any city in the world. São Paulo has become the largest city of South America and the second-largest metropolitan area of Latin America after Mexico City. The challenges facing these two cities because of their rapid growth are also confronting other Latin American cities.

Urban Challenges

One of the most serious challenges facing Latin American cities is poverty. Many people who left their rural homes expected to find jobs in the city. Many of the cities, however, were already overcrowded, and jobs often proved scarce, especially for the unskilled. As a result, as many as one-half of the people of working age in an overcrowded city like São Paulo or Mexico City might be unemployed.

Meeting Special Needs

Inefficient Readers Scanning is a useful technique for readers who need help in locating unfamiliar vocabulary. Review the section's Key Terms: ecosystem, deforestation, slash-and-burn farming, and reforestation. Then ask students to scan Section 2 to locate these words in bold type. Have them copy the words and their definitions.

Housing is another challenge. The number of people living in urban areas often exceeds the number of houses or apartments. Even if more good housing were available, many city dwellers could not afford it. Consequently, every major city has its slum areas, called by a different name from one city to another—*favelas* in São Paulo, *barriadas* in Bogotá, *villas miserias* in Buenos Aires. In these places people often live in shacks made of cardboard, asbestos panels, or sheets of metal, often without electricity, running water, underground sewer systems, or sanitary facilities.

In many urban areas, air pollution has also become a serious problem. Millions of automobiles, trucks, buses, and other vehicles clog city streets, creating serious traffic jams and congestion, and sending massive amounts of exhaust fumes into the air. Along with the pollutants from industrial smokestacks, these fumes badly pollute the air. In Mexico City the air pollution is so serious that people with breathing problems cannot always go outside, and the use of automobiles must be restricted.

Poorer urban residents also have difficulty getting enough food to eat. Many cannot afford to buy food, and in the city they do not have a place to grow their own.

Geographic Themes

Place: Havana, Cuba
Cuba's Communist policies led to shortages of goods for many people living in Havana and other Cuban cities. *What challenges have faced other Latin American cities?*

Solutions for One City

Latin American political leaders are aware of the problems of their cities and are trying to solve them. The Mexican government, for example, has carried out several efforts to improve the quality of life in Mexico City.

The government is encouraging businesses to relocate outside the city and is promoting tourism so that more jobs will be created. Mexico is also working to improve agriculture so that many former farm workers will be encouraged to leave the city and return to the countryside.

In an effort to cut down on the number of automobiles in Mexico City, a new subway system is being built. A new water system is being constructed to help overcome the city's water problems. The city has planted millions of trees, not only to help beautify urban areas but also to help purify the air.

Section 2 Review

Checking for Understanding

1. **Define** ecosystem, deforestation, slash-and-burn farming, reforestation.
2. **Locating Places** Where is the second-largest city in the world located?
3. **Human/Environment Interaction** What activities have contributed to deforestation in the Amazon River basin?
4. **Region** What are four challenges faced by many Latin American cities?

Critical Thinking

5. **Making Comparisons** In what ways are the challenges facing the major cities in your country the same as those facing major cities in Latin America?

RETEACH

Have students complete Workbook Activity 10-2 found in the TCR.

ENRICH

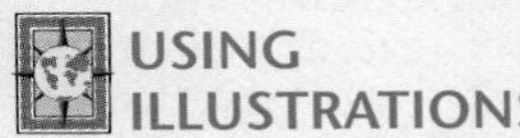

Have students complete Enrichment Activity 10 in the TCR.

CLOSE

Sum up the main idea of each subhead in a sentence. Scramble the words in the sentences and have students unscramble them.

USING ILLUSTRATIONS

PLACE Despite the challenges, 72 percent of all Cubans live in cities.

Answer to Caption: *poverty, lack of housing, pollution, and crime*

NATIONAL GEOGRAPHIC SOCIETY

EYE ON THE ENVIRONMENT POSTER SERIES

Display the three posters that discuss tropical rain forests—*Overview*, *Focus Amazonia*, and *A Global Look*. Discussion questions and Activities are presented on page 15 of the Teacher's Guide.

ANSWERS TO SECTION 2 REVIEW

1. **ecosystem:** complex variety of life in a delicately balanced environment; **deforestation:** the cutting down and clearing of trees; **slash-and-burn farming:** clearing and burning forests for use as farmland; **reforestation:** the planting of young trees or the seeds of trees
2. Mexico City
3. construction of highways and access roads, clearing of forests for settlements, development of ranches, and the commercial use of trees for lumber and other products
4. poverty, housing shortages, air pollution, and crime
5. Answers will vary but may focus on jobs, crime, education, population growth, and availability of housing.

TEACH

Say: "Suppose you are planning a vacation. In a travel agency, you see three posters. One poster shows banana trees; the second displays flowering cactus plants; the third shows maple trees in full fall color. What climate does each picture represent?" *(tropical, desert, and temperate climates respectively)* "How did you draw this conclusion?" *(The plants in each photo grow in those climates.)* Explain: "Because plants adapt to particular climates, geographers use them to identify various climatic regions, which are illustrated on vegetation maps. What aspects of human life are related to natural vegetation?" *(food sources, economic resources)*

Skills Practice
For additional practice, have students complete Skill Activity 10 in the TCR.

MAP & GRAPH SKILLS

Reading a Vegetation Map

Suppose you are traveling by car in the eastern United States. Beginning in northern Maine, you see vast stretches of evergreen trees such as pine, fir, and spruce. Farther south, the evergreen trees will mix with broad-leaved trees such as oak, hickory, maple, and aspen. At the southernmost tip of Florida, you will see palm trees and other tropical plants. Traveling from north to south, you have passed through several different vegetation zones, which can be shown on a **vegetation map.**

REVIEWING THE SKILL

Vegetation maps illustrate the kinds of plants that naturally grow in a given area. Because climate largely determines the vegetation of an area, there are many similarities between climate and vegetation maps. For example, evergreen trees, such as firs and spruces, grow in cool climates because their needle-like leaves can withstand cold temperatures. In the year-round warmth of the tropics, evergreens with broad leaves, such as palm trees, banana trees, and rubber trees, can grow. Between these two extremes, broad-leaved deciduous trees predominate. Like tropical species, these trees have broad leaves, but they shed them in autumn to endure cold winters. In dry climates, grasses and shrubs predominate because there is insufficient water to support tree growth.

Extremely cold or dry climates may have little or no vegetation at all.

When reading a vegetation map, study the map key carefully to determine what kinds of plants predominate in each area. Boundaries between vegetation zones are approximate because plants merge gradually with border areas usually having plants from both zones. To read a vegetation map, apply the following steps:

- Study the map key to identify the vegetation zones included on the map.
- Find examples of each vegetation zone on the map.
- Look at other aspects of the area's geography such as landforms, latitude, oceans, and climate zones to explain the vegetation patterns.

PRACTICING THE SKILL

Use the vegetation map to answer the following questions:

1. What vegetation zones are shown on this map?
2. What kind of vegetation grows nearest to the Equator in South America?
3. What vegetation zone is represented by the color yellow?
4. What color represents the areas of temperate grasslands?
5. Which vegetation zone(s) would be well suited for grazing livestock? Why?
6. How do you explain the lack of vegetation on the west coast of South America?

For additional practice in this skill, see Practicing Skills on page 208 of the Chapter 10 Review.

ANSWERS TO PRACTICING THE SKILL

1. tropical rain forest, chaparral, deciduous and mixed deciduous-coniferous forest, coniferous forest, tropical grassland, temperate grassland, desert scrub and desert waste, highland
2. tropical rain forest
3. desert scrub and desert waste
4. orange
5. tropical and temperate grasslands; they provide ample vegetation for grazing animals
6. Rain carried southwest drops on the eastern side of the Andes, leaving the west side very dry.

1 SECTION: Living in Latin America

Coffee farm in Colombia

KEY TERMS

developing country (p. 195)
export (p. 195)
cash crop (p. 195)
campesinos (p. 196)
latifundia (p. 196)
minifundia (p. 196)
service industry (p. 196)
maquiladoras (p. 197)

SUMMARY

- The economies of many Latin American countries are based on agriculture.
- There are two major classes of farms in Latin America—*latifundia* and *minifundia.*
- Most Latin American countries have been slow to industrialize because of lack of funds, a skilled workforce, and raw materials and energy sources.
- Latin America and some nations outside the region are interdependent due to Latin America's desire to industrialize.
- The development of transportation and communication networks in Latin America has been slowed because of cost and physical barriers.

2 SECTION: People and Their Environment

KEY TERMS

ecosystem (p. 202)
deforestation (p. 202)
slash-and-burn farming (p. 202)
reforestation (p. 203)

SUMMARY

- Large areas of the Amazon River basin are suffering from deforestation.
- Road construction, small-scale farming, large-scale ranching, and the commercial exploitation of trees have all contributed to the deforestation of the Amazon rain forest.
- There is need for new methods, better planning, and stronger government regulation to help solve the problems of the Amazon rain forest and develop the resources without seriously harming the environment.
- The rapid growth of some Latin American cities has led to environmental and social problems.
- Latin American governments are aware of the problems facing large cities and are working to solve them.

Logging in the Amazon basin

CHAPTER 10 HIGHLIGHTS

USING THE CHAPTER 10 HIGHLIGHTS

Use the Chapter 10 Highlights to preview, review, condense, or reteach the chapter.

PREVIEW/REVIEW

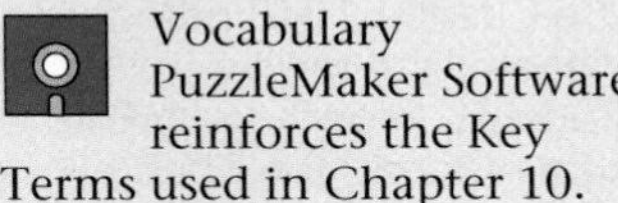

Vocabulary PuzzleMaker Software reinforces the Key Terms used in Chapter 10.

Student Self-Test and Review Software allows students to review Chapter 10 content.

CONDENSE

Have students read the Chapter 10 Highlights.

 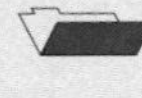

Have students listen to the Chapter 10 Audiocassettes in the TCR. Spanish Audiocassettes are also available.

Assign the Chapter 10 Audiocassette Activity and give students the Chapter 10 Audiocassette Quiz.

Have students complete the Guided Reading Activities for Chapter 10 in the TCR. Spanish Guided Reading Activities are also available.

RETEACH

Have students complete Reteaching Activity 10 in the TCR. Spanish Reteaching Activities are also available.

Map Activity

Identify and Locate Copy and distribute page 25 from the Outline Map Resource Book. Have students label the countries on the map of South America, locate different areas of economic activity, create a symbol for products produced in each area, and draw the symbols on the map. Refer them to the map on page 197 for help. Also, remind them to add a key to explain their symbols.

GLENCOE TECHNOLOGY

Videodisc

Use Chapter 10 MindJogger Videoquiz to review students' knowledge before administering the Chapter 10 Test.

MINDJOGGER VIDEOQUIZ

Chapter 10
Disc 2 Side A

The MindJogger Videoquiz is also available on videocassette.

ANSWERS

Reviewing Key Terms

1. cash crop
2. *latifundia*
3. developing countries
4. *campesinos*
5. export
6. service industries
7. reforestation
8. deforestation
9. slash-and-burn farming

Reviewing Facts

10. agriculture
11. cost and physical barriers such as rugged terrain and dense vegetation
12. Deforestation may cause a dangerous warming effect, an imbalance in the world's water cycle, and the extinction of many plant and animal species.
13. Students may answer poverty, housing shortages, pollution, or crime.

chapter 10 REVIEW

Reviewing Key Terms

Choose the vocabulary term that best completes each of the sentences below. Write your answers on a separate sheet of paper.

developing countries (p. 195)
export (p. 195)
cash crop (p. 195)
campesinos (p. 196)
latifundia (p. 196)
service industries (p. 196)
deforestation (p. 202)
slash-and-burn farming (p. 202)
reforestation (p. 203)

Section 1

1. Bananas produced to sell or trade with someone else are a _____.
2. Large estates owned by families or corporations are known as _____.
3. Countries in the process of becoming industrialized are called _____.
4. People who live in the countryside are known as _____.
5. To send a product to other countries for sale or trade is to _____.
6. Industries that provide personal services for others are _____.

Section 2

7. _____ is the practice of planting young trees or the seeds of trees where the forest land has been stripped.
8. The cutting down and clearing of forest land is known as _____.
9. The process of cutting down plants and stripping trees of bark and then burning it all is known as _____.

Reviewing Facts

Section 1

10. On what is the economy of many Latin American countries based?
11. What has slowed the development of communication networks in Latin America?

Section 2

12. What are some concerns people have about the deforestation of the Amazon River basin?
13. What is one of the most serious challenges facing Latin American cities?

Critical Thinking

14. **Drawing Conclusions** Why is the Panama Canal important?
15. **Predicting Consequences** What do you think will be the future of the Amazon River basin? Give reasons for your answer.

Geographic Themes

16. **Human/Environment Interaction** Why are Latin American transportation and communications systems not more highly developed?
17. **Human/Environment Interaction** How has rapid urban growth caused environmental problems?

Practicing Skills

Reading a Vegetation Map

Refer to the vegetation map on page 206.

18. Compare the vegetation in the northern and southern parts of South America.
19. How does the vegetation change farther inland from the southeastern coastline?

Using the Unit Atlas

Refer to the physical geography section of the Unit Atlas on pages 154–155.

20. What South American country is a leader in emerald mining?
21. Where is the source of the Amazon River?

Critical Thinking

14. It promotes trade between the Atlantic and Pacific coasts by eliminating the long route around South America.
15. Answers will vary but may focus on the role of political leaders, business leaders, scientists, and environmentalists in finding ways to use and protect the resources of the Amazon basin.

Geographic Themes

16. Natural barriers, the cost of building good highways, and the use of waterways—a cheaper means of transportation—stand in the way of development.
17. In overcrowded urban areas, millions of automobiles and other vehicles emit fumes, leading to increased air pollution.

Projects

Individual Activity

Select one of Latin America's overcrowded cities, and imagine that you are a city planner for that city. Write a plan for the mayor, who has asked you to help resolve some of the city's problems.

Cooperative Learning Activity

The Pan-American Highway connects the east and west coasts of Latin America and provides a route through much of the region. Working in a group of six, divide the route among group members. Each group member should find four or five interesting facts about the places through which his or her section of the route passes. Group members should share the facts with each other. Then, as a group, prepare a poster that shows the route with the most interesting facts written next to the appropriate places on the map.

Writing About Geography

Narration

Words can have different meanings to different people. Write four definitions of the concept of deforestation as each of these people might define it: a Native American who has grown up and still lives in the Amazon rain forest; a logger; a small-scale migrant farmer; a Brazilian government official. Then, write a paragraph discussing how the definitions are similar and how they are different. Use your journal, text, and library resources for help.

Locating Places

LATIN AMERICA: POLITICAL GEOGRAPHY

Match the letters on the map with the places of Latin America. Write your answers on a separate sheet of paper.

1. Brazil
2. Mexico
3. Costa Rica
4. Belém
5. Isthmus of Panamá
6. Bogotá
7. Lima
8. Santiago
9. Mexico City
10. São Paulo

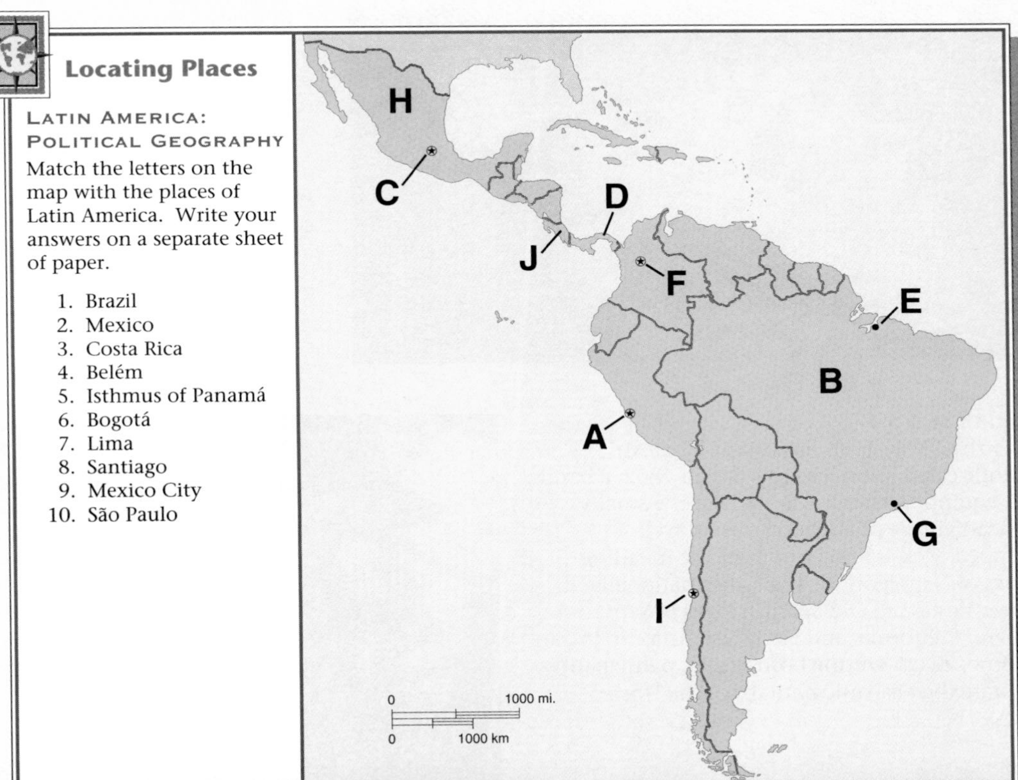

Chapter 10 Review

Practicing Skills

18. The northern area has rain forests, mixed forests, and some savanna areas. The southern tip is drier and has scrub forests and desert.

19. The coastal area has tropical rain forests. Farther inland, the vegetation changes to mixed forests and then savanna and scrub forests.

Using the Unit Atlas

20. Colombia

21. The Andes in Peru

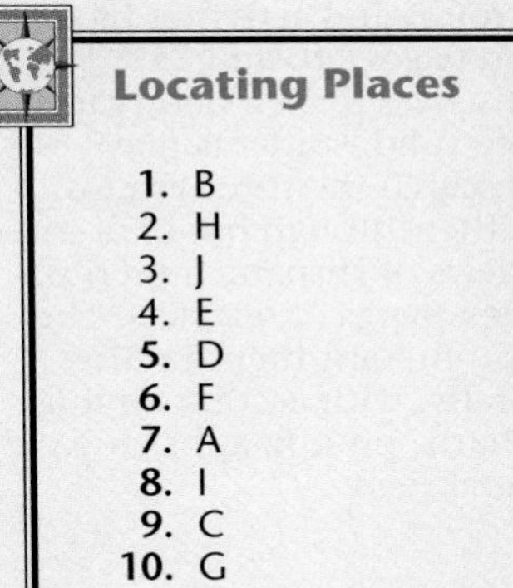

Locating Places

1. B
2. H
3. J
4. E
5. D
6. F
7. A
8. I
9. C
10. G

Chapter Bonus Test Question

This question may be used for extra credit on the chapter test. Choose the letter of the correct response.

How would a manufacturer in Medellin, Colombia, most likely ship his products to Lima, Peru?

(1) by boat on the Amazon River

(2) by truck on the Pan-American Highway

(3) on a barge through the Panama Canal

(4) in a freight car on a railway

Answer: (2)

FOCUS

Write the word *Hispanic* on the board. Ask students to tell how the term applies to the people and cultures presented on pages 210 and 211. *(Hispanic people are those descended from the early Spanish immigrants to the Americas.)*

TEACH

L1 Compare and Contrast Although Hispanic cultures share some qualities, each is distinct and unique. Have students find and list likenesses and differences in the groups and activities pictured on pages 210 and 211. To discover if their observations are valid, students may research the three groups, either through books or interviews of Hispanic American classmates or teachers. They can present their findings orally, with accompanying charts, photographs, and cultural items.

Latin America and the United States

LATIN AMERICAN CELEBRATIONS

Mexican Americans are the largest Hispanic group living in the United States today. They are the third-largest ethnic group in the United States. Many other people of Hispanic cultural heritage also live in the United States. Two of the largest groups are Puerto Rican Americans and Cuban Americans.

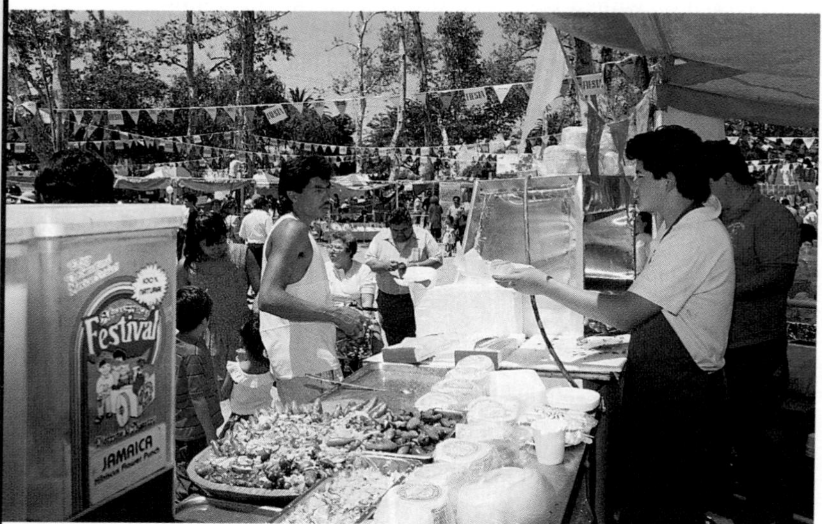

MEXICAN AMERICAN FIESTAS are woven into the fabric of life in the American Southwest. Filled with food, dancing and singing, colorful costumes, and decorations, a fiesta is a joyous time. Parades, processions, and fireworks also are often part of fiestas.

CINCO DE MAYO, the Fifth of May, is an important Mexican patriotic celebration. On this day in 1862, a band of ill-equipped, starving farmers in the small Mexican village of Puebla drove off well-equipped, well-trained troops of the invading armies of Napoleon III. Two other nationally known fiestas are Old Spanish Days in Santa Barbara, California, and Fiesta San Antonio in San Antonio, Texas. During both fiestas, participants celebrate the Hispanic heritage of the United States.

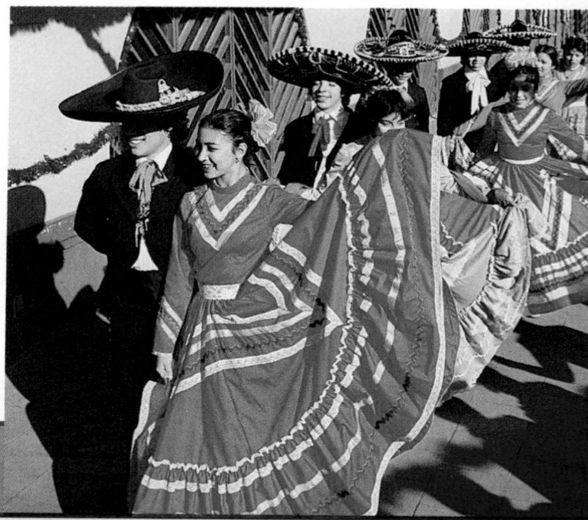

Making the Connection

Culture Organize students into three groups, and assign each group a Hispanic American culture. Have students research music, dance, art, cuisine, and any other cultural area of their choosing. Have groups plan and prepare a cultural "hands on" display: they may serve foods of the culture, play music, present a dance, share a piece of art, read a poem, produce a poster of a culturally well-known Hispanic entertainer. Encourage students to be creative, as well as culturally accurate.

Geography Connection

ASSESS

Have students answer the Checking for Understanding questions on page 211.

CLOSE

Have students determine the accuracy and completeness of their beginning definition of *Hispanic*.

Suggest that they expand their definition, adding significant supporting details from the article.

DID YOU KNOW?

In the 1990 census, Hispanic Americans were the second largest minority in the United States. A 1993 census projected that by the year 2010, Hispanic Americans would make up 14 percent of the U.S. population.

▲ **PUERTO RICAN AMERICAN FESTIVALS** celebrate saints' days and other special occasions. Like Mexican American fiestas, Puerto Rican festivals feature plenty of food and drink, music, fireworks, and parades.

▲ **CUBAN AMERICAN FESTIVITIES** bring family and friends together to sing and toast with *sidra espa ola*, a type of apple cider.

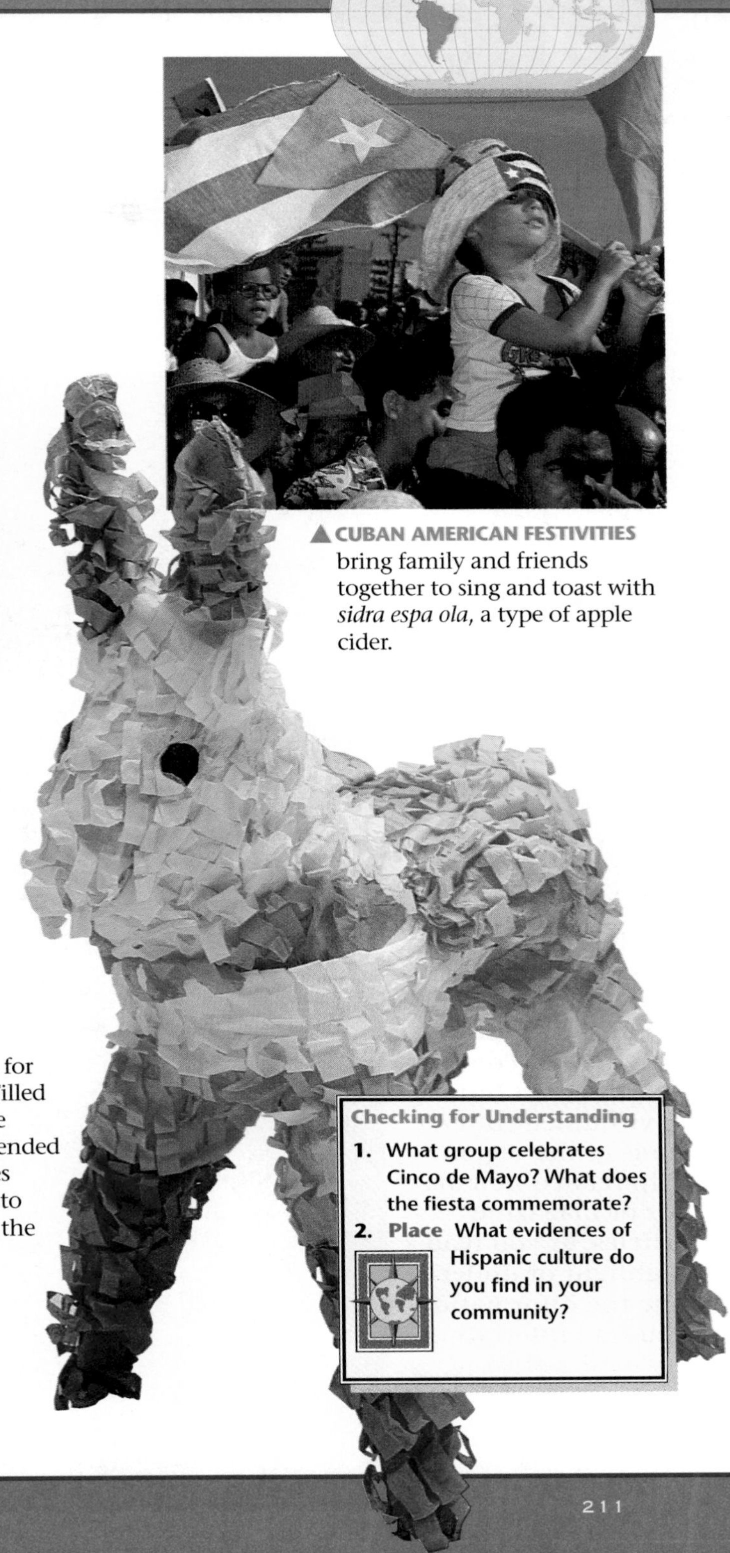

A PIÑATA ▶ is the centerpiece of any fiesta for Mexican American children. Filled with small gifts and candy, the brightly colored *piñata* is suspended in the air. Children, sometimes blindfolded, take turns trying to break it. Everyone wins when the treats finally shower down.

Checking for Understanding

1. What group celebrates Cinco de Mayo? What does the fiesta commemorate?
2. **Place** What evidences of Hispanic culture do you find in your community?

ANSWERS TO CHECKING FOR UNDERSTANDING

1. Mexicans; Mexican farmers in Puebla drove out Napoleon's invading army.
2. Answers will vary, but students should find examples of Hispanic culture discussed in Chapter 10.

Introducing
UNIT 4

UNIT OVERVIEW

The three chapters in this unit introduce students to the physical geography and peoples of Europe. Various aspects of European life—such as the economy, lifestyles, and human/environment interaction—are also presented.

GEOGRAPHY JOURNAL

Activity Students may choose to follow two or three specific countries in the news. They may also focus on one of the topics listed.

In addition to the sources suggested in the Student Edition, students may interview foreign exchange students, language teachers, or friends and family who have traveled to Europe.

Using their journals, students should compare and contrast life in Europe with life in the United States.

- This journal activity provides the basis for the "Writing About Geography" exercise in the Chapter Review.

- The Geography Journal may be used as an integral part of Performance Assessment.

Videodisc

STV: WORLD GEOGRAPHY, VOLUME 2

Side 2, Chapter 2
Frames 00001-47934
Title: ***Europe*** **(in its entirety)**
Subject: Tour Europe and explore how Europeans have changed their landscape to meet their needs

UNIT
4

Europe

David Doubilet

GeoJournal Activity

While studying Europe, collect current information about the physical geography, economy, cultures, and human-environment interactions of the region. Clip related newspaper or magazine articles; as you read, highlight or underline the information you find interesting.

212

Where in the World . . . .

Have students look at the map of Europe on pages A12 and A13. Display Unit Map Overlay Transparency 4-5 and ask the following questions: What body of water touches the coastlines of the western European nations? *(Atlantic Ocean)* The northern nations? *(Arctic Ocean)* What continent lies south of Europe? *(Africa)* What continent borders the eastern nations of Europe? *(Asia)* In what direction would you travel from Europe to reach the United States? *(west)* What body of water do you cross when you travel from Europe to the United States? *(Atlantic Ocean)* If you wanted to travel from Europe to South America, in what direction would you go? *(southwest)*

Picturing the World

Sunlight strikes the Charles Bridge and the curving roof of the National Theater in Prague, the capital of the newly-formed Czech Republic. Like other major European cities, Prague, located on the Vltava River in central Europe, has served as a political, academic, and cultural center for hundreds of years. Today's European city manages to combine Old World charm with modern conveniences. Look on the map on page 225.

1. What other capital cities are located on rivers?
2. Why did cities develop along rivers?

Picture Atlas CD-ROM Enrichment Corner

Many interesting bridges and buildings have been built over and along rivers in major European cities. Gather the following seven photographs for a Handbook of Architectural Styles: the Tower Bridge and the Houses of Parliament in London; the Louvre and Notre Dame in Paris; the Vltava River in Prague; the "old bridge" in Florence, Italy; and the Danube River in Budapest, Hungary. Read the photo captions and then answer the following questions:

1. How many bridges span the Thames River in London?
2. The Louvre is located on the north bank of which river?
3. What is the architectural style of the Cathedral of Notre Dame?

For many resources pertaining to Europe (including a clickable map maintained by the GeoWeb project), contact the following address:

World Wide Web
http://www.helsinki.fi/~aunesluo/eueng.html

GLENCOE TECHNOLOGY

Videodisc

REUTERS ISSUES IN GEOGRAPHY

Chapter 3
Disc 1 Side A
Title: ***Europe: United or Divided***
Subject: Forces that bring together and divide the European community

CD-ROM

PICTURE ATLAS OF THE WORLD
See page T38 for an additional CD-ROM activity to enrich Unit 4, Europe.

0:00 OUT OF TIME?

If time does not permit teaching each chapter in this unit, you may use the Chapter Highlights and the Audiocassettes that include a 1-page activity and a 1-page test for each chapter.

ANSWERS TO PICTURING THE WORLD

1. Lisbon, London, Paris, Rome, Ljubljana, Zagreb, Vienna, Budapest, Warsaw, Bratislava, Belgrade
2. Answers may include: for irrigation, for transportation, for trade, and so on.

Enrichment Corner Answers

1. 28
2. Seine River
3. Gothic style

LESSON PLAN
Unit 4 Atlas

These features and activities may be used as an introduction to the unit or as teaching tools throughout the course of the unit.

FOCUS

Ask students to use the maps on pages 214–215 to estimate the number of countries on the European continent. Write estimates on the board. Then have students analyze the relationship between a country's size and its population density.

TEACH

Implement Foods Around the World 3 as a class activity.

Have students complete Unit Map Overlay Transparency Activity 4 in the TCR.

GLENCOE TECHNOLOGY

Videodisc

Use the following to introduce or enrich Unit 4:

GEOGRAPHY AND THE ENVIRONMENT
THE INFINITE VOYAGE
Crisis in the Atmosphere

Chapter 9
Disc 2 Side A

Title: ***Energy Conservation: Changes in Switzerland***
Subject: Electric-car technology allows autos to run off of batteries that are recharged from solar panels

UNIT 4 ATLAS

EUROPE
Cultural Geography

EXPLORING CULTURAL DIVERSITY

1. *What nations make up the European continent?*
2. *What areas of Europe are the most heavily populated? Most sparsely populated?*
3. *What is the approximate population of Europe?*

From the 1200s to the early 1900s, **Austria** was the center of a huge empire that included much of central and eastern Europe. Today it is a small landlocked country.

Iceland has the oldest legislature in the world, the *Althing*.

Switzerland has three official languages: German, French, and Italian.

The Olympic Games began in **Greece** about 776 B.C. as part of religious festivals.

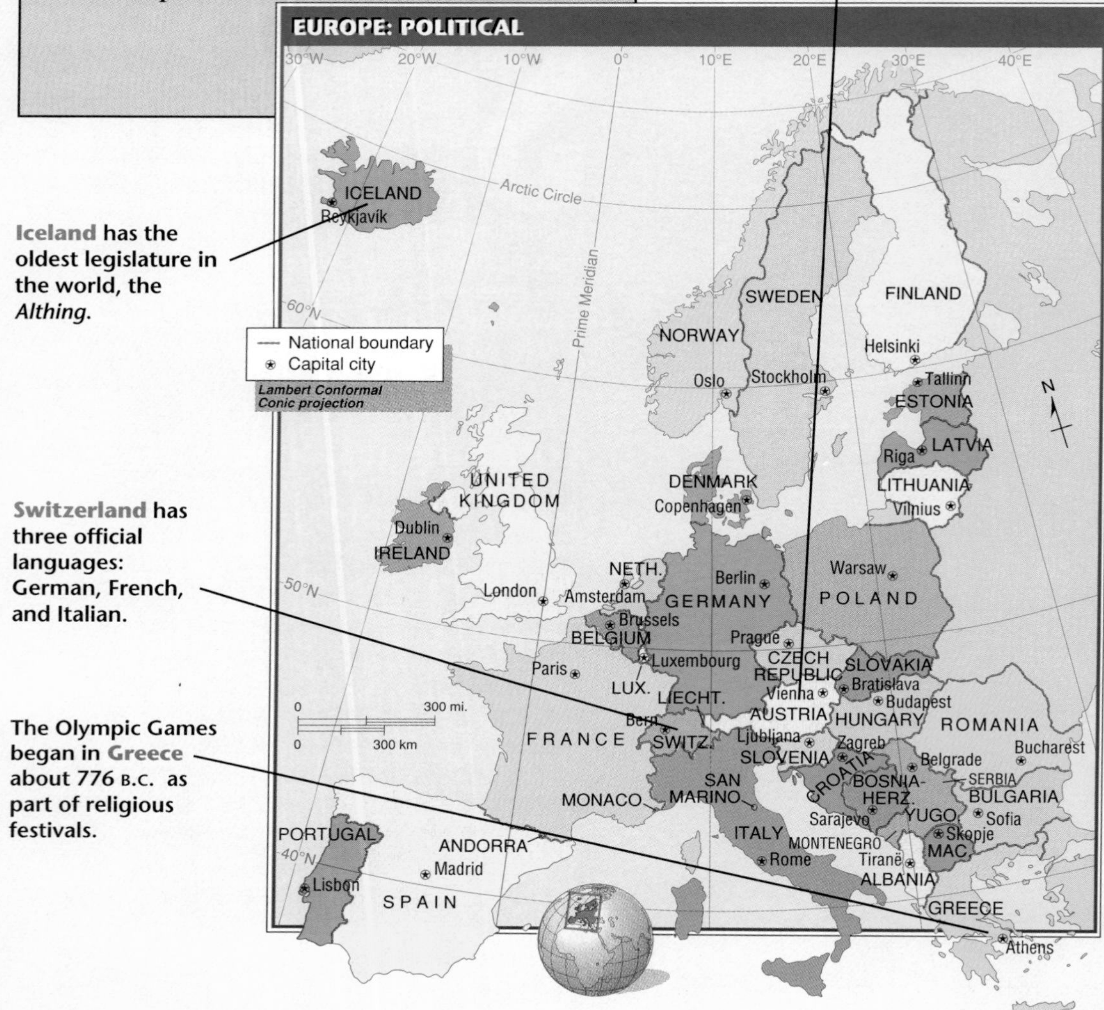

Classroom Resources for Unit 4

BLACKLINE MASTERS:
Geography Simulation 4

TRANSPARENCIES:
Unit Map Overlay Transparency 4

MULTIMEDIA:
***World Music:** Cultural Traditions, Lesson 3*

Picture Atlas of the World

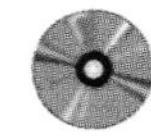

Geography and the Environment
Reuters Issues in Geography
STV: World Geography, Volume 2

Testmaker

Images of the World Poster Set

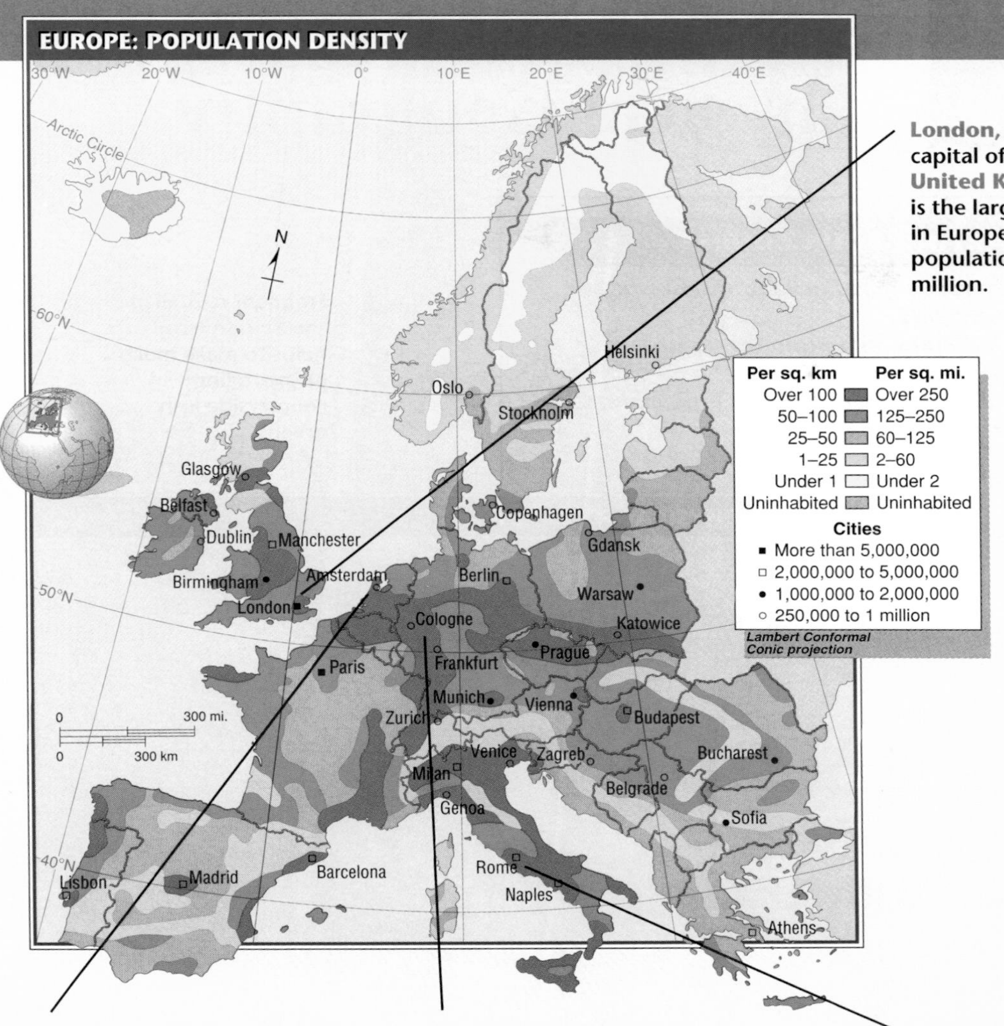

London, the capital of the **United Kingdom,** is the largest city in Europe. It has a population of 9.1 million.

The Netherlands is one of the most densely populated countries in Europe, with an average of more than 1,000 people per square mile.

Germany has experienced a rapid flight from farms into towns and cities; the rural population dropped from about 23 percent in 1950 to about 15 percent in 1993.

Vatican City, located within the city of Rome, is the center of the Roman Catholic Church and is the world's smallest populated nation. Only about 1,000 people live there.

Population: Europe and the United States

Europe*

United States

= 50,000,000

*Does not include Russia and Eurasian Republics
Source: 1994 World Population Data Sheet

Europe has twice as many people as the United States.

LESSON PLAN
Unit 4 Atlas

Play World Music: Cultural Traditions, Lesson 3. Have students do the Lesson 3 activity.

ASSESS

Have students answer the Exploring Cultural Diversity questions on page 214.

EXPLORING CULTURAL DIVERSITY

This feature may be used to introduce students to the cultural geography of Europe. Use questions to stimulate class discussion and help students become familiar with the region. Accept reasonable answers based on the maps, graph, and captions.

CLOSE

Have students compare their estimates of the number of countries with the actual count. *(37)* Ask them to summarize the relationship between size and population density. *(the smaller the country, the greater its population density)*

CD-ROM

PICTURE ATLAS OF THE WORLD

You and your students can view the streets of London, the moors of the United Kingdom, the vineyards of Germany, and the hillsides of Greece by clicking the "Video" button of selected countries.

Map and Graph Activity

Human/Environment Interaction

Explain that Europe is the most densely populated continent. Ask students to figure the average population density of the European countries, using the population comparison graph and the number of countries on the map. Have them list the positive and negative effects of population density on the geography, natural resources, and quality of life in Europe.

Ask each student to research one or two countries and find out the actual population density, its effects, and how the countries cope with the effects. Have students share their information in chart form. After students have presented their data, guide them to form generalizations about Europe's population density and the methods of coping and control.

LESSON PLAN
Unit 4 Atlas

These features and activities may be used as an introduction to the unit or as teaching tools throughout the course of the unit.

FOCUS

To introduce the physical geography of Europe, have students complete the Unit Map Overlay Transparency 4 Activity in the TCR.

TEACH

Human/ Environment Interaction Remind students that geography is the study of how people interact with the earth and its resources. Ask them to recall from previous units ways in which physical geography can affect our lives.

Map Activity Have students identify the latitudes and longitudes for Europe and its main landforms. *(highlands, mountains, plains)* Explain that highlands might be hills or plateaus. Ask students to speculate on ways that the lives of Europeans might be affected by this geographical location and these landforms.

Implement Geography Simulation 4 as a class activity.

UNIT 4 ATLAS

EUROPE
Physical Geography

CHARTING YOUR COURSE

1. *Is Europe's coastline long or short, jagged or straight?*
2. *What major mountain ranges are located in Europe?*
3. *What are three of Europe's principal natural resources?*

Frequent rainfall in the British Isles helps to make much of the rolling countryside lush green.

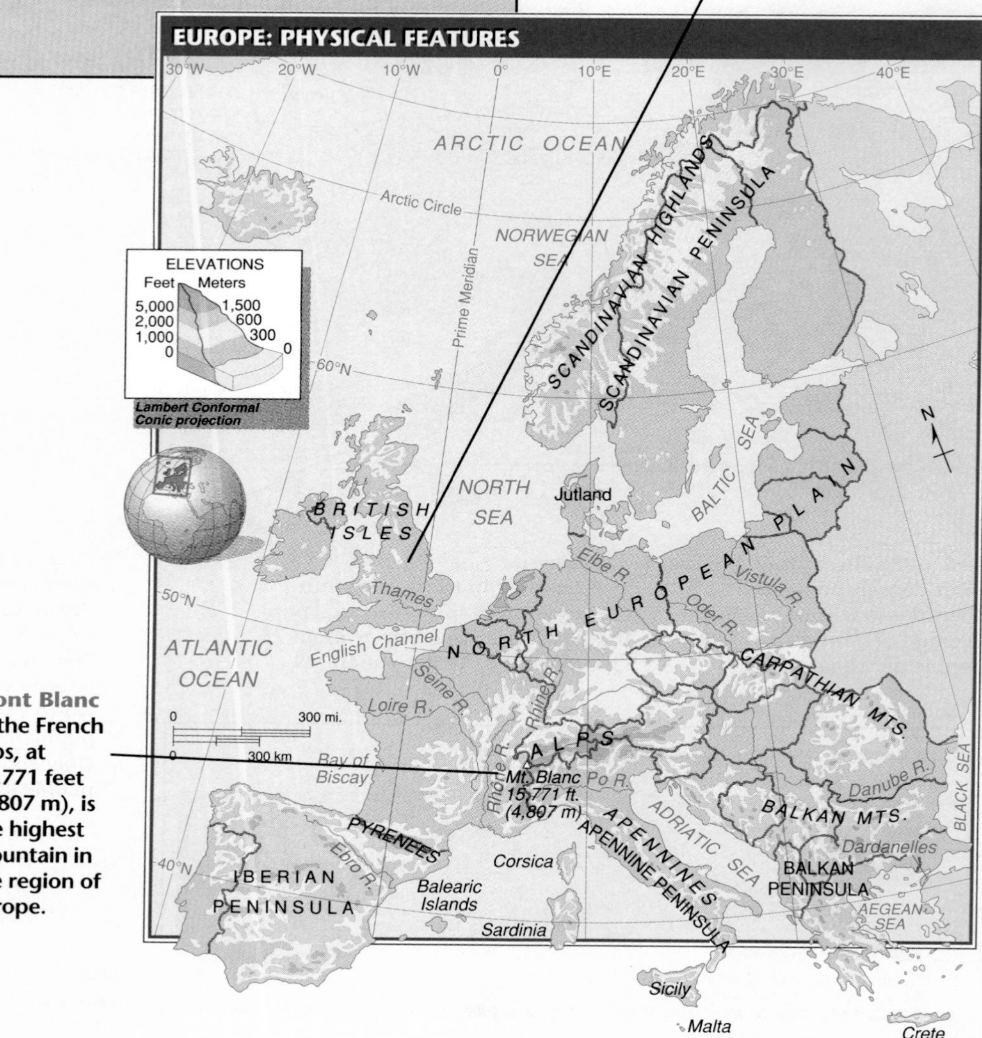

Mont Blanc in the French Alps, at 15,771 feet (4,807 m), is the highest mountain in the region of Europe.

Map and Graph Activity

Guide students to recognize that Europe includes several broad expanses of land with no apparent natural resources. Ask them to identify the landform of these open areas. *(plains)* Ask students to speculate on what resources might be found in these areas. *(farmland, grazing pasture)*

Ask each student to research the agricultural output of one or two countries. Have students record in their journals or on index cards the percentage of land used in agriculture, the main crops, and the location of agricultural/pasturage land. Provide a time for students to share their information and establish Europe's farming and livestock production areas. Suggest that they save the information for doublechecking as they progress through the unit.

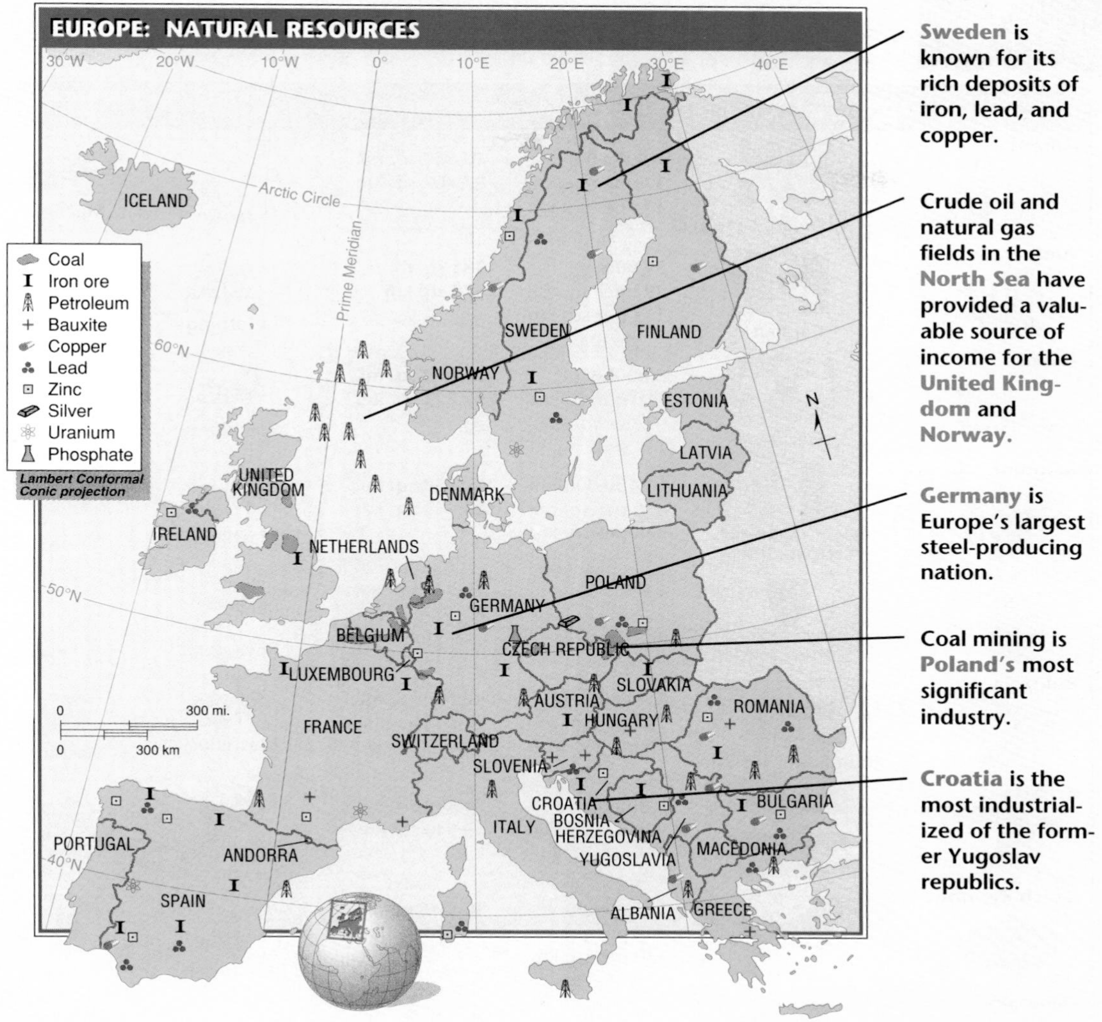

Sweden is known for its rich deposits of iron, lead, and copper.

Crude oil and natural gas fields in the **North Sea** have provided a valuable source of income for the **United Kingdom** and **Norway.**

Germany is Europe's largest steel-producing nation.

Coal mining is **Poland's** most significant industry.

Croatia is the most industrialized of the former Yugoslav republics.

Europe: Physical Profile

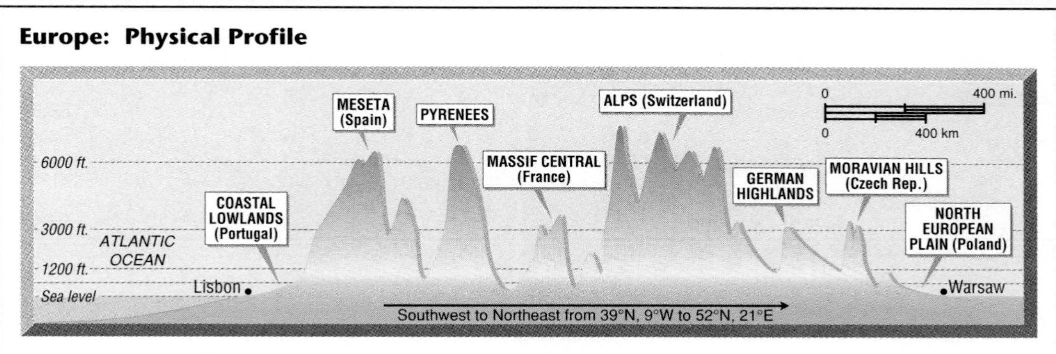

ASSESS

Have students answer the Charting Your Course questions on page 216.

CHARTING YOUR COURSE

This feature may be used to introduce students to the physical geography of Europe. Use questions to stimulate class discussion and help students become familiar with the region. Accept reasonable answers based on the maps, graph, and captions.

CLOSE

Ask for students' initial impressions of Europe and its peoples. Ask which maps and diagrams helped form these impressions.

IMAGES OF THE WORLD POSTER SET

Display the poster of Europe. Have students hypothesize about the climate zone and population density of each photo.

Map Activity

Resources Have students incorporate the list of natural resources on page 217 into a chart that includes the countries where those resources are found and the uses for the resources. After students locate the countries on the map, they can verify their identification by checking an encyclopedia, atlas, or other appropriate source.

LESSON PLAN
Unit 4 Atlas

These features and activities may be used as teaching tools throughout the course of the unit.

Ways of the World

EUROPE In many European countries, guests bring their hostess an uneven number of fresh flowers. An even number is considered unlucky. (Red roses are given only to indicate romantic love.)

DID YOU KNOW?

Throughout Europe, the legacy of the ancient Romans can still be found. Many European highways follow routes laid out by Roman engineers. The Roman language of Latin provided the roots of modern French, Spanish, Portuguese, Italian, and Romanian.

Ways of the World

EUROPE Most Europeans eat in the "continental" style: the fork stays in the left hand and the knife in the right. Proper manners also include keeping the hands above the table. In times past, hands under the table meant a person was hiding something. Now it is simply considered impolite.

UNIT 4 ATLAS

COUNTRY PROFILE

COUNTRY* AND CAPITAL	FLAG AND LANGUAGES	POPULATION	LANDMASS	PRINCIPAL PRODUCTS EXPORT	PRINCIPAL PRODUCTS IMPORT
Albania (Tirane)	Albanian, Greek	3,400,000 321 per sq. mi. 124 per sq. km	10,580 sq. mi. 27,402 sq. km	Fuels	Machinery
Andorra (Andorra la Vella)	Catalan	54,000 291 per sq. mi. 113 per sq. km	185 sq. mi. 479 sq. km	Clothing	Electronics
Austria (Vienna)	German	8,000,000 250 per sq. mi. 97 per sq. km	31,940 sq. mi. 82,725 sq. km	Machinery	Machinery
Belgium (Brussels)	Flemish, French, German, Italian	10,100,000 850 per sq. mi. 328 per sq. km	11,750 sq. mi. 30,433 sq. km	Machinery	Machinery
Bosnia and Herzegovina (Sarajevo)	Serbo-Croatian	4,600,000 223 per sq. mi. 86 per sq. km	19,740 sq. mi. 51,127 sq. km	Machinery	Fuels
Bulgaria (Sofia)	Bulgarian, Turkish	8,400,000 197 per sq. mi. 76 per sq. km	42,680 sq. mi. 110,541 sq. km	Machinery	Machinery
Croatia (Zagreb)	Croatian	4,800,000 220 per sq. mi. 85 per sq. km	21,830 sq. mi. 56,540 sq. km	Machinery	Machinery
Czech Republic (Prague)	Czech	10,300,000 337 per sq. mi. 130 per sq. km	30,590 sq. mi. 79,228 sq. km	Chemicals	Chemicals
Denmark (Copenhagen)	Danish	5,200,000 311 per sq. mi. 120 per sq. km	16,630 sq. mi. 42,372 sq. km	Machinery	Machinery
Estonia (Tallinn)	Estonian, Russian	1,500,000 91 per sq. mi. 35 per sq. km	17,410 sq. mi. 45,092 sq. km	Textiles	Textiles
Finland (Helsinki)	Finnish, Swedish	5,100,000 43 per sq. mi. 17 per sq. km	117,610 sq. mi. 304,610 sq. km	Metals	Fuels

*Country maps not drawn to scale.

Country Profile Activity

Economics Although Europe as a whole enjoys a higher standard of living than other world regions, western Europe is wealthier than eastern Europe.

Assign one or two countries to each student. Ask them to write these topics on index cards: GDP (gross domestic product), per capita income, life expectancy, available education, and literacy rate. Suggest that students research these topics by consulting encyclopedias, atlases, world almanacs, and other resources. Have them record their findings on the cards.

Require that students also determine the role geography plays in the country's economic standing. For example, excellent harbors and a long coastline are the basis for Norway's

COUNTRY* AND CAPITAL	FLAG AND LANGUAGES	POPULATION	LANDMASS	PRINCIPAL PRODUCTS EXPORT	PRINCIPAL PRODUCTS IMPORT
France (Paris)	French	58,000,000 273 per sq. mi. 105 per sq. km	212,390 sq. mi. 550,090 sq. km	Machinery	Machinery
Germany (Berlin)	German	81,200,000 602 per sq. mi. 232 per sq. km	134,930 sq. mi. 349,469 sq. km	Machinery	Machinery
Greece (Athens)	Greek	10,400,000 206 per sq. mi. 79 per sq. km	50,520 sq. mi. 130,847 sq. km	Food	Machinery
Hungary (Budapest)	Hungarian	10,300,000 287 per sq. mi. 111 per sq. km	35,650 sq. mi. 92,334 sq. km	Food	Machinery
Iceland (Reykjavík)	Icelandic	300,000 8 per sq. mi. 3 per sq. km	38,710 sq. mi. 100,259 sq. km	Fish	Ships
Ireland (Dublin)	English, Irish (Gaelic)	3,600,000 135 per sq. mi. 52 per sq. km	26,600 sq. mi. 68,894 sq. km	Machinery	Machinery
Italy (Rome)	Italian	57,200,000 504 per sq. mi. 195 per sq. km	113,540 sq. mi. 294,069 sq. km	Machinery	Machinery
Latvia (Riga)	Latvian	2,500,000 108 per sq. mi. 42 per sq. km	24,980 sq. mi. 64,491 sq. km	Machinery	Textiles
Liechtenstein (Vaduz)	German, Alemannic dialect	30,000 500 per sq. mi. 194 per sq. km	60 sq. mi. 155 sq. km	Machinery	Machinery
Lithuania (Vilnius)	Lithuanian	3,700,000 147 per sq. mi. 57 per sq. km	25,210 sq. mi. 65,294 sq. km	Machinery	Petroleum
Luxembourg (Luxembourg)	French, German, Luxembourgisch	400,000 404 per sq. mi. 156 per sq. km	990 sq. mi. 2,564 sq. km	Metals	Metals
Macedonia (Skopje)	Macedonian	2,100,000 211 per sq. mi. 82 per sq. km	9,930 sq. mi. 25,719 sq. km	Clothing	Food

*Country maps not drawn to scale.

Global Gourmet

Hot dogs originated in Germany as frankfurters: German smoked sausages. The American name "hot dog" was adopted during World War I. During that time, many Americans considered it unpatriotic to use German names for food.

DID YOU KNOW?

The world-popular French cuisine is famous for its sauces, soups, crisp breads, and pastries. French standards were one of the earliest gauges of fine cooking. The first French cookbooks date back to the Middle Ages.

Ways of the World

GREECE Ancient Greeks believed that a stranger might be a disguised god or goddess. Thus, they were kind to all strangers. The Greek tradition of hospitality to all continues to this day.

DID YOU KNOW?

Iceland heats most of its homes and hothouses with hot water pumped directly from its many hot springs.

economy, which is based on shipping and trade. Norway's land is not particularly suitable for farming, since it is mainly a high, mountain-covered plateau.

Provide time for students to share their findings. As they present their information, arrange the index cards down the side of a bulletin board, from wealthiest to poorest nations. Lead students to discover that the less wealthy European nations are in eastern Europe (Poland, Czech Republic, Slovakia, Hungary, Romania, Bulgaria, Macedonia, Croatia, Bosnia-Herzegovina, and so on).

LESSON PLAN
Unit 4 Atlas

These features and activities may be used as teaching tools throughout the course of the unit.

DID YOU KNOW?

Monaco is the world's second smallest independent state: only 0.6 square miles (1.6 sq. km), about the size of New York City's Central Park. It has the highest population density of any country: 49,520 people per square mile (14,856 per sq. km).

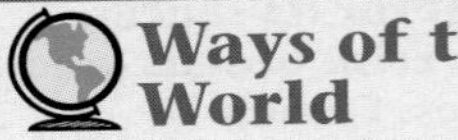

Ways of the World

NORWAY Women in Norway are a strong force in national politics. They make up one third of parliamentary members and 40 percent of the labor force. Their influence has helped Norway develop strong child care and educational and family programs.

DID YOU KNOW?

Finland has one of the world's cleanest environments. Helsinki, the capital, is called the White City of the North because of its cleanliness and its buildings of white native granite.

UNIT 4 ATLAS

COUNTRY PROFILE

COUNTRY* AND CAPITAL	FLAG AND LANGUAGES	POPULATION	LANDMASS	PRINCIPAL PRODUCTS EXPORT	PRINCIPAL PRODUCTS IMPORT
Malta (Valletta)	Maltese, English	400,000 3,125 per sq. mi. 1,286 per sq. km	120 sq. mi. 311 sq. km	Machinery	Machinery
Monaco (Monaco)	French	29,712 49,520 per sq. mi. 14,856 per sq. km	.6 sq. mi. 1.6 sq. km		
Netherlands (Amsterdam)	Dutch	15,400,000 1,175 per sq. mi. 454 per sq. km	13,100 sq. mi. 33,929 sq. km	Machinery	Machinery
Norway (Oslo)	Norwegian	4,300,000 36 per sq. mi. 14 per sq. km	118,470 sq. mi. 306,837 sq. km	Fuels	Machinery
Poland (Warsaw)	Polish	38,600,000 328 per sq. mi. 127 per sq. km	117,550 sq. mi. 304,455 sq. km	Machinery	Machinery
Portugal (Lisbon)	Portuguese	9,900,000 279 per sq. mi. 108 per sq. km	35,500 sq. mi. 91,945 sq. km	Textiles	Motor Vehicles
Romania (Bucharest)	Romanian, Hungarian, German	22,700,000 254 per sq. mi. 98 per sq. km	88,930 sq. mi. 230,329 sq. km	Fuels	Raw Materials
San Marino (San Marino)	Italian	20,000 1,000 per sq. mi. 384 per sq. km	20 sq. mi. 52 sq. km	Wine	Crude Oil
Slovakia (Bratislava)	Slovak	5,300,000 282 per sq. mi. 109 per sq. km	18,790 sq. mi. 48,667 sq. km	Machinery	Petroleum
Slovenia (Ljubljana)	Slovenian, Serbo-Croatian	2,000,000 254 per sq. mi. 98 per sq. km	7,820 sq. mi. 20,256 sq. km	Machinery	Machinery
Spain (Madrid)	Spanish, Catalan, Basque, Galician	39,200,000 203 per sq. mi. 78 per sq. km	192,830 sq. mi. 499,430 sq. km	Transport Equipment	Machinery
Sweden (Stockholm)	Swedish	8,800,000 55 per sq. mi. 21 per sq. km	158,930 sq. mi. 411,629 sq. km	Machinery	Machinery

*Country maps not drawn to scale.

Country Profile Activity

Interdependence Direct students to study the Export-Import columns on pages 218–221 for a few moments. Then suggest that they work in pairs or small groups to construct a trade dynamic using any four countries. Present the following as a beginning frame:

(Country)		(Country)	
Export	Import	Export	Import
(xxxx)	(xxxx)	(xxxx)	(xxxx)
(Country)		**(Country)**	
Export	Import	Export	Import
(xxxx)	(xxxx)	(xxxx)	(xxxx)

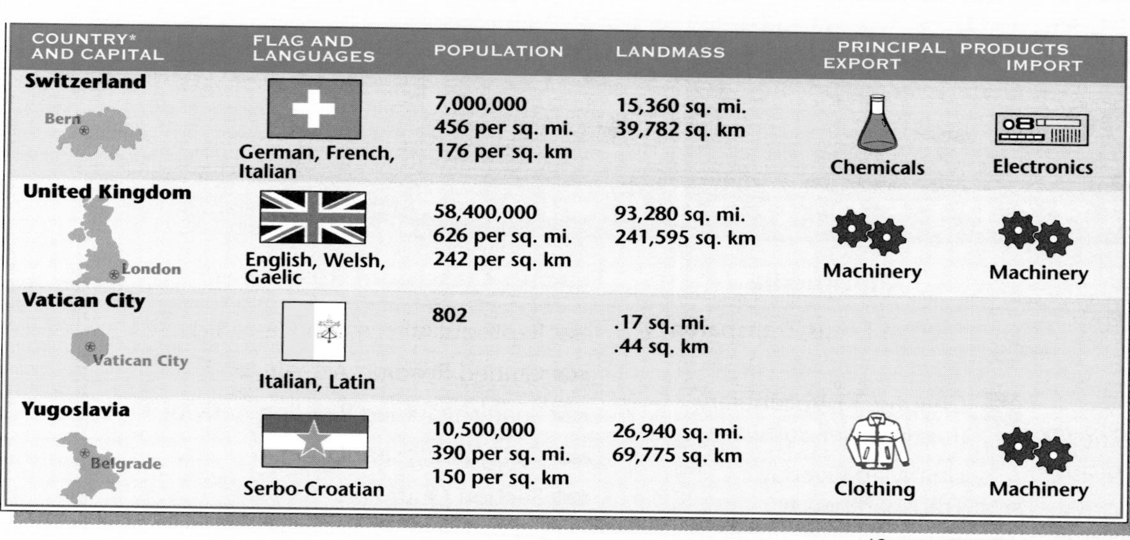

COUNTRY* AND CAPITAL	FLAG AND LANGUAGES	POPULATION	LANDMASS	PRINCIPAL PRODUCTS EXPORT	IMPORT
Switzerland Bern	German, French, Italian	7,000,000 456 per sq. mi. 176 per sq. km	15,360 sq. mi. 39,782 sq. km	Chemicals	Electronics
United Kingdom London	English, Welsh, Gaelic	58,400,000 626 per sq. mi. 242 per sq. km	93,280 sq. mi. 241,595 sq. km	Machinery	Machinery
Vatican City Vatican City	Italian, Latin	802	.17 sq. mi. .44 sq. km		
Yugoslavia Belgrade	Serbo-Croatian	10,500,000 390 per sq. mi. 150 per sq. km	26,940 sq. mi. 69,775 sq. km	Clothing	Machinery

*Country maps not drawn to scale.

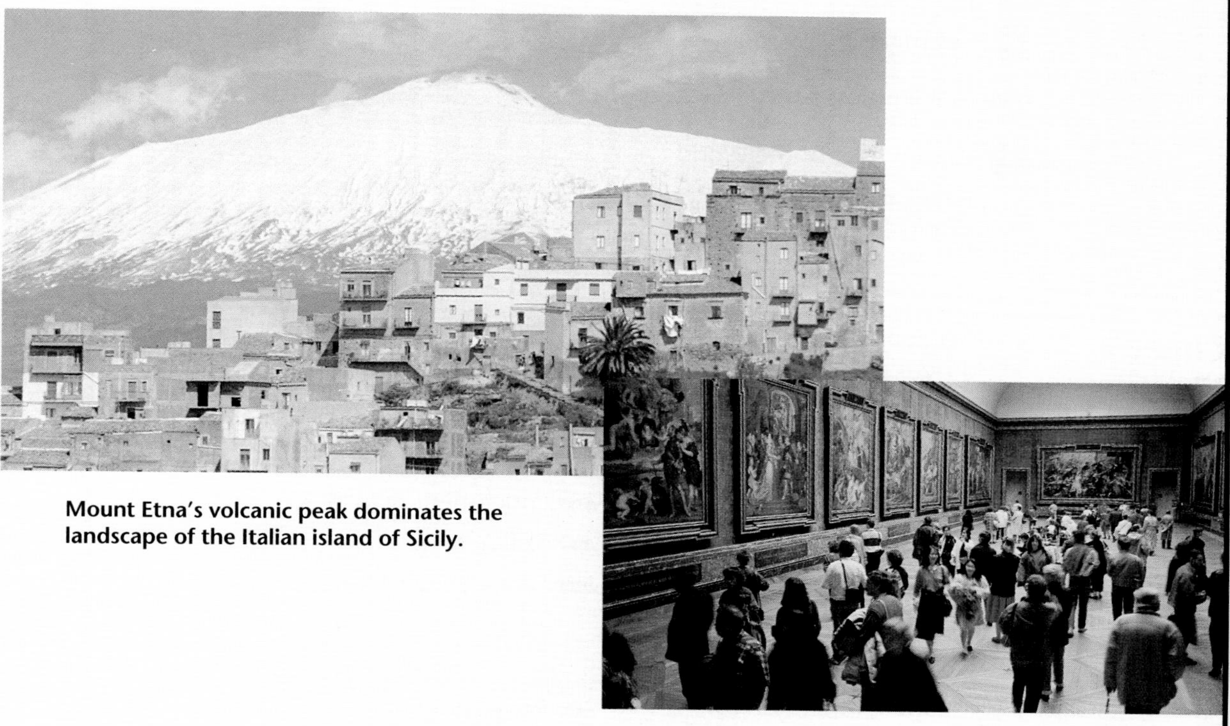

Mount Etna's volcanic peak dominates the landscape of the Italian island of Sicily.

The Louvre, in Paris, France, is considered one of the greatest art museums in the world.

Global Gourmet

A smorgasbord includes cold and warm dishes, meats, fishes, salads, dinner breads, desserts—all presented in buffet style. Swedish immigrants introduced this custom to the United States in the 1700s and 1800s.

Ways of the World

SWITZERLAND
Although Switzerland has much ethnic and religious diversity, its citizens are united under a strong federal government whose motto is "Unity, yes; uniformity, no." This attitude extends to its international relationships: Switzerland is politically neutral and not a member of the United Nations.

Ways of the World

ENGLAND The English do not like people to stand too close during conversations. They use a conservative approach with new acquaintances. Many English find Americans too casual, particularly in their use of the English language. In fact, some English do not consider the language spoken in the United States the same as the language they speak.

Have students show trade flow with arrows. Remind them that each country must be able to provide its citizens with necessities such as food and clothing, as well as jobs. Have students check that they have selected countries that can meet all of these needs, including goods for industrialization.

After students finish their dynamics, they might establish "trade ties" with other pairs or groups. Discuss how trade fosters interdependence among European countries.

Students may conclude by researching the European Union to learn its purpose and accomplishments.

CHAPTER 11

PLANNING GUIDE

The Physical Geography of Europe

CHAPTER ORGANIZER

Daily Lesson Objectives	Multimedia	Teacher Classroom Resources
SECTION 1 The Land 1. Describe the features that characterize Europe's coastline. 2. Locate the mountains and plains areas of Europe. 3. Identify the natural resources found in Europe.	Section Focus Transparency 11-1 Chapter 11 Vocabulary PuzzleMaker Software Unit Map Overlay Transparency 4-5 Geography and the Environment Testmaker STV: Restless Earth Picture Atlas of the World Physical Geography of the World Transparencies 21–30	Reproducible Lesson Plan 11-1 Guided Reading Activity 11-1 Spanish Guided Reading Activity 11-1 Geography Simulation 4 Section Quiz 11-1
SECTION 2 The Climate and Vegetation 1. Discuss how latitude and longitude and water bodies affect Europe's climate regions. 2. Recognize why Europe's natural vegetation has changed over the centuries.	Section Focus Transparency 11-2 Unit Map Overlay Transparencies 4-2 and 4-3 Political Map Transparency 4 Testmaker Geography and the Environment	Reproducible Lesson Plan 11-2 Guided Reading Activity 11-2 Spanish Guided Reading Activity 11-2 Workbook Activity 11-2 Enrichment Activity 11 Skill Activity 11 Section Quiz 11-2
CHAPTER REVIEW AND EVALUATION	Chapter 11 English (or Spanish) Audiocassettes MindJogger Videoquiz Testmaker Student Self-Test and Review Software	Reteaching Activity 11 Spanish Reteaching Activity 11 Chapter 11 Test Form A and Form B

0:00 *If time does not permit teaching the entire chapter, summarize using the Chapter 11 Highlights on page 235, and the Chapter 11 English (or Spanish) Audiocassettes. Review students' knowledge using the Glencoe MindJogger Videoquiz.*

KEY TO ABILITY LEVELS

Teaching strategies have been coded for varying learning styles and abilities.

L1 **BASIC** activities for all students

L2 **AVERAGE** activities for average to above-average students

L3 **CHALLENGING** activities for above-average students

LEP **LIMITED ENGLISH PROFICIENCY** activities

Performance Assessment

Making Comparisons Using maps of Europe and the United States and Canada and data from Chapters 5 and 11, students should search for physical features in Europe that are similar to those in the United States and Canada. They should list these physical features in T-charts. Students should then predict lifestyles in different areas of Europe.

Students should then take part in a scenario in which people in certain areas of the United States and Canada must emigrate due to a sudden natural phenomenon. Organize students into groups, and have each group formulate a plan for moving people to various locales in Europe. Each group could present a plan in the form of letters, a governmental booklet, or an "alert" newscast.

POSSIBLE RUBRIC FEATURES: Content information, concept attainment, ability to recognize relationships and draw conclusions, organization and clarity of ideas, viability of proposals

For additional professional and classroom resources, see Chapter Resources, pages T46–T51.

TEACHER'S CORNER

INDEX TO NATIONAL GEOGRAPHIC MAGAZINE

The following articles may be used for research relating to this chapter:

- "Volcanoes: Crucibles of Creation," by Noel Grove, December 1992.
- "Main-Danube Canal: Linking Europe's Waterways," by Bill Bryson, August 1992.
- "Switzerland: The Clockwork Country," by John J. Putman, January 1986.
- "Iberia's Vintage River," by Marion Kaplan, October 1984.
- "The Mediterranean: Sea of Man's Fate," by Rick Gore, December 1982.
- "The Civilizing Seine," by Charles McCarry, April 1982.
- "Striking It Rich in the North Sea," by Rick Gore, April 1977.

NATIONAL GEOGRAPHIC SOCIETY PRODUCTS AVAILABLE FROM GLENCOE

To order the following products for use with this chapter, contact your local Glencoe sales representative or call Glencoe at 1-800-334-7344:

- *Picture Atlas of the World* (CD-ROM)
- *STV: North America* (Videodisc)
- *STV: World Geography, South America and Antarctica* (Videodisc)
- *STV: Rain Forest* (Videodisc)
- *ZipZapMap! World* (Software)
- *GeoBee* (Software)
- *Images of the World* (Posters)
- *Eye on the Environment* (Posters)
- *Physical Geography of the World* (Transparencies)
- *Picture Atlas of Our 50 States* (Book)

ADDITIONAL NATIONAL GEOGRAPHIC SOCIETY PRODUCTS

To order the following products for use with this chapter, call National Geographic Society at 1-800-368-2728:

- *Geography of Europe Series,* "Northern Europe," "Western Europe," "Central Europe," "Southern Europe." (Filmstrip)
- *Nations of the World Series,* "East Germany," "West Germany." (Video)

PERFORMANCE ASSESSMENT

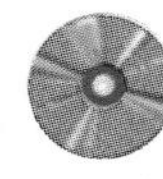

Refer to the Planning Guide on page 222B for a Performance Assessment Activity for this chapter. See the *Performance Assessment Activities* booklet for additional suggestions.

CHAPTER OBJECTIVES

1. **Identify** the four major landforms found in Europe.
2. **Explain** how Europe's location and physical features have affected its climate.

GLENCOE TECHNOLOGY

Videodisc

Use Chapter 11 MindJogger Videoquiz to preview chapter content.

MINDJOGGER VIDEOQUIZ

Chapter 11
Disc 2 Side A

The MindJogger Videoquiz is also available on videocassette.

chapter 11 The Physical Geography of Europe

CHAPTER FOCUS

Geographic Setting

The continent of Europe is a large peninsula with a long, irregular coastline. Europe's northern location and closeness to the sea result in a diversity of climates and kinds of vegetation.

Geographic Themes

Section 1 The Land

PLACE The continent of Europe consists of fertile plains interrupted by mountains.

Section 2 The Climate and Vegetation

LOCATION Europe's latitude and location relative to the sea affect its climate regions.

▲ Photograph: *Rolling meadows in southern England*

EXTRA CREDIT PROJECT

Script Have students work in groups to create scripts for an educational television program or travelogue about Europe. Ask them to use the map on page 225 to group the European countries into clusters of two to five countries. Then have each group prepare a script for one set of countries. If possible, have students record their narrations on audiotape or videotape. Consider videotaping large photographs or posters to accompany the narrations.

1 SECTION
The Land

SETTING THE SCENE

Read to Discover . . .
- the features of Europe's coastline.
- the characteristics of Europe's mountains and plains.
- the kinds of natural resources found in Europe.

Key Terms
- fjord
- polder
- peat

Identify and Locate
Eurasia, Scandinavian Peninsula, Iberian Peninsula, Balkan Peninsula, British Isles, Sicily, Alpine mountain system, North European Plain, Rhine River, Danube River, North Sea, English Channel

Gijón, Spain

¡Hola, amigos!
My family and I are spending our summer vacation in Gijón, a beautiful seaport in the northern region of Spain called Asturias. This region is known as the Switzerland of Spain because of its green valleys and tall snowy peaks. ¡Hasta pronto!
José María González

Europe's varied mountains, islands, and unusually long, irregular coastline offer many vacation sites like the ones described in José's postcard. Most of Europe lies within 300 miles (483 km) of a seacoast. This closeness to the sea has helped to fashion the history of its nations and the cultures of its peoples.

PLACE

Peninsulas and Islands

The continent of Europe is a giant peninsula that extends westward from northwestern Asia. Some geographers refer to this large landmass as Eurasia. The European continent curves in and out in a series of large and small peninsulas. For this reason, Europe often has been called "a peninsula of peninsulas."

The Northern Peninsulas

Norway and Sweden make up the Scandinavian Peninsula in northern Europe. During the Ice Ages, glaciers along the Norwegian coastline cut deep valleys to the ocean. When the ice sheets retreated, the sea filled in the valleys, called **fjords** (fee•YORDZ). The deep waters of the fjords provide fine harbors surrounded by rocky cliffs topped with thick forests.

Jutland, the northern peninsula opposite the Scandinavian Peninsula, is the major geographic feature of Denmark. Great sandy beaches extend along the western coast of Jutland. The marshes in the southwest result from the tides of the North Sea. Jutland's east-

LESSON PLAN
Chapter 11, Section 1

FOCUS

SECTION OBJECTIVES
1. **Describe** the features that characterize Europe's coastline.
2. **Locate** the mountains and plains areas of Europe.
3. **Identify** the natural resources found in Europe.

ABOUT THE POSTCARD
José likes to hike in the mountains and sail on the Bay of Biscay on his vacation.

BELLRINGER MOTIVATIONAL ACTIVITY
Project the Section 1 Focus Transparency and have students answer the questions.

PRETEACHING VOCABULARY
Explain that *fjords* are deep bays and long, narrow inlets along the coastline of Norway. Ask if students know of areas in the United States where inlets like fjords are located. *(coasts of Maine and Alaska)*

Use the Vocabulary PuzzleMaker Software to create a crossword or word search puzzle.

DID YOU KNOW?
Iceland is located at the meeting point of the North American and Eurasian continental plates. Its unique combination of glaciers and hot springs earned it the title "Land of Ice and Fire."

Classroom Resources for Section 1

BLACKLINE MASTERS:
Reproducible Lesson Plan 11-1
Geography Simulation 4
Guided Reading Activity 11-1
Section Quiz 11-1

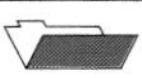
TRANSPARENCIES:
Section Focus Transparency 11-1
Unit Map Overlay Transparency 4-5
Physical Geography of the World Transparencies 21–30

MULTIMEDIA:

Vocabulary PuzzleMaker Software
Testmaker

Geography and the Environment STV: Restless Earth

Picture Atlas of the World

TEACH

GUIDED PRACTICE

Display Unit Map Overlay Transparency 4-5. Provide a list of physical features, such as peninsula, island, plain, mountain, river, and lake. Ask students to locate and identify an example of each feature found in Europe. **LEP**

Implement Geography Simulation 4 as a class activity.

USING ILLUSTRATIONS

PLACE Many steep-walled fjords have thick woods and roaring waterfalls. Slivers of fertile land lie at the foot of fjord walls.

Answer to Caption: *Glaciers carved valleys into the coastline; melting water from glaciers filled the valleys.*

GLENCOE TECHNOLOGY

Videodisc

Use the following to enrich Chapter 11:

GEOGRAPHY AND THE ENVIRONMENT
THE INFINITE VOYAGE
Living with Disaster

Chapter 5
Disc 3 Side A

Title: ***Earthquakes: A Turbulence Beneath the Earth***
Subject: The nature and cause of earthquakes is explained through animation

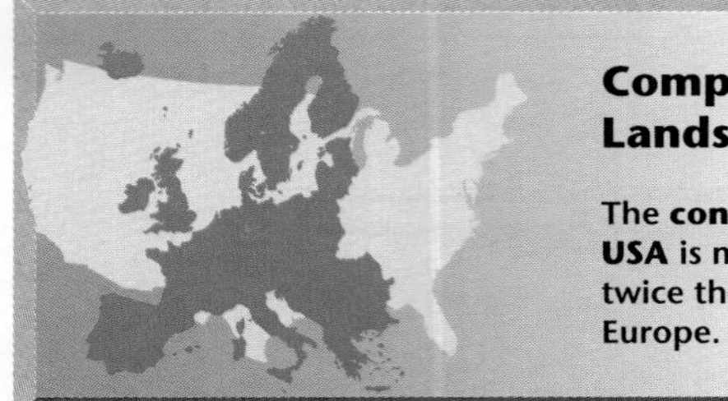

Comparing Lands

The **continental USA** is more than twice the size of Europe.

ern coast consists of rolling hills indented by narrow inlets.

The Southern Peninsulas

Spain and Portugal are located on southern Europe's Iberian Peninsula. Most of the Iberian Peninsula is a large, semiarid plateau. Sun-drenched plains stretch along the peninsula's western and southern coasts. The forested Pyrenees Mountains rise sharply along the northern coast and follow the border with France.

The Apennine Peninsula, which forms Italy, extends like a giant boot into the Mediterranean Sea. The interior of the southern part of the peninsula consists of mountains. The northern part is largely plains. Cliffs line the coast.

The former Yugoslav republics, Albania, Bulgaria, Greece, Romania, and the European part of Turkey occupy most of the Balkan Peninsula in southeastern Europe. The Black Sea, the Bosphorus, the Sea of Marmara, the Dardanelles Strait, and the Aegean Sea border the peninsula on the east. Like the Apennine Peninsula, the Balkan Peninsula is mountainous and is sometimes subject to earthquakes and volcanic activity.

Atlantic Islands

The island country of Iceland lies just south of the Arctic Circle in the North Atlantic Ocean. Grassy lowlands stretch along Iceland's coast, but the land rises sharply to form a large plateau that covers most of the island. Lying

Geographic Themes

Region: Scandinavian Peninsula

Long narrow inlets called fjords are common along the mountainous Norwegian coast of the Scandinavian Peninsula. *How were fjords formed?*

Cooperative Learning Activity

Organize the class into four groups. Assign each group one of the following geographic features: seas, islands, peninsulas, or mountains. Have each group list examples of its assigned feature in Europe.

Ask each group member to choose one item on the list to research. Encourage students to use encyclopedias and other references to determine the location of the feature, its importance to the region, and other relevant information. Each group should then construct a chart of this information and explain it to the class. Consider displaying the completed charts for future reference.

EUROPE: PHYSICAL-POLITICAL

ELEVATIONS
Feet / Meters
5,000 / 1,500
2,000 / 600
1,000 / 300
0 / 0

National boundary
Capital city

Conic Projection

Focus on Geographic Themes

1. **Movement:** How does the Rhine River contribute to Germany's economy?
2. **Region:** What mountain chain extends through the Italian Peninsula?
3. **Region:** What body of water separates the United Kingdom from Denmark?
4. **Place:** What city is the capital of Portugal?

Meeting Special Needs

Study Strategy Students who have difficulty preparing for tests may benefit from creating their own study guides. Have students outline Section 1, using subheads as major headings and noting important points beneath each heading. Students can use these study guides when preparing for the section review.

USING MAPS

Answers:
1. It connects industrial cities to Rotterdam on the North Sea; **2.** Apennines; **3.** North Sea; 4. Lisbon

Map Skills Practice
Reading a Map Which country has more lowland areas: Norway or Sweden? *(Sweden; Norway is almost completely mountainous)* What body of water borders Europe on the east? *(Black Sea)*

L1 Geography: Location Place slips of paper with the names of European countries in a box. Have each student choose a slip and write a detailed description of that country's location. As volunteers read their descriptions, have other students identify the country.

L2 Comparing Have students investigate and compare Europe's Atlantic islands and Mediterranean islands. Discuss possible bases of comparison, such as climate, physical features, size, economic activities, and political status.

Videodisc

STV: RESTLESS EARTH

Side 1, Chapter 2
Frames 14560-37468
Title: ***Volcanoes in Iceland* (in its entirety)**
Subject: Describes how volcanic activity has influenced human activity in Iceland

INDEPENDENT PRACTICE

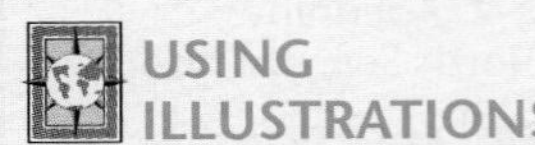

Guided Reading Have students complete Guided Reading Activity 11-1 in the TCR. **LEP**

USING ILLUSTRATIONS

MOVEMENT With 35 major ports, the Danube has the largest shipping volume of any European river. Commercial ships and barges carry agricultural goods, chemicals, steel, and other products.

Answer to Caption: *the Hungarian Basin*

MULTICULTURAL PERSPECTIVE

Culturally Speaking
Switzerland's location in the center of western Europe has influenced the development of its diverse culture. Switzerland shares borders with four countries and has four official languages: German, French, Italian, and Romansch.

CD-ROM

PICTURE ATLAS OF THE WORLD
You and your students can see and hear the sights and sounds of Europe by clicking the "Photos" and "Essay" buttons of selected countries.

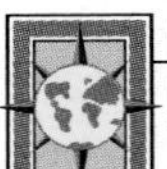

Geographic Themes

Place: Danube River, Hungary
The Danube River, one of Europe's most important waterways, flows through Budapest, the capital of Hungary. *What plains area does the Danube cross?*

astride the Mid-Atlantic Ridge, Iceland is an area of volcanoes, hot springs, and geysers. Because of Iceland's far-northern location, large glaciers are found next to volcanoes and hot springs.

The British Isles, which lie northwest of the European mainland, consist of two large islands, Great Britain and Ireland, and thousands of smaller islands. Mountain ranges, plateaus, and deep valleys cover most of northern and eastern Great Britain, while low hills and gently rolling plains dominate in the south. Ireland, often called the Emerald Isle, is a lush green land of cool temperatures and abundant rainfall. In many places, the rugged coastline of the British Isles rises in rocky cliffs that drop to deep bays.

Mediterranean Islands

Major islands south of Europe include the Balearic Islands, Corsica, Sardinia, Sicily, and Malta. These islands generally are rugged, mountainous places, but their warm climate and beautiful scenery attract many tourists. Many Greek islands are chiefly hills and fertile valleys.

PLACE

Mountains and Plains

Europe is essentially plains interrupted by mountains running through its interior and along its northern and southern edges.

Mountain Regions

Rugged highlands run from the northern part of the British Isles through the Scandinavian Peninsula. These Northwest Mountains include some of the oldest rock formations on the earth. The Central Uplands extend from the Iberian Peninsula through France and Germany to eastern Europe. This rocky, barren

Critical Thinking

Drawing Conclusions Ask students to study the map on page 225. Note that it shows landforms, rivers, and national boundaries. Ask them to use the map to draw conclusions about ways that geographic features such as mountains, rivers, and seas have helped determine national boundaries. Encourage students to consider how these features may cut off certain regions or protect them from invasions. Have students write their conclusions and then discuss them with the class.

Geographic Themes

Place: Mont Blanc, French Alps

Mont Blanc rises 15,771 feet (4,807 m) and is the highest mountain in the Alps. Its peak is always snow-covered. *Where is the Alpine mountain system located?*

region includes low mountains and high plateaus with scattered forests.

The Alpine mountain system extends across southern Europe from Spain to the Balkan Peninsula. It branches into Russia and some of the Eurasian republics in the region of the Caspian Sea. The Alpine mountain system is higher and younger than those of the Northwest Mountains region and the Central Uplands. Several mountain ranges, including the Alps and the Carpathians, make up the Alpine system. The Alps, however, make up the largest part. These world-famous peaks cover most of Switzerland and Austria and parts of Italy and France. The snowcapped Alps provide some of the world's most spectacular scenery as well as uncounted challenges for expert skiers and accomplished mountain climbers. A British mountain climber offers this description:

The Alps stretch in a tight-drawn bow for five hundred miles [805 km], from the Mediterranean to the Adriatic; a mountainspine which has helped to determine the history of Europe throughout the ages and which today provides the most developed playground in the world. It was also the birthplace of both mountaineering and skiing as sports.

Plains Regions

Europe's broad, fertile plains curve around the highlands. The vast North European Plain stretches from the southeastern United Kingdom and western France more than 1,800 miles (2,896 km) eastward to Poland. An extension of the plain reaches into Ukraine, Belarus, and Russia.

USING ILLUSTRATIONS

LOCATION Mont Blanc is located near the border of France and Italy.

Answer to Caption: *It extends across southern Europe and branches into Russia and some Eurasian republics.*

L2 Comparing Have students make a chart comparing Europe's major rivers. For each river they should include the source, direction of flow, outlet, and other facts. Some students might also construct a bar graph to compare the lengths of the rivers.

DID YOU KNOW?

The Loch Ness monster is a large sea creature that many people believe lives in Loch Ness, a lake in northern Scotland. The animal, nicknamed Nessie, supposedly has flippers, one or two humps, and a long slender neck. Reported sightings date back as far as A.D. 565.

Extending the Content

Earth Science Many of the world's best-known glaciers are in Europe. The Mer de Glace on Mont Blanc and the Aletsch Glacier are in the Alps. The Jostedal Glacier in Norway covers about 300 square miles (780 sq. km) and is the largest glacier on the European continent. Students may wish to research the formation and movement of glaciers.

USING ILLUSTRATIONS

MOVEMENT The United Kingdom and Norway own most of the North Sea's gas and oil reserves. Natural gas from under the sea is piped ashore to the United Kingdom and Germany.

Answer to Caption: *eastern Europe, especially Bulgaria and Romania*

L2 Sequence Have students create a chart or other graphic to indicate the sources of energy Europeans have used throughout history. Encourage students to find out how Europeans developed and used each source.

ASSESS

CHECK FOR UNDERSTANDING

Assign Section 1 Review as homework or an in-class activity.

MEETING LESSON OBJECTIVES

Each objective below is tested by the questions that follow it in parentheses.

1. **Describe** the features that characterize Europe's coastline. *(3)*
2. **Locate** the mountains and plains areas of Europe. *(2)*
3. **Identify** the natural resources found in Europe. *(4, 5)*

Geographic Themes

Human/Environment Interaction: North Sea Oil and Gas Fields
Europe's richest oil and natural gas fields are found in the North Sea between Scotland and Norway. *What other area of Europe has oil and natural gas resources?*

Most of the North European Plain is rolling land with isolated hills or low mountains. In the Netherlands, people pumped out the water to reclaim land that once was covered by the sea. The **polders**, or drained areas, became rich farmland like many other parts of the North European Plain.

Other plains regions are located in parts of Italy and the Iberian Peninsula and among the mountain ranges of eastern Europe. The Hungarian Basin is a treeless stretch of land noted for agriculture and horse-raising. In general, fertile soils and ease of movement have made the plains regions the most populated areas in Europe.

MOVEMENT

Rivers and Lakes

Many of Europe's rivers flow from interior mountain and highland areas to the coasts. They provide water to irrigate farmland and to produce electricity. Today, as in the past, Europe's rivers play an important role as transportation links between the interior and the coast. Europe does not have many large lakes similar to the Great Lakes in North America. A large number of lakes, however, are located in Sweden and Finland.

Rivers

Europe's rivers have differing characteristics. The rivers in Scandinavia are short and do not provide easy connections between cities. In the heartland of western and eastern Europe, however, relatively long rivers provide links between inland areas as well as to the sea. The Rhine is the most important river in western Europe. It flows from Switzerland, along the border of France and then north through Germany and the Netherlands, connecting many industrial cities to the busy port of Rotterdam on the North Sea. The Danube, which flows 1,776 miles (2,858 km) from Germany's Black Forest to the Black Sea, is eastern Europe's most important waterway. Each year, ships and barges carry millions of tons of cargo on the Danube. The major rivers of the Iberian Peninsula are too narrow and shallow

Cooperative Learning Activity

Have small groups prepare presentations about Europe's mineral resources. Assign each of the following minerals to a group: copper, lead, zinc, bauxite, potash, and uranium. The group should be prepared to explain where the mineral is found, how it is processed, and how it is used.

for large ships. Britain's Thames River, on the other hand, allows oceangoing ships to reach the port of London.

Lakes

Many lakes formed in the Scandinavian countries and Finland when melting glaciers retreated after the last Ice Age. Lakes cover about one-twelfth of Sweden, and Finland's interior plateau is called the Lake Plateau. Some of western and eastern Europe's most popular recreation areas center around lakes famous for their natural beauty. Located on the border between France and Switzerland, the clear blue waters of Lake Geneva mirror the Alpine peaks that surround it. The shores of Lake Como in northern Italy are lined with fertile vineyards and fine gardens. Hungary's Lake Balaton provides a scenic attraction among gently rolling hills and low mountains.

HUMAN/ENVIRONMENT INTERACTION

Natural Resources

Minerals rank among Europe's most important natural resources. Many mineral deposits are found in the plains and mountain areas of the European mainland. Others are located in the highlands of the British Isles and in the countries of southwestern Europe.

Iron and Coal

Europe, the birthplace of modern industry, has considerable amounts of coal and iron ore. These resources are considered the traditional necessities of an industrial society because they are used together to make steel. The major iron ore deposits are found in northeastern France, western Germany, northern Sweden, and the Balkan Peninsula. The major coal deposits are in the British Isles, the Ruhr district in western Germany, northern France, Belgium, the Czech Republic, and Poland.

Other Energy Sources

Resources that provide fuel for homes and factories in Europe vary widely. **Peat**, a kind of vegetable matter usually composed of mosses, was traditionally burned as fuel in some western European homes. Today Europeans largely rely on such energy sources as coal, oil, gas, and nuclear and hydroelectric power. The discovery and development of vast oil and natural gas reserves under the North Sea in the 1960s and 1970s greatly increased western Europe's energy sources. Eastern Europe also has oil and natural gas resources, especially in Bulgaria and Romania. Fast-flowing streams and rivers throughout the continent provide good sources of power for electricity. The world's first tidal power plant began operating in France in the 1960s. This plant uses the power of incoming and outgoing tides to provide electricity.

Other Mineral Resources

Two of Europe's major resources are bauxite, a source of aluminum, and potash, an element used in fertilizer. Bauxite deposits are found in southern France, Hungary, and the former Yugoslav republics, while potash is located in France, Germany, and Spain. Other minerals mined in Europe include copper, lead, zinc, uranium, gold, and silver. Many of Europe's industrial and transportation centers developed near mineral deposits.

SECTION 1 REVIEW

Checking for Understanding

1. **Define** fjord, polder, peat.
2. **Locating Places** Where are Europe's major mountain regions located?
3. **Region** What are three characteristics of Europe's coastline?
4. **Human/Environment Interaction** What are Europe's major energy sources?

Critical Thinking

5. **Drawing Conclusions** How did Europe's rivers contribute to the development of its industries?

EVALUATE

Assign the Section 1 Quiz in the TCR.

Use the Testmaker to create a customized quiz for Section 1.

RETEACH

Have students list the countries of Europe and identify major landforms, rivers, and lakes in each one.

ENRICH

Challenge students to find out how the movement of continental plates, glacial action, and volcanic activity have shaped the geography of Europe. Provide time to share their findings.

CLOSE

Have students write a postcard to José, recommending a vacation spot in their own region.

PHYSICAL GEOGRAPHY OF THE WORLD TRANSPARENCIES

Display and discuss the physical features of the following transparencies:

21. Surtsey, Iceland
22. Rock of Gibraltar
23. Gathering Peat, Ireland
24. Oil Rig, North Sea
25. Fjord, Norway
26. Matterhorn, Switzerland/Italy
27. Black Forest, Germany
28. Danube River, Hungary
29. Great European Plain, Lithuania
30. Crete, Greece

ANSWERS TO SECTION 1 REVIEW

1. **fjord:** deep, water-filled valley carved by glaciers along Norway's coast; **polder:** area of the Netherlands' coast reclaimed from the sea; **peat:** vegetable matter burned as fuel
2. Northwest Mountains extend from the northern part of the British Isles through the Scandinavian Peninsula; Central Uplands extend from the Iberian Peninsula through France and Germany to eastern Europe; Alpine Mountain System stretches across southern Europe from Spain to the Caspian Sea.
3. peninsulas, islands, bays, and inlets
4. peat, oil, natural gas, fast-flowing streams, and tides
5. Europe's rivers link the interior with coastal ports.

LESSON PLAN
Chapter 11, Section 2

FOCUS

SECTION OBJECTIVES

1. **Discuss** how latitude and longitude and water bodies affect Europe's climate regions.
2. **Recognize** why Europe's natural vegetation has changed over the centuries.

BELLRINGER MOTIVATIONAL ACTIVITY

Project the Section 2 Focus Transparency and have students answer the questions.

PRETEACHING VOCABULARY

Explain that *mistral* comes from a French word; *sirocco* comes from Italian; and *foehn* is a German word. Ask students why these three terms for wind come from different languages. *(Each kind of wind affects the region where the language is spoken.)*

USING ILLUSTRATIONS

REGION The Po Valley is Italy's richest and most modern agricultural region. It is also the country's most densely populated area.

Answer to Caption: *Europe's northern latitude and its location near large bodies of water*

SECTION 2

The Climate and Vegetation

SETTING THE SCENE

Read to Discover . . .
- how latitude and water bodies affect Europe's climate regions.
- why Europe's natural vegetation has changed over the centuries.

Key Terms
- mistral
- sirocco
- permafrost
- foehn
- avalanche
- chaparral

Identify and Locate
Gulf Stream, North Atlantic Drift, Climate regions: marine west coast, Mediterranean, humid continental, humid subtropical, steppe, subarctic, tundra, highland

Europe's climates vary from the tundra and subarctic regions of Iceland, Scandinavia, and Finland to the Mediterranean coasts of Italy, Spain, and Greece. Its diverse vegetation includes the dark fir and spruce trees of Germany's Black Forest as well as the short grasses and scattered shrubs of Spain's dry, central plateau, the Meseta. In Europe, as in other parts of the world, climate and vegetation patterns are closely linked. Europe's northern latitude and its location near large bodies of water are major factors in determining the diversity of its climates and vegetation.

Geographic Themes

Place: Po River Valley, Italy
The Po River valley of northern Italy is an area of productive farms and factories. *What two major factors help shape the diversity of Europe's climate and vegetation?*

REGION

Europe's Climate Regions

In spite of Europe's northern location, most of the continent has a mild climate. The climate in many parts of Europe is milder than that of other places in the world at about the same latitude. For example, January temperatures in Frankfurt, Germany, are warmer than those in Winnipeg, Canada, or in Irkutsk in the Asian part of Russia. Yet all three cities are about the same distance from the Equator. Europe's peninsular location in relation to the sea helps explain its relatively mild climate.

Major Climate Regions

A large part of western Europe has a marine west coast climate. This climate region extends from the Arctic Circle to the Alps and from Ireland to the western parts of Poland, the Czech Republic, and Hungary. Places in this climate region enjoy moderate tempera-

Classroom Resources for Section 2

BLACKLINE MASTERS:
Reproducible Lesson Plan 11-2
Guided Reading Activity 11-2
Spanish Guided Reading Activity 11-2
Workbook Activity 11-2
Skill Activity 11
Section Quiz 11-2

TRANSPARENCIES:
Section Focus Transparency 11-2
Unit Map Overlay Transparencies 4-2, 4-3
Political Map Transparency 4

MULTIMEDIA:
Testmaker

Geography and the Environment

tures in both summer and winter, and they receive between 20 and 40 inches (51 and 102 cm) of precipitation each year.

Northwest Europe's temperate, moist climate is caused by winds that blow across the continent from the Atlantic Ocean. The Gulf Stream and the North Atlantic Drift are powerful ocean currents that bring warm water from the Gulf of Mexico and the middle part of the Atlantic Ocean near the Equator to the west coast of Europe. Prevailing westerly winds, blowing over these currents, carry warm air across the continent. Even the Norwegian coast, which lies in northern Europe, remains ice-free in winter as a result of this climate pattern.

Most of southern Europe has a Mediterranean climate. Places in this part of the continent have hot, dry summers and mild, rainy winters. Southern Europe receives less yearly precipitation than northwestern Europe, because the Alpine mountain system and shifting air pressure belts during summer block the moist Atlantic winds. In winter, however, winds from the Mediterranean bring moderate rainfall. Local winds in this region sometimes cause changes in the normal weather pattern. The **mistral**, a strong, northerly wind from the Alps, may bring very cold air to southern France. **Siroccos,** hot winds from the North African deserts of Libya, can bring desert air and dust.

Most of eastern and northern Europe has a humid continental climate. This climate region includes the eastern parts of Poland, Hungary, the Czech Republic, Slovakia, Romania, and Bulgaria. The southern parts of Sweden and Finland also have a humid continental climate. Warm ocean currents have little influence on the climate because of the distance from the North Atlantic. Therefore, places in the humid continental climate region have greater differences between summer and winter temperatures than places in western and southern Europe.

EUROPE: CLIMATE REGIONS

Steppe
Mediterranean
Humid subtropical
Marine west coast
Humid continental
Subarctic
Highland

Lambert Conformal Conic projection

Focus on Geographic Themes

1. **Region:** What climate regions are found in Scandinavia?
2. **Movement:** Why does northwestern Europe have a milder climate than eastern Europe?
3. **Region:** What climate region includes eastern Switzerland and western Austria?
4. **Place:** What kind of climate region is found in central Italy?

Other Climates

Several other climates are found in small areas of Europe. A humid subtropical region stretches from northern Italy to the central part of the Balkan Peninsula. Parts of Spain's Meseta have a steppe, or partly dry, climate.

Most of Iceland and the northern parts of Scandinavia and Finland have subarctic and tundra climates. Places in these climate regions have long, bitterly cold winters and short, cool summers. Tundra and subarctic regions have **permafrost**, soil that is often permanently frozen below the surface.

The Alps have a highland climate with generally colder temperatures and more pre-

TEACH

GUIDED PRACTICE

L2 Environment Have students compare Unit Map Overlay Transparencies 4-2 and 4-3. Ask them to describe the relationship between Europe's climate regions and vegetation.

CURRICULUM CONNECTION

EARTH SCIENCE

Western Europe experiences avalanches, but its location and climate protect it from many other weather-related disasters, such as hurricanes and tornadoes.

L3 Apply Have students identify a place in Europe and in North America at about the same latitude. Direct them to compare both average temperatures and explain reasons for any differences in climate.

USING MAPS

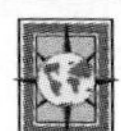

Answers:
1. marine west coast, humid continental, subarctic;
2. Warm ocean currents and westerly winds provide a moderate climate for northwest Europe.
3. highlands;
4. Mediterranean

Map Skills Practice

Reading a Map Which part of Europe has a steppe climate? *(southeast coast of Spain)*

Cooperative Learning Activity

Organize students into six groups. Assign one of the following locations and seasons to each group: Ireland—Summer; Hungary—Winter; Italy—Summer; Finland—Winter; Spain—Summer; Greece—Winter. Instruct each group to plan a vacation to its assigned location during the season specified. Have groups be sure to list the kinds of clothing they would take with them, based on the seasonal climate.

INDEPENDENT PRACTICE

Guided Reading Have students complete Guided Reading Activity 11-2 in the TCR. LEP

USING MAPS

Answers:
1. parts of Scandinavia and Latvia and Lithuania, the Alps, northeastern Poland; **2.** deciduous and mixed forests; **3.** Iberian Peninsula and along Mediterranean coast; **4.** Spain and Romania

Map Skills Practice
Comparing Maps Compare the maps on pages 231 and 232. What climate produces deciduous forests in northern and western Europe? *(marine west coast)*

ASSESS

CHECK FOR UNDERSTANDING

Assign Section 2 Review as homework or an in-class activity.

MEETING LESSON OBJECTIVES

Each objective below is tested by the questions that follow it in parentheses.
1. Discuss how latitude and longitude and water bodies affect Europe's climate regions. *(1, 3)*
2. Recognize why Europe's natural vegetation has changed over the centuries. *(2, 4)*

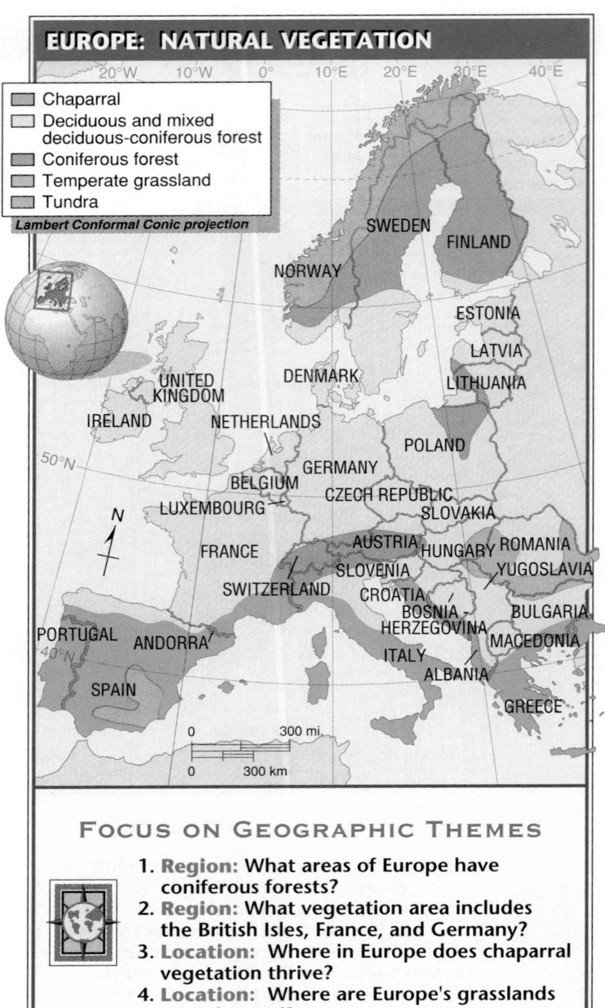

FOCUS ON GEOGRAPHIC THEMES

1. **Region: What areas of Europe have coniferous forests?**
2. **Region: What vegetation area includes the British Isles, France, and Germany?**
3. **Location: Where in Europe does chaparral vegetation thrive?**
4. **Location: Where are Europe's grasslands areas located?**

cipitation than nearby lowland areas. Sudden changes can occur, however, when dry winds called **foehns** (FUHNZ) blow down from the mountains. Foehns can cause an **avalanche**, a mass of ice, snow, or rock sliding down a mountainside.

HUMAN/ENVIRONMENT INTERACTION

Europe's Vegetation

The natural vegetation of Europe consists of forests, grasslands, and tundra plants. These types of vegetation are closely linked to the climate regions. Over the centuries, changing climate patterns have affected vegetation, but people have caused even greater changes.

Natural Vegetation Patterns

Deciduous forests, trees that lose their leaves, are the natural vegetation of Europe's marine west coast climate region. These forests include ash, beech, elm, maple, and oak trees that provide spectacular autumn color. Coniferous forests, needle-leaf evergreen trees consisting of fir, larch, pine, and spruce, are common in northern Europe and in mountain areas. Mediterranean climates support broad-leaved evergreens, such as the cork oak tree and the olive tree. Such trees are well suited to the dry summers of this climate region. Their tough, waxy leaves conserve moisture. Unlike other broad-leaved trees, they do not lose their leaves in autumn.

Parts of the North European Plain consist of grasslands. The height of the grasses is related to the amount of rainfall in the region. Fertile areas with tall grasses cover most of the western plain. Dry areas where only short grasses grow are found in Hungary and parts of the Iberian Peninsula. The hot, dry summers of the Mediterranean area produce **chaparral**, or shrubs and short trees. The tundra region near Europe's Arctic coast supports little vegetation. Mosses, small shrubs, and colorful wildflowers cover the tundra during the brief summer, however. The upper slopes of the Alps resemble tundra and support similar kinds of vegetation.

Human Interaction

Europeans cut down most of the natural forests that once covered large parts of the continent. They cleared the land for agriculture and industry and used the timber for fuel and building materials. Today, much of the once-forested land is occupied by urban areas and farms. Farmers also use parts of the tundra and high mountains as grazing land.

Great pine and spruce forests still cover parts of Scandinavia and Finland. Forests also cover parts of Poland, Slovakia, and the Czech

Meeting Special Needs

Language Delayed A troublesome challenge for students with language difficulties is asking their teachers questions. Form small groups and ask group members to practice developing questions, using the text under the heading "Europe's Vegetation." Praise groups for producing many, varied questions.

COMPARING CLIMATE REGIONS

Europe and the United States

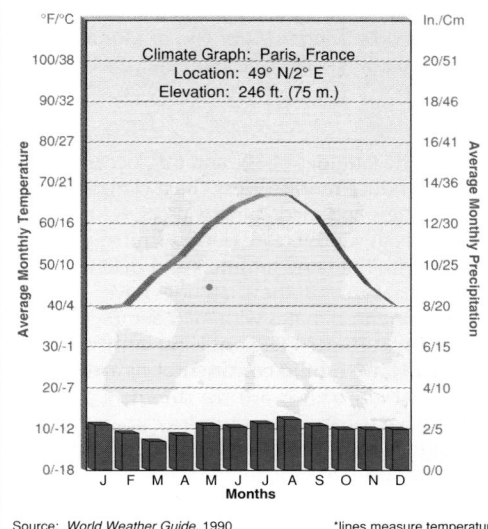

Climate Graph: Paris, France
Location: 49° N/2° E
Elevation: 246 ft. (75 m.)

°F/°C: 100/38, 90/32, 80/27, 70/21, 60/16, 50/10, 40/4, 30/-1, 20/-7, 10/-12, 0/-18
Average Monthly Temperature
In./Cm: 20/51, 18/46, 16/41, 14/36, 12/30, 10/25, 8/20, 6/15, 4/10, 2/5, 0/0
Average Monthly Precipitation
J F M A M J J A S O N D
Months

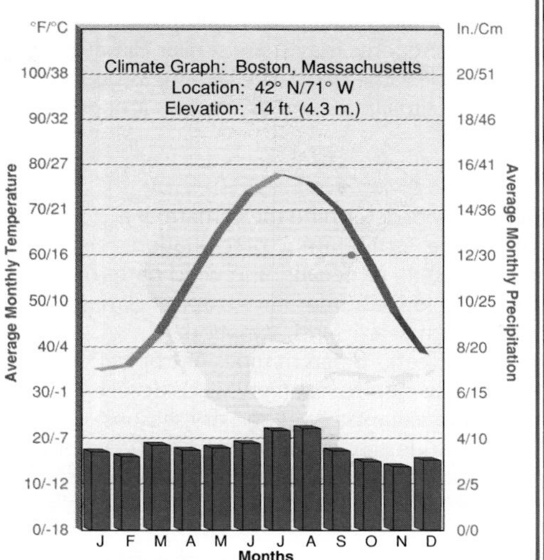

Source: *World Weather Guide*, 1990

*lines measure temperature/bars measure precipitation

GRAPH STUDY

The climate graphs above show the average monthly temperatures and the average monthly precipitation in Paris, France, and in Boston, Massachusetts. ***What is the average January temperature and precipitation in each city?***

Republic. Lumbering is an important industry in these European forest regions.

Some European governments regulate the cutting of trees to protect forests. In Germany's Black Forest, for example, new trees are planted to replace trees that are cut for timber.

Air pollution from Europe's industries and automobiles, however, poses a serious threat to forests as well as to other natural vegetation. In many industrialized countries, such as Germany, Belgium, Poland, and the Czech Republic, auto and factory pollution has brought widespread disaster to many woodlands. For example, scientists estimate that more than 20 percent of forests in the Czech Republic have been either killed or irreversibly damaged as a result of unregulated pollution.

SECTION 2 REVIEW

Checking for Understanding

1. **Define** mistral, sirocco, permafrost, foehn, avalanche, chaparral.
2. **Locating Places** In which country is the Black Forest located?
3. **Region** What type of climate is found in northwestern Europe?

Critical Thinking

4. **Determining Cause and Effect** How has human interaction with the environment changed vegetation patterns in Europe?

ANSWERS TO SECTION 2 REVIEW

1. **mistral:** strong north wind from the mountains that brings cold air to southern France; **sirocco:** hot wind that brings desert air from Africa to western Europe's Mediterranean coast; **permafrost:** soil that is often permanently frozen below ground; **foehn:** dry wind that blows down from the mountains in Alpine areas; **avalanche:** mass of ice, snow, or rock sliding down a mountainside; **chaparral:** shrubs and short trees
2. Germany
3. marine west coast climate
4. People cut down forests in much of Europe and used the land for agriculture.

EVALUATE

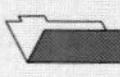 Assign the Section 2 Quiz in the TCR.

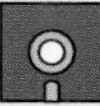 Use the Testmaker to create a customized quiz for Section 2.

USING GRAPHS

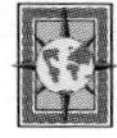 ***Answers:*** Paris 40°F (4°C), 2 in. (5 cm); Boston 35°F (2°C), 3.8 in. (9.5 cm)

 ***Skills Practice***

Interpreting a Graph
Why does Paris have a cooler summer than Boston? *(Paris is at a higher elevation; its temperatures are affected by ocean currents and winds.)*

RETEACH

 Have students complete Reteaching Activity 11 in the TCR.

ENRICH

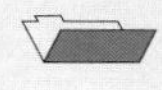 Have students complete Enrichment Activity 11 in the TCR.

CLOSE

Ask students how climate affects life in different parts of Europe.

GLENCOE TECHNOLOGY

 **Videodisc**

GEOGRAPHY AND THE ENVIRONMENT
THE INFINITE VOYAGE
Crisis in the Atmosphere

Chapter 9
Disc 2 Side A
Title: ***Energy Conservation: Changes in Switzerland***
Subject: Electric-car technology allows autos to run off of batteries that are recharged from solar panels

TEACH

Ask students about their own climatic region: What seasons do we have? What are average temperatures during these seasons? How much precipitation do we have? When do we have the most and the least precipitation? How does the climate affect the economy, social activities, food, dress, housing, and so on?

Direct students to read the skill on page 234. Ask: "Which climates are in the middle latitudes?" *(marine west coast, Mediterranean, humid subtropical, humid continental)* "Which climate has the coldest winters?" *(humid continental)*

Skills Practice For additional practice, have students complete Skill Activity 11 in the TCR.

MAP & GRAPH SKILLS

Reading a Climate Map

Climate is a main factor determining how people dress, live, work, and play in a particular region. People on different continents may share similar climates. For example, people living in Wyoming or Montana must survive the same harsh, dry climate as people in western China. By reading a climate map, you can discover these similarities and differences among regions.

REVIEWING THE SKILL

Several factors determine the climate of a region: latitude, temperature, precipitation, altitude, proximity to oceans, and wind patterns. Regions in the low latitudes have tropical climates, which are warm year-round. Variation in precipitation creates different types of tropical climates such as **rain forest** (very wet), **desert** (very dry), and **savanna** (wet and dry seasons).

Middle-latitude climates have seasonal variations in temperature. On the west coast of continents between the latitudes of 30° and 60°, ocean breezes produce **marine west coast** climates with cool summers and mild damp winters. Near the tropics, ocean winds create **humid subtropical** climates with hot rainy summers and mild winters. Other coastal areas in these latitudes have **Mediterranean** climates with mild damp winters and hot dry summers. Regions lying farther north and inland have **humid continental** climates with cold snowy winters and warmer summers. Polar regions have **subarctic** and **tundra** climates with bitterly cold winters and short cool summers.

Steppe (or semidesert) climates are dry but have more rainfall than deserts; these occur all over the globe. **Highland**, or mountain, climates vary with elevation.

On a climate map, different colors represent various climate regions. The map key explains the color code. To read a climate map, apply the following steps:

- Identify the area covered in the map.
- Study the key to identify the climate regions on the map.
- Locate the regions in each climate zone.
- Draw conclusions about the climate similarities and differences among regions.

EUROPE: CLIMATE REGIONS

Steppe
Mediterranean
Humid subtropical
Marine west coast
Humid continental
Subarctic
Highland

Lambert Conformal Conic projection

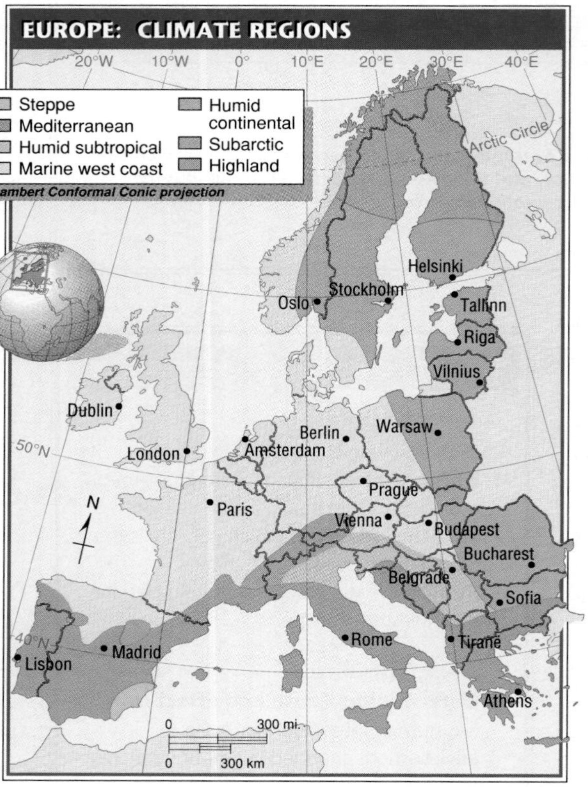

PRACTICING THE SKILL

Use the map to answer the following questions about climate maps:

1. What geographic area does this map cover?
2. Name two European cities that share a Mediterranean climate.
3. What kind of climate is shared by most of the countries in northwestern Europe?
4. Which region has the coolest climate?
5. Describe the climate in Sofia and Riga.

For additional practice in this skill, see Practicing Skills on page 236 of the Chapter 11 Review.

ANSWERS TO PRACTICING THE SKILL

1. Europe
2. possible answers: Lisbon, Madrid, Rome, Tiranë, Athens
3. marine west coast
4. Scandinavia
5. humid continental—cold winters and warm summers

HIGHLIGHTS

Section 1: The Land

Key Terms

fjord (p. 223)
polder (p. 228)
peat (p. 229)

The Danube River at Budapest, Hungary

Summary

- The continent of Europe is a huge peninsula that extends westward from the landmass of Eurasia.
- Europe has a long, irregular coastline with many peninsulas and islands surrounded by different seas.
- Europe consists of plains surrounded by mountains along its northern and southern edges.
- Rivers play an important role as transportation routes linking the interior of Europe with coastal ports.
- Europe has major coal, iron ore, oil, and natural gas deposits.

Section 2: The Climate and Vegetation

Key Terms

mistral (p. 231)
sirocco (p. 231)
permafrost (p. 231)
foehn (p. 232)
avalanche (p. 232)
chaparral (p. 232)

Po River valley in northern Italy

Summary

- Because of warm ocean currents, much of Europe has milder climates than other parts of the world at similar northern latitudes.
- Northwestern Europe has a marine west coast climate, with moderate temperatures in both summer and winter.
- Most of southern Europe has a Mediterranean climate with mild, rainy winters and hot, dry summers.
- The interior of Europe experiences more extreme seasonal temperatures than other parts of the continent.
- Europe's natural vegetation is influenced by climate and human interaction.

Map Activity

Identify and Locate Display Political Map Transparency 4. Point to a country. Have students identify it and describe its physical characteristics and climate.

CHAPTER 11 HIGHLIGHTS

USING THE CHAPTER 11 HIGHLIGHTS

Use the Chapter 11 Highlights to preview, review, condense, or reteach the chapter.

PREVIEW/REVIEW

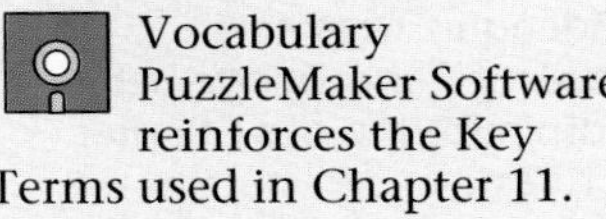

Vocabulary PuzzleMaker Software reinforces the Key Terms used in Chapter 11.

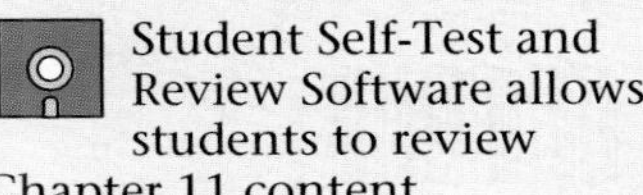

Student Self-Test and Review Software allows students to review Chapter 11 content.

CONDENSE

Have students read the Chapter 11 Highlights.

Have students listen to the Chapter 11 Audiocassettes in the TCR. Spanish Audiocassettes are also available.

Assign the Chapter 11 Audiocassette Activity and give students the Chapter 11 Audiocassette Quiz.

 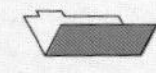

Have students complete the Guided Reading Activities for Chapter 11 in the TCR. Spanish Guided Reading Activities are also available.

RETEACH

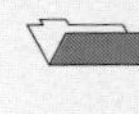

Have students complete Reteaching Activity 11 in the TCR. Spanish Reteaching Activities are also available.

GLENCOE TECHNOLOGY

Videodisc

Use Chapter 11 MindJogger Videoquiz to review students' knowledge before administering the Chapter 11 Test.

MINDJOGGER VIDEOQUIZ

Chapter 11
Disc 2 Side A

The MindJogger Videoquiz is also available on videocassette.

ANSWERS

Reviewing Key Terms

1. peat
2. fjord
3. polder
4. avalanche
5. sirocco
6. foehn
7. mistral
8. permafrost
9. chaparral

Reviewing Facts

10. The continent of Europe is a large peninsula extending from the Eurasian landmass. The irregular coastline of Europe is made up of many peninsulas.

11. Alps

12. in Norway, Spain, and the Balkan Peninsula

13. The Gulf Stream and the North Atlantic Drift bring warm water from the Gulf of Mexico to the west coast of Europe. Westerly winds, warmed by the current, blow across the continent and produce a mild climate.

14. Forests were cleared for agriculture.

chapter 11 REVIEW

Reviewing Key Terms

Choose the vocabulary term that best completes each of the sentences below. Write your answers on a separate sheet of paper.

fjord (p. 223)
polder (p. 228)
peat (p. 229)
mistral (p. 231)
sirocco (p. 231)
permafrost (p. 231)
foehns (p. 232)
avalanche (p. 232)
chaparral (p. 232)

SECTION 1

1. Some homes in western Europe burn _____ for fuel.
2. Along Norway's coast, a deep water-filled valley called a _____ may be used as a harbor.
3. A _____ is land that people in the Netherlands have reclaimed from the sea.

SECTION 2

4. The word _____ refers to ice, snow, or rock sliding down a mountainside.
5. A wind called the _____ brings desert air to the Mediterranean coast of western Europe.
6. A _____ is a warm, dry wind in Alpine areas.
7. Cold air is brought from the Alps to southeastern France by the _____.
8. _____ is soil that often is permanently frozen below the surface.
9. The hot, dry summers of the Mediterranean area produce shrubs and short trees known as _____.

Reviewing Facts

SECTION 1

10. Why is Europe called "a peninsula of peninsulas"?
11. Which mountains form the largest part of the Alpine system?
12. Where are Europe's major iron ore deposits located?

SECTION 2

13. How do the Gulf Stream and the North Atlantic Drift affect Europe's climate?
14. How has northwestern Europe's natural vegetation changed over time?

Critical Thinking

15. **Drawing Conclusions** Europe has a diversity of peoples and cultures. How might geographical factors have shaped this diversity?
16. **Expressing Problems Clearly** How has human interaction affected Europe's environment?

Geographic Themes

17. **Movement** How have rivers aided Europe's economic development?
18. **Region** What vegetation is found in the Mediterranean climate region?

Practicing Skills

Reading a Climate Map

Refer to the climate map on page 234.

19. Which climate regions do not occur in Europe? Explain why.
20. Compare climates in northern Europe and southern Europe.

Using the Unit Atlas

Refer to the physical geography section of the Unit Atlas on pages 216–217.

Critical Thinking

15. Mountain barriers separated people. Groups of people developed different ways of life based on the climate and resources of their regions.

16. People changed the vegetation patterns of Europe. Industrial pollution poses a threat to Europe's environment.

Geographic Themes

17. Many rivers connect major cities. They also provide transportation routes from the interior of the continent to coastal ports.

18. chaparral, broadleaf evergreens

21. What body of water affects the climate of northwestern Europe?
22. What points in Europe are higher than 5,000 feet (1,500 m) above sea level?

Projects

Individual Activity

Choose a city in Europe and prepare typical January and July weather forecasts for the location you choose. Present your forecasts to the class. You may use weather maps, charts, or graphs in your presentation.

Cooperative Learning Activity

Work in groups of four to do additional research on one of the regions of Europe described in this chapter and that you have described in your journal. Examples include the Iberian Peninsula, the Scandinavian Peninsula, the Alpine mountain system, or the North European Plain. Each member of the group should be responsible for reporting about one of the following topics: land features, water bodies, plants and animals, or human/environment interaction. Combine the reports to make a booklet or a display about the region.

Writing About Geography

Description

Imagine that you are in charge of an advertising campaign to attract tourists to Europe. Choose an area that you have learned about in this chapter and have described in your journal records. Write a 30-second television commercial that will encourage American tourists to visit that place. If possible, videotape your commercial.

Locating Places

EUROPE: PHYSICAL GEOGRAPHY

Match the letters on the map with the places and physical features of Europe. Write your answers on a separate sheet of paper.

1. British Isles
2. Rhine River
3. Sicily
4. Apennine Mountains
5. Danube River
6. Mediterranean Sea
7. Scandinavian Peninsula
8. Crete
9. Iberian Peninsula
10. Balkan Peninsula

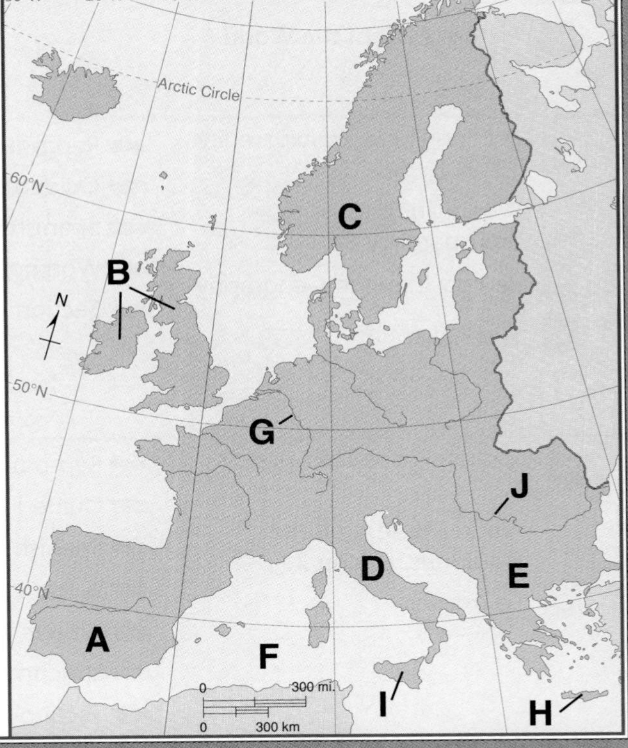

Chapter 11 Review

Practicing Skills

19. There are no tropical climates in Europe because it lies north of the Tropic of Cancer. There are no extensive deserts in Europe because most of the continent lies close to large bodies of water that bring moisture to the land.

20. Northern Europe generally has a much cooler and wetter climate than the Mediterranean countries, which have mild wet winters and hot dry summers.

Using the Unit Atlas

21. Atlantic Ocean

22. Meseta, Pyrenees, Alps

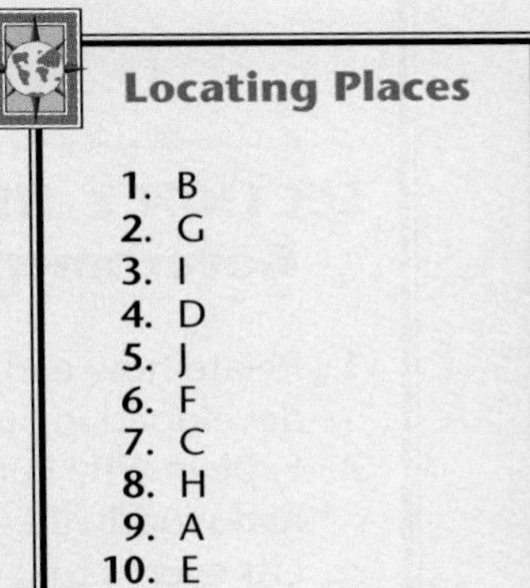

Locating Places

1. B
2. G
3. I
4. D
5. J
6. F
7. C
8. H
9. A
10. E

Chapter Bonus Test Question

This question may be used for extra credit on the chapter test.

Western Europe is called the birthplace of modern industry. What geographic factors promoted industrial development?

(Answer: Europe has deposits of coal and iron ore. It also has a long coastline and many navigable rivers to aid transportation of resources and goods.)

CHAPTER 12

PLANNING GUIDE

The Cultural Geography of Europe

CHAPTER ORGANIZER

Daily Lesson Objectives	Multimedia	Teacher Classroom Resources
SECTION 1 Population Patterns 1. Compare the differences and similarities among Europeans. 2. Relate how Europe's physical geography influences population distribution. 3. Explain why population patterns in Europe have changed.	Section Focus Transparency 12-1 Unit Map Overlay Transparency 4-1 World Cultures Transparency 5 Chapter 12 Vocabulary PuzzleMaker Software Testmaker Picture Atlas of the World	Reproducible Lesson Plan 12-1 Guided Reading Activity 12-1 Spanish Guided Reading Activity 12-1 Workbook Activity 12-1 Performance Assessment Activity 12 Section Quiz 12-1
SECTION 2 History and Government 1. Relate how early civilizations developed in Europe. 2. Explain why European cultures had worldwide influence. 3. List events that led to the creation of a new Europe.	Section Focus Transparency 12-2 World Cultures Transparency 6 Reuters Issues in Geography Testmaker	Reproducible Lesson Plan 12-2 Guided Reading Activity 12-2 Spanish Guided Reading Activity 12-2 Workbook Activity 12-2 Section Quiz 12-2
SECTION 3 Cultures and Lifestyles 1. Compare European languages, religions, and art forms. 2. Discuss the quality of life in European countries. 3. Explain how European lifestyles reflect cultural traditions.	Section Focus Transparency 12-3 World Music: Cultural Traditions, Lesson 3 Testmaker	Reproducible Lesson Plan 12-3 Guided Reading Activity 12-3 Spanish Guided Reading Activity 12-3 World Literature Reading 3 Writers' Guidebook Lesson 3 Enrichment Activity 12 Section Quiz 12-3
CHAPTER REVIEW AND EVALUATION	Chapter 12 English (or Spanish) Audiocassettes MindJogger Videoquiz Testmaker Student Self-Test and Review Software	Reteaching Activity 12 Spanish Reteaching Activity 12 Chapter 12 Test Form A and Form B

0:00 *If time does not permit teaching the entire chapter, summarize using the Chapter 12 Highlights on page 257, and the Chapter 12 English (or Spanish) Audiocassettes. Review students' knowledge using the Glencoe MindJogger Videoquiz.*

KEY TO ABILITY LEVELS

Teaching strategies have been coded for varying learning styles and abilities.

L1 **BASIC** activities for all students

L2 **AVERAGE** activities for average to above-average students

L3 **CHALLENGING** activities for above-average students

LEP **LIMITED ENGLISH PROFICIENCY** activities

Performance Assessment

Learning About Culture Have students take part in a simulation in which they assume the roles of potential exchange students who want to study in Europe. Direct them through the decision-making process of deciding whether or not they should study overseas. The process should begin with the development of a personal criteria. Students should consider as criteria the ways in which their education in Europe would differ from that in the United States and Canada. Some research may be required.

Students should individually produce a product in the form of a proposal to either the school administration, school board, or their parents justifying their decision.

POSSIBLE RUBRIC FEATURES: Content information, compare/contrast and persuasive abilities, decision-making process steps, research skills

For additional professional and classroom resources, see Chapter Resources, pages T46–T51.

TEACHER'S CORNER

NATIONAL GEOGRAPHIC SOCIETY

INDEX TO NATIONAL GEOGRAPHIC MAGAZINE

The following articles may be used for research relating to this chapter:

- "Venice: More Than A Dream," by Erla Zwingle, February 1995.
- "The Hanseatic League: Europe's First Common Market," by Edward Von Der Porten, October 1994.
- "The Light at the End of the Chunnel," by Cathy Newman, May 1994.
- "Czechoslovakia: The Velvet Divorce," by Thomas J. Abercrombie, September 1993.
- "Sweden: In Search of a New Model," by Don Belt, August 1993.
- "The Iceman: Lone Voyager from the Copper Age," by David Roberts, June 1993.
- "Europe Faces an Immigrant Tide," by Peter Ross Range, May 1993.
- "Man Against the Sea: The Oosterschelde Barrier," by Larry Kohl, October 1986.
- "The Byzantine Empire: Rome of the East," by Merle Severy, December 1983.
- "The World of Luther," by Merle Severy, October 1983.

NATIONAL GEOGRAPHIC SOCIETY PRODUCTS AVAILABLE FROM GLENCOE

To order the following products for use with this chapter, contact your local Glencoe sales representative or call Glencoe at 1-800-334-7344:

- *Picture Atlas of the World* (CD-ROM)
- *STV: World Geography, Africa and Europe* (Videodisc)
- *ZipZapMap! World* (Software)
- *GeoBee* (Software)
- *Images of the World* (Posters)
- *Eye on the Environment* (Posters)
- *Physical Geography of the World* (Transparencies)
- *Picture Atlas of Our 50 States* (Book)

ADDITIONAL NATIONAL GEOGRAPHIC SOCIETY PRODUCTS

To order the following products for use with this chapter, call National Geographic Society at 1-800-368-2728:

- *Geography of Europe Series*, "Northern Europe," "Western Europe," "Central Europe," "Southern Europe." (Filmstrip)
- *Democratic Goverment Series*, "France," "Germany," "United Kingdom." (Video)
- *Europe: The Road to Unity* (Video)
- *Nations of the World Series*, "East Germany," "West Germany." (Video)

Introducing
CHAPTER 12

PERFORMANCE ASSESSMENT

Refer to the Planning Guide on page 238B for a Performance Assessment Activity for this chapter. See the *Performance Assessment Activities* booklet for additional suggestions.

CHAPTER OBJECTIVES

1. **Explain** Europe's population patterns.
2. **Examine** the worldwide influence of European cultures.
3. **Compare** European lifestyles.

GLENCOE TECHNOLOGY

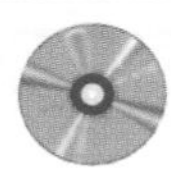

Videodisc

Use Chapter 12 MindJogger Videoquiz to preview chapter content.

MINDJOGGER VIDEOQUIZ

Chapter 12
Disc 2 Side A

The MindJogger Videoquiz is also available on videocassette.

chapter 12 The Cultural Geography of Europe

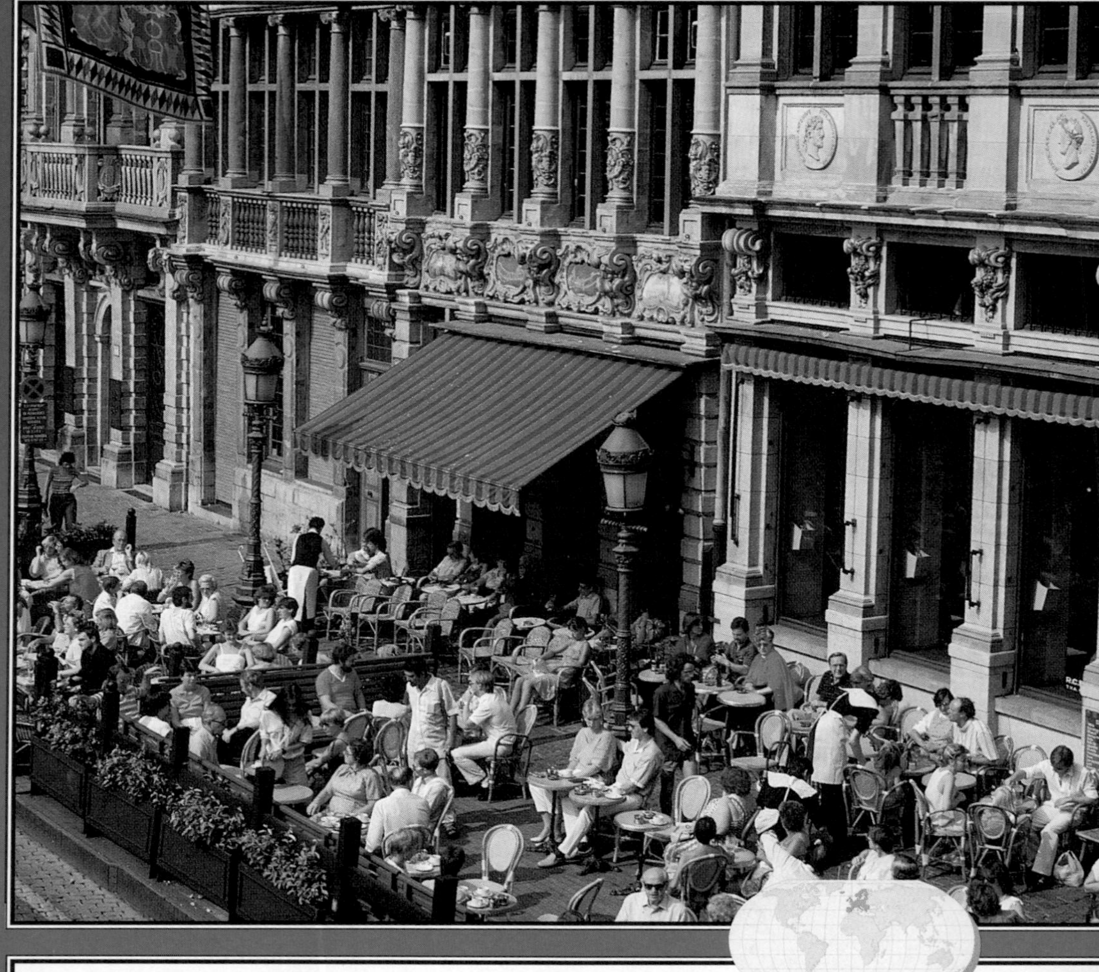

CHAPTER FOCUS

Geographic Setting

Europe's geographic features influenced population patterns and the development of its civilizations. Closeness to the sea favored exploration and trade.

Geographic Themes

Section 1 Population Patterns
PLACE Geography and climate help to make Europe one of the world's most densely populated areas.

▲ Photograph: *Bustling cafe in Kraków, Poland*

Section 2 History and Government
MOVEMENT European culture has spread around the world.

Section 3 Cultures and Lifestyles
PLACE European lifestyles reflect many cultural differences.

EXTRA CREDIT PROJECT

Culture Have students prepare a European Cultures Festival. Students who have European ancestry might investigate their own cultural heritage. Other students may choose a European culture to study. Suggest that students bring examples of traditional costumes, foods, music, and/or crafts to share with the class. Provide time for the festival at the conclusion of the chapter.

1 SECTION
Population Patterns

SETTING THE SCENE

Read to Discover . . .
- the differences and similarities among Europeans.
- how Europe's physical geography influences population distribution.
- why population patterns in Europe have changed.

Key Terms
- multicultural
- refugee

Identify and Locate
Spain, France, United Kingdom, Sweden, Belgium, Germany, Bosnia-Herzegovina, Vatican City, San Marino, Paris, London, Brussels

Balassagyarmat, Hungary

Szia! I live in Balassagyarmat, a town in Hungary. After school is finished for the day, I eat lunch. In the afternoon I spend time with friends, or in school organizing parties, competitions, working on the school newspaper, or with student council. In our spare time my friends and I like to play soccer, basketball, volleyball, or handball. Bye for now.
Eszter Visler

Eszter Visler's postcard reflects the typical lifestyle of a present-day European teenager. She comes from Hungary, a European nation that recently became a democracy after years of Communist rule. Hungary consists mainly of one ethnic group. Almost 95 percent of Hungarians are descended from the Magyars who settled the area in the late A.D. 800s. Other European nations, however, think of themselves as **multicultural**—having more than one culture. Europe is home to more than 30 countries, whose peoples speak some 50 different languages. In recent years, Europeans have been working toward unity. For centuries, however, conflict and competition have been far more characteristic. One of the challenges facing Europe today is dealing with the differences among its peoples.

REGION

Human Characteristics

Europe's diverse population reflects a long history of migrations throughout the Continent. Most Europeans are descended from various Indo-European and Mediterranean peoples who settled the Continent centuries ago. Europe's population also includes more recent immigrants from Asia, Africa, and the Caribbean who arrived during this century.

European Differences

In some European countries, most people belong to the same ethnic group. For example, more than 90 percent of the people in Sweden

LESSON PLAN
Chapter 12, Section 1

FOCUS

SECTION OBJECTIVES

1. **Compare** the differences and similarities among Europeans.
2. **Relate** how Europe's physical geography influences population distribution.
3. **Explain** why population patterns in Europe have changed.

ABOUT THE POSTCARD

Eszter also likes to dance, go to movies, visit museums, and sit by the fire talking with her friends.

BELLRINGER MOTIVATIONAL ACTIVITY

Project the Section 1 Focus Transparency and have students answer the questions.

PRETEACHING VOCABULARY

Discuss the meaning of *multicultural (having more than one culture)*. Ask students to suggest some advantages and disadvantages of having a multicultural society. *(Possible advantages: learning different ways of doing things; becoming tolerant of different beliefs. Possible disadvantages: conflict)*

Use the Vocabulary PuzzleMaker Software to create a crossword or word search puzzle.

Classroom Resources for Section 1

BLACKLINE MASTERS:
Reproducible Lesson Plan 12-1
Guided Reading Activity 12-1
Workbook Activity 12-1
Performance Assessment Activity 12
Section Quiz 12-1

TRANSPARENCIES:
Section Focus Transparency 12-1
World Cultures Transparency 5
Unit Map Overlay Transparency 4-1

MULTIMEDIA:

Vocabulary PuzzleMaker Software
Testmaker

Picture Atlas of the World

TEACH

GUIDED PRACTICE

L1 Geography: Region Display Unit Map Overlay Transparency 4-1. Have students identify densely populated areas and sparsely populated areas. Ask them to form a hypothesis to explain population patterns in Europe. Then have them read the explanation in the text to determine if their hypotheses were correct.

USING ILLUSTRATIONS

PLACE Sarajevo, the capital of Bosnia-Herzegovina, is famous for the products of its silversmiths and carpet weavers. Its many mosques were built by Turks who ruled the city for about 400 years.

Answer to Caption: *brutal warfare; being driven from their homes*

INDEPENDENT PRACTICE

Guided Reading Have students complete Guided Reading Activity 12-1 in the TCR. **LEP**

NATIONAL GEOGRAPHIC SOCIETY

CD-ROM

PICTURE ATLAS OF THE WORLD

Population figures for each European country can be found by clicking the "Stats" button.

are Swedes, descendants of Germanic and other groups that settled the Scandinavian Peninsula centuries ago. They share a common cultural background, the Swedish language, and the Lutheran religion. In other countries, the population consists of a few or a variety of different ethnic groups. Belgium, for example, has two leading ethnic groups—the Flemings and the Walloons. The Flemings make up about 55 percent of Belgium's population, and the Walloons make up about 30 percent. The Flemings are descendants of Germanic groups who invaded present-day Belgium during the A.D. 400s. The Walloons trace their ancestry to the Celts who lived in the area during the Germanic invasion. Flemings and Walloons share a common faith in Roman Catholicism, but language differences have led to bitter relations between them. Both groups, however, have managed to keep their disputes from endangering Belgium's national unity.

In other cases, however, tensions among European ethnic groups have led to violent conflict. In the early 1990s, the Balkan Peninsula became a battleground between ethnic groups in former Yugoslavia. Religious and ethnic differences among Serbs, Croats (KRO•atz), and Bosnian Muslims erupted in brutal warfare in newly independent Bosnia-Herzegovina. The Serbs, and to a lesser extent the Croats, carried out a policy they referred to as "ethnic cleansing" in which residents considered to be enemies were driven from their homes in captured areas. As a result, more than a million people became **refugees**—people who flee to a foreign country for safety.

Geographic Themes

Place: Sarajevo, Bosnia-Herzegovina
In the early 1990s, fighting among various ethnic groups reduced Sarajevo to a war zone. *What problems have the Bosnian people faced since independence?*

Since the 1960s, large numbers of immigrants have arrived in western Europe. Some come from former European colonies; others come from less prosperous parts of the Continent. North Africans from the former French colonies of Morocco, Algeria, and Tunisia have migrated to France. Immigrants from former French colonies in Southeast Asia have also come to live and work in France. Germany and other countries in Central Europe have admitted large numbers of people from Turkey and Greece, as well as from former Yugoslavia. These immigrants were welcomed at first because western Europe had a labor shortage. In recent years, however, economic and cultural differences have led to increased tensions between "old" and "new" Europeans. As a result of attacks on Turks by extremist groups, Germany, in 1993, decided to place limits on the flow of immigrants.

European Similarities

In spite of division and conflict, Europeans share several common attitudes and values. Most Europeans regard the family as the center of their social and economic lives. They also value the importance of the past and take pride in the cultural achievements of their ancestors. Most Europeans expect government to play an important role in running the economy of their nation and in providing for their welfare. These similarities make it increasingly possible for people to think of themselves as Europeans as well as members of ethnic or national groups.

Cooperative Learning Activity

Organize students into six groups and assign one of the following European cities to each group: Paris, London, Rome, Madrid, Berlin, or Budapest. Members of each group should prepare an article for a book about Europe's largest cities. Topics should include population, history, economy, and famous landmarks. Have the groups combine their articles. Reproduce copies of the "book" for each student.

Geographic Themes

Region: Alpine Europe

This picturesque village is nestled in an Alpine valley in the Austrian province of Tyrol. *How does the population of Europe's Alpine region compare with that of other parts of the continent?*

PLACE

Population Distribution

Europe is smaller than any continent except Australia. Only Asia, however, has a larger population and is more densely populated than Europe. In the mid-1990s, Europe's population was about 514 million. Germany, with more than 81 million people, ranked as Europe's most heavily populated country. Vatican City, with about 1,000 people, had the smallest population of any country in the world.

If Europe's population were distributed evenly throughout the Continent, the average population density would be 264 people per square mile (102 people per sq. km). In Europe, of course, as in all other continents, the population is not distributed evenly. Most of Europe has far less than the average population density. Some parts of the Continent, however, are among the world's most densely populated areas.

Sparsely Populated Areas

Population distribution is closely related to physical geography. Compare the population density map on page 215 with the physical features map on page 216. Notice that mountainous regions are less populated than plains regions. For example, the population density in much of the Alpine mountain system is less than 60 persons per square mile (25 persons per sq. km). The rugged highlands of northern Scotland are another sparsely populated area.

Climate also plays a role in determining population density. Compare the population density map with the climate map on page 231. Notice that the dry, barren regions of the Iberian Peninsula have a sparse population. The most sparsely populated areas of Europe include parts of the Scandinavian Peninsula and Iceland. Subarctic and tundra climates make these regions nearly uninhabited.

Densely Populated Areas

Some European countries have a high population density because of their small sizes. For

USING ILLUSTRATIONS

PLACE Tyrol is a popular summer and winter vacation spot.

Answer to Caption: *The Alpine region is sparsely populated.*

L3 Write Have students write a letter to the editor of a newspaper in a major European city. The purpose of the letter is to express an opinion about modernization of the city. Encourage students to support their opinions with sound reasoning.

Have students complete World Cultures Transparency 5 Activity in the TCR.

ASSESS

CHECK FOR UNDERSTANDING

Assign Section 1 Review as homework or an in-class activity.

MEETING LESSON OBJECTIVES

Each objective below is tested by the questions that follow it in parentheses.

1. **Compare** the differences and similarities among Europeans. *(3)*
2. **Relate** how Europe's physical geography influences population distribution. *(4)*
3. **Explain** why population patterns in Europe have changed. *(5)*

Meeting Special Needs

Reading Disability Students with reading problems often are helped by having a specific purpose for reading. Focused reading exercises present a limited goal. They force the reader to make judgments about the applicability of the material to the question. Have students read "Urbanization" to find out why most Europeans live in urban areas.

EVALUATE

Assign the Section 1 Quiz in the TCR.

Use the Testmaker to create a customized quiz for Section 1.

RETEACH

Have students list three ways in which Europeans are different from Americans and three ways in which they are similar.

ENRICH

Suggest that students investigate forms of greeting in different European countries. Have them report their findings to the class.

CLOSE

Ask students to write a postcard to Eszter Visler describing popular styles of dress among U.S. teenagers.

example, San Marino, a small country that is surrounded by Italy, covers only 20 square miles (52 sq. km). With a population of more than 20,000 people, San Marino has a population density of about 1,000 people per square mile (384 people per sq. km).

In general, the areas of Europe with average or higher than average population density share one or more of the following characteristics: favorable climate, plains, fertile soil, mineral resources, and inland waterways. One of the most densely populated parts of Europe extends from the United Kingdom into France and across the North European Plain into the Czech Republic and Poland. Another densely populated area extends from southeastern France into the Apennine Peninsula.

These regions contain some of the world's richest farmland. Although Europe's total agricultural area is less than half as large as that of North America, the total yearly production of European farms about equals that of North American farms. Europe's high crop yields, however, result from advanced farming techniques rather than a large number of farmers. Farming areas generally have fewer people than other parts of Europe's densely populated regions.

Industrialization and the location of mineral resources influenced population distribution in Europe. Urbanization is linked closely to industrialization. As a result of these two factors, the greatest concentration of Europe's people today live in and near its major cities.

MOVEMENT

Urbanization

Beginning in the late 1700s, the Industrial Revolution transformed Europe from an agricultural society to an industrial society. Between 1750 and 1900, many countries in western Europe became industrialized. Industrialization in eastern Europe increased rapidly after World War II but still lags behind western Europe.

By the early 1990s, about three-fourths of Europe's population lived in urban areas. According to the U. S. Bureau of the Census estimates, 2 European cities—Paris and London—ranked among the world's 20 largest urban areas in 1994. Other European cities with large populations include Milan and Rome, Italy; Madrid and Barcelona, Spain; Essen and Berlin, Germany; Budapest, Hungary; and Athens, Greece.

Europe's large cities, like cities everywhere, face the challenges of overcrowding and pollution. In spite of these problems, European cities provide a unique combination of old and new ways of life. Landmarks that date back hundreds of years stand near fast-food restaurants and shopping malls.

Many Europeans oppose the modernization of their historic cities. In the early 1990s, massive development projects were undertaken in Brussels, Belgium. One reporter summarized public opinion about the changes:

Brussels . . . is a pleasant city in which to live, even though much of its charm has been mauled by the new, modern, nondescript office buildings that have sprouted everywhere and are crowding out much that is Old World in a city that built its first, fortified walls in the 13th century.

SECTION 1 REVIEW

Checking for Understanding

1. **Define** multicultural, refugee.
2. **Locating Places** Where do the Walloons live?
3. **Region** What common attitudes and values do most Europeans share?
4. **Place** What are the characteristics of Europe's most densely populated areas?

Critical Thinking

5. **Drawing Conclusions** Why does western Europe have more densely populated areas and more large cities than eastern Europe?

ANSWERS TO SECTION 1 REVIEW

1. **multicultural:** having more than one culture; **refugee:** a person who flees to a foreign country for safety
2. Belgium
3. Most Europeans regard family as the center of their lives. They value the importance of the past and take pride in their ancestors' achievements. They expect government to run the economy and provide for their welfare.
4. favorable climate, plains, fertile soil, mineral resources, and/or inland waterways
5. The climate and physical features of western Europe support large populations. Industrialization and urbanization took place much earlier in western Europe than in eastern Europe.

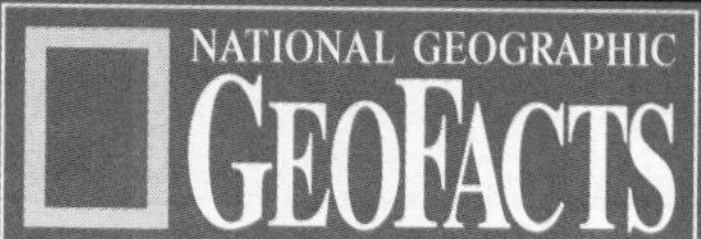

TEACH

Explain to students that Monaco is an independent principality encompassing only about 370 acres (150 hectares). Have students find Monaco's location on the map on page 243 and ask them what they think Monaco's economy relies on and why. *(Tourism—because of Monaco's mild climate, its location on the Mediterranean Sea, and its natural harbor. The world-famous gambling casino at Monte Carlo also draws many tourists every year.)*

DID YOU KNOW?

San Marino claims to be Europe's oldest existing state. Tourism and the sale of postage stamps are San Marino's principal sources of income.

NATIONAL GEOGRAPHIC GEOFACTS

What is the smallest country on earth?

MONACO
FRANCE
Monte Carlo
Mediterranean Sea
0.6 SQ MI

SAN MARINO
ITALY
San Marino
20 SQ MI

VATICAN CITY
ROME
St. Peter's Basilica
0.2 SQ MI

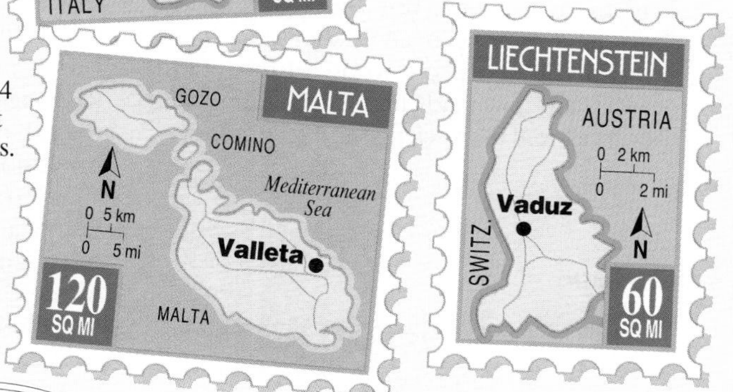

MALTA
GOZO
COMINO
Mediterranean Sea
Valletta
120 SQ MI

LIECHTENSTEIN
AUSTRIA
SWITZ.
Vaduz
60 SQ MI

ANDORRA
FRANCE
SPAIN
Andorra La Vella
185 SQ MI

Vatican City, at only 0.2 square miles (0.4 sq. km), is the world's tiniest country. It could fit within the U. S. Capitol grounds.

Vatican City is one of Europe's "postage stamp" countries, so called because of their small size and their special stamps.

Though tiny dots on the map, some of these countries have a global reach. Vatican City is the center of the world's largest religious body, the Roman Catholic Church. Liechtenstein counts more companies than citizens; its banks have outlets from New York to Hong Kong. Andorra is a kind of Hong Kong of the Pyrenees, with duty-free shops attracting about 10 million tourists a year.

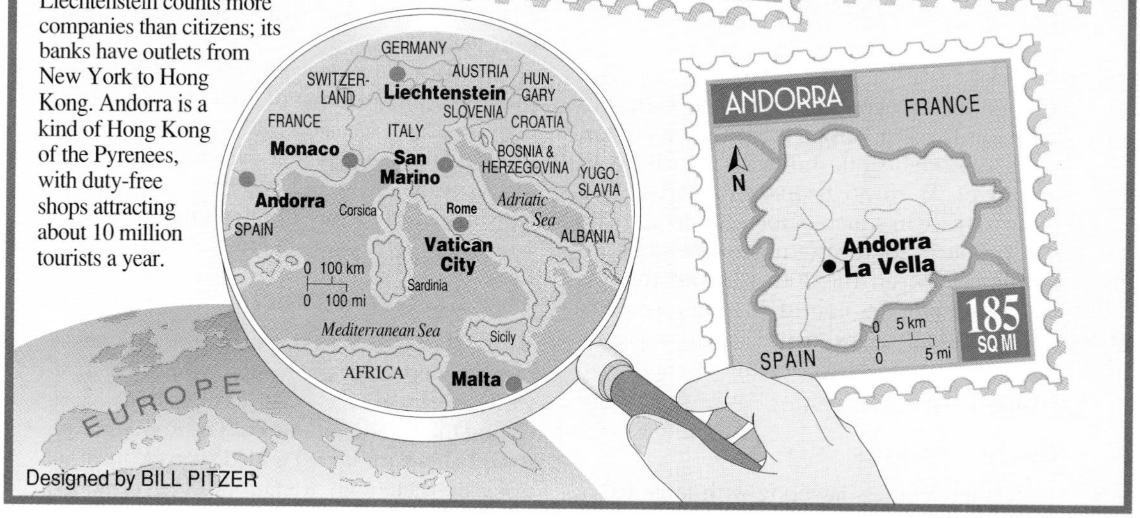

Designed by BILL PITZER

CHAPTER 12 243

FOCUS

SECTION OBJECTIVES

1. **Relate** how early civilizations developed in Europe.
2. **Explain** why European cultures had worldwide influence.
3. **List** events that led to the creation of a new Europe.

BELLRINGER MOTIVATIONAL ACTIVITY

Project the Section 2 Focus Transparency and have students answer the questions.

PRETEACHING VOCABULARY

Have students work with a partner to create a crossword puzzle using the Key Terms. Then have each pair of students exchange puzzles with another pair of students. Creating and completing puzzles will reinforce the meanings of the Key Terms. **LEP**

DID YOU KNOW?

The Maastricht Treaty, signed in 1993, was a step toward political and economic unity in Europe. Major goals included a common currency and a central bank.

SECTION

2 History and Government

SETTING THE SCENE

Read to Discover . . .
- how early civilizations developed in Europe.
- why European cultures had worldwide influence.
- what events led to the creation of the New Europe.

Key Terms
- city-state
- feudalism
- Crusades
- Renaissance
- Reformation
- communism
- Holocaust
- cold war

Identify and Locate
Greece, Roman Empire, Byzantine Empire, European Union

Through colonization, immigration, and trade, European civilization has had a powerful influence on world history. Europeans made great advances in learning and the arts as well as in science and technology.

MOVEMENT

The Development of European Civilizations

Scientific evidence suggests that early humans lived in Europe more than a million years ago. Prehistoric hunters, who lived in groups of 25 to 30 people, wandered from place to place in search of food. By about 6000 B.C., people in southeastern Europe had begun farming. Between the 300s B.C. and the A.D. 500s, great empires flourished in Europe. During the Middle Ages, major religions greatly influenced the development of European civilizations.

Early Peoples

A huge chinless jawbone with large teeth, discovered in Germany in 1907, led scientists to conclude that prehistoric people lived in that area about 650,000 years ago. A painting on a wall in a cave in Lascaux in southwestern France provides a record of prehistoric life in that area around 30,000 B.C. Clues such as these have helped anthropologists determine how and when civilizations began in Europe.

With the development of farming, early Europeans no longer had to move in search of food. Europe's first cities developed from some of these early farming villages. Between 6000 B.C. and 3000 B.C., farming spread from Southwest Asia to southeastern Europe and then to all but the dense northern forest regions of the Continent.

The first European civilization began on the Aegean Islands east of present-day Greece. Between 3000 B.C. and 1400 B.C., peoples in this region developed a system of writing. They became skilled craftworkers and traders who spread their way of life along the southern and western coasts of Europe.

The Classical World

Two later Mediterranean civilizations developed as models for the western world. The first was ancient Greece, which reached its peak during the 400s and 300s B.C. The Romans borrowed Greek ideas and added many contributions of their own to European civilization. The Roman Empire reached the height of its power between 27 B.C. and A.D. 180.

Classroom Resources for Section 2

BLACKLINE MASTERS:
Reproducible Lesson Plan 12-2
Guided Reading Activity 12-2
Workbook Activity 12-2
Section Quiz 12-2

TRANSPARENCIES:
Section Focus Transparency 12-2
World Cultures Transparency 6

MULTIMEDIA:

Testmaker

Reuters Issues in Geography

Geography played an important role in the development of Greek civilization. The mountainous landscape separated ancient Greeks in independent communities called **city-states**. Each city-state had its own way of life, but the Greeks were united by a common language and culture. Greek city-states established the first democratic governments. Except for women and enslaved persons, who could not vote, more people had a voice in these governments than in any earlier civilization. Greek art, literature, drama, and philosophy as well as mathematics and medicine spread across the Mediterranean world.

People called Etruscans (i•TRUHS•kuhnz) built a trading empire in Italy during the 800s B.C. Around 500 B.C., Rome, a city under Etruscan control, revolted and established a republic. By A.D. 117, Roman conquerors expanded their empire into half of Europe, much of the Middle East, and the north coast of Africa.

The Romans imitated Greek art and literature. They borrowed Greek science and architecture. Roman government, however, influenced many cultures. Roman engineers built a vast network of roads, aqueducts, and bridges throughout the empire.

Christianity became the official religion of the Roman Empire in A.D. 380. By the end of that century, the empire split into two parts—the West Roman Empire and the East Roman, or Byzantine, Empire. During the A.D. 400s, Germanic tribes from north of the West Roman Empire overthrew Roman rule in present-day Spain, Italy, France, and the United Kingdom. About a century later, Slavic peoples migrated from Ukraine into eastern and central Europe and the Balkan Peninsula. The Slavs lived in peace with the eastern Romans, or Byzantines. Over the next few centuries, the Slavs and Germans accepted Christianity and adopted aspects of Greek-Roman culture.

THE ROMAN EMPIRE, A.D. 117

FOCUS ON GEOGRAPHIC THEMES

1. **Place:** What body of water did most of the Roman Empire's territory border?
2. **Location:** On what peninsula was the city of Rome located?
3. **Movement:** About how many miles separate Rome from Byzantium?

The Middle Ages

With the collapse of the West Roman Empire's government, western Europe entered the Middle Ages. During this period, from about A.D. 500 to 1500, **feudalism**—a system in which powerful lords gave land to nobles in return for pledges of loyalty—replaced centralized government. The Roman Catholic Church, the western branch of Christianity, became the most powerful force in Europe. The Church introduced Roman government and justice to the Germanic peoples who had settled much of western Europe. Cathedrals and monasteries became the only centers of learning. Monks copied ancient Greek and Roman manuscripts.

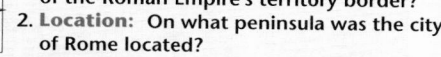

The Byzantine Empire influenced the cultures of southeastern Europe and the Middle East spreading to Italy, Spain, and the north coast of Africa. The Byzantines preserved ancient Greek and Roman cultures. Eastern Orthodoxy, the Byzantine form of Christianity, spread as missionaries converted the Slavs in eastern Europe. In the 1000s, the Christian Church split into two separate bodies: the Roman Catholic Church and Eastern Orthodox Church.

Islam, a religion based on belief in one God, was preached by the prophet Muhammad in Arabia during the early A.D. 600s. The followers of Islam, known as Muslims, spread their religion through Southwest Asia, North

TEACH

GUIDED PRACTICE

L1 Sequence Help students create a large time line along one or more walls in the classroom. The time line should represent the development of civilizations in Europe from around 15,000 B.C. to the present. As students read this section, have them add events at the appropriate places on the time line.

USING MAPS

Answers:
1. Mediterranean Sea; **2.** Italian; **3.** about 750 miles

Map Skills Practice

Reading a Map How far north did the Roman Empire extend in A.D. 117? *(England)*

GLENCOE TECHNOLOGY

Videodisc

Use the following to enrich Chapter 12:

REUTERS ISSUES IN GEOGRAPHY

Chapter 3
Disc 1 Side A

Title: ***Europe: United or Divided***
Subject: Forces that bring together and divide the European community

Cooperative Learning Activity

Organize students into six groups and assign each one a group of European countries that are clustered near each other. For example, one group might study Estonia, Latvia, and Lithuania. Another group might study France, Belgium, Luxembourg, Germany, and the Netherlands. Have the group members research to find out how the area's natural features influenced the historical development of the countries and important events in their history. Then create new groups that include one member from each of the original groups. Each of the new groups should hold a discussion in which each member reports on an area. After the discussions, the class should come together to share insights.

USING ILLUSTRATIONS

PLACE Chartres Cathedral is a masterpiece of Gothic architecture with stained-glass windows and tall, slender columns. The Romanian monastery is an example of Byzantine architecture. The frescoes—wall paintings—remind passers-by of their faith.

Answer to Caption: *Roman Catholicism and Eastern Orthodoxy*

L3 Creating Charts Have students create a chart comparing Europe's major religions: Roman Catholicism, Eastern Orthodoxy, and Islam. Discuss bases of comparison such as founder, number of members, and major beliefs.

MULTICULTURAL PERSPECTIVE

Culturally Speaking
The word *Gothic* was a term of disapproval by authors and writers who wanted to revive the classical styles of Greece and Rome. They associated the complicated Gothic style with the Goths, a Germanic people who had destroyed much classical art during the 400s.

Geographic Themes

Place: France and Romania
France's Chartres Cathedral (left) and Romania's Moldovita monastery (right) reflect the Christian heritage of the Middle Ages. *What were the two major branches of Christianity during this time?*

Africa, and Spain, contributing much to the culture of Europe. Muslims spread the Chinese inventions of paper and gunpowder and the Hindu system of numerals and expanded mathematics, medicine, and astronomy. They developed distinctive Islamic arts and founded many universities.

MOVEMENT

The Spread of European Civilizations

Beginning in the 1000s, western European forces carried out the **Crusades**—a series of religious wars to win Palestine from Muslim rule. Europeans failed to win permanent control of the area but did extend trade routes to the eastern Mediterranean. The increased trade renewed European interest in other parts of the world. Beginning in the early 1300s, the **Renaissance**—a 300-year period of learning and the arts—brought about great advancements in European civilization.

Renaissance

During the Middle Ages, European culture centered around the powerful Roman Catholic Church. During the Renaissance, scholars and artists were influenced by the cultures of ancient Greece and Rome. They stressed the importance of people and their lives in the present world. Writers described human feelings, artists created lifelike paintings and sculptures, and architects designed nonreligious buildings.

A religious movement called the **Reformation** lessened the power of the Roman

Meeting Special Needs

Inefficient Readers Students often profit by using a form of rapid "reading" called scanning to locate specific information. Model this procedure for students by sliding your finger down the middle of a column rapidly. Demonstrate scanning as a way to find all the dates mentioned under "The Spread of European Civilizations." Then time students as they scan the rest of Section 2.

Catholic Church and led to the beginnings of Protestantism. By the mid-1500s, separate Protestant churches were dominant in much of Europe.

The Renaissance and Reformation encouraged scientific advancements and world exploration. The invention of movable type in printing spread new ideas faster and easier.

Exploration

During the Middle Ages, Europe lagged behind China and the Islamic Empire in economic development. In the 1400s the Portuguese searched for new trade routes to Asia around Africa. Financed by Spain, the Italian explorer Christopher Columbus reached the Americas in the late 1400s. During the 1500s and 1600s, many European nations sent out exploration expeditions. They set up colonies in lands discovered by their explorers, often destroying the cultures already thriving there.

Trade with colonies in the Americas, Australia, Asia, and Africa brought great wealth and power to European nations. Trade also increased Europe's global influence.

MOVEMENT

A Changing Europe

By the early 1700s, wars and the building of empires had developed powerful European nations. During the next 200 years, however, economic and political revolutions swept the Continent. World wars changed the map of Europe as well as the balance of power in the world. By the 1990s, a new Europe had emerged.

Revolutions

The Industrial Revolution began in Great Britain in the 1700s and rapidly spread. Power-driven machinery and new methods of production transformed life in Europe. Industrial cities and improved transportation and communication developed. The Industrial Revolution also caused the growth of a prosperous middle class of merchants and factory owners. Factory workers, however, were poorly paid and lived under crowded, unhealthy conditions. These social problems in 1848 led to the birth of **communism**—an economic

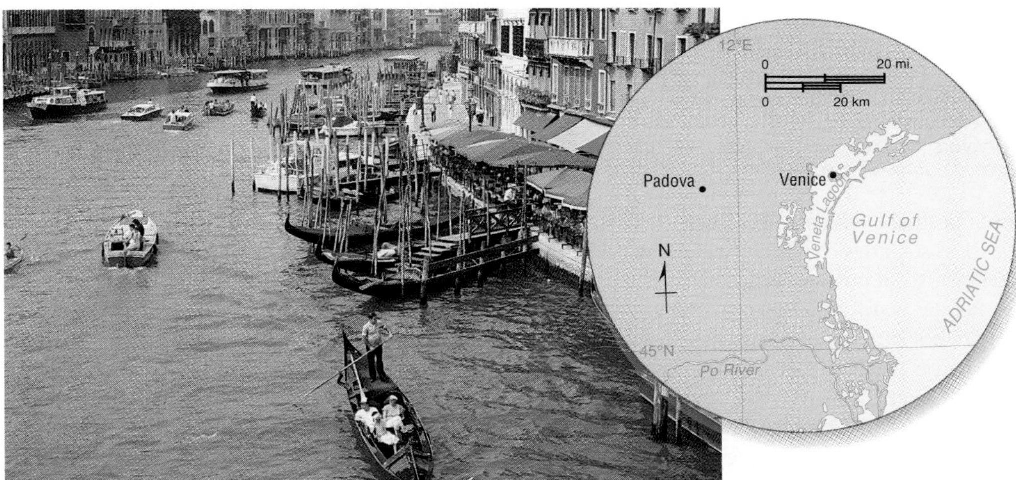

Geographic Themes

Location: Venice, Italy

Venice was a major port and cultural center during the Middle Ages and the Renaissance. Today it is still an important city of Italy. *On what body of water is Venice located?*

Chapter 12, Section 2

INDEPENDENT PRACTICE

Guided Reading Have students complete Guided Reading Activity 12-2 in the TCR. **LEP**

USING ILLUSTRATIONS

PLACE Venice, which lies on about 120 islands, has canals instead of streets.

Answer to Caption: Adriatic Sea

L2 Creating Charts Have students make a flow chart or other type of graphic organizer to show the causes and effects of the following events: Industrial Revolution, French Revolution, World War I, World War II, the cold war.

L3 Write Have students analyze the completed time line that they created for this section. Ask them to choose one event that they consider most significant in terms of one of the geographic themes: location, place, human/environment interaction, movement, or region. Instruct students to write a one-page explanation of the geographic significance of the event they chose.

Critical Thinking

Analyzing Information Organize students into four groups and provide each group with an outline map of Europe, found on page 30 of the Outline Map Resource Book. Have members of the first group color code their map to show the Allies and the Central Powers in World War I. Have the second group show Allied Powers and Axis Powers in World War II. Have the third group indicate the Eastern bloc and the Western bloc during the cold war. Have the fourth group show members of the European Union at the present time. Display the four maps and ask students to analyze geographic reasons for the different twentieth-century political and economic alliances among European countries.

USING ILLUSTRATIONS

MOVEMENT Beginning in 1939, the Nazis conquered one European nation after another. They thereby gained control of the Jewish populations in these countries.

Answer to Caption: *Germany's Nazi leaders*

ASSESS

CHECK FOR UNDERSTANDING

Assign Section 2 Review as homework or an in-class activity.

MEETING LESSON OBJECTIVES

Each objective below is tested by the questions that follow it in parentheses.

1. **Relate** how early civilizations developed in Europe. *(2)*
2. **Explain** why European cultures had worldwide influence. *(4)*
3. **List** events that led to the creation of a new Europe. *(5)*

EVALUATE

Assign the Section 2 Quiz in the TCR.

Use the Testmaker to create a customized quiz for Section 2.

RETEACH

Have students outline the material in Section 2 using the headings as main ideas.

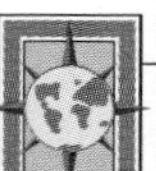

Geographic Themes

Place: Buchenwald, Germany

Holocaust concentration camps, such as Buchenwald, were liberated by Allied armies at the end of World War II. The condition of the survivors shocked the liberators. *Who planned and carried out the Holocaust?*

and political system designed to establish classless societies in which workers would control industrial production.

People wanting a voice in the government began political revolutions in Europe. In the 1600s the English Parliament passed a Bill of Rights that limited the powers of the monarch. The French Revolution in 1789 made France a republic and spread the ideals of democracy. During the 1800s, uprisings took place in Spain, Italy, Greece, Belgium, and Poland. By 1900, most European nations had democratic constitutions that guaranteed some human rights.

Conflict and Division

In the first half of the 1900s, two major wars resulted in great changes in Europe. European competition for colonies and economic power, the desire for independence, and secret military alliances led to World War I. As a result of that war, from 1914 to 1918, several central and eastern European nations won independence.

Unresolved problems from World War I and a worldwide economic depression enabled dictators Adolf Hitler and Benito Mussolini to gain control of Germany and Italy. Following aggressive territorial expansion by these two nations, World War II broke out in 1939. After it ended in 1945, most of Europe and all but a few of the world's nations had been involved. One of the horrors of World War II was the **Holocaust**, the mass killing of 6 million European Jews and others by Germany's Nazi leaders.

World War II brought the downfall of Western Europe as the center of world power. Most Eastern European governments came under Communist control, creating the **cold war**—a power struggle between the Communist world, led by the Soviet Union, and the non-Communist world, led by the United States. A divided Germany became a symbol of the cold war conflict because of Communist East Germany and non-Communist West Germany.

During the cold war, governments in Eastern Europe and Western Europe differed significantly. Western Europe had a commitment to democracy and private ownership of the economy. In Eastern Europe, the Communist party allowed people little voice in government, the society, or the economy.

Cooperation and Unity

In the 1980s, reform movements swept Eastern Europe. People in Poland, Hungary, Czechoslovakia, East Germany, Romania, and Bulgaria demanded more freedom. In 1989 and 1990, free elections in many countries ended Communist control. In 1990, East and West Germany were united into a single, non-Communist nation.

Extending the Content

Political Systems The Interparliamentary Union (IPU) is a non-governmental association that promotes international cooperation among democratic parliaments. According to the IPU, Germany's 662-member Bundestag is the largest democratically elected parliament in the world. Several other European countries also have large parliaments: British House of Commons—651 members; Italian Parliament—630 deputies; French National Assembly—577 delegates. Students can compare and contrast these or other European parliaments and report their findings to the class.

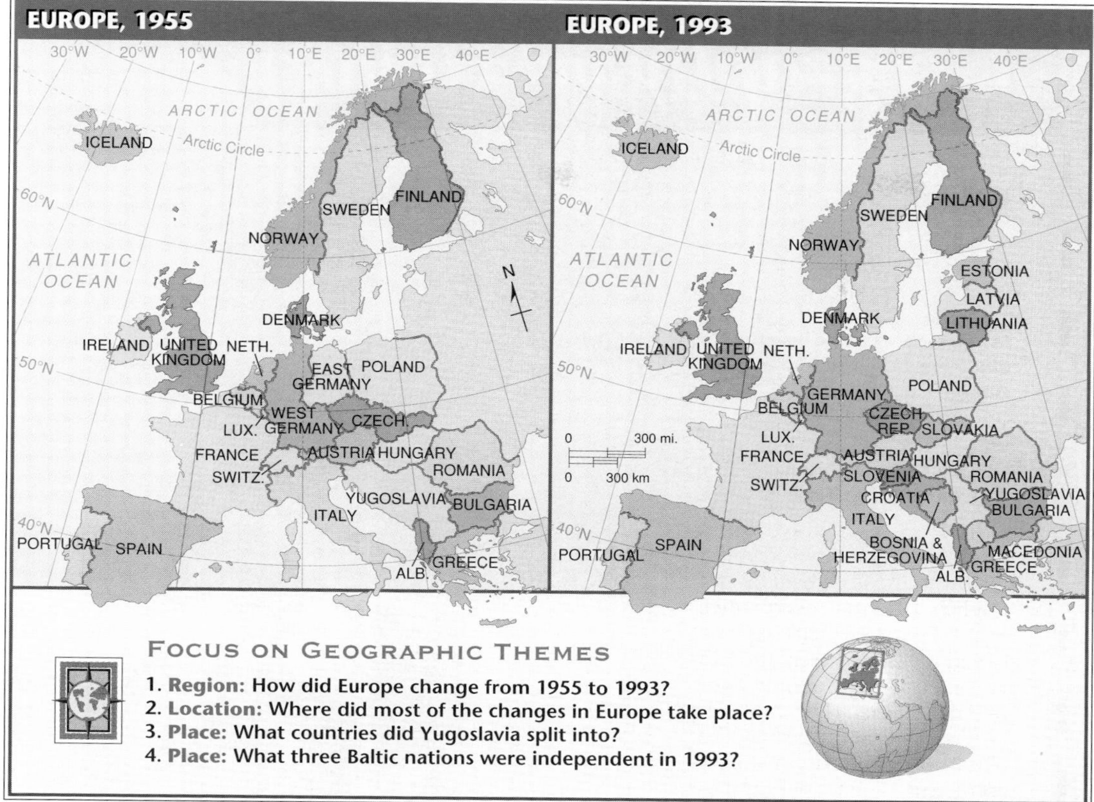

Focus on Geographic Themes

1. **Region:** How did Europe change from 1955 to 1993?
2. **Location:** Where did most of the changes in Europe take place?
3. **Place:** What countries did Yugoslavia split into?
4. **Place:** What three Baltic nations were independent in 1993?

Changes also occurred in Western Europe. Belgium, France, Italy, Luxembourg, the Netherlands, and West Germany in 1958 banded closer together in the European Community (EC)—an economic unit forming a single market for their resources. By 1990, Denmark, Ireland, the United Kingdom, Greece, Portugal, Spain, and the new united Germany had joined the others in the European Union. Turkey, Malta, and Cyprus were associate members.

The European Union worked to create a new Europe in which goods, services, workers, and money could move freely among countries. As a result, nations have increased their national incomes, total value of goods and services produced, and volume of trade. The opposition of some nations to a central all-European government, however, has blocked greater political and social unity.

Section 2 Review

Checking for Understanding

1. **Define** city-state, feudalism, Crusades, Renaissance, Reformation, communism, Holocaust, cold war.
2. **Locating Places** What area had the Romans conquered by A.D. 117?
3. **Movement** How did Renaissance art differ from that of the Middle Ages?
4. **Movement** How did European cultures spread to other parts of the world?

Critical Thinking

5. **Expressing Problems Clearly** Why did the nations of Europe lack unity during the cold war era?

ENRICH

Have students investigate and prepare a report on how the map of Europe has changed in the last 1,000 years. They may use a historical atlas to find maps to illustrate their reports.

CLOSE

Have students find examples of European influence in their community. *(Gothic-style churches or other buildings, ethnic restaurants or festivals, government)*

USING MAPS

Answers:
1. boundaries changed, countries were added; **2.** eastern Europe; **3.** Slovenia, Croatia, Bosnia-Herzegovina, Macedonia; **4.** Estonia, Latvia, Lithuania

Map Skills Practice
Reading a Map What European country became united? *(Germany)*

ANSWERS TO SECTION 2 REVIEW

1. city-state: independent community in ancient Greece; **feudalism:** system in which lords gave land to nobles in return for loyalty; **Crusades:** series of wars to free Palestine from Muslim rule; **Renaissance:** period of renewed interest in learning and the arts; **Reformation:** religious movement that led to Protestantism; **communism:** system in which workers control production; **Holocaust:** killing of 6 million Jews by the Nazis; **cold war:** power struggle between Communist and non-Communist world
2. half of Europe, Middle East, north Africa
3. Renaissance art was lifelike and based on present; Middle Ages art focused on religion.
4. by exploration, colonization, and trade
5. limited the freedoms and rights of the people

TEACH

Tell students that some of the British view the Chunnel with apprehension. Many do not want a physical link to mainland Europe. The British Isles have existed in what the British often termed "splendid isolation." Some worry that the Chunnel will make it easier for continental Europeans to take British jobs. Others worry that along with people and products will also come foreign cultures, and political unrest and terrorism.

Location What natural barriers have protected the British Isles and kept them in "splendid isolation"? *(English Channel, Atlantic Ocean)* What positive effects might "splendid isolation" have on a country? Negative effects?

Extending the Content

The Chunnel The Chunnel is the world's longest underwater tunnel system, connecting Calais, France, to Folkestone, England. At almost $16 billion, it also ranks as the most expensive, privately financed engineering project in history. Consisting of two train tunnels with a third smaller service tunnel sandwiched in between, the Chunnel offers travelers the option of taking a regular passenger train or a train that carries vehicles.

The last time that the British Isles were joined to mainland Europe was at the end of the last Ice Age, before water from melting ice covered the land bridge that linked them.

Geography and History

CHUNNEL VISION

As you read, examine how the Chunnel is expected to change Europe.

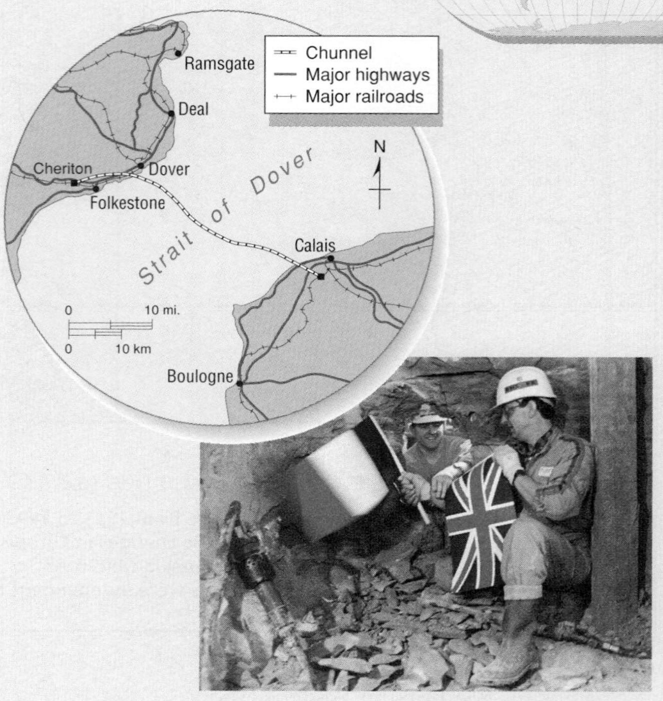

British and French workers celebrated completion of the Chunnel. It is hoped that the new Chunnel can offer a crucial economic link between the United Kingdom and the rest of Europe.

A Dream Come True

In 1993, the United Kingdom and France, separated for thousands of years by the English Channel, were once again "joined." Linking the island country to mainland Europe was the Channel Tunnel, nicknamed the Chunnel.

For many Europeans, the Chunnel represents a dream come true. The French in particular have worked for an under-the-seabed tunnel to the United Kingdom. On one occasion, the British actually began to dig. However, fear of military attack from the Continent halted construction.

In 1984, however, both the French and British governments agreed to connect the two nations. Eurotunnel, a private Anglo-French corporation, proposed the winning plan and raised money for construction.

In 1987, huge laser-guided, computerized boring machines called "moles" began digging, one from the French side, the other from the English side of the Channel. Digging was finished by mid-1991, and the three tunnels were open in 1993.

Far-Reaching Changes

The most obvious change the Chunnel brought is the length of time to travel between London and Paris. The trip took 6 hours by boat and train; now trains will speed through the Chunnel, covering the distance in half the time.

By the year 2003, the Chunnel is expected to carry more than 120,000 people between the United Kingdom and France each day. At night, tons of freight will move through it. The continental nations expect the Chunnel to allow the United Kingdom to fully join Europe.

Checking for Understanding

1. **How does the Chunnel affect the geography of Europe?**
2. **Human/Environment**

Interaction What changes is the Chunnel expected to cause?

ANSWERS TO CHECKING FOR UNDERSTANDING

1. The Chunnel links the island country of the United Kingdom to the European mainland.
2. The Chunnel will cut the amount of time needed to cross the English Channel; will move hundreds of thousands of people and tons of freight between the United Kingdom and Europe. Many think the Chunnel will help the United Kingdom become more involved in European affairs.

3 SECTION
Cultures and Lifestyles

SETTING THE SCENE

Read to Discover . . .
- the differences and similarities among European languages, religions, and art forms.
- the quality of life in European countries.
- how European lifestyles reflect cultural traditions.

Key Terms
- dialect
- language family
- romanticism
- realism
- impressionism
- welfare state

Identify and Locate
Athens, Rome, Venice, Vienna, Language groups: Balto-Slavic, Germanic, Romance, Greek, Albanian, Celtic, Uralic

Differences in European ways of life were influenced by culture and tradition, economic development, and political systems. Rural people followed more traditional ways of life than urban people did. Industrialization and urbanization increased the gap between northern and southern Europe. Political factors produced different lifestyles in Eastern and Western Europe. People in Western Europe did not experience the limits placed on the artistic, economic, political, and social freedoms of people by Communist-controlled governments in Eastern European countries.

PLACE

Cultural Expressions

Language, religion, and art are culture traits—characteristics of a culture. Through these traits, people express their ideas and values. A study of European languages, religions, and art forms reveals some similarities and some differences.

Languages

In Europe there are about 50 different languages and more than a hundred **dialects**, or local forms of languages. Almost all these languages belong to the Indo-European language family. A **language family** is a group of related languages that developed from an earlier language.

The Indo-European family has three major branches in Europe. Most people in eastern Europe speak Balto-Slavic languages, which include Bulgarian, Czech, Polish, Slovak, and Serbo-Croatian. Most northern Europeans speak Germanic languages, such as Danish, English, German, Dutch, Norwegian, and Swedish. The Romance languages, spoken mostly in southern Europe, include French, Italian, Spanish, Portuguese, and Romanian. Other Indo-European branches are Greek, Albanian, and Celtic, which includes Irish Gaelic, Scots Gaelic, Welsh, and Breton. Basque, Finnish, and Hungarian are European languages that belong to the Uralic family.

Many European countries have one or more official languages, those recognized by the government, and other minority languages. Romanian is the official language in Romania, but Hungarian or German is also spoken. Switzerland has three official languages—German, French, and Italian. Almost 70 percent of the Swiss people, however, speak Swiss-German; and people in some eastern mountain valleys speak Romansch.

LESSON PLAN
Chapter 12, Section 3

FOCUS

SECTION OBJECTIVES

1. Compare European languages, religions, and art forms.
2. Discuss the quality of life in European countries.
3. Explain how European lifestyles reflect cultural traditions.

BELLRINGER MOTIVATIONAL ACTIVITY

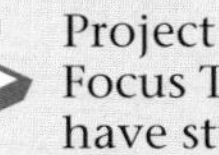

Project the Section 3 Focus Transparency and have students answer the questions.

PRETEACHING VOCABULARY

Display examples of art that reflect romanticism, realism, or impressionism. Ask students to make a list of words to describe each style of art. **LEP**

DID YOU KNOW?

The scientific study of language started in the 1700s. German scholars compared the world's languages and noted relationships among them. Today, the science of linguistics deals with the history and development of language groups.

Classroom Resources for Section 3

BLACKLINE MASTERS:
Reproducible Lesson Plan 12-3
World Literature Reading 3
Writers' Guidebook Lesson 3
Section Quiz 12-3

TRANSPARENCIES:
Section Focus Transparency 12-3

MULTIMEDIA:

Testmaker

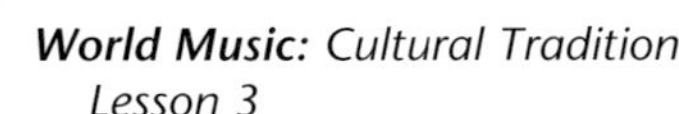

World Music: *Cultural Traditions, Lesson 3*

TEACH

GUIDED PRACTICE

L2 Linguistics Explain that languages within the same language family often have similar terms for basic words. Have students choose one of the branches of the Indo-European language family. Instruct them to find out the words for the following in each of the languages in that branch: *mother, father, child, day, night.* Then have students construct a chart to show similarities and differences among these terms in the major European languages.

USING MAPS

Answers:
1. Britain, Scandinavian Peninsula, north central Europe; **2.** Scotland, Ireland, Wales, and northwest France; **3.** eastern Europe, northern Balkan Peninsula

Map Skills Practice

Reading a Map What languages are spoken on the Iberian Peninsula? *(Portuguese, Spanish, Basque, Catalan)*

L3 Making Judgments Pose the following question for students to consider: Should governments subsidize education and health care? Direct students to write a paper defending their answer to the question. Provide time for students with opposing views to read their papers.

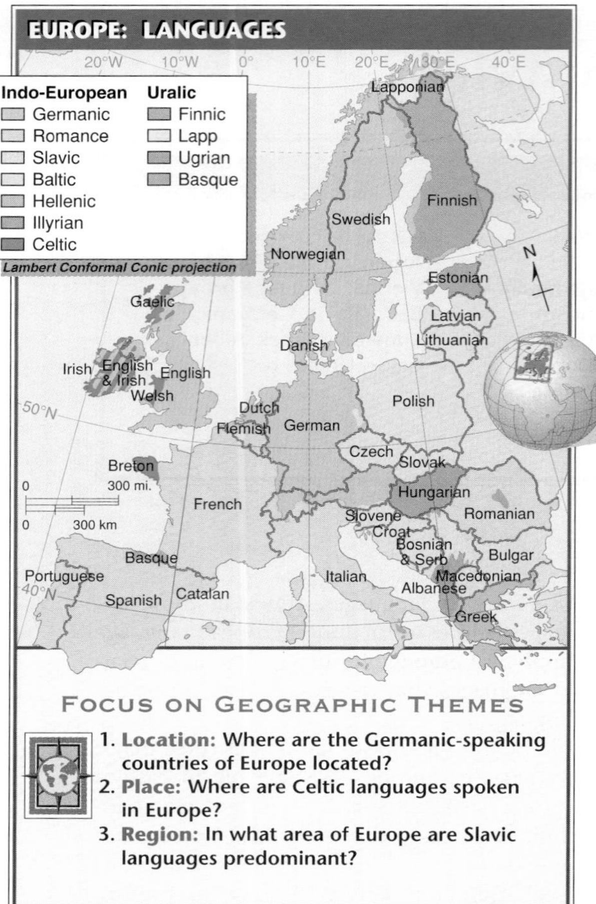

FOCUS ON GEOGRAPHIC THEMES

1. **Location:** Where are the Germanic-speaking countries of Europe located?
2. **Place:** Where are Celtic languages spoken in Europe?
3. **Region:** In what area of Europe are Slavic languages predominant?

Religions

Today some European countries are almost totally Christian (Roman Catholic, Protestant, or Eastern Orthodox) or Muslim. Others have a diversity of Christian and non-Christian faiths.

Most of Europe's Christians are Roman Catholics who live primarily in the southern areas of western Europe and the northern areas of eastern Europe. Protestantism is dominant in northern Europe, while Eastern Orthodoxy is strongest in the southern part of eastern Europe. Many Muslims live in Albania, Bosnia-Herzegovina, and Bulgaria; and Jews live in most European countries.

With the collapse of communism, religious freedom has been restored to many east European people.

Religious differences in Europe sometimes have resulted in violence. Recently, bitterness between Catholics and Protestants has caused conflict in Northern Ireland. Conflict between Christians and Muslims has played a role in the violent warfare in Croatia and Bosnia-Herzegovina.

Many historians believe that Christian ideas and values encouraged economic, political, and scientific developments and art forms in Europe.

The Arts

The art of Europe reflects its history as well as the ideas and values of its people and cultures, which have spread around the world. Europe's churches and temples show the development of architecture and major religions. The Parthenon in Athens and the Pantheon in Rome are examples of temples built by ancient Europeans. The cathedral in Cordoba, Spain, shows the influence of the Moors who spread Islam to Spain. The Basilica of St. Mark in Venice, Italy, and the Church of the Holy Apostles in Salonika, Greece, are examples of Byzantine art that reflect the spread of Eastern Orthodox beliefs. Notre Dame Cathedral in Paris is an example of Gothic architecture, which flourished from the mid-1100s to the 1400s. This style of construction enabled builders to substitute stained-glass windows for large portions of the walls.

During the Renaissance, European artists began to deal with everyday subjects as well as religious themes. The works of Leonardo da Vinci and Michelangelo Buonarotti influenced generations of artists.

After the Renaissance new art forms emerged. Opera and symphony developed in Europe during the 1600s and 1700s. **Romanticism** developed in Europe in the late 1700s and early 1800s. This artistic style tried to show feelings and emotions. **Realism**—an artistic style that tried to portray life as it really

Cooperative Learning Activity

Organize the class into five groups and assign one of the following topics to each group: painting, sculpture, music, literature, or architecture. Members of each group must prepare a 20-minute presentation on European artists or works in their subject area. Students may choose to discuss several styles or examples, or they may prepare an in-depth study on one artist or work of art. Group members should decide what methods of presentation to use.

was—developed during the mid-1800s. It was followed later in the century by French **Impressionism**—a style that showed the natural appearance of objects and light using dabs or strokes of primary colors.

Artists in the 1900s searched for new forms and styles. Sculptures and paintings became more abstract. A European artist who influenced modern art was the Spanish painter Pablo Picasso. In architecture, the Bauhaus school of design in Germany was influential worldwide.

REGION

Quality of Life

In general, Europeans who live in urban areas or in northern and western regions have a higher standard of living than those who live in rural areas or in southern and eastern regions. Literacy rate, life expectancy, and health care also indicate a region's quality of life.

Education

Respect for education is a traditional European value. The quality of education in Europe, whose people are among the world's best educated, is linked to the economy. Nations with a high standard of living can afford to improve schools and provide specialized training for students. Very few European nations have literacy rates below 90 percent.

The number of years of compulsory, or required, school attendance varies from country to country. In Portugal children must attend school for only 6 years. The United Kingdom requires 12 years of schooling. Some European school systems provide preparation for college or vocational training.

Europe has some of the world's finest universities, several of which date from the Middle Ages. Europe's famous schools include Cambridge and Oxford in England; the University of Bologna in Italy; the University of Heidelberg in Germany; the University of Vienna in Austria; Jagiellonian University in Kraków, Poland; and the Sorbonne, or the University of Paris, in France.

Health Care

Good nutrition and health care have given Europeans high life expectancies. The 1993 average life expectancy for all Europeans was 69.3 years for men and 76.9 years for women, the highest of any continent. Western European countries have a high average infant survival rate of 992 per 1,000, with eastern Europe's rate slightly lower.

One measure of health care is the ratio of population to doctors in a nation. In the world, the ratio is 740 people per doctor. In Europe, the average is 300 people per doctor.

Almost all European governments subsidize, or help pay for, health-care services. Some countries have a national health insurance that provides complete tax-supported medical care. Other countries provide more limited low-cost medical care through taxes.

The Role of Government

European governments generally play a major role in their nations' economies. They may operate airlines, railroads, electric companies, telephone companies, and other public services.

Most European governments provide some social welfare programs. In **welfare states**, such as the United Kingdom, Norway, and Sweden, the government assumes major responsibility for the welfare of its people. In the United Kingdom, for example, a child's elementary, high school, and often, university education is paid for by the government. In Norway, the government guarantees all employed people an annual four-week paid vacation and rent aid if they have more than one child. In Sweden, every family receives an allowance for each child under 16 and for secondary school or university students. Newlyweds can obtain government loans for home furnishings. Single parents with low incomes receive allowances for family vacations.

CURRICULUM CONNECTION

ECONOMICS

In the early 1990s, industrialized European nations experienced the worst recession in 60 years. As a result, most EU governments increased taxes and reduced benefits.

INDEPENDENT PRACTICE

Guided Reading Have students complete Guided Reading Activity 12-3 in the TCR. Spanish Guided Reading Activities are also available. **LEP**

L2 Compare Assign one or more European countries to each student. Tell students to consult an almanac or other reference to find out the average life expectancy, average infant survival rate, and ratio of population to doctors in their assigned country or countries. Then have students use the data to create a graph. Have students analyze the graph to determine regional differences in the quality of life in Europe.

ASSESS

CHECK FOR UNDERSTANDING

Assign Section 3 Review as homework or an in-class activity.

Meeting Special Needs

Inefficient Readers Students with problems decoding unfamiliar words often skip over them. However, they often are successful in defining the words based on the context of the sentence. Ask students to scan Section 3 for words that are unfamiliar to them. Have them write the words in their notebooks and interpret the meanings from context. Some words that may need definition and review are: *tradition, diversity, flourished, ratio,* and *destination.*

MEETING LESSON OBJECTIVES

Each objective below is tested by the questions that follow it in parentheses.

1. Compare European languages, religions, and art forms. *(1, 3, 5)*

2. Discuss the quality of life in European countries. *(2)*

3. Explain how European lifestyles reflect cultural traditions. *(4)*

USING ILLUSTRATIONS

MOVEMENT Soccer, as it is played today, developed in England during the 1800s.

Answer to Caption: *rugby football, tennis, skiing, swimming, rowing, hiking, bicycling*

USING GRAPHS

Skills Practice

Reading a Graph How does the percentage of Europeans who are Roman Catholic compare with the percentage of those of other religions? *(More than half are Roman Catholic.)*

EVALUATE

Assign the Section 3 Quiz in the TCR.

Use the Testmaker to create a customized quiz for Section 3.

Europe: Religions

Roman Catholic	262,026,000
Protestant	73,766,000
Orthodox	36,080,000
Other Christian*	40,918,000
Jewish	1,466,000
Muslim	12,545,000
Nonreligious	69,825,000
Other religions	1,466,000

Roman Catholic 52.4%
Protestant 14.8%
Orthodox 7.2%
Other Christian* 8.2%
Muslim 2.5%
Nonreligious 14.0%
Jewish 0.3%
Other religions 0.6%

*mainly Anglican (Church of England)
Source: *World Almanac,* 1993

PLACE

Lifestyles

Cultural and economic differences have produced a wide variety of lifestyles in Europe. But these differences have diminished as industrialization has brought a more common culture to many places. Many Hungarian farm families live in small stucco houses with tile roofs. The Lapps, a nomadic people in northern Scandinavia, for six months of the year live in cone-shaped tents and move frequently in search of food for their reindeer herds.

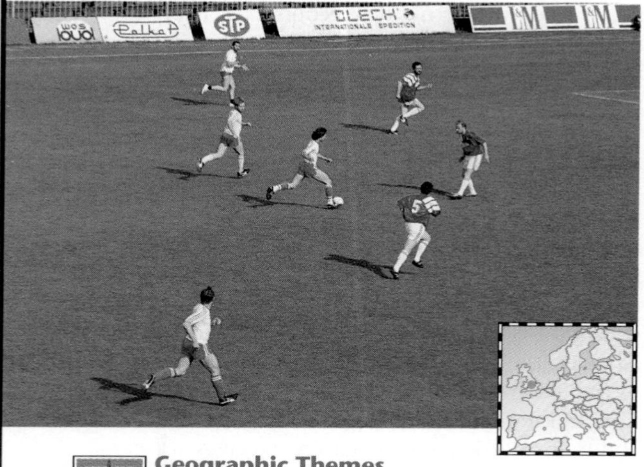

Geographic Themes

Place: London, United Kingdom

Athletic events, especially soccer matches, draw large crowds in Europe, and fans passionately root for their local teams. *What other recreational activities do Europeans enjoy?*

Home Life

In most European cultures, life centers around the extended family. Even when young people move away from home, they often maintain close family ties.

By the 1980s, many European women had begun to work outside the home. In the early 1990s, 42 percent of the workforce in Europe consisted of women. According to a survey in 1991, more than half of Europeans took a vacation at least once a year. July and August were the most popular vacation months, and seaside resorts were popular destinations.

Sports and Recreation

Soccer is the national sport in Europe, and many countries have professional soccer leagues. Rugby football also is a popular team sport, especially in the United Kingdom, France, and Ireland. Many Europeans play tennis for recreation, and the British tournament at Wimbledon is a major championship.

Communist governments in Eastern Europe required schoolchildren to play sports. Those with special talent were enrolled in rigorous sports training programs which produced many Olympic champions.

Many Europeans enjoy outdoor activities. Skiing and other winter sports are popular in the Alpine regions. Swimming, rowing, and hiking are favorite pastimes in many parts of Europe. Many young people take bicycling or hiking trips throughout Europe and spend the nights at inexpensive inns called youth hostels.

Critical Thinking

Drawing Conclusions Review the common attitudes and values that most Europeans share. *(importance of family, pride in achievements of the past, reliance on government)* Have students draw conclusions about how European lifestyles reflect these attitudes and values. Hold a class discussion in which students can share their insights.

Geographic Themes

Place: Athens, Greece

The ancient Greeks built the Parthenon and fashioned beautiful pottery. *What other ancient people set standards of cultural excellence in the Mediterranean region of Europe?*

Celebrations

European celebrations include family gatherings for special occasions. Traditional celebrations include eating special foods, wearing national costumes, and performing folk dances. Greeks celebrate Easter with a lamb feast. On Swedish St. Lucia Day, December 13, young girls dressed in white awaken their families with hot coffee and buns. In Poland, the Christmas celebration includes breaking and eating an *oplatek*—a thin wafer made of wheat flour and water.

Most European countries celebrate festivals to honor historical events. For example, Bastille Day, celebrated in France on July 14, commemorates the storming of Bastille prison in 1789 and the start of the French Revolution. A military parade, street dancing, and fireworks mark the occasion throughout the country.

Section 3 Review

Checking for Understanding

1. **Define** dialect, language family, romanticism, realism, impressionism, welfare state.
2. **Locating Places** What are three European countries that are welfare states?
3. **Region** In what ways has religion both unified and divided Europe?
4. **Place** How do European festivals reflect cultural traditions?

Critical Thinking

5. **Predicting Consequences** Are recent political and economic developments in Europe likely to produce greater similarities or differences in ways of life? Why do you think so?

Using Illustrations

PLACE The Parthenon, a Greek temple built to honor Athena, stands on a hill called the Acropolis. Athena, the goddess of warfare, wisdom, and arts, is depicted on the vase.

Answer to Caption: *Romans*

RETEACH

Have students complete Reteaching Activity 12 in the TCR.

ENRICH

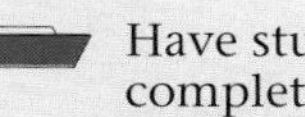

Have students complete Enrichment Activity 12 in the TCR.

CLOSE

Hold the European Cultures Festival that students prepared for their extra credit project.

ANSWERS TO SECTION 3 REVIEW

1. **dialect:** local form of a language; **language family:** group of languages that developed from a single earlier language; **romanticism:** style that stresses emotions; **realism:** style that portrays life as it is; **impressionism:** style that tries to show the natural appearance of things; **welfare state:** nation whose government assumes major responsibility for the welfare of its people
2. United Kingdom, Norway, and Sweden
3. Shared beliefs encouraged economic, political, and scientific advancements. Religious differences led to violence.
4. Festivals include traditional foods, clothing, dancing, music, and customs.
5. likely will produce greater similarities in lifestyles because of increased unity in the European Union

Teaching Skills

TEACH

Have the class choose a topic of interest. Have each student write a statement about this topic. Have several volunteers write their statements on the chalkboard. Then ask: "If we put these statements into a paragraph, what would be its main idea?" Have students develop a main idea statement. Explain that this statement is the topic sentence for the paragraph. Ask: "Why is a topic sentence important?" *(It clarifies the main idea of the paragraph for both writer and reader.)*

Direct students to read the skill on page 256.

Skills Practice

For additional practice, have students complete Lesson 3 in the Writer's Guidebook.

STUDY AND WRITING SKILLS

Writing a Topic Sentence

Writing is a basic survival skill in today's society. In school, you must write reports and answer essay questions. Some college applications require an essay about your goals and background. As adults, you may have to write letters for a wide range of business problems, such as applying for jobs and complaining about faulty products or poor services. Although typewriters and computers can simplify the mechanics of writing, you still must master the art of writing clear, readable prose.

REVIEWING THE SKILL

Most prose writing is divided into paragraphs. A *paragraph* is a group of sentences that develop a single main idea. In most paragraphs, a *topic sentence* states the main idea.

Although the topic sentence often appears at the beginning of a paragraph, it may appear at the end or within the paragraph. Sometimes, a paragraph has no topic sentence directly stating its main idea. Instead, the main idea is implied by the material in the other sentences.

To write a topic sentence, apply the following steps:

- Read the paragraph to identify its main idea.
- Reread the paragraph sentence by sentence. For each sentence, ask yourself: "Would the other sentences tie together and make sense without this sentence?" If the answer to the question is no, then you have probably identified the topic sentence stating the main idea.
- If the paragraph has no topic sentence, write a sentence stating the paragraph's main idea.
- Reread the entire paragraph. Be sure that each sentence directly relates to and supports the main idea stated in the topic sentence.

PRACTICING THE SKILL

Read the following paragraphs. Write a topic sentence for each paragraph. Topic sentences may or may not appear in the paragraphs.

1. Europeans share several common values. Most Europeans regard the family as the center of their social and economic lives. They also value the past and take pride in the achievements of their ancestors. Most Europeans expect government to play an important role in providing for their welfare.
2. For centuries, scientific ideas and principles had been held to be true because the Greek philosopher Aristotle had said they were true. At first Renaissance thinkers substituted the Greek physician Galen's authority for Aristotle's. But in pitting one authority against another, they opened a door to freedom. As the 1500s progressed, people began to base scientific truths on observation and experimentation.
3. My eyes delighted in the architecture of Prague. The city has been beautifully restored. Prague is a rich city, not merely in relics of the Habsburg monarchs, but in a contemporary prosperity. The Czech economy is a little shaky nowadays, but it does not show in the cafés stocked with pastries and cakes.

For additional practice in this skill, see Practicing Skills on page 259 of the Chapter 12 Review.

ANSWERS TO PRACTICING THE SKILL

1. Europeans share several common values.
2. The topic sentence does not appear in the paragraph. Students should write a topic sentence that states the following main idea: "During the 16th century, people replaced traditional beliefs about the world with new ideas based on scientific observation and reasoning."
3. Prague is a rich city, not merely in relics of the Habsburg monarchs, but in a contemporary prosperity.

chapter 12

HIGHLIGHTS

Section	Key Terms	Summary
1 Population Patterns	**multicultural** (p. 239) **refugee** (p. 240)	• The diversity of Europe's population reflects a history of migrations throughout the Continent. • Europe's physical features, climate, and resources influenced population distribution. • As a result of industrialization, nearly three-fourths of Europe's population lives in urban areas.

War-ravaged Sarajevo, Bosnia-Herzegovina

Section	Key Terms	Summary
2 History and Government	**city-state** (p. 245) **feudalism** (p. 245) **Crusades** (p. 246) **Renaissance** (p. 246) **Reformation** (p. 246) **communism** (p. 247) **Holocaust** (p. 248) **cold war** (p. 248)	• Greek and Roman civilizations served as models for the western world. • Scientific advancements during the Renaissance made it possible for Europeans to explore distant parts of the world. • European civilization spread to other continents through trade, colonization, and immigration. • After World War II, Europe became the center of the cold war, which divided Communist-controlled Eastern Europe from non-Communist Western Europe. • The European Union promotes economic unity among the nations of Europe.

Grand Canal in Venice, Italy

Section	Key Terms	Summary
3 Cultures and Lifestyles	**dialect** (p. 251) **language family** (p. 251) **romanticism** (p. 252) **realism** (p. 252) **impressionism** (p. 253) **welfare state** (p. 253)	• Differences in European ways of life reflect culture and tradition, economic development, and political systems. • Most European governments play a major role in providing for the welfare of their citizens. • Industrialization and urbanization have diminished differences in European lifestyles.

CHAPTER 12 HIGHLIGHTS

USING THE CHAPTER 12 HIGHLIGHTS

Use the Chapter 12 Highlights to preview, review, condense, or reteach the chapter.

PREVIEW/REVIEW

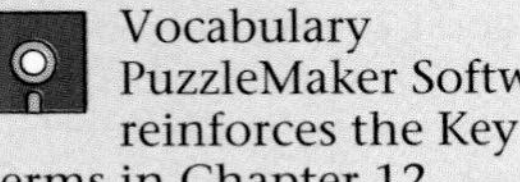

Vocabulary PuzzleMaker Software reinforces the Key Terms in Chapter 12.

Student Self-Test and Review Software allows students to review Chapter 12 content.

CONDENSE

Have students read the Chapter 12 Highlights.

Have students listen to the Chapter 12 Audiocassettes in the TCR. Spanish Audiocassettes are also available.

Assign the Chapter 12 Audiocassette Activity and give students the Chapter 12 Audiocassette Quiz.

Have students complete the Guided Reading Activities for Chapter 12 in the TCR. Spanish Guided Reading Activities are also available.

RETEACH

Have students complete Reteaching Activities for Chapter 12 in the TCR. Spanish Reteaching Activities are also available.

Map Activity

Identify and Locate Display Unit Map Overlay Transparency 4-4. Point to a country and have students identify it. Then ask students to recall facts about the population patterns, history and government, and cultures and lifestyles of that country.

GLENCOE TECHNOLOGY

Videodisc

Use Chapter 12 MindJogger Videoquiz to review students' knowledge before administering the Chapter 12 Test.

MINDJOGGER VIDEOQUIZ

Chapter 12
Disc 2 Side A

The MindJogger Videoquiz is also available on videocassette.

chapter 12 REVIEW

Reviewing Key Terms

Choose the vocabulary term that best completes each of the sentences below. Write your answers on a separate sheet of paper.

refugees (p. 240)
city-states (p. 245)
feudalism (p. 245)
Renaissance (p. 246)
communism (p. 247)
Holocaust (p. 248)
cold war (p. 248)
dialect (p. 251)
romanticism (p. 252)
impressionism (p. 253)
welfare states (p. 253)

SECTION 1

1. ____ are people who flee to a foreign country for safety.

SECTION 2

2. The mass killing of 6 million European Jews in World War II is known as the ____.
3. After World War II, ____ became the dominant political movement in Eastern Europe.
4. Ancient Greeks settled in independent communities called ____.
5. The ____ was a period of renewed interest in learning that brought advancements in European arts.
6. The ____ refers to the power struggle between the Soviet Union and the United States.
7. A system in which powerful lords gave land to nobles in return for pledges of loyalty was known as ____.

SECTION 3

8. The term ____ refers to a local form of a language.
9. Artists influenced by ____ tried to show emotions in their work.
10. In ____, governments assume major responsibility for education and health care.
11. ____ emphasized the natural appearance of objects and light.

Reviewing Facts

SECTION 1

12. Which parts of Europe are most densely populated?

SECTION 2

13. What were some accomplishments of ancient Greek civilization?

SECTION 3

14. How do European governments provide for the welfare of their people?

Critical Thinking

15. **Drawing Conclusions** What similarities create the strongest connections among Europeans?
16. **Analyzing Information** How did religion influence the development of Europe during the Middle Ages?
17. **Making Generalizations** How has urbanization diminished differences among European lifestyles?

Geographic Themes

18. **Movement** How did the Industrial Revolution change population patterns in Europe?
19. **Movement** How did the Crusades and the Renaissance encourage the spread of European civilization?
20. **Region** How does the quality of life differ in urban/rural, northern/southern, eastern/western regions of Europe?

ANSWERS

Reviewing Key Terms

1. refugees
2. Holocaust
3. communism
4. city-states
5. Renaissance
6. cold war
7. feudalism
8. dialect
9. romanticism
10. welfare states
11. impressionism

Reviewing Facts

12. One densely populated area extends from the United Kingdom into France and across the North European Plain into the Czech Republic and Poland. Another extends from southeastern France into the Apennine Peninsula.

13. The first democratic governments were established in Greek city-states. The Greeks created lasting works of art, literature, drama, and philosophy. Greek scientists made great advances in mathematics and medicine.

14. Most European governments subsidize health-care services. Many provide free education and other social welfare programs.

Critical Thinking

15. Europeans share certain common attitudes and values, such as the importance of family, the value of the past, and the responsibility of government for the welfare of the people.

16. The Roman Catholic Church introduced Roman ideas of government to Germanic peoples. The Byzantines preserved Greek culture and organized ancient Roman laws. Muslims spread knowledge of Asian cultures and made advances in mathematics, medicine, and astronomy.

17. People who live in urban areas have less traditional lifestyles than people in rural areas do. They live in similar kinds of housing, work in similar jobs, and participate in similar activities.

Practicing Skills

Writing a Topic Sentence

Refer to the skills activity on page 256. What is the topic sentence in the first paragraph of the skills activity?

Using the Unit Atlas

Refer to the cultural geography section of the Unit Atlas on pages 214–215.

21. What nation divided after World War II was reunited in 1990?
22. When and where were the first Olympics held?

Projects

Individual Activity

Make a chart of some simple words common to many languages such as days of the week or numbers. Refer to a dictionary to find the origin of language for each. Write a generalization about European languages.

Cooperative Learning

Form small groups. Choose one era in European history such as Classical Civilizations, Renaissance, or 20th Century. Each group member should research three events related to the topic. Plot all the events on a time line to create an overview of European history.

Writing About Geography

Cause and Effect

Using your journal record and other references, write an essay explaining the factors that helped spread European civilization to other parts of the world. Include the role of geography and be as specific as possible.

Locating Places

EUROPE: EUROPEAN UNION

Match the letters on the map with the names of members of the European Union. Write your answers on a separate sheet of paper.

1. Belgium
2. France
3. Italy
4. Luxembourg
5. Netherlands
6. Denmark
7. Ireland
8. United Kingdom
9. Greece
10. Portugal
11. Spain
12. Germany

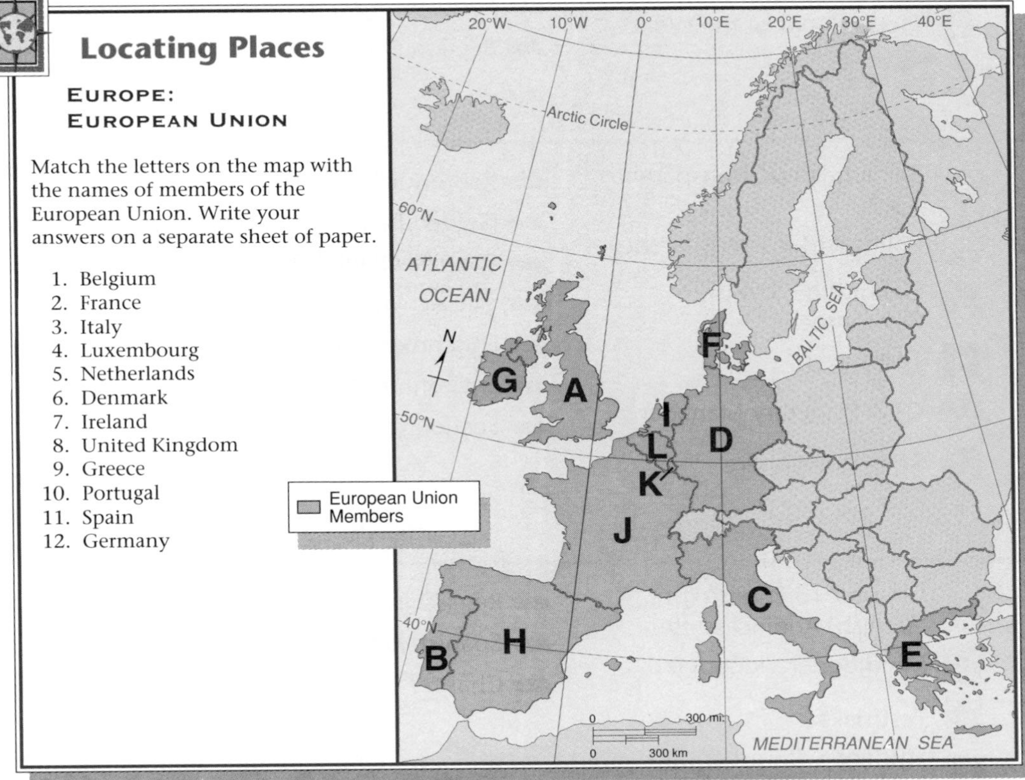

Chapter 12 Review

Geographic Themes

18. people left farming to seek jobs in factories; Europe's urban populations increased greatly

19. The Crusades led to the establishment of trade routes to the Middle East and gave Europeans a renewed interest in other parts of the world. The Renaissance brought about advancements in technology that enabled Europeans to explore distant lands.

20. In general, people who live in urban areas or in northern and western regions of Europe have a higher standard of living than people who live in rural areas or in southern and eastern Europe.

Practicing Skills

The topic sentence is "Writing is a basic survival skill in today's society."

Using the Unit Atlas

21. Germany
22. Greece, 776 B.C.

Locating Places

1. L
2. J
3. C
4. K
5. I
6. F
7. G
8. A
9. E
10. B
11. H
12. D

Chapter Bonus Test Question

This question may be used for extra credit on the chapter test.

How did Europe's geographic setting influence the development and spread of its civilizations?

(Answers: Europe's closeness to the sea favored exploration and trade. European civilizations spread as nations conquered other parts of the world and established colonies.)

CHAPTER 13

PLANNING GUIDE
Europe Today

CHAPTER ORGANIZER

Daily Lesson Objectives	Multimedia	Teacher Classroom Resources
SECTION 1 Living in Europe 1. Point out the effects of changing economies in eastern and western Europe. 2. Discuss the major economic activities in Europe. 3. Explain how communication and transportation systems link most parts of Europe.	Section Focus Transparency 13-1 Chapter 13 Vocabulary PuzzleMaker Software Political Map Transparency 4 Testmaker Picture Atlas of the World	Reproducible Lesson Plan 13-1 Guided Reading Activity 13-1 Spanish Guided Reading Activity 13-1 Workbook Activity 13-1 Performance Assessment Activity 13 Outline Map Resource Book, p. 30 Foods Around the World 3 Section Quiz 13-1
SECTION 2 People and Their Environment 1. Analyze the causes and effects of environmental pollution in Europe. 2. Explain why cleanup and reduction of pollution requires cooperation among European governments. 3. Identify steps Europeans are taking to protect the environment.	Section Focus Transparency 13-2 Political Map Transparency 4 Geography and the Environment Testmaker GTV: Planetary Manager STV: Atmosphere	Reproducible Lesson Plan 13-2 Guided Reading Activity 13-2 Spanish Guided Reading Activity 13-2 Skill Activity 13 Enrichment Activity 13 Environmental Issue 4 Section Quiz 13-2
CHAPTER REVIEW AND EVALUATION	Chapter 13 English (or Spanish) Audiocassettes MindJogger Videoquiz Testmaker Student Self-Test and Review Software	Reteaching Activity 13 Spanish Reteaching Activity 13 Chapter 13 Test Form A and Form B

0:00 *If time does not permit teaching the entire chapter, summarize using the Chapter 13 Highlights on page 277, and the Chapter 13 English (or Spanish) Audiocassettes. Review students' knowledge using the Glencoe MindJogger Videoquiz.*

KEY TO ABILITY LEVELS

Teaching strategies have been coded for varying learning styles and abilities.

L1 **BASIC** activities for all students

L2 **AVERAGE** activities for average to above-average students

L3 **CHALLENGING** activities for above-average students

LEP **LIMITED ENGLISH PROFICIENCY** activities

Performance Assessment

International Trade Group students to represent various countries in the culture regions previously studied in this text. These groups should then decide with which European countries they might become trading partners, what goods would be traded, what means of transportation would be used, and the possible environmental effects of trading with the designated partners. Students might use resource maps, text information, or other sources to determine the needs of their particular areas. Individual country trade laws and aspects of NAFTA, the EU, and other international economic associations should also be considered. Students should then write trade agreements modeled on those of nations and international organizations.

POSSIBLE RUBRIC FEATURES: Content information, research skills, concept attainment, decision-making skills, collaborative skills, communication skills, application and analysis skills

For additional professional and classroom resources, see Chapter Resources, pages T46–T51.

TEACHER'S CORNER

INDEX TO NATIONAL GEOGRAPHIC MAGAZINE

The following articles may be used for research relating to this chapter:

- "East Europe's Dark Dawn: The Iron Curtain Rises to Reveal a Land Tarnished by Pollution," by Jon Thompson, June 1991.
- "Berlin's Ode to Joy," by Priit J. Vesilind, April 1990.
- "High Tech: The Future is Now," by Michael E. Long, July 1989.
- "Are the Swiss Forests in Peril?" by Christian Mehr, May 1989.
- "Air: An Atmosphere of Uncertainty," by Noel Grove, April 1987.
- "The Incredible Potato," by Robert E. Rhoades, May 1982.
- "Acid Rain: How Great a Menace?" by Anne LaBastille, November 1981.

NATIONAL GEOGRAPHIC SOCIETY PRODUCTS AVAILABLE FROM GLENCOE

To order the following products for use with this chapter, contact your local Glencoe sales representative or call Glencoe at 1-800-334-7344:

- *Picture Atlas of the World* (CD-ROM)
- *STV: World Geography, Africa and Europe* (Videodisc)
- *ZipZapMap! World* (Software)
- *GeoBee* (Software)
- *Images of the World* (Posters)
- *Eye on the Environment* (Posters)
- *Physical Geography of the World* (Transparencies)
- *Picture Atlas of Our 50 States* (Book)

Introducing
CHAPTER 13

chapter 13 Europe Today

PERFORMANCE ASSESSMENT

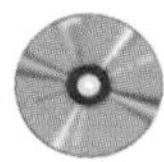

Refer to the Planning Guide on page 260B for a Performance Assessment Activity for this chapter. See the *Performance Assessment Activities* booklet for additional suggestions.

CHAPTER OBJECTIVES

1. **Explain** how the European Union and the nations of eastern Europe adjusted to changing economies.
2. **Describe** the effects of acid rain, air pollution, and water pollution on Europe's environment and economy.

GLENCOE TECHNOLOGY

Videodisc

Use Chapter 13 MindJogger Videoquiz to preview chapter content.

MINDJOGGER VIDEOQUIZ

Chapter 13
Disc 2 Side B

The MindJogger Videoquiz is also available on videocassette.

CHAPTER FOCUS

Geographic Setting

The physical closeness of European nations creates shared responsibility for the causes of pollution and the problems involved in cleanup.

Geographic Themes

Section 1 Living in Europe

REGION The European Union and the nations of eastern Europe adjusted to changing economies in the early 1990s.

▲ Photograph: *Port at Barcelona, Spain*

Section 2 People and Their Environment

HUMAN/ENVIRONMENT INTERACTION Acid rain, air pollution, and water pollution affect Europe's environment and economy.

EXTRA CREDIT PROJECT

Bulletin Board Have students research trade between Europe and the United States. Have them make lists of goods that are imported from Europe and exported to Europe. Encourage them to be as specific as possible. For example, tires from Akron, Ohio, to Florence, Italy; watches from Zurich, Switzerland, to Minneapolis, Minnesota. Have students combine their findings to create a large poster or bulletin-board display.

1 SECTION

Living in Europe

SETTING THE SCENE

Read to Discover . . .

- the effects of changing economies in eastern and western Europe.
- the major economic activities in Europe.
- how communication and transportation systems link most parts of Europe.

Key Terms

- heavy industry
- light industry
- organic farming
- mixed farming
- farm cooperative
- collective farm
- state farm
- consumer goods
- tariff

Identify and Locate

Rhine River, Ruhr, Lorraine-Saar district, Main-Danube Canal, Bavaria

V. INTERNATIONALE GARTENBAUAUSSTELLUNG 1993 STUTTGART
100
Deutsche Bundespost

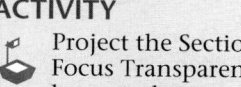

Munich, Germany

Golt mitrander. I'm excited because today my sister and I will go for a train trip on the new ICE (Intercity Express Train) to visit our uncle in Esslingen. We'll also look around in Stuttgart, but we'll use underground transportation in order to avoid heavy city traffic. On Monday, Uncle Hans will show us around in the Mercedes-Benz plant where he works as a technical engineer.

Tschüs

Rebekka Prapler

Rebekka Prapler describes the ease of travel in Germany, Europe's most economically powerful country. Since World War II, most Europeans have experienced rising standards of living and have had greater opportunity to travel at home and abroad. Meanwhile, Europe's diverse nationalities and ethnic groups have taken steps toward greater continental unity. In spite of this progress, national antagonisms still remain to trouble Europe's political life.

The economies of Europe, like its populations, are diverse and changing. More than half the land in Europe is used for farming. Europe also has 5 of the world's top 10 manufacturing nations. The European Union (EU) is a major economic unit with a greater volume of trade than any one country in the world. Eastern European economies are undergoing major changes as their governments adapt to growing democracy and economic reform.

REGION

Changing Economies

While the 12 nations of the European Union took steps toward economic unity in the early 1990s, eastern European nations struggled to adjust to free enterprise. Both regions experienced the realization that change is difficult. Their peoples looked to the dawning of the 21st century in a mood of hope mixed with concern.

Classroom Resources for Section 1

BLACKLINE MASTERS:

Reproducible Lesson Plan 13-1
Guided Reading Activity 13-1
Spanish Guided Reading Activity 13-1
Workbook Activity 13-1
Foods Around the World 3
Outline Map Resource Book, p. 30
Performance Assessment Activity 13
Section Quiz 13-1

TRANSPARENCIES:

Section Focus Transparency 13-1
Political Map Transparency 4

MULTIMEDIA:

Vocabulary PuzzleMaker Software
Testmaker

Picture Atlas of the World

LESSON PLAN
Chapter 13, Section 1

FOCUS

SECTION OBJECTIVES

1. Point out the effects of changing economies in eastern and western Europe.
2. Discuss the major economic activities in Europe.
3. Explain how communication and transportation systems link most parts of Europe.

ABOUT THE POSTCARD

Rebekka and her sister will also travel to Marbach to tour the poet Friedrich Schiller's birthplace.

BELLRINGER MOTIVATIONAL ACTIVITY

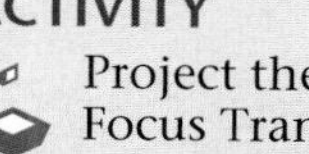

Project the Section 1 Focus Transparency and have students answer the questions.

PRETEACHING VOCABULARY

Have students look up the meanings of the Key Terms. Then list the following clues on the chalkboard and have students write the Key Term associated with each clue: tax *(tariff)*, factory machinery *(heavy industry)*, household items *(consumer goods)*, food processing *(light industry)*. **LEP**

Use the Vocabulary PuzzleMaker Software to create a crossword or word search puzzle.

CD-ROM

PICTURE ATLAS OF THE WORLD

Click the "Stats" button to learn more about the economies of countries in Europe.

TEACH

GUIDED PRACTICE

L1 Geography: Human/ Environment Interaction Display Political Map Transparency 4. Have students relate each Key Term that refers to economic activity to locations on the map. **LEP**

USING MAPS

Answers:
1. Ireland, United Kingdom, Portugal, Spain, France, Luxembourg, Belgium, Netherlands, Germany, Denmark, Italy, Greece; **2.** in western Europe; **3.** Ireland, United Kingdom

Map Skills Practice
Reading a Map What geographic feature aids the movement of goods to and from the European Union? *(coastlines)*

L2 Economies Have students create a chart comparing the economies of eastern and western Europe.

DID YOU KNOW?

Hungarians want to join the European Union. School curricula have been changed to emphasize a relationship with the West. Hungarians hope the change will give students an advantage in international business careers.

European Union

In 1950 France proposed closer links among Europe's coal and steel industries. The move was seen as a first step toward a united Europe. Over the years more steps were taken toward that goal, but not until the 1990s did most Europeans agree that such a goal could be reached.

Different traditions and points of view, however, made unity within the European Union difficult to achieve. Members defeated the proposal for a single European currency, but most of the proposed single-market measures were adopted into law. Results, however, failed to meet expectations. Forecasters had predicted overall economic growth, but Europe—along with the rest of the industrialized world—plunged into a recession.

In an effort to make their products competitive in a world market, many European companies cut costs by cutting jobs. Some economists proposed that governments also reduce or eliminate costly social welfare programs. Many Europeans oppose such measures, which they think would only increase hardships during a time of rising unemployment. The European Union continues to work toward the goal of a stronger single economy in spite of the difficulties brought on by change.

THE EUROPEAN UNION

FOCUS ON GEOGRAPHIC THEMES

1. **Region:** What countries are members of the European Union?
2. **Location:** Where are most of the Union's member countries located?
3. **Place:** What two European Union members are island nations?

Eastern Europe

For more than 40 years, Communist governments closely tied to the Soviet Union controlled Eastern European industries. Central planners made all decisions about what goods to produce and how to produce them. Industries generally employed many more workers and managers than they needed. Many factories lacked modern technology, such as automation, pollution controls, and energy conservation equipment.

To compete in a free market economy, eastern European industries must overcome the obstacles of outdated equipment and inefficient methods. Many workers must be laid off or retrained. Industries need to build new facilities with modern technology and adopt energy conservation methods to reduce pollution. The new democratic governments are seeking investments and financial aid from western Europe as well as from other parts of the world. Eastern Europeans have realized that change is costly as well as difficult.

REGION

Agriculture and Industry

Europe has some of the world's most fertile and productive farmland. Many European farmers use advanced scientific methods and

Cooperative Learning Activity

Organize students into six groups and assign several European countries to each group. Have students consult encyclopedias and other references to find out the major products of each country assigned to them. Provide each group with an outline map from the Outline Map Resource Book, page 30. Have students design symbols for major products and place them in appropriate places on their maps. Compare the completed maps and ask students to draw conclusions about the relationship between geography and major products of European countries.

farming equipment. They annually add fertilizers to the soil and plant a variety of crops to maintain the land's fertility.

More Europeans earn a living from farming than from any other single economic activity. The percentages of workers engaged in farming varies dramatically from one country to another, however. In highly industrialized countries, such as the United Kingdom and Belgium, less than 2 percent of the labor force works in agriculture. In Poland and Greece, almost 30 percent of the labor force is engaged in farming.

Economic Expansion

Europe is the birthplace of modern industry. Beginning in the late 1700s, the Industrial Revolution helped lay the foundation of Europe's economic growth and global influence. The increased productivity and lower costs brought by the use of machines slowly raised European living standards. Meanwhile, as markets at home and abroad expanded, several European countries became leading industrial centers of the world.

The development of industry is often linked to the availability of raw materials. In the 1800s and early 1900s, the largest coal and iron-ore deposits in Europe provided bases for the growth of **heavy industry**—the manufacture of machinery and equipment needed for factories and mines. Today, a series of large-scale industrial areas now stretch from the United Kingdom to Poland. These industrial centers include the Ruhr and Middle Rhine districts in Germany, the Lorraine-Saar district in France, the Po Basin in Italy, and the Upper Silesia-Moravia district in Poland and the Czech Republic. Vast deposits of mineral wealth have helped to make such nations as France and Germany leaders in manufacturing.

Nations lacking industrial raw materials, such as the Netherlands and Denmark, specialize in **light industry**, such as textiles or food processing. Service industries employ a large percentage of the workforce in most European nations. Switzerland, for example, has prospered from banking and finance.

Geographic Themes

Place: Stuttgart, Germany

Coal, iron, and steel have made Germany's Ruhr and Middle Rhine districts leading industrial centers. *Where are most of Europe's industrial centers located?*

Food Production

Europe leads the world in the production of barley, oats, potatoes, rye, and sugar beets. Wheat, the major grain crop, grows in most European nations. Citrus fruits, dates, and figs grow in the Mediterranean region. Nations in that region also produce most of the world's olives. Grapes grown in southern Europe are used to make much of the world's wine. Dairy farming is important in Denmark, the United Kingdom, and the Netherlands. Some of the world's finest breeds of cattle and sheep are raised in western Europe.

Europeans generally produce most of their own food supply. Imports consist mostly of tropical foods, such as cocoa and coffee. Nations that specialize in a few farm products trade among themselves for the foods they need. In addition to farming, the European fishing industry provides an important part of the Continent's food. Denmark and Norway rank among the world's leading fishing nations.

USING ILLUSTRATIONS

LOCATION About 85 percent of Germans live in cities and towns. Berlin, with a population of 3.5 million, is the largest city and the official capital. The southern cities of Munich and Stuttgart rank as the fastest-growing cities in Germany. Industrial expansion and technology have spurred this growth.

Answer to Caption: *in northwestern and central Europe*

L3 Compare Have students compare privately owned industries and farms with those owned by government. Bases of comparison include production/yields, prices, incentives, and benefits to workers/farmers. Ask students to predict the consequences of eastern Europe's change to private ownership of land and industry. *(Answers should indicate that changes created high prices and unemployment but should improve production and provide greater incentives for farmers/workers.)*

DID YOU KNOW?

The Netherlands exports 59 percent of the world's cut flowers, primarily to Germany, France, and the United Kingdom. Dutch floral exports to the United States total $100 million annually.

Meeting Special Needs

Learning Disabilities Students with learning problems often need help organizing and classifying material. Have them create a large chart with the following headings: Heavy Industry, Light Industry, Agriculture, Services. Have students reread the material from the text and list the facts they consider important under the appropriate heading. Then have each student choose one of the headings and write a paragraph using the facts listed on the chart.

MULTICULTURAL PERSPECTIVE

Culturally Speaking
French is an important international language. It is second only to English in use between nations for business and diplomacy.

USING GRAPHS

Answers:
20.7%; 19.7%

Skills Practice

Interpreting a Graph How does the European Union's share of imports and exports compare with that of the United States? *(EU exports exceed those of the U.S.; EU imports are only slightly less than those of the U.S.)*

INDEPENDENT PRACTICE

Guided Reading Have students complete Guided Reading Activity 13-1 in the TCR. **LEP**

L2 Mathematics Have students choose three European countries. Ask them to create circle graphs to show the percentages of each country's workforce engaged in different occupations. Display and compare the graphs.

Have students complete Performance Assessment Activity 13 in the TCR.

Farming Techniques

Soil and climate play a major role in determining the kinds and amounts of crops produced in a region. European farmers also have found ways to make the best use of their limited agricultural area. Farmers rely on **organic farming**—the use of natural substances to enrich the soil—as well as chemical fertilizers to increase crop yields. **Mixed farming**—raising several kinds of crops and livestock on the same farm—is common practice in parts of western Europe. Most farmers in western Europe own their land, and the average farm covers about 30 acres (12.2 ha). In Belgium and the United Kingdom, many farmers rent their land from private land owners. **Farm cooperatives**—organizations in which farmers share in growing and selling farm products—help farmers reduce their costs and increase profits.

Farming, like other aspects of life in eastern Europe, has undergone change in recent times. Under Communist control, all farms were owned by the government. On **collective farms**, the farmers received wages plus a share of products and profits. **State farms** were managed by government officials, and farmers did not share in the profits. Outdated farm machinery and methods, combined with a lack of incentive, resulted in poor crop yields. With the growth of democracy in the region, countries have begun to encourage private control of agricultural production and private ownership of the land.

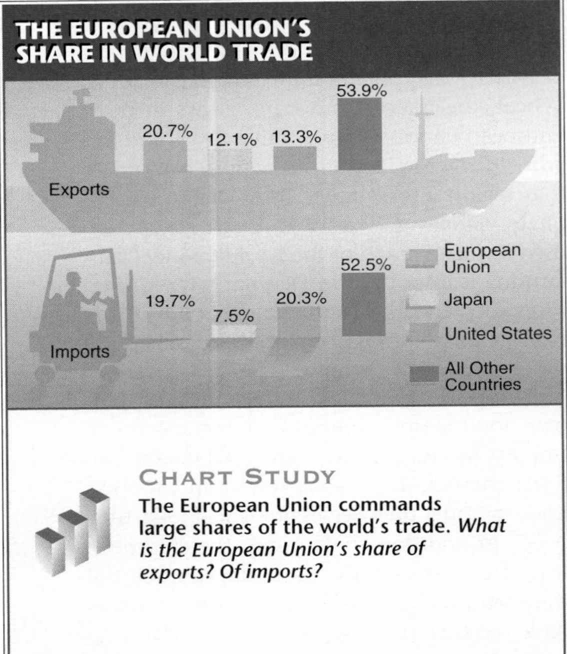

CHART STUDY

The European Union commands large shares of the world's trade. ***What is the European Union's share of exports? Of imports?***

Manufacturing

France, the United Kingdom, Italy, Poland, and Germany rank among the world's leaders in manufacturing. These nations are among the leading steel producers and automobile manufacturers in the world. Switzerland is noted for the high quality of its watches and other precision instruments. The Czech Republic and Poland are major manufacturers of machinery and chemicals.

In western Europe, most industries are privately owned. In eastern Europe, however, state-owned industries under the former Communist governments, emphasized heavy industry. As a result, few factories in Communist countries produced **consumer goods**—household goods, shoes, and clothing that individuals buy. In recent years, factories have switched to private ownership. Foreign companies have begun to buy or start new businesses in this region. Changing conditions have resulted in high prices and unemployment as eastern European governments struggle to stabilize their economies.

Services and Trade

Service industries employ nearly 60 percent of the labor force in western European countries. International banking and insurance rank among Europe's top service industries. Switzerland and the United Kingdom are leaders in these fields. Belgium serves as the headquarters for hundreds of international companies.

Tourism is another large service industry in Europe. The United Kingdom, France, Spain, Germany, Switzerland, Italy, and Austria are among the world's leading tourist nations. Barriers to travel among European nations

Critical Thinking

Analyzing Information Have students relate the economic activities of European countries to the five themes of geography. *(For example, agriculture is related to place and to human/environment interaction. Manufacturing may be related to place, movement, and human/environment interaction.)* Instruct students to work independently, then provide time for them to share their insights.

generally have been eliminated. People living in the European Union can travel freely among member nations. The collapse of communism in eastern Europe resulted in the removal of travel barriers in that region as well.

European Union members no longer pay a **tariff,** or tax, on goods traded among themselves. This policy encouraged bargain hunters to seek the best buys on consumer goods in neighboring countries. The single-market economy of the EU has made it the world's largest importer and exporter.

Before 1989, most Eastern European countries belonged to the Council for Mutual Economic Assistance (COMECON). Members of COMECON traded primarily among themselves for needed goods. For example, Romania traded coal to Czechoslovakia in exchange for manufactured goods. Since eastern European nations have switched to market economies, trade with other nations has increased.

EUROPE: ECONOMIC ACTIVITY

- Nomadic herding
- Forestry
- Commercial farming
- Subsistence farming
- Manufacturing and trade
- Commercial fishing

Lambert Conformal Conic projection

FOCUS ON GEOGRAPHIC THEMES

1. **Location:** Where does most of Europe's manufacturing and trade occur?
2. **Place:** What is the major form of economic activity in Portugal?
3. **Region:** In what area of Europe is forestry a major industry?

MOVEMENT

Communication and Transportation

Almost all of Europe's communication and transportation systems are government-owned. Although the quality varies from one region to another, these systems are among the best in the world. Modern communications systems link most parts of Europe with each other and with other parts of the world. Networks of highways, railways, waterways, and airline routes crisscross the Continent.

Communication Links

Many European nations belong to the International Telecommunications Satellite Organization (Intelsat). This international system uses communications satellites for the worldwide broadcast and reception of television programs. A television network called *Eurovision* links most western European countries, and a similar network called *Intervision* operates in eastern Europe. These networks sometimes exchange television programs.

Telephone service varies throughout the Continent. France, for example, has one telephone for every two people. The Czech Republic has one telephone for every four people, and in Poland the ratio is one telephone for every eight people. Within the European Union, rates generally are high and vary greatly from one government-owned telephone company to another. A call from Spain to Denmark, for example, costs twice as much as a call from Denmark to Spain.

Books, magazines, and newspapers are published throughout Europe. The growth of democracy has reduced or eliminated government censorship of printed materials in east-

L2 Geography: Location Challenge students to find out which European countries have the longest coastlines. *(Answers include Norway—eighth longest in the world; Greece—eleventh longest in the world.)* Then have students investigate which economic activities of these countries are linked to their coastlines. *(fishing, shipbuilding, trade, tourism)*

L2 Communications Have students obtain copies of European newspapers and magazines. Then have them compare the European publications with similar publications in the United States. Provide time for students to share their findings.

USING MAPS

Answers:
1. in northern and central Europe;
2. commercial farming;
3. Scandinavia

Map Skills Practice

Comparing Maps What are the major economic activities in EU countries? *(commercial farming, manufacturing and trade)*

L3 Transportation Provide copies of the map on page 30 of the Outline Map Resource Book. Tell students to indicate major ports, major railroad centers, and major airports. Have students analyze geographic influences on transportation centers.

Extending the Content

Service Industries Banking ranks as one of Switzerland's leading industries. Because of the nation's neutrality, its banks are considered the safest in the world. Swiss banks attract depositors from all over the world. Accounts are identified by a number known only to the depositor and a few bank officials. Except in criminal investigations, a Swiss bank employee who reveals information about secret accounts can be fined and imprisoned.

Global Gourmet

Belgian chocolates not only are world famous but are also one of the nation's main food exports—$605 million in 1990. The European love of chocolate, however, can be traced back to the court of the Aztec emperor Moctezuma II in the early 1500s. The Spanish conquistador Hernando Cortés is credited with introducing chocolate to Europe.

USING ILLUSTRATIONS

MOVEMENT Germans must attend expensive and rigorous driver training schools to get a driver's license. There is no speed limit on parts of the autobahn, but all other roads have strict limits.

Answer to Caption: mountains

ASSESS

CHECK FOR UNDERSTANDING

Assign Section 1 Review as homework or an in-class activity.

MEETING LESSON OBJECTIVES

Each objective below is tested by the questions that follow it in parentheses.

1. **Point out** the effects of changing economies in eastern and western Europe. *(5)*
2. **Discuss** the major economic activities in Europe. *(3)*
3. **Explain** how communication and transportation systems link most parts of Europe. *(2, 4)*

ern European countries. Many Europeans read daily newspapers. Sweden, with about 570 copies sold daily for every 1,000 people, leads the world in newspaper readership. Some European newspapers, such as *The Times* of London and *Le Monde* of Paris, are read by people in many parts of the world.

Highways and Railways

A well-developed system of highways and roads links all major cities in Europe. Germany's four-lane superhighways, called *autobahnen,* are among Europe's best roads. Bridges and tunnels carry traffic over or through the barriers posed by physical features. For example, the St. Gotthard Road Tunnel cuts through the Alps in central Switzerland. It is 10.14 miles (16.32 km) long, which makes it one of the world's longest road tunnels.

There are more automobile owners in Europe than in any other part of the world except the United States. The percentage of car owners is greater in western Europe than in eastern Europe. Bicycles and motorcycles provide popular forms of transportation for many Europeans.

Geographic Themes

Movement: Central European Superhighways Germany has about 3,900 miles (6,500 km) of four-lane superhighways. *What major physical obstacle has been overcome in building highways in central Europe?*

Trucks carry much of the freight in many western European countries. France, the United Kingdom, Germany, Spain, Italy, and Belgium rely on trucks for transporting goods. Road signs make use of pictures and symbols instead of words so that travelers from any country can understand traffic instructions.

Europe has about one-fourth of the total railroad trackage in the world. Railroads are a major means of freight and passenger transportation throughout the Continent. In eastern Europe, railroads provide the link between areas rich in natural resources and major industrial centers. Rail lines connect almost all the Continent's major cities. Railroad stations provide easy access to downtown and suburban areas. Tunnels carry rail traffic through Europe's mountains.

France's *trains á grande vitesse* (TGVs), which means "very fast trains," are the fastest in the world. TGVs travel at an average speed of 170 miles (270 km) per hour, but they can reach a top speed of 235 miles (380 km) per hour. Powered by smokeless, silent electricity, TGVs are much less harmful to the environment than are most other forms of transportation. Relatively low fares make TGVs more economical as well as more efficient than airline travel.

Major Transportation Centers

Most of Europe's major cities are railroad centers. Many of them have major airports as well. Airports in London, Frankfurt, Paris, Rome, Amsterdam, Stockholm, Zurich, Copenhagen, and Munich rank among the busiest in the world. European airlines fly throughout the Continent, but much of Europe's air traffic consists of international flights.

Europe handles more than half the world's international shipping. The Continent's long coastline influenced the seafaring tradition of many countries. Most of the world's largest merchant fleets belong to European countries. Europe also has many bustling ports. These include London; Rotterdam, in the Netherlands; Antwerp, Belgium; Genoa, Italy; Le Havre and Marseilles, France; and Gdansk, Poland.

Cooperative Learning Activity

Organize students into five groups and assign one of the following forms of transportation to each group: highways, waterways, railways, shipping, and airlines. Have members of each group research their assigned topic. Instruct them to find out how extensively the form of transportation has been developed in Europe, what plans for the future exist, and what problems need to be solved. Create new groups with one member from each of the original groups for the purpose of sharing knowledge of European transportation systems.

Waterways

Europe's rivers and canals form an important transportation system. Waterways carry passenger traffic, but they are more important for transporting freight. The Rhine River and its tributaries carry a greater volume of freight than any other river system in Europe. The Rhine River provides access to the North Sea for industrial centers in Switzerland, France, Belgium, Germany, and the Netherlands.

Canals link Europe's major waterways. For example, the Kiel Canal cuts across the part of Germany that occupies the Jutland Peninsula and shortens the route between the North Sea and the Baltic Sea. Canals also connect the Oder and the Vistula rivers in Poland and provide links between the Oder River and rivers in western Europe. The Main-Danube Canal in Germany links hundreds of inland ports from the North Sea to the Black Sea. The ambitious project, completed in 1992, sparked much controversy. Some people think that the amount of trade on the canal will not meet expectations. They consider the Main-Danube Canal an "extravagant folly." Environmentalists argue that construction of the canal upset the balance of nature in Bavaria's Altmuhl Valley. Reinhard Grebe, landscape architect for the canal, defends his plan to preserve the natural beauty of the region:

> *The engineers wanted to make the canal straight and build roads down both sides of it. It would have destroyed the valley utterly. We insisted that they make the canal look more natural, that they give it backwaters for the protection of wildlife, that they keep one side free of traffic and build a bikeway instead. . . .*

The long-range economic impact of the Main-Danube Canal remains unknown. The extraordinary effort to make the canal fit the landscape, however, expresses Europeans' growing concern for their environment.

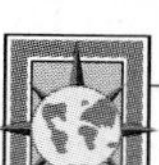

Geographic Themes

Movement: France's Rail System
The French rail network, including the famous TGV lines, forms a cobweb pattern with Paris as the hub. *Why are the TGVs much less harmful to the environment than other trains?*

Section 1 Review

Checking for Understanding

1. **Define** heavy industry, light industry, organic farming, mixed farming, farm cooperative, collective farm, state farm, consumer goods, tariff.
2. **Locating Places** What two major bodies of water does the Main-Danube Canal link?
3. **Region** From what economic activity do most Europeans earn a living?
4. **Movement** Why are railroads a major means of transportation in Europe?

Critical Thinking

5. **Making Comparisons** How do the problems of forming a single-market economy in the European Union differ from those of adjusting to free enterprise in eastern Europe?

EVALUATE

Assign the Section 1 Quiz in the TCR.

Use the Testmaker to create a customized quiz for Section 1.

USING ILLUSTRATIONS

MOVEMENT The first TGV began operating between Paris and Lyon in 1981. Today, these high-speed trains link Paris with several cities in France and in Switzerland.

Answer to Caption: *TGVs are powered by smokeless, silent electricity.*

RETEACH

Have students write one review question for each heading in this section. Have them exchange papers and answer the questions.

ENRICH

Suggest that interested students research European automobiles that are popular in the United States, then make an illustrated poster, identifying the cars and where they are manufactured.

CLOSE

Have students write a postcard to Rebekka Prapler, describing travel in the United States.

ANSWERS TO SECTION 1 REVIEW

1. **heavy industry:** manufacture of factory machinery; **light industry:** manufacture of consumer goods; **organic farming:** use of natural substances to enrich soil; **mixed farming:** raising several kinds of crops on the same farm; **farm cooperative:** organization that collects and sells farm products; **collective farm:** government-owned farm; **state farm:** Communist-controlled farm; **consumer goods:** goods that individuals buy; **tariff:** tax on traded goods
2. North Sea and Black Sea
3. farming
4. rail lines link resources with major industrial centers; connect Europe's major cities
5. In the EU, different points of view make unity difficult. In eastern Europe, industries have to update their methods.

FOCUS

Have students recall stories about floods that they may have read about or seen on the news or on television. Ask them to share particularly vivid images or memories. Then have students suggest methods for protecting homes, wildlife, and land from flooding.

TEACH

L1 Location Use Unit Map Overlay Transparency 4-5 to familiarize students with the location of the coastline of the Netherlands, the English Channel, and the North Sea.

L2 Debate Have students debate whether the environmentalists' demand was unfair in view of the necessity for saving human lives.

L3 Technology Have students research the various methods that the Dutch have developed through the centuries to retake their land from the sea. Have them present their findings either in a series of captioned illustrations or models.

L3 Research Have students research the marine life of the Netherlands coast, then create a chart presenting information about each species. Students may include species name, description, primary food, and purpose and/or contribution in the ecological environment.

PROTECTING THE NETHERLANDS

I was here about 18 years ago, going through this new land, and I couldn't believe my eyes. I realized what had been accomplished, but seeing all this virgin country with the soil very bumpy and the steam actually coming out of it like primeval land was like witnessing the dawn of creation. Just incredible. . . . To see it now in its final form is a miracle, really. Nowhere else in the world can you see something like this.

Hank Fisher in *Sea Frontiers* May-June 1989

On the night of February 1, 1953, a raging Atlantic sea storm roared toward the European coastline, pushing a storm surge before it. Hitting the English Channel, the surge had nowhere to go. It coupled with the heavy spring tide of the North Sea, forming a 15-foot-high (4.6 m) wall of water. The frothing waves crashed over and through the dikes and dams of Zeeland Province in the southwest corner of the Netherlands. Engulfing the entire area, the surge killed nearly 2,000 people and thousands of animals and livestock, washed away some 50,000 homes, and destroyed thousands of acres of farmland.

To protect Holland "once and for all" from other such tragedies, the Dutch set up the Delta Works Project. The project called for building barriers to seal off and protect the inlets of Holland's southwestern coast.

THE ISSUE

The Dutch planned to seal off three of the four Rhine-Maas tributaries that empty into the sea through Holland's southwestern corner. The fourth tributary would remain open, so that the shipping port of Antwerp would not be disrupted.

As construction progressed during the 1960s and 1970s, however, conservationists increasingly raised objections to closing off the third tributary. Its unique environment is a rich breeding ground for fish as well as an abundant source of mussels and oysters. In addition, this area is one of Europe's most important havens for migratory birds.

THE BACKGROUND

For centuries, the Dutch have waged war against the seas that batter the land and erode the country's coastlines. Early Dutch settlers reclaimed the delta land by building mounds of clay and peat. Then they built simple crude dams to protect the land from the rivers' flow, and dikes to keep out the sea.

Over the centuries, the Dutch worked continuously to improve and perfect their dam-and-dike system. By the mid-1900s, more than 1,800 miles (2,896 km) of dams and dikes protected the country.

To protect Holland "once and for all" from other such tragedies, the Dutch set up the Delta Works Project. The project called for building barriers to seal off and protect the inlets of Holland's southwestern coast.

The tragedy of 1953, however, proved to many how inade-

Extending the Content

Barrier Before the gates and pillars of the barrier system could be erected, engineers had to figure out a way to prevent erosion of the seabed. If the seabed was washed away during storms, parts of the barrier would shift and settle, and the gates would be destroyed.

Dutch engineers constructed mats of willow and brushwood, sometimes an acre in size, which were floated out to the desired place for a dike. The mats were sunk and stabilized with tons of stones, sand, and clay to make a dike.

Between the layers are synthetic fabrics; when the fabrics have rotted away, the foundation under the barrier will be a "natural" one of sand and stones. Huge steel pins hold the layers together. Each of the 65 mattresses that make up the barrier's foundation is 656 by 138 feet (200 by 42 meters), and weighs 5,500 tons.

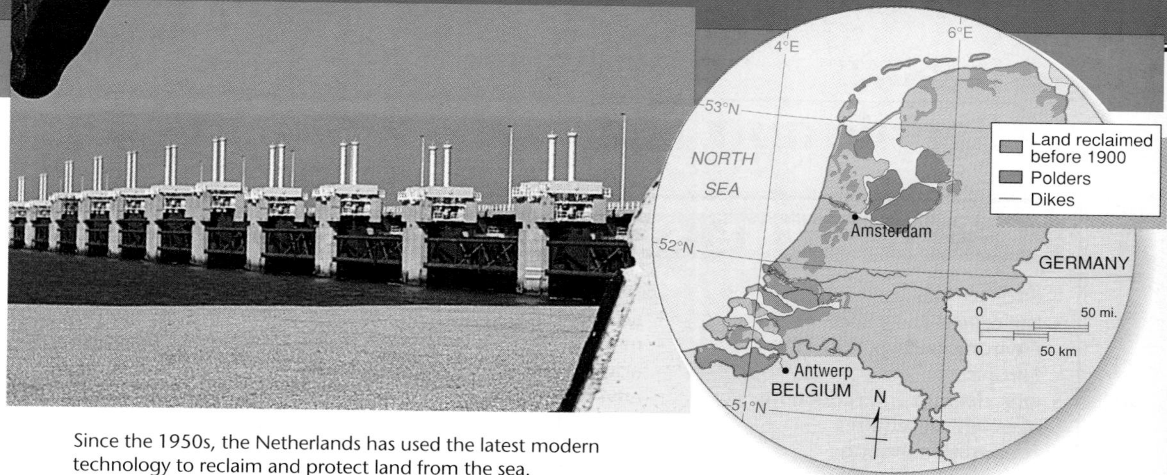

Since the 1950s, the Netherlands has used the latest modern technology to reclaim and protect land from the sea.

quate the system was. The Delta Project offered the protection many thought necessary. By 1972, two of the major southwestern inlets had been closed. Work had started on the third and widest tributary. Environmentalists and oyster farmers, however, were opposed to the plan and had enough support to halt the barrier's construction.

THE POINTS OF VIEW

Environmentalists pointed out that the abundant plant and animal life for which the third tributary is famous was at risk. Should this particular inlet be blocked, ecologists warned, it would turn into a stagnant, brackish lake, and the wildlife would eventually die. Oyster farmers protested that a barrier would also destroy the rich seabeds that provided them with their income.

Supporters of the barrier believed that to leave the third tributary open defeated the very purpose of the barrier. The area through which it flowed was the most vulnerable to devastating storms.

THE ISSUE TODAY

The Dutch parliament called a halt to the barrier's construction in the mid-1970s and ordered studies. In 1978, after two years of research, parliament ordered a seemingly impossible compromise: Build a barrier that will usually stay open, but can be closed in as little as an hour.

Today, an open barrier guards the third tributary's inlet. More than 2 miles long, it consists of 65 gigantic concrete pillars. Hanging like curtains between the pillars are 62 steel gates. Each gate measures as much as 138 feet (42 m) wide, 18 feet (5.5 m) thick, and 39 feet (11.9 m) high and weighs nearly 500 tons (453.5 metric tons). Each supporting pillar is about 12 stories high and weighs almost 18,000 tons (16,326 metric tons).

The gates remain open except for once or twice a year when high tides threaten the land. Thus, the barrier does not threaten the ecological balance or the tidal movement that supports it. Each gate is tested every month to ensure the entire system's workability.

The Netherlands appears safe from the sea for some years to come. In the meantime, the Dutch are "exporting" their skills to developing nations of Latin America, Africa, and Asia. They are also keeping in mind the future of their own country. They hope to be ready with bigger dikes and pumps if global warming causes the seas to rise, as some scientists predict.

Reviewing the Case

1. **Why was the Delta Project undertaken?**
2. **Who had concerns about the barrier at the third tributary?**
3. **Human/Environment**  **Interaction How were the concerns of the conservationists handled?**

Case Study

DID YOU KNOW?

More than a million tons of concrete were used in the construction of the Delta Project's barriers.

ASSESS

Have students answer the Reviewing the Case questions on page 269.

CLOSE

Share with students additional information from the Extending the Content box, then ask for comments on the technology involved in creating the barrier system.

ANSWERS TO REVIEWING THE CASE

1. The Delta Project was undertaken to prevent disastrous flooding of the Netherlands during sea storms.
2. Environmentalists were concerned that the plant and animal life in the third tributary would be in danger of dying out if the tributary was blocked.
3. The Dutch government called a halt to the barrier's construction, conducted a two-year study, then ordered the building of a barrier that would stay open most of the time, but could be closed in case of an emergency.

LESSON PLAN
Chapter 13, Section 2

FOCUS

SECTION OBJECTIVES

1. **Analyze** the causes and effects of environmental pollution in Europe.
2. **Explain** why cleanup and reduction of pollution requires cooperation among European governments.
3. **Identify** steps Europeans are taking to protect the environment.

BELLRINGER MOTIVATIONAL ACTIVITY

Project the Section 2 Focus Transparency and have students answer the questions.

PRETEACHING VOCABULARY

Review the suffix *-ist,* meaning "one who." Then have students infer the meanings of the two Key Terms that end with that suffix—biologist *(one who studies biology, or living things)* and environmentalist *(one who is concerned with the environment).* **LEP**

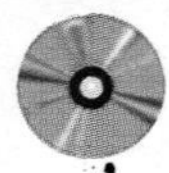

Videodisc

GTV: PLANETARY MANAGER

Side 2, Chapter 1
Frames 2-5929
Title: ***Up, Up, and Away?***
Subject: Consequences of air pollution

GTV: PLANETARY MANAGER

Side 2, Chapter 2
Frames 5931-12204
Title: ***Greenhouse of Eden***
Subject: The greenhouse effect and air pollution

SECTION 2

People and Their Environment

THE ENVIRONMENT

SETTING THE SCENE

Read to Discover . . .

- the causes and effects of environmental pollution in Europe.
- why cleanup and reduction of pollution requires cooperation among European governments.
- what steps Europeans are taking to protect the environment.

Key Terms

- acid rain
- meltwater
- acid deposition
- environmentalist
- biologist

Identify and Locate

Black Forest, Mediterranean Sea, Strait of Gibraltar, Lake Balaton

In spite of social, political, and economic differences, all Europeans have one thing in common—the environment. Environmental problems affect all Europeans regardless of their traditions, the country they live in, or their standard of living. Europeans, like people everywhere, face the challenge of resolving these growing problems.

HUMAN/ENVIRONMENT INTERACTION

Environmental Pollution

As in North America, **acid rain**, or precipitation carrying large amounts of pollutants, has damaged millions of acres of Europe's forests, destroyed wildlife, and hastened the erosion of historic buildings. Air pollution covers the land with soot, poisons the crops, and endangers the health of many Europeans. Water pollution threatens not only the beauty of the seas, rivers, and lakes but also the wildlife that these bodies of water support. Poor farming practices and lack of proper sewage treatment threaten Europe's drinking water as well.

Acid Rain

In the 1960s, industrial firms in several European countries built high smokestacks to carry pollution away from industrial sites. The method worked, but the pollution directed away from factories drifted into other countries. These kinds of pollutants combine with water vapor in the atmosphere and fall to the earth in what has been termed acid rain. In the 1970s, scientists began to observe the effects of acid rain on Europe's forests. Needles or leaves turned yellow and fell. As trees sickened, insects and disease took over.

The problems caused by acid rain are widespread. In western Germany, acid rain has damaged about one-third, or more than 5 million acres (2 million ha) of the Black Forest. Forests in Austria, Switzerland, and France also have been damaged. Acid rain has drifted north from the industrial belt of Europe to Scandinavia. Forests in Norway and Sweden show the withering effects of high-sulfur-content rain.

Classroom Resources for Section 2

BLACKLINE MASTERS:
Reproducible Lesson Plan 13-2
Environmental Issue 4
Skill Activity 13
Enrichment Activity 13
Section Quiz 13-2

TRANSPARENCIES:
Section Focus Transparency 13-2
Political Map Transparency 4

MULTIMEDIA:
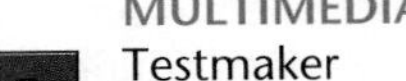
Testmaker

Geography and the Environment
GTV: Planetary Manager
STV: Atmosphere

In winter, snow carries the industrial pollution to the earth. In spring, the **meltwater**—the result of melting snow and ice—flows into rivers and lakes. The high concentration of acid in the meltwater destroys fish. Almost all fish are gone from lakes in the southern part of Norway. Scientists estimate that nearly one-fifth of Sweden's lakes are mostly or entirely without fish. The damage is costly. In Germany alone, scientists estimate the acid-rain damage to trees, lakes, and rivers at more than $1 billion each year.

Automobile exhaust also adds acid-forming compounds to the atmosphere. Scientists believe that **acid deposition**—wet or dry acid pollution that falls to the earth—damages more than the natural environment. Europe's historic buildings, such as the Acropolis in Greece, the Tower of London, and Cologne Cathedral in Germany, are among the buildings that have been affected by the corrosive effects of this acid. A Danish architect described the effects of acid deposition: "These buildings are melting away like sugar candy." Statues, bridges, and stained-glass windows also are showing the harmful effects of this kind of pollution.

Air Pollution

The nations of eastern Europe are paying the price for the inefficient factories once run by their Communist governments. Most plants derived their power from burning soft brown coal. This kind of coal is plentiful in the region, but it pollutes the air heavily. Smokestacks belched soot, sulfur, and carbon dioxide into the air by the hundreds of tons. As a result, Poland, Romania, and the Czech Republic are among the most polluted nations on the earth. Industrial pollution has ruined much of the food grown in that region of Europe. Houses, trees, grass, and even animals turn black from the soot. The poor quality of the air endangers the health of the people living there. Children in the northern part of the Czech Republic are sent away from home for one month each year for health reasons.

The problems of air pollution also affect industrial nations in western Europe. The people of the Netherlands drive the most cars per square mile (sq. km) and burn the most fossil fuel per person in Europe. As a result, levels of air pollution in the Netherlands cause concern for human health.

Global Warming

Air pollution, like other environmental concerns, has far-reaching effects. Some **environmentalists**—people concerned with the quality of the environment—believe that old factories, such as those in eastern Europe, are one of the many causes of the greenhouse effect. These factories burn coal, which releases carbon dioxide into the atmosphere. The carbon dioxide traps the sun's heat near the earth's surface. Over a period of time, this greenhouse effect could result in an increase in the earth's average temperature.

The long-range effects of possible global warming remain unknown. Many environmentalists believe that a rise in the earth's temperature would melt parts of the icy regions at the North and South Poles. As a result, the level of the oceans would rise. Among the possible consequences for Europe would be the flooding of some coastal lands. As a result,

Geographic Themes

Human/Environment Interaction: The Czech Republic
Heavy industrialization of the Czech Republic during the Communist era has led to the destruction of many forests by acid rain. *What other countries have had forests damaged by acid rain?*

TEACH

GUIDED PRACTICE

L1 Cause and Effect Have students create a diagram to show the causes and effects of acid rain. Have them label the diagram using appropriate Key Terms. **LEP**

 Implement Environmental Issue 4 as a class activity.

USING ILLUSTRATIONS

REGION These spruce forests, located in the Jizerske Mountains, are in a protected landscape region.

Answer to Caption: *Germany, Austria, Switzerland, France, Norway, and Sweden*

DID YOU KNOW?

Former Romanian leader Nicolae Ceausescu carried out a deliberate policy of concentrating pollution in towns such as Copsa Mica, which is known as "black town." Factories were built without tall chimneys so that pollution would stay in the town. As a result, a large percentage of residents are chronically ill.

L2 Environment Display Political Map Transparency 4. Have students locate areas of Europe affected by acid rain and air pollution. Then ask students to formulate a hypothesis about wind patterns on the Continent.

Cooperative Learning Activity

Organize students into groups of four or five. Have each group choose an issue related to environmental pollution in Europe. Ask group members to create a poster, a bumper sticker, a slogan, or a radio commercial designed to make people aware of the problem. Have students establish criteria for judging the works. Then have the class vote on which work is most effective in creating public awareness.

L2 Geography: Human/ Environment Interaction Display Political Map Transparency 4. Have students identify coastal cities on the Mediterranean Sea and rivers that flow into the sea. Discuss causes and effects of water pollution in this region.

USING ILLUSTRATIONS

HUMAN/ENVIRONMENT INTERACTION Most of the water in Poland's rivers is undrinkable, and 50 percent of river water is so toxic it corrodes industrial machinery.

Answer to Caption: *Environmentalists believe that coal-burning factories release carbon dioxide into the atmosphere, trapping the sun's heat near the earth's surface—the greenhouse effect.*

L3 Debate Organize students into four teams. Pose the following propositions for informal debate: 1) The European Union should aid eastern European nations in solving environmental problems; 2) industrial nations in other parts of the world should aid eastern European nations in solving environmental problems.

CURRICULUM CONNECTION

MEDICINE

Lead poisoning poses a major medical problem in coal mining and industrial regions of eastern Europe. Doctors' records show that most babies are born with amounts of lead in their bodies that are twice as high as the safe limit.

millions of people from low-lying areas would crowd into other regions of the Continent.

Water Pollution

Every European country that borders the Mediterranean Sea uses it for recreation and transportation. These countries also use it for waste disposal. Coastal cities dump millions of tons of raw and partially treated sewage into the Mediterranean. Floating garbage, blown from landfills or thrown directly into the sea, creates an unsightly mess.

In the past, bacteria in the Mediterranean Sea were able to break down most of the wastes that the sea received. In recent times, however, growing populations and tourism along the coast have increased the environmental problems of the Mediterranean. Small tides and weak currents tend to keep pollution where people discharge it. The Mediterranean Sea, open to the Atlantic only through the narrow Strait of Gibraltar, takes almost a century to renew itself completely.

Coastal cities are not the only sources of water pollution in the Mediterranean region. Hundreds of rivers flow into the Mediterranean Sea. These rivers carry into the sea pesticides from Greek farms, detergents from Spanish homes, and industrial pollutants from French factories. These forms of pollution contaminate marine and animal life and create health hazards for people.

Oil and floating garbage pollute beaches, greatly decreasing tourism. Most of the countries that border the Mediterranean depend on tourists' money. A decrease in tourism would hurt the economies of France, Spain, Italy, and Greece. All European countries that border the Mediterranean Sea share responsibility for cleanup and protection of this vital resource.

Water pollution affects Europe's rivers and lakes as well as its coastal waters. Hungary's Lake Balaton, one of the largest freshwater

Geographic Themes

Human/Environment Interaction: Kraków, Poland

This huge steel mill near Kraków is the largest industrial plant—and the greatest polluter—in Poland. *How do factories such as this one contribute to the greenhouse effect?*

Meeting Special Needs

Poor Learners Most students are familiar with the study system known as "SQ3R" (Survey, Question, Read, Recite, Review), but those with reading and learning problems may have difficulty surveying information. One task involved in surveying is predicting what kind of information will be given in a piece of text. Ask students to consider whether the text under each subhead in this section will 1) explain causes of environmental pollution, 2) discuss effects of pollution, or 3) describe solutions for environmental pollution.

lakes in Europe, has been threatened by industrial pollution. Industries in western Europe dump wastes into rivers, such as the Meuse and the Rhine. These rivers, in turn, carry the pollutants into the North Sea. Pollution levels in the coastal region from the Netherlands to Denmark have doubled over the past few decades.

Pollution from agricultural sources has affected the drinking water in many parts of Europe. Chemical and organic fertilizers seep into the groundwater, making it unfit for humans to drink. Lack of proper sewage treatment adds to the problem. Nearly 25 percent of Hungary's towns and cities do not have safe supplies of drinking water.

HUMAN/ENVIRONMENT INTERACTION

Efforts to Reduce Pollution

European citizens and government leaders share concern over growing environmental problems. They recognize their responsibility to preserve the environment for future generations. They also understand the economic impact of pollution—on the one hand, the loss of tourists; and on the other, the high cost of cleanup.

Concern for the Environment

Europeans share a long history of concern for the environment. Efforts to control air pollution date back to the Middle Ages. The English Parliament placed bans on burning coal in 1253. During the nineteenth century, Great Britain developed laws to control air pollution, health, and safety.

A sense of national heritage makes Europeans feel responsible for protecting and preserving the environment for future generations. This concern for the future makes many Europeans willing to take action to reduce pollution. At the United Nations Conference on Environment and Development in June 1992, European policy makers pushed for strong measures to reduce greenhouse gases.

Geographic Themes

Human/Environment Interaction: London
Throughout Europe, restorers must repair many historic buildings and monuments damaged by air pollution. *How are Europeans affected by industrial pollution?*

Other nations were less willing to act because the outcome of global climate change is uncertain.

Europeans also share a respect for nature. People who live in densely populated areas value an opportunity to get away from urban areas and enjoy the natural landscape. Those who live in sparsely populated areas often depend on the natural environment to support their way of life.

Europeans' idea of a natural environment differs somewhat from that concept in other parts of the world. Europe has few, if any, areas that have not been changed by human interaction. Over the centuries, people cleared the forests for farms, then paved over the farms to build factories and cities. They dug canals to connect rivers and tunneled through mountains to connect roads and rail lines. Although their environment has been modified greatly by humans, Europeans want to preserve their landscapes for future generations.

Critical Thinking

Predicting Consequences Have students create a diagram to show causes and effects of global warming. Discuss the possibility of polar ice melt. Then have students make predictions about how a rise in the level of the oceans would affect Europe. *(flooding of coastal lands)* Have them choose one area of Europe that would be affected by their prediction. Ask them to write a news bulletin describing the predicted consequences in that area.

INDEPENDENT PRACTICE

Guided Reading Have students complete Guided Reading Activity 13-2 in the TCR. **LEP**

USING ILLUSTRATIONS

PLACE Westminster Abbey in London is a national church of the United Kingdom that dates from the 1200s. It is an example of French Gothic style.
Answer to Caption:
Health problems; damage to forests, water resources, and wildlife; and erosion of historic buildings are related to pollution.

L2 Geography: Human/Environment Interaction Have students create web diagrams to show the efforts Europeans are making to reduce pollution. They should create one web for each of the following environmental problems: air pollution, water pollution, and acid rain. Students should write the problem in the center of the web and fill in the surrounding circles with solutions.

GLENCOE TECHNOLOGY

Videodisc

GEOGRAPHY AND THE ENVIRONMENT
THE INFINITE VOYAGE
Crisis in the Atmosphere

Chapter 8
Disc 2 Side A
Title: ***Energy Conservation as a Means to Reduce Carbon Dioxide Levels***
Subject: New window designs and improved light bulbs that are energy efficient

PLACE Lake Balaton, located in western Hungary, is surrounded by low, rounded mountains called the Transdanubian Central Highlands.

Answer to Caption: *Industrial and agricultural pollution have made much of Hungary's water unfit for humans to drink.*

ASSESS

CHECK FOR UNDERSTANDING

Assign Section 1 Review as homework or an in-class activity.

MEETING LESSON OBJECTIVES

Each objective below is tested by the questions that follow it in parentheses:

1. **Analyze** the causes and effects of environmental pollution in Europe. *(3, 4)*
2. **Explain** why cleanup and reduction of pollution requires cooperation among European governments. *(2, 5)*
3. **Identify** steps Europeans are taking to protect the environment. *(5)*

EVALUATE

Assign the Section 2 Quiz in the TCR.

Use the Testmaker to create a customized quiz for Section 2.

RETEACH

Have students complete Reteaching Activity 13 in the TCR.

Geographic Themes

Place: Lake Balaton, Hungary

Lake Balaton, the largest lake in central Europe, is one of Hungary's most popular recreation areas. *How has Lake Balaton been affected by pollution?*

Cleanup Efforts

In recent decades, Europeans have enacted several programs to counteract acid rain. Germany has passed laws to ensure that all cars built after 1986 have smog-control devices. Environmentalists have promoted lower speed limits to reduce harmful emissions from automobiles. Many western European cities have protected buildings and works of art with acid-resistant coatings. Lime has been used to lower the acid level in Scandinavian lakes. **Biologists**—scientists who study plant and animal life—are trying to raise fish that can tolerate higher acid levels.

Denmark has become a leader in attempts to control environmental pollution. Wastewater treatment plants have reduced pollution levels in some cities by 60 percent. Denmark also identified more than 3,000 hazardous waste sites and has begun to clean up these areas. Hungary's efforts to improve water quality has reduced pollution levels in Lake Balaton by half. The Netherlands accomplished its goal of reducing air pollution by 50 percent from 1980 to 1995.

Since 1975, European governments have joined forces to tackle the pollution of the Mediterranean Sea. The United Nations' Mediterranean Action Plan (MAP) involved 17 nations in developing strict laws against pollution. As a result, the waters off some Mediterranean beaches have been made suitable again for swimming. The success of MAP made the program a model for other cooperative efforts. In 1992, many European nations signed a pledge to combat global warming by reducing greenhouse gases.

Plans for the Future

Local governments are taking steps to reduce pollution. For example, Naples, Marseille, and Athens are among several cities in the Mediterranean area that are planning major new sewage systems. Portugal is planning to construct a new system to properly handle toxic waste.

The task of cleaning up the environment and reducing pollution requires continued cooperation among all levels of European gov-

Extending the Content

Conservation Pollution and commercial whaling have pushed many species of whales to the brink of extinction. In the 1980s, seafaring nations agreed to a worldwide ban on whaling. The United States threatened economic sanctions against Iceland and Norway if they persist in killing whales commercially. Norway, under pressure from communities that are dependent on whaling, continues its pro-whaling fight.

Geographic Themes

Place: Brussels, Belgium

Brussels, an important EU center, often hosts meetings dealing with Europe's environmental concerns. *What environmental decision was made in Brussels by the EU in 1993?*

ernments. Citizens must be made aware of the problems, and policy makers must enact legislation to provide solutions. The enormous cost of cleanup makes progress slow. The estimated cost of cleaning up air pollution in eastern Europe, for example, ranges from $200 billion to $500 billion. The cost of providing adequate sewage treatment for cities in the Mediterranean region could be from $25 billion to $100 billion.

The highly industrialized nations of the European Union cause about 70 percent of the Mediterranean's problems. EU members have pledged funds to help developing nations reduce pollution. Their plan calls for the Mediterranean to be cleaned by 2025.

In 1992, European Union representatives at a United Nations environmental conference in Dublin, Ireland, set goals for improving the quality of Europe's stream, river, and lake waters. That same year, European environment ministers agreed in Brussels to limit cross-border shipments of hazardous industrial wastes within the European Union.

Eastern Europeans are seeking financial aid to control pollution. They look to the EU for help because the air pollution from eastern factories threatens western Europe as well. American companies have offered technology, expertise, and investment to help modernize eastern European factories. Such efforts point out not only the economic impact but also the global aspects of Europe's environmental concerns.

Section 2 Review

Checking for Understanding

1. **Define** acid rain, meltwater, acid deposition, environmentalist, biologist.
2. **Locating Places** Which European nations border the Mediterranean Sea?
3. **Human/Environment Interaction** What are the effects of acid rain in Europe?
4. **Human/Environment Interaction** What are the causes of pollution of the Mediterranean Sea?

Critical Thinking

5. **Identifying Central Issues** Why does cleanup and preservation of the environment require the cooperation of European nations?

ANSWERS TO SECTION 2 REVIEW

1. **acid rain:** precipitation containing pollutants; **meltwater:** result of melting snow and ice; **acid deposition:** wet or dry acid pollution that falls to the earth; **environmentalist:** person concerned with the quality of the environment; **biologist:** scientist who studies plants and animals
2. Spain, France, Monaco, Italy, Greece, the Yugoslav republics, and Albania
3. It has damaged forests, destroyed wildlife, and hastened the erosion of historic buildings and artwork.
4. sewage and solid wastes from coastal cities, oil from tankers, industrial pollution and pesticides carried from northern Europe by rivers
5. Pollution does not stop at national boundaries. All European nations suffer the effects of pollution.

ENRICH

Have students complete Enrichment Activity 13 in the TCR.

USING ILLUSTRATIONS

PLACE Brussels is a center of international economic and political activity.

Answer to Caption: *EU nations agreed to limit cross-border shipments of hazardous industrial wastes.*

CLOSE

Provide a large sheet of paper or space on the chalkboard on which students can write slogans expressing their attitudes about pollution.

Videodisc

GTV: PLANETARY MANAGER

Side 2, Chapter 5
Frames 25236-31905
Title: ***Tidy World***
Subject: Solid wastes and how we might clean up the earth

GTV: PLANETARY MANAGER

Side 2, Chapter 4
Frames 18754-25234
Title: ***Holy Smoke!***
Subject: The use and abuse of fossil fuels

STV: ATMOSPHERE

Side 1, Chapter 2
Frames 31674-33803
Title: ***The Atmosphere in Action***
Subject: Greenhouse effect

TEACH

Show the class several print advertisements and have students analyze the accuracy of the claims. Ask: "Why is it important to analyze information in advertisements?" *(Because ads try to sell products, they may not present the product objectively.)* Say: "Similarly, it is important to analyze the purpose and accuracy of all kinds of information."

Direct students to read the skill on page 276. Then ask: "What is the difference between a primary and secondary source?" *(Primary sources are created by eyewitnesses to events; secondary sources are created after events occurred.)* "What are some examples of primary sources?" *(letters, journals, photographs, speeches, interviews)* "How can you analyze the content of a document?" *(Determine who created it, when and where it was created, its topic, and its purpose.)*

Skills Practice
For additional practice, have students complete Skill Activity 13 in the TCR.

CRITICAL THINKING SKILLS

Analyzing Information

In modern society, television, radio, computer networks, newspapers, magazines, and advertisements constantly bombard us with information. Amid this clamor for our attention, how can we learn to analyze information to determine what is truly useful and accurate?

REVIEWING THE SKILL

There are two basic types of information sources: primary sources and secondary sources. *Primary sources* are those created by eyewitnesses to events. For example, interviews or letters written by survivors of an earthquake are primary sources. Other examples of primary sources include diaries, speeches, and photographs. *Secondary sources*, on the other hand, are accounts generally created by scholars and writers after a period of time has elapsed following the event. Secondary sources often synthesize information from several sources. For example, a book about earthquakes all over the world would be a secondary source.

After determining the nature of the source, try to answer the following questions about it: Who created it? When was it created? Who and what is it about? Where does it take place? Why was it created? What is its purpose? Answering these questions will help you to understand the content of the information, and determine how accurate it is. Finally, always look for footnotes and references that identify information sources used to create the document.

To analyze information, apply the following steps:

- Determine whether the information is a primary or secondary source.
- Identify who created the document and when it was created.
- Examine the content of the document to answer these questions: Who and what is it about? Where does it take place? Why was it created, or what is its purpose? What are the main ideas?
- Look for references explaining the sources used to produce the document or information.

PRACTICING THE SKILL

Read the following excerpt on European efforts to improve the environment. Then answer the questions below:

On the waste management front, Denmark has emerged as a model by banning throwaway beverage containers, thus sharply reducing garbage generation. By forcing a shift to refillable containers, it has cut the energy invested in beverage containers by two-thirds or more and lowered air and water pollution accordingly. Employment, meanwhile, may have increased, because reusing beverage containers is more labor-intensive than manufacturing new ones.

Among the industrial countries, the Netherlands has pioneered the use of bicycles for personal transportation. With a bicycle fleet of 12 million for a population of 15 million, this compact country has more than twice as many bicycles as cars. In Groningen, the largest city in northern Netherlands, bicycles already account for half of all trips. . . . Using a combination of grants and taxes, the goal is to get more people out of their cars and onto bicycles for shorter trips and into trains for longer ones.

1. Is this a primary or secondary source of information?
2. What is the topic of this document?
3. According to this document, what are some European countries doing to improve the quality of the environment?
4. What European country has pioneered the use of bicycles for personal transportation?

For additional practice in this skill, see Practicing Skills on page 278 of the Chapter 13 Review.

ANSWERS TO PRACTICING THE SKILL

1. secondary source
2. efforts by European countries to reduce pollution
3. Denmark outlawed throwaway containers. The Netherlands uses taxes and grants to encourage people to ride bicycles and trains to reduce automobile pollution.
4. the Netherlands

chapter 13 HIGHLIGHTS

1 SECTION Living in Europe

Assembly line in Germany

KEY TERMS

heavy industry (p. 263)
light industry (p. 263)
organic farming (p. 264)
mixed farming (p. 264)
farm cooperative (p. 264)
collective farm (p. 264)
state farm (p. 264)
consumer goods (p. 264)
tariff (p. 265)

SUMMARY

- The 12 nations of the European Union worked toward economic unity in spite of difficulties brought on by change.
- Eastern European countries struggled to adjust to a free market economy after more than 40 years of Communist control.
- Europe has diverse economies based on agriculture, manufacturing, and services.
- Europe's communication and transportation systems are among the best in the world.
- Railroads are a major means of freight and passenger transportation throughout Europe.

2 SECTION People and Their Environment

KEY TERMS

acid rain (p. 270)
meltwater (p. 271)
acid deposition (p. 271)
environmentalist (p. 271)
biologist (p. 274)

SUMMARY

- Acid rain has damaged forests, wildlife, and buildings in many parts of Europe.
- Air pollution from factories in various parts of Europe endangers health and contributes to the greenhouse effect.
- Pollution from industrial wastes, sewage, garbage, and oil threatens the Mediterranean Sea and the wildlife the sea supports.
- Europeans share a concern for the environment and a sense of responsibility for future generations.
- European nations have taken steps to reduce pollution and clean up the environment.

Czech forest damaged by acid rain

CHAPTER 13 HIGHLIGHTS

USING THE CHAPTER 13 HIGHLIGHTS

Use the Chapter 13 Highlights to preview, review, condense, or reteach the chapter.

PREVIEW/REVIEW

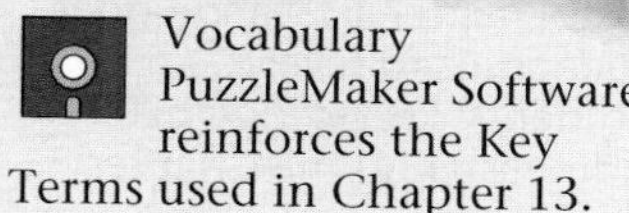

Vocabulary PuzzleMaker Software reinforces the Key Terms used in Chapter 13.

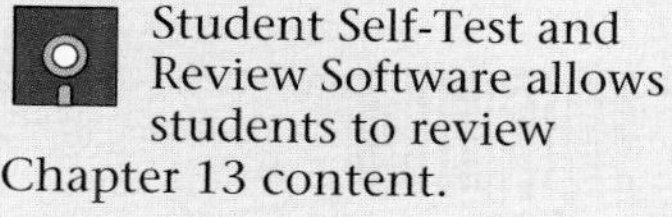

Student Self-Test and Review Software allows students to review Chapter 13 content.

CONDENSE

Have students read the Chapter 13 Highlights.

Have students listen to the Chapter 13 Audiocassettes in the TCR. Spanish Audiocassettes are also available.

Assign the Chapter 13 Audiocassette Activity and give students the Chapter 13 Audiocassette Quiz.

Have students complete the Guided Reading Activities for Chapter 13 in the TCR. Spanish Guided Reading Activities are also available.

RETEACH

Have students complete Reteaching Activity 13 in the TCR. Spanish Reteaching Activities are also available.

Map Activity

Identify and Locate Display Political Map Transparency 4. Have students point to a location and identify the major environmental problems of that area.

GLENCOE TECHNOLOGY

Videodisc

Use Chapter 13 MindJogger Videoquiz to review students' knowledge before administering the Chapter 13 Test.

MINDJOGGER VIDEOQUIZ

Chapter 13
Disc 2 Side B

The MindJogger Videoquiz is also available on videocassette.

ANSWERS

Reviewing Key Terms

1. heavy industry
2. organic farming
3. consumer goods
4. mixed farming
5. light industry
6. meltwater
7. acid deposition
8. acid rain

Reviewing Facts

9. More Europeans earn a living from farming than any other economic activity.
10. Tunnels carry road and rail traffic through mountains. Canals provide links between major waterways.
11. Winds carry pollution from industrial areas to other countries. Meltwater carries acid deposition into rivers and lakes. Acid rain destroys forests and wildlife and damages buildings and works of art.
12. The Mediterranean is open to the Atlantic only through the narrow Strait of Gibraltar. Small tides and weak currents keep pollution from being flushed out of the Mediterranean.

chapter 13 REVIEW

Reviewing Key Terms

Choose the vocabulary term that best completes each of the sentences below. Write your answers on a separate sheet of paper.

heavy industry (p. 263)
light industry (p. 263)
organic farming (p. 264)
mixed farming (p. 264)
consumer goods (p. 264)
acid rain (p. 270)
meltwater (p. 271)
acid deposition (p. 271)

SECTION 1

1. Communist governments in Eastern Europe emphasized _____, or the manufacture of machinery for factories and mines.
2. Farmers who rely on _____ use natural substances to enrich the soil.
3. Household goods, shoes, and clothing that individuals buy are called _____.
4. _____ is the raising of several kinds of crops and livestock on the same farm.
5. _____ involves the production of consumer goods.

SECTION 2

6. The result of melting snow and ice is called _____.
7. Scientists believe that _____ damages buildings as well as the natural environment.
8. Precipitation containing pollutants is called _____.

Reviewing Facts

SECTION 1

9. What is the single most important occupation in Europe?
10. How did Europeans overcome the barriers to transportation posed by physical geography?

SECTION 2

11. Why are the problems caused by acid rain so widespread?
12. Why does pollution tend to remain in the Mediterranean Sea?

Critical Thinking

13. **Drawing Conclusions** Why did changing economies in both eastern and western Europe result in unemployment?
14. **Making Predictions** What might happen to Europe as a result of global warming?

Geographic Themes

15. **Movement** Why are France's TGVs more economical and more efficient than other forms of transportation?
16. **Human/Environment Interaction** What steps have been taken to reduce water pollution in European countries?

Practicing Skills

Analyzing Information

Refer to the excerpt in the Analyzing Information skill on page 276.

17. What is the purpose of this document?
18. Do you think this information is factually correct? What leads you to this conclusion?

Using the Unit Atlas

Refer to the physical geography section of the Unit Atlas on pages 216–217.

19. What recently-discovered natural resources have helped the economies of the United Kingdom and Norway?
20. What country is Europe's largest steel producer?

Critical Thinking

13. To make their products competitive in a world market, western European companies cut costs by cutting jobs. To compete in a free-market economy, eastern European industries have to overcome inefficiency by laying off large numbers of workers.
14. Europe would lose coastal lands if global warming caused the level of the oceans to rise. Millions of people from low-lying areas would move to other regions of the Continent.

Geographic Themes

15. TGVs are the fastest trains in the world. They are powered by electricity, so they are less harmful to the environment than are most other forms of transportation. Relatively low fares make TGVs economical as well as efficient.

Projects

Individual Activity

Create a diagram or a flow chart illustrating the effects of pollution in Europe. Find or draw pictures showing how acid deposition, air pollution, and water pollution affect the European environment.

Cooperative Learning Activity

Organize into groups of three. Plan a European trip that includes travel through three countries. Have one member of the group determine the approximate cost of traveling by automobile. Have another member determine the cost of the trip by train. Have the third member of your group determine the cost of traveling by bicycle and staying in youth hostels. Use maps and travel guides. Compare the results of your research.

Writing About Geography

Argumentation

Imagine that you are a member of Europe's environmental policy community. You must convince other members to enact policies based on your views about global warming. Choose the role of someone who favors immediate action or of someone who prefers to take a "wait-and-see" approach. Write an argument that will convince others to accept your views. Use your journal and other references as you develop your argument.

Locating Places

MEDITERRANEAN REGION

Match the letters on the map with the places of the Mediterranean Region. Write your answers on a separate sheet of paper.

1. Mediterranean Sea
2. Italy
3. Greece
4. Strait of Gibraltar
5. Spain
6. France
7. Adriatic Sea
8. Sicily
9. Corsica
10. Sardinia

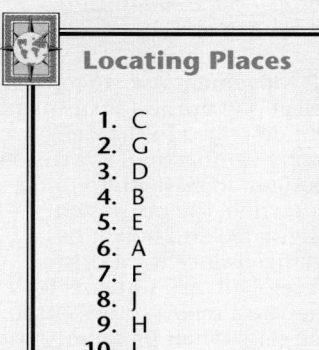

Chapter Bonus Test Question

This question may be used for extra credit on the chapter test.

How have the changing economies of eastern European nations affected environmental issues?

(Answer: To compete in a free-market economy, eastern European industries must build new factories with modern technology. These factories will help reduce pollution and conserve energy.)

Chapter 13 Review

16. Mediterranean countries have worked to clean up beaches and coastal waters. Nations agreed to develop strict laws against pollution. Several coastal cities are planning new sewage systems.

Practicing Skills

17. to provide information about policies used in Europe to control pollution.

18. Yes; the author provides references to sources of factual information, so these sources can be checked for accuracy.

Using the Unit Atlas

19. oil and natural gas

20. Germany

Locating Places

1. C
2. G
3. D
4. B
5. E
6. A
7. F
8. J
9. H
10. I

Geography Connection

FOCUS

Have students scan the photographs and bold type headings on pages 280–281 and write three questions that come to mind about the material they are going to read. Have them also vote for the section that they think will be most interesting.

TEACH

L2 Discussion Music is an important part of most cultures throughout the world. Ask students what role music plays in American culture. Encourage students to give specific examples from their lives. *(Ceremonies: birthday celebrations, sports, religious, government or patriotic events, holidays; Social: choirs, bands, parties, leisure activities)*

L2 Movement Ask students to select one musical instrument not described in the Geography Connection. Have each student do research to find out where the instrument originated and how it has changed since it was first developed. Ask students to prepare a report to present to the class. Their presentations might include pictures of the instrument in various forms or music recordings that they can play for the class. After the presentations, have the students discuss how instruments that originated in one country might have found their way to other countries.

GEOGRAPHY CONNECTION *The United States and Europe*

BEETHOVEN, THE BEATLES, AND BEYOND

European instruments, composers, and performers have long appealed to a wide variety of American musical tastes. Our European musical heritage began with simple instruments and tunes brought by the first colonists to these shores. Europe's influence continues to be felt in music today.

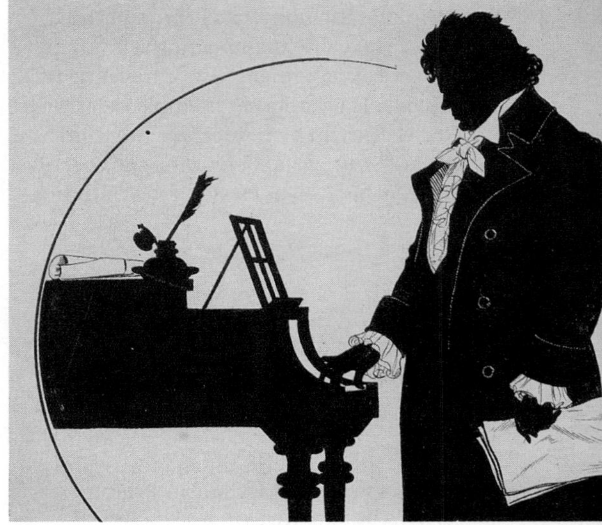

▲**THE FIDDLE** has long been a basic instrument of American country music. Also called the violin, the instrument as we know it today originated near Venice in the mid-1500s. Italian master craftsman Antonio Stradivari perfected the violin in the 1600s and 1700s; one of his instruments is nearly priceless today.

◀**ANTONÍN DVOŘÁK**, a Czech composer, first became popular among Americans in the late 1800s. The success of his music in the United States brought him to New York City in the 1890s to become director of the National Conservatory of Music. His American experiences inspired him to compose his most famous symphony, which he titled *From the New World*.

Making the Connection

Songs Suggest that students write new lyrics to a popular song that they think would appeal to a mixed audience of Americans and Europeans. Students can use the clippings they have collected during their study of the unit, as well as information from the unit, to get ideas for song subjects. Remind students, too, that European teenagers are interested in many of the same things that American teenagers find interesting.

For students who like a challenge, have them write original melodies.

◀ **THE BEATLES,** a band from Liverpool, England, gave a new direction to rock and roll during the 1960s. Previous rock and roll had been based on a strong beat. The Beatles' music, however, emphasized highly imaginative and memorable melodies and lyrics. Their fantastic success changed American music. Although the group broke up in 1970, lead singer Paul McCartney continues to be a strong influence on music as a composer and a performer.

UDWIG VAN BEETHOVEN, the 18th-century German composer, is practically an American household name. "He will give the world something worth listening to," said Mozart when he first heard Beethoven perform. Beethoven fulfilled Mozart's prophecy, creating grand musical works filled with passionate emotion. In recent times, American composers have used some of Beethoven's most famous passages as themes in rock and roll.

U2, an Irish rock group, has been popular with American audiences. Rock/country/western music has its roots in European folk music. Rock music was also influenced by the spirituals and blues style of African Americans, whose musical traditions have become well known in Europe.

◀ **THE GUITAR** comes from Spain and probably was introduced to America by the Spanish in the 1500s. Today's guitar-playing methods also were developed by a Spanish musician in the late 1800s. The acoustic guitar was important in early American rock and roll. The electric guitar, an American refinement, is now popular with rock musicians around the world.

Checking for Understanding

1. How has European music influenced the United States?
2. **Movement** Which European musical contribution has had the greatest effect on your life?

Geography Connection

ASSESS

Have students answer the Checking for Understanding questions on page 281.

CLOSE

Ask students to reread the questions they formulated prior to reading, and note answers where appropriate. Have students suggest resources for locating answers to those questions that were not answered by material from the article.

Then point out to students that Beethoven composed his music about two centuries ago, Dvořák a century ago, and the Beatles decades ago. People around the world continue to be moved by the music of all three. Ask students to discuss what makes music or a composition enduring and/or internationally popular. Ask them also to select contemporary composers or performers that they think will become as famous and as enduring as the three presented here. Have them support their opinions.

DID YOU KNOW?

The music that the Beatles wrote in the 1960s and 1970s is considered "classic" rock.

ANSWERS TO CHECKING FOR UNDERSTANDING

1. European composers have created famous musical works that are part of the cultural heritage of the United States; Europeans invented and perfected the violin and guitar, which are popular instruments used in American music; the Beatles emphasized melody and creative lyrics; European folk music gave rise to American country-western music.
2. Answers will vary.

UNIT OVERVIEW

The three chapters that comprise this unit introduce students to the physical geography and peoples of Russia and the Eurasian republics. Various aspects of the region's life—such as the economy, lifestyles, and human/environment interaction—are also presented.

GEOGRAPHY JOURNAL

Activity As students collect their newspaper articles, encourage them to look for relationships between the areas listed. For example, students may note that an article about a physical feature may also comment on that feature's economic or cultural effects.

Have students use their articles to create a time line in their journals of events and changes that occur in Russia and the Eurasian republics during their study of the unit.

• This journal activity provides the basis for the "Writing About Geography" exercise in the Chapter Review.

• The Geography Journal may be used as an integral part of Performance Assessment.

Videodisc

STV: WORLD GEOGRAPHY, VOLUME 1

Side 1, Chapter 1
Frames 00002-47133
Title: *Asia* **(in its entirety)**
Subject: Presents geographic characteristics, plants, animals, and people of Asia

UNIT 5

Russia and the Eurasian Republics

GeoJournal Activity

While studying Russia and the Eurasian republics, clip newspaper and magazine articles related to the physical features, cultures, politics, economy, and human-environment interactions of the region. Jot down recent changes occurring in any of the above categories.

282

Where in the World . . . .

Have students look at the map on pages A14–A15 in which Russia and the Eurasian republics are highlighted. Display Unit Map Overlay Transparency 5-5 and ask students the following questions: On what oceans does Russia have coastlines? *(Arctic, Pacific)* On what two continents does Russia lie? *(Europe, Asia)* Which republics are in Europe? *(Belarus, Ukraine, Moldova, Georgia, Armenia)* In Asia? *(Azerbaijan, Turkmenistan, Uzbekistan, Kazakhstan, Tajikistan, Kyrgyzstan)* What body of water provides the region with an outlet to the Mediterranean Sea? *(Black Sea)* What body of water surrounded by the republics has no outlet to an ocean? *(Caspian Sea)* What country borders southeastern Russia? *(China)* Which region of Russia is closest to the United States? *(northeastern corner)*

Picturing the World

Lavish mosaics grace the Church of the Resurrection, located in the Russian city of St. Petersburg. Founded by Russian tsar Peter the Great in 1703, St. Petersburg was built as a gateway to the West. Most Russians are members of the Russian Orthodox Church, a branch of the Eastern Orthodox Church. Many political changes have occurred in Russia since the founding of St. Petersburg. Power shifted in 1917 from the tsars to the Communists, who ruled until the breakup of the Soviet Union in 1991.

1. (a.) What is an icon? (b.) Do you see any in the picture on pages 282-83?
2. Now look at the picture on page 317. What was the Communist view toward religion?
3. How has that view changed?

Picture Atlas CD-ROM Enrichment Corner

Explore the Eurasian republics. Divide into five groups and choose one of the following republics: Ukraine, Belarus, Kazakhstan, Armenia, or Georgia. Read the essays and browse the photographs and captions, vital statistics, maps, and other features on the CD-ROM for information. As a group, present a comprehensive electronic report on one of the republics to the class.

interNET CONNECTIONS

For information about Russia, contact the following address:

World Wide Web
http://www.kiae.su/www/wtr/kremlin/begin.html

CD-ROM

PICTURE ATLAS OF THE WORLD
Turn to page T39 for an additional CD-ROM activity to enrich Unit 5, Russia and the Eurasian republics.

GLENCOE TECHNOLOGY

Videodisc

REUTERS ISSUES IN GEOGRAPHY

Chapter 4
Disc 1 Side A
Title: ***Russia: Managing Resources***
Subject: Resources of Russia and how they are affected by geographic, economic, and historic factors

ANSWERS TO PICTURING THE WORLD

1. (a) an intricate religious image; (b) yes, in the windows and mosaics
2. Communists thought people should be atheists. Many houses of worship were destroyed.
3. A religious revival occurred after Gorbachev allowed more religious freedom.

0:00 OUT OF TIME?

If time does not permit teaching each chapter in this unit, you may use the Chapter Highlights and Audiocassettes that include a 1-page activity and a 1-page test for each chapter.

LESSON PLAN
Unit 5 Atlas

These features and activities may be used as an introduction to the unit or as teaching tools throughout the course of the unit.

FOCUS

Have students recall that this group of countries lies on two continents. Have them also recall which countries are in Europe, and which in Asia. Ask students to speculate how geographical location might impact on the countries' cultures.

TEACH

Location As students read the facts presented, have them determine whether the fact is an outgrowth of the country's geographical location. Ask them to share their reasoning.

Implement Foods Around the World 4 as a class activity.

Have students complete the Political Map Transparency 5 Activity in the TCR.

Have students complete Unit Atlas Activity 5B.

UNIT 5 ATLAS

RUSSIA AND THE Cultural Geography

EXPLORING CULTURAL DIVERSITY

1. ***What areas of Russia and the Eurasian republics are most sparsely populated? Most heavily populated?***
2. ***What nations border the Black Sea?***
3. ***What cities in the region have more than 2 million people?***

Siberia covers 75 percent of Russia. However, only 22 percent of the Russian people live there. The weather is too harsh for most people.

The Armenians are among Europe's oldest ethnic groups. They have inhabited the area east and south of the Black Sea since the 600s B.C.

During ancient times, the cities of Tashkent, Samarkand, and Khiva in Uzbekistan were crossroads where the cultures and products of Europe, Southwest Asia, China, and India met.

The Kazakhs and the Kyrgyz are descendants of the nomadic Mongol herders who first settled the area.

Classroom Resources for Unit 5

BLACKLINE MASTERS:
World Literature Reading 4
Foods Around the World 4
Environmental Issue 5

TRANSPARENCIES:
Unit Map Overlay Transparency 5
Political Map Transparency 5
World Cultures Transparencies 7, 8
World History and Art Transparency 5

MULTIMEDIA:

World Music: *Cultural Traditions, Lesson 4*

Reuters Issues in Geography
STV: World Geography, Volume 1

Testmaker

Picture Atlas of the World

Images of the World Poster Set

Belarus has one of the fastest growing urban populations.

About 33 percent of the **Ukrainian** people live in rural areas.

About half of the region's population is **Russian,** and **Ukrainians** make up another 15 percent. The remaining 35 percent is composed of people from more than 100 ethnic groups.

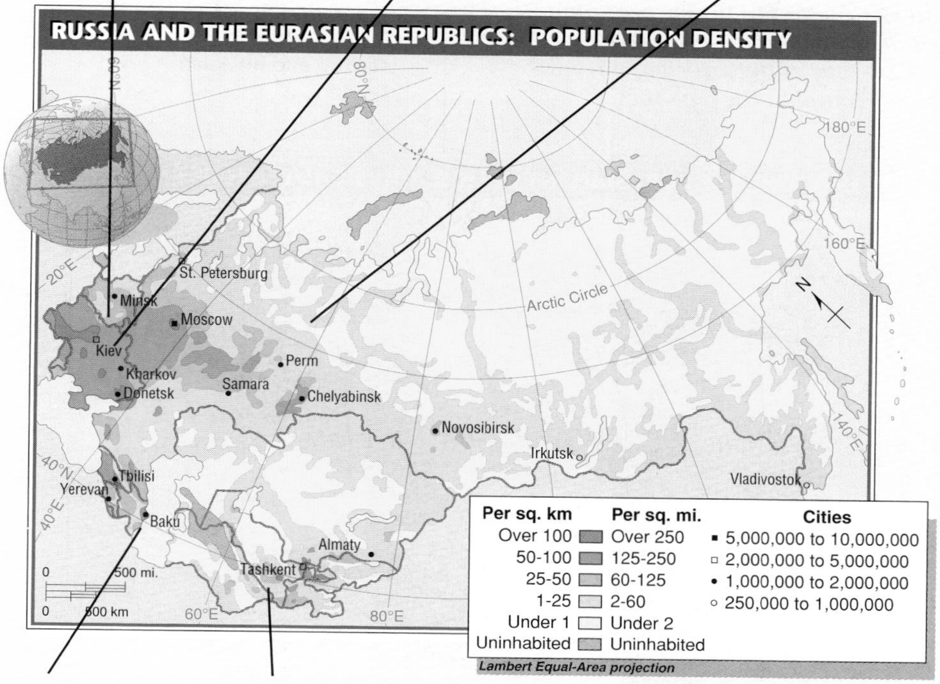

RUSSIA AND THE EURASIAN REPUBLICS: POPULATION DENSITY

Per sq. km	Per sq. mi.
Over 100	Over 250
50-100	125-250
25-50	60-125
1-25	2-60
Under 1	Under 2
Uninhabited	Uninhabited

Cities
- 5,000,000 to 10,000,000
- 2,000,000 to 5,000,000
- 1,000,000 to 2,000,000
- 250,000 to 1,000,000

Lambert Equal-Area projection

Azerbaijan is almost 50 percent urbanized.

Turkic peoples, including the Azeris, Uzbeks, Kazakhs, Kyrgyz, and Turks, live in central Asia.

Population: Russia and the Eurasian Republics and the United States

Russia and the Eurasian Republics

United States

= 50,000,000

Source: Population Reference Bureau, Inc., 1994

The combined population of **Russia and the Eurasian Republics** is just slightly greater than that of the United States.

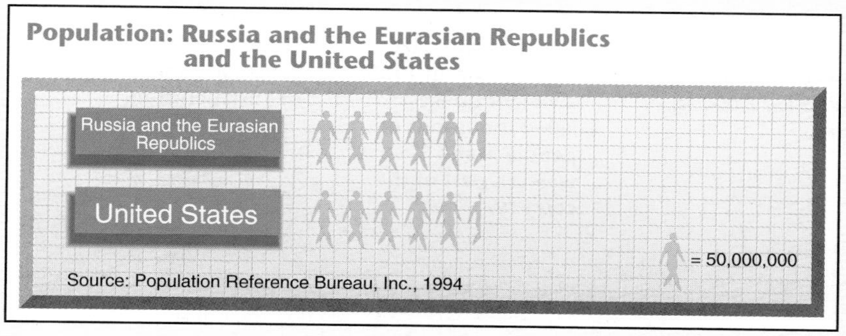

LESSON PLAN Unit 5 Atlas

Have students complete World Cultures Transparencies 7 and 8 Activities in the TCR.

Have students complete World Literature Reading 4 in the TCR.

Play World Music: Cultural Traditions, Lesson 4, and have students complete the Lesson 4 activity.

ASSESS

Have students answer the Exploring Cultural Diversity questions on page 284.

EXPLORING CULTURAL DIVERSITY

This feature may be used to introduce students to the cultural geography of Russia and the Eurasian republics. Use questions to stimulate class discussion and help students become familiar with the region. Accept reasonable answers based on the maps, graph, and captions.

CLOSE

Have students summarize the information from pages 284–285 that they consider most important to their understanding of the cultural geography of Russia and the Eurasian republics.

Map and Graph Activity

Assign a country to pairs or small groups of students. Using almanacs and world fact books, have students find out the major cultural groups of each country, as well as the group's percentage of the country's total population. Have students share their findings and create a table and circle graph showing the diverse cultural make-up of Russia and the Eurasian republics. Have students also use their shared information to discover which cultural group has a sizable percentage in each republic. *(Russians)*

LESSON PLAN
Unit 5 Atlas

These features and activities may be used as an introduction to the unit or as teaching tools throughout the course of the unit.

FOCUS

Have students determine the approximate latitudes and longitudes within which Russia and the Eurasian republics lie. *(latitudes: about 75°N–40°N; longitudes 20°E–180°E)*

Encourage students to turn back to the maps on pages A4–A11 to compare the relative size of this unit's regions with those they have previously studied. Ask for comparison/contrast comments.

TEACH

To introduce students to the physical geography of Russia and the Eurasian republics, have students complete the Unit Map Overlay Transparency 5 Activity in the TCR.

Implement Geography Simulation 5 as a class activity.

NATIONAL GEOGRAPHIC SOCIETY

CD-ROM

PICTURE ATLAS OF THE WORLD

You and your students can learn about the physical features, music, economy, and population of Russia and the Eurasian republics by selecting "Asia" on the main menu.

UNIT 5 ATLAS

RUSSIA AND THE Physical Geography

CHARTING YOUR COURSE

1. *Use the map to determine which of the republics are landlocked.*
2. *What two major landforms are found in Russia and the Eurasian republics?*
3. *What are four of the principal natural resources found in the republics?*

The Ural Mountains run north to south, separating Russia into a European section and an Asian section.

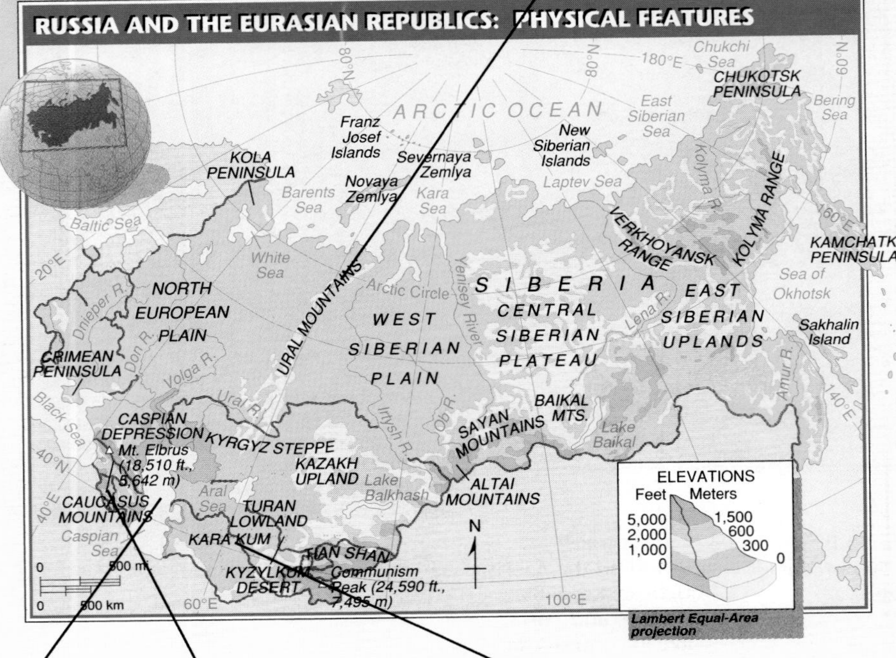

The Caspian Sea, the world's largest inland lake, covers 143,630 square miles (372,000 sq. km).

Armenia lies in a seismic region where earthquakes often occur. In 1988 a violent quake killed thousands of people in the western part of the country.

The Kara Kum, one of central Asia's largest deserts, covers the country of Turkmenistan.

Map Activity

Organize students into four groups and assign four natural resources to each group. Designate a time period, then have students use the two maps as well as the physical profile to compose descriptive sentences that tell the geographic locations of each assigned resource. Require students to find and describe all locations for each resource. When time is up, have groups share their location descriptions only, while other groups try to determine the resource. (Example: *This mineral can be found in quantities on the southeastern shores of the Caspian Sea.* Answer: *petroleum)*

When the resource is identified, have students determine how clear and accurate the description was.

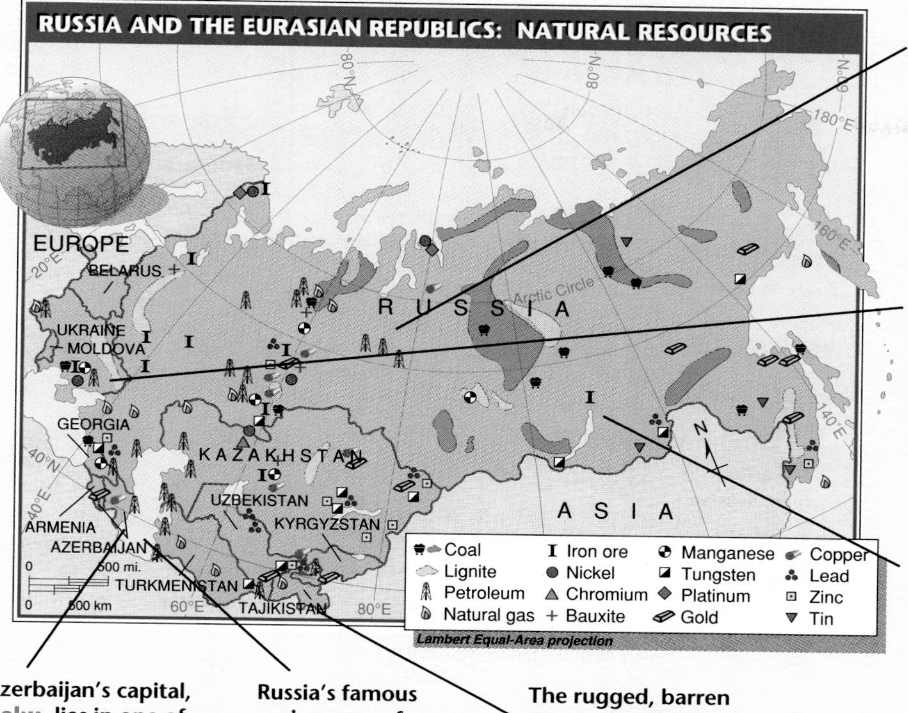

The West Siberian Plain is the world's largest flat region. Covered with swamps and marshes, the area is too flat to drain well.

The region's richest soils lie in the **Black Earth Belt,** which extends from western Ukraine to southwestern Siberia.

Russia is the world's largest country, covering almost a third of the continent of Europe and almost half of the continent of Asia.

Azerbaijan's capital, **Baku,** lies in one of the world's major oil-producing areas.

Russia's famous caviar comes from sturgeon caught in the **Caspian Sea.** Caviar is salted sturgeon eggs.

The rugged, barren **Pamirs** in Tajikistan are called *Bam i Dunya,* meaning "roof of the world." The area is the meeting place of four major Asian mountain ranges.

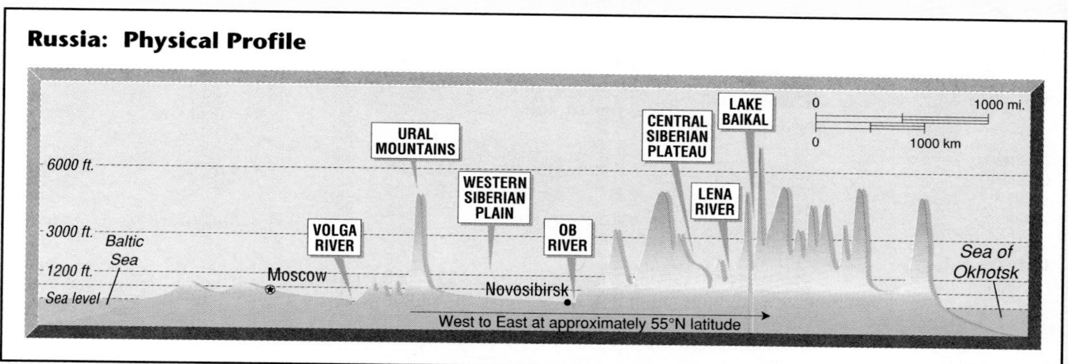

Map Activity

Interdependence Organize the class into pairs or small groups and assign a country to each. Have students use almanacs, encyclopedias, and other appropriate sources to learn what resources each country contributes to Russia, as well as what resources Russia provides in return. Allow time for students to share their information. Lead students to formulate generalizations about the areas of mutual exchange and dependence between Russia and the Eurasian republics.

LESSON PLAN Unit 5 Atlas

ASSESS

Have students answer the Charting Your Course questions on page 286.

CHARTING YOUR COURSE

This feature may be used to introduce students to the physical geography of Russia and the Eurasian republics. Use questions to stimulate class discussion and help students become familiar with the region. Accept reasonable answers based on the maps, graph, and captions.

CLOSE

Have students determine the location of mineral resources that would be difficult to recover, and tell why. Have them also comment on how they used the maps and diagram to gain a clear picture of the region's physical geography.

DID YOU KNOW?

Although Russia has more land than any other country on the earth, much of it is too cold, too dry, or too rugged for crop production.

NATIONAL GEOGRAPHIC SOCIETY

IMAGES OF THE WORLD POSTER SET

Display the poster "Russia and the Eurasian Republics." Have students hypothesize about the climate zone and population density of each photo.

These features and activities may be used as teaching tools throughout the course of the unit.

Ways of the World

RUSSIA To drop anything in the street—even an old movie ticket—is illegal and extremely offensive to the Russian sense of neatness.

DID YOU KNOW?

Russia, Belarus, Ukraine, and Moldova are the most industrialized, urbanized and westernized of the republics. These four have the slowest growth rates among the republics. The republics that lie along the Asian border have fast-growing population rates similar to economically developing countries.

Ways of the World

RUSSIA *Glasnost* has enabled the Russian people to be much more open and able to express their friendliness and curiosity. They are eager to learn about other countries, as well as find out how other countries view them.

UNIT 5 ATLAS

COUNTRY PROFILE

COUNTRY* AND CAPITAL	FLAG AND LANGUAGES	POPULATION	LANDMASS	PRINCIPAL PRODUCTS EXPORT	PRINCIPAL PRODUCTS IMPORT
Armenia Yerevan	Armenian	3,700,000 322 per sq. mi. 124 per sq. km	11,500 sq. mi. 29,785 sq. km	Machinery	Machinery
Azerbaijan Baku	Azeri, Turkish	7,400,000 222 per sq. mi. 86 per sq. km	33,400 sq. mi. 86,506 sq. km	Food	Food
Belarus Minsk	Belorussian, Russian	10,300,000 129 per sq. mi. 50 per sq. km	80,200 sq. mi. 207,718 sq. km	Machinery	Machinery
Georgia Tbilisi	Georgian, Russian	5,500,000 204 per sq. mi. 79 per sq. km	26,900 sq. mi. 69,671 sq. km	Food	Machinery
Kazakhstan Almaty	Kazakh, Russian	17,100,000 16 per sq. mi. 6 per sq. km	1,049,200 sq. mi. 2,717,428 sq. km	Raw Materials	Raw Materials
Kyrgyzstan Bishkek	Kyrgyz	4,500,000 59 per sq. mi. 23 per sq. km	76,600 sq. mi. 198,394 sq. km	Machinery	Light Industrial Products
Moldova Chisinau	Romanian, Ukranian	4,400,000 311 per sq. mi. 120 per sq. km	14,170 sq. mi. 36,700 sq. km	Food	Machinery
Russia Moscow	Russian	147,800,000 23 per sq. mi. 9 per sq. km	6,592,800 sq. mi. 17,075,352 sq. km	Fuels	Machinery
Tajikistan Dushanbe	Tadzhik, Russian	5,900,000 107 per sq. mi. 41 per sq. km	55,300 sq. mi. 143,227 sq. km	Aluminum	Chemicals
Turkmenistan Ashkhabad	Turkmen, Russian	4,100,000 21 per sq. mi. 8 per sq. km	188,500 sq. mi. 488,215 sq. km	Natural Gas	Machinery
Ukraine Kiev	Ukrainian	51,500,000 221 per sq. mi. 85 per sq. km	233,100 sq. mi. 603,729 sq. km	Machinery	Machinery
Uzbekistan Tashkent	Uzbek	22,100,000 128 per sq. mi. 49 per sq. km	172,700 sq. mi. 447,293 sq. km	Cotton	Food

*Country maps not drawn to scale.

Country Profile Activity

Culture Have students identify and list the characteristics of a culture (ethnic group, language, religions, literacy rate, form of government, education, per capita income, degree of urbanization, economy base). Organize students into pairs or small groups. Assign a country to each group. Using appropriate sources, have students note the cultural characteristics of their assigned countries in brief phrases and numbers. Specify a sharing time and provide an area of bulletin board or chalkboard with the label *Eurasian Republic.* As students share their findings, have them decide whether the cultural character of the republic is European or Asian and list it either under *Euro* or *Asian.* Encourage students to form generalizations about the two sets of republics.

Winters in Moscow, Russia's capital, are severe—with plenty of snow and bitterly cold temperatures.

Vast areas of tundra stretch across the northern part of Russia.

The ideas of Russian revolutionary leader Vladimir Lenin shaped the political and cultural life of Russia and the Eurasian republics from 1917 until the early 1990s.

Russian czars and czarinas built beautiful palaces in St. Petersburg during the period of the Russian Empire.

289

Global Gourmet

Borscht—beet soup—is a Russian favorite introduced to the United States by Russian immigrants. Made primarily with beets and onions, variations include potatoes, cabbages, and/or carrots. Those are the vegetables that are part of everyday life in Russia.

DID YOU KNOW?

Now that communism no longer requires the Russians to be totally obedient, most are searching for new social values. Used to obeying the government without argument, they must now learn to discuss and compromise, to be personally creative, and to take risks.

Country Profile Activity

Government Have students identify the Russian leaders mentioned on page 289. *(czars, czarinas, revolutionary Lenin)* Have them briefly research the powers that both kinds of Russian leaders have had, and what powers have been left to the people. Using their research, have students suggest reasons for the difficulties the country is having moving to a democratic form of government. *(Students should show awareness that the Russians, both leaders and people, are not used to working together to determine and carry out governmental tasks.)*

CHAPTER 14

PLANNING GUIDE

The Physical Geography of Russia and the Eurasian Republics

CHAPTER ORGANIZER

Daily Lesson Objectives	Multimedia	Teacher Classroom Resources
SECTION 1 The Land 1. Describe the major landforms in Russia and the Eurasian Republics.	Section Focus Transparency 14-1 Chapter 14 Vocabulary PuzzleMaker Software Unit Map Overlay Transparency 5-5 Political Map Transparency 5 Testmaker STV: World Geography, Volume 1 Picture Atlas of the World Physical Geography of the World Transparencies 31–40	Reproducible Lesson Plan 14-1 Guided Reading Activity 14-1 Spanish Guided Reading Activity 14-1 Workbook Activity 14-1 Performance Assessment 14 Geography Simulation 5 Section Quiz 14-1
SECTION 2 The Climate and Vegetation 1. Discuss the major climates found in Russia and the Eurasian republics. 2. Compare the kinds of natural vegetation in different climate regions of Russia and the Eurasian republics.	 Section Focus Transparency 14-2 Unit Map Overlay Transparencies 5, 5-3 Reuters Issues in Geography Testmaker	Reproducible Lesson Plan 14-2 Guided Reading Activity 14-2 Spanish Guided Reading Activity 14-2 Workbook Activity 14-2 Enrichment Activity 14 Skill Activity 14 Section Quiz 14-2
CHAPTER REVIEW AND EVALUATION	Chapter 14 English (or Spanish) Audiocassettes MindJogger Videoquiz Testmaker Student Self-Test and Review Software	Reteaching Activity 14 Spanish Reteaching Activity 14 Outline Map Resource Book, p. 34 Chapter 14 Test Form A and Form B

0:00 *If time does not permit teaching the entire chapter, summarize using the Chapter 14 Highlights on page 301, and the Chapter 14 English or Spanish Audiocassettes. Review students' knowledge using the Glencoe MindJogger Videoquiz.*

KEY TO ABILITY LEVELS

Teaching strategies have been coded for varying learning styles and abilities.

L1 **BASIC** activities for all students

L2 **AVERAGE** activities for average to above-average students

L3 **CHALLENGING** activities for above-average students

LEP **LIMITED ENGLISH PROFICIENCY** activities

Performance Assessment

Portfolios Have each student develop a portfolio of news clippings about Russia and the Eurasian republics. Students should use the headings and subheadings in Chapters 14, 15, and 16 as guides for organizing their portfolios. Each newspaper or magazine clipping should be accompanied by a short summary detailing how the item reflects change in the region. Snippets from newscasts may be summarized and documented by date, title, and network as a source. At the end of Chapter 14, students should examine their portfolios for evidence of physical features, climate, or vegetation.

Organize the class into groups. Students should share their portfolio data to create a fuller bank of knowledge. If a group has not found any relevant news regarding geography, they should devise strategies for uncovering any current developments in this area. These might include letters, phone calls, and interviews. Student portfolios should continue through Chapters 15 and 16.

POSSIBLE RUBRIC FEATURES: Content information, portfolio organization and contents, evaluation and summarization skills, collaboration skills, relevance of research, written communication skills

For additional professional and classroom resources, see Chapter Resources, pages T46–T51.

TEACHER'S CORNER

NATIONAL GEOGRAPHIC SOCIETY

INDEX TO NATIONAL GEOGRAPHIC MAGAZINE

The following articles may be used for research relating to this chapter:

- "A Russian Voyage: From the White to the Black Sea," by Miles Clark, June 1994.
- "Kamchatka: Russia's Land of Fire and Ice," by Bryan Hodgson, April 1994.
- "The World's Great Lake: Russia's Lake Baikal," by Don Belt, June 1992.
- "Siberia: In from the Cold," by Mike Edwards, March 1990.
- "Ukraine," by Mike Edwards, May 1987.

NATIONAL GEOGRAPHIC SOCIETY PRODUCTS AVAILABLE FROM GLENCOE

To order the following products for use with this chapter, contact your local Glencoe sales representative or call Glencoe at 1-800-334-7344:

- *Picture Atlas of the World* (CD-ROM)
- *STV: World Geography, Asia and Australia* (Videodisc)
- *ZipZapMap! World* (Software)
- *GeoBee* (Software)
- *Images of the World* (Posters)
- *Eye on the Environment* (Posters)
- *Physical Geography of the World* (Transparencies)
- *Picture Atlas of Our 50 States* (Book)

ADDITIONAL NATIONAL GEOGRAPHIC SOCIETY PRODUCTS

To order the following products for use with this chapter, call National Geographic Society at 1-800-368-2728:

- *The Soviet World in Transition,* "Geography," "History." (Filmstrip)

Introducing CHAPTER 14

PERFORMANCE ASSESSMENT

Refer to the Planning Guide on page 290B for a Performance Assessment Activity for this chapter. See the *Performance Assessment Activities* booklet for additional suggestions.

CHAPTER OBJECTIVES

1. **Name** three interconnected plains and numerous mountain ranges that form the major landscapes of Russia and the Eurasian republics.
2. **Explain** how the climate and vegetation of Russia and the Eurasian republics are affected by their northern location and their distance from the sea.

GLENCOE TECHNOLOGY

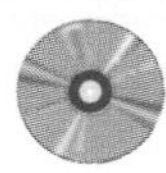

Videodisc

Use Chapter 14 MindJogger Videoquiz to preview chapter content.

MINDJOGGER VIDEOQUIZ

Chapter 14
Disc 2 Side B

The MindJogger Videoquiz is also available on videocassette.

NATIONAL GEOGRAPHIC SOCIETY

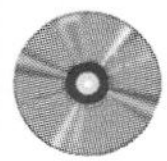

Videodisc

STV: WORLD GEOGRAPHY, VOLUME 1

Side 1, Chapter 1
Frames 1185-6885
Title: *Asia*
Subject: Overview

chapter 14 The Physical Geography of Russia and the Eurasian Republics

CHAPTER FOCUS

Geographic Setting

Together Russia and the Eurasian republics stretch almost halfway around the world. Diverse climate and vegetation zones extend across the broad expanse.

Geographic Themes

Section 1 The Land

PLACE Three interconnected plains and numerous mountain ranges form the major landscapes of Russia and the Eurasian republics.

▲ Photograph: *Towering Caucasus Mountains, Georgia*

Section 2 The Climate and Vegetation

LOCATION The climates and vegetation of Russia and the Eurasian republics are affected by their northern location and their distance from the sea.

EXTRA CREDIT PROJECT

Write a Book Challenge interested students to write ABC books about Russia and the Eurasian republics. For items with names beginning with letters not covered in the chapter, refer the students to an encyclopedia. Tell them to model their illustrations after Russian folk art or decorative Ukrainian Easter eggs. Donate their books to an elementary school library.

1 SECTION The Land

SETTING THE SCENE

Read to Discover . . .
- **the major landforms in Russia and the Eurasian republics.**

Key Terms
- **chernozem**
- ***kums***

Identify and Locate
North European Plain, West Siberian Plain, Caucasus Mountains, Black Sea, Caspian Sea, Aral Sea, Volga River, Dnieper River

Siberia, Russia

Zdravstvuy!
I was born in the Altai Mountains in the southwestern part of Siberia. I often come back here to spend my summer vacation. I enjoy hiking in the mountains where you can see glaciers on the distant mountaintops, drink crystal-clear and ice-cold water from rapid streams, and breathe the sweet air of Alpine meadows. Come and see for yourself!
Best wishes, Vladimir Marchenkov

Vladimir Marchenkov comes from Siberia, the eastern part of Russia. Russia and the Eurasian republics together cover 8,534,370 square miles (22,104,018 sq. km) of territory. They are more than the size of Canada, the United States, and Mexico combined. Territorial size and a diversity of landforms have affected the development of these countries.

PLACE

Plains Areas

Three plains connect Europe and Asia. The North European Plain, the West Siberian Plain, and the Turan Lowland stretch eastward from Poland to the Yenisey (yeh•nuh•SAY) River.

The North European Plain

The North European Plain is the center of economic life for almost three-fourths of the people of Russia and the Eurasian republics. The region's rich black topsoil called **chernozem** (cher•nuh•ZYAWM) makes Ukraine one of Europe's best farming areas. Three large cities—Moscow and St. Petersburg in Russia and Kiev in Ukraine—are located in the region. Its major rivers are the Volga, the Dniester (NEES•tuhr), the Dnieper (NEE•puhr), and the Don.

The West Siberian Plain

East of the Ural Mountains lies the world's largest area of flat land. Most of its one million square miles (2.6 million sq. km) is swamps, marshes, and frozen land unsuitable for farm-

LESSON PLAN
Chapter 14, Section 1

FOCUS

SECTION OBJECTIVE

1. **Describe** the major landforms in Russia and the Eurasian republics.

ABOUT THE POSTCARD

Although Vladimir has been to many beautiful places, he is always drawn to the Altai Mountains in Siberia, where he can see clearly the myriad of stars in the night sky.

BELLRINGER MOTIVATIONAL ACTIVITY

Project the Section 1 Focus Transparency and have students answer the questions.

PRETEACHING VOCABULARY

Have students scan the section for the pronunciations of *chernozem* and various place names. Ask volunteers to pronounce the words aloud.

Use the Vocabulary PuzzleMaker Software to create a crossword or word search puzzle.

CD-ROM

PICTURE ATLAS OF THE WORLD
See the physical geography of Russia and the Eurasian republics by clicking the "Photos" button of selected countries.

Classroom Resources for Section 1

BLACKLINE MASTERS:
- Reproducible Lesson Plan 14-1
- Geography Simulation 5
- Guided Reading Activity 14-1
- Spanish Guided Reading Activity 14-1
- Workbook Activity 14-1
- Performance Assessment Activity 14
- Section Quiz 14-1

TRANSPARENCIES:
- Section Focus Transparency 14-1
- Unit Map Overlay Transparency 5-5
- Political Map Transparency 5
- Physical Geography of the World Transparencies 31–40

MULTIMEDIA:

Vocabulary PuzzleMaker Software
Testmaker

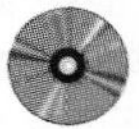

STV: World Geography, Volume 1

Picture Atlas of the World

TEACH

GUIDED PRACTICE

L1 Locate Have students locate and draw landforms and bodies of water from the section on the Political Map Transparency 5. Project Unit Map Overlay Transparency 5-5 to check their work.

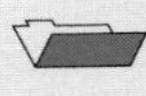

Implement Geography Simulation 5 as a class activity.

USING ILLUSTRATIONS

LOCATION A higher natural border than the Urals are the Tian Shan Mountains between Kyrgyzstan and China. The uniforms of border guards there include skis.

Answer to Caption: *between Europe and Asia*

Global Gourmet

Because Armenian soil is so rocky, scientists predict that one-fifth of all Armenian plants, including fruits and vegetables, will be grown hydroponically—in gravel rather than soil—by the year 2000.

MULTICULTURAL PERSPECTIVE

Cultural Diffusion
Natural barriers have discouraged invaders but also have isolated Russia from cultural events, such as the Renaissance and the Reformation.

Geographic Themes

Location: Ural Mountains
The Ural Mountains, an old range of rounded peaks, contain rich mineral resources. *Where are the Ural Mountains located?*

ing. The northern two-thirds is evergreen forest and swamp.

The Turan Lowland

Between the Caspian Sea and the Tian Shan (tee•AHN SHAHN) mountain range, the Turan Lowland has a few areas irrigated for agriculture. The rest is dune-covered ***kums,*** or deserts. The Kara Kum, or black sand desert, occupies most of Turkmenistan. The Kyzylkum (ky•zuhl•KUHM), or red sand desert, covers half of Uzbekistan.

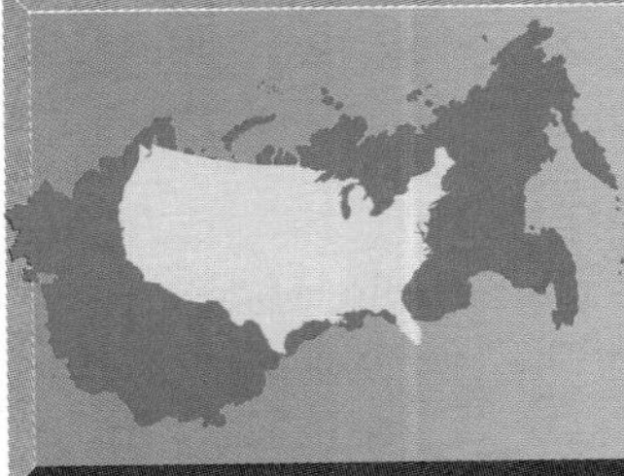

Comparing Lands

The continental USA is a little less than three and a half times smaller than Russia and the Eurasian republics.

PLACE

Mountains and Plateaus

Mountain ranges and plateaus punctuate the landscape of Russia and the Eurasian republics. The Carpathian Mountains bordering Ukraine and the Caucasus (KAW•kuh•suhs) in the southwest are extensions of the Alpine mountain system of Europe. Thickly covered with pines and other trees, the Caucasus form the Russian frontier with Azerbaijan and Georgia.

Mount Elbrus, in the Caucasus, rises 18,510 feet (5,642 m). Communism Peak, in the Pamirs on the eastern border of Tajikistan, at 24,590 feet (7,495 m) is the region's highest elevation. The Tian Shan, meaning "heavenly mountains" in Chinese, is a towering system covering much of Kyrgyzstan. It includes some of the world's largest glaciers.

The mineral-rich Ural Mountains, worn down by streams and wind erosion, rise only a few thousand feet. Stretching 1,500 miles

Cooperative Learning Activity

Suggest that interested students research chernozem and other soils of the world and make a chart showing their different characteristics, such as color and texture. Suggest that, along with the chart, they display models, such as simulated permafrost (mud left in the freezer) or a profile of soil found in their community. For sources, refer them to the *Readers' Guide to Periodical Literature.*

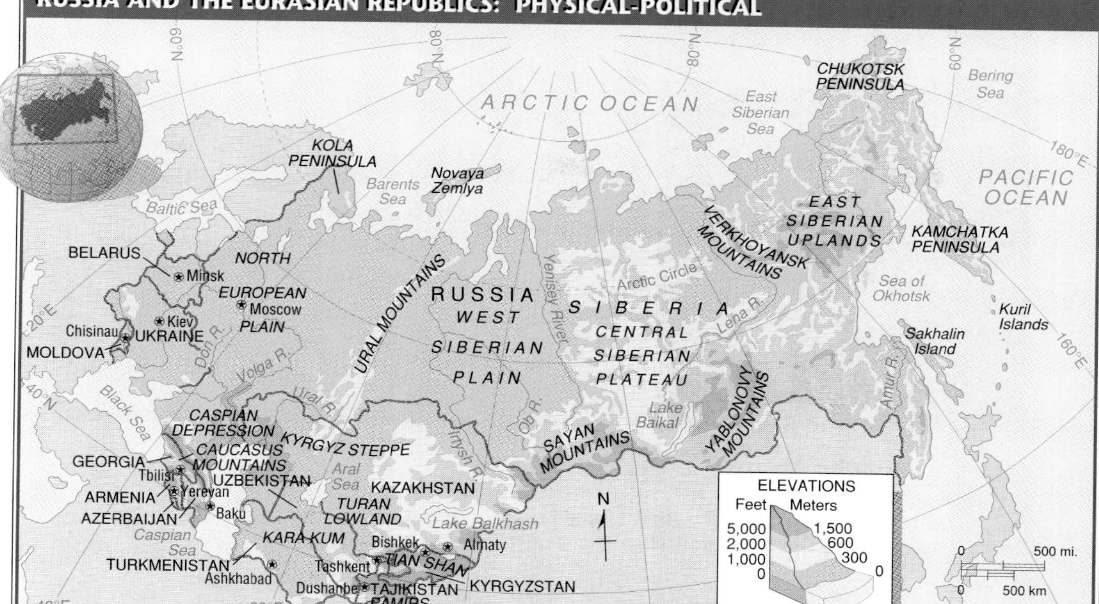

Focus on Geographic Themes

1. **Region:** What three republics are located in the region of the Caucasus Mountains?
2. **Place:** What city is the capital of the Ukraine?
3. **Movement:** What sea lies south of Russia and Ukraine?
4. **Place:** What desert area lies in Turkmenistan?

(2,414 km) from the Arctic Ocean to near the Aral Sea, the Urals divide European Russia and Siberia.

The East Siberian Uplands form the largest region of Siberia. This wilderness of forests, mountains, and plateaus extends to the Pacific Ocean. To the west, the Central Siberian Plateau slopes upward as you move from the Arctic Ocean to the Sayan and Baikal mountains. Fast-running streams have cut deep canyons in these plateaus.

REGION

Seas and Lakes

Russia and the Eurasian republics contain many seas and lakes. Ice-covered most of the year, the White, the Barents, the Kara, the Laptev, the East Siberian, and the Chukchi seas all border northern Russia. The Sea of Okhotsk (oh•KAHTSK) and the Bering Sea border on the northeast. The Black Sea—a warm water sea—touches Russia, Georgia, and Ukraine and flows south into the Mediterranean.

Nestled among the republics of Azerbaijan, Russia, Kazakhstan, and Turkmenistan is the Caspian Sea. The largest inland body of water in the world is really a saltwater lake. Although four rivers flow into it, the Caspian Sea is shrinking from evaporation. The Aral Sea is also shrinking because Soviet policies allowed its waters to be overused for irrigation.

Lake Baikal (by•KAHL) in Siberia is the oldest and deepest lake in the world. Called in Russian folk songs a "glorious and sacred sea," it holds one-fifth of the earth's total freshwater supply.

INDEPENDENT PRACTICE

Guided Reading Have students complete Guided Reading Activity 14-1 in the TCR. **LEP**

Have students complete Performance Assessment Activity 14 in the TCR.

L2 Making a Graph Have interested students make a picture graph comparing the lengths of the rivers listed in the section with the lengths of other major rivers in the rest of the world. Refer them to an almanac for the facts they need.

USING MAPS

Answers: **1.** Georgia, Armenia, Azerbaijan; **2.** Kiev; **3.** Black Sea; **4.** Kara Kum

Map Skills Practice

Reading a Map Which area has the highest elevation—the West Siberian Plain, the Central Siberian Plateau, or the East Siberian Uplands? *(the East Siberian Uplands)*

CURRICULUM CONNECTION

ART

Ukrainians decorate their Easter eggs with symbols that reflect their resources. For example, a border of wheat stands for the harvest, and a stylized deer for prosperity.

DID YOU KNOW?

In the former Soviet Union, little attention was paid to the environment. As a result, 20 kinds of mammals, 38 kinds of birds, and 530 kinds of plants are threatened species in Russia and the Eurasian republics.

Meeting Special Needs

Slow Readers The ability to scan for the location of specific information will help slow readers work more efficiently. Explain that the purpose of scanning is to locate specific information rapidly. Then select one student to demonstrate the scanning procedure. Ask students to scan the subhead "Natural Resources" on page 294 to find where in the region the largest reserves of natural gas and oil are found *(west of the Ural Mountains)* and how much of the region is forestland *(one-third).*

USING ILLUSTRATIONS

LOCATION Even tributaries of the Volga act as highways for trade. For centuries, lumberjacks have used the Kama River to carry logs to sawmills.

Answer to Caption: *The source is the Valdai Hills and the outlet is the Caspian Sea.*

USING ILLUSTRATIONS

PLACE The Black Sea is important for trade and recreation. Goods flow from the Black Sea to the Mediterranean and back again.

Answer to Caption: *The Black Sea is a warm water sea.*

ASSESS

CHECK FOR UNDERSTANDING

Assign Section 1 Review as homework or an in-class activity.

MEETING LESSON OBJECTIVE

The objective below is tested by the question that follows it in parentheses.

1. Describe the major landforms in Russia and the Eurasian republics. *(2)*

DID YOU KNOW?

Lake Baikal's ecosystem includes 1,500 types of plants and animals found nowhere else.

Geographic Themes

Location: The Volga River

Although the Volga River is frozen for almost four months of the year, it handles almost half of Russia's river-freight traffic. *Where are the source and the outlet of the Volga?*

HUMAN/ENVIRONMENT INTERACTION

Rivers

Long navigable rivers, connected to seas and other rivers by canals, have played a major role in Russian and Eurasian trade and development. Some flow eastward, like the Amur, which forms part of Russia's border with China. Others, like the Ural and the Volga, flow southward. Many that flow northward, such as the Lena, Ob, and Yenisey, are frozen much of the year.

The Dnieper, the Western Dvina, the Dniester, the Don, and the Volga cross the plains. Called *Matushka Volga,* or "Mother Volga," the longest river in European Russia flows 2,193 miles (3,528.5 km) from Russia's Valdai Hills to the Caspian Sea. Although frozen for four to six months each year, this river provides hydroelectric power, municipal water supplies, and water for industries and irrigation. For centuries the Volga has been a major highway for trade and communications.

The only large river of Siberia that does not flow northward is the Amur. Its river valley is the only major food-producing area in eastern Siberia. Four Siberian rivers are among the 12 largest in the world—the Lena, the Ob, the Yenisey, and the Irtysh (ihr•TISH).

Geographic Themes

Place: Black Sea Coast

A mild climate and beautiful scenery make the Black Sea coast a popular vacation spot. *What makes the Black Sea unique among the seas that touch Russia and other republics?*

REGION

Natural Resources

Russia and the Eurasian republics are rich in natural resources. Russia is the world's largest producer of manganese and chromium

Critical Thinking

Making Predictions Assign each student one of the following minerals found in Russia and the Eurasian republics: coal, copper, silver, gold, lead, salt, tin, tungsten, zinc, iron ore, asbestos, chromium, bauxite, antimony, manganese, sulfur, and sodium sulfate. Have the students report to the class on the minerals' uses. Then ask the class to predict what kinds of industries the region has, based on its mineral resources. (For example, coal, iron ore, manganese, nickel, chromium and tungsten are used in the production of steel and steel alloys. Students may predict that the region has steel mills.) Have the students compare their predictions with listings of industries for Russia and the Eurasian republics in an encyclopedia.

and the second-largest producer of gold. Together Russia, Kazakhstan, and Ukraine contain almost 20 percent of the world's known coal and lignite reserves. The Tyumen field in the West Siberian Plain produces more oil in a day than any country except the United States and Saudi Arabia. Russia is the world's leading exporter of natural gas.

Minerals and Energy

Almost every mineral used by industry is found in Russia and the Eurasian republics. The region leads in coal, copper, and silver production and ranks second in production of gold, lead, salt, tin, tungsten, and zinc. Iron ore, nickel, asbestos, chromium, bauxite, antimony, manganese, and precious stones are in abundance. Turkmenistan has the world's largest deposits of sulfur and sodium sulfate.

Nearly all the republics have natural gas and oil. The main oil-producing areas are the Tyumen and Volga-Urals fields in Russia and the Baku field in Azerbaijan. Russia is a leading producer of hydroelectric power. A series of power stations along the Volga and at Bratsk on the Angara River are among the world's largest.

Soils, Forests, Wildlife, and Fish

The Black Earth Belt stretches from western Ukraine to southwestern Siberia. Its rich black chernozem makes the region a leading producer of wheat, rye, oats, barley, and sugar beets. Fertile soil made Ukraine the former Soviet Union's breadbasket for years.

About one-third of Russia and the Eurasian republics is forestland. Hardwood forests cover about one-fourth of the republic of Belarus. The region's vast forests with larch, pine, fir, linden, elm, and other trees account for about one-fifth of the world's timber.

Eastern Siberia is home to the majestic Siberian tiger, an endangered species. Other wildlife in the region include bear, fox, reindeer, elk, lynx, deer, wolf, wildcat, sable, and boar.

Fish are a key regional resource—salmon from the Pacific coast area; herring, cod, and halibut from the Barents Sea; and carp and sturgeon from the Caspian Sea.

Geographic Themes

Human/Environment Interaction: Baku, Azerbaijan

The major source of wealth for the economy of Azerbaijan is oil. The Caspian Sea near Baku has many oil refineries. *What are the two major oil-producing areas in Russia?*

SECTION 1 REVIEW

Checking for Understanding

1. **Define** chernozem, *kums.*
2. **Locating Places** What are the three major plains areas of Russia and the Eurasian republics?
3. **Region** What are two common characteristics of most rivers in Russia and the Eurasian republics?
4. **Region** What are five natural resources found in Russia and the Eurasian republics?

Critical Thinking

5. **Making Comparisons** In what ways are Lake Baikal and the Caspian Sea the same? How are they different? What does the future hold for these two lakes and the people who rely on them for a living?

ANSWERS TO SECTION 1 REVIEW

1. **chernozem:** rich black topsoil on the European plain; ***kums:*** dune covered deserts in Turkmenistan and Uzbekistan
2. the North European Plain, the West Siberian Plain, and the Turan Lowlands
3. Most flow northward and are frozen for much of the year.
4. minerals, energy resources, soils, wildlife, and fish
5. Both lakes are inland bodies of water. The Caspian is a shrinking saltwater lake called a sea in central Asia while Baikal is a deep freshwater lake in Siberia. Answers will vary, but students should point out the hazards of developing or using these bodies of water without environmental safeguards.

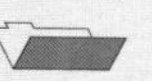

USING ILLUSTRATIONS

HUMAN/ENVIRONMENT INTERACTION Besides oil, Azerbaijan produces grain, cotton, rice, silk, iron, copper, lead, and zinc.

Answer to Caption: *the Tyumen and Volga-Urals fields*

EVALUATE

Assign the Section 1 Quiz in the TCR.

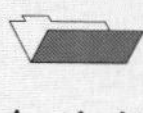

Use the Testmaker to create a customized quiz for Section 1.

RETEACH

Have students complete Workbook Activity 14-1 found in the TCR.

ENRICH

Invite a speaker from the local zoo to talk to the class about Eastern Siberian wildlife, including Siberian tigers, reindeer, sables, and wolves.

CLOSE

Have students write a postcard to Vladimir, telling him about a favorite summer vacation.

PHYSICAL GEOGRAPHY OF THE WORLD TRANSPARENCIES

Display and discuss the physical features of the following transparencies:

31. Caspian Sea at Baku, Azerbaijan
32. El'brus, Georgia
33. Volga River, Russia
34. Ural Mountains
35. Aral Sea, Kazakhstan
36. Steppe, Kazakhstan
37. Taiga, Russia
38. Lake Baikal, Russia
39. Tundra, Russia
40. Tolbachik, Russia

LESSON PLAN
Chapter 14, Section 2

FOCUS

SECTION OBJECTIVES

1. Discuss the major climates found in Russia and the Eurasian republics.
2. Compare the kinds of natural vegetation in different climate regions of Russia and the Eurasian republics.

BELLRINGER MOTIVATIONAL ACTIVITY

Project the Section 2 Focus Transparency and have students answer the questions.

PRETEACHING VOCABULARY

Tell the students that permafrost is a kind of soil. Next, ask them to hypothesize about what kind of soil it is. Then have them scan the section to find the meaning of permafrost and compare it to their hypotheses.

USING ILLUSTRATIONS

PLACE Salts and sand blown from the dried-up Aral Sea have added to the desertification of Turkmenistan, home of the Kara Kum.

Answer to Caption: *Its vegetation supports nomadic herds of sheep, goats, and camels.*

SECTION 2

The Climate and Vegetation

SETTING THE SCENE

Read to Discover . . .
- the major climates found in Russia and the Eurasian republics.
- the kinds of natural vegetation in different climate regions of Russia and the Eurasian republics.

Key Terms
- permafrost
- tundra
- taiga
- steppe

Identify and Locate
Arctic Circle, Odessa, Siberia, Kara Kum, Climate regions: humid continental, subarctic, steppe, desert, humid subtropical, Mediterranean

The vast size of Russia and the Eurasian republics has an important impact on their climate. Within their borders is a diversity of natural vegetation, including tundra, forest, grassland, and desert.

Geographic Themes
Place: Kara Kum, Central Asia
In the Kara Kum, the temperature has been known to rise above 120°F (48.9°C). *How does much of the vegetation of the Kara Kum compare with other desert areas?*

REGION

Climate Regions of Russia and the Eurasian Republics

The lack of mountains near lowlands and a northern location influence the climate of Russia and the Eurasian republics. About 75 percent of the region is located farther north than the United States, excluding Alaska. Like parts of Canada, the far northern part of Russia is within the Arctic Circle.

Most of the republics lie well within the continent, far from the moderating influences of the sea. This leads to a wide range of annual temperatures. Verkhoyansk, located at about 68°N latitude, has been called the "cold pole of the world" because of its bitter winter temperatures. Without mountains to shelter them, lowland areas receive the full impact of sultry summer winds and frigid winter storms.

Kinds of Climate

Two major climates—humid continental and subarctic—are found in most of Russia and the Eurasian republics. The range between temperature highs and lows is the widest in the world. While summers may be hot or warm, they are always short, and winters are

Classroom Resources for Section 2

BLACKLINE MASTERS:
Reproducible Lesson Plan 14-2
Guided Reading Activity 14-2
Enrichment Activity 14
Workbook Activity 14-2
Skill Activity 14
Section Quiz 14-2

TRANSPARENCIES:
Section Focus Transparency 14-2
Unit Map Overlay Transparencies 5, 5-3

MULTIMEDIA:

Testmaker

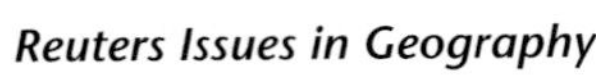

Reuters Issues in Geography

RUSSIA AND THE EURASIAN REPUBLICS: CLIMATE REGIONS

EUROPE, BELARUS, MOLDOVA, UKRAINE, GEORGIA, ARMENIA, AZERBAIJAN, KAZAKHSTAN, UZBEKISTAN, TURKMENISTAN, KYRGYZSTAN, TAJIKISTAN, RUSSIA, ASIA, Arctic Circle

Dry
- Steppe
- Desert

Mid-Latitude
- Humid subtropical
- Humid continental
- Mediterranean

High Latitude
- Tundra
- Subarctic
- Highland

Lambert Equal-Area projection

FOCUS ON GEOGRAPHIC THEMES

1. **Region: What climate region is found in the far north of Russia?**
2. **Place: In what climate region is Belarus located?**
3. **Region: What climate region extends around the north coast of the Black Sea?**
4. **Location: Where are highland areas found?**

always long and cold. More than half of the land is covered with snow six months a year. About half has **permafrost**, a permanently frozen layer of soil beneath the ground. In the words of one writer, "Indeed, so cold does it get that almost all of the . . . northern coast is never entirely free of ice, and even the southern port of Odessa on the Black Sea is frozen in for six weeks or so each winter."

Range of Climates

In the far north, the landscape is dominated by the vast treeless plains called **tundra.** In winter, when the northern part of the earth is tipped away from the sun, the sky stays dark for long periods. In summer there is daylight for weeks. The cold is the fiercest in northeastern Siberia. Temperatures there have been known to drop as low as –90°F (–68°C).

In the subarctic **taiga,** the vast woodland that begins where the tundra ends, summers are reasonably warm. Yet a deep blanket of snow often cloaks the land for as long as eight months of the year.

In contrast, the desert regions of central Asia have cold winters and long, hot summers. In July, for example, daytime temperatures average about 90°F (32°C) and have been known to rise above 120°F (49°C) in the shade.

In the North European Plain, summers are warm. Winters are cold, but not so painfully cold as farther north. More precipitation falls in summer than in winter, giving rise to conditions favorable for agriculture.

TEACH

GUIDED PRACTICE

L1 Classify On the chalkboard, list and number names of vegetation from the section. Then project Unit Map Overlay Transparency 5 and have students assign each number on the chalkboard to a climate zone on the transparency. Use Unit Map Overlay Transparency 5-3 to check their work.

INDEPENDENT PRACTICE

Guided Reading Have students complete Guided Reading Activity 14-2 in the TCR. **LEP**

USING MAPS

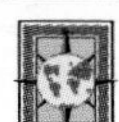

Answers: **1.** tundra; **2.** humid continental; **3.** steppe; **4.** between the Black and Caspian seas

Map Skills Practice

What climate regions lie on the eastern coast of the Caspian Sea? *(desert and steppe)*

GLENCOE TECHNOLOGY

Videodisc

Use the following to enrich Chapter 14:

REUTERS ISSUES IN GEOGRAPHY

Chapter 4
Disc 1 Side A
Title: ***Russia: Managing Resources***

Cooperative Learning Activity

Have students create a multimedia experience of a vegetation region in the chapter. Suggest they bring a pop-up tent to class (or improvise a tent from a sheet and clothesline), make transparencies from pictures of landforms and wildlife in a region such as the taiga or tundra, and tape simulated sounds, such as whistling winds or howling wolves. Then tell the students to invite the rest of the class into the theater, to project the pictures onto the tent walls, and to play the sounds that go with the pictures.

USING GRAPHS

Answers:
In Moscow, the average August temperature is 65°F (18.5°C) and the average precipitation is 3 inches (7.5 cm). In Minneapolis, the average August temperature is 71°F (21.5°C) and the average precipitation is 3.5 inches (9 cm).

ASSESS

CHECK FOR UNDERSTANDING

Assign Section 2 Review as homework or an in-class activity.

MEETING LESSON OBJECTIVES

Each objective below is tested by the questions that follow it in parentheses.

1. Discuss the major climates found in Russia and the Eurasian republics. *(2, 3)*

2. Compare the kinds of natural vegetation in different climate regions of Russia and the Eurasian republics. *(2, 4, 5)*

EVALUATE

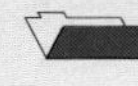

Assign the Section 2 Quiz in the TCR.

COMPARING CLIMATE REGIONS

Russia and the United States

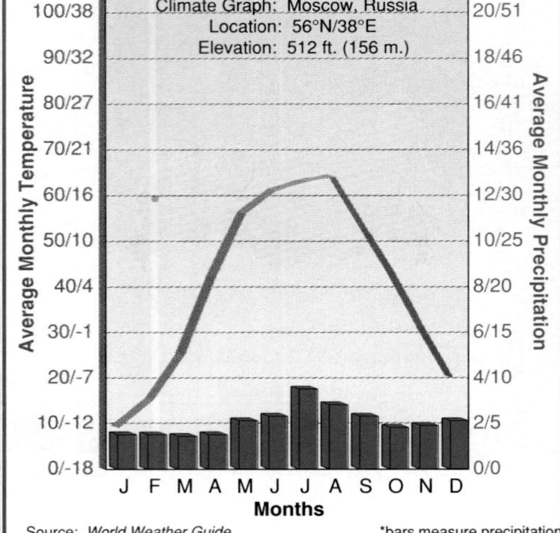

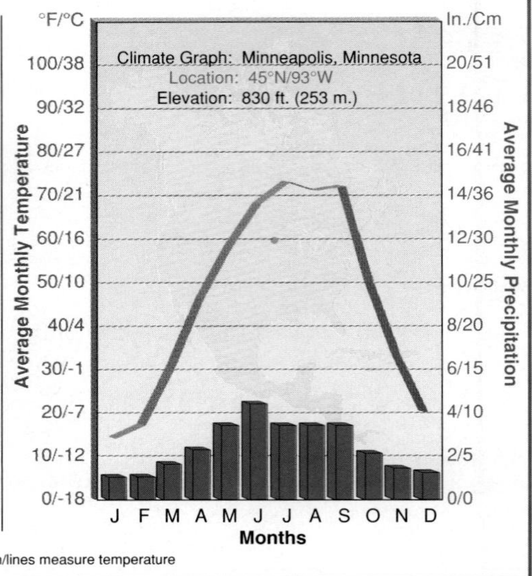

Source: *World Weather Guide*

*bars measure precipitation/lines measure temperature

GRAPH STUDY

The climate graph above shows the average monthly temperature and the average monthly precipitation in Minneapolis, Minnesota, and Moscow, Russia. *What is the average August temperature and precipitation in each city?*

In the wide grassy plains known as **steppes** that stretch from the western shores of the Black Sea to the Altai Mountains, winter is a time when frosty northern winds pile the snow in drifts across the frozen earth. In summer, rainfall is uncertain and, as one writer explains:

> *The sun of the steppelands is like a boiling kettle, pouring yellow boiling water over your back.*

Other climates prevail in scattered parts of Russia and the Eurasian republics. The Black Sea coast of Georgia has a humid subtropical climate suitable for growing cotton, tea, citrus fruits, and tobacco. The Crimean Peninsula has a Mediterranean climate in which citrus fruits, winter grains, and vegetables thrive.

PLACE

Vegetation

Many kinds of vegetation can be found in this region. In western Georgia, Azerbaijan, and Turkmenistan, for example, a person can see subtropical vegetation such as citrus fruits. At the far eastern end of the Black

Meeting Special Needs

Inefficient Readers Students with problems decoding unfamiliar words or familiar words used in unfamiliar ways often skip over them. Many times, however, they are successful in comprehending words based on their context. Ask students to scan Section 2 for words with which they are unfamiliar. Ask them to write these words and to guess at the meanings based on the context. Some words that may need definition or review are *moderating, dominated, prevail, encompasses, barren,* and *pedestrians.*

Sea, there are rich tea plantations and a subtropical rain forest. Seven natural vegetation zones run roughly from west to east across the vast territory. These zones are tundra, taiga, mixed forest, wooded steppe, steppe, semidesert, and desert.

Tundra

Tundra is the northernmost vegetation zone. The soil beneath the tundra is always frozen, but different kinds of low grasses, reeds, and mosses still grow.

Taiga and Mixed Forest

South of the tundra is the taiga—the coniferous forest belt. The largest forest region in the world, it stretches from Finland to the Sea of Okhotsk. One writer refers to these large forests as "one of the mightiest features of our planet."

In past decades, many furbearing animals lived in the forests. Mink and Russian sable pelts sold for a great deal of money—a source of wealth for many generations. Today the animals are fewer in number, and the wealth rests more in timber. In some places the forest has been cleared, and farmers have cultivated crops. The soil, however, is not very good, and the growing season is short.

To the south of the taiga is a mixed forest with both coniferous trees and deciduous trees. It encompasses much of Belarus and eventually joins with forests of central Europe.

Steppe Areas

The northern areas of the steppes border the southern edge of the mixed forest. This strip of steppes alternates thick clumps of trees with wide open spaces. The rest of the steppe is largely grassland.

Semidesert and Desert

The semidesert and desert south of the steppes have little vegetation. The hot, dry climate makes much of the area barren. Large stretches of bare rock and sandy dunes dominate drought-resistant shrubs and cacti. In the Kara Kum, however, vegetation supports nomadic herds of sheep, goats, and camels. The valleys of the Syr and Amu Darya rivers in Uzbekistan have been irrigated. In these regions melons, rice, and cotton grow.

Geographic Themes

Place: Irkutsk, Siberia

Warmly dressed pedestrians are on their way to work on a typical winter morning in Siberia. *How does the cold climate affect the soil in Siberia and other parts of Russia?*

SECTION 2 REVIEW

Checking for Understanding

1. **Define** permafrost, tundra, taiga, steppe.
2. **Locating Places** In what part of Russia and the Eurasian republics are the steppes located?
3. **Region** What two general kinds of climate prevail in most of Russia and the Eurasian republics?
4. **Place** How does the vegetation of the tundra compare with that of the taiga?

Critical Thinking

5. **Making Generalizations** What generalization can you make about climate and vegetation in Russia and the Eurasian republics? Relate this generalization to human activity, particularly agriculture.

RETEACH

Have students complete Reteaching Activity 14 in the TCR.

ENRICH

Have students complete Enrichment Activity 14 in the TCR.

CLOSE

Suggest that students dramatize a Russian folktale, e.g., "The Wicked Stepmother," in which climate plays a part.

USING ILLUSTRATIONS

PLACE Russians call the fur hats they wear in frigid weather *ushanki.*

Answer to Caption: *More than one-half the land is covered with snow six months a year and about half has permafrost.*

ANSWERS TO SECTION 2 REVIEW

1. **permafrost:** permanently frozen layer of soil beneath the ground; **tundra:** vast treeless plains; **taiga:** vast woodland; **steppe:** wide grassy plains
2. north of the Black and Caspian seas to the Altai Mountains
3. humid continental and subarctic
4. The tundra has no trees, and the taiga is a coniferous forest.
5. Answers will vary but should indicate that climate and vegetation are interrelated and that the vegetation areas follow the climate. Agriculture is profoundly affected by the region's northern location, distance from the moderating effects of seas and oceans, and sharp variations in temperature.

Teaching Skills

TEACH

Ask: "In what town or city do we live?" Explain that a city, town, or township is the smallest unit of government, or political unit. Ask: "What is the next larger political unit in which we live?" *(county)* Have students name their county and then their state and country. Point out that political maps illustrate the boundaries between political units.

Direct students to read the skill on page 300. Ask: "What are boundaries between nations called?" *(international boundaries)* "What causes political maps to change?" *(Political boundaries change due to war, new alliances, and independence movements.)*

Skills Practice For additional practice, have students complete Skill Activity 14 in the TCR.

MAP & GRAPH SKILLS

Interpreting a Political Map

As you travel, you may see signs indicating that you have left one town, county, or state and entered the next. Lines drawn to separate towns, counties, states, and nations are called *political boundaries* because they divide areas controlled by different governments. A **political map** illustrates these divisions and relationships.

Reviewing the Skill

On political maps of large areas, lines indicate boundaries between countries, or *international boundaries.* Political maps often also include cities and selected natural features, such as large bodies of water and major rivers.

Unlike physical maps, which remain fairly constant over time, political maps change as political relationships evolve. By comparing political maps from different periods of history, you can see changes in political relationships over time.

To interpret a political map, apply the following steps:

- Read the map title to find out what geographic area it covers and what time period the map reflects.
- Identify the countries or other political units named on the map.
- Identify capitals and major cities.

Practicing the Skill

Use the map below to answer the following questions about political maps:

1. Which countries separate Russia from the rest of Europe?
2. What is the capital of Kazakhstan? Of Ukraine?
3. Which countries border the Black Sea?
4. Which two cities lie farthest east on this map?

For additional practice in this skill, see Practicing Skills on page 302 of the Chapter 14 Review.

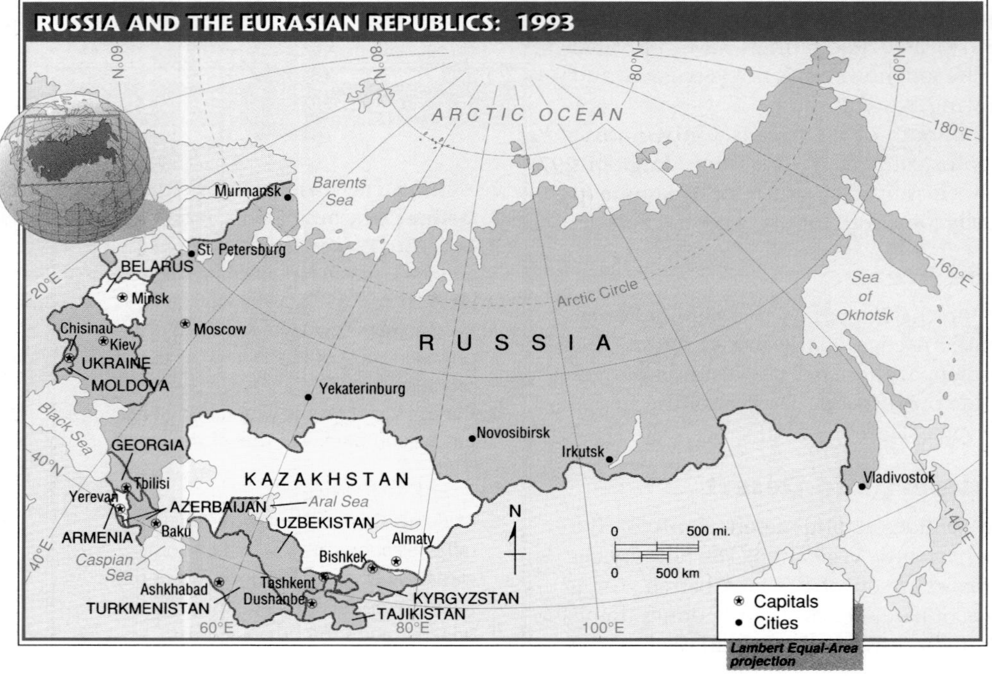

ANSWERS TO PRACTICING THE SKILL

1. Belarus, Ukraine, Moldova
2. Almaty; Kiev
3. Ukraine, Georgia, Russia
4. Irkutsk, Vladivostok

chapter 14 HIGHLIGHTS

Section	Key Terms	Summary
1 The Land	**chernozem** (p. 291) ***kums*** (p. 292)	• The land occupied by Russia and the Eurasian republics spans two continents—Europe and Asia. • Plains areas cover the greatest part of Russia and the Eurasian republics. • Numerous mountain ranges, uplands, plateaus, and inland bodies of water are scattered throughout Russia and the Eurasian republics. • All of the republics except Russia, Georgia, and Ukraine are landlocked. • Most of the rivers of the region flow northward and are frozen for much of the year. • Minerals, energy resources, fertile soils, forests, wildlife, and fish are abundant in Russia and the Eurasian republics.

The Ural Mountains—the divide between Europe and Asia

Section	Key Terms	Summary
2 The Climate and Vegetation	**permafrost** (p. 297) **tundra** (p. 297) **taiga** (p. 297) **steppe** (p. 298)	• Because of their northern location, distance from large bodies of water, and lack of mountains near lowland areas, most areas of Russia and the Eurasian republics have a humid continental or subarctic climate. • More than half the land of Russia and the Eurasian republics is covered with snow for much of the year. Permafrost (permanently frozen subsoil) is found beneath about 40 percent of the area of Russia and the Eurasian republics. • Throughout the region summers are short, and winters are very long and very cold. • Natural vegetation varies, ranging from treeless tundra in the north to densely wooded taiga in the center to barren desert in the south.

A winter morning in Siberia, the eastern half of Russia

Map Activity

Identify and Locate Distribute page 34 from the Outline Map Resource Book. Tell students to locate and label landforms and bodies of water and to shade climate regions on the map as they reread Chapter 14. Suggest that they make a key to explain the shades that show climates.

CHAPTER 14 HIGHLIGHTS

USING THE CHAPTER 14 HIGHLIGHTS

Use the Chapter 14 Highlights to preview, review, condense, or reteach the chapter.

PREVIEW/REVIEW

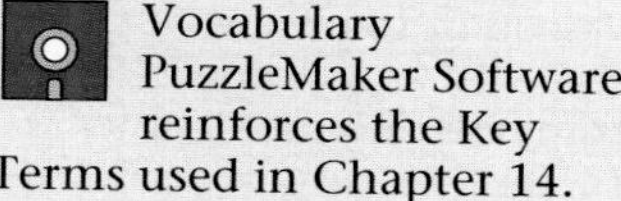

Vocabulary PuzzleMaker Software reinforces the Key Terms used in Chapter 14.

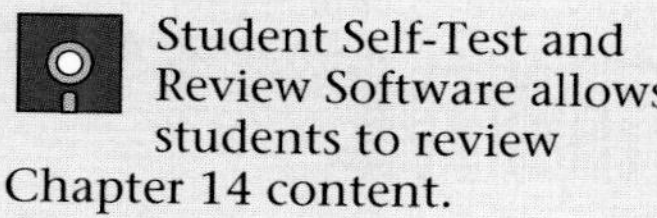

Student Self-Test and Review Software allows students to review Chapter 14 content.

CONDENSE

Have students read the Chapter 14 Highlights.

Have students listen to the Chapter 14 Audiocassettes in the TCR. Spanish Audiocassettes are also available.

Assign the Chapter 14 Audiocassette Activity and give the students the Chapter 14 Audiocassette Quiz.

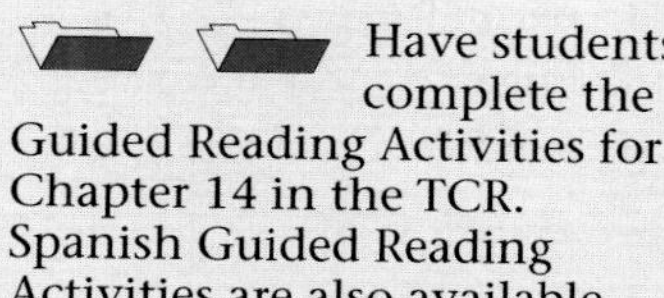

Have students complete the Guided Reading Activities for Chapter 14 in the TCR. Spanish Guided Reading Activities are also available.

RETEACH

Have students complete Reteaching Activity 14 in the TCR. Spanish Reteaching Activities are also available.

GLENCOE TECHNOLOGY

Videodisc

Use Chapter 14 MindJogger Videoquiz to review students' knowledge before administering the Chapter 14 Test.

MINDJOGGER VIDEOQUIZ

Chapter 14
Disc 2 Side B

The MindJogger Videoquiz is also available on videocassette.

ANSWERS

Reviewing Key Terms

1. chernozem
2. *kums*
3. steppes
4. permafrost
5. taiga
6. tundra

Reviewing Facts

7. the Ural Mountains
8. Russia, Georgia, and the Ukraine
9. It provides hydroelectric power, municipal water supplies, and water for industries and irrigation. The Volga is located in European Russia.
10. the widest in the world, from −90°F (−68°C) to 120°F (49°C)
11. tundra, taiga, mixed forest, wooded steppe, steppe, semidesert, and desert
12. semidesert and desert

chapter 14 REVIEW

Reviewing Key Terms

Choose the vocabulary term that best completes each of the sentences below. Write your answers on a separate sheet of paper.

chernozem (p. 291) tundra (p. 297)
kums (p. 292) taiga (p. 297)
permafrost (p. 297) steppes (p. 298)

SECTION 1

1. The rich black topsoil of the North European Plain is called ____.
2. A few areas of the Turan Lowland are agriculturally productive, but most of the plain is ____.

SECTION 2

3. Wide grassy plains called ____ cover southern Russia and Ukraine.
4. ____ is the permanently frozen layer of soil that lies beneath the ground.
5. A deep blanket of snow often cloaks the ____ for many months of the year.
6. Vast treeless plains called ____ dominate the landscape of the far northern regions of Russia.

Reviewing Facts

SECTION 1

7. Which mountains form a natural dividing line between European Russia and Siberia?
8. Which republics have direct access to the seas?
9. What functions does the Volga River fulfill for the people of Russia? Where is the Volga River located?

SECTION 2

10. How much of a range is there between temperature highs and lows in Russia and the Eurasian republics?
11. What are the seven vegetation zones found in Russia and the Eurasian republics?
12. What two vegetation zones are south of the steppe?

Critical Thinking

13. **Drawing Conclusions** Most of the people of Russia and the Eurasian republics make their homes on a Russian extension of the North European Plain. What reasons can you give for this?
14. **Determining Cause and Effect** Why are the climates of Russia and the Eurasian republics so harsh?

Geographic Themes

15. **Region** What kinds of natural resources are abundant in Russia and the Eurasian republics?
16. **Place** What vegetation is found in the tundra?

Practicing Skills

Interpreting a Political Map

Refer to the political map on page 300.

17. What is the capital of Georgia?
18. What seas border Kazakhstan?

Using the Unit Atlas

Refer to the physical geography section of the Unit Atlas on pages 286–287.

19. What mountains in Tajikistan are called the "roof of the world"?
20. What natural resource is found in Baku?

Projects

Individual Activity

Rivers have always played an important role in Russia and the Eurasian republics. Re-

Critical Thinking

13. Answers will vary but should indicate that the North European Plain has temperate weather conditions, major rivers, rich soil, productive industrial plants, and large urban centers.
14. because of their global location, their distance from large bodies of water, and the lack of mountains near their lowland areas

Geographic Themes

15. minerals, energy resources, fertile soils, forests, wildlife, and fish
16. lichens and different kinds of low grasses, reeds, and mosses

search a major river of the region. Then imagine that you are on a ship traveling from one end of the river to the other and write a poem describing the physical features, environment, climate, vegetation, and human activity in the areas through which you journey.

Cooperative Learning Activity

Work in a group of seven. Each group member will research a different vegetation zone of Russia and the Eurasian republics and present to the other group members what he or she learned. Then group members will work together to construct a poster that will illustrate what it might be like to live in each of the region's vegetation zones.

Writing About Geography

Proposal

Suppose you are a Russian. A foreign automobile manufacturer plans to open a plant in Russia or in one of the Eurasian republics and has asked you to recommend one or two areas in which to build the plant. Write a letter to the company president that includes your recommendations and an argument to support those recommendations. Use your journal, text, and magazine and newspaper articles as references in writing your letter.

Locating Places

THE PHYSICAL GEOGRAPHY OF RUSSIA AND THE EURASIAN REPUBLICS

Match the letters on the map with the places and physical features of Russia and the Eurasian republics. Write your answers on a separate sheet of paper.

1. Ural Mountains
2. Caucasus Mountains
3. Kazakhstan
4. Tian Shan
5. Siberia
6. East Siberian Uplands
7. Arctic Ocean
8. Bering Sea
9. Caspian Sea
10. Volga River

Chapter 14 Review

Practicing Skills

17. Tbilisi
18. Caspian and Aral seas

Using the Unit Atlas

19. Pamirs
20. oil

Locating Places

1. B
2. E
3. G
4. F
5. H
6. I
7. J
8. D
9. A
10. C

Chapter Bonus Test Question

This question may be used for extra credit on the chapter test.

What climate regions does the Volga pass through from its source to its outlet in the Caspian Sea?

(Answer: humid continental and steppe)

CHAPTER 15

PLANNING GUIDE

The Cultural Geography of Russia and the Eurasian Republics

CHAPTER ORGANIZER

Daily Lesson Objectives	Multimedia	Teacher Classroom Resources
SECTION 1 Population Patterns 1. Identify the diverse peoples who live in Russia and the Eurasian republics. 2. Explain where most people of Russia and the Eurasian republics live and why.	Section Focus Transparency 15-1 Chapter 15 Vocabulary PuzzleMaker Software World Cultures Transparency 7 Unit Map Overlay Transparencies 5, 5-1 Testmaker STV: World Geography, Volume 1	Reproducible Lesson Plan 15-1 Guided Reading Activity 15-1 Spanish Guided Reading Activity 15-1 Foods Around the World 4 Section Quiz 15-1
SECTION 2 History and Government 1. Locate the peoples who populated and created early Russia. 2. Discuss the rule of the czars. 3. Examine the rise and fall of the Soviet Union. 4. Describe the new independence of Russia and the Eurasian republics.	Section Focus Transparency 15-2 Political Map Transparency 5 World Cultures Transparency 7 Testmaker	Reproducible Lesson Plan 15-2 Guided Reading Activity 15-2 Spanish Guided Reading Activity 15-2 Workbook Activity 15-2 Vocabulary Activity 15 Section Quiz 15-2
SECTION 3 Cultures and Lifestyles 1. Name the religions practiced in Russia and the Eurasian republics. 2. Cite changes in education in Russia and the Eurasian republics. 3. Appreciate the arts of Russia and the Eurasian republics. 4. Characterize life and leisure in Russia and the Eurasian republics.	World Cultures Transparency 8 World Music: Cultural Traditions, Lesson 4 Testmaker Picture Atlas of the World	Reproducible Lesson Plan 15-3 Guided Reading Activity 15-3 Spanish Guided Reading Activity 15-3 Workbook Activity 15-3 Skill Activity 15 World Literature Reading 4 Section Quiz 15-3
CHAPTER REVIEW AND EVALUATION	Chapter 15 English (or Spanish) Audiocassettes MindJogger Videoquiz Testmaker Student Self-Test and Review Software	Reteaching Activity 15 Spanish Reteaching Activity 15 Chapter 15 Test Form A and Form B

0:00 *If time does not permit teaching the entire chapter, summarize using the Chapter 15 Highlights on page 323, and the Chapter 15 English (or Spanish) Audiocassettes. Review students' knowledge using the Glencoe MindJogger Videoquiz.*

KEY TO ABILITY LEVELS

Teaching strategies have been coded for varying learning styles and abilities.

L1 **BASIC** activities for all students

L2 **AVERAGE** activities for average to above-average students

L3 **CHALLENGING** activities for above-average students

LEP **LIMITED ENGLISH PROFICIENCY** activities

Performance Assessment

Portfolios Students should continue working on their individual portfolios about change in Russia and the Eurasian republics. Additions related to Chapter 15 should focus on news about ethnic diversity, population shifts, government, religion, the arts, sports, and holidays.

As in Chapter 14, groups of students should meet to consolidate data and to plan for acquiring data for areas not filled. As an additional item for the portfolios, have students consult almanacs and add current information on population, diversity, and religion. They should depict the data in the form of bar graphs. As with the articles, students should summarize how the information reflects change in the region.

POSSIBLE RUBRIC FEATURES: Content information, portfolio organization and contents, evaluation and summarization skills, collaboration skills, relevance of research, written communication skills

For additional professional and classroom resources, see Chapter Resources, pages T46–T51.

TEACHER'S CORNER

NATIONAL GEOGRAPHIC SOCIETY

INDEX TO NATIONAL GEOGRAPHIC MAGAZINE

The following articles may be used for research relating to this chapter:

- "A Mummy Unearthed from the Pastures of Heaven," by Natalya Polosmak, October 1994.
- "St. Petersburg: Capital of the Czars," by Steve Raymer, December 1993.
- "A Broken Empire: After the Soviet Union's Collapse," by Mike Edwards, March 1993.
- "The Bolshevik Revolution: Experiment that Failed," by Dusko Doder, October 1992.
- "Mother Russia on a New Course," by Mike Edwards, February 1991.
- "Inside the Kremlin," by Jon Thompson, January 1990.
- "The Baltic: Arena of Power," by Priit J. Vesilind, May 1989.
- "The World of Tolstoy," by Peter T. White, June 1986.
- "Peoples of the Arctic," by Priit J. Vesilind, February 1983.

NATIONAL GEOGRAPHIC SOCIETY PRODUCTS AVAILABLE FROM GLENCOE

To order the following products for use with this chapter, contact your local Glencoe sales representative or call Glencoe at 1-800-334-7344:

- *Picture Atlas of the World* (CD-ROM)
- *STV: World Geography, Asia and Australia* (Videodisc)
- *ZipZapMap! World* (Software)
- *GeoBee* (Software)
- *Images of the World* (Posters)
- *Eye on the Environment* (Posters)
- *Physical Geography of the World* (Transparencies)
- *Picture Atlas of Our 50 States* (Book)

ADDITIONAL NATIONAL GEOGRAPHIC SOCIETY PRODUCTS

To order the following products for use with this chapter, call National Geographic Society at 1-800-368-2728:

- *The Soviet World in Transition*, "Geography," "History." (Filmstrip)
- *The Rise and Fall of the Soviet Union* (Video)
- *Russia: After the U.S.S.R.* (Video)
- *Voices of Leningrad* (Video)

chapter 15 The Cultural Geography of Russia and the Eurasian Republics

PERFORMANCE ASSESSMENT

Refer to the Planning Guide on page 304B for a Performance Assessment Activity for this chapter. See the *Performance Assessment Activities* booklet for additional suggestions.

CHAPTER OBJECTIVES

1. **Realize** that Russia and the Eurasian republics once made up the world's third most populous nation.
2. **Point out** how, from the 1200s through much of the 1900s, autocratic rulers expanded first Russian and then Soviet territory in all directions.
3. **Discuss** why, since the fall of communism, culture in Russia and the Eurasian republics has been changing.

GLENCOE TECHNOLOGY

Videodisc

Use Chapter 15 MindJogger Videoquiz to preview chapter content.

MINDJOGGER VIDEOQUIZ

Chapter 15
Disc 2 Side B

The MindJogger Videoquiz is also available on videocassette.

CHAPTER FOCUS

Geographic Setting

In the early 1990s, a number of independent republics arose in the area once occupied by the Russian Empire and later, the Soviet Union.

▲ Photograph: *Busy shoppers in St. Petersburg, Russia*

Geographic Themes

Section 1 Population Patterns
PLACE Russia and the Eurasian republics once made up the world's third most populous nation.

Section 2 History and Government
REGIONS From the 1200s through much of the 1900s, autocratic rulers expanded first Russian and then Soviet territory in all directions.

Section 3 Cultures and Lifestyles
HUMAN/ENVIRONMENT INTERACTION Since the fall of communism, culture in Russia and the Eurasian republics has been changing.

EXTRA CREDIT PROJECT

Time Line Have interested students research the history of communism in Russia and reduce it to about twenty main events. Direct the students to depict these events with drawings and descriptions in a time line on a long strip of paper. Display the time line in the classroom and refer to it as you read the history of Russia and the Eurasian republics in the second section.

1 SECTION Population Patterns

SETTING THE SCENE

Read to Discover . . .
- the diverse peoples who live in Russia and the Eurasian republics.
- where most people of Russia and the Eurasian republics live and why.

Key Terms
- ethnic group
- nationalities

Identify and Locate
Russia, Ukraine, Belarus, Moldova, Azerbaijan, Kazakhstan, Uzbekistan, Tajikistan, Caucasus, Armenia, Georgia, Turkmenistan, Ural Mountains, Moscow, St. Petersburg, Kiev, Tashkent

Moscow, Russia
My name is Anton Alexeev and I live in an apartment in Moscow. The school that I attend is really small. We have a total of about 1,000 students and we have all grades—from first grade through eleventh grade. We have just 11 years in school. In my free time I hang out with my friends, ride bikes, and go to the park and to parties.
Anton Alexeev

Конфетница, 1896–1908 Сухарница 1844 РОССИЯ Rossija 1993 250 РУБ.

Anton Alexeev is Russian and lives in Russia, the largest of the republics in a culture region known as Russia and the Eurasian republics. The vast lands of Russia and the Eurasian republics are home to diverse peoples.

PLACE

Ethnic Diversity

Each people, or **ethnic group,** has its own unique heritage, customs, beliefs, and language. When Russia and the Eurasian republics were all part of the Soviet Union, boundaries were based on one of the country's major ethnic groups, or **nationalities.**

Language

During the Soviet era, Russian was the official language and was taught in all Soviet schools. It was the native language, however, of only about one-half of the people. Today Russian is still spoken and read in most of the republics, but now each republic has its own official language. The more than 100 nationalities who live in the region speak many hundreds of different languages.

Many people in Russia and the Eurasian republics are of Slavic background and speak languages that belong to the Indo-European family. Others are of Turkic background and speak one of the Turkic languages, which are part of the Ural-Altaic (YOR•uh•lal•TAY•ik) family. Still others speak either an Indo-European or Turkic language like Caucasian.

Russians, Ukrainians, and Belarusians, for example, are Slavs. Uzbeks, Kazakhs, Turkmenis, and most other peoples of the republics in central Asia are in the Turkic group. Georgians and Armenians, on the other hand, are Caucasian peoples and speak distinctive languages.

LESSON PLAN Chapter 15, Section 1

FOCUS

SECTION OBJECTIVES

1. **Identify** the diverse peoples who live in Russia and the Eurasian republics.
2. **Explain** where most people of Russia and the Eurasian republics live and why.

ABOUT THE POSTCARD

Anton also tells us that the most popular sport in Moscow today is karate.

BELLRINGER MOTIVATIONAL ACTIVITY

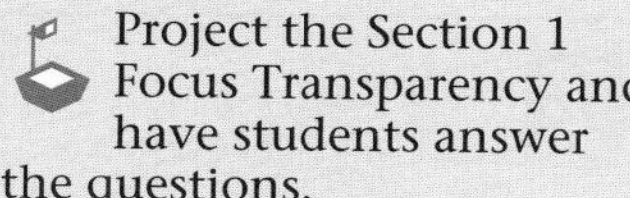

Project the Section 1 Focus Transparency and have students answer the questions.

PRETEACHING VOCABULARY

Have students read the meanings of *ethnic group* and *nationalities* on page 305 and then complete this analogy: an ethnic group is to a nationality what a language groups map is to a *(political map).*

Use the Vocabulary PuzzleMaker Software to create a crossword or word search puzzle.

Ways of the World

RUSSIA When Russians ask "How are you?" *(Kak dela?)* they expect a detailed reply. They consider rude anyone who asks the question and does not wait for a full response.

Classroom Resources for Section 1

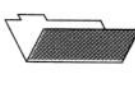

BLACKLINE MASTERS:
Reproducible Lesson Plan 15-1
Foods Around the World 4
Section Quiz 15-1

TRANSPARENCIES:
Section Focus Transparency 15-1
World Cultures Transparency 7
Unit Map Overlay Transparencies 5, 5-1

MULTIMEDIA:
Vocabulary PuzzleMaker Software
Testmaker

STV: World Geography, Volume 1

TEACH

GUIDED PRACTICE

 Implement Foods Around the World 4 as a class activity.

L1 Identify After students read the material under "Distribution and the Environment," project Unit Map Overlay Transparency 5. Ask volunteers to "X" the region where the population density is low and to circle the region where the population density is high. Project Unit Map Overlay Transparency 5-1 to check their accuracy.

USING ILLUSTRATIONS

REGION An inflation rate of 80 percent a month considerably hobbled Ukrainians' buying power in 1993.

Answer to Caption: *Russia and Belarus*

MULTICULTURAL PERSPECTIVE

Culturally Speaking Most Russians younger than 40 years of age speak English because it is taught in Russian schools beginning in the third grade. In fact, Russia has more teachers of English than the United States has students of Russian.

The Slavs

Of all the ethnic groups in Russia and the Eurasian republics, the Slavs are most numerous. During their early history, all Slavs in the region shared a common cultural identity. In time, the different types of Slavs in different places developed customs and languages distinct from the others. The Slavs living in the south near the city of Kiev became known as Ukrainians. Those inhabiting the west near present-day Poland were called Belarusians. Another group of Slavs living in the north near the city of Moscow became known as Russians.

Together the Slavs now make up the greater part of the population of three of the European republics—Russia, Ukraine, and Belarus. The greatest number live in Russia, where 83 percent of the population are actually ethnic Russians, people who follow Russian customs and speak Russian as their first language.

There is only one Eurasian republic in which the Slavs are not the majority—Moldova. Sixty-four percent of the people are Moldovans, most of them Romanians who came originally from the Bessarabia region of Romania. They speak Romanian and follow Romanian customs.

Turkic Peoples

With the exception of the Azeri, whose land—now the Republic of Azerbaijan—was for several centuries part of the Persian Empire, most Turkic peoples live in the republics of central Asia. They are Uzbeks, Kazakhs, Kyrgyz, Tatars, and Turks, and each is different from the other in a number of ways. But they all have one thing in common—language. All speak some form of a Turkic language. Almost all are Muslim, followers of the religion of Islam.

The Uzbeks are the largest group of Turkic people in the republics and the second-largest in the world. Only the Turks of Turkey form a larger group. Of all the Turkic peoples of the republics, only one—the Kazakhs—are a minority in their own country. For many years, more Russians than Kazakhs have lived in Kazakhstan. Since the end of the Soviet era,

Geographic Themes

Place: Ukraine

Ukrainians shop for goods and produce in a Kiev department store. Nearly 52 million people live in the republic of Ukraine. *What Slavic republics border Ukraine?*

Cooperative Learning Activity

Have a group of students make a puzzle of Russia and the Eurasian republics. Suggest that the group project Unit Map Overlay Transparency 5-4 on a sheet of poster board and trace the borders of the countries. Tell them to label the countries, using pages A14 and A15 as their guide, and then cut apart the poster board along the countries' borders. Then direct the group to make and label cardboard figures representing ethnic groups in the different countries. Refer the group to pictures in the chapter and other sources for models. Challenge the rest of the class to assemble the puzzle and to place the figures in their correct countries.

Geographic Themes

Human/Environment Interaction: Russia

For centuries, the Slavic peoples of Russia, Ukraine, and Belarus have used timber from the forests to build *izbas*, or cottages. *What Eurasian republic in the region is not Slavic?*

however, thousands of Russians have returned to Russia.

Another large non-Turkic group in the central Asian republics is the Tajiks, who make up most of the population of Tajikistan. They are descendants of Iranian-speaking people who entered central Asia many centuries ago. The Tajiks speak a language much like Farsi, the major language of Iran.

Caucasian Peoples

One large group of diverse peoples are classified as Caucasian. "The Caucasus presents a living museum of languages and peoples who have lived there since pre-history," says a leading regional writer. Most of these peoples, though, are relatively few in number except for the Armenians, Georgians, and Azeris.

The Armenians, who migrated to the Caucasus many centuries ago, once had a kingdom that stretched from the Mediterranean to the Caucasus. Today the Armenians make up more than 90 percent of the population of Armenia, the smallest of the republics. The Armenians speak their own language and have had their own alphabet and literature for more than 15 centuries.

The Armenian language is very different from the one spoken by Georgians. The Georgian language, also with its own alphabet, is considered a Caucasian language, which means that the Georgians probably originally came from the Caucasus. Language is one of the things in which Georgians take great pride. "Three divine gifts have been bestowed on us by our ancestors: language, homeland, faith," said one Georgian poet.

Like the Armenians, most Georgians are Christians and have their own church. Both are proud that their lands are among the world's oldest Christian countries. Armenia converted to Christianity around A.D. 300. Georgia did the same about 30 years later.

INDEPENDENT PRACTICE

Guided Reading Have students complete Guided Reading Activity 15-1 in the TCR. **LEP**

Have students complete Performance Assessment Activity 15 in the TCR.

Have students complete World Cultures Transparency 7 Activity in the TCR.

Have students complete Unit Map Overlay Transparency 5 Activity in the TCR.

L2 Write a Puzzle Ask interested students to make crossword puzzles using the names of ethnic groups and nationalities from the section. Have them include a list of ACROSS and DOWN clues. Distribute copies of the best puzzles.

L3 Record Ask volunteers to tape the pronunciations of the names of the Eurasian republics and of the ethnic groups who live there. Refer them to immigrants from the region for help.

USING ILLUSTRATIONS

HUMAN/ENVIRONMENT INTERACTION Rural homes in Russia are generally larger than city apartments, but they lack running water.

Answer to Caption: *Moldova*

Meeting Special Needs

Inefficient Readers Students with reading problems often have difficulty differentiating main ideas from details. Teach them to skim for a main idea in the subsection titled "The Slavs." Have students tell in their own words what the subsection is about. *(the distribution of Slavs in Russia and the Eurasian republics)* Next, have them read the first sentence of the subsection. Point out that the main idea of a paragraph often is stated in its first sentence. Then have students state the main idea of the subsection. *(The Slavs are most numerous of all the ethnic groups in Russia and the Eurasian republics.)*

USING ILLUSTRATIONS

LOCATION Almost 2.8 million people live in Kiev—about the same as in Dallas. But the population density in Kiev is more than 7 times that in Dallas.

Answer to Caption:
Most live where they have access to water, a moderate climate, and fertile soil.

ASSESS

CHECK FOR UNDERSTANDING

Assign Section 1 Review as homework or an in-class activity.

MEETING LESSON OBJECTIVES

Each objective below is tested by the questions that follow it in parentheses.

1. **Identify** the diverse peoples who live in Russia and the Eurasian republics. *(3)*
2. **Explain** where most people of Russia and the Eurasian republics live and why. *(2, 4, 5)*

Global Gourmet

Qurut is a favorite dish of herders in Kyrgyzstan. To make it, hard, dried yogurt is mixed with water to form a paste and then bits of fat and bread are added to the paste as it cooks.

HUMAN/ENVIRONMENT INTERACTION

Population Density and Distribution

More than 285 million people live in Russia and the Eurasian republics. Armenia, with about 3.7 million people, and Turkmenistan, with about 4.1 million, have the smallest populations of all the republics. Russia, still the largest country in the world in area, also has the region's largest population—148 million.

Density

More than 285 million people translates into a population density of about 33 persons per square mile (about 13 persons per sq. km). There are not many people in the region compared to the number living in a square mile or kilometer in other parts of the world.

Take the United States, for example. Together Russia and the Eurasian republics are about two and one-half times its size. Yet the population of the United States is only about 26 million less than that of Russia and the other republics. This means that the population of the United States is a little more than twice as dense, with 74 persons per square mile (about 28 persons per sq. km).

Distribution and the Environment

The population of Russia and the Eurasian republics is far from evenly distributed. Many people live in some areas, while hardly any live in others.

Environment has much to do with where people have chosen to live or not live. East of the Ural Mountains, for example, where the climate is harsh and much of the land is mountains or deserts, the population density is low.

However, this is not the case west of the Ural Mountains, between the Baltic and Black seas. Here is where most people of the region

Geographic Themes

Location: Kiev, Ukraine

Kiev, the capital of Ukraine, is located on the banks of the Dnieper River, the major waterway of the republic. *How does environment affect where people live?*

Critical Thinking

Making Comparisons Repeat for the class the Georgian poet's saying on page 307: "Three divine gifts have been bestowed on us by our ancestors: language, homeland, faith." Next, direct the students to make charts with language, homeland, and faith across the top of the page and the names of the ethnic groups from the section along the left side. Suggest that they draw lines to create columns under the heads and rows next to the names. Then, have students fill the spaces with the names of language families, countries, and religions. When the students have completed their charts, ask them to predict which groups get along and which have conflicts.

Geographic Themes

Place: Armenia

Armenians gather at a monument to remember the millions of their people who perished in the 1915 Holocaust at the hands of the Ottoman Turks. *What is the capital of the republic of Armenia?*

live, and where the population is most dense. The majority of the large cities and major industrial centers are located in this area, including the three largest cities of the region—Moscow, St. Petersburg, and Kiev. The climate of this western part is the most moderate and cooperative, and here the richest and most fertile farmland lies.

A great many cities dot Russia and the Eurasian republics, especially in the western part. Many cities originally grew up along major rivers because even during the coldest part of the year people and goods could move along them. Even today, all three of the largest cities are linked to major waterways through rivers and canals. In the Caucasus region, the Armenian capital of Yerevan is located on the banks of the Razdan River in the Ararat Valley.

SECTION 1 REVIEW

Checking for Understanding

1. **Define** ethnic group, nationalities.
2. **Locating Places** In what part of the region is population the most dense?
3. **Region** What are three major ethnic groups of Russia and the Eurasian republics?
4. **Place** What are the three largest cities in Russia and the Eurasian republics?

Critical Thinking

5. **Drawing Conclusions** Why are some areas of Russia and the Eurasian republics more densely populated than others?

ANSWERS TO SECTION 1 REVIEW

1. **ethnic group:** group of people with its own unique heritage, customs, beliefs, and language; **nationalities:** ethnic groups on which Russia and the Eurasian republics' political boundaries are based.
2. west of the Ural Mountains, between the Baltic and Black seas
3. Slavs, Turkic peoples, and Caucasian peoples
4. Moscow, St. Petersburg, and Kiev
5. Answers will vary but should indicate that people settled in areas that had moderate climates, good soil, and access to waterways.

EVALUATE

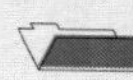

Assign the Section 1 Quiz in the TCR.

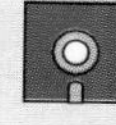

Use the Testmaker to create a customized quiz for Section 1.

RETEACH

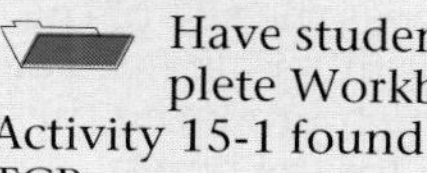

Have students complete Workbook Activity 15-1 found in the TCR.

ENRICH

Have students research a nearby Eastern Orthodox church and later have them write essays comparing it with other places of worship in the community.

CLOSE

Have students write a postcard to Anton telling him about their school.

USING ILLUSTRATIONS

REGION Knowledge of Turkish inhumanity was widespread. The United States formally protested the massacres of Armenians in 1916.

Answer to Caption: Yerevan

NATIONAL GEOGRAPHIC SOCIETY

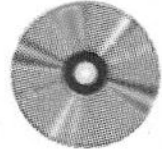

Videodisc

STV: WORLD GEOGRAPHY, VOLUME 1

Side 1, Chapter 1
Frames 13631-17712
Title: *Asia*
Subject: Interior and North Asia

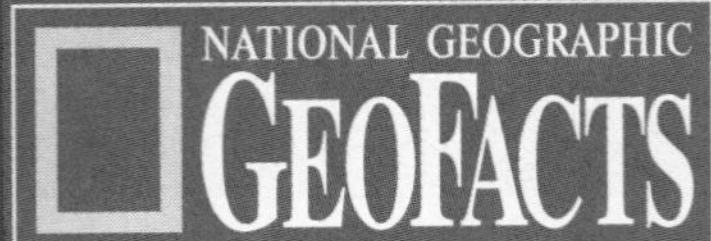

TEACH

According to the *Environmental Almanac* compiled by the World Resources Institute, the most contaminated site in the United States is the Hanford Plant in Hanford, Washington. This plant was the site of the world's first full-scale nuclear reactor, which produced the plutonium for the bomb dropped on Nagasaki, Japan, on August 9, 1945. More than half of the nation's nuclear wastes are stored at the Hanford Plant. The cost of cleaning up the nuclear waste there is estimated to be at least $57 billion.

Have students research the human and environmental problems caused by the reactors at the Hanford Plant as well as at plants at Savannah River near Aiken, South Carolina; Idaho National Engineering Laboratory near Idaho Falls, Idaho; and Fernald near Cincinnati, Ohio.

NATIONAL GEOGRAPHIC GEOFACTS

Where is the most polluted place on earth?

The shore of a small lake in Russia's heavily industrialized Ural Mountains is considered the most contaminated spot in the world. "No place else on earth can you just stand, and get a lethal dose in an hour," says American physicist Thomas B. Cochran of the Natural Resources Defense Council. A dose of radiation from Lake Karachay would kill a person within weeks.

In the early 1950s, the lake became the repository for radioactive wastes from the nearby nuclear-weapons production complex at Chelyabinsk. When the lake shrank in a 1967 drought, thousands were exposed to wind-borne radioactive dust.

The world's second most polluted place is also found in Russia, at Tomsk. Russian scientists recently disclosed that the former Soviet Union and now Russia have been pumping billions of gallons of radioactive liquid waste directly into the ground at three widely dispersed sites near rivers. The earth around the Tomsk and Krasnoyarsk sites probably contains more nuclear waste than the Karachay area, but is not as accessible or exposed.

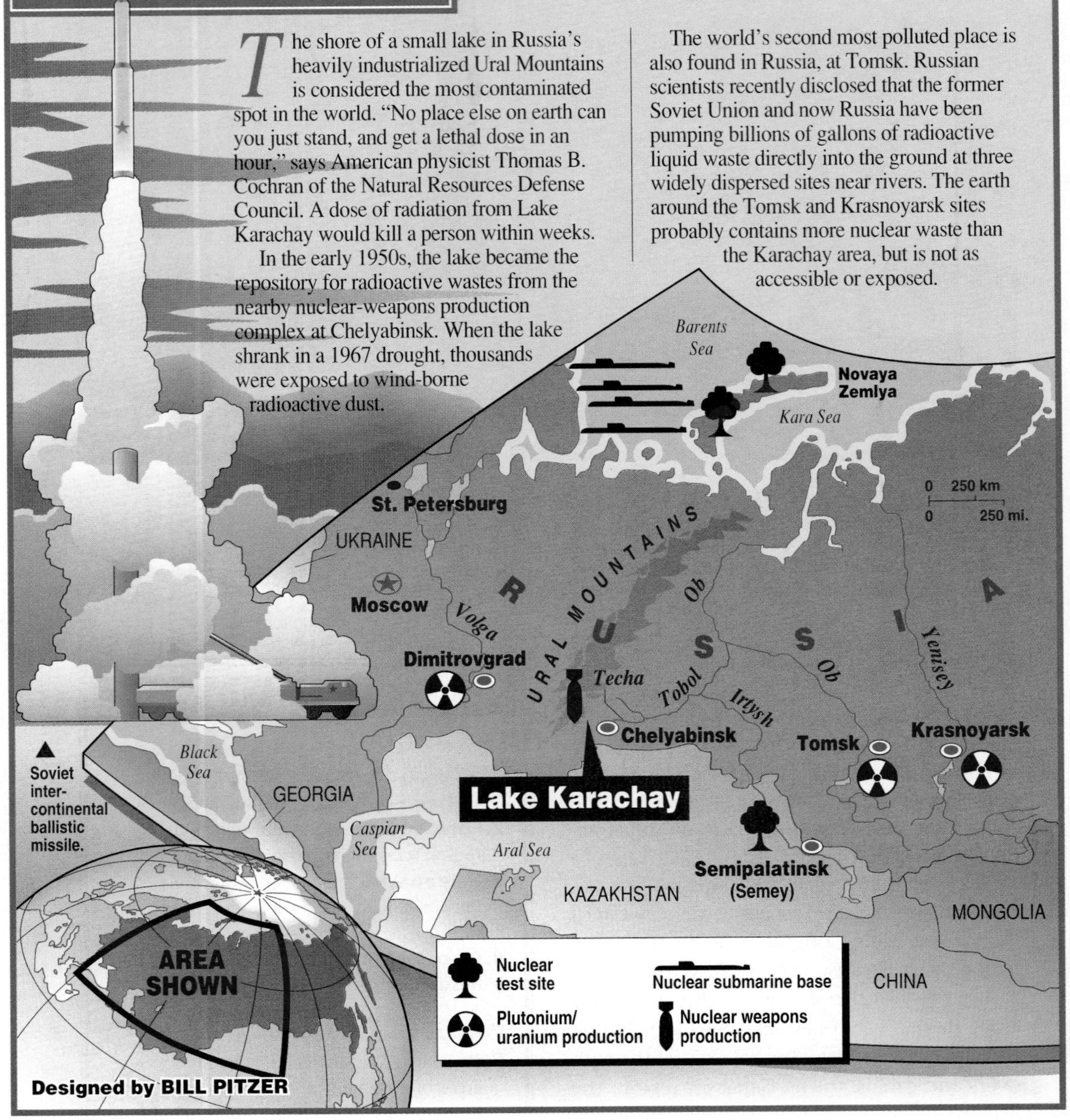

Barents Sea
Novaya Zemlya
Kara Sea
St. Petersburg
UKRAINE
Moscow
Volga
URAL MOUNTAINS
RUSSIA
Ob
Yenisey
Dimitrovgrad
Techa
Tobol
Irtysh
Chelyabinsk
Tomsk
Krasnoyarsk
Lake Karachay
Black Sea
GEORGIA
Caspian Sea
Aral Sea
KAZAKHSTAN
Semipalatinsk (Semey)
MONGOLIA
CHINA
0 250 km
0 250 mi.
Soviet intercontinental ballistic missile.
AREA SHOWN
Nuclear test site
Nuclear submarine base
Plutonium/uranium production
Nuclear weapons production

Designed by BILL PITZER

2 SECTION History and Government

SETTING THE SCENE

Read to Discover . . .
- the peoples who populated and created early Russia.
- the rule and power of the czars.
- the rise and fall of the Soviet Union.
- the new independence of Russia and the Eurasian republics.

Key Terms
- czar
- serf
- socialism
- russification
- communism
- *perestroika*
- *glasnost*

Identify and Locate
Dnieper River, Baltic Sea, Volga River, Caspian Sea, Kiev, Moskva River, Moscow, Siberia, St. Petersburg

Russia and the Eurasian republics have a long history as rich and diverse as the land and the peoples who occupy it. Over thousands of years, different peoples have come and gone. Each has left its mark on the land, and each, in turn, was influenced by the land, the climate, and the environment.

MOVEMENT

Early Peoples and States

In ancient times, people were living in and farming much of the land that is now Russia and the Eurasian republics. Over time, different groups came and went. Some were hunters and gatherers, others were nomads, and still others were farmers. Said one Russian expert:

> *The picture we obtain from the written sources is that of a bewildering procession of tribes and nations which every few centuries succeed each other on the steppes, only to sweep each other off the map.*

River Settlers and Towns

Among the many groups who over the centuries cut through the mountain passes and crossed the valleys and plains of the region were Slavs, who came from the northernmost part of eastern Europe. Over time they spread throughout the western part of the region. Some settled near the Dnieper River, which was part of a chain of waterways that led to the Baltic Sea. Others settled near the Volga River, which was a trade route to the Caspian Sea. Before long the Slavs built trading towns along the rivers. These towns became links in a trade route that joined the Slavs with peoples in the Mediterranean, western Europe, and Scandinavia.

In the 800s, fierce warrior-traders from Scandinavia, called Varangians, settled near the Dnieper and the Volga. The area they settled became known as Kievan Rus. In time one of their leaders set up the first state in the region at Kiev, a trading town on the Dnieper.

By the 900s the Varangians had adopted the Slavs' language and many of their customs and had organized the trading towns into city-states. Before long the Slavs organized into a loose union in which each city-state was ruled by a prince. Kiev became the capital and its ruler the Grand Prince.

LESSON PLAN
Chapter 15, Section 2

FOCUS

SECTION OBJECTIVES

1. **Locate** the peoples who populated and created early Russia.
2. **Discuss** the rule and power of the czars.
3. **Examine** the rise and fall of the Soviet Union.
4. **Describe** the new independence of Russia and the Eurasian republics.

BELLRINGER MOTIVATIONAL ACTIVITY

Project the Section 2 Focus Transparency and have students answer the questions.

PRETEACHING VOCABULARY

Have students write meanings of *social* and *commune* on the chalkboard. Next, explain that the suffix *-ism* means "system or theory." Then have them combine the meanings of the words with the meaning of the suffix and predict whether the combinations come close to the definitions of socialism and communism in the section.

Classroom Resources for Section 2

BLACKLINE MASTERS:
Reproducible Lesson Plan 15-2
Guided Reading Activity 15-2
Workbook Activity 15-2
Outline Map Resource Book, p. 34
Section Quiz 15-2

TRANSPARENCIES:
Section Focus Transparency 15-2
Political Map Transparency 5
World Cultures Transparency 7

MULTIMEDIA:

Testmaker

TEACH

GUIDED PRACTICE

L1 Sequence On the chalkboard, list historical events from the section in random order. Then have volunteers number the events in the order that they happened.

L2 Debate Invite students to come up with arguments that Peter the Great, Joseph Stalin, and Boris Yeltsin might have used to defend their form of government. Have them present a debate and then ask the class to vote for the most convincing speaker.

USING ILLUSTRATIONS

PLACE The stone walls of the Kremlin reach 70 feet (21 meters) high and include 19 towers.

Answer to Caption: *Ivan III*

DID YOU KNOW?

The "mad monk" Rasputin was the only person who could control the hemophilia of Alexis—son of the last Russian czar, Nicholas II. As a result, Rasputin had considerable influence over the czarevich's parents as well as the government of Russia. His policies fueled discontent and hastened the czar's downfall.

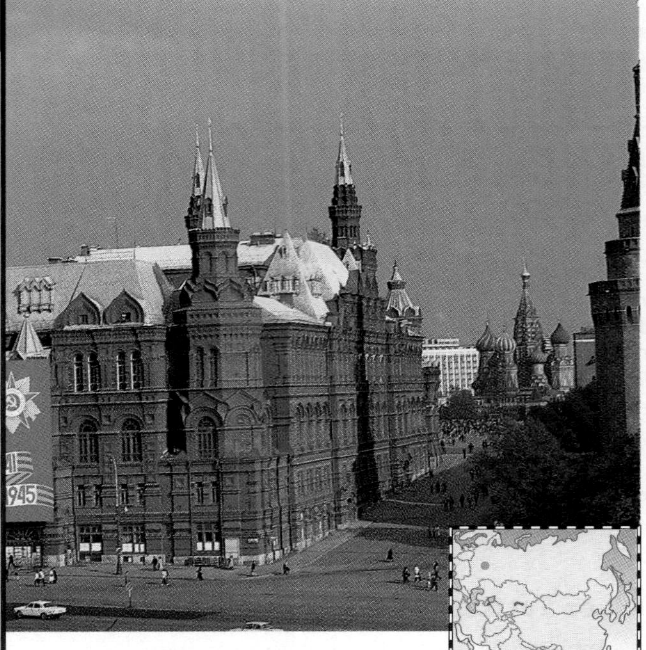

Geographic Themes

Place: Red Square, Moscow

Early Russian rulers built a huge fortress called the Kremlin in the heart of Moscow. It later became the seat of government and a religious center. *Who was the first Russian czar?*

Mongols

In the early 1200s warriors known as Mongols invaded from central Asia and destroyed Kiev. Ultimately they conquered much of the Slav territories and made them part of their vast empire. Although they allowed the Slavs self-rule, they continued to control the area for more than 200 years, cutting many of the Slavs off from European civilization.

When the Mongols first overran Kiev, many Slavs living there had fled into nearby forests. Later some of those people settled along the Moskva River. In time their settlement grew into the city of Moscow, known then as Muscovy (muh•SKOH•vee). For nearly two centuries, its princes kept peace with the Mongol rulers. Finally, in the 1400s, a Grand Prince of Muscovy named Ivan conquered other Slavic princes, set up a Russian state, and drove out the Mongols.

PLACE

The Rule of the Czars

Ivan became Ivan III, later known as Ivan the Great, the first **czar**, or supreme ruler, of all Russia. Moscow became the religious and political center of Russia.

In the late 1500s, Russia began to expand its territory and kept on expanding for the next several hundred years. With the new territories came new non-Russian peoples.

A Window to the West

Europeans had made many achievements. They moved forward and left Russia far behind, especially in scientific knowledge and technology. Then, in the late 1600s, Czar Peter I came to power determined to modernize Russia and make it into a European nation.

Peter made war to get some of the things he wanted. From Sweden, for example, he won the seaports he needed along the Baltic Sea to give his country access to major sea routes and increase its trade with northwest and Mediterranean Europe. His hard-won seaports could be used year-round.

Under Peter, who came to be known as Peter the Great, Russia's territory expanded, its naval strength increased, its trade multiplied, and a new capital city—St. Petersburg—was carved out of the wilderness. Built on land along the Gulf of Finland, St. Petersburg was Peter's "window to the West."

Seeds of Discontent

By the late 1800s, the Russian people were tired of war and resentful of the iron rule of the czars and their secret police. Peasants and **serfs**, laborers owned by nobles and bound to the land, lived in poverty and were treated like enslaved persons. The life of factory workers in the cities was not much better. Many thinkers were unhappy as well. They favored **socialism**, a philosophy that called for ownership of all land and factories by peasants and workers.

Cooperative Learning Activity

Distribute index cards and assign a different person or group from the section to each student. (If the section does not include enough names, obtain more from recent news reports about Russia and the Eurasian republics.) Instruct the students to write four clues to the identity of their group or person, including a clue to the person's or group's beliefs or values. After the students complete their cards, tell them to read their clues to other class members, who can score 4 points if they guess the name of the group or person on the first clue, 3 points if they guess correctly on the second clue, and so on. Have students keep track of their own points. After the students have asked their questions of one another, find out who earned the most points.

Geographic Themes

Place: St. Petersburg, Russia

During the 1700s and 1800s, Russian czars built beautiful palaces on the outskirts of St. Petersburg. *Why did Peter the Great move the capital from Moscow to St. Petersburg?*

Frustrated and discontented, many Russians took to heart the writings of a German philosopher, Karl Marx. He believed that in time the conflict between landowners and the working class would lead to a workers' revolution that would spread all over the world. Out of this revolution, he said, would arise a new, classless society.

The few reforms the czars made—freeing the serfs and promoting education—were not enough. To unify the people, the government began a program of **russification** that required everyone in the empire to speak Russian and to become Eastern Orthodox Christians. The policy only made matters worse.

World War I brought more hardship—and more protests. Food, clothing, fuel, weapons, and ammunition all were in short supply. Thousands of striking factory workers demanding "bread and freedom" overran the streets of Petrograd, previously St. Petersburg. After a few days, the government called in the army to end the demonstrations. Most of the soldiers, though, ended up joining the demonstrators. Finally, in March 1917, the czar abdicated, and the rule of the czars came to an end.

PLACE

The Soviet Era

The new government did not last. In November 1917, a group of revolutionaries known as Bolsheviks (BOHL•shuh•viks) took over the city of Petrograd and proclaimed a socialist revolution.

Birth of a New Nation

The Bolsheviks set up a new government headed by a revolutionary named Vladimir Ilyich Lenin. Lenin, whose political ideas were based on the teachings of Karl Marx, promised the Russian people "peace, land, and bread." His government withdrew from World War I, moved the capital back to Moscow, took control of industry and church property, and promised workers an eight-hour workday.

Not all Russians agreed with **communism,** the teachings of Marx and Lenin, and war soon broke out between the Bolsheviks—Reds—and anti-Bolsheviks—Whites. In 1921 the Bolsheviks, now known as Communists, won the war. The next year they established a new nation—the Union of Soviet Socialist Re-

Meeting Special Needs

Inefficient Readers Scanning a passage before reading can help students develop a time frame for events or ideas that are presented. Have students scan material under "The Soviet Era" for time markers such as the words "In November 1917 . . ." in the first paragraph. Other examples are "In 1921 . . ." in the third paragraph, "In the later 1920s . . ." in the fourth paragraph, "By the end of 1940, . . . " in the fifth paragraph, ". . . well into the 1980s" in the sixth paragraph, and "In 1985 . . ." in the seventh paragraph.

INDEPENDENT PRACTICE

Guided Reading Have students complete Guided Reading Activity 15-2 in the TCR. **LEP**

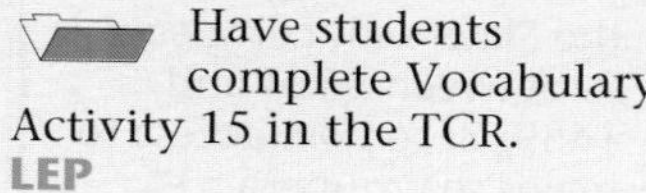

Have students complete Vocabulary Activity 15 in the TCR. **LEP**

L3 Research Have interested students research events that happened in other parts of the world at the same time as the events on the chalkboard in the sequencing activity under "Guided Practice." Ask that they record these on parallel time lines that cover two or three regions other than Russia and the Eurasian republics.

USING ILLUSTRATIONS

MOVEMENT Catherine the Great, a successor of Peter, admired French theories about equality. After the French Revolution, however, she persecuted the thinkers whose views she once espoused.

Answer to Caption: *to make the capital accessible to Europe*

ASSESS

CHECK FOR UNDERSTANDING

Assign Section 2 Review as homework or an in-class activity.

USING MAPS

Answers:
1. Slavic towns became links in a trade route that joined the Slavs with Europeans. **2.** between 1524 and 1689; **3.** to gain access to major sea routes and to increase trade

Map Skills Practice
Reading a Map To what important sea did Russians gain access between 1689 and 1917? *(the Black Sea)*

MEETING LESSON OBJECTIVES

Each objective below is tested by the questions that follow it in parentheses.
1. Locate the peoples who populated and created early Russia. *(2)*
2. Discuss the rule and power of the czars. *(3, 5)*
3. Examine the rise and fall of the Soviet Union. *(4)*
4. Describe the new independence of Russia and the Eurasian republics. *(1)*

EVALUATE

Assign the Section 2 Quiz in the TCR.

Use the Testmaker to create a customized quiz for Section 2.

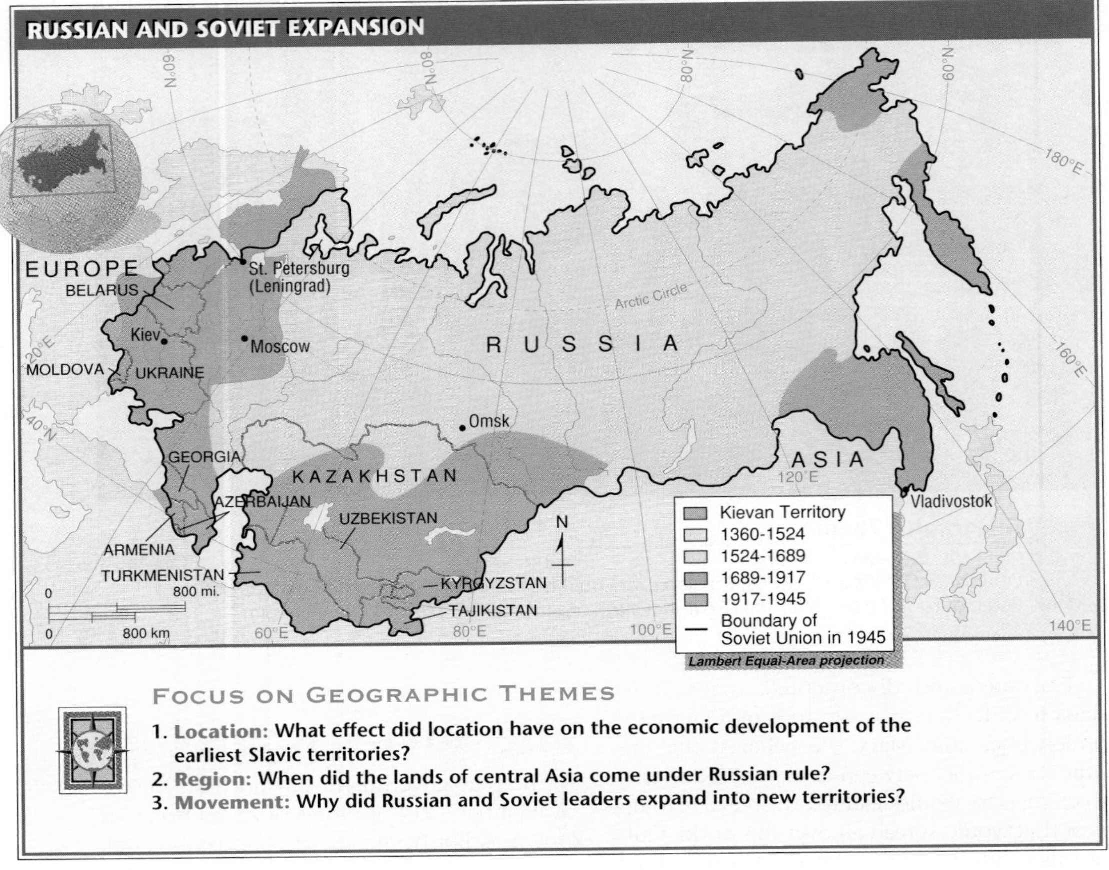

FOCUS ON GEOGRAPHIC THEMES

1. **Location:** What effect did location have on the economic development of the earliest Slavic territories?
2. **Region:** When did the lands of central Asia come under Russian rule?
3. **Movement:** Why did Russian and Soviet leaders expand into new territories?

publics (USSR), or Soviet Union. Made up of Russia, Ukraine, Byelorussia, and the Transcaucasus, its capital was Moscow.

Building and Expanding the Communist State

In the late 1920s a new leader, Joseph Stalin, came to power and set about making the Soviet Union one of the world's greatest industrial powers. To accomplish this goal, his government took control of industrial and farm production. Millions of people, however, died or were sent to labor camps as Stalin ruthlessly strengthened his hold over the country.

By the end of 1940, the Soviet Union was a nation of 15 republics. By the middle of the next year, the Soviets found themselves under attack by the Germans, caught in another world war. The war took more than 30 million Soviet lives, but the nation came out of it stronger than ever. The Soviets had expanded their territory and spread communism to eastern Europe.

Now a superpower in competition with the United States, the Soviet Union became involved in a cold war with non-Communist countries, a war in which it sought world influence by any means short of total war. The cold war continued well into the 1980s.

In 1985 a new leader, Mikhail Gorbachev, took power. He thought that the country could not survive without "restructuring," which he called ***perestroika*** (pehr•ehs•TROY•kah), and a new openness, or ***glasnost.*** Gorbachev's reforms were not enough.

Critical Thinking

Drawing Conclusions Tell the students that during Alexander II's reign, a revolutionary group of Nihilists advocated terrorism to speed the demise of Russian society so a new society could be built in its place. Another revolutionary group called *narodniks* urged the peasants to revolt. In 1856 Alexander II said: "Better to abolish serfdom from above than to wait till it begins to abolish itself from below." In 1861 he freed the serfs and offered them state loans to buy farms. Why did Alexander free the serfs? *(to avoid revolution)* What more might Alexander and his successors have done to prevent the eventual overthrow of the czar? *(Answers will vary but students may say that the czars could have given the people some say in their government.)*

REGION

New Republics

By 1990 many people were dissatisfied with the way communism was working. By the end of the year, the Baltic republics of Latvia, Lithuania, and Estonia had declared their independence, and all the other republics had declared some freedoms.

In the summer of 1991, the Soviet republic of Russia held its first democratic election for president. The new president, Boris Yeltsin, backed Gorbachev when some others turned against him and tried to strengthen the government, but it was too late to save the Soviet Union. By mid-December, all the republics had declared their independence.

Russia's Yeltsin met with the leaders of Ukraine and Belarus, and they announced that they had united to form a new community—the Commonwealth of Independent States (CIS)—in which each member republic was independent and had its own government and constitution. They invited all the other republics to join. By late December all the former Soviet republics except Latvia, Lithuania, Estonia, and Georgia had done so, making the CIS the largest federation of separate republics in the world. In 1992 Azerbaijan left the CIS, but later rejoined. Georgia also became a member. Today the Soviet Union and the cold war belong to the past, and the "new" republics are trying to come to terms with the changes brought by their independence.

In Russia, Yeltsin introduced economic reforms to move the economy toward free enterprise. A better future was promised to the Russian people; but in the short term, the reforms brought increased hardships. Taking advantage of widespread dissatisfaction, extreme nationalists and Communists tried to undermine Yeltsin, while Yeltsin sought to increase his powers.

In 1993 Yeltsin succeeded in blocking a Communist attempt to seize control of the government. A few months later, however, voters gave only partial support to Yeltsin. They approved a new constitution granting him sweeping powers, but many of them protested against reforms by electing anti-Yeltsin candidates—mostly extreme nationalists and Communists—to the Russian parliament. Analysts predicted continued political instability as Yeltsin and his parliamentary opponents competed for control of Russia.

Geographic Themes

Place: Moscow, Russia

After the collapse of the Soviet Union, Boris Yeltsin emerged as the leader of Russia. *What organization replaced the Soviet Union?*

Section 2 Review

Checking for Understanding

1. **Define** czar, serf, socialism, russification, communism, *perestroika, glasnost.*
2. **Locating Places** Where did the Slavs and Varangians settle?
3. **Movement** Why did Peter the Great want to acquire land along the Baltic Sea?
4. **Place** What did the Soviets gain from World War II?

Critical Thinking

5. **Expressing Problems Clearly** Why were most Russians discontented under czarist rule?

RETEACH

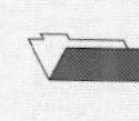

Have students complete Workbook Activity 15-2 found in the TCR.

ENRICH

Ask students why they agree or disagree with the following passage from Leo Tolstoy's *War and Peace:* "The subject of history is the life of peoples and of humanity. To catch and pin down in words—that is, to describe directly the life, not only of humanity, but even of a single people, appears to be impossible."

CLOSE

Ask students when and where in Russia and the Eurasian republics they would go if they could time-travel.

USING ILLUSTRATIONS

PLACE Strobe Talbott, a top Russia specialist, said that the large support for Yeltsin's foes in the 1993 election showed that Yeltsin stressed reforming the economy over improving the lives of Russians.

Answer to Caption: the Commonwealth of Independent States

ANSWERS TO SECTION 2 REVIEW

1. **czar:** supreme ruler of all Russia; **serf:** laborer bound to estates of wealthy landowners; **socialism:** philosophy that called for ownership of land and factories by peasants and workers; **russification:** czarist order requiring all people to speak Russian and become Christians; **communism:** teachings of Marx and Lenin; ***perestroika:*** Mikhail Gorbachev's name for the restructuring of the Soviet Union; ***glasnost:*** a new openness
2. near the Dnieper and Volga rivers
3. to give Russia access to major sea routes and trade with western Europe
4. the opportunity to expand their territory and to spread communism to eastern Europe
5. Most czars were harsh rulers and unwilling to make reforms; most people had few rights and little freedom.

Geography and History

The Unconquerable Russian Winter

As you read, examine how natural forces affected Napoleon's efforts to conquer Russia.

In the spring of 1812, French ruler Napoleon Bonaparte began an assault on Russia. Napoleon had signed an alliance with Russia's czar, Alexander I, in 1807. Alexander, however, had not stopped trade with Great Britain, as the pact demanded. Napoleon decided that Alexander needed to be taught a lesson.

Napoleon and his troops retreat from Moscow to face the long and bitter Russian winter.

To Moscow

Leading an army of more than 600,000, Napoleon crossed into Russia from Poland, over the Nieman River. The Russians, outnumbered 3 to 1, fought fiercely and retreated slowly, destroying anything that Napoleon might have used as supplies for his troops. Led deeper and deeper into Russia, Napoleon found his supply lines getting longer, thinner, and less reliable. It was also getting later in the year: winter was approaching.

Napoleon and his forces pursued the Russians all the way to Moscow. When he arrived, however, Napoleon found himself the conqueror of a burning, deserted ruin. The Russians had set fire to Moscow and relocated to St. Petersburg. It took the French army a month to stop the flames.

The Russian Winter Wins

During that month, Napoleon offered Czar Alexander a truce. However, the Russian winter had set in. Knowing the Russian winter as Napoleon did not, the czar refused.

The days grew colder; supplies dwindled. When Napoleon learned that thousands of his soldiers were suffering from frostbite and freezing to death, he ordered his troops to abandon Moscow.

During the retreat, the horrendous cold and blinding snowstorms of Russia's winter killed more than 90,000 of the 100,000 troops that left Moscow. A scant 9,000 straggled into Poland during the winter months. The Russian winter accomplished what Europe's leaders could not: Napoleon's defeat.

Checking for Understanding

1. **How did the Russians use the size of their country to defeat Napoleon?**
2. **Location How did Russia's location help defeat Napoleon?**

TEACH

Using the map on pages A14–A15, have students locate Napoleon's entrance point to Russia and figure the distance between that point and Moscow. Remind them that, while the distance may not seem great today, Napoleon did not have the support of modern war technology.

Have students also trace supply routes on the map on pages A12–A13 that Napoleon might have used to bring men and supplies from France.

Place What geographical feature protected Moscow from Napoleon's assault? *(its great distance from Napoleon's point of entry into Russia)*

Extending the Content

Napoleon Napoleon once stated his own vision of his military future: "The object of war is victory. The object of victory is conquest. And the object of conquest is occupation. When I see an empty throne, I feel the urge to sit on it."

When Napoleon attacked Russia, he controlled Spain, France, Italy, Switzerland, Germany, Austria, and Poland. To finance the wars that gave him these conquests, he had sold the Louisiana Territory to a fledgling United States in 1803.

ANSWERS TO CHECKING FOR UNDERSTANDING

1. Napoleon had hoped to conquer the Russians at or close to the Russian-Polish border. However, the Russians refused to surrender, even though badly outnumbered. They continued to fight, leading Napoleon's troops deeper and deeper into Russia, closer to Moscow, but farther and farther away from his main supply centers.

2. Russia lies much farther north than France or any other country that Napoleon ruled. He was unaware of, and unprepared for, the harshness of the Russian winter.

3 SECTION Cultures and Lifestyles

SETTING THE SCENE

Read to Discover . . .
- the religions practiced in Russia and the Eurasian republics.
- changes in education in Russia and the Eurasian republics.
- the arts of Russia and the Eurasian republics.
- life and leisure in Russia and the Eurasian republics.

Key Terms
- atheist
- icon
- patriarch
- pogrom
- socialist realism

Identify and Locate
Black Sea, Kiev, Baltic Sea, Belarus, Mtskheta, Yerevan, Amu Darya, Syr Darya, Crimea, Minsk, Chisinau, Moldova

For the more than 70 years that the Soviets were in power, they tried to convince the peoples of Russia and the Eurasian republics to abandon their religious beliefs. They made Russian the language of all the schools and worked to glorify communism. They influenced everything from the holidays celebrated to the quality of life. Now everything is different.

REGION

Religion

The Soviets thought that the peoples of the republics should be **atheists**, or nonbelievers, and closed down or destroyed many houses of worship. In 1988, when Mikhail Gorbachev allowed more religious freedom, people of all ages flocked to religious services. The religious revival has continued in the post-Communist era.

Christianity

Many people who practice a religion in Russia and the Eurasian republics practice some form of Christianity. Although some Christians are Protestant or Roman Catholic, most belong to the Eastern Orthodox Church, which is made up of separate, self-governing churches. Most Russians, for example, are members of the Russian Orthodox Church, and most Ukrainians belong to the Ukrainian Orthodox Church. A cornerstone of both is the use of **icons**, or intricate religious images, many of which are hundreds of years old.

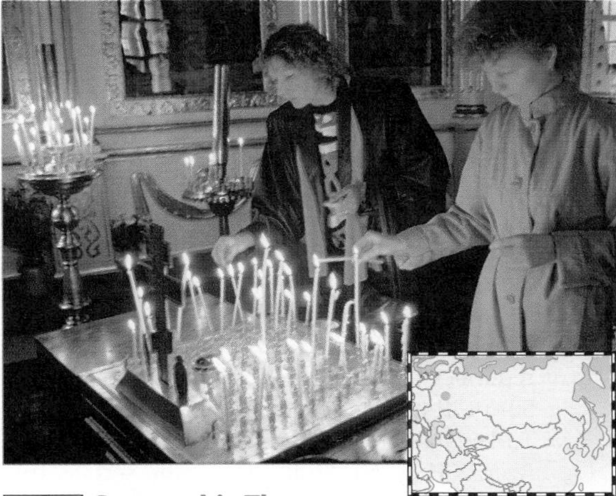

Geographic Themes
Place: Moscow, Russia
Russian Orthodox worshippers pray in one of Moscow's newly restored churches. *What art form plays an important role in Russian and Ukrainian Orthodox worship?*

LESSON PLAN
Chapter 15, Section 3

FOCUS

SECTION OBJECTIVES

1. **Name** the religions practiced in Russia and the Eurasian republics.
2. **Cite** changes in education in Russia and the Eurasian republics.
3. **Appreciate** the arts of Russia and the Eurasian republics.
4. **Characterize** life and leisure in Russia and the Eurasian republics.

BELLRINGER MOTIVATIONAL ACTIVITY

Project the Section 3 Focus Transparency and have students answer the questions.

USING ILLUSTRATIONS

PLACE Examples of grand churches in the region are Santa Sophia in Kiev and the Cathedral of St. Basil in Moscow.

Answer to Caption: *icons*

DID YOU KNOW?

The oldest known chess pieces—from the second century A.D.—were found in the region of Russia and the Eurasian republics.

Classroom Resources for Section 3

BLACKLINE MASTERS:
Reproducible Lesson Plan 15-3
Guided Reading Activity 15-3
Workbook Activity 15-3
World Literature Reading 4
Skill Activity 15
Section Quiz 15-3

TRANSPARENCIES:
World Cultures Transparency 8

MULTIMEDIA:

Testmaker

World Music: *Cultural Traditions, Lesson 4*

Picture Atlas of the World

PRETEACHING VOCABULARY

Ask students what *icon* means in computer jargon. Then tell them to read the section to find out the word's meaning to Eastern Orthodox Christians.

TEACH

GUIDED PRACTICE

L1 Compare In one column on a sheet of paper, have each student describe education under the Soviet government in Ukraine, Moldova, and Azerbaijan. In a second column, have them describe the changes the new independent governments have made.

USING GRAPHS

Skills Practice

How many more Christians than Muslims live in Russia and the Eurasian republics? *(twice as many or 50,498,000 more)*

DID YOU KNOW?

Directors Tarkovsky, Hutseev, and Dovzhenko made great movies despite Soviet restrictions on the arts, but the best known Soviet director was Sergei Eisenstein. His 1925 silent film *Potemkin* is a classic.

CD-ROM

PICTURE ATLAS OF THE WORLD

Hear the various languages of Russia and the Eurasian republics by clicking the "Speech" button of selected countries in the Asia region.

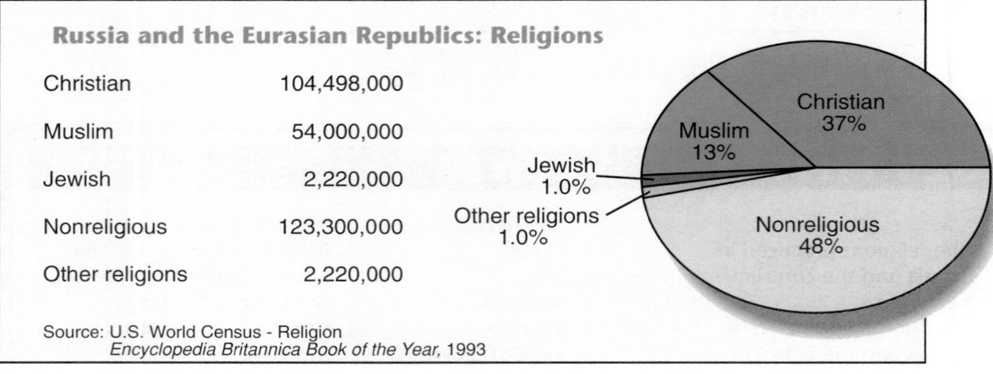

Russia and the Eurasian Republics: Religions

Religion	Number
Christian	104,498,000
Muslim	54,000,000
Jewish	2,220,000
Nonreligious	123,300,000
Other religions	2,220,000

Source: U.S. World Census - Religion
Encyclopedia Britannica Book of the Year, 1993

Two other republics, Georgia and Armenia, have strong national churches whose membership grew even under Soviet rule. The center of Georgian Orthodoxy is Sveti Tskhoveli, the Pillar of Life church in Mtskheta, still in use today. Most Armenians, both in Armenia and in neighboring Azerbaijan, belong to the Armenian Apostolic Church. Although its rites are similar to Eastern Orthodox rites, the Armenian Church was founded in the 300s. Like Eastern Orthodox churches, it has a leader called a **patriarch.** The patriarch lives in a monastery not far from the Armenian capital of Yerevan.

Islam

Islam has the second-largest number of followers in the region. Most Muslims live in the central Asian republics of Tajikistan, Uzbekistan, Turkmenistan, and Kyrgyzstan. Together the republics of the region have a Muslim population of 54 million. Most Kazakhs and Azeris also are Muslims. So are most people in the area of Ukraine called the Crimea.

Most Muslims in Russia and the Eurasian republics belong to a sect of Islam known as Sunni, the same sect as those of Saudi Arabia, Turkey, and Afghanistan. An exception is the Azeris. They are Shiite, the same sect as the Muslims of Iran.

Judaism

Over many centuries the Jews in the region suffered from prejudice and discrimination. In czarist Russia Jews were allowed to settle only certain areas, and they were often the target of organized persecution and massacres known as **pogroms.** This persecution continued under the Soviets and became particularly brutal when the invading Nazis shipped hundreds of thousands of Jews to death camps.

In recent years large numbers of Jews have been emigrating, often to Israel or the United States. Some, however, have fought hard to keep their religious and cultural identity and want to stay where they are.

PLACE

Education

The region's literacy rate is extremely high. This high rate is largely the result of the former Soviet rulers' emphasis on free education from grade school through college and the requirement that all children go to school for at least 10 years.

The Soviet Legacy

After independence the republics faced some education-related problems that they have been working to resolve. Most textbooks, for example, must be replaced because they are outdated and were written from the Soviet Communist point of view. Some of the schools need repairs. Others do not have plumbing or running water. Many are short of supplies, especially modern equipment like computers.

Cooperative Learning Activity

Organize the class into groups and give each group a copy of the following brain teaser:

D E
A B C

1. The composer of *Swan Lake* is next to B.
2. Fyodor Dostoyevsky, the author of *Crime and Punishment*, is also next to B.
3. The composer to the left of Tchaikovsky wrote the opera *Boris Godunov.*
4. The exiled author who refused to adopt socialist realism is to the right of Anton Chekhov, the author of *Three Sisters.*

Which name goes with each letter? *(A—Fyodor Dostoyevsky, B—Modest Mussorgsky, C—Peter Tchaikovsky, D—Anton Chekov, E—Aleksandr Solzhenitsyn)* The first group to figure out the correct answers wins.

As under the Soviets, there are several different kinds of schools students can attend. Vocational schools teach skills such as plumbing or carpentry; technical schools prepare students for jobs in areas like medicine or teaching; and some schools offer courses in farming or language skills. Which kind of high school a student goes to depends on how well he or she does on a national exam that every student must take at the end of ninth grade.

Local and Regional Needs

Since becoming independent, most republics have been making changes that reflect their own local and regional needs. Ukraine, for example, revised the courses taught and made Ukrainian—instead of Russian—the language of the classroom. Children now start school when they are 6 years old and cannot quit until they have finished the ninth grade. High school graduates may go on to a vocational school, an institute, or a university.

Moldova, where most of the people are of Romanian heritage, has taken steps to reverse Soviet efforts to stifle Romanian culture. The Soviets, for example, did not allow the Romanian language to be used in the schools, and gave Russian and Ukrainian students in Moldova first choice of institutions of higher education. Now Romanian is the language of the schools, and the Moldovan educational system has close ties with the Romanian one.

Armenia's leaders also have been reforming their educational system. In Armenia most children start school when they are 6 years old. The government has opened many elementary schools, but there is still a shortage of high schools. Students do not have to pay for their university education, but there is not enough space for every student. Only those who pass difficult exams are admitted.

In Azerbaijan, where there are thousands of elementary and high schools and more than a dozen institutions of higher learning, religion has been returned to the schools. Copies of the Quran, the holy text of Islam, have been provided by some countries in Southwest Asia. Iran is even sending Islamic teachers to provide religious instruction.

REGION

The Arts

Russia and the Eurasian republics have a strong cultural tradition that dates back to times long past. The modern governments are attempting to encourage the arts as symbols of national pride.

The Golden Years

The truly golden age of culture—a time when Russian painters, musicians, composers, and writers created works recognized and admired all over the world—was the 1800s and early 1900s.

During this period, Russian painters like Ilya Repin and Isaak Levitan used their talents not only to portray historical and contemporary scenes but also the beauty of the Russian countryside. In the early 1900s, Kasimir Malevich, Wasily Kandinsky, and other artists contributed to the rise of modern art. Meanwhile, Russian composers produced outstanding

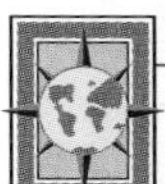

Geographic Themes

Human/Environment Interaction: Fabergé Egg Russia's most famous jeweler, Carl Fabergé, crafted a series of these elaborate eggs from gold, silver, enamel, and precious stones. *When was Russia's golden age of culture?*

INDEPENDENT PRACTICE

Guided Reading Have students complete Guided Reading Activity 15-3 in the TCR. **LEP**

Have students complete World Cultures Transparency 8 Activity in the TCR.

Have students complete World Literature Reading 4 in the TCR.

USING ILLUSTRATIONS

PLACE One of Fabergé's most remarkable works was a tiny gold clockwork model of the Trans-Siberian Express. The passenger cars had crystal windows and the engine's headlight was a ruby. The whole train was housed in a gold egg engraved with a map of the railroad.

Answer to Caption: *in the 1800s and early 1900s*

CURRICULUM CONNECTION

MUSIC

In 1936 Russian composer Sergey Prokofiev wrote **Peter and the Wolf*****—a fairy tale for a narrator and an orchestra—to instruct children how to identify instruments by their sound.***

DID YOU KNOW?

Under Soviet rule, the government required people to attend parades on May Day to show their solidarity as Communists. Russians still observe the holiday but attendance is now optional.

Meeting Special Needs

Superficial Readers Transition words and key words in the text help focus readers' attention. Students who read superficially often need help to notice these "markers." Have students skim the material under the subhead "Local and Regional Needs" with you as you point to these words: "Since," "for example," and "Now." Discuss the use of these words and the kind of information students might expect to follow such words. Have students skim the material under "The Golden Years" to find other transition or key words.

USING ILLUSTRATIONS

REGION The Uzbeks' history includes conquests by the Mongols in 1220 and by the Russians in the 1800s.

Answer to Caption: *because the new governments espouse freedom and individual enterprise*

USING ILLUSTRATIONS

PLACE Russian artist Marc Chagall depicted his village of Vitebsk in pictures such as "Maternity."

Answer to Caption: *They punished artists who did not go along with socialist realism.*

ASSESS

CHECK FOR UNDERSTANDING

Assign Section 3 Review as homework or an in-class activity.

MEETING LESSON OBJECTIVES

Each objective below is tested by the questions that follow it in parentheses.

1. **Name** the religions practiced in Russia and the Eurasian republics. *(2)*
2. **Cite** changes in education in Russia and the Eurasian republics. *(4)*
3. **Appreciate** the arts of Russia and the Eurasian republics. *(5)*
4. **Characterize** life and leisure in Russia and the Eurasian republics. *(5)*

Geographic Themes

Region: Central Asia

The people of Uzbekistan in central Asia enliven their festivities with traditional folk dancing. *Why do modern governments encourage the arts?*

musical works. Peter Tchaikovsky composed the dramatic *1812 Overture,* the light and playful *Nutcracker Suite,* and the romantic *Swan Lake* and *Sleeping Beauty;* Nikolay Rimsky-Korsakov wrote many of his symphonies and ballets; and Modest Mussorgsky composed the opera *Boris Godunov.*

Above all, this was an age of great Russian and Ukrainian writers who rank among the best in the history of world literature—Leo Tolstoy, Fyodor Dostoyevsky, Anton Chekhov, Ivan Turgenev, Alexander Pushkin, Nikolay Gogol, Maxim Gorky. Most wrote about the society, politics, and events of their times, mirroring both the extravagant life led by the rich and the sufferings of the poor.

Geographic Themes

Place: Outdoor Art Exhibit, St. Petersburg

Today Russian artists can freely paint and exhibit their works. *What was the artistic policy of Russia's former Communist leaders?*

Contemporary Times

The people kept their passion for culture in Soviet times, and artists of all kinds continued to contribute. The Soviet government, however, severely limited artistic freedom.

The government believed that a work of art had to agree with and praise everything Soviet and ignore any Soviet faults. Writers, painters, and other artists who did not go along with this type of art, known as **socialist realism,** were punished in a number of different ways. Alexander Solzhenitsyn, for example, was forced to leave the country because his books criticized the government.

When the Soviet Union ceased to exist, so did most of the restrictions on artists. Now artists in Russia and the Eurasian republics have the freedom to be artistic, to freely express, exhibit, and publish their ideas and beliefs.

Critical Thinking

Distinguishing Fact from Opinion On the chalkboard, copy the following quote by Alexander Solzhenitsyn: "Literature transmits incontrovertible condensed experience . . . from generation to generation. In this way literature becomes the living memory of a nation." Allow students to look up unfamiliar words and to rewrite the quote in their own words. Then ask if they can use American literature to prove Solzhenitsyn's statement. To help them, give examples such as *Innocents Abroad* by Mark Twain, *Uncle Tom's Cabin* by Harriet Beecher Stowe, *Look Homeward Angel* by Thomas Wolfe, *Grapes of Wrath* by John Steinbeck, and *Death in the Family* by James Agee. After the students list several titles, ask if the quote states a fact or an opinion. Have them give reasons for their answers.

REGION

Life and Leisure

During Soviet rule, the people of the region knew with some certainty what they could and could not do and what to expect or not expect. Whether they lived in the city or the countryside, lifestyle was controlled by the Soviet government.

Way of Life

Under the new regimes, many people in the rural areas still cling to traditional ways. Uzbeks, for example, use the same farming methods that their ancestors used hundreds of years ago.

In the cities, most people live in high-rise apartments, often under crowded conditions. Even though the Soviets built huge numbers of new apartments over the years, there still are not enough to go around, especially in the large cities.

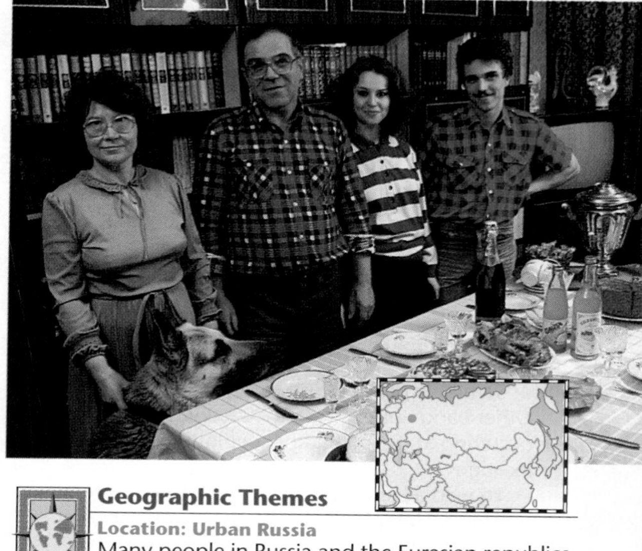

Geographic Themes

Location: Urban Russia
Many people in Russia and the Eurasian republics still have to cope with housing shortages. *In what kind of dwellings do most urban residents live?*

Leisure-time Activities

The people of Russia and the Eurasian republics enjoy many different activities during their free time, from watching television to playing chess in the park to going to a concert, a lecture, a seminar, the theater, or a movie. Almost everyone enjoys reading, especially now that they can buy books, magazines, and newspapers that the Soviets once banned.

Many people enjoy outdoor activities such as skiing, ice skating, hiking, camping, mountain climbing, and hunting. They also relish sports like soccer, ice hockey, and tennis.

Holidays and Celebrations

In most republics, families and friends enjoy celebrating holidays and other special occasions. During these festivities, they enjoy generous amounts of food and drink.

Holidays and celebrations are characterized by the blending of old folk practices with newer traditions. Most ethnic groups have their own traditional dances, costumes, and folk music, which are part of the festivities.

On May 1—May Day—when many nations traditionally celebrated the arrival of spring, people in the former Soviet Union celebrated the Communists and their achievements. Since independence, though, fireworks are set off, and people celebrate both the worker and the arrival of spring.

Section 3 Review

Checking for Understanding

1. **Define** atheist, icon, patriarch, pogrom, socialist realism.
2. **Locating Places** What are the major religions of Russia and the Eurasian republics?
3. **Place** In what ways did the Soviets restrict religious freedom?
4. **Place** What education-related problems do the Eurasian republics face?

Critical Thinking

5. **Making Generalizations** What generalization might you make about the role of the arts in Russia and the Eurasian republics?

EVALUATE

Assign the Section 3 Quiz in the TCR.

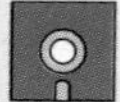
Use the Testmaker to create a customized quiz for Section 3.

USING ILLUSTRATIONS

LOCATION In urban apartments, a family of three or four often lives in one room.

Answer to Caption: *high-rise apartments*

RETEACH

Have students complete Reteaching Activity 15 in the TCR.

ENRICH

Have students complete Enrichment Activity 15 in the TCR.

CLOSE

Have students complete World Music: Cultural Traditions, Lesson 4 activity in the TCR.

CD-ROM

PICTURE ATLAS OF THE WORLD
View the Russian circus by clicking the "Video" button of Russia.

ANSWERS TO SECTION 3 REVIEW

1. **atheist:** nonbeliever; **icon:** intricate religious image; **patriarch:** leader of the Armenian Apostolic Church; **pogrom:** organized persecution and massacre of Jews; **socialist realism:** belief that a work of art had to agree with and praise everything Soviet
2. Christianity and Islam
3. They closed down or destroyed many houses of worship, and they persecuted Jews.
4. Most textbooks must be replaced because they are outdated, some schools need repairs, others do not have plumbing or running water, and many are short of supplies, especially modern equipment such as computers.
5. Answers will vary but should point out the continuing importance of the arts over the centuries despite limitations or restrictions placed on them.

Teaching Skills

TEACH

Have the class create a bar graph. Count the numbers of students with the following eye color: blue, brown, other. On the chalkboard, draw a bar graph, placing eye color labels along the horizontal axis (x-axis) and numbers of students on the vertical axis (y-axis). Identify the axes. Have volunteers draw each bar to its correct height. Ask: "What does this graph accomplish?" *(It compares various groups.)* Explain: "Bar graphs also compare the same group at different times." Use Graph A in the Chapter 15 skill as an example.

Skills Practice For additional practice, have students complete Skill Activity 15 in the TCR.

MAP & GRAPH SKILLS

Reading a Bar Graph

Graphs illustrate numerical data and relationships in a clear visual format. One of the most common ways to show statistical information is the **bar graph.**

REVIEWING THE SKILL

In a bar graph, bars of various lengths represent different quantities. The bars can be drawn vertically or horizontally. In either arrangement, labels on the two axes of the graph identify what the bars represent.

Some bar graphs illustrate changes over time. Other bar graphs compare measurements occurring at the same time, but in different locations.

To read a bar graph, apply the following steps:

- Read the graph title to identify the subject of the graph.
- Study the information presented on the horizontal and vertical axes and the use of colors on the graph.
- Compare the lengths of the bars and look for relationships among the data.

PRACTICING THE SKILL

Use the graphs below to answer the following questions:

1. In what year were the populations of Moldova and Tajikistan about equal?
2. In 1991, which country had a larger population?
3. According to Graph A, which country is growing more quickly?
4. Of the countries shown in Graph B, which country is growing most slowly? Which is growing most quickly?
5. In which countries does population grow at a rate of less than 1 percent each year?

For additional practice in this skill, see Practicing Skills on page 324 of the Chapter 15 Review.

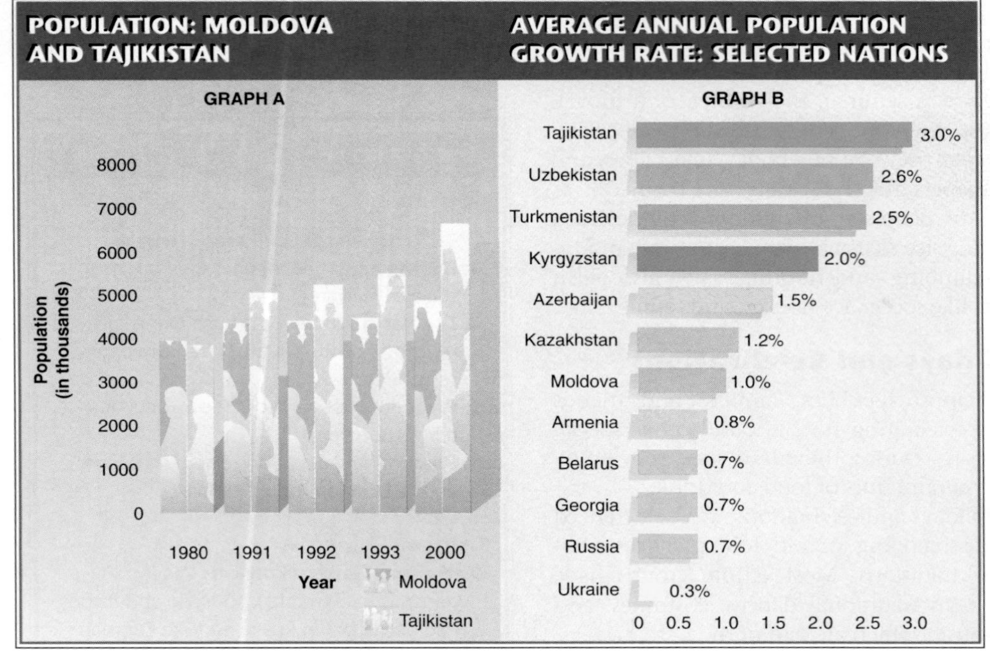

ANSWERS TO PRACTICING THE SKILL

1. 1980
2. Tajikistan
3. Tajikistan
4. Ukraine; Tajikistan
5. Ukraine, Russia, Georgia, Belarus, Armenia

chapter 15

HIGHLIGHTS

Section 1: Population Patterns

Key Terms

ethnic group (p. 305)
nationalities (p. 305)

Summary

- Both Russia and each of the Eurasian republics has its own official language.
- Three major ethnic groups—Slavs, Turkic peoples, and Caucasian peoples—live in Russia and the Eurasian republics.
- Population is not evenly distributed across Russia and the Eurasian republics.
- In the past most of the people of Russia and the Eurasian republics lived in the countryside; today they live in the city.

Panoramic view of Kiev, Ukraine

Section 2: History and Government

Key Terms

czar (p. 312)
serf (p. 312)
socialism (p. 312)
russification (p. 313)
communism (p. 313)
perestroika (p. 314)
glasnost (p. 314)

Summary

- The first Slavic state in the region grew out of the settlements of the Slavs and the Varangians.
- Under the czars, Russia became one of the largest empires in the world.
- In the early 1900s the Russian Empire became a new nation called the Union of Soviet Socialist Republics, which for more than 70 years was under Communist rule.
- All of the former republics of the Soviet Union, which ceased to exist in the early 1990s, are now independent states.

Moscow's Red Square and Kremlin

Section 3: Cultures and Lifestyles

Key Terms

atheist (p. 317)
icon (p. 317)
patriarch (p. 318)
pogrom (p. 318)
socialist realism (p. 320)

Summary

- The three major religions of Christianity, Islam, and Judaism, as well as a number of other faiths, are now practiced openly in Russia and the Eurasian republics.
- The people of Russia and the Eurasian republics have strong cultural traditions and are devoted to the arts. They have diverse lifestyles and enjoy a variety of different celebrations.

Folk dancers in central Asia

CHAPTER 15 HIGHLIGHTS

USING THE CHAPTER 15 HIGHLIGHTS

Use the Chapter 15 Highlights to preview, review, condense, or reteach the chapter.

PREVIEW/REVIEW

Vocabulary PuzzleMaker Software reinforces the Key Terms used in Chapter 15.

Student Self-Test and Review Software allows students to review Chapter 15 contents.

CONDENSE

Have students read the Chapter 15 Highlights.

Have students listen to the Chapter 15 Audiocassettes in the TCR. Spanish Audiocassettes are also available.

Assign the Chapter 15 Audiocassette Activity and give students the Chapter 15 Audiocassette Quiz.

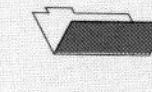 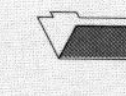

Have students complete the Guided Reading Activities for Chapter 15 in the TCR. Spanish Guided Reading Activities are also available.

RETEACH

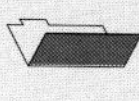

Have students complete Reteaching Activity 15 in the TCR.

Map Activity

Identify and Locate Distribute copies of page 34 of the Outline Map Resource Book. Using the Atlas maps at the beginning of the unit and maps from the chapter, have the students identify and label Russia and the Eurasian republics as well as the major cities mentioned in the chapter.

GLENCOE TECHNOLOGY

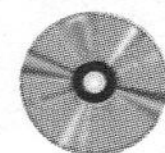

Videodisc

Use Chapter 15 MindJogger Videoquiz to review students' knowledge before administering the Chapter 15 Test.

MINDJOGGER VIDEOQUIZ

Chapter 15
Disc 2 Side B

The MindJogger Videoquiz is also available on videocassette.

ANSWERS

Reviewing Key Terms

1. nationalities
2. ethnic group
3. czar
4. socialism
5. *glasnost*
6. patriarch
7. pogroms

Reviewing Facts

8. Moldova
9. the republics of central Asia
10. Boris Yeltsin
11. Georgia
12. the Eastern Orthodox Church
13. the 1800s and early 1900s, when Russian painters, composers, and writers created works recognized and admired all over the world

chapter 15 REVIEW

Reviewing Key Terms

Choose the vocabulary term that best completes each of the sentences below. Write your answers on a separate sheet of paper.

ethnic group (p. 305)
nationalities (p. 305)
czar (p. 312)
socialism (p. 312)
glasnost (p. 314)
patriarch (p. 318)
pogroms (p. 318)

Section 1

1. Under the Soviets, republics were based on ____.
2. Slavs make up the largest ____ in Russia and the Eurasian republics.

Section 2

3. For more than 400 years the supreme ruler of all Russia was the ____.
4. The Bolsheviks believed in the philosophy of ____.
5. The new "openness" in the Soviet Union in the late 1980s was known as ____.

Section 3

6. The world leader of the Armenian Apostolic Church is called a ____.
7. The organized persecution and massacres suffered by Jews in czarist Russia are known as ____.

Reviewing Facts

Section 1

8. In which European republic are Slavs in the minority?
9. Where do most Turkic peoples of Russia and the Eurasian republics live?

Section 2

10. Who was Russia's first democratically elected president?
11. Which former Soviet republic did not become a member of the CIS?

Section 3

12. To what church do most Christians in the former Soviet Union belong?
13. To what does the phrase "Russia's golden age of culture" refer?

Critical Thinking

14. **Making Comparisons** What do Armenians and Georgians have in common? In what ways are they different?
15. **Analyzing Information** Explain why you agree or disagree with this statement: "The Soviet experience was 70 years on the road to nowhere."
16. **Making Comparisons** In what ways is education in Russia and the Eurasian republics like that in your town? In what ways is it different?

Geographic Themes

17. **Human/Environment Interaction** Where did many of the cities of Russia and the Eurasian republics originally develop?
18. **Place** How did the city of Moscow come into existence?
19. **Movement** What invasion disrupted Slavic links to Europe?

Practicing Skills

Reading a Bar Graph

Refer to the bar graphs on page 322. How does Graph B support the information presented in Graph A? In which sections of Russia and the Eurasian republics is the population growing most rapidly?

Critical Thinking

14. Both are Caucasian peoples, have their own alphabet, speak their own language, have been Christians since the fourth century. The Armenians migrated to the Caucasus many centuries ago while the Georgians probably came from there originally.

15. Answers will vary but should point out the advances made under communism as well as the calamities that occurred.

16. Answers will vary but should use textbooks, equipment, age of students, multiculturalism, and other aspects of education mentioned in the chapter as bases for comparison.

Using the Unit Atlas

Refer to the cultural geography section of the Unit Atlas on pages 284–285.

20. Why do so few people live in Siberia?
21. What central Asian cities were ancient crossroads of trade?
22. What is the second-largest group of people in Russia and the Eurasian republics?

Cooperative Learning Activity

Working in a group of five, have each member do research to determine what territory Russia acquired during one of these periods: 1400–1500, 1500–1600, 1600–1700, 1800–1900, 1900–1945. Then, as a group, using a different color to represent each period, construct a map showing Russian expansion.

Writing About Geography

Comparison

Select two capital cities, one in a republic west of the Ural Mountains and the other in a republic east of the Ural Mountains. Using your journal record and resources available in your school or public library, research both cities. Then write a one-page comparison of the two cities.

Projects

Individual Activity

Select one of the writers named in the chapter. Research the writer's life and then read one of his works. Then write a brief review of the work.

Locating Places

THE PHYSICAL GEOGRAPHY OF RUSSIA AND THE EURASIAN REPUBLICS

Match the letters on the map with the places and physical features of Russia and the Eurasian republics. Write your answers on a separate sheet of paper.

1. Black Sea
2. Moldova
3. Moscow
4. St. Petersburg
5. Kiev
6. Dnieper River
7. Baltic Sea
8. Yerevan
9. Yenisey River
10. Volga River

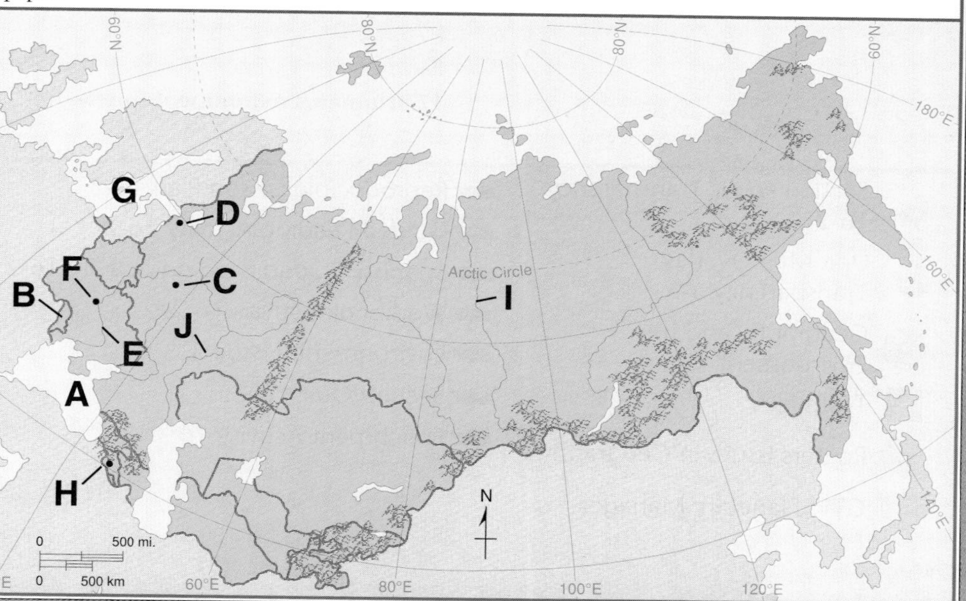

Chapter 15 Review

Geographic Themes

17. along major rivers

18. People who fled Kiev when the Mongols overran the city settled along the Moskva River, and Moscow grew out of the settlement.

19. the Mongol invasion from Central Asia

Practicing Skills

Graph B shows that Tajikistan has the highest population growth rate; this supports the projected population figures for the year 2000 shown in Graph A. Population growth is the most rapid in the Central Asian republics and most stable in the European republics.

Using the Unit Atlas

20. because of the cold climate

21. Tashkent, Samarkand, Khiva

22. the Kazakhs and the Kyrgyz

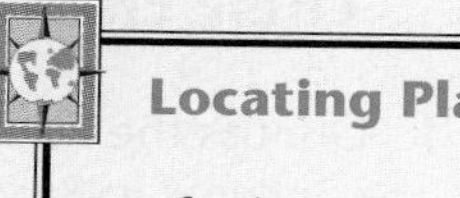

Locating Places

1. A
2. B
3. C
4. D
5. F
6. E
7. G
8. H
9. I
10. J

Chapter Bonus Test Question

This question may be used for extra credit on the chapter test.

Karl Marx wrote that "the theory of the Communists may be summed up in the single sentence: Abolition of private property." How did the government under Lenin and Stalin carry out this ideal?

(Answer: Lenin's government took control of industry and church property. Stalin's government took control of industrial and farm production.)

CHAPTER 16

PLANNING GUIDE

Russia and the Eurasian Republics Today

CHAPTER ORGANIZER

Daily Lesson Objectives	Multimedia	Teacher Classroom Resources
SECTION 1 Living in Russia and the Eurasian Republics 1. Describe the economies of Russia and the Eurasian republics before and after independence. 2. Compare agriculture and industry in Russia and the Eurasian republics before and after independence. 3. Examine the communication and transportation systems of Russia and the Eurasian republics. 4. Identify the economic ties that bind Russia and the Eurasian republics.	Section Focus Transparency 16-1 Chapter 16 Vocabulary PuzzleMaker Software Unit Map Overlay Transparency 5 Testmaker Picture Atlas of the World GTV: Planetary Manager Reuters Issues in Geography	Reproducible Lesson Plan 16-1 Guided Reading Activity 16-1 Spanish Guided Reading Activity 16-1 Workbook Activity 16-1 Performance Assessment Activity 16 Section Quiz 16-1
SECTION 2 People and Their Environment 1. Discuss the nuclear disaster and concerns in Russia and the Eurasian republics. 2. Specify environmental problems affecting some bodies of water in Russia and the Eurasian republics. 3. Analyze effects of industrial and pesticide pollution in Russia and the Eurasian republics.	Section Focus Transparency 16-2 Unit Map Overlay Transparency 5-5 Geography and the Environment Testmaker Reuters Issues in Geography GTV: Planetary Manager	Reproducible Lesson Plan 16-2 Guided Reading Activity 16-2 Spanish Guided Reading Activity 16-2 Workbook Activity 16-2 Environmental Issue 5 Section Quiz 16-2 Enrichment Activity 16
CHAPTER REVIEW AND EVALUATION	Chapter 16 English (or Spanish) Audiocassettes MindJogger Videoquiz Testmaker Student Self-Test and Review Software	Reteaching Activity 16 Spanish Reteaching Activity 16 Outline Map Resource Book, p. 34 Chapter 16 Test Form A and Form B

0:00 *If time does not permit teaching the entire chapter, summarize using the Chapter 16 Highlights on page 343, and Chapter 16 English (or Spanish) Audiocassettes. Review students' knowledge using the Glencoe MindJogger Videoquiz.*

KEY TO ABILITY LEVELS

Teaching strategies have been coded for varying learning styles and abilities.

L1 **BASIC** activities for all students

L2 **AVERAGE** activities for average to above-average students

L3 **CHALLENGING** activities for above-average students

LEP **LIMITED ENGLISH PROFICIENCY** activities

Performance Assessment

Portfolios Students should continue adding news articles about change in Russia and the Eurasian republics to their individual portfolios. The data for Chapter 16 should focus on economic and environmental concerns. At the end of the chapter, students should be provided time to fill in needed information. Each student should be paired with a partner to select ten items that they would like to remain in their portfolios for assessment. The criteria for choosing the items should be (a.) items that show a comprehensive view of change throughout the entire region and reflect all relevant areas of geographic study; (b.) specific examples of dramatic change; and (c.) developments that may indicate further change in the future. Students should conclude by writing an essay on change in the region, supporting conclusions with information from the chapters and their portfolios.

POSSIBLE RUBRIC FEATURES: Content information, portfolio organization and contents, evaluation and summarization skills, collaboration skills, relevance of research, written communication skills

For additional professional and classroom resources, see Chapter Resources, pages T46–T51.

TEACHER'S CORNER

NATIONAL GEOGRAPHIC SOCIETY

INDEX TO NATIONAL GEOGRAPHIC MAGAZINE

The following articles may be used for research relating to this chapter:

- "Chernobyl: Living With the Monster," by Mike Edwards, August 1994.
- "Lethal Legacy: Pollution in the Former U.S.S.R.," by Mike Edwards, August 1994.
- "Hard Harvest on the Bering Sea," by Bryan Hodgson, October 1992.
- "The Aral: A Soviet Sea Lies Dying," by William S. Ellis, February 1990.
- "Living With Radiation," by Charles E. Cobb, Jr., August 1989.
- "Chernobyl—One Year After," by Mike Edwards, May 1987.

NATIONAL GEOGRAPHIC SOCIETY PRODUCTS AVAILABLE FROM GLENCOE

To order the following products for use with this chapter, contact your local Glencoe sales representative or call Glencoe at 1-800-334-7344:

- *Picture Atlas of the World* (CD-ROM)
- *STV: World Geography, Asia and Australia* (Videodisc)
- *ZipZapMap! World* (Software)
- *GeoBee* (Software)
- *Images of the World* (Posters)
- *Eye on the Environment* (Posters)
- *Physical Geography of the World* (Transparencies)
- *Picture Atlas of Our 50 States* (Book)

Introducing CHAPTER 16

PERFORMANCE ASSESSMENT

Refer to the Planning Guide on page 326B for a Performance Assessment Activity for this chapter. See the *Performance Assessment Activities* booklet for additional suggestions.

CHAPTER OBJECTIVES

1. **Understand** that Russia and the Eurasian republics are moving toward various free enterprise economies.
2. **Recognize** that pollution is a matter of great concern throughout Russia and the Eurasian republics.

GLENCOE TECHNOLOGY

Videodisc

Use Chapter 16 MindJogger Videoquiz to preview chapter content.

MINDJOGGER VIDEOQUIZ

Chapter 16
Disc 2 Side B

The MindJogger Videoquiz is also available on videocassette.

CD-ROM

PICTURE ATLAS OF THE WORLD

You and your students can find economic and population figures for Russia and the Eurasian republics by clicking the "Stats" button of selected countries.

chapter 16 Russia and the Eurasian Republics Today

CHAPTER FOCUS

Geographic Setting

Most of the heavy industry of Russia and the Eurasian republics is located north of the Black Sea and in the Ural Mountains, where energy resources and raw materials are readily available.

Geographic Themes

Section 1 Living in Russia and the Eurasian Republics

PLACE Russia and the Eurasian republics are trying to move away from the single, centrally controlled economy to various free enterprise economies.

Section 2 People and Their Environment

HUMAN/ENVIRONMENT INTERACTION The badly damaged and heavily polluted environment is a matter of great concern throughout Russia and the Eurasian republics.

▲ Photograph: *Street vendors in Bukhara, Uzbekistan*

EXTRA CREDIT PROJECT

Board Game Have interested students create a board game that could help people from Russia and the Eurasian republics learn about capitalism. Suggest that students call the game "Capital Pursuit."

They can make up questions similar to these: What Scot arrived in Pittsburgh at age 13, started work at $1.20 a week, and ended up earning $25 million a year as head of his own steel company? *(Andrew Carnegie)* What law states that when the price of a product increases, its manufacturer increases production? *(law of supply)*

Refer students to history and economics textbooks for facts about capitalism. They can write the question on one side of a card and the answer on the other side.

1 SECTION

Living in Russia and the Eurasian Republics

SETTING THE SCENE

Read to Discover . . .

- how the economies of Russia and the Eurasian republics changed after independence.
- how agriculture and industry in Russia and the Eurasian republics changed after independence.
- how the communication and transportation systems of Russia and the Eurasian republics work.
- what economic ties bind Russia and the Eurasian republics.

Key Terms

- command economy
- consumer goods
- black market
- market economy
- *sovkhozes*
- *kolkhozes*

Identify and Locate

Kazakhstan, Baku, Baltic Sea, White Sea, Don River, Black Sea, Vladivostok, Lake Baikal, Amur River, Polotsk, Mozyr, Tbilisi

Fergana, Uzbekistan

Dobry dyen, I am writing to you from my summer house in the mountains. It is cool up here, even when it is hot down in the valley. Yesterday we had a picnic by a beautiful waterfall. The water comes from a large glacier on the mountain and flows down into the valley. Please come visit me sometime.

Your friend,
Tatyana Yeremenko

УЗБЕКИСТОН 1993 UZBEKISTAN 5'00 Remiz pendulinus

Tatyana Yeremenko writes from Uzbekistan, a Eurasian republic that relies on irrigation for its productive agriculture. For many decades, the economies of Russia, Uzbekistan, Ukraine, and the other Eurasian republics were in the hands of the Soviets. The Soviets ran their vast nation as a single economy, one of the largest centrally planned economies in the world. Today, however, each republic is moving at its own rate, trying to make its own way, and struggling to develop its own separate economic path.

REGION

Changing Economies

As Russia and the Eurasian republics make the transition to generally free enterprise economies, they must meet the challenges of providing sufficient food and jobs for their citizens. They must also compete successfully in world markets by producing goods efficiently and cost-effectively.

LESSON PLAN
Chapter 16, Section 1

FOCUS

SECTION OBJECTIVES

1. **Describe** the economies of Russia and the Eurasian republics before and after independence.
2. **Compare** agriculture and industry in Russia and the Eurasian republics before and after independence.
3. **Examine** the communication and transportation systems of Russia and the Eurasian republics.
4. **Identify** the economic ties that bind Russia and the Eurasian republics.

ABOUT THE POSTCARD

Tatyana buys grapes and watermelon for her picnics at the farmers' market in town.

BELLRINGER MOTIVATIONAL ACTIVITY

Project the Section 1 Focus Transparency and have students answer the questions.

PRETEACHING VOCABULARY

Read the definitions of *command economy* and *market economy*. Ask students which describes the United States economy. *(market economy)*

Use the Vocabulary PuzzleMaker Software to create a crossword or word search puzzle.

Classroom Resources for Section 1

BLACKLINE MASTERS:
Reproducible Lesson Plan 16-1
Guided Reading Activity 16-1
Spanish Guided Reading Activity 16-1
Workbook Activity 16-1
Performance Assessment Activity 16
Section Quiz 16-1

TRANSPARENCIES:
Section Focus Transparency 16-1
Unit Map Overlay Transparency 5

MULTIMEDIA:

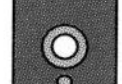

Vocabulary PuzzleMaker Software
Testmaker

Picture Atlas of the World

GTV: Planetary Manager
Reuters Issues in Geography

TEACH

GUIDED PRACTICE

L1 Describe On the chalkboard, write "In the Soviet economy . . . " to the left and "In the new economies . . . " to the right. Ask students to use details from page 328 to finish these sentences, describing the economies before and after independence. Have volunteers write their sentence endings under the appropriate headings.

L1 Compare Have students write phrases that describe *sovkhozes* and *kolkhozes* on the chalkboard. (Examples: "state-owned and run," "machinery belongs to the government," "workers paid for items produced") Then ask students to match each phrase with one that describes a similar aspect of American farming.

USING ILLUSTRATIONS

PLACE Prices in Russia and the Eurasian republics may seem low to us. In 1993 Moscow shoppers paid 36 cents for a half pound of butter. However, Russians at the poverty level earn only $14 a month.

Answer to Caption: *They had to do without things or pay high prices on the black market.*

Geographic Themes

Place: Minsk, Belarus

Belarusian shoppers make purchases in a Minsk department store. *During the Soviet period, what problems did shoppers face in finding food or clothing?*

The Soviet Command Economy

Under the Soviets, Russia and the Eurasian republics had what is known as a **command economy**, an economy in which some central authority makes economic decisions. The Soviet government owned most of the banks, factories, land, mines, and transportation systems. It decided what and how much to produce, how to go about producing, and who would benefit. It also planned and controlled the distribution and pricing of most goods.

Most people worked for the state. While there was no unemployment, no one was paid very much. The government's main concern was heavy industry, the manufacture of such goods as machinery, electric generators, tanks, and military hardware. It was not particularly interested in services or **consumer goods** such as bicycles, shoes, and toys.

This attitude helped make the Soviet Union a leading industrial giant. At the same time, it meant that very often people had to do without many things. Often people could find some items on the **black market**, the illegal market where goods were sold at much higher prices than those set by the government. Very few Soviet citizens, however, could afford to pay the inflated prices.

When Mikhail Gorbachev came to power in the mid-1980s, he admitted what most people had known for some time—the strictly state-controlled system was not working. Gorbachev wanted to move toward a **market economy** like the one in the United States, a free enterprise economy in which businesses are privately owned and what people buy or do not buy determines what and how much is produced.

So, as part of his policy of perestroika, or restructuring, Gorbachev began cutting back the central government's rigid economic controls and allowing local leaders to make more decisions. He also allowed Soviet citizens to start small- and medium-sized businesses and encouraged investment from the West. Even though other reforms followed, they could not save the Soviet system.

The New Economies

When Russia and the other republics became independent, each moved to take charge of its own economy. For each, this has meant a certain amount of burden and pain.

Of all the republics, Russia has probably moved the fastest to create a market economy and private enterprise. State-set prices for most goods were lifted the first week of January 1992. The effect was startling. In no time at all prices skyrocketed by as much as 350 percent. By the end of the month, however, more goods had begun to appear in stores, and prices had started to come down a little. The same year, a plan to turn over state businesses to private owners was initiated.

Although this and other economic reforms represented progress, they have caused hardship for many Russians. The salaries of most Russian workers have not kept pace with rising prices. Food and clothing are still not as plentiful as they should be. Workers are no longer guaranteed employment, and some businesses have had to close their doors. Other republics face many of the same problems.

Cooperative Learning Activity

Have pairs of students draw two-panel cartoons illustrating some aspect of the Russian and Eurasian economies before and after independence.

For example, a "before" panel might show a disgruntled Russian shopper who has enough rubles to buy shoes at state-set prices but must select from shoes that are all for left feet. The "after" panel might show the same shopper, who is still disgruntled. Now there are many shoes to choose from, but the shopper does not have enough rubles to pay the inflated prices. You might illustrate this cartoon on an acetate sheet and project it as an example.

HUMAN/ENVIRONMENT INTERACTION

Agriculture and Industry

Under the Soviets, the government controlled agriculture and industry. In its efforts to make the Soviet Union one of the leading industrial countries of the world, the government pushed steadily forward, ignoring the wants and needs of its people.

The Soviet System

Under the Soviets, most farmers worked on huge state-owned-and-run farms called ***sovkhozes*** or on large collective farms called ***kolkhozes***. The state paid sovkhoz workers wages for the number of items they produced, all of which they turned over to the government. Peasant families worked the kolkhoz. Each family had its own home, household goods, a few animals, and a small plot of land. Everything else, from livestock to buildings to machinery, belonged to the government, which for a set price bought a specific amount of everything the workers produced.

Government control was as strong—or stronger—when it came to industry. Government was the only employer. People worked where the government told them and accepted the wages the government was willing to pay. Government agencies ran the factories. In

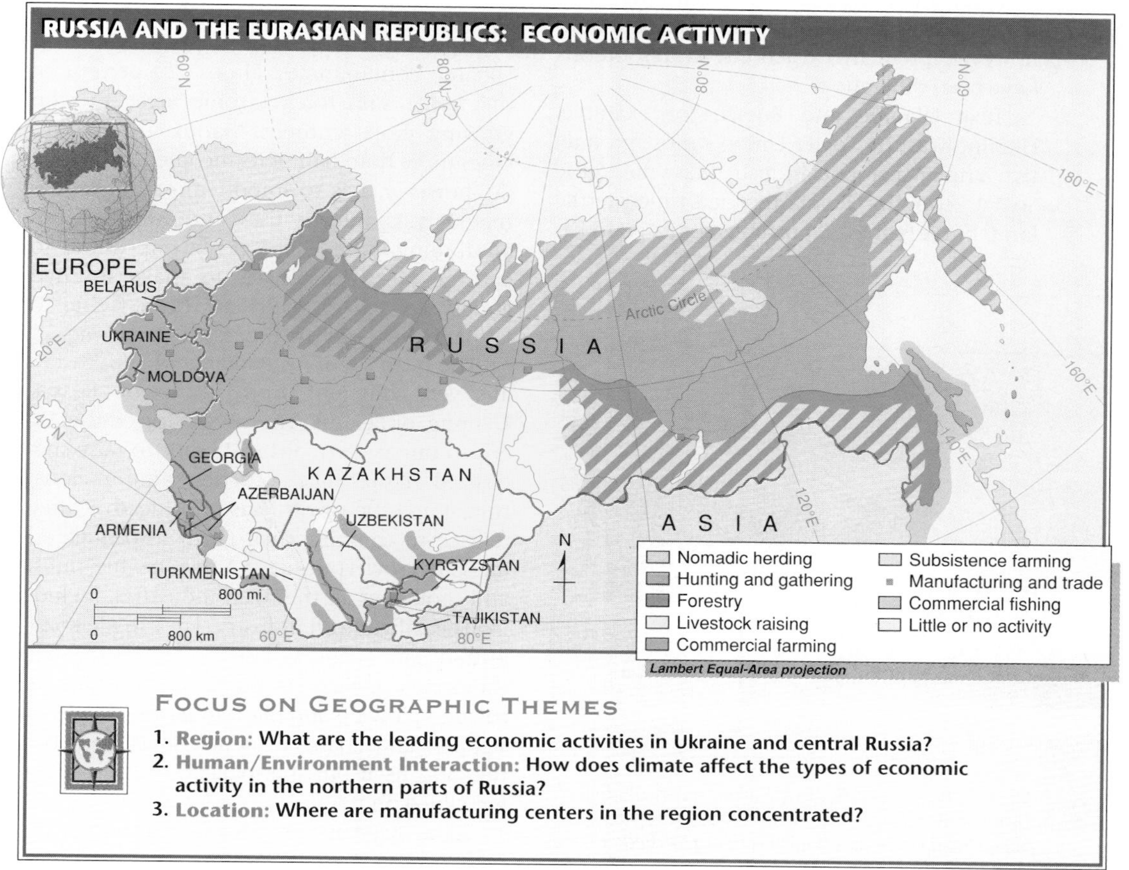

FOCUS ON GEOGRAPHIC THEMES

1. **Region:** What are the leading economic activities in Ukraine and central Russia?
2. **Human/Environment Interaction:** How does climate affect the types of economic activity in the northern parts of Russia?
3. **Location:** Where are manufacturing centers in the region concentrated?

USING MAPS

Answers:
1. commercial farming, forestry, manufacturing, and trade; **2.** The climate is too cool for farming so northern Russians herd, hunt, or gather instead. **3.** in western and central Russia and the Ukraine

Map Skills Practice
Where in Russia is subsistence farming a leading economic activity? *(southeast)*

Global Gourmet

Mutton is a favorite meat in Tajikistan, but in 1993 few could afford it. Due to almost daily inflation of 350 percent in late November, about two pounds of mutton (one kilogram) cost 9,450 rubles. The average salary was 8,000 rubles a month.

CURRICULUM CONNECTION

LITERATURE

Russian poet Andrei A. Voznesensky exhibited what he called "Videoms" in the Pushkin Museum in Moscow. One of his favorite sounded like "Money-moneymoneymonyema." Nyema means "nothing" in Russian, and that is what many Russians think they get for their money.

Meeting Special Needs

Inefficient Readers Acting out situations can help weak readers. Have some students act as Soviet government officials, while others take the roles of Soviet farmers, factory managers, and workers. Ask the "officials" to explain and defend government control of agriculture and industry. *(Students should point out that the state provided security by paying the workers on sovkhozes and supplying livestock, buildings, and machinery to peasants on kolkhozes.)*

Have the farmers, factory workers, and managers explain the shortcomings of the Soviet system and outline changes they would like to see. *(Students should mention the lack of motivation under the Soviet system and the greater freedom under* perestroika.*)*

INDEPENDENT PRACTICE

Guided Reading Have students complete Guided Reading Activity 16-1 in the TCR. **LEP**

Have students complete Performance Assessment Activity 16 in the TCR.

Have students complete Workbook Activity 16-1 in the TCR.

Have students complete Unit Map Overlay Transparency 5 Activity in the TCR.

L2 Write an Editorial Ask interested students to write editorials for a newspaper in Russia, Ukraine, Belarus, Azerbaijan, or Kazakhstan. They should praise changes in the government's attitude toward farming or decry the treatment of farmers under the Soviets.

REGION Ukraine is Europe's leading producer of grain, cattle, dairy products, and sugar.

Answer to Caption: *about one-third*

most cases workers were paid not for the number of hours they worked but for the number of "pieces" they produced.

Both agriculture and industry suffered because workers were not motivated. They had no reason to be because all decisions were made for them, including exactly how much they had to produce within a given time. For many years, factory managers were not even allowed to buy raw materials on their own.

Change came first under perestroika. Factory managers were given much greater freedom to decide what and how much to produce. Farmers were encouraged to leave the state-run farms and lease land, equipment, buildings, and other property from the government.

Changing Farms and Factories

Reform and change continued after independence. Because each republic was different, however, problems, reactions, and solutions have been different as well.

Take Ukraine and Russia, for example. Ukraine was the Soviet Union's most productive farm area, and its industry was vital to the Soviet economy. Russia too had much fertile land, but it had to import most of its grain because its farms did not produce well. At the same time, though, Russia had some of the world's largest steel mills, automobile and truck factories, and chemical plants.

Geographic Themes

Region: Ukrainian Steppes

Ukraine is a rich agricultural area that provides grain to Russia and the other Eurasian republics. *How much of Ukraine's land is being farmed or used as pasture?*

Today both Ukraine and Russia want people to have their own farms and are encouraging foreign investment in industry. About one-third of Ukraine's land is being farmed or used as pasture, and Ukrainian coal and iron-ore mines supply raw materials to plants in several major industrial centers. Meanwhile, Russian farms still are not producing well, and most Russian factories have been finding it hard to compete with the better-equipped, more up-to-date, and more progressive Asian and European firms.

Belarus has many of the same goals as Russia and Ukraine but a slightly different set of circumstances and problems. Until a few years ago, more than one-third of its land was being farmed. Then, in 1986, radiation from the damaged Chernobyl nuclear plant located in Ukraine contaminated almost 20 percent of the fertile soil, forcing some areas to stop growing crops entirely. Manufacturing provides more than half of its income. The republic, however, has to import most of the raw materials its industry uses, and most factories are finding it very hard, if not impossible, to get the parts they need to make finished goods. The government has been trying to help industry, but the process is a slow one.

The histories of Azerbaijan and Kazakhstan are very different from those of Russia, Ukraine, or Belarus. The Soviets forced the Azeris to put aside traditional crops to raise specialized crops like peaches and melons, threatened them with prison or death if they refused to combine their farms into huge estates to grow cotton for Soviet textile mills, and took over all the Azeri industries, including the valuable oil industry. They made Kazakhstan part of the Virgin Lands project, sent thousands of Russian and Ukrainian farmers there to plow up and plant millions of acres of steppes, and changed for all times not only the land itself but the makeup of the people who lived on it.

Today Azerbaijan earns a fair amount of export income from agriculture, especially from

Critical Thinking

Analyzing Information Write the following quote from Vladimir Ilyich Lenin on the chalkboard: "If we lose the Ukraine, we lose our heads."

Ask students what they think Lenin meant. Then tell them to find details that support or refute his statement. They might consult the textbook, encyclopedias, or newspapers as sources of facts. Ask them to use these facts to decide whether Lenin's statement was true or false. Have them explain their decisions.

cotton, and Kazakhstan is an important grain-producing area. Azerbaijan has developed a large-scale petrochemical industry, and the port city of Baku is fast becoming an important shipbuilding hub. The government of Kazakhstan, meanwhile, is pressing hard and fast to put industry in the hands of private owners. The government also has opened the border with China in the hope that Chinese businesspeople will consider doing business in Kazakhstan.

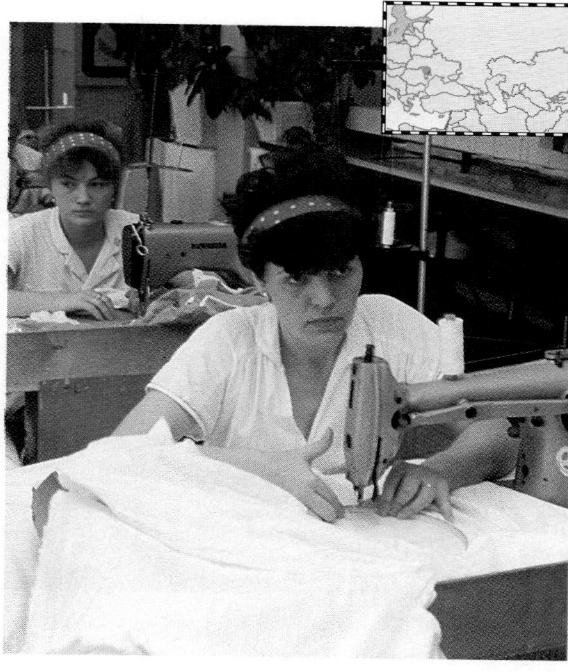

Geographic Themes

Movement: Moldova's Economy and Trade
These garment workers are manufacturing clothing in a factory in Chisinau, the capital of Moldova. *What major challenge do factories in the former Soviet Union face from abroad?*

MOVEMENT

Communications and Transportation

There is a saying that a nation is only as strong as its systems of communications and transportation. In Russia and the Eurasian republics, the communications systems are not as highly developed as the governments would like, and railroads are still the major means of transportation.

Communications

Under the Soviets, the government owned and controlled all the mass-communication networks from newspapers and magazines to postal, telegraph, and telephone services. Censorship committees reviewed everything and made sure that there was no criticism of the government. The media was a way to manipulate the news and put forth Communist views and beliefs. The people and news reporters from other countries got their information from a special Soviet news agency called Tass that dispensed official government statements and commentary.

With independence came greater freedom of expression. For the most part, now there is little or no government censorship. People can read books, newspapers, and magazines that once were banned because of their content, because the author was not in favor with the Communists, or simply because they were "foreign" or the wrong kind of influence.

Rivers and Canals

Russia and the Eurasian republics have many waterways—both natural and artificial. For many centuries, these waterways were the chief transportation system.

Ships loaded and unloaded their cargoes at Georgian and Ukrainian ports along the Black Sea. With most northern ports closed for almost half the year because of ice, the Black Sea was a major and vital Soviet shipping route. The Ukrainian docks alone handled a tenth of the Soviet Union's ocean freight.

Rivers and canals were—and still are—important links in the system. Belarus and Ukraine are just two of the republics that still depend on a network of canals and rivers for transportation of raw materials and goods. The Volga River, for example, is connected to other rivers by a seemingly endless system of inland waterways.

L3 Give a Speech Suggest that a student read Vyacheslav Mikhailovich Molotov's autobiography to find out how he helped his friend Joseph Stalin create an artificial famine to break the resistance of Ukrainian farmers to collectivized farming. Then have the student give a speech that Molotov might have given to justify his and Stalin's actions.

USING ILLUSTRATIONS

LOCATION Moldova's major industries are textiles, canning, and wine making.

Answer to Caption: *They must compete with better-equipped, up-to-date Asian and European firms.*

MULTICULTURAL PERSPECTIVE

The gifts Russians appreciate most from abroad are T-shirts, blue jeans, rock records, country and western music tapes, chewing gum, and baseball caps.

DID YOU KNOW?

In Moscow, taxi fares are negotiable, and the subway is clean and efficient.

Extending the Content

Economy The Ukrainian government wants to change to a market economy slowly. In 1990 the government employed 82 percent of all workers. Another 13.4 percent worked on collective farms. Many of the rest worked in producers' cooperatives—non-agricultural private businesses.

Many government workers may find the transition to private industry difficult, but for other Ukrainians private industry has a strong appeal. Under *perestroika,* the number of cooperatives jumped from 1,843 in January 1988 to 34,823 in January 1991. About half these cooperatives were involved in construction and industry, and most produced handicrafts. The other half engaged in services and trade.

ASSESS

CHECK FOR UNDERSTANDING

Assign Section 1 Review as homework or an in-class activity.

MEETING LESSON OBJECTIVES

Each objective below is tested by the questions that follow it in parentheses.

1. **Describe** the economies of Russia and the Eurasian republics before and after independence. *(2, 5)*
2. **Compare** agriculture and industry in Russia and the Eurasian republics before and after independence. *(5)*
3. **Examine** the communication and transportation systems of Russia and the Eurasian republics. *(3)*
4. **Identify** the economic ties that bind Russia and the Eurasian republics. *(4)*

USING ILLUSTRATIONS

MOVEMENT To cross Russia by train takes seven days on the Trans-Siberian Railroad.

Answer to Caption: *It is a major means of transportation east of the Ural Mountains.*

EVALUATE

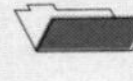

Assign the Section 1 Quiz in the TCR.

Use the Testmaker to create a customized quiz for Section 1.

Geographic Themes

Movement: Trans-Siberian Railroad

The Trans-Siberian, built during the 1890s and early 1900s, is the longest railroad in the world. *How has the Trans-Siberian helped in the development of Russia?*

Roads and Rails

Roads provide vital transportation links in the region today. In some areas, such as the Caucasus, roads provide the only access to the outside world. Because of the mountains, most freight is carried by road in Armenia. Azerbaijan and Georgia have rail networks on which they tend to depend, but they too have many places reachable only by road.

Even so, in many republics, including Russia, good roads, especially paved ones, are still scarce. A major highway system does link Moscow with some of the other major cities, but there are not all that many cars and much of the system is used for trucking. In reality, the trucks do not move much freight, less than 10 percent of the total. Most of what they do carry is farm products or manufactured goods that are not going very far. In winter, the trucks often use frozen rivers as roadways, especially in Siberia.

Railroads are the major means of transportation, one that the republics are committed to maintaining. One-tenth of the world's railway tracks crisscross the region. The area has the longest railroad in the world—the Trans-Siberian—that stretches from Vladivostok across China and Siberia to the Ural Mountains and north of China from Khabarovsk to Kuenga.

Planes and Pipelines

The Soviet Union was the first country to use jet airplanes for passenger traffic, although the Communists discouraged or regulated travel for most Soviet citizens. Since the republics became independent, travel restrictions have been lifted, and the network of air routes are heavily used. Moldova, for example, has direct flights from its capital city of Chisinau to Bucharest, Romania, making it easier for Moldovan companies to move their exports to foreign markets. Aeroflot, the national airline of Russia and the republics, carries both passengers and cargo to most major cities in the

Critical Thinking

Drawing Conclusions On the chalkboard, copy the following republics and their major products:

Russia: chemicals, building materials, machine steel, cars, trucks, wheat, barley, rye, potatoes, sugar beets
Ukraine: wheat, sugar beets, iron, oil, chemicals, machinery
Belarus: chemicals, agricultural machinery, paper, building materials, potatoes, livestock
Moldova: wines, tobacco, grain, vegetables

Ask students to draw conclusions about ways these republics are interdependent. As an example, point out that Belarus needs steel from Russia to produce machinery.

republics and to many countries outside the region, including the United States.

Pipelines have also become much more important as a means of transporting oil and natural gas. The Soviets laid thousands of miles of pipeline, some to carry oil to countries in eastern Europe and some to transport natural gas within their own country. Many of these pipelines are in independent republics. Belarus, for example, controls an important pipeline through which Russia pumps its oil westward to central Europe. Along this pipeline Belarusian refineries at Polotsk and Mozyr process the crude oil for fuel. In Azerbaijan, Soviet-built pipelines carry refined oil from Baku to Batumi and transport natural gas from Karadag to Akstafa and to Tbilisi in Georgia.

REGION

Interdependence

Shortly before the Soviet Union collapsed, one reporter offered this information to her readers:

Both Soviet and Western economists warn that a total break now from the giant, if tottering, Soviet economy would only leave individual republics scrambling for survival. Decades of Moscow's central planning have ensured that the republics are interdependent in every economic sphere: energy, food, consumer goods, light and heavy industry.

Russia and the Eurasian republics soon discovered the truth of the economists' warning. They knew that they had inherited a flawed economic system that could not produce enough goods to satisfy the needs of all their people. They soon found out that it also was a system in which no single republic was totally independent. For example, one republic might have industries but no raw materials or parts, while another republic had the raw materials or parts but no industries. One by one, the republics concluded that interdependence was necessary for survival.

Belarus, for example, does not have enough oil and natural gas fuels, but Russia has an abundance of these resources. As a result, much of Belarus's economy hinges on exchanging goods with Russia and Belarus's other neighbor–Ukraine.

Moldova's economy also depends on trade with Ukraine and Russia. When the Soviet Union fell apart, its currency—the ruble—became far less valuable. Rubles were also the currency of Moldova. Because the rubles are worth so little, factory managers in Moldova can no longer buy the raw materials they need with them. So they have had to depend on bartering with other republics.

Other republics have similar dependence on their neighbors. Ukraine, for example, must import oil. Armenia needs petroleum and natural gas, as well as metals, farm machinery, and some consumer goods. Kazakhstan depends on Russia for the chemicals and other products its factories need.

Section 1 Review

Checking for Understanding

1. **Define** command economy, consumer goods, black market, market economy, *sovkhozes, kolkhozes.*
2. **Locating Places** What were two of the early changes in industry and agriculture under the Soviets?
3. **Movement** What is the major means of transportation in Russia and the Eurasian republics?
4. **Region** For what does Ukraine have to depend on the other republics?

Critical Thinking

5. **Making Comparisons** In what ways is the market economy preferred by the independent republics different from the Soviet economy?

RETEACH

Have the students outline the section by using its subheads as main ideas and adding details from the paragraphs.

ENRICH

Display pictures of old and new American and European trains. A good source is the *Antique Locomotives Coloring Book* (Dover Publications). Have students try to find a model similar to the Trans-Siberian Railroad pictured in this section.

CLOSE

Write a postcard to Tatyana, describing your favorite picnic location.

DID YOU KNOW?

Since 1988, Russia's oil production has declined by one-third because of inefficient oil wells and leaking pipelines.

ANSWERS TO SECTION 1 REVIEW

1. **command economy:** economy in which a central authority makes the decisions; **consumer goods:** goods people buy; **black market:** illegal market with high-priced goods; **market economy:** economy based on supply and demand and privately owned businesses; ***sovkhozes:*** state-owned farms where workers were paid for the items they produced; ***kolkhozes:*** collective farms worked by peasant families
2. Factory managers make production decisions, and farmers lease land and other property from the government.
3. railroads
4. oil
5. Answers may vary but should indicate that the Soviet economy was not based on supply and demand and private ownership.

FOCUS

Ask students to read the quote and describe some industrial uses of water. Have them hypothesize about the effects of widespread water loss to a region. List their speculations on the board, or have students write them in their journals.

TEACH

L1 Location Use Unit Map Overlay Transparency 5-5 to show the location of the Aral Sea and the Uzbekistan and Kazakhstan regions.

L2 Express Opinions Ask students to explain whether they agree with the Russian government's support of the cotton industry rather than the fishing industry.

L2 Cause-Effect Have students compose a cause-effect outline to explain the Aral Sea situation.

DID YOU KNOW?

Salt and other materials blowing off the Aral's dry seabed have shortened life expectancy and led to high death rates for mothers and newborns, as well as caused many infectious respiratory and eye diseases, hepatitis, throat cancer, and severe anemia.

Videodisc

GTV: PLANETARY MANAGER

Side 2, Chapter 6
Frames 31907-38777
Title: *Dust in the Wind*
Subject: Time travel shows the consequences of overgrazing, excessive irrigation, and deforestation

CASE STUDY

THE DYING ARAL SEA

We need water not only for the population and farms but also for industrial development. The intellectuals sitting at desks understand the ecological slogans, but they fail to understand the needs of the people working on the farms.

Viktor Dukhovnyi, Director of the Central Asian Scientific Research Institute for Irrigation, *National Geographic*, February 1990

The Aral Sea lies in central Asia in the republics of Kazakhstan and Uzbekistan. In 1960 the Aral covered 25,660 square miles (66,459 sq. km) and had a fragile, but rich environment. The huge, inland saltwater lake provided a healthy living for the fishing communities around its shores.

By the 1980s, when the Soviet Union (now the Commonwealth of Independent States) opened its doors under the policy of *glasnost*, or openness, the Aral Sea had shrunk to a third of its former size. The delicate environment had disappeared, every marine plant and animal replaced with salt-coated sand. The fishing industry was a shadow of what it had once been, and people living near the lake were suffering from severe health problems.

THE ISSUE

Scientists claimed that water from the Amu Darya River, the sea's source, had been diverted for irrigating cotton and rice farms. For 30 years, very little water had been flowing into the Aral. To restore the sea, they said, the water must be allowed to flow along its original course back into the Aral Sea.

Government officials said that it was impossible to return the full flow of the Amu Darya to the Aral Sea. They pointed to the 3 million acres (about 1.2 million hectares) of irrigated land on either side of the canal. The irrigation, they said, had made once-arid land productive, growing about half of the former Soviet Union's cotton crop. In addition, the diverted water had increased the acres planted with rice and fruits.

THE BACKGROUND

The Aral is an inland saltwater sea with no outlet. It is fed by two rivers, the Amu Darya and Syr Darya. The freshwater from these two rivers held the Aral's water and salt levels in perfect balance.

In the early 1960s, the Soviet central government decided to make the Soviet Union self-sufficient in cotton and increase rice production. Government officials ordered the

A stranded ship lies beached on the shrinking coastline of the Aral Sea.

Extending the Content

Human/Environment Interaction At one time, the 24 native fish species in the Aral Sea produced 3 percent of the Soviet Union's annual fish catch. The sea also provided 60,000 jobs at the fishery of Muynak, Uzbekistan, on the southern shore.

As the Aral Sea began to diminish, the Soviet government went to great expense to keep the cannery operational and preserve the area's primary livelihood. For example, frozen fish were shipped from the Soviet Union's northern sea ports to the Muynak fishery. The strategy proved unsuccessful. By 1990, the fishery employed just 900 workers. Muynak is now a forsaken, landlocked town 20 miles from the water.

Over the past few decades, the Aral Sea has experienced a severe drop in water level, its shoreline receded, and its salt content increased.

additional amount of needed water to be taken from the two rivers that feed the Aral Sea.

Raushan Tuliagakov, a member of the Committee to Save the Aral Sea, said, "We knew the problem as far back as 1960, but we were not allowed to speak out."

Large dams were built across both rivers, and an 850-mile (1,368-km) central canal with a far-reaching system of feeder canals was created. When the irrigation system was completed, millions of acres along both sides of the main canal were flooded.

During the next 30 years, the Aral Sea experienced a severe drop in water level, its shoreline receded, and its salt content increased. The marine environment became hostile to the sea life in it, killing the plants and animals. As the marine life died, the fishing industry suffered.

THE POINTS OF VIEW

Since the mid-1980s, scientists have spoken out more strongly for saving the Aral Sea. Agricultural officials, however, say that it is impossible to demolish the canal system. Too many farmers depend on the income from cotton. Argues an official, "We could [reduce by half the amount of land being irrigated]. But we have to think of the people who depend on the irrigation for work. What will they do then? What will they eat?"

THE ISSUE TODAY

Government leaders have said that the amount of land for cotton will be reduced and large amounts of water will be pumped back into the Aral Sea until the year 2005. The government, however, has also indicated that the welfare of the cotton farmers must come first. Exported cotton is a major source of income.

Most scientists believe that the Aral Sea cannot ever be as it was before. The best they hope for is some sort of stabilization of the sea and the survival of the rivers' two deltas. Saving the deltas could lead to new commercial fishing activity.

Reviewing the Case

1. **Who is involved in the concern over the Aral Sea?**
2. **Human/Environment Interaction**  **How did governmental policy damage the Aral Sea?**

Case Study

ASSESS

Have students answer the Reviewing the Case questions on page 335.

CLOSE

Have students reread the speculations they made earlier. Ask for changes and additions. Then share **Extending the Content** and the following information. Encourage students to add facts to their lists:

Prior to the 1960s, the Aral Sea helped regulate the region's weather and wind. Great dust storms now ravage the area. Scientists estimate that the 43 million tons (39 million metric tons) of salt and poison whipped up annually are carried as far away as the Arctic Ocean. Daily temperatures around the Aral Sea now exceed 100° for extended periods.

Encourage students to locate the contaminated area on the map on pages A14–A15.

GLENCOE TECHNOLOGY

 **Videodisc**

REUTERS ISSUES IN GEOGRAPHY

Chapter 4
Disc 1 Side A

Title: ***Russia: Managing Resources***

Subject: Resources of Russia and how they are affected by geographic, economic, and historic factors

ANSWERS TO REVIEWING THE CASE

1. Russian agricultural officials, scientists who want to save the Aral Sea, cotton farmers, people in the fishing industry
2. The Russian government ordered that the rivers feeding the Aral Sea be used to irrigate millions of acres of cotton and rice fields. With the rivers diverted, the Aral Sea's water level dropped, its salt content increased, and its marine life died.

LESSON PLAN
Chapter 16, Section 2

FOCUS

SECTION OBJECTIVES

1. **Discuss** the nuclear disaster and concerns in Russia and the Eurasian republics.
2. **Specify** environmental problems affecting some bodies of water in Russia and the Eurasian republics.
3. **Analyze** effects of industrial and pesticide pollution in Russia and the Eurasian republics.

BELLRINGER MOTIVATIONAL ACTIVITY

Project the Section 2 Focus Transparency and have students answer the questions.

PRETEACHING VOCABULARY

Tell students that the ending *-cide* comes from the Latin "kill." Ask them to think of words with this ending. *(suicide, homicide)* Then have them suggest the meaning of *pesticide.*

DID YOU KNOW?

In 1992, Ukraine's chief epidemiologist reported a 900 percent increase in leukemia near the Chernobyl nuclear power plant.

GLENCOE TECHNOLOGY

Videodisc

REUTERS ISSUES IN GEOGRAPHY

Chapter 4
Disc 1 Side A

Title: ***Russia: Managing Resources***

Subject: Resources of Russia and how they are affected by geographic, economic, and historic factors

SECTION 2

People and Their Environment

THE ENVIRONMENT

SETTING THE SCENE

Read to Discover . . .

- how nuclear disaster and other concerns have affected Russia and the Eurasian republics.
- how environmental problems affect some bodies of water in Russia and the Eurasian republics.
- about the effects of industrial and pesticide pollution in Russia and the Eurasian republics.

Key Terms

- industrialize
- polluted
- pesticide

Identify and Locate

Tian Shan Mountains, Chernobyl, Kiev, Belarus, Ust-Kamenogorsk, Metsamov, Nayirit, Semipalatinsk, Caspian Sea, Lake Sevan, Radzan River, Lake Baikal, Central Siberian Plateau, Dniester River, Bishkek, Yerevan

Almost from the time they took over, the Soviets pushed to **industrialize**, or develop industry, and to make their nation a world power. In the process they neglected and abused the environment. Rivers and lakes, urban areas and rural areas, even the air people breathe—all have been very badly damaged, in some cases permanently. This pollution, most of it caused by the long-term Soviet emphasis on heavy industry, has put millions of people in the republics at risk and made public health a matter of great concern.

HUMAN/ENVIRONMENT INTERACTION

Nuclear Energy

Under the Soviets, a number of different kinds of energy were used as sources of fuel. One of these was nuclear energy, which the government championed as an economical source of fuel. The uranium the Soviets needed to power any nuclear plants they might build lay in their own country, much of it in the area northwest of the Black Sea and in the Tian Shan range.

Committed to nuclear energy as a major source of electric power, in 1986 the Soviets were building 18 new nuclear power stations. They already had other nuclear power stations and two nuclear heat supply stations, each intended to generate enough heat for a city of about 400,000. All that came to a halt—some of it permanently—because of an accident at a nuclear power station in a small Ukrainian town called Chernobyl.

Disaster at Chernobyl

In 1986 Chernobyl was a small, quiet town in northern Ukraine about 60 miles (96 km) from Kiev. It was also the site of one of the Soviet Union's nuclear power stations. On April 26, at a little before 1:30 A.M., an explosion ripped apart a nuclear reactor at the station. The blast started more than 30 fires and released tons of radioactive particles into the atmosphere.

Two days later, scientists in Sweden discovered increased amounts of radiation in the air over their country and began asking questions. It turned out that the Soviet government already knew about the explosion but had not told the public about it or warned them of the dangers it had brought. Because people were not evacuated at once, about 100,000 people in the vicinity were exposed to deadly levels of radiation. Most of those peo-

Classroom Resources for Section 2

BLACKLINE MASTERS:
Reproducible Lesson Plan 16-2
Environmental Issue 5
Section Quiz 16-2
Enrichment Activity 16

TRANSPARENCIES:
Section Focus Transparency 16-2
Unit Map Overlay Transparency 5-5

MULTIMEDIA:

Testmaker

Geography and the Environment
Reuters Issues in Geography
GTV: Planetary Manager

ple probably will die prematurely from radioactivity-related diseases.

Aftermath of Chernobyl

The great cloud of radioactive dust released at Chernobyl poisoned a vast area of northwestern Europe. Thousands of people, many of them children, suffer from cancer, blood diseases, and stomach disorders because of the increased radiation in the area. Each year some young Ukrainians are sent to northern Europe and to the United States for a few months to lower the levels of radiation in their bodies.

Chernobyl no longer exists as a populated town. It was evacuated and its houses and trees bulldozed and buried beneath its contaminated soil. The destroyed reactor was put in a special steel and cement building. It is unlikely that anyone will ever be able to live in Chernobyl again, even in the very distant future.

It is estimated that there were 2 million victims of Chernobyl. Many of them live in Belarus, where the wind carried 70 percent of the fallout. Here too much of the soil was contaminated and many people infected with cancer, stomach diseases, breathing ailments, and other serious illnesses. Thousands of acres of rich farmland cannot be used and hundreds of villages cannot be inhabited. Farmers have been told that it is no longer safe to grow crops in some of the soil on their farms. Because the demand for food keeps growing, however, they keep on raising vegetables, fruits, and livestock in soil they know is not safe. Villagers still eat food from their gardens, and many still live in homes and villages they have been told were poisoned by radiation.

After Belarus became independent, the government started to monitor radiation levels. When they found villages where the levels were high enough to indicate contamination, the government made people leave. Experts calculate that the accident at Chernobyl caused radiation ailments in 2 million Belarusians, 500,000 of them children. To help treat all these people, the government also built new clinics that specialize in treating radiation poisoning.

Nuclear Concerns

What happened at Chernobyl made people stop and think about the dangers of nuclear power and led Belarusians, Ukrainians,

Geographic Themes

Place: Chernobyl, Ukraine

The atomic explosion at the Chernobyl nuclear plant killed scores of people and released a radioactive cloud that contaminated surrounding farmland. *What will be the long-term effects of Chernobyl?*

TEACH

GUIDED PRACTICE

 Implement Environmental Issue 5 as a class activity.

L1 Discuss After the class reads "Nuclear Energy" on pages 336–338, discuss why the Chernobyl disaster happened. *(The reactors were not designed well and lacked spare parts.)* Ask if students think a similar disaster could occur in the United States.

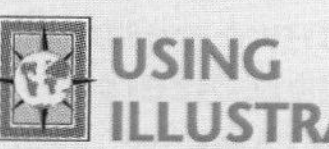

USING ILLUSTRATIONS

PLACE The concrete encasing the Chernobyl reactor is cracking. Radiation may be leaking into the atmosphere again.

Answer to Caption: *Millions will die prematurely or suffer from radiation-linked ailments.*

GLENCOE TECHNOLOGY

Videodisc

Use the following to enrich Chapter 16:

GEOGRAPHY AND THE ENVIRONMENT
THE INFINITE VOYAGE
Living With Disaster

Chapter 7
Disc 3 Side A

Title: ***Documenting Tragedy—Developing a Cure: Soviet Armenia***

Cooperative Learning Activity

Have each student write the first part of an "if" statement relating to the Chernobyl disaster or other nuclear concerns of Russia and the Eurasian republics. Copy the following on the chalkboard as examples:

1. If the Soviet government had immediately warned the public about the explosion . . .
2. If the Chernobyl accident had not happened when it did . . .

Organize the class into pairs. Ask each pair to choose one of its "if" statements and finish it. Add these examples to the board:

1. . . . 100,000 people would not have been exposed to deadly radiation levels.
2. . . . nuclear power plants that were being built or planned would have been completed.

Ask pairs to share completed sentences.

INDEPENDENT PRACTICE

Guided Reading Have students complete Guided Reading Activity 16-2 in the TCR. **LEP**

Have students complete Workbook Activity 16-2 in the TCR.

Have students complete Vocabulary Activity 16 in the TCR.

DID YOU KNOW?

Farmers in Moldova use six times more pesticides and fertilizers than farmers in California.

USING ILLUSTRATIONS

HUMAN/ENVIRONMENT INTERACTION The Caspian Sea has become polluted, probably by pesticide and fertilizer run-off from fields in Turkmenistan and Kazakhstan.

Answer to Caption: *Water used for irrigation was diverted from the sea.*

DID YOU KNOW?

Nuclear weapon facilities often produce more nuclear wastes than weapons. When Ukraine removed the warheads from 17 of its 46 SS-24 missiles in 1993 and promised to deactivate the rest, environmentalists and advocates of disarmament were both encouraged.

and others to hold protests against nuclear plants and weapons. It was because of these efforts that some reactors completed by the Soviets never opened, and some still in the planning stages were never built. In 1990, when an explosion at the Ulba nuclear fuel processing plant at Ust-Kamenogorsk released beryllium gas into the air, 60,000 people demanded that the plant be closed.

Many Russians are now speaking out against some of the older nuclear power stations in their republic. They say that because the reactors were not well designed in the first place and lack needed spare parts, the reactor plants could become dangerous to operate. Armenians are also expressing their views about two nuclear power plants in their republic, one at Metsamov and one at Nayirit. Even though some of the Metsamov reactors have been shut down, many people still doubt the wisdom of having nuclear power stations in a nation known to have earthquakes.

For some, nuclear weapons and testing are also a cause for concern. For many years the Soviets developed and stocked up on nuclear weapons. When the Soviet Union broke up, what would happen to those weapons became a major—and a controversial—issue. The four republics that now have nuclear weapons—Russia, Ukraine, Belarus, and Kazakhstan—agreed that before any one republic could use the weapons it had to have the consent of the other three.

This, however, has not changed the damage that past nuclear testing has already done in certain areas. One is the Semipalatinsk area of Kazakhstan, where the Soviets once had nuclear bases. Kazakhstan is believed to still have several thousand nuclear warheads within its borders. The Soviet army tested its nuclear weapons in the Semipalatinsk area and its chemical and biological weapons in other places in the republic. In 1989 a Semipalatinsk Oblast Peace Committee announced that there had been radiation leaks in the area as a result of nuclear weapons testing. It will be years before all traces of contamination will be gone.

Geographic Themes

Human/Environment Interaction: Caspian Sea
The Caspian Sea, the largest inland body of water in the world, is an important source of a fish called sturgeon. *How has human activity contributed to the shrinking of the Caspian Sea?*

HUMAN/ENVIRONMENT INTERACTION

Water Problems

The Soviet emphasis on heavy industry and desire to grow certain crops where there was not enough water for them took its toll on some of the rivers, lakes, and seas of Russia and the Eurasian republics. In some cases, water levels have shrunk drastically, endangering the plant, fish, and animal life and changing the nearby landscape. In other cases, the water is being **polluted**, contaminated by harmful substances.

The many industries and farms in the Volga River basin, for example, use huge amounts of river water. Much of that water ends up back in the Volga with different kinds of pollutants discharged by the industries and farms. A fast-flowing river can purify itself. Because so many dams slow the Volga's flow, however, the river remains polluted.

Shrinking of the Caspian Sea and Lake Sevan

The Caspian Sea lies on the border between Europe and Asia, bounded on the west by Rus-

Meeting Special Needs

Inefficient Organizers Have students scan the section for names of polluted bodies of water, their locations, and the kinds of pollutants.

Then have them construct and complete a chart similar to the one shown here. Copy it on the chalkboard as an example:

Body of Water	*Location*	*Pollutants*
Lake Sevan	northeastern Armenia	organic wastes

Geographic Themes

Human/Environment Interaction: Lake Baikal

Lake Baikal, the world's deepest lake, is more than 5,315 feet (1,620 m) at its deepest point. *What are the major causes of the pollution problems affecting Lake Baikal?*

sia and Azerbaijan, on the north by Russia and Kazakhstan, and on the east by Kazakhstan and Turkmenistan. Lake Sevan, one of the highest lakes in the world, lies in northeastern Armenia and is surrounded by the Caucasus Mountains. The two bodies of water share a common problem—they have been shrinking.

Kazakhstan and the other central Asian republics do not get much rain. So their land had to be irrigated to grow the cotton and other crops the Soviets demanded of them and to yield the hay and fodder they needed to feed their animals during the winter. Much of the water used for irrigation was diverted from the Caspian Sea. From 1960 to the mid-1970s, the water level of the Caspian dropped 8 feet (2.4 m). Although since then it has risen a little, several thousand square miles have dried up.

Lake Sevan also suffered because its waters were steadily drained over a long period of time. The lake feeds the Radzan River. For more than 60 years, Armenians have drawn water from the river to power hydroelectric stations and to irrigate their farms. In the 1970s concern about the loss of water in the lake led the Soviets to build a tunnel to reroute water to the lake from the Arpa River in Azerbaijan. Even with the tunnel, the water level kept going down. At the same time, organic waste from nearby cities and towns polluted the lake. In the late 1980s, plans were made to build a pipeline to keep the wastes out of the Radzan River. Although the pipeline will help keep the water clean, it will not solve the problem of water level, which by the early 1990s had dropped almost 20 feet (6 m).

Pollution of Lake Baikal

Lake Baikal lies on the southern edge of the Central Siberian Plateau. It holds a huge volume of water that influences the weather around it, making the area nearest the lake warmer in winter and cooler in summer than areas farther away from the lake.

L2 Locate Have students project and trace Unit Map Overlay Transparency 5-5. Ask them to label the Caspian Sea, Lake Sevan, Radzan River, Lake Baikal, and the Dneister River. Display the map as students read pages 339 and 340.

USING ILLUSTRATIONS

HUMAN/ENVIRONMENT INTERACTION Geographers prevented further pollution of Lake Baikal by warning that mining and processing the phosphorus-containing ore nearby would damage the lake.

Answer to Caption: *toxic chemicals from a pulp and paper mill and fertilizers from farms*

Global Gourmet

Fish are important in the Russian diet. A favorite breakfast is fish served in compressed cakes. Most festive meals begin with *zukuski—an* appetizer of fish, meat, and pickles.

DID YOU KNOW?

Uzbekistan produces so much cotton that Russians call it "the white gold of Uzbekistan."

Critical Thinking

Predicting Consequences Tell students that Uzbekistan produced 62 percent of all the cotton grown in the Soviet Union but now hopes to reduce the percentage of land devoted to cotton. According to Renat S. Nazarov, director of cotton for the Uzbekistan Ministry of Agriculture, farmers are replacing pesticides with biological methods. They are also lining irrigation ditches with concrete to prevent wasting water.

Ask students to predict changes in the environment if the farmers of the central Asian republics continue to take better care of the land. *(Answers will vary but students may point out that pollution from pesticides will be reduced and water sources such as the Aral Sea may recover.)*

ASSESS

CHECK FOR UNDERSTANDING

Assign Section 2 Review as homework or an in-class activity.

MEETING LESSON OBJECTIVES

Each objective below is tested by the questions that follow it in parentheses.

1. **Discuss** the nuclear disaster and concerns in Russia and the Eurasian republics. *(2, 3)*
2. **Specify** environmental problems affecting some bodies of water in Russia and the Eurasian republics. *(4, 5)*
3. **Analyze** effects of industrial and pesticide pollution in Russia and the Eurasian republics. *(5)*

EVALUATE

Assign the Section Quiz 16-2 in the TCR.

Use the Testmaker to create a customized quiz for Section 2.

USING ILLUSTRATIONS

HUMAN/ENVIRONMENT INTERACTION Pollution is a true threat to people's lives. In Hungary, air pollution causes 1 in 17 deaths. An hour's stroll through Budapest's polluted streets is as bad for the lungs as smoking 20 cigarettes! In the Ukrainian city of Odessa, the cancer rate has soared 27 percent since 1975, probably because the city's drinking water comes from the very polluted Dniester River.

Answer to Caption: *Factories dump toxic wastes into almost every river.*

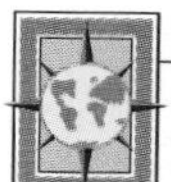

Geographic Themes

Human/Environment Interaction: Yerevan, Armenia

Air pollution from nearby industries has eroded many buildings in Yerevan, Armenia. *How has the development of industry contributed to the pollution of waterways in Russia and the Eurasian republics?*

About 40 years ago, a huge paper and pulp mill that had grown up along the southwestern shore of the lake began to spill toxic chemicals into its waters. On top of this, rivers flowing into the lake were depositing farm fertilizers and other poisonous chemicals. All this pollution upset the chemical balance of the lake, posing a real threat to plants and animals.

In the late 1980s, Soviet writers and scientists urged the government to stop pollution. They wanted equipment installed to reduce the amount of waste the paper and pulp factory was emptying in the lake. In 1987 the pulp plant was ordered to stop polluting the lake. Not long after, plans to build other factories along the shores of the lake were halted. The next step, to be taken by the Russian government in the 1990s, is to make the factories already on the shores of the lake convert to cleaner production processes—or to tear them down completely.

HUMAN/ENVIRONMENT INTERACTION

Pollution

Pollution affects more than just the rivers, lakes, and other bodies of water of Russia and the Eurasian republics. It affects the land and the air as well. Just about every feature of the physical and natural environment of the region has suffered because of the Soviet passion to industrialize and to grow more, different, bigger, and better crops.

Under the Soviets, factories dumped toxic wastes into almost every river of Russia and the Eurasian republics. In 1983, for example, when a dam on a tributary of the Dniester River in Ukraine collapsed, hazardous wastes from a fertilizer plant poured into the river. The wastes poisoned the waters that ran downstream through Moldova to the Black Sea, killing fish and putting at risk Moldovans who had to get their water from the Dniester.

Extending the Content

Weapons Nuclear weapons are not the only weapons that have damaged the environment in Russia and the Eurasian republics. World War II-era factories that produced chemical weapons did not protect employees, dumped contaminated water into rivers, and burned dangerous substances such as mustard gas at open sites.

Chemist Lev Fyodorov, president of the Union for Chemical Safety, said: "Only two people who worked at the shop No. 4 in Chapayevsk, (a central Russian town) where they produced mustard gas, remain alive. Just two women from shop No. 5 where artillery shells were filled with gas, have survived. The rest are all dead."

Because soft brown coal was plentiful in the region, most Soviet factories burned it even though they knew it polluted the air. Because most factory smokestacks did not have pollution-preventing equipment or devices, they released incredible amounts of soot, sulfur, and carbon dioxide. The wind carried the pollution to other areas. Emissions from smokestacks in Ukrainian and Romanian factories, for example, drifted over Moldova, adding to the pollutants already released into the air by Moldovan factories.

Soviet industries dumped wastes wherever they wanted—even after the Soviets passed laws that were supposed to keep such things from happening. Republics like Moldova that accepted toxic wastes for landfills that did not meet international sanitary regulations only made an already-bad problem worse.

No republic has escaped the effects of the different kinds of pollution associated with industry. People in Kazakhstan, for example, suffer from health problems linked to toxic chemicals in the atmosphere. The chemicals are there because planners in Moscow insisted on building up heavy industry in Kazakhstan. The increase in infant mortality in Kazakhstan has been linked directly to the pollution problem as well. In Kyrgyzstan, too, the development of heavy industry has polluted the air. In Bishkek, for example, the concentration of benzopyrene in the atmosphere is more than 10 times greater than what it should be.

One of the most polluted of all the cities of Russia and the Eurasian republics, though, is Yerevan, the capital of Armenia. Three-fifths of Armenia's industries are located in and around the city, and most are devoted to kinds of heavy industry that produce significant pollution—synthetic rubber, fertilizers, chemicals, nonferrous metals, and equipment.

Not all of the pollution comes from factories. In some areas, much of it is from **pesticides,** chemicals used to kill insects, rodents, and other pests. To rid cotton, vegetables, and fruits of insects and other pests that were destroying them, Soviet farmers began spraying and dumping huge quantities of pesticides on their fields. This went on for more than 30 years. By the 1990s most farmers all across the region were doing it. Banning certain pesticides did not stop some farmers from using them. DDT, one of the most deadly pesticides, was officially banned by the Soviet Union—as well as most other countries—more than two decades ago. But Azeri farmers, who produce more cotton than anyone else in the Caucasus, still spray strong doses of it on their crops.

Geographic Themes

Region: Central Asia

The growing of cotton is an important agricultural activity in central Asia. *What major source of pollution affects farmers in Russia and the Eurasian republics?*

SECTION 2 REVIEW

Checking for Understanding

1. **Define** industrialize, polluted, pesticide.
2. **Locating Places** What happened at Chernobyl in 1986?
3. **Movement** Why were so many people in Belarus affected by the accident at Chernobyl?
4. **Human/Environment Interaction** What caused the water levels of the Caspian Sea and Lake Sevan to drop?

Critical Thinking

5. **Determining Cause and Effect** What was the major cause of the environmental problems of Russia and the Eurasian republics?

ANSWERS TO SECTION 2 REVIEW

1. **industrialize:** develop industry; **polluted:** contaminated by harmful substances; **pesticide:** chemical used to kill insects, rodents, and other pests
2. A nuclear reactor exploded and released tons of radioactive particles into the atmosphere.
3. because the wind carried 70 percent of the fallout to Belarus
4. long-term drainage and diversion of the water for irrigation
5. the Soviet drive to industrialize

RETEACH

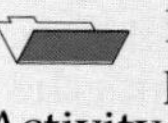

Have students complete Reteaching Activity 16 in the TCR.

USING ILLUSTRATIONS

HUMAN/ENVIRONMENT INTERACTION

Uzbekistan's economy depends largely on cotton, which is mainly exported outside the republic.

Answer to Caption: *pesticides*

ENRICH

Have students complete Enrichment Activity 16 in the TCR.

CLOSE

Ask students to name environmental challenges and solutions discussed in the section. List their responses on the board.

Videodisc

GTV: PLANETARY MANAGER

Side 2, Chapter 7
Frames 38779-41076
Title: ***Water, Water Everywhere***
Subject: Amount of available drinking water

GTV: PLANETARY MANAGER

Side 2, Chapter 8
Frames 41078-46201
Title: ***Shall We Gather at the River?***
Subject: Everyday sources of water pollution and how we can clean up our water

TEACH

After students read the skill on page 342, discuss the differences between fact and opinion.

Have each student write three facts on one index card and three opinions on another card. Collect the cards.

Select several judges and organize the other students into two teams. Have the judges read statements from the cards. The teams will decide if each one is a fact or an opinion. Score points for correct responses.

Skills Practice
Have students complete Skill Activity 16 in the TCR.

CRITICAL THINKING SKILLS

Distinguishing Fact From Opinion

Suppose you overhear the following conversation between two girls who are eating ice cream cones.

Tanya: This is absolutely the best chocolate ice cream in the city!

Lisa: Is that a fact? Well, yesterday I had another kind of chocolate ice cream, and it was much better. It was creamier and richer. This isn't even in the same league.

Tanya: But this chocolate is so dark. This is definitely the best. It's a fact.

Is it? Although Tanya and Lisa claim to know the facts about chocolate ice cream, they are actually expressing opinions. It's important to know the differences between them.

REVIEWING THE SKILL

Facts are statements that can be checked for accuracy. They explain what happened, when and where it happened, who was involved, and so on. However, not all factual statements are true or correct. For example, read the following statement: "In 1989 Russia produced almost 50 million metric tons of iron ore." Because you can check the accuracy of this statement in government reports, almanacs, and other sources, it is a fact. In this case, however, the statement is incorrect. Russia produced almost 96 million metric tons in that year.

Opinions, on the other hand, are statements of feelings, emotions, and beliefs. It is impossible to check their accuracy. For example, suppose someone says, "The breakup of the Soviet Union is the most exciting political change of the 1990s."

Although this statement expresses the speaker's beliefs, no one can prove or disprove it. Therefore, it is an opinion, not a fact. Opinions often begin with phrases such as, *I believe, probably, it seems,* or *in my view.* They often contain qualifying words such as *may, might, could, should, ought,* and superlatives such as *best, worst, greatest, outstanding,* and *extraordinary.*

To distinguish facts from opinions, apply the following steps:

- Identify facts by looking for verifiable statements such as names, dates, places, numbers, and specific actions. Often facts answer the questions *who? what? where?* and *when.*
- Identify opinions by looking for statements expressing beliefs or feelings. Often, they contain phrases such as *I believe* or *In my view*, or qualifiers and superlatives.

PRACTICING THE SKILL

For each statement below, write **F** if it is a fact, or **O** if it is an opinion. Explain each answer.

1. By mid-1991, Russian oil production was down to 7.8 million barrels a day, 17 percent below the rate in 1988.
2. In all likelihood, Soviet carbon emissions will continue to fall in the next few years.
3. The accident at the Chernobyl nuclear reactor could result in hundreds of thousands more cancer deaths.
4. Nuclear power is the most dangerous environmental threat in the world today.
5. In 1967, a hot, windy summer dried up Lake Karachay, a dumping site for Soviet nuclear waste in the 1950s; radioactive dust spread contamination to 41,000 people.

For additional practice in this skill, see Practicing Skills on page 344 of the Chapter 16 Review.

342 UNIT 5

ANSWERS TO PRACTICING THE SKILL

1. *F.* Production rates and percentages can be checked for accuracy.
2. *O.* The qualifier "in all likelihood" indicates that this is an opinion, or projection of what may happen.
3. *O.* The qualifier "could" indicates that this is an opinion.
4. *O.* The superlative "the most dangerous" indicates that this is an opinion.
5. *F.* Figures and events can be checked for accuracy.

chapter 16

HIGHLIGHTS

Section	Key Terms	Summary
1 Living in Russia and the Eurasian Republics	**command economy** (p. 328) **consumer goods** (p. 328) **black market** (p. 328) **market economy** (p. 328) ***sovkhozes*** (p. 329) ***kolkhozes*** (p. 329)	• For many decades, Russia and the Eurasian republics constituted a single economy controlled by the Soviet government. • Upon becoming independent, each republic took charge of its own economy and is trying to move toward a market economy. • Russia and the other republics all are taking steps to privatize agriculture and industry. • Independence brought greater freedom of expression to the communications systems and most forms of media. • Although waterways, roads, and railways remain vital methods of transportation for freight and passengers, airlines and pipelines are growing in importance. • Because they were parts of the Soviet system for so long, Russia and the Eurasian republics today are not totally independent of one another.
2 People and Their Environment	**industrialize** (p. 336) **polluted** (p. 338) **pesticide** (p. 341)	• In their push to industrialize, the Soviets neglected and abused the environment. • Committed to nuclear power as an economical source of electric power, the Soviets built numerous nuclear power stations in various parts of the nation. • The Chernobyl disaster led to doubts and protests about nuclear energy and weapons. • Pollution caused by heavy industry and the use of pesticides presents a major problem for Russia and the Eurasian republics.

Farmers harvesting wheat in Kazakhstan

Fishing in the Caspian Sea

CHAPTER 16 HIGHLIGHTS

USING THE CHAPTER 16 HIGHLIGHTS

Use the Chapter 16 Highlights to preview, review, condense, or reteach the chapter.

PREVIEW/REVIEW

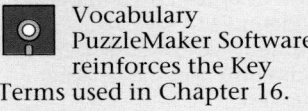

Vocabulary PuzzleMaker Software reinforces the Key Terms used in Chapter 16.

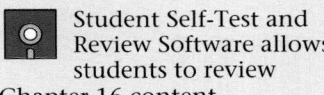

Student Self-Test and Review Software allows students to review Chapter 16 content.

CONDENSE

Have students read the Chapter 16 Highlights.

Have students listen to the Chapter 16 Audiocassettes in the TCR. Spanish Audiocassettes are also available.

Assign the Chapter 16 Audiocassette Activity and give the students the Chapter 16 Audiocassette Quiz.

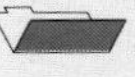 

Have students complete the Guided Reading Activities for Chapter 16 in the TCR. Spanish Guided Reading Activities are also available.

RETEACH

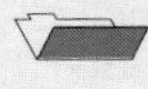 

Have students complete Reteaching Activity 16 in the TCR. Spanish Reteaching Activities are also available.

Map Activity

Identify and Locate Copy and distribute page 34 of the Outline Map Resource Book. On the map, have students locate and label the following bodies of water: Baltic Sea, Black Sea, Lake Baikal, Caspian Sea, and Lake Sevan.

Then have them draw and label the following rivers: Don River, Amur River, Radzan River, and Dniester River. Refer the class to the Atlas maps at the beginning of the unit for help.

chapter 16 REVIEW

GLENCOE TECHNOLOGY

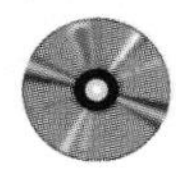

Videodisc

Use Chapter 16 MindJogger Videoquiz to review students' knowledge before administering the Chapter 16 Test.

MINDJOGGER VIDEOQUIZ

Chapter 16
Disc 2 Side B

The MindJogger Videoquiz is also available on videocassette.

Reviewing Key Terms

Choose the vocabulary term that best completes each of the sentences below. Write your answers on a separate sheet of paper.

consumer goods (p. 328)
black market (p. 328)
kolkhozes (p. 329)
industrialize (p. 336)
polluted (p. 338)
pesticides (p. 341)

SECTION 1

1. Most Soviet citizens could not afford to buy goods on the ____.
2. In the Soviet Union large collective farms were called ____.
3. People in Russia and the Eurasian republics still suffer from a shortage of ____.

SECTION 2

4. Heavy industry has ____ many rivers in Russia and the Eurasian republics by dumping toxic wastes in their waters.
5. To kill insects destroying their crops, farmers in Russia and the Eurasian republics use ____.
6. In their drive to ____, the Soviets severely damaged the environment.

Reviewing Facts

SECTION 1

7. What was the role of the Soviet government in the economy?
8. Which republic has moved the fastest to create a market economy?
9. In what ways have communications changed since independence?

SECTION 2

10. What concerns some Russians and Armenians about nuclear power plants?
11. What four independent republics now have nuclear weapons?
12. How did Lake Baikal, on the Central Siberian Plateau, become polluted?

Critical Thinking

13. **Analyzing Information** Do you think it is important for the independent republics to cooperate with one another? Explain your answer.
14. **Expressing Problems Clearly** How have factories contributed to pollution in Russia and the other republics?

Geographic Themes

15. **Movement** How have railroads aided economic development in the region?
16. **Human/Environment Interaction** How has industrialization affected the environment of Russia and the Eurasian republics?

Practicing Skills

Distinguishing Fact From Opinion

For each statement below, write **F** if it is a fact, or write **O** if it is an opinion. Explain each answer.

17. The collapse of the centrally controlled economies in Russia and the Eurasian republics is a plus for the global environment.
18. The nuclear physicist appointed to supervise the cleanup at Chernobyl estimates that this process has already claimed between 5,000 and 7,000 lives.

Using the Unit Atlas

Refer to the physical geography section of the Unit Atlas on pages 286–287.

19. What Asiatic part of Russia is rich in mineral deposits?

ANSWERS

Reviewing Key Terms

1. black market
2. *kolkhozes*
3. consumer goods
4. polluted
5. pesticides
6. industrialize

Reviewing Facts

7. It owned nearly everything, decided what and how much to produce, and planned and controlled the distribution and pricing of most goods.
8. Russia
9. Republics have greater freedom of expression, little or no censorship, new newspapers, more televisions and telephones. The governments no longer manipulate the news.
10. Russians think older nuclear plants could be dangerous because they are poorly designed and lack spare parts; Armenians think nuclear plants should not be in earthquake zones.
11. Russia, Ukraine, Belarus, Kazakhstan
12. A paper and pulp mill spilled toxic chemicals into it, and rivers carried fertilizers and other chemicals into it.

Critical Thinking

13. Answers will vary but should point out that under the Soviet government, the republics became dependent on one another for resources and so need to cooperate at least until they can become self-sufficient.
14. by dumping toxic wastes everywhere, using a polluting type of coal, and not using pollution-preventing equipment

Geographic Themes

15. Railroads opened up new areas, linked areas rich in natural resources with urban centers, and moved freight and passengers from one place to another.
16. It has polluted and damaged the environment.

20. What body of water is the center of the sturgeon fishing industry?

Projects

Individual Activity

Imagine that you are an American entrepreneur interested in investing in a business in Russia or one of the other republics. Write a letter to your banker that indicates in which republic the business is located, what kind of business it is, and why you think it would be a good investment.

Cooperative Learning Activity

Working in a group of six, two people will research the history and routes of the Trans-Siberian Railroad, while two others research the history and routes of the Baikal-Amur Mainline (BAM). For each railroad, one person should be prepared to take the role of a construction worker and the other that of a passenger. The remaining two students will take the roles of news reporters and interview the others for a television documentary titled *Adventures in Railroading.*

Writing About Geography

Cause and Effect

Imagine that you are captain of a barge that carries freight along a waterway in one of the republics. Research the waterway and what has happened to it and to the surrounding area over the last 50 years. Then write a letter to the president of the republic explaining how industrialization and/or agriculture have changed the waterway for better or for worse.

Locating Places

THE PHYSICAL GEOGRAPHY OF RUSSIA AND THE EURASIAN REPUBLICS

Match the letters on the map with the places and physical features of Russia and the Eurasian republics. Write your answers on a separate sheet of paper.

1. Baku
2. Don River
3. Vladivostok
4. Lake Baikal
5. Kiev
6. Amur River
7. Kazakhstan
8. Yerevan
9. Chernobyl
10. Caspian Sea

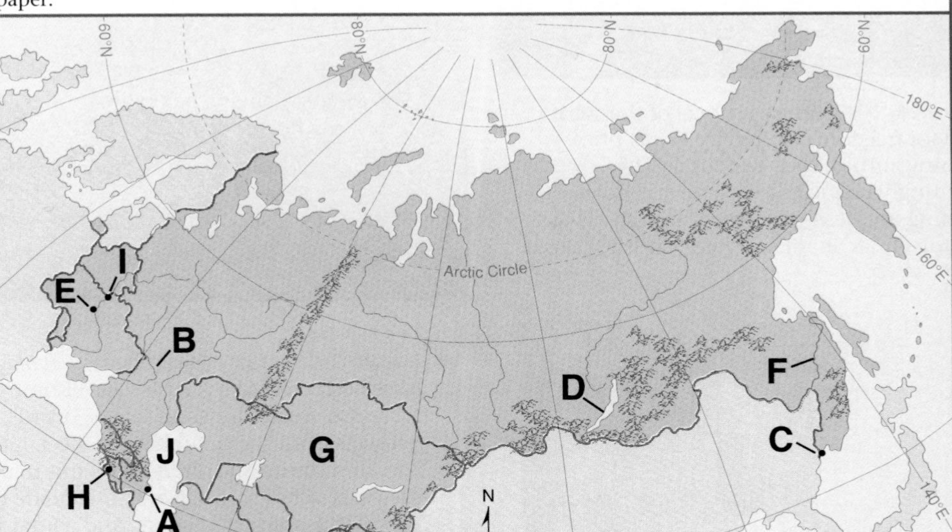

Chapter 16 Review

Practicing Skills

17. O; The statement cannot be proved with facts and so expresses an opinion.

18. F; This statement can be verified and so states a fact.

Using the Unit Atlas

19. Siberia

20. the Caspian Sea

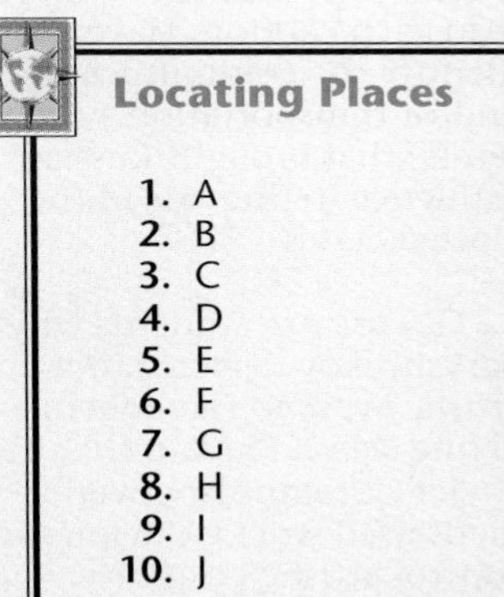

Locating Places

1. A
2. B
3. C
4. D
5. E
6. F
7. G
8. H
9. I
10. J

Chapter Bonus Test Question

This question may be used for extra credit on the chapter test. Choose the letter of the correct response.

Which of the following statements does NOT refer to Kazakhstan?

(1) The Soviet army tested nuclear and chemical weapons there.

(2) Russian and Ukrainian farmers came there to plow up millions of acres of steppes.

(3) Radiation from the Chernobyl plant contaminated 20 percent of the fertile soil.

(4) Little rain falls there so the land has to be irrigated to grow cotton.

Answer: (3)

Geography Connection

FOCUS

Ask students to scan the titles and photographs on pages 346 and 347 and define the term *fine arts*. List several definitions on the board and create a composite definition.

TEACH

L1 Movement Invite students to apply the geographic theme of movement as they read each caption. Have them identify the communications and/or transportation system(s) that brought Russian influence to fine arts in the United States.

L2 Discuss Ask students why Baryshnikov defected. *(for artistic freedom)* Have them define *defect*. Explain that the Soviet Communist government used strict guidelines to control artistic creativity. Only works praising Soviet Communist life were permitted. Criticism of the guidelines or government was not allowed. Ask students if they agree with this policy. Discuss the role they think government should play concerning the fine arts.

Russia and the Eurasian Republics and the United States

THE FINE ARTS

Russian artists have influenced many areas of the fine arts in the United States—music, ballet, modern dance, literature, poetry, film, painting, sculpture. Russians have applied their deep love of the lyrical and the beautiful to create works of enduring significance.

▲ ***DR. ZHIVAGO*** is a timeless novel of the spirit's need for freedom, written by Nobel prize-winning author Boris Pasternak. The hauntingly poetic tale became an Oscar-winning, modern-day American film classic starring Omar Sharif and Julie Christie (1965).

◀ **INNOVATIVE SCULPTURES** called *assemblages* have been created by Louise Nevelson. Nevelson creates in wood scraps, boards, leftovers from Victorian houses, steel, lucite, and aluminum. She often uses paint to unify the parts of her works. Nevelson Square in New York City is named after her, and contains seven mammoth steel sculptures.

Making the Connection

Research Have students plan and present a "Russian Connection" celebration. Ask small groups to review and choose several Pasternak poems, passages from *Dr. Zhivago,* a Tchaikovsky composition, art works by Kandinsky or Chagall, or works by other Russian artists who have defected from their native land. As groups present their selections to the class, require that they explain the reasons for their choices.

After the presentations, guide students to comment on the works as a whole and form any generalizations. If time allows, encourage students to try sketching or painting a memoir of the celebration in the style of Kandinsky or Chagall.

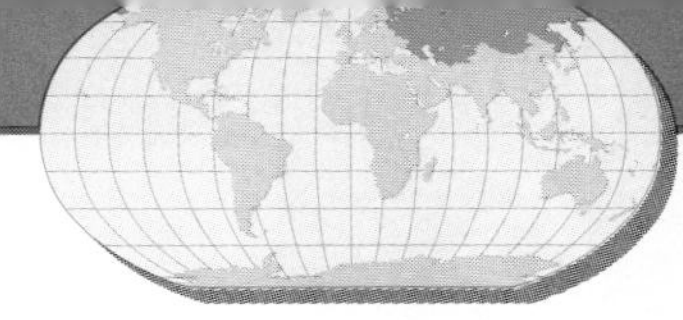

MIKHAIL BARYSHNIKOV, a Russian ballet dancer who settled in the United States, delighted his audiences with his flying leaps into the air. Famous for this dynamic style, Baryshnikov executed his moves with great brilliance and daring. He defected to the West in 1974, discontented with the lack of freedom and the limits that the Soviet Union placed on his dancing. Joining the American Ballet Theater, Baryshnikov gave his imagination and style full rein.

RUSSIAN COMPOSER PETER TCHAIKOVSKY produced works that have become classical standards. Instantly recognizable to most Americans are his orchestral composition, *Nutcracker Suite,* and his three ballets, *Swan Lake, Sleeping Beauty,* and *The Nutcracker.*

MODERN ART movements were led by Wassily Kandinsky and Marc Chagall. Kandinsky's clear, pure colors and free-form shapes and lines earned him recognition as the first abstract expressionist. Chagall transformed the "shattered" techniques of the cubists to create graceful, dreamlike surrealist art.

GEORGE BALANCHINE aroused affection and loyalty from every dancer he developed and the millions of fans who loved his ballets. Just a year after arriving in the United States, he cofounded the School of American Ballet, guiding and nurturing it until it became the famed New York City Ballet. Balanchine remained with the ballet from its cofounding in 1934 to his death in 1983, creating more than 200 ballets.

Checking for Understanding

1. Who are two Russian dancers who have influenced American ballet?
2. **Movement** Who are three artists who influenced modern American art?

Geography Connection

ASSESS

Have students answer the Checking for Understanding questions on page 347.

CLOSE

Ask students to reread the class definition of *fine arts* and suggest any necessary changes. Have a volunteer check an encyclopedia definition. Ask students why they think the people featured are considered fine artists.

Suggest that students research these artists to learn what caused them to leave Russia.

DID YOU KNOW?

George Balanchine developed a new style of ballet called *neo-classic.* His dances are notable for quick, strong movements and changes of direction. An extraordinarily innovative choreographer, Balanchine often used his works to showcase dancing and the study of movement.

CD-ROM

PICTURE ATLAS OF THE WORLD

You can hear the music of the balalaika by clicking the "Music" button of Russia.

ANSWERS TO CHECKING FOR UNDERSTANDING

1. George Balanchine, Mikhail Baryshnikov
2. Wassily Kandinsky, Marc Chagall, Louise Nevelson

UNIT OVERVIEW

The three chapters that comprise this unit introduce students to the physical geography and peoples of North Africa and Southwest Asia. Various aspects of the region's life—such as the economy, lifestyles, and human/environment interaction—are also presented.

GEOGRAPHY JOURNAL

Activity Have students choose one event that interests them particularly and research the background. Suggest that they present outlines of their findings to the class, as well as be prepared to answer questions.

- This journal activity provides the basis for the "Writing About Geography" exercise in the Chapter Review.
- The Geography Journal may be used as an integral part of Performance Assessment.

GLENCOE TECHNOLOGY

Videodisc

Use the following to introduce or enrich Unit 6:

REUTERS ISSUES IN GEOGRAPHY

Chapter 5
Disc 1 Side A

Title: ***North Africa and Southwest Asia: The Influence of Oil and Water***

Subject: How oil and water affect life in the region and events around the world

UNIT 6

North Africa and Southwest Asia

Mehmet Biber/Ajans Biber

GeoJournal Activity

In your study of North Africa and Southwest Asia, read newspapers and magazines, and listen to television and radio broadcasts about events affecting the environment, politics, cultures, and daily life of the region. Make a brief list of the items in your journal.

348

Where in the World . . . .

Have students look at the map on pages A16–A17 in which North Africa and Southwest Asia are highlighted. Display Unit Map Overlay Transparency 6-5 and ask students the following questions: Which ocean forms part of northern Africa's coastline? *(Atlantic)* What bodies of water form the coastlines of the Arabian Peninsula? *(Red Sea, Gulf of Aden, Persian Gulf, Gulf of Oman, Arabian Sea)* What continent is north of Africa? *(Europe)* What is North Africa's only river system? *(Nile)* Southwest Asia's *(Tigris and Euphrates)* What areas appear to have no internal source of water? *(all North Africa except Egypt; all Southwest Asia, except Turkey and Iraq)* Which is the most direct route to the United States from Africa? *(west across the Atlantic Ocean)*

Picturing the World

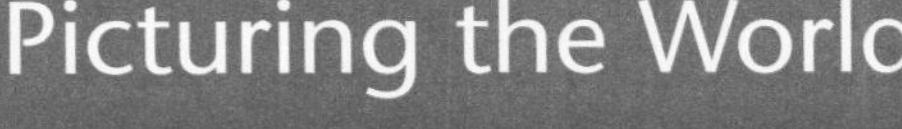

Pilgrims crowd the sacred mosque at Makkah (Mecca) in Saudi Arabia, birthplace of the Prophet Muhammad. The draped Kaaba, in the center of the mosque, is the most sacred shrine of Islam. The vast majority of the people of North Africa and Southwest Asia are followers of Islam. Muslims are divided into two main groups: Sunni Muslims and Shiite Muslims. Look at the graph on page 382.

1. Muslims form what percentage of the region's population?
2. What are the only two countries in the region that do not follow Islam?

Picture Atlas CD-ROM Enrichment Corner

Research the populations of the following countries: Egypt, Iraq, Kuwait, Libya, Morocco, Saudi Arabia, and Tunisia. Look at the population projection graph and figure out how many millions of people are projected to be added to each of these countries by the year 2025. (Round off your answers to the nearest million.) Make a bar graph of your findings. (See page 20 for more information on graphs.) Based on your graph, answer the following questions:

1. Which country will add the most people?
2. Which country will add the fewest?
3. Which country is projected to triple its population?

349

Information about North Africa and Southwest Asia can be found at the following address:

World Wide Web
http://www.pol.umu.se/html/ac/islam.htm

NATIONAL GEOGRAPHIC SOCIETY

CD-ROM

PICTURE ATLAS OF THE WORLD
See page T40 for an additional CD-ROM activity to enrich Unit 6, North Africa and Southwest Asia.

0:00 OUT OF TIME?

If time does not permit teaching each chapter in this unit, you may use the Chapter Highlights and the Audiocassettes that include a 1-page activity and a 1-page test for each chapter.

ANSWERS TO PICTURING THE WORLD

1. 93 percent
2. Israel and Cyprus

Enrichment Corner Answers

1. Egypt
2. Kuwait
3. Libya

These features and activities may be used as an introduction to the unit or as teaching tools throughout the course of the unit.

FOCUS

Ask students to study the maps on pages 350–351 for a moment, then suggest what seems to be the determining factor in population distribution in North Africa and Southwest Asia.

TEACH

Deduce As students read each fact, have them deduce which of the five geographic themes supports the statement.

Implement Foods Around the World 5 as a class activity.

Have students complete the Political Map Transparency 6 Activity in the TCR.

Have students complete Unit Map Overlay Transparency 6 Activity in the TCR.

Have students complete World Cultures Transparencies 9 and 10 Activities in the TCR.

Have students complete World Literature Reading 5 in the TCR.

UNIT 6 ATLAS

NORTH AFRICA AND Cultural Geography

EXPLORING CULTURAL DIVERSITY

1. ***What areas of the region are most heavily populated? Most sparsely populated?***
2. ***What nations are in the region?***
3. ***What cities in North Africa and Southwest Asia have more than 5 million people?***

Aleppo, Syria, has been an important trading center since the 1500s BC.

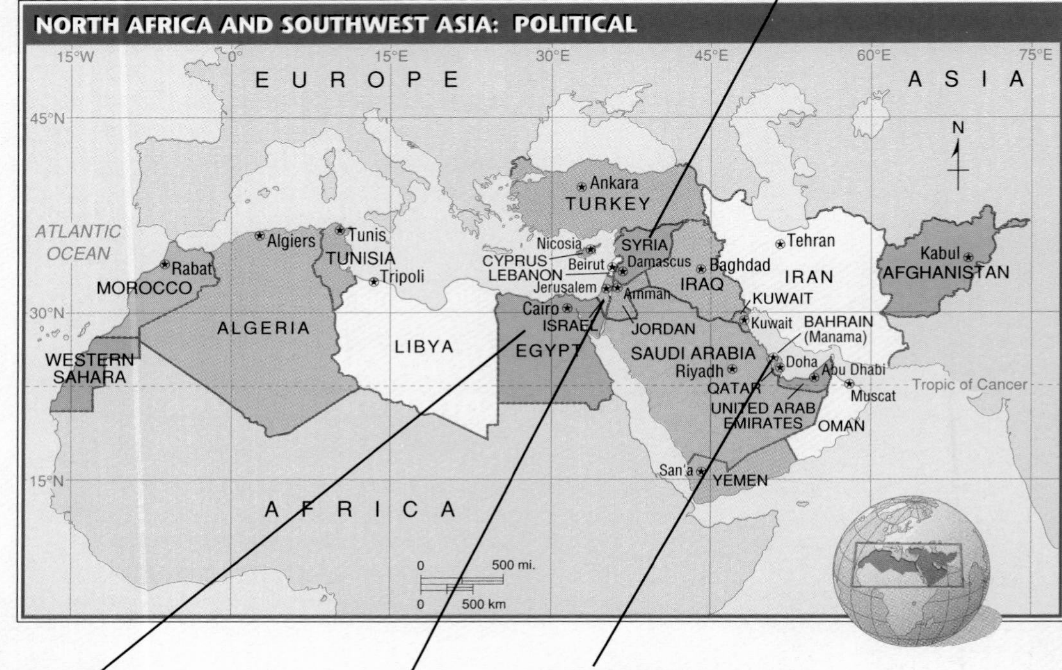

Because of its strategic location, Egypt is important in world transportation.

In 1950, Israel passed the Law of the Return allowing any Jew to settle in the country. Since then, Jews from all over the world have relocated to Israel.

Bahrain has one of the highest standards of living in the Persian Gulf area.

Many bedouins, Arab nomads who live in Southwest Asia, are giving up their traditional nomadic lifestyle to move to the city.

350 UNIT 6

Classroom Resources for Unit 6

BLACKLINE MASTERS:
Geography Simulation 6
World Literature Reading 5
Environmental Issue 6

TRANSPARENCIES:
Unit Map Overlay Transparency 6
Political Map Transparency 6
World Cultures Transparencies 9, 10

MULTIMEDIA:

World Music: *Cultural Traditions, Lesson 5*

Reuters Issues in Geography

Testmaker

Picture Atlas of the World

Images of the World Poster set

People have lived in present-day **Algeria** for at least 40,000 years.

The **Sahara** is very sparsely populated.

Egypt's **Nile River Valley** is one of the world's most heavily populated areas.

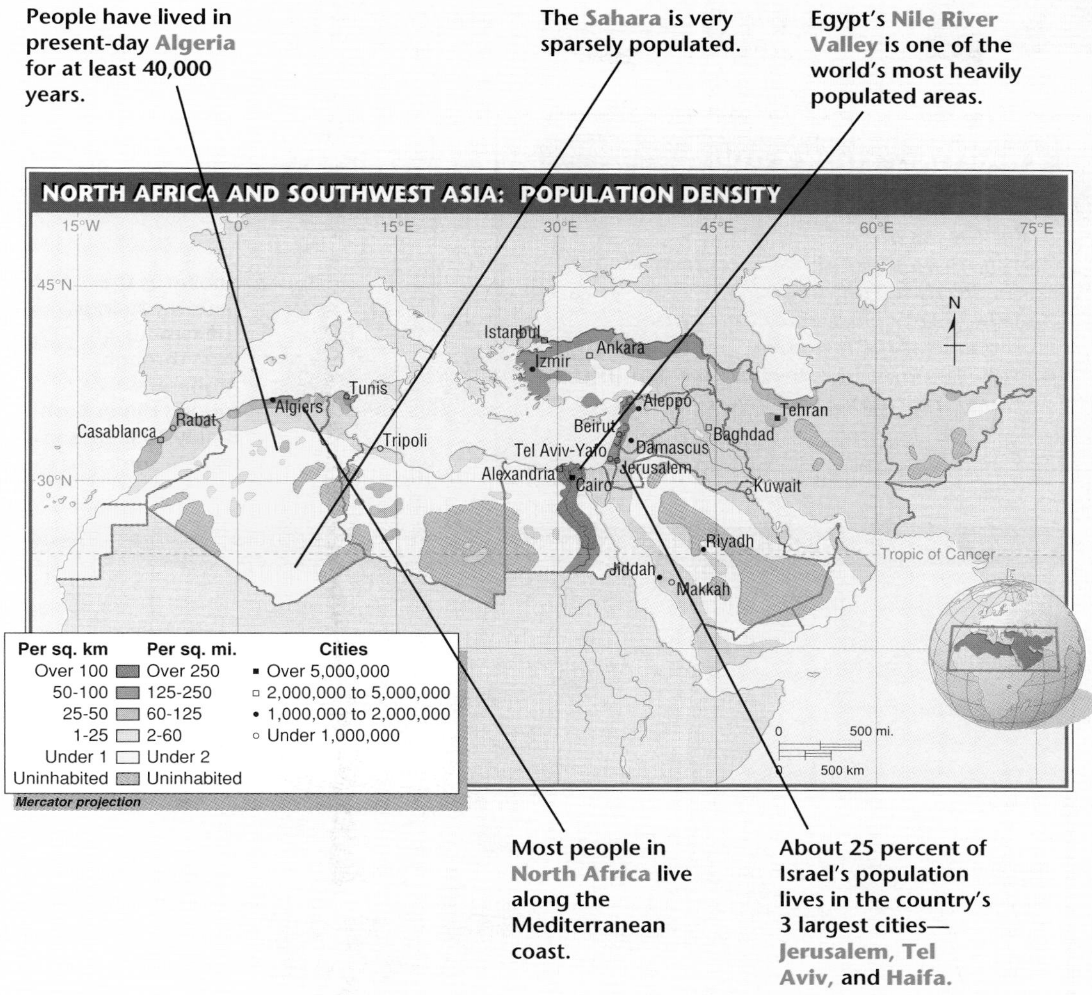

Most people in **North Africa** live along the Mediterranean coast.

About 25 percent of Israel's population lives in the country's 3 largest cities—**Jerusalem, Tel Aviv,** and **Haifa.**

North Africa and Southwest Asia have about 70 million more people than the United States.

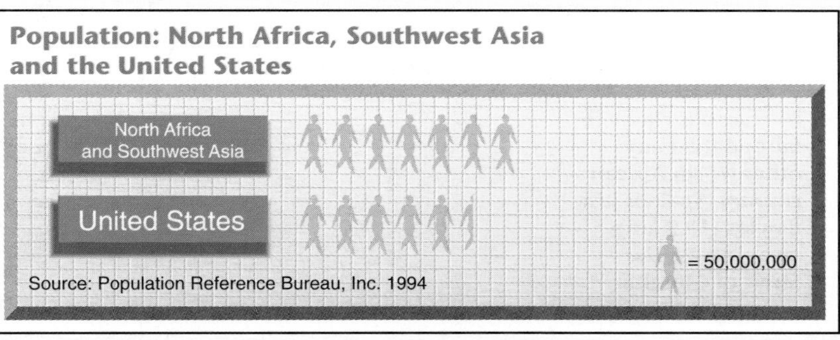

Map and Graph Activity

Culture Assign a country to each student or pair of students. Have them use appropriate sources to discover the ethnic and religious groups in each country, as well as the percentage each group makes up of the country's total population. Have students illustrate their findings in either bar or circle graph form. Provide a time to pool information; lead students to identify the area's major and minority ethnic groups and religions. Encourage students to speculate on how such differences could affect the region.

LESSON PLAN Unit 6 Atlas

Play World Music: Cultural Traditions, Lesson 5, and have students complete the Lesson 5 activity.

ASSESS

Have students answer the Exploring Cultural Diversity questions on page 350.

EXPLORING CULTURAL DIVERSITY

This feature may be used to introduce students to the cultural geography of North Africa and Southwest Asia. Use questions to stimulate class discussion and help students become familiar with the region. Accept reasonable answers based on the maps, graph, and captions.

CLOSE

Ask students to reread each fact quickly, and predict which might be explained by the physical maps on the upcoming pages.

GLENCOE TECHNOLOGY

Videodisc

Use the following to introduce or enrich Unit 6:

REUTERS ISSUES IN GEOGRAPHY

Chapter 5
Disc 1 Side A

Title: ***North Africa and Southwest Asia: The Influence of Oil and Water***

Subject: How oil and water affect life in the region and events around the world

LESSON PLAN
Unit 6 Atlas

These features and activities may be used as an introduction to the unit or as teaching tools throughout the course of the unit.

FOCUS

Allow students a moment to study the maps, then ask students to try to answer any of the questions formulated at the end of the previous lesson. Have students share such questions and answers.

TEACH

Cause and Effect Have students recall their suggestions concerning the determining factor in the region's population distribution. Ask them to formulate a cause/effect statement(s) about the physical geography that explains the uneven distribution.

To introduce students to the physical geography of North Africa and Southwest Asia, have students complete Unit Atlas Activity 6A in the TCR.

Implement Geography Simulation 6 as a class activity.

CD-ROM

PICTURE ATLAS OF THE WORLD

You and your students can see and read about the physical features of North Africa and Southwest Asia by clicking the "Photos" and "Essay" buttons of individual countries in the region.

UNIT 6 ATLAS

NORTH AFRICA AND Physical Geography

CHARTING YOUR COURSE

1. *What bodies of water provide coastlines for the region?*
2. *What two natural resources are found in the Persian Gulf area?*
3. *What is the most abundant natural resource of the region?*
4. *What mountain ranges are located in North Africa and Southwest Asia?*

Known as the gateway to India, the famous Khyber Pass through Afghanistan's rugged Hindu Kush is only 10 feet (3 m) wide in some places.

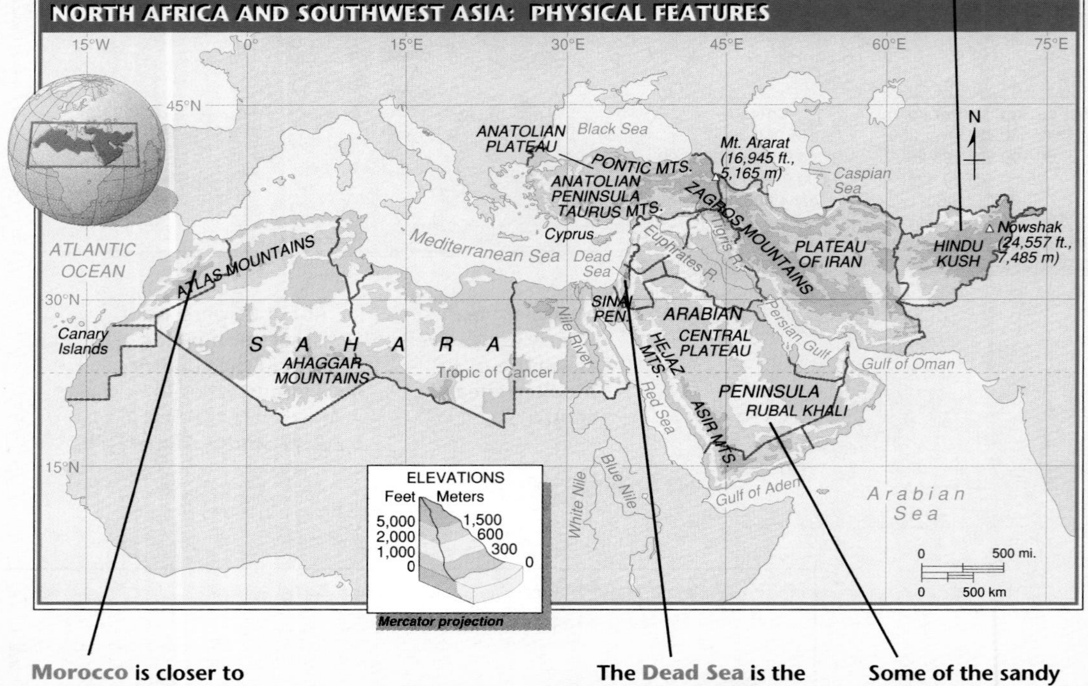

Morocco is closer to Europe than any other North African country. Spain is just 8 miles (12.9 km) away, across the Strait of Gibraltar.

The Dead Sea is the earth's saltiest body of water—about nine times saltier than the oceans.

Some of the sandy areas of the Arabian Peninsula are so large they are called "sand seas."

Map Activity

Interpendence Assign a country to one or two students; have students use appropriate sources to find out and list each country's trading partners, imports, and exports. Provide a time for sharing information. After all students have contributed their findings, ask students to formulate generalizations concerning the region's main imports, exports, and trading partners. Have students also discuss what effects local wars and disagreements could have on each country's economy.

Morocco has about two-thirds of the world's known phosphate reserves.

Cotton is Egypt's most important crop.

Oman is one of the world's hottest countries.

NORTH AFRICA AND SOUTHWEST ASIA: NATURAL RESOURCES

Petroleum
Natural gas
Iron ore
Copper
Lead
Zinc
Manganese
Phosphate

Lambert Equal-Area projection

A variety of crops grow in the Fertile Crescent, a region of rich, fertile soil between the Tigris and Euphrates rivers.

The Arabian Peninsula supplies the world with one-fourth to one-third of all oil produced.

North Africa and Southwest Asia: Physical Profile

West to East at approximately 30°N latitude

LESSON PLAN
Unit 6 Atlas

ASSESS

Have students answer the Charting Your Course questions on page 352.

CHARTING YOUR COURSE

This feature may be used to introduce students to the physical geography of North Africa and Southwest Asia. Use questions to stimulate class discussion and help students become familiar with the region. Accept reasonable answers based on the maps, graph, and captions.

CLOSE

Ask students to suggest what natural resources are scarce in this world region, and to support their answers with evidence from the maps.

DID YOU KNOW?

Saudi Arabia has almost 26 percent of the world's proven oil reserves.

IMAGES OF THE WORLD POSTER SET

Display the poster of "North Africa and Southwest Asia." Have students hypothesize about the climate zone and population density of each photo.

Map Activity

Place Have students, individually or in pairs, research agricultural areas of North Africa and Southwest Asia, as well as the methods used to bring water to the areas. Have them illustrate their findings on a physical map of the region, labeling countries, rivers, and water usage methods. Encourage them to also note the percentage of arable land in each country, then figure an average percentage for the entire region.

These features and activities may be used as teaching tools throughout the course of the unit.

DID YOU KNOW?

Written history begins with the records of ancient Egypt.

DID YOU KNOW?

Damascus, the capital of Syria, is the oldest continuously inhabited city on the globe—4,000 years.

Ways of the World

TURKEY To begin or end a meal, a diner often says *Afiyet Olsun*—"May what you eat bring you well-being."

DID YOU KNOW?

As the site of the Tigris-Euphrates River, Iraq is the birthplace of the world's first city-states.

DID YOU KNOW?

Bahrain is the headquarters of the U.S. Central Command, and the docking and refining base for the U.S. Navy contingent that has been patrolling the Persian Gulf since 1949.

COUNTRY PROFILE

COUNTRY* AND CAPITAL	FLAG AND LANGUAGES	POPULATION	LANDMASS	PRINCIPAL PRODUCTS EXPORT	PRINCIPAL PRODUCTS IMPORT
Afghanistan Kabul	Pushtu, Dari Persian	17,800,000 71 per sq. mi. 27 per sq. km	251,770 sq. mi. 652,084 sq. km	Fruits & Nuts	Machinery
Algeria Algiers	Arabic, Berber	27,900,000 30 per sq. mi. 11 per sq. km	919,590 sq. mi. 2,381,738 sq. km	Petroleum	Machinery
Bahrain Manama	Arabic, Farsi, Urdu	600,000 2,308 per sq. mi. 892 per sq. km	260 sq. mi. 673 sq. km	Petroleum	Petroleum
Cyprus Nicosia	Greek, Turkish, English	756,000 212 per sq. mi. 82 per sq. km	3,570 sq. mi. 9,246 sq. km	Citrus Fruits	Machinery
Egypt Cairo	Arabic, English	58,900,000 152 per sq. mi. 59 per sq. km	384,340 sq. mi. 995,440 sq. km	Petroleum	Machinery
Iran Tehran	Farsi, Turkish, Kurdish, Arabic	61,200,000 97 per sq. mi. 38 per sq. km	631,660 sq. mi. 1,635,999 sq. km	Petroleum	Motor Vehicles
Iraq Baghdad	Arabic, Kurdish	19,900,000 118 per sq. mi. 45 per sq. km	168,870 sq. mi. 437,373 sq. km	Fuels	Machinery
Israel Jerusalem	Hebrew, Arabic	5,400,000 688 per sq. mi. 266 per sq. km	7,850 sq. mi. 20,332 sq. km	Machinery	Diamonds
Jordan Amman	Arabic	4,200,000 122 per sq. mi. 47 per sq. km	34,340 sq. mi. 88,941 sq. km	Phosphates	Food
Kuwait Kuwait	Arabic	1,300,000 189 per sq. mi. 73 per sq. km	6,880 sq. mi. 17,819 sq. km	Petroleum	Machinery
Lebanon Beirut	Arabic, French	3,600,000 911 per sq. mi. 352 per sq. km	3,950 sq. mi. 10,231 sq. km	Jewelery	Machinery
Libya Tripoli	Arabic	5,100,000 7 per sq. mi. 3 per sq. km	679,360 sq. mi. 1,759,542 sq. km	Petroleum	Food

*Country maps not drawn to scale.

Country Profile Activity

Culture/Sequence Have students choose a country and complete a brief overview of the country's history. In their journals, have students note the approximate date of the country's settlement, groups who were important in the country's history, and contributions to world culture. Have students transfer their data to index cards, using concise phrases. As students present their material, arrange the cards, as far as possible, in an accurate time line. When all students have contributed, lead students to a realization of the region's rich cultural heritage.

COUNTRY* AND CAPITAL	FLAG AND LANGUAGES	POPULATION	LANDMASS	PRINCIPAL PRODUCTS EXPORT	PRINCIPAL PRODUCTS IMPORT
Morocco** Rabat	Arabic, Berber	28,600,000 166 per sq. mi. 64 per sq. km	172,320 sq. mi. 446,309 sq. km	Food	Crude Oil
Oman Muscat	Arabic	1,900,000 23 per sq. mi. 9 per sq. km	82,030 sq. mi. 212,458 sq. km	Petroleum	Machinery
Qatar Doha	Arabic, English	500,000 122 per sq. mi. 47 per sq. km	4,250 sq. mi. 11,008 sq. km	Petroleum	Machinery
Saudi Arabia Riyadh	Arabic	18,000,000 21 per sq. mi. 8 per sq. km	830,000 sq. mi. 2,149,700 sq. km	Petroleum	Machinery
Syria Damascus	Arabic, Kurdish, Armenian, Turkish	14,000,000 197 per sq. mi. 76 per sq. km	71,070 sq. mi. 184,071 sq. km	Petroleum	Food
Tunisia Tunis	Arabic, French	8,700,000 143 per sq. mi. 55 per sq. km	59,980 sq. mi. 155,348 sq. km	Clothing	Textiles
Turkey Ankara	Turkish, Kurdish	61,800,000 208 per sq. mi. 80 per sq. km	297,150 sq. mi. 769,619 sq. km	Textiles	Machinery
United Arab Emirates Abu Dhabi	Arabic	1,700,000 53 per sq. mi. 20 per sq. km	32,280 sq. mi. 83,605 sq. km	Petroleum	Machinery
Yemen San'a	Arabic	12,900,000 63 per sq. mi. 24 per sq. km	203,850 sq. mi. 527,972 sq. km	Coffee	Food

**Morocco claims the Western Sahara area but other countries do not accept this claim.

*Country maps not drawn to scale.

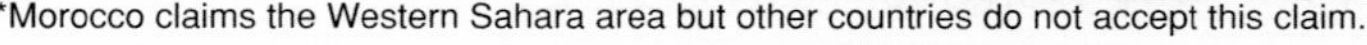

The rulers of the ancient Persian Empire built a magnificent capital at Persepolis.

Global Gourmet

Egyptians like preparing elaborate and expensive meals for their guests. In return, guests do not eat everything on the plate. By leaving a little food, the guest signals compliments to the host for providing so well.

DID YOU KNOW?

Although Israel is poor in natural resources, and averages less than five inches of rainfall a year, it produces most of its own food through improved irrigation techniques and soil conservation.

Ways of the World

OMAN Laws exist against ugliness that distresses the sultan. A person can be fined for driving a dirty car or leaving a building unpainted.

DID YOU KNOW?

Jordan's largest source of income is the billions of dollars sent home by Jordanians working in other Arab countries.

Country Profile Activity

Political Systems Assign each student or pair of students a country. Using appropriate sources, have students quickly find the country's official name, title of the country's leader, his or her powers, and the form of government the country claims. Have students list this information in columns on the chalkboard. When every country has been accounted for, have students survey the table and generalize on the role of religion, as well as the power of the leader, in the region. Be sure that students also note the one exception—Israel—and speculate on the effects this difference might have.

CHAPTER 17

PLANNING GUIDE

The Physical Geography of North Africa and Southwest Asia

CHAPTER ORGANIZER

Daily Lesson Objectives	Multimedia	Teacher Classroom Resources
SECTION 1 The Land 1. Locate the seas and coastal areas of North Africa and Southwest Asia. 2. Discuss the mountains and plateaus in North Africa and Southwest Asia. 3. Identify the kinds of natural resources found in North Africa and Southwest Asia.	Section Focus Transparency 17-1 Unit Map Overlay Transparencies 1-8, 6-2 Reuters Issues in Geography Testmaker Chapter 17 Vocabulary PuzzleMaker Software STV: World Geography, Volume 1 STV: World Geography, Volume 2 Picture Atlas of the World Physical Geography of the World Transparencies 41–50	Reproducible Lesson Plan 17-1 Guided Reading Activity 17-1 Spanish Guided Reading Activity 17-1 Workbook Activity 17-1 Performance Assessment 17 Chapter 17 Vocabulary Activity Geography Simulation 6 Section Quiz 17-1
SECTION 2 The Climate and Vegetation 1. Identify three types of climate found in North Africa and Southwest Asia. 2. Explain how mountain ranges influence rainfall in coastal regions of North Africa and Southwest Asia. 3. Describe the type of vegetation found in North Africa and Southwest Asia.	Section Focus Transparency 17-2 Unit Map Overlay Transparencies 6-3, 6-5 Testmaker STV: World Geography, Volume 2	Reproducible Lesson Plan 17-2 Guided Reading Activity 17-2 Spanish Guided Reading Activity 17-2 Workbook Activity 17-2 Writer's Guidebook Lessons 4, 5 Enrichment Activity 17 Section Quiz 17-2
CHAPTER REVIEW AND EVALUATION	Chapter 17 English (or Spanish) Audiocassettes MindJogger Videoquiz Testmaker Student Self-Test and Review Software	Reteaching Activity 17 Spanish Reteaching Activity 17 Chapter 17 Test Form A and Form B

0:00 *If time does not permit teaching the entire chapter, summarize using the Chapter 17 Highlights on page 367, and the Chapter 17 English (or Spanish) Audiocassettes. Review students' knowledge using the Glencoe MindJogger Videoquiz.*

KEY TO ABILITY LEVELS

Teaching strategies have been coded for varying learning styles and abilities.

L1 **BASIC** activities for all students

L2 **AVERAGE** activities for average to above-average students

L3 **CHALLENGING** activities for above-average students

LEP **LIMITED ENGLISH PROFICIENCY** activities

Performance Assessment

Environmental Adaptation Take students through a simulation in which they assume the roles of oil company executives and employees. Using resource maps and other sources, groups of students should locate an area of North Africa and Southwest Asia for their oil company. Each group should then research the physical features and climate of the area.

Upon completion of this research, each group should take the role of executives and make a presentation to the rest of the class in which they promote their company's need to relocate to the culture region. In each presentation, class members who are not part of the presenting group will assume the roles of employees whom the company is trying to persuade to relocate. Aspects of the physical geography and the ways in which humans could meet the region's environmental challenges should be included in a discussion between "executives" and "employees."

POSSIBLE RUBRIC FEATURES: Content information, concept attainment, collaborative skills, argumentation skills, problem analysis, communication skills

For additional professional and classroom resources, see Chapter Resources, pages T46–T51.

TEACHER'S CORNER

NATIONAL GEOGRAPHIC SOCIETY

INDEX TO NATIONAL GEOGRAPHIC MAGAZINE

The following articles may be used for research relating to this chapter:

- "The Desert Sea," by David Doubilet, November 1993.
- "The Persian Gulf: Living in Harm's Way," by Thomas J. Abercrombie, May 1988.
- "Journey Up the Nile," by Robert Caputo, May 1985.
- "The Mediterranean: Sea of Man's Fate," by Rick Gore, December 1982.
- "Egypt's Desert of Promise," by Farouk El-Baz, February 1982.
- "The Desert: An Age-old Challenge Grows," by Rick Gore, November 1979.

NATIONAL GEOGRAPHIC SOCIETY PRODUCTS AVAILABLE FROM GLENCOE

To order the following products for use with this chapter, contact your local Glencoe sales representative or call Glencoe at 1-800-334-7344:

- *Picture Atlas of the World* (CD-ROM)
- *STV: World Geography, Asia and Australia* (Videodisc)
- *STV: World Geography, Africa and Europe* (Videodisc)
- *ZipZapMap! World* (Software)
- *GeoBee* (Software)
- *Images of the World* (Posters)
- *Eye on the Environment* (Posters)
- *Physical Geography of the World* (Transparencies)
- *Picture Atlas of Our 50 States* (Book)

ADDITIONAL NATIONAL GEOGRAPHIC SOCIETY PRODUCTS

To order the following products for use with this chapter, call National Geographic Society at 1-800-368-2728:

- *The Water's Edge: Life Along the Great Rivers*, "The Amazon," "The Mississippi," "The Nile." (Filmstrip)
- *Nations of the World Series*, "Egypt," "Israel." (Video)

Introducing
CHAPTER 17

chapter 17 The Physical Geography of North Africa and Southwest Asia

PERFORMANCE ASSESSMENT

Refer to the Planning Guide on page 356B for a Performance Assessment Activity for this chapter. See the *Performance Assessment Activities* booklet for additional suggestions.

CHAPTER OBJECTIVES

1. **Describe** the major landforms found in North Africa and Southwest Asia.
2. **Explain** the relationship between climate and vegetation in the region.

GLENCOE TECHNOLOGY

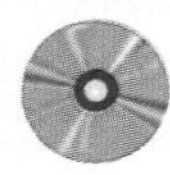

Videodisc

Use MindJogger to preview chapter content.

MINDJOGGER VIDEOQUIZ

Chapter 17
Disc 3 Side A

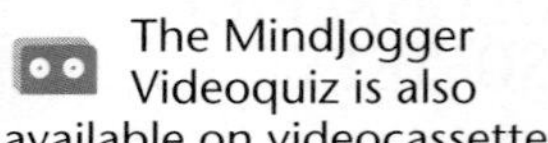

The MindJogger Videoquiz is also available on videocassette.

NATIONAL GEOGRAPHIC SOCIETY

Videodisc

STV: WORLD GEOGRAPHY, VOLUME 1

Side 1, Chapter 1
Frames 00002-47133
Title: ***Asia*** **(in its entirety)**

STV: WORLD GEOGRAPHY, VOLUME 2

Side 1, Chapter 1
Frames 00001-49739
Title: ***Africa*** **(in its entirety)**

CHAPTER FOCUS

Geographic Setting

The region of North Africa and Southwest Asia spans a vast area from Morocco to Afghanistan and from the Mediterranean Sea to the Sahara. Its heartland consists of the lands of Southwest Asia that stretch from Turkey to Saudi Arabia.

Geographic Themes

Section 1 The Land

PLACE The region of North Africa and Southwest Asia is at least three-fourths desert and semiarid lands. Mountains are found in North Africa, Turkey, and northern Iraq and Iran.

Section 2 The Climate and Vegetation

LOCATION Coastal areas, western Turkey, and northern Iran receive enough rainfall for agriculture.

▲ Photograph: *Farmland reclaimed from the desert, Israel*

EXTRA CREDIT PROJECT

Poster Interested students might investigate the plant and animal life of North Africa and Southwest Asia. They should research how plants and animals adapt to the region's climate. Students might prepare illustrated posters or booklets to share with the class.

1 SECTION
The Land

SETTING THE SCENE

Read to Discover . . .
- the seas and coastal areas of North Africa and Southwest Asia.
- the mountains and plateaus in North Africa and Southwest Asia.
- the kinds of natural resources found in North Africa and Southwest Asia.

Key Terms
- seismic
- alluvial-soil deposit
- delta
- wadi
- phosphate

Identify and Locate
Arabian Peninsula, Sinai Peninsula, Anatolian Peninsula, Sahara, Hindu Kush Mountains, Atlas Mountains, Nile River, Tigris River, Euphrates River

Nazareth, Israel

I was born in Nazareth, a small Israeli city with a lot of history. Many of our streets, houses, and churches are very old. A half-hour from Nazareth is the city of Haifa, located by the Mediterranean Sea at the foot of Mt. Carmel. I have lived here for most of my life. Bishara Baransi

Bishara Baransi describes the historical heritage of his home city in Israel, one of the many countries in the culture region of North Africa and Southwest Asia. Although this region has some of the oldest cities in the world, many people may imagine North Africa and Southwest Asia as expanses of sand dunes stretching to the horizon. This vast and complex part of the world, however, contains relatively few extended areas of sand dunes; much of the deserts consist of gravelly surfaces. River lowlands and the coasts of the Mediterranean Sea, the Caspian Sea, and the Persian Gulf contain plains that can be farmed if rainfall is adequate or irrigation is used.

From Morocco and the Atlantic Ocean on the west to Afghanistan in the east and from the Mediterranean Sea on the north across the Sahara to the south, the region covers about 5.5 million square miles (14.2 million sq. km)—more than 10 percent of the earth's total land surface. In this area are found the world's largest desert as well as the world's longest river, in addition to the sites of two of the world's earliest civilizations. Due to its location around the southern and eastern coasts of the Mediterranean Sea, the region has served as the crossroads of Europe, Africa, and Asia for centuries.

PLACE

Peninsulas and Seas

Two peninsulas and three bodies of water make up the central area of North Africa and Southwest Asia. The largest peninsula is

LESSON PLAN
Chapter 17, Section 1

FOCUS

SECTION OBJECTIVES
1. **Locate** the seas and coastal areas of North Africa and Southwest Asia.
2. **Discuss** the mountains and plateaus in North Africa and Southwest Asia.
3. **Identify** the kinds of natural resources found in North Africa and Southwest Asia.

ABOUT THE POSTCARD
After school, Bishara works in a restaurant as a cook and a waiter.

BELLRINGER MOTIVATIONAL ACTIVITY
Project the Section 1 Focus Transparency and have students answer the questions.

PRETEACHING VOCABULARY
Teach the meanings of the words delta *(triangular shaped land at a river's mouth)* and wadi *(dry river bed)*. Help students understand that similar geographic features are found in many regions of the world. For example, have them compare the Nile Delta with the Mississippi Delta. Also, have students compare the wadis of North Africa with the arroyos of the American Southwest.

Use the Vocabulary PuzzleMaker Software to create a crossword or word search puzzle.

CD-ROM

PICTURE ATLAS OF THE WORLD
You and your students can see and read about the physical features of North Africa and Southwest Asia by clicking the "Photos" and "Essay" buttons of individual countries in the region.

Classroom Resources for Section 1

BLACKLINE MASTERS:
- Geography Simulation 6
- Performance Assessment Activity 17
- Section Quiz 17-1

TRANSPARENCIES:
- Section Focus Transparency 17-1
- Unit Map Transparencies 1-8, 6-2
- Physical Geography of the World Transparencies 41–50

MULTIMEDIA:

- Vocabulary PuzzleMaker Software
- Testmaker

- *Reuters Issues in Geography*
- *STV: World Geography, Volume 1*
- *STV: World Geography, Volume 2*

- *Picture Atlas of the World*

TEACH

GUIDED PRACTICE

L1 Recall List the following geographic features on the chalkboard: peninsula, sea, plateau, mountain, desert, river. Call on students to define each term and/or describe the characteristics of each feature. **LEP**

Implement Geography Simulation 6 as a class activity.

Display Unit Map Overlay Transparency 6-2. Have students identify and locate the fertile areas of the region. *(plains along the coasts of the Mediterranean Sea, Caspian Sea, and Persian Gulf; Nile River valley, Tigris-Euphrates valley)* Ask students to formulate a hypothesis about why these areas are fertile. *(availability of water)*

NATIONAL GEOGRAPHIC SOCIETY

Videodisc

STV: WORLD GEOGRAPHY, VOLUME 1

Side 1, Chapter 1
Frames 6886-13594
Title: *Asia*
Subject: Southwest Asia

STV: WORLD GEOGRAPHY, VOLUME 2

Side 1, Chapter 1
Frames 07986-12726
Title: *Africa*
Subject: Northern Africa: The Sahara

Side 1, Chapter 1
Frames 12728-14986
Title: *Africa*
Subject: Northern Africa: The Sahel

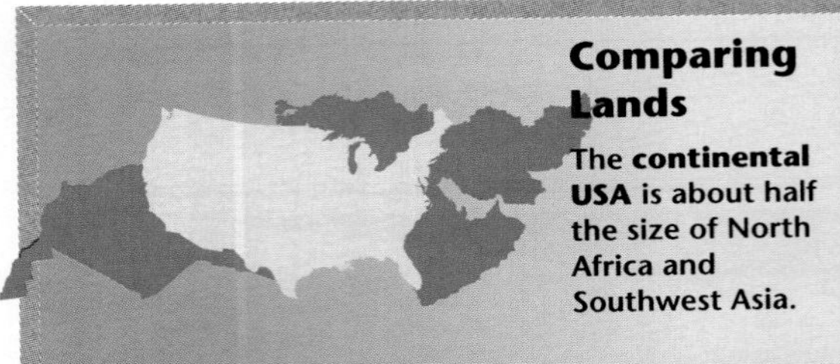

Comparing Lands

The continental USA is about half the size of North Africa and Southwest Asia.

the Arabian Peninsula in Southwest Asia. The Red Sea borders this peninsula on the west. The Persian Gulf lies on the east. The peninsula's southern borders are the Gulf of Aden and the Arabian Sea.

Stretching into the Red Sea is the smaller Sinai Peninsula. To the north lies the Anatolian Peninsula bordered by the Black Sea, the Aegean Sea, and the Mediterranean Sea.

The Dead Sea, located at the mouth of the Jordan River, forms part of the border between Israel and Jordan. The Dead Sea is actually a landlocked, saltwater lake. Its shore, which lies about 1,312 feet (400 m) below sea level, is the lowest place on the earth's surface. The Dead Sea is the saltiest body of water in the world—about 9 times as salty as the ocean.

PLACE

Coasts, Mountains, and Plateaus

Fertile coastal plains are found along the Mediterranean coasts of North Africa and Southwest Asia. Other fertile areas are found along the coasts of the Caspian Sea and the Persian Gulf.

The Mountains of Southwest Asia

Mountains cover much of North Africa and Southwest Asia. Along the west coast of the Arabian Peninsula they divide into two groups. In the north are the Hejaz and to the south are the Asir Mountains, which have taller peaks. Rainfall averaging more than 19 inches (50 cm) a year in the Asir region makes it the most suitable area for agriculture on the Arabian Peninsula. East of the Asir mountain range lies the Central Plateau where the average annual rainfall ranges from 0 to 4 inches (0 to 10 cm).

The eastern shore of the Mediterranean Sea includes mountain chains. On the Anatolian Peninsula, along the Black Sea are the Pontic Mountains. The Taurus Mountains lie along the Mediterranean or Turkey's southern border. Between these ranges lies the Anatolian Plateau with an elevation that ranges from 2,000 to 5,000 feet (610 to 1,524 m) above sea level. In eastern Turkey, Ararat, an isolated mountain with two peaks, rises 16,945 feet (5,165 m) above sea level.

East of the Anatolian Peninsula, the Zagros Mountains form the western border of the Plateau of Iran, a large desert plateau that stands about 3,000 feet (914 m) above sea level. North of the plateau and directly south of the Caspian Sea lie the Elburz Mountains.

The Zagros and the Taurus Mountains are along a belt of frequent and often severe **seismic**, or earthquake, activity. Earthquakes also occur in North Africa. Perhaps the area of greatest hazard is Iran, which has experienced numerous earthquakes in the last 40 years.

At the easternmost part of the region, in Afghanistan, lies the Hindu Kush mountain range. Some of these mountains rise to heights of 23,000 feet (7,010 m) or more.

The Mountains of North Africa

Along the Mediterranean coast in Morocco and Algeria lies Africa's longest mountain range, the Atlas Mountains. The Atlas Mountains cause greater rainfall on their northern flanks, making the coastal areas of western North Africa more suitable for human settlement. A smaller, isolated mountain range known as the Ahaggar (uh•HAGH•uhr) crosses southern Algeria.

HUMAN/ENVIRONMENT INTERACTION

Rivers

Rivers provide water and deposit rich soil in the otherwise dry desert regions of North Africa and Southwest Asia. The largest

Cooperative Learning Activity

Organize students into six groups and assign one of the following geographic features to each group: peninsulas, gulfs, seas, rivers, mountains, deserts. Members of each group must identify all examples of their assigned feature in North Africa and Southwest Asia. In addition, students should write an accurate description of the location of each feature. They should indicate the country or countries in which the feature is located and tell why the feature is significant to the region. Provide time for groups to share information.

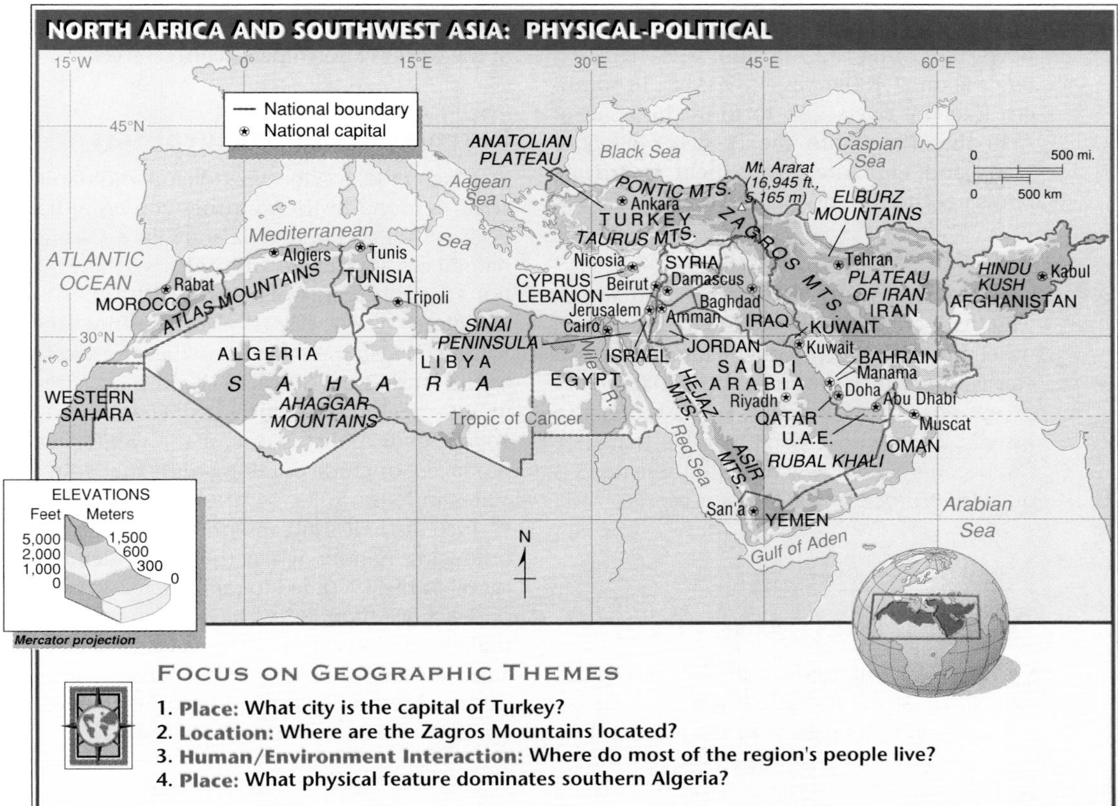

FOCUS ON GEOGRAPHIC THEMES

1. **Place:** What city is the capital of Turkey?
2. **Location:** Where are the Zagros Mountains located?
3. **Human/Environment Interaction:** Where do most of the region's people live?
4. **Place:** What physical feature dominates southern Algeria?

of these rivers are the Nile in northern Africa and the Tigris and Euphrates (yu•FRAT•EEZ) rivers of Southwest Asia.

The Nile

The Nile River, which flows 4,160 miles (6,693 km), is the longest river in the world. Beginning near the Equator, the Nile flows through Egypt to the Mediterranean Sea.

For thousands of years, the Nile River has benefited Egypt. The fertile strip of land along its banks was the site of one of the world's earliest civilizations. Today, the Nile River valley, which makes up 3 percent of the land area of Egypt, is home to more than 90 percent of the Egyptian people.

In ancient times the predictable annual floods allowed farmers to plant their crops in the rich soil deposited by the Nile. These **alluvial-soil deposits**—sand and mud deposited by the flowing water—formed a **delta.** A delta is a section of land at a river's mouth that looks like the Greek letter *delta* (Δ). Modern dams, such as the Aswan High Dam, now control the river's flow, reducing the deposits of alluvial soil. The dams, however, extend irrigation and allow planting of more than one crop a year.

The Tigris and Euphrates Rivers

Several thousand years ago, a series of civilizations developed in Mesopotamia, which means "land between two rivers." These civilizations thrived in the fertile valley between the Tigris and the Euphrates.

Both rivers originate in the mountains of eastern Turkey and flow southeast through

Meeting Special Needs

Language Delayed Students with problems decoding (figuring out) words often skip over proper nouns. Help students use respellings of these words, which appear in parentheses in the text, as a guide to pronunciation.

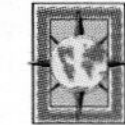

Display Unit Map Overlay Transparency 1-8. Ask students to compare the petroleum reserves of North Africa and Southwest Asia with those of other world regions. Then ask what they might infer about the economic importance of petroleum to North Africa and Southwest Asia. *(Answers should indicate that this region has most of the world's known petroleum reserves.)*

USING MAPS

Answers:
1. Ankara; **2.** eastern Turkey through western Iran; **3.** in coastal areas and in Nile River valley; **4.** Ahaggar Mountains

Map Skills Practice

Reading a Map What body of water separates Africa from the Arabian Peninsula? *(Red Sea)*

INDEPENDENT PRACTICE

Guided Reading Have students complete Guided Reading Activity 17-1 in the TCR. **LEP**

GLENCOE TECHNOLOGY

Videodisc

Use the following to introduce or enrich Unit 6:

REUTERS ISSUES IN GEOGRAPHY

Chapter 5
Disc 1 Side A

Title: ***North Africa and Southwest Asia: The Influence of Oil and Water***
Subject: How oil and water affect life in the region and events around the world

MULTICULTURAL PERSPECTIVE

Cultural Heritage
Many North Africans and Southwest Asians consider it an insult to point the bottom of one's foot at another person.

USING ILLUSTRATIONS

MOVEMENT At Khartoum, the White Nile from Sudan joins the Blue Nile from Ethiopia. North of Khartoum, the river is called simply the Nile.

Answer to Caption:
Fertile land along the river could be used for farming.

ASSESS

CHECK FOR UNDERSTANDING

Assign Section 1 Review as homework or an in-class activity.

MEETING LESSON OBJECTIVES

Each objective below is tested by the questions that follow it in parentheses.

1. **Locate** the seas and coastal areas of North Africa and Southwest Asia. *(3)*
2. **Discuss** the mountains and plateaus in North Africa and Southwest Asia. *(2, 3)*
3. **Identify** the kinds of natural resources found in North Africa and Southwest Asia. *(5, 6)*

EVALUATE

Assign the Section 1 Quiz in the TCR.

Use the Testmaker to create a customized quiz for Section 1.

Syria and Iraq. The Euphrates, the longer river, flows 1,700 miles (2,735 km). The Tigris extends about 1,180 miles (1,899 km). In southern Iraq the rivers join to form the Shatt al Arab that flows into the Persian Gulf. The Tigris and Euphrates rivers help to irrigate farms in otherwise dry Southwest Asia.

Streambeds

Many streams in North Africa and Southwest Asia are not permanent. In the desert, water runoff from infrequent rainstorms creates **wadis,** which are streambeds that are dry except during a heavy rain. Wadis become so heavily laden with eroded material that they can become mud flows. Water in these flows is quickly absorbed by the land surface.

HUMAN/ENVIRONMENT INTERACTION

Natural Resources

The most important natural resources in North Africa and Southwest Asia are petroleum and natural gas. Current estimates are that the region contains more than 60 percent of the world's known petroleum reserves.

Petroleum and Natural Gas

Much of the region's petroleum and natural gas is found in the countries bordering the Persian Gulf and in Algeria and Libya. Oil and natural gas, for the present time, give these nations the appearance of being wealthy.

Before World War II, North Africa and Southwest Asia produced less than 5 percent of the world's oil. Since 1945, oil production in the region has increased dramatically. Today Saudi Arabia is one of the world's top producers of crude oil along with the United States and Russia.

Increased wealth came to the region's oil-producing nations when the global demand for oil in the 1970s led to rapid increases in oil prices. Since then, prices have fallen as industrialized nations have reduced consumption and searched for other energy sources. The result has been a slowdown in economic development among some nations in the region.

Geographic Themes

Place: Nile River Valley, Egypt
The Nile River cuts a lush, green valley through Egypt's vast desert landscape. *How has the Nile River benefited the people of Egypt?*

Critical Thinking

Drawing Conclusions Ask students to list different characteristics that define regions. *(physical features, climate, economic activities, culture)* Then ask students to draw conclusions about why North Africa and Southwest Asia are considered a region. *(Answers include similar landforms, location, climate, and culture.)* Ask students why this region is called a "crossroads." *(It joins Europe, Asia, and Africa.)*

Geographic Themes

Location: Atlas Mountains

Phosphate rock, iron ore, and manganese are mined in the Atlas Mountains, Africa's longest mountain range. *Where are the Atlas Mountains located?*

Other Minerals

In addition to petroleum and natural gas, North Africa and Southwest Asia have mineral resources. Iron ore, copper, lead, manganese, and zinc are found from Morocco to Afghanistan. For many years most deposits in the area were thought to be modest by world standards. Recent discoveries of iron ore and copper deposits in North Africa and Southwest Asia indicate that the region may have up to 10 percent of the world's iron ore reserves.

In addition to other mineral deposits in the region, **phosphate**—a chemical compound often used in fertilizers—is present in some areas. Phosphate is important to many nations, such as Morocco, which ranks third in world phosphate production.

Although exports of the region's resources, particularly oil, have added prosperity to the region, farming and raising livestock remain the major occupations of most people. These activities are directly affected by the region's climates and vegetation.

Section 1 Review

Checking for Understanding

1. **Define** seismic, alluvial-soil deposit, delta, wadi, phosphate.
2. **Locating Places** Through what countries does the Atlas mountain range extend?
3. **Region** What are the three land features characteristic of North Africa and Southwest Asia?
4. **Human/Environment Interaction** How do the major rivers of North Africa and Southwest Asia benefit the people in the region?
5. **Region** What is the most important natural resource in the region?

Critical Thinking

6. **Predicting Consequences** How might economic development in the nations of North Africa and Southwest Asia change in the future? Support your answer.

Answers to Section 1 Review

1. **seismic:** earthquake activity; **alluvial-soil deposit:** soil made up of sand and mud deposited by flowing water; **delta:** triangular section of land at a river's mouth; **wadi:** stream bed formed during heavy rains; **phosphate:** chemical compound used in fertilizer
2. Morocco, Algeria
3. peninsulas, plateaus, mountains
4. They provide fertile river valleys.
5. petroleum
6. If more alternate energy sources are developed by industrialized nations, oil revenues might decline and economic development will slow down.

Using Illustrations

HUMAN/ENVIRONMENT INTERACTION Farming is practiced on terraced fields along streams in the High Atlas of central Morocco.

Answer to Caption: *along the Mediterranean coast in Morocco and Algeria*

RETEACH

Have students work with a partner to make a list of important landforms and rivers in North Africa and Southwest Asia and locate each feature on a map of the region.

ENRICH

Ask interested students to research the history of the Sahara and explain to the class how the desert was formed and why it has expanded.

CLOSE

Have students write a postcard to Bishara. Suggest that they ask questions about how the environment of Southwest Asia affects his way of life.

National Geographic Society

Physical Geography of the World Transparencies

Display and discuss the physical features of the following transparencies:

41. Atlas Mountains, Morocco
42. Sahara in North Africa
43. Dakhla Oasis, Egypt
44. Nile River, Egypt
45. Jordan River, Israel
46. Dead Sea, Israel
47. Hindu Kush, Afghanistan
48. Mount Ararat, Turkey
49. Tigris River, Iraq
50. Persian Gulf

FOCUS

SECTION OBJECTIVES

1. **Identify** three types of climate found in North Africa and Southwest Asia.
2. **Explain** how mountain ranges influence rainfall in coastal regions of North Africa and Southwest Asia.
3. **Describe** the types of vegetation found in North Africa and Southwest Asia.

BELLRINGER MOTIVATIONAL ACTIVITY

Project the Section 2 Focus Transparency and have students answer the questions.

PRETEACHING VOCABULARY

Tell students that the word *cereal* comes from Ceres, the goddess of grain, the harvest, and agriculture in Roman mythology. Ask them to name cereal grains. *(corn, oats, wheat, rice, barley)*

CURRICULUM CONNECTION

EARTH SCIENCE

Water that occurs at oases generally comes from precipitation in distant mountains or hills. The water seeps into the ground and flows toward low places in the desert. Soil in desert regions is generally fertile when water is available.

Videodisc

STV: WORLD GEOGRAPHY, VOLUME 2

Side 1, Chapter 1
Frames 07986-12726
Title: *Africa*
Subject: Northern Africa: The Sahara

SECTION 2

The Climate and Vegetation

SETTING THE SCENE

Read to Discover . . .
- the three types of climate found in North Africa and Southwest Asia.
- how mountain ranges influence rainfall in coastal regions of North Africa and Southwest Asia.
- the types of vegetation found in North Africa and Southwest Asia.

Key Terms
- oasis
- cereal
- pastoralism

Identify and Locate
Sahara, Rubal Khali, Black Sea, Caspian Sea, Climate regions: desert, Mediterranean, steppe, highland

A characteristic common to most of North Africa and Southwest Asia is the scarcity of water. Most parts of the region average 10 inches (25 cm) of precipitation or less each year. The area north of the Elburz Mountains in Iran, however, receives an abundant annual rainfall. Another well-watered area is the southern edge of the Caspian Sea, which receives more than 78 inches (198 cm) of rainfall per year.

These differences in climatic conditions affect the nature of the region's vegetation as well as the economic way of life of most of the population.

REGION

Climate Regions of North Africa and Southwest Asia

In many parts of North Africa and Southwest Asia precipitation averages 10 inches (25 cm) or less each year. Deserts are widespread throughout the region. Three other types of climate regions also are present. These are the Mediterranean, steppe, and highland climates.

Desert Climate

Deserts cover about 50 percent of North Africa and Southwest Asia. Lebanon, Cyprus, and Turkey are the only countries with no desert areas. The Sahara, the largest desert in the world, covers most of North Africa—about 3.5 million square miles (9 million sq. km).

The Sahara and other deserts in the region have sparse vegetation. Farming, however, occurs where water for irrigation is found. **Oases**—places in the desert where water is present—make small-scale agriculture possible in the Sahara. A traveler, arriving at an oasis in North Africa, made the following observation:

We wandered . . . through lush groves of palms. There are about a quarter of a million palms in the oasis, but unlike most Saharan oases there is a wide variety of other crops. . . . As one goes through the groves every so often one comes upon one of the two hundred and eighty springs. . . . Young . . . boys play by the springs, diving off the walls sending sluggish ripples across the thick surface of the water. It seems a happy place.

Classroom Resources for Section 2

BLACKLINE MASTERS:
Reproducible Lesson Plan 17-2
Guided Reading Activity 17-2
Workbook Activity 17-2
Writer's Guidebook Lessons 4, 5
Enrichment Activity 17
Section Quiz 17-2

TRANSPARENCIES:
Section Focus Transparency 17-2
Unit Map Overlay Transparencies 6-3, 6-5

MULTIMEDIA:

Testmaker

STV: World Geography, Volume 2

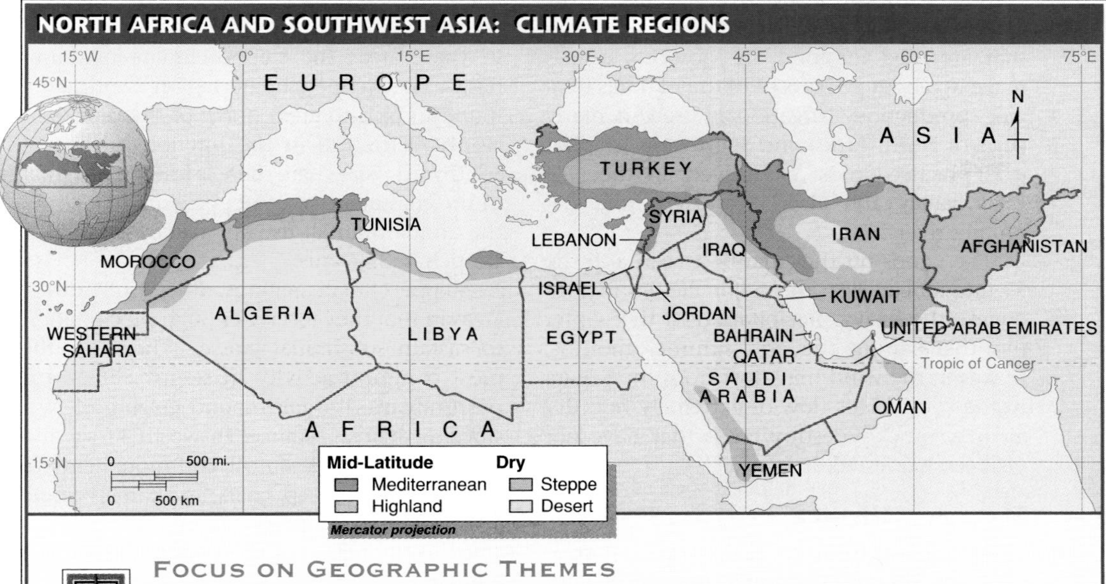

FOCUS ON GEOGRAPHIC THEMES

1. **Region:** What is the dominant climate region in North Africa and Southwest Asia?
2. **Location:** Where are Mediterranean climate regions located?
3. **Human/Environment Interaction:** What effect might climate have on patterns of human settlement in the region?

Some oases scattered across the Sahara are quite large and serve as sites for villages, towns, and in some instances, cities.

The deserts of North Africa and Southwest Asia have limited areas of dunes. More extensive are rocky gravel areas called "desert pavement." For example, less than 10 percent of the Sahara is sand; the rest consists of desert pavement, mountains, and exposed barren rock.

The desert with the largest area of sand in the region is the Rubal Khali, or Empty Quarter, in the southern part of the Arabian Peninsula. The Rubal Khali is one of several deserts and covers about 250,000 square miles (650,000 sq. km) or about one-quarter of the total land area of the Arabian Peninsula.

Mediterranean and Highland Climates

The Mediterranean climate is a variably wet and dry climate found in upland areas of the region as well as on the coastal plains of the Mediterranean Sea, the Black Sea, the Caspian Sea, and in the Tigris-Euphrates Valley. A Mediterranean climate region consists of hot, dry summers and cool, rainy winters. At times during the winter months, it can become relatively cold, particularly at higher elevations.

Coastal and highland areas near mountain ranges usually receive the most rainfall. This rainfall is the result of moist, warm air driven off the sea by prevailing westerly winds during the winter months. As the moist air reaches the mountains, it rises, cools, and the moisture condenses and falls to the earth as rain. The coastal area in North Africa near the Atlas Mountains, for example, averages more than 30 inches (76 cm) of rain each year. The southern coast of the Caspian Sea often has an average annual rainfall of more than twice that amount.

Areas receiving more than 14 inches (35 cm) of rainfall a year can grow certain crops

TEACH

GUIDED PRACTICE

L1 Environment Ask students to describe a desert. List responses on the chalkboard. Then call on a volunteer to read aloud the quote on page 362 from a traveler in the Sahara. Discuss reasons why this description may differ from students' descriptions. *(The traveler has firsthand knowledge; the quote describes an oasis, which differs from the usual desert environment.)* **LEP**

Display Unit Map Overlay Transparencies 6-3 and 6-5. Have students explain how mountain ranges influence climate patterns in North Africa and Southwest Asia. *(Moist air rises over mountain ranges, cools, and produces precipitation along coastal areas.)*

USING MAPS

Answers:
1. desert; **2.** coasts of Morocco, Algeria, Lebanon, Tunisia, Turkey, Syria; eastern Iraq; western Iran; **3.** Areas with desert climates are sparsely populated.

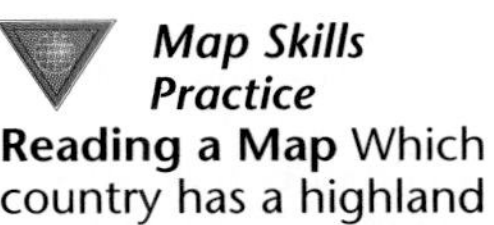
Map Skills Practice
Reading a Map Which country has a highland climate? *(Afghanistan)*

Cooperative Learning Activity

Organize students into three groups and assign each group one of the following climate regions: desert, Mediterranean, or steppe. Instruct members of each group to identify a location in North Africa or Southwest Asia within their assigned climate region. Tell students to prepare a weather forecast for that location. Students should consult references for information about average temperatures and precipitation. Suggest that they prepare weather maps and other visual aids to go with their presentation. Provide time for each group to present its forecast.

INDEPENDENT PRACTICE

Guided Reading Have students complete Guided Reading Activity 17-2 in the TCR. **LEP**

USING MAPS

Answers:
1. coastal areas and Turkey, Iran, Afghanistan; **2.** northern Iraq and Syria, southern Turkey, western Iran; **3.** coasts of Morocco, Algeria, Tunisia, Turkey, Syria, Lebanon

Map Skills Practice
Reading a Map In what country are tropical grasslands found? *(Algeria)*

ASSESS

CHECK FOR UNDERSTANDING

Assign Section 2 Review as homework or an in-class activity.

MEETING LESSON OBJECTIVES

Each objective below is tested by the questions that follow it in parentheses.
1. Identify three types of climate found in North Africa and Southwest Asia. *(3)*
2. Explain how mountain ranges influence rainfall in coastal regions of North Africa and Southwest Asia. *(4)*
3. Describe the types of vegetation found in North Africa and Southwest Asia. *(5)*

without irrigation. Many farmers grow **cereals**—grains, such as barley, oats, or wheat, that are used for food. In Morocco, cereals make up about 40 percent of the nation's total crop production. Irrigation is used in many parts of North Africa and Southwest Asia, but it is practiced most extensively in the Nile River valley and along the Tigris and Euphrates rivers.

The winds off the Atlantic Ocean and the Mediterranean Sea are major factors in producing the heavy precipitation in the winter months. During the arid summer months, however, the wind may flow from the Sahara to the south. This flow of extremely hot, dry air may quickly destroy crops that have not yet been harvested.

Steppe Climate

As distance from the region's coastal areas increases, the average yearly amount of rainfall decreases. Land suitable for farming gives way to grassy areas used for grazing livestock. In these areas the steppe climate predominates. The steppe climate region is primarily found in upland areas north of the deserts in North Africa and in the interior of parts of Southwest Asia where there is less rainfall than in the coastal areas. In steppe climate regions, the annual rainfall usually averages less than 14 inches (35.6 cm).

Steppe climate regions differ from desert areas in that they receive enough precipitation to sustain substantial grasses. Therefore, the most common activity in steppe climates is **pastoralism**—the raising and grazing of livestock. In many instances in North Africa and Southwest Asia, the most common herds of livestock are of sheep, goats, and camels. Some current estimates place the number of livestock in the region at more than 300 million animals.

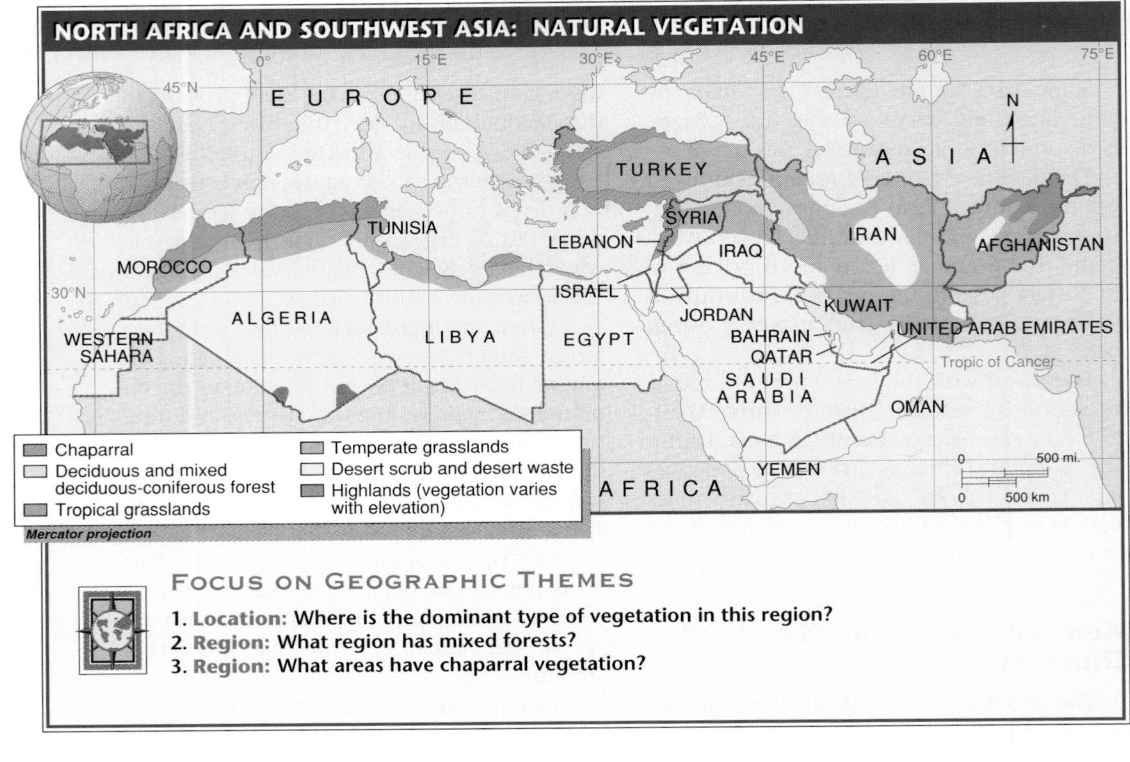

FOCUS ON GEOGRAPHIC THEMES

1. Location: Where is the dominant type of vegetation in this region?
2. Region: What region has mixed forests?
3. Region: What areas have chaparral vegetation?

Meeting Special Needs

Sequencing Problems Students with verbal sequencing problems have special difficulty forming concise summaries of information. Have students read and summarize the material under "Natural Vegetation." Discuss the techniques they used to create the summaries. Explain that this skill is important for note taking and taking tests.

Geographic Themes

Region: Mediterranean Coast of Turkey

Coastal areas of North Africa and Southwest Asia receive more rainfall than many interior areas of the region. *What type of climate is found along the region's coasts?*

HUMAN/ENVIRONMENT INTERACTION

Natural Vegetation

Natural vegetation in North Africa and Southwest Asia varies according to soil conditions and climate. The region's natural vegetation ranges from forests to grasses and shrubs to sparse desert vegetation.

Forest areas usually are found in higher elevations that have more abundant rainfall, as in the Atlas Mountains in North Africa and the highland areas of Turkey. In desert areas, on the other hand, vegetation is rare and in most cases nonexistent except around oases.

In recent years, natural vegetation in North Africa and Southwest Asia has declined. The needs of growing populations have led to an increase in the demand for agricultural and animal food products. To meet these demands, forests have been cleared for cultivation, and grasses and shrubs in steppe regions have suffered from overgrazing.

SECTION 2 REVIEW

Checking for Understanding

1. **Define** oasis, cereal, pastoralism.
2. **Locating Places** Which North African nations contain parts of the Sahara?
3. **Region** What are four climates found in North Africa and Southwest Asia?
4. **Region** How do mountain ranges along coastal areas in North Africa and Southwest Asia affect the climate?
5. **Human/Environment Interaction** Why is pastoralism common in the steppe areas of North Africa and Southwest Asia?

Critical Thinking

6. **Making Comparisons** Why do the farming techniques in some of the region's coastal areas differ from what is practiced in the Nile River valley?

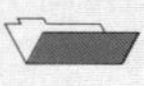

USING ILLUSTRATIONS

LOCATION The city of Kas overlooks the Mediterranean Sea.

Answer to Caption: *Mediterranean*

EVALUATE

Assign the Section 2 Quiz in the TCR.

Use the Testmaker to create a customized test for Section 2.

RETEACH

Have students complete Reteaching Activity 17 in the TCR.

ENRICH

Have students complete Enrichment Activity 17 in the TCR.

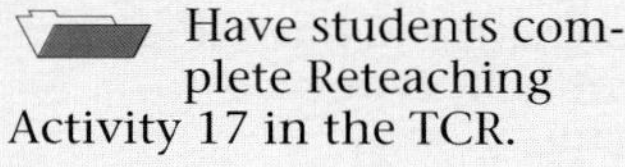

CLOSE

Have students write a paragraph explaining how climate affects ways of life in North Africa and Southwest Asia.

ANSWERS TO SECTION 2 REVIEW

1. **oasis:** desert place where water is present; **cereal:** grain used for food; **pastoralism:** the raising and grazing of livestock
2. Morocco, Algeria, Tunisia, Libya, Egypt
3. desert, Mediterranean, steppe, highland
4. Warm, moist air off the water rises over mountain ranges and cools, and the condensed moisture falls to the earth as rain, thus producing the Mediterranean climate.
5. Cultivation is difficult with little precipitation, but vegetation in the area is suitable for grazing.
6. Rainfall in coastal areas is adequate for farming. Irrigation is commonly used along the Nile.

TEACH

Duplicate and distribute copies of a paragraph that is organized chronologically. After reading the paragraph, have students identify the main idea and topic sentence, supporting details, and transitional words.

Ask: "How is this paragraph organized?" *(in the order of time)* Explain: "There are many ways to organize paragraphs. Some paragraphs begin with the most important idea and proceed to the least important. Others describe cause-and-effect relationships or compare things." Distribute a second paragraph and have students identify its type of organization.

Skills Practice
For additional practice, have students complete Lessons 4 and 5 in the Writer's Guidebook.

STUDY AND WRITING SKILLS

Writing a Paragraph

Imagine reading a chapter in this textbook that has not been divided into paragraphs. Most readers would give up after a few pages as the print blurred before their eyes and the ideas blurred in their minds. By visually marking the beginning and end of each idea, paragraphs help readers follow the writer's thoughts.

REVIEWING THE SKILL

The paragraph is the basic unit of prose writing. The American Heritage Dictionary defines a paragraph as, "a distinct division of a written work or composition that expresses a thought or point relevant to the whole but is complete in itself; it may consist of a single sentence or several sentences." Notice the main points of the definition: 1) a paragraph must express a complete thought; 2) that thought must relate to the composition as a whole; and 3) paragraphs can be any length.

A well-written paragraph displays four characteristics. First, it expresses only one main idea, which is usually (though not always) stated in a topic sentence. Second, the other sentences support and develop the main idea. Third, the sentences advance the main idea step-by-step, so the reader can easily follow the writer's thoughts. Fourth, transitional words and phrases clarify relationships among sentences in the paragraph, and between each paragraph and the paragraphs that precede and follow it. Examples of transitional words and phrases include: *first, next, finally, also, therefore, because, however,* and *instead.*

Writing clear, well-organized paragraphs enables you to express your ideas so that any reader can share and understand your thoughts.

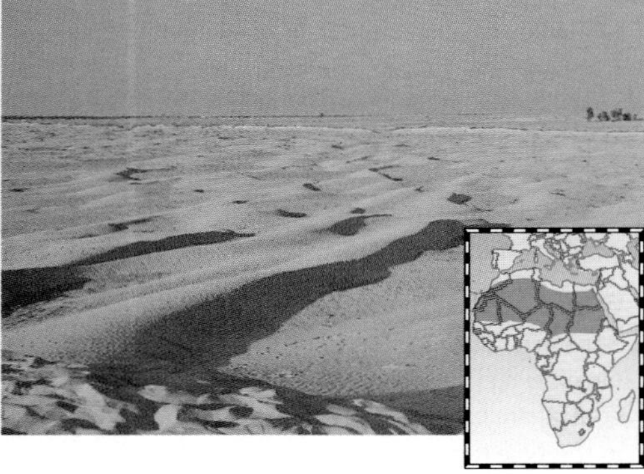

To help you write effective paragraphs, apply the following steps:

- State the main idea of the paragraph as a topic sentence.
- Choose details that support or explain the main idea.
- Arrange the sentences in a logical sequence to help the reader follow your thoughts.
- Use transitional words and phrases to clarify relationships within the paragraph and within the composition as a whole.

PRACTICING THE SKILL

A. The sentences below discuss the relationship between landforms, wind patterns, and climate in North Africa. After reading the sentences, arrange them into a paragraph with a topic sentence, supporting details, a logical sequence, and transitional words as needed.

1. This moisture-laden air rises as it crosses the coastal mountain ranges.
2. The largest desert in the world, the Sahara, has been formed by these natural forces.
3. As the air rises, it cools off, dropping most of its moisture on the windward side of the mountains.
4. In North Africa, landforms and wind patterns strongly affect climate.
5. On one side of the mountains, little or no rain falls, creating a desert climate.
6. The rainfall produces a Mediterranean climate with warm, dry summers and cool, wet winters.
7. As the prevailing winds sweep eastward across the Mediterranean Sea, the air picks up moisture.

B. Choose a main idea that is related to the material in Chapter 17. Write a paragraph about this main idea, using a topic sentence, supporting details, and transitional words as needed.

For additional practice in this skill, see Practicing Skills on page 368 of the Chapter 17 Review.

ANSWERS TO PRACTICING THE SKILL

A. Paragraphs should appear as follows: In North Africa, landforms and wind patterns strongly affect climate. As the prevailing winds sweep eastward across the Mediterranean Sea, the air picks up moisture. This moisture-laden air rises as it crosses the coastal mountain ranges. As the air rises, it cools off, dropping most of its moisture on the windward side of the mountains. The rainfall produces a Mediterranean climate with warm, dry summers and cool, wet winters. On one side of the mountains, little or no rain falls, creating a desert climate. The largest desert in the world, the Sahara, has been formed by these natural forces.

B. Paragraphs should include topic sentences, supporting details, and transitional words.

chapter 17

HIGHLIGHTS

SECTION	KEY TERMS	SUMMARY
1 The Land	**seismic** (p. 358) **alluvial-soil deposit** (p. 359) **delta** (p. 359) **wadi** (p. 360) **phosphate** (p. 361)	• The region of North Africa and Southwest Asia stretches from Morocco in the west to Afghanistan in the east and covers more than 10 percent of the earth's total land surface. • North Africa and Southwest Asia have a number of peninsulas and several seas. • Rainfall in North Africa and Southwest Asia varies widely, ranging from less than 4 inches (10 cm) on some plateaus to far heavier amounts in some highland areas. • The fertile Nile River valley and the area near the Tigris and Euphrates rivers provide land where agriculture flourishes. • Petroleum and natural gas, two of the most important natural resources of North Africa and Southwest Asia, provide substantial revenues to some nations in the region.

Atlas Mountains of North Africa

SECTION	KEY TERMS	SUMMARY
2 The Climate and Vegetation	**oasis** (p. 362) **cereal** (p. 364) **pastoralism** (p. 364)	• The four climate regions in North Africa and Southwest Asia are the desert, the Mediterranean, the steppe, and the highland. • Much of the farming in North Africa and Southwest Asia occurs along the coastal areas where rainfall is more prevalent than in other areas of the region. • In recent years the clearing of land for farming and the overgrazing of steppe areas have taken their toll on natural vegetation except in a few areas where there is more abundant rainfall.

Mediterranean coast of Turkey

Map Activity

Identify and Locate Provide each student with a copy of the outline map found on page 37 of the Outline Map Resource Book. Have students label the following from memory: Arabian Peninsula, Sinai Peninsula, Anatolian Peninsula, Mediterranean Sea, Red Sea, Black Sea, Persian Gulf.

CHAPTER 17 HIGHLIGHTS

USING THE CHAPTER 17 HIGHLIGHTS

Use the Chapter 17 Highlights to preview, review, condense, or reteach the chapter.

PREVIEW/REVIEW

Vocabulary PuzzleMaker Software reinforces the Key Terms used in Chapter 17.

Student Self-Test and Review Software allows students to review Chapter 17 content.

CONDENSE

Have students read the Chapter 17 Highlights.

Have students listen to the Chapter 17 Audiocassettes in the TCR. Spanish Audiocassettes are also available.

Assign the Chapter 17 Audiocassette Activity and give the students the Chapter 17 Audiocassette Quiz.

Have students complete Guided Reading Activities for Chapter 17 in the TCR. Spanish Guided Reading Activities are also available.

RETEACH

Have students complete Reteaching Activity 17 in the TCR. Spanish Reteaching Activities are also available.

GLENCOE TECHNOLOGY

Videodisc

Use Chapter 17 MindJogger Videoquiz to review students' knowledge before administering the Chapter 17 Test.

MINDJOGGER VIDEOQUIZ

Chapter 17
Disc 3 Side A

The MindJogger Videoquiz is also available on videocassette.

ANSWERS

Reviewing Key Terms

1. delta
2. seismic
3. alluvial-soil deposits
4. wadi
5. pastoralism
6. cereal
7. oases

Reviewing Facts

8. Arabian Peninsula
9. in Egypt
10. Tigris and Euphrates
11. in North Africa
12. hot, dry summers and cool, wet winters
13. grasses and shrubs

chapter 17 REVIEW

Reviewing Key Terms

Choose the vocabulary term that best completes each of the sentences below. Write your answers on a separate sheet of paper.

seismic (p. 358)
alluvial-soil deposits (p. 359)
delta (p. 359)
wadi (p. 360)
oases (p. 362)
cereal (p. 364)
pastoralism (p. 364)

Section 1

1. The _____ is the area at the mouth of the Nile River.
2. Some mountain areas in parts of North Africa and Southwest Asia are centers of _____ activity.
3. Before modern dams, the Nile River left _____ along its banks as it flowed to the Mediterranean Sea.
4. A _____ is a dry streambed in the desert that carries water only for a short time during infrequent rainstorms.

Section 2

5. In steppe regions a common economic activity is _____.
6. The growing of _____ is most common in coastal areas of the region where rainfall is heavier.
7. Across the dry Sahara, scattered _____ provide water and shade.

Reviewing Facts

Section 1

8. What is the largest peninsula in the region of North Africa and Southwest Asia?
9. Where is the world's longest river?
10. What rivers provide a fertile farming area in Iraq?

Section 2

11. Where is the world's largest desert?
12. What are the characteristics of the Mediterranean climate in North Africa and Southwest Asia?
13. What natural vegetation is usually found in the steppe areas?

Critical Thinking

14. **Drawing Conclusions** How do the region's resources affect North Africa and Southwest Asia's position in the world?
15. **Determining Cause and Effect** How are increased cultivation and overgrazing linked to population growth in North Africa and Southwest Asia?

Geographic Themes

16. **Movement** What natural land features affect the movement of people in North Africa?
17. **Human/Environment Interaction** What technology has contributed to the concentration of people in the Nile River valley?

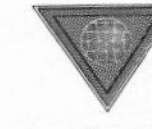

Practicing Skills

Writing a Paragraph

Refer to the Writing a Paragraph skill activity on page 366. Find a paragraph in Chapter 17 that contains all the elements of an effective paragraph. On a separate sheet of paper, rewrite this paragraph. Then, write the paragraph's topic sentence. If it has no topic sentence, write your own. Next, list the supporting details in the paragraph. Finally, write any transitional words and phrases found in the paragraph.

Critical Thinking

14. Large reserves of oil and natural gas make North Africa and Southwest Asia important to industrialized nations.
15. As the population has grown, the demand for more food and animal products has led to increases in land under cultivation and the size of livestock herds.

Geographic Themes

16. mountain ranges and the Sahara
17. Dams that control flooding provide for year-round crops.

Using the Unit Atlas

Refer to the physical geography section of the Unit Atlas on pages 352–353.

18. What is the region's highest point?

Projects

Individual Activity

An oil crisis faced the United States and other industrialized nations during the 1970s. Research the events and the outcome of this crisis and write a brief report on its effects in the United States.

Cooperative Learning Activity

Working together in a group of four or five students, research and plan an imaginary trip across the Sahara. Each student should take responsibility for one important factor involved in the trip. For example, plan the transportation to be used, the number of helpers needed, the supplies, and the best route to take.

When individual planning is complete, each group may discuss the arrangements and present a final report to the class.

Writing About Geography

Description

Imagine that you are traveling along the Nile River. Write a letter to your best friend describing your journey from Khartoum north to the delta. Use your text, journal, and travel books to describe what you see. In your letter, discuss the climate and physical features of the river valley.

Locating Places

THE PHYSICAL GEOGRAPHY OF NORTH AFRICA AND SOUTHWEST ASIA

Match the letters on the map with the places and physical features of North Africa and Southwest Asia. Write your answers on a separate sheet of paper.

1. Persian Gulf
2. Nile River
3. Mediterranean Sea
4. Arabian Peninsula
5. Caspian Sea
6. Red Sea
7. Black Sea
8. Atlas Mountains
9. Gulf of Aden
10. Sahara

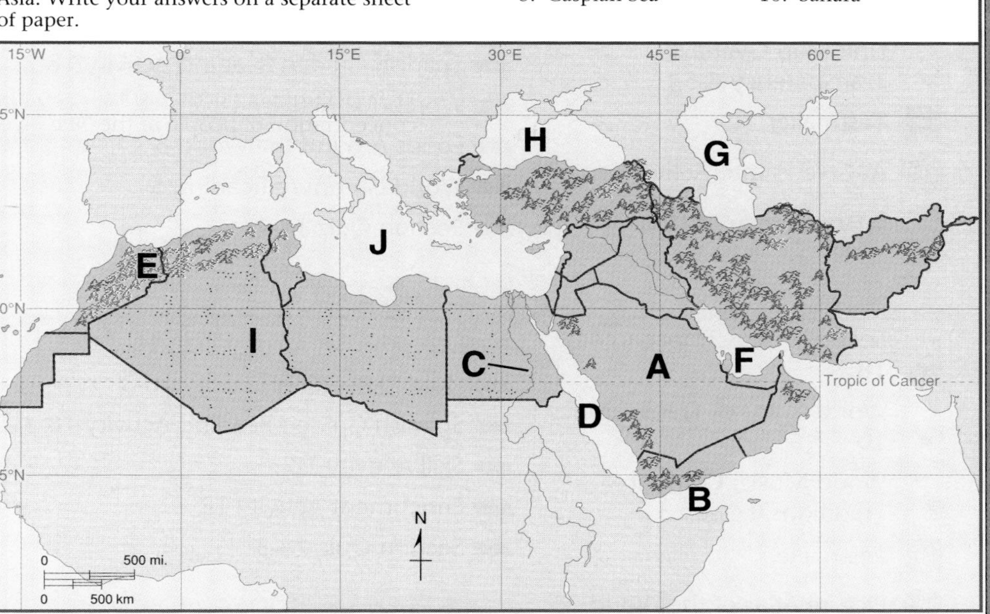

Chapter 17 Review

Practicing Skills

Answers will vary depending on the paragraph that students selected.

Using the Unit Atlas

18. Hindu Kush

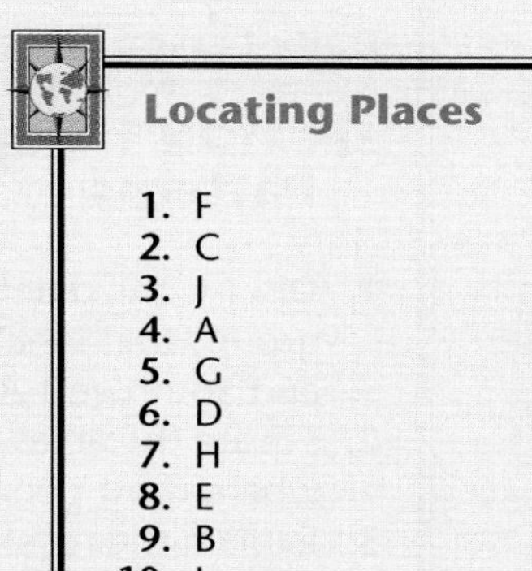

Locating Places

1. F
2. C
3. J
4. A
5. G
6. D
7. H
8. E
9. B
10. I

Chapter Bonus Test Question

This question may be used for extra credit on the chapter test.

How has the location of North Africa and Southwest Asia made the region historically significant?

(Answer: The location of North Africa and Southwest Asia around the southern and eastern coasts of the Mediterranean Sea has made the region the crossroads of Europe, Asia, and Africa for centuries.)

CHAPTER 18

PLANNING GUIDE

The Cultural Geography of North Africa and Southwest Asia

CHAPTER ORGANIZER

Daily Lesson Objectives	Multimedia	Teacher Classroom Resources
SECTION 1 Population Patterns 1. Discuss the different ethnic groups that inhabit North Africa and Southwest Asia. 2. Locate the areas in the region where most people live. 3. Explain the recent trend toward urbanization.	Section Focus Transparency 18-1 Unit Map Overlay Transparency 6-1 Chapter 18 Vocabulary PuzzleMaker Software Political Map Transparency 6 Testmaker ABCNews InterActive™	Reproducible Lesson Plan 18-1 Guided Reading Activity 18-1 Spanish Guided Reading Activity 18-1 Workbook Activity 18-1 Performance Assessment Activity 18 Section Quiz 18-1
SECTION 2 History and Government 1. Describe the natural environment of two of the world's earliest civilizations. 2. Compare three of the world's major religions. 3. Discuss influences created by the interactions of different peoples in the region.	Section Focus Transparency 18-2 Unit Map Overlay Transparency 6-5 Testmaker ABCNews InterActive™ GTV: Planetary Manager	Reproducible Lesson Plan 18-2 Guided Reading Activity 18-2 Spanish Guided Reading Activity 18-2 Workbook Activity 18-2 Foods Around the World 5 World Literature Reading 5 Section Quiz 18-2
SECTION 3 Cultures and Lifestyles 1. Explain the impact of religion on the development of North Africa and Southwest Asia. 2. Compare ways of life in North Africa and Southwest Asia. 3. Describe the geographic factors that have contributed to the region's standard of living.	Section Focus Transparency 18-3 World Cultures Transparency 10 World Music: Cultural Traditions, Lesson 5 Testmaker Picture Atlas of the World	Reproducible Lesson Plan 18-3 Guided Reading Activity 18-3 Spanish Guided Reading Activity 18-3 Skill Activity 18 Enrichment Activity 18 Section Quiz 18-3
CHAPTER REVIEW AND EVALUATION	Chapter 18 English (or Spanish) Audiocassettes MindJogger Videoquiz Testmaker Student Self-Test and Review Software	Reteaching Activity 18 Spanish Reteaching Activity 18 Chapter 18 Test Form A and Form B

0:00 *If time does not permit teaching the entire chapter, summarize using the Chapter 18 Highlights on page 387, and the Chapter 18 English (or Spanish) Audiocassettes. Review students' knowledge using the Glencoe MindJogger Videoquiz.*

KEY TO ABILITY LEVELS

Teaching strategies have been coded for varying learning styles and abilities.

L1 **BASIC** activities for all students

L2 **AVERAGE** activities for average to above-average students

L3 **CHALLENGING** activities for above-average students

LEP **LIMITED ENGLISH PROFICIENCY** activities

Performance Assessment

Correcting Stereotypes Have students investigate the stereotypes that Americans often have about the people of North Africa and Southwest Asia. Groups of students should first develop a list of survey questions based on their predicted misconceptions that Americans might hold. Surveys should then be conducted (by random sample if possible in order to integrate mathematics) and conclusions drawn. Graphic material should be developed in order to visually present the acquired information.

Students should then develop the script for a documentary about the region's people and lifestyles that rectifies the stereotypes found through the survey. The script itself or an actual play or tape of the documentary may serve as a product. Individual students should write their reflections of the process they followed and what they learned about people of the culture region and about those at home.

POSSIBLE RUBRIC FEATURES: Content information, prediction and inference skills, research abilities (surveying), graph skills, organization and communication skills, collaborative skills, summarization skills

For additional professional and classroom resources, see Chapter Resources, pages T46–T51.

TEACHER'S CORNER

INDEX TO NATIONAL GEOGRAPHIC MAGAZINE

The following articles may be used for research relating to this chapter:

- "Age of Pyramids: Egypt's Old Kingdom," by David Roberts, January 1995.
- "Turkey: Struggles for Balance," by Thomas B. Allen, May 1994.
- "Cairo: Glamorous Heart of Eygpt," by Peter Theroux, April 1993.
- "Who Are the Palestinians?" by Tad Szulc, June 1992.
- "Iraq: Crucible of Civilization," by Merle Severy, May 1991.
- "Woman of Saudi Arabia," by Marianne Alireza, October 1987.
- "Morocco's Ancient City of Fez," by Harvey Arden, March 1986.
- "Iran Under the Ayatollah," by Michael Coyne, July 1985.
- "Israel: Searching for the Center," by Priit J. Vesilind, July 1985.
- "Saudi Arabia: The Kingdom and Its Power," by Robert Azzi, September 1980.

NATIONAL GEOGRAPHIC SOCIETY PRODUCTS AVAILABLE FROM GLENCOE

To order the following products for use with this chapter, contact your local Glencoe sales representative or call Glencoe at 1-800-334-7344:

- *Picture Atlas of the World* (CD-ROM)
- *STV: World Geography, Asia and Australia* (Videodisc)
- *STV: World Geography, Africa and Europe* (Videodisc)
- *ZipZapMap! World* (Software)
- *GeoBee* (Software)
- *Images of the World* (Posters)
- *Eye on the Environment* (Posters)
- *Physical Geography of the World* (Transparencies)
- *Picture Atlas of Our 50 States* (Book)

ADDITIONAL NATIONAL GEOGRAPHIC SOCIETY PRODUCTS

To order the following products for use with this chapter, call National Geographic Society at 1-800-368-2728:

- *The Middle East*, "Lands of the Middle East," "Religion and Culture," "The 20th Century: Imperialism, Nationalism, and Independence," "The 20th Century: Modernization," "The 20th Century: The Recent Years—Conflict and the Search for Solutions." (Filmstrip)
- *Nations of the World Series*, "Egypt," "Israel." (Video)

PERFORMANCE ASSESSMENT

Refer to the Planning Guide on page 370B for a Performance Assessment Activity for this chapter. See the *Performance Assessment Activities* booklet for additional suggestions.

CHAPTER OBJECTIVES

1. **Recognize** that movement and interaction of people in this region have led to ethnic diversity.
2. **Point out** that the region's people have settled near sources of water.
3. **Explain** that Southwest Asia is the birthplace of Judaism, Christianity, and Islam.

GLENCOE TECHNOLOGY

Videodisc

Use Chapter 18 MindJogger Videoquiz to preview chapter content.

MINDJOGGER VIDEOQUIZ

Chapter 18
Disc 3 Side A

The MindJogger Videoquiz is also available on videocassette.

chapter 18 The Cultural Geography of North Africa and Southwest Asia

CHAPTER FOCUS

Geographic Setting

The culture region of North Africa and Southwest Asia has been the crossroads for people from Asia, Africa, and Europe who have adopted ways of life necessary for survival in a harsh environment.

Geographic Themes

Section 1 Population Patterns
MOVEMENT The movement and interaction of people in the region have led to ethnic diversity.

Section 2 History and Government
REGION The region's people have settled near water sources.

Section 3 Cultures and Lifestyles
PLACE Southwest Asia is the birthplace of Judaism, Christianity, and Islam.

▲ Photograph: *Cairo, Egypt*

EXTRA CREDIT PROJECT

Research Have students research and report on ideas or inventions that were introduced to the world by the early civilizations of North Africa and Southwest Asia—Sumerians, Egyptians, Phoenicians, or Persians. Tell students to focus on developments that still exist in some form today. *(Topics include 60-second minute and 60-minute hour, paper, irrigation canals, writing systems, calendar based on 365-day year, alphabet with letters that stand for sounds.)*

1 SECTION

Population Patterns

SETTING THE SCENE

Read to Discover . . .
- the different ethnic groups that inhabit North Africa and Southwest Asia.
- the areas in the region where most of the people live.
- the recent trend toward urbanization.

Key Term
- ethnic diversity

Identify and Locate
Maghreb, Cairo, Bahrain, Israel, Libya, Iran, Iraq, Tehran, Damascus, Baghdad, Kuwait, Riyadh, Istanbul, Jerusalem

Tehran, Iran

I would like to tell you about one of our holidays, called Norose. It was established by an ancient empire, and it begins on the first day of each new year. On this day we visit relatives and neighbors. Children receive gifts of money and candy. We also have 15 days of vacation beginning on the first day of the new year. This is one of my favorite holidays.

Your friend,
Sorush Firouzmandi

Sorush Firouzmandi, who lives in Iran, describes one of the many festivals celebrated by the peoples of North Africa and Southwest Asia. North Africa and Southwest Asia is a complex culture region with a mixture of racial and ethnic groups, languages, religions, cultures, and lifestyles.

PLACE

Human Characteristics

For centuries, North Africa and Southwest Asia has served as the crossroads for the people of Africa, Europe, and Asia. As a result, the region has much **ethnic diversity**—a difference in peoples based on their origins, languages, customs, or beliefs.

Arabs

The vast majority of the people of North Africa and Southwest Asia are Arabs. Most Arabs are Muslims who practice Islam. Their culture, especially the Arabic language, has had a profound impact on the entire region.

Before the spread of Islam in the 600s, Arabic-speaking peoples lived in the Arabian Peninsula and some areas north of the peninsula. Not all Arabic-speaking people, however, trace their roots to the Arabian Peninsula. Many are descendants of such ancient groups as the Canaanites, the Babylonians, and the Egyptians, all of whom became Arab by learning Arabic. Today Arabs live in 21 countries in the region, including the Maghreb—the area of North Africa now comprised of Tunisia, Algeria, and Morocco.

LESSON PLAN
Chapter 18, Section 1

FOCUS

SECTION OBJECTIVES

1. **Discuss** the different ethnic groups that inhabit North Africa and Southwest Asia.
2. **Locate** the areas in the region where most people live.
3. **Explain** the recent trend toward urbanization.

ABOUT THE POSTCARD

Sorush also tells us that Norose is his favorite holiday. He has many happy memories of these celebrations throughout the years.

BELLRINGER MOTIVATIONAL ACTIVITY

Project the Section 1 Focus Transparency and have students answer the questions.

PRETEACHING VOCABULARY

Present the Key Term *ethnic diversity.* Ask students to guess at its meaning. Then read the first sentence under "Human Characteristics." Ask students if the sentence gives a clue to the meaning of the term. Finally, have students find the meaning of the term in the text. LEP

Use the Vocabulary PuzzleMaker Software to create a crossword or word search puzzle.

ABCNEWS INTERACTIVE™

Videodisc

IN THE HOLY LAND

Side One, Chapter 3
Frame 2471

Title: ***Ted Koppel: The Holy Land***
Subject: Introduction to the geography and history of the Holy Land

Classroom Resources for Section 1

BLACKLINE MASTERS:
Reproducible Lesson Plan 18-1
Guided Reading Activity 18-1
Workbook Activity 18-1
Performance Assessment Activity 18
Section Quiz 18-1

TRANSPARENCIES:
Section Focus Transparency 18-1
Unit Map Overlay Transparency 6-1
Political Map Transparency 6

MULTIMEDIA:
Vocabulary PuzzleMaker Software
Testmaker

ABCNews InterActive™

TEACH

GUIDED PRACTICE

L1 Geography: Place Display Unit Map Overlay Transparency 6-1. Have students identify the areas with greatest population density. Then have them determine what these areas have in common. *(water)*

USING ILLUSTRATIONS

The two men standing behind President Clinton are King Hussein of Jordan (left) and Egyptian President Hosni Mubarak (right).

Answer to Caption: *Arabs live in 21 countries in the region.*

MULTICULTURAL PERSPECTIVE

Culturally Speaking
Cultural interactions among Southwest Asians and Europeans resulted in Arabic and Persian words becoming part of the English language. These include *algebra, bazaar, coffee, cotton, guitar, lemon, lute, sofa, taffeta,* and *tambourine.*

USING ILLUSTRATIONS

PLACE During biblical times, the Western Wall formed part of the Jews' Holy Temple. It is about 160 feet (49 m) long and 40 feet (12 m) high.

Answer to Caption: *Israel and Judah*

Geographic Themes

Place: Israel
In October 1995 Israeli Prime Minister Yitzhak Rabin (left) and Palestinian leader Yasser Arafat (right) signed the West Bank Accord, which handed over most Arab-populated areas of Israel to Palestinian control. Several weeks later, on November 4, 1995, Rabin was assassinated by an Israeli Jew who wanted to stop the peace process. *How many countries of the region are predominantly Arab?*

Israelis

About 5 million people of the region are Israelis, citizens of the country of Israel. Of these, about 4.1 million are Jewish and 0.9 million are Arab.

Israeli Jews trace their ancestral roots to the Hebrews, who settled the region in ancient times and believed that God had given them the land as a permanent home. Over the centuries, wars and persecution drove many of the Jews, as the descendants of the Hebrews were called, to settle in other countries. Their religious identity, however, kept alive their links to their ancient homeland until Israel was founded as a Jewish homeland in 1948.

The Arabs of the region, however, did not want a Jewish state on territory that had been their homeland for centuries. As a result, conflict broke out between Arabs and Jews. It brought severe hardship to all the people, including the Palestinians, or the Arabs living in territory on which Israel was established. Today, however, peace agreements between Is-

Geographic Themes

Place: Western Wall, Jerusalem
Devout Jews from all over the world pray before the Western Wall, which was part of the Jews' holy temple during ancient times. *What two kingdoms formed the ancient homeland of the Hebrews?*

Cooperative Learning Activity

Organize students into six groups and assign one of the following peoples to each group: Arabs, Israelis, Turks, Iranians and Afghanis, Cypriots, or Armenians and Kurds. Instruct members of each group to investigate the culture of their assigned peoples. They should find out about customs such as family life, eating, greetings, visiting, dating, and/or business. Provide time for a "cultural exchange" during which students can share information about the peoples of North Africa and Southwest Asia.

rael and Palestinian leaders have led to greater self-rule for Palestinians in the area.

Turks

The people of Turkey are a blend of the many people who have lived for centuries in Southwest Asia. The most notable of these were the Ottoman Turks, whose empire ruled much of the eastern Mediterranean world for more than 600 years.

The Turks are not Arab, but like the Arabs, most practice Islam. They also speak their own Turkish language and have developed a culture that blends Turkish, Islamic, and Western elements.

Iranians and Afghanis

Today more than 60 million people live in Iran, once called Persia. The term *Iran* means "land of the Aryans," and many Iranians believe they are descendants of the Aryans, Indo-Europeans who migrated into the region from southern Russia about 1000 B.C. Iranians today speak Farsi, an Indo-European language that is distantly related to English. Most Iranians practice a form of Islam known as Shiism.

On the eastern border of Iran is Afghanistan, another of the non-Arab countries in the region. Afghanistan is a country of many ethnic groups that reflect the centuries of migrations and invasions of different peoples. A common adherence to Islam is the thread that helps hold the country together.

Cypriots

Another non-Arab nation in North Africa and Southwest Asia is the island nation of Cyprus. The people of Cyprus include a Greek majority and a significant Turkish minority. After the island gained independence from the United Kingdom, a violent civil war erupted between the two groups. Today Cyprus remains a divided nation of Greeks and Turks.

Armenians and Kurds

The region also includes two large ethnic groups—the Armenians and the Kurds. For many years, both groups have struggled to form their own countries.

Before World War I, most Armenians lived in Turkey. During the Greek-Turkish conflict, an estimated 1 million Armenians were massacred, deported, or died of illness at the hands of the Turks. The survivors fled, many settling in other parts of Southwest Asia as well as Europe and the United States. Recently, Armenians have celebrated the independence of the Armenian republic in the former Soviet Union.

The Kurds live in the border region separating Turkey, Iraq, Iran, Syria, and the former Soviet Union. They call their land Kurdistan, but their efforts to win self-rule have been repeatedly crushed.

HUMAN/ENVIRONMENT INTERACTION

Water and Population

Most of the people of North Africa and Southwest Asia live near water. People live along seacoasts, rivers, or near highlands, and near oases. For example, most Egyptians live along the Nile River or near the Suez Canal. In Iraq, many people live in the Tigris-Euphrates Valley.

The environment in these areas makes it possible to grow crops and raise animals. Drinking water is also readily available in these locations. Farming, mining, fishing, and trading are the major economic activities.

The desert areas of North Africa and Southwest Asia are largely unpopulated except for the cities, where oil-related industries provide jobs. Nomadic herders live in or near the desert oases.

PLACE

Population Densities and Growth

The most populous countries in the region are Turkey, Egypt, and Iran. Each of these countries has a population of more than 50 million. Morocco, Algeria, Iraq, Saudi Arabia, and Afghanistan have populations ranging between about 17 million and 28 million. The

INDEPENDENT PRACTICE

Guided Reading Have students complete Guided Reading Activity 18-1 in the TCR. **LEP**

L2 Geography: Location/ Place Have students work in pairs to make information cards about the major cities of the region. On one side of the card, students should list the name of the city and describe its location. On the other side of the card, they should list important facts about the city. Have partners use the cards to quiz each other about the cities and to locate each city on a map.

ASSESS

CHECK FOR UNDERSTANDING

Assign Section 1 Review as homework or an in-class activity.

MEETING LESSON OBJECTIVES

Each objective below is tested by the questions that follow it in parentheses.

1. Discuss the different ethnic groups that inhabit North Africa and Southwest Asia. *(3)*

2. Locate the areas in the region where most people live. *(2)*

3. Explain the recent trend toward urbanization. *(4, 5)*

Meeting Special Needs

Language Disability Many students with language difficulties have trouble finding the relationships among words that set up the sequence of the ideas. Explain that good notes require careful attention to these relationships. Read aloud the material under "Urbanization." Stop after each sentence to ask if there were key words or transition words presented. Point out the use of "since," "however," and "as a result." Demonstrate how these words signal a sequence of events.

USING ILLUSTRATIONS

PLACE A view of Istanbul from Golden Horn Harbor shows the Süleymaniye Mosque in the background.

Answer to Caption: *Islam*

EVALUATE

Assign the Section 1 Quiz in the TCR.

Use the Testmaker to create a customized quiz for Section 1.

RETEACH

Display Political Map Transparency 6. Have students identify the most populous areas of the region. Then ask them to summarize information about the different groups of people who live there.

ENRICH

Have interested students investigate how one of the major cities in this region reflects the cultures of the people. They might present a mini-travelogue to share their findings.

CLOSE

Have students write a postcard to Sorush. Suggest that they describe an American celebration.

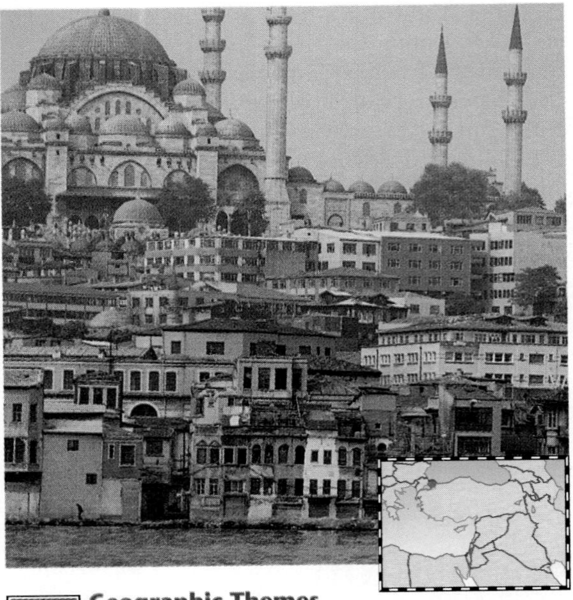

Geographic Themes

Location: Istanbul, Turkey

Istanbul's location near the point where the Black Sea meets the Mediterranean Sea has made it an important trading city. *What religion do most Turks practice?*

remaining countries have populations of roughly 13.5 million or fewer. Tiny Bahrain on the Persian Gulf is the most densely populated, with about 2,000 people per square mile (772 per sq. km).

Overall the populations of the countries of the region currently total about 350 million and are growing at a rapid rate. The result is that citizens in a number of countries already are finding it hard to find jobs and are migrating to other nations to work. This migration serves as a safety valve for some nations, but changing conditions, such as a reduction in oil production, could lead to a decline in the need for foreign workers and become a source of unrest.

PLACE

Urbanization

Many great cities once existed in North Africa and the Middle East. For centuries, however, the region's population was rural rather than urban. Since World War II, most of the major oil-and-gas-producing countries, however, have rapidly become urbanized.

Urban growth has been due, in part, to rural villagers moving to the cities in search of a better life. This population shift, however, has caused problems because the cities have grown faster than have the means of supplying food and housing. As a result, food and housing shortages have become problems in some cities.

Cairo is one of the region's largest cities with more than 10 million people. Located on the Nile River, Cairo is the capital as well as the cultural and economic center of Egypt. Alexandria, Egypt's other major city, is a seaport on the Mediterranean Sea.

The other major cities in North Africa are all located on the coast. They include Tripoli, the capital of Libya; Tunis, the capital of Tunisia; Algiers, the capital of Algeria; and Casablanca in Morocco.

The major cities in the eastern part of the region are Tehran, the capital of Iran; Baghdad, the capital of Iraq; and Istanbul in Turkey. This area also includes two cities that originally developed around oases—Syria's capital, Damascus, and Saudi Arabia's capital, Riyadh (ree•AHD).

SECTION 1 REVIEW

Checking for Understanding

1. **Define** ethnic diversity.
2. **Locating Places** Where in the region are the largest concentrations of people?
3. **Place** What different peoples make up the region?
4. **Movement** What has been the trend in the distribution of population in North Africa and Southwest Asia since World War II?

Critical Thinking

5. **Analyzing Information** What challenges does a growing population bring to the region?

ANSWERS TO SECTION 1 REVIEW

1. **ethnic diversity:** differences in groups of people based on their origins, languages, customs, or beliefs
2. along rivers and in coastal areas
3. Arabs, Israelis, Turks, Cypriots, Kurds, and Armenians
4. movement from rural to urban areas
5. Because of a limited amount of farmland, a scarcity of water, and a lack of industrial jobs, the rapidly growing population is a threat to the region's resources.

NATIONAL GEOGRAPHIC
GEOFACTS

Where is the lowest point on earth?

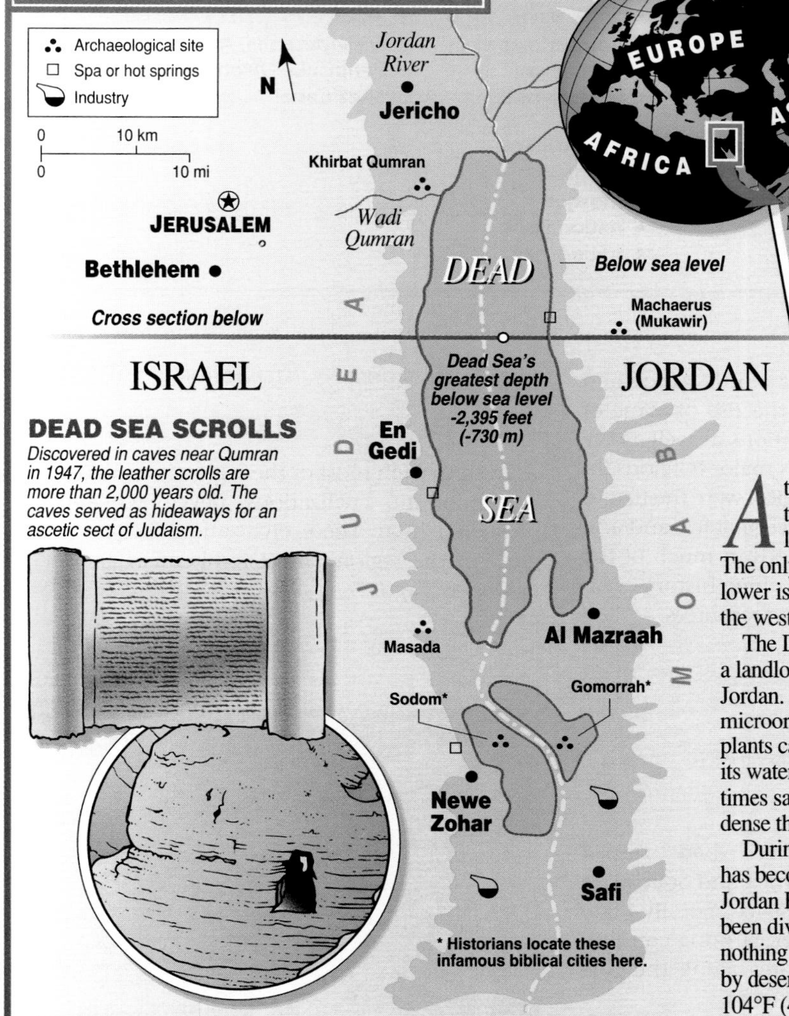

Archaeological site
Spa or hot springs
Industry

N

0 10 km
0 10 mi

Jordan River
Jericho
Khirbat Qumran
JERUSALEM
Wadi Qumran
Bethlehem
DEAD SEA
Below sea level
Machaerus (Mukawir)
Cross section below
ISRAEL
JORDAN
JUDEA
MOAB
Dead Sea's greatest depth below sea level -2,395 feet (-730 m)
En Gedi
Masada
Al Mazraah
Sodom*
Gomorrah*
Newe Zohar
Safi
* Historians locate these infamous biblical cities here.

EUROPE
ASIA
AFRICA

LEBANON
Damascus
SYRIA
GOLAN HEIGHTS
Sea of Galilee
ISRAEL
WEST BANK
JORDAN
Mediterranean Sea
Jericho
Amman
Jerusalem
Dead Sea
GAZA STRIP
Occupied by Israel
EGYPT
0 25 km
0 25 mi

DEAD SEA SCROLLS

Discovered in caves near Qumran in 1947, the leather scrolls are more than 2,000 years old. The caves served as hideaways for an ascetic sect of Judaism.

At 1,312 feet (400 m) below sea level, the shore of the Dead Sea is the lowest point on the earth's surface. The only place where land is known to be lower is completely covered by ice, a spot in the western part of Antarctica.

The Dead Sea is not really a sea at all, but a landlocked lake split between Israel and Jordan. It is not really dead either; microorganisms can live in it. Fish and plants cannot live in the Dead Sea because its water is the saltiest on the planet—nine times saltier than the ocean. The sea is so dense that swimmers cannot sink.

During the past 50 years, the Dead Sea has become even saltier and smaller. The Jordan River, a source of freshwater, has been diverted for agriculture, leaving nothing to balance the evaporation caused by desert air temperatures that often top 104°F (40°C).

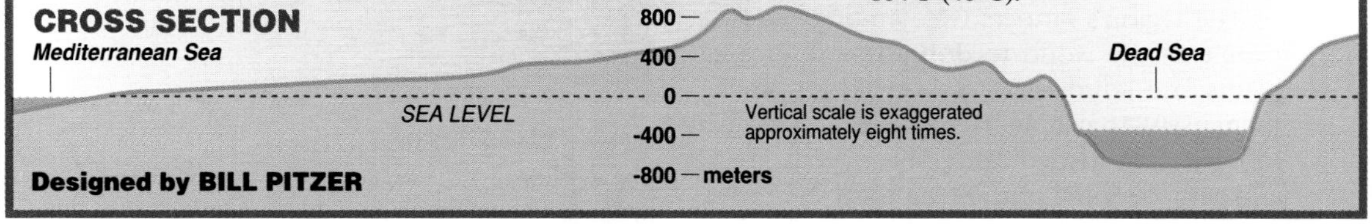

CROSS SECTION

Mediterranean Sea
Dead Sea
800
400
0
SEA LEVEL
-400
-800 meters
Vertical scale is exaggerated approximately eight times.

Designed by BILL PITZER

TEACH

Archaeologists found the Dead Sea Scrolls stored in jars. Tell students that the Dead Sea Scrolls include almost all of the books of the Old Testament. They also include descriptions of life in the community near which the Scrolls were found. Some of these manuscripts explain how one became a member of the community and rules that governed daily life.

Have students work together to write similar rules for their own lives and community. Explain that you would like to place students' manuscripts in a time capsule, which may be discovered 2,000 years from now. Have students decide in what type of container (jar, metal box, milk jug, and so on) their manuscripts should be stored.

LESSON PLAN
Chapter 18, Section 2

FOCUS

SECTION OBJECTIVES

1. **Describe** the natural environment of two of the world's earliest civilizations.
2. **Compare** three of the world's major religions.
3. **Discuss** influences created by the interactions of different peoples in the region.

BELLRINGER MOTIVATIONAL ACTIVITY

Project the Section 2 Focus Transparency and have students answer the questions.

PRETEACHING VOCABULARY

Have students find the definitions for the Key Terms in the text. Then call on volunteers to use one of the terms in a sentence. LEP

USING ILLUSTRATIONS

HUMAN/ENVIRONMENT INTERACTION Statues of Ramses II guard the Abu Simbel temple near the Nile River. The monument was moved to higher ground during construction of the Aswan High Dam.

Answer to Caption: *calendar with a 365-day year; hieroglyphics*

Videodisc

IN THE HOLY LAND

Side One, Chapter 9
Frame 9487

Title: *Three Religions*
Subject: Introduction to Islam, Christianity, and Judaism

SECTION 2

History and Government

SETTING THE SCENE

Read to Discover . . .
- the natural environment of two of the world's earliest civilizations.
- the nature of three of the world's major religions.
- the influences created by the interaction of different peoples in the region.

Key Terms
- domesticate
- cuneiform
- hieroglyphics
- qanat
- monotheism
- prophet
- mosque
- nationalism
- nationalize

Identify and Locate
Mesopotamia, Arabian Peninsula, Ottoman Empire, Suez Canal

The culture region of North Africa and Southwest Asia saw the rise of some of the world's greatest civilizations as well as the birth of three of the world's major religions. In addition, farmers of the region were the first to raise many of the cereals, vegetables, and animals still used as staple foods in much of the world. The region also has a long history of intense conflicts over land and resources.

HUMAN/ENVIRONMENT INTERACTION

Early Peoples

Hunters and gatherers had settled throughout North Africa and Southwest Asia by the end of the last Ice Age. By 6000 B.C., about 4,000 years later, farming communities had spread to the area along the Nile River and the Mediterranean Sea.

The region's farmers were among the first people in the world to **domesticate**, or take plants and animals from the wild and make them useful to people. These early farmers also captured and herded cattle, sheep, goats, pigs, and camels. Some of these animals were used for food. Farmers used the hides of some other animals to make clothes and shelters.

HUMAN/ENVIRONMENT INTERACTION

Early Civilizations

Even though most of the region is semiarid, important civilizations developed and prospered here. These civilizations began to grow in the region's most fertile areas about 6,000 years ago.

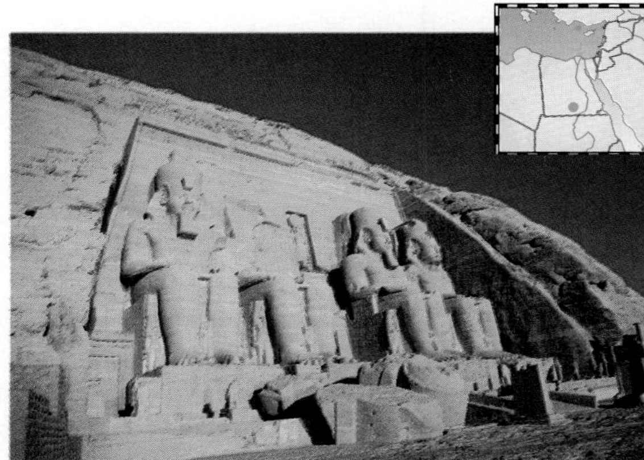

Geographic Themes
Place: Abu Simbel Monument, Egypt
The ancient Egyptians built monuments and pyramid tombs for their rulers. *What were other achievements of ancient Egyptian civilization?*

Classroom Resources for Section 2

BLACKLINE MASTERS:
- Reproducible Lesson Plan 18-2
- Guided Reading Activity 18-2
- Spanish Guided Reading Activity 18-2
- Workbook Activity 18-2
- Foods Around the World 5
- World Literature Reading 5
- Section Quiz 18-2

TRANSPARENCIES:
- Section Focus Transparency 18-2
- Unit Map Overlay Transparency 6-5

MULTIMEDIA:

- Testmaker

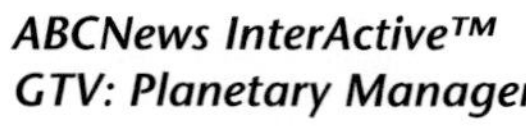

ABCNews InterActive™
GTV: Planetary Manager

Mesopotamia

The Sumerian civilization was one early society that developed in Mesopotamia, the area between the Tigris and Euphrates rivers. Mesopotamia's warm climate allowed the Sumerians to raise crops year-round. Irrigation canals and flood-control dikes were used to bring the nearby river water to the land. Efforts to improve water distribution led to progress in the study of mathematics, engineering, and soil science. The Sumerians kept records by carving wedge-shaped symbols on wet clay tablets. These tablets were then baked and hardened. This writing system is called **cuneiform.**

Egypt

Egyptian civilization grew along the Nile River. Because of sophisticated irrigation methods and the alluvial-soil deposits resulting from the annual flooding of the Nile, farmers could grow 2 or 3 crops each year. The Egyptians' cultural achievements included building pyramids as tombs for their rulers and developing a calendar with a 365-day year. In addition, the Egyptians developed a form of picture writing called **hieroglyphics.**

Later Civilizations

The Phoenician civilization arose along the Mediterranean coast of present-day Israel and Lebanon. The Phoenicians' most important achievement was the development of an alphabet in which letters stood for sounds. This alphabet formed the basis for the alphabet used throughout much of the Western world today.

During the 500s B.C., the Persian Empire developed. The Persian Empire extended from beyond the eastern border of the region to the Nile River and the Aegean Sea. Realizing that irrigation water for their settlements would evaporate if carried across the desert in surface canals, the Persians constructed a system of **qanats,** or underground canals, to carry water from the mountains across the desert to farmlands.

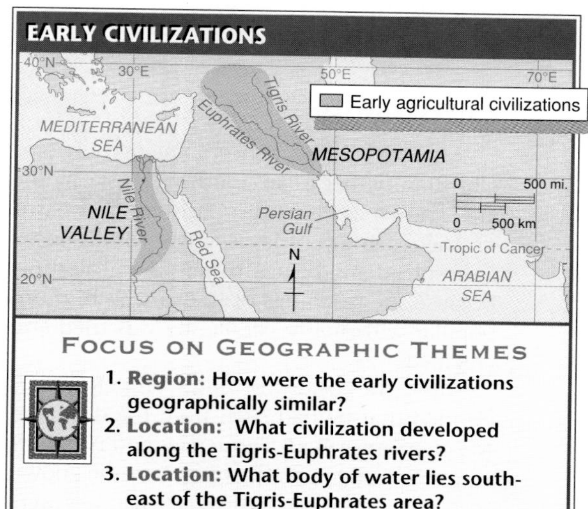

FOCUS ON GEOGRAPHIC THEMES

1. **Region:** How were the early civilizations geographically similar?
2. **Location:** What civilization developed along the Tigris-Euphrates rivers?
3. **Location:** What body of water lies southeast of the Tigris-Euphrates area?

The Sumerians, Egyptians, Phoenicians, Persians, and other empires to the west and to the east had many cultural and economic exchanges. Because of these exchanges, North Africa and Southwest Asia became known as the crossroads of civilization.

REGION

The Birthplace of Three Major Religions

Three of the world's major religions began in Southwest Asia. One of the earliest, Judaism, developed as the religion of the Hebrews.

Judaism

Once a nomadic people, the Hebrews established the kingdoms of Israel and Judah along the eastern coast of the Mediterranean Sea. There they made the city of Jerusalem their capital and religious center. The followers of Judaism, called Jews, based their religion on **monotheism**—the belief in one God. In addition, Judaism taught the importance of obedience to God's laws and the creation of a just

TEACH

GUIDED PRACTICE

L1 Geography: Place Display Unit Map Overlay Transparency 6-5. Have students locate the region where the following civilizations began: Sumerian *(Mesopotamia),* Egyptian *(along the Nile),* Phoenician *(Mediterranean coast of Israel and Lebanon).* Have them identify the region that was part of the Persian Empire *(eastern border of the region to the Nile River and the Aegean Sea).*

Implement Foods Around the World 5 as a class activity.

Global Gourmet

In many countries of North Africa and Southwest Asia, food is eaten with the fingers. Only the right hand is used for eating and for passing dishes of food.

USING MAPS

Answers: **1.** developed in river valleys; **2.** Sumerians; **3.** Persian Gulf

Map Skills Practice

Drawing Conclusions How did location and environment aid the development of civilizations? *(Warm climate and fertile soils provided a reliable food supply.)*

Cooperative Learning Activity

Organize students into four groups and assign one of the following civilizations to each group: Sumerians, Egyptians, Phoenicians, or Persians. Group members should investigate the way of life developed by each civilization, concentrating on how the people adapted to the environment of the region. Provide time for sharing insights. Then discuss how these civilizations helped make North Africa and Southwest Asia a crossroads of culture.

INDEPENDENT PRACTICE

Guided Reading Have students complete Guided Reading Activity 18-2 in the TCR. **LEP**

USING MAPS

Answers: **1.** Spain and southeastern Europe; **2.** Medina and Makkah; **3.** Baghdad

Map Skills Practice

Reading a Map What bodies of water likely aided the spread of Islam? *(Answers include Arabian Sea, Mediterranean Sea, Persian Gulf, Red Sea, Caspian Sea, Black Sea)*

Have students complete World Literature Reading 5 in the TCR.

L1 Compare Have students list the present-day countries of North Africa and Southwest Asia. Then have them find out what system of government each country has. Have students classify the countries according to their political systems.

L3 Research Have students locate Palestine. Ask them to research how areas known as the West Bank and the Gaza Strip have caused continuing conflict between Arab and Israeli peoples.

CURRICULUM CONNECTION

SOCIOLOGY

During the reign of Queen Hatshepsut (c. 1500–1480 B.C.), Egyptian women had more rights than any other women in the ancient world. They had full legal rights and could inherit, own, and sell property without their husband's permission.

society. Books based on these laws and on the history of the Jews make up the Hebrew Bible.

Christianity

Another of the region's major religions, Christianity, began in Southwest Asia in the area known as Palestine. Christianity is based on the teachings of Jesus, a Jew who traveled and spread his beliefs throughout Palestine. Because the teachings of Jesus made him unpopular with many people, he was tried and crucified.

After the death of Jesus, his followers claimed that he had risen from the dead and was the Son of God. Those Jews and non-Jews who followed Jesus's teachings became known as Christians. Many Christian teachings were detailed in books about Jesus and the early churches, which Christians added to the Hebrew Bible. The new books are called the New Testament.

Islam

Another major religion that emerged in Southwest Asia, and the religion followed by the vast majority of the people in North Africa and Southwest Asia today, was Islam. This religion began in the Arabian Peninsula about A.D. 600 with Muhammad, a merchant of the city of Makkah (Mecca). Believing that he was God's **prophet**, or messenger, Muhammad proclaimed that people should change their ways of living and believe in the one true God. It is estimated that today as many as one-fifth of the world's people are Muslims—a term from an Arabic word meaning "those who submit to the will of God." Muslims pay close attention to the rules of their faith that are set down in the Islamic holy book, the Quran. They pray in **mosques**—houses of public worship.

By the A.D. 800s, Islam had spread to North Africa, South Asia, Southwest Asia, and parts

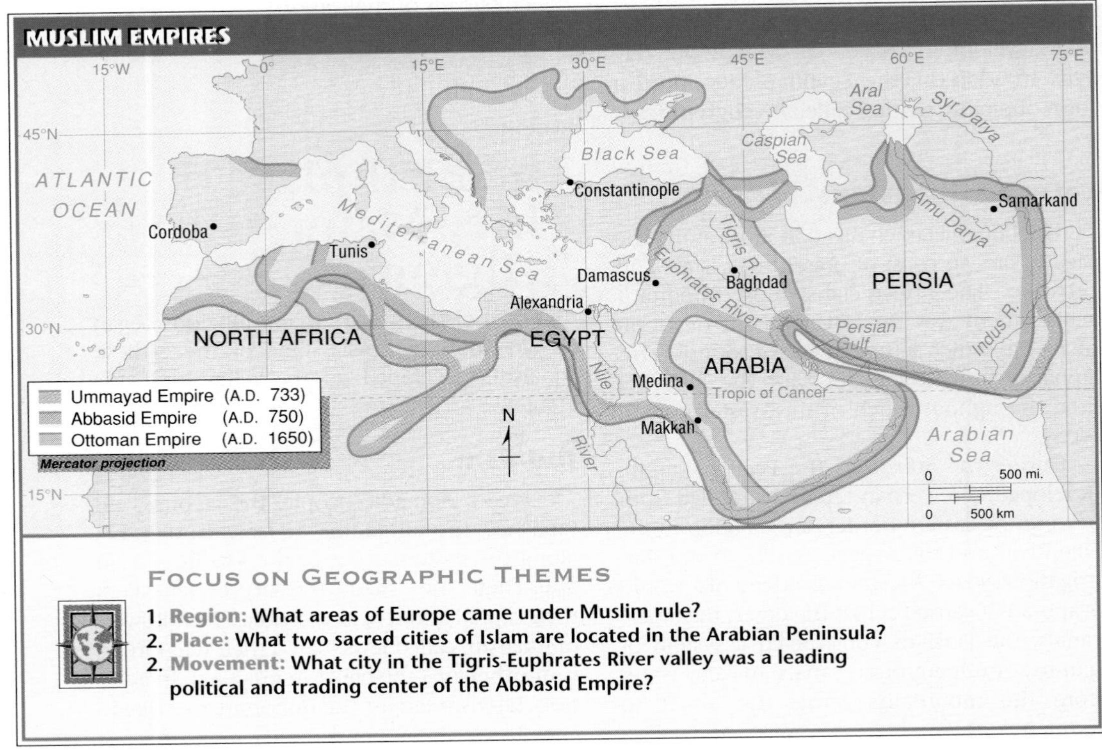

FOCUS ON GEOGRAPHIC THEMES

1. **Region: What areas of Europe came under Muslim rule?**
2. **Place: What two sacred cities of Islam are located in the Arabian Peninsula?**
2. **Movement: What city in the Tigris-Euphrates River valley was a leading political and trading center of the Abbasid Empire?**

Meeting Special Needs

Visual Learners For visual learners, a diagram is an especially useful note-taking tool to help students remember relationships among cultures. From the text under "The Birthplace of Three Major Religions," have students create three web diagrams: one for Judaism, one for Christianity, and one for Islam. Ask students to fill in each web with facts about the religion in the center of that diagram. Then have students compare the webs and draw lines connecting similarities, such as monotheism.

of Europe. Islamic scholars, particularly those in the Muslim empires of North Africa and Southwest Asia, made important contributions in the natural sciences, medicine, astronomy, and mathematics. They introduced the Arabic number system, based on the numerals 0 to 9, into the region. The scholars also translated Greek writings into Arabic.

THE MIDDLE EAST AFTER WORLD WAR I

FOCUS ON GEOGRAPHIC THEMES

1. **Region: What areas of the region were under British administration?**
2. **Place: What European country administered Syria?**

REGION

The Modern Era

Over the years, the Muslim empires of North Africa and Southwest Asia began to decline. By the late 1800s, the region was largely under the control of Europeans. The region's decline was due in part to the many wars fought on its lands. Some major conflicts included the Crusades and the Mongol invasions.

Another reason for the decline was the lack of resources, such as minerals, wood, and coal. The region lacked many of the raw materials needed to fuel an industrial revolution such as the one that took place in Europe.

The peoples of the region chafed under European control. During the 1800s a well-educated urban middle class developed. Trained in European ways, the new middle class accepted European ideas about **nationalism**, or the right of each people to have its own independent nation. This development stirred nationalistic feelings that provided the basis for the modern nations that have been carved out of the region.

Independence

The continuing rise of nationalism after World Wars I and II gradually brought an end to direct European rule. By the 1960s most of the Arab countries in North Africa and Southwest Asia had achieved independence. European nations, however, often controlled the newly independent countries' economies. To counter the European presence, some countries seized European property. Iran, Iraq, and Libya, for example, **nationalized**, or placed under government control, the foreign-owned oil companies in their countries.

Not all the newly independent nations in the region were Arab or Muslim. Many Jews had returned to Palestine since World War I, and in 1948 the United Nations agreed to create the state of Israel. Arab opposition to Israel's existence and Israel's concerns for its security led to a series of wars. An ongoing issue in the Arab-Israeli dispute is the status of the Palestinians, who want a separate homeland in areas occupied by Israeli forces in the 1967 Arab-Israeli war. In 1993, a considerable move toward peace in the region was taken when Israel and the Palestinians agreed to a peace settlement. The agreement called for eventual Palestinian self-rule in return for Arab recognition of Israel's right to nationhood.

Other trouble spots in the region also have led to armed conflicts. In Lebanon there have been continuing struggles between Christians and Muslims over control of the government.

Critical Thinking

Drawing Conclusions Pose the following question for students to consider: Has religion been a unifying or a dividing force in North Africa and Southwest Asia? Ask students to write their answer, supporting their opinion with facts from the text or other references. Provide time for students with differing viewpoints to discuss their ideas.

USING MAPS

Answers:
1. Palestine, Trans-Jordan, Iraq;
2. France

Map Skills Practice
Reading a Map What group of people opposed Israel's claim to nationhood? *(Arabs)*

ASSESS

CHECK FOR UNDERSTANDING

Assign Section 2 Review as homework or an in-class activity.

MEETING LESSON OBJECTIVES

Each objective below is tested by the questions that follow it in parentheses.
1. Describe the natural environment of two of the world's earliest civilizations. *(2, 5)*
2. Compare three of the world's major religions. *(1)*
3. Discuss influences created by the interactions of different peoples in the region. *(3, 4)*

ABCNEWS INTERACTIVE™

Videodisc

IN THE HOLY LAND

Side One, Chapter 10
Frame 13273

Title: ***Ted Koppel: History of Hatred***
Subject: A history of the conflict between Jews and Arabs

USING ILLUSTRATIONS

PLACE The Israeli flag displays the Star of David—an ancient Jewish symbol, and the colors of a *tallit* (prayer shawl).
Answer to Caption: *rise of nationalism*

EVALUATE

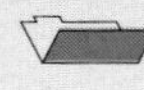

Assign the Section 2 Quiz in the TCR.

Use the Testmaker to create a customized quiz for Section 2.

RETEACH

List the four major headings from this section on the chalkboard. Under each heading, have students write the Key Terms that apply to that part of the text. Then have them use the Key Terms to review the main ideas of each subsection.

ENRICH

Have students find out how the Rosetta stone provided a key to the language of ancient Egypt.

CLOSE

Ask students if they think North Africa and Southwest Asia are still a crossroads of civilization. *(Answers will vary but should reflect reasoning.)*

ABCNEWS INTERACTIVE™

Videodisc

IN THE HOLY LAND

Side One, Chapter 11
Frame 14633

Title: *Timeline*
Subject: A step-by-step history of the Holy Land, 1878–1988

Geographic Themes

Place: Tel Aviv, Israel

Israelis celebrate their country's independence day. *What development in the 20th century led to the emergence of independent countries in the region?*

In addition, border conflicts, such as the conflict between Iraq and Iran that led to years of warfare, still exist.

The most recent dispute arose in 1990 after Iraq invaded its oil-rich neighbor Kuwait. Iraq's invasion and occupation of Kuwait ended only after a coalition of nations led by the United States expelled the Iraqi forces and forced Saddam Hussein, Iraq's president, to withdraw his army.

Today's Governments

The independent nations of North Africa and Southwest Asia have several different types of governments. Monarchs rule eight of the nations in the region. Other types of government include Israel's parliamentary democracy, Egypt's republic with a strong national government and a president, Libya's military dictatorship, and Iran's government based on Islamic laws.

SECTION 2 REVIEW

Checking for Understanding

1. **Define** domesticate, cuneiform, hieroglyphics, qanat, monotheism, prophet, mosque, nationalism, nationalize.
2. **Locating Places** What rivers were the bases for the Mesopotamian and Egyptian civilizations?
3. **Movement** Why was North Africa and Southwest Asia called the crossroads of civilization?
4. **Region** How are the governments of North Africa and Southwest Asia organized?

Critical Thinking

5. **Drawing Conclusions** Why was the domestication of plants and animals so important to the founding of permanent settlements?

ANSWERS TO SECTION 2 REVIEW

1. **domesticate:** making wild plants and animals useful to people; **cuneiform:** Sumerian writing system; **hieroglyphics:** Egyptian picture writing; **qanat:** underground canal; **monotheism:** belief in one God; **prophet:** messenger of God; **mosque:** Muslim place of worship; **nationalism:** people's right to have their own nation; **nationalize:** to place under government control
2. Nile, Tigris, and Euphrates rivers
3. many cultural exchanges between the region and lands to the east and west
4. Eight nations are monarchies. Israel is a parliamentary democracy. Libya is a military dictatorship. Iran's government is based on Islamic laws.
5. The domestication of plants and animals enabled farmers to settle in one area.

Geography and History

The Sahara: Growing or Shifting?

Farmers living in grasslands bordering the Sahara have built shelter belts to prevent soil from being blown away and to control the movement of sand into their fields. Efforts to control the effects of desertification, however, have not always met with success.

As you read, examine how the Sahara has changed and may change in the future.

Region

The vast, dry Sahara covers about 3.5 million square miles (9 million sq. km)—an area roughly equal to the size of the continental United States. At the Sahara's center are volcanic mountains. Plains broken by plateaus and boulders surround the mountains; at the very edge of the Sahara are seas of sand dunes.

A Glorious Green Past

The Sahara as it is today gives no hint that in the past grasslands and forests covered the region. Geologists have determined that the Sahara's climate slowly began to change about 10,000 years ago. By about 4000 B.C., an arid region had appeared at the center of the once fertile area.

The climate continued to slowly dry out through the centuries. People living in the area also contributed to the desert's growth by practicing *shifting cultivation*. They cut down trees in an area, uprooted the shrubs for firewood and building materials, and let their herds overgraze. When they had depleted the resources of an area, the people moved on to another place. With no ground cover to protect the soil in the abandoned area, the desert took over, increasing its size.

Population Overload

Desertification of the Sahara continues today at an even more alarming rate than in the past. Beginning in the 1940s, foreign aid and enhanced technology increased the population living on the edges of the Sahara. The human activities that contribute to desertification have increased: uprooting bushes and grass, cutting down trees, overgrazing. In the late 1970s, scientists reported that the Sahara was "growing" in a southward direction of 2 to 6 miles (3 to 10 km) a year.

Important new studies in the early 1990s suggested that the Sahara's southward movement might be more like a sea tide, shifting back and forth within a 145-mile (269-km) zone, rather than a permanent increase. Scientists cautioned, however, that whatever natural activity may be taking place, it does not alter the need to change the human behavior in the region.

Checking for Understanding

1. Study the illustration at the top of the page. How has the Sahara region changed since the end of the Ice Age?
2. **Human/Environment Interaction** How have humans contributed to the Sahara's growth?

ANSWERS TO CHECKING FOR UNDERSTANDING

1. Since the end of the Ice Age, the Sahara has expanded.
2. Human populations along the Sahara's edge cut down trees, uproot bushes and grass, and let their herds overgraze the land. These activities destroy the ground cover that protects the topsoil, allowing the desert to take over.

Geography and History

TEACH

Ask students to compose comparison/contrast sentences about the Sahara and the United States' southwestern deserts. Encourage students to look back at photographs in Unit 2. Share the information in Extending the Content, then ask students to answer the following question.

Human/Environment Interaction How would human behavior have to change in order to slow or stop further desertification of the Sahara? *(Vegetation should be left to grow; other means of economic survival would have to be found to replace the farming and herding of the area.)*

Extending the Content

The Sahel The tidal-like movement of the Sahara takes place in a region called the Sahel that borders the desert's southern edge. The Sahel has had no big rains since 1968, and the Sahara appears to be encroaching in areas where villagers once grew crops or raised cattle. Millions have starved to death, while others have left their villages to build a life elsewhere. In some areas of the Sahel, sand dunes have buried entire villages.

Videodisc

GTV: PLANETARY MANAGER

Side 2, Chapter 6
Frames 31907-38777
Title: *Dust in the Wind*
Subject: Time travel shows the consequences of overgrazing, excessive irrigation, and deforestation

FOCUS

SECTION OBJECTIVES

1. Explain the impact of religion on the cultural and political development of North Africa and Southwest Asia.
2. Compare three different ways of life in North Africa and Southwest Asia.
3. Describe the geographic factors that have contributed to the region's standard of living.

BELLRINGER MOTIVATIONAL ACTIVITY

Project the Section 3 Focus Transparency and have students answer the questions.

PRETEACHING VOCABULARY

Inform students that the word *ziggurat* means "pinnacle" or "mountaintop." In ancient Mesopotamian cities, the ziggurat towered above other structures. **LEP**

USING GRAPHS

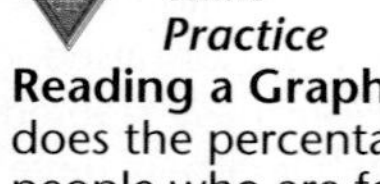

Skills Practice

Reading a Graph How does the percentage of people who are followers of Islam compare with that of other religions in North Africa and Southwest Asia? *(93% of the people are Muslims)*

SECTION 3 Cultures and Lifestyles

SETTING THE SCENE

Read to Discover . . .
- the impact of religion on the cultural and political development of North Africa and Southwest Asia.
- three different ways of life for most people in North Africa and Southwest Asia.
- the geographic factors that have contributed to the region's standard of living.

Key Terms
- ziggurat
- bedouin
- *sūq*

Identify and Locate
Lebanon, Cyprus, United Arab Emirates

Religion is an important unifying element within each of the cultures of North Africa and Southwest Asia. These cultures have also been enriched by contact with the peoples of the three continents for which this region has been a crossroads.

REGION

Religion

The great majority of people in the region follow Islam. The religion influences the language, arts, government, and lifestyles of its followers. Islam is the major religion of all the countries in the region with the exception of Israel and Cyprus.

Even though Judaism and Christianity have their roots in the region, only a small percentage of the current population is either Jewish or Christian. Although Algeria and Morocco have some Jewish residents, the overwhelming majority of Jews in the region live in Israel.

The countries of Lebanon and Cyprus have large Christian populations. The majority of the Lebanese Christians are Maronites, which is a branch of Roman Catholicism. In contrast, most Cypriot Christians follow the Eastern Orthodox faith.

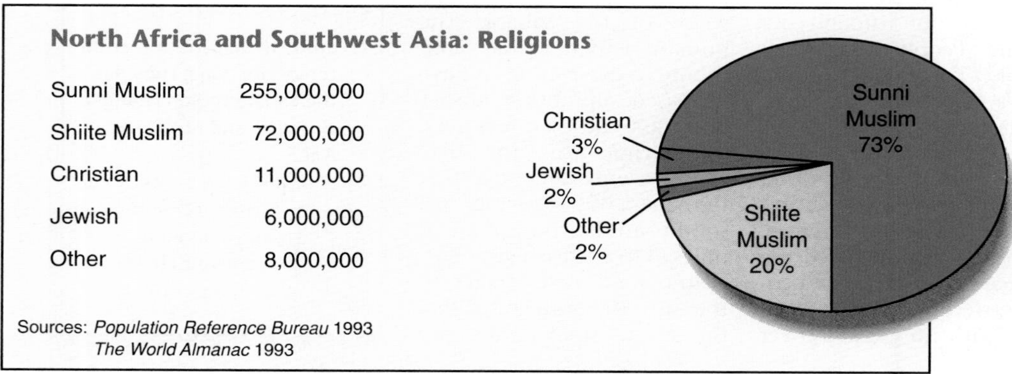

Classroom Resources for Section 3

BLACKLINE MASTERS:
Reproducible Lesson Plan 18-3
Guided Reading Activity 18-3
Enrichment Activity 18
Skill Activity 18
Section Quiz 18-3

TRANSPARENCIES:
Section Focus Transparency 18-3
World Cultures Transparency 10

MULTIMEDIA:

Testmaker

***World Music:** Cultural Traditions, Lesson 5*

Picture Atlas of the World

Geographic Themes

Location: Grand Mosque, Saudi Arabia

The Grand Mosque, the center of worship for all Muslims, stands in the heart of Makkah, the holiest city of Islam. *What art forms do Muslim artists use in mosques and other public buildings?*

REGION

Languages

Because the Quran was originally written in Arabic, non-Arab Muslims often learned Arabic in order to read the Quran. Thus, as more people converted to Islam, Arabic became the region's main language. Other major languages include Hebrew in Israel, Berber in southern Morocco and Algeria, Turkish in Turkey and Cyprus, Greek in Cyprus, Pushtu in Afghanistan, and Farsi in Iran.

REGION

The Arts

The arts of North Africa and Southwest Asia are based on the achievements of early civilizations. Later, Judaism, Christianity, and Islam provided inspiration for architects, writers, and artists. Today, the arts reflect the influence of East and West as well as the old and the new.

Architecture and Art

The region's early civilizations produced fine metal craftswork and stone sculptures. These civilizations, however, were best known for their architecture. In Mesopotamia large temples—**ziggurats**—made of mud brick rose in step-like fashion above the flat landscape. In Egypt large blocks of stone were painstakingly fitted to form the towering pyramids. The Persians later built great palaces of stone decorated with beautifully patterned woven textiles.

The best-known forms of Islamic architecture are its mosques and palaces. Because Islam did not encourage the images of living figures in religious art, artists have used geometric patterns and floral designs to decorate buildings. Beautiful writing is also often used for decoration. Many mosques are decorated with passages from the Quran.

Literature

The region's strong oral tradition has made epics and poetry the dominant literature

Cooperative Learning Activity

Organize students into groups of four or five. Instruct members of each group to investigate ways in which the arts of North Africa and Southwest Asia reflect religious influences. Students may present an in-depth study of one example or they may find several different examples. They may create models or drawings or obtain illustrations to go with their reports. Provide time for groups to share their work.

TEACH

GUIDED PRACTICE

L2 Contrast Have students draw a ladder illustrating standards of living in North Africa and Southwest Asia. Each rung of the ladder represents a way of life in the region, with the highest standard of living at the top. Have students fill in information about the countries, economies, and lifestyles for each standard of living represented on the ladder.

USING ILLUSTRATIONS

MOVEMENT All Muslims are required to make a pilgrimage to Makkah at least once.

Answer to Caption: *geometric patterns and floral designs*

DID YOU KNOW?

Many nations in North Africa and Southwest Asia have set up programs to encourage Bedouin settlement. Some governments give Bedouins land on which to farm and raise livestock. Others build housing projects for Bedouins.

Have students complete World Music: Cultural Traditions, Lesson 5 activity in the TCR.

CD-ROM

PICTURE ATLAS OF THE WORLD

You and your students can hear the various languages of the people in this region by clicking the "Speech" button of selected countries.

INDEPENDENT PRACTICE

Guided Reading Have students complete Guided Reading Activity 18-3 in the TCR. **LEP**

Have students complete World Cultures Transparency 10 Activity in the TCR.

USING ILLUSTRATIONS

PLACE This *sūq* is located in Akko, Israel. The Panorama shopping center is on Mt. Carmel in Haifa, Israel.

Answer to Caption: *wheat, barley, rice*

ASSESS

CHECK FOR UNDERSTANDING

Assign Section 3 Review as homework or an in-class activity.

MEETING LESSON OBJECTIVES

Each objective below is tested by the questions that follow it in parentheses.

1. **Explain** the impact of religion on the cultural and political development of North Africa and Southwest Asia. *(2, 3)*
2. **Compare** three different ways of life in North Africa and Southwest Asia. *(5)*
3. **Describe** the geographic factors that have contributed to the region's standard of living. *(4)*

NATIONAL GEOGRAPHIC SOCIETY

CD-ROM

PICTURE ATLAS OF THE WORLD

Students can view life on the Nile, camel riders, and Mevlevi dancers by clicking the "Video" button for Egypt, Saudi Arabia, and Turkey.

among the Arabs and other Muslim peoples. The epic *Shahnameh (King of Kings)* describes heroic events in early Persian history. A well-known example of another kind of literature is the *Arabian Nights*—a collection of Arab, Indian, and Persian stories. These stories often reflect life in the early period of the Muslim empires.

Today poets and writers in many parts of the region deal with the problems of change in traditional society. Much of the modern literature also has nationalistic themes. Many new rhythms and rhyme patterns in recent poetry reflect the increased influence of the West.

REGION

Varying Ways of Life

During the 1900s the way of life of the people of North Africa and Southwest Asia has changed dramatically. Since 1900 the population of the region has grown rapidly. This growth has led to many lifestyle changes as more people have moved from rural to urban areas. Current estimates are that less than 50 percent of the region's people cultivate the land and that only a very small percent are **bedouins**, or desert nomads.

Standards of Living

Countries in the region with economies based on manufacturing and trade or oil, such as Israel and Qatar, enjoy a relatively high standard of living. Many countries, however, have poverty-stricken populations. Population growth in such countries as Afghanistan and Egypt has surpassed economic growth. As a result, economic systems often cannot provide people with basic necessities.

Most hospitals in the region are government-owned. In addition, medical care in many of the wealthy oil-producing countries is free. Medical treatment, however, is available mainly in the region's towns and cities. There also is a shortage of doctors in many countries. These factors contribute to low life expectancies in much of the region.

Geographic Themes

Place: Southwest Asian Markets

In many cities of the region, the traditional *sūq* provides a marked contrast to modern department stores. *What are the staple foods of North Africa and Southwest Asia?*

Meeting Special Needs

Mixed Learners Some students learn best visually. Others are auditory learners. Many are "mixed" learners who use a combination of auditory and visual materials in order to learn. Ask students to look at and think about the information they get from the pictures in Section 3. Ask students if the pictures or the text provides them with more information. Then ask how the kind of information they can get from pictures is different from the kind they can get from the text.

Meeting Human Needs

Methods of meeting the needs of the people vary throughout the region. Housing, for example, differs from country to country. In many areas the people live without running water and electric lights. As a result, people must carry water from pumps and use lanterns or candles for light.

In some cities, such as Jerusalem, many of the buildings are made of stone and are hundreds of years old. Farmers and rural workers in North Africa and Southwest Asia usually live in tin or stone structures, or shelters made from wood and iron. A writer describes a typical Egyptian rural home:

> *Houses, mostly flat roofed, are generally built around a courtyard and face south to absorb the winter sun. Within the compact enclosure live dozens of people of all ages with their water buffalo, cattle, an ox or camel, an ass, and a few scrawny chickens. Furniture, if it exists at all, is sparse, and the average hut is furnished only with a crude grass mat or carpet to cover the earthen floor. Bread is the staff of peasant life, supplemented by some vegetables. Occasionally, on festive days such as the Prophet's [Muhammad's] birthday, there are eggs, meat, and fruit.*

The staple foods of the region consist of wheat, barley, and rice, sometimes supplemented by meat, dairy products, fruits, and vegetables. People often buy food at a ***sūq,*** or an enclosed marketplace.

Many of the people of the region wear traditional long, loose cotton clothing. They also wear a head covering to reflect the hot sunlight. In many cities, however, people wear clothing like that found in North America and Europe.

Education

Primary education is free, and enrollment is increasing in the region. Many students complete both primary and secondary school, and a small percentage enroll in universities. Well-known institutions of higher learning in the region include Cairo's University of Al-Azhar, which was founded in A.D. 970. It is one of the oldest universities in the world.

Leisure Time

Family ties are important to the people of the region. Family hospitality is taken very seriously, and leisure time is often spent visiting and entertaining family members.

Popular sports include soccer, hunting, and fishing. Board games such as backgammon are popular in some countries. The people also enjoy going to movies and watching television.

Religious holidays are important throughout the region. *Īd al Adha,* or the Feast of Sacrifice, is a very important Muslim celebration during which many Muslims go on pilgrimage to Makkah. Such Jewish holidays as Passover, Yom Kippur, and Hanukkah and such Christian holidays as Christmas and Easter are observed in some countries in the region.

SECTION 3 REVIEW

Checking for Understanding

1. **Define** ziggurat, bedouin, *sūq.*
2. **Locating Places** What ancient civilization built pyramids?
3. **Region** Why does the art of the region use geometric patterns, floral designs, and beautiful writing?
4. **Human/Environment Interaction** What economic factors have enabled some countries in the region to enjoy a high standard of living?

Critical Thinking

5. **Making Generalizations** Why did the cultures in the region often borrow from each other and from cultures outside the region?

EVALUATE

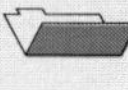 Assign the Section 3 Quiz in the TCR.

 Use the Testmaker to create a customized quiz for Section 3.

RETEACH

Have students complete Reteaching Activity 18 in the TCR.

ENRICH

Have students complete Enrichment Activity 18 in the TCR.

CLOSE

Have students identify changes that have taken place in the way of life of people in North Africa and Southwest Asia since 1900. Then ask them to classify each change as positive or negative. Discuss differences of opinion.

 **CD-ROM**

PICTURE ATLAS OF THE WORLD

Listen to musicians in **Cairo,** folk tunes from **Morocco** and **Turkey,** the "nay" and "tanbur" in **Iraq,** and the **Israeli** song "Hope" by clicking the "Music" button of the countries in bold type.

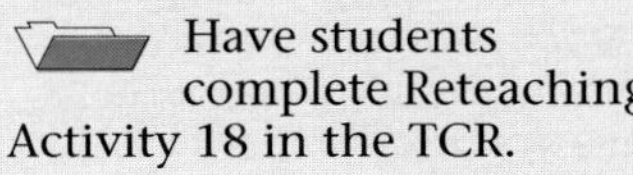

ANSWERS TO SECTION 3 REVIEW

1. **ziggurat:** Sumerian step-like pyramid; **Bedouin:** desert nomad; ***sūq:*** enclosed marketplace
2. Egypt
3. Islam does not encourage artists to draw images of living figures in religious art.
4. economies based on manufacturing and trade, especially the production of oil
5. Trade brought them in contact.

TEACH

Have students read the skill on page 386. Say: "Describe the difference between general-purpose and special-purpose maps." *(General-purpose maps include basic physical and political information; special-purpose maps describe particular subjects.)* "What special-purpose maps have you used in earlier skill lessons?" *(cartogram, vegetation map, climate map)* "What is the subject of the special-purpose map on page 386?" *(literacy rates in the countries of Southwest Asia)* Have students identify the values represented by various colors on the map. Discuss these questions: How would the quality of life differ in countries with high and low literacy rates? What causes these differences?

Skills Practice
For additional practice, have students complete Skill Activity 18 in the TCR.

MAP AND GRAPH SKILLS

Interpreting a Special-Purpose Map

Maps fall into two basic categories: general-purpose maps and special-purpose maps. General-purpose maps contain the most basic physical and/or political information about a region, such as international boundaries, major cities, rivers, large bodies of water, and key physical features. Maps that illustrate information on specialized subjects, or themes, are called special-purpose maps, or thematic maps.

REVIEWING THE SKILL

A special-purpose map can illustrate almost any kind of information. It can contain physical, political, economic, climatic, historic, or cultural information—almost anything that can be expressed geographically.

To interpret a special-purpose map, apply the following steps:

- Read the map title to determine the subject and purpose of the map.
- Read all the labels to identify the geographic region and other information listed on the map.
- Identify each symbol and color shown in the map key.
- Locate each symbol and color on the map.
- Form hypotheses and generalizations based on the map information.

PRACTICING THE SKILL

Use the map below to answer the following questions:

1. What is the subject of the map?
2. What geographic region is shown on the map?
3. What do the colors represent?
4. What percentage of the population of Iran can read and write?
5. In which country is the literacy rate 40–50 percent?
6. Which countries have the highest literacy rate?

For additional practice in this skill, see Practicing Skills on page 388 of the Chapter 18 Review.

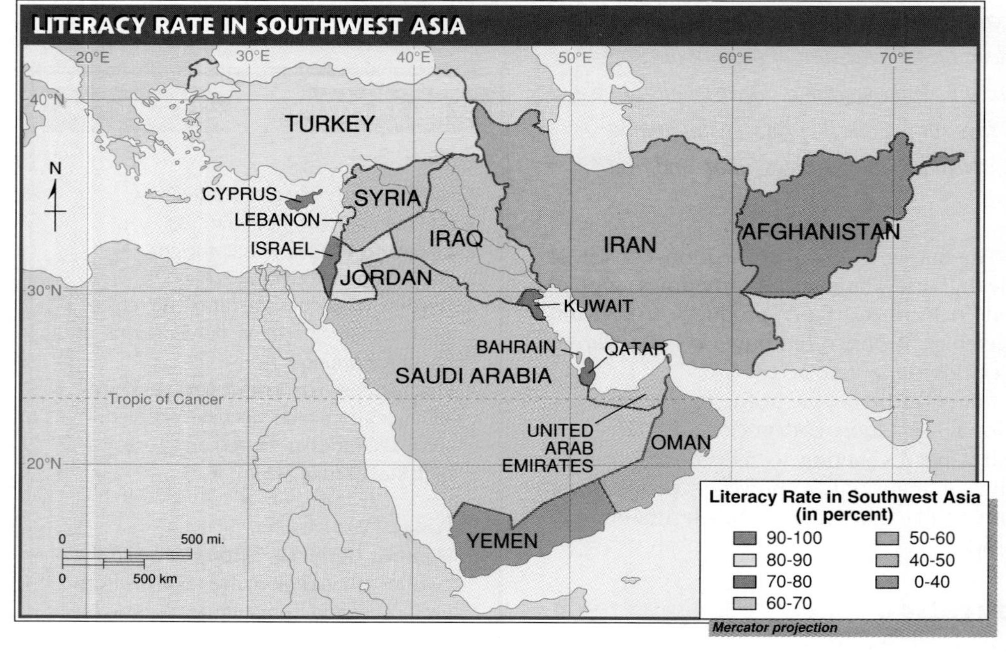

ANSWERS TO PRACTICING THE SKILL

1. literacy rates, or the percentage of people who can read and write
2. Southwest Asia
3. percentages of literate people in each country
4. 50–60%
5. Oman
6. Israel and Cyprus

chapter 18

HIGHLIGHTS

1 Section: Population Patterns

Key Terms

ethnic diversity (p. 371)

Istanbul's mosques and palaces along the Golden Horn harbor

Summary

- The culture region of North Africa and Southwest Asia has been a crossroads for the peoples and cultures of Asia, Africa, and Europe.
- The heaviest concentrations of population in North Africa and Southwest Asia are in coastal and river valley areas where water is available.
- Rapid population growth and rising urbanization have characterized the region since World War II.

2 Section: History and Government

Israelis celebrate their Independence Day

Key Terms

domesticate (p. 376)
cuneiform (p. 377)
hieroglyphics (p. 377)
qanat (p. 377)
monotheism (p. 377)
prophet (p. 378)
mosque (p. 378)
nationalism (p. 379)
nationalize (p. 379)

Summary

- North Africa and Southwest Asia was the birthplace of two of the world's earliest civilizations—Mesopotamia and Egypt—and three of the world's major religions—Judaism, Christianity, and Islam.
- After centuries of European influence, independent states arose in North Africa and Southwest Asia during the 1900s.

3 Section: Cultures and Lifestyles

Key Terms

ziggurat (p. 383)
bedouin (p. 384)
sūq (p. 385)

Makkah's Grand Mosque, Islam's holiest shrine

Summary

- Islam and the Arabic language have been the primary unifying forces in North Africa and Southwest Asia.
- The people living in countries based on manufacturing and trade generally enjoy a high standard of living. The people living in countries where the economies are based on agriculture, however, have a lower standard of living.
- Family relationships are important to people in the region. Popular leisure activities include soccer, hunting, and fishing.

CHAPTER 18 HIGHLIGHTS

USING THE CHAPTER 18 HIGHLIGHTS

Use the Chapter 18 Highlights to preview, review, condense, or reteach the chapter.

PREVIEW/REVIEW

Vocabulary PuzzleMaker Software reinforces the Key Terms used in Chapter 18.

Student Self-Test and Review Software allows students to review Chapter 18 content.

CONDENSE

Have students read the Chapter 18 Highlights.

Have students listen to the Chapter 18 Audiocassettes in the TCR. Spanish Audiocassettes are also available.

Assign the Chapter 18 Audiocassette Activity and give students the Chapter 18 Audiocassette Quiz.

Have students complete Guided Reading Activities for Chapter 18 in the TCR. Spanish Guided Reading Activities are also available.

RETEACH

Have students complete Reteaching Activity 18 in the TCR. Spanish Reteaching Activities are also available.

Map Activity

Identify and Locate Using Political Map Transparency 6, ask students to locate the site of each illustration on page 387. Have them write a caption for each picture that incorporates an understanding of one of the main ideas of the chapter.

GLENCOE TECHNOLOGY

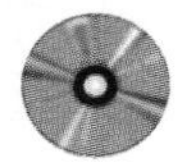

Videodisc

Use Chapter 18 MindJogger Videoquiz to review students' knowledge before administering the Chapter 18 Test.

MINDJOGGER VIDEOQUIZ

Chapter 18
Disc 3 Side A

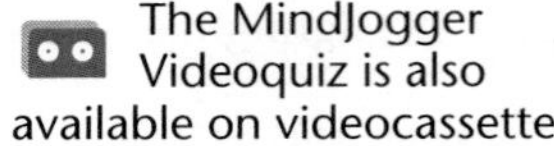

The MindJogger Videoquiz is also available on videocassette.

ANSWERS

Reviewing Key Terms

1. ethnic diversity
2. cuneiform
3. prophet
4. mosque
5. qanats
6. ziggurats
7. Bedouin

Reviewing Facts

8. Most of the region's population lives along the rivers, in or near highlands, in or near oases, and along the coasts. These locations make it possible for people to obtain drinking water, grow crops, and raise animals.

9. Cairo, Egypt, on the Nile River; Alexandria, Egypt, on the Mediterranean Sea; Istanbul, Turkey, on the Bosporus; Baghdad, Iraq, on the Tigris

10. Fertile land was available in the river valleys.

11. Judaism, Islam, and Christianity

12. mosques

13. entertaining family and friends, sports, hunting, fishing, playing board games, watching movies and television

chapter 18 REVIEW

Reviewing Key Terms

Choose the vocabulary term that best completes each of the sentences below. Write your answers on a separate sheet of paper.

ethnic diversity (p. 371)
cuneiform (p. 377)
qanats (p. 377)
prophet (p. 378)
mosque (p. 378)
ziggurats (p. 383)
bedouin (p. 384)

SECTION 1

1. Differences in groups of people based on their national origins, languages, customs, beliefs, and/or religions is known as ____.

SECTION 2

2. The Sumerian writing system was called ____.
3. Muslims regard Muhammad as a ____, or messenger, of God.
4. A Muslim house of worship is known as a ____.
5. The Persians constructed a system of ____, or underground canals, to carry water from the mountains across the deserts.

SECTION 3

6. The Sumerians built step-like pyramids called ____.
7. A desert nomad is often called a ____.

Reviewing Facts

SECTION 1

8. How are population patterns in North Africa and Southwest Asia affected by the environment?
9. What large cities in the region are located near or on bodies of water?

SECTION 2

10. Why did two early civilizations originate in North Africa and Southwest Asia?
11. What are the three major religions that originated in the region?

SECTION 3

12. What was the outstanding architectural achievement of Islamic civilization?
13. How do the people of North Africa and Southwest Asia spend their leisure time?

Critical Thinking

14. **Drawing Conclusions** Why do most of the people in North Africa and Southwest Asia live in areas near water?
15. **Predicting Consequences** What might have been the future of the nations in North Africa and Southwest Asia if there had not been the discovery of oil?
16. **Analyzing Information** What factors account for varying standards of living in North Africa and Southwest Asia?

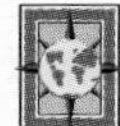

Geographic Themes

17. **Movement** How has the movement of peoples into North Africa and Southwest Asia affected its cultures?
18. **Location** Why did early civilizations develop in the Tigris-Euphrates and Nile river valleys?
19. **Region** How is the Islamic influence reflected in the languages of the region?

Practicing Skills

Interpreting a Special-Purpose Map

Refer to the special-purpose map on page 386.

20. Which countries have literacy rates of 40 percent or below?

Critical Thinking

14. Water makes it possible to grow crops and raise animals; drinking water is available.

15. A typical answer might be that people in the various nations in the region might have suffered economic hardships because of the lack of industrialization and modernization.

16. A typical answer might be that the lack of large-scale industrialization and agricultural modernization have left some countries with too few well-paying jobs and limited agricultural production. Other nations in the region have prospered from oil production, manufacturing, or trade.

21. Why do you think North Africa and Southwest Asia have such wide differences in literacy rates?

Using the Unit Atlas

Refer to the cultural geography section of the Unit Atlas on pages 350–351.

22. Where do most people in Algeria live?
23. What city is a major religious center for Jews, Christians, and Muslims?

Projects

Individual Activity

Select one North African country for study. Research that nation's population growth, and write a brief report about how that growth is affecting the way people live.

Cooperative Learning Activity

Working together in a small group, put together a meeting of representatives from each of four or five oil-producing nations. Each group member will research and report to the rest of the group on his or her nation's oil production and revenues and how the revenue should be spent. Upon completion, the report can be compiled and an overall summary can be presented to the entire class.

Writing About Geography

Description

Imagine you are traveling for your hometown newspaper in Saudi Arabia to write about the way of life and the type of housing of the people in one of the major cities Your description should include the effects of the climate on the way people live.

Locating Places

THE POLITICAL GEOGRAPHY OF NORTH AFRICA AND SOUTHWEST ASIA

Match the letters on the map with the places in North Africa and Southwest Asia. Write your answers on a separate sheet of paper.

1. Suez Canal
2. Riyadh
3. Istanbul
4. Iran
5. Tehran
6. Israel
7. Cairo
8. Cyprus
9. Tripoli
10. Casablanca

Chapter 18 Review

Geographic Themes

17. It has produced the ethnic and cultural diversity of the region, with Arab culture being predominate.

18. Mesopotamia's climate allowed Sumerians to grow crops year round. The use of irrigation and the alluvial-soil deposits from the annual flooding of the Nile allowed farmers to grow two or three crops each year.

19. Because the Quran was originally written in Arabic, non-Arab Muslims learned Arabic in order to read the Quran. Arabic became the region's main language.

Practicing Skills

20. Yemen and Afghanistan

21. Countries that have oil-based economies have more money to spend on education. Industrialized countries have a higher standard of living than other countries.

Using the Unit Atlas

22. northern coastal area

23. Jerusalem

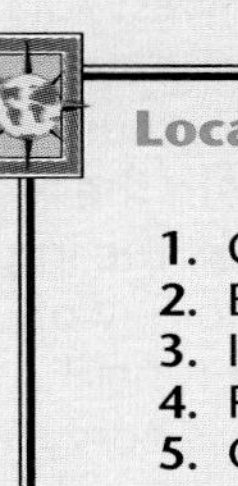

Locating Places

1. C
2. E
3. I
4. F
5. G
6. D
7. B
8. H
9. A
10. J

Chapter Bonus Test Question

This question may be used for extra credit on the chapter test.

Defend or reject the following statement: Islam is the single greatest unifying influence among the peoples of North Africa and Southwest Asia.

(Answer: Students who defend the statement may point out that Islam is the major religion of the region. It influences the languages, arts, governments, and customs of the people. Those who reject the statement may argue that many Jews and Christians live in the region. Religion has been a source of conflict among peoples in North Africa and Southwest Asia.)

North Africa and Southwest Asia Today

CHAPTER ORGANIZER

Daily Lesson Objectives	Multimedia	Teacher Classroom Resources
SECTION 1 Living in North Africa and Southwest Asia 1. Summarize the effects of geography on economic activity in North Africa and Southwest Asia. 2. Explain how recent industrial growth in the region is related to natural resources. 3. Discuss the role of service industries and governments in the economies of North Africa and Southwest Asia.	Section Focus Transparency 19-1 Chapter 19 Vocabulary PuzzleMaker Software Testmaker	Reproducible Lesson Plan 19-1 Guided Reading Activity 19-1 Spanish Guided Reading Activity 19-1 Workbook Activity 19-1 Performance Assessment Activity 19 Outline Map Resource Book, p. 32 Section Quiz 19-1
SECTION 2 People and Their Environment 1. Explain how the scarcity of water challenges North Africa and Southwest Asia. 2. Describe steps being taken to utilize groundwater and sea water in the region. 3. Discuss the impact of war and technology on the region's environment. 4. Discuss how the control of river water can affect the environment.	Section Focus Transparency 19-2 Reuters Issues in Geography Testmaker Picture Atlas of the World	Reproducible Lesson Plan 19-2 Guided Reading Activity 19-2 Spanish Guided Reading Activity 19-2 Enrichment Activity 19 Skill Activity 19 Section Quiz 19-2
CHAPTER REVIEW AND EVALUATION	Chapter 19 English (or Spanish) Audiocassettes MindJogger Videoquiz Testmaker Student Self-Test and Review Software	Reteaching Activity 19 Spanish Reteaching Activity 19 Outline Map Resource Book, p. 32 Chapter 19 Test Form A and Form B

0:00 *If time does not permit teaching the entire chapter, summarize using the Chapter 19 Highlights on page 403, and the Chapter 19 English (or Spanish) Audiocassettes. Review students' knowledge using the Glencoe MindJogger Videoquiz.*

KEY TO ABILITY LEVELS

Teaching strategies have been coded for varying learning styles and abilities.

L1 **BASIC** activities for all students

L2 **AVERAGE** activities for average to above-average students

L3 **CHALLENGING** activities for above-average students

LEP **LIMITED ENGLISH PROFICIENCY** activities

Performance Assessment

International Involvement The United States has sometimes taken political or military action in order to protect its interests in North Africa and Southwest Asia. Have groups of students research some of these interventions and write about how American actions were influenced by the culture region's environment, economy, natural resources, and transportation routes.

In their groups, students should share their opinions about each of the American involvements in the region. Each individual should then develop a position statement about how the United States should respond in any future crisis. Students might research the views of current and former American political leaders to find support for their positions. Quotes from these leaders could be incorporated in their position statements.

POSSIBLE RUBRIC FEATURES: Content information, concept attainment, research skills, ability to recognize relationships and draw conclusions, collaborative skills, argumentation skills, writing skills, decision-making process steps

For additional professional and classroom resources, see Chapter Resources, pages T46–T51.

TEACHER'S CORNER

NATIONAL GEOGRAPHIC SOCIETY

INDEX TO NATIONAL GEOGRAPHIC MAGAZINE

The following articles may be used for research relating to this chapter:

- "Water: The Middle East's Critical Resource," by Priit J. Vesilind, May 1993.
- "Persian Gulf Pollution: Assessing the Damage One Year Later," by Sylvia A. Earle, February 1992.
- "After the Storm," by Thomas Canby, August 1991.

NATIONAL GEOGRAPHIC SOCIETY PRODUCTS AVAILABLE FROM GLENCOE

To order the following products for use with this chapter, contact your local Glencoe sales representative or call Glencoe at 1-800-334-7344:

- *Picture Atlas of the World* (CD-ROM)
- *STV: World Geography, Asia and Australia* (Videodisc)
- *STV: World Geography, Africa and Europe* (Videodisc)
- *ZipZapMap! World* (Software)
- *GeoBee* (Software)
- *Images of the World* (Posters)
- *Eye on the Environment* (Posters)
- *Physical Geography of the World* (Transparencies)
- *Picture Atlas of Our 50 States* (Book)

Introducing
CHAPTER 19

PERFORMANCE ASSESSMENT

Refer to the Planning Guide on page 390B for a Performance Assessment Activity for this chapter. See the *Performance Assessment Activities* booklet for additional suggestions.

CHAPTER OBJECTIVES

1. **Describe** ways of life in North Africa and Southwest Asia.
2. **Explain** efforts to improve the region's supply of water for drinking and for irrigation.

GLENCOE TECHNOLOGY

Videodisc

Use Chapter 19 MindJogger Videoquiz to preview chapter content.

MINDJOGGER VIDEOQUIZ

Chapter 19
Disc 3 Side A

The MindJogger Videoquiz is also available on videocassette.

chapter 19 North Africa and Southwest Asia Today

CHAPTER FOCUS

Geographic Setting

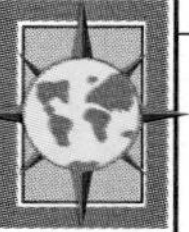

Because of the unequal distribution of fertile lands, rainfall, and natural resources, wealth and standards of living vary from one nation to another in North Africa and Southwest Asia.

Geographic Themes

Section 1 Living in North Africa and Southwest Asia
REGION The culture region of North Africa and Southwest Asia includes some of the world's wealthiest and poorest nations.

▲ Photograph: *Harbor of Haifa, Israel*

Section 2 People and Their Environment
HUMAN/ENVIRONMENT INTERACTION Arid conditions in the region have led to technological and scientific efforts to improve the supply of water for drinking and for irrigation.

EXTRA CREDIT PROJECT

Documentary Have students research the Persian Gulf War of 1991. Direct them to find out how the environment affected the troops and how warfare affected the environment. They might also investigate cultural differences between the international troops and the inhabitants of the region. Have students present mini-documentaries about the Gulf War by creating a bulletin-board display with pictures and articles.

1 SECTION

Living in North Africa and Southwest Asia

SETTING THE SCENE

Read to Discover . . .

- the effects of geography on economic activity in North Africa and Southwest Asia.
- how recent industrial growth in North Africa and Southwest Asia is related to natural resources.
- the role of service industries and governments in the economies of North Africa and Southwest Asia.

Key Terms

- petrochemical
- service industry
- gross domestic product (GDP)

Identify and Locate

Kuwait, United Arab Emirates, Black Sea, Bahrain, Persian Gulf

Saudi Arabia

Salam (peace),
Although a large part of my country is desert, by using efficient irrigation systems we produce and export agricultural products such as wheat and dates. Oil is our main resource and our major income. While oil is our main energy source, we also use solar energy.
Abdullah Alhamdan

The economies of the nations within the culture region of North Africa and Southwest Asia vary greatly. Abdullah Alhamdan comes from Saudi Arabia, one of the wealthiest nations. Some of the nations, however, are poor. The reasons for these differences are related to geography or history.

PLACE

Meeting Food Needs

Producing food for the rapidly growing population of North Africa and Southwest Asia is a major concern.

Agriculture

Only a small portion of the region is suitable for crops or grazing, although a large percentage of the people in poorer nations work in agriculture. Only 15 percent of Afghanistan's land is arable, yet about 75 percent of its workers are farmers. In wealthier nations, such as Kuwait, only about 5 percent of the workforce raises crops or livestock. Farmers and herders in the region often live and work separately.

In areas having a Mediterranean climate, cereal crops, citrus fruits, grapes, and dates are important products. Egypt, Saudi Arabia, Iraq, Iran, and Algeria are the largest producers of

LESSON PLAN
Chapter 19, Section 1

FOCUS

SECTION OBJECTIVES

1. **Summarize** the effects of geography on economic activity in North Africa and Southwest Asia.
2. **Explain** how recent industrial growth in the region is related to natural resources.
3. **Discuss** the role of service industries and governments in the economies of North Africa and Southwest Asia.

ABOUT THE POSTCARD

Although Abdullah's native language is Arabic, he also speaks and writes in English.

BELLRINGER MOTIVATIONAL ACTIVITY

Project the Section 1 Focus Transparency and have students answer the questions.

PRETEACHING VOCABULARY

Have students find the meanings of the Key Terms in the text. Then ask them to make a list of industries based on petrochemicals and a list of service industries. Help them understand how all these industries are related to a nation's gross domestic product. Ask what other factors are included in the GDP. *(agriculture, manufacturing)*

Use the Vocabulary PuzzleMaker Software to create a crossword or word search puzzle.

Classroom Resources for Section 1

BLACKLINE MASTERS:
Reproducible Lesson Plan 19-1
Guided Reading Activity 19-1
Spanish Guided Reading Activity 19-1
Workbook Activity 19-1
Performance Assessment Activity 19
Outline Map Resource Book, p. 32
Section Quiz 19-1

TRANSPARENCIES:
Section Focus Transparency 19-1

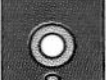

MULTIMEDIA:
Vocabulary PuzzleMaker Software
Testmaker

TEACH

GUIDED PRACTICE

L2 Geography: Place Have students create a chart to illustrate how physical features, climate, and resources affect economic activities in North Africa and Southwest Asia.

USING CHARTS

Answers: 26%; 3%

Skills Practice

Interpreting a Chart Which country has the largest total land area? *(Algeria)* Which country has the greatest percentage of arable land? *(Turkey)*

CURRICULUM CONNECTION

GEOLOGY

Many geologists believe that petroleum was formed from the remains of organisms that died millions of years ago. According to this theory, water covered much more of the earth's surface in the past than it does today. The remains of tiny organisms settled to the bottom of the ocean and were compressed to form the rock in which oil is found.

dates. Egypt exports cotton to countries in Asia, Europe, and North America.

Livestock

Another source of food for the people of the region is an estimated 330 million livestock, mostly cattle and sheep.

The effect of climate on livestock is seen by comparing two countries: Turkey and Saudi Arabia. Turkey is one of the region's leading producers of livestock, largely because it has adequate rainfall and its land is suitable for grazing. Saudi Arabia, in contrast, has almost 3 times as much land but most of it is desert. As a result, it produces only about 10 percent as much livestock as Turkey.

Fishing

The fishing industry, which provides only about 2 percent of the world's fish, is another source of food. Tuna, sardines, and sturgeon are caught in the Mediterranean Sea, Black Sea, Caspian Sea, and the Persian Gulf. The region's two largest producers of fish are Turkey and Morocco.

PLACE

Industrial Growth

The most important natural resource in North Africa and Southwest Asia is petroleum, with the region producing about 25 percent of the world's supply.

Oil, Natural Gas, and Mining

The wealth from oil has brought industrial growth throughout the region. Iran and Saudi Arabia have large oil-refining and oil-shipping facilities. Some countries have developed industries that use **petrochemicals**—products derived from petroleum or natural gas—to make fertilizers, medicines, plastics, and paints. Less than 5 percent of the oil produced is refined in the region. Most is exported in crude form to industrialized countries.

Natural gas has also advanced the region's industrial growth by powering steel-making, textile, and diamond-cutting industries. This economic growth has provided thousands of jobs and helped improve the standard of living for many people in the region.

LAND USE IN SELECTED COUNTRIES OF NORTH AFRICA AND SOUTHWEST ASIA

Country	Total Land Area sq. mi.	(sq. km)	Arable Land	Forests and Woodlands	Herding
			(as a percentage of the total land area of each country)*		
Afghanistan	251,770	(652,084)	20	5	75
Algeria	919,590	(2,381,738)	3	2	15
Egypt	384,340	(995,441)	3	*	*
Iran	631,660	(1,635,999)	9	11	27
Israel	7,850	(20,332)	21	6	40
Jordan	34,340	(88,941)	4	1	1
Lebanon	3,950	(10,231)	29	7	1
Morocco	172,320	(446,309)	19	12	28
Saudi Arabia	830,000	(2,149,700)	1	1	40
Tunisia	59,980	(155,348)	32	4	20
Turkey	297,150	(769,619)	35	26	12

Columns will not total 100 percent as some land uses are omitted
*Less than 1 percent
Sources: *World Population Data Sheet of the Population Reference Bureau, Inc., 1994; The Cambridge Atlas of the Middle East; Britannica Year Book, 1993*

CHART STUDY

The climate of North Africa and Southwest Asia directly affects land use in the region. The amount of arable land and the land that can support forest and woodlands is usually relatively small. ***What percentage of Turkey's land is forested? What percentage of Egypt's land is suitable for farming?***

Cooperative Learning Activity

Assign one or more countries in North Africa and Southwest Asia to each student. Then have students form groups of four or five. Each student is responsible for writing a want ad for a job opening in the assigned country or countries. *(for example, a farmer in Iraq, a fisher in Morocco, a worker for an oil refinery in Saudi Arabia)* Have members of each group compare their want ads and write a generalization about economic activities in the region.

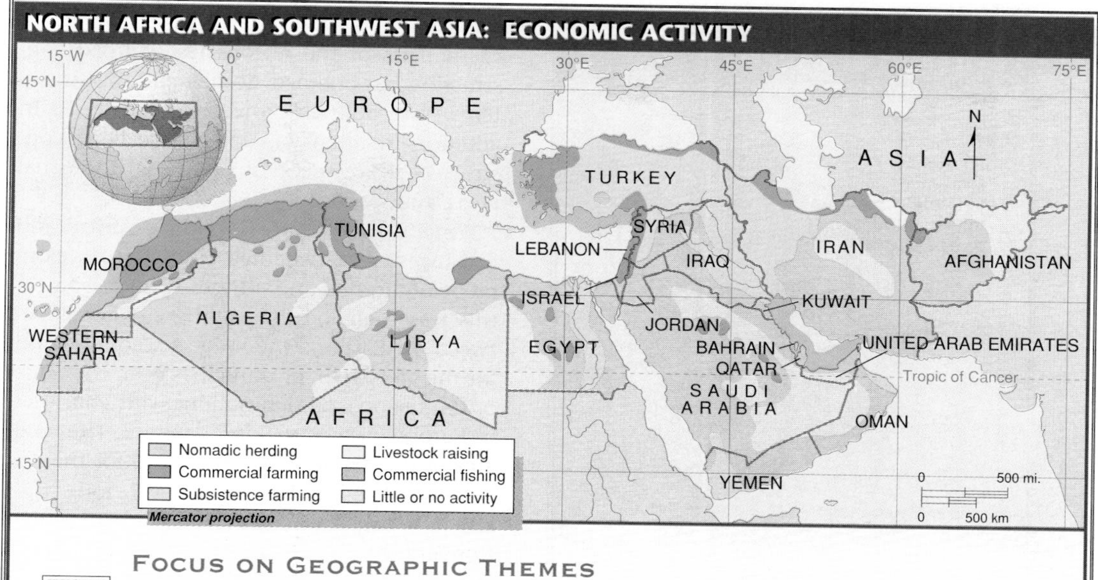

Focus on Geographic Themes

1. **Human/Environment Interaction: What are the leading economic activities along the coast of North Africa?**
2. **Region: In what areas is subsistence farming an important activity?**
3. **Region: Where does livestock raising take place?**

Service Industries

The businesses that provide services—banking, insurance, financial services, or tourism—are known as **service industries.** These industries also play an important role in the economies of this region. In Bahrain the banking, real estate, and insurance industries provide more than 60 percent of that nation's **gross domestic product (GDP)**—the value of the goods and services created in a country in a year.

One important service industry—because of the region's historical importance and closeness to Europe—is tourism. Over the years the region's ancient monuments and religious sites have drawn millions of visitors.

Tourism, however, has not grown rapidly in all nations. Some governments discourage outside influences. Regional conflicts, political upheavals, and violence in parts of the region have also affected tourism.

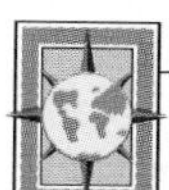

Geographic Themes

Movement: Jidda Airport, Saudi Arabia
Oil revenue has enabled Saudi Arabia to build modern transportation facilities, such as this airport in the city of Jidda. *What service industries have developed in the region?*

USING MAPS

Answers: **1.** commercial fishing, nomadic herding, commercial farming; **2.** along the Nile River, most of Turkey and Iraq, western Iran; **3.** northeastern Iran, western Turkey

Map Skills Practice
Reading a Map What economic activity takes place in every country in the region except Lebanon? *(nomadic herding)*

INDEPENDENT PRACTICE

Guided Reading
Have students complete Guided Reading Activity 19-1 in the TCR. **LEP**

USING ILLUSTRATIONS

LOCATION Jidda is a major port on the Red Sea. It is also the location of one of Saudi Arabia's three international airports.
Answer to Caption: *banking, real estate, insurance, tourism*

MULTICULTURAL PERSPECTIVE

Cultural Heritage
Many businesses in North Africa and Southwest Asia close during the midday heat and open again in the late afternoon. Muslim businesses are closed on Fridays.

Meeting Special Needs

Learning Disability To help learning disabled students, illustrate the use of headings and subheadings as a means of understanding the main ideas of a section. For example, use the first heading to ask: "How do people in North Africa and Southwest Asia meet food needs?" Students should use subheads to answer: "Agriculture, livestock, fishing." Have students ask and answer similar questions based on the remaining headings and subheadings in Section 1.

USING DIAGRAMS

Answers: Middle East; Western Europe

Skills Practice

Interpreting a Diagram About how much greater are Middle East oil reserves than those of the rest of the world? *(The Middle East has almost twice as much oil as the rest of the world combined.)*

L3 Geography: Movement Provide each student with a copy of the map found on page 32 of the Outline Map Resource Book. Students should use resource books to find and label regional waterways, major ports, airports, highways, and pipelines.

ASSESS

CHECK FOR UNDERSTANDING

Assign Section 1 Review as homework or an in-class activity.

MEETING LESSON OBJECTIVES

Each objective below is tested by the questions that follow it in parentheses.

1. Summarize the effects of geography on economic activity in North Africa and Southwest Asia. *(2, 3)*

2. Explain how recent industrial growth in the region is related to natural resources. *(4, 5)*

3. Discuss the role of service industries and governments in the economies of North Africa and Southwest Asia. *(4, 5)*

WORLD OIL RESERVES IN BILLIONS OF BARRELS

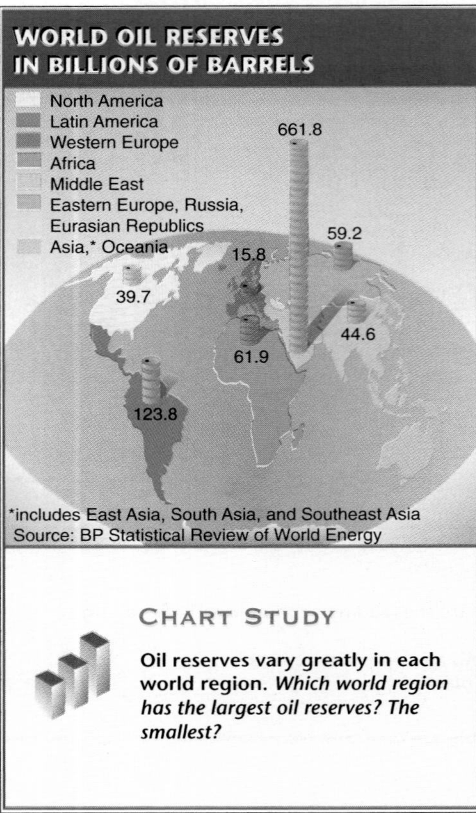

*includes East Asia, South Asia, and Southeast Asia
Source: BP Statistical Review of World Energy

CHART STUDY

Oil reserves vary greatly in each world region. *Which world region has the largest oil reserves? The smallest?*

MOVEMENT

Transportation and Communication

North Africa and Southwest Asia's systems of transportation and communication are growing rapidly. Most development is concentrated in the eastern Mediterranean area.

Roads and Highways

The most extensive road systems are found in Iran, Turkey, and Egypt where roads connect the major cities with oil fields and seaports. Iran, with 94,072 miles of roads (151,485 km), is the leader. Mountainous and desert land have made it costly to build roads in some areas. The increased number of vehicles and the need to link cities, however, has continued to increase highway development.

Railroads and Airlines

In parts of the region new railroad construction has boomed. Some rapid transit systems were built in crowded urban areas. In addition, national rail lines have been constructed to connect urban areas, industrial areas, and seaports.

After World War II, North Africa and Southwest Asia benefited from the development of airports and airlines. One reason for this was their location at the crossroads between the East and the West. A second reason for the growth of air traffic has been the trade of the region's oil-rich nations with countries in Europe, Asia, and North America. The total area of the region is a third reason for the development of airlines. Relatively long distances separate one nation or urban center from another.

Waterways and Pipelines

Inland waterways, with the exception of the Nile River and the Suez Canal, play a far lesser role in the movement of goods and people in this region. The Tigris and the Euphrates rivers are too shallow for large boats. Although the Shatt al Arab, formed where the two rivers meet, is deeper, its control has been a matter of dispute between Iraq and Iran for years.

An elaborate system of pipelines is the major means of transporting oil. Pipelines transport oil to seaports on the Mediterranean Sea, where the huge oil tankers that are too large to pass through the Suez Canal dock.

Communication Systems

Television and radio communication systems are developing rapidly in some areas of North Africa and Southwest Asia. Newspapers are also a major means of communication although the number varies widely from country to country.

Telephone communication is difficult in some areas, because of vast stretches of desert. New technology, especially that of solar-powered radiophones, is opening telephone service to more people.

Critical Thinking

Drawing Conclusions Have students list the geographic factors that influence economies in North Africa and Southwest Asia. *(climate, soil, landforms, water resources, mineral resources)* Then have them explain how these factors have contributed to the great differences in wealth and standards of living among nations in the region. *(Answers should indicate the importance of petroleum to the economies of the region.)*

CRUDE OIL PRODUCTION IN SELECTED COUNTRIES OF NORTH AFRICA AND SOUTHWEST ASIA

Country	1991 Crude Oil Reserves (in barrels)	1990 Crude Oil Production (in metric tons)	1991 Crude Oil Production (in metric tons)
Algeria	9,200,000,000	56,673,000	58,454,000
Egypt	4,500,000,000	43,805,000	45,264,000
Iran	92,800,000,000	157,084,000	166,024,000
Iraq	100,000,000,000	100,681,000	14,876,000
Kuwait	97,000,000,000	58,729,000	9,567,000
Libya	22,800,000,000	65,990,000	73,567,567
Saudi Arabia	260,000,000,000	321,928,000	409,839,000
United Arab Emirates	98,100,000,000	102,004,000	117,940,000

Sources: Energy Information/U.S. Dept. of Energy; *Statesman's Year Book* 1992-1993

CHART STUDY

The nations of North Africa and Southwest Asia have the largest known oil reserves of any world region. *Which nation has the largest known reserves? Which nation had the smallest crude oil production in 1990? In 1991?*

MOVEMENT

Interdependence

The wealthier countries have helped their poor neighbors by providing foreign aid, trade concessions, and development loans. This aid has built hospitals, schools, and roads.

In 1960, five oil-producing countries—Iran, Iraq, Kuwait, Saudi Arabia, and Venezuela—formed the Organization of Petroleum Exporting Countries (OPEC). This organization was formed to give these oil-producing nations greater control over the production and price of oil. In the 1970s OPEC placed and later cancelled an embargo on the shipment of oil to the United States and other industrial countries, to raise the price of oil. More recently, the large supply of oil and a worldwide recession has forced the price of oil to fall.

SECTION 1 REVIEW

Checking for Understanding

1. **Define** petrochemical, service industry, gross domestic product (GDP).
2. **Locating Places** From what bodies of water do most countries of this region obtain fish?
3. **Place** Why is Turkey the leading producer of livestock?
4. **Movement** What are the three reasons for the growth of airlines in the region?

Critical Thinking

5. **Drawing Conclusions** Why do you think only 5 percent of the oil produced in this region is refined there?

EVALUATE

Assign the Section 1 Quiz in the TCR.

Use the Testmaker to create a customized quiz for Section 1.

USING GRAPHS

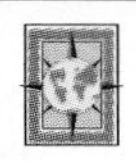

Answers:
Saudi Arabia; Egypt; Kuwait

Skills Practice

Interpreting a Graph
Which nations decreased crude oil production in 1991? *(Iraq and Kuwait)* What event in 1990 influenced oil production in these nations? *(Iraq's invasion of Kuwait)*

RETEACH

Have students use the headings in this section to outline the material.

ENRICH

Have students find out how the Israelis have cultivated the Negev Desert. Provide time for them to share their findings.

CLOSE

Have students write a postcard to Abdullah, describing their region's resources.

ANSWERS TO SECTION 1 REVIEW

1. **petrochemical:** product made from petroleum or natural gas; **service industry:** business that provides services; **gross domestic product:** the value of goods and services created in a country in a year
2. Mediterranean Sea, Black Sea, Persian Gulf, Caspian Sea
3. It has adequate rainfall and its land is suitable for grazing.
4. location at the crossroads between East and West; oil trade with Europe, Asia, and North America; total area of the region
5. Possible reasons include the cost of refining oil and the fact that there are so many different petroleum products.

FOCUS

Have students hold a brief discussion on the kinds and prices of bottled water available at local supermarkets. Have them discuss how their spending habits would change if it became necessary for them to buy water.

TEACH

L1 Identify Have students use a map and identify other countries in the region which could also suffer from lack of freshwater.

L2 Research Have students learn more about the process of *desalination,* how the process could help countries in North Africa and Southwest Asia, and which countries have desalinizing plants.

L3 Debate Have students debate whether Syria and Iraq are justified in their fears concerning Turkey.

GLENCOE TECHNOLOGY

Videodisc

Use the following to further student understanding of the water problem in North Africa and Southwest Asia:

REUTERS ISSUES IN GEOGRAPHY

Chapter 5
Disc 1 Side A

Title: ***North Africa and Southwest Asia: The Influence of Oil and Water***
Subject: How oil and water affect life in the region and events around the world

THE WAR FOR WATER

"In the year 2000, water will be more expensive than oil."

Joyce Starr, founder of the Global Water Summit Initiative, a private study group

In 1974, the flow of the Euphrates River into Iraq slowed from a roaring 1,185 cubic yards (907 cu. m) a second to a trickle of just 75 cubic yards (57 cu. m) a second. President Saddam Hussein prepared to invade Syria, convinced that Syrians were pirating an unfair share of the region's scanty water resources. Only last-minute peacemaking efforts by a third party, Saudi Arabia, stopped hostilities from breaking out.

In actuality, Iraq's dwindling water supply was caused by a combination of natural events, none of them intentionally war-like.

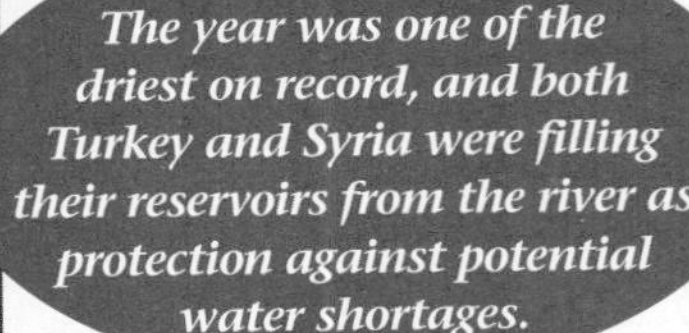

The year was one of the driest on record, and both Turkey and Syria were filling their reservoirs from the river as protection against potential water shortages.

THE ISSUE

Iraq's dwindling water supply, however, was an early sign of the crisis now facing the three countries: insufficient water for their populations.

To ensure its water supply, Turkey is building a series of huge dams on the Euphrates. These dams will slow the water flow into Syria.

Syria also is building dams on the Euphrates. The dams will further reduce the water that Iraq receives.

THE BACKGROUND

Of the three countries, only Turkey receives frequent and consistent rainfall, and that rainfall occurs only in its northern mountains. The well-watered mountains, in turn, give rise to the Tigris and Euphrates rivers.

Originating in Turkey, the Euphrates River provides irrigation water for the Anatolian highlands, where most of Turkey's farms are located. The reservoirs from the dams also provide electricity for Turkey's expanding industries and cities.

Most of Syria's rural people are farmers who raise a variety of crops for a living. Syria's rainfall, however, is too light and inconsistent to provide the needed amount for the country's extensive farmlands. So Syria, too, uses the Euphrates to provide irrigation water. In addition, the dams will provide electricity for the country.

A hydroelectric dam on Syria's portion of the Euphrates River

Extending the Content

Human/Environment Interaction
"Population growth in regions of limited natural water supply—in the Middle East, parts of Central America, North Africa, and the western United States—has resulted in serious water shortages." (*The UN Chronicle,* June 1992) Assign each world region listed in the quote to a group of students. Have students research the environment, finding out where the area's natural water supply comes from, why the area's population has increased, how the increased population has impacted on the water supply, and what solutions are being sought. Have students present their findings in short reports that include appropriate graphics, locator maps, illustrations, photographs, charts, tables, and graphs.

EUPHRATES RIVER VALLEY

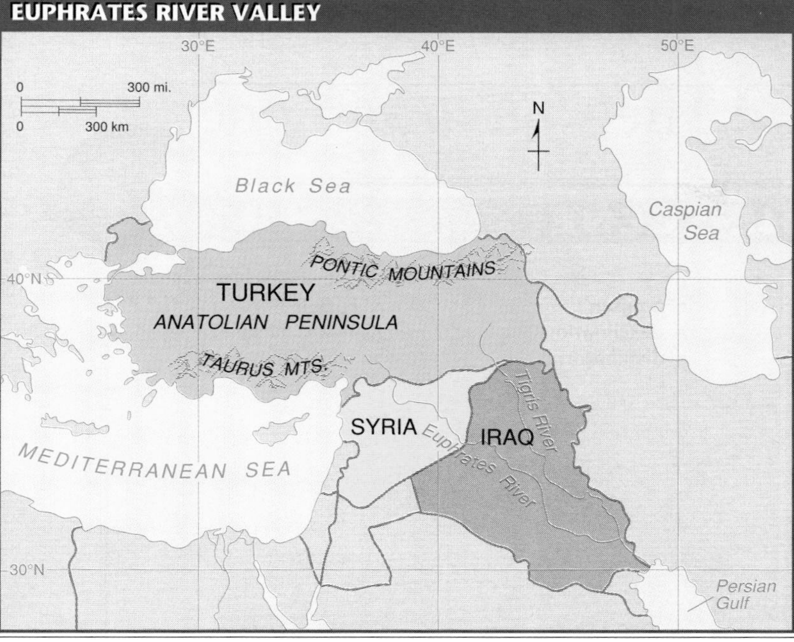

Iraq receives little rain. Its sole sources of water are the Tigris and Euphrates rivers, both of which flow through the country and join to empty into the Persian Gulf. Turkish and Syrian dams will reduce the amount of water flowing to Iraq by 50 to 80 percent.

THE POINTS OF VIEW

The Turks defend their right to use the rivers that rise within their borders to improve economic and social conditions. They hope to turn most of the Anatolian Peninsula into farmland. Crops grown there must feed Turkey's growing population, they say.

Syria retorts that Turkey does not own the entire Euphrates River. Syrian officials point out that not only will they lose water from the reduced flow, but that more will be lost through evaporation from the Turkish reservoirs.

Like Syria, Iraq accuses Turkey of using water to control the politics and economics of the surrounding countries. Isolated from its neighbors by its leaders, the country seems ready to take a militant stand if its water supply is drastically reduced.

THE ISSUE TODAY

Water management experts and negotiators for the three countries feel that a number of practices could ease the crisis.

Iraq uses desalinated, or salt-free, water for domestic purposes. Current desalination techniques, however, are expensive, so the country, along with allies, is working to develop extremely low-cost salt removal technology. All three countries need to repair existing equipment, improve their irrigation and water conservation techniques, and expand their water recycling. The countries also need to grow some crops that do not require so much water.

These are only short-term solutions, water management experts say. Recent expansion of populations, along with the demand for a higher standard of living, strain a water supply that cannot be increased and whose cycle cannot be changed.

Southwest Asia's water crisis cannot be separated from the population crisis. So far, though, most political and religious leaders have failed to address this issue. Until the overpopulation problem is solved, experts maintain, no long-term solution to the water shortage is possible.

Reviewing the Case

1. What nations are concerned about the water supply from the Tigris and Euphrates rivers?
2. **Human/Environment Interaction** What concerns do the Syrians and Iraqis have about Turkey?

ANSWERS TO REVIEWING THE CASE

1. Turkey, Syria, Iraq
2. Syrians and Iraqis are concerned that Turkey might cut off the water flow from the Tigris and Euphrates or use the water supply to control local politics.

Case Study

ASSESS

Have students answer the Reviewing the Case questions on page 397.

CLOSE

Have students discuss how high a price they would be willing to pay if water became scarce or how much they could do without if water were rationed and how they would conserve water.

DID YOU KNOW?

A 1993 UN report provided these statistics on water around the world: 1.2 billion people currently lack access to clean drinking water, 2.2 billion live without sewage systems and two-thirds of the world's households must fetch water from outside their home.

NATIONAL GEOGRAPHIC SOCIETY

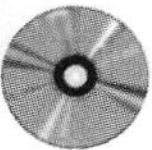

Videodisc

GTV: PLANETARY MANAGER

Side 2, Chapter 7
Frames 38779-41076
Title: ***Water, Water Everywhere***
Subject: Amount of available drinking water

EYE ON THE ENVIRONMENT POSTER SERIES

Display the three posters that discuss the scarcity of water—*Overview*, *Focus Middle East*, and *A Global Look*. Discussion questions and activities are presented on page 19 of the Poster Series Teacher's Guide.

FOCUS

SECTION OBJECTIVES

1. Explain how the scarcity of water challenges North Africa and Southwest Asia.
2. Describe steps being taken to utilize groundwater and sea water in the region.
3. Discuss the impact of war and technology on the region's environment.
4. Discuss how the control of river water can affect the environment.

BELLRINGER MOTIVATIONAL ACTIVITY

Project the Section 2 Focus Transparency and have students answer the questions.

PRETEACHING VOCABULARY

Have students find the meaning of the word *aquifer* in context. *(underground layer of rock that contains water)* Explain that the word comes from the Latin roots *aqua* (water) and *fer* (to bear).

DID YOU KNOW?

NASA space shuttles have been used to locate arable land and underground aquifers. This technology may help solve some water problems in North Africa and Southwest Asia.

SECTION 2

People and Their Environment

THE ENVIRONMENT

SETTING THE SCENE

Read to Discover . . .
- **the challenges facing the culture region of North Africa and Southwest Asia because of the scarcity of water.**
- **the steps being taken to utilize groundwater and sea water in the region.**
- **the environmental effects of the Persian Gulf War.**
- **how efforts to control the flow of river water can affect the environment.**

Key Terms
- **aquifer**
- **desalination**
- **distillation**

Identify and Locate
Libya, Tripoli, Persian Gulf, Iraq, Kuwait, Saudi Arabia, Aswan High Dam

Because almost 70 percent of the earth is covered by water, we often think that water is an abundant natural resource. About 97 percent of the world's water, however, is salty and not usable in many instances. In certain regions of the world, the issue of freshwater for people is a serious problem.

REGION

Need for Water

Some experts predict that by the year 2050 about 10 billion people will be living on the earth. By that time, without some human action, an increased population will be forced to share approximately the same amount of water as is now available.

Water Resources

According to the United Nations, about 1.2 billion people worldwide cannot obtain clean water to drink. It also is estimated that about two-thirds of the world's households must find water outside of their homes. Meanwhile, in the United States, people use approximately 300 billion gallons of water each day.

In most parts of North Africa and Southwest Asia, providing freshwater for drinking and for irrigation is often difficult. The need for water has been fulfilled by rivers and oases and wells that draw water from **aquifers**—underground layers of porous rock, gravel, or sand that contain water. These aquifers have been used as sources of water for thousands of years. The increase in the use of this groundwater, however, has increased with the region's growing population.

The only major freshwater rivers in North Africa and Southwest Asia are the Nile, Tigris, and Euphrates rivers. Thus, only the nations of Turkey, Egypt, Iraq, and Syria have abundant fresh river water to meet their irrigation needs. Israel gets much of its irrigation water from the Jordan River through an elaborate complex of human-made canals that take freshwater from north to south. The remaining nations in the region have to turn to a few smaller rivers and to other sources of water.

Classroom Resources for Section 2

BLACKLINE MASTERS:
Reproducible Lesson Plan 19-2
Skill Activity 19
Section Quiz 19-2
Guided Reading Activity 19-2
Spanish Guided Reading Activity 19-2
Enrichment Activity 19

TRANSPARENCIES:
Section Focus Transparency 19-2

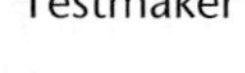

MULTIMEDIA:
Testmaker

Reuters Issues in Geography

Picture Atlas of the World

The "Great Human-Made River"

The most ambitious effort to find water in recent years is Libya's "great human-made river." This project, a multibillion-dollar-pipeline, will carry water from two large aquifers beneath the Sahara to farm areas near the Mediterranean coast. Recently, a 13-foot (4-m) diameter pipeline was completed and now carries freshwater across eastern Libya to the growing coastal population. The second phase of the project will lengthen this pipeline. Another pipeline in western Libya will carry water from the desert aquifer to areas near Tripoli, the nation's capital.

A number of scientists question the long-term value of this human-made river. They believe that the aquifers in Libya and neighboring countries are in danger of being drained. They also claim that pumping aquifers near the Mediterranean coast could draw in salt water from the sea or salt from the surrounding land.

Desalination

There has been an increased search for other water sources in the region. The most widely used method is **desalination**—the removal of salt from seawater.

Desalination was used to provide fresh drinking water during World War II. United States naval ships had simple desalination units that boiled salt out of seawater.

Today it is estimated that the world's desalination plants can produce about 3.4 billion gallons (12.8 billion l) of freshwater a day. In North Africa and Southwest Asia desalination was first tried in Israel and then in other countries. About 60 percent of the world's water-producing capacity—the production of more than 2 billion gallons (7.6 billion l) a day—takes place in this region.

Recent improvements in desalination have moved beyond the simple **distillation**—the boiling and condensing of water—and producing freshwater has decreased in price. Nevertheless the cost can still be too great for

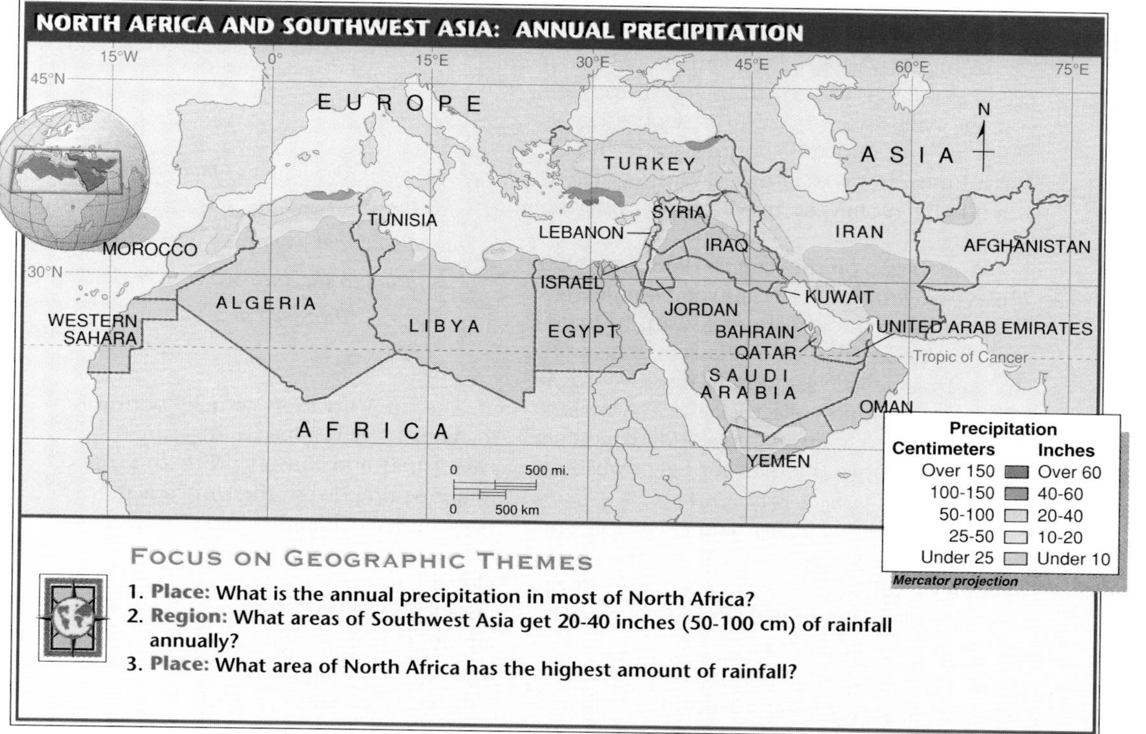

FOCUS ON GEOGRAPHIC THEMES

1. **Place:** What is the annual precipitation in most of North Africa?
2. **Region:** What areas of Southwest Asia get 20-40 inches (50-100 cm) of rainfall annually?
3. **Place:** What area of North Africa has the highest amount of rainfall?

Cooperative Learning Activity

Organize students into three groups and assign one of the following topics to each group: rivers, aquifers, or sea water. Instruct members of each group to research their topic to find out how these resources provide water for the people of North Africa and Southwest Asia. Each group should prepare a presentation for the class, using maps, diagrams, or other graphic aids.

TEACH

GUIDED PRACTICE

L1 Compare Have students find out the average annual precipitation in the region where they live. Then have them compare that amount with the amount of annual precipitation in North Africa and Southwest Asia. Discuss how annual precipitation affects a region's economy.

USING MAPS

Answers:
1. Under 10 in. (25 cm); **2.** Turkey, parts of western Iran, part of Yemen; **3.** coast of Algeria

Map Skills Practice
Reading a Map Based on the map, which country in the region has the least problem related to lack of precipitation? *(Turkey)*

INDEPENDENT PRACTICE

Guided Reading Have students complete Guided Reading Activity 19-2 in the TCR. **LEP**

GLENCOE TECHNOLOGY

Videodisc

Use the following to enrich Chapter 19:

REUTERS ISSUES IN GEOGRAPHY

Chapter 5
Disc 1 Side A

Title: ***North Africa and Southwest Asia: The Influence of Oil and Water***
Subject: How oil and water affect life in the region and events around the world

L2 Write Have students list the goals for building the Aswan High Dam. Then have them list the positive and negative effects of the dam. Ask students to write an essay explaining whether they think the gains outweigh the problems caused by the dam.

ASSESS

CHECK FOR UNDERSTANDING

Assign Section 2 Review as homework or an in-class activity.

MEETING LESSON OBJECTIVES

Each objective below is tested by the questions that follow it in parentheses.

1. **Explain** how the scarcity of water challenges North Africa and Southwest Asia. *(5)*
2. **Describe** steps being taken to utilize groundwater and sea water in the region. *(2, 3)*
3. **Discuss** the impact of war and technology on the region's environment. *(4)*
4. **Discuss** how the control of river water can affect the environment. *(4)*

EVALUATE

 Assign the Section 2 Quiz in the TCR.

 Use the Testmaker to create a customized test for Section 2.

some nations. The oil-rich nations along the Persian Gulf have been among the few countries able to afford desalination.

About 3,500 desalination plants operate in some 105 world countries. Many nations around the Persian Gulf are dependent upon their desalination plants for water.

HUMAN/ENVIRONMENT INTERACTION

Environmental Concerns

In recent decades, the introduction of new technology and the destructive effects of war have heightened environmental concerns in the region. In some instances a nation's action to harness nature, such as the building of dams for hydroelectricity, has caused problems for the environment. This was true in Egypt with the construction of the Aswan High Dam.

The Aswan High Dam

In the early 1950s, President Gamal Abdel Nasser of Egypt wanted to build a huge dam on the Nile River at Aswan in Upper Egypt. After having difficulty borrowing the necessary funds from wealthier countries, Egypt found the money to move ahead with the project.

Work began on the dam in 1958 about 600 miles (955 km) south of Cairo and 4 miles (6.5 km) south of an old dam at Aswan. In building the Aswan High Dam, Nasser's goals were to control the Nile's floods, to improve irrigation, and to supply electricity to the nation. He also wanted to create the world's largest artificial lake above the dam for Egypt's fishing industry.

The 364-foot (111-m) dam was successful in meeting these goals. Nearly 3 million acres (about 1.2 million ha) were opened to irrigation. The dam also provided nearly 50 percent of Egypt's electrical power.

In spite of these successes, the project had negative effects on the environment. Before the dam's construction, the annual Nile floods had deposited fertile alluvial soil along the river banks. Now, the soil was trapped above the dam. Egyptian farmers soon faced the problem of using expensive fertilizers to maintain the land's fertility. The dam also prevented the annual floods from washing away salt from the soil.

The dam also affected humans and their livestock. Following its completion, there was an increase in diseases and death caused by parasites. These parasites lived in the Nile waters and formerly were washed toward the sea.

Although the Aswan Dam has had some negative effects upon the environment, geographers point out that these must be weighed against the gains. With aid from other nations and international organizations, Egypt is overcoming many of the difficulties created by the dam.

The Persian Gulf War

Another area of the region that has faced environmental challenges is the Persian Gulf. A reporter who flew into the Persian Gulf area immediately after the Persian Gulf War ended wrote about the war's effect on the environment:

> *The Gulf War's legacy of pollution has been felt the world over and has left millions in the Middle East wondering whether their air is fit to breathe, their water fit to drink, their food fit to eat.*

The Iraqi invasion of neighboring Kuwait in August 1990 capped a lingering dispute between Iraq and Kuwait. With the support of major world powers, the United Nations Security Council demanded Iraq's immediate withdrawal from Kuwait but was ignored. After a global ban on trade with Iraq had been imposed, the United Nations called for massive air attacks and ground attacks against the Iraqis. The international effort, led by the United States, ended with Iraq's army greatly reduced.

Meeting Special Needs

Reading Disability Many reading comprehension questions require students to restate what they have read. Model a restating strategy for students. Have them read the first sentence under the heading "Environmental Concerns." Demonstrate restating: "People have become more concerned about the environment because of new technology and the harmful effects of war." Have students practice this strategy by restating other sentences from this section.

Geographic Themes

Human/Environment Interaction: Persian Gulf
During the Persian Gulf War, Iraqi oil spills brought danger to the wildlife and vegetation of the region. *What other effect did the conflict have on the environment?*

Unfortunately for the region, the Iraqi forces set fire to a large number of Kuwait's oil wells before being driven out of that country. Huge black clouds of smoke polluted the area. Iraqi troops also dumped an estimated 250 million gallons (950 million l) of Kuwait's oil into the Persian Gulf.

The total effect of the Persian Gulf War on the environment is still being studied by scientists and environmentalists. Thousands of fish and other forms of marine life died when the oil spill spread for 350 miles (563 km) along the Gulf coastline. Most environmentalists believe that the shallowness of the Persian Gulf—the average depth is about 110 feet (about 30.5 m) deep—will delay the recovery of much of the area's marine life. The pools of oil left in Kuwait after the oil-well fires were put out have also threatened millions of birds.

Section 2 Review

Checking for Understanding

1. **Define** aquifer, desalination, distillation.
2. **Locating Places** What area in Libya receives water from the "human-made river"?
3. **Human/Environment Interaction** Why are so many desalination plants found in the Persian Gulf?
4. **Human/Environment Interaction** What were the environmental effects of the Aswan High Dam and the Persian Gulf War?

Critical Thinking

5. **Identifying Central Issues** How is the relationship between population and the supply of freshwater a problem in North Africa and Southwest Asia?

RETEACH

Have students complete Reteaching Activity 19 in the TCR.

ENRICH

Have students complete Enrichment Activity 19 in the TCR.

Using Illustrations

PLACE Iraqi troops set fire to hundreds of oil wells in Kuwait. Dense smoke filled the sky as the wells burned out of control.

Answer to Caption: *air pollution, water pollution, destruction of land and crops*

CLOSE

If possible, invite someone who served in Operation Desert Storm to share firsthand experiences and insights with the class.

CD-ROM

PICTURE ATLAS OF THE WORLD
You and your students can see the burning oil wells in Kuwait by clicking the "Video" button of Kuwait.

ANSWERS TO SECTION 2 REVIEW

1. **aquifer:** underground layer of rock that contains water; **desalination:** the removal of salt from sea water; **distillation:** the boiling and condensation of water
2. the coastal area
3. The oil-rich nations in the area can afford to produce needed water through desalination.
4. The Aswan Dam has decreased the soil's fertility, increased salt in the soil, and increased diseases. The Gulf War produced air and water pollution.
5. The supply of water for drinking and irrigation is scarce. As the population increases, so does the need for water.

Teaching Skills

TEACH

Have students write "Similarities" and "Differences" in separate columns on a sheet of paper. Then say: "Choose a person such as a brother, sister, cousin, or friend, but not another member of the class. Write five similarities and five differences between you and this person." Ask volunteers to share observations, and have the class identify the qualities compared—such as age, physical characteristics, interests, abilities, and so on.

Have students read the skill on page 402. Then ask: "Why are comparisons useful?" *(Possible answers: to make choices, to understand how things are alike and different)* "How does Egypt's population differ from the other countries in the chart?" *(much larger)* Have students identify other similarities and differences in the chart.

Skills Practice For additional practice, have students complete Skill Activity 19 in the TCR.

CRITICAL THINKING SKILLS

Making Comparisons

Suppose you want to buy a portable compact disc (CD) player, and you must choose among three models. To make this decision, you would probably compare the three models according to various qualities or characteristics such as features, price, sound quality, weight, and so on. By making comparisons, you will figure out which model is best for you.

REVIEWING THE SKILL

Making comparisons involves identifying similarities and differences between two or more things. As long as two things share one common quality, they can be compared. In the example above, all the objects were CD players, so they shared many common qualities. However, you could compare a CD player with an audiocassette player. Even though they are different kinds of machines, both are kinds of audio equipment. When making comparisons, apply the following steps:

- Decide what items will be compared.
- Determine which characteristics you will use to compare them.
- Identify similarities and differences in these characteristics.
- If possible, look for causes that explain the similarities and differences.

PRACTICING THE SKILL

Study the chart below. Then answer the following questions.

1. Which countries are compared in the chart?
2. What characteristics are used to compare these countries?
3. What are the two smallest countries in population size? Which country is growing the fastest in population?
4. Which countries have about the same literacy rate?
5. How are Egypt, Kuwait, and Saudi Arabia all similar in their exports?

For additional practice in this skill, see Practicing Skills on page 404 of the Chapter 19 Review.

COMPARING SELECTED COUNTRIES OF NORTH AFRICA AND SOUTHWEST ASIA

	1994 Population (millions)	Annual % Population Growth Rate	Literacy Rate	Annual Oil Production (metric tons)	Major Imports	Major Exports
Egypt	58.9	2.3	48%	45.264m	Foodstuffs Machinery	Petroleum products Cotton products
Iraq	19.9	3.7	60%	14.876m	Machinery Vehicles	Fuels Energy
Israel	5.4	1.5	92%	250m in reserves (oil bearing shale)	Consumer goods Fuels	Machinery Chemicals
Kuwait	1.3	3.3	74%	9.567m	Machinery Manufactured goods	Petroleum products Machinery
Saudi Arabia	18.0	3.2	62%	409.839m	Machinery Foodstuffs	Petroleum products

Sources: *The Statesman's Year Book*, 1992-1993; The Population Reference Bureau, Inc., 1994

ANSWERS TO PRACTICING THE SKILL

1. Egypt, Iraq, Israel, Kuwait, Saudi Arabia
2. 1994 population, annual population growth rate, literacy rate, annual oil production, major imports, major exports
3. Israel and Kuwait; Iraq
4. Iraq and Saudi Arabia
5. All export petroleum products.

chapter 19 HIGHLIGHTS

1 Section: Living in North Africa and Southwest Asia

Key Terms

petrochemical (p. 392)
service industry (p. 393)
gross domestic product (GDP) (p. 393)

Summary

- Although the region has limited arable land, a relatively large percentage of the people are engaged in some type of agriculture.
- The raising of livestock and fishing are two other sources of needed food in the region.
- The level of industrialization is uneven among the nations of the region with a higher level usually found in many of the oil-producing nations.
- The need to connect urban and economic centers with each other has led to a recent growth in transportation and communication systems.
- Although there has been an increase in the interdependence among the nations of the region, disputes and warfare have disrupted some of the region's economies.

Airport in Jidda, Saudi Arabia

2 Section: People and Their Environment

Key Terms

aquifer (p. 398)
desalination (p. 399)
distillation (p. 399)

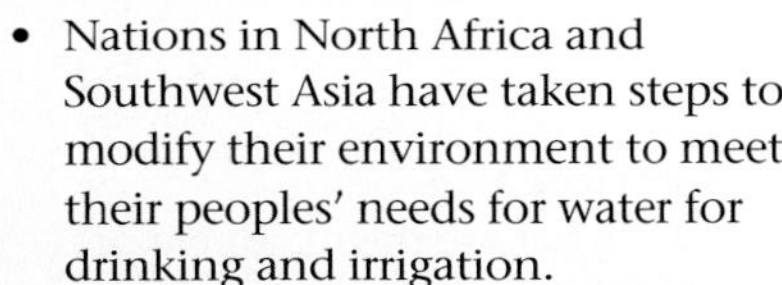

Summary

- Nations in North Africa and Southwest Asia have taken steps to modify their environment to meet their peoples' needs for water for drinking and irrigation.
- River water needed for extensive irrigation is scarce in most of the nations in the region.
- Desalination is widely used to provide water, particularly in the Arabian Peninsula.
- The Aswan High Dam has brought benefits to Egypt, but it has also had negative effects upon the environment.
- The Persian Gulf War severely damaged the natural environment in the Persian Gulf area.

Burning oil spills in the Persian Gulf

CHAPTER 19 HIGHLIGHTS

USING THE CHAPTER 19 HIGHLIGHTS

Use the Chapter 19 Highlights to preview, review, condense, or reteach the chapter.

PREVIEW/REVIEW

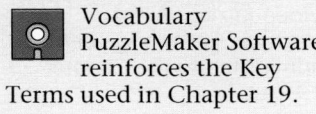

Vocabulary PuzzleMaker Software reinforces the Key Terms used in Chapter 19.

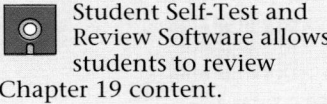

Student Self-Test and Review Software allows students to review Chapter 19 content.

CONDENSE

Have students read the Chapter 19 Highlights.

Have students listen to the Chapter 19 Audiocassettes in the TCR. Spanish Audiocassettes are also available.

Assign the Chapter 19 Audiocassette Activity and give students the Chapter 19 Audiocassette Quiz.

Have students complete the Guided Reading Activities for Chapter 19 in the TCR. Spanish Guided Reading Activities are also available.

RETEACH

Have students complete Reteaching Activity 19 in the TCR. Spanish Reteaching Activities are also available.

Map Activity

Identify and Locate Display Unit Map Overlay Transparency 6-4. Call on student volunteers to identify one of the countries and state one fact about its economy or environment. Continue until each country in the region has been identified.

GLENCOE TECHNOLOGY

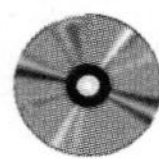
Videodisc

Use Chapter 19 MindJogger Videoquiz to review students' knowledge before administering the Chapter 19 Test.

MINDJOGGER VIDEOQUIZ

Chapter 19
Disc 3 Side A

The MindJogger Videoquiz is also available on videocassette.

ANSWERS

Reviewing Key Terms

1. service industries
2. gross domestic product
3. petrochemicals
4. distillation
5. aquifers
6. desalination

Reviewing Facts

7. dates and cotton
8. dry climate and desert land
9. They want to avoid outside influences.
10. about 97 percent
11. a pipeline in Libya built to carry water from large aquifers beneath the Sahara to farms near the Mediterranean coast
12. The cost is too high.

chapter 19 REVIEW

Reviewing Key Terms

Choose the vocabulary term that best completes each of the sentences below. Write your answers on a separate sheet of paper.

petrochemicals (p. 392)
service industries (p. 393)
gross domestic product (GDP) (p. 393)
aquifers (p. 398)
desalination (p. 399)
distillation (p. 399)

SECTION 1

1. Banking and insurance are two types of ____.
2. A nation's ____ is an indication of that nation's goods and services created in a year.
3. ____ are products produced from petroleum.

SECTION 2

4. ____ was an early method used to create salt-free water.
5. Oases and wells draw water from ____.
6. Freshwater is produced by ____, which removes salt.

Reviewing Facts

SECTION 1

7. What are the major export crops of Iraq and Egypt?
8. Why does Saudi Arabia produce so little livestock?
9. Why is tourism discouraged by some countries in the region?

SECTION 2

10. What percentage of the world's water is salty?
11. What, and where, is the "great human-made river" project?
12. Why is the desalination process not used to provide water for irrigation in poorer nations?

Critical Thinking

13. **Expressing Problems Clearly** Explain why the need for industrialization is so important in some nations in North Africa and Southwest Asia.
14. **Determining Cause and Effect** How has the production of oil caused changes in the natural environment in parts of the region?

Geographic Themes

15. **Location** How has the region's location affected transportation?
16. **Region** What is a desperately needed but scarce natural resource in North Africa and Southwest Asia?

Practicing Skills

Making Comparisons

Refer to the chart on page 402.

17. Which characteristic shows the widest differences among these countries—oil production or population?
18. How would you explain these differences?
19. Compare literacy rates among the countries. What relationship do you find between these characteristics?

Using the Unit Atlas

Refer to the physical geography section of the Unit Atlas on pages 352–353.

20. What is the most important resource of the countries in the Arabian Peninsula?
21. What large body of water is the saltiest body of water on the earth?
22. What is the highest point in the region?

Critical Thinking

13. The growing population and limited land available for farming make industrialization necessary to provide jobs.
14. It has provided money for desalination plants and has led to warfare that polluted the environment.

Geographic Themes

15. The region's location at a crossroads between East and West has increased the need for airlines and other means of transportation.
16. water

Projects

Individual Activity

You have learned about the importance of the process of desalination in providing freshwater for North Africa and Southwest Asia. Research current developments in the process. Write a brief report describing some of the new and more efficient methods of desalination that are being used or developed today.

Cooperative Learning Activity

Working in a group of four, have a meeting of representatives of nations that are members of OPEC. Each student will represent a different member nation. Each representative should prepare a written statement of his or her nation's position on the amount and the price of oil to be produced next year. Once each representative has prepared a written statement of his or her country's position, the group should try to reach a decision on pricing policy that should be presented to the class as a whole.

Writing About Geography

Cause and Effect

Imagine that you are a farmer in Egypt. Write a letter to a close friend in another country explaining how the construction of the Aswan High Dam has affected you and others living in your area. Use your journal, text, encyclopedias, travel books, and other reference books to help you in your research.

Locating Places

THE PHYSICAL/POLITICAL GEOGRAPHY OF NORTH AFRICA AND SOUTHWEST ASIA

Match the letters on the map with the places and physical features of North Africa and Southwest Asia. Write your answers on a separate sheet of paper.

1. Nile River
2. Suez Canal
3. Libya
4. Arabian Peninsula
5. Turkey
6. Kuwait
7. Shatt al Arab
8. Jordan
9. Morocco
10. Persian Gulf

Chapter 19 Review

Practicing Skills

17. oil production
18. Oil production is based on availability of the resource and access to modern technology.
19. A high literacy rate is related to a higher level of economic development.

Using the Unit Atlas

20. oil
21. Dead Sea
22. Nowshak in Afghanistan

Locating Places

1. C
2. D
3. B
4. F
5. G
6. I
7. H
8. E
9. A
10. J

Chapter Bonus Test Question

This question may be used for extra credit on the chapter test.

How has the distribution of petroleum resources affected the political, social, and economic development of North Africa and Southwest Asia?

(Answers will vary but should indicate the following understandings: Oil resources have widened the gap between rich and poor nations, fostered interdependence, increased world trade and outside influences, produced conflicts, raised standards of living, and harmed the environment.)

Geography Connection

FOCUS

Ask students to tell which foods are part of their regular diets, which are familiar, which they've never enjoyed, and those they would like to try.

TEACH

L1 Rank Have students list those foods that all class members have eaten, then vote for the favorite.

L2 Language Arts Write the names of the foods presented on slips of paper. Fold the slips, then organize students into small groups and have each group choose a slip. Allow students five or ten minutes to write a mouthwatering description, then let each group read their description while other groups guess the food being described.

L2 Survey Have students compose a questionnaire concerning familiarity with foods from North Africa and Southwest Asia. Encourage students to conduct a random survey of the school's student body to determine how well-known these foods are.

L3 Interview Students may arrange an interview or a tour with the owner or chef of a restaurant that serves North African or Southwest Asian food. Have students prepare a list of questions beforehand.

GEOGRAPHY CONNECTION

North Africa and Southwest Asia and the United States

NORTH AFRICAN AND SOUTHWEST ASIAN CUISINE

Southwest Asian and North African cuisine has contributed several favorites to the American menu. The distinct flavor and taste most often comes from spices that are not often found in American foods: ginger, marjoram, and curry.

◀ **PITA BREAD,** or pita pockets, as many Americans call them, has become a great favorite with sandwich-loving Americans. A wheat bread baked in thin flat cakes, pita cakes puff out in the middle to form a pocket. The hungry diner can stuff any assortment of ingredients into the bread to make a handy, hearty meal. Pita bread is often accompanied by *tabbouleh* and *hummus*.

TABBOULEH ▶ is a salad of chopped tomatoes, green and white onions, radishes, parsley, and mint dressed up with *burghul*, a final ingredient that adds a nut-like flavor and a chewy texture.

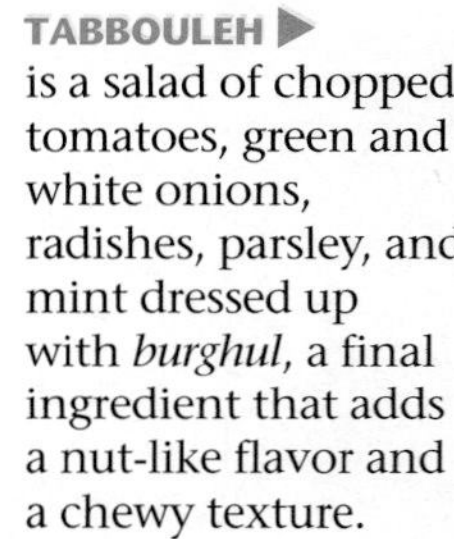

◀ **BAKLAVA** is a favorite of Americans with a sweet tooth. Baklava is a rich pastry made of finely chopped nuts—pistachio or walnuts—baked between thin layers of dough. The pastry is drenched with honey or syrup flavored with cinnamon and lemon juice.

Making the Connection

Diversity Using cookbooks, have students explore North African and Southwest Asian foods and customs further. Encourage them to note unfamiliar ingredients, particularly spices. Suggest they plan a tasting party, then let them choose several simple, typical recipes that have the spices particular to the region's cooking. Students might be able to arrange time for cooking with the home economics department or the school's kitchen. Students may also prefer to simply discover the smell and taste of curry, marjoram, and ginger, or purchase and sample already prepared foods.

▲ **COUSCOUS** is a North African dish of finely ground wheat meal combined with salted water to make a kind of pasta. Americans and North Africans alike top a bowl of couscous with powdered sugar and nuts to make a sumptuous dessert.

▲ **SHISH KABOB** is one of the best known "American" foods from Southwest Asia and North Africa. It consists of skewered cubes of succulent spiced meat alternating with chunks of vegetables or fruit. The name comes from the Turkish words *sis* meaning "sword" or "skewer," and *kebab*, meaning "lamb" or "mutton." Americans generally substitute beef, their favorite meat, for lamb.

◀ **YOGURT** is another Southwest Asian staple that Americans enjoy. Yogurt, a tart source of nutrients with few calories, is the preferred form of milk in Southwest Asia. Americans use yogurt as a basis for salad dressings and dips, mix it with fruit for a light dessert, and eat it right out of the carton. Many Americans also enjoy frozen yogurt as a treat.

Checking for Understanding

1. What ingredients make North African and Southwest Asian cooking unique?
2. **Place** Which of the foods shown are offered by restaurants in your area?

Geography Connection

ASSESS

Have students answer the Checking for Understanding questions on page 407.

CLOSE

Entertain comments about the differences between foods from North Africa and Southwest Asia and the more common dishes that the students eat regularly. Have them formulate several generalizations about the foods of the region.

DID YOU KNOW?

Southwest Asians, who prefer yogurt to any other form of milk, maintain it has extraordinary nutritional properties. Yogurt, they say, lengthens life, confers good looks, supports the soul, aids the complexion, and cures sunburn, ulcers, and malaria.

ANSWERS TO CHECKING FOR UNDERSTANDING

1. ginger, marjoram, curry
2. Answers will vary.

UNIT OVERVIEW

The three chapters that comprise this unit introduce students to the physical geography and peoples of Africa south of the Sahara. Aspects of the region's life—such as the economy, lifestyles, and human/environment interaction—are also presented.

GEOGRAPHY JOURNAL

Activity Students may choose to target one or two countries, or they may divide the region by quadrants or by physical geographic characteristics.

In addition to sources listed in the Student Edition, students may check atlases, almanacs, and other references.

At the end of the month, have students review their calendar notes and formulate generalizations about the topic they chose. Ask them to enter these generalizations in their journals.

•This journal activity provides the basis for the "Writing About Geography" exercise in the Chapter Review.

•The Geography Journal may be used as an integral part of Performance Assessment.

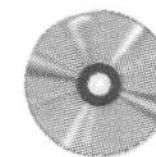

Videodisc

STV: WORLD GEOGRAPHY, VOLUME 2

Side 1, Chapter 1
Frames 00001-49739
Title: *Africa* **(in its entirety)**
Subject: Describes the geographic contrasts and how people and animals have affected the natural environment of Africa

UNIT 7

Africa South of the Sahara

Frans Lanting

GeoJournal Activity

On a piece of poster-board, make a calendar for the month you will be studying this region. Make the boxes large enough for notes. Each day, record something that you learned about Africa south of the Sahara. After each entry, list the source of information, such as text, TV and radio reports, magazines, and newspaper articles.

408

Where in the World . . . .

Have students look at the map on page A19 in which Africa south of the Sahara is highlighted. Display Unit Map Overlay Transparency 7-5 and ask the following questions: What body of water lies on Africa's west coast? *(Atlantic Ocean)* East coast? *(Indian Ocean)* What appear to be the two largest African rivers south of the Sahara? *(Nile, Zaire)* What countries appear to have no internal fresh-water source? *(Mauritania, Chad, Guinea Bissau, Gambia, Sierra Leone, Liberia, Côte d'Ivoire, Togo, Benin, Cameroon, Equatorial Guinea, São Tomé and Príncipe, Gabon, Rwanda, Burundi, Tanzania, Zimbabwe, Botswana, Swaziland, Madagascar)* What countries are affected by the Sahara? *(Mauritania, Mali, Niger, Chad, Sudan, Eritrea)*

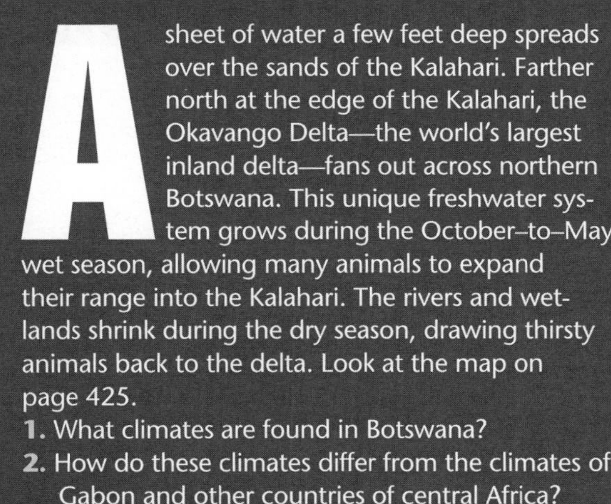

Picturing the World

A sheet of water a few feet deep spreads over the sands of the Kalahari. Farther north at the edge of the Kalahari, the Okavango Delta—the world's largest inland delta—fans out across northern Botswana. This unique freshwater system grows during the October–to–May wet season, allowing many animals to expand their range into the Kalahari. The rivers and wetlands shrink during the dry season, drawing thirsty animals back to the delta. Look at the map on page 425.

1. What climates are found in Botswana?
2. How do these climates differ from the climates of Gabon and other countries of central Africa?
3. How do you think wildlife survive in the harsh climate of Botswana?

Picture Atlas CD-ROM Enrichment Corner

Create a photo album of animal life of Africa south of the Sahara. Include the following photographs: bullfrog and lionesses in Botswana; rhinos in Kenya; elephants in Namibia; buffalo in South Africa; savanna in Tanzania. Read the captions and identify the following:

1. A famous animal reserve in South Africa
2. An animal that estivates
3. A national park in Tanzania larger than the state of Connecticut

Then divide into groups to search for more wildlife facts on the CD-ROM and create a Jeopardy game to test other groups' knowledge of African wildlife.

409

ANSWERS TO PICTURING THE WORLD

1. steppe and desert
2. Central African countries experience mostly tropical climates.
3. They hibernate during the dry months.

Enrichment Corner Answers

1. Kruger National Park
2. frog
3. Serengeti National Park

interNET CONNECTIONS

Information about Africa south of the Sahara can be found at the following address:

gopher://gopher.adp.wisc.edu/11/.class/.african

GLENCOE TECHNOLOGY

Videodisc

Use the following to introduce or enrich Unit 7:

REUTERS ISSUES IN GEOGRAPHY

Chapter 6
Disc 1, Side A

Title: ***Sub-Saharan Africa: Preserving Its Legacy***
Subject: Preservation of African wildlife habitats as a world issue

CD-ROM

PICTURE ATLAS OF THE WORLD

See page T41 for an additional CD-ROM activity that enriches Unit 7, Africa south of the Sahara.

0:00 OUT OF TIME?

If time does not permit teaching each chapter in this unit, you may use the Chapter Highlights and the Audiocassettes that include a 1-page activity and a 1-page test for each chapter.

LESSON PLAN
Unit 7 Atlas

These features and activities may be used as an introduction to the unit or as teaching tools throughout the course of the unit.

FOCUS

Ask students to read the country names on the map on page 410 and share what they know about the countries. Encourage students to add any cultural knowledge they have about Africa south of the Sahara.

TEACH

Apply Ask students to apply what they have learned about cultural geography to offer reasons why Africa south of the Sahara forms a world region. List several of their speculations on the chalkboard.

Implement Foods Around the World 6 as a class activity.

Have students complete Unit Atlas Activity 7B in the TCR.

Have students complete World Cultures Transparencies 11 and 12 in the TCR.

Have students complete World Literature Reading 6 in the TCR.

UNIT 7 ATLAS

AFRICA
Cultural Geography

EXPLORING CULTURAL DIVERSITY

1. *What areas of Africa south of the Sahara are most heavily populated? Most sparsely populated?*
2. *What nations make up Africa south of the Sahara?*

Ethiopian tradition says that Ethiopia's first emperor, Menelik I, was the son of the Biblical Queen of Sheba and Israel's King Solomon.

Mali was home to three great trading empires: Ghana, Mali, and Songhai.

Liberia is Africa's oldest republic. It was settled by African Americans freed from slavery.

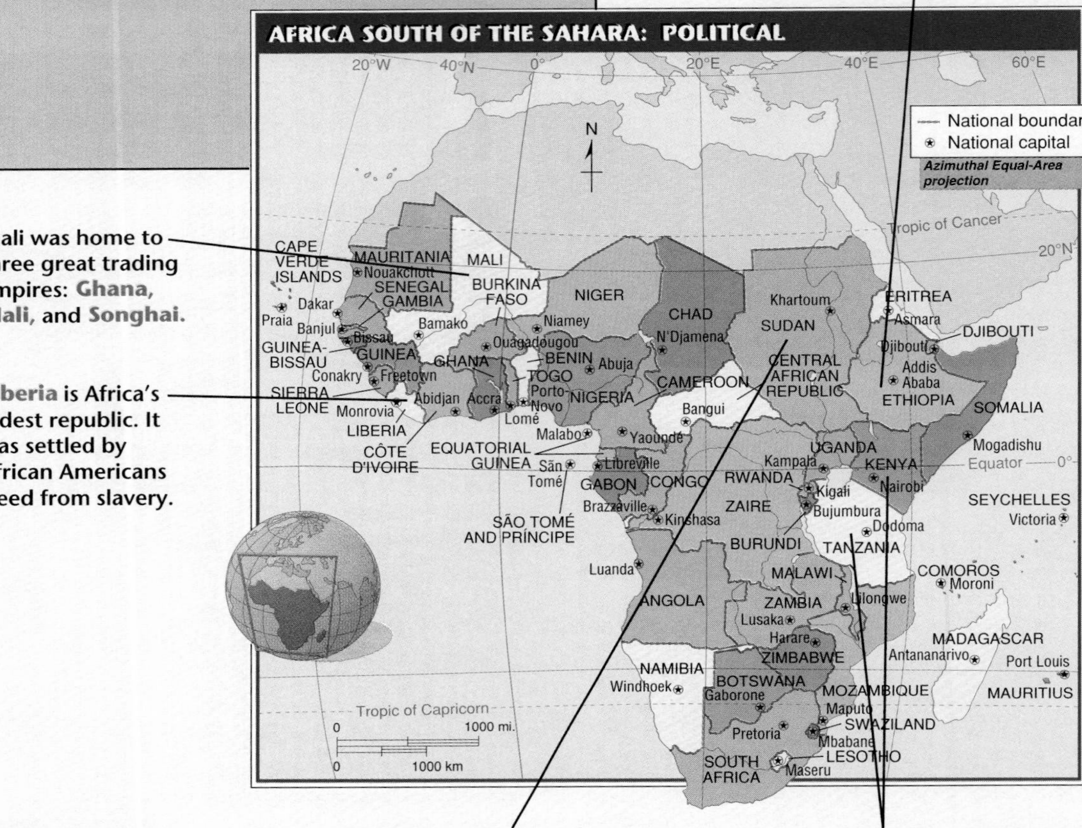

The oldest bones and fossils ever discovered have been found in eastern and southern sites in Africa. These findings give Africa the title "birthplace of the human race."

In Sudan, African blacks are a majority and live in the south; Arab Muslims live in the north and central regions.

Arab and European minorities live along the coasts of Kenya and Tanzania.

Classroom Resources for Unit 7

BLACKLINE MASTERS:
Geography Simulation 7
Environmental Issue 7
Foods Around the World 6
World Literature Reading 6

TRANSPARENCIES:
Unit Map Overlay Transparency 7
World Cultures Transparencies 11, 12

MULTIMEDIA:

World Music: *Cultural Traditions, Lesson 6*

Reuters Issues in Geography
STV: World Geography, Volume 2

Testmaker

Images of the World Poster Set

Picture Atlas of the World

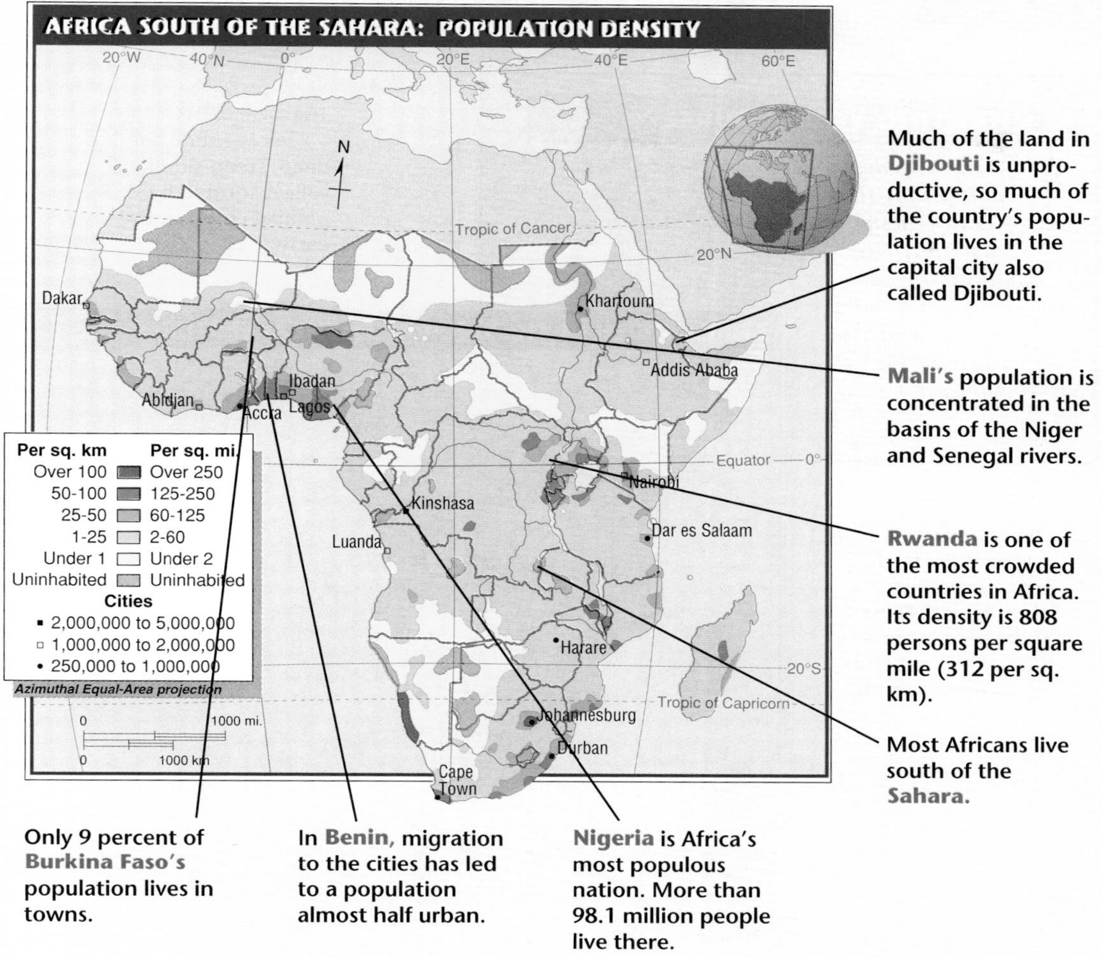

Much of the land in **Djibouti** is unproductive, so much of the country's population lives in the capital city also called Djibouti.

Mali's population is concentrated in the basins of the Niger and Senegal rivers.

Rwanda is one of the most crowded countries in Africa. Its density is 808 persons per square mile (312 per sq. km).

Most Africans live south of the **Sahara.**

Only 9 percent of **Burkina Faso's** population lives in towns.

In **Benin,** migration to the cities has led to a population almost half urban.

Nigeria is Africa's most populous nation. More than 98.1 million people live there.

Population: Africa South of the Sahara and the United States

Africa

United States

= 50,000,000

Source: Population Reference Bureau, Inc., 1994

Africa south of the Sahara has more than twice as many people as the United States.

LESSON PLAN Unit 7 Atlas

Play World Music: Cultural Traditions, Lesson 6, and have students complete the Lesson 6 activity.

ASSESS

Have students answer Exploring Cultural Diversity on page 410.

EXPLORING CULTURAL DIVERSITY

This feature may be used to introduce students to the cultural geography of Africa south of the Sahara. Use questions to stimulate class discussion and help students become familiar with the region. Accept reasonable answers based on the maps, graph, and captions.

CLOSE

Have students read their earlier speculations and make any needed changes, based on the maps.

CD-ROM

PICTURE ATLAS OF THE WORLD

You and your students can learn about the physical features, music, economy, and population of Africa south of the Sahara by selecting "Africa" on the main menu.

Map and Graph Activity

Diversity Assign one or two countries to each student. Ask students to find out the names of ethnic groups in these countries. Have them write the name of each group on a slip of paper. Provide a large wall map of Africa south of the Sahara. Have students read the name of each group and attach it to the appropriate country.

Have students keep a running tally of the number of different groups. After all students have contributed, make a final tally of ethnic groups that live south of the Sahara. Discuss what effects the large number of groups could have on the region.

LESSON PLAN
Unit 7 Atlas

These features and activities may be used as an introduction to the unit or as teaching tools throughout the course of the unit.

FOCUS

To introduce students to the physical geography of Africa south of the Sahara, have them complete Unit Map Overlay Transparency 7 Activity in the TCR.

TEACH

Identify After students study the map on page 412, ask them to cite the physical geographic features that correspond to the areas of light population on page 411.

Apply/Predict Have students recall the kind of areas that usually produce mineral or agricultural resources and predict the agricultural areas south of the Sahara. Students might also explain why certain areas produce mineral resources.

Implement Geography Simulation 7 as a class activity.

DID YOU KNOW?

About 70 percent of all Africans south of the Sahara live in rural villages.

UNIT 7 ATLAS

AFRICA
Physical Geography

CHARTING YOUR COURSE

1. *What two desert areas are located in southern Africa?*
2. *What two mountains are located in eastern Africa?*
3. *What are three natural resources found in Africa south of the Sahara?*

The **Great Rift Valley** is a series of deep, steep-sided valleys formed by parallel cracks in the earth.

The eastern and southern areas of Africa are called **High Africa.** Most of the area is more than 3,000 feet (910 m) above sea level.

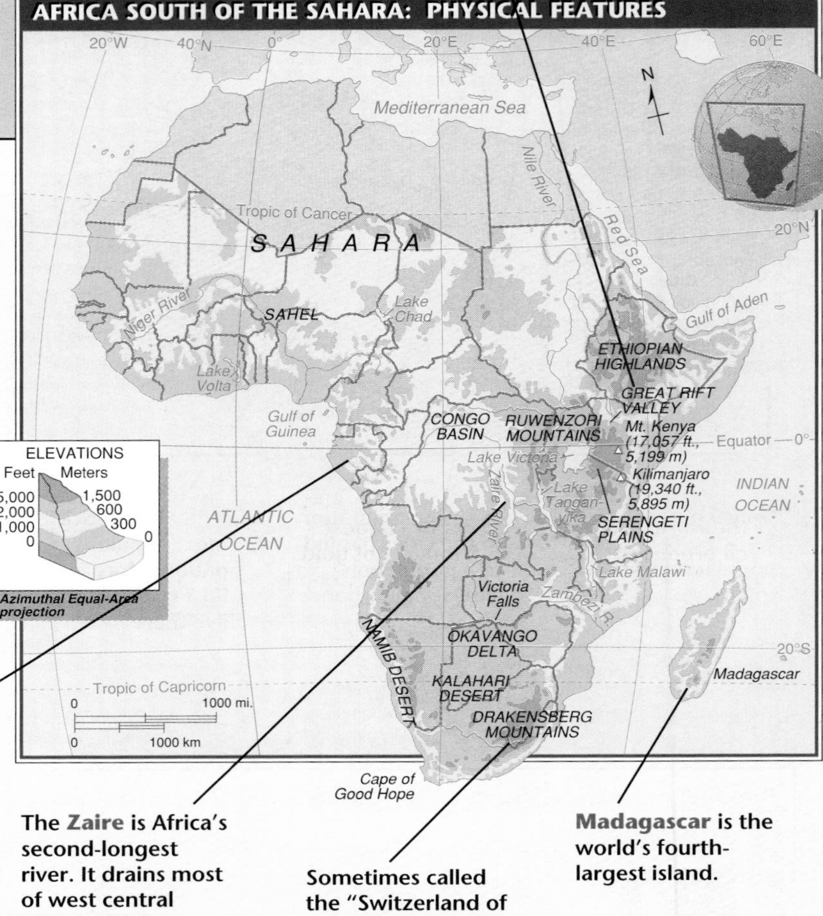

Cape of Good Hope

The **Equator** runs through the middle of Africa. About 90 percent of the continent lies within the tropics, giving Africa the largest tropical area of any other continent.

The **Zaire** is Africa's second-longest river. It drains most of west central Africa, winding through rain forests.

Sometimes called the "Switzerland of southern Africa," **Lesotho** is famous for the scenery in its beautiful Drakensberg and Maloti mountains.

Madagascar is the world's fourth-largest island.

412 UNIT 7

Map Activity

Cause/Effect Organize students into six small groups and assign each group a fact from page 412. Tell them to use the fact as the topic sentence for a three- or four-sentence paragraph that expands or explains the topic. Encourage them to gather more information from the school library or classroom research materials. Have each group read its completed paragraph aloud for the class, or post the paragraphs where everyone can read them.

SOUTH OF THE SAHARA

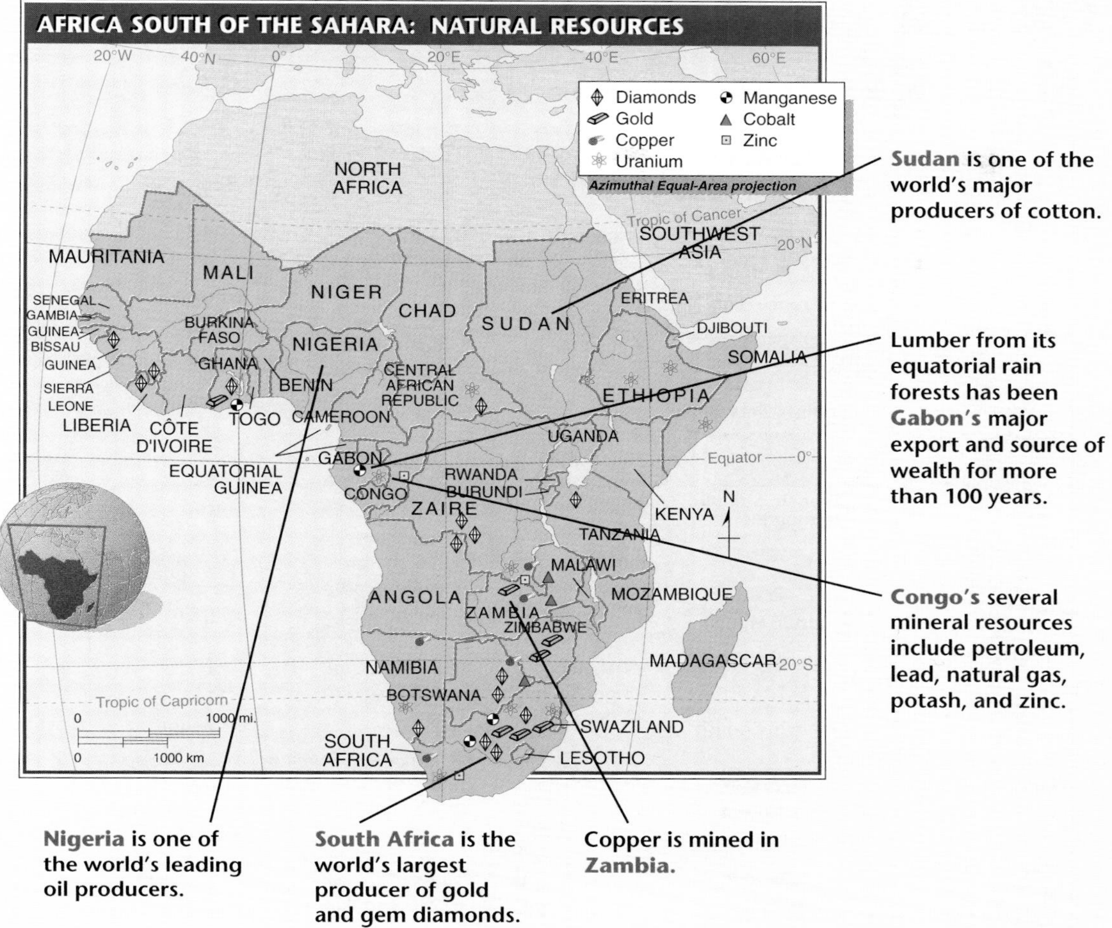

Sudan is one of the world's major producers of cotton.

Lumber from its equatorial rain forests has been **Gabon's** major export and source of wealth for more than 100 years.

Congo's several mineral resources include petroleum, lead, natural gas, potash, and zinc.

Nigeria is one of the world's leading oil producers.

South Africa is the world's largest producer of gold and gem diamonds.

Copper is mined in **Zambia.**

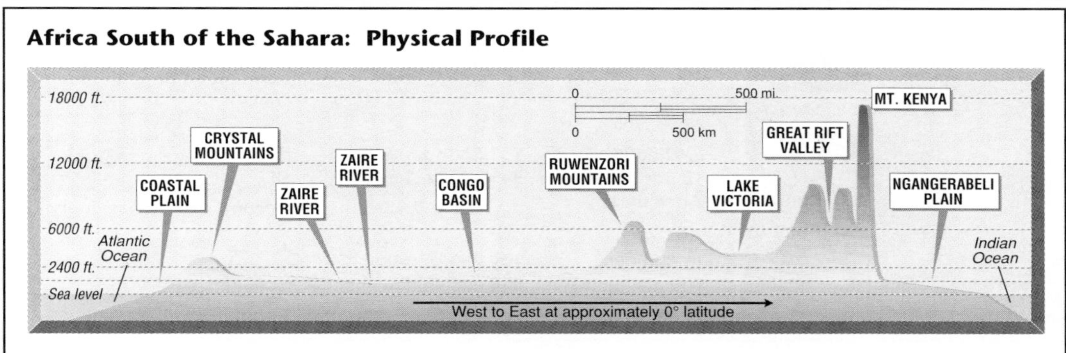

Map Activity

Predict After students have studied the maps on pages 412–413, have them work as a class to predict which areas will be farming regions. Ask them to support their predictions with evidence from the maps and diagram and from previous lessons. Ask students to copy the predictions in their journals and review them as they proceed through the unit or at the end of the unit.

At the appropriate time, discuss any predictions that were incorrect. Be sure that students understand why the facts do not support these predictions. In some cases, students' logic may be correct, but insufficient knowledge of the region may have led to faulty predictions.

LESSON PLAN Unit 7 Atlas

ASSESS

Have students answer the Charting Your Course questions on page 412.

CHARTING YOUR COURSE

This feature may be used to introduce students to the physical geography of Africa south of the Sahara. Use questions to stimulate class discussion and help students become familiar with the region. Accept reasonable answers based on the maps, graph, and captions.

CLOSE

Challenge students to volunteer adjectives that they think describe and/or characterize the physical geography of Africa south of the Sahara.

DID YOU KNOW?

Africa is literally "cracking up." The split is occurring along the Great Rift Valley. Parts of eastern Africa appear to be pulling away from the main mass of the continent.

GLENCOE TECHNOLOGY

Videodisc

Use the following to introduce or enrich Unit 7:

REUTERS ISSUES IN GEOGRAPHY

Chapter 6
Disc 1, Side A

Title: ***Sub-Saharan Africa: Preserving Its Legacy***
Subject: Preservation of African wildlife habitats as a world issue

LESSON PLAN
Unit 7 Atlas

These features and activities may be used as teaching tools throughout the course of the unit.

DID YOU KNOW?

Botswana has offered safety, tolerance, and freedom to refugees of civil wars in neighboring countries.

Ways of the World

MALAWI People in Malawi determine their ancestry and descent from their mothers. Couples quite often set up their homes near the wife's mother.

Ways of the World

ETHIOPIA In Ethiopia, marriage is considered the union of two families. For this reason, most people leave the choice of their spouse to their parents.

DID YOU KNOW?

Comoros is a leading producer of *ylang-ylang*, a substance used in manufacturing perfume.

UNIT 7 ATLAS

COUNTRY PROFILE

COUNTRY* AND CAPITAL	FLAG AND LANGUAGES	POPULATION	LANDMASS	PRINCIPAL PRODUCTS EXPORT	PRINCIPAL PRODUCTS IMPORT
Angola (Luanda)	Portuguese, Bantu	11,200,000 23 per sq. mi. 9 per sq. km	481,350 sq. mi. 1,246,697 sq. km	Fuels	Transport Equipment
Benin (Porto-Novo)	French, Fon	5,300,000 124 per sq. mi. 48 per sq. km	42,710 sq. mi. 110,619 sq. km	Cotton	Textiles
Botswana (Gaborone)	English, Setswana	1,400,000 6 per sq. mi. 2 per sq. km	218,810 sq. mi. 566,718 sq. km	Diamonds	Transport Equipment
Burkina Faso (Ouagadougou)	French, Sudanic languages	10,100,000 95 per sq. mi. 37 per sq. km	105,710 sq. mi. 273,789 sq. km	Cotton	Machinery
Burundi (Bujumbura)	Rundi, French	6,000,000 606 per sq. mi. 234 per sq. km	9,900 sq. mi. 25,641 sq. km	Coffee	Machinery
Cameroon (Yaoundé)	French, English	13,100,000 73 per sq. mi. 28 per sq. km	179,690 sq. mi. 465,397 sq. km	Petroleum	Machinery
Cape Verde Islands (Praia)	Portuguese	400,000 256 per sq. mi. 99 per sq. km	1,560 sq. mi. 4,040 sq. km	Bananas	Food
Central African Republic (Bangui)	French, local dialects	3,100,000 13 per sq. mi. 5 per sq. km	240,530 sq. mi. 622,973 sq. km	Diamonds	Food
Chad (N'Djamena)	French, Arabic	6,500,000 13 per sq. mi. 5 per sq. km	486,180 sq. mi. 1,259,206 sq. km	Cotton	Petroleum
Comoros (Moroni)	Arabic, French	500,000 581 per sq. mi. 224 per sq. km	860 sq. mi. 2,227 sq. km	Vanilla	Rice
Congo (Brazzaville)	French, Kongo, Teke	2,400,000 18 per sq. mi. 7 per sq. km	131,850 sq. mi. 341,492 sq. km	Petroleum	Machinery
Côte d'Ivoire (Yamoussoukro, Abidjan)	French, Akan	13,900,000 109 per sq. mi. 42 per sq. km	122,780 sq. mi. 318,000 sq. km	Food	Petroleum

*Country maps not drawn to scale.

Country Profile Activity

Economics Assign a country or two to each student. Have students research and record on index cards each countries' GDP, GDP per capita, sectors of the economy, and percentages of workers employed in each sector. Provide an area where students can display their findings. Have them put the countries in order from most to least prosperous, arranging their index cards in that order.

Ask students to comment on the prosperity of Africa south of the Sahara in comparison with other world regions they have studied.

COUNTRY* AND CAPITAL	FLAG AND LANGUAGES	POPULATION	LANDMASS	PRINCIPAL PRODUCTS EXPORT	PRINCIPAL PRODUCTS IMPORT
Djibouti Djibouti	French, Arabic	600,000 67 per sq. mi. 26 per sq. km	8,950 sq. mi. 23,200 sq. km	Livestock	Food
Equatorial Guinea Malabo	Spanish, Fang, Bubi	400,000 37 per sq. mi. 14 per sq. km	10,830 sq. mi. 28,050 sq. km	Food & Livestock	Food and Beverages
Eritrea Asmara	Native languages	3,500,000 73 per sq. mi. 28 per sq. km	48,260 sq. mi. 124,993 sq. km	Coffee	Food
Ethiopia Addis Ababa	Amharic, Tigre, Galla	55,200,000 146 per sq. mi. 57 per sq. km	376,830 sq. mi. 975,990 sq. km	Coffee	Machinery
Gabon Libreville	French, Bantu	1,100,000 11 per sq. mi. 4 per sq. km	99,490 sq. mi. 257,679 sq. km	Petroleum	Machinery
Gambia Banjul	English, Mandinka, Wolof	1,100,000 285 per sq. mi. 110 per sq. km	3,860 sq. mi. 9,997 sq. km	Peanuts	Food
Ghana Accra	English, Ewe, Akan, Mossi	16,900,000 190 per sq. mi. 73 per sq. km	88,810 sq. mi. 230,018 sq. km	Cocoa Products	Machinery
Guinea Conakry	French, Peul, Mande	6,400,000 67 per sq. mi. 26 per sq. km	94,930 sq. mi. 245,869 sq. km	Bauxite	Petroleum
Guinea-Bissau Bissau	Portuguese, Crioulo	1,100,000 101 per sq. mi. 39 per sq. km	10,860 sq. mi. 28,127 sq. km	Cashews	Transport Equipment
Kenya Nairobi	Swahili, English, Kikuyu	27,000,000 122 per sq. mi. 47 per sq. km	219,960 sq. mi. 569,696 sq. km	Tea	Machinery
Lesotho Maseru	English, Sotho	1,900,000 162 per sq. mi. 63 per sq. km	11,720 sq. mi. 30,355 sq. km	Machinery	Clothing
Liberia Monrovia	English, native dialects	2,900,000 78 per sq. mi. 30 per sq. km	37,190 sq. mi. 96,322 sq. km	Iron Ore	Machinery

*Country maps not drawn to scale.

Global Gourmet

Africans introduced new fruits and vegetables to the Americas, including yams, okra, watermelon, collard, and black-eyed peas. They also introduced a more nutritional cooking method: African cooks used the liquid in which vegetables had been cooked as the basis for soups and stews, rather than throwing it out. Thus, more nutrients were retained.

DID YOU KNOW?

Gambia is the home of Kunta Kinte, hero of *Roots* and author Alex Haley's ancestor.

DID YOU KNOW?

Lesotho's high altitude effectively prohibits the existence of many common African diseases.

Ways of the World

GUINEA-BISSAU
Guinea-Bissauans may seem shy to Westerners because they do not often make eye contact during conversations. Avoiding eye contact is a sign of respect in this culture.

Country Profile Activity

Health Profile Have students research one or two countries (perhaps the same countries as in the activity on page 414). On index cards, have students record each country's birthrate, infant deaths per thousand, life expectancy, and any common health characteristics of the population.

Involve students in deciding how to rank the countries; then have them do so. Discuss whether there is a connection between each country's economic profile and its health profile.

LESSON PLAN
Unit 7 Atlas

These features and activities may be used as teaching tools throughout the course of the unit.

DID YOU KNOW?

Madagascar was a favorite base for pirates in the 1600s and 1700s. One frequent visitor was the notorious Scot Captain Kidd.

Ways of the World

MALI Malians are usually polite and friendly and rarely confrontational. They tend to handle misunderstandings and disagreements with humorous, teasing comments.

Ways of the World

KENYA Kenya's social systems are group-oriented; the group with the highest value is the family. Someone who doesn't keep close ties with his or her family is considered rebellious.

NATIONAL GEOGRAPHIC SOCIETY

IMAGES OF THE WORLD POSTER SET

Display the poster "Africa South of the Sahara." Have students hypothesize about the climate zone and population density of each photo.

UNIT 7 ATLAS

COUNTRY PROFILE

COUNTRY* AND CAPITAL	FLAG AND LANGUAGES	POPULATION	LANDMASS	PRINCIPAL PRODUCTS EXPORT	PRINCIPAL PRODUCTS IMPORT
Madagascar (Antananarivo)	Malagasy, French	13,700,000 61 per sq. mi. 24 per sq. km	224,530 sq. mi. 581,533 sq. km	Coffee	Machinery
Malawi (Lilongwe)	Chewa, English, Lomwe, Yao	9,500,000 262 per sq. mi. 101 per sq. km	36,320 sq. mi. 94,069 sq. km	Tobacco	Machinery
Mali (Bamako)	French, Bambara, Senufo	9,100,000 19 per sq. mi. 7 per sq. km	471,120 sq. mi. 1,220,201 sq. km	Cotton	Machinery
Mauritania (Nouakchott)	French, Arabic, Hassanya Arabic	2,300,000 6 per sq. mi. 2 per sq. km	395,840 sq. mi. 1,025,226 sq. km	Fish	Machinery
Mauritius (Port Louis)	English, French Creole, Bhojpuri	1,100,000 1,549 per sq. mi. 598 per sq. km	710 sq. mi. 1,839 sq. km	Clothing	Machinery
Mozambique (Maputo)	Portuguese, Makua, Malawl	15,800,000 52 per sq. mi. 20 per sq. km	302,740 sq. mi. 784,097 sq. km	Shrimp	Food
Namibia (Windhoek)	Afrikaans, English	1,600,000 5 per sq. mi. 2 per sq. km	317,870 sq. mi. 823,283 sq. km	Minerals	Petroleum
Niger (Niamey)	French, Fulani, Hausa	8,800,000 18 per sq. mi. 7 per sq. km	489,070 sq. mi. 1,266,691 sq. km	Uranium	Machinery
Nigeria (Abuja)	English, Hausa, Yoruba, Ibo	98,100,000 279 per sq. mi. 108 per sq. km	351,650 sq. mi. 910,774 sq. km	Petroleum	Machinery
Rwanda (Kigali)	French, Rwanda	7,700,000 808 per sq. mi. 312 per sq. km	9,530 sq. mi. 24,683 sq. km	Coffee and Tea	Machinery
São Tomé & Príncipe (São Tomé)	Portuguese	100,000 270 per sq. mi. 104 per sq. km	370 sq. mi. 958 sq. km	Cocoa	Food
Senegal (Dakar)	French, Wolof, Serer, Peul	8,200,000 110 per sq. mi. 43 per sq. km	74,340 sq. mi. 192,541 sq. km	Peanut Oil	Machinery

*Country maps not drawn to scale.

416 UNIT 7

Country Profile Activity

Education Have students find out the literacy rate and education requirements of one or two assigned countries. (Students could continue to research the same countries assigned previously, adding this information to the data they have already gathered.)

Ask students to speculate on the relationship between each country's literacy rate and its economic and health profiles. After students have shared their thoughts, have them work together to compose an opinion on the relationships among the three areas.

COUNTRY* AND CAPITAL	FLAG AND LANGUAGES	POPULATION	LANDMASS	PRINCIPAL PRODUCTS EXPORT	IMPORT
Seychelles Victoria	Portuguese	400,000 256 per sq. mi. 99 per sq. km	1,560 sq. mi. 4,040 sq. km	Bananas	Food
Sierra Leone Freetown	English Native Languages	4,600,000 166 per sq. mi. 64 per sq. km	27,650 sq. mi. 71,614 sq. km	Rutile	Food & Livestock
Somalia Mogadishu	Somali, Arabic	9,800,000 40 per sq. mi. 15 per sq. km	242,220 sq. mi. 627,350 sq. km	Livestock	Petroleum
South Africa Pretoria	Afrikaans, English, Nguni	41,200,000 87 per sq. mi. 34 per sq. km	471,440 sq. mi. 1,221,030 sq. km	Gold	Machinery
Sudan Khartoum	Arabic, Dinka, Nubian, Nuer	28,200,000 31 per sq. mi. 12 per sq. km	917,370 sq. mi. 2,375,988 sq. km	Cotton	Machinery
Swaziland Mbabane	Swazi, English	800,000 120 per sq. mi. 47 per sq. km	6,640 sq. mi. 17,198 sq. km	Sugar	Machinery
Tanzania Dodoma	Swahili, English	29,800,000 87 per sq. mi. 34 per sq. km	342,100 sq. mi. 886,039 sq. km	Coffee	Machinery
Togo Lomé	French, Gur and Kwa languages	4,300,000 205 per sq. mi. 79 per sq. km	21,000 sq. mi. 54,390 sq. km	Phosphates	Machinery
Uganda Kampala	English, Swahili, Luganda	19,800,000 257 per sq. mi. 99 per sq. km	77,050 sq. mi. 199,560 sq. km	Coffee	Sugar
Zaire Kinshasa	French, Kongo, Luba, Mongo	42,500,000 49 per sq. mi. 19 per sq. km	875,520 sq. mi. 2,267,597 sq. km	Copper	Machinery
Zambia Lusaka	English, Bantu	9,100,000 32 per sq. mi. 12 per sq. km	287,020 sq. mi. 743,382 sq. km	Copper	Machinery
Zimbabwe Harare	English, Shona, Sinde bele	11,200,000 75 per sq. mi. 29 per sq. km	149,290 sq. mi. 386,661 sq. km	Tobacco	Machinery

*Country maps not drawn to scale.

Global Gourmet

Peanuts and peanut butter from the Americas are great favorites in the cuisines of many African countries. In Nigeria, for example, chunky peanut butter is the flavoring of Nigerian Peanut Soup.

DID YOU KNOW?

In southern Sudan, the rainy season may last up to nine months or may not come at all. Sudan experienced three droughts between 1985 and 1991.

DID YOU KNOW?

Tanzania is one of Africa's most peaceful countries. About 120 ethnic groups comprise its population; however, no single group is large enough to control the country.

DID YOU KNOW?

Tanzania's Kilimanjaro (19,340 feet [5,895 m]) is the highest point in Africa south of the Sahara. The lowest point is Lake Assal (512 feet [156 m] below sea level) in Djibouti.

Country Profile Activity

Issues Ask students to think for a few moments about the statistics they have collected in the previous activities. Then challenge them to formulate questions they think face all or most African countries south of the Sahara. List the questions on the board as students suggest them.

At the end of the discussion, copy the questions on a sheet of paper and post it with the information already displayed. As students proceed through the unit, encourage them to note when their questions about this world region match those questions the area's leaders and people are asking themselves.

CHAPTER 20 PLANNING GUIDE

The Physical Geography of Africa South of the Sahara

CHAPTER ORGANIZER

Daily Lesson Objectives	Multimedia	Teacher Classroom Resources
SECTION 1 The Land 1. Name the major landforms in Africa south of the Sahara. 2. Locate the physical barriers to inland travel in Africa south of the Sahara. 3. Explain how topography affects the water systems of Africa south of the Sahara.	Section Focus Transparency 20-1 Chapter 20 Vocabulary PuzzleMaker Software Unit Map Overlay Transparencies 1-4, 7, 7-4, 7-5 Geography and the Environment Testmaker STV: World Geography, Volume 2 Picture Atlas of the World Physical Geography of the World Transparencies 51–60	Reproducible Lesson Plan 20-1 Guided Reading Activity 20-1 Spanish Guided Reading Activity 20-1 Workbook Activity 20-1 Geography Simulation 7 Section Quiz 20-1
SECTION 2 The Climate and Vegetation 1. List the climate regions and vegetation patterns in Africa south of the Sahara. 2. Describe how elevation and rainfall affect climate in Africa south of the Sahara.	Section Focus Transparency 20-2 Unit Map Overlay Transparencies 7, 7-2, 7-3 Testmaker STV: World Geography, Volume 2 Geography and the Environment	Reproducible Lesson Plan 20-2 Guided Reading Activity 20-2 Spanish Guided Reading Activities 20-2 Workbook Activity 20-2 Vocabulary Activity 20 Skill Activity 20 Enrichment Activity 20 Section Quiz 20-2
CHAPTER REVIEW AND EVALUATION	Chapter 20 English (or Spanish) Audiocassettes MindJogger Videoquiz Testmaker Student Self-Test and Review Software	Reteaching Activity 20 Spanish Reteaching Activity 20 Outline Map Resource Book, p. 36 Chapter 20 Test Form A and Form B

0:00 *If time does not permit teaching the entire chapter, summarize using the Chapter 20 Highlights on page 429, and the Chapter 20 English (or Spanish) Audiocassettes. Review students' knowledge using the Glencoe MindJogger Videoquiz.*

KEY TO ABILITY LEVELS

Teaching strategies have been coded for varying learning styles and abilities.

L1 **BASIC** activities for all students

L2 **AVERAGE** activities for average to above-average students

L3 **CHALLENGING** activities for above-average students

LEP **LIMITED ENGLISH PROFICIENCY** activities

Performance Assessment

Survival in Varying Environments Give students a simulated problem-solving task related to the physical geography of sub-Saharan Africa. Organize students into groups, and have group members portray themselves as survivors of plane crashes in different areas of the region. Each group should consider the following:

(1) How would you determine your location?
(2) What is the physical description of the location?
(3) What survival problems do you expect there?
(4) What might you likely find in the ruins of the plane or in your personal belongings that could assist you in your survival efforts?
(5) How would you travel to safety? By what means and through what natural features?

Products may take the form of oral presentations with visual aids including maps, illustrations, flowcharts, or other relevant props.

POSSIBLE RUBRIC FEATURES: Content information, concept attainment, problem-solving process steps, oral presentation skills, collaborative skills, creative and divergent thinking skills

For additional professional and classroom resources, see Chapter Resources, pages T46–T51.

TEACHER'S CORNER

NATIONAL GEOGRAPHIC SOCIETY

INDEX TO NATIONAL GEOGRAPHIC MAGAZINE

The following articles may be used for research relating to this chapter:

- "Africa's Skeleton Coast," by Des and Jen Bartlett, January 1992.
- "Zaire River: Lifeline for a Nation," by Robert Caputo, November 1991.
- "Africa's Great Rift," by Curt Stager, May 1990.
- "The Living Sands of the Namib," by William J. Hamilton III, September 1983.
- "Rain Forests: Nature's Dwindling Treasures," by Peter T. White, January 1983.
- "Diamonds: The Incredible Crystal," by Fred Ward, January 1979.

NATIONAL GEOGRAPHIC SOCIETY PRODUCTS AVAILABLE FROM GLENCOE

To order the following products for use with this chapter, contact your local Glencoe sales representative or call Glencoe at 1-800-334-7344:

- *Picture Atlas of the World* (CD-ROM)
- *STV: World Geography, Africa and Europe* (Videodisc)
- *ZipZapMap! World* (Software)
- *GeoBee* (Software)
- *Images of the World* (Posters)
- *Eye on the Environment* (Posters)
- *Physical Geography of the World* (Transparencies)
- *Picture Atlas of Our 50 States* (Book)

Introducing
CHAPTER 20

chapter
20

The Physical Geography of Africa South of the Sahara

PERFORMANCE ASSESSMENT

Refer to the Planning Guide on page 418B for a Performance Assessment Activity for this chapter. See the *Performance Assessment Activities* booklet for additional suggestions.

CHAPTER OBJECTIVES

1. **Recognize** that Africa south of the Sahara rises from west to east in a series of plateaus, the dominant landform on the continent.
2. **Discuss** how climate regions in Africa south of the Sahara range from steamy rain forests to tropical grasslands to arid deserts.

GLENCOE TECHNOLOGY

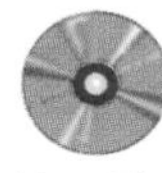

Videodisc

Use Chapter 20 MindJogger Videoquiz to preview chapter content.

MINDJOGGER VIDEOQUIZ

Chapter 20
Disc 3 Side A

The MindJogger Videoquiz is also available on videocassette.

CD-ROM

PICTURE ATLAS OF THE WORLD

Have students click the "Essay," "Photos," and "Stats" buttons of select African countries to see and read about their physical features and climates.

CHAPTER FOCUS

Geographic Setting

Africa south of the Sahara comprises an area more than twice the size of the continental United States. It includes diverse landforms and climates.

Geographic Themes

Section 1 The Land

PLACE Africa south of the Sahara rises from west to east in a series of plateaus, the dominant landform on the continent.

Section 2 The Climate and Vegetation

REGION Climate regions in Africa south of the Sahara range from steamy rain forests to tropical grasslands to arid deserts.

▲ Photograph: *Cape Town, South Africa*

EXTRA CREDIT PROJECT

Slide Presentation Ask interested students to make slides showing landforms and water bodies in Africa south of the Sahara. Tell them to photograph pictures from the chapter and other books and magazines. Have a local photographer show the students how to shoot flatwork (steady the camera with a holder and flatten the artwork with a glass plate) and to mount slides.

Encourage students to arrange the features on the slides in some logical order, such as north to south or east to west. Have them include slides of outline maps of Africa indicating where the features are located. Tell them to include a script that identifies and describes the features.

1 SECTION
The Land

SETTING THE SCENE

Read to Discover . . .
- the major landforms in Africa south of the Sahara.
- the physical barriers to inland travel in Africa south of the Sahara.
- how topography affects the water systems of Africa south of the Sahara.

Key Terms
- escarpment
- cataract
- fault

Identify and Locate
Eastern Highlands, Drakensberg Mountains, Ruwenzori Mountains, Kilimanjaro, Great Rift Valley, Lake Victoria, Lake Tanganyika, Lake Malawi, Lake Volta, Lake Chad, Nile River, Zaire River, Niger River, Zambezi River, Victoria Falls

Nairobi, Kenya
Jambo! Yesterday we left Nairobi and drove to the Great Rift Valley. On the way, we viewed the beautiful, snow-capped Mt. Kenya and Mt. Kilimanjaro. From the top of the valley, I could see dense forests. Thorny trees and shrubs lined the way as we descended to the bottom of the valley. What a magnificent scene!
Umbisa Gusa
3/-
Lake Turkana
HOMO HABILIS
2 million years
Origins of Mankind
Kenya

Africa south of the Sahara includes almost 50 countries, or about one-third of all countries on the earth. In his postcard, Umbisa Gusa describes the varied landscape of Kenya, a country in East Africa. Kenya, however, represents only a small portion of the huge African landmass that occupies almost one-fifth of the earth's total land area.

PLACE

Landforms

As the world's second-largest continent, Africa is a land of immense diversity. The desert expanse of the Sahara, the largest desert in the world, blankets much of the northern third of the continent. Sub-Saharan Africa also includes about 9 million square miles (23 million sq. km) of huge plateaus, mountains, and valleys.

Continent of Plateaus

Many geographers describe Africa as a gigantic plateau. Narrow coastal plains that extend inland less than 20 miles (32 km) edge most of the continent. Until recent times, this sudden rise in land prevented easy access to the interior of Africa. One plateau follows the other as the land rises from west to east in a series of steps. Separating the plateaus are steep cliffs or slopes known as **escarpments.**

The highest and broadest plateaus and steepest escarpments lie in the south and east. Here rivers spill over escarpments in thunder-

Classroom Resources for Section 1

BLACKLINE MASTERS:
Geography Simulation 7
Section Quiz 20-1

TRANSPARENCIES:
Section Focus Transparency 20-1
Unit Map Overlay Transparencies 1-4, 7, 7-4, 7-5
Physical Geography of the World Transparencies 51–60

MULTIMEDIA:

Vocabulary PuzzleMaker Software
Testmaker

Geography and the Environment
STV: World Geography, Volume 2

Picture Atlas of the World

LESSON PLAN
Chapter 20, Section 1

FOCUS

SECTION OBJECTIVES

1. **Name** the major landforms in Africa south of the Sahara.
2. **Locate** the physical barriers to inland travel in Africa south of the Sahara.
3. **Explain** how topography affects the water systems of Africa south of the Sahara.

ABOUT THE POSTCARD

Umbisa hopes next to travel to Mombasa, a town along the Indian Ocean.

BELLRINGER MOTIVATIONAL ACTIVITY

Project the Section 1 Focus Transparency and have students answer the questions.

PRETEACHING VOCABULARY

Read aloud several dictionary definitions for *fault*. Then ask the class to predict which meaning defines the word as it is used in the section.

Use the Vocabulary PuzzleMaker Software to create a crossword or word search puzzle.

Videodisc

STV: WORLD GEOGRAPHY, VOLUME 2

Side 1, Chapter 1
Frames 42895-48595
Title: *Africa*
Subject: Southern Africa: The South

TEACH

GUIDED PRACTICE

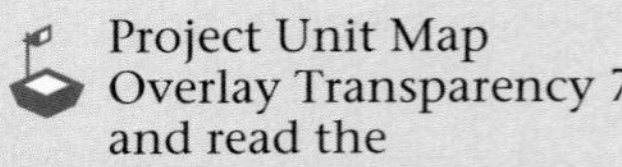

Implement Geography Simulation 7 as a class activity.

Project Unit Map Overlay Transparency 7 and read the "Landforms" section on pages 419 and 420 aloud. As each landform or lake is described, have a student locate it on the map. Project Unit Map Overlay Transparency 7-5 to check the students' accuracy.

INDEPENDENT PRACTICE

Guided Reading Have students complete Guided Reading Activity 20-1 in the TCR. **LEP**

L2 Make a Graph Have a student compare the lengths of these rivers in a bar graph:

RIVER	LENGTH
Zaire	2,700 miles (4,344 km)
Nile	4,160 miles (6,693 km)
Niger	2,600 miles (4,183 km)
Zambezi	2,200 miles (3,540 km)

GLENCOE TECHNOLOGY

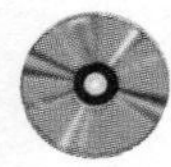

Videodisc

Use the following to enrich Chapter 20:

GEOGRAPHY AND THE ENVIRONMENT
THE INFINITE VOYAGE
To the Edge of the Earth

Chapter 3
Disc 1 Side B

Title: ***Exploring Volcanoes: To the Center of the Earth***

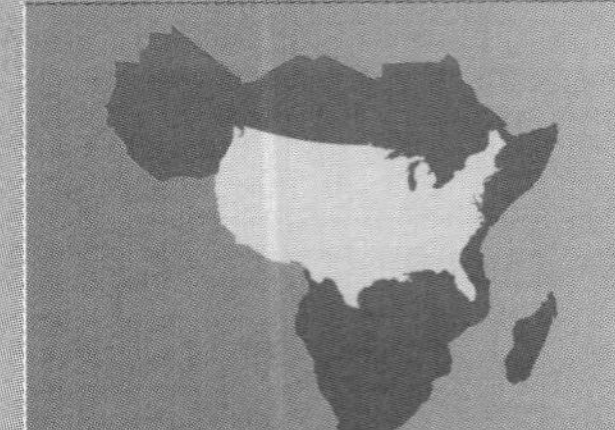

Comparing Lands

The **continental USA** is about three times smaller than Africa south of the Sahara.

ing waterfalls, or **cataracts**, as they plunge toward the Atlantic or Indian oceans.

Because of its plateaus, Africa boasts the highest overall elevation of any other continent. In Europe, only about half the land lies at more than 500 feet (152 m) above sea level. In the region south of the Sahara, the average elevation is more than 2,000 feet (610 m) above sea level.

Mountains and Highlands

Despite its high elevations, Africa possesses surprisingly few mountains. With the exception of the Atlas Mountains in northwestern Africa, it has only scattered peaks. South of the Sahara, most mountains are found in the eastern highlands that reach from Ethiopia almost to the Cape of Good Hope.

The Drakensberg Mountains rim the edge of the southeastern plateau, while the Ruwenzori Mountains border Uganda and Zaire. The snow-clad peaks of the Ruwenzori seem to float in the sky, causing Africans to call them Mountains of the Moon.

The cone-shaped volcanic peaks of Kenya and Tanzania include Mount Kenya and Kilimanjaro, Africa's highest mountain. Each year, thousands of climbers try to reach its summit 19,340 feet (5,895 m) above the east African plateau.

The Great Rift Valley

Kilimanjaro perches on the edge of the Great Rift Valley, one of the world's natural wonders. This valley stretches from the Jordan River in Southwest Asia to the Zambezi River in Mozambique. In East Africa, it slashes a Y-shaped trench more than 3,500 miles (5,631 km) long and creates bold escarpments more than a mile high.

Scientists believe the Great Rift Valley emerged when Africa was part of a huge supercontinent they call Pangaea. Violent movements below the earth's crust began to rip Pangaea apart about 180 million years ago. Huge chunks of land drifted away from one another, creating the present-day continents.

The tremendous pressure on land surfaces caused cracks, or **faults**, and pushed up mountains. For 20 to 35 million years, East Africa seethed with volcanic activity. Another gigantic volcano to the west of Kilimanjaro blew its top and collapsed in on itself, creating the immense Ngorongoro Crater.

PLACE

Water Systems

Landforms shaped millions of years ago have influenced the water systems of Africa. Cuts in the Great Rift Valley form the continent's largest lakes, while the longest rivers all rise in the steplike plateaus. Because of high escarpments, rapids and waterfalls at the edge of the continent block easy inland travel by river.

A Chain of Lakes

A double chain of lakes lies in the Great Rift Valley. Lake Victoria—surrounded by Kenya, Tanzania, and Uganda—is the second-largest freshwater lake in the world and the source of the White Nile. To the southwest, Tanganyika reaches 420 miles (676 km) in length, making it the world's longest freshwater lake.

Surrounded by Tanzania, Mozambique, and Malawi is Lake Malawi, the third-greatest lake in Africa. Many types of fish, some that exist in no other place, live in Lake Malawi.

Few other lakes exist outside the Great Rift Valley. In West Africa, the people of Ghana built a dam across the Volta River to form Lake Volta. To the northeast lies Lake Chad. With no natural outlet to the sea, Lake Chad loses its water to evaporation and seepage.

Cooperative Learning Activity

Ask a student to trace Unit Map Overlay Transparency 1-4, cut out each state, trace each state twice on cardboard, cut out the cardboard states, and label them. Then project Unit Map Overlay Transparency 7-4 and demonstrate the relative size of these African countries by placing states within their borders.

For example, show that Ethiopia is almost twice the size of Texas by placing two outlines of Texas within that country's borders. Demonstrate that South Africa is slightly larger than Texas, New Mexico, and Oklahoma combined by placing those states inside that country. Challenge students to hypothesize which states equal the area of an African country and to test their hypotheses with the patterns and the transparency.

AFRICA SOUTH OF THE SAHARA: PHYSICAL-POLITICAL

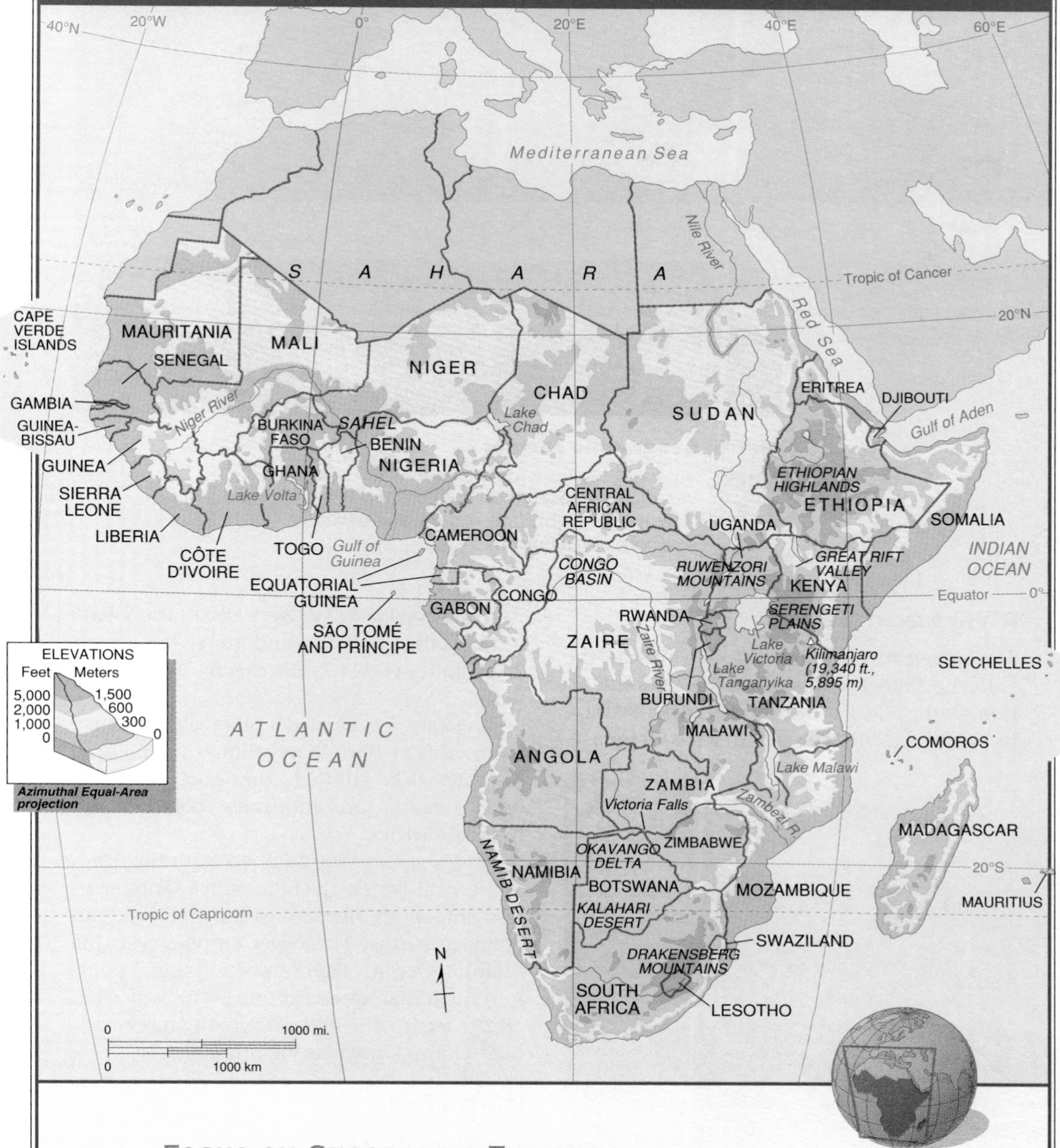

40°N 20°W 0° 20°E 40°E 60°E

Mediterranean Sea
S A H A R A
Nile River
Tropic of Cancer
Red Sea
20°N
CAPE VERDE ISLANDS
MAURITANIA
MALI
NIGER
CHAD
SUDAN
SENEGAL
GAMBIA
GUINEA-BISSAU
GUINEA
SIERRA LEONE
LIBERIA
Niger River
BURKINA FASO
SAHEL
Lake Chad
BENIN
NIGERIA
GHANA
Lake Volta
CÔTE D'IVOIRE
TOGO
Gulf of Guinea
EQUATORIAL GUINEA
SÃO TOMÉ AND PRÍNCIPE
CAMEROON
CENTRAL AFRICAN REPUBLIC
ERITREA
DJIBOUTI
Gulf of Aden
ETHIOPIAN HIGHLANDS
ETHIOPIA
SOMALIA
UGANDA
CONGO BASIN
RUWENZORI MOUNTAINS
GREAT RIFT VALLEY
KENYA
INDIAN OCEAN
Equator 0°
GABON
CONGO
RWANDA
SERENGETI PLAINS
ZAIRE
Zaire River
Lake Victoria
Lake Tanganyika
Kilimanjaro (19,340 ft., 5,895 m)
SEYCHELLES
BURUNDI
TANZANIA
MALAWI
COMOROS
ATLANTIC OCEAN
ANGOLA
Lake Malawi
ZAMBIA
Victoria Falls
Zambezi R.
MADAGASCAR
OKAVANGO DELTA
ZIMBABWE
NAMIBIA
NAMIB DESERT
BOTSWANA
20°S
MOZAMBIQUE
MAURITIUS
Tropic of Capricorn
KALAHARI DESERT
SWAZILAND
DRAKENSBERG MOUNTAINS
SOUTH AFRICA
LESOTHO
N
0 1000 mi.
0 1000 km

ELEVATIONS
Feet Meters
5,000 1,500
2,000 600
1,000 300
0 0

Azimuthal Equal-Area projection

FOCUS ON GEOGRAPHIC THEMES

1. **Movement:** Which waterway forms the border between Zambia and Zimbabwe?
2. **Place:** Which country is completely surrounded by South Africa?
3. **Place:** In what nation is Kilimanjaro?
4. **Location:** Where are the areas of highest elevation in Africa?

USING MAPS

Answers:
1. Zambezi River;
2. Lesotho;
3. Tanzania;
4. Atlas Mountains in northwestern Africa, Eastern Highlands from Ethiopia almost to the Cape of Good Hope, Drakensberg Mountains at the edge of the southeastern plateau, Ruwenzori Mountains on the border of Uganda and Zaire, and the volcanic peaks of Kenya and Tanzania

Map Skills Practice

Where are the lowlands in sub-Saharan Africa located? *(along the coasts)*

CURRICULUM CONNECTION

EARTH SCIENCE

Display a periodic table of elements and have students circle gold, copper, uranium, manganese, cobalt, and zinc—the elements that are resources in Africa south of the Sahara.

ASSESS

CHECK FOR UNDERSTANDING

Assign Section 1 Review as homework or an in-class activity.

CD-ROM

PICTURE ATLAS OF THE WORLD

Click the "Video" button of Botswana to see the wildlife of the Linyanti River.

Meeting Special Needs

Poor Visual Observers Students with visual-spatial processing problems may have difficulty interpreting maps. Since information is often presented in map form in geography, these students need to strengthen their skills in reading and interpreting maps.

Direct students to the physical-political map above. Have them note the explanation of the map's colors in the map key. Then ask them to write a summary of the information shown on the map.

MEETING LESSON OBJECTIVES

Each objective below is tested by the questions that follow it in parentheses.

1. **Name** the major landforms in Africa south of the Sahara. *(2)*
2. **Locate** the physical barriers to inland travel in Africa south of the Sahara. *(3)*
3. **Explain** how topography affects the water systems of Africa south of the Sahara. *(4, 5)*

EVALUATE

Assign the Section 1 Quiz in the TCR.

Use the Testmaker to create a customized quiz for Section 1.

USING ILLUSTRATIONS

HUMAN/ENVIRONMENT INTERACTION Niagara Falls is less than half as high as Victoria Falls.

Answer to Caption: *They offer tremendous potential for hydroelectricity.*

USING ILLUSTRATIONS

REGION The only river system in North America longer than the Zaire is the Mississippi-Missouri.

Answer to Caption: *Nile, Niger, and Zambezi*

NATIONAL GEOGRAPHIC SOCIETY

CD-ROM

PICTURE ATLAS OF THE WORLD

You and your students can view the "Zaire Highway" by clicking the "Video" button of Zaire.

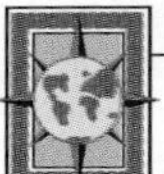

Geographic Themes

Human/Environment Interaction: Victoria Falls

Victoria Falls, located on the Zambezi River, measure 350 feet (107 m) in height. *How might waterfalls affect Africa's future economic development?*

Rivers and Basins

Four great rivers slice through Africa—the Nile, the Zaire, the Niger, and the Zambezi. Although the Nile lies mostly in northern Africa, its White Nile branch starts in Lake Victoria.

Geographic Themes

Region: Zaire River, Central Africa

Many villages and markets thrive along the banks of central Africa's Zaire River. *What three other major rivers are located in Africa?*

The largest river system south of the Sahara is the Zaire. It twists and turns for almost 2,700 miles (4,344 km), crossing the Equator twice.

The Zaire has created a huge saucer-shaped basin. Almost 10 million gallons (38 million l) of water flow through the Zaire each second, creating an enormous potential for hydroelectricity.

The Niger and the Zambezi form the third- and fourth-largest rivers in Africa. Tributaries feed into both rivers, creating hollowed-out drainage basins. The Niger empties into the Atlantic Ocean. The Zambezi, which pours into the Indian Ocean at one point, widens to 18,297 feet (5,577 m) before plunging down a huge chasm known as Victoria Falls.

Waterfalls

During the rainy season, millions of gallons of water crash over Victoria Falls. Clouds of spray splash more than 1,640 feet (500 m) into the air. David Livingstone, the first European explorer to see the falls, named them after the British queen.

Victoria Falls, more than twice the height of Niagara Falls, joins dozens of smaller water-

Critical Thinking

Determining Cause and Effect List the natural resources of Africa south of the Sahara on the board: diamonds, gold, copper, oil, uranium, manganese, cobalt, and zinc. Have students note those they consider valuable.

Explain that valuable resources can cause problems. For example, in the 1870s the United States government forced the Sioux onto reservations after miners found gold on Sioux land. Point out that some ancestors of South Africa's rulers were from Great Britain. Have students hypothesize why the British took over South Africa and how South Africa's resources caused problems for native Africans.

Geographic Themes

Place: The Great Rift Valley, East Africa
The Great Rift Valley cuts a deep gash through the landscape of East Africa. *How was the Great Rift Valley formed?*

falls in offering tremendous potential for the development of hydroelectricity.

HUMAN/ENVIRONMENT INTERACTION

Natural Resources

Africa south of the Sahara is rich in resources. In South Africa and Zaire, miners extract diamonds from some of the biggest deposits on the earth. Some geologists believe that more than half the world's gold comes from South Africa and the Great Rift Valley. Central Africa, especially Zambia and Zaire, yields reserves of copper. Nigeria controls 3 percent of the world's known oil reserves. Other parts of the continent hold pockets of industrial minerals, such as uranium, manganese, cobalt, and zinc.

Africans have begun to tap two other sources of energy—waterfalls and the sun. Hydroelectric power and solar energy hold the keys to the continent's future development.

SECTION 1 REVIEW

Checking for Understanding

1. **Define** escarpment, cataract, fault.
2. **Locating Places** What major landform dominates Africa south of the Sahara?
3. **Location** Where is the Great Rift Valley?
4. **Region** What major lakes and rivers lie south of the Sahara?

Critical Thinking

5. **Expressing Problems Clearly** Explain what resources in Africa hold the answer to how to meet the continent's future energy needs.

ANSWERS TO SECTION 1 REVIEW

1. **escarpment:** steep cliff or slope; **cataract:** rapid or waterfall; **fault:** crack in the earth's crust
2. plateau
3. It stretches from the Jordan River in Southwest Asia to the Zambezi River in Mozambique.
4. Lakes Victoria, Malawi, and Chad; the Nile, Zaire, Zambezi, and Niger rivers
5. The scarcity of fuel, such as oil and coal, has led Africans to look increasingly toward hydroelectric and solar energy.

RETEACH

Make copies of the section and cut the paragraphs apart. (Omit subheads.) Give each small group a set of section pieces. Have groups put the paragraphs in order and write headings for each subsection.

ENRICH

Tell the students about David Livingstone: In 1840 this Scot went as a medical missionary to Africa, where he advocated abolition of the slave trade. In 1873 he died while searching for the source of the Nile. His followers buried his heart beneath a tree and carried his remains to Westminster Abbey in London.

CLOSE

Have students write to Umbisa, telling him where they would like to travel.

USING ILLUSTRATIONS

PLACE The Great Rift Valley is a fertile agricultural area in Kenya.

Answer to Caption: *Great pressure on land surfaces caused the crack.*

NATIONAL GEOGRAPHIC SOCIETY

PHYSICAL GEOGRAPHY OF THE WORLD TRANSPARENCIES

Display and discuss the physical features of the following transparencies:

51. Namib Desert, Namibia
52. Sahel, Niger
53. Rain Forest, Zaire
54. Zaire River, Zaire
55. Okavango Delta, Botswana
56. Cape of Good Hope, South Africa
57. Lake Victoria in East Africa
58. Great Rift Valley, Kenya
59. Serengeti Plain, Tanzania
60. Kilimanjaro, Tanzania

LESSON PLAN
Chapter 20, Section 2

FOCUS

SECTION OBJECTIVES

1. **List** the climate regions and vegetation patterns in Africa south of the Sahara.
2. **Describe** how elevation and rainfall affect climate in Africa south of the Sahara.

BELLRINGER MOTIVATIONAL ACTIVITY

Project the Section 2 Focus Transparency and have students answer the questions.

PRETEACHING VOCABULARY

Explain that *tropical savanna* is a grassland with scattered trees. Display pictures of the American prairie and plains. Ask the students which one is more like the African savanna. *(the prairie)*

Videodisc

STV: WORLD GEOGRAPHY, VOLUME 2

Side 1, Chapter 1
Frames 39250-42850
Title: *Africa*
Subject: Southern Africa: The Namib

STV: WORLD GEOGRAPHY, VOLUME 2

Side 1, Chapter 1
Frames 36055-39155
Title: *Africa*
Subject: Southern Africa: The Kalahari

SECTION 2

The Climate and Vegetation

SETTING THE SCENE

Read to Discover . . .
- the climate regions and vegetation patterns in Africa south of the Sahara.
- how elevation and rainfall affect climate in Africa south of the Sahara.

Key Terms
- savanna
- leach

Identify and Locate
Tropic of Cancer, Tropic of Capricorn, Namib Desert, Kalahari Desert, Okavango Delta, Sahel, Serengeti Plain, Climate regions: desert, steppe, tropical savanna, tropical rain forest

Painting a picture of the African landscape is much like weaving a piece of *kenta* cloth. This highly prized cloth of western Africa is made of long strips of fabric woven together in vivid patterns. Each strip is distinctly different. Yet it forms part of a pattern instantly recognized by most Africans. Like kenta cloth, the landscape of Africa is made up of distinct climate regions with their own characteristic forms of vegetation. These regions are woven together into a pattern shaped by Africa's location in the tropics.

Such climatic variations are partially explained by elevation. The combination of high plateaus, lowland coastal areas, and large interior basins strongly influence climate patterns. Higher elevations generally mean cooler climates. Wetter climates are found along escarpments that force rain-heavy clouds to drop their moisture. Such is the case with Zaire. Moisture-carrying clouds sweep inland until they run into the escarpment at the edge of the towering eastern plateau. As a result, rain falls more heavily in Zaire than in neighboring Tanzania.

LOCATION

A Diverse Continent

Three tropical latitudes define the location of Africa south of the Sahara—the Tropic of Cancer, the Tropic of Capricorn, and the Equator. The Tropic of Cancer crosses the countries that line the southern edge of the desert. The Tropic of Capricorn extends through the southern tip of the continent. In between these two latitudes runs the Equator. No other continent on the earth straddles all three tropical latitudes.

Although all of Africa lies within 35 degrees of the Equator, the continent has great variations in climate and vegetation. Areas of steamy rain forests, desert and steppe areas, and milder climates are all found in Africa.

REGION

Climate Regions

Climate regions with distinct vegetation patterns lie both north and south of the Equator. A trip toward the Equator from either the Tropic of Cancer or the Tropic of Capricorn goes through four main climate regions: desert, steppe, tropical savanna, and tropical rain forest.

Deserts

Deserts cover a larger percentage of Africa than any other continent—about two-fifths of its land area. The Sahara sprawls across north-

Classroom Resources for Section 2

BLACKLINE MASTERS:
Reproducible Lesson Plan 20-2
Guided Reading Activity 20-2
Workbook Activity 20-2
Vocabulary Activity 20
Enrichment Activity 20
Skill Activity 20
Section Quiz 20-2

TRANSPARENCIES:
Section Focus Transparency 20-2
Unit Map Overlay Transparencies 7, 7-2, 7-3

MULTIMEDIA:
Testmaker

STV: World Geography, Volume 2
Geography and the Environment

ern Africa from the Atlantic Ocean to the Red Sea. In southern Africa, the Namib Desert blankets the coast of Namibia. On the southern plateau to the west stretches the Kalahari Desert. About the size of Italy, the Kalahari covers most of Botswana.

Little rain ever falls on the deserts of Africa. The complex system of escarpments and plateaus keeps rain-laden clouds from reaching interior areas. Except for scattered cactuses and thorny shrubs, the deserts, where temperatures soar to 120°F (48.9°C), are barren. At night, heat escapes until temperatures cool to 50°F (10°C) or lower.

Desert Oases

Most oases are created by groundwater close to the surface. On the northern edge of the Kalahari Desert, however, the world's largest inland delta blooms. The delta is formed by the Okavango River. Spilling out of the highlands of distant Angola, the Okavango River spreads a sheet of water over the Kalahari sands until it disappears into the desert. The vegetation in the delta supports a variety of wildlife. "The delta," commented one scientist, "returns the pulse of life to the 'great thirstland' of the Kalahari."

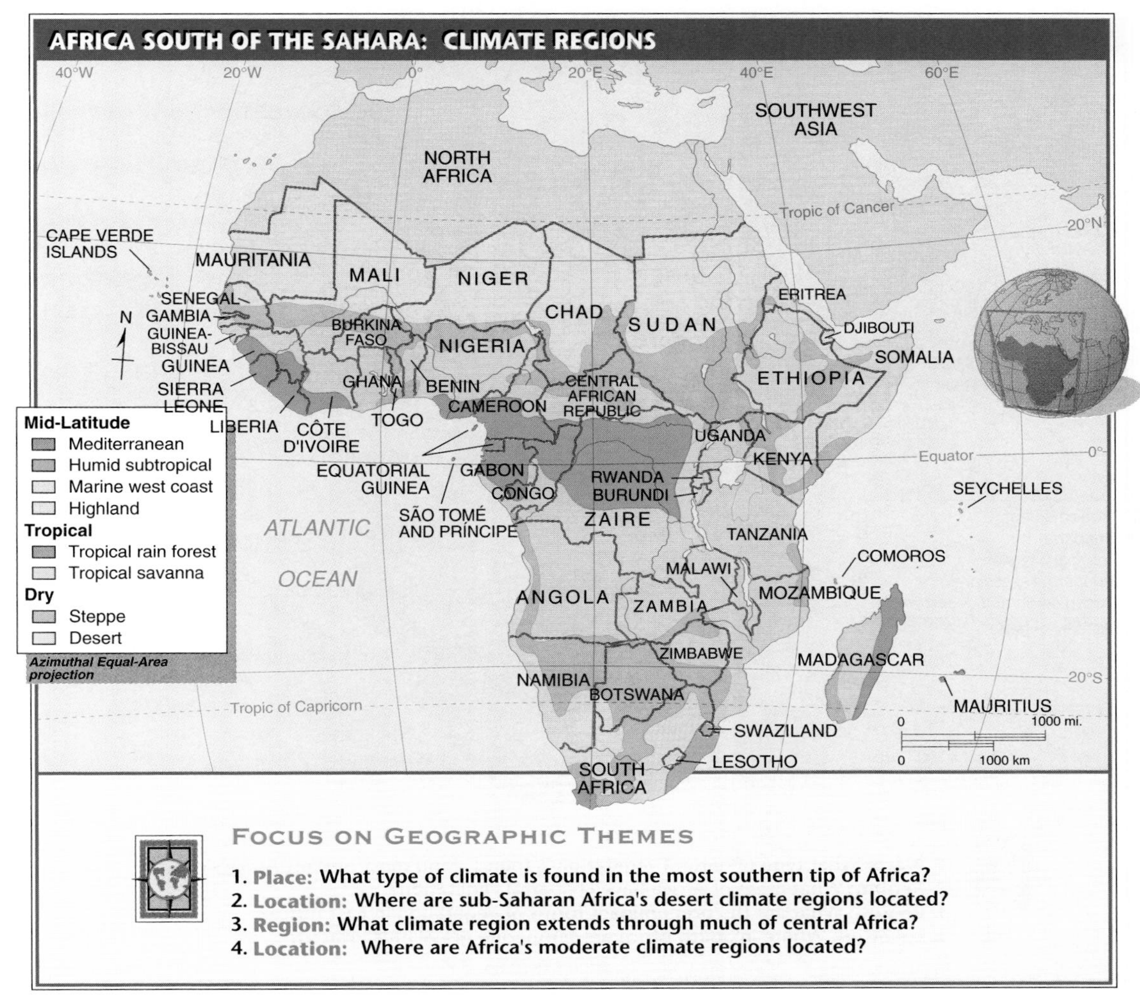

FOCUS ON GEOGRAPHIC THEMES

1. **Place:** What type of climate is found in the most southern tip of Africa?
2. **Location:** Where are sub-Saharan Africa's desert climate regions located?
3. **Region:** What climate region extends through much of central Africa?
4. **Location:** Where are Africa's moderate climate regions located?

TEACH

GUIDED PRACTICE

L1 Interpret a Map Assign each student a country from sub-Saharan Africa. Ask each person to locate the country on the map on page 425, identify its climate regions, and describe the location of each region.

INDEPENDENT PRACTICE

Guided Reading Have students complete Guided Reading Activity 20-2 in the TCR. **LEP**

Have students complete Vocabulary Activity 20 in the TCR.

Have students complete Unit Map Overlay Transparency 7 Activity in the TCR.

USING MAPS

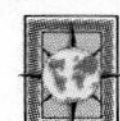

Answers:
1. Mediterranean; **2.** the coast of Namibia and the southern plateau to the west, covering much of Botswana; **3.** tropical; **4.** highlands of Kenya and the southern tip of Africa

Map Skills Practice
What part of Madagascar has a tropical rain forest climate? *(the east coast)*

ASSESS

CHECK FOR UNDERSTANDING

Assign Section 2 Review as homework or an in-class activity.

MULTICULTURAL PERSPECTIVE

Cultural Diffusion
During the late 1500s, Dutch settlers introduced hogs to Mauritius. Many hogs escaped and bred. These feral hogs destroyed the eggs of dodos—birds unique to the island. Dodos soon became extinct.

Cooperative Learning Activity

Help the students make a double-layer puzzle. Project Unit Map Overlay Transparency 7-2 on a large poster board and have a student trace the map and color the vegetation zones. Also have a student trace the map outline on corrugated cardboard and cut along the outline, preserving the outside portion.

Project Unit Map Overlay Transparency 7-3 on another piece of corrugated cardboard. Have a student trace the map, color the climate regions, and cut along the borders of the countries. Paste the corrugated cardboard with the Africa-shaped hole over the vegetation map. Piece together the climate map inside the cutout. Remember to include the map keys on the puzzle. When students remove a country, they can see what kind of vegetation grows in each climate region.

MEETING LESSON OBJECTIVES

Each objective below is tested by the questions that follow it in parentheses.

1. List the climate and vegetation patterns in Africa south of the Sahara. *(2)*

2. Describe how elevation affects climate in Africa south of the Sahara. *(3)*

EVALUATE

Assign the Section 2 Quiz in the TCR.

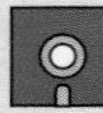

Use the Testmaker to create a customized quiz for Section 2.

USING MAPS

Answers:

1. desert scrub and desert waste; **2.** the tip of South Africa; **3.** tropical forest and tropical grassland; **4.** the area around Lesotho

Map Skills Practice

Drawing Conclusions In what areas of sub-Saharan Africa is herding livestock most likely important? *(the northern and west central areas)*

NATIONAL GEOGRAPHIC SOCIETY

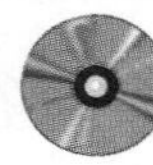

Videodisc

STV: WORLD GEOGRAPHY, VOLUME 2

Side 1, Chapter 1
Frames 12728-14986
Title: ***Africa***
Subject: Northern Africa: The Sahel

Side 1, Chapter 1
Frames 30988-36010
Title: ***Africa***
Subject: Southern Africa: The Savanna

The Sahel

Beyond the parched deserts stretch the steppe grasslands. The western part of this area is often referred to as the Sahel, from an Arabic word that means "coast." The Sahel lies between the desert and the more fertile grasslands to the south. Its climate alternates between a long, dry season and a short, wet season. Unfortunately, in recent years the rainy seasons have almost disappeared from the Sahel. A persistent drought has brought misery, famine, and hardship to much of the region.

Tropical Savanna

Beyond the drought-ridden steppes stretch the **savannas,** or tropical grasslands containing scattered trees. The savannas also alternate between wet and dry seasons. They, however, receive considerably more rain than the Sahel. In the wetter savannas of the southern plateaus, between 30 and 60 inches (76 and 152 cm) of rain falls annually.

In some parts of the savannas, which provide grazing for livestock and wild game, elephant grass grows to more than 15 feet (4.5 m) tall. To protect wildlife, governments have cre-

AFRICA SOUTH OF THE SAHARA: NATURAL VEGETATION

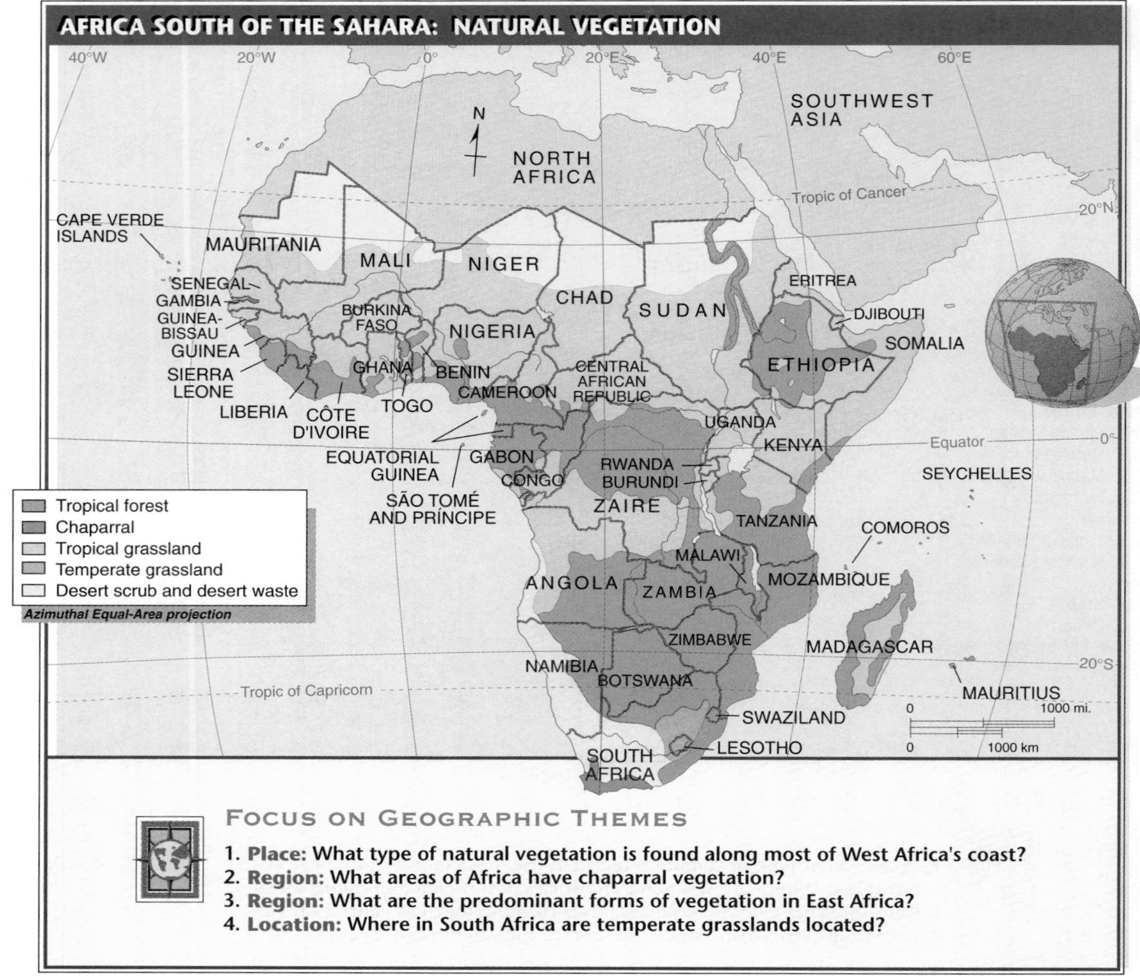

Focus on Geographic Themes

1. **Place:** What type of natural vegetation is found along most of West Africa's coast?
2. **Region:** What areas of Africa have chaparral vegetation?
3. **Region:** What are the predominant forms of vegetation in East Africa?
4. **Location:** Where in South Africa are temperate grasslands located?

Meeting Special Needs

Poor Learners Most students are familiar with the study system known as "SQ3R" (Survey, Question, Read, Recite, Review), but those with reading and learning problems often have difficulty surveying information. One task involved in surveying is predicting what kind of information will be given in a piece of text. Guide students to recognize that the first paragraph under each main head makes general statements and the rest of the subsection gives detailed information.

Geographic Themes

Human/Environment Interaction: The Sahel

Grazing and farming lands in the Sahel have been gradually swallowed up by the advancing Sahara. *How have changes in climate affected the people of the Sahel?*

ated huge game preserves such as Tanzania's Serengeti Plains and Kenya's Nairobi National Park.

Tropical Rain Forests

Many non-Africans imagine Africa as a land of vast tropical rain forests. The steamy tropical rain forest climate region, however, covers only about 8 percent of Africa and is centered mostly on the Equator. Here temperatures hover around 80°F (27°C), and rain falls daily.

The heavy rains **leach,** or wash away, many nutrients from the soil. The rain forests provide poor farmland but are rich in other vegetation. Yet the rain forests face destruction. Cocoa, rubber, and palm-oil plantations take more and more land. Logging companies that seek valuable hardwood trees have increased their harvesting. As is the case with rain forests elsewhere in the world, this climate region may someday disappear.

Moderate Climates

The map on page 425 shows pockets of moderate climates in the highlands of Kenya and the southern tip of Africa. These heavily populated areas have fertile soil, adequate rain, and a favorable climate—all good conditions for farming.

Section 2 Review

Checking for Understanding

1. **Define** savanna, leach.
2. **Locating Places** What are the main climate regions that run north and south from the Equator?
3. **Place** How do elevation and rainfall affect climate in sub-Saharan Africa?
4. **Human/Environment Interaction** Why might the rain forests of Africa face possible destruction?

Critical Thinking

5. **Determining Cause and Effect** Explain the causes of the climate problem in the Sahel and its effect on human and animal life.

ANSWERS TO SECTION 2 REVIEW

1. **savanna:** tropical grasslands having rainy and dry seasons; **leach:** to wash away nutrients from the soil
2. desert, steppe, tropical savanna, and tropical rain forest
3. Higher elevations result in cooler climates; plentiful rainfall yields lusher vegetation.
4. Cocoa, rubber, and palm-oil plantations cover more and more land, and logging companies have increased their harvesting.
5. Rainy seasons have almost disappeared from the Sahel. The resulting drought has brought misery, famine, and hardship to the region.

USING ILLUSTRATIONS

HUMAN/ENVIRONMENT INTERACTION Overgrazing, overcultivating, and drought all contribute to desertification.

Answer to Caption: *Drought has brought misery, famine, and hardship.*

RETEACH

Have students complete Reteaching Activity 20 in the TCR.

ENRICH

Have students complete Enrichment Activity 20 in the TCR.

CLOSE

Have each student name a country in sub-Saharan Africa and vegetation that grows there.

Videodisc

STV: RAIN FOREST

Side 1, Chapter 1
Frames 00002-08879
Title: ***Introduction*** **(in its entirety)**
Subject: Introduction to climatic conditions and animals of the rain forest

STV: RAIN FOREST

Side 2, Chapter 6
Frames 33538-49359
Title: ***Upward and Onward*** **(in its entirety)**
Subject: Hundreds of thousands of unique life forms, and the possibility of their extinction due to the destruction of the rain forest

TEACH

Write the words "reliable" and "unreliable" on the chalkboard. Then ask: "What makes a person reliable or unreliable?" *(A reliable person fulfills most obligations and promises; an unreliable person does not.)* Summarize by saying, "A reliable person can be trusted. Similarly, sources of information may be reliable or unreliable. What makes a source reliable?"

Have students read the skill on page 428. Ask: "What factors indicate the reliability of a source?" *(expertise in the subject, purpose of the information, biases and opinions)* Have students explain how to use each factor to determine reliability. Point out mainstream publications are usually reliable sources because they maintain high standards of accuracy.

Skills Practice For additional practice, have students complete Skill Activity 20 in the TCR.

GLENCOE TECHNOLOGY

Videodisc

GEOGRAPHY AND THE ENVIRONMENT
THE INFINITE VOYAGE
To the Edge of the Earth

Chapter 5
Disc 1 Side B
Title: ***The Tropical Rain Forest***
Subject: Rain forests support lush vegetation even though the soil is poor in nutrients

CRITICAL THINKING SKILLS

Evaluating Information

Remember the old expression: "Don't believe everything you read"? It's always important to question and evaluate the accuracy and reliability of information.

REVIEWING THE SKILL

There are two main purposes for evaluating information—to determine its relevance and its reliability. First, analyze the purpose and nature of the information. Decide whether it is a primary or secondary source. Both kinds of sources can provide valid information, but each has limitations. For example, primary sources (those written by eyewitnesses to events) may seem more accurate than secondary sources. However, because the author of a primary source was directly involved in the events, he or she may be less objective and more biased than a secondary source.

Second, for any kind of source, you must evaluate its *reliability*. In determining reliability, consider these factors: 1) Is this source an expert on the topic? A meteorologist may be a reliable source of information on weather, but not on sports. 2) What is the purpose of the information? A source that wants to persuade you to buy something or do something is less reliable than a source that just provides information. 3) Is the source biased, or influenced by strong beliefs and opinions? For example, two people with different political views may watch the same speech on television, but their political biases may produce very different accounts of the speech. To evaluate sources, apply the following steps:

- Determine whether it is a primary or secondary source.
- Evaluate reliability by asking these questions: Does the source know this topic well? What is the purpose? What are the biases?
- Compare the information with other sources to see if they support or contradict each other.

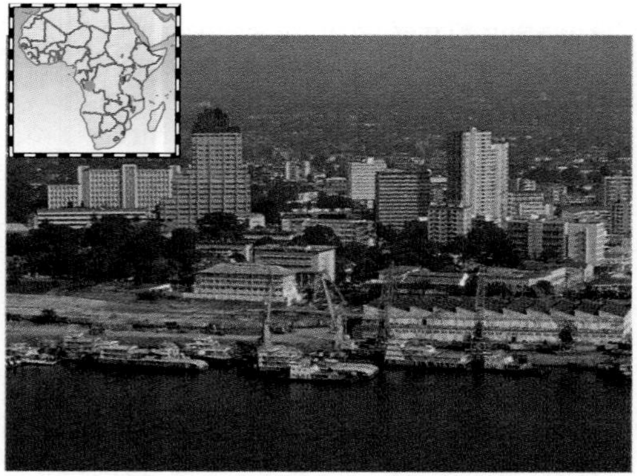

Kinshasa, Zaire

PRACTICING THE SKILL

Africa has extensive river systems that have played an important role in the continent's history and development. The Zaire River is Africa's second-longest river. Below, a writer discusses the river, and a part of the land through which it winds. Read the excerpt, and answer the following questions:

1. Is this a primary or secondary source? Why?
2. Is the writer an expert on the topic discussed? Why or why not?
3. Do you think the information about the river and its environment is reliable? Why or why not?

At Kisangani the river, now called Zaire, begins its long easy curl through the central forest. As it bends around toward the southwest, the river widens to 9 miles [14.5 km], its glassy waters dotted with myriad islands. Kinshasa lies at the head of Livingstone Falls, actually 220 miles [354 km] of cataracts and rapids where the river crashes through the Crystal Mountains, the western rim of the Congo Basin. The ocean port, Matadi, lies at the foot of the falls.

Now called the bas fleuve (lower river), it once again spreads out, wide and deep enough for oceangoing ships to sail down the final hundred miles to the Atlantic. But the river doesn't stop there. The current is so strong that its brown waters are hurled nearly a hundred miles into the sea and have gouged a 4,000-foot [1,200-m] canyon in the ocean floor.[1]

For additional practice in this skill, see Practicing Skills on page 430 of the Chapter 20 Review.

[1] Source: Robert Caputo. "Lifeline for a Nation–Zaire River" in NATIONAL GEOGRAPHIC, November, 1991, p. 29.

ANSWERS TO PRACTICING THE SKILL

1. probably a primary source because it is a first-person narrative
2. Although his credentials aren't listed, he seems to know many facts on the topic.
3. It is probably reliable because it was published in a well-respected magazine.

chapter 20

HIGHLIGHTS

1 The Land

Key Terms

escarpment (p. 419)
cataract (p. 420)
fault (p. 420)

Summary

- A series of steplike plateaus dominates lands south of the Sahara.
- High elevations and a narrow coastal plain have historically hindered travel to the interior of Africa.
- The Great Rift Valley slices through East Africa and affects the landforms of nations from Ethiopia to Mozambique.
- Most of Africa's large freshwater lakes nestle in cuts in the Great Rift Valley.
- Four major river systems tumble over escarpments in dramatic rapids and falls as they spill off the continent.

Village and market along the Zaire River in central Africa

2 The Climate and Vegetation

Key Terms

savanna (p. 426)
leach (p. 427)

Summary

- Although most of Africa lies in the tropics, it still exhibits diverse climates and vegetation.
- Elevation and rainfall are the main factors influencing climate variations in sub-Saharan Africa.
- The main climate regions in Africa south of the Sahara include: desert, steppe, tropical savanna, and tropical rain forest.
- Africa has an abundance of mineral wealth, but it lacks the fuels to develop it.
- Deserts and steppes cover more than two-thirds of the land surface in Africa.

Desertification in western Africa

CHAPTER 20 HIGHLIGHTS

USING THE CHAPTER 20 HIGHLIGHTS

Use the Chapter 20 Highlights to preview, review, condense, or reteach the chapter.

PREVIEW/REVIEW

Vocabulary PuzzleMaker Software reinforces the Key Terms used in Chapter 20.

Student Self-Test and Review Software allows students to review Chapter 20 content.

CONDENSE

Have students read the Chapter 20 Highlights.

 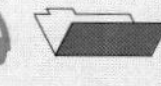

Have students listen to the Chapter 20 Audiocassettes in the TCR. Spanish Audiocassettes are also available.

Assign the Chapter 20 Audiocassette Activity and give students the Chapter 20 Audiocassette Quiz.

Have students complete the Guided Reading Activities for Chapter 20 in the TCR. Spanish Guided Reading Activities are also available.

RETEACH

Have students complete Reteaching Activity 20 in the TCR. Spanish Reteaching Activities are also available.

Map Activity

Identify and Locate Copy and distribute page 36 of the Outline Map Resource Book. On the map, have students locate, draw, and label the following features: the Drakensberg Mountains, Kilimanjaro, the Great Rift Valley, Lake Victoria, the Nile River, the Zaire River, the Zambezi River, and Victoria Falls.

Ask students to shade the desert and tropical rain forest regions of Africa south of the Sahara. Remind them to include a map key. Refer the students to the maps on page 425 and in the Unit Atlas for help.

Chapter 20 Review

GLENCOE TECHNOLOGY

Videodisc

Use Chapter 20 MindJogger Videoquiz to review students' knowledge before administering the Chapter 20 Test.

MINDJOGGER VIDEOQUIZ

Chapter 20
Disc 3 Side A

The MindJogger Videoquiz is also available on videocassette.

ANSWERS

Reviewing Key Terms

1. escarpments
2. faults
3. cataracts
4. leach
5. savanna

Reviewing Facts

6. because of the step-like plateaus that follow one another from east to west
7. Tremendous pressure from violent movements of the earth's crust caused cracks in the earth's surface.
8. because of the many cataracts and the sharp rise in elevation from coast to coast
9. It is the only region to lie across all three tropical latitudes.
10. High elevations produce cool climates.
11. grasses and scattered trees
12. A tributary of the Zambezi flows into and ends in the Kalahari.
13. the spread of plantations and logging

chapter 20 REVIEW

Reviewing Key Terms

Choose the vocabulary term that best completes each of the sentences below. Write your answers on a separate sheet of paper.

escarpment (p. 419)
cataract (p. 420)
fault (p. 420)
savanna (p. 426)
leach (p. 427)

SECTION 1

1. Steep cliffs or slopes that separate plateaus in Africa are called ____.
2. The Great Rift Valley developed when volcanic activity created ____ in the earth's crust.
3. Because of Africa's plateaus, most rivers tumble off waterfalls or ____.

SECTION 2

4. ____ relates to the rain forests of Africa.
5. An area of grasslands with scattered trees is called a ____.

Reviewing the Facts

SECTION 1

6. Why do some geographers refer to Africa as a "continent of plateaus"?
7. What forces helped create the Great Rift Valley?
8. Why has it been historically difficult to travel into the interior of Africa by river?

SECTION 2

9. Why is Africa south of the Sahara said to be the most tropical region on the earth?
10. Why do the Kenya highlands have a milder climate than northern Zaire?
11. What vegetation exists in the tropical savannas?
12. How was a delta able to form on the sands of the Kalahari Desert?
13. What forces threaten the rain forests of Africa?

Critical Thinking

14. **Analyzing Information** Many myths surround African mountains. What geographic data help explain the awe in which many mountains are held?
15. **Making Comparisons** Choose two climate regions in Africa south of the Sahara. How are they different? How are they alike?

Geographic Themes

16. **Movement** What geographic factors discouraged the exchange of ideas between Europe and sub-Saharan Africa until recent times?
17. **Location** How does location set Africa apart as a continent?

Practicing Skills

Evaluating Information

Refer to the Evaluating Information skill on page 428.

18. What biases might this source have about Africa?
19. How is the account of the Zaire River supported by the text of Chapter 20?

Using the Unit Atlas

Refer to the physical geography section of the Unit Atlas on pages 412–413.

20. What river drains most of west central Africa?
21. About what percentage of Africa has a tropical climate?

Projects

Individual Activity

Because of its great elevation, Kilimanjaro includes many climates. Research Kilimanjaro

Critical Thinking

14. Answers will vary but may include that snowcapped mountains in a tropical land probably inspired myths.
15. Students should mention rainfall, elevation, vegetation, and so on.

Geographic Themes

16. the sudden rise in land and the waterfalls that prevented easy access inland
17. It is the only continent to lie within all three tropical latitudes.

and write a short description of what climbers might see on their way to the summit.

Cooperative Learning Activity

Each summer, trucks carry European students across the continent of Africa. With a group of three or four classmates, design a three-month tour that takes students from Khartoum, Sudan, to Cape Town, South Africa that focuses on the vegetation areas of Africa. Prepare an information packet on each area crossed. The packets should include travel tips and, if possible, maps.

Writing About Geography

Cause and Effect

Imagine you are a geographer from Kenya invited to write and deliver a paper on the Great Rift Valley to the National Council of Geographic Education. Using your journal, text, and other references, write a descriptive paper about the valley's major characteristics. Be sure your paper explains the links between present-day physical features and ancient volcanic activity.

Locating Places

AFRICA SOUTH OF THE SAHARA: PHYSICAL GEOGRAPHY

Match the letters on the map with the physical features of Africa south of the Sahara. Write your answers on a separate sheet of paper.

1. Lake Chad
2. Okavango Delta
3. Zaire River
4. Great Rift Valley
5. Lake Tanganyika
6. Zambezi River
7. Kilimanjaro
8. Lake Victoria
9. Kalahari Desert
10. Lake Malawi

Chapter 20 Review

Practicing Skills

18. The author describes a beautiful, wild river. Others might describe the same river in a negative way.

19. Section 1 states that the Zaire River is the largest river system south of the Sahara and that it has created a huge basin.

Using the Unit Atlas

20. the Zaire River

21. about 90 percent

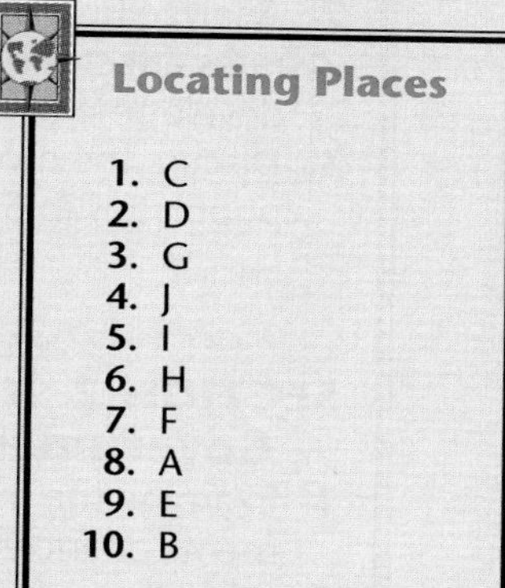

Locating Places
1. C
2. D
3. G
4. J
5. I
6. H
7. F
8. A
9. E
10. B

Chapter Bonus Test Question

This question may be used for extra credit on the chapter test.

Why might pockets of minerals and precious metals in the interior of sub-Saharan Africa be difficult to reach and carry out?

(Answer: The sudden rise in land and the rapids and waterfalls at the edge of the continent prevent easy access to the interior by river or roadway. For the same reasons, ore could not be shipped out easily by river or roads.)

CHAPTER 21

PLANNING GUIDE

The Cultural Geography of Africa South of the Sahara

CHAPTER ORGANIZER

Daily Lesson Objectives	Multimedia	Teacher Classroom Resources
SECTION 1 Population Patterns 1. Identify the major population trends in sub-Saharan Africa. 2. Analyze how economic growth rates affect Africa's population development. 3. Discuss the diverse peoples who populate sub-Saharan Africa.	Section Focus Transparency 21-1 Chapter 21 Vocabulary PuzzleMaker Software Unit Map Overlay Transparencies 1-10, 7 Testmaker STV: World Geography, Volume 2 Picture Atlas of the World	Reproducible Lesson Plan 21-1 Foods Around the World 6 Guided Reading Activity 21-1 Spanish Guided Reading Activity 21-1 Workbook Activity 21-1 Section Quiz 21-1
SECTION 2 History and Government 1. Examine the major accomplishments of ancient peoples in sub-Saharan Africa. 2. Describe how European rule disrupted patterns of life. 3. Summarize the challenges facing sub-Saharan Africa.	Section Focus Transparency 21-2 Political Map Transparency 7 Testmaker Picture Atlas of the World	Reproducible Lesson Plan 21-2 Guided Reading Activity 21-2 Spanish Guided Reading Activity 21-2 Vocabulary Activity 21 Workbook Activity 21-2 Section Quiz 21-2
SECTION 3 Cultures and Lifestyles 1. Name the cultural factors that help define sub-Saharan Africa as a region. 2. Relate how language and religion have contributed to diversity. 3. Illustrate the ways in which sub-Saharan art forms have touched upon the world. 4. Explain the obstacles to universal education.	Section Focus Transparency 21-3 World Cultures Transparencies 11, 12 World Music: Cultural Traditions, Lesson 6 Testmaker Picture Atlas of the World	Reproducible Lesson Plan 21-3 Guided Reading Activity 21-3 Spanish Guided Reading Activity 21-3 Workbook Activity 21-3 Enrichment Activity 21 World Literature Reading 6 Skill Activity 21 Section Quiz 21-3
CHAPTER REVIEW AND EVALUATION	Chapter 21 English (or Spanish) Audiocassettes MindJogger Videoquiz Testmaker Student Self-Test and Review Software	Reteaching Activity 21 Spanish Reteaching Activity 21 Chapter 21 Test Form A and Form B

0:00 *If time does not permit teaching the entire chapter, summarize using the Chapter 21 Highlights on page 447, and the Chapter 21 English (or Spanish) Audiocassettes. Review students' knowledge using the Glencoe MindJogger Videoquiz.*

KEY TO ABILITY LEVELS

Teaching strategies have been coded for varying learning styles and abilities.

L1 **BASIC** activities for all students

L2 **AVERAGE** activities for average to above-average students

L3 **CHALLENGING** activities for above-average students

LEP **LIMITED ENGLISH PROFICIENCY** activities

Performance Assessment

Planning Industrial Growth Ask students to assume that they are entrepreneurs who would like to be involved in the industrial development of sub-Saharan Africa. Organize the class into groups, and assign each group a country in the culture region. Using physical, resource, and population maps, students in each group should select one or more industrial products in which they would like to invest in the country. These products should reflect a need of the people in the country.

Student groups should also decide on a location for building manufacturing plants, attracting new workers, and implementing a new invention. Each group should present its proposal to the rest of the class, which will assume the role of investors. The "investors" should ask specific questions that the presenting group will use for revision purposes.

POSSIBLE RUBRIC FEATURES: Content information, concept attainment, decision-making process skills, collaborative and communication skills, argumentation skills, creative abilities

For additional professional and classroom resources, see Chapter Resources, pages T46–T51.

TEACHER'S CORNER

INDEX TO NATIONAL GEOGRAPHIC MAGAZINE

The following articles may be used for research relating to this chapter:

- "The Twilight of Apartheid: Life in Black South Africa," by Charles E. Cobb, Jr., February 1993.
- "Botswana: The Adopted Land," by Arthur Zich, December 1990.
- "Oasis of Art in the Sahara," by Henri Lhote, August 1987.
- "Madagascar: A World Apart," by Alison Jolly, February 1987.
- "Senegambia—A Now and Future Nation," by Michael and Aubine Kirtley, August 1985.
- "Ethiopia: Revolution in an Ancient Empire, by Robert Caputo, May 1983.
- "The Ivory Coast—African Success Story," by Michael and Aubine Kirtley, July 1982.
- "Namibia: Nearly a Nation?" by Bryan Hodgson, June 1982.
- "Sudan: Arab-African Giant," by Robert Caputo, March 1982.

NATIONAL GEOGRAPHIC SOCIETY PRODUCTS AVAILABLE FROM GLENCOE

To order the following products for use with this chapter, contact your local Glencoe sales representative or call Glencoe at 1-800-334-7344:

- *Picture Atlas of the World* (CD-ROM)
- *STV: World Geography, Africa and Europe* (Videodisc)
- *ZipZapMap! World* (Software)
- *GeoBee* (Software)
- *Images of the World* (Posters)
- *Eye on the Environment* (Posters)
- *Physical Geography of the World* (Transparencies)
- *Picture Atlas of Our 50 States* (Book)

ADDITIONAL NATIONAL GEOGRAPHIC SOCIETY PRODUCTS

To order the following products for use with this chapter, call National Geographic Society at 1-800-368-2728:

- *South Africa: After Apartheid* (Video)

chapter 21 The Cultural Geography of Africa South of the Sahara

PERFORMANCE ASSESSMENT

Refer to the Planning Guide on page 432B for a Performance Assessment Activity for this chapter. See the *Performance Assessment Activities* booklet for additional suggestions.

CHAPTER OBJECTIVES

1. **Infer** that overpopulation in sub-Saharan Africa has resulted, in part, from an uneven distribution of people and natural resources.
2. **Appreciate** that the region's history has been characterized by movements of people.
3. **Recognize** that history and beliefs help bind together sub-Saharan Africa.

GLENCOE TECHNOLOGY

Videodisc

Use Chapter 21 MindJogger Videoquiz to preview chapter content.

MINDJOGGER VIDEOQUIZ

Chapter 21
Disc 3 Side B

The MindJogger Videoquiz is also available on videocassette.

CHAPTER FOCUS

Geographic Setting

Africa south of the Sahara constitutes the third most populous—and fastest-growing—region in the world. More than 550 million people from some 2,000 distinct groups populate the land.

Geographic Themes

Section 1 Population Patterns
PLACE Overpopulation in sub-Saharan Africa has resulted, in part, from an uneven distribution of people and natural resources.

Section 2 History and Government
MOVEMENT The region's history has been characterized by movements of people.

Section 3 Cultures and Lifestyles
REGION History and beliefs help bind together sub-Saharan Africa.

▲ Photograph: *Village market in Zaire*

EXTRA CREDIT PROJECT

Stage a Musical Have interested students write and perform a musical skit about African history or life in Africa today. Tell them to accompany the words and actions with the kinds of music discussed in the chapter. For instance, they might play African cuts from Paul Simon's "Graceland" or an album by an African group such as Mahlathini and the Mahotella Queens. Suggest that they look for the music at the library. Also suggest that they research African textiles and try to simulate African designs in costumes for the musical.

1 SECTION Population Patterns

SETTING THE SCENE

Read to Discover . . .
- the major population trends in sub-Saharan Africa.
- how economic growth rates affect Africa's population development.
- the diverse peoples who populate sub-Saharan Africa.

Key Terms
- gross domestic product (GDP)
- per capita income
- urbanization
- ethnic group

Identify and Locate
Rwanda, Chad, Gabon, Lagos, Johannesburg, Cape Town

Gonder, Ethiopia

My family and I celebrate Christmas Day by going to church. The men wear white pants, a long white shirt and a white scarf. Women wear long white dresses decorated with fringe or embroidery. We give presents to our friends and family. I like to give people fresh flowers.

Alemu Getachew

Africa south of the Sahara boasts one of the world's youngest populations. About half the region's people are no more than 15 years old. One of Africa's many teenagers wrote the postcard on this page. Alemu Getachew describes the people of Ethiopia—only a small part of the 570 million people who live in sub-Saharan Africa, the third-most populous region in the world.

REGION

A Region of Variety

Sub-Saharan Africa claims the world's highest birthrate and the world's shortest life expectancy. The region has the world's highest population growth rate and the world's lowest economic growth rate. It possesses some of the world's most densely populated areas and some of the world's least densely populated areas. These are but a few of the characteristics of the population in sub-Saharan Africa today.

A Booming Population

With a high infant mortality and a short life expectancy, Zaire's population grows at 3.3 percent a year. In 1994 its population stood at more than 42.5 million. The example of Zaire is repeated throughout the region. As the decade of the 1990s began, the annual growth rate for Africa south of the Sahara stood at about 3 percent. If sub-Saharan Africa keeps growing at its present rate, experts predict that the region's population will double in less than 20 years.

LESSON PLAN
Chapter 21, Section 1

FOCUS

SECTION OBJECTIVES

1. **Identify** the major population trends in sub-Saharan Africa.
2. **Analyze** how economic growth rates affect Africa's population development.
3. **Discuss** the diverse peoples who populate sub-Saharan Africa.

ABOUT THE POSTCARD

Alemu also likes to share a big Christmas dinner with his family and friends. A favorite dish is chicken stew and homemade bread.

BELLRINGER MOTIVATIONAL ACTIVITY

Project the Section 1 Focus Transparency and have students answer the questions.

PRETEACHING VOCABULARY

Have selected students make up meanings for the Key Terms. Read the made-up and real meanings to the class, and have students vote for those they think are correct. Students earn a point for each correct vote they cast. Those who made up meanings earn a point for each vote their definition receives.

Use the Vocabulary PuzzleMaker Software to create a crossword or word search puzzle.

NATIONAL GEOGRAPHIC SOCIETY

Videodisc

STV: WORLD GEOGRAPHY, VOLUME 2

Side 1, Chapter 1
Frames 625-4765
Title: *Africa*
Subject: Overview

Classroom Resources for Section 1

BLACKLINE MASTERS:
Reproducible Lesson Plan 21-1
Foods Around the World 6
Guided Reading Activity 21-1
Workbook Activity 21-1
Section Quiz 21-1

TRANSPARENCIES:
Section Focus Transparency 21-1
Unit Map Overlay Transparencies 1-10, 7

MULTIMEDIA:

Vocabulary PuzzleMaker Software
Testmaker

STV: World Geography, Volume 2

Picture Atlas of the World

TEACH

GUIDED PRACTICE

 Implement Foods Around the World 6 as a class activity.

L1 Make a Circle Graph Help students illustrate the distribution of ethnic groups in South Africa's population of 40.6 million. On acetate strips, write the following labels: 74% black ethnic groups, 14% descendants of Europeans, 9% mixed descendants of Europeans, blacks, and Asians, 3% descendants of Asian laborers. On Unit Map Overlay Transparency 1-10, divide the blank circle graph into parts that correspond to the percentages above and project the transparency. Have students match the labels with the correct parts and add a title to the graph.

USING ILLUSTRATIONS

PLACE Dakar also could be considered a national health center. Seventy percent of the doctors in Senegal practice there.

Answer to Caption: *for mild climate and easy access to water and fertile soil*

Geographic Themes

Place: Dakar, Senegal

Dakar, the capital of Senegal, is a modern port city of West Africa that has undergone tremendous growth in population. *Why do most sub-Saharan Africans settle in coastal areas?*

Uneven Population Density

If Africa's population were spread out evenly across the continent, there would be about 30 people per square mile. This compares favorably to the 170 per square mile (66 per sq. km) packed into western Europe. Africa's population, however, is not evenly distributed. An estimated 808 people per square mile (312 per sq. km) squeeze into Rwanda, while only 6 people per square mile (2 per sq. km) fill Namibia and Botswana.

Such uneven population distribution is closely linked to the region's physical geography. Desert and arid steppes cover nearly two-thirds of Africa. As a result, most sub-Saharan Africans crowd along the coast of western Africa, around the lakes of eastern Africa, and along the coast of southeastern Africa. They are lured to these areas by easy access to water, fertile soil, and mild climates good for farming. In describing Rwanda, the world's eleventh most densely populated nation, an expert on Africa writes:

The rugged, spectacularly beautiful hills and mountains of Rwanda are tiered like giant staircases. On each level . . . a family clan lives and farms. The dirt roads that wind through the valleys and across the hills are as busy as the sidewalks of New York's Fifth Avenue during lunch hour, a shoulder-to-shoulder procession of pedestrians. . . .

HUMAN/ENVIRONMENT INTERACTION

Population and Economics

Africa's limited farmland has strained the ability of governments to feed their people. In recent years, huge expanses of land have been exhausted through intensive cultivation, loss of soil fertility, and crippling droughts. United Nations officials estimate that food production in sub-Saharan Africa has dropped 20 percent since 1970. Yet the region's population has nearly doubled. Although some 70 percent of sub-Saharan Africans work as farmers, they are producing less and eating less.

Famine and poor nutrition claim many lives, especially infants and young children. Impure water is another cause of death. Only about 37 percent of sub-Saharan Africans have clean water to drink. Diseases are widespread. Insects such as the tsetse fly carry viruses that kill cattle, horses, and people. Acquired Immunodeficiency Syndrome (AIDS), a worldwide disease, has reached epidemic proportions in sub-Saharan Africa. The situation is worsened by a lack of both doctors to treat disease and up-to-date equipment to test and screen blood.

Sub-Saharan Africa suffers the lowest standards of living in the world. While the region's population grows at 3 percent, its economy limps ahead at about 1.5 percent. The 550 million people of sub-Saharan Africa generate a combined **gross domestic product (GDP)**, or total output of goods and services within a

Cooperative Learning Activity

Have a group of students compare the populations of the countries mentioned on pages 434 and 435 by drawing a pictograph on the chalkboard. Tell them to make different colored stick figures to represent different numbers of people, such as a red figure for 1 million people, a blue figure for 100,000 people, and so on. Supply the students with colored chalk and the following data:

COUNTRY	POPULATION
Botswana	1,400,000
Chad	6,500,000
Gabon	1,100,000
Namibia	1,600,000
Rwanda	7,700,000

country or region, of about $150 billion. This is roughly the same GDP as Belgium, a nation of about 10 million people.

Standards of living vary widely in the region. In Chad, the **per capita income**, or average per person income, hovers around $220. Gabon, on the other hand, enjoys a per capita income of $4,450, which is based upon oil and mining. Yet even Gabon lags far behind the $20,880 per capita income of Belgium. The low per capita incomes of sub-Saharan Africa translate into too little capital to develop the health care, food production, and industry necessary to improve the overall standard of living.

MOVEMENT

Rapid Urbanization

Although Africa is the least urbanized of any continent, it is urbanizing at the world's fastest rate. In 1950, only about 35 million Africans lived in cities. By the year 2000, population experts predict that 350 million will live in cities. In less than 50 years, the number of urban Africans will have increased 10 times!

Most of the cities in sub-Saharan Africa lie on the coast, along major rivers, or near sources of valuable resources. They grew up largely as trading centers. Lagos, Nigeria, start-

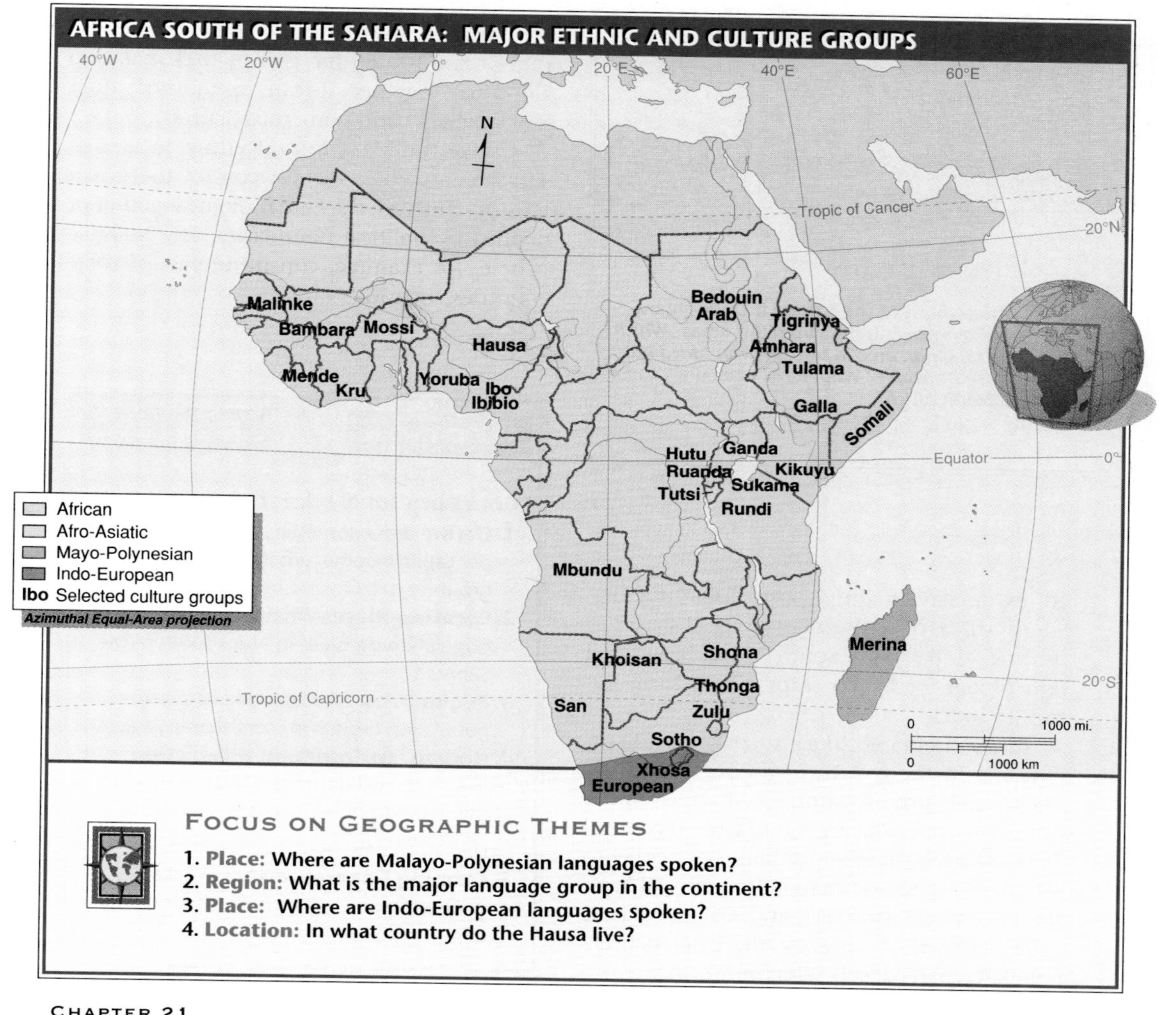

FOCUS ON GEOGRAPHIC THEMES

1. **Place:** Where are Malayo-Polynesian languages spoken?
2. **Region:** What is the major language group in the continent?
3. **Place:** Where are Indo-European languages spoken?
4. **Location:** In what country do the Hausa live?

INDEPENDENT PRACTICE

Guided Reading Have students complete Guided Reading Activity 21-1 in the TCR. **LEP**

Have students complete Unit Map Overlay Transparency 7 Activity in the TCR.

ASSESS

CHECK FOR UNDERSTANDING

Assign Section 1 Review as homework or an in-class activity.

MEETING LESSON OBJECTIVES

Each objective below is tested by the questions that follow it in parentheses.

1. **Identify** the major population trends in sub-Saharan Africa. *(3)*
2. **Analyze** how economic growth rates affect Africa's population development. *(2, 4)*
3. **Discuss** the diverse peoples who populate sub-Saharan Africa. *(5)*

USING MAPS

Answers:
1. Madagascar; **2.** African; **3.** southern South Africa and Lesotho; **4.** Nigeria

Map Skills Practice

Interpreting a Map To which language group does the Somalis' language belong? *(Afro-Asiatic)*

Meeting Special Needs

Language Deficient Students with language problems often have difficulty seeing differences in similar words. The objectives for this section require students to identify, analyze, and discuss. Point out that identifying usually involves listing, analyzing requires drawing conclusions based on information in the reading, and discussing requires giving details about a topic. Provide opportunities for identification, analysis, and discussion in the context of normal lesson-time conversation.

EVALUATE

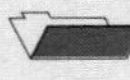 Assign the Section 1 Quiz in the TCR.

 Use the Testmaker to create a customized quiz for Section 1.

RETEACH

 Have students complete Workbook Activity 21-1 found in the TCR.

ENRICH

To show the mixed emotions a move to the city evokes for Africans, read excerpts from *Weep Not, Child* by Ngugi wa Thiong'o.

CLOSE

Have students write a postcard to Alemu, describing any special clothing they might wear for a holiday.

USING CHARTS

 *Answers:* Lagos; Cape Town, Johannesburg, Durban

Skills Practice
How many cities in sub-Saharan Africa have populations greater than 2 million? *(three)*

 **CD-ROM**

PICTURE ATLAS OF THE WORLD
Click the "Video" button of Tanzania to view the Masai and Serengeti National Park.

AFRICA SOUTH OF THE SAHARA: METROPOLITAN AREAS

City and Country	Population*
Lagos, Nigeria	7,998,000
Kinshasa, Zaire	3,747,000
Abidjan, Côte d'Ivoire	2,700,000
Cape Town, South Africa	1,900,000
Johannesburg, South Africa	1,900,000
Dakar, Senegal	1,700,000
Addis Ababa, Ethiopia	1,600,000
Dar es Salaam, Tanzania	1,400,000
Ibadan, Nigeria	1,300,000
Luanda, Angola	1,100,000
Durban, South Africa	1,100,000
Lusaka, Zambia	982,000
Nairobi, Kenya	959,000
Accra, Ghana	949,000
Maputo, Mozambique	931,000

*Cities with population of 900,000 or more, based on available estimates
Source: *The World Almanac,* 1995

CHART STUDY

Africa south of the Sahara includes many rapidly growing metropolitan areas. ***Which metropolitan area in sub-Saharan Africa has the most people? What large cities are located in South Africa?***

ed as a slave-trading post. Johannesburg, South Africa, owes its origins to gold strikes in the area. Cape Town, South Africa, began as a port of call for Dutch ships sailing from Europe to India.

Today trade continues to play an important role in the growth of the region's cities. But so does **urbanization,** or the movement of people from rural areas into cities. Economic hardships have driven millions of people to seek new opportunities in cities such as Lagos, Nairobi, Accra, Kinshasa, and Dar es Salaam. Urban areas now comprise the most densely populated parts of sub-Saharan Africa.

PLACE

Population Diversity

Wide differences between rural and urban Africans have increased the diversity of an already incredible mix of people. Anyone who thinks of Africans as a homogeneous, or similar, mass of people is mistaken. East Africa, for example, provides home to many Asians and a variety of *mzungu,* or whites, from more than a dozen nations, including the United States. It is also home to hundreds of African **ethnic groups,** or people with similar histories and cultures.

The Maasai, for example, form one of the 70 ethnic groups that make up Kenya and the more than 100 ethnic groups that make up Tanzania. Together Africans speak more than 800 languages and numerous dialects.

Unlike the Maasai, most ethnic groups in sub-Saharan Africa do not control their own territory. Instead, they are brought together or divided by political boundaries. The Malinke people, for example, constitute part of three countries, instead of one.

SECTION 1 REVIEW

Checking for Understanding

1. **Define** gross domestic product (GDP), per capita income, urbanization, ethnic group.
2. **Locating Places** What factors determine population densities in Africa south of the Sahara?
3. **Region** What overall trend characterizes population growth in sub-Saharan Africa?
4. **Human/Environment Interaction** How is the economic growth rate linked to the standard of living in Africa?

Critical Thinking

5. **Forming Generalizations** What valid generalization can you form about the mix of people in sub-Saharan Africa?

ANSWERS TO SECTION 1 REVIEW

1. **gross domestic product:** total output of goods and services within a country or region; **per capita income:** average per person income; **urbanization:** movement of people from rural areas into cities; **ethnic group:** people with similar histories and cultures
2. Population densities are determined by access to water, fertile soil, and mild climate.
3. a more than 3.2 percent annual growth rate despite high infant mortality and short life expectancy
4. The low economic growth results in too little capital for health care, food production, and industry necessary to improve the standard of living.
5. Answers will vary but may include that political boundaries bring together or divide ethnic groups in sub-Saharan Africa.

NATIONAL GEOGRAPHIC GEOFACTS

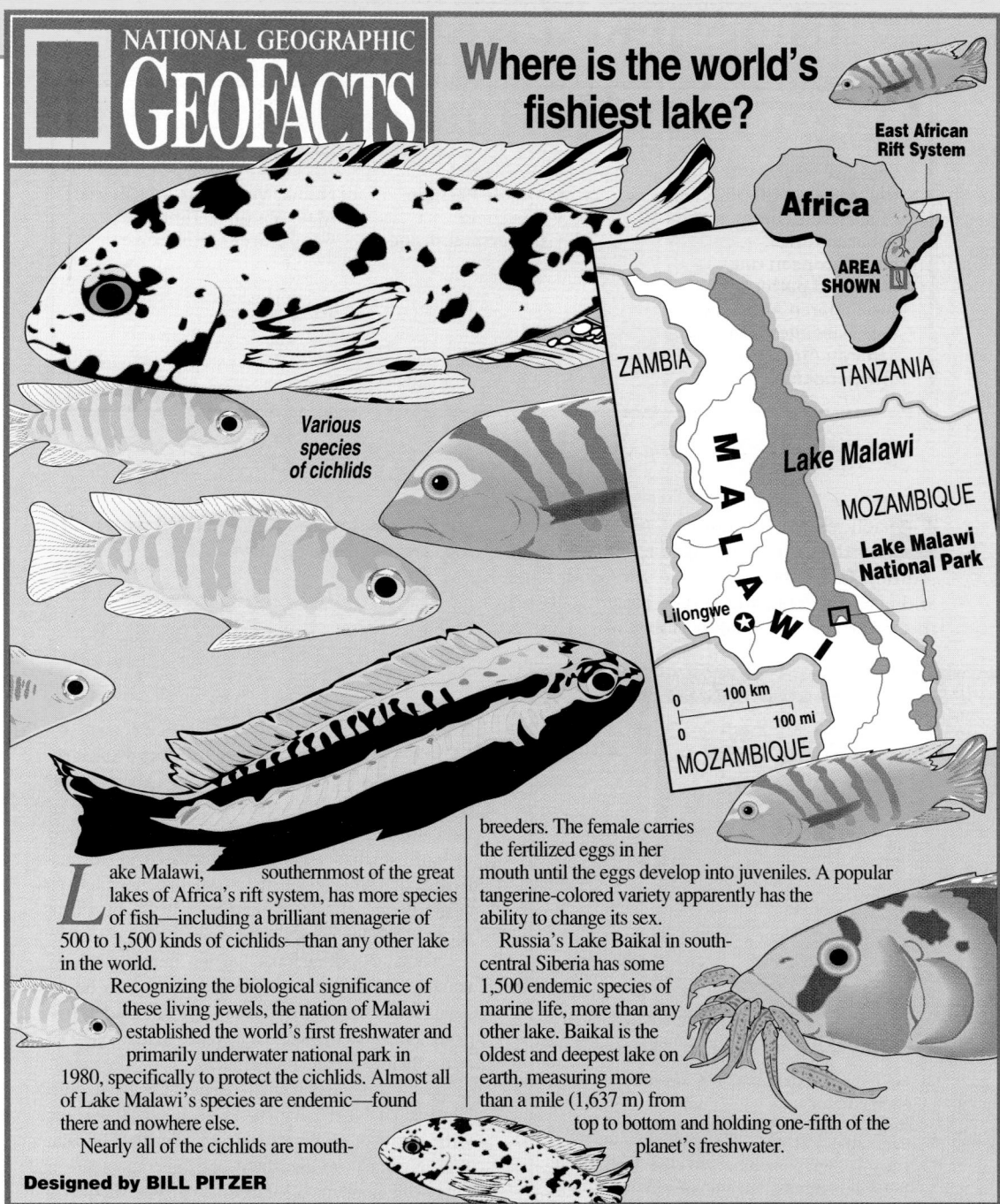

Where is the world's fishiest lake?

Lake Malawi, southernmost of the great lakes of Africa's rift system, has more species of fish—including a brilliant menagerie of 500 to 1,500 kinds of cichlids—than any other lake in the world.

Recognizing the biological significance of these living jewels, the nation of Malawi established the world's first freshwater and primarily underwater national park in 1980, specifically to protect the cichlids. Almost all of Lake Malawi's species are endemic—found there and nowhere else.

Nearly all of the cichlids are mouth-breeders. The female carries the fertilized eggs in her mouth until the eggs develop into juveniles. A popular tangerine-colored variety apparently has the ability to change its sex.

Russia's Lake Baikal in south-central Siberia has some 1,500 endemic species of marine life, more than any other lake. Baikal is the oldest and deepest lake on earth, measuring more than a mile (1,637 m) from top to bottom and holding one-fifth of the planet's freshwater.

Designed by BILL PITZER

TEACH

Ask students to raise their hands if they own pet fish. For those students that do have an aquarium, ask what kinds of fish live in it. Among the better known of many aquarium fish are the firemouth, the Jack Dempsey, the oscar, the discus, and the angelfish. Tell students that these fish are cichlids, many of which come from Lake Malawi.

Have interested students visit a pet store or aquarium to identify how many types of fish originated either in Lake Malawi or another African source.

LESSON PLAN
Chapter 21, Section 2

FOCUS

SECTION OBJECTIVES

1. **Examine** the major accomplishments of ancient peoples in sub-Saharan Africa.
2. **Describe** how European rule disrupted patterns of life in sub-Saharan Africa.
3. **Summarize** the challenges facing sub-Saharan Africa since independence.

BELLRINGER MOTIVATIONAL ACTIVITY

Project the Section 2 Focus Transparency and have students answer the questions.

PRETEACHING VOCABULARY

Tell students to find "universal" and "suffrage" in the dictionary and combine the meanings to define "universal suffrage."

USING MAPS

Answers: **1.** in what is now Sudan; **2.** Ghana, Mali, and Songhai; **3.** gold

Map Skills Practice
Reading a Map Where do most of the trade routes begin? *(Mediterranean Sea)*

SECTION 2

History and Government

SETTING THE SCENE

Read to Discover . . .
- the major accomplishments of ancient peoples in sub-Saharan Africa.
- how European rule disrupted patterns of life in sub-Saharan Africa.
- the challenges facing sub-Saharan Africa since independence.

Key Terms
- Middle Passage
- apartheid
- universal suffrage

Identify and Locate
Nubia, Meroë, Axum, Ghana, Mali, Songhai, Timbuktu, Bantu, Great Zimbabwe

Each year, a handful of travelers heads northeast out of Agadiz, Niger. Their journey takes them past the Air Mountains and across the blazing Tenere Desert. Beyond the desert lie the Djabo Mountains. Here a guide leads travelers to caves filled with paintings created some 6,000 years ago.

EARLY STATES

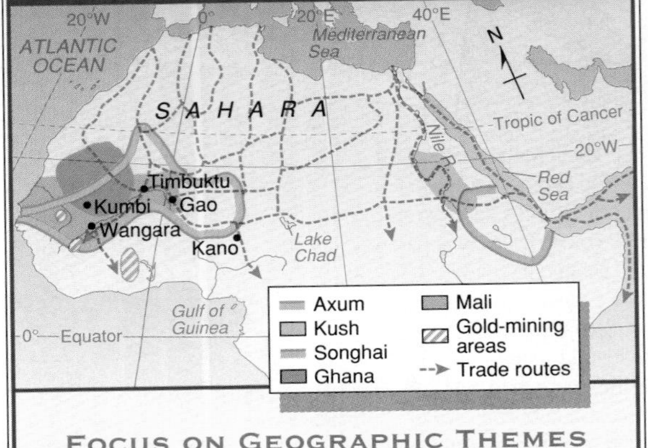

FOCUS ON GEOGRAPHIC THEMES

1. **Location:** Where was the kingdom of Kush located?
2. **Region:** What three kingdoms ruled in West Africa at different periods?
3. **Human/Environment Interaction:** What natural resource was mined in West Africa?

PLACE

African Civilizations

The Djabo cave painters lived at a remarkable time in African history. About 5500 B.C., the fish-filled rivers and plentiful game of the Sahara lured settlers. Early peoples learned to harvest the seeds of wild grasses and domesticate, or tame, animals. Such practices led to agriculture—the cornerstone for building more complex societies.

About 2000 B.C., the Sahara began to grow warmer and drier. People slowly migrated in search of more favorable lands. These migrants helped diffuse, or spread, knowledge of agriculture throughout Africa.

The Egyptians founded the first great civilization of North Africa. In time, they fought with another civilization to the south—Nubia. The Nubian civilization centered around a kingdom known as Kush and thrived until the 700s when armies from a rival trading kingdom—Axum—captured the capital of Meroë.

Classroom Resources for Section 2

BLACKLINE MASTERS:
- Reproducible Lesson Plan 21-2
- Guided Reading Activity 21-2
- Spanish Guided Reading Activity 21-2
- Vocabulary Activity 21
- Workbook Activity 21-2
- Section Quiz 21-2

TRANSPARENCIES:
- Section Focus Transparency 21-2
- Political Map Transparency 7

MULTIMEDIA:

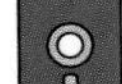

Testmaker

Picture Atlas of the World

At the same time, a series of trading kingdoms—Ghana, Mali, and Songhai—emerged one after the other in West Africa. The power and wealth of these kingdoms rested on control of the trans-Saharan trade, and they thrived until the late 1500s when Moroccans overpowered the Songhai.

Meanwhile, several states developed in eastern and southern Africa. These states traced their origins to a group of people called the Bantu who over the centuries fanned out over much of Africa in one of the largest migrations in history. The Bantus built several great central African states, including the kingdoms of Kongo, Luba, and Lunda. In southeastern Africa, a Bantu people called the Shona built the trading empire of Monomotapa.

MOVEMENT

European Colonization

In the 1600s and 1700s, Europeans eagerly traded with African societies. Finally, in the 1800s, Europeans seized almost the entire continent.

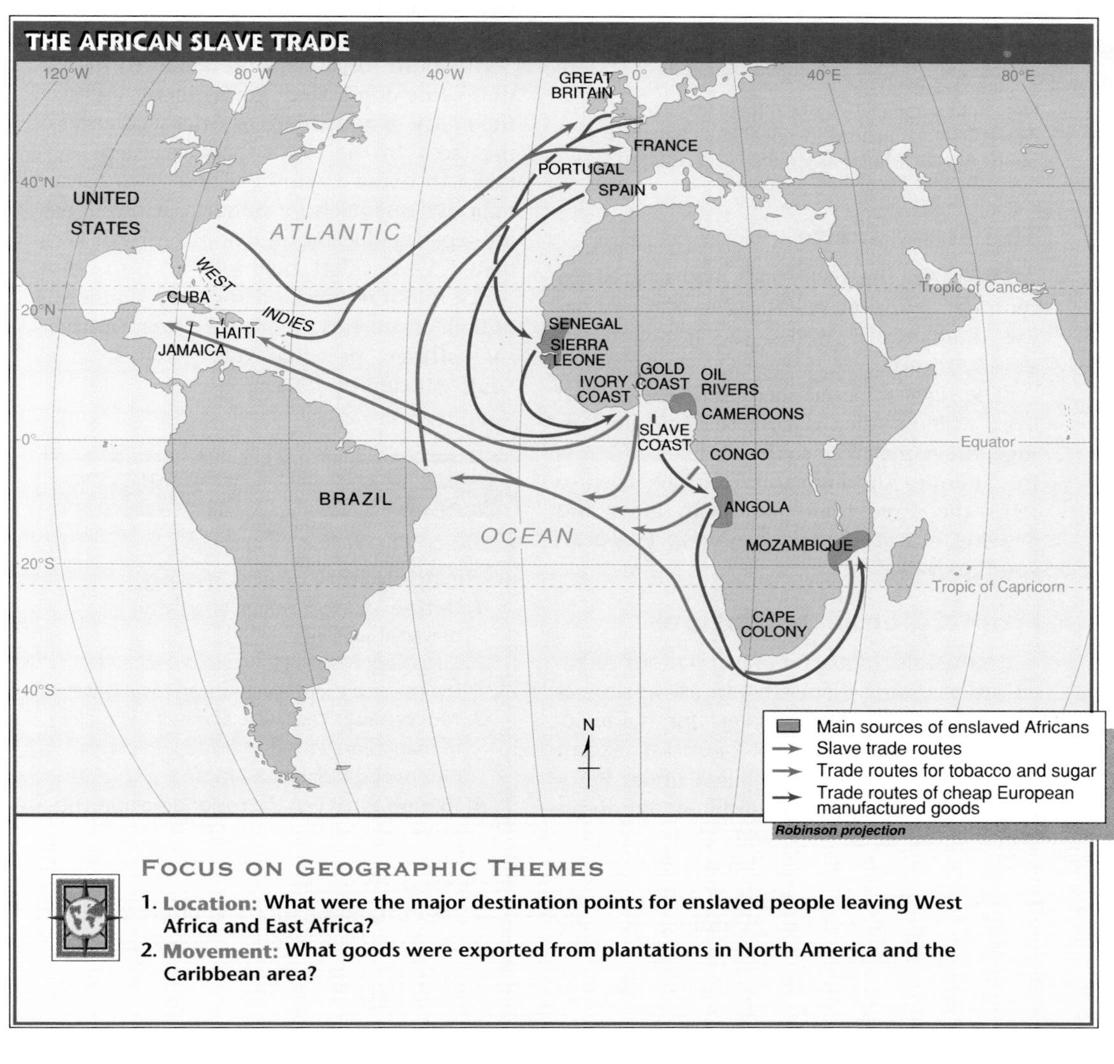

FOCUS ON GEOGRAPHIC THEMES

1. **Location: What were the major destination points for enslaved people leaving West Africa and East Africa?**
2. **Movement: What goods were exported from plantations in North America and the Caribbean area?**

Chapter 21, Section 2

TEACH

GUIDED PRACTICE

L1 Sequence List events from the section. As students read, have them find the year each occurred.

INDEPENDENT PRACTICE

Guided Reading Have students complete Guided Reading Activity 21-2 in the TCR. **LEP**

USING MAPS

Answers: **1.** Brazil, the Caribbean, Central America; **2.** tobacco, sugar

Map Skills Practice

Inferring Information Why did traders carry manufactured goods to Africa? (to trade for enslaved persons)

ASSESS

CHECK FOR UNDERSTANDING

Assign Section 2 Review as homework or an in-class activity.

MEETING LESSON OBJECTIVES

Each objective below is tested by the questions that follow it in parentheses.

1. Examine the major accomplishments of ancient peoples in sub-Saharan Africa. *(2)*
2. Describe how European rule disrupted patterns of life in sub-Saharan Africa. *(3, 4)*
3. Summarize the challenges facing sub-Saharan Africa since independence. *(5)*

Cooperative Learning Activity

Tell students that in 1652 the Dutch East India Company established a supply base at the Cape of Good Hope in what is now South Africa and that, soon after, European settlers arrived. Then read this excerpt from a Dutch diary: "(The Khoikhoi, a native people) strongly insisted that we had been appropriating more and more of their land . . . . They asked if they would be allowed to do such a thing supposing they went to Holland . . . ." Then say, "In 1652 the Khoikhoi of South Africa set up a supply base in Amsterdam. What happened next?" Let the class continue the story by having each student contribute a sentence or two. Appoint a secretary to record the class version of what may have happened if Africans had settled in Europe.

EVALUATE

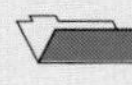 Assign the Section 2 Quiz in the TCR.

 Use the Testmaker to create a customized quiz for Section 2.

RETEACH

 Have students complete Workbook Activity 21-2 found in the TCR.

ENRICH

Show scenes from the movie *Cry Freedom* to give the class a view of South Africa under apartheid.

CLOSE

Ask students to name events in other world regions that happened around the same times as events in this section.

 **USING ILLUSTRATIONS**

REGION In 1984 another South African, Archbishop Desmond Tutu, received the Nobel Peace Prize for trying to change his country nonviolently.

Answer to Caption: *apartheid*

 **CD-ROM**

PICTURE ATLAS OF THE WORLD

You and your students can see apartheid's legacy by clicking the "Video" button of South Africa.

 **Geographic Themes**

Region: South Africa

Nelson Mandela *(right)* won the 1993 Nobel Peace Prize for promoting peaceful change in South Africa. *What policy ended as a result of his and others' actions?*

The Slave Trade

Although the slave trade had existed for centuries, European colonization of the Americas dramatically swelled the traffic in enslaved Africans.

The slave trade claimed countless African lives. Millions died during the **Middle Passage,** the name given to the terrible trip across the Atlantic. Although some Africans tried to resist the slave trade, European guns and growing African dependence upon European goods prevailed.

From Colonies to Nations

In the mid-1800s, European nations divided Africa among themselves to use as sources of raw materials and markets for manufactured goods. By 1914, all of Africa, except Liberia and Ethiopia, had fallen under European control. Africans endured European domination until they won their independence in the mid- to late 1900s. For example, Ghana became independent in 1957, Nigeria in 1960, Kenya in 1963, Zimbabwe in 1980, and Namibia in 1990.

PLACE

Challenges for the Future

The colonial legacy has created many serious problems for sub-Saharan Africans. The political boundaries the Europeans established cut across ethnic lines, grouping diverse peoples under the same government. These groupings often led to civil wars. The colonial system caused most of the region to be underdeveloped. Few European nations prepared their colonies for independence. As a result, lack of political experience contributed to the rise of one-party states backed by the military.

In South Africa, tension remained high as the white-dominated government enforced the policy of **apartheid,** or strict separation of the races. In the 1990s, however, steps were taken to remove apartheid and work toward majority rule. Nelson Mandela, a prominent anti-apartheid leader, and South African President F. W. de Klerk held talks to turn South Africa into a nonracial democracy. One result of their efforts was the pledge to grant **universal suffrage,** or equal voting rights, to all South Africans by 1994.

SECTION 2 REVIEW

Checking for Understanding

1. **Define** Middle Passage, apartheid, universal suffrage.
2. **Locating Places** How did location affect the rise of ancient west African kingdoms?
3. **Movement** What were some of the major human migrations that helped shape the history of sub-Saharan Africa?
4. **Region** What was the major development in Africa after World War II?

Critical Thinking

5. **Determining Cause and Effect** What is the connection between colonial rule and some of the problems facing sub-Saharan Africa today?

ANSWERS TO SECTION 2 REVIEW

1. **Middle Passage:** the Atlantic journey of enslaved Africans; **apartheid:** forced separation of the races; **universal suffrage:** equal voting rights
2. Most ancient African kingdoms lay at the crossroads of trade.
3. the movement of hunters, herders, and farmers out of the Sahara; the movement of Bantus across much of Africa; the forced migration of Africans across the Atlantic
4. the end of European colonial rule and the rise of independent African nations
5. Answers may vary but should include that European-established boundaries led to civil wars, the colonial system caused most of the region to be underdeveloped, and lack of political experience contributed to the rise of one-party states.

ɿeography and History

ꟻRICA: EUROPEAN COLONIES

ɔu read, examine how ɒpean colonial rule affected ɑ.

uring the 1800s, the In- rial Revolution swept ugh western Europe, fuel- a policy of colonial ex- sion. Newly industrialized ntries needed raw materi- or their factories and mar- for their manufactured ds. By colonizing, they d acquire both while also easing their share of glob- ɔwer. Africa was one of the s targeted for expansion.

ɒpeans in Africa

uring the late 1800s, Por- l, Spain, Italy, France, the nerlands, and Great Bri- began strengthening r hold on Africa. For the 40 years, European gov- nents engaged in efforts ontrol the most profitable ons of the region. During mid-1920s, most of Africa still under European con-

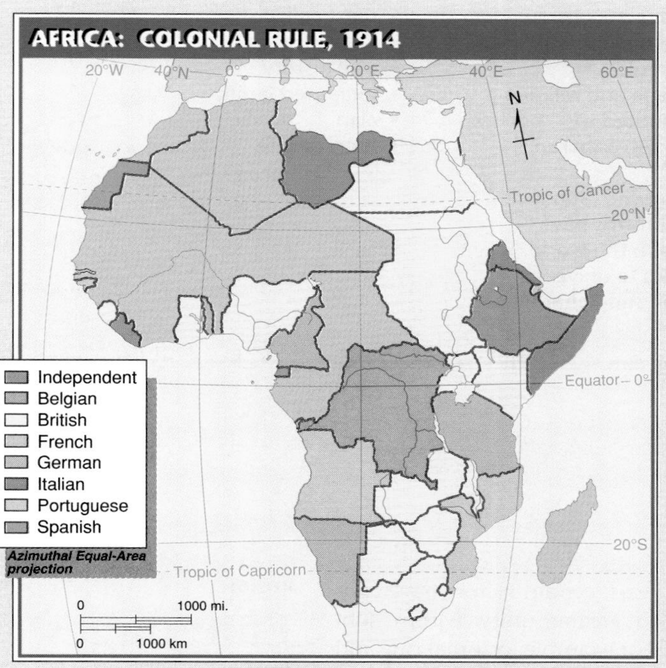

Beginning around 1870, the major European powers began a mad scramble to divide Africa, establish colonies, and exploit the wealth of natural resources found there. By 1914 only two African countries—Liberia and Ethiopia—had managed to escape European control.

cts of Colonial Rule

ɿropean governments cre- colonial units arbitrarily, no regard for the ethnic nelands of the people in regions. Colonial bound- often cut across ethnic ɿelands. European admin- tors gave little thought to aring Africans for future pendence. Economic sys- s tied to production for d markets replaced the African system of production only for family or local community needs. Christian missionaries challenged beliefs and practices long a part of African life.

Colonial rule also offered expanded educational opportunities to Africans. As some Africans became politically aware, they led the demand for a share in governing. Finally, in the 1950s and 1960s, educated Africans also led independence movements that ended European rule.

Checking for Understanding

1. **Why did European nations colonize Africa?**
2. **Regions Study the map.**  **What problem can be foreseen from the colonial divisions?**

Geography and History

TEACH

Explain to students that until the late 1800s, Europeans had only been interested in establishing coastal trading and slave stations. The continent's large rivers were too difficult to sail into the interior; the coasts had very few good harbors.

 **Place** Considering Africa's geography, what problems might Europeans have encountered in colonizing the continent? *(difficulty in finding hospitable sites for towns, harbors; problems in transporting building materials)*

Extending the Content

"Darkest Africa" This phrase was commonly used by Europeans and Americans during the 1800s and reflected Westerners' ignorance about the interior of Africa south of the Sahara. Most were "in the dark" about the geography and culture of this world region, seeing it mainly as a large obstacle when sailing to India.

ANSWERS TO CHECKING FOR UNDERSTANDING

1. to obtain raw materials for their factories and open new markets for their manufactured goods
2. lack of unity in government, language, culture, and economy

LESSON PLAN
Chapter 21, Section 3

FOCUS

SECTION OBJECTIVES

1. Name the cultural factors that help define sub-Saharan Africa as a region.
2. Relate how language and religion have contributed to diversity in sub-Saharan Africa.
3. Illustrate the ways in which sub-Saharan art forms have touched upon the world.
4. Explain the obstacles to universal education in sub-Saharan Africa.

BELLRINGER MOTIVATIONAL ACTIVITY

Project the Section 3 Focus Transparency and have students answer the questions.

PRETEACHING VOCABULARY

Explain that *lingua franca* means "universal language." Ask students to hypothesize about why Africans would need a *lingua franca* when each group has its own language.

MULTICULTURAL PERSPECTIVE

Cultural Diffusion
Ethiopia and the Judaeo-Christian tradition go back even further than A.D. 300. The Bible refers to Ethiopia and Ethiopians no fewer than 41 times.

CD-ROM

PICTURE ATLAS OF THE WORLD
Listen to the languages of Africa by clicking the "Speech" button of selected countries.

SECTION 3

Cultures and Lifestyles

SETTING THE SCENE

Read to Discover . . .
- the cultural factors that help define sub-Saharan Africa as a region.
- how language and religion have contributed to diversity in sub-Saharan Africa.
- the ways in which sub-Saharan art forms have touched upon the world.
- the obstacles to universal education in sub-Saharan Africa.

Key Terms
- mass culture
- *lingua franca*
- oral history
- extended family
- clan
- literacy rate

Identify and Locate
Sierra Leone

In recent years, certain factors have contributed to greater unity within sub-Saharan Africa. For example, colonial rule and the push for independence now form a part of the histories of most sub-Saharan nations. Also, the wider availability of television and radio has helped create a **mass culture**, or popular culture promoted by the media. In addition, sub-Saharan Africans share some common beliefs, such as the importance of family ties.

Yet despite such similarities, great diversity still exists throughout the region. In many ways, the African people are as diverse as the African landscape itself. Sometimes, they are even more diverse! Consider the city of Freetown, Sierra Leone. Its population of 469,000 includes Lebanese, Indians, Europeans, the descendants of enslaved Africans, and members of 18 ethnic groups. All these various people—their cultures and their lifestyles—help shape the human geography of sub-Saharan Africa.

REGION

Languages

Today Africans speak more than 800 languages and numerous dialects. Some of these languages originated in Africa. Others were brought to Africa by Arabs, Europeans, and other foreigners. Some African languages consist of a mixture of African and foreign words. Swahili, for example, is a major African language that is a mix of languages. Its main root is Bantu, but over the centuries, Arabic and Portuguese words have been added. Today Swahili serves as a ***lingua franca,*** or universal language, spoken throughout much of East Africa. It allows the people of Uganda, Rwanda, Kenya, Tanzania, and the Congo to understand each other. Such widespread use of Swahili helps define East Africa as a region.

The colonial powers imported new languages that helped Africans speak to the outside world and with one another. English is an

Classroom Resources for Section 3

BLACKLINE MASTERS:
Reproducible Lesson Plan 21-3
World Literature Reading 6
Skill Activity 21
Section Quiz 21-3

TRANSPARENCIES:
Section Focus Transparency 21-3
World Cultures Transparencies 11, 12

MULTIMEDIA:

Testmaker

World Music: *Cultural Traditions, Lesson 6*

Picture Atlas of the World

example. Although many of these languages serve as the official languages of nations, a wide variety of ethnic languages remain in use. Language experts classify the region's many languages into three families—African, Afro-Asiatic, and Malayo-Polynesian. African languages are the most widely spoken. These include some 300 Bantu languages used in central, eastern, and southern Africa. The main Afro-Asiatic languages are the Arabic and Berber spoken in the region's northwest corner. Indo-European languages are those imported by colonial powers. In South Africa, people speak English and Afrikaans, the language of early Dutch settlers.

REGION

Religions

In describing the religion of Nigeria's Igbo, an enslaved African named Olaudah Equiano wrote:

As to religion, [we] . . . believe that there is one Creator of all things, and that he lives in the sun, . . . and governs all events, especially our deaths.

The religious beliefs described by Equiano form part of some of Africa's many traditional religions. Although each ethnic group might have its own religion, these tend to have some beliefs in common. Like the Igbo, most traditional religions believe in a supreme Creator and several lesser gods.

Islam and Christianity constitute the other two major religions in sub-Saharan Africa. The largest number of Muslims, or followers of Islam, can be found along the Swahili coast and in areas once held by the kingdoms of Mali and Songhai. Ethiopia embraces both Islam and Christianity. Christianity arrived in Ethiopia with missionaries and traders in the A.D. 300s. Christianity came to other nations with the European colonial powers. After independence, some Africans formed new churches that blended Christianity and traditional African religions.

REGION

The Arts

During the course of their history, sub-Saharan Africans have developed an incredible variety of art forms—from the Djabo cave paintings to the Kente cloth of West Africa to the multi-rhythmic music of traditional dances. African artists have worked in many mediums and in many styles. Because of the forced migration of enslaved Africans to other parts of the world, these styles have been widely diffused throughout the Americas, the Caribbean, and parts of Europe and Asia.

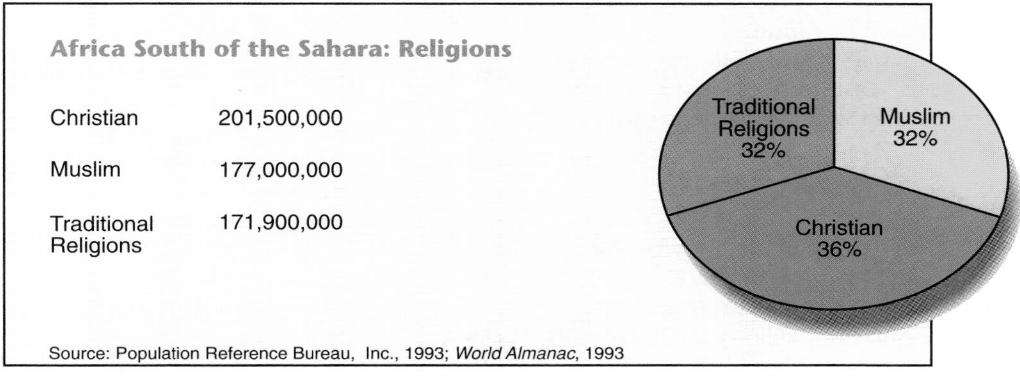

TEACH

GUIDED PRACTICE

L1 Compare Ask students to recall a comparable English proverb for each of these Swahili proverbs:

When fortune knocks at the door, you have to open the door yourself. *(When opportunity knocks, answer.)*

He who cultivates millet does not harvest beans. *(You reap what you sow.)*

Stretch your legs according to your bed. *(Don't get too big for your britches.)*

INDEPENDENT PRACTICE

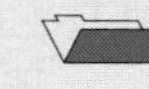

Guided Reading Have students complete Guided Reading Activity 21-3 in the TCR. **LEP**

CURRICULUM CONNECTION

SOCIOLOGY ***Americans generally believe that their ancestors lived in extended families. However, research shows that several generations rarely lived together because life expectancy was so short. In Massachusetts cities about 100 years ago, women could expect to live only 37 years and men 41.***

USING GRAPHS

Skills Practice What is the dominant religion in sub-Saharan Africa? *(Christianity)*

Cooperative Learning Activity

On the chalkboard, copy the following sub-Saharan African customs:
KENYA
Some groups greet one another by slapping palms and then gripping each other's cupped fingers.
ZIMBABWE
People show thanks and politeness by clapping.

Suggest that students adopt these customs for a day. When the class meets again, discuss the reactions of friends, families, and classmates to the students' use of African customs.

ASSESS

CHECK FOR UNDERSTANDING

Assign Section 3 Review as homework or an in-class activity.

MEETING LESSON OBJECTIVES

Each objective below is tested by the questions that follow it in parentheses.

1. Name the cultural factors that help define sub-Saharan Africa as a region. *(2)*
2. Relate how language and religion have contributed to diversity in sub-Saharan Africa. *(3)*
3. Illustrate the ways in which sub-Saharan art forms have touched upon the world. *(4)*
4. Explain the obstacles to universal education in sub-Saharan Africa. *(5)*

EVALUATE

Assign the Section 3 Quiz in the TCR.

Use the Testmaker to create a customized quiz for Section 3.

HUMAN/ENVIRONMENT INTERACTION In addition to drums, Africans play bells, whistles, gourd xylophones, and other instruments.

Answer to Caption: *blues, jazz, and rock*

Geographic Themes

Region: West Africa

Traditional dances and music in West Africa often are featured at annual festivals to honor ancestors. *What American forms of music have been inspired by African music?*

Painting, Sculpture, Weaving

African masks, sculptures, and weavings can be seen in museums and in everyday life. Modern European artists such as Pablo Picasso drew inspiration from the abstract masks of the Yoruba of Nigeria. The bronze castings of the Benin are known around the world. So are the many types of textiles designed by Africans. Prized by Africans and non-Africans alike are Ghana's Kente cloth, Nigeria's *adire* cloth, and East Africa's Konga cloth—complete with a Swahili proverb on each piece.

Music

Music forms a part of everyday life for Africans. Africans traditionally use music to bring order to life and to express themselves spiritually. Music also relieves the toil of work such as planting, hoeing, or harvesting.

Today the musical rhythms and instruments of Africa can be heard in popular music throughout the United States. Both the blues and jazz owe their origins to styles carried to the Americas by enslaved Africans. Even contemporary rock 'n' roll stars freely borrow from Africa. Sting, Paul Simon, and David Byrne are but a few of the artists who have looked to Africa for inspiration.

Literature

Much of the history and many of the stories of sub-Saharan Africa have been preserved in **oral history,** or the legends passed down orally from generation to generation. In more recent times, the region has produced prize-winning poets, novelists, and playwrights. In recent years, two Africans have claimed the Nobel Prize in Literature—Wole Soyinka of Nigeria (1986) and Nadine Gordimer of South Africa (1991).

PLACE

Varied Lifestyles

A journey through an African nation such as Kenya reveals the variety of lifestyles within the region. Kenya's dozens of ethnic groups all have their own customs. Wide differences also exist between rural and urban dwellers. In Nairobi, people usually wear clothes similar to those in the United States. In Maasailand, on the other hand, people wear loose-fitting clothes and brilliant jewelry.

Africans tend to share one important way of life in common. Most place great emphasis on family ties. Africans still strongly value **extended families,** or households made up of several generations. Although urbanization has made it more difficult to preserve the extended family, it is still not uncommon to find family compounds filled with relatives from grandparents to grandchildren to even great-grandchildren.

In some places, families are organized into **clans,** or large groups of people related to each other. Clan members help safeguard an ethnic

Meeting Special Needs

Language Delayed One of the most common problems of students with language difficulties is an inability to ask questions of their teachers. Form small groups to practice developing questions. The text under the heading "Varied Lifestyles" on pages 444 and 445 is rich in information of both a general and specific nature. Reward the group that produces the most varied questions.

Geographic Themes

Place: Ndebele Village, South Africa
Many Africans, even those living in urban areas, maintain close connections with their families and ancestral villages. *What kind of family ties do many Africans value?*

group's traditions by passing them from one generation to the next. As in other parts of the developing world, many people also believe large families help relieve economic hardship by providing more workers. Such beliefs have made it difficult for governments to curb Africa's booming population.

REGION

Looking Ahead

The young people growing up in Africa south of the Sahara today face many challenges. Since independence, more children are attending public school. **Literacy rates**, or the ability to read and write, have risen. Still, the ideal of even an elementary education remains beyond the reach of many people.

A number of obstacles have undermined popular education. The most serious is the low standard of living. Many people simply cannot afford to send children to school. Also, some parents believe their children will profit more from survival skills, such as hunting or farming. As a result, literacy rates in sub-Saharan Africa remain the lowest in the world.

To give the region's children a more hopeful future, governments are using innovative methods to chip away at monumental problems. Television, for example, has become one of the region's most effective teaching tools.

Section 3 Review

Checking for Understanding

1. **Define** mass culture, *lingua franca,* oral history, extended family, clan, literacy rate.
2. **Locating Places** What are some of the factors that have helped unify sub-Saharan Africa as a region in recent years?
3. **Region** How do language and religion increase diversity within sub-Saharan Africa?
4. **Movement** How have sub-Saharan Africans influenced global culture?

Critical Thinking

5. **Determining Cause and Effect** What is the connection between low standards of living and low literacy rates in sub-Saharan Africa?

RETEACH

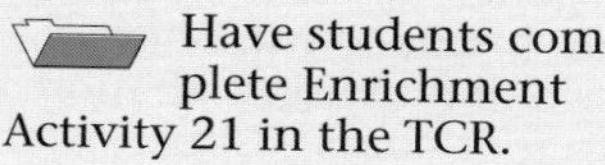

Have students complete Reteaching Activity 21 in the TCR.

ENRICH

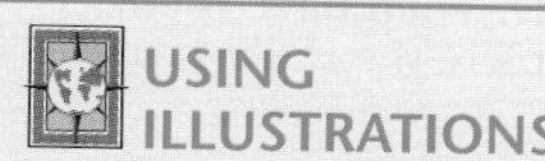

Have students complete Enrichment Activity 21 in the TCR.

CLOSE

Distribute magazines and ask students to find examples of sub-Saharan African influence.

USING ILLUSTRATIONS

PLACE Most Nigerians leave their villages, but keep track of where other villagers have gone.

Answer to Caption: *extended families and clans*

ANSWERS TO SECTION 3 REVIEW

1. **mass culture:** popular culture promoted by the media; ***lingua franca:*** universal language; **oral history:** legends of a people passed down orally; **extended family:** family made up of several generations; **clan:** a large group of related people; **literacy rate:** the percentage of people able to read and write
2. shared historical experiences, the rise of mass culture, and shared values
3. Hundreds of languages and many religions help diversify the culture.
4. Sub-Saharan Africans have inspired European artists, contributed to American music, and introduced prized textile designs.
5. Families with a low standard of living cannot afford to send children to school and emphasize survival skills over academic skills.

Teaching Skills

TEACH

Survey the students on this question: How many hours of television do you watch on school nights? Use these categories: a) less than one hour; b) one to two hours; c) two to four hours; d) more than four hours. Using this data, have students determine the percentage of each group to the whole. Convert these findings into a circle graph on the chalkboard. Point out that circle graphs illustrate the relationship of parts to a whole. Then have them complete the skill on page 446.

Skills Practice For additional practice, have students complete Skill Activity 21 in the TCR.

MAP & GRAPH SKILLS

Reading a Circle Graph

Suppose you must give a report that analyzes student participation in various extracurricular activities. First, you conduct a survey to find out how many students participate in sports, clubs, arts groups, and so on. After compiling this data, you must find a good way to present the information quickly, clearly, and concisely. One excellent format would be a **circle graph**.

REVIEWING THE SKILL

Circle graphs illustrate numerical information and the relationship of parts to a whole. Because it looks like a pie cut into slices, a circle graph is also called a pie graph. The complete circle represents the whole group, while each slice, or wedge, represents a fraction of the whole expressed in percentages.

When reading a circle graph, apply the following steps:

- Read the graph title to determine the subject.
- Study the labels and key to understand what each part of the graph represents.
- Compare the sizes of the parts to draw conclusions about the subject.

PRACTICING THE SKILL

Study the circle graphs below and then answer the following questions:

1. What are the subjects of the circle graphs?
2. What color represents the Luo people and their language?
3. What percentage of Kenyans are speakers of Luhya?
4. What percentage of Kenyans belong to ethnic groups other than those listed specifically on the graph?
5. What is the most striking similarity between the percentages shown on the two graphs?

For additional practice in this skill, see Practicing Skills on page 448 of the Chapter 21 Review.

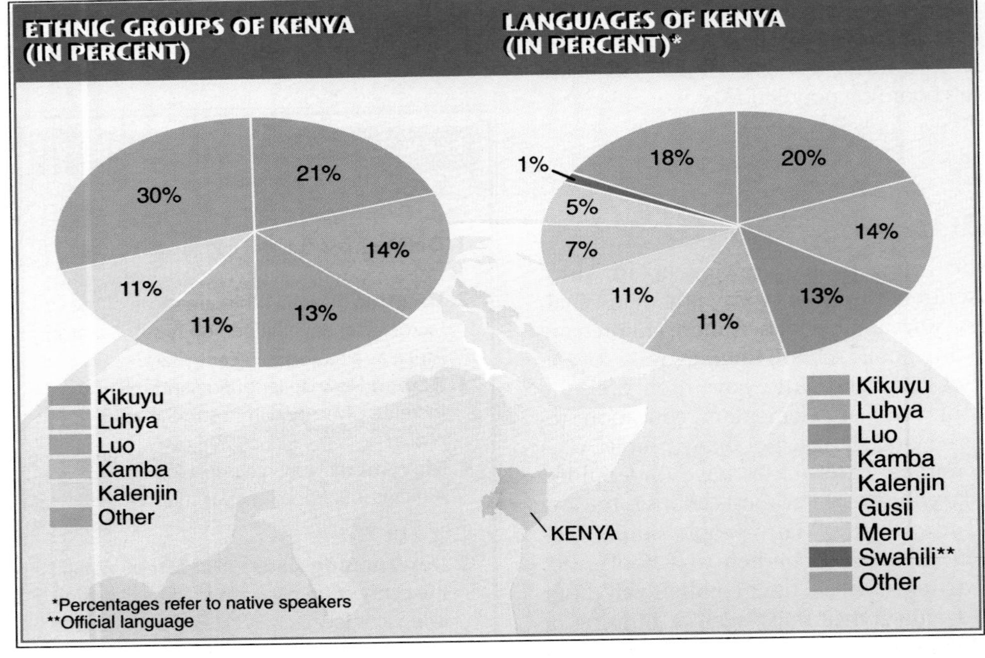

ANSWERS TO PRACTICING THE SKILL

1. The composition of Kenyan society according to major ethnic and language groups
2. green
3. 14%
4. about 30%
5. The Kikuyu, Luhya, Luo, Kamba, and Kalenjin groups account for about the same percentages in each graph.

chapter 21

HIGHLIGHTS

Section	Key Terms	Summary
1 Population Patterns  West African urban scene	**gross domestic product (GDP)** (p. 434) **per capita income** (p. 435) **urbanization** (p. 436) **ethnic group** (p. 436)	• With more than 570 million people, sub-Saharan Africa is the third most populous region in the world. • The uneven distribution of people in sub-Saharan Africa is linked to the region's physical geography. • Inadequate food, water, and health care contribute to short life expectancies in sub-Saharan Africa. • Sub-Saharan Africa is urbanizing faster than any other region in the world. • More than 2,000 ethnic groups, speaking some 800 languages, make up the population of Africa south of the Sahara.
2 History and Government  South African leader Nelson Mandela	**Middle Passage** (p. 440) **apartheid** (p. 440) **universal suffrage** (p. 440)	• The movement of the Bantu south from Niger formed one of the largest human migrations in history. • European colonization remapped traditional ethnic territories. • Most of Africa's nations have won independence since the 1960s. • In the 1990s, South Africans began to dismantle apartheid.
3 Cultures and Lifestyles  Nigerians celebrating annual festival	**mass culture** (p. 442) ***lingua franca*** (p. 442) **oral history** (p. 444) **extended family** (p. 444) **clan** (p. 444) **literacy rate** (p. 445)	• Sub-Saharan Africa's many languages and variety of religions contribute to the region's diversity. • Sub-Saharan Africans have influenced the artistic cultures of the world. • One of the biggest challenges facing sub-Saharan African governments is how to raise literacy rates.

CHAPTER 21 HIGHLIGHTS

USING THE CHAPTER 21 HIGHLIGHTS

Use the Chapter 21 Highlights to preview, review, condense, or reteach the chapter.

PREVIEW/REVIEW

 Vocabulary PuzzleMaker Software reinforces the Key Terms used in Chapter 21.

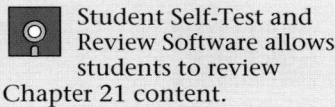

 Student Self-Test and Review Software allows students to review Chapter 21 content.

CONDENSE

Have students read the Chapter 21 Highlights.

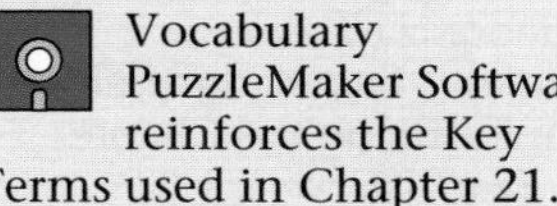 Have students listen to the Chapter 21 Audiocassettes in the TCR. Spanish Audiocassettes are also available.

Assign the Chapter 21 Audiocassette Activity and give students the Chapter 21 Audiocassette Quiz.

  Have students complete Guided Reading Activities for Chapter 21 in the TCR. Spanish Guided Reading Activities are also available.

RETEACH

 Have students complete Reteaching Activity 21 in the TCR. Spanish Reteaching Activities are also available.

Map Activity

Identify and Locate Distribute copies of page 37 of the Outline Map Resource Book. Using the Atlas maps at the beginning of the unit and maps from the chapter, have the students identify and label the countries south of the Sahara.

GLENCOE TECHNOLOGY

Videodisc

Use Chapter 21 MindJogger Videoquiz to review students' knowledge before administering the Chapter 21 Test.

MINDJOGGER VIDEOQUIZ

Chapter 21
Disc 3 Side B

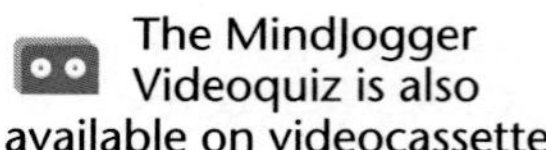

The MindJogger Videoquiz is also available on videocassette.

ANSWERS

Reviewing Key Terms

1. per capita income
2. urbanization
3. ethnic group
4. Middle Passage
5. apartheid
6. *lingua franca*
7. literacy rate

Reviewing Facts

8. the rapid growth rate or the high number of births

9. diverse geography, many ethnic groups, many languages, and so on.

10. Nubia, Ghana, Mali, Songhai, Kongo, Luba, Lunda, Monomotapa

11. South Africa now has universal suffrage.

12. African, Afro-Asiatic, and Malayo-Polynesian

13. traditional African religions, Islam, Christianity, and a blend of African and Christian beliefs

chapter 21 REVIEW

Reviewing Key Terms

Choose the vocabulary term that best completes each of the sentences below. Write your answers on a separate sheet of paper.

per capita income (p. 435)
urbanization (p. 436)
ethnic group (p. 436)
Middle Passage (p. 440)
apartheid (p. 440)
lingua franca (p. 442)
literacy rate (p. 445)

SECTION 1

1. The average annual earnings per person of a nation's population is called the ____.
2. The movement of people from rural areas into cities is known as ____.
3. People with similar histories and cultures are known as an ____.

SECTION 2

4. Millions of Africans died during the ____, the name given to the terrible trip across the Atlantic.
5. The forced separation of races in South Africa was called ____.

SECTION 3

6. Swahili is an example of a ____, or universal language, spoken in East Africa.
7. When a large number of people can read and write, a nation is said to have a high ____.

Reviewing Facts

SECTION 1

8. What trend most accurately characterizes population growth in sub-Saharan Africa?
9. What factor(s) account for the diverse population patterns in sub-Saharan Africa?

SECTION 2

10. What ancient kingdoms and empires grew up in East and West Africa?
11. How will the end of apartheid affect government in South Africa?

SECTION 3

12. What are the three major language groups in sub-Saharan Africa?
13. What religions are practiced in Africa today?

Critical Thinking

14. **Predicting Consequences** What effect do you think migration from rural areas to cities has had on traditional ways of life?
15. **Analyzing Information** What role do you think trade played in early African societies?
16. **Making Comparisons** Music has given the people of sub-Saharan Africa a sense of identity. Do you think this is unique to Africa? Why or why not?

Geographic Themes

17. **Place** How has physical geography affected population densities in sub-Saharan Africa?
18. **Movement** How did climate changes in the Sahara affect population patterns in the region?
19. **Region** How has language helped define East Africa as a region?

Practicing Skills

Reading a Circle Graph

Refer to the circle graphs on page 446.

20. What percentage of Kenyans are speakers of Swahili?
21. What is the largest single ethnic group in Kenya?
22. What percentage of Kenyans are speakers of Gusii?

Critical Thinking

14. Urbanization may break up extended families and clans.

15. Trade increased the power and wealth of early African societies but also caused wars between them.

16. Answers will vary but students may point out that Europeans and North Americans also identify with traditional music of their ancestors.

Geographic Themes

17. The population is unevenly distributed, people tend to live in mild climates and near water and fertile soil.

18. As the Sahara grew warmer and drier, people migrated in search of new lands.

19. Although many languages are spoken throughout East Africa, most people there speak Swahili as well.

23. Which 2 ethnic groups each make up about 11 percent of Kenya's population?

Using the Unit Atlas

Refer to the cultural geography section of the Unit Atlas on pages 410–411.

24. What is the most populous nation in Africa?
25. What nation is Africa's oldest republic?
26. What is the approximate population of Africa south of the Sahara?

Projects

Individual Activity

You learned about the incredible variety of art forms in sub-Saharan Africa. Pick one of the art forms mentioned in the chapter—painting, sculpture, masks, weaving, music, poetry, or literature. Then, using an encyclopedia or a book on Africa, look up this art form. Pick one example of this art form and prepare an audio/visual report.

Cooperative Learning Activity

In small groups, pick two nations in sub-Saharan Africa. Using an almanac, prepare population graphics of the nations chosen. When all the student teams are done, form a committee to bind the information together alphabetically.

Writing About Geography

Description

Write a vivid description of Africa south of the Sahara based on the information recorded in your journal activity calendar. Illustrate your description with sketches based on pictures found in the text and other sources.

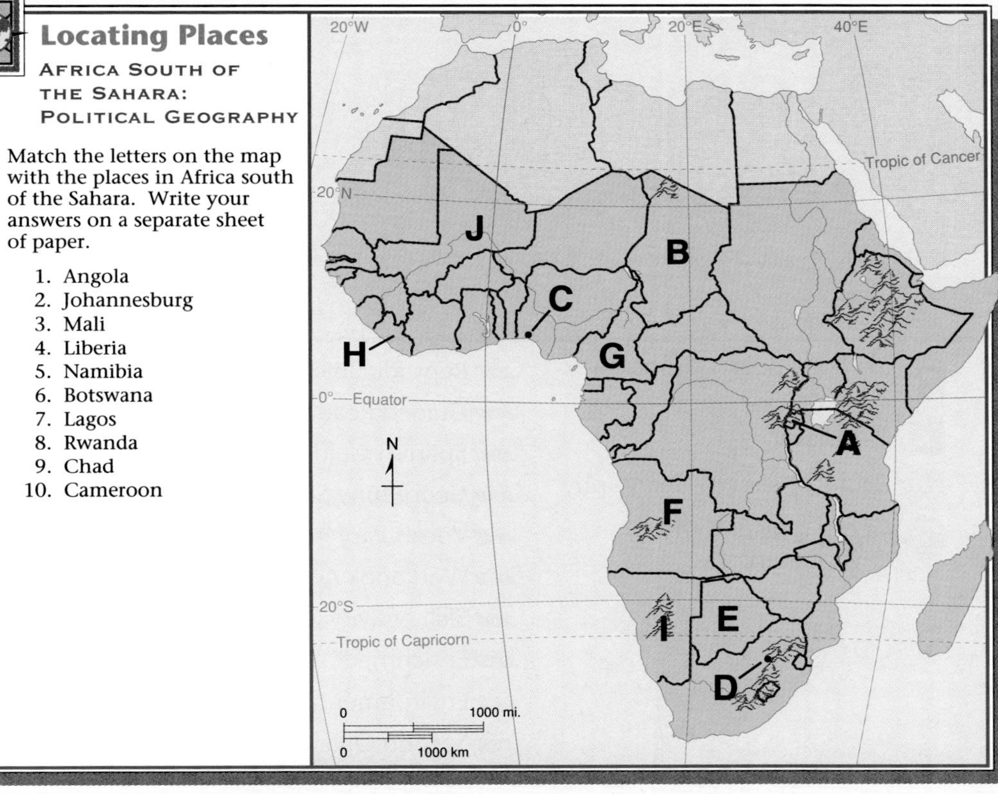

Locating Places

AFRICA SOUTH OF THE SAHARA: POLITICAL GEOGRAPHY

Match the letters on the map with the places in Africa south of the Sahara. Write your answers on a separate sheet of paper.

1. Angola
2. Johannesburg
3. Mali
4. Liberia
5. Namibia
6. Botswana
7. Lagos
8. Rwanda
9. Chad
10. Cameroon

Chapter 21 Review

Practicing Skills

20. 1 percent
21. Kikuyu
22. 7 percent
23. Kamba and Kalenjin

Using the Unit Atlas

24. Nigeria
25. Liberia
26. about 550 million

Locating Places

1. F
2. D
3. J
4. H
5. I
6. E
7. C
8. A
9. B
10. G

Chapter Bonus Test Question

This question may be used for extra credit on the chapter test.

How did the colonial system prevent African countries south of the Sahara from developing industry?

(Answer: Colonial powers used African raw materials for European industries and made Africans dependent on manufactured goods from Europe.)

CHAPTER 22

PLANNING GUIDE

Africa South of the Sahara Today

CHAPTER ORGANIZER

Daily Lesson Objectives	Multimedia	Teacher Classroom Resources
SECTION 1 Living in Africa South of the Sahara 1. Identify the major types of economic activities in sub-Saharan Africa. 2. Describe the obstacles that face industrial development of Africa south of the Sahara. 3. Explain how colonialism hindered the growth of transportation and trade in sub-Saharan Africa. 4. Name the most common form of communication in Africa south of the Sahara.	Section Focus Transparency 22-1 Chapter 22 Vocabulary PuzzleMaker Software Geography and the Environment Testmaker	Reproducible Lesson Plan 22-1 Guided Reading Activity 22-1 Spanish Guided Reading Activity 22-1 Workbook Activity 22-1 Performance Assessment Activity 22 Section Quiz 22-1
SECTION 2 People and Their Environment 1. Discuss how hunger in Africa south of the Sahara is related to human interaction with the environment. 2. Examine the reasons many plants and animals in the region face destruction. 3. Illustrate the efforts sub-Saharan Africans have taken to offset decades of famine and war.	Section Focus Transparency 22-2 Testmaker Reuters Issues in Geography Geography and the Environment	Reproducible Lesson Plan 22-2 Guided Reading Activity 22-2 Spanish Guided Reading Activity 22-2 Geography Simulation 7 Vocabulary Activity 22 Workbook Activity 22-2 Skill Activity 22 Enrichment Activity 22 Environmental Issue 7 Section Quiz 22-2
CHAPTER REVIEW AND EVALUATION	Chapter 22 English (or Spanish) Audiocassettes MindJogger Videoquiz Testmaker Student Self-Test and Review Software	Reteaching Activity 22 Spanish Reteaching Activity 22 Outline Map Resource Book, p. 37 Chapter 22 Test Form A and Form B

0:00 *If time does not permit teaching the entire chapter, summarize using the Chapter 22 Highlights on page 463, and the Chapter 22 English (or Spanish) Audiocassettes. Review students' knowledge using the Glencoe MindJogger Videoquiz.*

KEY TO ABILITY LEVELS

Teaching strategies have been coded for varying learning styles and abilities.

L1 **BASIC** activities for all students

L2 **AVERAGE** activities for average to above-average students

L3 **CHALLENGING** activities for above-average students

LEP **LIMITED ENGLISH PROFICIENCY** activities

Performance Assessment

Problem Solving People in many areas of sub-Saharan Africa are facing challenges as a result of war, social upheaval, and environmental change. International organizations and foreign governments have been trying to help in these crises. Ask students to brainstorm the problems facing sub-Saharan Africa and to develop a list of possible sources to contact in an effort to identify various outreach programs. Students should choose one program to research and then carry out the following steps:

(1) Explain what is currently being done.
(2) Predict the relative success of the program.
(3) Explain the role of the United States in the effort.
(4) Make recommendations to the appropriate parties.

Students should write and communicate their ideas to the agencies, organizations, or governments involved in the project.

POSSIBLE RUBRIC FEATURES: Content information, problem-solving skills, communication skills, research skills, application skills

For additional professional and classroom resources, see Chapter Resources, pages T46–T51.

TEACHER'S CORNER

NATIONAL GEOGRAPHIC SOCIETY

INDEX TO NATIONAL GEOGRAPHIC MAGAZINE

The following articles may be used for research relating to this chapter:

- "Tragedy Stalks the Horn of Africa," by Robert Caputo, August 1993.
- "Elephants: Out of Time, Out of Space," by Douglas H. Chadwick, May 1991.
- "Africa's Sahel: The Stricken Land," by William S. Ellis, August 1987.
- "The Serengeti: The Glory of Life," by Shana Alexander, May 1986.
- "Somalia's Hour of Need," by Robert Paul Jordan, June 1981.

NATIONAL GEOGRAPHIC SOCIETY PRODUCTS AVAILABLE FROM GLENCOE

To order the following products for use with this chapter, contact your local Glencoe sales representative or call Glencoe at 1-800-334-7344:

- *Picture Atlas of the World* (CD-ROM)
- *STV: World Geography, Africa and Europe* (Videodisc)
- *ZipZapMap! World* (Software)
- *GeoBee* (Software)
- *Images of the World* (Posters)
- *Eye on the Environment* (Posters)
- *Physical Geography of the World* (Transparencies)
- *Picture Atlas of Our 50 States* (Book)

Introducing
CHAPTER 22

PERFORMANCE ASSESSMENT

Refer to the Planning Guide on page 450B for a Performance Assessment Activity for this chapter. See the *Performance Assessment Activities* booklet for additional suggestions.

CHAPTER OBJECTIVES

1. **Understand** that the one-crop economies created under colonialism discouraged the development of regional trade and transportation within sub-Saharan Africa.
2. **Recognize** that over the past century, human interaction with the environment has contributed to the problem of hunger in Africa south of the Sahara.

GLENCOE TECHNOLOGY

Videodisc

Use Chapter 22 MindJogger Videoquiz to preview chapter content.

MINDJOGGER VIDEOQUIZ

Chapter 22
Disc 3 Side B

The MindJogger Videoquiz is also available on videocassette.

chapter 22 Africa South of the Sahara Today

CHAPTER FOCUS

Geographic Setting

The economy of Africa south of the Sahara, or sub-Saharan Africa, rests heavily on agriculture and the export of raw materials. Efforts to industrialize have been hindered by the legacy of colonialism, a lack of capital, and pressing environmental concerns.

Geographic Themes

Section 1 Living in Africa South of the Sahara
REGION The one-crop economies created under colonialism discouraged the development of regional trade and transportation within sub-Saharan Africa.

Section 2 People and Their Environment
HUMAN/ENVIRONMENT INTERACTION Over the past century, human interaction with the environment has contributed to the problem of hunger in Africa south of the Sahara.

▲ Photograph: *Downtown Harare, Zimbabwe*

EXTRA CREDIT PROJECT

Demonstrate Refer interested students to page 459. Have them read about how Ethiopian farmers plant seedlings to prevent erosion. Point out that plants stop desertification not only by holding soil in place but also by releasing moisture into the air. Ask the students to demonstrate this fact by performing the following experiment:

(1) Set a houseplant in a clear plastic bag large enough not to crush the plant. Tie the bag shut.
(2) After 24 hours, check the bag and observe the moisture.

Tell the class that a houseplant releases 1½ pints of water into the air every 24 hours.

SECTION 1

Living in Africa South of the Sahara

SETTING THE SCENE

Read to Discover . . .

- the major types of economic activities in sub-Saharan Africa.
- the obstacles that face industrial development of Africa south of the Sahara.
- how colonialism hindered the growth of transportation and trade in sub-Saharan Africa.
- the most common form of mass communication in Africa south of the Sahara.

Key Terms

- cash crop
- commercial farming
- subsistence farming
- shifting farming
- sedentary farming

Identify and Locate

Transvaal, Dar es Salaam, Great Uhuru Railroad, Shaba Province

Johannesburg, South Africa

Although my family has an automobile, most South Africans use public transport. Because of the unnatural policies of apartheid, vast portions of the population have been forced to live far from their places of work. Over the years, the train and bus services have not been able to keep up with the demand. Mini-bus taxis have become a major form of transport.

Maurice R. DeVries

Maurice DeVries describes recent advances in transportation in South Africa. He notes it is one area of life in sub-Saharan Africa that has undergone change in recent years. Likewise, Lydiah Macharia and her family in Kenya are coping with new situations. In Kikuyu tradition, Lydiah Macharia's father will leave his tea plantation to his sons. He broke with tradition, however, when he encouraged his daughters to follow careers. Two of Lydiah's sisters became doctors. Lydiah works as a labor manager for a railroad and has used her earnings to buy land in the Great Rift Valley.

HUMAN/ENVIRONMENT INTERACTION

Agriculture

Lydiah Macharia hired several workers to till her land. She grows tea—one of Kenya's leading exports. Although Kenya is more industrialized than most nations in Africa south of the Sahara, its economy still relies on agriculture from which most Kenyans earn their living.

Colonial Legacy

Most African nations still suffer from the economies created by colonial rule, which

LESSON PLAN
Chapter 22, Section 1

FOCUS

SECTION OBJECTIVES

1. **Identify** the major types of economic activities in sub-Saharan Africa.
2. **Describe** the obstacles that face industrial development of Africa south of the Sahara.
3. **Explain** how colonialism hindered the growth of transportation and trade in sub-Saharan Africa.
4. **Name** the most common form of communication in Africa south of the Sahara.

ABOUT THE POSTCARD

Maurice lives in Cape Town, and writes that his city contains the best elements of both country and city living.

BELLRINGER MOTIVATIONAL ACTIVITY

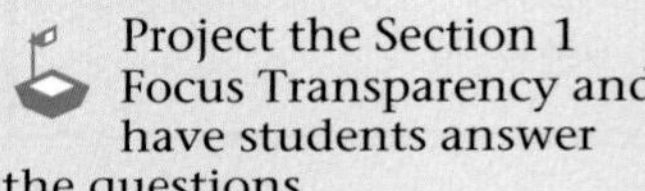

Project the Section 1 Focus Transparency and have students answer the questions.

PRETEACHING VOCABULARY

Read aloud the definition of *sedentary* from the dictionary and ask students to hypothesize about the meaning of *sedentary farming* based on the definition of *sedentary*. Then ask which Key Term sounds like the opposite of sedentary farming. *(shifting farming)*

Use the Vocabulary PuzzleMaker Software to create a crossword or word search puzzle.

Classroom Resources for Section 1

BLACKLINE MASTERS:
Reproducible Lesson Plan 22-1
Guided Reading Activity 22-1
Performance Assessment Activity 22
Section Quiz 22-1

TRANSPARENCIES:
Section Focus Transparency 22-1

MULTIMEDIA:

Vocabulary PuzzleMaker Software
Testmaker

Geography and the Environment

TEACH

GUIDED PRACTICE

L1 Make a Graph Copy a skeleton graph with PRODUCTS along the vertical axis, PERCENT along the horizontal axis, and PERCENTAGE OF THE WORLD'S SUPPLY FROM SUB-SAHARAN AFRICA at the top. Distribute the graph to the class. Have students complete the bar graph using facts from page 452.

USING CHARTS

Answer: 80 percent

Skills Practice

Reading a Chart Which country on the chart has the greatest percentage of workers in agriculture? *(Rwanda)*

USING ILLUSTRATIONS

HUMAN/ENVIRONMENT INTERACTION Coffee provides 80 to 90 percent of Burundi's export earnings.

Answer to Caption: It is grown for profit.

DID YOU KNOW?

Nigeria and Madagascar are among the world's top 20 rice producers.

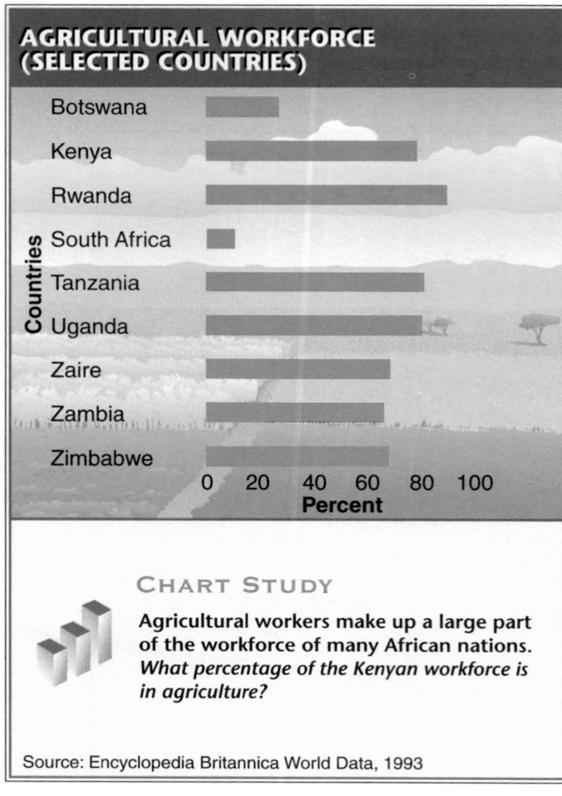

CHART STUDY

Agricultural workers make up a large part of the workforce of many African nations. ***What percentage of the Kenyan workforce is in agriculture?***

Source: Encyclopedia Britannica World Data, 1993

they have tried to balance since gaining independence. Europeans used sub-Saharan Africa as a resource base. As a result, sub-Saharan Africans produced only one or two **cash crops**, or crops grown for a profit.

Ghana still depends heavily on the sale of cacao. Burundi depends on coffee. Such reliance on one product is filled with risks. An unfavorable growing season or a drop in prices on the world market can adversely affect a nation's entire economy.

Farming Methods

Only a few people work at **commercial farming**, or farming organized as a business. Most plantations that produce crops for export are owned, at least in part, by companies outside the region.

Despite their small number, commercial farms provide the bulk of cash crops in sub-Saharan Africa. The plantations that dot the region produce almost 75 percent of the world's palm oil, 80 percent of the peanuts, 75 percent of the cacao, and 66 percent of the world's sisal—a vegetable fiber used for making rope.

Most sub-Saharan Africans work at **subsistence farming**, or agriculture that provides just for the needs of a family or village. Some peoples, such as the Maasai, practice nomadic herding. Others support themselves by **shifting farming**, a method in which farmers move every one to three years to find better soil. Yet other farmers depend on **sedentary farming**, or farming conducted at permanent settlements. All farmers face problems caused by overgrazing, exhausted soil, and a lack of technology.

The region's population is booming, and the majority of people lack the technology to increase food production. Chemical fertilizers and farm machinery would help boost crop yields, yet few nations can afford these aids to cultivation. Hunger has become a fact of life for countless subsistence farmers.

Geographic Themes

Human/Environment Interaction: East Africa

Coffee, grown on plantations, is one of the most important agricultural products of East Africa. *Why is coffee considered a cash crop?*

Cooperative Learning Activity

Remind students that chemical fertilizers pollute. Then have a group research less harmful and expensive alternatives for enriching exhausted soil. Assign one of the following topics related to the problem or the solution to each group member: monoculture, salination, desertification, sustainable agriculture, organic farming, organic fertilizer, crop rotation, strip farming, and integrated pest management. Refer the members to *Environmental Literacy: Everything You Need to Know About Saving Our Planet* by H. Steven Dashefsky for information on their topic. Then have them report their findings on a sheet of paper and arrange the reports on a free-standing, three-sided display board entitled FARMING IN SUB-SAHARAN AFRICA: WHAT IS WRONG AND WAYS TO FIX IT.

HUMAN/ENVIRONMENT INTERACTION

Forests and Seas

Forests cover almost 25 percent of Africa. These forests yield many valuable hardwood trees—Rhodesian teak, ebony, African walnut, and rosewood. Transportation systems and capital, however, are needed to develop a lumber industry. Currently, only coastal nations with rain forests export much lumber, accounting for less than 10 percent of the world's supply. The rain forests are also being cleared for farmland and fuel at an alarming rate. Their destruction has created a major environmental problem for the region and the world.

Commercial fishing has also developed slowly in sub-Saharan Africa. Few nations can afford to build fleets of ocean trawlers. The most profitable commercial fishing exists along the southwestern coast. Fish canned and exported from there include tuna, sardines, anchovies, and mackerel.

AFRICA SOUTH OF SAHARA: ECONOMIC ACTIVITY

20°W 40°N 0° 20°E 40°E 60°E
Tropic of Cancer 20°N
Equator 0°
20°S Tropic of Capricorn
N
0 1000 mi.
0 1000 km

- Nomadic herding
- Livestock raising
- Commercial farming
- Subsistence farming
- Commercial fishing
- Little or no activity

Azimuthal Equal-Area projection

FOCUS ON GEOGRAPHIC THEMES

1. **Region:** In which region of Africa is economic activity most developed?
2. **Place:** What is the dominant economic activity in Somalia?
3. **Region:** What type of farming is practiced in most of Africa?

HUMAN/ENVIRONMENT INTERACTION

Mining

Mining is an important—and difficult—economic activity in the region. Miners cope with hazardous conditions, long hours, and time away from their families.

Despite the risks thousands of black South Africans work in the mines. Their wages help support families in impoverished rural areas.

South Africa boasts a fortune of mineral wealth. A gold deposit more than 300 miles (483 km) long arcs across the Transvaal, a grassy plateau. It accounts for almost half of the world's known reserves of gold. South Africa is also a world leader in the production of gem diamonds, platinum, and minerals such as chromium, vanadium, and manganese.

South Africa's mineral wealth has made it one of the richest nations in the region, with a 1992 gross domestic product (GDP) of almost $115 billion. Most profits, however, have gone to foreign investors or companies owned by white South Africans. Little money has trickled down to black South Africans. This has caused wide gaps in the standard of living. In the late 1980s, for example, black South Africans earned a yearly per capita income of $1,467 compared to $7,276 enjoyed by white South Africans.

Resources are not spread evenly over the region, causing economic imbalances and overdependence on a single resource. Most deposits lie along the Atlantic coast and south of the Equator. Guinea has one of the world's largest deposits of bauxite, Zaire has large quantities of diamonds and important copper, and Nigeria has huge reserves of oil. Nigeria is the only sub-Saharan member of the Organization of Petroleum Exporting Countries (OPEC).

L1 List After students read page 453, have a student list a resource important to the sub-Saharan African economy on the chalkboard. Then have the student pass the chalk to another student who also must list a resource, and so on, until all the resources from page 453 are listed.

INDEPENDENT PRACTICE

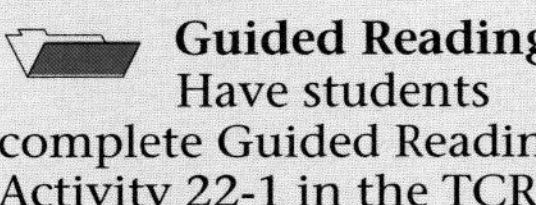

Guided Reading Have students complete Guided Reading Activity 22-1 in the TCR. **LEP**

USING MAPS

Answers: **1.** southern Africa; **2.** nomadic herding; **3.** subsistence

Map Skills Practice

Reading a Map What does the map show about desert areas in sub-Saharan Africa? *(They have little or no economic activity.)*

GLENCOE TECHNOLOGY

Videodisc

Use the following to enrich Chapter 22:

GEOGRAPHY AND THE ENVIRONMENT
THE INFINITE VOYAGE
The Keepers of Eden

Chapter 8
Disc 1 Side A

Title: ***Preserves of Endangered Species: San Diego and Kenya***

Meeting Special Needs

Study Strategy Model the use of the "Question" component of studying for students who are not fluent in asking questions. Explain that this exercise is part of a study routine and should be practiced whenever reading for information in a text. Read aloud the first sentence of each paragraph under the heading "Mining." For the first paragraph ask, "Why is mining in the region difficult?" For the second paragraph ask, "Why do thousands of South Africans work in the mines?" Have students form other questions using the first sentences of the paragraphs that follow in the section.

ASSESS

CHECK FOR UNDERSTANDING

Assign Section 1 Review as homework or an in-class activity.

MEETING LESSON OBJECTIVES

Each objective below is tested by the questions that follow it in parentheses.

1. Identify the major types of economic activities in sub-Saharan Africa. *(1, 3)*
2. Describe the obstacles that face industrial development of Africa south of the Sahara. *(2, 4)*
3. Explain how colonialism hindered the growth of transportation and trade in sub-Saharan Africa. *(5)*
4. Name the most common form of communication in Africa south of the Sahara.

EVALUATE

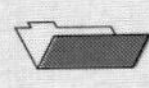
Assign the Section 1 Quiz in the TCR.

Use the Testmaker to create a customized quiz for Section 1.

USING ILLUSTRATIONS

MOVEMENT Cameroon, for instance, has 686 miles (1,104 km) of railroad track or one mile (1.609 km) of track for every 262 square miles (678.6 sq. km) of the country's area.

Answer to Caption: *They need ground routes to coastal ports.*

PLACE

Industrialization

Manufacturing plays a relatively small role in Africa's economy. In the past, colonial rulers obtained raw materials in Africa for their home industries and left Africa industrially undeveloped.

Today many sub-Saharan nations, such as Nigeria, have used foreign loans to industrialize. Despite an abundance of raw materials, few nations have industrial centers to process them. Therefore, most sub-Saharan nations continue to act as supply bases for the industrial world.

Manufacturing

In 1993 manufacturing accounted for only about 14.4 percent of the region's entire GDP. Manufacturing, however, contributed between 38 and 44 percent of the GDP in South Africa, Swaziland, Zimbabwe, and Zambia. This was offset by the low industrial outputs of Uganda (7.4 percent), Niger (7 percent), and Guinea (less than 1 percent).

Geographic Themes

Movement: Southern Africa

Since independence, African countries have worked to improve means of transportation. *Why have landlocked countries sought to build railroads and pipelines?*

Obstacles

Obstacles to industrialization include a lack of capital, political turmoil between or within nations, and not enough skilled workers or transportation systems. The region's great hydroelectric potential also remains largely untapped.

Such conditions have forced much of Africa south of the Sahara into a cycle of poverty. Nations spend scarce revenues on feeding an ever-growing population and rely heavily on trade with industrial nations, such as the United States, Japan, and the colonial powers of Europe.

To break this dependency, some nations have attempted to form regional trading associations such as the Economic Community of West African States (ECOWAS). Others have acted on their own. For example, Nigeria has tried to further its economic growth by lifting taxes on goods shipped by landlocked nations to its ports.

MOVEMENT

Transportation and Communication

Efforts by sub-Saharan Africa to develop good transportation or communication systems have not been highly successful. Outside of cities, few paved roads exist. In rural areas travelers have to search for telephones and often must use long-wave radio transmitters. Railway and airplane travel are the most successful means of spanning the region.

Railroad Travel

Each day trains traveling the Kenya National Railroad leave Nairobi for coastal cities such as Mombasa. The 12-hour journey is considered one of the world's great train rides.

This world-famous railroad was built by the British before Kenyan independence. It spans the rugged terrain that separates the highlands from the coast to allow hauling of raw materials to port. Other colonial powers built railroads for the same purpose.

Critical Thinking

Predicting Consequences Have students imagine that, like in Chad, only 1 out of every 1,114 people in their community had access to a telephone, that fewer people had televisions, and that the only form of communication was one radio per family. Ask them to write an essay about how their lives would be different. Have them explain the disadvantages of limited communications, but also urge them to come up with advantages as well.

Improving Transportation

Since independence, many obstacles have hindered efforts to improve transportation. Wars and lack of funds have caused a decline of existing highways and railroads. The region's size and unfavorable terrain have made it difficult to build new routes. The region also has few harbors and navigable rivers.

For most nations air travel has overcome geographic barriers. Government-owned airlines have set up international and domestic service. International airports are found in Addis Ababa, Ethiopia; Nairobi, Kenya; Johannesburg, South Africa; and Dakar, Senegal.

Landlocked nations have also sought ground routes to coastal ports. Oil is transported through pipelines across Tanzania, Zambia, Sudan, South Africa, and Nigeria.

To transport freight, several nations have built railroads. The most successful is the Great Uhuru (Tanzam) Railroad. It connects the mineral-rich Shaba Province in southeastern Zaire to Dar es Salaam, Tanzania, a distance of about 1,153 miles (1,855 km). Many other overland routes, however, have been stopped or closed by warfare or a lack of funds.

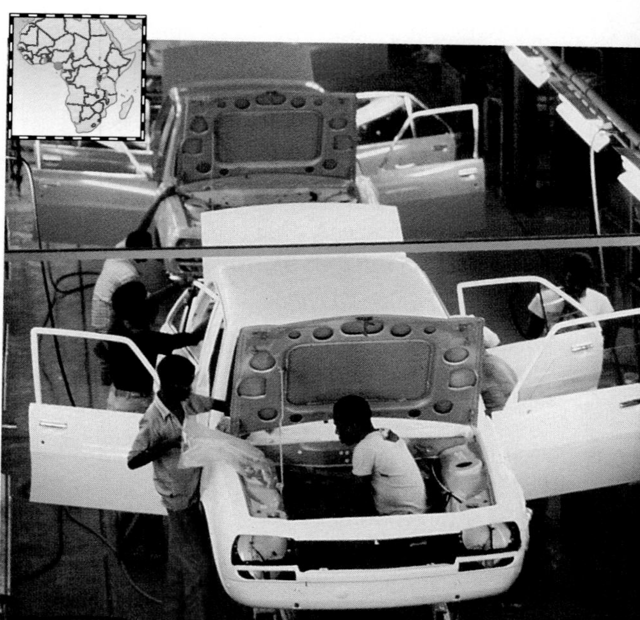

Geographic Themes

Region: Nigeria

Factories in Nigeria produce a wide variety of goods. Manufacturing, however, employs only a small number of Nigerians. *What percent of Africa's GDP comes from manufacturing?*

Mass Communications

The scarcity of newsprint and the low literacy rates have limited the number of newspapers and magazines printed in the region south of the Sahara. Telephone service also is limited with the most extensive systems found in urban areas. In Chad only 1 out of every 1,114 people has access to a telephone. Even in Kenya, telephones average only about 1 per every 96 people.

The most effective means of communication in sub-Saharan Africa is radio. In Kenya, 1 out of 6 people owns a radio. In Chad, 1 out of 4.3 people owns one. Most important news is broadcast over the radio.

Television broadcasting, however, has grown slowly. Television stations offer a variety of programs, including popular reruns from the United States. Although televisions remain confined largely to urban areas, some governments are experimenting with television as an educational tool.

Section 1 Review

Checking for Understanding

1. **Define** cash crop, commercial farming, subsistence farming, shifting farming, sedentary farming.
2. **Locating Places** Why do few transportation networks link sub-Saharan Africa as a region?
3. **Human/Environment Interaction** What are the most common forms of agricultural production in Africa south of the Sahara?
4. **Region** Why do sub-Saharan Africans share unequally in the region's mineral wealth?

Critical Thinking

5. **Expressing Problems Clearly** What are the most critical obstacles facing economic development in Africa south of the Sahara?

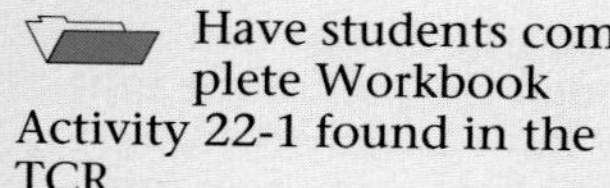

RETEACH

Have students complete Workbook Activity 22-1 found in the TCR.

ENRICH

Ask volunteers to "radio broadcast" recent stories about sub-Saharan Africa from newspapers. Supply a toy microphone as a prop.

CLOSE

Have students write a postcard to Maurice, describing the transportation where they live.

USING ILLUSTRATIONS

PLACE Nigerian factories also produce processed food and textiles.

Answer to Caption:
14.4 percent

ANSWERS TO SECTION 1 REVIEW

1. **cash crop:** crop raised for profit; **commercial farming:** farming organized as a business; **subsistence farming:** farming to feed a family or village; **shifting farming:** when farmers move in search of more fertile soil; **sedentary farming:** when farmers stay in one place
2. because colonial powers had little interest in developing regional trade, the purpose of railroads was to haul raw materials to port
3. nomadic herding, shifting farming, and sedentary farming
4. Foreigners kept profits from South African mining, and minerals are spread unevenly throughout the region.
5. lack of capital and skilled workers, low literacy rates, political instability, and trading patterns imposed by colonialism

FOCUS

Ask students to skim through the part of the unit they have already read, noting heads, photographs, and captions. Have them offer reasons why a rural African might want to move to a large city. List some of their speculations on the chalkboard.

TEACH

Use Unit Map Overlay Transparency 7-5 to familiarize students with the location of Nigeria and Lagos.

L2 Culture Have students research to find common cultural beliefs held by rural Nigerians of different ethnic groups. Ask students to provide the reasons behind these beliefs.

L3 Debate Have students debate the ending quote, either agreeing or disagreeing. Require that they provide support for their opinions from material they have read in the unit.

Moving to Lagos

Hundreds of millions of Africans are lurching between an unworkable Western present and a collapsing African past . . . they [must] sort out new connections with their families, their tribes, and their countries.

Blain Harden, "Nigeria: Africa's Great Black Hope," *World Monitor,* August 1990

Lagos, Nigeria's capital, is the country's financial hub and headquarters of western European businesses in the country.

Factories in Lagos turn out a wide variety of items including foodstuffs, beverages, paint, soaps, textiles, and parts for auto assembly. Much of the wealth that comes from the country's petroleum, tin, coal, and iron resources is concentrated in Lagos.

THE ISSUE

Every year Lagos attracts thousands of people, mostly rural farmers, from the Nigerian countryside. To them, the city promises employment and a better way of life.

Since the 1960s, the population of Lagos has almost tripled—from a little less than 500,000 to about 8 million in the early 1990s.

This overwhelming population growth presents grim challenges for Lagos, as well as for thousands of displaced rural Africans.

THE BACKGROUND

In the mid-1960s, petroleum reserves were discovered along Nigeria's coast. During the next decade, oil exports brought a period of rapid economic growth to the country. Lagos took on the atmosphere of a boomtown.

As Lagos boomed, however, agriculture declined. Severe droughts in the early 1970s reduced crop production drastically. Many migrants from rural areas flocked to the city, hoping to improve their standard of living. At the time Lagos's businesses required more workers, both skilled and unskilled. Hundreds of thousands profited from the petroleum earnings.

Then, in the early 1980s, the oil bubble burst. World demand for petroleum dropped sharply as consumers in Western nations reacted to foreign oil prices by introducing energy conservation programs. Nigeria's foreign earnings from oil dropped also. The country's foreign debt increased; Lagos's factories slowed production or stopped altogether for lack of imported raw materials.

Thousands of workers lost their jobs and could not find others. Agriculture was depressed even further. During the mid- and late-1980s, more and more farmers found they could not support themselves, and joined the thousands seeking work in Lagos.

This overwhelming population growth presents grim challenges for Lagos, as well as for thousands of displaced rural Africans.

Slum dwellings sprang up along the outskirts of Lagos. Unemployment was high, and the crime rate increased. In addition, agricultural production further decreased as farmers left their lands to find work in the city. By the early 1990s, Lagos was overwhelmed by an economy gone sour and a population that had tripled.

Extending the Content

Government Nigeria has a complex, diversified, and—despite the decline in the importance of oil—a potentially strong economy and democratic government. Have students research the country's history since gaining independence from Great Britain, noting the diversity of economic sectors and the status of education. Have students also update the government's move from a military leadership to democracy. Lead them to discuss whether they think positive factors in Nigeria's economy and government will affect the situation in Lagos, as well as the country in general. Require that students support their opinions with evidence.

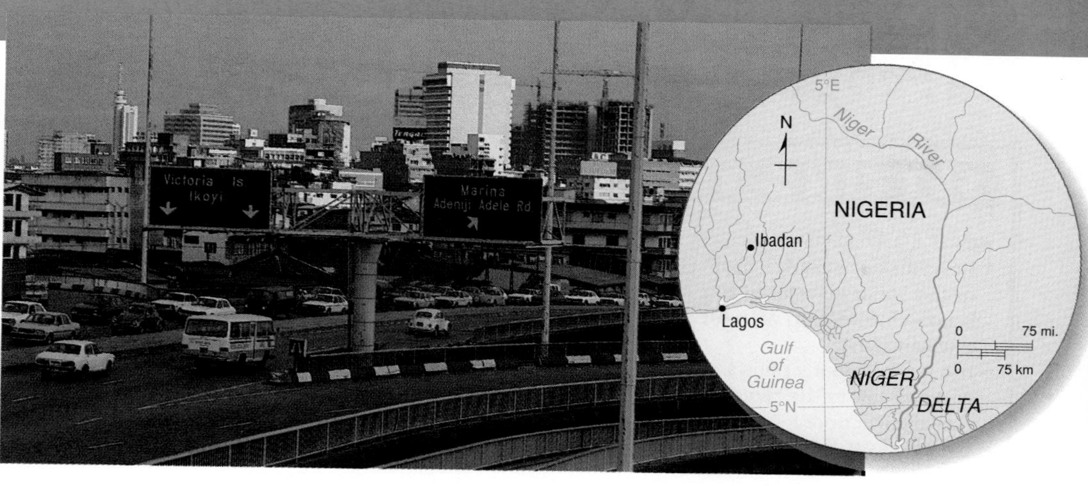

Lagos is Nigeria's chief port. High-rise buildings and overcrowded residential areas dominate the city's landscape.

THE POINTS OF VIEW

Many African leaders say that Lagos's overpopulation is part of a larger problem, that of the loss of Nigeria's traditional society. Nigeria's economic success has weakened the traditional agricultural society. Books and newspapers promoting opportunities in the cities are readily available. Even those who do not migrate to the city are becoming antagonistic to old values.

Others point out that Nigeria's population is increasing so rapidly that none of the economic gains since the 1960s could possibly keep pace. They add that a belief in a large family is one that is held in common by many of Nigeria's ethnic groups. Large families are no longer economically necessary, say these experts, yet the government has done little to develop family planning.

THE ISSUE TODAY

Overpopulation in Lagos remains a serious problem. Overcrowding has led to poor housing, a lack of good water and sanitation, and shortages of electricity and other public services. Such conditions also increase already poor health problems due to mosquitos, which breed in the city's many ponds and swampy areas. In addition, the ponds have long been used as garbage dumps, and both the land and water have become polluted.

The national government has begun water reclamation projects, and educational facilities are expanding. The government has also developed agricultural cooperatives and better markets for local surpluses. More money has been made available for investment in agriculture.

Nigerian leaders agree, however, that the runaway growth of Lagos and the country's other cities is linked directly to a loss of village life. They believe many Nigerians are torn between the old way of life and the hurried and often unrewarding pursuit of Western goals. Nigerian statesman Olusagan Obasanjo voices the hope of many Africans: "I believe that for us in Africa, our salvation lies in our own hands and nowhere else. Only we can be the architects of our future; as we have been the architects of our misfortune by and large for the past quarter of a century."

Reviewing the Case

1. What events contributed to the overpopulation in Lagos?
2. **Human/Environment Interaction** What are some problems Lagos faces because of overpopulation?

DID YOU KNOW?

The Nigerians have a rich history as African artists. The oldest known African sculptures were created by the Nok as far back as 500 B.C. The Nok worked in terra cotta, sculpting figures from 1 inch (2.54 cm) to life size.

ASSESS

Have students answer the Reviewing the Case questions on page 457.

CLOSE

Have students summarize the causes and effects of the overpopulation problems in Lagos.

ANSWERS TO REVIEWING THE CASE

1. an oil boom in the late 1960s and through the 1970s; severe drought in the 1970s; depression of the agricultural market in the 1980s
2. inadequate water due both to increasing population as well as pollution of water supply from garbage dumping; inadequate housing; poor sanitation methods; rise in disease

LESSON PLAN
Chapter 22, Section 2

FOCUS

SECTION OBJECTIVES

1. **Discuss** how hunger in Africa south of the Sahara is related to human interaction with the environment.
2. **Examine** the reasons many plants and animals in the region face destruction.
3. **Illustrate** the efforts sub-Saharan Africans have taken to offset decades of famine and war.

BELLRINGER MOTIVATIONAL ACTIVITY

Project the Section 2 Focus Transparency and have students answer the questions.

PRETEACHING VOCABULARY

Read the definitions of *desertification* and *deforestation* and have the students hypothesize about how the two are linked in sub-Saharan Africa. Then have them read page 458 to find support for their hypotheses.

MULTICULTURAL PERSPECTIVE

Culturally Speaking
Somalia is in some ways a rare case of homogeneity. Most Somalis are Sunni Muslims, and all speak the same language.

SECTION 2

People and Their Environment

THE ENVIRONMENT

SETTING THE SCENE

Read to Discover . . .
- how hunger in Africa south of the Sahara is related to human interaction with the environment.
- the reasons many plants and animals in the region face destruction.
- the efforts sub-Saharan Africans have taken to offset decades of famine and war.

Key Terms
- desertification
- deforestation
- extinction
- habitat
- poaching
- ecotourism

Identify and Locate
Somalia, Horn of Africa, Madagascar, Serengeti Plain, Sahel

In late 1992 a Somalian woman named Muslima Aden Abdulrahman watched her mother and daughter die. A few days later, her 7-year-old son died. Muslima told a reporter:

> *I have buried all my family. Almost everyone from my village is dead. I have no more tears left.*

Within weeks Muslima also died. Like her mother and children, she starved to death. Between 1991 and 1993, more than 350,000 Somalians suffered the same fate. In recent times similar stories have come out of other nations south of the Sahara. Since the 1970s, starvation and poverty have become all too familiar experiences for millions of nomadic herders and subsistence farmers of the region.

PLACE

The Shadow of Famine

The causes of famine in sub-Saharan Africa are complex and varied. As you have read, a booming population, a lack of capital, and overdependence on cash crops all contribute to food shortages. Two other factors also rob millions of sub-Saharan Africans of food—expansion of the desert and civil war.

Desertification

In the past 100 years, a band of desert more than 93 miles (150 km) wide has crept into the countries of Mauritania, Mali, Niger, Chad, and Sudan. Humans have been largely responsible for the **desertification**, or the transformation of arable land into desert, in the Sahel. Overgrazing, overplanting, and destruction of trees have left the land dangerously exposed to erosion.

Classroom Resources for Section 2

BLACKLINE MASTERS:
Reproducible Lesson Plan 22-2
Vocabulary Activity 22
Skill Activity 22
Enrichment Activity 22
Geography Simulation 7
Environmental Issue 7
Section Quiz 22-2

TRANSPARENCIES:
Section Focus Transparency 22-2

MULTIMEDIA:

Testmaker

Reuters Issues in Geography
Geography and the Environment

A series of recent droughts have added to the misery. Two droughts in the Sahel—one from 1968 to the early 1970s and one in the early 1980s—turned farmland into wasteland. They wiped out nearly half the area's cattle. As the 1990s began, the United Nations Food and Agriculture Organization (FAO) reported 20 million people were on the brink of starvation.

Civil War

From the 1970s into the 1990s, civil war has been among the biggest human causes of famine on the Horn of Africa, the eastern bulge of land that juts into the Indian Ocean. Here political upheavals combined with droughts to create widespread suffering. Food became a weapon as rival factions battled each other in Sudan, Eritrea, Ethiopia, and Somalia. Armies burned the fields of suspected enemies. Relief agencies such as the Red Cross sent in food, only to see up to half of it stolen by rebels or corrupt warlords.

Starvation and bloodshed created millions of refugees. Famine and disease swept through many refugee camps. The situation became so critical in Somalia that the United Nations intervened in 1992. Led by 25,000 troops from the United States, the United Nations sent in a peacekeeping force made up of units from 22 nations. Armed with guns and food, the soldiers tried to stop rival warlords from interrupting food shipments to a starving nation.

HUNGER IN AFRICA

Calories per person per day
- High (more than 3,000)
- Adequate (2,500-2,999)
- Low (2,000-2,499)
- Very Low (less than 1,999)
- No data

Azimuthal Equal-Area projection

FOCUS ON GEOGRAPHIC THEMES

1. **Region:** What countries of East Africa are most seriously affected by food shortages?
2. **Region:** What is the status of the food supply in most countries of central Africa along the Equator?

PLACE

Battling Hunger

To combat hunger sub-Saharan Africans have focused on 2 tasks—restoring their battered environment and keeping the peace. The examples of Ethiopia and Eritrea show how these efforts have borne fruit. For almost 30 years, rebellion tore Ethiopia apart. For equally as long, Eritrea fought to break free of Ethiopia. At the beginning of the 1990s, the guns quieted in both nations as Eritrea finally gained its independence. As farmers went back to their land, they sought to undo the damage of drought and war.

To stop erosion, farmers in the northern Ethiopian province of Tigray terraced more than 250,000 acres (about 101,250 ha) of land. They also planted 42 million seedlings, or young trees, to hold soil in place. Using hand tools, they built earthen dams to store precious rain water. In 1992 fields in Tigray bloomed with crops such as barley, wheat, and a local grain called teff. In neighboring Eritrea farmers produced such abundant crops that the government reduced its requests for relief in 1993 by 50 percent.

The success of Ethiopia and Eritrea have held out hope for other nations. A sense of self-respect has returned. "We can make a good life," explained one Eritrean farmer with quiet pride. "All we need is rain and peace."

TEACH

GUIDED PRACTICE

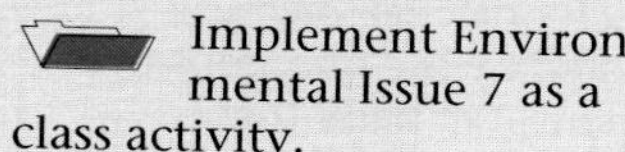
Implement Environmental Issue 7 as a class activity.

L1 Interdependence Invite a Red Cross representative to tell the class about the agency's relief work around the world, including sub-Saharan Africa. Have students prepare questions about how geography affects the work of the Red Cross.

INDEPENDENT PRACTICE

Guided Reading Have students complete Guided Reading Activity 22-2 in the TCR. **LEP**

USING MAPS

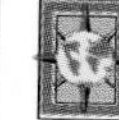
Answers:
1. Sudan, Eritrea, Somalia, Ethiopia, and Mozambique;
2. between 2,000 and 2,499 calories per person per day

Map Skills Practice
Reading a Map Where do the best-fed people in sub-Saharan Africa live? *(South Africa)*

ASSESS

CHECK FOR UNDERSTANDING

Assign Section 2 Review as homework or an in-class activity.

Cooperative Learning Activity

Write to the Dian Fossey Gorilla Fund at 45 Inverness Drive East, Englewood, CO 80112-5480 to order "Can Rwandans, Mountain Gorillas and Tourists Coexist?"—a curriculum package that incorporates geography themes, scientific concepts, and negotiation skills. Use the package to help your students explore the dilemma of people and endangered mountain gorillas sharing the same space.

Chapter 22, Section 2

MEETING LESSON OBJECTIVES

Each objective below is tested by the questions that follow it in parentheses.

1. **Discuss** how hunger in Africa south of the Sahara is related to human interaction with the environment. *(2)*
2. **Examine** the reasons many plants and animals in the region face destruction. *(5)*
3. **Illustrate** the efforts sub-Saharan Africans have taken to offset decades of famine and war. *(3, 4)*

EVALUATE

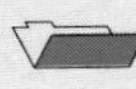
Assign the Section 2 Quiz in the TCR.

Use the Testmaker to create a customized quiz for Section 2.

USING CHARTS

Answers: Botswana, Rwanda, South Africa, Tanzania, and Zimbabwe

Skills Practice

Drawing Conclusions What does setting aside land for reserves suggest about the values of a country? *(that the country values wildlife)*

CURRICULUM CONNECTION

FRENCH

Côte d'Ivoire, named after the elephant herds that once roamed there, means "ivory coast" in French.

HUMAN/ENVIRONMENT INTERACTION

Saving the Forests

South of the Sahel, sub-Saharan Africans face another struggle. As this century draws to a close, the region is losing its tropical rain forests at a rate of about 3.2 million acres (1.3 million ha) per year. Since 1900 Côte d'Ivoire (Ivory Coast) has lost almost 70 percent of its rain forest. Madagascar has lost 75 percent.

Causes of **deforestation**, or destruction of forests, vary. Côte d'Ivoire cuts down many hardwood trees for export. In Madagascar, farmers burn forests to clear land for farming or grazing. Throughout sub-Saharan Africa, people cut trees for fuel.

The destruction of rain forests in Africa and elsewhere in the world has created a global problem. Plants turn carbon dioxide (CO_2) into oxygen. As the rain forests are destroyed, the amount of CO_2 rises. This gas allows the sun's rays to reach the earth. Carbon dioxide also holds in much more heat than oxygen. As a result, deforestation has very likely made the planet hotter, affecting growing seasons, rainfall patterns, and sea levels.

Destruction of the rain forests has also placed many plant and animal species at risk. Of the 200,000 plant and animal species on Madagascar, almost three-fourths exist nowhere else in the world. Deforestation is also the reason more than 20 animal species on Madagascar face **extinction**, or disappearance, from the earth.

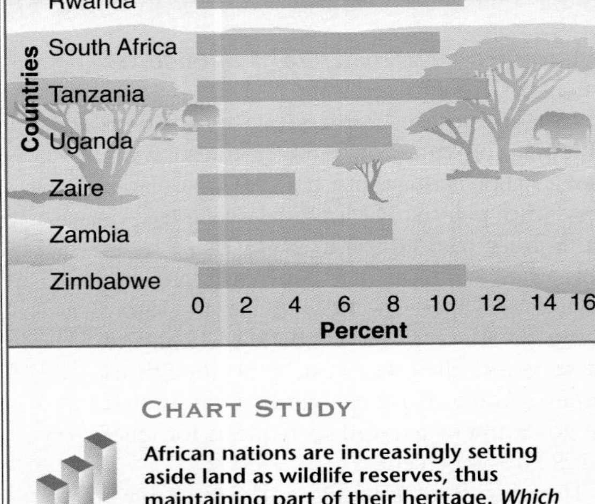

CHART STUDY

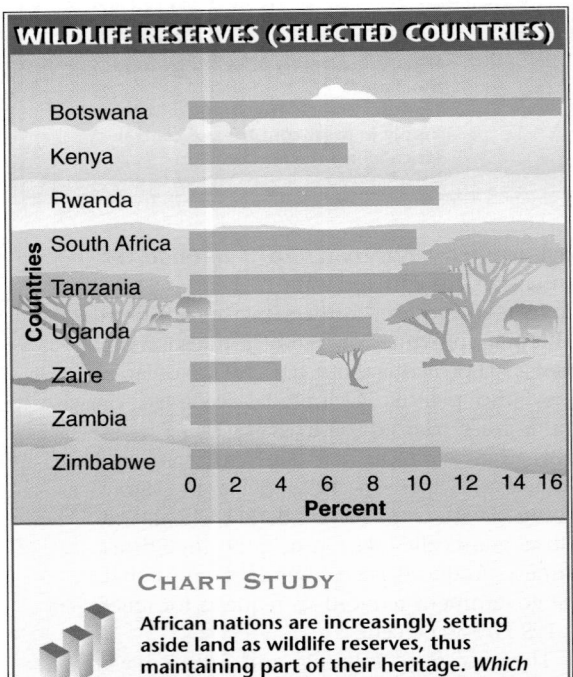

African nations are increasingly setting aside land as wildlife reserves, thus maintaining part of their heritage. ***Which nations have preserved 10 percent or more of their land as reserves?***

HUMAN/ENVIRONMENT INTERACTION

Conflicts Over Land Use

Protection of rain forests and endangered wildlife have raised difficult questions about land use. As the population of Africa south of the Sahara grows, nomadic herders and farmers have increasingly cut into forests. They have also pushed onto savanna grasslands that provide homes to Africa's huge herds of game. The lands on which these herds thrive are the same lands needed to feed and house Africa's people.

At the beginning of the 1970s, almost 70,000 black rhinos roamed across sub-Saharan Africa. By the early 1990s, only about 3,000 could be found. Other endangered animals included the African elephant, Cape Mountain zebra, and mountain gorilla.

Such animals are endangered for a number of reasons. First, humans have pushed into the animals' natural **habitats**, or living areas. Second, in recent decades hunters in greater numbers have tracked down game for sport and profit. The rhino and elephant have suffered heavily from **poaching**, or illegal hunting. Rhino horns and ivory from elephant tusks bring high prices on the world market.

To save endangered species, some nations have created huge game preserves, such as Tanzania's Serengeti National Park, Kenya's Masai Mara, or Rwanda's Parcs des Volcans.

Meeting Special Needs

Study Strategy Learning-disabled students often have difficulty generalizing the use of a strategy from one situation to another. They need to have periodic review of both the steps of the strategy they are using and the procedures that are used in each step. Tell students that in this section they are going to use a study strategy independently. Have each student make a chart to self-evaluate each of the following: Did I skim for the title, headings, main ideas? Did I ask questions? Did I answer my questions? Then have them use the chart after finishing each subhead in the section.

Geographic Themes

Human/Environment Interaction: Madagascar Rain Forest
Many rare plant and animal species thrive in the rain forests of Madagascar, an island off the coast of southeast Africa. *What development poses a threat to their existence?*

These preserves lure millions of tourists into East Africa every year. **Ecotourism**, or tourism based on the environment, brought more than $420 million into Kenya in 1989 alone.

Despite the profits earned from such preserves, many sub-Saharan Africans object to them. "People are too desperate," explained one park official. "They need food in their stomach." To win support for conservation, governments have tried to give rural peoples an economic stake in the preserves. Zimbabwe and Zambia, for example, use money from ecotourism to build local clinics and schools.

REGION

Toward the Future

In the 1950s and 1960s, sub-Saharan Africans won political independence. In the 2000s, their foremost task will be to win economic independence.

As sub-Saharan Africans look ahead to the next century, they are searching for ways to take charge of the region. Most agree that the time has come to shake off foreign dependency. In late 1992 Ugandan President Yoweri Museveni issued a challenge to the region:

> *We have to go back to the year 1500 [prior to colonialism], where we left off building an African economy, able to produce its own food, its own tools, its own weapons. . . . In short, we have to rely on ourselves.*

Section 2 Review

Checking for Understanding

1. **Define** desertification, deforestation, extinction, habitat, poaching, ecotourism.
2. **Locating Places** How has growth of the desert affected life in the Sahel?
3. **Region** What was the connection between civil war and the famines of the 1980s?
4. **Human/Environment Interaction** What steps have sub-Saharan Africans taken to preserve the environment?

Critical Thinking

5. **Identifying Central Issues** What is the central issue involved in the debate over the creation of game preserves?

Answers to Section 2 Review

1. **desertification:** destruction of vegetation, causing the desert to spread; **deforestation:** destruction of trees; **extinction:** disappearance of a species; **habitat:** area in which plants, animals, or humans live; **poaching:** illegal hunting; **ecotourism:** tourism based on environmental interests
2. It has caused widespread hunger, and put pressure on farmers to give up traditional farming methods.
3. They increased the hardships caused by droughts and desertification. Rival groups burned fields and stole food.
4. terracing land, planting seedling trees, building dams, and wildlife reserves
5. whether scarce land should be used to protect endangered species or to provide space and food for the booming population

RETEACH

Have students complete Reteaching Activity 22 in the TCR.

ENRICH

Have students complete Enrichment Activity 22 in the TCR.

CLOSE

Have students write and illustrate a children's story about an endangered animal from the section.

USING ILLUSTRATIONS

HUMAN/ENVIRONMENT INTERACTION Scientists suspect that some of the plant species found on Madagascar may be the source of miracle medicines.

Answer to Caption: *Farmers clear forests for farming and grazing.*

GLENCOE TECHNOLOGY

Videodisc

REUTERS ISSUES IN GEOGRAPHY

Chapter 6
Disc 1 Side A

Title: ***Sub-Saharan Africa: Preserving Its Legacy***
Subject: Preservation of African wildlife as a world issue

GEOGRAPHY AND THE ENVIRONMENT
THE INFINITE VOYAGE
The Keepers of Eden

Chapter 8
Disc 1 Side A

Title: ***Preserves of Endangered Species: San Diego and Kenya***

TEACH

Have students read the skill on page 462. Say: "Compare the purposes of vegetation maps and land-use maps." *(Vegetation maps describe natural plant life; land-use maps show human uses of the land and its resources.)* Have students identify the economic activities in the map on page 462. Point out the broad bands of land use—nomadic herding in northern Africa, tropical crop agriculture in central Africa, ranching in southern Africa. Ask: "How does climate affect land use in Africa?" *(The Sahara is too dry to support agriculture or large-scale ranching; tropical plants grow in the rain forest climate near the Equator; ranching prevails in the south where it is cooler and grasslands abound.)*

Skills Practice For additional practice, have students complete Skill Activity 22 in the TCR.

MAP & GRAPH SKILLS

Reading a Land-Use Map

In an earlier chapter, you learned that vegetation maps describe the natural plant life in different environments. Few places on the earth, however, are still untouched by the economic activities of humans. A **land-use map** illustrates how humans use land and other natural resources to make a living.

REVIEWING THE SKILL

Like other maps, land-use maps employ colors and symbols to represent various human uses of the land. The map key describes the meaning of each color and symbol on the map. Usually, colors show general activities such as crop farming, herding, ranching, and forestry. Symbols or labels often identify more particular kinds of information. For example, a color may show farming activities over a broad region, while a label or symbol may name the most important crop in that region.

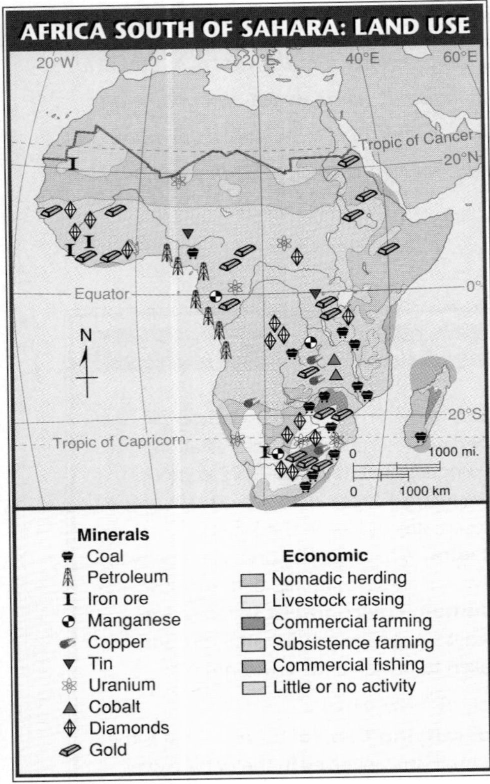

To interpret a land-use map, first read the title and the key to identify the region and activities illustrated in the map. Then find examples of each color and symbol on the map. By comparing a land-use map with a climate or vegetation map, you can see how humans have used the natural environment and how the environment has influenced the economic development of the region.

To read a land-use map, apply the following steps:

- Read the map title to identify the region shown on the map.
- Using the map key, identify the various land uses shown on the map.
- Determine which economic activities take place in each area of the region. Look for areas where similar activities occur.
- Compare a land-use map with a climate or vegetation map to draw conclusions about how natural conditions have affected human activities.

PRACTICING THE SKILL

Use the land-use map of Africa to answer the following questions:

1. What color represents commercial farming?
2. What do the following symbols represent?

3. Which part of Africa includes ranches? What animals are raised on these ranches?
4. What minerals are found in southern Africa?
5. Which part of sub-Saharan Africa has petroleum reserves?

For additional practice in this skill, see Practicing Skills on page 464 of the Chapter 22 Review.

ANSWERS TO PRACTICING THE SKILL

1. dark green
2. coal, tin, copper
3. southern Africa; cattle and sheep
4. manganese, petroleum, gold, tin, diamonds
5. west central coast near the Equator

chapter 22

HIGHLIGHTS

SECTION	KEY TERMS	SUMMARY
1 Living in Africa South of the Sahara	**cash crop** (p. 452) **commercial farming** (p. 452) **subsistence farming** (p. 452) **shifting farming** (p. 452) **sedentary farming** (p. 452)	• Most sub-Saharan nations depend on the export of one or two cash crops. • The majority of sub-Saharan Africans work as subsistence farmers. • Mineral deposits, as well as the profits from their export, are spread unevenly throughout Africa south of the Sahara. • Industrialization is hindered by a lack of capital and a shortage of skilled workers. • To reduce foreign dependence some nations are developing regional trade and transportation systems.

Coffee plantation in Kenya

SECTION	KEY TERMS	SUMMARY
2 People and Their Environment	**desertification** (p. 458) **deforestation** (p. 460) **extinction** (p. 460) **habitat** (p. 460) **poaching** (p. 460) **ecotourism** (p. 461)	• Desertification, drought, and war have contributed to hunger in sub-Saharan Africa. • In the 1990s Ethiopia and Eritrea took steps to restore their battered environment. • Destruction of the rain forests is a global problem. • Increasing human population and hunting has placed some African wildlife at risk of extinction. • To win rural support of game preserves, some nations have shared the profits of ecotourism. • As sub-Saharan Africans head into the next century, they hope to win economic independence.

A lemur in the Madagascar rain forest

CHAPTER 22 HIGHLIGHTS

USING THE CHAPTER 22 HIGHLIGHTS

Use the Chapter 22 Highlights to preview, review, condense, or reteach the chapter.

PREVIEW/REVIEW

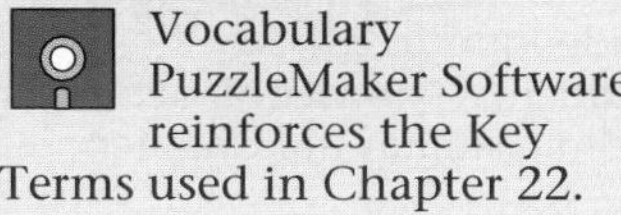

Vocabulary PuzzleMaker Software reinforces the Key Terms used in Chapter 22.

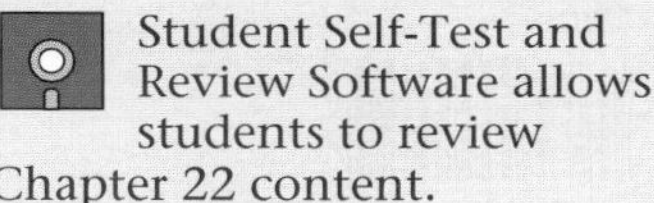

Student Self-Test and Review Software allows students to review Chapter 22 content.

CONDENSE

Have students read the Chapter 22 Highlights.

Have students listen to the Chapter 22 Audiocassettes in the TCR. Spanish Audiocassettes are also available.

Assign the Chapter 22 Audiocassette Activity and give the students the Chapter 22 Audiocassette Quiz.

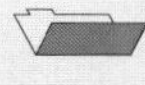 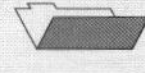

Have students complete Guided Reading Activities for Chapter 22 in the TCR. Spanish Guided Reading Activities are also available.

RETEACH

Have students complete Reteaching Activity 22 in the TCR. Spanish Reteaching Activities are also available.

Map Activity

Identify and Locate Copy and distribute page 37 of the Outline Map Resource Book. On the map, have students label the countries with wildlife reserves. Then tell them to make up a symbol representing a reserve, draw and identify the symbol in a corner of the map, and copy it on the labeled countries. Refer them to the chart on page 460 for the countries' names.

GLENCOE TECHNOLOGY

Videodisc

Use Chapter 22 MindJogger Videoquiz to review students' knowledge before administering the Chapter 22 Test.

MINDJOGGER VIDEOQUIZ

Chapter 22
Disc 3 Side B

The MindJogger Videoquiz is also available on videocassette.

chapter 22 REVIEW

Reviewing Key Terms

Choose the vocabulary term that best completes each of the sentences below. Write your answers on a separate sheet of paper.

cash crops (p. 452)
commercial farming (p. 452)
subsistence farming (p. 452)
shifting farming (p. 452)
desertification (p. 458)
deforestation (p. 460)
extinction (p. 460)
habitat (p. 460)
poaching (p. 460)
ecotourism (p. 461)

SECTION 1

1. Crops raised and sold for a profit are known as _____.
2. _____ supports the needs of an individual family or village.
3. Farmers who practice _____ move often to more fertile soil.
4. Farming established as an organized business is _____.

SECTION 2

5. _____ threatens to destroy the rain forests.
6. The illegal hunting of endangered animals is known as _____.
7. Tourism based on the environment is known as _____.
8. An animal's living area is its _____.
9. The disappearance of a plant or animal from the earth is _____.
10. Transforming arable land into desert is _____.

Reviewing Facts

SECTION 1

11. What are the key cash crops exported from this region?
12. What factors have discouraged a lumber industry in Africa?
13. What economic imbalances affect mining in sub-Saharan Africa?
14. Why has this region been slow to industrialize?
15. How did colonialism affect transportation in Africa?
16. Why is radio the most effective form of mass communication?

SECTION 2

17. Why did the United Nations intervene in Somalia in 1992?
18. What are some of the causes of deforestation in the region?
19. How have some rural farmers conserved the region's wildlife?

Critical Thinking

20. **Making Generalizations** How has political instability in Africa south of the Sahara contributed to its lack of capital?
21. **Analyzing Information** Based on the quote by Yoweri Museveni on page 461, what is one leading cause of current economic problems?

Geographic Themes

22. **Region** What economic traits do many nations of sub-Saharan Africa share?
23. **Human/Environment Interaction** How has the human population boom affected the region's wildlife?

Practicing Skills

Reading a Land-Use Map

Refer to the land-use map on page 462.

24. Compare the land-use map with the climate map on page 425. Do herding and livestock ranching take place in drier or wetter regions? Explain why.
25. Where in Africa does Mediterranean agriculture take place? Explain why.

ANSWERS

Reviewing Key Terms

1. cash crops
2. subsistence farming
3. shifting agriculture
4. commercial farming
5. deforestation
6. poaching
7. ecotourism
8. habitat
9. extinction
10. desertification

Reviewing Facts

11. peanuts, palm oil, coffee, cacao, sisal, cotton, tea, rubber, bananas
12. lack of transportation and capital
13. unequal distribution of profits, uneven distribution of minerals, overdependence on a single mineral
14. because of terms imposed under colonialism, lack of capital and skilled workers, inadequate transportation, political instability, and reluctance of foreign investors to invest in the region
15. Colonial powers built roads and railroads to carry raw materials to ports rather than to serve regional trade.
16. because of low literacy rates and the limited use of televisions
17. to help the people through drought, famine, and civil war
18. export of hardwood trees, burning of forests to clear land for farming and grazing, use of wood for fuel
19. by supporting preserves in return for money from ecotourism to build clinics and schools

Critical Thinking

20. It has discouraged investors from risking capital to develop business in sub-Saharan Africa.
21. colonialism, a system that created dependence on foreign powers

Using the Unit Atlas

Refer to the physical geography section of the Unit Atlas on pages 412–413.

26. What natural resources are mined in Zambia?
27. What country is the world's largest producer of gold and gem diamonds?

Projects

Individual Activity

You learned about the effects of drought and civil war on Somalia. Using the *Readers' Guide to Periodical Literature,* research Somalia after the 1992 arrival of UN troops. Write a news story about your findings and post it.

Cooperative Learning Activity

Working in groups, research endangered animals in Africa south of the Sahara. Consult a variety of resources and present your findings on an outline map.

Writing About Geography

Argumentation

Review text material and your journal notes about the debate over creation of African game preserves. Put yourself in the place of a government official of Kenya, Tanzania, or Rwanda. Decide whether more or less land should be set aside for big game. Present your arguments as you would to a group of subsistence farmers.

Locating Places

AFRICA SOUTH OF THE SAHARA: PHYSICAL/POLITICAL GEOGRAPHY

Match the letters on the map with the places and physical features of Africa south of the Sahara. Write your answers on a separate sheet of paper.

1. Mauritania
2. Nigeria
3. Madagascar
4. Eritrea
5. Côte d'Ivoire
6. Sudan
7. Zambia
8. Nairobi
9. Dar es Salaam
10. Somalia

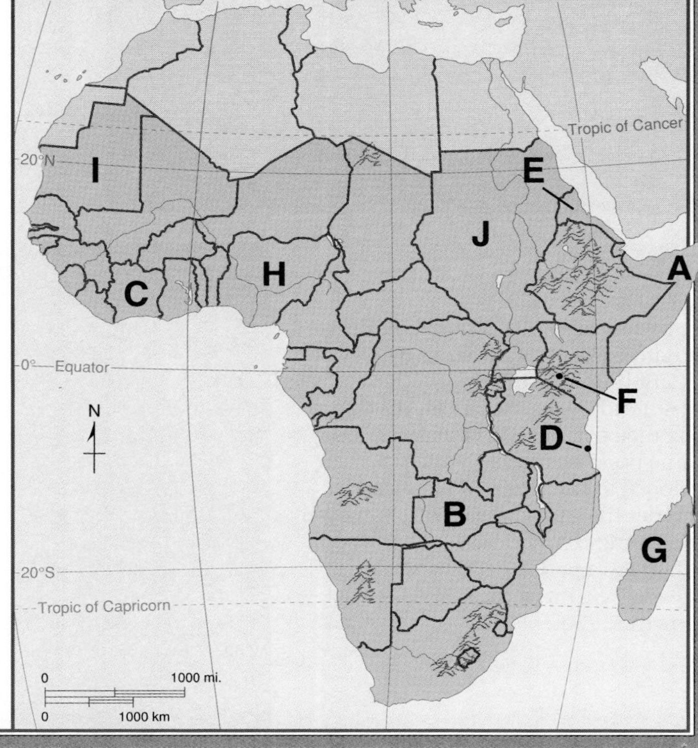

Chapter 22 Review

Geographic Themes

22. a heavy reliance on subsistence farming, economic patterns set in the colonial period, and relying upon a single cash crop or resource
23. Wildlife and farmers compete for the same land.

Practicing Skills

24. in drier regions because the livestock graze on the sparse grasses that grow there
25. on the northwest coast and southern tip of Africa, prevailing winds bring enough moisture in winter to produce citrus fruits, olives, grapes, and other Mediterranean crops

Using the Unit Atlas

26. copper, gold, cobalt
27. South Africa

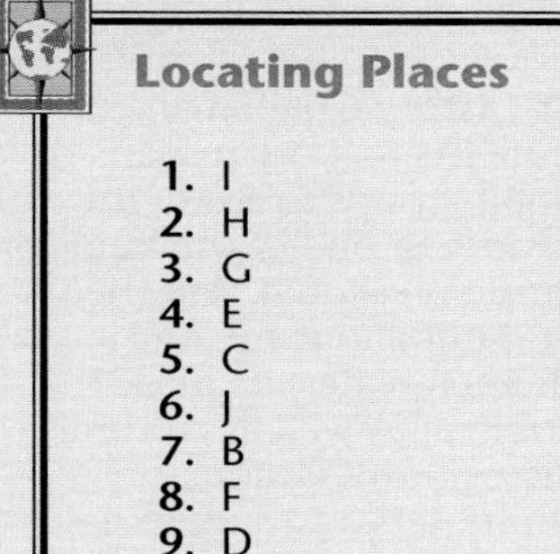

Locating Places

1. I
2. H
3. G
4. E
5. C
6. J
7. B
8. F
9. D
10. A

Chapter Bonus Test Question

This question may be used for extra credit on the chapter test.

How might developing sub-Saharan Africa's potential for hydroelectric energy help slow deforestation?

(Answer: Hydroelectricity could replace wood for fuel, and fewer trees would be cut.)

FOCUS

Ask students to scan the boldfaced headings of each caption. Then ask them for names of singers or composers associated with each kind of music.

TEACH

L1 Explain Have students compare and contrast the rhythms of the kinds of music presented in the selection. Ask students also to describe the difference between music with African roots and music with European roots.

L2 Research Suggest that students research the kinds of percussion instruments that Africans use, as well as the kinds used in African American music. Students can share their information by means of captioned photographs, taped or live demonstrations, or in a poem.

L3 History Challenge students to work in pairs or small groups to study the history of one of the kinds of music presented. Ask them to find out about the music's characteristics, its place in political as well as cultural history, and famous composers and singers associated with the style. Ask them to share findings in an informal talk, with examples of the music as support.

GEOGRAPHY CONNECTION

Africa South of the Sahara and the United States

THE BEAT GOES ON

Strong rhythms form the core of African music—the music of the peoples who live south of the Sahara. Strong African rhythms beat through many kinds of American music, enriching our musical heritage.

◀ **SPIRITUALS** were the earliest American music with an African rhythm. Deeply emotional religious songs, spirituals developed in the southern United States among enslaved Africans who added the rhythms of their lost homeland to southern biblical preaching. Spirituals became famous worldwide after the 1870s, when Nashville's Fisk University Jubilee Singers toured the United States and Europe. Today spirituals, such as "Swing Low, Sweet Chariot," "Go Down, Moses," and "Deep River," are standards of American music.

CALYPSO AND REGGAE ▶ were two forms of African-based music that entered the United States by way of the Caribbean. During the 1950s calypso, with its lively African rhythm, lilting melody, and island dialects, became popular. Reggae, which developed in the 1960s in Jamaica, combines the African beat with Jamaican folk music and American blues and soul. The Jamaican performer Bob Marley made reggae a hit in the United States during the 1970s.

Making the Connection

Movement Encourage students to find out more about contemporary African music, as well as *salsa*, the Latin American offshoot of African music. Suggest that they visit the audiovisual department of the local library for examples of both kinds of music. Allow time for students to share and discuss the music. Have them listen carefully, noting the likenesses and differences to African American music. As they do so, tell them that most African music features very complex rhythms, with drums as the most prominent instrument. Have students identify these characteristics in contemporary African music; ask if they think these characteristics are true of *salsa* and African American music. Have them support their opinions with examples.

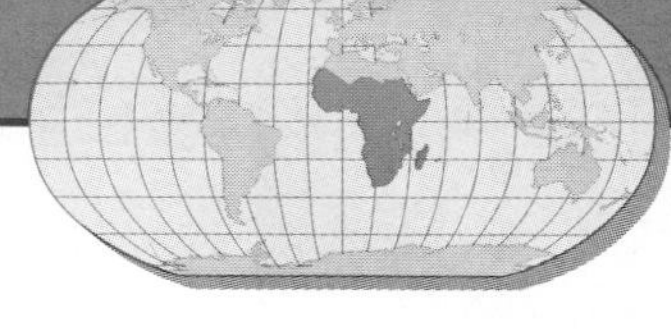

◀ **RAGTIME AND DIXIELAND** arose out of blues and jazz in the early 1900s. Jazz quartets led to big band jazz in the 1920s. In 1932, bandleader Duke Ellington introduced "swing," jazz with an easy-going, relaxed rhythm. The "boogie woogie" beat also appeared in the 1930s.

ROCK 'N' ROLL ▶ made its entry in the mid-1950s when blues composer and singer Chuck Berry heightened the beat and turned out a new sound. Rock and roll led on through soul of the late 1960s and heavy metal of the 1970s. From the 1970s and into the 1990s, the African beat exploded into the insistent recurring rhythmic pattern of rap.

▼ **BLUES AND JAZZ** became popular after 1900. Blues is a highly creative personal statement, a musical response to an experience or circumstances of life. Like blues, jazz is also a highly creative musical form, because it allows the performer complete freedom to invent and vary a piece of music as it is played.

Checking for Understanding

1. What kinds of music have developed from African roots?
2. **Movement** How was the African beat brought to the United States?

ANSWERS TO CHECKING FOR UNDERSTANDING

1. spirituals, blues, jazz, ragtime, Dixieland, swing, boogie woogie, rock, soul, heavy metal, rap

2. Enslaved Africans brought their rhythms with them when they were brought to the United States.

Geography Connection

ASSESS

Have students answer the Checking for Understanding questions on page 467.

CLOSE

Share the information below; invite comments on ways this deeply emotional feeling shows itself, either in a composer's words or melody or in the manner in which an entertainer performs the songs. Ask students to speculate on other experiences that might add an element of emotion to African American music.

DID YOU KNOW?

African peoples south of the Sahara use music in every area of their lives. It is a particularly important ingredient in religious ceremonies, festivals, and social rituals. Many Africans believe that music serves as a link with the spirit world.

UNIT OVERVIEW

The three chapters that comprise this unit introduce students to the physical geography and peoples of South Asia. Various aspects of the region's life—such as the economy, lifestyles, and human/environment interaction—are also presented.

GEOGRAPHY JOURNAL

Activity Students may wish to organize themselves in small groups, with each group responsible for a different medium: television news programs, news magazines, newspapers, and so forth.

At the unit's end, students may work together to compose summaries of the current events in the region.

•This journal activity provides the basis for the "Writing About Geography" exercise in the Chapter Review.

•The Geography Journal may be used as an integral part of Performance Assessment.

CD-ROM

PICTURE ATLAS OF THE WORLD

You and your students can view and read about the physical and cultural features of South Asia by clicking the "Photo," "Essay," and "Stats" buttons of selected South Asian countries.

UNIT 8

South Asia

GeoJournal Activity

While you are studying about South Asia, keep a journal of recent developments in the region. Organize the material in your journal into the following categories: Physical Geography, Cultures and Lifestyles, Economy and Environment.

468

Where in the World . . . .

Have students look at the map on page A19 in which South Asia is highlighted. Display Unit Map Overlay Transparency 8-5 and ask students the following questions: What mountain range separates South Asia from the main part of the continent? *(Himalayas)* What body of water lies on the western coast of India? *(Arabian Sea)* On the eastern coast? *(Bay of Bengal)* Directly south? *(Indian Ocean)* A traveler flying directly east from India to get to the United States would cross what continent? *(Southeast Asia)* Directly west? *(Africa)* What continent is south of South Asia? *(Antarctica)* What is the region's major river? *(Ganges)*

Picturing the World

Sherpa porters and their yaks help launch another expedition in the lofty peaks of the Himalaya range in Nepal. The world's highest mountain range, the Himalaya extend for some 1,500 miles (2,410 km) to form the northern boundary of South Asia. Look at the map on page 472.

1. What is the name and elevation of the highest peak in the Himalaya?
2. What is the highest peak in the world?
3. Now read about the people of Nepal on page 492. Where did the ancestors of the Sherpa and other Nepalese originally come from?
4. What event made the Sherpa famous worldwide?

Picture Atlas CD-ROM Enrichment Corner

South Asia has one of the highest concentrations of people and one of the most diverse populations in the world. Create a file on the religions and languages of the six countries in South Asia. (See the *Picture Atlas of the World* User's Guide on how to use the Collector button.) Read the essays, research the vital statistics, and listen to the spoken languages. Gather items from many parts of the CD-ROM and create an electronic report to explain the complex ethnic patterns of South Asia.

ANSWERS TO PICTURING THE WORLD

1. Mount Everest; 29,028 ft. (8,848 m)
2. Mount Everest
3. Mongolia
4. Their mountaineering skills helped in the first conquest of Mount Everest.

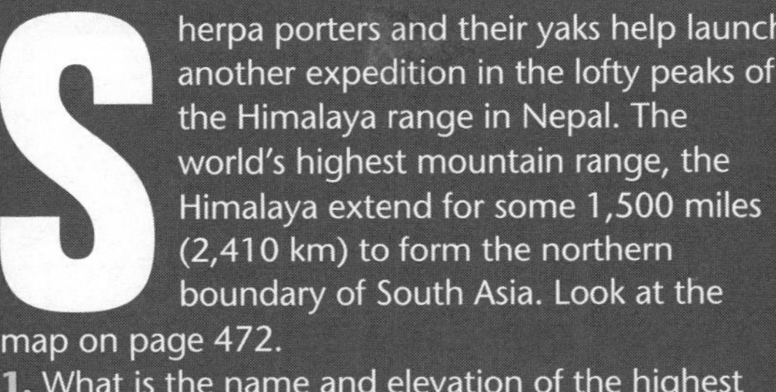

The Center for South Asian Studies at the University of Virginia has a web site. Contact it at the following address:

World Wide Web
http://www.virginia.edu/~soasia

CD-ROM

PICTURE ATLAS OF THE WORLD
See page T42 for an additional CD-ROM activity to enrich Unit 8, South Asia.

GLENCOE TECHNOLOGY

Videodisc

REUTERS ISSUES IN GEOGRAPHY

Chapter 7
Disc 1 Side A

Title: ***South Asia: Preserving the Himalayas***
Subject: Physical processes that operate in the region, and how human choices affect the environment

0:00 OUT OF TIME?

If time does not permit teaching each chapter in this unit, you may use the Chapter Highlights and Audiocassettes that include a 1-page activity and a 1-page test for each chapter.

LESSON PLAN
Unit 8 Atlas

These features and activities may be used as an introduction to the unit or as teaching tools throughout the course of the unit.

FOCUS

Ask students to study the maps on pages 470–471 for a moment, then ask for comments on the population density and distribution of the area. Encourage students to compare the population density and distribution of South Asia with other world regions. Have students turn back to the maps in previous Unit Openers to help them with their comparisons.

TEACH

Implement Foods Around the World 7 as a class activity.

Have students complete the Political Map Transparency 8 Activity in the TCR.

Have students complete World Cultures Transparencies 13 and 14 in the TCR.

Have students complete World Literature Reading 7 in the TCR.

Have students complete the Unit Atlas Activity 8B in the TCR.

UNIT 8 ATLAS

SOUTH ASIA
Cultural Geography

EXPLORING CULTURAL DIVERSITY

1. *What areas of South Asia are most heavily populated? Most sparsely populated?*
2. *What nations make up South Asia?*

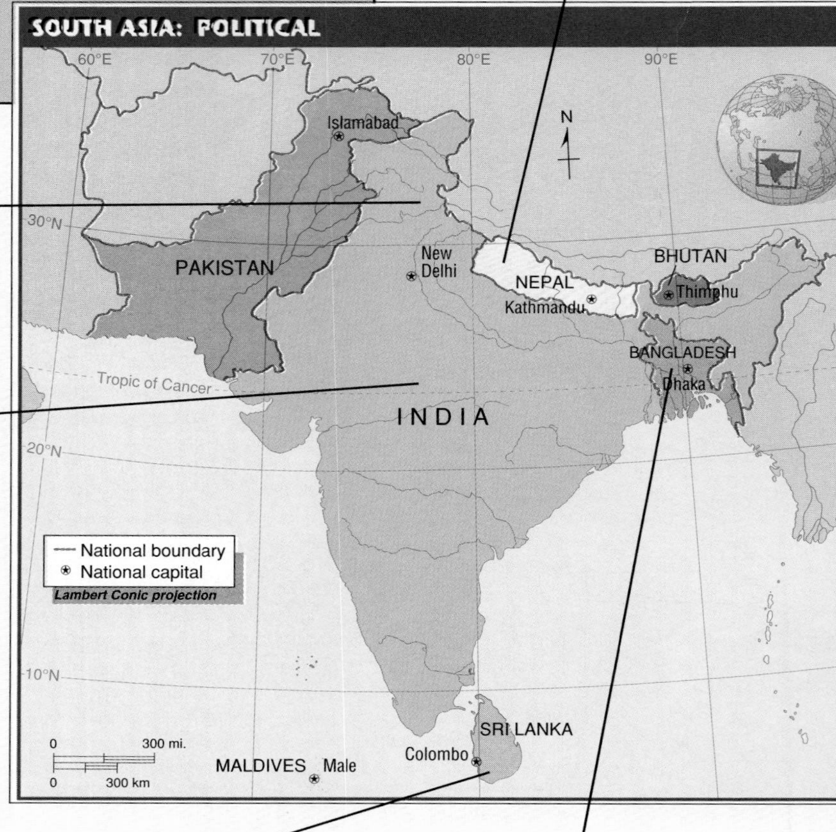

A well-known myth of the **Himalayas** tells of the Abominable Snowman, a beast with a large apelike body and a human face.

The state of **Kashmir** has been the scene of a Muslim-Hindu struggle since 1947.

India's people speak 14 major languages and hundreds of regional dialects.

Sri Lanka, which means "resplendent land," is home to Buddhist Sinhalese and Hindu Tamils. Continuing bitter relations between the two groups have caused much turmoil on the beautiful island.

Until 1971 **Bangladesh** was the eastern part of Pakistan. Following a short civil war, the nation declared its independence and changed its name.

Classroom Resources for Unit 8

BLACKLINE MASTERS:
Geography Simulation 8
Foods Around the World 7
World Literature Reading 7

TRANSPARENCIES:
Unit Map Overlay Transparency 8
Political Map Transparency 8
World Cultures Transparencies 13, 14

MULTIMEDIA:

***World Music:** Cultural Traditions, Lesson 7*

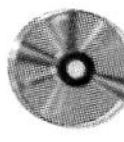
Reuters Issues in Geography

Testmaker

Picture Atlas of the World

Images of the World Poster Set

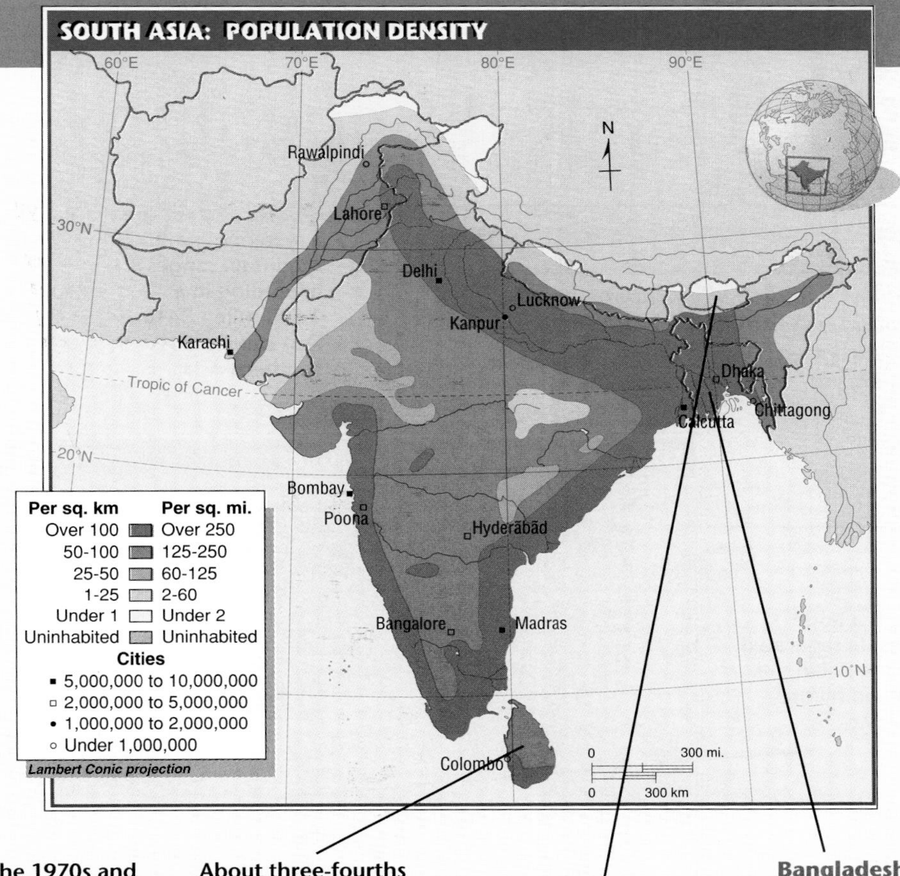

During the 1970s and 1980s, **India's** population increased by about 14 million every year. Overpopulation has caused serious overcrowding.

About three-fourths of all **Sri Lankans** live in rural agricultural villages.

Most of **Bhutan's** population live in the fertile valleys that run north and south among the country's mountain ranges.

Bangladesh has a high birthrate and a relatively small area, resulting in a population density of about 2,320 per square mile (895/sq. km). More than 85 percent of the people are rural farmers.

Population: South Asia and the United States

South Asia

United States

= 50,000,000

Source: Population Reference Bureau, Inc., 1994

South Asia has more than four times as many people as the United States.

LESSON PLAN
Unit 8 Atlas

Play World Music: Cultural Traditions, Lesson 7, and have students complete the Lesson 7 activity.

ASSESS

Have students answer the Exploring Cultural Diversity questions on page 470.

EXPLORING CULTURAL DIVERSITY

This feature may be used to introduce students to the cultural geography of South Asia. Use questions to stimulate class discussion and help students become familiar with the region. Accept reasonable answers based on the maps, graph, and captions.

CLOSE

Ask students to speculate on the kinds of challenges that the region might face, based on the information shown.

GLENCOE TECHNOLOGY

Videodisc

REUTERS ISSUES IN GEOGRAPHY

Chapter 7
Disc 1 Side A

Title: ***South Asia: Preserving the Himalayas***

Subject: Physical processes that operate in the region, and how human choices affect the environment

Map and Graph Activity

Regions Lead students to note that the two general challenges faced by South Asia are internal disagreements and overpopulation. Have them find the current population in each country, and the reason(s) for the dissension. Have them jot down the information in the section of their journals designated for their unit journal activity. As they read the unit, have them add appropriate information. They can use the statistics and information in their summaries.

LESSON PLAN
Unit 8 Atlas

These features and activities may be used as an introduction to the unit or as teaching tools throughout the course of the unit.

FOCUS

To introduce students to the physical geography of South Asia, have students complete Unit Map Overlay Transparency 8 Activity in the TCR.

TEACH

Ask students to generalize about South Asia's physical geography and speculate about effects on the region's economic activities.

Map Activity Have students compose questions and answers about the region, using the material presented in the graphics on pages 472–473. Have each student read one of their answers and let their classmates formulate the question that accompanies it.

Simulation Have students complete the Unit 8 Geography Simulation found in the TCR.

Have students complete Unit Atlas Activity 8A in the TCR.

IMAGES OF THE WORLD POSTER SET

Display the poster of "Asia." Have students hypothesize about the climate zone and population density of each photo.

UNIT 8 ATLAS

SOUTH ASIA
Physical Geography

CHARTING YOUR COURSE

1. *What two high mountain peaks are found in South Asia?*
2. *What large island is located east of Cape Comorin?*

The Himalayas are a system of parallel mountain ranges extending in a 1,500-mile (2,410-km) curve across southern Asia.

India is a huge peninsula separated from the Asian mainland by the Himalayas.

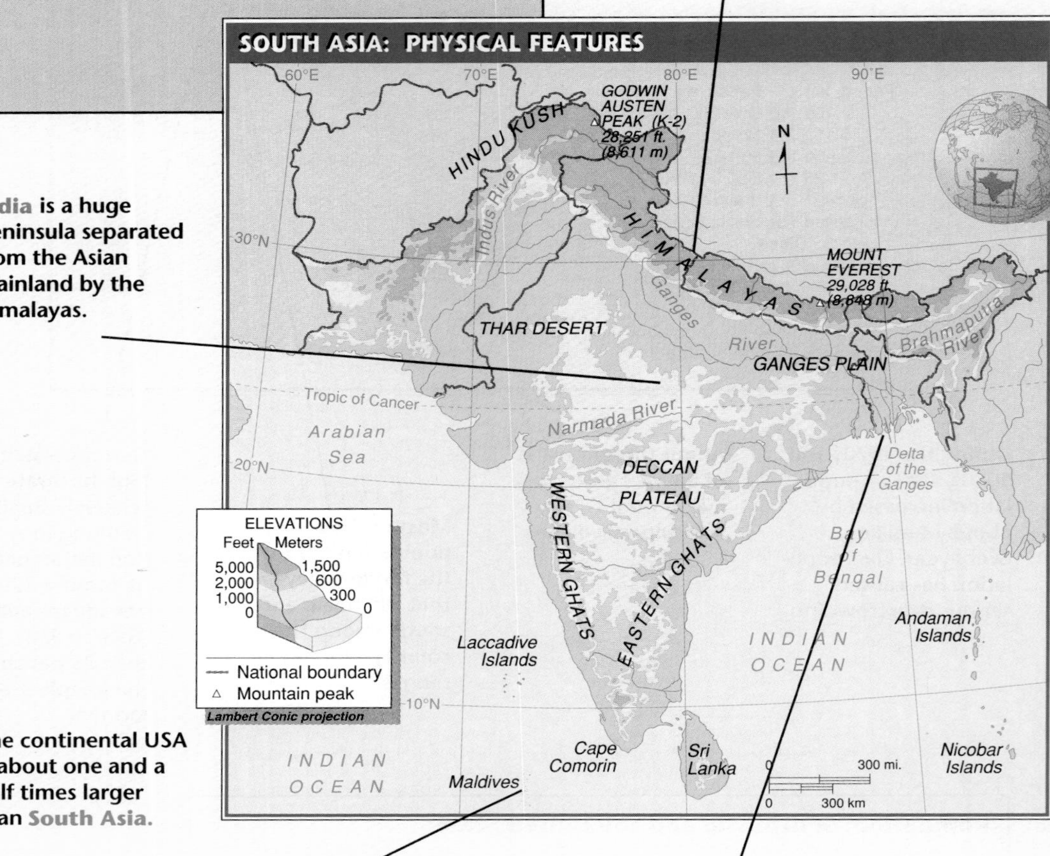

The continental USA is about one and a half times larger than South Asia.

The country of the Maldives consists of about 1,200 coral islands, none of which cover more than 5 square miles (3 sq. km).

Bangladesh has the largest river delta in the world, where the Ganges and Brahmaputra rivers empty into the Indian Ocean.

Map Activity

Place, Natural Resources Have students compare South Asia's physical geography and natural resources to other world regions they have studied. Encourage them to return to previous Unit Openers and use the maps there to help them make comparison and contrasting descriptive statements. When they have finished their study, organize them into small groups, and have them find out whether South Asia's mineral resources are developed or undeveloped and why. Have them add the information to that in their journals.

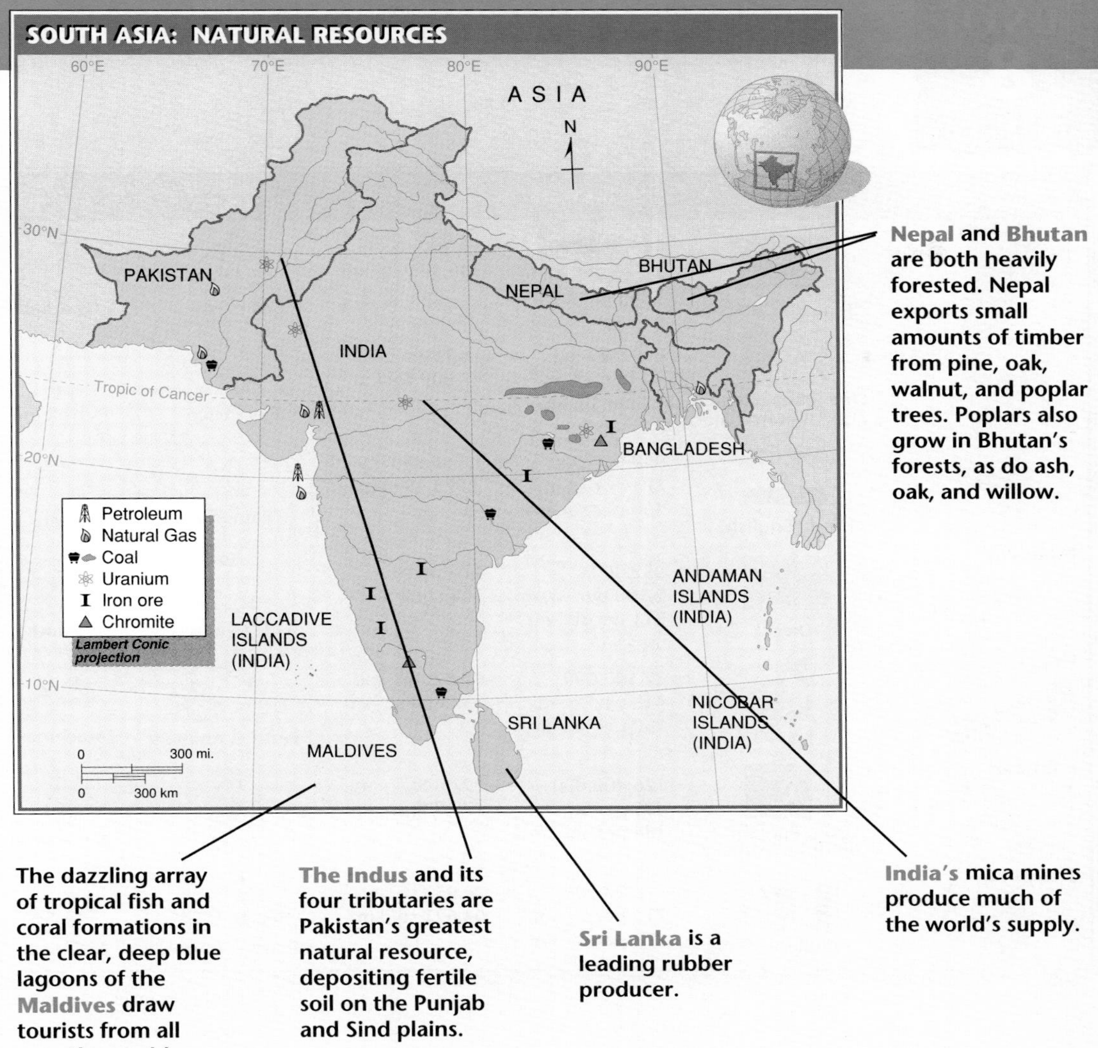

Nepal and **Bhutan** are both heavily forested. Nepal exports small amounts of timber from pine, oak, walnut, and poplar trees. Poplars also grow in Bhutan's forests, as do ash, oak, and willow.

The dazzling array of tropical fish and coral formations in the clear, deep blue lagoons of the **Maldives** draw tourists from all over the world.

The Indus and its four tributaries are Pakistan's greatest natural resource, depositing fertile soil on the Punjab and Sind plains.

Sri Lanka is a leading rubber producer.

India's mica mines produce much of the world's supply.

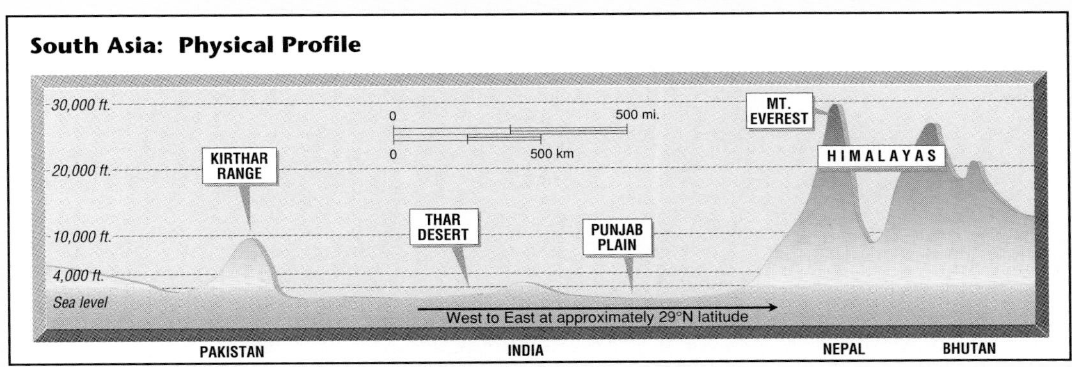

Map Activity

Geographical Profile Using the graphics on pages 472–473, as well as completed map transparencies, have students create concise but complete geographical profiles for the countries of South Asia. Encourage them to work as a group to identify and list the data they want to include in their profiles. Then allow them to organize themselves into smaller groups, choose a country, and compose a profile. Display completed profiles in an appropriate place for all students to share.

LESSON PLAN
Unit 8 Atlas

ASSESS

Have students answer the Charting Your Course questions on page 472.

CHARTING YOUR COURSE

This feature may be used to introduce students to the physical geography of South Asia. Use questions to stimulate class discussion and help students become familiar with the region. Accept reasonable answers based on the maps, graph, and captions.

CLOSE

Ask students to make predictions about what they think they will learn concerning the physical geography and natural resources of the region. Ask for supporting evidence from the graphics on pages 472–473.

DID YOU KNOW?

South Asia covers about 10 percent of the Asian continent; India covers 75 percent of the region.

GLENCOE TECHNOLOGY

Videodisc

REUTERS ISSUES IN GEOGRAPHY

Chapter 7
Disc 1 Side A

Title: ***South Asia: Preserving the Himalayas***
Subject: Physical processes that operate in the region, and how human choices affect the environment

LESSON PLAN
Unit 8 Atlas

These features and activities may be used as teaching tools throughout the course of the unit.

DID YOU KNOW?

Nepal has almost 3,000 Hindu and Buddhist shrines, attesting to the importance of religion in the country.

Ways of the World

BANGLADESH Bangladeshis are very polite. When they are not able to attend a social gathering, they still say they'll try to come. Saying "no" may be a sign that the host's friendship is not valued.

Ways of the World

SRI LANKA The country's religions play an important role in what Sri Lankans eat. All religious groups avoid items likely to cause spiritual pollution. Food is considered a prime source of potential pollution because it enters the body. Sri Lankans who practice strict Buddhism do not eat any kind of animal flesh. Hindus do not eat beef or pork, and Muslims do not eat pork.

UNIT 8 ATLAS

COUNTRY PROFILE

COUNTRY* AND CAPITAL	FLAG AND LANGUAGES	POPULATION	LANDMASS	PRINCIPAL PRODUCTS EXPORT	IMPORT
Bangladesh Dhaka	Bengali, Chakma	116,600,000 2,320 per sq. mi. 895 per sq. km	50,260 sq. mi. 130,173 sq. km	Garments	Yarns & Fabrics
Bhutan Thimphu	Dzongkha, Nepali and Tibetan dialects	800,000 44 per sq. mi. 17 per sq. km	18,150 sq. mi. 47,009 sq. km	Electricity	Petroleum
India New Delhi	Hindi, English,	919,900,000 801 per sq. mi. 309 per sq. km	1,147,950 sq. mi. 2,973,191 sq. km	Diamonds	Fuels
Maldives Male	Divehi	252,000 2,100 per sq. mi. 811 per sq. km	120 sq. mi. 311 sq. km	Clothing	Food
Nepal Kathmandu	Nepali	22,100,000 418 per sq. mi. 162 per sq. km	52,820 sq. mi. 136,804 sq. km	Food & Animals	Machinery
Pakistan Islamabad	Urdu, Punjabi, Sindhi, Pushtu	126,400,000 425 per sq. mi. 164 per sq. km	297,640 sq. mi. 770,888 sq. km	Textiles	Petroleum
Sri Lanka Colombo	Sinhalese, Tamil	17,900,000 717 per sq. mi. 277 per sq. km	24,950 sq. mi. 64,621 sq. km	Food & Animals	Machinery

*Country maps not drawn to scale.

Country Profile Activity

Geographic Themes As students read the caption of each photograph on pages 474–475, have them locate the place where the photograph was taken on the maps on pages 473–474. Have them also identify any statements on pages 471–472 that they think explain or expand the photos. Encourage them to identify any of the other four geographic themes that they consider represented by the photographs.

◀ Beautiful frescoes line the walls of a Buddhist temple in Sri Lanka.

▲ Nepal's capital of Kathmandu has many outdoor markets in its traditional neighborhoods.

▼ The coasts of southern India and Sri Lanka are lined with beautiful beaches and tropical vegetation.

▼ India's Thar Desert receives about 10 inches (25 cm) of rain each year.

▲ Calcutta, India, is one of the busiest and most important port cities in Asia.

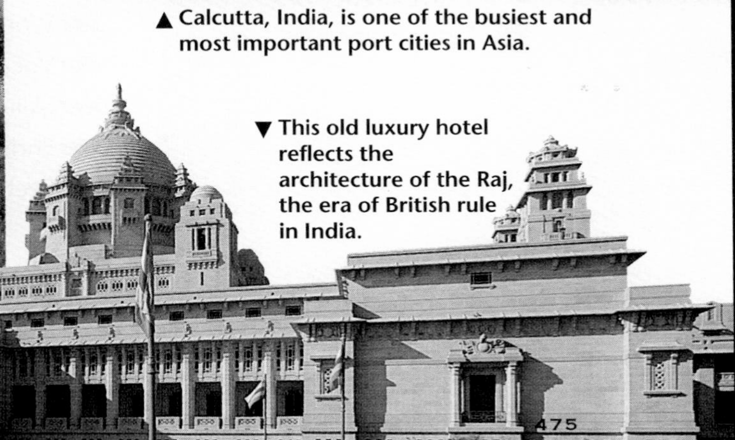

▼ This old luxury hotel reflects the architecture of the Raj, the era of British rule in India.

Country Profile Activity

Opinion Allow students a few moments to look back over the Unit Opener and Unit Atlas pages. Encourage them, too, to recall any maps and journal entries they made during the unit's introduction activities.

Then have them write a paragraph or two stating their first impressions of South Asia. Some students may prefer to compose free verse poetry or quickly jot down free associative phrases. Have them save their first impressions to reread and revise at the unit's end.

Global Gourmet

Bananas originally came from South Asia. Arab traders brought bananas into Egypt, where they gained popularity throughout Africa and Europe. In the fifteenth century, Portuguese traders brought the fruit from Africa to the West Indies and the Americas.

DID YOU KNOW?

Bhutan has strong ties with India. The larger country handles the smaller's foreign affairs and defense, and is helping the small nation improve its industries and train its workers.

Ways of the World

INDIA Indian Hindu women often wear a *bindi,* or red dot, on their foreheads. Traditionally, the *bindi* was a sign of femininity, gracefulness, and marital status. In modern times, however, the dot has become an optional beauty aid; its color often matches the wearer's outfit.

DID YOU KNOW?

Pakistan's many cultural groups, each with its own customs and language, have made it difficult for the country to become strong and unified.

CHAPTER 23

PLANNING GUIDE

The Physical Geography of South Asia

CHAPTER ORGANIZER

Daily Lesson Objectives	Multimedia	Teacher Classroom Resources
SECTION 1 The Land 1. Identify the mountains, plateaus, and plains of South Asia. 2. Explain the importance of the region's great river systems. 3. List the natural resources of South Asia.	Section Focus Transparency 23-1 Chapter 23 Vocabulary PuzzleMaker Software Political Map Transparency 8 Geography and the Environment Testmaker STV: World Geography, Volume 1 Picture Atlas of the World Physical Geography of the World Transparencies 61, 63, 64	Reproducible Lesson Plan 23-1 Guided Reading Activity 23-1 Spanish Guided Reading Activity 23-1 Workbook Activity 23-1 Geography Simulation 8 Section Quiz 23-1
SECTION 2 The Climate and Vegetation 1. Describe the climate regions of South Asia. 2. Explain the importance of seasonal rains.	Section Focus Transparency 23-2 Unit Map Overlay Transparency 8-3 Testmaker	Reproducible Lesson Plan 23-2 Guided Reading Activity 23-2 Spanish Guided Reading Activity 23-2 Workbook Activity 23-2 Vocabulary Activity 23 Skill Activity 23 Enrichment Activity 23 Section Quiz 23-2
CHAPTER REVIEW AND EVALUATION	Chapter 23 English (or Spanish) Audiocassettes MindJogger Videoquiz Testmaker Student Self-Test and Review Software	Reteaching Activity 23 Spanish Reteaching Activity 23 Chapter 23 Test Form A and Form B

0:00 *If time does not permit teaching the entire chapter, summarize using the Chapter 23 Highlights on page 487, and the Chapter 23 English (or Spanish) Audiocassettes. Review students' knowledge using the Glencoe MindJogger Videoquiz.*

KEY TO ABILITY LEVELS

Teaching strategies have been coded for varying learning styles and abilities.

L1 **BASIC** activities for all students

L2 **AVERAGE** activities for average to above-average students

L3 **CHALLENGING** activities for above-average students

LEP **LIMITED ENGLISH PROFICIENCY** activities

Performance Assessment

Relating Narrative and Physical Geography

Have students complete a creative-thinking task involving the physical features of South Asia. Brainstorm and discuss with students epic novels in which the characters travel through many locales and experience many types of adventures. Have the class decide on a time period, a scenario for an epic journey, and a set of characters, including names and descriptions, for a class novel.

Organize the class into groups and assign each a South Asian country. Each group should match a list of physical features with possible adventures for the characters as they travel through the country. Groups should discuss and elaborate their ideas before each individual selects one scenario to write for a chapter in an adventure book. Groups should sequence their chapters before sharing them with the class, which will then sequence the entire novel. A person or committee may be assigned to write an introduction and conclusion. The book should be published by editing and binding the final copies.

POSSIBLE RUBRIC FEATURES: Content information, concept attainment, cause/effect skills, narrative writing, creative thinking, collaborative skills

For additional professional and classroom resources, see Chapter Resources, pages T46–T51.

TEACHER'S CORNER

INDEX TO NATIONAL GEOGRAPHIC MAGAZINE

The following articles may be used for research relating to this chapter:

- "Long Journey of the Brahmaputra," by Jere Van Dyk, November 1988.
- "The Mighty Himalaya: A Fragile Heritage," by Barry C. Bishop, November 1988.
- "Monsoons: Life Breath of Half the World," by Priit J. Vesilind, December 1984.
- "The Forgotten Face of Everest," by Andrew Harvard, July 1984.
- "By Rail Across the Indian Subcontinent," by Paul Theroux, June 1984.
- "The Desert: An Age-old Challenge Grows," by Rick Gore, November 1979.

NATIONAL GEOGRAPHIC SOCIETY PRODUCTS AVAILABLE FROM GLENCOE

To order the following products for use with this chapter, contact your local Glencoe sales representative or call Glencoe at 1-800-334-7344:

- *Picture Atlas of the World* (CD-ROM)
- *STV: World Geography, Asia and Australia* (Videodisc)
- *ZipZapMap! World* (Software)
- *GeoBee* (Software)
- *Images of the World* (Posters)
- *Eye on the Environment* (Posters)
- *Physical Geography of the World* (Transparencies)
- *Picture Atlas of Our 50 States* (Book)

ADDITIONAL NATIONAL GEOGRAPHIC SOCIETY PRODUCTS

To order the following products for use with this chapter, call National Geographic Society at 1-800-368-2728:

- *Return to Everest* (Video)

Introducing
CHAPTER 23

chapter 23 The Physical Geography of South Asia

PERFORMANCE ASSESSMENT

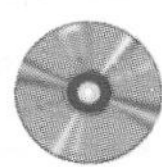

Refer to the Planning Guide on page 476B for a Performance Assessment Activity for this chapter. See the *Performance Assessment Activities* booklet for additional suggestions.

CHAPTER OBJECTIVES

1. **Explain** how the river systems of South Asia influence land use in the region.
2. **Describe** the effects of seasonal winds and landforms on South Asia's climate and vegetation.

GLENCOE TECHNOLOGY

Videodisc

Use Chapter 23 MindJogger Videoquiz to preview chapter content.

MINDJOGGER VIDEOQUIZ

Chapter 23
Disc 3 Side B

The MindJogger Videoquiz is also available on videocassette.

NATIONAL GEOGRAPHIC SOCIETY

Videodisc

STV: WORLD GEOGRAPHY VOLUME 1

Side 1, Chapter 1
Frames 6886-13594
Title: *Asia*
Subject: Southwest Asia

CHAPTER FOCUS

Geographic Setting

South Asia includes the large, diamond-shaped peninsula that forms the southern part of the Asian continent. This peninsula is separated from the main part of Asia by the towering, snow-capped Himalayas, Karakorams, and the Hindu Kush.

Geographic Themes

Section 1 The Land

PLACE The river systems of South Asia form the world's largest continuous floodplain. These fertile valleys were home to one of the world's earliest civilizations and are still an area of great agricultural abundance.

▲Photograph: *Mountain village in the Himalayas, Nepal*

Section 2 The Climate and Vegetation

LOCATION South Asia's climate and vegetation are strongly affected by seasonal winds. These winds bring the rains on which the region's farmers depend. Landforms, such as mountains and hills, have a powerful effect on where and how heavily the rains fall.

EXTRA CREDIT PROJECT

Relief Map Have students work individually, in pairs, or in small groups to create a relief map of South Asia. Maps should include major landforms and bodies of water. Students should paint their map, label major physical features, and create a key to indicate elevation.

SECTION 1

The Land

SETTING THE SCENE

Read to Discover . . .

- the mountains, plateaus, and plains of South Asia.
- the importance of the region's great river systems.
- the seasons of South Asia.
- the natural resources of South Asia.

Key Terms

- subcontinent
- alluvial plain
- mica

Identify and Locate

Himalayas, Vindhya Mountains, Western Ghats, Eastern Ghats, Deccan Plateau, Chota Nagpur Plateau, Ganges River, Indus River, Brahmaputra River

Laxmi chamari, Bangladesh

Assalamu-alaikum.
I am spending my vacation in the tiny village of Laxmi chamari. Now it is raining season and the many rivers and marshy areas are filled to the brim. Every day I go out in a boat to enjoy the vast green paddy fields. The plants waver gracefully when the wind blows over them.

Md. Afsar Ali

বাংলাদেশ
SAVE THE TIGER
50P
BANGLADESH

Afsar Ali writes from Bangladesh, one of the seven countries that make up the culture region of South Asia. Separated by mountains from the rest of Asia, South Asia is often called a **subcontinent**, a landmass like a continent, only smaller. It is rimmed by three large bodies of water—the Arabian Sea to the west, the Indian Ocean to the south, and the Bay of Bengal to the east. The peninsula is about 1.7 million square miles (4.4 million sq. km), and almost 75 percent of this land belongs to India. The other nations of South Asia include Pakistan, which is located along the northwest edge of the peninsula, and the small kingdoms of Nepal and Bhutan, which are in the mountains of the northeast. Bangladesh lies at the head of the Bay of Bengal, and Sri Lanka and the Maldives are island nations south of the Indian subcontinent.

PLACE

Mountains and Plateaus

Mountains and plateaus dominate the far northern landscape of South Asia. They include some of the highest mountain ranges in the world.

The Himalayas

About 60 million years ago, when the earth's continents were still forming, a part of east Africa broke loose and began to drift slowly northward. When it rammed into Asia, the force of the collision caused the land to crumple up into a vast mountain range—the Himalayas. More than 1,000 miles (1,609 km) long and hundreds of miles wide, this range

LESSON PLAN
Chapter 23, Section 1

FOCUS

SECTION OBJECTIVES

1. **Identify** the mountains, plateaus, and plains of South Asia.
2. **Explain** the importance of the region's great river systems.
3. **List** the natural resources of South Asia.

ABOUT THE POSTCARD

Afsar tells us that Laxmi chamari is located about 300 miles (483 km) south of the Himalayas and about 200 miles (322 km) north of the Bay of Bengal.

BELLRINGER MOTIVATIONAL ACTIVITY

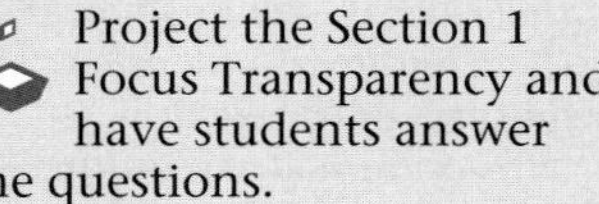

Project the Section 1 Focus Transparency and have students answer the questions.

PRETEACHING VOCABULARY

Display Political Map Transparency 8. Have students locate the South Asia region. Define the term *subcontinent (a landmass like a continent, only smaller).* Discuss why South Asia is called a subcontinent. *(It is separated from the rest of Asia by mountains.)*

Use the Vocabulary PuzzleMaker Software to create a crossword or word search puzzle.

Classroom Resources for Section 1

BLACKLINE MASTERS:
Reproducible Lesson Plan 23-1
Guided Reading Activity 23-1
Geography Simulation 8
Section Quiz 23-1

TRANSPARENCIES:
Section Focus Transparency 23-1
Political Map Transparency 8
Physical Geography of the World Transparencies 61, 63, 64

MULTIMEDIA:

Vocabulary PuzzleMaker Software
Testmaker

Geography and the Environment
STV: World Geography, Volume 1

Picture Atlas of the World

TEACH

GUIDED PRACTICE

L1 Geography: Location Have students play a quiz game to reinforce the physical geography of South Asia. Call on a student to describe the location of a country, body of water, or landform in South Asia. *(Example: a body of water located east of the subcontinent)* Then call on a volunteer to identify the feature by asking a question. *(Example: What is the Bay of Bengal?)* **LEP**

CURRICULUM CONNECTION

GEOLOGY
Plate tectonics is the theory that explains how the Himalayas and other features of the earth's surface formed. According to this theory, the earth has an outer shell made up of many rigid pieces. These tectonic plates move on a layer of rock that is under such heat and pressure that it is capable of flow. The Himalayas formed when two plates collided, and one piled on top of the other.

GLENCOE TECHNOLOGY

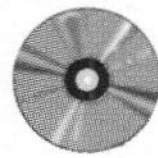

Videodisc

Use the following to enrich Chapter 23:

GEOGRAPHY AND THE ENVIRONMENT
THE INFINITE VOYAGE
Crisis in the Atmosphere

Chapter 3
Disc 2 Side A
Title: ***Our Future Climate***

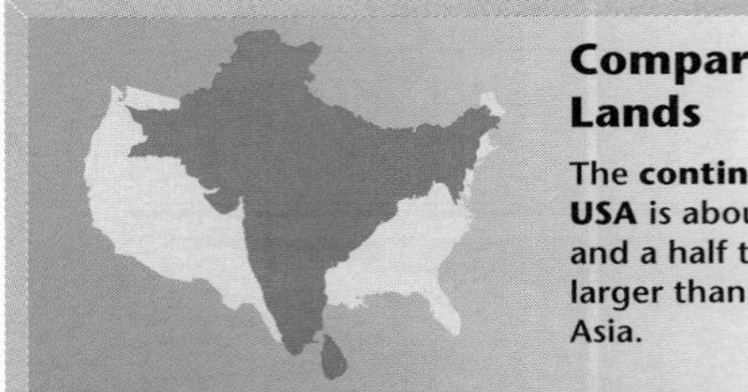

Comparing Lands

The **continental USA** is about one and a half times larger than South Asia.

contains some of the highest mountains in the world, including jagged peaks on which the snow never melts. The most famous of these is Mount Everest, the world's highest peak, which rises to 29,028 feet (8,848 m) above sea level. A writer describes the awesome sight of the Himalayas in the following way:

> *To the north a deep tumult of swirling gray was all that could be seen of the Himalaya. At dusk, white egrets [birds] flapped across the sunken clouds, now black with rain; on earth, the dark had come. Then, 4 miles above these mud streets of the lowlands, at a point so high as to seem overhead, a luminous whiteness shown—the light of snows. Glaciers loomed. . . .*

Other Northern Ranges

The Himalayas meet the Karakoram Mountains in the northernmost part of South Asia. Farther west, the mountains of the Hindu Kush complete the chain. Together, these northern ranges create a formidable barrier between the Indian subcontinent and the rest of Asia. In the past, invaders from the north could only enter the region through a few narrow passes. The mountain kingdoms of Bhutan and Nepal managed to remain isolated from the outside world until well into this century.

Vindhya Mountains

The Vindhya Mountains lie across the center of the Indian subcontinent. These mountains were also created by the shock of the collision between South Asia and the rest of the Asian continent. Although the Vindhya are not as lofty as the Himalayas, they separated the people of northern and southern India and contributed to the development of two very different cultures.

The Ghats and the Deccan Plateau

Forming a triangle at the base of the Indian peninsula are two chains of rugged hills and eroded mountains called the Eastern Ghats and the Western Ghats. Sandwiched between the Eastern and Western Ghats is the main tableland of South Asia—the Deccan Plateau. Here the hills are flat-topped and steep-sided. In the past, lava flowed over the plateau, creating rich, black soil. Because the coastal ranges keep the moisture-laden seasonal winds from reaching the interior, the Deccan Plateau is relatively arid.

Other Plateaus

In the northeastern part of the peninsula lies the Chota Nagpur Plateau, where the rounded hills are covered with forests of bamboo and teak. The other plateaus of South Asia include the stony tablelands that border the northwestern deserts and the humid Karnataka Plateau in the southwest, where herds of wild elephants range through dense rain forests.

Plains

Spreading between the Himalayas and the Deccan Plateau are South Asia's northern plains. Much of this vast lowland area is fertile farmland, watered by the region's three great river systems. As a result, most of South Asia's population lives on these plains.

PLACE

Major River Systems

High in the Himalayas are the sources of South Asia's three great river systems: the Indus, the Brahmaputra, and the Ganges. The

Cooperative Learning Activity

Organize students into seven groups and assign one of the nations of South Asia to each group. Instruct group members to create a geographic profile of their assigned country. Information should include location, boundaries, major landforms, major bodies of water, and resources. When groups have completed their work, form new groups with one student from each of the original groups. Have the new groups share the geographic profiles of the countries.

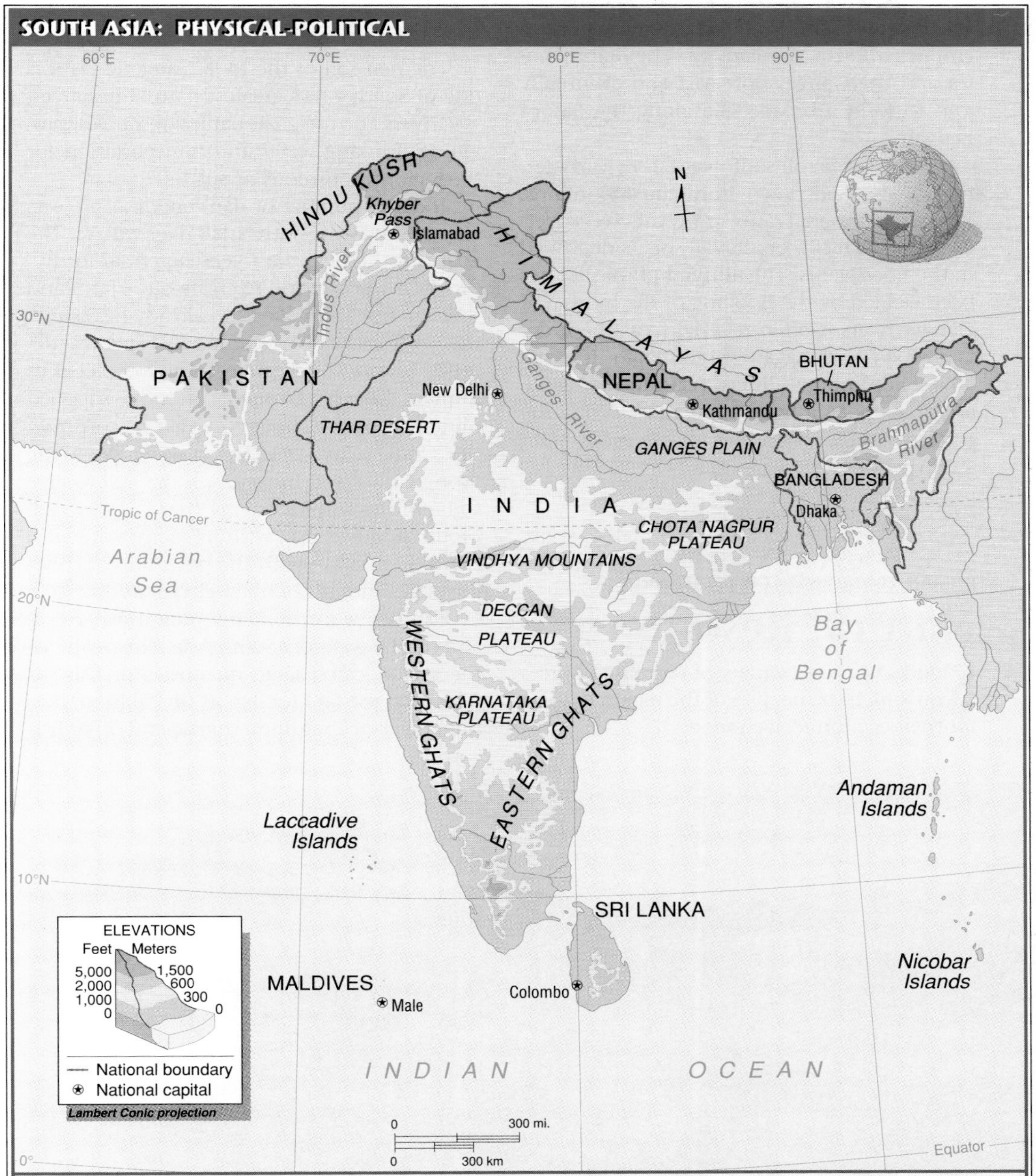

SOUTH ASIA: PHYSICAL-POLITICAL

60°E 70°E 80°E 90°E
30°N 20°N 10°N 0°
HINDU KUSH
Khyber Pass
Islamabad
HIMALAYAS
Indus River
PAKISTAN
New Delhi
Ganges River
NEPAL
Kathmandu
BHUTAN
Thimphu
Brahmaputra River
THAR DESERT
GANGES PLAIN
BANGLADESH
Dhaka
Tropic of Cancer
INDIA
CHOTA NAGPUR PLATEAU
Arabian Sea
VINDHYA MOUNTAINS
DECCAN PLATEAU
Bay of Bengal
WESTERN GHATS
KARNATAKA PLATEAU
EASTERN GHATS
Andaman Islands
Laccadive Islands
SRI LANKA
Nicobar Islands
MALDIVES
Male
Colombo
INDIAN OCEAN
Equator
N

ELEVATIONS
Feet Meters
5,000 1,500
2,000 600
1,000 300
0 0
— National boundary
⊛ National capital
Lambert Conic projection

0 300 mi.
0 300 km

FOCUS ON GEOGRAPHIC THEMES

1. **Place:** What city is the capital of Sri Lanka?
2. **Movement:** Into what sea does the Indus River empty?
3. **Location:** Where is the highest elevation in South Asia?
4. **Region:** What ranges extend along the coasts of southern India?

Meeting Special Needs

Attention Deficiency Students who have difficulty paying attention in class because of attention deficit disorder may benefit from special classroom interventions. For example, set a time limit for a task. Ask students to read the text "Natural Resources" in five minutes. When students have finished reading, discuss whether the time limit helped them pay attention.

USING MAPS

Answers:
1. Colombo; **2.** Arabian Sea; **3.** Mount Everest in the Himalayas; **4.** Western Ghats and Eastern Ghats

Map Skills Practice
Reading a Map Why does most of South Asia's population live on India's northern plains? *(Much of the rest of South Asia is mountainous; the fertile plains are watered by the region's three great river systems.)*

DID YOU KNOW?

A deadly earthquake struck Maharashtra in west central India in September 1993. While most earthquakes occur at the edges of geological plates, this one struck in the middle. The high death toll, estimated at 20,000, resulted from the region's dense population and low-quality construction of housing.

Implement Geography Simulation 8 as a class activity.

INDEPENDENT PRACTICE

Guided Reading Have students complete Guided Reading Activity 23-1 in the TCR. **LEP**

MULTICULTURAL PERSPECTIVE

Culturally Speaking
The name *Himalaya* means "House of Snow" in Sanskrit. Snow on the peaks never melts.

L3 Research Have students find out about mountain climbing in the Himalayas. Some students might research the expedition of Sir Edmund Hillary. Others might find out about the Sherpas who work as guides for expeditions.

USING ILLUSTRATIONS

LOCATION The city of Dhaka is west of the Meghna River in the delta region of Bangladesh.

Answer to Caption:
Ganges and Brahmaputra

ASSESS

CHECK FOR UNDERSTANDING

Assign Section 1 Review as homework or an in-class activity.

MEETING LESSON OBJECTIVES

Each objective below is tested by the questions that follow it in parentheses.

1. **Identify** the mountains, plateaus, and plains of South Asia. *(3)*
2. **Explain** the importance of the region's great river systems. *(5)*
3. **List** the natural resources of South Asia. *(4)*

EVALUATE

Assign the Section 1 Quiz in the TCR.

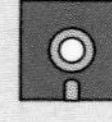

Use the Testmaker to create a customized quiz for Section 1.

CD-ROM

PICTURE ATLAS OF THE WORLD

Click India's "Video" button to see Hindus celebrate the New Year by bathing in the Ganges River.

Indus flows mostly through Pakistan and empties into the Arabian Sea. The Brahmaputra and the Ganges flow east and eventually join to form a broad delta along the Bay of Bengal.

As the rivers roll southward, they carry fertile soil washed down from the mountains. When the seasonal rains strike, the rivers overflow, and rich silt, or alluvial soil, is deposited in the floodplains. The **alluvial plain** that has been created by the flooding of the Indus and Ganges rivers is often referred to as the Indo-Gangetic (IN•duh•gan•JET•ik) Plain. It is the largest continuous alluvial plain in the world, and it supports a huge population. Along the eastern Ganges, densities reach more than 1,000 people per square mile.

HUMAN/ENVIRONMENT INTERACTION

Natural Resources

South Asia has a variety of natural resources on which the peoples of the region depend for their economic livelihood.

Soil and Water

The rich soil of the Indo-Gangetic Plain is one of South Asia's greatest natural resources. The rivers also are great natural resources, providing drinking water and transportation for the region's enormous population.

Today a number of dam-building projects are underway in South Asia's river valleys. The goal is to harness the rivers' potential for hydroelectric power and to create more farmland through irrigation. Pakistan already has one of the world's largest hydroelectric plants. Recently another such project was completed in Bhutan. The government of India supplied Bhutan with the money needed to construct the Chukha hydroelectric project along the Wong Chu River. In return, India will receive some of the surplus energy that is generated. Mountainous Nepal, with its many waterfalls, is another nation with the potential for creating large amounts of hydroelectricity.

Fish thrive in the many inland waterways and coastal waters of South Asia. The people of the region catch large quantities of fish for their own use and for export. In Pakistan, herring, mackerel, sardines, sharks, and other fish

Geographic Themes

Movement: Bangladesh

Many rivers and streams flow through Bangladesh and serve as the country's chief transportation routes. *What two rivers form a broad delta along the Bay of Bengal?*

Critical Thinking

Determining Cause and Effect Have students create a flow chart to show how mountains and rivers of South Asia have affected climate, settlement patterns, and land use in the region. *(Example: Rivers carry rich soil from the mountains to the plains. Many people live on the plains. The fertile soil is suitable for farming.)*

are caught in the Arabian Sea. India is also a major fishing nation. A variety of fish—mackerel, sardines, shrimp, and shark—are caught in the surrounding seas. Indians catch *Bombay duck*, a small fish that is dried and used as a relish. The rivers of India yield carp and catfish.

Energy Resources

South Asia has few significant oil reserves. Some known reserves are located along India's northwestern coast and near the Ganges Delta. There are also petroleum reserves in northern Pakistan, and offshore exploration is taking place in the Arabian Sea.

Natural gas fields are found in southern Pakistan and in the Ganges Delta area of India. Central and eastern India and southern Pakistan have some coal deposits. A major uranium deposit is located in India, north of the Eastern Ghats. Bangladesh has few energy resources other than several small deposits of natural gas and some low-grade coal.

Minerals

Minerals are scattered throughout the region. Large iron-ore deposits are found in the eastern part of the Deccan Plateau. India is one of the world's leading iron-ore exporters. South Asia also has deposits of manganese, chromite, coal, iron ore, and gypsum. Many of these resources still await development. India provides nine-tenths of the world's supply of **mica**, which is needed to manufacture electrical equipment. Nepal is another producer of mica. Small amounts of copper and gold are found in the Himalayas.

Sri Lanka is one of the world's largest producers of graphite. It is also famous for its beautiful gemstones. More than 40 different varieties of precious and semiprecious stones are mined on the island. The most valuable of these are sapphires and rubies. Sri Lanka has no known deposits of coal, oil, copper, or other resources that can be used for fuel or in industry.

Timber

Another important resource of South Asia is timber. India's rain forests produce woods such as sal and teak. India also produces a prized, sweet-smelling timber called sandalwood. Forests cover much of Bhutan, and the government of Bhutan is doing its best to protect this precious natural resource. Nepal's forests, also an important resource, have been severely reduced by overcutting. To protect Sri Lanka's forests, the export of timber from that country has been banned since 1977.

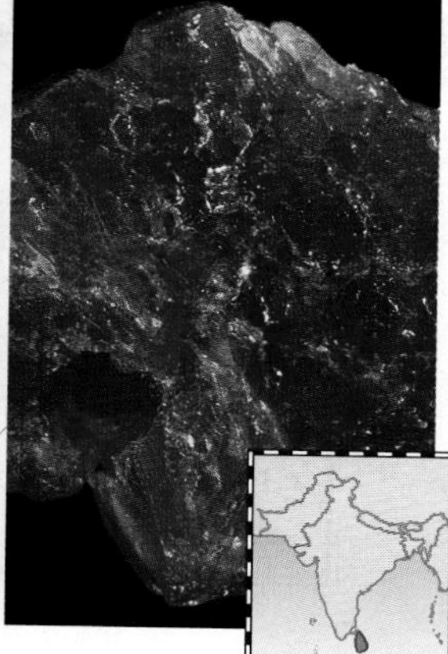

Geographic Themes

Human/Environment Interaction: Sri Lanka
Sapphires and rubies come from the same mineral—corundum. Corundum with chromium oxide produces rubies. A trace of iron and titanium results in blue sapphires. *What other mineral does Sri Lanka produce?*

SECTION 1 REVIEW

Checking for Understanding

1. **Define** subcontinent, alluvial plain, mica.
2. **Locating Places** What three bodies of water surround South Asia?
3. **Place** What is the major mountain range along South Asia's northern border?
4. **Human/Environment Interaction** What are three mineral resources of South Asia?

Critical Thinking

5. **Understanding Cause and Effect** Why are population densities so high in the Indo-Gangetic Plain?

ANSWERS TO SECTION 1 REVIEW

1. **subcontinent:** landmass like a continent, only smaller; **alluvial plain:** floodplain on which rich silt has been deposited; **mica:** mineral used in the manufacture of electrical equipment
2. Arabian Sea, Indian Ocean, Bay of Bengal
3. Himalayas
4. Answers include iron ore, manganese, ilmenite, mica, copper, gold, graphite, gemstones.
5. Fertile soils produce substantial crops and support large populations.

USING ILLUSTRATIONS

HUMAN/ENVIRONMENT INTERACTION A ruby's color may be pink or deep bluish-red. Sapphires come in a rainbow of colors, but blue sapphires are the most prized. Star sapphires—the most precious of all the blues—reflect light as white, glowing, starlike rays.

Answer to Caption: *graphite*

RETEACH

Have students write one question based on each subheading in this section. Then have them work with a partner to answer each other's questions.

ENRICH

Have students research and report on the animals of South Asia. These include elephants, yaks, cobras, Bengal tigers, and mongooses.

CLOSE

Have students write a postcard to Afsar describing the climate in the region where they live.

PHYSICAL GEOGRAPHY OF THE WORLD TRANSPARENCIES

Display and discuss the physical features of the following transparencies:

61. Great Indian Desert, Pakistan
63. Mount Everest, Nepal/China
64. Brahmaputra River, Bangladesh

LESSON PLAN
Chapter 23, Section 2

FOCUS

SECTION OBJECTIVES

1. Describe the climate regions of South Asia.
2. Explain the importance of seasonal rains.

BELLRINGER MOTIVATIONAL ACTIVITY

Project the Section 2 Focus Transparency and have students answer the questions.

PRETEACHING VOCABULARY

Tell students that the word *monsoon* comes from an Arabic word for "season."

All cyclones have winds that spiral in toward the center. Severe tropical cyclones with winds of 74 miles (119 km) per hour or more are called hurricanes or typhoons, depending on where they form. **LEP**

DID YOU KNOW?

Nepal has its own calendar with the new year in mid-April. The Buddhist calendar, used in Sri Lanka, is based on phases of the moon; every full moon day is a holiday.

SECTION 2

The Climate and Vegetation

SETTING THE SCENE

Read to Discover . . .

- the climate regions of South Asia.
- the importance of the seasonal rains.

Key Terms

- monsoon
- cyclone

Identify and Locate

Climate regions: highland, desert, steppe, tropical rain forest, tropical savanna

South Asia lies at about the same distance from the Equator as the Sahara and the other great deserts of the world. South Asia has a hot climate and a number of deserts, yet it also contains rain forests full of exotic orchids, fields of golden sunflowers, and mountainsides covered with birch trees and flowering shrubs.

REGION

South Asia's Climate Regions

South Asia is divided into five major climate regions: highland, desert, steppe, tropical rain forest, and tropical savanna.

Highland Climate

The coldest climates of South Asia are found at the northern edge of the subcontinent, in the snowy Himalayan peaks along the border of Tibet. At lower elevations of the Himalayas, the climate is mild, or temperate. In the Himalayan foothills, temperatures are actually quite warm.

Desert and Steppe Climates

A desert climate region is found along the Indus River. The land to the east of the Indus River is called the Thar Desert, or the Great Indian Desert.

A steppe climate region, made up of semiarid grasslands, surrounds the desert climate region, except along the coast. There is also a narrow strip of steppe that runs north and south through the center of the peninsula, between the Western Ghats and Eastern Ghats.

Tropical Climates

Tropical rain forest climate regions, with a variety of trees, are found along the western coast of the Indian subcontinent, near the Ganges Delta, and in the southwestern part of Sri Lanka. Tropical savanna regions, grasslands with both wet and dry seasons, surround the steppe climate area between the Ghats and are found in the remainder of Sri Lanka.

Monsoons

The climate of South Asia is greatly affected by **monsoons**, or seasonal winds. Between October and May, the winter winds blow from the north and northeast and are dry. As summer nears, temperatures gradually rise. The heated air also rises. As the air rises, a change in the wind direction is triggered. Moist air from the ocean replaces the rising air over the land. Winds blow from the Indian Ocean in the south and southwest between June and September, carrying warm, moist air. During this time, heavy rains provide the region with the largest portion of its yearly precipitation. The map on page 520 shows the difference between the winter and summer monsoons.

Classroom Resources for Section 2

BLACKLINE MASTERS:
Reproducible Lesson Plan 23-2
Guided Reading Activity 23-2
Vocabulary Activity 23
Workbook Activity 23-2
Skill Activity 23
Enrichment Activity 23
Section Quiz 23-2

TRANSPARENCIES:
Section Focus Transparency 23-2
Unit Map Overlay Transparency 8-3

MULTIMEDIA:

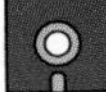

Testmaker

The rainfall is heaviest in the eastern part of South Asia as the winds sweep up the eastern side of the peninsula. One spot in the northeast of India near Shillong receives an average of 450 inches (1,140 cm) of rain each year. Once the wind reaches the Himalayas, it is forced west across the region. Most of the precipitation falls near the mountains. The rain decreases as the winds cross the region to the west.

With a large number of South Asia's population dependent on the land, rainfall crucially affects lives. Each year millions anxiously wait and watch for the monsoon crossing the subcontinent. Most parts of South Asia receive only one spell of rain yearly, and the early part of the year is dry in most places. January is the coldest month, with temperatures below 60°F (15.6°C) in northern India. The temperature, however, rises sharply in the early spring, and by May, it often exceeds 100°F (37.8°C) in the Indo-Gangetic Plain. Thus, the people yearn for the rains.

SOUTH ASIA: CLIMATE REGIONS

60°E 70°E 80°E 90°E
30°N
Tropic of Cancer
20°N
Equator
N
ASIA
PAKISTAN
NEPAL
BHUTAN
INDIA
BANGLADESH
LACCADIVE ISLANDS (INDIA)
ANDAMAN ISLANDS (INDIA)
SRI LANKA
MALDIVES
0 300 mi.
0 300 km

Tropical
- Tropical rain forest
- Tropical savanna

Dry
- Steppe
- Desert

Mid-Latitude
- Humid subtropical
- Highland

Lambert Conical projection

FOCUS ON GEOGRAPHIC THEMES

1. **Place: Which three climate regions dominate southern South Asia?**
2. **Location: Where are tropical rain forest climate regions located?**
3. **Region: What climate dominates the northernmost part of the region?**

Geographic Themes
Region: India
Farms cover more than half of India. Rice is the major crop, making India the world's second-largest rice producer after China. *How do monsoons affect the growing of rice?*

When the monsoon arrives, it is greeted with joyous song and dance. In southwestern India, forests of teak and bamboo turn green again. In Bangladesh, farmers plant their rice. The monsoon, unfortunately, does not benefit all South Asians equally. The dry Deccan Plateau receives little rain, even in monsoon season. Parts of western Pakistan may receive no rain at all for several years in a row. In low-lying Bangladesh, the monsoon rains frequently cause disastrous floods that ruin crops and kill livestock and people. Yet without the monsoons, farming in South Asia would suffer greatly.

TEACH

GUIDED PRACTICE

L2 Climate Patterns Display Unit Map Overlay Transparency 8-3. Have students indicate the direction of monsoons in winter and in summer. Discuss how monsoons affect the climate in South Asia.

USING ILLUSTRATIONS

HUMAN/ENVIRONMENT INTERACTION Farmers plant rice seeds densely in small seedbeds and transplant seedlings to a flooded field after several weeks. In developing countries like Bangladesh, this work is done by hand.

Answer to Caption: *Monsoons provide the precipitation that is necessary for rice.*

USING MAPS

Answers: **1.** tropical rain forest, tropical savanna, steppe; **2.** southwestern Sri Lanka, west coast of India, near the Ganges Delta; **3.** highland

Map Skills Practice

Reading a Map Which parts of South Asia have a dry climate year-round? *(northwestern India and much of Pakistan)*

Cooperative Learning Activity

Organize students into groups of three or four. Assign to each group, or have each group choose, a major city in South Asia. Instruct students to prepare a climate graph showing average monthly temperature and precipitation for their city. Display completed graphs for reference.

INDEPENDENT PRACTICE

Guided Reading Have students complete Guided Reading Activity 23-2 in the TCR. **LEP**

USING MAPS

Answers: **1.** tropical forest; **2.** northwestern; **3.** highland

Map Skills Practice

Comparing Maps How is vegetation related to climate in the northern part of the region? *(Highland climate produces different vegetation at various elevations.)*

ASSESS

CHECK FOR UNDERSTANDING

Assign Section 2 Review as homework or an in-class activity.

MEETING LESSON OBJECTIVES

Each objective below is tested by the questions that follow it in parentheses.
1. Describe the climate regions of South Asia. *(2)*
2. Explain the importance of seasonal rains. *(3, 4)*

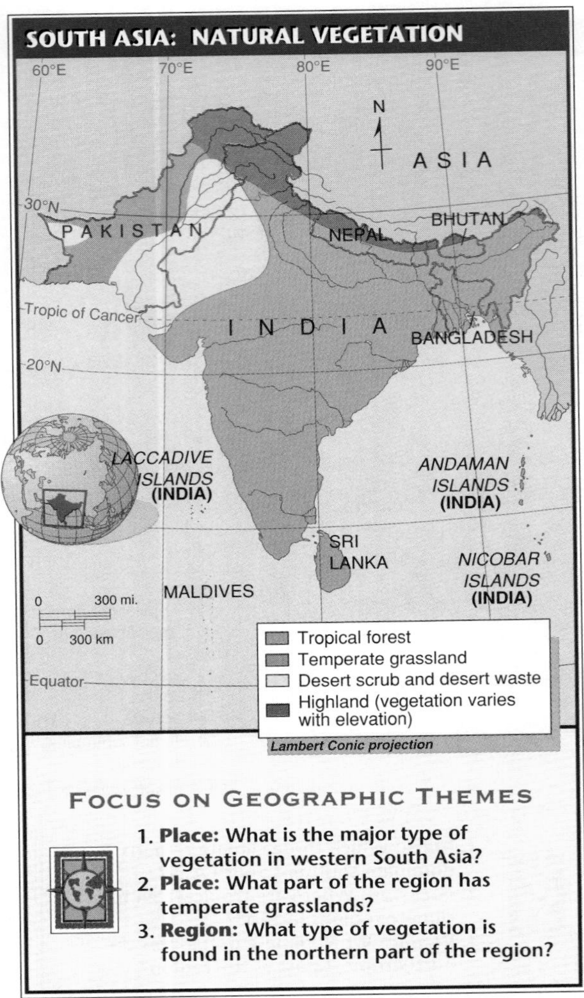

FOCUS ON GEOGRAPHIC THEMES

1. **Place:** What is the major type of vegetation in western South Asia?
2. **Place:** What part of the region has temperate grasslands?
3. **Region:** What type of vegetation is found in the northern part of the region?

Cyclones

Bangladesh is also dramatically affected by cyclones. A **cyclone** is a storm marked by high winds and heavy rains. Because Bangladesh is a low-lying coastal region, the violent surges of seawater typical of cyclones often cause major disasters by submerging productive farmland and causing rivers to overflow into villages and fields. In 1991, a cyclone roaring in from the Bay of Bengal pounded the country's southern coast, killing at least 131,000 people and causing losses amounting to $1.7 billion.

HUMAN/ENVIRONMENT INTERACTION

Vegetation

The natural vegetation of South Asia varies from one climate region to another, depending on rainfall and temperature. Long ago most of the region was probably covered with forests. Over the centuries, however, trees have been cut down for firewood and shelter and to create cropland and fields for grazing. Today only about one-sixth of the subcontinent is forested. Of this land much is covered with low, thorny scrub rather than tall trees.

Forests

When the southwestern monsoons sweep along India's west coast, they encounter the Western Ghats and drop much of their moisture. This plentiful rainfall produces a band of rain forest, dense with coconut palms and teak. Rain forests full of towering ebony trees and magnificent orchids cover much of Sri Lanka, and similar forests grow on a small section of India's southeastern coast and along the Bay of Bengal. All of these rain forests lie in the path of the monsoon.

Surrounding India's west coast rain forests are woodlands that contain a mixture of deciduous and coniferous trees. A band of temperate mixed forest extends along the northern border of the peninsula. Mixed tropical forests thrive in the damp, hot climate of Bangladesh. Bamboo and trees, such as mango and palm, grow throughout most of Bangladesh. Valuable teak forests are located in the Chittagong Hills in the southeast, while mangrove trees and other tropical plants thrive in the Sundarbans, a swampy region in the southwest.

Because the Western and Eastern Ghats prevent much rain from reaching the center of India, the climate of the Deccan Plateau and the northern plains is drier than that of the coastal regions. As a result, the natural vegetation of India's interior is tropical dry deciduous forest, rather than a type of woodland that requires more rainfall.

Meeting Special Needs

Attention Deficiency The following strategy may make students with attention problems more aware of their attending behaviors. Have students divide a sheet of paper into two columns titled "On-task" and "Off-task." Call out "check" at intervals as students silently read Section 2. Students should put a check in the proper column to indicate whether they were paying attention to their reading or their minds were wandering. At the end of the exercise, ask students to evaluate their attention and try to determine what interfered with their reading.

COMPARING CLIMATE REGIONS

India and the United States

Climate Graph: Delhi, India
Location: 29° N/77° E
Elevation: 714 ft. (218 m)

Climate Graph: Houston, Texas
Location: 30° N/95° W
Elevation: 41 ft. (12.5 m)

°F/°C: 100/38, 90/32, 80/27, 70/21, 60/16, 50/10, 40/4, 30/-1, 20/-7, 10/-12, 0/-18 — Average Monthly Temperature

In./Cm.: 20/51, 18/46, 16/41, 14/36, 12/30, 10/25, 8/20, 6/15, 4/10, 2/5, 0/0 — Average Monthly Precipitation

J F M A M J J A S O N D — Months

Source: *World Weather Guide*, 1990

*lines measure temperature/bars measure precipitation

GRAPH STUDY

The climate graphs show the average monthly temperature and the average monthly precipitation in Delhi, India, and Houston, Texas. ***What is the average December temperature and precipitation in each city?***

Scrub and Grassland

The northwestern part of the Indian peninsula is extremely arid. Annual rainfall is less than 20 inches (51 cm) a year. The natural vegetation of this region is desert scrub—a mix of low trees and grasses. Some parts of this region can be used for grazing livestock, while other areas are wasteland. Irrigation projects, however, have made some parts of this desert area near the Indus River suitable for growing grains.

Grasslands and thick stands of bamboo are found in the foothills of the Himalayas. At higher elevations there are lovely alpine meadows, blooming with pink and blue flowers in spring. At the highest elevations of the mountains, however, there is little or no vegetation.

SECTION 2 REVIEW

Checking for Understanding

1. **Define** monsoon, cyclone.
2. **Locating Places** In which climate region is Sri Lanka located?
3. **Place** Why does the Deccan Plateau receive little of the monsoon rains?
4. **Place** Why does the monsoon often cause flooding in Bangladesh?

Critical Thinking

5. **Making Comparisons** How does the vegetation of northwestern India and western Pakistan compare with that of Bangladesh?

EVALUATE

Assign the Section 2 Quiz in the TCR.

Use the Testmaker to create a customized test for Section 2.

RETEACH

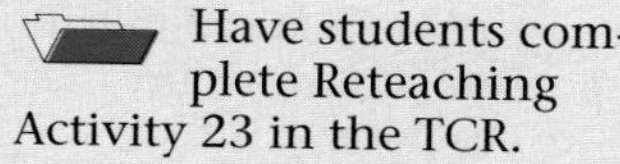
Have students complete Reteaching Activity 23 in the TCR.

USING GRAPHS

Answers: Delhi: About .5 in. (1.2 cm), 60°F (16°C); Houston: 4.5 in. (11.2 cm), 55°F (13°C).

Skills Practice

Interpreting a Graph How does rainfall in Houston differ from that in Delhi? *(Houston's average rainfall does not differ significantly from month to month. Delhi receives most of its rainfall from June to September.)*

ENRICH

Have students complete Enrichment Activity 23 in the TCR.

CLOSE

Ask students to write a paragraph stating how their life would be different if they lived in one of the climate regions of South Asia.

ANSWERS TO SECTION 2 REVIEW

1. **monsoon:** seasonal wind; **cyclone:** powerful storm characterized by high winds and strong rains
2. tropical rain forest
3. Coastal ranges prevent the moisture-laden winds from reaching the Deccan Plateau.
4. Most of Bangladesh is a low-lying coastal region.
5. Much of northwest India and western Pakistan has dry scrub vegetation. Bangladesh is covered with teak forests, bamboo, mango, palm, and other tropical vegetation.

TEACH

Have students draw conclusions by participating in this theater game. Divide the class into small groups. Have each group choose a location that they would like to "portray." These locations should be kept secret from other groups. Each group will use actions (no words or sounds) to portray this location. To show a supermarket, for example, students may push shopping carts, choose items from shelves, and run a cash register.

Have each group present its scene to the class. After each scene, the audience draws conclusions about the location. Have students identify clues (actions) that helped them determine the location.

Skills Practice
For additional practice, have students complete Skill Activity 23 in the TCR.

CRITICAL THINKING SKILLS

Drawing Conclusions

Suppose you come home from school and decide to put on your favorite jeans. But your jeans, which lie near an open window, are damp. The windowsill is wet, too. Putting these facts together, you conclude that it must have rained, and the jeans got wet because they were near the open window.

REVIEWING THE SKILL

In this example, you were **drawing conclusions.** You used facts, experience, and insight to form judgments about events. Drawing conclusions allows you to understand indirectly stated ideas and events, so you can apply your knowledge to a wider range of situations.

Often, however, people draw incorrect conclusions. In the example above, perhaps your brother or sister spilled water on your jeans. Maybe the jeans were washed, but not completely dried. To determine the accuracy of your conclusion, gather information that will prove or disprove it. In this case, you could find out if it had rained that day, or whether the jeans had been washed, or if anyone had spilled something on them.

When drawing conclusions, apply the following steps:

- Review the facts that are stated directly.
- Use your own knowledge, experience, and insight to form conclusions about them.
- Find information that proves or disproves your conclusions.

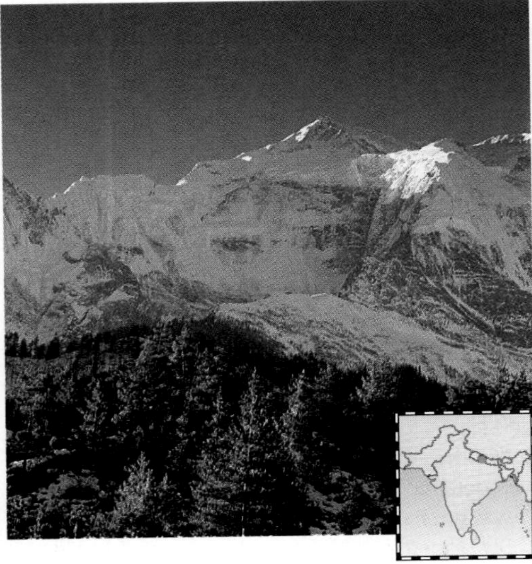

PRACTICING THE SKILL

Read the following excerpt from the diary of a mountain climber. A member of an all-woman expedition, she describes her ascent to the summit of Annapurna in the Himalayas of Nepal. Then answer the questions below.

Vera Komarkova and I and the Sherpas Mingma Tsering and Chewang Rinjing, rope together and start off shortly before 7:00 A.M. *. . . I am breathing six times for each step. . . . Our oxygen tanks are only good for six hours; we must get as high as possible before starting to use them.*

After climbing steadily for two and a half hours, we slow to a crawl. Time for oxygen . . . We don't talk as we climb higher. All our energy and concentration go into the steady, monotonous plod that is taking us toward our goal. There is still no wind, but we can see plumes of snow blowing off the summit in the winter gale. . . . Just below the summit pyramid the snow is again very deep, and our pace drags. But soon there is less snow, and the walking gets easier. . . . We traverse three or four bumps, and finally there we are. . . . The summit of Annapurna I at last! At 3:30 P.M. *on October 15, 1978, we are at 26,504 feet on top of the world's tenth highest mountain — on top of the world.*[1]

1. What conclusion can you draw about the weather conditions on this day?
2. What evidence do you have to support this conclusion?
3. Why did the climbers walk so slowly?
4. What evidence do you have to support this conclusion?

For additional practice in this skill, see Practicing Skills on page 488 of the Chapter 23 Review.

[1] Source: *Annapurna, A Woman's Place,* Arlene Blum. Sierra Club Books, San Francisco, 1980, pp. 213–214.

ANSWERS TO PRACTICING THE SKILL

1. cold, not windy
2. The author says, "There is still no wind." Also, they are walking through snow; they are climbing to 26,000 feet where it is always cold. She says there is a winter gale blowing off the summit.
3. lack of oxygen
4. The author says she took six breaths per step, had to wait as long as possible to use oxygen tanks; even with oxygen, they had very little energy in the thin mountain air.

chapter 23 HIGHLIGHTS

1 Section: The Land

Key Terms

subcontinent (p. 477)
alluvial plain (p. 480)
mica (p. 481)

Brahmaputra River Delta in Bangladesh

Summary

- South Asia consists of a large peninsula with an island near its southern tip. The peninsula is also known as a subcontinent, a large landmass smaller than a continent.
- South Asia is bordered by the Himalayas in the north, the Arabian Sea on the west, the Indian Ocean on the south, and the Bay of Bengal on the east.
- Most of the region's people live on the northern plains, an agriculturally rich area.
- South Asia has three great river systems and the world's largest alluvial plain.
- South Asia has few significant oil reserves, but some natural gas, coal, and uranium. The region also has a number of substantial mineral deposits, including iron ore and mica.

2 Section: The Climate and Vegetation

Key Terms

monsoon (p. 482)
cyclone (p. 484)

Indian farmer planting rice

Summary

- South Asia has highland, desert, steppe, and tropical climates.
- The monsoon is a seasonal change in wind direction that brings heavy rains to much of South Asia between June and September.
- South Asia's vegetation is affected by altitude, rainfall, and human activity.
- South Asia was once largely covered by forests. Today only a small portion of the land is forested.

Map Activity

Identify and Locate Provide a copy of page 34 of the Outline Map Resource Book for each student. Have students label the following on their maps: Himalayas, Arabian Sea, Indian Ocean, Bay of Bengal; Pakistan, India, Nepal, Bhutan, Bangladesh, Sri Lanka, and Maldives.

CHAPTER 23 HIGHLIGHTS

USING THE CHAPTER 23 HIGHLIGHTS

Use the Chapter 23 Highlights to preview, review, condense, or reteach the chapter.

PREVIEW/REVIEW

Vocabulary PuzzleMaker Software reinforces the Key Terms used in Chapter 23.

Student Self-Test and Review Software allows students to review Chapter 23 content.

CONDENSE

Have students read the Chapter 23 Highlights.

Have students listen to the Chapter 23 Audiocassettes in the TCR. Spanish Audiocassettes are also available.

Assign the Chapter 23 Audiocassette Activity and give the students the Chapter 23 Audiocassette Quiz.

Have students complete Guided Reading Activities for Chapter 23 in the TCR. Spanish Guided Reading Activities are also available.

RETEACH

Have students complete Reteaching Activity 23 in the TCR. Spanish Reteaching Activities are also available.

Chapter 23 Review

GLENCOE TECHNOLOGY

Videodisc

Use Chapter 23 MindJogger Videoquiz to review students' knowledge before administering the Chapter 23 Test.

MINDJOGGER VIDEOQUIZ

Chapter 23
Disc 3 Side B

The MindJogger Videoquiz is also available on videocassette.

ANSWERS

Reviewing Key Terms

1. alluvial plain
2. mica
3. subcontinent
4. cyclone
5. monsoon

Reviewing Facts

6. Himalayas
7. Eastern Ghats and Western Ghats
8. in the Himalayas
9. to create hydroelectricity and to bring more land under cultivation through irrigation
10. Sri Lanka
11. in the northern Himalayas
12. along India's west coast and in Sri Lanka
13. Winds blow from the south and southwest.
14. Trees have been cut for firewood and to provide land for farming and grazing.
15. southern part

chapter 23 REVIEW

Reviewing Key Terms

Choose the vocabulary term that best completes each of the sentences below. Write your answers on a separate sheet of paper.

subcontinent (p. 477)
alluvial plain (p. 480)
mica (p. 481)
monsoon (p. 482)
cyclone (p. 484)

SECTION 1

1. Silt from a flooding river is deposited in the ____ .
2. ____ is a mineral used in the manufacture of electrical equipment.
3. The Indian peninsula is often called a ____ .

SECTION 2

4. A severe storm marked by heavy rains and strong winds is a ____ .
5. ____ refers to seasonal reversals in wind direction.

Reviewing Facts

SECTION 1

6. In what mountain range is Mount Everest located?
7. What are the names of the two mountain ranges that form a triangle at the base of the Indian peninsula?
8. Where are the sources of the Indus, the Ganges, and the Brahmaputra rivers?
9. What are the two goals of the dam-building projects in South Asia?
10. Which country in South Asia is known for its gemstones?

SECTION 2

11. Where are the coldest climates of South Asia found?
12. Name two locations in South Asia where tropical rain forests exist.
13. From which direction do winds blow during the June-to-September monsoon season?
14. Why have many of South Asia's forests disappeared?
15. In what part of Nepal are grains cultivated?

Critical Thinking

16. **Understanding Cause and Effect** In what way are the Himalayas responsible for the richness of the agricultural soil in the Indian subcontinent's northern plains?
17. **Making Comparisons** State the advantages and disadvantages the monsoon brings to the people of South Asia.

Geographic Themes

18. **Human/Environment Interaction** How have the inhabitants of the arid regions of western Pakistan adapted their lifestyle in response to the climate and vegetation?
19. **Location** Where do the monsoon rains strike hardest?

Practicing Skills

Drawing Conclusions

Refer to the skills feature on page 486.

20. What equipment did Vera bring on her mountain climb?
21. What conclusion can you draw about her physical reaction to the climb?
22. What evidence do you have to support this conclusion?

Using the Unit Atlas

Refer to the physical geography section of the Unit Atlas on pages 472–473.

Critical Thinking

16. Rivers carry rich soil from the mountains. When seasonal rains cause rivers to overflow, the alluvial soil is deposited on the plains.

17. The monsoons bring most of the region's annual precipitation and make farming possible. However, they also cause flooding and loss of life, especially in Bangladesh.

Geographic Themes

18. They have become nomadic herders.

19. along the eastern coast of the peninsula

23. Where is the world's largest river delta? What two rivers form this delta?
24. What is a major natural resource of Sri Lanka?

Projects

Individual Activity

You have learned about the diversity of the physical features of South Asia. Choose one of the seven nations of the region and research the interrelationships among its physical features, climate, and vegetation.

Cooperative Learning Activity

Working in a small group, trace the path of a typical monsoon across South Asia. Research when and where the monsoon rains fall, and how they affect the different regions along their path. Present your findings to the rest of the class using maps and other visual aids (such as charts showing rainfall and/or calendars) as well as written descriptions.

Writing About Geography

Description

Imagine that you are a tourist visiting the plains of northern India for the first time. It is May, and the land is hot and dry. Describe the dust, the heat, and the vegetation. Then describe the coming of the monsoon rains and their effect on the rivers, vegetation, and people of the area. Use your journal record and other references in writing your description.

Locating Places

SOUTH ASIA: PHYSICAL GEOGRAPHY

Match the letters on the map with the places and physical features of South Asia. Write your answers on a separate sheet of paper.

1. Deccan Plateau
2. Himalayas
3. Arabian Sea
4. Nepal
5. Indus River
6. Pakistan
7. Thar Desert
8. Ganges River
9. Bay of Bengal
10. Brahmaputra River

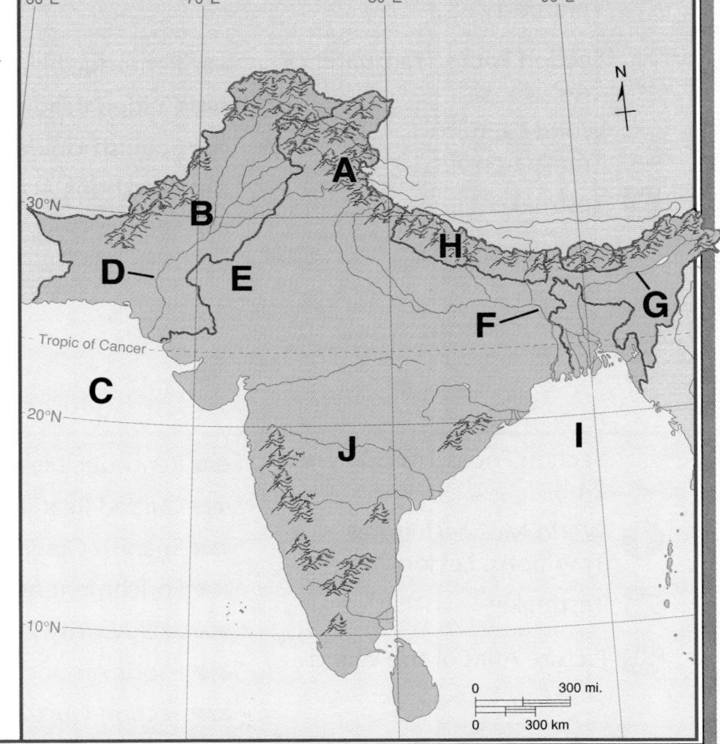

Chapter 23 Review

Practicing Skills

20. oxygen tanks
21. The climb was difficult.
22. They slowed to a crawl, needed all their energy and concentration to climb, and their pace dragged in the deep snow.

Using the Unit Atlas

23. Indo-Gangetic Plain in northern India; Indus and Ganges rivers
24. graphite

Locating Places

1. J
2. A
3. C
4. H
5. D
6. B
7. E
8. F
9. I
10. G

Chapter Bonus Test Question

This question may be used for extra credit on the chapter test.

Why do the climates of South Asia include both desert and tropical rain forest regions?

(Answer: Monsoons influence the climates. Dry winds blow from the north and northeast. Moist winds blow from the south and southwest. Coastal ranges prevent moisture-laden winds from reaching the interior.)

CHAPTER 24

PLANNING GUIDE

The Cultural Geography of South Asia

CHAPTER ORGANIZER

Daily Lesson Objectives	Multimedia	Teacher Classroom Resources
SECTION 1 Population Patterns 1. Identify the ethnic groups of South Asia. 2. Describe population density and distribution in South Asia. 3. Compare rural and urban life in the region.	Section Focus Transparency 24-1 Chapter 24 Vocabulary PuzzleMaker Software World Music: Cultural Traditions, Lesson 7 Testmaker STV: World Geography, Volume 1	Reproducible Lesson Plan 24-1 Guided Reading Activity 24-1 Spanish Guided Reading Activity 24-1 Workbook Activity 24-1 Performance Assessment Activity 24 World Literature Reading 7 Section Quiz 24-1
SECTION 2 History and Government 1. Discuss the early civilizations that developed in South Asia. 2. Compare the characteristics of Hinduism and Buddhism. 3. Identify the empires established in South Asia. 4. Explain how South Asians achieved independence.	Section Focus Transparency 24-2 World Cultures Transparencies 13, 14 Testmaker	Reproducible Lesson Plan 24-2 Guided Reading Activity 24-2 Spanish Guided Reading Activity 24-2 Workbook Activity 24-2 Section Quiz 24-2
SECTION 3 Cultures and Lifestyles 1. List the languages and religions of South Asia. 2. Contrast rural and urban lifestyles in South Asia. 3. Discuss the arts and celebrations of South Asia.	Section Focus Transparency 24-3 World Music: Cultural Traditions, Lesson 7 Testmaker Picture Atlas of the World	Reproducible Lesson Plan 24-3 Guided Reading Activity 24-3 Spanish Guided Reading Activity 24-3 Enrichment Activity 24 Skill Activity 24 Foods Around the World 7 Section Quiz 24-3
CHAPTER REVIEW AND EVALUATION	Chapter 24 English (or Spanish) Audiocassettes MindJogger Videoquiz Testmaker Student Self-Test and Review Software	Reteaching Activity 24 Spanish Reteaching Activity 24 Chapter 24 Test Form A and Form B

0:00 *If time does not permit teaching the entire chapter, summarize using the Chapter 24 Highlights on page 507, and the Chapter 24 English (or Spanish) Audiocassettes. Review students' knowledge using the Glencoe MindJogger Videoquiz.*

KEY TO ABILITY LEVELS

Teaching strategies have been coded for varying learning styles and abilities.

L1 **BASIC** activities for all students

L2 **AVERAGE** activities for average to above-average students

L3 **CHALLENGING** activities for above-average students

LEP **LIMITED ENGLISH PROFICIENCY** activities

Performance Assessment

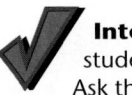

Interviewing for Concept Attainment Assess student understanding through an interview process. Ask the following questions:

(1) What have you learned about South Asia today?

(2) Tell me about the way people live in South Asia.

Progress to more specific questions with follow-ups:

(3) What noticeable effects did British rule in South Asia have on the region's people today?

(4) How would South Asia be different if Africans had ruled the region instead of Europeans?

(5) What is your opinion about the domination of a group of people by a foreign power?

Conclude with questions about the student's own learning, such as:

(6) What were the most interesting concepts you learned?

POSSIBLE RUBRIC FEATURES: Content information, concept attainment, critical thinking skills, communication skills

For additional professional and classroom resources, see Chapter Resources, pages T46–T51.

TEACHER'S CORNER

INDEX TO NATIONAL GEOGRAPHIC MAGAZINE

The following articles may be used for research relating to this chapter:

- "Bombay: India's Capital of Hope," by John McCarry, March 1995.
- "High Road to Hunza," by John McCarry, March 1994.
- "Bhutan: Kingdom in the Clouds," by Bruce W. Bunting.
- "Searching for India: Along the Grand Trunk Road," by Harvey Arden, May 1990.
- "Population, Plenty, and Poverty," by Paul L. Ehrlich and Anne H. Ehrlich, December 1988.
- "At the Crossroads of Katmandu," by Douglas H. Chadwick, July 1987.
- "New Delhi: Mirror of India," by Bryan Hodgson, April 1985.
- "When the Moguls Ruled India," by Mike Edwards, April 1985.
- "Pakistan Under Pressure," by William S. Ellis, May 1981.

NATIONAL GEOGRAPHIC SOCIETY PRODUCTS AVAILABLE FROM GLENCOE

To order the following products for use with this chapter, contact your local Glencoe sales representative or call Glencoe at 1-800-334-7344:

- *Picture Atlas of the World* (CD-ROM)
- *STV: World Geography, Asia and Australia* (Videodisc)
- *ZipZapMap! World* (Software)
- *GeoBee* (Software)
- *Images of the World* (Posters)
- *Eye on the Environment* (Posters)
- *Physical Geography of the World* (Transparencies)
- *Picture Atlas of Our 50 States* (Book)

Introducing
CHAPTER 24

chapter 24 The Cultural Geography of South Asia

PERFORMANCE ASSESSMENT

Refer to the Planning Guide on page 490B for a Performance Assessment Activity for this chapter. See the *Performance Assessment Activities* booklet for additional suggestions.

CHAPTER OBJECTIVES

1. **Describe** population patterns in South Asia.
2. **Discuss** the two religions that began in South Asia.
3. **Compare** lifestyles in South Asia.

GLENCOE TECHNOLOGY

Videodisc

Use Chapter 24 MindJogger Videoquiz to preview chapter content.

MINDJOGGER VIDEOQUIZ

Chapter 24
Disc 3 Side B

The MindJogger Videoquiz is also available on videocassette.

CHAPTER FOCUS

Geographic Setting

Throughout history many peoples have entered South Asia through the mountain ranges of the north and then dispersed throughout the Indian subcontinent. The result is a rich diversity of peoples, languages, and traditions.

Geographic Themes

Section 1 Population Patterns
REGION Throughout South Asia people tend to cluster in the fertile plains and lowlands.

Section 2 History and Government
MOVEMENT Two great religions, Hinduism and Buddhism, began in South Asia.

Section 3 Cultures and Lifestyles
HUMAN/ENVIRONMENT INTERACTION Lifestyles, education, and health care all vary in South Asia depending on whether people live in urban or rural environments.

▲ Photograph: *Jewelry vender in Rajasthan, India*

EXTRA CREDIT PROJECT

Culture Have students find examples of South Asian art, music, foods, crafts, and/or tradtional dress. Provide time to display and discuss students' exhibits.

SECTION 1

Population Patterns

SETTING THE SCENE

Read to Discover . . .
- the ethnic groups of South Asia.
- the density and distribution of population in South Asia.
- differences between rural and urban life in the region.

Key Term
- jati

Identify and Locate
Indo-Gangetic Plain, Thar Desert, Calcutta, Bombay, Delhi, Dhaka, Islamabad

50 nP TIGER भारत INDIA

Bangalore, India

Bangalore is a very busy, cosmopolitan city. People from all over the globe have settled here permanently. You can see children playing cricket, soccer, and field hockey wherever there is empty space. Movies are the major source of recreation, but sometimes it is impossible to get a ticket unless bought in advance. Flower shows and gardens are very popular and numerous in Bangalore.

Your friend,
Azeez Haque

Azeez Haque's description of the hectic pace of life in Bangalore, India, is typical of urban areas in the culture region of South Asia. More than 1,204 million people—about 22 percent of the world's population—live in South Asia. India's population of about 920 million people ranks second in the world and constitutes more than 76 percent of the region's total population. Bangladesh and Pakistan are home to most of the region's remaining population.

PLACE

Human Characteristics

South Asia has one of the richest and most complex mixes of people in the world. The peoples of the region are divided by six major religions, hundreds of languages, and numerous social groupings.

India

In India a person's religion may be Hindu, Muslim, Buddhist, Sikh, Jain, or Christian. The person's ancestors may have entered India from Europe or Central Asia thousands of years ago, or the individual may be part of a group whose roots go back more than 8,000 years. If the individual is a Hindu, he or she will belong to one of hundreds of **jati**—social groups that define one's occupation and social standing.

Pakistan and Bangladesh

In Pakistan and Bangladesh, more than 9 out of 10 people are Muslims. In Pakistan there are at least 5 main ethnic groups, while in Bangladesh, virtually all of the people are Bengali.

Sri Lanka

Conflict divides Sri Lanka's two main ethnic groups—the Sinhalese and the Tamils. These

Classroom Resources for Section 1

BLACKLINE MASTERS:
Reproducible Lesson Plan 24-1
World Literature Reading 7
Guided Reading Activity 24-1
Workbook Activity 24-1
Performance Assessment Activity 24
Section Quiz 24-1

TRANSPARENCIES:
Section Focus Transparency 24-1

MULTIMEDIA:

Vocabulary PuzzleMaker Software
Testmaker

World Music: Cultural Traditions, Lesson 7

STV: World Geography, Volume 1

LESSON PLAN
Chapter 24, Section 1

FOCUS

SECTION OBJECTIVES

1. **Identify** the ethnic groups of South Asia.
2. **Describe** population density and distribution in South Asia.
3. **Compare** rural and urban life in the region.

ABOUT THE POSTCARD

Azeez tells us that the everyday scene in Bangalore includes streets full of people—walking, talking, on buses and scooters, riding in cars—accompanied by music blaring from nearby restaurants.

BELLRINGER MOTIVATIONAL ACTIVITY

Project the Section 1 Focus Transparency and have students answer the questions.

PRETEACHING VOCABULARY

Explain that a *jati* has its own customs and that members of a *jati* typically have only certain kinds of jobs. Although modern urban life has weakened this system, it remains an important culture trait in India.

Use the Vocabulary PuzzleMaker Software to create a crossword or word search puzzle.

Videodisc

STV: WORLD GEOGRAPHY, VOLUME 1

Side 1, Chapter 1
Frames 1185-6885
Title: *Asia*
Subject: Overview

TEACH

GUIDED PRACTICE

L1 Chart Have students make a chart on the chalkboard identifying ethnic groups in South Asia. Ask them to list one fact or characteristic about each group. Discuss how ethnic diversity affects the region.

USING ILLUSTRATIONS

PLACE Kathmandu is noted for its many graceful Hindu and Buddhist temples. Its major industry is tourism.

Answer to Caption: *Sherpas*

Have students complete World Literature Reading 7 in the TCR.

INDEPENDENT PRACTICE

Guided Reading Have students complete Guided Reading Activity 24-1 in the TCR. **LEP**

two groups inhabit different parts of the island, speak different languages, and practice different religions. The Sinhalese are Buddhist and the Tamils are Hindu. The Sinhalese are the majority, and they dominate the government of Sri Lanka. Many Tamils have pressured the government to create an independent Tamil state, and some have joined terrorist groups such as the Tamil Tigers.

Bhutan and Nepal

Most inhabitants of Bhutan and Nepal came originally from Mongolia and are quite different in appearance from the inhabitants of India. Tiny Nepal has one of the most complex ethnic patterns in the world. Probably the best-known Nepalese are the Sherpas, famous worldwide since their mountaineering skills helped in the first conquest of Mount Everest, the world's highest peak, located in the Himalayas.

PLACE

Population Density and Distribution

South Asia's overall population density is high—756 people per square mile (292 people per sq. km). This is about 7 times the world average. The rate of population growth in South Asia also is high. If growth continues at its present rate, the population of South Asia will double in less than 40 years.

Regional Variation

Although population densities are generally high in South Asia, they vary from one region to another. Factors such as climate, vegetation, and terrain have an impact on the number of people the land can support. Some of the most fertile farmland in South Asia is home to many thousands of people per square mile, while other areas, such as the glacier-

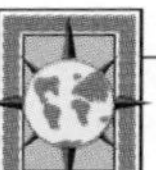

Geographic Themes

Place: Kathmandu, Nepal

Kathmandu, Nepal's capital and largest city, lies at the foot of the Himalayas. *What Nepalese are famous for their mountain-climbing skills?*

Cooperative Learning Activity

Organize students into seven groups and assign one of the countries of South Asia to each group. Have students create charts, graphs, and/or maps to illustrate the population characteristics of their assigned country. Information should include size of population, density, distribution, and ethnic diversity. Students may include additional information from other references.

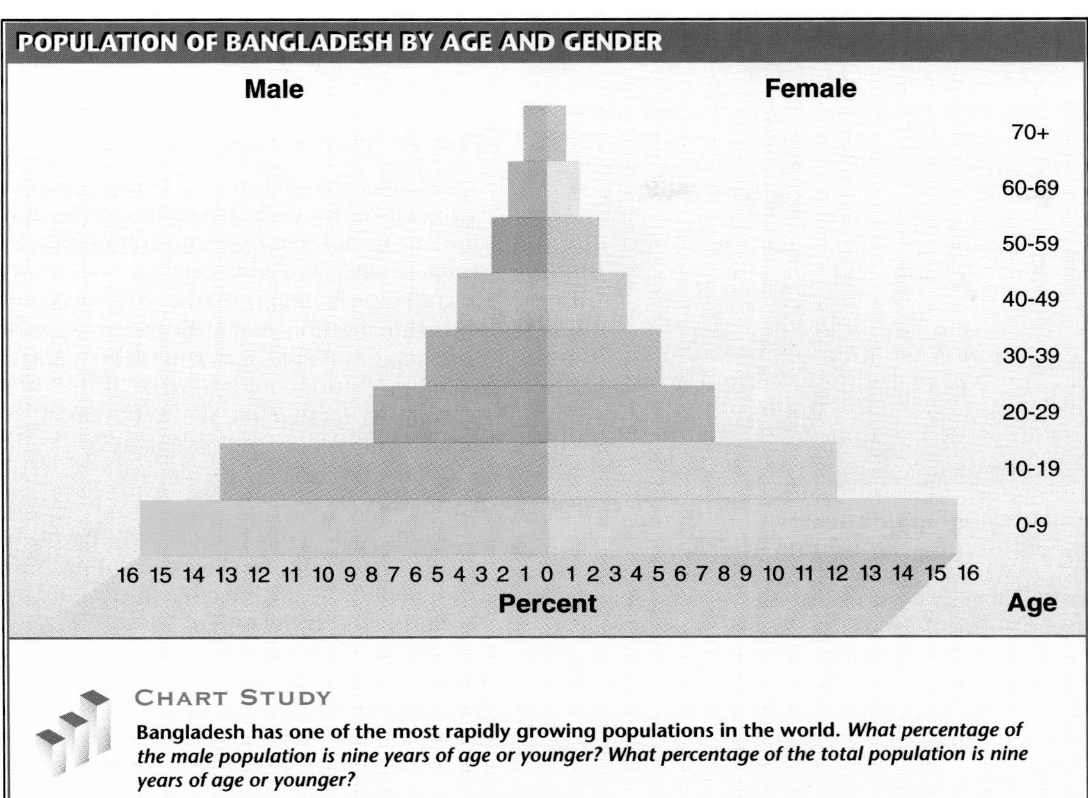

CHART STUDY

Bangladesh has one of the most rapidly growing populations in the world. ***What percentage of the male population is nine years of age or younger? What percentage of the total population is nine years of age or younger?***

dotted mountains of Nepal and Bhutan, can support only a few individuals per square mile.

Densely Populated Areas

The greatest concentration of people in South Asia is found on the fertile Indo-Gangetic Plain and along the monsoon-watered coasts of the peninsula. Because rice is an abundant and important food source, it is only natural that most South Asians live where rice is grown.

On Sri Lanka, tea and rubber are grown on large plantations. Because large plantations require large workforces, most of Sri Lanka's population live in rural villages.

The most densely populated country in the region is Bangladesh, with 2,320 people per square mile (895 people per sq. km). This is one of the highest population densities in the world. Having so many people packed into this tiny country creates serious problems. Despite rich alluvial soil and improved farming techniques, there is not enough food for all the people of Bangladesh. The situation is likely to be even more severe in the future. If the population continues to grow at its current rate, the population of Bangladesh will double in about 29 years.

Less Densely Populated Regions

India's Deccan Plateau is not as populous as the Indo-Gangetic Plain, but it is still home to an average of 125 to 250 people per square mile (48 to 97 people per sq. km).

The population of the Thar Desert is very sparse, and few people inhabit the mountainous western part of Pakistan.

USING GRAPHS

Answers:
16 percent; 31 percent

Skills Practice

Reading a Graph About what percentage of the total population is 70 years of age or older? *(about 2 percent)*

MULTICULTURAL PERSPECTIVE

Culturally Speaking
There are at least 300 languages in India. About 30 percent of the population speaks Hindi, which is one of 16 official languages in the country.

ASSESS

CHECK FOR UNDERSTANDING

Assign Section 1 Review as homework or an in-class activity.

MEETING LESSON OBJECTIVES

Each objective below is tested by the questions that follow it in parentheses.

1. **Identify** the ethnic groups of South Asia. *(1)*
2. **Describe** population density and distribution in South Asia. *(3, 5)*
3. **Compare** rural and urban life in the region. *(4)*

Meeting Special Needs

Poor Visual Observers Students with visual-spatial processing problems may have difficulty interpreting graphs. Direct students to the population graph on page 493. Ask several questions based on reading the graph. Then have students write a summary statement of the information shown on the graph.

EVALUATE

 Assign the Section 1 Quiz in the TCR.

 Use the Testmaker to create a customized quiz for Section 1.

USING ILLUSTRATIONS

PLACE In August 1995, the legislature of Maharashtra—the state in which Bombay is located—changed the name of Bombay to Mumbai.

Answer to Caption: *New Delhi*

RETEACH

Have students use the charts, graphs, and/or maps they prepared for the cooperative learning activity to review population characteristics of South Asia.

ENRICH

Ask interested students to research and report on the work of Mother Teresa, who won the Nobel Peace Prize for her work with the poor in Calcutta.

CLOSE

Have students write a postcard to Azeez, describing recreational activities in their community.

Geographic Themes

Place: Bombay, India

A bustling metropolis of 12 million people, Bombay is India's financial and film-making capital. *What is India's capital?*

The southernmost parts of Bhutan and Nepal have populations of about 25 to 60 people per square mile (10 to 23 people per sq. km), but in the northern areas of both countries—where elevations are higher—the density drops to fewer than 25 people per square mile (10 people per sq. km).

PLACE

Urbanization

The percentage of South Asians living in urban areas is generally low. The urban portion of the population ranges from as low as 5 percent in Bhutan to 28 percent in Pakistan. Urbanization, however, is an important aspect of life in the region. Currently almost 300 million people in South Asia live in cities.

Rapid Urban Growth

Many South Asians are migrating to urban areas in search of better jobs and higher wages. The rapid growth of cities presents an important challenge for the governments of the region. The cities are becoming overcrowded, and the increased population is putting a tremendous strain on public facilities such as schools and hospitals.

The Region's Largest Cities

Calcutta, located on a branch of the Ganges River, is India's largest city. People continue to flock there from the countryside in search of work. The grim slum areas of Calcutta contrast sharply with the city's bustling port, thriving iron and steel industries, efficient subway system, and handsome modern buildings.

Bombay, located on the Arabian Sea, is India's main western port. Millions of people from outlying areas pour into the city each day to work.

Delhi, India's third-largest city, traces its origins to the mid-1600s. Neighboring New Delhi, India's capital, is a modern city built by the British during the early 1900s.

The cities of Bangladesh are as crowded as the rest of that country. The capital, Dhaka, has more inhabitants per square mile than any city in the world except Lagos, Nigeria. In Islamabad, the capital of Pakistan, new housing developments are being built to accommodate the growing middle class.

SECTION 1 REVIEW

Checking for Understanding

1. **Define** jati.
2. **Locating Places** On what body of water is Bombay located?
3. **Place** Which is the most densely populated country of South Asia?
4. **Movement** What challenge have South Asia's cities faced in recent decades?

Critical Thinking

5. **Drawing Conclusions** Why are the Indo-Gangetic Plain and coastal areas the most densely populated parts of South Asia?

ANSWERS TO SECTION 1 REVIEW

1. **jati:** social group that define's one's occupation and social standing among Hindus
2. on the Arabian Sea
3. Bangladesh
4. overcrowding
5. Rice grown in these areas provides an abundant and important food source for the large population.

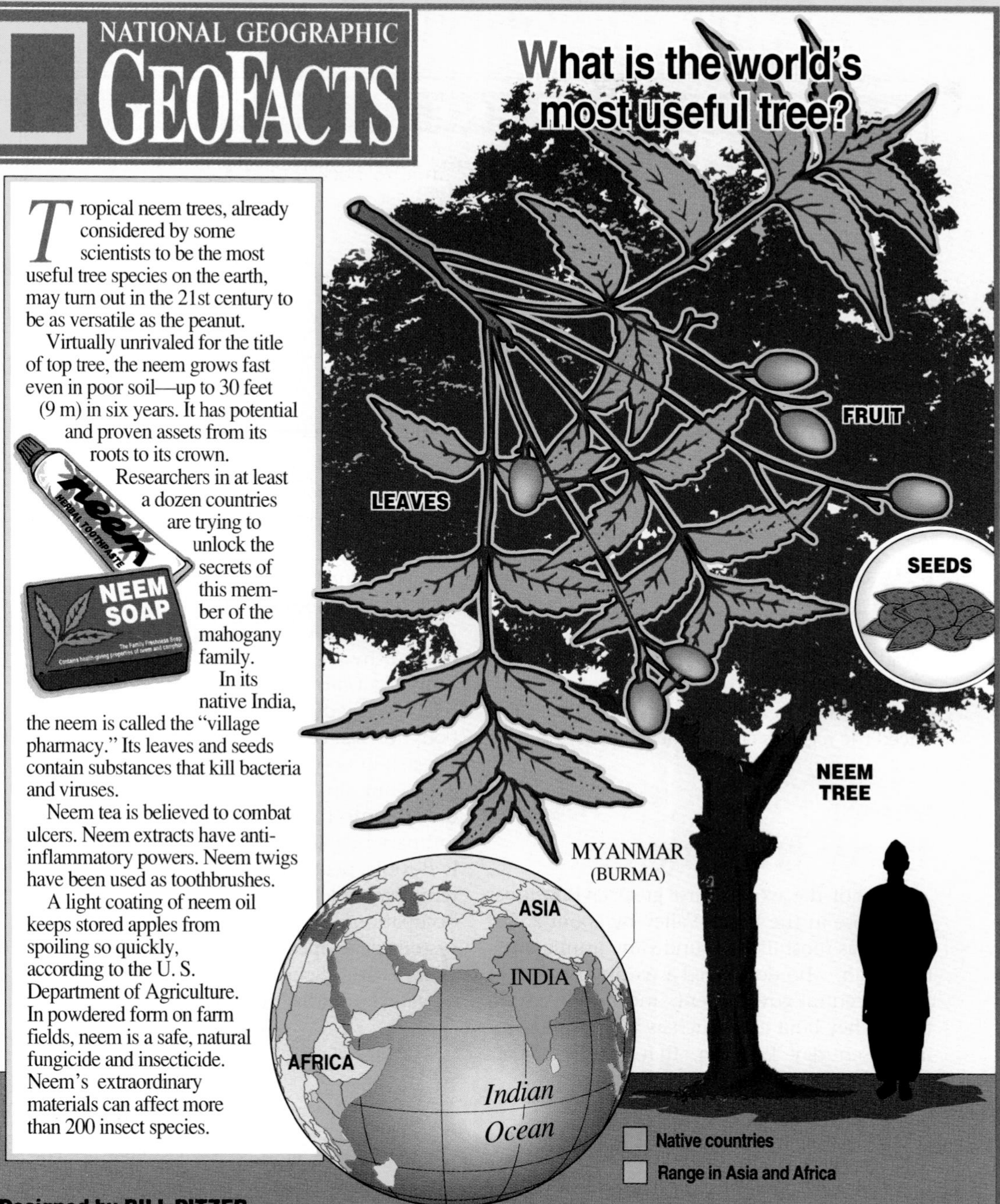

Tropical neem trees, already considered by some scientists to be the most useful tree species on the earth, may turn out in the 21st century to be as versatile as the peanut.

Virtually unrivaled for the title of top tree, the neem grows fast even in poor soil—up to 30 feet (9 m) in six years. It has potential and proven assets from its roots to its crown.

Researchers in at least a dozen countries are trying to unlock the secrets of this member of the mahogany family.

In its native India, the neem is called the "village pharmacy." Its leaves and seeds contain substances that kill bacteria and viruses.

Neem tea is believed to combat ulcers. Neem extracts have anti-inflammatory powers. Neem twigs have been used as toothbrushes.

A light coating of neem oil keeps stored apples from spoiling so quickly, according to the U. S. Department of Agriculture. In powdered form on farm fields, neem is a safe, natural fungicide and insecticide. Neem's extraordinary materials can affect more than 200 insect species.

NATIONAL GEOGRAPHIC GEOFACTS

TEACH

Have students list the uses of the neem tree as outlined in the feature on page 495. Interested students may write to the United States Department of Agriculture to learn more about the medicinal and agricultural advantages of the neem tree. Ask students if they can think of other products that are similarly used in multiple ways (e.g., spearmint, the peanut, lemon juice, and so on).

FOCUS

SECTION OBJECTIVES

1. **Discuss** the early civilizations that developed in South Asia.
2. **Compare** the characteristics of Hinduism and Buddhism.
3. **Identify** the empires established in South Asia.
4. **Explain** how South Asians achieved independence.

BELLRINGER MOTIVATIONAL ACTIVITY

Project the Section 2 Focus Transparency and have students answer the questions.

PRETEACHING VOCABULARY

Have students find the meanings of the Key Terms in context. Then challenge them to illustrate each term. **LEP**

CURRICULUM CONNECTION

SOCIOLOGY
People not belonging to the caste system and considered inferior were known as "untouchables." Since 1950, India's constitution has outlawed untouchability and granted equal status to all people.

SECTION 2

History and Government

SETTING THE SCENE

Read to Discover . . .
- **the early civilizations that developed in South Asia.**
- **the characteristics of Hinduism and Buddhism.**
- **how the British established an empire in the region.**
- **how South Asians achieved independence and established new governments.**

Key Terms
- **caste system**
- **dharma**
- **karma**
- **reincarnated**
- **nirvana**

Identify and Locate
Mohenjo-Daro, Hindu Kush, Gupta Empire, Maurya Empire, Mogul Empire, British India

Over the centuries the fertile Indo-Gangetic Plain of South Asia has attracted many groups of people. The first people to invade, the Aryans, had a lasting influence on all the others. Later invaders, including Muslims and Europeans, also significantly influenced the region's cultural development.

MOVEMENT

Early History

One of the world's first great civilizations arose in the Indus Valley by about 2500 B.C. It was most likely founded by immigrants from Iran, who developed a writing system, a strong central government, and rich overseas trade. They built cities such as Mohenjo-Daro, in present-day Pakistan, that boasted great wealth and sophisticated technology.

Environmental changes may have led to the decline of this great civilization between 1700 B.C. and 1500 B.C. Over time, the Indus River changed its course, flooding some cities. Other cities became stranded, far from the water on which they depended for irrigation and trade networks.

About the time the Indus Valley civilization was collapsing, a new group of people known as the Aryans entered the region from the northwest. Unlike the people who built Mohenjo-Daro, the Aryans left behind few artifacts. They did, however, hand down a great body of sacred literature called the Vedas. These four books tell about Aryan religious beliefs. They also explain how Aryan society was divided into three classes: nobles, priests, and ordinary people. At first these classes were fairly flexible; people of different groups could intermarry and individuals could change their occupations. Eventually, however, a rigid **caste system** developed in which people could not change their social status. The caste system prevailed in India for centuries.

PLACE

Religions

Two of the world's great religions—Hinduism and Buddhism—began in India. To understand Indian history and culture, it is important to understand the origins and the teachings of these religions.

Classroom Resources for Section 2

BLACKLINE MASTERS:
Reproducible Lesson Plan 24-2
Guided Reading Activity 24-2
Spanish Guided Reading Activity 24-2
Workbook Activity 24-2
Section Quiz 24-2

TRANSPARENCIES:
Section Focus Transparency 24-2
World Cultures Transparencies 13, 14

MULTIMEDIA:

Testmaker

Geographic Themes

Human/Environment Interaction: Indus River valley
The Indus River valley civilization centered around planned cities: Mohenjo-Daro (shown above) and Harappa. *What environmental changes led to the decline of the cities?*

Hinduism

Hinduism grew out of Aryan culture and incorporated the caste system first laid out in the Vedas. Hinduism is both a way of life and a set of beliefs.

Hindus believe that every individual must live according to her or his own **dharma** (DUHR•muh), or moral duty. All good actions are rewarded and bad deeds punished according to the law of **karma**. People are **reincarnated**, or reborn, repeatedly until they have overcome all their weaknesses and earthly desires. At that point, they are released from the cycle of rebirth.

Hinduism recognizes many gods and goddesses. Many Hindus see them as different forms of one being. Similarly, Hinduism sees all of the world's religions as different paths toward the same goal.

Buddhism

In approximately 563 B.C., in present-day Nepal, a prince was born—Siddhartha Gautama (sih•DAHR•tuh GAUT•uh•muh). As a man, he had everything he could want. Siddhartha's awareness of human suffering, however, made him unable to enjoy life, so he went on a pilgrimage. After years of spiritual searching and intense meditation, he perceived the true nature of human existence for the first time. In so doing, he became known as the Buddha, or the Awakened One.

Buddha spent the rest of his life trying to teach people that they suffer because they are overly attached to material things, and that to escape the chain of desire and suffering which leads to endless rebirth, one must live by certain rules. These rules include thinking clearly, acting wisely, and behaving kindly toward others.

Unlike Hinduism, Buddhism as preached by Buddha had no religious rituals. Buddha wanted to offer human beings a practical way out of their unhappiness. By following his guidelines, people could enter a state of great insight, calm, and happiness, which is called **nirvana** (nir•VAHN•uh).

TEACH

GUIDED PRACTICE

L2 Time line Help students create a time line of events from the rise of Indus Valley civilizations to the present. Suggest that they use long narrow strips of paper divided into increments representing centuries. They can indicate major events in each century, then connect the strips of paper to illustrate the scope of South Asia's history.

USING ILLUSTRATIONS

HUMAN/ENVIRONMENT INTERACTION The Indus people used baked or sun-dried bricks for building. This brick-lined depression may have been a bathing area.

Answer to Caption: *The course of the Indus River changed.*

INDEPENDENT PRACTICE

Guided Reading Have students complete Guided Reading Activity 24-2 in the TCR. **LEP**

ASSESS

CHECK FOR UNDERSTANDING

Assign Section 2 Review as homework or an in-class activity.

Cooperative Learning Activity

Organize students into seven groups and assign one of the countries of South Asia to each group. Instruct group members to find out what kind of government their assigned country has. They should prepare a chart or other graphic to use in explaining the government to the rest of the class.

USING MAPS

Answers:
1. Gupta Empire;
2. southern and northeastern India

Map Skills Practice

Reading a Map What geographic factors aided the cultural advances of the Gupta Empire? *(Possible answers include Ganges River; fertile soil of the Indo-Gangetic Plain.)*

USING ILLUSTRATIONS

PLACE Most Hindu temples have many shrines, each of which is dedicated to a god or goddess. Every day, Hindu priests wash and dress the sculptured images of these deities and bring them food.

Answer to Caption: *as different paths toward the same goal*

MEETING LESSON OBJECTIVES

Each objective below is tested by the questions that follow it in parentheses.

1. Discuss the early civilizations that developed in South Asia. *(2)*
2. Compare the characteristics of Hinduism and Buddhism. *(5)*
3. Identify the empires established in South Asia. *(3)*
4. Explain how South Asians achieved independence. *(4)*

MOVEMENT

Invasions and Empires

After the Aryans, many other groups of invaders entered South Asia through the Hindu Kush Mountain range in the northwest. The first invaders, the Maurya (MAU•ree•uh), established an empire that lasted from about 320 B.C. to 180 B.C. The last and greatest Mauryan emperor was named Asoka. Although officially a Hindu, he was impressed by Buddha's teachings and helped spread Buddhism.

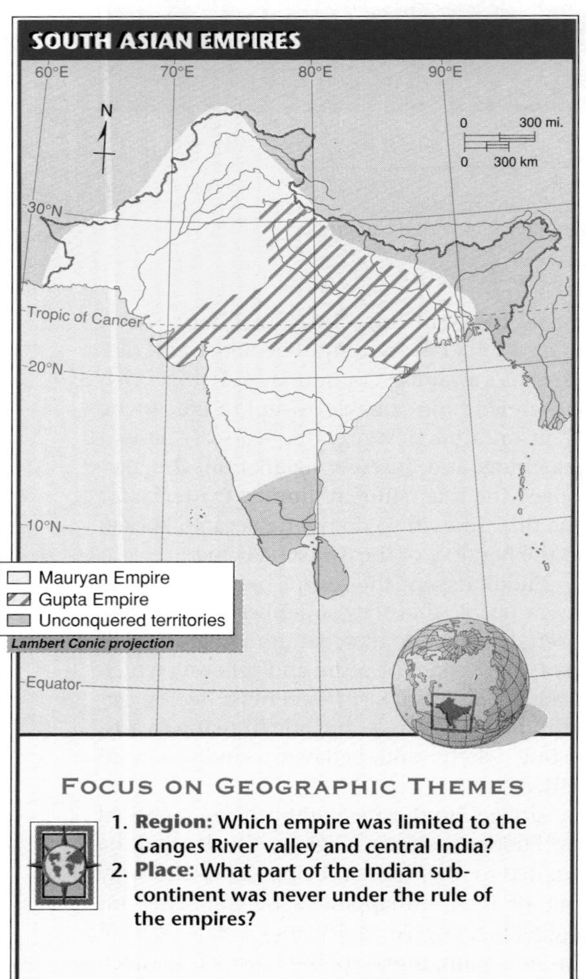

Focus on Geographic Themes

1. **Region:** Which empire was limited to the Ganges River valley and central India?
2. **Place:** What part of the Indian subcontinent was never under the rule of the empires?

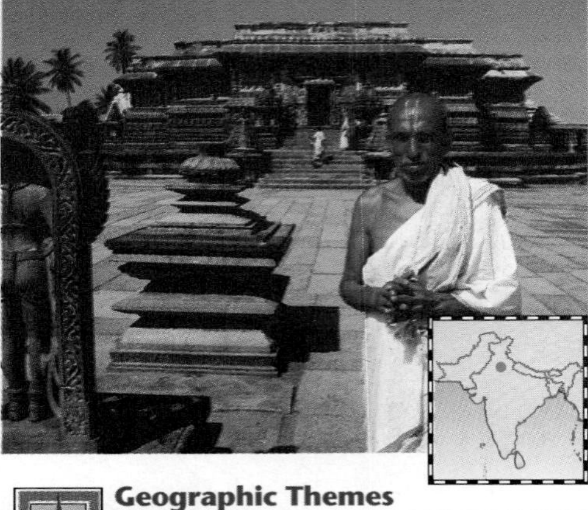

Geographic Themes

Region: South Asia
Even though there are Hindu priests and temples, Hindu worship and meditation are mostly centered in the home. *How does Hinduism regard other religions?*

About 500 years after the Mauryan Empire, the Gupta dynasty created a new empire in northern India. During the Gupta Empire, which lasted from about A.D. 320 to 550, India was one of the most advanced cultures in the world, excelling in the arts, science, and technology. The numerals we use today were most likely developed in India before being introduced to Europe by Arab traders.

Muslim merchants, adventurers, and missionaries first entered India in the 700s. By the 1100s, Muslim armies had conquered northern India. A succession of Muslim conquerors ruled the subcontinent for the next several centuries.

The final invaders were the Europeans who arrived about 1500. The Portuguese arrived first, and they came mainly to trade.

By the early 1600s, England had become the leading European power in South Asia, largely because of the success of its royal trading company, the East India Company. The company was so successful that by the mid-1700s it had occupied almost the entire region. Under the company's rule, changes were introduced, such as the reorganization of education, the introduction of the English language, and the development of a civil service.

Meeting Special Needs

Study Strategy Note-taking helps students consolidate and summarize information. Notes must be complete enough so that the information is clear when read. Have students read "Invasions and Empires" and take notes in their usual way. Then pair students and have them teach the information to each other based only on their notes. Ask students to evaluate the effectiveness of their notes.

PLACE

Modern South Asia

Today the countries of South Asia are independent of European control. Independence did not come easily, however.

Independence

Many people of South Asia wanted freedom from the United Kingdom. One leader of this group was a British-trained lawyer named Mohandas K. Gandhi. Gandhi believed that Indians should rely on nonviolent methods to persuade the British to leave India. Under his guidance, many Indians refused to buy British-made goods. Known as *Mahatma,* or "Great Soul," Gandhi was often imprisoned and went on a hunger strike.

By the end of World War II, the British were tired of fighting faraway conflicts and agreed to grant independence. In 1947 British India was divided into 2 independent states. Areas with a Muslim majority became part of the Muslim nation of Pakistan, while areas with a majority of Hindus became part of the nation of India. Under this plan, Pakistan consisted of 2 sections—East Pakistan and West Pakistan—separated by about 1,000 miles (1,609 km) of Indian territory.

The departure of the British brought other changes. One year after the division of British India, British-ruled Ceylon was granted independence. In 1972 the nation changed its name to Sri Lanka. In the northern part of the subcontinent, Bhutan and Nepal had always remained independent of the British.

Today's Governments

After independence, tensions arose between Muslims and Hindus. Muslims living in mostly Hindu India fled to Pakistan, while many Hindus in Pakistan migrated to India. Rioting broke out, and tens of thousands were killed. Problems also developed between the people of East and West Pakistan. In 1971, East Pakistan revolted and declared itself the independent nation of Bangladesh.

The current governments of South Asia include democracies and monarchies. India is a federal parliamentary republic. Sri Lanka and Bangladesh also have parliamentary systems. Pakistan today has a president who is elected indirectly by members of the legislature. Bhutan and Nepal are monarchies.

Geographic Themes
Region: India
Mohandas K. Gandhi led India toward independence from British rule. *What was Gandhi's background?*

SECTION 2 REVIEW

Checking for Understanding

1. **Define** caste system, dharma, karma, reincarnated, nirvana.
2. **Locating Places** In what part of South Asia were the first great cities built?
3. **Place** What was a major feature of each empire established in South Asia?
4. **Movement** What action did Mohandas K. Gandhi recommend in the struggle for independence?

Critical Thinking

5. **Making Comparisons** Compare and contrast Buddhism and Hinduism.

EVALUATE

Assign the Section 2 Quiz in the TCR.

Use the Testmaker to create a customized quiz for Section 2.

RETEACH

Have students write one paragraph about each illustration and the map in this section to review the main ideas.

USING ILLUSTRATIONS

PLACE Gandhi began a program of hand spinning and weaving to make India self-sufficient in cloth and to challenge the British textile industry.

Answer to Caption: He was a British-trained lawyer.

ENRICH

Have students find out more about the life and work of Mohandas Gandhi. Provide time for a class discussion.

CLOSE

Have each student complete the following statement: The most significant influence in South Asia's history has been . . . . Call on volunteers to share their answers.

ANSWERS TO SECTION 2 REVIEW

1. **caste system:** social system in India that divided people into four main groups; **dharma:** Hindu moral duty; **karma:** law which rewards good deeds and punishes bad deeds; **reincarnated:** reborn; **nirvana:** state of great happiness
2. Indus River valley
3. Maurya—spread Buddhism; Gupta—advancements in arts, science, technology; Muslims—ruled from 1100s to 1500s; British—organized education
4. nonviolent methods such as boycotts and hunger strikes
5. Both teach that people are reincarnated until they overcome their weaknesses. Buddhism has no religious rituals.

Geography and History

TEACH

Have students locate Nepal and Bhutan on the map on page 470. Ask students to speculate on geographic reasons for the countries' isolation. List answers on the chalkboard; return to check and discuss after students have read the selection.

Place How does the photograph support the fact of the geographic isolation of Nepal and Bhutan? *(few buildings, no people, buildings are not modern; countryside pictured appears to be unsettled and uncultivated; Himalayas tower in the background, almost like a wall)*

Extending the Content

Modernization As both countries have moved toward modernization, Bhutan has elected to do so at a slower pace than Nepal. The country is still considerably protected by the mountains, has few roads, and no modern highways.

Nepal has been forced to change much faster. Many Nepalis took part in India's struggle for independence and national self-rule. They introduced these ideals on returning to their homeland.

Geography and History

NEPAL AND BHUTAN: ISOLATED BY GEOGRAPHY

As you read, examine how Nepal and Bhutan were affected by their geography.

The Himalayas cover much of Nepal and Bhutan. The mountains have long, harsh winters and short, cool summers. Steep river valleys cut through the icy glaciers and snow. Buddhist monasteries and Hindu temples often are perched on hillsides overlooking the valleys.

Location

Cradled between the huge countries of India and China, and hidden among the imposing crags of the Himalayas, Nepal and Bhutan remained mysteries to much of the world for many centuries. Indeed, chroniclers in China refer to Bhutan as the "hidden holy land." Its present-day name came from British explorers who arrived in the mid-1770s.

Mountain Lands

Of the two countries, Bhutan is the more geographically isolated. Eight successive ranges of the Himalayas cut north to south across the tiny country, slicing it into a series of parallel valleys. The river systems that irrigate and drain the valleys provide additional obstacles that explorers or would-be invaders had to overcome.

Not until the early 1960s were roads completed across the country as well as farther south into India. Before that time, the few people who visited the country had the choice of the two methods of travel the Bhutanese themselves used: foot or horse. Most Bhutanese still travel by those two methods, while Bhutanese officials now use helicopters extensively.

Himalayan ranges cover the northern two-thirds of Nepal, forming the largest of the country's three parallel regions that run east and west. The remaining southern third of Nepal is divided into a strip of hills and river basins and a section that is part of India's Gangetic Plain. Steamy, tangled rain forest met intruders from the south; the freezing, hostile Himalayas met any challenge coming from the north.

Widening Contacts

During the late 1700s and early 1800s, the British increased their influence in both countries while strengthening their hold on India. Although the United Kingdom assumed control of the countries' foreign affairs and defense, it did not interfere with either nation's internal politics. Until the late 1950s, Bhutan and Nepal continued their isolation from world affairs. Since then, both nations have lessened their ties to the United Kingdom and have moved toward greater modernization.

Checking for Understanding

1. What geographical factors isolated Bhutan and Nepal?
2. **Movement** What changes have come to Nepal and Bhutan during this century?

ANSWERS TO CHECKING FOR UNDERSTANDING

1. In Bhutan, isolation was achieved by eight ranges of the Himalayas, as well as the river systems. In Nepal, a combination of the Himalayas in the north and jungle in the south effectively kept the world out.

2. Both countries rely less on the United Kingdom and have moved toward greater modernization, especially in transportation.

3 SECTION Cultures and Lifestyles

SETTING THE SCENE

Read to Discover . . .
- the languages and religions of South Asia.
- the contrasts between rural and urban lifestyles in South Asia.
- the arts and celebrations of South Asia.

Key Terms
- mantra
- sadhu
- raga
- tala

Identify and Locate
Taj Mahal, Golden Temple

South Asia's ethnic diversity and its long and complicated history have produced a rich culture. Although the region's standard of living tends to be low when measured in terms of material wealth or life expectancy, South Asians are surrounded by beautiful art and architecture, have access to a lively film industry, and celebrate hundreds of festivals each year.

PLACE

Languages

South Asia has a diversity of languages. India alone has 14 major languages and hundreds of regional dialects. Although English is commonly spoken in government and business, Hindi is the official language of India.

Indo-Aryan Languages

Most of the languages spoken in Pakistan, Bangladesh, and northern India fall into the Indo-Aryan family of languages. These include Hindi, Urdu, and Bengali. About half of the Indian people, especially in the north and central areas, speak Hindi as a first or second language. Urdu is the official language of Pakistan, and Bengali is the official language of Bangladesh. Hindustani, a language spoken in northern India, is a mixture of Hindi and Urdu. Nepali and Sinhalese, the official languages of Nepal and Sri Lanka, are Indo-Aryan languages as well.

Other Languages

About one-fifth of the people in southern India and Sri Lanka speak languages of the Dravidian family. The Dravidian languages include Tamil, Telegu, Kannada, and Malayalam. In northern South Asia, the languages spoken in Bhutan and Nepal reflect these countries' close ethnic and historic ties with central Asia.

PLACE

Religions

The major religions of South Asia are Hinduism, Islam, and Buddhism. Most of the people in India and Nepal practice Hinduism. There are also Hindus in Bhutan, Sri Lanka, Pakistan, and Bangladesh.

The majority of people in Pakistan and Bangladesh are Muslim. In India, Muslims are the largest single minority, exceeding 100 million.

Although Buddhism had its beginnings in South Asia, its overall influence has declined in the region. This has been primarily because of the flexibility of Hinduism, which has absorbed many of the teachings of Buddhism.

LESSON PLAN
Chapter 24, Section 3

FOCUS

SECTION OBJECTIVES

1. List the languages and religions of South Asia.
2. Contrast rural and urban lifestyles in South Asia.
3. Discuss the arts and celebrations of South Asia.

BELLRINGER MOTIVATIONAL ACTIVITY

Project the Section 3 Focus Transparency and have students answer the questions.

PRETEACHING VOCABULARY

Have students find the meanings of the Key Terms in context. Then have them classify the terms by asking which terms refer to religion? *(mantra, sadhu)*. Which terms refer to music? *(raga, tala)* **LEP**

DID YOU KNOW?

Nepal is the only official Hindu state in the world. About 88 percent of the population is Hindu.

Classroom Resources for Section 3

BLACKLINE MASTERS:
Reproducible Lesson Plan 24-3
Guided Reading Activity 24-3
Skill Activity 24
Enrichment Activity 24
Foods Around the World 7
Section Quiz 24-3

TRANSPARENCIES:
Section Focus Transparency 24-3

MULTIMEDIA:

Testmaker

World Music: Cultural Traditions, *Lesson 7*

Picture Atlas of the World

TEACH

GUIDED PRACTICE

L2 Compare Have students create a chart contrasting urban and rural lifestyles in South Asia. Based on the chart, have them identify the major problems South Asians face today.

Implement Foods Around the World 7 as a class activity.

USING MAPS

Answers: **1.** Indo-European; **2.** Nepal, Bhutan, Bangladesh, northeastern India; **3.** Dravidian

Map Skills Practice

Drawing Conclusions What does the variety of languages in South Asia indicate about the region's history? *(Many different groups of people settled in South Asia.)*

USING GRAPHS

Skills Practice

Interpreting a Graph How does the number of Hindus compare with that of followers of other religions in South Asia? *(There are more than twice as many Hindus as followers of all other religions combined.)*

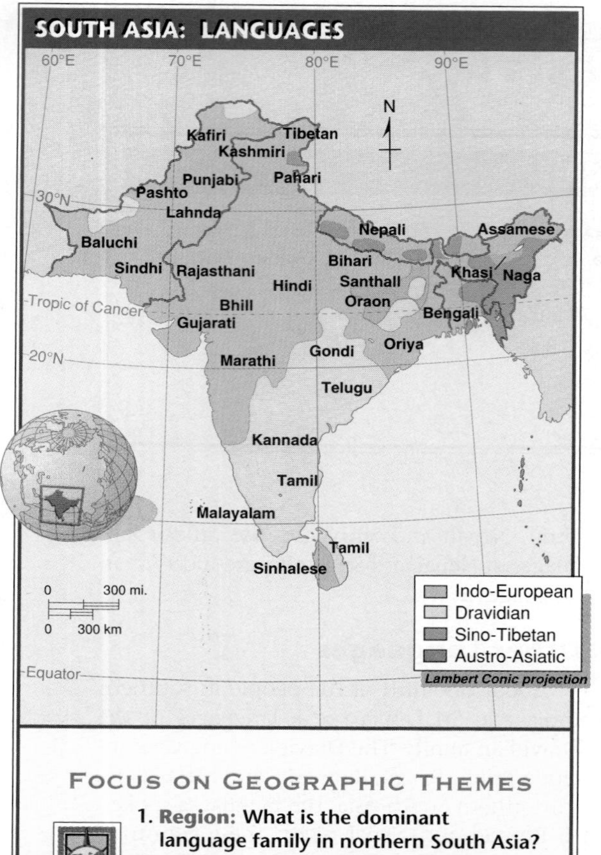

Focus on Geographic Themes

1. **Region:** What is the dominant language family in northern South Asia?
2. **Location:** Where are Sino-Tibetan languages spoken?
3. **Place:** To which language family does Tamil belong?

Buddhism, however, remains quite strong in Sri Lanka, Bhutan, and Nepal.

Two other religions of South Asia are Sikhism and Jainism. Jainism was founded in the 500s B.C. by a young Hindu teacher named Mahavira. Its chief characteristic is a belief in extreme nonviolence. Jains believe that every living thing has a soul, and that to kill even an insect is evil. Today, Jainism has over 3 million followers in India.

Sikhism was founded in the early 1500s by a teacher named Nanak. Nanak was interested in combining Hinduism and Islam into one united creed. Sikhs are monotheistic, like Muslims, and accept Hindu ideas on karma and reincarnation. Most of the 18 million Sikhs live in the northwestern part of India.

Another religion in South Asia is Christianity with about 28 million followers. Most Christians live in the south of India.

Influence of Religion

Religion has a powerful influence on daily life in South Asia. In Bhutan, prayer flags flap in the wind, sending out sacred messages called **mantras**. In India, Hindu teachers known as **sadhus** can be seen everywhere. Usually dressed in yellow robes, they carry just a bowl and a blanket and live on gifts from those who want to improve their karma. In India, where Hindus consider cattle sacred, thousands of cows roam the streets. In Pakistan women dress modestly as Islamic law requires.

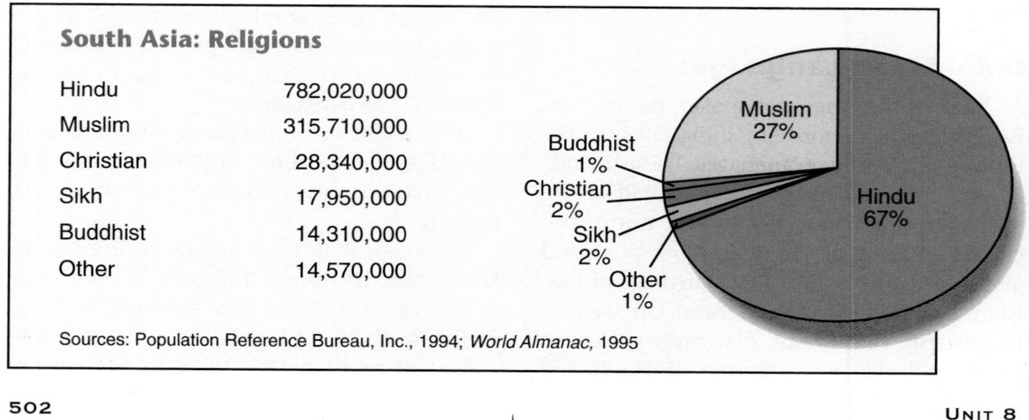

South Asia: Religions

Religion	Followers
Hindu	782,020,000
Muslim	315,710,000
Christian	28,340,000
Sikh	17,950,000
Buddhist	14,310,000
Other	14,570,000

Sources: Population Reference Bureau, Inc., 1994; *World Almanac*, 1995

Cooperative Learning Activity

Organize students into three groups and assign one of the following religions to each group: Hinduism, Buddhism, Islam. Have group members research their assigned religion and summarize the following facts about it: when and where it started, who founded it, what its major beliefs and rituals are, where in South Asia it is practiced today. Provide time for students to share information. Then discuss how each religion influences life in South Asia.

PLACE

The Arts

Like religion, the arts are an important aspect of life in South Asia. Even the humblest workers perform their tasks in an artistic way. For example, a spice or cosmetic stall in any Indian bazaar is a palette of dazzling colors piled in perfect pyramids by merchant vendors.

Architecture

One of the world's most famous buildings, the Taj Mahal, is in India. A Muslim emperor built it in the 1600s as a tomb for his beloved wife. The structure is made of white marble and has towers and domes in the Islamic style. Delicate screens, which allow air to circulate, are carved in the Hindu style.

Other outstanding architectural works include mosques in Pakistan and Bangladesh and the Golden Temple of the Sikhs in Amritsar (UHM•RIT•suhr), India. In Bhutan there are old fortified monasteries called dzong (dzawng) that developed as centers for Buddhist learning and art.

Music and Dance

Classical Indian dances are based on themes from Hindu mythology. There are numerous dance styles, each from a different region.

The style known as Bharata Natyam (bah•RAH•tah naht•yahm) is mainly danced in the south. The dancers are usually women, gorgeously dressed in bright silk saris and gold bracelets. The dances are long and elaborate, with complex hand gestures, rapid whirling, and stamping feet.

In the Kathakali (kah•thah•KAHL•lee) dances from India's west coast, the dancers wear huge, colorful masks and move violently. Very different is Manipuri, a gentle, swaying dance style from northeastern India.

Indian classical music is divided into two basic types: Hindustani—practiced in the North—and Karnatak—practiced in the South. The melody is called the **raga**, and the rhythm is called the **tala**. There is no harmony in Indian music, and improvisation plays an important role.

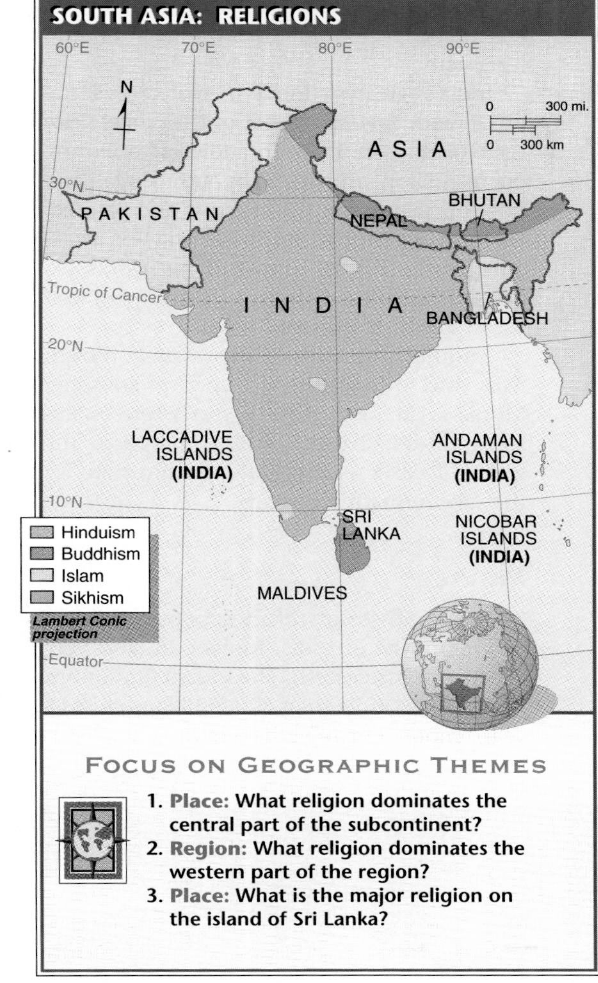

FOCUS ON GEOGRAPHIC THEMES

1. **Place: What religion dominates the central part of the subcontinent?**
2. **Region: What religion dominates the western part of the region?**
3. **Place: What is the major religion on the island of Sri Lanka?**

Literature

Two of India's most famous works of literature are the *Mahabharata* (muh•HAH•BHA•ruh•tuh) and the *Ramayana* (rah•MAH•yah•nuh). These two great epic poems were composed between about 1500 B.C. and 500 B.C. and are still frequently read aloud or used as the basis of dramas today.

The Mahabharata includes a shorter work known as the *Bhagavad Gita* (BAH•guh•vahd GEE•tuh), meaning "the lord's song." This

INDEPENDENT PRACTICE

Guided Reading Have students complete Guided Reading Activity 24-3 in the TCR. **LEP**

USING MAPS

Answers:
1. Hinduism;
2. Islam;
3. Buddhism

Map Skills Practice

Reading a Map Where do most of the followers of Sikhism live? *(northwestern India)*

L2 Architecture Have students photocopy or draw pictures of religious buildings in South Asia. Display the pictures and discuss differences in styles among Hindu, Buddhist, and Muslim buildings.

L3 Literature Have students read stories from the *Panchatantra,* a collection of Indian animal fables. Students should share the stories through dramatization, pantomime, or illustrations.

CD-ROM

PICTURE ATLAS OF THE WORLD

You and your students can hear the music of a sitar by clicking India's "Music" button.

Meeting Special Needs

Physical Disability Students who have difficulty with fine motor skills often are slow and inefficient writers. Teach these students to use an abridged note-taking system of writing only single words and associated facts. Practice this technique by having students read "The Arts" and write one-word notes for each main idea.

Have students complete World Music: Cultural Traditions, Lesson 7 activity in the TCR.

USING ILLUSTRATIONS

LOCATION The Taj Mahal stands at Agra in northern India, south of Delhi.

Answer to Caption: *as a tomb for the wife of a Muslim emperor*

ASSESS

CHECK FOR UNDERSTANDING

Assign Section 3 Review as homework or an in-class activity.

MEETING LESSON OBJECTIVES

Each objective below is tested by the questions that follow it in parentheses.

1. **List** the languages and religions of South Asia. *(2, 4)*
2. **Contrast** rural and urban lifestyles in South Asia. *(3, 4, 5)*
3. **Discuss** the arts and celebrations of South Asia. *(1)*

EVALUATE

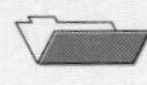

Assign the Section 3 Quiz in the TCR.

Use the Testmaker to create a customized quiz for Section 3.

RETEACH

Have students complete Reteaching Activity 24 in the TCR.

story takes place before a great battle and teaches people to fulfill their duties and not to fear death.

India's greatest modern writer was Rabindranath Tagore, winner of the Nobel Prize for Literature in 1913. In addition to writing poetry, fiction, and drama in both Bengali and English, Tagore composed music and painted. He lived at a time when South Asia was awakening from British rule, and his works expressed the cultural and patriotic ferment that was sweeping the region.

Another important modern writer of South Asia was Muslim poet and philosopher Muhammad Iqbal. Iqbal, who wrote extensively during the early 1900s, proposed the idea of Pakistan—a separate Muslim state for the subcontinent's Muslims.

Movies

Today movies are the most popular form of entertainment in India. Movies are also very popular in Bangladesh. The Indian film industry produces more than 800 full-length films a year—more than any other country.

Geographic Themes

Place: Taj Mahal

The white marbled Taj Mahal is considered one of the most beautiful buildings in the world. *Why was the Taj Mahal built?*

PLACE

Lifestyles

Lifestyles in South Asia, like those in many developing nations, are a complicated mixture of the traditional and the modern.

Urban and Rural Contrasts

The standard of living in the rural areas of South Asia is often low. The majority of the people are peasant farmers who must struggle to raise enough food to feed their families. Large extended families live in small villages and work on small farms nearby.

Prosperous people in the cities live very different lives. These people include business leaders, industrialists, political leaders, and large landowners. They live in high-rise apartments or small houses, drive cars, and enjoy the many cultural offerings.

Many of the cities' residents, however, have little chance to appreciate these luxuries. Millions live in the streets, spreading out their beds on the sidewalks each night. Others build flimsy shelters of bamboo.

Health

Because much of South Asia has a semitropical or tropical climate, such diseases as malaria and smallpox are widespread. Governments have made some progress against these diseases. Sri Lanka was one of the first developing nations to eliminate malaria, a disease spread by mosquitoes. Nepal has also eradicated the disease through insect spraying programs.

In Bhutan, life expectancy is the shortest in the region—only 46 years. Only Sri Lanka with its life expectancy of 70 years approaches the rates of developed countries such as Japan or the United States, where life expectancy exceeds 75 years.

The availability of clean water is a problem in much of South Asia. Therefore, water-borne diseases such as cholera and dysentery are still common. In Nepal, almost one-third of the babies die from dysentery before they reach their first birthday. Infant mortality is also very high in Bangladesh.

Critical Thinking

Determining Cause and Effect Have students create diagrams or flow charts to illustrate causes and effects of social problems in South Asia. Problems include poverty, disease, poor nutrition, and illiteracy. Display the diagrams and charts. Then have students propose solutions to the problems.

Food Needs

Another reason for the health problems that face South Asia is poor nutrition. It has been estimated that almost one-third of the people of this region do not get enough protein to eat. The reason is simple: they are too poor to afford a variety of foods.

Governments are doing what they can to improve food production and people's diets. In Nepal, government-sponsored reforms have taken farmland away from large landowners and put it in the hands of those who actually work it. The result has been increased production. Beginning in the 1960s, the Indian government began a many-sided campaign to increase the country's food supply. So far the campaign has been very successful.

Education

Improving education is essential to improving South Asia's standard of living. In most areas of South Asia, about one-third of the people over the age of 15 can read and write. In Sri Lanka, the literacy rate is very high—more than 86 percent. The government of India is committed to expanding educational opportunities. Today's literacy rate is twice what it was when the country first became an independent nation. Advances in education are also weakening the caste system, especially in the cities. Laws have also been passed giving the lowest social class—the untouchables—the same rights as other people.

Celebrations

An example of South Asia's rich and varied cultures are the region's many celebrations. Hindu festivals, such as Diwali, the festival of lights, are joyous, colorful occasions marked by ancient symbols and community togetherness. Muslims celebrate a great day of festivity at the end of Ramadan, the month during which they abstain from food and drink from dawn to dusk. The day is marked by visiting and feasting with friends, relatives, and neighbors. Buddhists widely celebrate the birth of Buddha, and Christians celebrate the traditional holidays of the Christian calendar.

Geographic Themes

Region: South Asia

The countries of South Asia are committed to improving education and raising their standards of living. *About how many people in South Asia over the age of 15 can read and write?*

SECTION 3 REVIEW

Checking for Understanding

1. **Define** mantra, sadhu, raga, tala.
2. **Locating Places** In what part of India are the Dravidian languages spoken?
3. **Place** What has been the greatest improvement in medical care in South Asia?
4. **Region** How does religion affect lifestyles in South Asia?

Critical Thinking

5. **Expressing Problems Clearly** How does unclean water affect the health of South Asians?

USING ILLUSTRATIONS

PLACE Punjab University in Chandigarh is one of more than 3,000 universities and colleges in India.

Answer to Caption: *about one third*

ENRICH

Have students complete Enrichment Activity 24 in the TCR.

CLOSE

Have students write a paragraph describing how South Asia's languages, religions, arts, and celebrations reflect its ethnic diversity.

CD-ROM

PICTURE ATLAS OF THE WORLD

View the Hindu and Buddhist religious art in Kathmandu by clicking Nepal's "Video" button.

ANSWERS TO SECTION 3 REVIEW

1. **mantra:** sacred message; **sadhu:** Hindu teacher; **raga:** melody in classical Indian music; **tala:** rhythm in Indian music
2. southern
3. elimination of malaria
4. Religion affects what people eat, what they wear, and their celebrations.
5. Unclean water spreads diseases such as cholera and dysentery that contribute to the high infant mortality rate.

Teaching Skills

TEACH

Say: "Suppose you join a swim team. Each week the coach tests the number of lengths you can swim in 30 minutes. Here are your scores for ten weeks." Write these scores on the chalkboard: 30, 32, 34, 32, 35, 38, 36, 36, 39, 40. Have students convert this data into a line graph; plot the weeks on the x-axis, and plot the swim scores on the y-axis. Then ask: "How does this graph illustrate your progress in swimming?" *(There were some dips and plateaus, but it shows gradual improvement over ten weeks.)*

Skills Practice For additional practice, have students complete Skill Activity 24 in the TCR.

MAP & GRAPH SKILLS

Reading a Line Graph

A line graph is an excellent tool for recording changes in data over time. On a line graph, time intervals (hours, weeks, years, etc.) are recorded on the horizontal axis, or **x-axis.** The vertical axis, or **y-axis,** shows numbers or units of measurement. These two axes form a grid.

REVIEWING THE SKILL

In plotting a line graph, for each time interval you must place a dot along the vertical axis showing what quantity occurred at that time. Then draw a line connecting the dots to show whether the numbers go up or down.

To read a line graph, apply the following steps:

- Read the graph title to determine its subject.
- Study the information on the x- and y-axes to identify the units of measurement and the time period.
- Look at the placement of dots on the grid.
- Study the movement of the line(s) on the graph to draw conclusions about trends over time.

PRACTICING THE SKILL

Use the graphs below to answer the following questions:

1. What is the topic of the graphs?
2. What time period is measured on these graphs?
3. What do the numbers on the y-axis represent?
4. What was the approximate population of each country in 1992?
5. Are the figures shown for the year 2000 actual or estimated? Explain your answer.

For additional practice in this skill, see Practicing Skills on page 508 of the Chapter 24 Review.

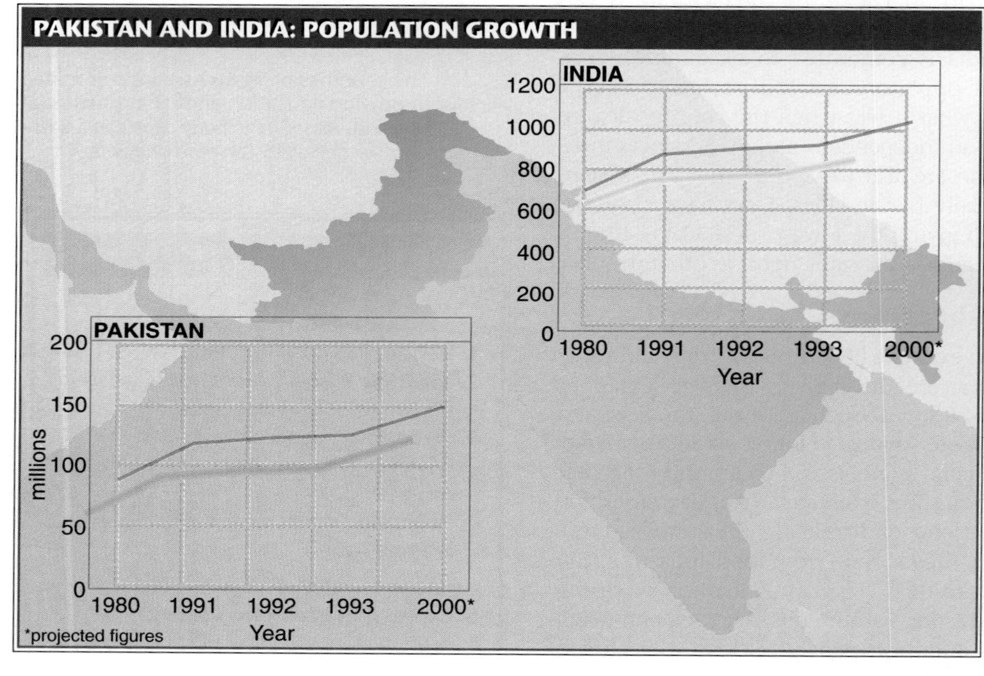

ANSWERS TO PRACTICING THE SKILL

1. population growth in India and Pakistan
2. 1980–2000, twenty years
3. millions of people
4. Pakistan—about 120,000,000; India—almost 900,000,000
5. They are estimated figures based on the continuation of current population trends.

chapter 24 HIGHLIGHTS

Section	Key Terms	Summary
1 Population Patterns  Victoria Railway Station, Bombay, India	**jati** (p. 491)	• South Asia is an ethnically diverse area. • Population density is greatest on the Indo-Gangetic Plain. • Although most South Asians live in rural areas, an increasing number are migrating to the cities in search of work.
2 History and Government  Hindu temple and priest	**caste system** (p. 496) **dharma** (p. 497) **karma** (p. 497) **reincarnated** (p. 497) **nirvana** (p. 497)	• The Indus Valley was home to one of the world's first great civilizations. • Many peoples have conquered South Asia, from the Aryans to the British. • Two of the world's great religions—Hinduism and Buddhism—originated in South Asia. • After World War II, the region achieved independence from the British Empire. • Today most of the people of South Asia elect their leaders.
3 Cultures and Lifestyles	**mantra** (p. 502) **sadhu** (p. 502) **raga** (p. 503) **tala** (p. 503)  Modern university class in India	• South Asians speak many different languages. India alone has 14 major languages and hundreds of dialects. • The main religions of South Asia are Hinduism, Islam, and Buddhism. People also practice Christianity, Jainism, and Sikhism. • In most of South Asia the standard of living is low and life expectancy is short. There have been improvements, however, in health care and education in recent years.

CHAPTER 24 HIGHLIGHTS

USING THE CHAPTER 24 HIGHLIGHTS

Use the Chapter 24 Highlights to preview, review, condense, or reteach the chapter.

PREVIEW/REVIEW

Vocabulary PuzzleMaker Software reinforces the Key Terms used in Chapter 24.

Student Self-Test and Review Software allows students to review Chapter 24 content.

CONDENSE

Have students read the Chapter 24 Highlights.

Have students listen to the Chapter 24 Audiocassettes in the TCR. Spanish Audiocassettes are also available.

Assign the Chapter 24 Audiocassette Activity and give students the Chapter 24 Audiocassette Quiz.

Have students complete Guided Reading Activities for Chapter 24 in the TCR. Spanish Guided Reading Activities are also available.

RETEACH

Have students complete Reteaching Activity 24 in the TCR. Spanish Reteaching Activities are also available.

Map Activity

Identify and Locate Provide each student with a copy of the map from page 34 of the Outline Map Resource Book. Instruct students to indicate densely populated areas. Students should also label the following cities: Calcutta, Bombay (Mumbai), Delhi, Dhaka, and Islamabad. Discuss how geography influences population distribution.

GLENCOE TECHNOLOGY

Videodisc

Use Chapter 24 MindJogger Videoquiz to review students' knowledge before administering the Chapter 24 Test.

MINDJOGGER VIDEOQUIZ

Chapter 24
Disc 3 Side B

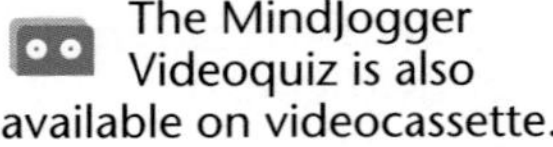

The MindJogger Videoquiz is also available on videocassette.

ANSWERS

Reviewing Key Terms

1. jati
2. dharma
3. caste system
4. raga
5. sadhu

Reviewing Facts

6. 22 percent
7. Dhaka
8. Aryans
9. endless rebirth
10. Islam
11. They are too poor to afford a variety of foods.

chapter 24 REVIEW

Reviewing Key Terms

Choose the vocabulary term that best completes each of the sentences below. Write your answers on a separate sheet of paper.

jati (p. 491)
caste system (p. 496)
dharma (p. 497)
sadhu (p. 502)
raga (p. 503)

SECTION 1

1. The term for a Hindu social division is ____.

SECTION 2

2. Hindus believe that each person must follow his or her moral duty, or ____.
3. India's ancient ____ consisted of four major groups.

SECTION 3

4. ____ is the melody of Indian classical music.
5. ____ are Hindu teachers.

Reviewing Facts

SECTION 1

6. South Asia is home to what percentage of the world's population?
7. Which capital is the second most densely populated city in the world?

SECTION 2

8. Which people passed on the body of literature known as the Vedas?
9. According to Buddha, what is the result of desiring things?

SECTION 3

10. What religion is followed by most of the people of Pakistan and Bangladesh?
11. Why do so many South Asians fail to eat enough protein?

Critical Thinking

12. **Cause and Effect** Why do few people live at high elevations in Nepal and Bhutan?
13. **Drawing Conclusions** What do the objects discovered at Mohenjo-Daro suggest about the people who created them?
14. **Expressing Problems Clearly** Why have the governments of South Asia been unable to improve urban living conditions?

Geographic Themes

15. **Region** How does the region's overall population density compare with the world average?
16. **Movement** From what direction did most invaders enter South Asia?
17. **Place** What is the *Baghavad Gita's* theme?

Practicing Skills

Reading a Line Graph

Refer to the line graph on page 506.

18. By how much did Pakistan's population grow from 1980 to 1991?
19. By how much is each country's population expected to increase in the 20-year period shown in the graphs?

Using the Unit Atlas

Refer to the cultural geography section of the Unit Atlas on pages 470–471.

20. From what country did Bangladesh win its independence? When?
21. What major social problem is India facing?

Critical Thinking

12. The regions are cold and cannot support a large population.
13. Answers may vary but should be based on the following understandings: engineering skill, concern for cleanliness and order.
14. because of the rapid growth of population

Geographic Themes

15. Population density in South Asia is about 7 times the world average.
16. from the northwest
17. It teaches people to fulfill their duties and not to fear death.

Projects

Individual Activity

You have learned about Hinduism, Buddhism, and Islam. Choose one of the religions and research one aspect of it in depth. You might examine its teachings on the deity, its rules for daily life, or its views on what happens after death. Write a report on what you learn.

Cooperative Learning Activity

Working in a small group, go to the library or media center. Have each person in the group research one topic related to South Asia, such as festivals, health, education, or ethnic diversity. Use the *Readers' Guide to Periodical Literature* to locate recent magazine articles on these subjects. Report on your findings to the rest of the class.

Writing About Geography

Description

Locate a book, magazine article, or encyclopedia entry about Mohenjo-Daro. Read the descriptions and study the pictures. Then describe Mohenjo-Daro as it would have looked to someone living there thousands of years ago. Using your journal record, compare the products of modern South Asia with those produced in the region's earliest civilization. What geographic factors account for any similarities or differences?

Locating Places

SOUTH ASIA: PHYSICAL GEOGRAPHY

Match the letters on the map with the places of South Asia. Write your answers on a separate sheet of paper.

1. Thar Desert
2. Sri Lanka
3. New Delhi
4. Calcutta
5. Nepal
6. Indus River
7. Hindu Kush
8. Bombay
9. Dhaka
10. Bhutan

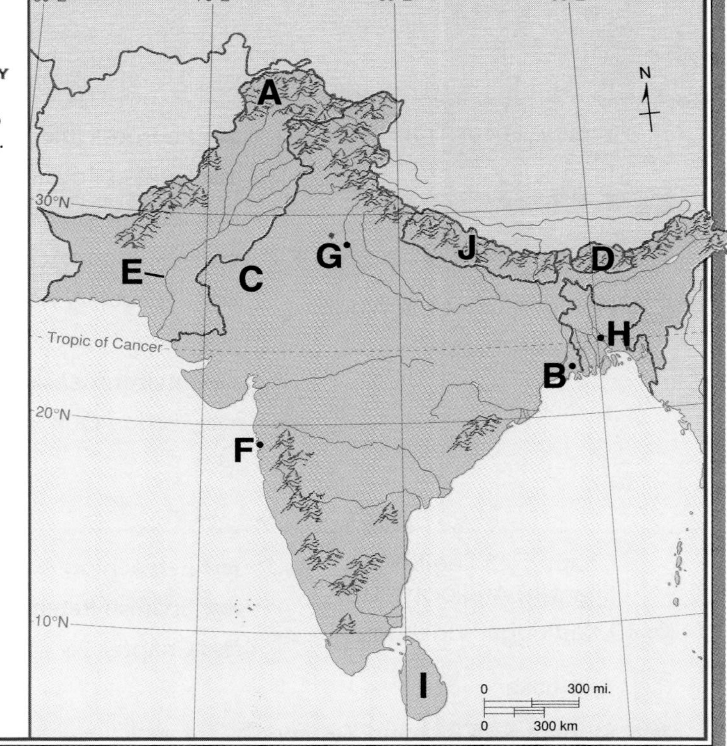

Chapter 24 Review

Practicing Skills

18. by about 30 million
19. India's will grow by about 300 million; Pakistan's will grow by about 70 million.

Using the Unit Atlas

20. Pakistan, 1971
21. overpopulation

Locating Places

1. C
2. I
3. G
4. B
5. J
6. E
7. A
8. F
9. H
10. D

Chapter Bonus Test Question

This question may be used for extra credit on the chapter test.

What problems contribute to a low standard of living in much of South Asia?

(Answer: The majority of people in rural areas are peasant farmers who must struggle to feed their families. In cities, millions live in the streets. The tropical climate and lack of clean water promote widespread diseases. Poor nutrition leads to a short life expectancy.)

South Asia Today

CHAPTER ORGANIZER

Daily Lesson Objectives	Multimedia	Teacher Classroom Resources
SECTION 1 Living in South Asia 1. Identify the major crops of South Asia. 2. Describe industrial development in South Asia. 3. Discuss mining and fishing resources of South Asia.	Section Focus Transparency 25-1 Chapter 25 Vocabulary PuzzleMaker Software Geography and the Environment Testmaker	Reproducible Lesson Plan 25-1 Guided Reading Activity 25-1 Spanish Guided Reading Activity 25-1 Workbook Activity 25-1 Performance Assessment Activity 25 Section Quiz 25-1
SECTION 2 People and Their Environment 1. Explain how people have affected South Asia's wildlife. 2. Discuss deforestation and reforestation in South Asia. 3. Describe how water use is changing in South Asia. 4. Discuss how activities such as tourism affect the environment.	Section Focus Transparency 25-2 Testmaker Reuters Issues in Geography Picture Atlas of the World	Reproducible Lesson Plan 25-2 Guided Reading Activity 25-2 Spanish Guided Reading Activity 25-2 Workbook Activity 25-2 Vocabulary Activity 25 Spanish Vocabulary Activity 25 Environmental Issue 8 Section Quiz 25-2
CHAPTER REVIEW AND EVALUATION	Chapter 25 English (or Spanish) Audiocassettes MindJogger Videoquiz Testmaker Student Self-Test and Review Software	Reteaching Activity 25 Spanish Reteaching Activity 25 Chapter 25 Test Form A and Form B

0:00 *If time does not permit teaching the entire chapter, summarize using the Chapter 25 Highlights on page 523, and the Chapter 25 English (or Spanish) Audiocassettes. Review students' knowledge using the Glencoe MindJogger Videoquiz.*

KEY TO ABILITY LEVELS

Teaching strategies have been coded for varying learning styles and abilities.

L1 **BASIC** activities for all students

L2 **AVERAGE** activities for average to above-average students

L3 **CHALLENGING** activities for above-average students

LEP **LIMITED ENGLISH PROFICIENCY** activities

Performance Assessment

Global Interdependence Have students assume the role of political leaders in different South Asian countries and research the economic, social, and environmental problems that these leaders are facing. They should use information from previous units or other sources to identify other countries or regions that are experiencing similar concerns. Using their research, students should develop a booklet in which they identify the similar areas and compare and contrast the problems of these areas with those of South Asia.

In the role of a South Asian leader, each student should then write a persuasive letter to a leader from another region in which he or she is asked to join with the South Asians in a global effort to solve common problems. The letters should demonstrate the information formulated earlier in the booklet. The class might then put on a simulated session of the United Nations. Student speakers should present information and employ persuasive reasoning to urge a global commitment to the solution of the problems.

POSSIBLE RUBRIC FEATURES: Content information, compare/contrast skills, persuasive writing and argumentation, communication skills, analysis skills

For additional professional and classroom resources, see Chapter Resources, pages T46–T51.

TEACHER'S CORNER

NATIONAL GEOGRAPHIC SOCIETY

INDEX TO NATIONAL GEOGRAPHIC MAGAZINE

The following articles may be used for research relating to this chapter:

- "Bangladesh: When the Water Comes," by Charles E. Cobb, Jr., June 1993.
- "Gatekeepers of the Himalaya," by Jim Carrier, December 1992.
- "India's Wildlife Dilemma," by Geoffrey C. Ward, May 1992.
- "Sacred Space, Sacred Time: India's Maha Kumbh Mela Draws Millions," by Tony Heiderer, May 1990.
- "Annapurna: Sanctuary for the Himalaya," by Galen Rowell, September 1989.
- "Heavy Hands on the Land," by Larry Kohl, November 1988.
- "They Stopped the Sea," by Hans Van Duivendijk, July 1987.
- "Monsoons: Life Breath of Half the World," by Priit J. Vesilind, December 1984.

NATIONAL GEOGRAPHIC SOCIETY PRODUCTS AVAILABLE FROM GLENCOE

To order the following products for use with this chapter, contact your local Glencoe sales representative or call Glencoe at 1-800-334-7344:

- *Picture Atlas of the World* (CD-ROM)
- *STV: World Geography, Asia and Australia* (Videodisc)
- *ZipZapMap! World* (Software)
- *GeoBee* (Software)
- *Images of the World* (Posters)
- *Eye on the Environment* (Posters)
- *Physical Geography of the World* (Transparencies)
- *Picture Atlas of Our 50 States* (Book)

Introducing
CHAPTER 25

chapter
25

South Asia Today

PERFORMANCE ASSESSMENT

Refer to the Planning Guide on page 510B for a Performance Assessment Activity for this chapter. See the *Performance Assessment Activities* booklet for additional suggestions.

CHAPTER OBJECTIVES

1. **Describe** major economic activities in South Asia.
2. **Explain** the effects of a rapidly expanding population on the environment of South Asia.

GLENCOE TECHNOLOGY

Videodisc

Use Chapter 25 MindJogger Videoquiz to preview chapter content.

MINDJOGGER VIDEOQUIZ

Chapter 25
Disc 4 Side A

The MindJogger Videoquiz is also available on videocassette.

CHAPTER FOCUS

Geographic Setting

The people who live in South Asia have adapted to a rich and varied geographic setting, which includes everything from isolated mountain valleys to a long coastline that is a crossroads for international trade.

Geographic Themes

Section 1 Living in South Asia

REGION **In most nations of South Asia, a large majority of the people still make their living in agriculture.**

▲ Photograph: *Indian girl celebrating the Festival of Lights*

Section 2 People and Their Environment

HUMAN/ENVIRONMENT INTERACTION **The rapidly expanding population of South Asia is placing an ever-increasing burden on the environment.**

EXTRA CREDIT PROJECT

Travel Itinerary Have students choose one country in South Asia that they would like to visit. Have them plan a travel itinerary that includes methods of travel, cities, and places of interest. Students should prepare a map showing their proposed travel route. They should also create an illustrated brochure describing their trip.

SECTION 1 Living in South Asia

SETTING THE SCENE

Read to Discover . . .
- the major crops of South Asia.
- the industries that are developing in South Asia.
- mining and fishing resources of South Asia.

Key Terms
- subsistence farming
- jute
- cash crop
- green revolution

Identify and Locate
Malabar Coast, Kathmandu Valley, Chittagong

Rawalpindi, Pakistan

My family lives in Rawalpindi, a city in northern Pakistan. About 65 percent of Pakistanis live on farms, but the country is rapidly setting up new industries. Communication by means of mail, telephone, and fax are reliable, and even the remotest areas are getting equipped with telephones and post offices.

Zia Raja

Rs.2 POSTAGE PAKISTAN پاکستان

Zia Raja describes the growth of industry in his homeland of Pakistan. In recent years the governments of India, Bangladesh, and the other nations in South Asia have also made tremendous progress toward modernizing their economies. India especially has increased agricultural output, slowed population growth, and established a broad and impressive industrial base. As a result, India ranks among the world's top 12 producers of goods and services. Yet India continues to have one of the world's lowest per capita incomes—about $310 a year. Furthermore, its output per person is quite low. In India—as throughout the region—traditional, labor-intensive methods are used in most occupations. As a result, the average individual produces and earns little.

HUMAN/ENVIRONMENT INTERACTION

Agriculture

Most people in South Asia make their living by farming. In India 70 percent of the population is engaged in farming; in Bangladesh the figure jumps to 80 percent. Most people practice **subsistence farming**—managing to produce just what they need to survive. These subsistence farmers use simple tools; a peasant plowing with a wooden harrow pulled by an ox is still a common sight throughout much of the region. Gradually, however, agriculture is changing as modern methods are introduced in the hopes of producing larger harvests. Some farmers now use tractors and irrigate their fields with water pumped from electric-powered wells.

LESSON PLAN
Chapter 25, Section 1

FOCUS

SECTION OBJECTIVES

1. **Identify** the major crops of South Asia.
2. **Describe** industrial development in South Asia.
3. **Discuss** mining and fishing resources of South Asia.

ABOUT THE POSTCARD

Zia Raja tells us that the economy of his country depends on receiving just the right amount of rain—enough to water the crops but not enough to cause floods and destroy them.

BELLRINGER MOTIVATIONAL ACTIVITY

Project the Section 1 Focus Transparency and have students answer the questions.

PRETEACHING VOCABULARY

Have students create a pictionary clue for each of the Key Terms in this section. Then have them work in pairs to identify the terms based on each other's clues.

Use the Vocabulary Puzzlemaker Software to create a crossword or word search puzzle.

Classroom Resources for Section 1

BLACKLINE MASTERS:
Reproducible Lesson Plan 25-1
Guided Reading Activity 25-1
Workbook Activity 25-1
Performance Assessment Activity 25
Section Quiz 25-1

TRANSPARENCIES:
Section Focus Transparency 25-1

MULTIMEDIA:

Vocabulary PuzzleMaker Software
Testmaker

Geography and the Environment

TEACH

GUIDED PRACTICE

L2 Economy Have students list ways South Asians have worked to improve their economies. *(trained farmers to use modern methods and equipment; encouraged industrial development)* Then have them list ways that developed countries have aided South Asian economies. *(tourism, foreign trade, foreign aid, and foreign-owned industries)*

USING ILLUSTRATIONS

PLACE Workers called tea pluckers pick the flushes—several leaves and a bud—from tea bushes by hand. A plucker can harvest about 40 pounds (18 kg) of tea leaves in a day.

Answer to Caption: *tea and rubber*

DID YOU KNOW?

The use of tea bags began in the United States in 1904. Thomas Sullivan, a New York City merchant, sent his customers samples of tea leaves in small silk bags. Customers began ordering the tea in bags after finding that the tea could be brewed easily with them.

Agricultural Conditions

South Asian farms vary in size from large plantations in Sri Lanka to small plots of land in India.

The Sri Lankan plantations were originally established by the British and the Dutch. Today on these plantations, skilled workers use advanced technology to produce tea, rubber, coconut, and other products for export.

Contrasting with the vast tea and rubber plantations are the region's small farms. In India more than one-third of the farms are less than one acre in area. Their small size is a result of traditional inheritance practices. It is the custom to divide a family's land equally among all the family's sons. As generations pass and the plots are divided and then further subdivided, plots grow smaller. A family may own several such plots, scattered around the village where the family lives. This makes farming difficult. In an attempt to solve this problem, some states in India have passed laws establishing a minimum size for farms.

Geographic Themes

Place: Sri Lanka

About three-fourths of all Sri Lankans live in villages and work on farms or plantations. *What agricultural products are exported from Sri Lanka?*

A Variety of Crops

The major food crop grown in South Asia is rice. Rice is grown chiefly in the tropical rain forest climate of the Ganges Delta and along the Malabar Coast—the western coast of the peninsula. India is the world's second-largest producer of rice. Tiny Bangladesh (about the size of Iowa) ranks fourth.

Wheat is a major crop of the Indo-Gangetic Plain. It is also the chief crop of the Indus Valley of Pakistan. Peanuts grown along the western coast of the peninsula are another important crop of the region.

Although rice is the major food crop of Bangladesh, **jute**—a fiber used to make string and cloth—is the country's major cash crop. When harvested, the slender stalks shine a dull gold color. Jute is called the "golden crop" for another reason: sales of this product account for 75 percent of all the money Bangladesh earns from exports.

Cotton is another important fiber crop grown in South Asia; India and Pakistan are world leaders in its production. India is also one of the world's largest producers of bananas, while citrus fruits are grown in the steppe areas of India, Pakistan, and Bangladesh.

India and Sri Lanka are two of the world's largest producers of tea. Originally grown in China, tea was introduced to India by British planters who brought plants and seeds from China. When workers on the Indian tea plantations began demanding better working conditions, the British set up new plantations in Ceylon (now Sri Lanka). When Sri Lanka gained its independence in 1948, the British planters moved on once again, but the plantations remain. The sale of tea abroad brings much-needed cash into Sri Lanka. So does the sale of rubber, the nation's second-largest plantation crop. The island's dependence on **cash crops**, however, forces it to import great quantities of rice to meet its people's food needs. This conflict—between growing the food crops a nation's people need to survive

Cooperative Learning Activity

Organize students into six groups and assign one of the following crops to each group: rice, tea, peanuts, jute, rubber, or cotton. Explain that these are among South Asia's major agricultural crops. Have group members research climate, soil type, length of growing season, and planting, cultivation, and harvesting methods. Have them find or draw pictures of the crop at various stages of growth, harvesting, and/or processing. Provide time for groups to share their information.

physically and growing the cash crops the country needs in order to survive in the global economy—exists throughout South Asia, as in many developing regions.

Improved Agricultural Practices

At the present growth rate, the population of South Asia will double in less than 40 years. Although government leaders—especially in India—have made efforts to slow the rate of population growth, they realize that agricultural production must rise dramatically if the region's people are to be adequately fed.

Government programs throughout South Asia are training farmers to use modern technology. These programs focus on how irrigation, insect control, and fertilization can raise productivity.

In some areas farmers are taught to plant two or more crops on the same piece of land in a single year. In Bangladesh, for example, farmers can harvest three crops of rice in most years. In the Kathmandu Valley of Nepal, farmers used to let their land lie fallow after harvesting their rice crops; now they plant a second crop of winter wheat. This method cannot work everywhere, however. In places where agriculture is dependent on the monsoon rains, growing more than one crop in a year is difficult. Also, farmers who have used traditional methods for centuries may be reluctant to experiment with new techniques; subsistence farmers have little room for error in their lives.

Education and government leadership are crucial—both to change attitudes and to teach specific new techniques. Agricultural research stations in Bhutan have led to the establishment of very successful fruit orchards. The government of Sri Lanka has encouraged rice production by paying high prices for rice and establishing new irrigation programs.

One of the most impressive achievements of recent years has been the **green revolution.** Worried by the rising threat of world hunger, plant breeders began in the 1960s to develop new and more productive varieties of rice, wheat, and maize. Asian rice growers planted the new varieties, and rice production increased by more than 60 percent between 1965 and 1985. Wheat yields in India increased by 50 percent. These new varieties, however, are more susceptible to disease than the old strains were. They also require expensive fertilizers and much irrigation. Despite these problems, the green revolution has allowed countries such as India to store grain surpluses and even export grain. Researchers are currently working to develop strains that can better resist diseases and drought.

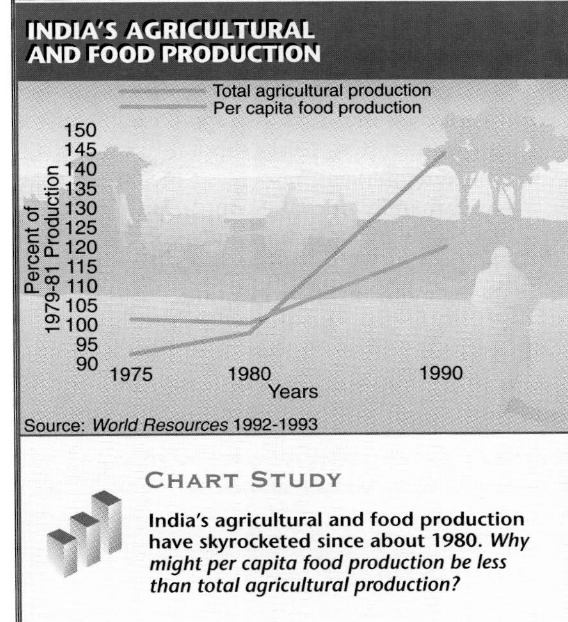

Source: *World Resources* 1992-1993

CHART STUDY

India's agricultural and food production have skyrocketed since about 1980. ***Why might per capita food production be less than total agricultural production?***

HUMAN/ENVIRONMENT INTERACTION

Mining and Fishing

South Asia consists of a peninsula and islands; naturally, fish are an important resource. Mining is also an important source of income.

Mining

Most of the mining in the region takes place on the Indo-Gangetic Plain and in east-

INDEPENDENT PRACTICE

Guided Reading Have students complete Guided Reading Activity 25-1 in the TCR. **LEP**

L2 Interdependence Challenge students to find examples of products in their homes or local stores that were grown or manufactured in South Asia. Provide a bulletin board or a large poster on which students can list or display findings.

USING GRAPHS

Answers: The population is growing more rapidly than agricultural production.

Skills Practice

Interpreting a Graph By about how much did India's total agricultural production increase between 1980 and 1990? *(50 percent)* By about how much did per capita food production increase during the same period? *(20 percent)*

GLENCOE TECHNOLOGY

Videodisc

Use the following to enrich Chapter 25:

GEOGRAPHY AND THE ENVIRONMENT
THE INFINITE VOYAGE
To the Edge of the Earth

Chapter 5
Disc 1 Side B

Title: ***The Tropical Rain Forest***

Meeting Special Needs

Mixed Learners Some students learn best through a combination of auditory and visual materials. Have students look at the pictures on pages 512 and 515. Then have them read the paragraphs that describe agriculture and industry in South Asia. Ask them if the pictures or the paragraphs provide them with more information. Have them compare the kinds of information they get from each source.

USING MAPS

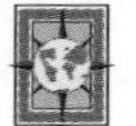

Answers:
1. near major cities and ports and along the Ganges River;
2. subsistence farming;
3. Sri Lanka, southern India, and northeastern India

Map Skills Practice

Reading a Map Why is there little or no economic activity in the northern part of the region? *(It is mountainous.)*

ASSESS

CHECK FOR UNDERSTANDING

Assign Section 1 Review as homework or an in-class activity.

MEETING LESSON OBJECTIVES

Each objective below is tested by the questions that follow it in parentheses.
1. Identify the major crops of South Asia. *(2, 3)*
2. Describe industrial development in South Asia. *(5)*
3. Discuss mining and fishing resources of South Asia. *(4)*

EVALUATE

Assign the Section 1 Quiz in the TCR.

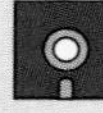

Use the Testmaker to create a customized quiz for Section 1.

RETEACH

Have students use headings and subheadings in the text to outline the material in this section.

ern India. India produces large amounts of mica, coal, and iron ore and also has significant deposits of bauxite, silver, and copper. Pakistan has some natural-gas deposits, and precious stones such as sapphires and rubies are mined in Sri Lanka. Bhutan possesses significant mineral resources, including coal, lead, marble, zinc, and copper. Unfortunately, problems in extracting and processing these minerals have so far prevented them from being mined in large quantities.

Fishing

Fishing is an important industry in Sri Lanka and Pakistan. Fresh and dried fish, as well as lobsters and shrimp, are important exports of Pakistan. In Bangladesh, fish are a primary food source for many people. The majority of farmers in rural Bangladesh fish during the flood season, and the nation's commercial fisheries industry, though new, is very successful. Japan is a major purchaser of shrimp and frogs' legs from Bangladesh.

SOUTH ASIA: ECONOMIC ACTIVITY

Nomadic herding
Commercial farming
Subsistence farming
Manufacturing and trade
Commercial fishing
Little or no activity

Lambert Conic projection

FOCUS ON GEOGRAPHIC THEMES

1. **Location:** Where does manufacturing and trade take place?
2. **Human/Environment Interaction:** What is the major economic activity in most of the region?
3. **Location:** Where does most commercial farming take place?

MOVEMENT

Industrial Growth

The pace of industrialization varies in South Asia. In India the process of industrialization was begun by the British. The nation's industries have traditionally been heavily regulated by the government. An easing of government regulations in the 1980s, however, led to a surge in development. At the other end of the spectrum is tiny Bhutan, which has remained isolated and undeveloped until recently. Government policy currently is to encourage development but to proceed very slowly, so that the nation's cultural heritage and natural resources are carefully preserved.

Light Industry

Light industry involves the production of consumer goods, such as bicycles, televisions, and textiles. Textile manufacturing is India's most important industry, and has been for hundreds of years. Roughly 24 million people are employed in India's textile industry, producing cotton, wool, and silk in an astonishing variety of colors and styles—embroidered, woven, painted, and tie-dyed. The garment industry is also thriving in Bangladesh. In 1979, the year Bangladesh first exported finished garments, the clothing industry earned $9 million in profits. Within just 10 years, profits had soared to $450 million.

Throughout South Asia many goods are manufactured by workers laboring in their own homes. Millions of these laborers weave

Critical Thinking

Drawing Conclusions Ask students to explain the effects of history and culture on agricultural conditions in South Asia. *(The British and Dutch established large plantations in Sri Lanka. Traditional inheritance practices have resulted in small plots in India because a family's land is divided equally among all the sons.)*

fabrics of cotton, rayon, and silk by hand. They also make shoes, jewelry, brassware, woodcarvings, furniture, bowls, and other goods. Because these home industries provide jobs for villagers, the government has always encouraged them. Today, many of the products made in these industries are sold in different parts of the world.

South Asia also has a number of privately owned small industries. These industries generally are plants that employ fewer than 100 workers and use simple machinery. They make such goods as bicycle parts, shoes, and carpets.

Heavy Industry

South Asia also has large-scale industries that specialize in heavy industrial production. These include or are related to mining, electric power, and iron and steel manufacturing. India manufactures steel, cement, and heavy machinery. Bangladesh produces cement, iron, and steel. Bangladesh also melts down and reuses steel from one of its most unusual industries—shipbreaking. Shipowners from all over the world send their old or crippled ships to the port of Chittagong, where workers scramble over the ships with sledgehammers and torches, ripping the structure apart. Manufacturing is not an important part of the economy of Sri Lanka, and in Bhutan there are only a few large industrial employers.

Until the early 1990s, when India moved to a free market economy, more than 200 of its large-scale industries were owned solely by the government. The rest were owned jointly by the government and private investors or were still in private hands.

Under the old economy, India did not welcome foreign investments. All foreign-brand products sold in India had to have Indianized names. Since 1992, however, foreign investment has been encouraged, and products may be sold under their own brand names.

Tourism

Tourism is important to the economies of several South Asian nations. Tourists are attracted to Nepal by the opportunities to hunt, photograph wildlife, and climb or trek in the Himalayas. Tourists are also drawn to exotic Bhutan, but their activities are carefully controlled by the government. Sri Lanka has many beautiful beaches and lovely hotels to attract tourists. Unfortunately, continuing violence between the Sinhalese and the Tamils has drastically reduced tourism on the island.

Geographic Themes

Place: India

India produces a variety of manufactured goods, including machines, tractors, cars, ships, and airplanes. *How many people are employed in India's textile industry?*

Section 1 Review

Checking for Understanding

1. **Define** subsistence farming, jute, cash crop, green revolution.
2. **Locating Places** What areas in India and Pakistan are known for growing wheat?
3. **Human/Environment Interaction** What are two problems with the new strains of wheat and rice being planted in South Asia?
4. **Place** Why is there little mining in Bhutan?

Critical Thinking

5. **Making Comparisons** Compare and contrast industrial development in India and Bhutan.

Using Illustrations

PLACE India's total industrial production is six times greater than it was in 1950.

Answer to Caption:
24 million

ENRICH

Have students research and report on the history of the textile industry in South Asia.

CLOSE

Have students write a postcard to Zia Raja describing an industry or agricultural region in or near their community.

ANSWERS TO SECTION 1 REVIEW

1. **subsistence farming:** growing just what one needs to survive; **jute:** fiber used to make string and cloth; **cash crop:** crop grown to aid the economy rather than to feed the people; **green revolution:** development and use of new, more productive varieties of rice, wheat, and maize
2. the Indo-Gangetic Plain in India; Indus Valley in Pakistan
3. more susceptible to disease than the old ones; require expensive fertilizers, irrigation
4. because of problems in extracting and processing minerals
5. The British industrialization of India grew rapidly in the 1980s after government deregulation. Isolated until recently, Bhutan's government regulates its development.

FOCUS

Allow students a moment to read the selection's title and look at the photographs. What are their thoughts about the photo on page 517?

TEACH

L1 Location Use Unit Map Overlay Transparency 8-5 to familarize students with the location of the Ganges River. Encourage students to count the number of cities on or near the Ganges.

L2 Research Have students use magazines, newspapers, and encyclopedias to update the cleanup program initiated by the government. Encourage discussion and understanding of the problems' magnitude faced by the Indian government.

NATIONAL GEOGRAPHIC SOCIETY

Videodisc

GTV: PLANETARY MANAGER

Side 2, Chapter 8
Frames 41078-46201
Title: ***Shall We Gather at the River?***
Subject: Everyday sources of water pollution and how we can clean up our water

The Ganges: Plagued by Pollution

The Ganges is more than a river. It is a phenomenal force that holds 5,000 years of history, culture, and tradition.

The Ganges River flows across the northern corner of India, beginning as a pair of headstreams in the Himalayas. The streams flow south-southeast, joining at Kanpur, then continue across India and Bangladesh to empty into the Bay of Bengal. The Ganges River flows a total length of 1,557 miles (2,507 km), providing water to southern Tibet, northern India, and the entire countries of Nepal and Bangladesh.

THE ISSUE

The Ganges is the most sacred river of the Hindus, India's major religious group. Every year, millions of pilgrims journey to bathe in its waters. Those waters, however, are heavily polluted, carrying industrial and human waste, as well as agricultural runoff.

THE BACKGROUND

According to the Hindu religion, the Ganges is the Hindu goddess Ganga, come to earth in the form of a river to redeem the souls of worthy men and women. To bathe in the waters of "Mother Ganges" is to be cleansed of all sins.

For years waste materials from distilleries, chemical manufacturers, fertilizer complexes, and the sewage from a steadily growing population have poured into the Ganges.

Millions of Hindus trek across India every year to bathe in the Ganges. Various points along the river provide flights of stairs, called *ghats,* down which pilgrims travel to reach the river. Many believers come, or are brought, especially to die in the Ganges. A believer so fortunate as to die while immersed in its waters is assured of a place in paradise.

"Mother Ganges" provides physical support as well as spiritual. The river and its tributaries drain a region of almost 400,000 square miles (1,040,000 sq. km). These lands have been fertilized continu-

Dams on South Asia's great river systems, especially the Ganges, supply electricity to the region's villages and factories.

Extending the Content

Culture Hinduism is the predominant religion in India and Nepal. The Hindu culture has given rise to India's caste system. Have students research Hinduism and the caste system, the system's effects on India, and the Indian government's efforts to end the caste system.

After students have shared their information, have them offer opinions on the positive and negative effects of the system. Encourage them also to compare and contrast the caste system with other cultural systems they have studied.

ously for centuries by nutrients from the river.

The Ganges and its tributaries support roughly 300 million people, more than the entire population of the United States. Most are rural farmers, living in villages of about 1,000 or fewer people that dot the fertile plain. Drinking water for the villages is provided by a few wells dug deeply enough to tap into groundwater. Washing and bathing are usually done in the river.

Although the Ganges runs through a primarily agricultural area, several major cities are located along its banks: the commercial center Allahabad, heavily industrialized Kanpur, and Patna, a rice-producing center. Delhi, one of the world's fastest-growing cities, spreads along a northwestern tributary. Most of these cities have 1 million or more inhabitants. Kanpur has more than 2 million people; Delhi has 8.7 million residents.

In the last 40 years, factories and chemical plants have developed in these cities, as well as along the river's banks. During the 1980s alone, more than 230 million gallons (872 million L) of untreated sewage were also emptied into the river every day.

THE POINTS OF VIEW

Observers point out that it is virtually impossible for many Hindus to comprehend pollution in the river's sacred waters. "A Hindu pilgrim has no knowledge of the fact that an average drop of water contains traces of cyanide, arsenic, lead, zinc, chromium, selenium and mercury," maintains photojournalist Raghubir Singh. Experts point out the continuing—and steadily increasing—pollution problems posed by India's expanding population and the advance of modern industrialization. The rapid population increase results from better preventive medical care and intensive public health measures. These, in turn, have produced a significant drop in infant deaths.

THE ISSUE TODAY

The Indian government has instituted ongoing efforts to reverse pollution in the Ganges. In 1986 a $250 million cleanup project was begun.

In addition, the government started an ambitious program of population control. Many claim it is the most ambitious in history. Radio and TV ads promote family planning programs. The government also makes generous payments to families who agree to have no more than 2 children.

Although population growth has decreased, the average couple still has 3 to 4 children. About 65,000 babies are born every day. The continued population growth, coupled with the extent of the pollution from which the Ganges is already suffering, cause many to think that the river is long past the point of ecological recovery.

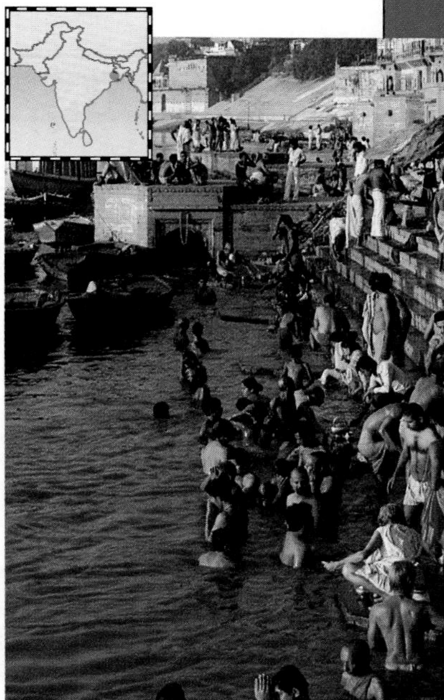

Some of India's largest cities, such as Calcutta and Varanasi, stand on the banks of the Ganges River. Pilgrims gather along the Ganges to perform ritual bathings.

Reviewing the Case

1. **What place does the Ganges River hold in the Hindu religion?**
2. **Human/Environment Interaction What factors contributed to the pollution of the Ganges?**

ASSESS

Have students answer the Reviewing the Case questions on page 517.

CLOSE

Ask students for opinions on the state of the Ganges; encourage them to offer suggestions for reversing the pollution.

DID YOU KNOW?

A Hindu believer fortunate enough to die while immersed in the waters of the Ganges is assured of a place in paradise. Hindu funeral services are held on the ghats; the dead are cremated and their ashes are scattered over the river. A shrine marks the river's source, a sacred ice cave in India's state of Uttar Pradesh.

EYE ON THE ENVIRONMENT POSTER SERIES

Display the three posters that discuss pollution—*Overview, Focus Europe,* and *A Global Look*. Present the activity "Wicked Water Pollutants" found on page 11 of the Poster Series Teacher's Guide.

ANSWERS TO REVIEWING THE CASE

1. Hindus believe the river to be sacred; the deity Ganga in water form come to the earth to save the blessed.

2. The river has been freely used as a dump for industrial, human, and agricultural waste.

FOCUS

SECTION OBJECTIVES

1. **Explain** how people have affected South Asia's wildlife.
2. **Discuss** deforestation and reforestation in South Asia.
3. **Describe** how water use is changing in South Asia.
4. **Discuss** how activities such as tourism affect the environment.

BELLRINGER MOTIVATIONAL ACTIVITY

Project the Section 2 Focus Transparency and have students answer the questions.

PRETEACHING VOCABULARY

List the Key Terms on the chalkboard. Have students listen, with their books closed, as you read the sentence from the text that defines each term, saying "blank" instead of the term. Have students write the Key Term they think fits in each sentence.

CURRICULUM CONNECTION

EARTH SCIENCE
Erosion caused by commercial logging on the lower slopes of the Himalayas has led to flash floods. During the 1970 monsoon, a 200-foot (70-meter) wall of water carried away entire villages, cattle, roads, and buses near Alaknanda in northern India.

SECTION 2

People and Their Environment

THE ENVIRONMENT

SETTING THE SCENE

Read to Discover . . .
- **how people have affected South Asia's wildlife.**
- **how both deforestation and reforestation are occurring.**
- **how water use is changing.**
- **how activities such as tourism affect the environment.**

Key Terms
- **deforestation**
- **trekker**
- **mangrove tree**
- **Chipko**

Identify and Locate
Sundarbans, Uttar Pradesh, Narmada River basin

As in all parts of the world, the environment of South Asia is affected in many ways by the human beings who inhabit the region. Because much of South Asia is so densely populated, the interaction between humans and the environment is especially intense.

HUMAN/ENVIRONMENT INTERACTION

Forests of South Asia

Centuries ago much of South Asia was covered with forests. Over time, much forestland has been converted into farmland or pastureland. Trees have been cut for firewood and shelter. Still, many forests survive—from the rain forests of Sri Lanka and the west coast of India to the deciduous forests of drier and cooler areas. Many experts doubt that these forests can be preserved if South Asia's population continues to expand at its present rate. They point out the severe effects of **deforestation**, or the loss of forests, and urge governments and individuals to conserve woodlands.

Deforestation

One expert estimates that half of the trees of northern India have been cut down in the past 30 years. Many trees have been cut by commercial timbering enterprises or to make way for other businesses, such as quarrying. Others have been slowly killed by impoverished villagers who use the leaves as fodder for their animals.

During the same period, almost one-third of Nepal's forests have been cut down. Nepalese farmers, pushed out of traditional farmlands because of the rising population, have been forced higher into the mountains. There they have cleared trees for farmland and grazing.

Tourists vastly increase the demand on firewood in Nepal and Bhutan. A single **trekker**, or mountain hiker, may use as much firewood as 10 Sherpas. Trekkers also leave litter and garbage behind on the once-pristine slopes of the Himalayas. To avoid these problems, the government of Bhutan closely supervises the tourists who enter the country.

Little of Sri Lanka's original vegetation remains untouched. Slash-and-burn methods of agriculture and illegal logging have caused rapid deforestation. In Bangladesh, using firewood as the main fuel has caused a severe loss of woodlands. The only forests left are in the Chittagong Hills—home to a small number of tribal people—and the Sundarbans, swampland full of **mangrove trees** along the Bay of Bengal.

Classroom Resources for Section 2

BLACKLINE MASTERS:
- Reproducible Lesson Plan 25-2
- Environmental Issue 8
- Guided Reading Activity 25-2
- Spanish Guided Reading Activity 25-2
- Vocabulary Activity 25
- Spanish Vocabulary Activity 25
- Section Quiz 25-2

TRANSPARENCIES:
Section Focus Transparency 25-2

MULTIMEDIA:

Testmaker

Reuters Issues in Geography

Picture Atlas of the World

Effects

The effects of deforestation can be devastating. Traditionally, dense mangroves in the Sundarbans have provided protection from cyclones and tidal waves that affect the coast of Bangladesh. As the mangroves are cut down, this defense is weakened. The forests in the Himalayas have acted like sponges—absorbing the heavy rains in the monsoon season and gradually releasing the moisture throughout the year. When these forests are cleared, heavy rains pour down the bare mountainsides. The water run-off causes serious monsoon flooding as far away as Bangladesh. Downpours wash topsoil off the mountains, sometimes causing dangerous landslides. Soil, carried along by streams and rivers, clogs dams with silt and alters the paths of the rivers.

Deforestation affects wildlife as well. As forests are cut down, animals such as tigers and elephants are slowly forced into smaller habitats. In the foothills of the Himalayas, a traditional honey hunter reports, "My grandfather took 600 nests a year. Last year we took 80." This is an example of the nature of human-environment relations. Human activity reduces the number of bee colonies, and then the people who depend on honey to make a living also suffer.

Deforestation of tropical rain forests is dangerous. These forests usually grow in poor soils. The trees' elaborate root systems efficiently absorb available nutrients and also hold the topsoil in place. The trees absorb and gradually release rainfall, and help keep the climate cooler than it would otherwise be. If the rain forests disappear, soil erodes, and climate changes occur.

Conservation

The people of Bhutan have taken steps to protect the nation's trees. The government supervises control of the forests, limiting commercial timbering and training citizens in forestry. Despite a high demand for Bhutan's wood products, roughly 70 percent of the landscape is still wooded. Pine trees have been planted on Nepalese hillsides to stop erosion. In Sri Lanka a reforestation program began in 1970, and the export of timber has been banned since 1977.

Geographic Themes

Human/Environment Interaction: Nepal

A Sherpa carries people and goods across the foothills of the Himalayas. *How have Nepalese farmers affected the environment of the foothills area?*

Cooperative Learning Activity

Organize students into three groups and assign one of the following topics to each group: forests, wildlife, water. Tell group members to research opposing viewpoints regarding the environmental issues surrounding their assigned topic in South Asia. Then ask them to propose ways to balance human needs with the need to preserve the environment.

TEACH

GUIDED PRACTICE

L2 Cause and Effect Direct students to create a flow chart on the chalkboard to illustrate the causes and effects of deforestation in South Asia. Discuss the impact on people, animals, and land in the region.

Implement Environmental Issue 8 as a class activity.

USING ILLUSTRATIONS

PLACE Sherpas raise yaks, a type of ox that thrives in high altitudes. As pack animals, yaks can carry a heavy load 20 miles (32 km) a day.

Answer to Caption: *They cleared trees for farmland.*

INDEPENDENT PRACTICE

Guided Reading Have students complete Guided Reading Activity 25-2 in the TCR. **LEP**

L2 Poster Have students work individually or in pairs to create a conservation poster for the Chipko movement. Provide time for students to share their work.

MULTICULTURAL PERSPECTIVE

Cultural Heritage

The Sherpas probably moved to Nepal from Tibet in the early 1500s. Their Tibetan heritage is indicated by their language and dress. Sherpas also practice Lamaism, a form of Buddhism that is the traditional religion of Tibet.

USING MAPS

Answers:
1. north and northeast; dry;
2. They provide heavy rainfall, which irrigates crops but also causes flooding.

Map Skills Practice

Reading a Map What is the source of moisture for the summer monsoons? *(Indian Ocean)*

ASSESS

CHECK FOR UNDERSTANDING

Assign Section 2 Review as homework or an in-class activity.

MEETING LESSON OBJECTIVES

Each objective below is tested by the questions that follow it in parentheses.
1. Explain how people have affected South Asia's wildlife. *(2, 3)*
2. Discuss deforestation and reforestation in South Asia. *(4, 5)*
3. Describe how water use is changing in South Asia. *(4)*
4. Discuss how activities such as tourism affect the environment. *(3)*

EVALUATE

Assign the Section 2 Quiz in the TCR.

Use the Testmaker to create a customized test for Section 2.

RETEACH

Have students complete Reteaching Activity 25 in the TCR.

In India the **Chipko**—or tree-hugger—movement was started by environmental activist Sunderlal Bahaguna, a former follower of Gandhi. The tree-hugger movement is devoted to saving the remaining forests of northern India. Bahaguna tells villagers about the importance of trees and teaches them land management and reforestation techniques. In some villages Chipko has opened nurseries and provided seedlings. Bahaguna has had success in showing impoverished villagers that trees must be preserved if erosion and drought are to be avoided. He also convinced then Prime Minister Indira Gandhi to halt commercial timbering in the Himalayan forests of Uttar Pradesh.

Wildlife

South Asia is home to spectacular wildlife. For example, elephants, water buffalo, and monkeys are found in Sri Lanka. Crocodiles and the magnificent Bengal tiger roam Bangladesh. Unfortunately, many of these animals are endangered in a rapidly changing environment, especially in forested areas.

Some animals of the region have become rare through overhunting. Others have been endangered as a result of the loss of habitat.

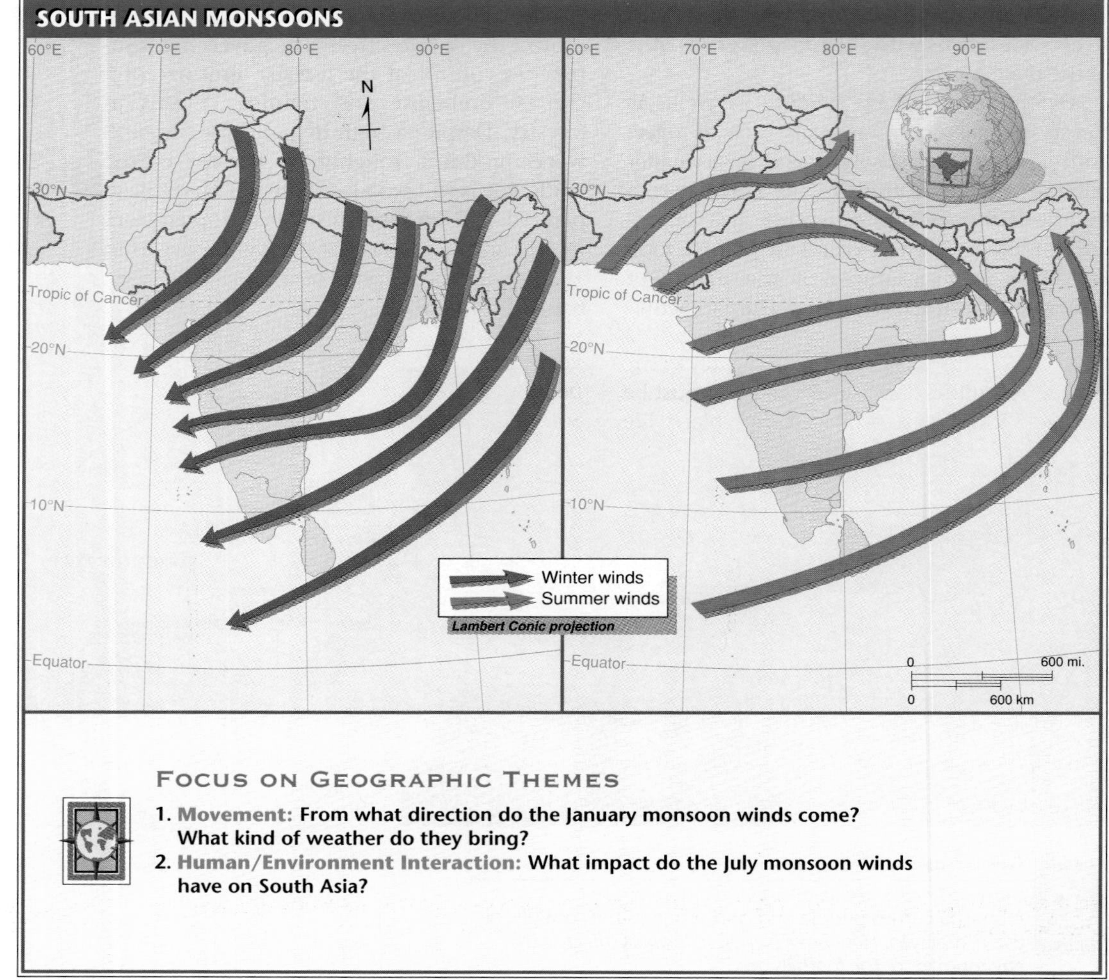

FOCUS ON GEOGRAPHIC THEMES

1. **Movement: From what direction do the January monsoon winds come? What kind of weather do they bring?**
2. **Human/Environment Interaction: What impact do the July monsoon winds have on South Asia?**

Meeting Special Needs

Learning Disability Students who have learning disabilities may benefit from having a specific purpose for listening. After students have read Section 2, lead a discussion about the material. Tell students to listen for words or phrases from the text. Tell them to write each word or phrase they hear that also appeared in the text. Use the following terms: deforestation, Sundarbans, bee colonies, mangrove trees, reforestation, Uttar Pradesh, water buffalo, Bengal tiger, Narmada River. Give extra credit to any student who gets them all right.

Deforestation and development projects, such as the construction of dams, have taken a severe toll on animal species.

In recent decades, the countries of South Asia have taken steps to protect animals. Governments have created wildlife reserves with help from international organizations. They also have passed laws to control hunting and development.

Geographic Themes

Human/Environment Interaction: Endangered Species

South Asian animals, such as this tiger, are facing extinction as humans have cleared forested areas for development. *What steps are being taken to protect South Asia's wildlife?*

HUMAN/ENVIRONMENT INTERACTION

Water

In South Asia, humans and the environment affect each other in relation to water. The people build dams, they irrigate, they pollute, and they change the courses of rivers and the effects of the monsoons.

Dams

Dams play a crucial role in irrigating dry areas and regulating the flow of water. The Tarbela Dam of Pakistan is the world's largest earthen dam. Built in the 1970s, this dam controls floods and holds water in reserve for irrigating Pakistan's crops during the driest months. Dams also produce hydroelectric power. To build a dam, however, land must be flooded. Wildlife is displaced and plant life destroyed.

Dams trap silt that otherwise would flow downstream, and dam reservoirs can be a source of waterborne disease. In a country such as India, where many people consider the rivers holy, dams are seen as interfering with the spiritual force of the water.

Narmada River Project

Plans to build a huge dam in India's Narmada River basin have met with both intense excitement and violent disapproval. Supporting the project are those who point out that the dam will generate large amounts of electricity and irrigate millions of acres of cropland. It will also control flooding during the monsoon months.

Opposing the dam are the thousands of tribal people who will be forced out of their villages when flooding begins, and environmental activists who point out that dams ruin soils and create health problems. This controversy is an example of the complex interdependence between the human residents of South Asia and their environment.

Section 2 Review

Checking for Understanding

1. **Define** deforestation, trekker, mangrove tree, Chipko.
2. **Locating Places** Where can the Bengal tiger still be found?
3. **Human/Environment Interaction** How do tourists affect the Himalayas?
4. **Region** How do forests prevent loss of topsoil?

Critical Thinking

5. **Drawing Conclusions** Why is it important for South Asians to preserve their forests?

ANSWERS TO SECTION 2 REVIEW

1. **deforestation:** loss of forests; **trekker:** mountain hiker; **mangrove tree:** tree that grows in swampland; **Chipko:** movement to preserve the remaining forests of northern India
2. in Bangladesh
3. They leave litter and use up large amounts of firewood.
4. Forests absorb heavy rains and prevent flooding that washes away topsoil.
5. Forests protect topsoil, provide habitat for wildlife, and produce wood for fuel and shelter.

USING ILLUSTRATIONS

PLACE The tiger's coloration helps conceal the animal in its environment. Although tigers can live in almost any climate, wild tigers are found only in Asia.

Answer to Caption: *Governments have created wildlife reserves and have passed laws to control hunting.*

ENRICH

Have students complete Enrichment Activity 25 in the TCR.

CLOSE

Have students share the travel itineraries they prepared for the Extra Credit Project.

GLENCOE TECHNOLOGY

Videodisc

REUTERS ISSUES IN GEOGRAPHY

Chapter 7
Disc 1 Side A

Title: ***South Asia: Preserving the Himalayas***

Subject: Physical processes that operate in the region, and how human choices affect the environment

NATIONAL GEOGRAPHIC SOCIETY

CD-ROM

PICTURE ATLAS OF THE WORLD

You and your students can see and hear the wildlife in India's Kanha Wildlife Preserve by clicking India's "Video" button.

Teaching Skills

TEACH

Conduct a brief survey about students' after-school activities. Questions may include: How many participate in sports teams and arts activities? How many have after-school jobs? How many hours do they watch television?

Record the data on the chalkboard, and have students write a statement summarizing these facts. Say: "These are generalizations, or general statements about a topic based on a group of facts. Why are generalizations useful?" *(They compile and organize facts about a topic.)* "Why are generalizations sometimes misleading?" *(Specific examples may not fit the generalization; generalizations based on incorrect facts can be misleading.)* Have students discuss inaccurate generalizations about teenagers.

Skills Practice For additional practice, have students complete Skill Activity 25 in the TCR.

CRITICAL THINKING SKILLS

Making Generalizations

Suppose you ask a friend to go roller blading. Your friend says, "I don't know. Luiz just twisted his knee on roller blades. Janet scraped up her arms and legs in a roller-blading accident. Roller blading is too dangerous." Whether you like it or not, your friend used these facts to form a **generalization**, or general statement, about roller blading. The generalization may be true or false. That depends largely on the accuracy of the supporting details.

Reviewing the Skill

Using knowledge and experiences, people form generalizations to explain and understand the world. Generalizations play a key part in many fields of study. By observing animals in their natural surroundings, biologists form generalizations, or hypotheses, about such things as how animals find food, rear their young, and defend against enemies. Forming generalizations based on observation, and then testing these theories against more evidence, is a cornerstone of the scientific method.

Although generalizations help us understand the world, they also can be misleading. For example, the generalization about roller blading was based on two incidents. But what really caused these roller-blading accidents? Were Luiz and Janet using proper equipment? Were they roller blading on busy streets? Were they wearing pads and helmets? To say that roller blading is always dangerous may be an **over generalization**, or a statement that is too broad. Perhaps proper equipment and precautions make it a far less dangerous sport. Whenever making generalizations, be sure that they are based on accurate supporting details. Use the following steps in making generalizations:

- Gather facts, examples, or statements related to the topic.
- Identify similarities or patterns among these facts.
- Use these similarities or patterns to form generalizations about the topic.
- Test your generalizations against other facts and examples.

Practicing the Skill

Write a generalization based on each group of statements that follow.

1.
   - Using simple hand tools and oxen-drawn plows, most South Asian subsistence farmers produce just enough food to feed their families.
   - Because many people in India believe that land must be divided equally among sons, farms are becoming smaller and less efficient.
   - Many South Asian farmers are reluctant to abandon traditional practices such as leaving the land fallow after harvest.
2.
   - Agricultural production in South Asia must rise to meet the nutritional demands of a rapidly growing population.
   - Increasing population severely limits the abilities of South Asian governments to provide services for their people.
   - To acquire more land, people in South Asia clear forests for planting and grazing, thus causing environmental problems such as soil erosion, habitat destruction, and climate change.

For additional practice in this skill, see Practicing Skills on page 524 of the Chapter 25 Review.

ANSWERS TO PRACTICING THE SKILL

1. Some traditional farming methods and beliefs limit agricultural productivity in South Asia.

2. Rapid population growth causes both economic and environmental problems in South Asia.

chapter 25

HIGHLIGHTS

1 SECTION Living in South Asia

KEY TERMS

subsistence farming (p. 511)
jute (p. 512)
cash crop (p. 512)
green revolution (p. 513)

SUMMARY

- Agricultural advances are helping South Asia produce enough food for its expanding population.
- Main food crops include rice and wheat; main cash crops include jute and tea.
- Mining, fishing, and tourism are significant sources of income in the region.
- Industry—both light and heavy—is expanding in the region.

Tea plantation in Sri Lanka

2 SECTION People and Their Environment

KEY TERMS

deforestation (p. 518)
trekker (p. 518)
mangrove tree (p. 518)
Chipko (p. 520)

Tiger reserve in India

SUMMARY

- Much of South Asia has been deforested by human beings seeking wood for fuel and shelter, and land for farming and grazing.
- Deforestation can lead to flooding, landslides, loss of valuable topsoil, loss of habitat for animals, and climate changes.
- Governments and individuals throughout South Asia are attempting to conserve and replant forests.
- Despite the loss of many animals due to overhunting and habitat loss, South Asians are working to maintain existing species in wildlife preserves and elsewhere.
- Water usage is controversial in South Asia for many reasons; dams are needed to control flooding and provide water for irrigation, but they also cause environmental problems.

CHAPTER 25 HIGHLIGHTS

USING THE CHAPTER 25 HIGHLIGHTS

Use the Chapter 25 Highlights to preview, review, condense, or reteach the chapter.

PREVIEW/REVIEW

Vocabulary PuzzleMaker Software reinforces the Key Terms used in Chapter 25.

Student Self-Test and Review Software allows students to review Chapter 25 content.

CONDENSE

Have students read the Chapter 25 Highlights.

Have students listen to the Chapter 25 Audiocassettes in the TCR. Spanish Audiocassettes are also available.

Assign the Chapter 25 Audiocassette Activity and give students the Chapter 25 Audiocassette Quiz.

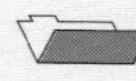 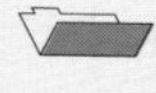

Have students complete Guided Reading Activities for Chapter 25 in the TCR. Spanish Guided Reading Activities are also available.

RETEACH

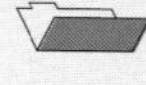

Have students complete Reteaching Activity 25 in the TCR. Spanish Reteaching Activities are also available.

Map Activity

Identify and Locate Provide each student with a copy of the map on page 34 of the Outline Map Resource Book. Have students indicate South Asia's major economic activities. Instruct them to design symbols for the activities and to create a key to explain the symbols.

GLENCOE TECHNOLOGY

Videodisc

Use Chapter 25 MindJogger Videoquiz to review students' knowledge before administering the Chapter 25 Test.

MINDJOGGER VIDEOQUIZ

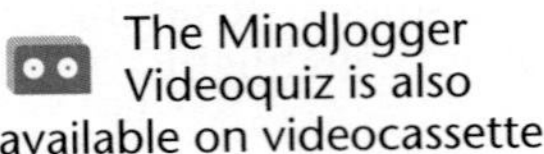

Chapter 25
Disc 4 Side A

The MindJogger Videoquiz is also available on videocassette.

ANSWERS

Reviewing Key Terms

1. jute
2. cash crop
3. green revolution
4. trekker
5. mangrove trees
6. Chipko
7. deforestation

Reviewing Facts

8. in agriculture
9. rice
10. textiles
11. Bhutan
12. because of a rapidly changing environment in forested areas
13. Many people consider rivers holy and think dams interfere with the spiritual force of the water.

chapter 25 REVIEW

Reviewing Key Terms

Choose the vocabulary term that best completes each of the sentences below. Write your answers on a separate sheet of paper.

jute (p. 512)
cash crop (p. 512)
green revolution (p. 513)
deforestation (p. 518)
trekker (p. 518)
mangrove trees (p. 518)
Chipko (p. 520)

SECTION 1

1. A fiber used to make rope and cloth is ____.
2. Something grown to make money rather than to use for one's own survival is known as a ____.
3. The development and use of new, high-yield grains is called the ____.

SECTION 2

4. A mountain hiker is known as a ____.
5. ____ grow in the swamplands of Bangladesh.
6. A movement to save the forests of northern India is called ____.
7. The loss of all the trees in an area is called ____.

Reviewing Facts

SECTION 1

8. How do the majority of people in South Asia make their living?
9. What is the major food crop of South Asia?
10. What is India's most important industry?

SECTION 2

11. Which South Asian country still has forests covering 70 percent of the land?
12. Why is the Bengal tiger endangered?
13. What religious reason do people in India have for opposing dam construction?

Critical Thinking

14. **Making Generalizations** What effect is modern technology having on the economy of South Asia?
15. **Expressing Problems** What are several ways in which expanding human populations are having negative effects on the environment of South Asia?

Geographic Themes

16. **Place** Where does most mining take place in India? What are the key minerals?
17. **Movement** How has Bhutan's isolation helped to preserve its environment?

Practicing Skills

Making Generalizations

18. Write a generalization based on the group of statements below.
    A. The government of Bhutan strictly controls commercial use of its forests.
    B. Nepal, Sri Lanka, and India employ reforestation projects to replace forests.
    C. South Asian governments have restricted hunting of endangered species, used experimental methods for removing large animals from populated areas, and established wildlife reserves.

Using the Unit Atlas

Refer to the physical geography section of the Unit Atlas on page 472–473.

19. What mineral is mined in India?
20. What is Pakistan's greatest natural resource?
21. What is South Asia's highest point?

Critical Thinking

14. Technology is making agriculture more productive and helping to industrialize the region.
15. Answers include causing deforestation, loss of habitat for animals, pollution, and litter.

Geographic Themes

16. on the Indo-Gangetic Plain and in eastern India; mica, coal, iron ore, bauxite, silver, copper
17. Isolation has preserved Bhutan from excessive industrial development, deforestation, and tourism.

Projects

Individual Activity

You have learned a little about the economic activities in the various nations of South Asia. Choose the nation that interests you most and research one form of economic activity. You might research the garment industry of India, the tourist business in Nepal, or shipbreaking in Bangladesh. Write a brief report on the subject.

Cooperative Learning Activity

Working in a small group, organize a debate on one of the aspects of the environmental issues in South Asia. For example, half of the group might assemble arguments and data to support the building of dams in the region, while the other half might compile arguments against dam-building. Each group should hold its debate in front of the rest of the class. Afterward, the class as a whole should evaluate the issue and try to form judgments.

Writing About Geography

Cause and Effect

Choose one aspect of human-environment interaction in South Asia and write an essay that shows how humans both cause changes in the environment and then are affected in turn by those changes. You may use your journal, text, encyclopedias, guide books, or magazine articles to help you write your essay.

Practicing Skills

18. Sample generalization: South Asian countries have started conservation programs to protect their natural resources.

Using the Unit Atlas

19. chromite
20. natural gas
21. Mount Everest

Locating Places

1. H
2. A
3. G
4. D
5. B
6. I
7. C
8. E
9. J
10. F

Locating Places

SOUTH ASIA: PHYSICAL GEOGRAPHY

Match the letters on the map with the places and physical features of South Asia. Write your answers on a separate sheet of paper.

1. Calcutta
2. Arabian Sea
3. Kathmandu Valley
4. Narmada River
5. Indus Valley
6. Ganges River
7. Indo-Gangetic Plain
8. Malabar Coast
9. Bay of Bengal
10. Himalayas

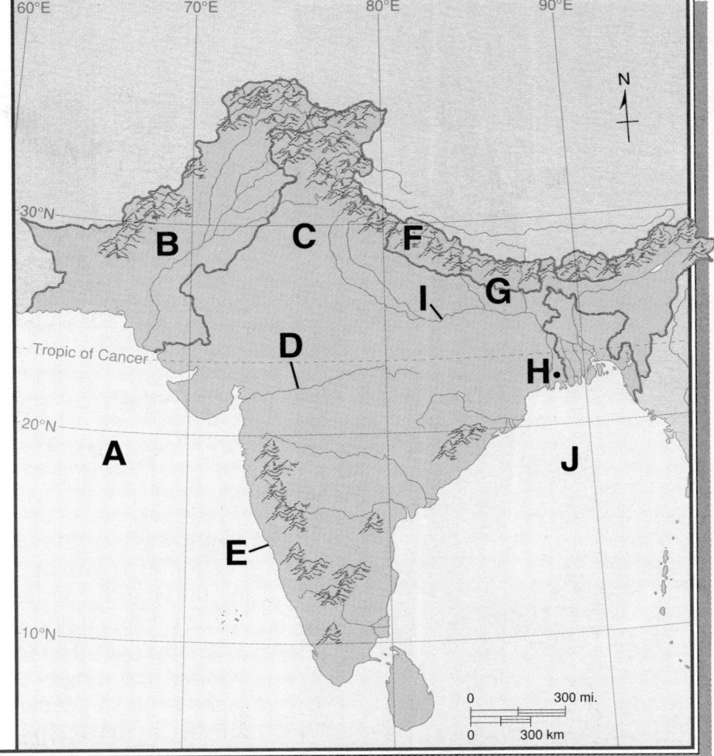

Chapter Bonus Test Question

This question may be used for extra credit on the chapter test.

What are the arguments for and against building dams in South Asia?

(Answer: Dams control floods, provide water for irrigation during dry months, and produce hydroelectricity. When dams are built, people are forced out of areas because of flooding. Wildlife is displaced, and plant life is destroyed. Dam reservoirs can be a source of disease.)

FOCUS

Take a class vote on how many students have worn an item of clothing made from one of the fabrics shown or a tie-dyed shirt. Encourage comments on what the wearer liked about the clothing item.

TEACH

L1 Location Have students locate Madras and Calcutta on the map on page A19. Encourage them to suggest routes that traders and merchants might have taken from the two cities back to European markets.

L2 Movement Calico was a staple fabric in the American colonies by the late 1700s. Have students speculate on communication and transportation systems that would have brought knowledge of calico to the colonies. Have students briefly research to learn if their speculations were correct.

L3 Research Encourage students to find out more about the fabrics presented on pages 526–527. They can look through catalogs for photographs of items made from the materials, noting the styles and prices. They may also be interested in visiting a local fabric store to examine the look, feel, and variety of fabrics. Allow time for students to share their findings.

GEOGRAPHY CONNECTION

South Asia and the United States

COTTONS, CASHMERE, AND TIE-DYE

South Asia's textile industry has an ancient past. Experts have dated some printed cottons of the region to 3000 B.C. The materials calico and chintz have been part of our heritage since colonial times. Cashmere, madras, and tie-dye appeared later in our fashion history, but have become popular and enduring favorites as well.

▲ **CHINTZ** is a cotton export from South Asia that quickly became an American favorite. A medium-weight cotton fabric with a soft, lustrous glaze, chintz has been used in home decorating since the 1700s. Its wide variety of colors and patterns, as well as its durability and easy care, keep it in demand.

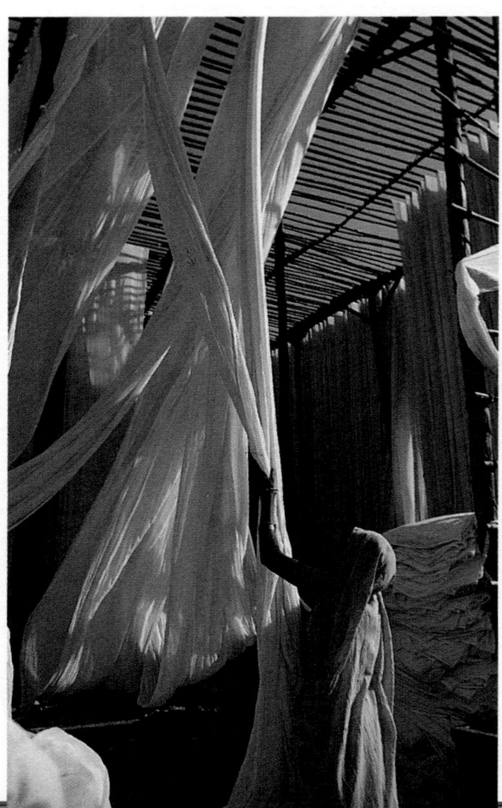

◀ **MADRAS** is a cotton fabric from South Asia that has found a place in American wardrobes. First produced in the Indian city of Madras, the fabric's strong bright designs are colored with vegetable dyes. The colors "bleed," or run, when washed, resulting in the soft, subtle coloring that is the fabric's trademark. Madras fabric reached the height of its popularity in the United States during the late 1950s and early 1960s.

Making the Connection

Culture Calico fabrics were great favorites with American pioneer women because of the wide range of colors and designs. Encourage students to find out more about the American craft of quilting through quilting books and magazines, as well as a visit to a local fabric store to view the many calico fabrics available. Interested students might design a quilted square or two.

Students might also be interested in trying their hands at tie-dying. Many easy-to-follow books with a number of tie-dye projects are available.

CALICO, a lightweight cotton fabric, originated in and was named for the Indian city of Calcutta. It quickly became one of the most popular products imported to the United Kingdom by the British-owned East India Company. Hundreds of designs and colors were eventually available in Europe and North America as a result of the Industrial Revolution. Fragments of cotton calicos became the basic ingredient of an American art form developed by pioneer women—the patchwork quilt. Colorful calicos remain a contemporary textile for shirts, blouses, and casual summer clothing.

▲ **CASHMERE,** a lightweight luxury fabric, is made from the fine, soft hair fibers that grow as the undercoat on goats in the Vale of Kashmir in northern South Asia. An especially supple and elegant textile, cashmere tops the list of the best dressed for coats and sweaters.

TIE-DYE ▶ refers to a special technique developed in central India to decorate fabrics. A length of fabric, usually cotton or silk, is twisted, and sections are tied with thread or rope before dying. Tie-dying most often produces spectacular circular or zigzag designs of brilliant hue. Fashion seekers prize tie-dye for its unique one-of-a-kind look.

Checking for Understanding

1. What South Asian textiles are part of American fashion?
2. **Movement** How did calico and chintz first get to the United States?

Geography Connection

ASSESS

Have students answer the Checking for Understanding questions on page 527.

CLOSE

Have students summarize the reasons for the popularity of the Indian fabrics shown.

DID YOU KNOW?

Calico, madras, and chintz are cotton textiles. British traders found out about cotton material in India in the 1600s; clothes made from it were much more comfortable for the traders than their own heavy English clothing. Cotton fabric quickly became one of the most popular products imported to England by the East India Trading Company. Its popularity soon spread to the American colonies, where the hot, humid New England summers and the southern climates assured its popularity.

ANSWERS TO CHECKING FOR UNDERSTANDING

1. calico, madras, chintz, cashmere, tie-dye
2. imported from England, where it was brought from South Asia by the East India Trading Company

UNIT OVERVIEW

The three chapters that comprise this unit introduce students to the physical geography and peoples of East Asia.

Various aspects of the region's life—such as the economy, lifestyles, and human/environment interaction—are also presented.

GEOGRAPHY JOURNAL

Activity As students collect articles, encourage them to look for cause/effect relationships between developments in one category and those in another. Have them jot down such relationships in their journals. At the unit's end, have students summarize or generalize about cause/effect in regional situations.

- This journal activity provides the basis for the "Writing About Geography" exercise in the Chapter Review.

- The Geography Journal may be used as an integral part of Performance Assessment.

CD-ROM

PICTURE ATLAS OF THE WORLD

You and your students can see and read about the physical features of East Asia by clicking the "Photos" and "Essay" buttons of selected countries.

0:00 OUT OF TIME?

If time does not permit teaching each chapter in this unit, you may use the Chapter Highlights and the Audiocassettes that include a 1-page activity and a 1-page test for each chapter.

UNIT 9

East Asia

GeoJournal Activity

While studying East Asia, follow news reports about the region either on television or in newspapers and magazines. Keep a record of the developments under the following categories: Environment, Culture and Daily Life, History and Government.

National Geographic photographer Jodi Cobb

528

Where in the World . . . .

Have students look at the map on pages A20–A21 in which East Asia is highlighted. Display Unit Map Overlay Transparency 9-5 and ask students the following questions: What body of water forms a coastline for the region? *(Pacific Ocean)* Which country is the region's northernmost? *(Mongolia)* Which countries lie within approximately the same latitudes as Mongolia? *(North Korea, Japan)* Which country is landlocked? *(Mongolia)* What rivers provide water for the mainland countries? *(Chang Jiang, Huang He)* Which countries are not on the mainland? *(Taiwan, Japan)*

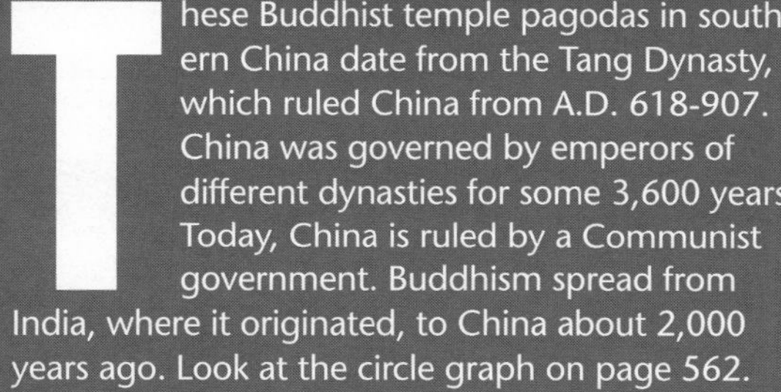

Picturing the World

These Buddhist temple pagodas in southern China date from the Tang Dynasty, which ruled China from A.D. 618-907. China was governed by emperors of different dynasties for some 3,600 years. Today, China is ruled by a Communist government. Buddhism spread from India, where it originated, to China about 2,000 years ago. Look at the circle graph on page 562.

1. What percentage of East Asians practice Buddhism?
2. Read to learn about the religions of East Asia. Why are so many East Asians considered as nonreligious in the chart?

Picture Atlas CD-ROM Enrichment Corner

Create a file of East Asia information. (See the *Picture Atlas of the World* User's Guide on how to use the Collector button.) Read the essays and vital statistics, look at the photos, map, and videos, and listen to the musical selections for each country. Make sure your file includes the following information:

1. Most heavily and sparsely populated nations
2. Where the majority of the people of East Asia live
3. Examples of cultural phenomena that date back more than a thousand years
4. National dishes or pastimes
5. Major physical features of the region
6. Major tourist sites of the region
7. Major problems in the region

529

ANSWERS TO PICTURING THE WORLD

1. 20 percent
2. because religious statistics are not available from the People's Republic of China

*inter*NET CONNECTIONS

The Land of Beauty—pictures of notable sites in China—can be found at the following address:

World Wide Web
http://www.cnd.org/Scenery/index.html

The Japan Information Network Web site is located at:

World Wide Web
http://www.ntt.jp/japan/index.html

CD-ROM

PICTURE ATLAS OF THE WORLD
You can find an additional CD-ROM activity to enrich Unit 9, East Asia, on page T43.

GLENCOE TECHNOLOGY

Videodisc

Use the following to introduce or enrich Unit 9:
REUTERS ISSUES IN GEOGRAPHY

Chapter 8
Disc 1 Side A

Title: ***China: The New Prosperity***
Subject: Changes taking place in the way goods and services are produced in the People's Republic of China

LESSON PLAN
Unit 9 Atlas

These features and activities may be used as an introduction to the unit or as teaching tools throughout the course of the unit.

FOCUS

Ask students to study the maps on pages 530–531 for a moment, then generalize on what appears to be the dominant population distribution characteristic.

TEACH

Implement Foods Around the World 8 as a class activity.

Have students complete World Cultures Transparencies 15 and 16 Activities in the TCR.

Have students complete World Literature Reading 8 in the TCR.

Play World Music: Cultural Traditions, Lesson 8, and have students complete the Lesson 8 activity.

DID YOU KNOW?

The enormous influence of China on its neighbors is one of East Asia's unifying influences. Most East Asians read a written language based on the Chinese ideographic system; most of China's neighbors also adapted Chinese techniques in metalworking, pottery, weapons, transportation, architecture, and agriculture.

UNIT 9 ATLAS

EAST ASIA
Cultural Geography

EXPLORING CULTURAL DIVERSITY

1. *What nations make up East Asia?*
2. *What areas of China are most heavily populated? Most sparsely populated?*
3. *What is the approximate population of East Asia?*
4. *What are the national capitals for the six nations of East Asia?*

During the 1200s, the **Mongols** built the largest empire in history, conquering the area from eastern Asia to eastern Europe.

The **Japanese** enjoy a mixture of Eastern and Western cultures. Their favorite spectator sports, for example, are baseball and sumo wrestling.

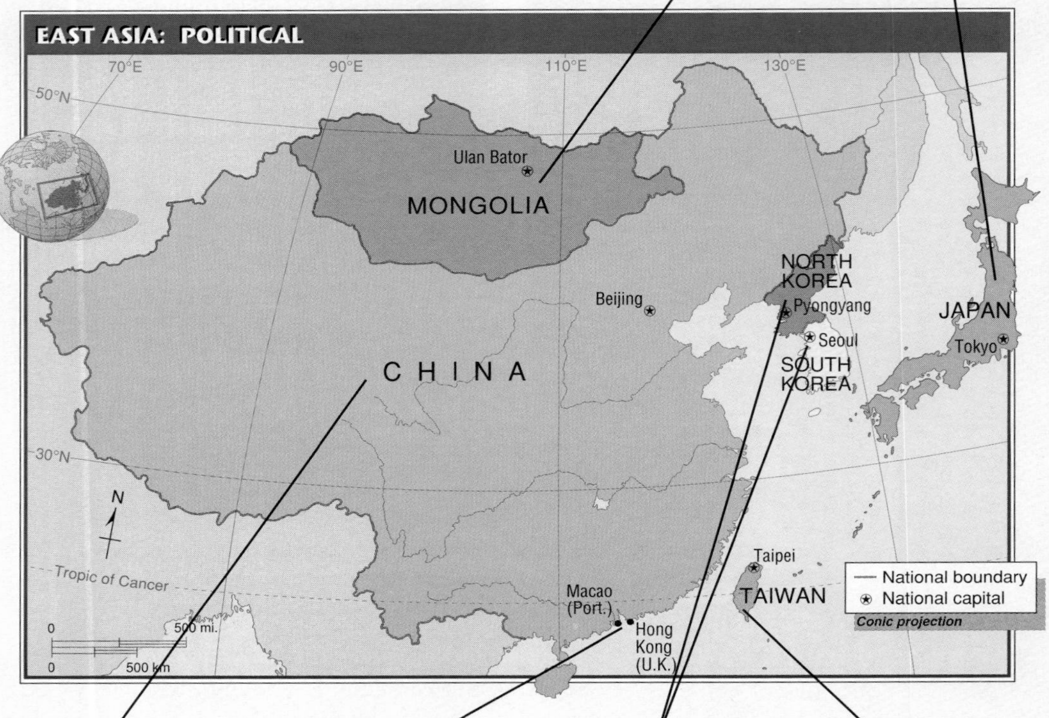

China's largest ethnic group is the Han nationality, which includes 94 percent of the population. The remaining 6 percent is divided among 50 ethnic groups.

The Chinese leased **Hong Kong** to the British for 99 years in 1898. Hong Kong will revert to Chinese rule in 1997.

North and South Korea are divided by a heavily policed 2.5 mile- (4.0 km-) wide demilitarized zone. The zone was established in 1953, after the Korean War.

The Chinese Nationalist government rules **Taiwan.**

530 UNIT 9

Classroom Resources for Unit 9

BLACKLINE MASTERS:
Geography Simulation 9
Environmental Issue 9
Foods Around the World 8
World Literature Reading 8

TRANSPARENCIES:
Unit Map Overlay Transparency 9
Political Map Transparency 9
World Cultures Transparencies 15, 16

MULTIMEDIA:

Picture Atlas of the World

World Music: *Cultural Traditions, Lesson 8*

Reuters Issues in Geography

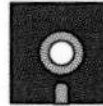
Testmaker

Images of the World Poster Set

Although almost 75 percent of all Chinese live in rural villages, **China** has at least 31 major cities with populations of 1 million or more. More than 90 percent of China's 1.2 billion people live crowded into one-sixth of the country's land.

About half of all people of **Mongolia** live and work on livestock farms.

About 70 percent of all Koreans live in cities. **South Korea,** however, has almost three times the number of large cities as **North Korea.**

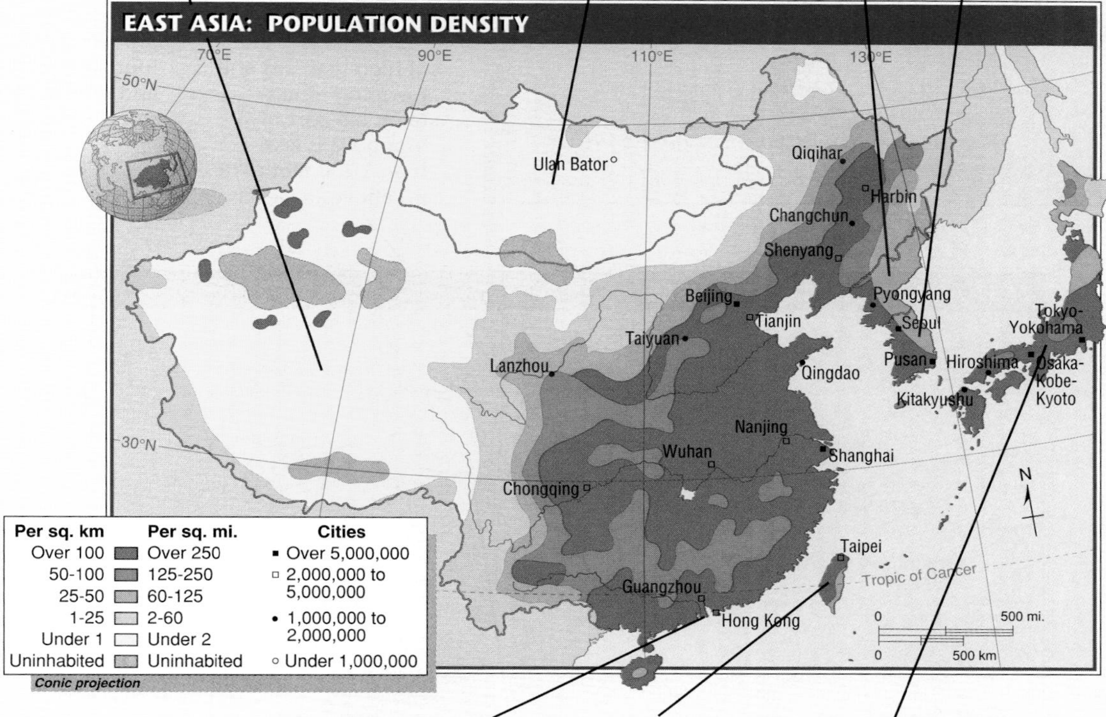

The majority of **Hong Kong's** people live in the capital, Victoria, and Kowloon. The cities are Hong Kong's major centers of economic activity.

Almost all of **Taiwan's** people live on the western third of the island, which is a coastal plain.

So much of **Japan's** land is covered with mountains and hills that its population of 125 million lives densely packed along the islands' coasts.

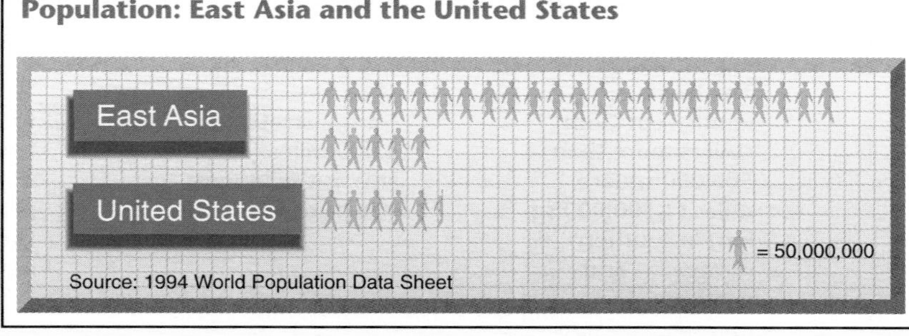

The population of East Asia is more than 5½ times that of the United States.

LESSON PLAN Unit 9 Atlas

ASSESS

Have students answer the Exploring Cultural Diversity questions on page 530.

EXPLORING CULTURAL DIVERSITY

This feature may be used to introduce students to the cultural geography of East Asia. Use questions to stimulate class discussion and help students become familiar with the region. Accept reasonable answers based on the maps, graph, and captions.

CLOSE

Ask students to predict what geographic features might account for the uneven population distribution in East Asia. List suggestions on the chalkboard to be reread when students have looked at the physical geography maps on the following two pages.

GLENCOE TECHNOLOGY

Videodisc

Use the following to introduce or enrich Unit 9:

REUTERS ISSUES IN GEOGRAPHY

Chapter 8
Disc 1 Side A

Title: ***China: The New Prosperity***

Subject: Changes taking place in the way goods and services are produced in the People's Republic of China

Map and Graph Activity

Culture/Movement Share the **Did You Know?** information from the side column on page 530. Organize the class into six groups, and assign each group a country. Further assign each student in the groups one of the following categories: literature and drama, arts and crafts, weapons, transportation, architecture, agriculture. Have students research their assigned topics, jotting down the country's achievements as well as the Chinese influence. Have students also discover how the Chinese influence arrived in the country.

Provide a time for students to share their information.

LESSON PLAN
Unit 9 Atlas

These features and activities may be used as an introduction to the unit or as teaching tools throughout the course of the unit.

FOCUS

Allow students a moment to study the maps on pages 532–533. Then ask them to give what appears to be the geographic reason for the population distribution on page 531.

TEACH

Map Activity Have students compose complex sentences by combining facts from page 532 with facts from page 533. For example: Rich deposits of coal, copper, gold, iron, and petroleum are mined in the high plateaus and towering mountains of Mongolia.

To introduce students to the physical geography of East Asia, have them complete Unit Map Overlay Transparency 9 Activity in the TCR.

Implement Geography Simulation 9 as a class activity.

Have students complete Unit Atlas Activity 9A in the TCR.

NATIONAL GEOGRAPHIC SOCIETY

IMAGES OF THE WORLD POSTER SET

Display the poster of "Asia." Have students identify the photos that show scenes of East Asia. (*Horse breeder, Mongolia; Traffic in Hong Kong*)

UNIT 9 ATLAS

EAST ASIA
Physical Geography

CHARTING YOUR COURSE

1. *What four large islands make up Japan?*
2. *What desert area is found in Mongolia and northern China?*
3. *What are three natural resources found in East Asia?*
4. *What is the highest point in East Asia?*

Mongolia is a land of high plateaus and towering mountains. No part of Mongolia is less than 1,700 feet (518 m) above sea level.

Japan consists of four large islands and thousands of smaller ones.

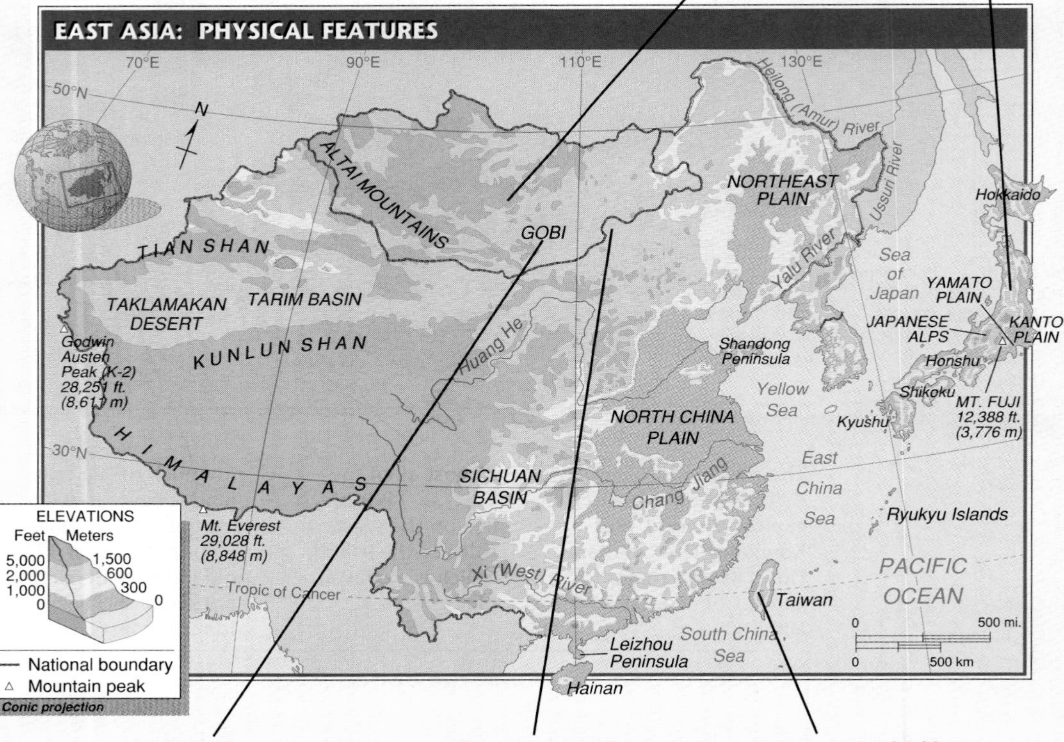

The treeless, windswept Gobi covers more than 500,000 square miles (1,300,000 sq. km) in southern Mongolia and northern China.

The Great Wall of China, stretching 4,000 miles (6,437 km), is the longest structure ever built.

Taiwan's thickly forested mountains blanket about half of the island. Many plunge sharply to the sea along the eastern coast.

Map Activity

Geography Organize students into small groups and assign a country to each group. Have groups find out each country's leading economic sectors, exports and imports, and trading partners. Have students enter the information in their journals, then jot down the physical geography features from the graphics on pages 532–533 that support the economic profile of the country.

Mongolia has rich deposits of coal, copper, gold, iron, and petroleum.

Anthracite (hard coal) and tungsten are **South Korea's** chief mining products.

Although **Japan** has few natural resources, it is a world industrial superpower. It imports most of its raw materials.

EAST ASIA: NATURAL RESOURCES

70°E 90°E 110°E 130°E 50°N 30°N

RUSSIA
MONGOLIA
CHINA
NORTH KOREA
SOUTH KOREA
JAPAN
ASIA
TAIWAN
MACAO
HONG KONG
Tropic of Cancer
N
0 500 mi.
0 500 km

Petroleum
Coal
Iron ore
Tin
Tungsten
Bauxite
Copper

Conic projection

The Sichuan Basin's mild climate and long growing season make it one of **China's** main agricultural regions.

An accessible location and excellent natural harbor have helped make **Hong Kong** a world center of trade, finance, manufacturing, and transportation.

Cedar, hemlock, and oak trees grow in **Taiwan's** forests, its most important natural resource.

China and the Korean Peninsula: Physical Profile

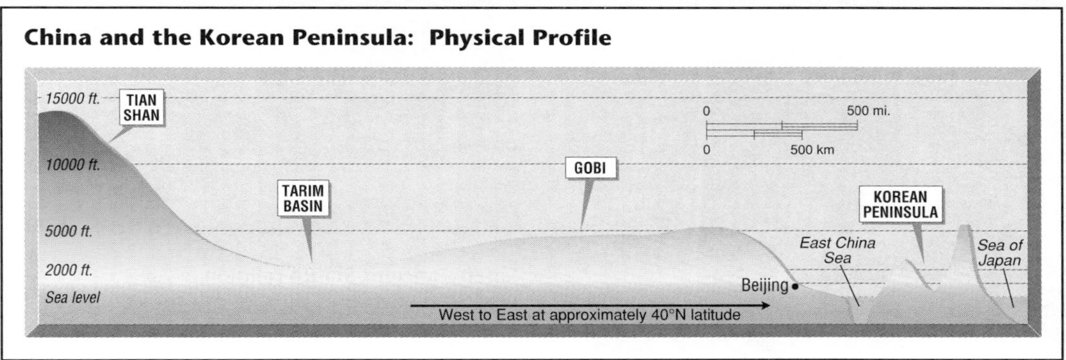

LESSON PLAN Unit 9 Atlas

ASSESS

Have students answer the Charting Your Course questions on page 532.

CHARTING YOUR COURSE
This feature may be used to introduce students to the physical geography of East Asia. Use questions to stimulate class discussion and help students become familiar with the region. Accept reasonable answers based on the maps, graph, and captions.

CLOSE

Ask students to suggest other regions of the world that have some of the same characteristics as this region.

DID YOU KNOW?

Like the United States, China has a "wild west"—western lands that are drier and more sparsely settled than its eastern lands. The western mountains and deserts are home to ethnic groups who raise livestock rather than plant crops.

DID YOU KNOW?

In Hong Kong, movies and television are the most popular forms of entertainment.

Map Activity

Comparison/Contrast Challenge students to learn more about the Gobi and the nomadic peoples who roam there. In their journals, have them record important facts about the desert and the nomadic lifestyle. Then have them write a two or three-paragraph comparison/contrast of the Gobi and the Sahara, and their peoples. Encourage students to return to Unit 6 as necessary for details.

These features and activities may be used as teaching tools throughout the course of the unit.

DID YOU KNOW?

Chinese is a *tonal* language: each written character can have five or six different meanings, depending on the tone used when the word is spoken. *Ma,* for example, can mean horse, mother, or function as a question mark, depending on the tone of voice in which it is uttered.

Ways of the World

CHINA When eating out in China, tipping is unnecessary. In fact, a tip is an insult: it is considered something that a superior does to an inferior.

Ways of the World

JAPAN Giving gifts in Japan is an extremely important matter. A gift is a comment on the feelings of the giver toward the recipient. Giving the right-priced gifts—the price is more important than the gift—to the right people at the end of a year sets the tone for the upcoming year.

UNIT 9 ATLAS

COUNTRY PROFILE

COUNTRY* AND CAPITAL	FLAG AND LANGUAGES	POPULATION	LANDMASS	PRINCIPAL PRODUCTS EXPORT	PRINCIPAL PRODUCTS IMPORT
China (Beijing)	Mandarin, Yue Wu Hakka, Xiang	1,192,000,000 331 per sq. mi. 128 per sq. km	3,600,930 sq. mi. 9,326,409 sq. km	Textiles	Machinery
Japan (Tokyo)	Japanese	125,000,000 859 per sq. mi. 331 per sq. km	145,370 sq. mi. 376,508 sq. km	Motor Vehicles	Fuels
Mongolia (Ulan Bator)	Mongolian	2,400,000 4 per sq. mi. 2 per sq. km	604,830 sq. mi. 1,566,510 sq. km	Minerals	Machinery
North Korea (Pyongyang)	Korean	23,100,000 497 per sq. mi. 192 per sq. km	46,490 sq. mi. 120,409 sq. km	Minerals	Petroleum
South Korea (Seoul)	Korean	44,500,000 1,170 per sq. mi. 452 per sq. km	38,120 sq. mi. 98,731 sq. km	Machinery	Machinery
Taiwan (Taipei)	Mandarin Chinese, Taiwanese, Hakka dialects	21,100,000 1,517 per sq. mi. 586 per sq. km	13,900 sq. mi. 36,001 sq. km	Machinery	Machinery

*Country maps not drawn to scale.

The Potala Palace in Lhasa, Tibet, was once home of the Dalai Lama, Tibet's exiled Buddhist leader.

Japan's ancient Shinto religion is still practiced at shrines throughout the country.

534 UNIT 9

Country Profile Activity

Economy Have students return to the economic information they researched for the physical geography lesson (page 532). Have them compare their information with the chart on page 534. Then have them speculate on the factors that determined the products to be listed as the country's principal imports and exports.

Taiwan has a booming industrial economy that exports products to other parts of the world.

Yurts, or tentlike structures, are common living quarters in the far western part of China.

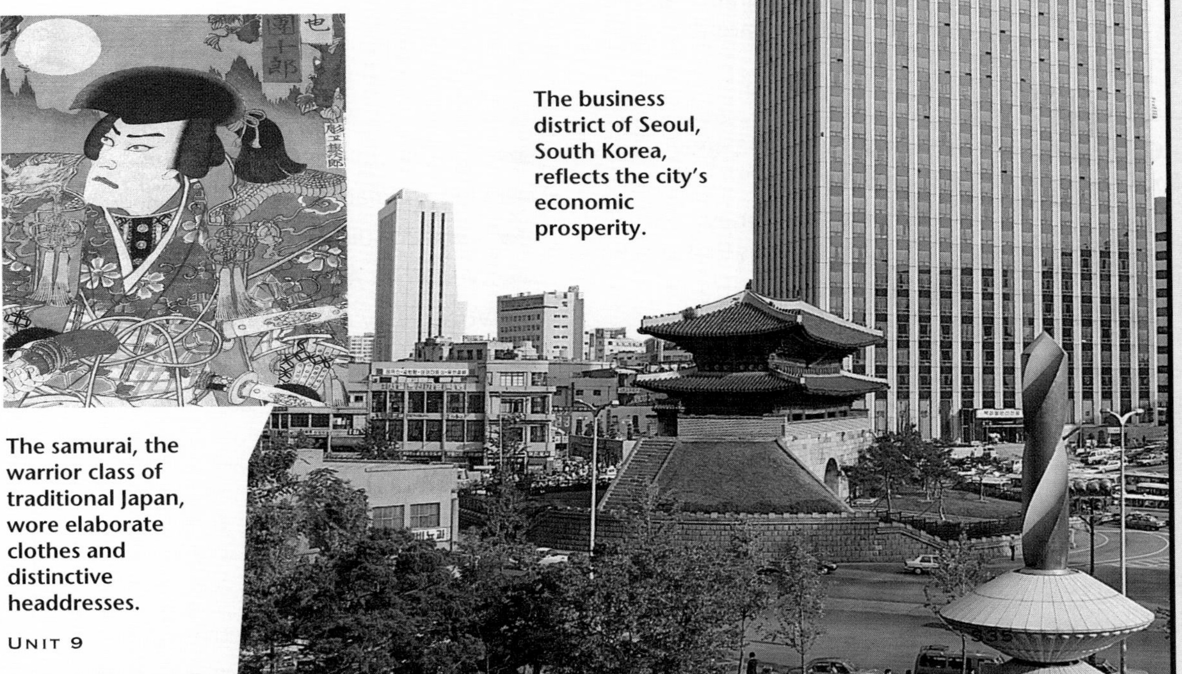

The business district of Seoul, South Korea, reflects the city's economic prosperity.

The samurai, the warrior class of traditional Japan, wore elaborate clothes and distinctive headdresses.

Global Gourmet

Pasta was first prepared in China at least 3,000 years ago, using rice and bean flour. Niccolo Polo, and his son Marco, brought back the recipe for pasta to Italy after their travels through China in the 1200s. The Italians gave it the name "spaghetti," meaning "little strings."

DID YOU KNOW?

Mongolian society is in a state of flux after decades of Communist rule. Communism demanded conformity; now, the growth of entrepreneurism is hindered by much fear of personal initiative and risk-taking. The government is looking for ways to help people understand that talent, differing opinions, and personal performance are important to a democratic society.

Ways of the World

NORTH KOREA North Koreans consider it impolite to eat with the fingers. They accept slurping soup and noodles: they feel it is the only practical way to eat hot food at the pace they are used to.

Country Profile Activity

Research/Culture Have students read aloud the caption under each photograph on pages 534–535 and locate the country mentioned on the map on page 530. Then allow students a few moments to choose a photograph and caption, study it, then compose at least three questions that they have about the photograph. For example, the caption about the Potala Palace might give rise to questions such as: *Where is Lhasa, Tibet? Why was the Dalai Lama exiled? What has happened to the Palace?* Have them also list several sources that they think might help them learn the answers. Have students return to their questions periodically as they work through the unit. If their questions are not answered by material in the unit, encourage students to look for the answers in the sources they listed.

CHAPTER 26

PLANNING GUIDE

The Physical Geography of East Asia

CHAPTER ORGANIZER

Daily Lesson Objectives	Multimedia	Teacher Classroom Resources
SECTION 1 The Land 1. Locate the variety of landscapes in East Asia. 2. Describe the importance of East Asian rivers. 3. Discuss natural resources of East Asia.	Section Focus Transparency 26-1 Chapter 26 Vocabulary PuzzleMaker Software Political Map Transparency 9 Unit Map Overlay Transparencies 9 and 9-5 Geography and the Environment Testmaker STV: World Geography, Volume 1 Physical Geography of the World Transparencies 62, 65, 70	Reproducible Lesson Plan 26-1 Guided Reading Activity 26-1 Spanish Guided Reading Activity 26-1 Workbook Activity 26-1 Section Quiz 26-1
SECTION 2 The Climate and Vegetation 1. Name the different climate regions in East Asia. 2. Explain how seasonal winds affect climates in East Asia. 3. Describe the kinds of plants and trees that grow in different parts of East Asia.	Section Focus Transparency 26-2 Unit Map Overlay Transparencies 9–2 and 9–3 Testmaker	Reproducible Lesson Plan 26-2 Guided Reading Activity 26-2 Spanish Guided Reading Activity 26-2 Workbook Activity 26-2 Vocabulary Activity 26 Skill Activity 26 Enrichment Activity 26 Section Quiz 26-2
CHAPTER REVIEW AND EVALUATION	Chapter 26 English (or Spanish) Audiocassettes MindJogger Videoquiz Testmaker Student Self-Test and Review Software	Reteaching Activity 26 Spanish Reteaching Activity 26 Outline Map Resource Book, p. 35 Chapter 26 Test Form A and Form B

0:00 *If time does not permit teaching the entire chapter, summarize using the Chapter 26 Highlights on page 547, and the Chapter 26 English (or Spanish) Audiocassettes. Review students' knowledge using the Glencoe MindJogger Videoquiz.*

KEY TO ABILITY LEVELS

Teaching strategies have been coded for varying learning styles and abilities.

L1 **BASIC** activities for all students

L2 **AVERAGE** activities for average to above-average students

L3 **CHALLENGING** activities for above-average students

LEP **LIMITED ENGLISH PROFICIENCY** activities

Performance Assessment

Travel Opportunities in East Asia Students should become travel editors for a large city newspaper in this simulation task. Have the class examine the travel sections of the Sunday newspapers of various cities. Students should determine the types of articles, data, and photos that are commonly used.

Groups of students should then develop a travel section for a country of East Asia. In their travel sections, groups should mention the physical features of the country that attract tourists as well as any that might pose obstacles to travel. Layouts may be done on oversized posterboards, by computer, or by cut and paste. Groups should share information, with each group reading and making comments through short "letters to the editor."

POSSIBLE RUBRIC FEATURES: Content information, descriptive writing, organizational skills, analysis and evaluation skills, collaborative skills, creative thinking

For additional professional and classroom resources, see Chapter Resources, pages T46–T51.

TEACHER'S CORNER

INDEX TO NATIONAL GEOGRAPHIC MAGAZINE

The following articles may be used for research relating to this chapter:

- "The Mekong: A Haunted River's Season of Peace," by Thomas O'Neill, February 1993.
- "Suruga Bay: In the Shadow of Mount Fuji," by David Doubilet, October 1990.
- "Above China," by Larry Kohl, March 1989.
- "China Passage," by Paul T. Theroux, March 1988.
- "Jade: Stone of Heaven," by Fred Ward, September 1987.
- "Monsoons: Life Breath of Half the World," by Priit J. Vesilind, December 1984.
- "The Japan Alps," by Charles McCarry, August 1984.
- "Bamboo, The Giant Grass," by Luis Marden, October 1980.

NATIONAL GEOGRAPHIC SOCIETY PRODUCTS AVAILABLE FROM GLENCOE

To order the following products for use with this chapter, contact your local Glencoe sales representative or call Glencoe at 1-800-334-7344:

- *Picture Atlas of the World* (CD-ROM)
- *STV: World Geography, Asia and Australia* (Videodisc)
- *ZipZapMap! World* (Software)
- *GeoBee* (Software)
- *Images of the World* (Posters)
- *Eye on the Environment* (Posters)
- *Physical Geography of the World* (Transparencies)
- *Picture Atlas of Our 50 States* (Book)

ADDITIONAL NATIONAL GEOGRAPHIC SOCIETY PRODUCTS

To order the following products for use with this chapter, call National Geographic Society at 1-800-368-2728:

- *The People's Republic of China*, "Introducing China Today," "Living and Working in China Today," "Chinese Arts and Culture." (Filmstrip)
- *China: Sichuan Province* (Video)
- *Nations of the World Series*, "Japan." (Video)

PERFORMANCE ASSESSMENT

Refer to the Planning Guide on page 536B for a Performance Assessment Activity for this chapter. See the *Performance Assessment Activities* booklet for additional suggestions.

CHAPTER OBJECTIVES

1. **Understand** that East Asia has a varied landscape.
2. **Appreciate** that East Asia's large landmass puts it in many different climate zones, from subarctic to tropical rain forest.

GLENCOE TECHNOLOGY

Videodisc

Use Chapter 26 MindJogger Videoquiz to preview chapter content.

MINDJOGGER VIDEOQUIZ

Chapter 26
Disc 4 Side A

The MindJogger Videoquiz is also available on videocassette.

chapter 26 The Physical Geography of East Asia

CHAPTER FOCUS

Geographic Setting

The culture region of East Asia includes much of the Asian mainland south of Russia, along with nearby islands. High inland mountains and plateaus separate mainland East Asia from the rest of the continent.

Geographic Themes

Section 1 The Land

PLACE East Asia has a varied landscape. Landforms range from towering mountains to barren deserts to rich river valleys.

▲ Photograph: *Mount Fuji, Japan*

Section 2 The Climate and Vegetation

LOCATION East Asia's large landmass puts it in many different climate zones, from subarctic to tropical rain forest. Location inland or near the coast also has a great effect on climates.

EXTRA CREDIT PROJECT

Prepare a Menu Have interested students prepare a menu for an imaginary Chinese restaurant. Tell the students that Chinese cuisine is divided into the four major regions of the country: the northern province of Hopei, usually represented by Peking dishes; the southern province of Kwantung, home of Cantonese dishes; the eastern region, including the city of Shanghai; and the western provinces of Szechwan and Hunan, sources of popular spicy dishes. For the names and descriptions of dishes from the four regions, refer them to local restaurants and Jennifer Brennan's *The Cuisines of Asia*, a cookbook.

1 SECTION The Land

SETTING THE SCENE

Read to Discover . . .
- the variety of landscapes in East Asia.
- the importance of East Asian rivers.
- the natural resources of East Asia.

Key Terms
- archipelago
- tsunami
- loess

Identify and Locate
Mongolia, Korean Peninsula, Japan, Taiwan, Huang He, Chang Jiang, Xi River, Plateau of Xizang, the Himalayas, Gobi, Tarim Basin, North China Plain, Hong Kong

Tokyo, Japan

Konnichiwa. My hometown, Tokyo, is very crowded. I live close to the Metropolitan Office, which is the most crowded place in Japan. There are a lot of advertising signs with bright blinking lights, so we hardly see the stars. But when it's a beautiful sunny day, I can see Mt. Fuji in the distance. Some people always speak ill of a big city but I like my city. Hope you'll come and visit me.
Ema Ito

This postcard from Japan mentions Mount Fuji, one of many amazing sights in the lands that make up East Asia. A few hundred miles away, Ema Ito would have seen a very different landscape. East Asia is a place of immense contrast—towering, snow-covered mountains in the west, barren deserts in the north, lush green fields in the southeast, and hundreds of islands.

PLACE

Land and Sea

The huge People's Republic of China dominates the geography of East Asia, occupying almost 3,600,000 square miles (9,326,000 sq. km)—about 81 percent of the land area. With about 1.2 billion people, China has the largest population of any nation.

Mongolia, north of China, covers more than 604,000 square miles (1,567,000 sq. km)—an area larger than Texas, New Mexico, Arizona, and Colorado combined. Its population, however, is only about 2,400,000.

The other countries in East Asia are Japan, North Korea, South Korea, and Taiwan. The region also includes the colonies of Hong Kong and Macao.

Peninsulas, Islands, and Seas

The smaller nations of East Asia are located on peninsulas and islands. These landforms divide this part of the Pacific Ocean into small seas.

The Korean Peninsula juts out from northern China, between the Sea of Japan and the Yellow Sea. To the southwest, between Japan and the mainland, is the East China Sea. Still farther south, beyond the island of Taiwan, the South China Sea lies between the Philippines and the peninsula of Southeast Asia.

LESSON PLAN
Chapter 26, Section 1

FOCUS

SECTION OBJECTIVES
1. Locate the variety of landscapes in East Asia.
2. Describe the importance of East Asian rivers.
3. Discuss natural resources of East Asia.

ABOUT THE POSTCARD
Ema is in eleventh grade and has many foreign teachers at his school who teach their native languages. Ema has been studying English since seventh grade.

BELLRINGER MOTIVATIONAL ACTIVITY
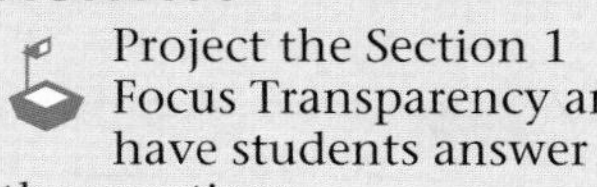
Project the Section 1 Focus Transparency and have students answer the questions.

PRETEACHING VOCABULARY
On the chalkboard, copy the Key Terms and their pronunciations: archipelago (AHR-kuh-PEL-uh-GOH), tsunami (tsu-NAH-mee), loess (LES).

Use the Vocabulary PuzzleMaker Software to create a crossword or word search puzzle.

NATIONAL GEOGRAPHIC SOCIETY

Videodisc

STV: WORLD GEOGRAPHY, VOLUME 1

Side 1, Chapter 1
Frames 17713-27588
Title: ***Asia***
Subject: Central and Eastern Asia

Side 1, Chapter 1
Frames 27589-42384
Title: ***Asia***
Subject: South and Southeast Asia

Classroom Resources for Section 1

BLACKLINE MASTERS:
Reproducible Lesson Plan 26-1
Guided Reading Activity 26-1
Section Quiz 26-1

TRANSPARENCIES:
Section Focus Transparency 26-1
Political Transparency 9
Unit Map Overlay Transparencies 9 and 9-5

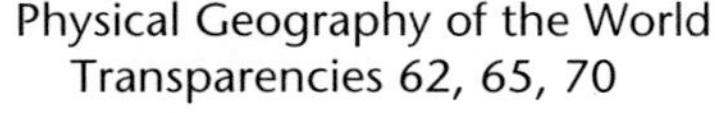
Physical Geography of the World Transparencies 62, 65, 70

MULTIMEDIA:
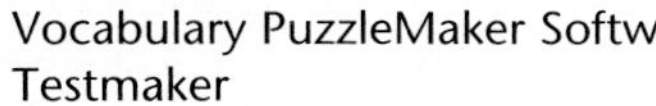
Vocabulary PuzzleMaker Software
Testmaker

Geography and the Environment STV: World Geography, Volume 1

TEACH

GUIDED PRACTICE

Implement Geography Simulation 9 as a class activity.

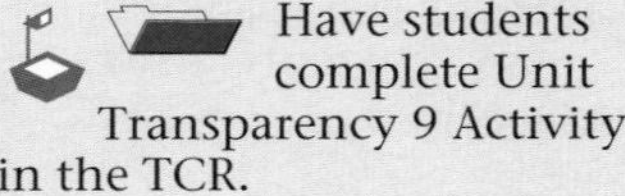

Project Unit Map Overlay Transparency 9 onto the chalkboard and have students locate and label the physical features from the section on the map. Project Unit Map Overlay Transparency 9-5 to check the students' accuracy.

INDEPENDENT PRACTICE

Guided Reading Have students complete Guided Reading Activity 26-1 in the TCR. **LEP**

Have students complete Unit Transparency 9 Activity in the TCR.

DID YOU KNOW?

Mountains cover one-third of China. Of the 14 highest mountain peaks in the world, 9 are in China or on its borders.

GLENCOE TECHNOLOGY

Videodisc

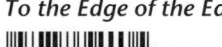

GEOGRAPHY AND THE ENVIRONMENT
THE INFINITE VOYAGE
To the Edge of the Earth

Chapter 3
Disc 1 Side B
Title: ***Exploring Volcanoes: To the Center of the Earth***
Subject: A manned submersible is used to study volcanic activity below the surface of the Pacific Ocean

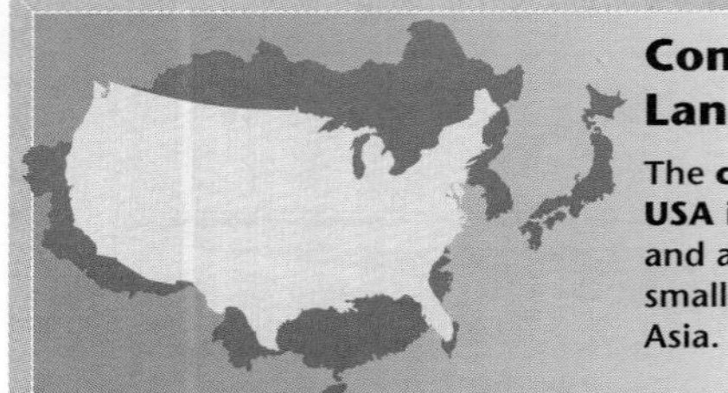

Comparing Lands

The **continental USA** is about one and a half times smaller than East Asia.

The Japanese Islands

Japan is an **archipelago**, a group of islands made up of four large, mountainous islands and thousands of smaller ones. Most of Japan's major cities are on the large island of Honshu. The other islands, from north to south, are Hokkaido (hah•KY•doh), Shikoku (shi•KOH•KOO), and Kyushu (kee•OO•shoo).

Other Islands

South from Japan, a curving arc of small islands sweeps toward the mainland of Asia. The Ryukyu (ree•YOO•KYOO) Islands end near Taiwan (ty•WAHN), a mountainous island about 100 miles (about 161 km) from the coast of mainland China. This island is the home of the Republic of China. This small country also includes 2 other offshore islands, Quemoy and Matsu, and an island chain called the Pescadores.

The island arc that includes Japan, the Ryukyus, Taiwan, and the Philippines is at a boundary where tectonic plates meet. The islands are part of the Pacific Rim's Ring of Fire, where violent earthquakes and volcanoes are frequent.

Volcanoes originally formed most of these islands. Japan still has about 50 active volcanoes, and more than 1,000 small earthquakes shake the country every year. Violent quakes occur less often but bring disaster to people and buildings. An undersea earthquake can send a huge **tsunami** (tsu•NAH•mee), or sea wave, crashing against the islands.

Macao and Hong Kong

Farther south, on the China coast, are two small European colonies on offshore islands and peninsulas. British Hong Kong and Portuguese Macao are both bustling commercial shipping ports.

REGION

Mountains and Lowlands

Mountain ranges and rugged highlands cover much of East Asia. The only large lowland areas are on the mainland, in eastern China.

The world's highest mountains mark the western edge of East Asia where many peaks soar more than 25,000 feet (7,620 m) high. This area is known as "the roof of the world." Mount Everest, the highest mountain in the world, is found here.

The region has several other mountain ranges. They fan out in different directions from this center. They include the Himalayas, the Karakoram Range, the Kunlun Shan, the Tian Shan, and the Altai Mountains.

The mountain ranges of Manchuria extend southward through the center of Korea. Coastal plains edge both sides of the peninsula. Japan is even more mountainous than Korea and also has coastal plains.

The highest plateau region in East Asia is the Plateau of Xizang, at elevations ranging from 13,000 to 15,000 feet (3,962 to 4,572 m)—higher than many mountain peaks in other places. North and east of the plateau are other rugged highlands, at elevations ranging from 3,300 to 6,500 feet (1,006 to 1,981 m). The huge Mongolian Plateau extends over much of Mongolia and parts of northern China.

Between the highlands are broad, flat basins. For example, the huge Tarim Basin lies between the Kunlun Shan and Tian Shan. It is part desert and part salt marshes. By contrast, much of Sichuan (SSU•CHWAN) province in southwestern China lies in a great fertile basin that is heavily cultivated.

Large parts of northwestern China and Mongolia are dry, windswept desert waste-

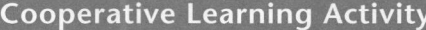

Cooperative Learning Activity

Organize the class into five groups and assign each group one of the following features or groups of features: mountains; rivers; plateaus; deserts, basins, and plains; and oceans and seas. Then tell each group to gather in a circle and pass a sheet of paper around the group. Each person should identify one East Asian example of the feature or features assigned. The student should name the feature, give its relative location, and add any additional information available from the textbook. After each student has written at least once, ask one member from each group to share the information with the class.

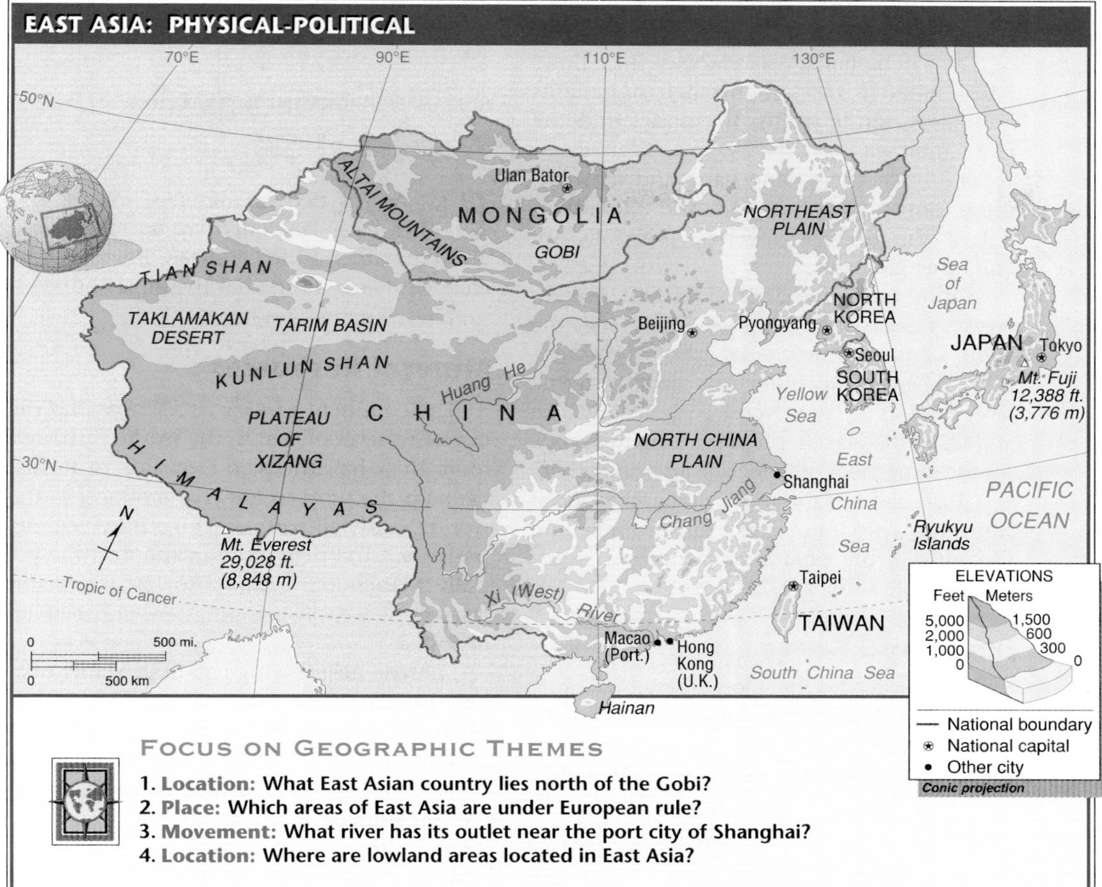

FOCUS ON GEOGRAPHIC THEMES

1. **Location: What East Asian country lies north of the Gobi?**
2. **Place: Which areas of East Asia are under European rule?**
3. **Movement: What river has its outlet near the port city of Shanghai?**
4. **Location: Where are lowland areas located in East Asia?**

lands. The sandy Taklamakan Desert and the treeless Gobi are among these deserts. The Gobi stretches across southern Mongolia and parts of China.

PLACE

River Systems

Extensive river systems have always been important on the mainland of East Asia. Chinese civilization began in these river valleys, and they are still crucial to China's economic well-being.

China's Rivers

China's major rivers begin in the highlands of the Plateau of Xizang and flow eastward to the sea. The northernmost is the Huang He (HWAHNG•HUH), which flows across the North China Plain and empties into the Yellow Sea. This river is known as the Yellow River because it carries tons of fine, yellowish-brown topsoil called **loess** (LES), which is blown from the western deserts into the air and water by winds. This rich soil, along with water from the river, makes the North China Plain a rich wheat-farming area.

The Huang He is also known as "China's sorrow." For thousands of years, the river's frequent and terrible floods have destroyed

USING MAPS

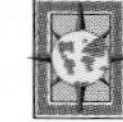

Answers:
1. Mongolia; **2.** Macao and Hong Kong; **3.** Chang Jiang; **4.** the Northeast and North China plains in China and along the coasts

Map Skills Practice
Reading a Map What mountains help form the boundary between southern China and the rest of Asia? *(the Himalayas)*

Global Gourmet

In the past, Japanese emperors set aside sections of Japan's Nagara River as private preserves for *ayu*—a sweet-tasting, troutlike fish that emperors and shoguns especially liked.

ASSESS

CHECK FOR UNDERSTANDING

Assign Section 1 Review as homework or an in-class activity.

DID YOU KNOW?

In 1995 explorers discovered what they termed "Stone Age" horses in a Tibetan valley. The ancient breed of horse resembled horses in prehistoric cave paintings. Scientists believe that the valley's 16,000-foot-high (4,877-m) walls kept the breed isolated from others, thus preserving its characteristics.

Meeting Special Needs

Language Delayed Students with language concept problems will need practice in categorizing information. Direct students' attention to headings in this section, "Mountains and Lowlands," "River Systems," and "Natural Resources." After reading each section, have students think of alternate titles such as "Ranges, Plateaus, and Basins," "The Economic Importance of Rivers," and "Riches on the Land and in the Water."

MEETING LESSON OBJECTIVES

Each objective below is tested by the questions that follow it in parentheses.

1. Locate the variety of landscapes in East Asia. *(2, 4)*

2. Describe the importance of East Asian rivers. *(3, 5)*

3. Discuss natural resources of East Asia. *(5)*

EVALUATE

Assign the Section 1 Quiz in the TCR.

Use the Testmaker to create a customized quiz for Section 1.

USING ILLUSTRATIONS

PLACE The northern agricultural area that the Huang He flows through produces wheat.

Answer to Caption: *It carries tons of yellowish-brown topsoil called loess.*

MULTICULTURAL PERSPECTIVE

Cultural Heritage

A Chinese myth tells about Pan Gu, the first man. According to the legend, "His hair became the forests and meadows, his perspiration the rain, his breath the wind, his voice the thunder—and his fleas our ancestors."

villages and towns, killing hundreds of thousands of people.

The Chang Jiang, Asia's longest river, flows 3,964 miles (6,378 km) through mountains and across fertile plains. It empties into the East China Sea.

The basin the Chang Jiang and its tributaries form is China's "rice bowl." More than half of China's crops grow here, especially rice and other grains.

A third major river, the Xi (SHEE), or West, crosses southeastern China and flows into the South China Sea near Guangzhou (GWANG•JOH). There it has built up a delta of fertile soil. Farmers in this warm region grow rice and other food crops, often growing two crops on the same piece of land, one after the other.

China also has the world's longest artificial waterway. The Grand Canal runs from Beijing (BAY•JING), the capital, to Hangzhou, a distance of 1,114 miles (1,792 km).

Japan and Korea

In contrast to the long rivers of China, Japan and Korea have many short, swift-flowing rivers that run from the mountains to the sea. They flow through deep valleys with forested hillsides, often forming spectacular waterfalls.

Geographic Themes

Place: Huang He Valley

The Huang He flows through one of China's important agricultural and industrial areas. *Why is the Huang He River also known as the Yellow River?*

HUMAN/ENVIRONMENT INTERACTION

Natural Resources

East Asia is rich in minerals, forests, and other resources, but they are distributed unevenly among the countries. Because of its great land area, China has the most abundant supplies of natural resources.

Mineral Resources

The continent of Asia, as a whole, has the largest reserves of coal in the world. Although more than half the world's coal is in Russia, China is the third-largest coal producer in the world. Nearly all parts of China have coal deposits, but the richest are in the north, especially Manchuria. China also has petroleum reserves as well as tin, tungsten, and bauxite deposits.

Like the neighboring region of Manchuria, the Korean Peninsula has good mineral resources. They include iron ore, coal, gold, and copper.

Japan is East Asia's leading industrial country, but mineral resources are scarce in its islands. It does have coal, copper, some iron ore, and a few other minerals. Still, Japan must import a variety of minerals.

Land and Forest Resources

Asia's many mountains provide little available land that is flat enough or rich enough for farming and growing food. In China, only about 11 percent of the land—most of it in the north—can be used for growing crops. Larger areas in western China and Mongolia are grasslands where animals can graze. The soil in much of north China's farmland is made up of thick deposits of loess blown from the Gobi. Loess can also pile up and form thick, rounded cliffs. Since ancient times, people in areas of northern China have dug cave homes in such loess cliffs.

Forests once covered huge areas of China, but over many centuries, the Chinese people have cut down trees for heating, building, and

Critical Thinking

Determining Cause and Effect Organize the class into three groups. Assign one of the following to each group: Mongolia, the eastern lowlands of China, or South Korea and Japan. Then ask each group to research the diet of the people in its area, focusing on local food-production activities. Ask each group to create a presentation that explains how climate, physical geography, and other natural factors affect what the people of the area eat.

Geographic Themes

Place: Inland Sea, Japan

Hundreds of hilly, wooded islands dot Japan's beautiful Inland Sea, which separates Honshu from Shikoku. *Why are the people of East Asia so dependent on the sea?*

other uses. Today, about 12 percent of the country is forested.

In Japan farmland is very scarce. Japanese farmers try to make good use of every inch of land, and they have the most efficient agriculture in Asia. While urban areas are crowded and farmland is scarce, most of the steep hillsides of Japan are still covered with thick forests. Some trees supply lumber for building.

Korea's best farmland is on the coastal plain in the south. Many trees have been cleared for farmland, but forests still grow in the mountains.

Farmers use about one-third of the land on the island of Taiwan, growing rice and tropical fruits like bananas and pineapples. About half of the island is thickly forested mountains.

Water and Ocean Resources

For thousands of years, farmers in East Asia have depended on water from the rivers for irrigating their fields. Where the weather is warm enough, irrigation lets farmers grow two or three crops a year. The rivers also carry fertile soil and deposit it on the flood plains and in deltas.

Because farmland is scarce throughout East Asia, island nations and coastal areas depend on the oceans as an important food source. Their fishing fleets bring back food both for people at home and for export. Japan is one of the world's two main fish producers, while China ranks third.

Section 1 Review

Checking for Understanding

1. **Define** archipelago, tsunami, loess.
2. **Locating Places** In what countries is the Gobi located?
3. **Place** What are China's three major rivers?
4. **Location** Which nations of East Asia are located on islands?

Critical Thinking

5. **Expressing Problems Clearly** How has the Huang He both helped and hurt the people of northern China?

RETEACH

Have students complete Workbook Activity 26-1 found in the TCR.

ENRICH

Order *sashimi* (uncooked fish) and *sushi* (cooked or uncooked fish with vinegar) from a local sushi bar or specialty grocery and have the class examine it.

CLOSE

Have students write a postcard to Ema, describing either a small or large city in the United States.

USING ILLUSTRATIONS

PLACE The Japanese harvest more than fish from the sea. An important ingredient in many Japanese dishes is *konbu*—giant kelp, or seaweed.

Answer to Caption: *Farmland is scarce so they depend on oceans for food.*

PHYSICAL GEOGRAPHY OF THE WORLD TRANSPARENCIES

Display and discuss the physical features of the following transparencies:

62. Plateau of Tibet, China
65. Gobi, Mongolia
70. Kobe, Japan

ANSWERS TO SECTION 1 REVIEW

1. **archipelago:** an island group; **tsunami:** sea wave caused by an undersea earthquake; **loess:** a fine, yellowish-brown topsoil
2. China and Mongolia
3. Huang He, Chang Jiang, Xi
4. Japan, Taiwan
5. The river deposits rich soil on farmland, but it also causes frequent and devastating floods.

FOCUS

SECTION OBJECTIVES

1. Name the different climate regions in East Asia.
2. Explain how seasonal winds affect climates in East Asia.
3. Describe the kinds of plants and trees that grow in different parts of East Asia.

BELLRINGER MOTIVATIONAL ACTIVITY

Project the Section 2 Focus Transparency and have students answer the questions.

PRETEACHING VOCABULARY

Explain that *typhoon* is the English version of a Chinese term *tai-fung*, which means "great wind."

DID YOU KNOW?

Mongolia is known as the "Land of Blue Sky" because it averages 257 cloudless days a year. Although the winters can be bitter, little snow falls because the climate is so dry.

CURRICULUM CONNECTION

BOTANY

Japanese city dwellers bring the countryside to their cramped living spaces by growing dwarfed trees called bonsai.

SECTION 2

The Climate and Vegetation

SETTING THE SCENE

Read to Discover . . .
- the different climate regions in East Asia.
- how seasonal winds affect climates in East Asia.
- the kinds of plants and trees that grow in different parts of East Asia.

Key Terms
- monsoon
- typhoon

Identify and Locate
Japan Current, Climate regions: humid continental, humid subtropical, steppe, desert, highland, tropical rain forest

East Asia has a large landmass. In latitude, it spans a greater range than the contiguous United States. Heilongjiang (HAY•LUNG•jee•AHNG) Province in northern Manchuria is about as far north as Hudson Bay in Canada, while the Chinese island of Hainan is at about the same latitude as Mexico City. As the *People's Republic of China Yearbook* says:

When Heilongjiang Province in the north is snow-bound in winter, it is stifling hot on the islands in the South China Sea. And when the sun rises over the Wusuli River in the east, it is still night on the Pamir Plateau in the west.

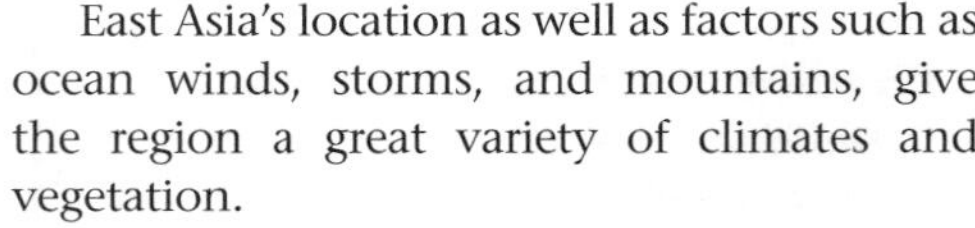

East Asia's location as well as factors such as ocean winds, storms, and mountains, give the region a great variety of climates and vegetation.

REGION

East Asia's Climate Regions

Much of East Asia is in one of the mid-latitude climate zones, while the rest is generally divided among highland, desert, and steppe climates. Small parts of northern Mongolia are subarctic. Small areas in southern China are tropical rain forest.

Monsoons

As in South Asia, the seasonal winds called **monsoons** have a great effect on East Asia's climate. In the summer, warm monsoon winds blow from the Pacific. They bring hot, humid weather and soaking downpours of rain, especially near the coast. Most rain falls between April and October.

In the fall and winter, the winds switch direction. Icy winds blow from Siberia and Mongolia. Because of these winds, winters in monsoon areas of China are colder and drier than in other countries at the same latitudes. When these cold winds blow across the Sea of Japan, however, they pick up moisture and bring heavy snow to northern Japan.

The monsoons are necessary to life in Asia, especially for farmers to grow crops. If the summer monsoons are late or do not bring enough rain, even the coastal plains in northern China may have droughts.

Violent hurricanes called **typhoons** also blow across coastal East Asia from the Pacific Ocean. Most occur between late August and October. High winds and heavy rains can do great damage, but typhoons also may bring welcome rain in the dry season.

Classroom Resources for Section 2

BLACKLINE MASTERS:
- Reproducible Lesson Plan 26-2
- Guided Reading Activity 26-2
- Spanish Guided Reading Activity 26-2
- Workbook Activity 26-2
- Vocabulary Activity 26
- Skill Activity 26
- Enrichment Activity 26
- Section Quiz 26-2

TRANSPARENCIES:
- Section Focus Transparency 26-2
- Unit Map Overlay Transparencies 9-2 and 9-3

MULTIMEDIA:

- Testmaker

Ocean Currents

Ocean currents also influence the climate of island countries in East Asia. The warm-water Japan Current flows along the southern and southeastern coasts of the Japanese islands, making winters milder there.

Along the coasts of Hokkaido, the northernmost island of Japan, the cold Okhotsk Current flows from the Arctic. It brings harsh, cold winters to Hokkaido.

Mid-latitude Climates

Southeastern China, southern Korea, Taiwan, and the southern islands of Japan have a humid subtropical climate. Summers here are

Geographic Themes

Place: Hokkaido, Japan
Winters are cold and snowy in the northern part of the Japanese archipelago. *What type of climate is found in southern Japan?*

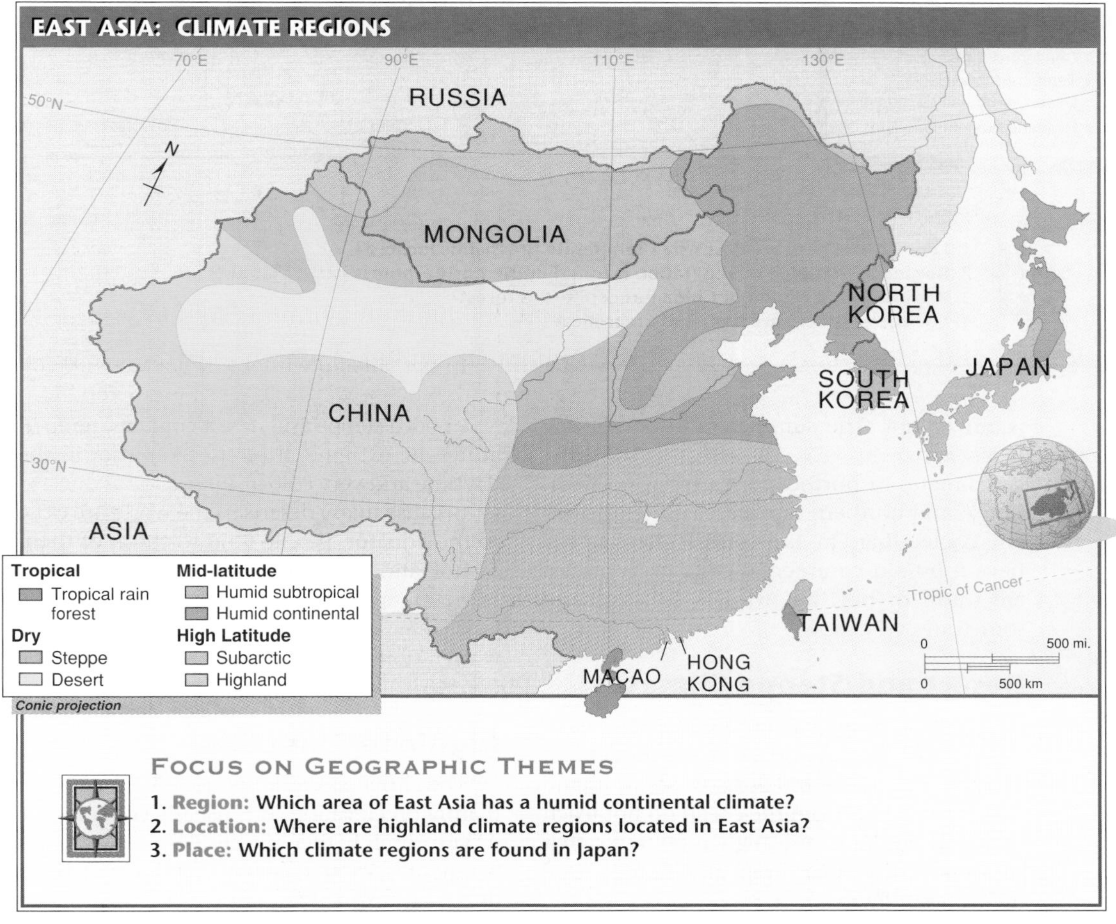

FOCUS ON GEOGRAPHIC THEMES

1. **Region:** Which area of East Asia has a humid continental climate?
2. **Location:** Where are highland climate regions located in East Asia?
3. **Place:** Which climate regions are found in Japan?

TEACH

GUIDED PRACTICE

L1 Identify After students read the section, have them identify the vegetation in each climate zone on Unit Map Overlay Transparency 9-3. Project Unit Map Overlay Transparency 9-2 to check the students' accuracy.

INDEPENDENT PRACTICE

Guided Reading Have students complete Guided Reading Activity 26-2 in the TCR. **LEP**

USING ILLUSTRATIONS

PLACE After a harsh winter, Japan celebrates Greenery Day on April 29.

Answer to Caption: *humid subtropical*

USING MAPS

Answers:
1. northeastern China, northern Japan, North Korea and the northern part of South Korea, and a small part of northeastern Mongolia;
2. southwestern China;
3. humid subtropical and humid continental

Map Skills Practice
Reading a Map What word describes the climate in most of Mongolia? *(dry)*

Cooperative Learning Activity

Tell students that *haiku* is an unrhymed Japanese lyric poem. *Haiku* has a fixed three-line form consisting of five, seven, and five syllables, respectively. Read the following *haiku* to the students.

Slender, silver grove
Bamboo, filtering sunlight
Whisper ancient myths.

Then have them select a photograph from the chapter and write a *haiku* about it. Tell them to focus on climate or vegetation shown in the picture. Make copies of the finished *haikus* and bind them into booklets. Distribute the booklets to the class.

ASSESS

CHECK FOR UNDERSTANDING

Assign Section 2 Review as homework or an in-class activity.

MEETING LESSON OBJECTIVES

Each objective below is tested by the questions that follow it in parentheses.

1. Name the different climate regions in East Asia. *(2)*

2. Explain how seasonal winds affect climates in East Asia. *(3, 4)*

3. Describe the kinds of plants and trees that grow in different parts of East Asia. *(5)*

EVALUATE

Assign the Section 2 Quiz in the TCR.

Use the Testmaker to create a customized quiz for Section 2.

USING MAPS

Answers:
1. Mongolia and northern China; **2.** coniferous forest; **3.** the northern border; **4.** western and south central China

Map Skills Practice

Reading a Map Where is desert vegetation in East Asia? *(central China)*

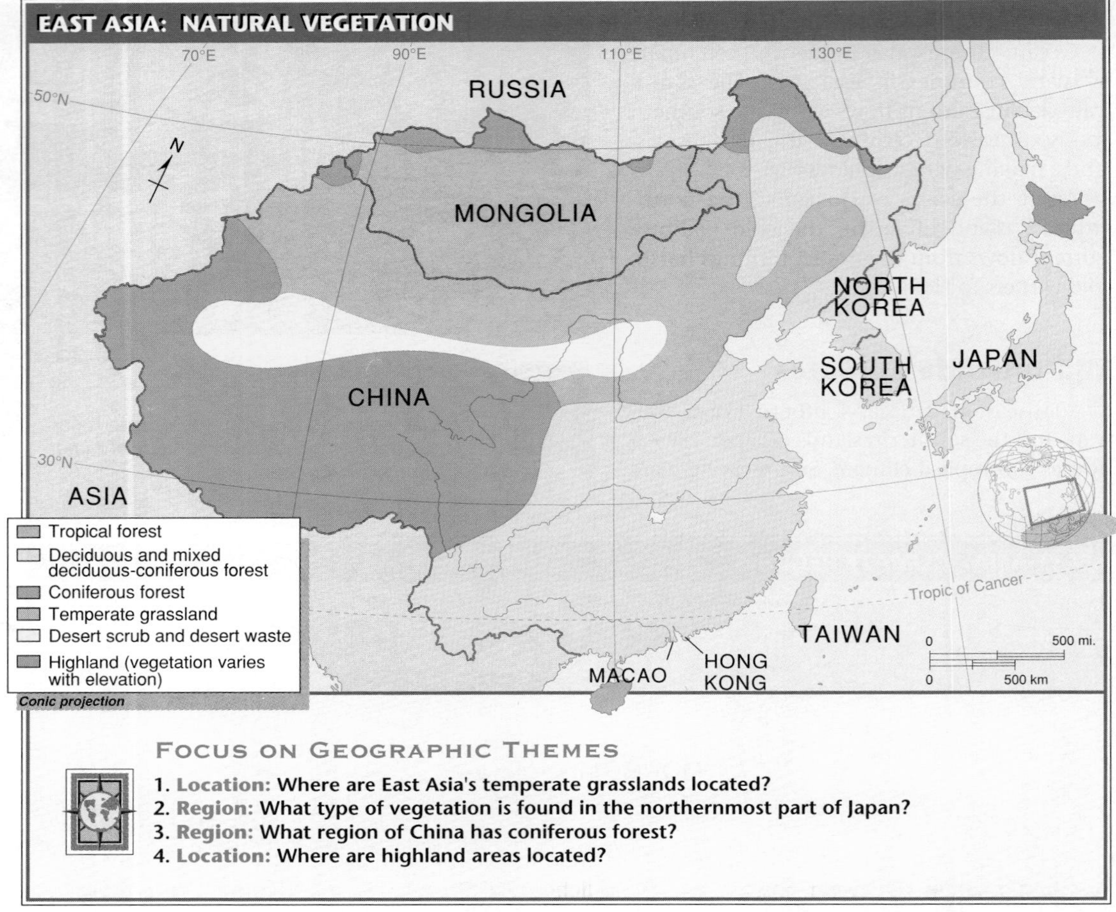

Focus on Geographic Themes

1. **Location: Where are East Asia's temperate grasslands located?**
2. **Region: What type of vegetation is found in the northernmost part of Japan?**
3. **Region: What region of China has coniferous forest?**
4. **Location: Where are highland areas located?**

warm or hot. The summer monsoons bring heavy rains.

Climates in northeastern China, northern Korea, and northern Japan are still temperate, but cooler than in the south. These places have a humid continental climate. Summers are warm or hot, but winters are cold and sometimes very snowy.

Desert and Steppe Climates

Much of Mongolia and the inland areas of northern China have dry climates—desert and steppe. These great arid areas lie so far inland that moist winds from the ocean do not reach them. In addition, the high mountains that surround these areas trap any rainfall that might reach them.

In both steppe and desert climates, temperatures are extreme. It often is very hot in the daytime and very cold at night.

Because many deserts in the world are close to the Equator, people tend to think of them as hot and dry. The Gobi and Taklamakan, however, are often cold and windy. While the Gobi may have summer heat waves, average winter temperatures there are only 10°F (–12°C).

Highland Climates

The climate in mountainous areas depends mainly on elevation. It is usually cool or cold. As you climb higher, the air temperature drops by about 3.5°F (2°C) every 1,000 feet (305 m) of elevation. For example, the Plateau of

Meeting Special Needs

Language Delayed Students with difficulty categorizing information will find it helpful to use a framework for comparing climate zones. Develop categories for these comparisons such as temperature, precipitation, and vegetation. Direct students in searching for information that might be included in these categories. Then point out that some information needed to complete this task is not included in Chapter 26.

Xizang averages more than 13,000 to 15,000 feet (3,962 to 4,572 m) in elevation. Even in summer, average temperatures there are only about 58°F (14°C).

Tropical Climates

A small strip of land along China's southern coast, part of Taiwan, and the island of Hainan have a tropical rain forest climate. Here it is hot year-round, with a rainy season brought by the summer monsoons.

Geographic Themes

Place: Southern China
A small part of southern China has a tropical climate with warm temperatures and plenty of rain. *How does the climate of northern China compare with that in southern China?*

REGION

East Asia's Vegetation

Forests once covered more of East Asia than they do today. Over thousands of years, however, forests have been cut for timber and cleared for farms. In many places, this has led to serious erosion problems on hillsides and along river valleys.

Vegetation in the Middle Latitudes

In the mid-latitude climate of most of East Asia, forests are a mix of needleleaf evergreen trees, or conifers; broad-leaved deciduous trees; and broad-leaved evergreens.

Both deciduous trees and broad-leaved evergreens grow in humid subtropical climates. Bamboos, which are not trees but tree-like grasses, grow in many warm areas of East Asia. Other valuable plants are the tea bush and the mulberry tree, whose leaves provide food for silkworms.

Tropical Vegetation

Where the climate is tropical, palms and tropical hardwoods grow along with broad-leaved evergreens and tropical fruits such as bananas. A lush rain forest covers much of the tropical island of Hainan.

Steppe and Highland Vegetation

Natural vegetation on the steppe is mainly grasses and a few trees. Many of the original forests have been cut, leaving grasses and shrubs that can grow in the dry climate.

The lower slopes of mountains may have small alpine meadows with grass, flowers, and trees. Above a certain elevation—the treeline—trees cannot grow. Vegetation is similar to that found on the tundra. Mosses and colorful lichens grow on the rocky slopes.

SECTION 2 REVIEW

Checking for Understanding

1. **Define** monsoon, typhoon.
2. **Locating Places** In what two climate zones is Japan located?
3. **Region** How do the monsoons affect climate in much of East Asia?
4. **Place** What are the summers like in southern Korea and southeastern China?

Critical Thinking

5. **Determining Cause and Effect** Why do northern China and Mongolia have a steppe climate and vegetation?

USING ILLUSTRATIONS

PLACE China's climate is similar to that in the United States.

Answer to Caption: *Northern China has steppe, humid continental, and subarctic climates, whereas southern China has humid subtropical and tropical rain forest climates.*

RETEACH

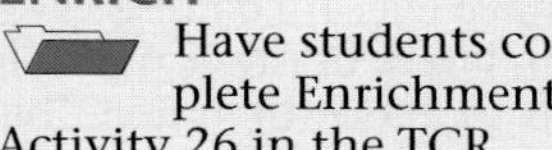

Have students complete Reteaching Activity 26 in the TCR.

ENRICH

Have students complete Enrichment Activity 26 in the TCR.

CLOSE

Ask a student to name an East Asian country, and have the class identify its climate types and vegetation.

ANSWERS TO SECTION 2 REVIEW

1. **monsoon:** seasonal wind; **typhoon:** hurricane that forms in the Pacific Ocean
2. humid continental and humid subtropical
3. Summer monsoon winds blow from the Pacific and bring heavy rain and hot weather; winter monsoons blow from Siberia and bring cold, usually dry, weather.
4. hot and humid with heavy rainfall
5. They are located far inland and get little moisture from the oceans, high mountains block rainfall, and countries at high latitudes are cool.

TEACH

Have students read the skill on page 546. Then ask: "What is the purpose of a contour map?" *(to show the shape of the land)* "What are isolines?" *(lines that connect all the points at the same elevation)* "How are steep areas shown on a contour map?" *(The isolines are close together.)*

If available, show students a contour map of a local geographic area such as a state park. Have students identify peaks, valleys, cliffs, plains, the direction of waterflow in rivers, and so on. Have them use the map to plan a hike. Ask students if they have ever hiked in a national park or other natural area. If so, have them describe the maps they used on this hike.

Skills Practice For additional practice, have students complete Skill Activity 26 in the TCR.

MAP & GRAPH SKILLS

Interpreting a Contour Map

If you went hiking in the mountains, what kind of map would help you find your way? A trail map would show the paths you could follow. But how would you know if the trail follows a gentle easy route, or cuts straight up the side of a mountain? To get this kind of information, you need a **contour map.**

REVIEWING THE SKILL

Contour maps use lines, called **isolines**, to describe the shape, or contour, of the landscape. Isolines connect all the points that are at the same elevation. The number on each isoline indicates its elevation. If you walked along one isoline, you would always be at the same height above sea level.

The relationship of the isolines to one another indicates the slope of the terrain. Where the lines are far apart, the land rises gradually. Where the lines are close together, the land rises steeply. Rivers often flow through valleys between mountains and hills. Because they outline the topography of an area, contour maps are also called **topographic maps.**

When interpreting a contour map, apply the following steps:

- Identify the area shown in the map.
- Read the labels on the isolines to determine how much the elevation increases with each line.
- Locate the highest and lowest points on the map.
- Figure out which areas have the most gradual and steepest grades.

PRACTICING THE SKILL

Study the contour map below and then answer the following questions:

1. What area is shown on the map?
2. What is the interval, or difference, between each isoline?
3. What is the highest point on Taiwan?
4. Which side of Taiwan has the steepest topography?
5. Which cities are located more than 1,000 feet (305 meters) above sea level?
6. If you were to hike to the top of Hsinkao Shan, what would be the most gradual route?
7. If you hiked straight up Hsinkao Shan from the city of Taitung, how many miles would you walk? On this route, how much elevation would you gain for every mile you walk?

For additional practice in this skill, see Practicing Skills on page 548 of the Chapter 26 Review.

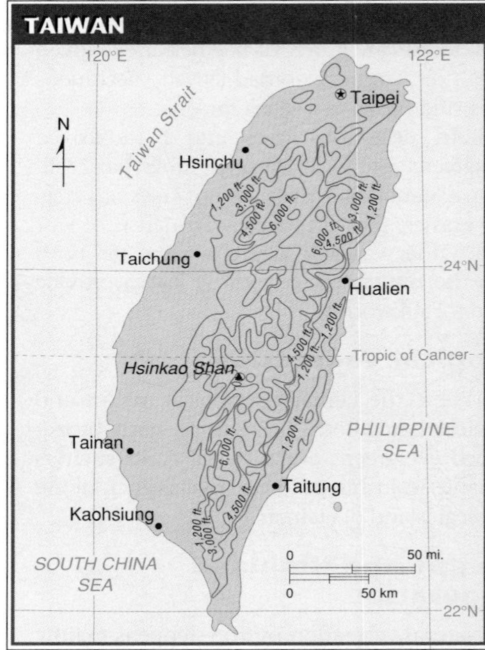

ANSWERS TO PRACTICING THE SKILL

1. Taiwan
2. first line is 1,200 feet (400 meters); next isoline is 1,800 feet (600 meters) higher; others are 1,500-foot (500 meter) intervals
3. Hsinkao Shan
4. east side
5. none
6. Although routes may vary, students should begin on the flat western plain, continue along the western side of mountain, and finally walk along the central ridge to the peak.
7. about 50 miles (75 km); about 100 feet per mile

chapter 26

HIGHLIGHTS

SECTION 1 The Land

KEY TERMS

archipelago (p. 538)
tsunami (p. 538)
loess (p. 539)

Japan's Inland Sea

SUMMARY

- The region of East Asia is made up of China, Mongolia, and North and South Korea on the continent of Asia, and two island nations, Japan and Taiwan.
- China occupies 90 percent of the land area in East Asia. Other nations occupy peninsulas and islands.
- Mainland East Asia has mountains and highlands in the west, plateaus and basins in the central and northern regions, and coastal plains in the east.
- Because so much of East Asia is mountainous, population and cities are densely crowded on the coastal plains.
- East Asia is rich in minerals, but they are unevenly distributed and sometimes poorly located.
- Because population pressure is high and farmland is limited, the ocean is an important food source for East Asia.

SECTION 2 The Climate and Vegetation

KEY TERMS

monsoon (p. 542)
typhoon (p. 542)

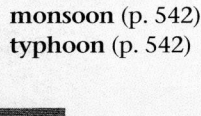

Tropical vegetation and village in southern China

SUMMARY

- East Asia has a wide variety of climates because of its great land area.
- Seasonal monsoon winds have a major influence on climates in East Asia.
- Much of East Asia is in the middle latitudes with humid continental or humid subtropical climates.
- Inland steppe and desert areas have dry climates with extremes of hot and cold temperatures.
- Many parts of East Asia, especially Japan, North and South Korea, and Taiwan, are thickly forested.

CHAPTER 26 HIGHLIGHTS

USING THE CHAPTER 26 HIGHLIGHTS

Use the Chapter 26 Highlights to preview, review, condense, or reteach the chapter.

PREVIEW/REVIEW

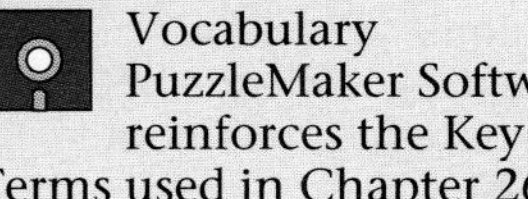

Vocabulary PuzzleMaker Software reinforces the Key Terms used in Chapter 26.

Student Self-Test and Review Software allows students to review Chapter 26 content.

CONDENSE

Have students read the Chapter 26 Highlights.

Have students listen to the Chapter 26 Audiocassettes in the TCR. Spanish Audiocassettes are also available.

Assign the Chapter 26 Audiocassette Activity and give the students the Chapter 26 Audiocassette Quiz.

Have students complete Guided Reading Activities for Chapter 26 in the TCR. Spanish Guided Reading Activities are also available.

RETEACH

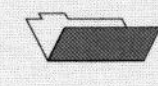 

Have students complete Reteaching Activity 26 in the TCR. Spanish Reteaching Activities are also available.

Map Activity

Identify and Locate Copy and distribute page 35 of the Outline Map Resource Book. On the map, have students locate and label China, Japan, North Korea, South Korea, Mongolia, Taiwan, the Gobi, the Himalayas, the Huang He, the Chang Jiang, the Xi River, and the Japan Current.

GLENCOE TECHNOLOGY

Videodisc

Use Chapter 26 MindJogger Videoquiz to review students' knowledge before administering the Chapter 26 Test.

MINDJOGGER VIDEOQUIZ

Chapter 26
Disc 4 Side A

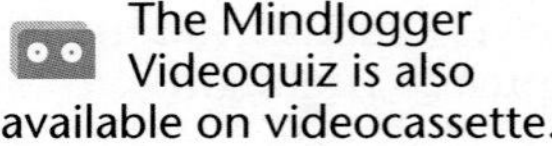

The MindJogger Videoquiz is also available on videocassette.

ANSWERS

Reviewing Key Terms

1. loess
2. tsunami
3. archipelago
4. typhoon
5. monsoon

Reviewing Facts

6. the Tibetan plateau
7. Huang He, Chang Jiang, Xi
8. Honshu
9. coal
10. Because farmland is scarce, the ocean is a valuable source of food.
11. In summer they blow from the warm oceans and bring warmth and moisture; in winter they blow from the cold mainland of Siberia and bring cold, dry air.
12. It warms the southern coast of Japan.
13. A humid subtropical climate has warm or hot summers and mild winters. Southeastern China, South Korea, Taiwan, and southern Japan
14. The steppe is dry, has cold winters and warm or hot summers, and grasses and scattered trees grow there.

chapter 26 REVIEW

Reviewing Key Terms

Choose the vocabulary term that best completes each of the sentences below. Write your answers on a separate sheet of paper.

archipelago (p. 538)
tsunami (p. 538)
loess (p. 539)
monsoon (p. 542)
typhoon (p. 542)

SECTION 1

1. Farmlands in eastern China are richer because of thick deposits of ____ carried by wind and water.
2. A ____ caused by an earthquake can do great damage to coastal areas.
3. Like Japan, the Ryukyu Islands are an ____ .

SECTION 2

4. In Asia, a violent tropical hurricane is known as a ____ .
5. China is cold and dry in the winter because of ____ winds from Siberia.

Reviewing Facts

SECTION 1

6. What highland area covers much of western China?
7. What are China's three great rivers?
8. Which is the largest and most densely populated of the Japanese islands?
9. What is China's richest energy resource?
10. Why are the oceans a valuable resource for East Asian countries?

SECTION 2

11. What is the pattern of monsoon winds in East Asia?
12. How does the Japan Current influence climate in Japan?
13. What are the characteristics of a humid subtropical climate? What parts of East Asia have this climate?
14. What are the climate and vegetation like on the steppes of East Asia?

Critical Thinking

15. **Predicting Consequences** China and East Asia are separated from the rest of Asia by steep mountains and highlands. How might this have affected the ways in which East Asian cultures developed?
16. **Making Comparisons** How do climate and vegetation differ between northern and southern China? Why?

Geographic Themes

17. **Interaction** How have the Huang He and Chang Jiang been important to the people of China?
18. **Location** What is the most important factor in the climate of a mountain region?

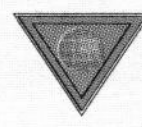

Practicing Skills

Interpreting a Contour Map

Refer to the contour map on page 546.

19. If you were to hike to the top of Hsinkao Shan, what would be the steepest route that you would take on your trip?
20. Look at the locations of the cities shown on the contour map. In what general areas are they located? Why are no major cities located on the central portion of the map?

Using the Unit Atlas

Refer to the cultural geography section of the Unit Atlas on pages 530–531.

21. Where do about 75 percent of most Chinese people live?
22. How vast was the Mongol Empire?
23. What kind of culture is dominant in Japan today?

Critical Thinking

15. Answers should point out that East Asians probably devised customs and cultures independent of outside influences.
16. Northern China has a humid continental climate with evergreens and broadleaf trees; southern China has a humid subtropical climate with deciduous and broadleaf evergreens. Differences depend on both latitude and the pattern of monsoons.

Geographic Themes

17. Both rivers bring good soil for farming and water for irrigation; they also have great floodplains where most Chinese live.
18. elevation or altitude

Projects

Individual Activity

You have read about the three great rivers that have been important in China. Choose one of those rivers—Huang He, Chang Jiang, or Xi—and research its individual profile: Where does it begin and end? Through what kind of terrain does it flow? How does the river influence the people who live near it? Has the river changed over time? How? Prepare a short oral or written report telling what you have discovered about the river.

Cooperative Learning Activity

Work with two or three classmates to prepare questions for a game of Geography Jeopardy that the whole class can play. As in the television quiz show, players are given the answer and must supply the question. Organize your "answers" into at least five different categories, such as "Rivers," "Begins with *T*," or "Climate Regions." For example, in the category "Begins with *T*," players might be given this answer: This island nation is located in the East China Sea. (The appropriate response is "What is Taiwan?")

Writing About Geography

Description

The environment of East Asia helped the peoples of the region to develop unique civilizations. Consult your journal, text, and reference sources to find out how landforms and bodies of water have shaped the countries of the region. Select one country and describe how its physical features might affect the lifestyles of its people.

Locating Places

EAST ASIA: PHYSICAL GEOGRAPHY

Match the letters on the map with the places and physical features of East Asia. Write your answers on a separate sheet of paper.

1. Tibetan Plateau
2. Mongolia
3. Korean Peninsula
4. Honshu
5. Yellow Sea
6. Huang He
7. Yangzi River
8. Taiwan
9. North China Plain
10. Himalayas

Chapter 26 Review

Practicing Skills

19. The steepest route would be from the northeast.

20. mountains; few, if any, inhabitants because of the high elevation

Using the Unit Atlas

21. rural villages

22. from eastern Asia to eastern Europe

23. a mixture of Eastern and Western cultures

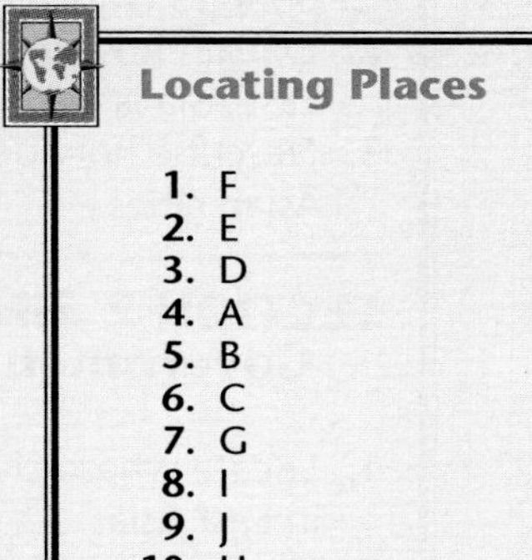
Locating Places

1. F
2. E
3. D
4. A
5. B
6. C
7. G
8. I
9. J
10. H

Chapter Bonus Test Question

This question may be used for extra credit on the chapter test. Choose the letter of the correct response.

Which place is hot year-round and covered with broadleaf evergreens?

(1) the island of Hainan
(2) northeastern China
(3) the island of Hokkaido
(4) northern Korea

(Answer: 1)

CHAPTER 27

PLANNING GUIDE

The Cultural Geography of East Asia

CHAPTER ORGANIZER

Daily Lesson Objectives	Multimedia	Teacher Classroom Resources
SECTION 1 Population Patterns 1. Name the different ethnic peoples who live in East Asia. 2. Explain how the population of East Asia is distributed. 3. Describe how people live in East Asian cities.	Section Focus Transparency 27-1 Chapter 27 Vocabulary PuzzleMaker Software Unit Map Overlay Transparency 9 Testmaker	Reproducible Lesson Plan 27-1 Guided Reading Activity 27-1 Spanish Guided Reading Activity 27-1 Workbook Activity 27-1 Performance Assessment Activity 27 Section Quiz 27-1
SECTION 2 History and Government 1. Locate where civilization began in East Asia. 2. Discuss how ideas spread from the Chinese Empire throughout East Asia. 3. Illustrate how East Asia has changed in the 20th century.	Section Focus Transparency 27-2 Political Map Transparency 9 Geography and the Environment Testmaker	Reproducible Lesson Plan 27-2 Guided Reading Activity 27-2 Spanish Guided Reading Activity 27-2 Workbook Activity 27-2 Vocabulary Activity 27 Section Quiz 27-2
SECTION 3 Cultures and Lifestyles 1. Identify the languages and the religions of the peoples of East Asia. 2. Analyze how standards of living differ among countries in East Asia. 3. Understand the importance of arts and leisure activities in the countries of East Asia.	Section Focus Transparency 27-3 World Cultures Transparencies 15 and 16 World Music: Cultural Traditions, Lesson 8 Testmaker Picture Atlas of the World	Reproducible Lesson Plan 27-3 Guided Reading Activity 27-3 Spanish Guided Reading Activity 27-3 Workbook Activity 27-3 Skill Activity 27 Enrichment Activity 27 Foods Around the World 8 World Literature Reading 8 Section Quiz 27-3
CHAPTER REVIEW AND EVALUATION	Chapter 27 English (or Spanish) Audiocassettes MindJogger Videoquiz Testmaker Student Self-Test and Review Software	Reteaching Activity 27 Spanish Reteaching Activity 27 Chapter 27 Test Form A and Form B

0:00 *If time does not permit teaching the entire chapter, summarize using the Chapter 27 Highlights on page 567, and the Chapter 27 English (or Spanish) Audiocassettes. Review students' knowledge using the Glencoe MindJogger Videoquiz.*

KEY TO ABILITY LEVELS

Teaching strategies have been coded for varying learning styles and abilities.

L1 **BASIC** activities for all students

L2 **AVERAGE** activities for average to above-average students

L3 **CHALLENGING** activities for above-average students

LEP **LIMITED ENGLISH PROFICIENCY** activities

Performance Assessment

Forecasting Problems Related to Culture Check for concept understanding by having students take part in a problem-solving simulation about East Asia. Organize students into groups, and have each group select an owner, manager, concierge, and security chief for a hypothetical hotel located in a particular country of the region. Have groups name their hotels and describe the types of hotels they will be running, and the advantages for travelers.

Students should brainstorm a list of the kinds of problems that they might characteristically have to solve for their guests. These problems should demonstrate their understanding of East Asia's physical and cultural geography presented in Chapters 26 and 27. Have students create a personal anecdote that expresses how they assisted one traveler.

POSSIBLE RUBRIC FEATURES: Content information, concept attainment, application skills, problem-solving skills, narrative writing skills, creative thinking, collaborative skills

For additional professional and classroom resources, see Chapter Resources, pages T46–T51.

TEACHER'S CORNER

INDEX TO NATIONAL GEOGRAPHIC MAGAZINE

The following articles may be used for research relating to this chapter:

- "Inner Japan," by Patrick Smith, September 1994.
- "Shanghai: Where China's Past and Future Meet," by William S. Ellis, March 1994.
- "Kyushu: Japan's Southern Gateway," by Tracy Dahlby, January 1994.
- "Taiwan: The Other China Changes Course," by Arthur Zich, November 1993.
- "Hong Kong: Countdown to 1997," by Ross Terrill, February 1991.
- "Japanese Women," by Deborah Fallows, April 1990.
- "Population, Plenty, and Poverty," by Paul L. Ehrlich and Anne H. Ehrlich, December 1988.
- "The South Koreans," by Boyd Gibbons, August 1988.
- "Tokyo: A Profile of Success," by William Graves, November 1986.
- "Sichuan: Where China Changes Course," by Ross Terrill, September 1985.

NATIONAL GEOGRAPHIC SOCIETY PRODUCTS AVAILABLE FROM GLENCOE

To order the following products for use with this chapter, contact your local Glencoe sales representative or call Glencoe at 1-800-334-7344:

- *Picture Atlas of the World* (CD-ROM)
- *STV: World Geography, Asia and Australia* (Videodisc)
- *ZipZapMap! World* (Software)
- *GeoBee* (Software)
- *Images of the World* (Posters)
- *Eye on the Environment* (Posters)
- *Physical Geography of the World* (Transparencies)
- *Picture Atlas of Our 50 States* (Book)

ADDITIONAL NATIONAL GEOGRAPHIC SOCIETY PRODUCTS

To order the following products for use with this chapter, call National Geographic Society at 1-800-368-2728:

- *The People's Republic of China,* "Introducing China Today," "Living and Working in China Today," "Chinese Arts and Culture." (Filmstrip)
- *China: Sichuan Province* (Video)
- *Democratic Government Series,* "Japan." (Video)
- *Hong Kong: A Family Portrait* (Video)
- *Nations of the World Series,* "Japan." (Video)

chapter 27 The Cultural Geography of East Asia

PERFORMANCE ASSESSMENT

Refer to the Planning Guide on page 550B for a Performance Assessment Activity for this chapter. See the *Performance Assessment Activities* booklet for additional suggestions.

CHAPTER OBJECTIVES

1. **Discuss** how East Asian cultures began in river valleys.
2. **Examine** how throughout much of history, Chinese influences spread throughout the region.
3. **Recognize** that, although Chinese influence has been strong, each country in East Asia has a unique culture.

GLENCOE TECHNOLOGY

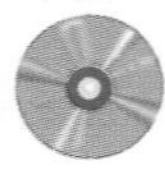

Videodisc

Use Chapter 27 MindJogger Videoquiz to preview chapter content.

MINDJOGGER VIDEOQUIZ

Chapter 27
Disc 4 Side A

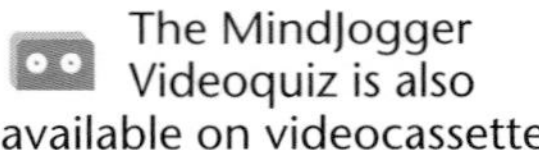

The MindJogger Videoquiz is also available on videocassette.

CHAPTER FOCUS

Geographic Setting

The geography of East Asia has greatly influenced how and where people live. The rugged mountains and plateaus are thinly populated, while the coastal plains are some of the most crowded places on the earth.

Geographic Themes

Section 1 Population Patterns
MOVEMENT East Asian cultures began in river valleys.

Section 2 History and Government
MOVEMENT Throughout much of history, Chinese influences spread throughout the region.

Section 3 Cultures and Lifestyles
REGION Although Chinese influence has been strong, each country in East Asia has a unique culture.

▲ Photograph: *Bustling Taipei, Taiwan*

EXTRA CREDIT PROJECT

Perform a Play Have interested students perform a play that they adapt from scenes in a movie about Japanese history. Suggest they draw material from Akira Kurosawa's *Ran,* about Japan's feudal period, or Steven Spielberg's *Empire of the Sun,* about a Japanese detention camp during World War II. Tell them to research *Noh* theater and to imitate its style and costumes in their play.

SECTION 1

Population Patterns

SETTING THE SCENE

Read to Discover . . .
- the different ethnic peoples who live in East Asia.
- how the population of East Asia is distributed.
- how people live in East Asian cities.

Key Terms
- ethnic group
- homogeneous
- megalopolis

Identify and Locate
Xizang (Tibet), Xinjiang, Taiwan, Hokkaido, Hong Kong, Tokyo, Yokohama

Chuncheon, South Korea

Ahnnounghaseyo! I live in Chuncheon, South Korea. In my spare time I enjoy hobbies such as swimming, playing the piano, singing, being with friends, reading, and taking long walks in the park. I like a variety of foods, such as Italian, Mexican, and American, but my favorite is Korean.

Sonmin Kim

Sonmin Kim describes the typical lifestyle of a teenager in South Korea, one of the countries in East Asia. East Asia is a region made up of many different religions, languages, and lifestyles. The majority of people in East Asia live in China, the world's most populous country.

PLACE

Human Characteristics

The East Asia culture region contains more than 1.5 billion people—a little more than 25 percent of the world's population. East Asians are members of many different **ethnic groups**—groups that share a common language, religion, ancestry, or a combination of such characteristics.

China

About 94 percent of the people of China belong to the group, or nationality, called the Han. They live mainly in eastern and southern China. The rest of China's 1.2 billion people belong to about 50 different ethnic groups. The non-Chinese peoples live mainly in the far north and west. Although they live in China, non-Chinese peoples such as the Tibetans have long cultural histories and traditions of their own.

Most of the people of Taiwan are Chinese, some of whom are descendants of Nationalist Chinese who fled the mainland after the defeat of the Nationalists by the Communists in

LESSON PLAN
Chapter 27, Section 1

FOCUS

SECTION OBJECTIVES

1. **Name** the different ethnic peoples who live in East Asia.
2. **Explain** how the population of East Asia is distributed.
3. **Describe** how people live in East Asian cities.

ABOUT THE POSTCARD

Sonmin lives in a small town surrounded by mountains, lakes, and the Soyang River. One of her favorite scenes in the area is of beautiful waterfalls.

BELLRINGER MOTIVATIONAL ACTIVITY

Project the Section 1 Focus Transparency and have students answer the questions.

PRETEACHING VOCABULARY

Explain to the class that homogenized milk is the same all through as opposed to non-homogenized milk which is part cream and part skim. Then ask students to hypothesize about what makes a people ethnically homogeneous. *(They are all the same.)*

Use the Vocabulary PuzzleMaker Software to create a crossword or word search puzzle.

Classroom Resources for Section 1

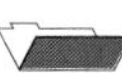

BLACKLINE MASTERS:
- Reproducible Lesson Plan 27-1
- Guided Reading Activity 27-1
- Spanish Guided Reading Activity 27-1
- Workbook Activity 27-1
- Performance Assessment Activity 27
- Section Quiz 27-1

TRANSPARENCIES:
- Section Focus Transparency 27-1
- Unit Map Overlay Transparency 9

MULTIMEDIA:

- Vocabulary PuzzleMaker Software
- Testmaker

TEACH

GUIDED PRACTICE

L1 Label Circle Graphs Help students recognize the rural/urban makeup of East Asian countries. On the chalkboard, copy the following data:
China: 27% urban
Japan: 77% urban
Mongolia: 58% urban
Then draw three unlabeled circle graphs, each reflecting the urban/rural makeup of a country listed on the board. Have students label each circle with the correct country and data.

USING ILLUSTRATIONS

PLACE About 45 percent of Japan's 125 million people live in three metropolitan areas: Tokyo, Osaka, and Nagoya.

Answer to Caption: *homogeneous*

Ways of the World

EAST ASIA When greeting others, the Japanese bow low, the Chinese nod or bow slightly, Mongolians shake hands, and Koreans bow and the men add a handshake.

a civil war that ended in 1949. A small minority are the original inhabitants of the island, who are related to the peoples of Indonesia.

Japan

Japan is ethnically **homogeneous**—of the same kind. That is, most Japanese belong to the same ethnic group. They share language, customs, and ancestry. Koreans are the largest minority group in Japan.

One minority ethnic group in Japan is the Ainu. They were probably the earliest inhabitants of the islands. When the present-day Japanese migrated from Asia, several thousand years ago, the Ainu gradually moved north. Today they live mostly on the island of Hokkaido.

Korea

Although Korea is now divided politically into North and South Korea, it had a long history as a unified nation until after World War II. The people of Korea are also a distinct ethnic group. People throughout the peninsula share a common ancestry, language, and appearance. Only about 35,000 people of foreign descent live in Korea. People of Chinese descent make up the largest non-Korean group.

Geographic Themes

Place: Tokyo, Japan

Japanese shoppers stroll on the Ginza, Tokyo's most famous street, which is known for its modern buildings and neon signs. *How are the Japanese described ethnically?*

Mongolia

The people of Mongolia are also homogeneous, with about 90 percent being Mongols. Mongols are divided into several tribes but share a common language and ancestry. About three-fourths belong to one tribe, the Khalkhas. A number of Mongol groups live across the border in northern China. Others live in Russia.

MOVEMENT

Population Distribution

Population is distributed very unevenly throughout East Asia, because much of the area is barren and mountainous. The dry, cold deserts and remote mountains are empty and almost uninhabited. The fertile river valleys and coastal plains, however, are some of the most crowded places on the earth.

China

China has almost 1.2 billion people, and more than 90 percent of them are crowded onto only one-sixth of the land. Most live in the fertile valleys and plains of China's three great rivers: the Huang He, Chang Jiang, and Xi. In this thickly settled part of China, average population density is more than 518 people per square mile (200 per sq. km).

Population is scarcest in the rugged western provinces of Xinjiang (SHIN•jee•AHNG) and Xizang. A few farmers and herders live on scattered oases.

Chinese government officials worry that the country's huge population may grow faster than the food supply. In the past, China often had serious famines in which thousands died of hunger. Today the government encourages smaller families. People with only one child are rewarded—perhaps with better income through reduced taxation or the chance to go to a good school.

Cooperative Learning Activity

Have students create first a table and then a pictograph comparing the population density of East Asian countries. On the chalkboard, copy the following incomplete table, leaving out the numbers in parentheses.

COUNTRY	POPULATION DENSITY People per square mile [sq. km]
China	(331 [128])
Japan	(859 [331])
South Korea	(1,170 [452])
Mongolia	(4 [2])
Taiwan	(1,517 [586])
Hong Kong	(14,000 [5,405])

Have students scan pages 552 and 553 for the data to complete the table. Then have them use the table to make a pictograph comparing the countries' population density.

Japan

Japan, with a much smaller land area, is even more crowded than China. Forested mountains cover the center of the Japanese islands. Most of its 125 million people, therefore, live in the valleys and on coastal plains at the base of the mountains. As in most other industrial nations, population growth is slow.

The average population density in Japan is about 850 people per square mile (328 per sq. km). Around large cities, however, population density is much greater.

Japan has few uninhabited areas like those in China. The northern island of Hokkaido, which is rural and mountainous, still has a population density of about 250 people per square mile (96 per sq. km).

Korea

In both North and South Korea, most people live on the coastal plains. The two nations are quite different, however.

Only about 34 percent of Koreans live in the north. Even though its population is growing rapidly, North Korea is short of workers. More than 3 million people have migrated to South Korea since the Korean War in the early 1950s.

The rest of the people of the divided peninsula live in South Korea, making it another crowded country. Average population density is about 1,170 people per square mile (452 per sq. km).

Mongolia

With much of its land covered by deserts and mountains, Mongolia's small population of 2.4 million is spread thinly over the broad steppes. Population density for the country as a whole is only about 4 people per square mile (2 per sq. km). About one-fourth of Mongolia's people live in the capital, Ulan Bator, which is located in a river basin.

Taiwan and Hong Kong

By contrast the island nation of Taiwan has a population density of about 1,517 people per square mile (586 per sq. km). As in Japan, most people live in cities on the coastal plain rather than in the wooded mountains in the center of the island.

The prosperous United Kingdom colony of Hong Kong includes two islands and mainland territory, a total of less than 400 square miles (1,036 sq. km). Almost 6 million people are squeezed into this small area—a density of about 14,000 people per square mile (5,405 per sq. km).

Geographic Themes

Place: Seoul, South Korea

Since the mid-1950s, South Korea's capital of Seoul has grown into a busy, modern city. *How does Seoul rank among the world's cities in terms of population and living conditions?*

HUMAN/ENVIRONMENT INTERACTION

Urbanization

The mountainous or dry nature of the land in East Asia and the attraction of cities have caused millions of people to crowd into large, urban industrial areas. Small farming villages, however, are still an important part of life in East Asia.

INDEPENDENT PRACTICE

Guided Reading Have students complete Guided Reading Activity 27-1 in the TCR. **LEP**

Have students complete Unit Map Overlay Transparency 9 Activity in the TCR.

ASSESS

CHECK FOR UNDERSTANDING

Assign Section 1 Review as homework or an in-class activity.

MEETING LESSON OBJECTIVES

Each objective below is tested by the questions that follow it in parentheses.

1. Name the different ethnic peoples who live in East Asia. *(1)*

2. Explain how the population of East Asia is distributed. *(3, 4, 5)*

3. Describe how people live in East Asian cities. *(2)*

USING ILLUSTRATIONS

PLACE South Korea is slightly larger than Indiana, where 5.6 million people live—less than one-third the population of Seoul.

Answer to Caption: *It is one of the largest and most crowded.*

Meeting Special Needs

Language Deficient Students with language problems often have difficulty seeing differences in similar words. The objectives for this section require students to name, explain, and describe. Point out that naming usually involves labeling people, places, or things; explaining means giving reasons or interpreting; and describing requires listing characteristics. Provide opportunities for naming, explaining, and describing in the context of normal lesson discussion.

EVALUATE

Assign the Section 1 Quiz in the TCR.

Use the Testmaker to create a customized quiz for Section 1.

RETEACH

Have students complete Workbook Activity 27-1 found in the TCR.

ENRICH

Help students appreciate the relatively cramped living conditions in Japan. Distribute floor plan grids of a three-room house and have students arrange pictures of the furniture and appliances necessary to accommodate a family of four.

CLOSE

Have students write a postcard to Sonmin, telling her about their favorite foods.

GLENCOE TECHNOLOGY

Videodisc

GEOGRAPHY AND THE ENVIRONMENT
THE INFINITE VOYAGE
To the Edge of the Earth

Chapter 2
Disc 1 Side B
Title: ***Exploring Tibet: The Gateway of Exchange***
Subject: Physiological adaptations, lifestyle, and nutritional habits of Tibetan nomads and Peruvians living at high altitudes

China

Only about one-fourth of China's people live in cities. The rest live and work on farms. However, since the country has more than 1 billion people, there are more than 35 major cities with populations well over 1 million. The largest cities are the seaport of Shanghai, with about 7 million, and Beijing, the capital, with about 6 million.

Like other cities in Asia, China's cities are very crowded. Population density in Shanghai, for example, is more than 87,000 people per square mile (33,590 per sq. km). At rush hour, thousands of bicycles fill the streets. People in cities live in crowded apartments, often behind a store or shop. Sometimes many families share what was once the private home and courtyard of a wealthy family.

Japan

Unlike China, Japan is very urbanized. This is not a new development. Even in the 1700s, city life flourished in Japan. In 1721 Edo, present-day Tokyo, had about 1 million people. Today more than three-fourths of the people in Japan live in cities.

About half of all Japan's people live in the crowded coastal corridor about 320 miles (515 km) long on the island of Honshu. This is the Tokaido **megalopolis**—a super-city that includes several large cities and the smaller cities near them.

The largest urban center in the corridor is the area around Tokyo-Yokohama, with a population of about 27 million in 1990. The other centers are Nagoya and the industrial areas of Osaka, Kobe, and Kyoto.

Japan's busy modern cities have glass and concrete skyscrapers and huge neon signs advertising cars, cameras, and watches. Private homes are small and crowded closely together. A suburban family of four typically lives in a three-room wooden house—with a tiny garden if they are lucky. An average city couple probably has a small, two-room apartment.

Korea

About two-thirds of the people in both North and South Korea live in cities. Seoul (SOHL), the capital of South Korea, had more than 16 million people in 1990, making it one of the world's largest—and most crowded—cities. Korean urban life first expanded after Japan seized control of the country in 1910. The Japanese brought industry to Korean cities and took much farmland away from farmers. As a result, many Koreans moved to the cities to find work. After World War II, the division of Korea into two countries, the Korean conflict, and the continued growth of industry furthered urbanization.

Today, population density in Seoul is about 46,000 per square mile (17,760 per sq. km)—4 times that of New York City. South Korea's cities are growing as many people move there in search of jobs.

Taiwan

On the island of Taiwan, too, about three-fourths of the people live in cities. The largest city is Taipei with a population of about 7 million. Taipei is the capital of Taiwan and a growing manufacturing center. The Chinese Nationalist government moved to Taipei in 1949 after the Chinese Communists conquered mainland China. Since then, the city and its suburbs have grown rapidly both in area and population.

SECTION 1 REVIEW

Checking for Understanding

1. **Define** ethnic group, homogeneous, megalopolis.
2. **Locating Places** Where is the Tokaido megalopolis located?
3. **Place** In what part of China does most of the population live?
4. **Place** Which has the greater population density—North or South Korea?

Critical Thinking

5. **Determining Cause and Effect** Why are some parts of East Asia overcrowded while others are almost uninhabited?

ANSWERS TO SECTION 1 REVIEW

1. **ethnic group:** people who share a common ancestry, language, religion, or combination of characteristics; **homogeneous:** describing something that is alike throughout; **megalopolis:** continuous urban area made up of several major cities and the nearby smaller cities
2. on the coast of Honshu
3. river valleys and coastal plains in the south and east
4. South Korea
5. Large parts of the region are too dry, desolate, or mountainous for many people to live there; they are crowded into the flatter, more fertile areas.

NATIONAL GEOGRAPHIC GEOFACTS

Where is the world's longest escalator?

Among the longest single escalators are two at Metro subway stations, one in downtown Moscow, the other in suburban Washington, D. C. The 115-foot (35-m) Wheaton, Maryland, escalator is the longest in the Western Hemisphere.

0 10 km
0 10 mi
Europe
Asia
China
Africa
Pacific Ocean
Indian Ocean
CHINA
Shenzhen
HONG KONG (U.K.)
South China Sea
Hong Kong Island
Victoria Harbor
ESCALATOR SYSTEM
Connaught Rd.
MID-LEVELS
CENTRAL
Queens Rd.
Des Voeux Rd.
Caine Rd.
Conduit Rd.
ESCALATOR
MOVING SIDEWALK

The world's longest escalator system is a half-mile-long (800-m) covered outdoor network that snakes through the crowded streets of Hong Kong.

It opened in October 1993 to ease rush-hour traffic congestion on densely populated Hong Kong Island. The series of moving sidewalks and escalators, with 23 exits and entrances, links the central business district with residences about midway up Victoria Peak.

The 28-million-dollar escalator network runs downward for the morning commute, and then reverses direction at 10 a.m. and runs uphill until its 10 p.m. closing. The entire ride, which is free, takes about 20 minutes. At least 27,000 people are expected to use the system every day.

Designed by BILL PITZER

TEACH

Remind students that Hong Kong has a population density of about 14,000 people per square mile (5,405 per sq. km). Imagine the traffic jams if even one-fourth of these people drove an automobile along Hong Kong's crowded urban congestion!

Point out how population density figures are calculated: the number of people is divided by the land area. Ask students to research the square miles (sq. km) of their community or state as well as its population. Then have students calculate the population density for their community or state.

LESSON PLAN
Chapter 27, Section 2

FOCUS

SECTION OBJECTIVES

1. **Locate** where civilization began in East Asia.
2. **Discuss** how ideas spread from the Chinese Empire throughout East Asia.
3. **Illustrate** how East Asia has changed in the 20th century.

BELLRINGER MOTIVATIONAL ACTIVITY

Project the Section 2 Focus Transparency and have students answer the questions.

PRETEACHING VOCABULARY

List the Key Terms on the chalkboard and their meanings on slips of paper. Give the slips to volunteers and have them pantomime the meanings. Tell the rest of the class to match each pantomime with a Key Term.

GLENCOE TECHNOLOGY

Videodisc

Use the following to enrich Chapter 27:

GEOGRAPHY AND THE ENVIRONMENT
THE INFINITE VOYAGE
To the Edge of the Earth

Chapter 2
Disc 1 Side B

Title: ***Exploring Tibet: The Gateway of Exchange***

SECTION 2
History and Government

SETTING THE SCENE

Read to Discover . . .
- where civilization began in East Asia.
- how ideas spread from the Chinese Empire throughout East Asia.
- how East Asia has changed in the 20th century.

Key Terms
- culture hearth
- dynasty
- clan
- shogun
- samurai

Identify and Locate
Huang He, North China Plain, Kyoto

Some of the world's longest continuous civilizations can be found in East Asia. Their history is filled with the rise and fall of powerful ruling families.

LOCATION

River Valley Civilization

The culture of East Asia began in China about 2000 B.C., in the valley of the Wei River, a major tributary of the Huang He. China is considered East Asia's **culture hearth**, the center from which ideas and traditions spread.

Dynasties

Recorded Chinese history begins about 1700 B.C. with the Shang (SHAHNG) **dynasty**, or ruling house. The Shang and all succeeding dynasties faced similar problems—rebellions by local lords, attacks by central Asian nomads, and natural disasters, such as floods or famine. When the government was stable, it could defend its people against these problems. Sooner or later, however, the dynasty would weaken and fall. People explained this event by saying that its rulers had lost "the mandate of heaven," the approval of the deities.

Imperial China

Shang rulers set up a city-state in the North China Plain. Evidence shows that the Shang were skillful metalworkers and had a writing system.

The Zhou (JAU) dynasty conquered the Shang in about 1100 B.C. and ruled for 900 years. During that time Chinese culture spread, trade increased, and China entered the Iron Age. China's best-known philosopher and teacher Kung Fu-tzu, known as Confucius (Konfuzi), lived during this time. Another philosophy, Daoism (DOW•ism) also appeared. The Zhou were followed by a series of powerful dynasties that expanded Chinese territory.

By 221 B.C. the Qin (CHIN) dynasty had established the Chinese Empire. It would continue to influence East Asia for centuries. The Great Wall, stretching about 4,000 miles (6,437 km) along China's northern border, was built in the Qin dynasty. Rulers of a later dynasty—the Tang—continued to make the empire larger. By 620 A.D. merchants, travelers, missionaries, and silk traders were taking Chinese culture to all of East Asia.

Classroom Resources for Section 2

BLACKLINE MASTERS:
Reproducible Lesson Plan 27-2
Guided Reading Activity 27-2
Workbook Activity 27-2
Vocabulary Activity 27
Section Quiz 27-2

TRANSPARENCIES:
Section Focus Transparency 27-2
Political Map Transparency 9

MULTIMEDIA:
Testmaker

Geography and the Environment

CHINESE EMPIRES

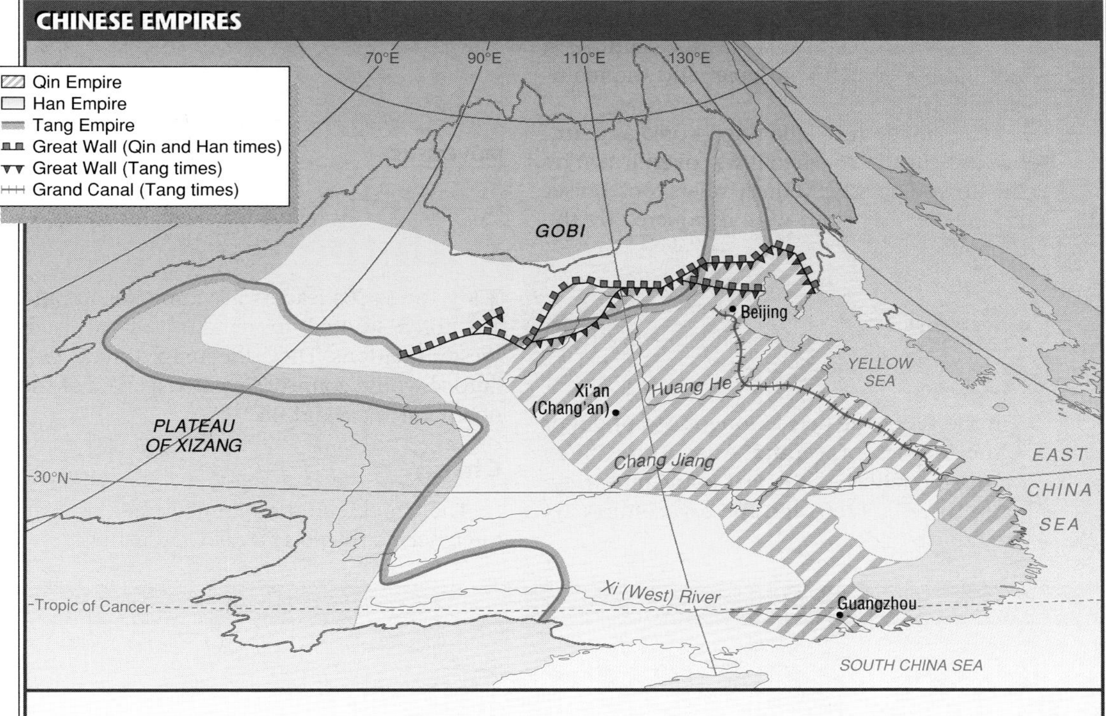

FOCUS ON GEOGRAPHIC THEMES

1. **Movement:** What barrier did the Chinese build to keep out nomadic invaders?
2. **Place:** Which rivers are linked by the Grand Canal?
3. **Place:** What city developed in central China under the empires?

PLACE

Japan and Korea

Many people borrowed Chinese ideas but shaped them to fit their own cultures.

Ancient Japan

The people of early Japan lived in **clans**, small tribal communities. From China and Korea, they learned metalworking and ways of growing rice in irrigated fields.

The Yamato people, whose main clan became the imperial family, ruled Japan by the A.D. 400s.

During the 500s and 600s, Japanese leaders sent students to China to learn technology, government, and the arts.

Feudal Japan

By the 1100s, local nobles and their armies were fighting to control Japan. The country's first military ruler, or **shogun**, took power in 1192. He was supported by professional soldiers, or **samurai**, who lived by a strict code of loyalty. Military dictators would rule Japan until the late 1800s.

TEACH

GUIDED PRACTICE

L1 Sequence Draw a line across the chalkboard and write a date along the line for every 200-year period between 2000 B.C. and A.D. 2000. As the students read the section, have volunteers record each event from their reading at the correct place along the line.

INDEPENDENT PRACTICE

Guided Reading Have students complete Guided Reading Activity 27-2 in the TCR. **LEP**

USING MAPS

Answers:
1. the Great Wall;
2. the Huang He and the Chang Jiang;
3. Xi'an or Chang'an

Map Skills Practice

Inferring Information Why do you think the Chinese dug the Grand Canal? *(to improve trade and transportation)*

Cooperative Learning Activity

Have students research the lives and accomplishments of the Mongol Khans, from Genghis Kahn through his sons and grandsons—Batu Khan, Mangu Khan, Kublai Khan, and Hulagu. Refer them to *The Discoverers* in which Daniel J. Boorstin makes the case that the Khans were courageous, versatile, and tolerant rather than barbaric. Tell the students to present their findings in an oral report. Suggest that they draw the Mongol rulers' family tree to use as a visual aid.

Korea

The Korean Peninsula was for centuries a cultural bridge between Japan and the mainland of Asia.

The kingdom of Silla ruled Korea as a unified state until 936 when it was overthrown by the Koryo Dynasty. Military rulers took power in the late 1100s but were conquered by the Mongols.

MOVEMENT

The Mongols

In the 1200s the fierce Mongols swept out of the steppes of central Asia, into China. Mongols established the first non-Chinese dynasty there in 1260, and the two cultures existed side by side.

Japanese samurai fought off two huge Mongol invasions in 1274 and 1281.

MOVEMENT

Contacts with the West

By the 1600s leaders in China, Japan, and Korea wanted to remain isolated from Western nations. They discouraged trade with Europe whose countries wanted a share of the rich trade in tea and silk.

China

The Chinese Empire limited trade with all foreigners to the port city of Guangzhou.

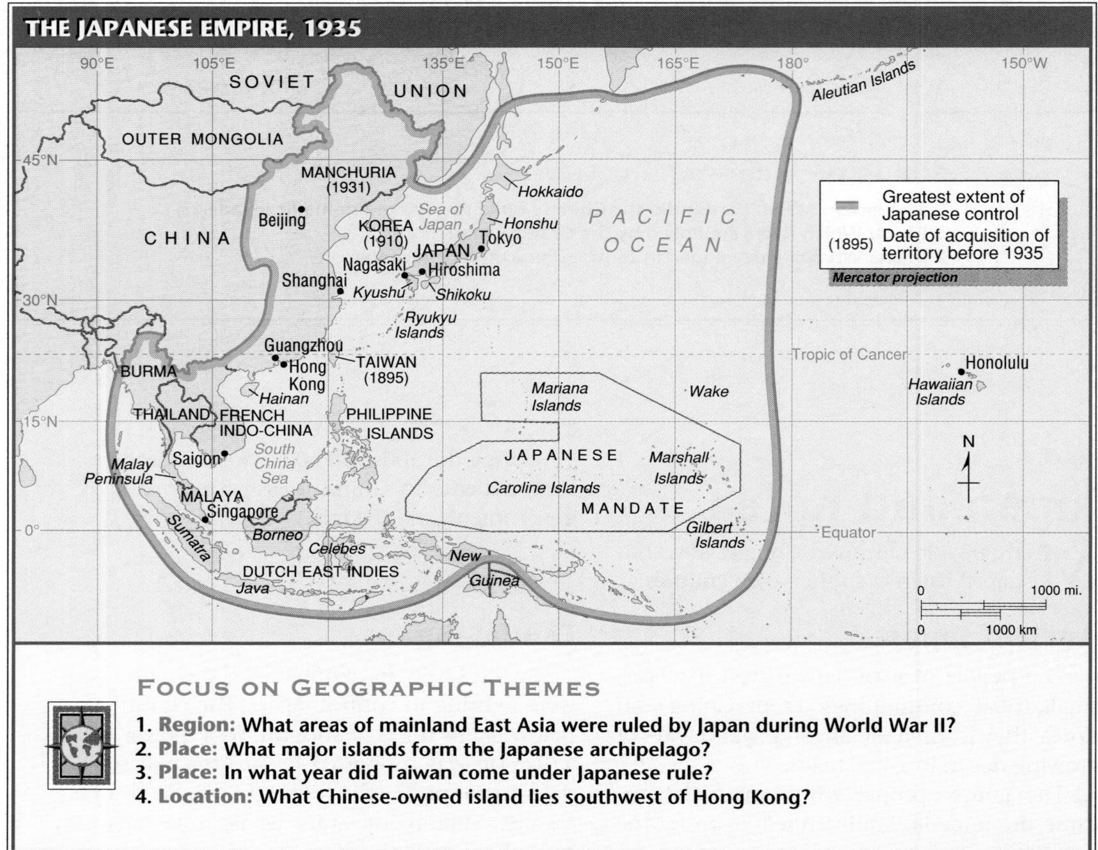

FOCUS ON GEOGRAPHIC THEMES

1. **Region:** What areas of mainland East Asia were ruled by Japan during World War II?
2. **Place:** What major islands form the Japanese archipelago?
3. **Place:** In what year did Taiwan come under Japanese rule?
4. **Location:** What Chinese-owned island lies southwest of Hong Kong?

ASSESS

CHECK FOR UNDERSTANDING

Assign Section 2 Review as homework or an in-class activity.

MEETING LESSON OBJECTIVES

Each objective below is tested by the questions that follow it in parentheses.

1. **Locate** where civilization began in East Asia. *(2)*
2. **Discuss** how ideas spread from the Chinese Empire throughout East Asia. *(3)*
3. **Illustrate** how East Asia has changed in the 20th century. *(4)*

USING MAPS

Answers:

1. Manchuria, Korea, eastern China, French Indo-china, Thailand, and most of Burma; **2.** Hokkaido, Honshu, Shikoku, and Kyushu; **3.** 1895; **4.** Hainan

Map Skills Practice

Drawing Conclusions Why was the conquest of Korea an important step toward the conquest of northeastern China? *(Korea acted as a bridge across which arms and communications could travel.)*

Meeting Special Needs

Language Delayed To help students with language concept delays, discuss the meaning of "cultural bridge" and "sphere of influence" in the class. Read aloud the portion under "Wars and Recovery" and ask why Japan might have experienced an "economic boom." Have students define "free enterprise" and tell why it is linked with the Mongolians' move toward democracy.

Eventually the United Kingdom, Germany, Russia, and France all forced trade treaties on China. They also made China give them "spheres of influence" in various parts of the country.

Japan

In 1853 United States steamships sailed into Tokyo Bay. Rather than fight, Japanese officials signed trade treaties with the United States and European nations.

Foreign influence gave the Japanese a chance to introduce changes. Japan quickly built factories and railroads and modernized its government, military forces, and economy. It also began to build an empire in Asia, taking over Korea and parts of Manchuria.

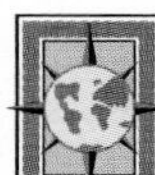

Geographic Themes

Region: China

In 1989, Chinese students unsuccessfully tried to limit the power of China's Communist government. *Who was the first Communist leader of China?*

MOVEMENT

War and Revolution

The 20th century involved East Asia in two world wars, brought two revolutions to China, and divided the Korean Peninsula.

Wars and Recovery

Japan aided the Allies in World War I, gaining Germany's former possessions in China and the Pacific. During World War II, Japan took over parts of China and Southeast Asia. After that war ended in its defeat, Japan lost its empire. In 1948, Korea, once its colony, was divided into pro-American South Korea and Communist-ruled North Korea.

Postwar Japan transformed itself into a democracy. Within a few decades, an economic boom made the country one of the richest in the world.

Revolutions in China

The Chinese Empire came to an end in 1911 when a Nationalist revolution led by Dr. Sun Yat-sen (SUN YAHT•SEN) overthrew the Manchu dynasty. In 1927 Chiang Kai-shek set up a Nationalist government, but his rival Communist Mao Zedong (MAU ZUH•DUNG), gained huge support from peasants.

During World War II, Nationalists and Communists together resisted Japan. At the end of the war, the two groups fought each other again. By 1949 the Communists set up the People's Republic of China on the mainland. The Nationalists fled to the island of Taiwan and set up the Republic of China.

In 1924 Mongolia set up a Communist government. After the fall of the Soviet Union, the Mongolians in the 1990s began to move toward democracy and free enterprise.

SECTION 2 REVIEW

Checking for Understanding

1. **Define** culture hearth, dynasty, clan, shogun, samurai.
2. **Locating Places** Where did East Asian civilization begin?
3. **Movement** What elements of Chinese culture did the Japanese borrow and adapt?
4. **Place** How did China's government change during the 20th century?

Critical Thinking

5. **Drawing Conclusions** Why would the East Asian nations want to be isolated from Western countries in the 1800s?

EVALUATE

Assign the Section 2 Quiz in the TCR.

Use the Testmaker to create a customized quiz for Section 2.

RETEACH

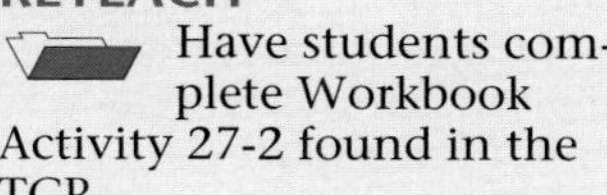

Have students complete Workbook Activity 27-2 found in the TCR.

ENRICH

Show scenes from the movie *The Last Emperor* to give the class a view of imperial China.

CLOSE

Read lines from the section such as "the first Communist leader of China" and "established the first non-Chinese dynasty," and have students name the groups or figures that the lines identify.

USING ILLUSTRATIONS

REGION The Communists hunted down and arrested an estimated 7,000 people involved in the 1989 rebellion.

Answer to Caption: *Mao Zedung*

ANSWERS TO SECTION 2 REVIEW

1. **culture hearth:** place where ideas originate and from which they spread; **dynasty:** ruling family or house; **clan:** family or tribal community; **shogun:** military dictator in feudal Japan; **samurai:** military class in Japan
2. in the valley of the Wei, a tributary of the Huang He
3. Buddhist religion, Confucian ideas of government, writing system, and art and architecture
4. The empire ended with the revolution in 1911. Communists and Nationalists fought until Communists won and established their government in 1949.
5. Answers will vary but may include that East Asians probably wanted to resist change and to ward off potential invaders.

TEACH

Tell students that late in 1993 and early in 1994, negotiations between the Chinese government and Hong Kong leaders became strained over the issue of how much freedom Hong Kong should retain. Have students update the Hong Kong situation from news stories on television, in newspapers, or in magazines.

Extending the Content

Hong Kong's Value
Hong Kong is very valuable economically to China. One-third of all Chinese imports and exports pass through Hong Kong's harbor. The area serves as a market for much of China's foodstuffs, water, raw materials, and manufactured products. The Chinese government owns many Hong Kong banks, department stores, and hotels. Many of Hong Kong's citizens are immigrants from southern China or descendants of immigrants from that region.

DID YOU KNOW?

Hong Kong is known as the "Pearl of the Orient," a tribute to the city's impressive beauty, magnificent harbor, and the energetic, hardworking people that have built Hong Kong into a major trade center.

Geography and History

Hong Kong: Harbor of Free Enterprise

As you read, examine the change facing Hong Kong.

Hong Kong is one of East Asia's busiest ports. Most of Hong Kong's people are Chinese, but the territory has been under British rule since the 1800s. In 1997, the United Kingdom will finally return Hong Kong to China.

Leading Asian Port

Hong Kong, on the southeast coast of China, has been a dependency of the United Kingdom since the 1840s. British officials approved and appointed by Britain's monarch control the government.

As a British dependency, Hong Kong has grown and prospered. An excellent natural harbor has made the territory a major Asian port. Hong Kong's low taxes and free port status—no duties are collected on imported goods—have made it a center of trade. More than 100 banks and 4 stock exchanges make Hong Kong Asia's second-largest international financial center.

Hong Kong has also become an industrial center, making use of a large and cheap labor force. More than 2 million tourists visit Hong Kong yearly, spending money that stimulates the economy.

A Change of Hands

Although Hong Kong has been governed by the United Kingdom, it is powerfully influenced by the neighboring Republic of China. Chinese citizens hold many of the government's lower offices, and 98 percent of Hong Kong's population is Chinese.

Through wars and treaties, Great Britain gained control of Hong Kong Island in 1842, then Kowloon peninsula in 1860. In 1898, China leased the New Territories to the United Kingdom for 99 years.

The Chinese Communists have governed China since 1949, but have never officially recognized the United Kingdom's control of Hong Kong. Neither have they opposed British rule.

Changing Hands Again

On July 1, 1997, the United Kingdom's 99-year lease of the New Territories expires, and all of Hong Kong will return to Chinese rule. In 1984 the two nations signed a joint declaration that pledged Hong Kong's return to China in 1997, but with a high degree of independence from the Chinese Communist regime.

Checking for Understanding

1. **Place** Study the map on this page. How does Hong Kong's coastline contribute to its success as a trading center?
2. How did the United Kingdom acquire control of Hong Kong?

ANSWERS TO CHECKING FOR UNDERSTANDING

1. Hong Kong's coastline is highly irregular, providing the area with fine natural harbors.

2. China leased Hong Kong to the United Kingdom in 1898 for a period of 99 years.

3 SECTION
Cultures and Lifestyles

SETTING THE SCENE

Read to Discover . . .
- the languages and religions of the peoples of East Asia.
- how standards of living differ among countries in East Asia.
- the importance of arts and leisure activities in the countries of East Asia.

Key Terms
- ideogram
- shamanism
- calligraphy
- haiku

Identify and Locate
Xizang (Tibet), Mongolia, Korea, Mount Fuji, Kyoto

The people of East Asia have a long and rich cultural tradition. The ideas of Confucianism, Daoism, Buddhism, and Shinto have been major influences. Communism has also had a major impact on the cultures of China, North Korea, and Mongolia.

REGION

Languages

People in East Asia speak languages from several different language families. The largest, Sino-Tibetan, which includes Chinese and Tibetan, is spoken by more than 1.1 billion people.

Chinese Languages

Chinese has many dialects, pronounced very differently from one another. Mandarin, the northern dialect, is the most widely spoken and is taught in schools.

The Chinese written language is based on **ideograms**, or pictorial characters, that each carry one meaning. When each character becomes a spoken syllable, however, it takes on a different meaning—these pronunciations form a dialect. Chinese languages are also tonal. The same syllable has different meanings depending upon tone and pitch. Other languages spoken in China include Mongolian, Manchu, and Uygur.

Japanese and Korean

Japanese and Korean languages are related. Learning to read and write Japanese is challenging because three different writing systems are used. The Japanese borrowed many ideograms from Chinese. Then, in the ninth century, two phonetic alphabets were invented to represent the actual sounds of Japanese.

Koreans have their own writing system developed by a 15th-century ruler.

PLACE

Religion

People in East Asia may follow more than one religion. Many Japanese, for example, practice both Buddhism and the traditional Japanese religion of Shinto. Confucian ideas have also influenced the entire region.

Communist governments in China and North Korea have discouraged religious practices, but many people have held to their beliefs. In China these beliefs can mean a blend of Buddhism or Christianity with Confucian and Daoist ideas. In the far western province of Xinjiang, the Uygurs are Muslims.

LESSON PLAN
Chapter 27, Section 3

FOCUS

SECTION OBJECTIVES

1. **Identify** the languages and the religions of the peoples of East Asia.
2. **Analyze** how standards of living differ among countries in East Asia.
3. **Understand** the importance of arts and leisure activities in the countries of East Asia.

BELLRINGER MOTIVATIONAL ACTIVITY

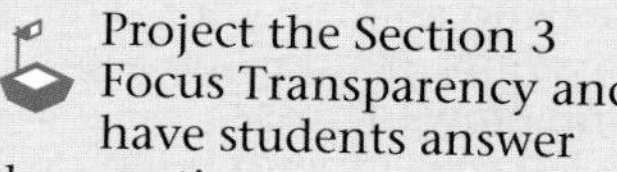
Project the Section 3 Focus Transparency and have students answer the questions.

PRETEACHING VOCABULARY

On the chalkboard, write *ideogram, calligraphy,* and *haiku* and display an example of each in random order. After the students read the section, have them match each term with the correct example.

CURRICULUM CONNECTION

MATH

The oldest known Chinese numerals were inscribed on bones and tortoise shells between the sixteenth and eleventh centuries B.C. Specific characters represented the units: tens, hundreds, thousands, and ten thousands.

Classroom Resources for Section 3

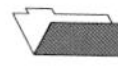
BLACKLINE MASTERS:
- Reproducible Lesson Plan 27-3
- Skill Activity 27
- Enrichment Activity 27
- Foods Around the World 8
- World Literature Reading 8
- Section Quiz 27-3

TRANSPARENCIES:
- Section Focus Transparency 27-3
- World Cultures Transparencies 15, 16

MULTIMEDIA:

- Testmaker

***World Music:** Cultural Traditions, Lesson 8*

Picture Atlas of the World

TEACH

GUIDED PRACTICE

 Implement Foods Around the World 8 as a class activity.

L1 Debate Read the following teachings of Confucius to the class:
(1) A youth, when at home, should be filial (like a son), and, when abroad, respectful to his elders.
(2) The relationship between superiors and inferiors is like that between the wind and the grass. The grass must bend when the wind blows across it.
(3) Let the emperor be emperor and the subject subject.

Allow students to explain what the teachings mean to them, to agree or disagree with each, and to try to convert others to their point of view.

USING DIAGRAMS

Skills Practice
What two religions have the most East Asian followers? *(Buddhism and Confucianism)*

CD-ROM

PICTURE ATLAS OF THE WORLD
View traditional ceremonies that open games in Urumqi, a Muslim city deep in Central Asia, by clicking China's "Video" button.

East Asia: Religions

Nonreligious[1]	700,000,000
Buddhist	277,000,000
Confucian	245,000,000
Shintoist[2]	108,000,000
Muslim	30,000,000
Christian	18,000,000
Daoist	4,280,000
Other	16,000,000

Daoist less than 1%; Other 1%; Christian 1%; Muslim 2%; Shintoist 8%; Confucian 18%; Buddhist 20%; Nonreligious 50%

[1]Religious statistics not available from People's Republic of China.
[2]Many Japanese practice both Shintoism and Buddhism.
Source: Population Reference Bureau, Inc., 1994; World Almanac, 1995

Many Koreans are Buddhists, with some ideas taken from Confucianism. Others follow **shamanism**, a belief in a leader who can communicate with spirits, or belong to the nationalistic sect called Chundo Kyo. About 20 percent of South Koreans are Christians.

Before Communist governments took power, Xizang (Tibet) and Mongolia were religious states led by Buddhist monks.

PLACE

Standards of Living

Standards of living in East Asia have steadily improved as these nations' economies have developed. Contrasts are still great, however—from glittering skyscrapers to mud houses in rural parts of the region.

Japan

Japan is the most modern and industrialized country in East Asia. In 1992 its average annual household income was $48,900, one of the highest in the world. Most Japanese live in cities where housing shortages are a continuing problem.

Consumer costs in Japan are high by American standards, but income is distributed more evenly. Japanese businesses emphasize teamwork and cooperation. A *sarariman*, the Japanese term for a white-collar worker, can usually enjoy the security of a lifetime job and good benefits. Breaking with tradition, many Japanese women now have professional careers.

Korea and Taiwan

Both South Korea and Taiwan have developed quickly into modern industrial nations, with rising standards of living.

Prosperity in Taiwan has improved living standards for both farmers and city dwellers.

China

Communist leaders in China have tried new approaches to running the economy, reforming land ownership, and increasing food production.

After the death of Mao Zedong, new leaders began to allow people to improve their own standard of living through opening businesses and working private farm plots.

PLACE

Education and Health

East Asians respect learning. Today elementary education is free and compulsory throughout the region. Opportunities for higher education have increased greatly since the 1950s.

Literacy

Japan has a long tradition of literacy. Today almost all Japanese adults can read and write. North and South Korea, and Taiwan also have literacy rates of more than 90 percent. In

Cooperative Learning Activity

Tell the class that Chinese students use abacuses to calculate math problems. Have students make their own abacuses from shoe boxes, florist wire, and craft beads. On the chalkboard, draw an abacus to guide them. Indicate that the first wire represents ones, the second tens, the third hundreds, and so on. Show that each wire has two counters at the top representing five units each and five counters at the bottom representing single units. Suggest that students use a different color for the top two counters in every row. After students complete their abacuses, pair them and have the members in each pair compete to see who can use an abacus to solve math problems more quickly.

Mongolia, 89 percent of the people can read and write.

Historically, only the wealthiest people in China were literate. Since the 1940s the Communist government has built more elementary schools and has started adult education. Today the literacy rate in China is about 76 percent.

Schools

Japan's demanding school system teaches students to work together and value cooperation. Students must finish ninth grade, attending school almost year-round. More than 90 percent of all students also finish high school, but a difficult entrance exam is required for most colleges or technical schools.

Advanced education has been one of the reasons for the economic development in much of East Asia.

Health Care

Better health care has caused life expectancies to rise and infant deaths to decline in East Asia. In general, the life expectancy for women is more than 70 years, and for men—65 years. Japan, with the most up-to-date medical facilities, has the longest life expectancies—82 years for women, and 76 years for men.

In the Communist countries, medical treatment is free. In Korea, Taiwan, and China both Western medical techniques and traditional herbal medicine and acupuncture are used.

PLACE

Leisure Time

People in East Asia participate in a variety of free-time enjoyments from music to sports. Family life is at the center of many activities.

Food

East Asia has many national and regional styles of cooking with some staple foods in common. Grains such as rice, wheat, and millet are basic foods, often made into noodles or dumplings. Asians eat less red meat than North Americans or Europeans, getting more

Geographic Themes

Region: Japan

Japanese workers at a Tokyo plant perform exercises before beginning a busy day. The Japanese workforce is one of the most highly skilled in the world. *What values does it stress?*

INDEPENDENT PRACTICE

Have students complete World Music: Cultural Traditions, Lesson 8 activity in the TCR.

USING ILLUSTRATIONS

REGION Some Japanese companies rely on their workers—and music. Certain bakers, brewers, and noodle makers claim that manufacturing foods to classical music makes them tastier.

Answer to Caption: *teamwork and cooperation*

ASSESS

CHECK FOR UNDERSTANDING

Assign Section 3 Review as homework or an in-class activity.

MULTICULTURAL PERSPECTIVE

Cultural Diffusion

The Japanese call battered, fried fish *tempura.* The name comes from the Latin words *Quattuor Tempora,* or Ember Days, when Catholics—including Portuguese traders in Japan—abstained from meat and instead ate seafood, which they fried in batter.

DID YOU KNOW?

Koreans treat each birthday after the sixtieth as a special occasion because it is considered a victory over death.

Meeting Special Needs

Language Delayed Give students who have difficulty asking questions of their teachers an opportunity to practice a skill introduced earlier in the textbook—formulating questions. Organize the class into small groups to develop questions. Have students focus on the text under the heading "Education and Health" on pages 562 and 563. Reward the groups that accomplish the following tasks: formulating the most questions and coming up with the most varied questions.

MEETING LESSON OBJECTIVES

Each objective below is tested by the questions that follow it in parentheses.

1. **Identify** the languages and the religions of the peoples of East Asia. *(2, 3)*
2. **Analyze** how standards of living differ among countries in East Asia. *(5)*
3. **Understand** the importance of arts and leisure activities in the countries of East Asia. *(4)*

EVALUATE

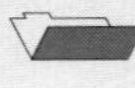 Assign the Section 3 Quiz in the TCR.

 Use the Testmaker to create a customized quiz for Section 3.

RETEACH

 Have students complete Reteaching Activity 27 in the TCR.

USING ILLUSTRATIONS

PLACE Seoul has the largest Presbyterian and Methodist congregations in the world.

Answer to Caption: *painting, sculpture, and pottery*

NATIONAL GEOGRAPHIC SOCIETY

 **CD-ROM**

PICTURE ATLAS OF THE WORLD

Have students click Japan's "Video" button to view a Bunraku puppet presentation.

protein from soybeans and fish. Many strict Buddhists are vegetarians.

Sports

East Asians enjoy many sports such as baseball, soccer, and volleyball. Olympic champions in skiing, swimming, gymnastics, table tennis, and other sports have come from this region. Many people, old and young, also practice traditional exercises and martial arts.

Ceremonies and Holidays

Several Asian philosophies and religions, such as Shinto and Zen Buddhism, require followers to celebrate rituals. Each Asian country also celebrates traditional ethnic and national holidays. Many celebrate the New Year according to the lunar calendar, in late January or early February.

MOVEMENT

Arts and Architecture

Chinese styles in art and architecture have influenced all of East Asia. Religion has also inspired much great art.

In 1966, communism changed the standards for Chinese arts with Mao Zedong's Cultural Revolution. It tried to wipe out the memory of centuries of art. After Mao died, however, many Chinese artists returned to traditional forms.

Painting, Sculpture, and Pottery

Daoism's emphasis on quiet contemplation of nature has influenced both Chinese

Geographic Themes

Place: Seoul, Korea

This Buddhist temple in Korea reflects the historical influence of Buddhism on the arts of East Asia. *In what arts do East Asians excel?*

Extending the Content

Movement Point out that the art, history, and geography of East Asia have influenced many Western artists. In the late 1800s, Impressionists such as Mary Cassatt and Vincent van Gogh imitated the look of Japanese woodblock prints in their paintings. More recently, moviemaker Bernardo Bertolucci recalled the splendor of imperial China in *The Last Emperor.* Even authors of children's books have not escaped the influence. Newbery Medal winner Katherine Paterson wrote about the tradition of puppet theaters in Japan in *The Master Puppeteer* and Ed Young has illustrated many Chinese folktales, including *The Terrible Nung Gwama* and *The Rooster's Horns.*

and Japanese painting. Many paintings include a verse or inscription done in **calligraphy**, the art of beautiful writing.

Japanese artists of the 1700s and early 1800s also developed a style of wood-block printing with vivid colors. Famous print artists, such as Hiroshige and Hokusai, influenced Western artists.

Asian sculptors have often portrayed the Buddha or traditional deities. Buddhist temples in Korea, China, and Japan contain many statues and images of stone, bronze, or jade.

Pottery makers worked in Japan as long ago as 10,000 B.C. During the Tang dynasty, Chinese potters learned how to make fine, thin porcelain called china. Korean potters in the Koryo dynasty were famous for their pale green celadon vases.

Music and Theater

East Asian music is based on a five-tone, or pentatonic, scale that has a melody line but no harmony. Music originally was used in temple rituals and to accompany dancers with flutes, drums, and gongs. Stringed instruments included the lute, guitar, and *koto*, a zither.

Traditional musical dramas, combining music and story, are popular. The Chinese perform opera, and the Japanese enjoy serious *Noh* plays, and the livelier Kabuki theater. Several countries have motion picture industries.

Literature

In about 1010, what is thought to be the world's first novel, *The Tale of Genji*, was written in Japan. The author was a noblewoman at the Heian court, Lady Murasaki Shikibu.

Poetry has long been important in East Asian culture, from the Chinese Confucian writing to the 17-syllable form of Japanese poetry, the **haiku**.

Architecture

Except for modern city skyscrapers, most East Asian architecture is based on simple wood construction, often with gracefully curved tile roofs. People also build with brick or stone if it is locally available. One common style is the pagoda, derived from Buddhist temples in India. It is a multistory building, with each story smaller than the one below.

Geographic Themes

Place: Tokyo, Japan
Lavish costumes and colorful stage sets characterize Kabuki theater, which has been popular in Japan for centuries. *What other type of play developed in traditional Japan?*

SECTION 3 REVIEW

Checking for Understanding

1. **Define** ideogram, shamanism, calligraphy, haiku.
2. **Locating Places** Where do people speak languages from the Sino-Tibetan family?
3. **Place** What religions are practiced by people in different parts of China?
4. **Place** When and where was the first real novel written? By whom?

Critical Thinking

5. **Making Generalizations** How have rising standards of living changed the lives of people in East Asia?

ENRICH

 Have students complete Enrichment Activity 27 in the TCR.

CLOSE

Write EAST ASIA vertically on the chalkboard and challenge students to copy a term from the section that begins with each letter. Start them off by writing *acupuncture* next to an *A* in *ASIA*.

USING ILLUSTRATIONS

PLACE A favorite entertainment in China is the shadow puppet show, a tradition that goes back hundreds of years.

Answer to Caption: *Noh plays*

NATIONAL GEOGRAPHIC SOCIETY

CD-ROM

PICTURE ATLAS OF THE WORLD
Listen to the music of China, South Korea, and Japan by clicking the "Music" button of the respective countries.

ANSWERS TO SECTION 3 REVIEW

1. **ideogram:** a pictorial character standing for a word; **shamanism:** belief in a leader who can communicate with spirits; **calligraphy:** the art of beautiful handwriting; **haiku:** Japanese verse form, usually with 17 syllables
2. China, Tibet, Taiwan
3. Buddhism, Confucianism, Daoism, and Christianity
4. about A.D. 1010 at the Heian court in Japan; Lady Murasaki, a noblewoman
5. Answers will include more opportunities for education and better health care.

TEACH

Ask students: "What is population density?" *(the number of people living in a given area)* Explain: "Population density determines a great deal about the lifestyle in a region."

Write these column headings on the chalkboard: urban center/rural area. Have students compare various aspects of living in densely and sparsely populated areas—such as housing, work activities, environmental quality, and so on. Discuss the population density of your local area and how it affects lifestyle. Then, have students read the skill on page 566 and discuss the factors determining population distribution patterns within a region.

Skills Practice For additional practice, have students complete Skill Activity 27 in the TCR.

MAP & GRAPH SKILLS

Reading a Population Density Map

In most countries, population is concentrated in particular areas—in cities, along coastlines, in moderate climates, near rivers, and so on. Because of uneven distribution, population density varies within each country.

REVIEWING THE SKILL

Population density is the number of people living in a square mile or square kilometer. A **population density map** illustrates the distribution of population in a given region. Mapmakers can show population density in two ways. On some maps, different colors represent various population densities. On other maps, a dot represents a particular number of people, such as 1,000 or 100,000. The number of dots clustered in an area indicates the population density.

When reading a population density map, apply the following steps:

- Study the map key to determine what the colors and symbols represent.
- Find the areas that have the greatest and least population density.
- Compare the map with other information about the region to draw conclusions about the causes and effects of the population density patterns in this area.

PRACTICING THE SKILL

Study the population density map below and then answer the following questions:

1. What does the color yellow represent?
2. What symbols stand for cities of more than 2,000,000 people?
3. Which areas of China are least densely populated?
4. What physical features affect population distribution in China?

For additional practice in this skill, see Practicing Skills on page 568 of the Chapter 27 Review.

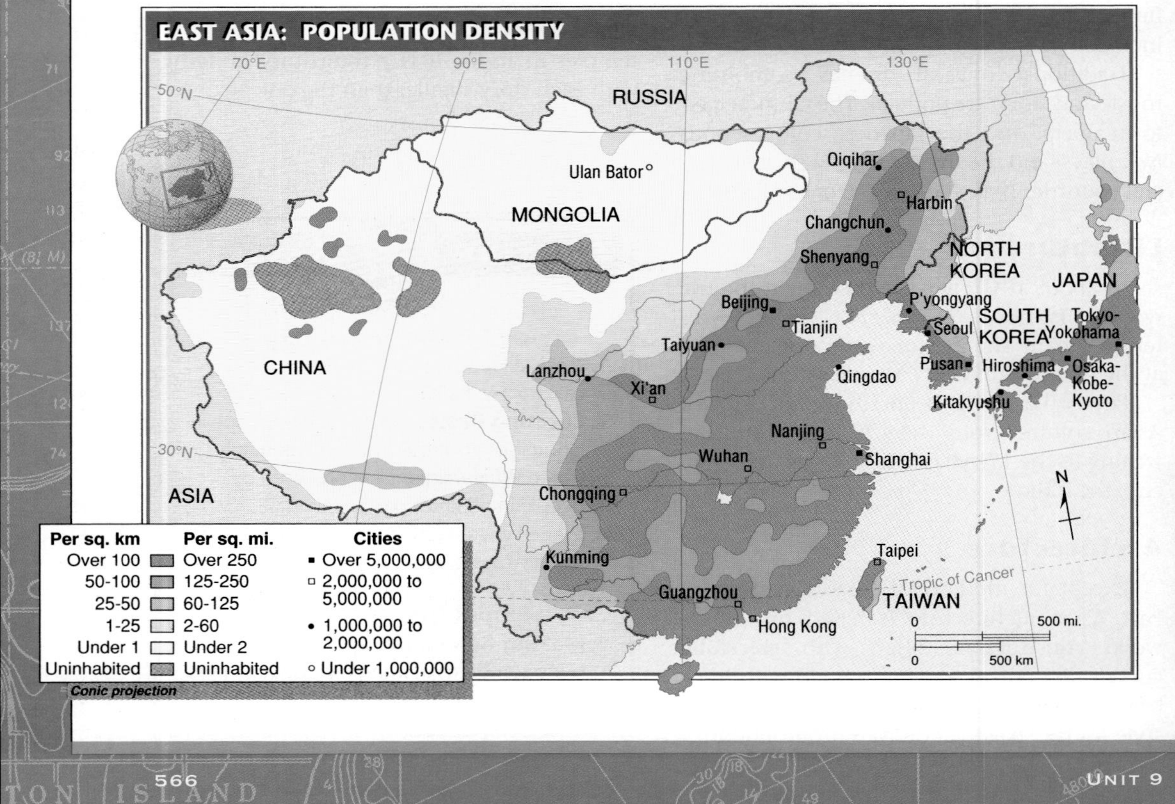

ANSWERS TO PRACTICING THE SKILL

1. population density of less than 2 people/sq. mi. (less than 1 person/sq.km)
2. a white and black square
3. north and far west
4. Population is most dense in the flat fertile river valleys, plains, and coastal areas of eastern China. Population is least dense in the high, dry, rugged mountainous country of the north and west where survival is more difficult.

chapter 27 HIGHLIGHTS

Section 1 Population Patterns

The Ginza, the main shopping street of Tokyo, Japan

Key Terms

ethnic group (p. 551)
homogeneous (p. 552)
megalopolis (p. 554)

Summary

- The people of East Asia belong to many different ethnic groups, the largest of which is the Han of China.
- Population in East Asia is unevenly distributed. It is concentrated in river valleys and on coastal plains.
- Japan is the most urbanized nation in East Asia; China remains predominantly rural with hundreds of millions of its citizens living in a nonurban setting.

Section 2 History and Government

Student protests in China, 1989

Key Terms

culture hearth (p. 556)
dynasty (p. 556)
clan (p. 557)
shogun (p. 557)
samurai (p. 557)

Summary

- East Asian culture began in the Huang He valley of China and spread to other countries in the region.
- Confucianism and Daoism, two influential schools of thought, developed in China about 500 B.C.; Buddhism was brought from India.
- The Chinese Empire dominated East Asia for several centuries.
- Contact with the West weakened China but led Japan to modernize.

Section 3 Cultures and Lifestyles

A Buddhist temple in Korea

Key Terms

ideogram (p. 561)
shamanism (p. 562)
calligraphy (p. 565)
haiku (p. 565)

Summary

- Sino-Tibetan languages are the most widely spoken in Asia, while Korean and Japanese are spoken in their native countries.
- Rising standards of living have brought improvements in education and health care.
- People in East Asia practice traditional arts and leisure activities but also enjoy modern recreations.

CHAPTER 27 HIGHLIGHTS

USING THE CHAPTER 27 HIGHLIGHTS

Use the Chapter 27 Highlights to preview, review, condense, or reteach the chapter.

PREVIEW/REVIEW

Vocabulary PuzzleMaker Software reinforces the Key Terms used in Chapter 27.

Student Self-Test and Review Software allows students to review Chapter 27 content.

CONDENSE

Have students read the Chapter 27 Highlights.

Have students listen to the Chapter 27 Audiocassettes in the TCR. Spanish Audiocassettes are also available.

Assign the Chapter 27 Audiocassette Activity and give the students the Chapter 27 Audiocassette Quiz.

 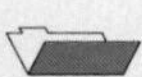
Have students complete Guided Reading Activities for Chapter 27 in the TCR. Spanish Guided Reading Activities are also available.

RETEACH

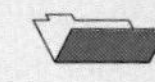 
Have students complete Reteaching Activity 27 in the TCR. Spanish Reteaching Activities are also available.

Map Activity

Identify and Locate Distribute copies of page 35 of the Outline Map Resource Book. Using the Atlas maps at the beginning of the unit and maps from the chapter, have the students identify and label the cities of Hong Kong, Tokyo, Nagoya, Osaka, Kobe, Kyoto, Yokohama, Seoul, Beijing, Shanghai, Taipei, and Ulan Bator.

GLENCOE TECHNOLOGY

Videodisc

Use Chapter 27 MindJogger Videoquiz to review students' knowledge before administering the Chapter 27 Test.

MINDJOGGER VIDEOQUIZ

Chapter 27
Disc 4 Side A

The MindJogger Videoquiz is also available on videocassette.

ANSWERS

Reviewing Key Terms

1. homogeneous
2. ethnic group
3. shogun
4. dynasty
5. calligraphy
6. haiku

Reviewing Facts

7. Japan, Korea, Mongolia
8. China
9. It adopted Western technology and ideas about government and the economy.
10. The Communists won a civil war and established the People's Republic of China in 1949.
11. Buddhism, Confucianism, and Shintoism
12. Japan

chapter 27 REVIEW

Reviewing Key Terms

Choose the vocabulary term that best completes each of the sentences below. Write your answers on a separate sheet of paper.

ethnic group (p. 551)
homogeneous (p. 552)
dynasty (p. 556)
shogun (p. 557)
calligraphy (p. 565)
haiku (p. 565)

SECTION 1

1. The population of Mongolia is quite _____ .
2. The largest _____ in China is the Han.

SECTION 2

3. Japan's feudal military leaders were called the _____ .
4. The Great Wall of China was built during the Qin _____ .

SECTION 3

5. _____ is an artful form of handwriting.
6. One Japanese verse form is the _____ .

Reviewing Facts

SECTION 1

7. Which countries in East Asia are the most homogeneous in ethnic groups?
8. Which country in East Asia has the largest percentage of rural people?

SECTION 2

9. How did Japan respond to contact with the West in the 1800s?
10. How did China's government change after World War II?

SECTION 3

11. What are the major religions in East Asia?
12. Which Asian nation has the highest standard of living?

Critical Thinking

13. **Drawing Conclusions** How has geography influenced population density and distribution in East Asia?
14. **Identifying Central Issues** How did Confucianism influence government and society in China?
15. **Making Generalizations** Why do you think Japanese schools emphasize cooperation and teamwork? How has this philosophy helped Japan's economic growth?

Geographic Themes

16. **Human/Environment Interaction** Why are the valleys and coastal plains of China and Japan such crowded areas?
17. **Location** Where was the original center of East Asian culture?
18. **Movement** What religious ideas traveled from China to Korea and Japan?

Practicing Skills

Reading a Population Density Map

Refer to the population density map on page 566.

19. Which of the following cities have fewer than 2 million people—Beijing, Nanjing, Xi'an, Guangzhou, Hong Kong, Kunming?
20. Along which major rivers lie the most densely populated areas of China?
21. What is the largest city in Taiwan?

Using the Unit Atlas

Refer to the physical geography section of the Unit Atlas on pages 532–533.

22. What geographic factors have made Hong Kong a world center of trade, manufacturing, and transportation?

Critical Thinking

13. Highlands cover the western part of the region, so most people are crowded into the valleys and plains in eastern China and on the coastal plains in other countries.

14. It encouraged respect for authority and led to choosing officials based on scholarship and merit.

15. because teamwork is important in Japanese society, business, and government; Everyone works together to accomplish Japan's economic goals.

Geographic Themes

16. because other parts of the region are too mountainous or too remote to farm and to live on

23. What is the Great Wall and why is it extraordinary?

Projects

Individual Activity

From your textbook or other sources about East Asian art and architecture, choose one object or building from China, Japan, or Korea. Then write several paragraphs about the object, explaining the creator's skill, the material used, and how it represents the creator's culture.

Cooperative Learning Activity

Flags often include important symbols. Divide the class into six groups to each research the flag of one nation: China, Japan, Taiwan, North Korea, South Korea, Mongolia. Each group should draw a picture of the flag, and research its symbols and what changes it may have gone through, to report to the class.

Writing About Geography

Argumentation

Imagine that you are a Japanese official in 1851 as an American fleet arrives in Tokyo Bay. How do you think the Japanese should respond to this development? Using your journal and other source materials, write a short essay in which you argue either *for* adapting Western technology and ideas or *against* accepting anything that comes from these intrusive foreigners. Highlight issues such as available resources, population pressure, international trade, and international relations.

Locating Places

EAST ASIA: PHYSICAL GEOGRAPHY

Match the letters on the map with the places in East Asia. Write your answers on a separate sheet of paper.

1. Taiwan
2. Mongolia
3. Tokyo
4. Chiang Jiang
5. Seoul
6. Taipei
7. Guangzhou
8. Ulan Bator
9. Shanghai
10. Beijing

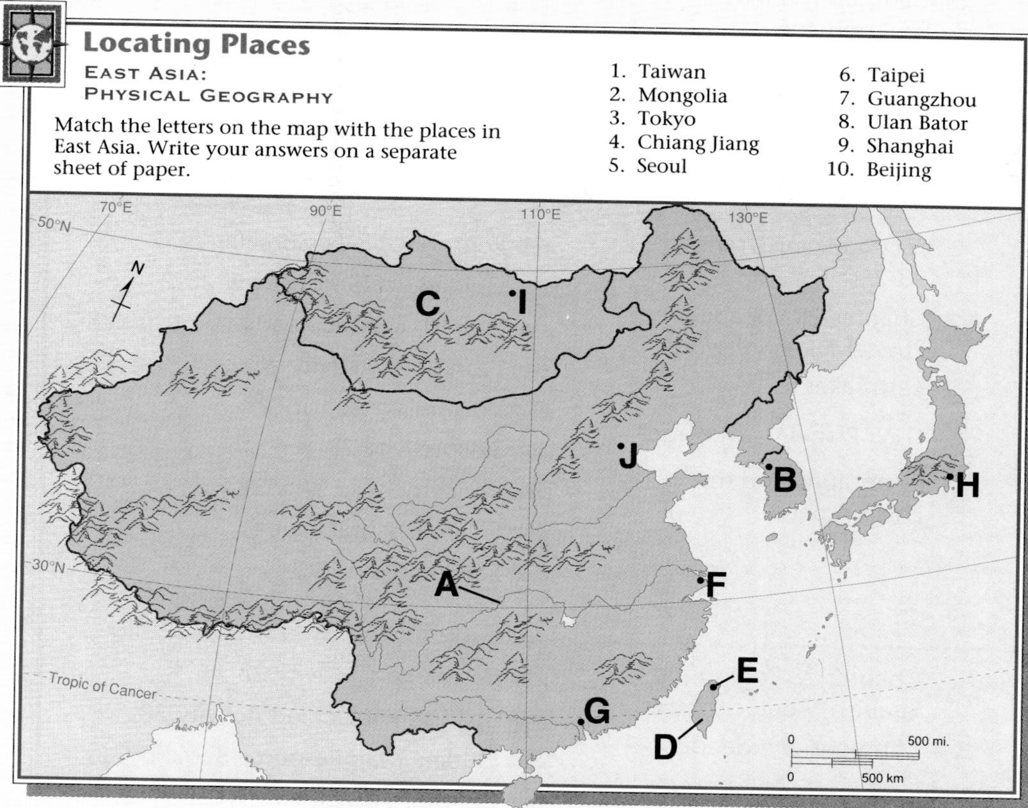

Chapter 27 Review

17. the Wei River, a tributary of the Huang He in China

18. Buddhism, Confucianism, Daoism

Practicing Skills

19. Kunming

20. Huang He to the north and the Chang Jiang and Chang rivers to the east

21. Taipei

Using the Unit Atlas

22. an accessible location and an excellent natural harbor

23. The Great Wall of China is 4,000 miles (7,408 km) long, the longest structure ever built.

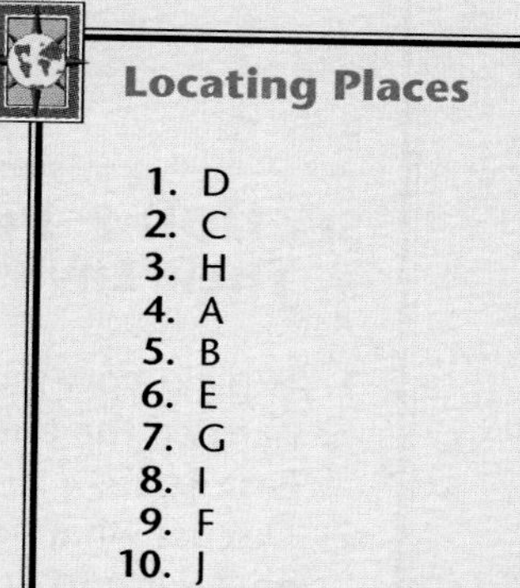

Locating Places

1. D
2. C
3. H
4. A
5. B
6. E
7. G
8. I
9. F
10. J

Chapter Bonus Test Question

This question may be used for extra credit on the chapter test. Choose the number of the correct response.

Which country has a Communist government, a mostly rural population, traditional herbal medicine and acupuncture, and a literacy rate of 76%?

(1) China
(2) Japan
(3) Taiwan
(4) North Korea

Answer: (1)

CHAPTER 28

PLANNING GUIDE

East Asia Today

CHAPTER ORGANIZER

Daily Lesson Objectives	Multimedia	Teacher Classroom Resources
SECTION 1 Living in East Asia 1. Appreciate the importance of agriculture and fishing in East Asian economies. 2. Analyze how smaller nations are challenging Japan's economic dominance in Asia. 3. Predict what the economic future holds for East Asia.	Section Focus Transparency 28-1 Chapter 28 Vocabulary PuzzleMaker Software Unit Map Overlay Transparency 1-9 Geography and the Environment Testmaker Reuters Issues in Geography Picture Atlas of the World	Reproducible Lesson Plan 28-1 Guided Reading Activity 28-1 Spanish Guided Reading Activity 28-1 Workbook Activity 28-1 Section Quiz 28-1
SECTION 2 People and Their Environment 1. Explain how industrialization has harmed the environment in East Asia. 2. Discuss what actions East Asians are taking to fight pollution and other environmental problems. 3. Examine how natural forces affect East Asia.	Section Focus Transparency 28-2 Chapter 28 Vocabulary PuzzleMaker Software Testmaker GTV: Planetary Manager Geography and the Environment	Reproducible Lesson Plan 28-2 Guided Reading Activity 28-2 Spanish Guided Reading Activity 28-2 Workbook Activity 28-2 Vocabulary Activity 28 Skill Activity 28 Enrichment Activity 28 Environmental Issue 9 Section Quiz 28-2
CHAPTER REVIEW AND EVALUATION	Chapter 28 English (or Spanish) Audiocassettes MindJogger Videoquiz Testmaker Student Self-Test and Review Software	Reteaching Activity 28 Spanish Reteaching Activity 28 Outline Map Resource Book, p. 35 Chapter 28 Test Form A and Form B

0:00 *If time does not permit teaching the entire chapter, summarize using the Chapter 28 Highlights on page 583, and Chapter 28 English (or Spanish) Audiocassettes. Review students' knowledge using the Glencoe MindJogger Videoquiz.*

KEY TO ABILITY LEVELS

Teaching strategies have been coded for varying learning styles and abilities.

L1 **BASIC** activities for all students

L2 **AVERAGE** activities for average to above-average students

L3 **CHALLENGING** activities for above-average students

LEP **LIMITED ENGLISH PROFICIENCY** activities

Performance Assessment

Predicting East Asia's Future Have students complete a trend study for economic and environmental issues affecting East Asia. Students should study and graph changes in population, trade, environment, and economic development. Students should then work in groups to study their data and use text information to predict what countries in the region will be like in another 50 years. They may address changes in government, economy, lifestyles, political boundaries, foreign relations, and so on.

Individual students in each group should present their views of the future with appropriate visual aids, such as maps, graphs, and posters. Other class members should pose questions to fully understand how the group reached its conclusions.

POSSIBLE RUBRIC FEATURES: Content information, concept attainment, research skills, generalization and prediction skills, pattern recognition, collaboration and communication skills

For additional professional and classroom resources, see Chapter Resources, pages T46–T51.

TEACHER'S CORNER

INDEX TO NATIONAL GEOGRAPHIC MAGAZINE

The following articles may be used for research relating to this chapter:

- "Rice: The Essential Harvest," by Peter T. White, May 1994.
- "In a Japanese Garden," by Bruce A. Coats, November 1989.
- "Soybean," by Fred Hapgood, July 1987.
- "Our Restless Planet Earth," by Rick Gore, August 1985.
- "Plight of the Bluefin Tuna," by Michael J. A. Butler, August 1982.

NATIONAL GEOGRAPHIC SOCIETY PRODUCTS AVAILABLE FROM GLENCOE

To order the following products for use with this chapter, contact your local Glencoe sales representative or call Glencoe at 1-800-334-7344:

- *Picture Atlas of the World* (CD-ROM)
- *STV: World Geography, Asia and Australia* (Videodisc)
- *ZipZapMap! World* (Software)
- *GeoBee* (Software)
- *Images of the World* (Posters)
- *Eye on the Environment* (Posters)
- *Physical Geography of the World* (Transparencies)
- *Picture Atlas of Our 50 States* (Book)

Introducing
CHAPTER 28

chapter 28 East Asia Today

PERFORMANCE ASSESSMENT

Refer to the Planning Guide on page 570B for a Performance Assessment Activity for this chapter. See the *Performance Assessment Activities* booklet for additional suggestions.

CHAPTER OBJECTIVES

1. **Understand** that most of the countries of East Asia depend heavily on both regional and international trade for their growth and prosperity.
2. **Recognize** that the intense concentration of people and industries in a small part of the region has had a severe impact on the environment.

GLENCOE TECHNOLOGY

Videodisc

Use Chapter 28 MindJogger Videoquiz to preview chapter content.

MINDJOGGER VIDEOQUIZ

Chapter 28
Disc 4 Side A

The MindJogger Videoquiz is also available on videocassette.

CHAPTER FOCUS

Geographic Setting

Like population, most agriculture and industry are concentrated in the river valleys and coastal plains of East Asia. The climate and terrain in much of the region make huge areas unsuitable for human habitation.

Geographic Themes

Section 1 Living in East Asia

MOVEMENT Most of the countries of East Asia depend heavily on both regional and international trade for their growth and prosperity.

▲ Photograph: *Farm market in Beijing, China*

Section 2 People and Their Environment

HUMAN/ENVIRONMENT INTERACTION The intense concentration of people and industries in a fairly small part of the region has had a severe impact on the natural environment.

EXTRA CREDIT PROJECT

Research Explain to students that the Japanese kill up to 330 minke whales annually for what they claim are "scientific studies," although some environmentalists believe that it is only a cover-up for commercial whaling. Point out that the minke whale is relatively plentiful. Then challenge interested students to find out which species of whales are considered endangered and what efforts are being made to save them. Have the students use their findings to create a display about whales.

1 SECTION Living in East Asia

SETTING THE SCENE

Read to Discover . . .
- the importance of agriculture and fishing in East Asian economies.
- how smaller nations are challenging Japan's economic dominance in Asia.
- what the economic future holds for East Asia.

Key Terms
- commune
- cooperative
- trading partner
- merchant marine

Identify and Locate
Xinjiang, Tian Shan, Shanghai, Hong Kong, Fujian (province), Wuhan, Guangzhou

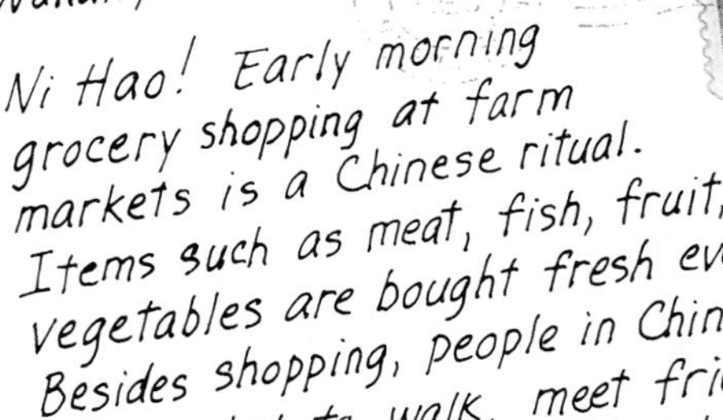

Wuhan, China

Ni Hao! Early morning grocery shopping at farm markets is a Chinese ritual. Items such as meat, fish, fruit, eggs and vegetables are bought fresh every day. Besides shopping, people in China come to the market to walk, meet friends, eat breakfast, or just watch the shoppers and farmers bargain for produce. Bing Liu

Bing Liu, who lives in central China, describes the importance of agriculture in Chinese daily life. Until recently most people in East Asia depended on agriculture for a living. Today industry and trade have become very important. Japan remains the leading industrial nation, but the Four Tigers—South Korea, Taiwan, Hong Kong, and Singapore (in Southeast Asia)—are becoming stronger economically.

HUMAN/ENVIRONMENT INTERACTION

Agriculture

Politics and economic development have changed farming styles in East Asia since the 1950s. Supplying enough food, however, remains crucially important.

China

China is the most agricultural of the nations of East Asia, with a huge land area and a growing population. More than 60 percent of the people in China work in agriculture. It is one of the world's leading producers of rice, wheat, and tea. Chinese farmers also produce large quantities of soybeans, cotton, jute, and silk. Livestock is an important product in the rugged western province of Xinjiang.

Since 1949, China's Communist government has made many changes in the country's agriculture. In the Great Leap Forward in 1958, farmers were organized into huge **communes,** collective farming communities whose members share work and products equally. An average commune had 5,000 households, divided into units called production brigades.

LESSON PLAN
Chapter 28, Section 1

FOCUS

SECTION OBJECTIVES

1. **Appreciate** the importance of agriculture and fishing in East Asian economies.
2. **Analyze** how smaller nations are challenging Japan's economic dominance in Asia.
3. **Predict** what the economic future holds for East Asia.

ABOUT THE POSTCARD

Bing tells us that many Chinese have pet birds that they "walk" around the market.

BELLRINGER MOTIVATIONAL ACTIVITY

Project the Section 1 Focus Transparency and have students answer the questions.

PRETEACHING VOCABULARY

Have students hypothesize about which Key Terms have similar meanings in the section. Then tell them to read the section to find out if their hypotheses are correct. *(commune and cooperative)*

Use the Vocabulary PuzzleMaker Software to create a crossword or word search puzzle.

NATIONAL GEOGRAPHIC SOCIETY

CD-ROM

PICTURE ATLAS OF THE WORLD
Click the "Stats" button of selected East Asian countries to learn about their economies and populations.

Classroom Resources for Section 1

BLACKLINE MASTERS:
Reproducible Lesson Plan 28-1
Guided Reading Activity 28-1
Workbook Activity 28-1
Section Quiz 28-1

TRANSPARENCIES:
Section Focus Transparency 28-1
Unit Map Overlay Transparency 1-9

MULTIMEDIA:

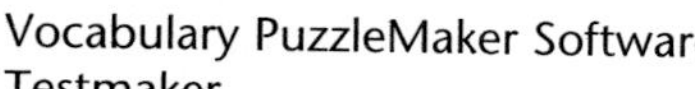

Vocabulary PuzzleMaker Software
Testmaker

Geography and the Environment
Reuters Issues in Geography

Picture Atlas of the World

TEACH

GUIDED PRACTICE

L1 Complete a Chart Make copies of the following incomplete chart. Omit the answers in parentheses.

COUNTRY	PRODUCTS
China	*(rice, wheat, tea, soybeans, cotton, jute, and silk)*
Japan	*(rice, vegetables, tea, and mulberry bushes)*
Korea	*(rice, other grains, potatoes, chickens, cattle, and pigs)*
Taiwan	*(rice, pineapples, bananas, tea, peanuts, and vegetables)*
Mongolia	*(sheep, goats, camels, cattle, milk, and wool)*

Distribute the copies to the class. Have students complete the chart with facts from pages 571 and 572.

USING ILLUSTRATIONS

REGION One hundred million Chinese farmers are underemployed or unemployed.

Answer to Caption: *more than 60 percent*

GLENCOE TECHNOLOGY

Videodisc

Use the following to enrich Chapter 28:

GEOGRAPHY AND THE ENVIRONMENT
THE INFINITE VOYAGE
Miracles by Design

Chapter 7
Disc 3 Side B

Title: *Ceramic Superconductors: Rapid Transportation*

Most peasants disliked the communes, and crop production fell, bringing famine. Since then, smaller farms and smaller groups of workers have been allowed. Many farmers also have private garden plots and sell extra crops or animals.

Japan

Because farmland is scarce in the Japanese islands, farmers use every inch of it carefully. In the warmer southern islands, they may plant and harvest three crops a year. Farmers terrace their fields and use machinery, fertilizers, and irrigation.

Most farms—usually about three acres—are family businesses. In some families, women and grandparents run the farm while men commute to city jobs.

Even with limited land, Japan grows all the rice, and many of the vegetables, that it needs. In higher areas, tea and mulberry bushes—to feed silkworms—are grown.

Korea

Much of the land in the Korean Peninsula is too rugged for farming. As industries and cities grow, fewer Koreans work in agriculture, causing farmers to depend on machines.

Rice is the main crop in both North and South Korea. South Korean farmers plant two crops of rice a year using special seeds and farming methods to produce high yields. They grow other grains and potatoes and raise farm animals such as chickens, cattle, and pigs.

Taiwan

Taiwanese farmers also terrace their fields to grow rice. Most farms there are only two or three acres. The warm climate lets farmers plant pineapples, bananas, tea, peanuts, and vegetables.

Mongolia

Most of the land in Mongolia, in north-central East Asia, is used for grazing herds of sheep, goats, camels, and cattle.

Until the early 1990s, Mongolia followed the Soviet Union as its economic model. Herders were organized into collectives with quotas for producing milk and wool. State farms also grew food for people and fodder for animals. Today Mongolian farmers are slowly moving toward free enterprise.

Geographic Themes

Region: Eastern China

China's farmers rely on human and animal labor as well as machinery. *What percent of China's people work in agriculture?*

HUMAN/ENVIRONMENT INTERACTION

Fishing

Three of the world's leading fishing nations are in East Asia—Japan, China, and South Korea.

Fishing is an important food source and export of the region. In China, people depend on freshwater fish while the Japanese catch and eat more seafood than any other people.

Commercial fishing is especially important for peninsular and island nations. Fleets of trawlers catch tons of snapper, tuna, squid, shrimp, and other seafood. Factory ships often travel along to clean and freeze the fish soon after it is caught.

Most Japanese fishing communities have organized **cooperatives,** or co-ops. Co-op members work together to buy boats, sell the catch, and provide housing and benefits for their members.

Cooperative Learning Activity

Have a group of students research cormorants—specially trained fishing birds. Tell them that the Japanese keep alive the tradition of fishing with cormorants in Kyoto's Arishiyama Park. Suggest that they present their findings in story form, perhaps as a cartoon they draw on a bleached filmstrip and show using a film projector. Remind them to prepare and recite a narration that explains what is happening in the cartoon.

POPULATION OF JAPAN BY AGE AND SEX

POPULATION OF CHINA BY AGE AND SEX

Male | Female | Age: 70+, 60-69, 50-59, 40-49, 30-39, 20-29, 10-19, 0-9 | Percentage: 14 13 12 11 10 9 8 7 6 5 4 3 2 1 0 1 2 3 4 5 6 7 8 9 10 11 12 13 14

CHART STUDY

Japan's population is stable, but China's population had been growing rapidly. In recent years, however, the Chinese government has attempted to reduce population growth. ***Using the population pyramid, determine whether the Chinese government has been successful at slowing population growth.***

MOVEMENT

Industry and Trade

Since the 1950s most nations of East Asia have become prosperous trading and industrial nations. Many have invited foreign investors.

Despite political differences regional nations are economically interdependent. Japan, Taiwan, and Hong Kong have all made investments in China, and state-owned Chinese companies have invested in Hong Kong.

Japan

Japan has long had flourishing industries, trade, and finance. As Japan became an imperial and military power in the 1890s, it developed heavy industries such as shipbuilding and steelmaking.

Recovering from World War II, Japan became Asia's economic miracle. Japanese

Geographic Themes

Region: South Korea

South Korea has one of the world's fastest-growing economies. A major industry is shipbuilding. *What is a major source of South Korea's prosperity?*

MULTICULTURAL PERSPECTIVE

Cultural Diversity

Although the most common rice produced and consumed in Asia is long-grain, which produces the best separation of grains after cooking, the Japanese prefer sticky short-grain rice because they can easily pick it up with chopsticks.

USING CHARTS

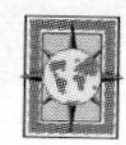

Answer: Yes, the youngest group is getting smaller.

Skills Practice

Drawing Conclusions How long ago do you think the government started its efforts to reduce the population? Explain how you arrived at your answer. *(between 10 and 20 years ago; Those between the ages of 10 and 20 form the largest part of the population, so the last time there was an increase rather than a decrease in birthrates was between 10 and 20 years ago.)*

USING ILLUSTRATIONS

REGION About one-fourth of all South Korean workers are in mining and manufacturing.

Answer to Caption: *trade with the United States and Japan*

Meeting Special Needs

Study Strategy Stress the "Question" component of studying for students who have difficulty formulating questions. Explain that this exercise should be practiced whenever the students read for information: Turn the first sentence of each paragraph into a question. Direct their attention to the first sentence under the heading "Japan." Then ask, "Why has Japan long had flourishing industries, trade, and finance?" Tell the students to look for the answer in the rest of the paragraph. *(As Japan became an imperial and military power in the 1890s, it developed heavy industries such as shipbuilding and steelmaking.)* Ask volunteers to formulate a question and an answer from the next paragraph.

INDEPENDENT PRACTICE

Guided Reading Have students complete Guided Reading Activity 28-1 in the TCR. **LEP**

L2 Compare Distribute copies of Unit Map Overlay Transparency 1-9 (a blank grid) and have students convert the data in the chart on page 575 into a bar graph comparing Japan's imports and exports over the years. Suggest that the students use different colors for the import and export bars.

USING MAPS

Answers:
1. near the coast and along rivers;
2. nomadic herding;
3. parts of western and southern China and northern North Korea;
4. Mongolia

Map Skills Practice
Reading a Map Which countries have mainly subsistence farming? *(China, North Korea, and South Korea)*

CURRICULUM CONNECTION

EARTH SCIENCE
North Korea has about 80 to 90 percent of all the Korean Peninsula's known mineral resources, which the nation has used to fuel its industrial growth.

industries such as Honda, Sony, and Toyota prospered. Japanese-made cars, VCRs, stereos, cameras, and other electronic equipment have a world market.

One reason for Japan's success is that its workers turn out more goods per hour than workers in Europe or the United States. Japanese-style management encourages workers to feel part of a team. Also, factories continually modernize their equipment.

Because Japan has few industrial raw materials, it depends on trade. Although the country is a major steelmaker, for example, it imports iron ore. It also imports some food and most energy fuels—coal, oil, and natural gas, for example.

Japan's export trade, on the other hand, is extremely successful with its **trading partners**—countries that buy from or sell to the Japanese. The United States is Japan's largest partner, with Europe and other East Asian countries also its customers.

Taiwan

The island of Taiwan—the Republic of China—depends on thousands of smaller businesses, which make textiles, appliances, and other goods. Many Taiwanese operate factories in China's Fujian province and in other countries where land is available, the workforce is large, and labor is cheap.

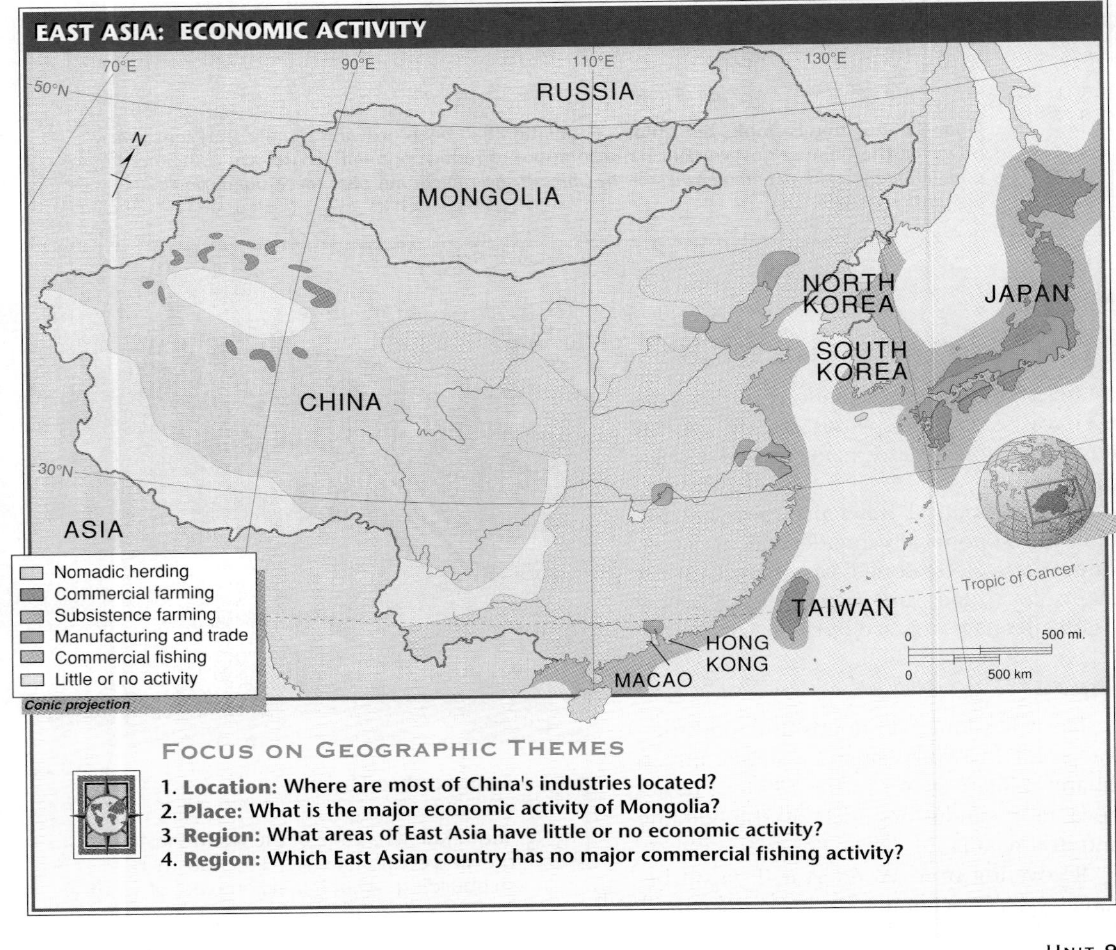

FOCUS ON GEOGRAPHIC THEMES

1. **Location:** Where are most of China's industries located?
2. **Place:** What is the major economic activity of Mongolia?
3. **Region:** What areas of East Asia have little or no economic activity?
4. **Region:** Which East Asian country has no major commercial fishing activity?

Critical Thinking

Making Comparisons Distribute copies of the following incomplete chart:

	UNITED STATES	CHINA	JAPAN
AGRICULTURE			
FISHING			
INDUSTRY AND TRADE			
TRANSPORTATION			
COMMUNICATION			

Instruct students to complete the chart with facts from the section and from a recent world almanac. After they finish, ask them to rank the three nations first, second, and third in each of the categories on the chart.

China and Hong Kong

Outdated technology, poor government planning, and a lack of skilled workers have all slowed industrial growth in the People's Republic of China. The government owns and runs most major industries. China's natural resources, however, make it a leading producer of coal, steel, and cement. In the 1990s, Chinese leaders proposed many changes in the economy, encouraging foreign investments.

Entrepreneurs from Hong Kong and Taiwan have invested billions of dollars in plants in the nearby mainland provinces of Fujian and Guangdong. Beijing and cities in Manchuria in northern China are centers for iron and steel, petrochemicals, and cars. Shanghai produces textiles, steel, and ships.

Many economists believe that "greater China"—the People's Republic, Taiwan, and Hong Kong—will become an economic giant with the return of Hong Kong to China in 1997.

Korea

"Greater Korea" is also expected to become an economic center. It would include North and South Korea as well as northern China and far eastern Russia.

South Korea is one of Asia's new economic powers. Its prosperity since the Korean War has come mainly from trade with the United States and Japan. South Korea exports electronic equipment, textiles, ships, steel, and cars and trucks.

The Communist government of North Korea, which has large mineral reserves, emphasizes heavy industry such as machinery, chemicals, and iron and steel.

Mongolia

Most industries in Mongolia are based on its livestock, farms, and forests. Factories make textiles from wool and leather shoes and coats from hides. They also process meat and milk products and make furniture, paper, and other wood products.

Before the fall of communism in Russia, Mongolia traded mainly with China and Soviet bloc countries. In the 1990s Mongolia began to move gradually toward capitalism.

JAPAN'S BALANCE OF TRADE

Year	Value of Imports (in billions of dollars)	Value of Exports (in billions of dollars)	Balance of Trade (in billions of dollars)
1978	79.3	97.5	+18.2
1979	110.7	103.0	-7.7
1980	140.5	129.9	-10.6
1981	152.0	143.3	-8.7
1982	139.0	132.0	-7.0
1983	126.0	146.0	+20.0
1984	136.5	170.1	+33.6
1985	130.0	177.0	+47.0
1986	126.4	209.2	+82.8
1987	149.5	229.2	+79.7
1988	187.4	264.9	+77.5
1989	210.8	275.2	+64.40
1990	234.8	286.9	+52.10
1991	236.7	314.5	+77.80

Source: *The Statesman's Yearbook*, 1992-1993 *Encyclopedia Britannica Yearbook*, 1993

CHART STUDY

Japan has maintained a positive balance of trade since 1983. *In what year did the value of Japan's exports start to exceed $200 billion?*

MOVEMENT

Transportation and Communication

Before air travel was common, rugged mountains isolated East Asia. Today every country in the region has at least one scheduled air service. Overland travel in mainland Asia, however, involves long journeys by railroad or road. Transportation and communication networks are concentrated in the heavily populated areas.

Water

Rivers in China are important routes from inland industrial cities to seaports. The Chiang

Chapter 28, Section 1

ASSESS

CHECK FOR UNDERSTANDING

Assign Section 1 Review as homework or an in-class activity.

MEETING LESSON OBJECTIVES

Each objective below is tested by the questions that follow it in parentheses.

1. Appreciate the importance of agriculture and fishing in East Asian economies. *(3)*

2. Analyze how smaller nations are challenging Japan's economic dominance in Asia. *(4)*

3. Predict what the economic future holds for East Asia. *(5)*

EVALUATE

Assign the Section 1 Quiz in the TCR.

Use the Testmaker to create a customized quiz for Section 1.

USING CHARTS

Answer: 1986

Skills Practice

Interpreting a Chart

During what years did Japan experience a trade deficit? *(1979, 1980, 1981, 1982)*

RETEACH

Have students complete Workbook Activity 28-1 found in the TCR.

Extending the Content

Place One of the oldest countries in the world, Mongolia changed from a totally nomadic culture to a partially agricultural and industrial nation with the help of the former Soviet Union. Today Mongolian manufacturers produce processed foods, textiles, chemicals, and cement. Other signs of Mongolia's development are its acquisition of modern communication systems: 1 out of each 18 Mongolians has a television, 1 out of each 7.5 has a radio, and 91 newspapers circulate for every 1,000 people.

ENRICH

Display a copy of a Chinese or Japanese book, magazine, or newspaper.

CLOSE

Have students write a postcard to Bing, describing grocery/market shopping.

USING ILLUSTRATIONS

PLACE Japan has 17,059 miles (27,448 km) of railroad track—more than 1 mile (1.6 km) for every 10 square miles (25.9 sq. km) of area.

Answer to Caption: *145 miles per hour (240 km per hour)*

GLENCOE TECHNOLOGY

Videodisc

REUTERS ISSUES IN GEOGRAPHY

Chapter 8
Disc 1 Side A
Title: ***China: The New Prosperity***
Subject: Changes taking place in the way goods and services are produced in the People's Republic of China

Geographic Themes

Region: Honshu, Japan
Japan's bullet-shaped, high-speed electric trains run the length of the main island of Honshu. *How fast can the bullet trains travel?*

Jiang is the longest navigable river and the major port of Shanghai lies at its mouth. Large oceangoing ships can travel upriver 680 miles (1,090 km) to the transportation center of Wuhan in central China.

Other major ports are also at the mouths of rivers: Tianjin (TYEN•JIN) on the Huang He, and Guangzhou, on the Xi River. The world's oldest and longest artificial waterway, the Grand Canal, connects the Chiang Jiang and the Huang He.

Much of the trade of East Asian nations depends on their **merchant marine,** ships that engage in commerce. The leading nation is Japan, with a merchant fleet of nearly 10,000 ships, the second largest in the world. Japan's coast, especially the Inland Sea, has many fine harbors. Major ports are Yokohama, Kobe (KOH•bee), and Nagoya.

Land Travel

Japan has had busy highways since the 1600s. Railroads were an important part of Japan's drive toward modernization in the late 1800s. Today Japanese railway systems include high-speed trains, known as bullet trains, that can travel at 145 miles per hour (240 kmph).

Outside Japan few East Asians own cars. Railroads are important for long-distance travel, especially for the great distances within China. In the northwest a major railway line links Beijing with the Trans-Siberian Railway in Russia. Locally, buses connect towns. In rural areas people still travel by animal-drawn carts. Bicycles are popular everywhere.

North Korean railroads link that country with China. Railroads connect major South Korean cities. South Korea also built new highways for the 1988 Olympic Games held in Seoul.

Communications

In the Communist nations of East Asia, governments keep tight control of communications media. China's largest newspaper is the *People's Daily,* the official paper of the Communist Party.

Access to mass communications varies with a country's standard of living. Most people in Japan and Taiwan own television sets; a typical Chinese working family, on the other hand, is lucky to have a radio.

The Japanese have more than 125 daily newspapers, 2,000 magazines, and a large book publishing industry. A Tokyo paper, *Asahi Shimbun,* has a circulation of 11 million copies a day, the largest in the world.

SECTION 1 REVIEW

Checking for Understanding

1. **Define** commune, cooperative, trading partner, merchant marine.
2. **Locating Places** What Chinese port city is located on the Chiang Jiang?
3. **Place** What are China's major food crops?
4. **Movement** Why is trade important to Japan's prosperity?

Critical Thinking

5. **Analyzing Information** Why are the nations of East Asia interdependent in spite of their political differences?

ANSWERS TO SECTION 1 REVIEW

1. **commune:** government-organized farming community including thousands of households whose members share work and benefits; **cooperative:** voluntary organization whose members share work and benefits; **trading partner:** nation that buys from or sells to another nation; **merchant marine:** a country's fleet of ships used in commerce
2. Shanghai
3. wheat, rice, tea
4. because it lacks natural resources and raw materials for industry
5. Economic growth has led the countries to invest in one another, especially in places where land is available and labor is cheap.

2 SECTION People and Their Environment

THE ENVIRONMENT

SETTING THE SCENE

Read to Discover . . .
- how industrialization has harmed the environment in East Asia.
- what actions East Asians are taking to fight pollution and other environmental problems.
- how natural forces affect East Asia.

Key Terms
- acid rain
- chlorofluorocarbon

Identify and Locate
Beijing, Guangzhou, Guangdong

In terms of the environment, the people of East Asia have paid a high price for economic growth and prosperity. Industry and development have caused serious pollution problems. The region is also subject to natural disasters such as floods and earthquakes.

HUMAN/ENVIRONMENT INTERACTION

Environmental Concerns

In many parts of East Asia, industrial growth has seemed so important that its effects on the environment have been largely ignored. This has created serious environmental problems that affect not only this region but the entire world.

China

Coal is an inexpensive fuel—and China has huge reserves of it. As China works to industrialize, coal provides about 70 percent of its energy, running factories and heating homes. Burning coal, however, causes serious air pollution, especially in industrial cities. In Beijing where the air is already polluted by wind-blown dust, coal adds soot and poisonous fumes. In regions of China devoted to heavy industry, large numbers of people suffer from lung disease.

Burning coal gives off sulfur dioxide, a major ingredient of **acid rain**. When sulfur dioxide and other acids mix with water in the air, the rain that falls can be more acid than vinegar. It damages trees and can kill wildlife in lakes and rivers. Acid rain is a serious problem in the industrial region of southeast China, especially Guangdong, Guangxi, and Guizhou provinces. Winds spread acid rain across the sea to Japan's forests.

As China industrializes, problems with polluted water and toxic wastes increase. Thousands of acres of forests are cleared every year, adding to desert land and making floods worse. Government policies such as the Great Leap Forward caused damage to the environment by neglect. Although China has laws regulating pollution, they often are not enforced.

As a nation industrializes, its people tend to use more goods, consume more energy, and create more waste. Because China has more than 1 billion people, its continuing econom-

Classroom Resources for Section 2

BLACKLINE MASTERS:
Reproducible Lesson Plan 28-2
Environmental Issue 9
Guided Reading Activity 28-2
Spanish Guided Reading Activity 28-2
Workbook Activity 28-2
Vocabulary Activity 28
Skill Activity 28
Enrichment Activity 28
Section Quiz 28-2

TRANSPARENCIES:
Section Focus Transparency 28-2

MULTIMEDIA:
Testmaker

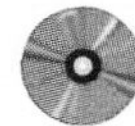

GTV: Planetary Manager
Geography and the Environment

LESSON PLAN
Chapter 28, Section 2

FOCUS

SECTION OBJECTIVES

1. **Explain** how industrialization has harmed the environment in East Asia.
2. **Discuss** what actions East Asians are taking to fight pollution and other environmental problems.
3. **Examine** how natural forces affect East Asia.

BELLRINGER MOTIVATIONAL ACTIVITY

Project the Section 2 Focus Transparency and have students answer the questions.

PRETEACHING VOCABULARY

Have a student read the first paragraph in the right column on page 577 about acid rain. Then display a twig that has been soaked in vinegar for several days next to a control twig from the same bush or tree.

NATIONAL GEOGRAPHIC SOCIETY

Videodisc

GTV: PLANETARY MANAGER

Side 2, Chapter 1
Frames 2-5929
Title: ***Up, Up, and Away?***
Subject: Consequences of air pollution

GTV: PLANETARY MANAGER

Side 2, Chapter 4
Frames 18754-25234
Title: ***Holy Smoke!***
Subject: The use and abuse of fossil fuels

TEACH

GUIDED PRACTICE

Implement Environmental Issue 9 as a class activity.

INDEPENDENT PRACTICE

Guided Reading Have students complete Guided Reading Activity 28-2 in the TCR. **LEP**

ASSESS

CHECK FOR UNDERSTANDING

Assign Section 2 Review as homework or an in-class activity.

USING ILLUSTRATIONS

PLACE Concentrations of air pollutants in Tokyo, Osaka, and Yokohama have increased over the past decade.

Answer to Caption: *Japan encouraged industries to prevent pollution and passed strict pollution-control laws.*

GLENCOE TECHNOLOGY

Videodisc

GEOGRAPHY AND THE ENVIRONMENT
THE INFINITE VOYAGE
To the Edge of the Earth

Chapter 3
Disc 1 Side B
Title: ***Exploring Volcanoes: To the Center of the Earth***
Subject: A manned submersible is used to study volcanic activity below the surface of the Pacific Ocean

ic growth will have a great impact on the world's environment.

Japan

Japan is highly industrialized and very crowded. Waste products from factories, plus the trash of a rich "throwaway society," have polluted the air and water.

For many years the Japanese were criticized for ignoring the environmental problems their technologies were creating. In the 1970s, however, the Japanese government began to encourage industries to prevent pollution. Today its pollution-control laws are among the world's strictest.

Japanese industries sought new technologies to clean up or prevent air and water pollution. Japan soon became efficient in using energy. Of all the industrialized nations, it produces the least carbon dioxide, which contributes to the greenhouse effect. The United States, on the other hand, produces the most carbon dioxide, about 24 percent of the world total.

In the 1990s Japan became a world leader in environmental issues. It urged other nations to reduce their emissions of carbon dioxide and **chlorofluorocarbons**, or CFCs. These substances, found in liquid coolants, destroy parts of the earth's protective ozone layer. Japan also offered "clean" technology and financial help for environmental projects to neighboring East Asian countries and other developing nations.

Other Countries

Rapid economic growth also brought environmental problems in Korea and Taiwan. In Taiwan, for example, computer factories were producing toxic waste, and petrochemical plants polluted river water. Both countries took steps to regulate industries.

Conservation

Other threats to the environment in East Asia are caused by growing populations, overfishing, and trade in rare animal products. Carved elephant ivory is valued in Asian art, and rhinoceros horn is used in traditional medicine. Yet both animals are endangered.

Japan has been criticized worldwide for some of its fishing methods. It is one of the few countries in the world that still hunts whales. In 1991 Japan agreed to stop fishing with drift nets, huge deep-sea nets that drastically lowered fish populations and killed anything caught in them, including dolphins and birds.

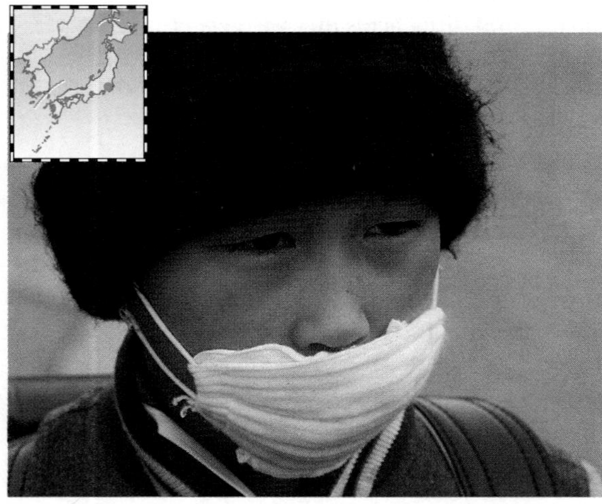

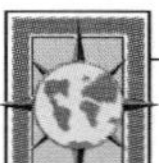
Geographic Themes
Place: Tokyo, Japan
Some Japanese often wear masks on days when pollution is severe. *How has Japan sought to improve the environment of East Asia?*

REGION

Natural Disasters

Because of its geography, East Asia constantly faces catastrophic natural disasters. Throughout its history, China has had to deal with disastrous floods on the Huang He and the Chiang Jiang. A young Chinese worker in 1969 described how the government and commune members worked to control floods:

We don't fear flood and we don't fear drought! That 1961 flood was the last. . . . We've deepened and widened and straightened the Wei [River]. We have a network of drainage and irrigation

Cooperative Learning Activity

Read the following excerpt from Midori Yamanouchi's account of a Tokyo earthquake:

All around, the bamboo was trembling and rustling. I was afraid. Bamboo is supposed to be a safe place during an earthquake because its roots twine together so tight that the earth can't split open beneath you and the trees can't fall on you. But it was shaking so much I wasn't sure. When I got to our house, I found all the neighbors in our backyard because we had the best bamboo grove anywhere around. Everybody stayed right there from noon, when the earthquake began, until almost midnight.

Have students compare the passage with earthquake experiences they have had or accounts they have read related to the California earthquake of 1994.

Geographic Themes

Place: Huang He valley, China

Because the Huang He often floods over a large area and causes great destruction, it has been called "China's sorrow." *How have the Chinese sought to control floods?*

canals and channels that can carry off or bring in water quickly. From source to mouth the work of harnessing the Yellow River [Huang He] is going ahead. That settles the danger of flood.

Several parts of China also suffer from frequent, damaging earthquakes. Typhoons often devastate coastal areas.

The island nations of East Asia are part of the Pacific Ocean's Ring of Fire. Located at plate boundaries where the earth's crust sometimes shifts, this region has frequent earthquakes and volcanic activity. Japan has about 50 active volcanoes and many hot springs from underground sources.

Every year Japan has about 1,500 small earthquakes. The most devastating, in 1923, destroyed large parts of Tokyo and Yokohama and killed about 130,000 people. Earthquakes on the sea floor can be equally serious for coastal areas. In 1993 an earthquake sent huge tsunami crashing onto the shores of Hokkaido and nearby small islands.

Section 2 Review

Checking for Understanding

1. **Define** acid rain, chlorofluorocarbon.
2. **Locating Places** In what part of China is the problem of acid rain most serious?
3. **Place** What is the Ring of Fire?
4. **Human/Environment Interaction** What kinds of natural disasters are a threat to East Asia?

Critical Thinking

5. **Predicting Consequences** Why will China's continued economic growth have an effect on the world environment?

MEETING LESSON OBJECTIVES

Each objective below is tested by the questions that follow it in parentheses.

1. **Explain** how industrialization has harmed the environment in East Asia. *(2)*
2. **Discuss** what actions East Asians are taking to fight pollution and other environmental problems. *(5)*
3. **Examine** how natural forces affect East Asia. *(3, 4)*

EVALUATE

Assign the Section 2 Quiz in the TCR.

Use the Testmaker to create a customized quiz for Section 2.

RETEACH

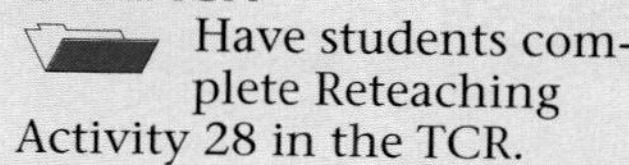

Have students complete Reteaching Activity 28 in the TCR.

ENRICH

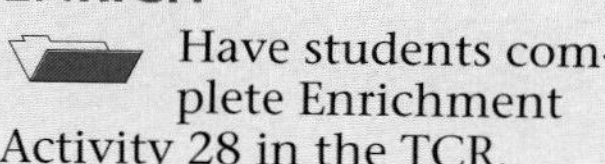

Have students complete Enrichment Activity 28 in the TCR.

CLOSE

Name items from the section, such as the bullet train and *People's Daily*, and have students identify the East Asian country associated with each.

USING ILLUSTRATIONS

PLACE In 1887, 900,000 people died in a Huang He flood.

Answer to Caption: They enlarged and straightened the Wei and dug canals and channels to control the water flow.

ANSWERS TO SECTION 2 REVIEW

1. **acid rain:** rainwater that has mixed with chemicals in the air; **chlorofluorocarbon:** substance that damages the earth's ozone layer
2. southeast China
3. A region that is located at plate boundaries where the earth's crust sometimes shifts and so has frequent earthquakes and volcanic activity.
4. earthquakes, volcanoes, tsunami, and typhoons
5. People in more developed countries use more energy and goods and create more wastes. Since China has so many people, the impact will be very great.

FOCUS

Ask students to scan the photos and captions of the selection, then recall the size and population of Japan. Ask them for predictions of effects of earthquakes in that country. Write responses on the chalkboard.

TEACH

L1 Location Use Political Transparency 9 to familiarize students with the location of Japan.

L2 Location Have students recall the cause of earthquakes and identify other regions of the world that are prone to these disasters.

GLENCOE TECHNOLOGY

Videodisc

GEOGRAPHY AND THE ENVIRONMENT
THE INFINITE VOYAGE
Living With Disaster

Chapter 5
Disc 3 Side A
Title: ***Earthquakes: A Turbulence Beneath the Earth***
Subject: The nature and cause of earthquakes is explained through animation

GEOGRAPHY AND THE ENVIRONMENT
THE INFINITE VOYAGE
Living With Disaster

Chapter 10
Disc 3 Side A
Title: ***Adapting to the Nature of Volcanoes: Sakurajima***
Subject: The city of Kagoshima, Japan, copes with the more than 200 yearly eruptions of a nearby volcano

CASE STUDY

TROUBLESOME TREMORS

I never had much, but what I had, I lost it all.

Fujiharu Hatsuzuka, 63-year-old fisher who survived a 1993 earthquake in northern Japan.

On January 17, 1995, a 7.5-magnitude earthquake struck central Japan, demolishing the city of Kobe, the country's second-largest port. Within minutes the quake triggered landslides and raging firestorms. More than 6,000 people were killed, another 250,000 were made homeless, and the city experienced nearly $120 billion in damage. The quake was the worst to hit Japan in seven decades.

More than 94,000 buildings and houses were demolished in Kobe when a devastating earthquake struck the city in early 1995.

THE ISSUE

The 1995 quake was one of about 1,500 that shake Japan every year. Building construction and city planning are areas of intense interest as the Japanese study ways to minimize the devastating effects of major earthquakes.

THE BACKGROUND

Japan lies in a region where three huge plates of the earth's surface crunch against one another. The collisions are continuous, accounting for the thousands of earthquakes that are part of Japan's geological make-up.

Most quakes are short tremors. Every few years, however, a serious quake occurs. Major crunches usually cause several other natural catastrophes, such as landslides and tsunami.

Through the centuries the Japanese have developed housing that is remarkably resilient to quakes. Most famous is the traditional Japanese house—one story, of wood, constructed on a sturdy skeletal frame. The frames are able to sustain the repeated shocks of frequent earthquakes. Luckily, Japan has tremendous timber resources, so wooden houses can be quickly and easily rebuilt.

Although wooden houses can withstand a quake's jolts, they are vulnerable to the firestorms that often occur in conjunction with quakes.

Traditional Japanese cooking is done over an open charcoal fire: the earth's shaking upsets the stoves, spilling smoldering charcoal on the floor, which

Extending the Content

Place Encourage students to find out about the earthquake that struck Japan in 1923, demolishing the capital of Tokyo. Suggest that students look for dramatic photographs, first-person accounts, and statistics to help them better understand the experience. Also, encourage them to find out how long it took to rebuild Tokyo completely. Allow time for an informal sharing; the class may want to discuss which photographs and statistics are the most informative.

catches fire. Tokyo's 1923 quake—the century's worst—began during lunch hour. Overturned cookstoves fired the rubble, producing two great walls of fire that pushed fleeing crowds into the Sumida River.

To reduce the chance of fire, brick construction was introduced in the early 1890s. By the turn of the century, Japanese architects had learned how to strengthen brick walls with steel frame construction, build with composite brick-and-steel frame structures, and use reinforced concrete.

Through the centuries the Japanese have developed housing that is remarkably resilient to quakes.

THE POINTS OF VIEW

Although several construction techniques now exist for quake-proofing buildings, some Japanese architects say that such construction is not used as widely as it could be. In addition, say these architects, no time is ever given to examine ways in which destruction from a quake could be lessened through better city planning. Says a leading architect, "Our authorities only recognize the need for reconstruction and clearance after a catastrophe. They see no necessity to prevent the recurrence of catastrophes by a new program of building."

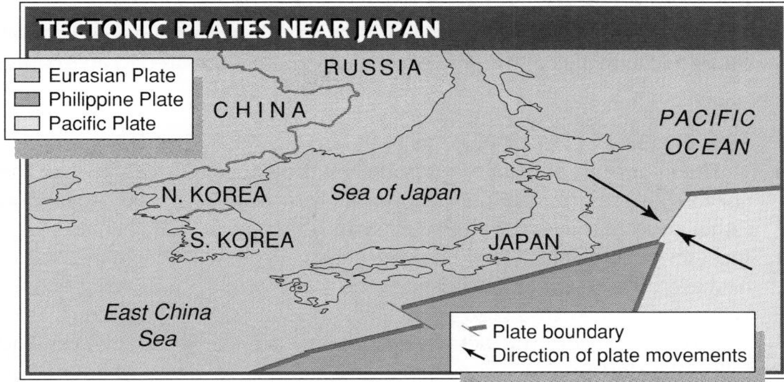

Experts also point out that Japan's urban population is rapidly increasing. More people crowding in the cities means potentially more victims during a quake.

THE ISSUE TODAY

Japan continues to build. While more concrete buildings are going up, they do not necessarily replace wooden houses. Most are built in addition to wooden housing.

Charcoal stoves have been replaced by kerosene for heating and bottled gas for cooking. Unfortunately, both are much more highly flammable than charcoal.

Engineers and earthquake scientists are working together to design buildings that will not collapse during a quake. Cities have passed strict zoning laws requiring tall buildings to conform to certain rigorous standards. Japanese citizens participate in frequent earthquake drills. Many families keep survival kits ready. Fire extinguishers are handy everywhere, even in buses and taxicabs.

Experts admit, however, that a large quake could demolish buildings—wooden or cement—by the thousands. As many as one-half million people could die.

Reviewing the Case

1. Why does Japan have many earthquakes?
2. What steps have the Japanese taken to minimize earthquake damage?
3. **Human/Environment Interaction**  What nongeographical problem contributes to earthquake damage in Japan?

ASSESS

Have students answer the Reviewing the Case questions on page 581.

CLOSE

Have students offer any other suggestions for preparing for earthquakes.

DID YOU KNOW?

In addition to the danger of fire with an earthquake, Japan also often faces the destruction of *tsunami.* If the earthquake is undersea, the sea floor's shifting rocks create a wave in the water. The wave can begin small in the deep ocean water, but as it travels toward the shore, it can develop into a towering wall of water.

 **Videodisc**

STV: RESTLESS EARTH

Side 1, Chapter 3
Frames 37503-51201
Title: ***Spreading and Subduction*** **(in its entirety)**
Subject: Describes how geologic action of spreading is detaching coastal East Africa from its mother continent, and how subduction, the action of one plate moving underneath another, is causing earthquakes in Japan

ANSWERS TO REVIEWING THE CASE

1. Japan lies in a region where three of the earth's plates come together. The plates are constantly bumping each other, producing earthquakes.
2. They have designed earthquake-proof homes and buildings; they have earthquake drills; and they keep emergency supplies ready.
3. Japan's population is increasing, which means an increased death rate in the event of an earthquake.

Teaching Skills

TEACH

Write the following economic activities on the chalkboard: farming, ranching, fishing, mining, trade, manufacturing, and services. Ask students to identify the activities performed by most people in their region. Have students summarize the "dominant economic activities." Then ask: "Why are these economic activities dominant in our area?" *(Students should identify physical factors such as climate, resources, landforms, and so on.)* Explain: "By examining these relationships, we discover how physical factors shape human life." Ask students to find news articles describing the effects of environmental change on a city's or region's economy.

Skills Practice For additional practice, have students complete Skill Activity 28 in the TCR.

MAP & GRAPH SKILLS

Reading an Economic Activity Map

Most people in any region practice one or two basic types of economic activity—the dominant economic activities of that region. These can be illustrated in an **economic activity map.**

REVIEWING THE SKILL

The economic activity maps in this textbook use colors to represent dominant economic activities. Other sources may use patterns or symbols to represent economic activities. In all maps, however, the key or legend defines the colors and symbols.

To read an economic activity map, apply the following steps:

- Read the map title to identify the geographic region shown by the map.
- Study the map key to understand all colors, symbols, and patterns used on the map.
- Study the map to determine what activities dominate the economy of each area.
- Compare the map with maps showing landforms, climate, and resources of the region to draw conclusions about the interaction of humans and the environment.

PRACTICING THE SKILL

Use the map below to answer the following questions:

1. What color represents subsistence agriculture? Manufacturing and trade?
2. What economic activity dominates eastern China?
3. How do landforms and climate determine the economic activity in eastern China?
4. In what areas do most people practice nomadic herding? Why is there little agriculture in these regions?
5. What activities dominate Japan's economy?
6. How has Japan's physical geography influenced its economy?

For additional practice in this skill, see Practicing Skills on page 584 of the Chapter 28 Review.

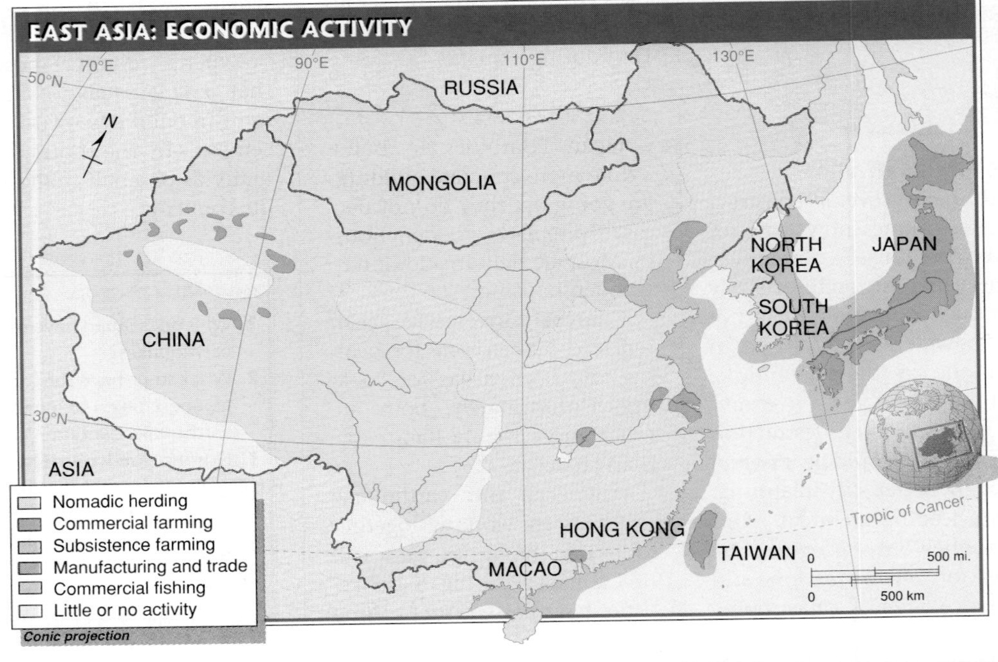

ANSWERS TO PRACTICING THE SKILL

1. light green; red
2. commercial farming
3. Eastern China has ideal conditions for intensive agriculture—flat, rolling plains, fertile soil from river floodplains, and ample rainfall.
4. northern and western China, Mongolia; These areas have rugged mountains and high plateaus with little rainfall.
5. agriculture, manufacturing and trade, fishing
6. Japan's mountainous terrain limits agriculture to the lower elevations. Because it is an island country surrounded by good harbors and fishing banks, its economy depends primarily on trade, fishing, and manufacturing.

chapter 28

HIGHLIGHTS

Section	Key Terms	Summary
1 Living in East Asia	**commune** (p. 571) **cooperative** (p. 572) **trading partner** (p. 574) **merchant marine** (p. 576)	• East Asia was once mainly agricultural, but trade and industry have brought prosperity and economic growth to most of its nations. • A majority of Chinese people still work in agriculture, following policies set by the Communist government. • Fishing is important both for food and for export. • Japan is East Asia's leading industrial nation but is being challenged by Taiwan and South Korea. • Trade and business investment bring together capitalist and Communist countries in East Asia. • Ships and railroads are important links within East Asia; transportation is most developed in the eastern part of the region.

Japanese bullet train

Section	Key Terms	Summary
2 People and Their Environment	**acid rain** (p. 577) **chlorofluorocarbon** (p. 578)	• Rapid industrial growth in East Asia has caused air and water pollution and toxic wastes; such environmental problems were ignored for several decades. • Japan has become a leader in protecting and cleaning up the environment, with strict anti-pollution laws. • China's huge population increases the impact of its economic development on the environment. • East Asia is subject to natural disasters such as flooding, earthquakes, tsunami, and typhoons.

Chinese town on the banks of the Huang He

Map Activity

Identify and Locate Copy and distribute page 35 of the Outline Map Resource Book. On the map, have students locate and label Yokohama, Kobe, Nagoya, Guangzhou, Shanghai, and Hong Kong. Then tell them to shade the industrial areas of East Asia. Refer them to the map on page 574 for the locations of manufacturing and trade in East Asia.

CHAPTER 28 HIGHLIGHTS

USING THE CHAPTER 28 HIGHLIGHTS

Use the Chapter 28 Highlights to preview, review, condense, or reteach the chapter.

PREVIEW/REVIEW

Vocabulary PuzzleMaker Software reinforces the Key Terms used in Chapter 28.

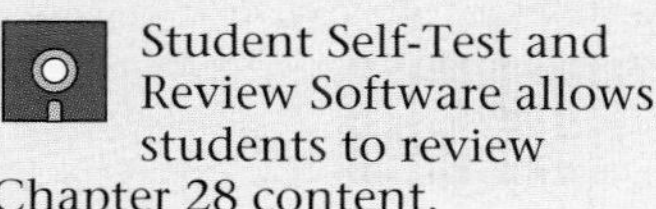

Student Self-Test and Review Software allows students to review Chapter 28 content.

CONDENSE

Have students read the Chapter 28 Highlights.

Have students listen to the Chapter 28 Audiocassettes in the TCR. Spanish Audiocassettes are also available.

Assign the Chapter 28 Audiocassette Activity and give the students the Chapter 28 Audiocassette Quiz.

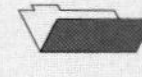 

Have students complete Guided Reading Activities for Chapter 28 in the TCR. Spanish Guided Reading Activities are also available.

RETEACH

Have students complete Reteaching Activity 28 in the TCR. Spanish Reteaching Activities are also available.

GLENCOE TECHNOLOGY

Videodisc

Use Chapter 28 MindJogger Videoquiz to review students' knowledge before administering the Chapter 28 Test.

MINDJOGGER VIDEOQUIZ

Chapter 28
Disc 4 Side A

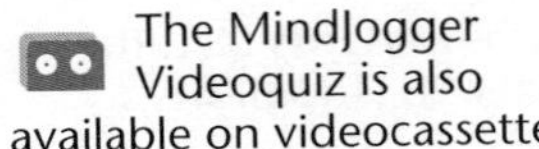

The MindJogger Videoquiz is also available on videocassette.

ANSWERS

Reviewing Key Terms

1. trading partner
2. cooperative
3. merchant marine
4. commune
5. chlorofluorocarbons
6. acid rain

Reviewing Facts

7. rice
8. raw materials because Japan does not have the raw materials to support its industries such as steelmaking
9. Taiwanese industries tend to be small or middle-sized while those in Japan and Korea are large.
10. Land is available and labor is cheap.
11. coal; Burning coal pollutes the air and contributes to acid rain.
12. encouraged industries to prevent pollution and passed strict anti-pollution laws
13. They lie in the Ring of Fire, a region along the earth's plate boundaries.

chapter 28 REVIEW

Reviewing Key Terms

Choose the vocabulary term that best completes each of the sentences below. Write your answers on a separate sheet of paper.

commune (p. 571)
cooperative (p. 572)
trading partner (p. 574)
merchant marine (p. 576)
acid rain (p. 577)
chlorofluorocarbons (p. 578)

SECTION 1

1. South Korea is a major ____ of Japan's.
2. Members of a farming or fishing ____ voluntarily work together to share the work and the profits.
3. Japan's ____ carries its exports to other countries.
4. During the Great Leap Forward, several thousand farm households were organized into a single ____.

SECTION 2

5. The greatest danger to the earth's ozone layer comes from ____.
6. ____ endangers forests in China and neighboring countries.

Reviewing Facts

SECTION 1

7. What is the most important food crop in North and South Korea?
8. What kinds of things must Japan import? Why?
9. How do industries in Taiwan differ from those in Japan and Korea?
10. Why do businesses in Taiwan and Hong Kong invest in factories in mainland China?

SECTION 2

11. What is the most important energy source in China? How does this affect the environment?
12. What steps has Japan taken to solve environmental problems?
13. Why are earthquakes and volcanoes common in the islands of East Asia?

Critical Thinking

14. **Making Predictions** How might "greater China"—China, Taiwan, and Hong Kong—challenge Japan's economic power?
15. **Identifying Central Issues** Why did pollution problems develop in industrialized East Asia?

Geographic Themes

16. **Location** Why is fishing important and necessary for the people of East Asia?
17. **Human/Environment Interaction** How does acid rain in China affect pollution in Japan?

Practicing Skills

Reading An Economic Activity Map

Refer to the map on page 582.

18. How has physical geography affected the location of manufacturing and trade centers in China?
19. In which parts of East Asia is fishing an important economic activity?
20. Compare the map on page 582 with the climate map of East Asia on page 543. How would you explain areas of little or no economic activity?

Using the Unit Atlas

Refer to the physical geography section of the Unit Atlas on pages 532–533.

21. Describe the physical makeup of Japan.

Critical Thinking

14. Hong Kong and Taiwan have business skills and money to invest; China has land, labor, natural resources, and a potential market of a billion people.
15. Most countries focused on building their economies and ignored the environmental problems that increased industrialization caused.

Geographic Themes

16. They live on the seacoast or along rivers and many have limited farmlands.
17. Winds spread acid rain across the seas to Japan's forests.

22. What are the major natural resources of Mongolia?
23. What is China's main agricultural area? What makes it good for growing crops?

Projects

Individual Activity

You have learned how important trade is to the nations of East Asia. Research and write a brief report about the imports and exports of one country or territory. Try to answer these questions: Does the country import/export mostly food and agricultural products or industrial goods? What does this show about the country and its people?

Cooperative Learning Activity

The United States is an important trading partner for East Asia. Work with four or five classmates to find out what products from East Asia you use every day. Check all parts of your homes and schools for products. Make a group list of what you find to share with the class.

Writing About Geography

Comparison

Imagine that you are a reporter making a tour of farming communities in two or more places in East Asia—for example, Taiwan and China, or two distinct regions of China. Write a short news article comparing and contrasting the farms and farm families. You may want to compare the size of farms, farming methods, crops grown, or other factors. Use your journal record to help you write your article.

Locating Places

EAST ASIA: PHYSICAL GEOGRAPHY

Match the letters on the map with the places and physical features of East Asia. Write your answers on a separate sheet of paper.

1. Shanghai
2. Tian Shan
3. Hong Kong
4. Guangzhou
5. Yokohama
6. Mongolia
7. Taiwan
8. Grand Canal
9. North Korea
10. Nagasaki

Chapter 28 Review

Practicing Skills

18. Most manufacturing and trade areas are located along coasts and rivers.
19. all coastal areas except the western coasts of North Korea and South Korea
20. The areas with little or no economic activity have desert or highland climates.

Using the Unit Atlas

21. four large islands and thousands of smaller ones
22. coal, copper, gold, iron, and petroleum
23. Sichuan Basin; its mild climate and long growing season

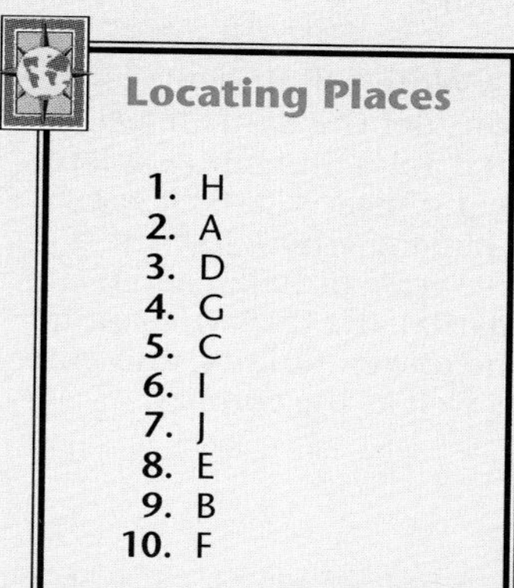

Chapter Bonus Test Question

This question may be used for extra credit on the chapter test.

Give an example that illustrates each of the following characteristics of the Japanese and their way of life: fast-paced, well-informed, environmentally conscious.

(Answers will vary but may include bullet trains; many newspapers, magazines, and a large book publishing industry; strict pollution-control laws.)

FOCUS

Invite any students that are currently studying or have studied a martial art to share information with the class. Also ask students for their general impressions of the martial arts; list these on the chalkboard.

TEACH

L1 Discussion Lead students to note the wide range of different-aged people in the photographs. Ask them to supply reasons for participating in martial arts. Encourage them to discuss the impression given of the martial arts in popular movies and television, and how this image might differ from reality.

L2 Write Ask students to consider the term "martial arts" for a moment; explain that it means "arts of war." Challenge them to write a free verse or haiku about martial arts that will capture the power, fluidity, and grace as well as the combat.

East Asia and the United States

THE MARTIAL ARTS

Martial arts is a catch-all phrase identifying various fighting methods developed from ancient Asian combat skills. Experts believe that the martial arts began as forms of exercise and self-defense practiced by Buddhist monks in India and Tibet. The monks then introduced the skills in China; from there, they spread to Korea and Japan. Today, hundreds of martial arts systems and styles exist.

The most popular martial arts in the United States are tae kwan do, karate, kung fu, and judo. Millions of Americans participate for recreation, physical fitness, or competition.

▲ **THE AMERICAN MARTIAL ARTS** system advocates that practitioners pick and choose from all available techniques to find the most practical and realistic for personal use. Since the introduction of judo, Americans have embraced hundreds of styles and substyles of East Asian martial arts.

JUDO ▶ gets its name from the Japanese words *ju* (gentle) and *do* (way). Judo uses no hand or foot blows; rather, its purpose is to neutralize an opponent with various throws and locks. The "gentle way" refers to the participant's use of pretended weakness to take an opponent off balance.

Making the Connection

Research Encourage students to choose one of the martial arts presented and find out about its history and style. Remind them that as well as books, they might also want to interview a martial arts instructor. Suggest that they also consider inviting a martial arts participant to speak to the class. Allow students to plan the time for pooling information and any demonstrations.

KARATE is a Japanese term: *kara* is most often translated "empty"; *te* means "hand." The name refers to the sport's beginning: Originally, karate skills were hand-and-foot blows learned by soldiers as defense if they became weaponless ("empty-handed") during battle. Today, the term includes any martial art using hand-and-foot blows as basic techniques. Japanese karate employs hard, quick, powerful blows. Introduced in the United States in the 1940s, karate has more American participants than anywhere else in the world.

TAE KWAN DO, or Korean karate, is by far the favorite of all the martial arts. Known as the art of kicking and punching, this sport combines the abrupt movements of Japanese karate with the circular movement patterns of kung fu. The Koreans added their own touches—spectacular jumping and spinning kicks—which punctuate tae kwan do performances.

KUNG FU—Chinese karate—is the best known of the Chinese martial arts. Kung fu practitioners incorporate their blows and kicks into a flowing, circular motion.

Checking for Understanding

1. What martial arts are popular in the United States?
2. **Movement** How did martial arts spread from India and Tibet to China?

Geography Connection

ASSESS

Have students answer the Checking for Understanding questions on page 587.

CLOSE

Have students summarize how the martial arts spread to the United States.

DID YOU KNOW?

All kung fu and karate systems use similar hitting and kicking techniques. Differences among them are stylistic. Two basic schools, or methods, are the "hard," which emphasizes power and strength, and the "soft," which trains for speed and precision.

ANSWERS TO CHECKING FOR UNDERSTANDING

1. karate, kung fu, tae kwan do, judo
2. demonstrated to Chinese by Buddhist monks from India and Tibet

UNIT OVERVIEW

The three chapters that comprise this unit introduce students to the physical geography and peoples of Southeast Asia. Aspects of the region's life—such as the economy, lifestyles, and human/environment interaction—are also presented.

GEOGRAPHY JOURNAL

Activity Students can clip and save appealing photographs with well-worded captions, along with unusual adjectives, adverbs, or phrases they encounter. At the unit's end, have them use this vocabulary collection in a journal entry describing one of the Southeast Asian countries they "visited" on their journey through the unit.

- This journal activity provides the basis for the "Writing About Geography" exercise in the Chapter Review.

- The Geography Journal may be used as an integral part of Performance Assessment.

CD-ROM

PICTURE ATLAS OF THE WORLD

You and your students can see and read about the physical features of Southeast Asia by clicking the "Photos" and "Essay" buttons of selected countries in the region.

0:00 OUT OF TIME?

If time does not permit teaching each chapter in this unit, you may use the Chapter Highlights and the Audiocassettes that include a 1-page activity and a 1-page test for each chapter.

UNIT 10

Southeast Asia

GeoJournal Activity

While studying Southeast Asia, keep track of photo images and descriptions about the region published in newspapers and magazines. Record your thoughts about each photo and description in your journal.

588

Where in the World . . . .

Have students look at the map on pages A22–A23 in which Southeast Asia is highlighted. Display Unit Map Overlay Transparency 10-5 and ask the following questions: What body of water lies west of the region? *(Indian Ocean)* What body of water lies west of the Philippines? *(South China Sea)* Which country is partly mainland, partly island? *(Malaysia)* What countries are on the mainland? *(Myanmar, Laos, Thailand, Cambodia, Vietnam)* What countries are islands? *(Singapore, Indonesia, Philippines)* What rivers flow through the region? *(Mekong, Irrawaddy, Hong, Salween)*

Picturing the World

Boats mob a canal of the Mekong River Delta in southern Vietnam. The Mekong River begins in China and flows 2,600 miles (4,183 km) through Myanmar, Laos, Thailand, Cambodia, and Vietnam. The river has few bridges, no industrial centers, and is the least developed of Asia's great rivers. Look at the map on page 591.

1. Where do most Laotians live, and what crop do they grow?
2. Now look at the map on page 592. What are other major rivers in Southeast Asia?

Picture Atlas CD-ROM Enrichment Corner

Rivers are very important for communication and transportation on the mainland of Southeast Asia. Create a file of photographs showing life along these rivers. (See the *Picture Atlas of the World* User's Guide on how to use the Collector button.) Include the following photographs: the Irrawaddy River in Myanmar; the houses on a canal in Bangkok and the barges on the Chao Phraya River in Thailand; gold panning in Laos; the Mekong Delta in Vietnam; and the Mekong River in Cambodia. Get together in groups. Use the information in the photo captions in your file and any other sources you can find to write questions about the rivers of Southeast Asia that will challenge your classmates in other groups.

589

ANSWERS TO PICTURING THE WORLD

1. Most Laotians live along the Mekong River and its tributaries. Most Laotians grow rice.
2. Irrawaddy River, Salween River, Red River, Chao Phraya River

interNET CONNECTIONS

For information about Vietnam—the Vietnam War, contemporary data, and links to other resources on the Web—contact the following address:

World Wide Web
http://grunt.space.swri.edu/visit.htm

CD-ROM

PICTURE ATLAS OF THE WORLD
You will find an additional CD-ROM activity to enrich Unit 10, Southeast Asia, on page T44.

GLENCOE TECHNOLOGY

Videodisc

Use the following to introduce or enrich Unit 10:

REUTERS ISSUES IN GEOGRAPHY

Chapter 9
Disc 1 Side A

Title: ***Southeast Asia: Patterns of Migration***
Subject: Migration of a family from a rural area of Thailand to the city of Bangkok

These features and activities may be used as an introduction to the unit or as teaching tools throughout the course of the unit.

FOCUS

Ask students to study the maps on pages 590–591 for a moment. Then have students formulate sentences telling where the population is most dense in each country.

TEACH

Implement Foods Around the World 9 as a class activity.

Have students complete the Political Map Transparency 10 Activity in the TCR.

Have students complete Unit Atlas Activity 10B.

Have students complete World Cultures Transparencies 17 and 18 Activities in the TCR.

Have students complete World Literature Reading 9 in the TCR.

Play World Music: Cultural Traditions, Lesson 9, and have students complete the Lesson 9 activity.

UNIT 10 ATLAS

SOUTHEAST ASIA Cultural Geography

EXPLORING CULTURAL DIVERSITY

1. *What areas of Southeast Asia are the most heavily populated? Most sparsely populated?*
2. *What nations make up Southeast Asia?*
3. *What cities in Southeast Asia have more than 2 million people?*
4. *What countries of Southeast Asia are made up of islands?*

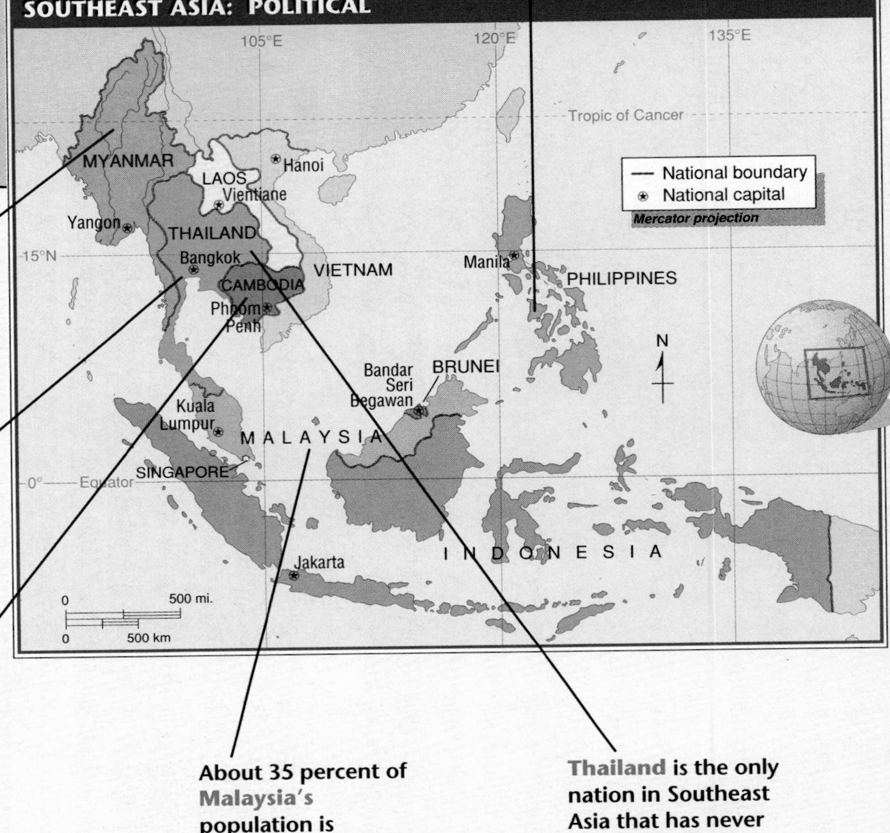

After nearly 400 years of Spanish colonial rule, **the Philippines** was governed by the United States from 1898 to 1946.

Houses in **Myanmar** (Burma) are built on poles above the ground to protect the inhabitants against floods and wild animals.

Bangkok, Thailand's capital, has more than 300 Buddhist temples.

Cambodia has faced almost constant warfare since the 1960s.

About 35 percent of **Malaysia's** population is Chinese, most of whom live in cities.

Thailand is the only nation in Southeast Asia that has never been ruled by a Western power.

Classroom Resources for Section 2

BLACKLINE MASTERS:
Geography Simulation 10
Environmental Issue 10
World Literature Reading 9
Foods Around the World 9

TRANSPARENCIES:
Unit Map Overlay Transparency 10
Political Map Transparency 10
World Cultures Transparencies 17 and 18

MULTIMEDIA:

Picture Atlas of the World

World Music: Cultural Traditions, Lesson 9

Reuters Issues in Geography

Testmaker

Images of the World Poster Set

About four-fifths of Thailand's population lives in rural areas.

Most Laotians live along the Mekong River and its tributaries and grow rice.

Fertile plains created by the Mekong River's floodwaters are home to most Cambodians.

About 65 percent of Brunei's people live in urban areas.

SOUTHEAST ASIA: POPULATION DENSITY

Per sq. km	Per sq. mi.
Over 100	Over 250
50-100	125-250
25-50	60-125
1-25	2-60
Under 1	Under 2
Uninhabited	Uninhabited

Cities
- Over 10,000,000
- 2,000,000 to 10,000,000
- 1,000,000 to 2,000,000
- Under 1,000,000

Mercator projection

With a population of almost 200 million, Indonesia is the fourth most populous country in the world, after China, India, and the United States.

Only about 900 of the Philippines's 7,000 islands are inhabited.

About half of the Philippines's population of 69 million live on the island of Luzon.

Population: Southeast Asia and the United States

Southeast Asia

United States

= 50,000,000

Source: 1994 World Population Data Sheet

Southeast Asia has one and a half times as many people as the United States.

LESSON PLAN Unit 10 Atlas

ASSESS

Have students answer the Exploring Cultural Diversity questions on page 590.

EXPLORING CULTURAL DIVERSITY
This feature may be used to introduce students to the cultural geography of Southeast Asia. Use questions to stimulate class discussion and help students become familiar with the region. Accept reasonable answers based on the maps, graph, and captions.

CLOSE

Have students predict, based on the size of the region and the proximity of the countries, what kind of cultural geography they expect to find.

GLENCOE TECHNOLOGY

Videodisc

Use the following to introduce or enrich Unit 10:

REUTERS ISSUES IN GEOGRAPHY

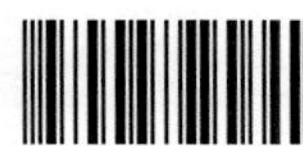

Chapter 9
Disc 1 Side A

Title: ***Southeast Asia: Patterns of Migration***
Subject: Migration of a family from a rural area of Thailand to the city of Bangkok

Map and Graph Activity

Culture Have students, working individually or with partners, extend their end-of-the-lesson predictions by adding a logical extension to each fact presented on pages 590 and 591. For example, an extension to the statement about Bangkok might predict that the main religion in Thailand is Buddhism. Allow time for students to share and discuss their predictions.

LESSON PLAN
Unit 10 Atlas

These features and activities may be used as an introduction to the unit or as teaching tools throughout the course of the unit.

FOCUS

To introduce the physical geography of Southeast Asia, have students complete Unit Map Overlay Transparency 10 Activity in the TCR.

TEACH

Human/ Environment Interaction Note the predominance of water in the region. Ask students to think of positive and negative ways the presence of so much water could affect the region and the population.

Map Activity Encourage students to find physical factors that account for the population distribution shown on page 591. Also ask them to find physical factors that explain the distribution of natural resources shown on page 593.

Implement Geography Simulation 10 as a class activity.

DID YOU KNOW?

Vietnam, Laos, and Cambodia are sometimes referred to as *Indochina*. The term reflects the two huge lands on either side of Southeast Asia: India and China.

UNIT 10 ATLAS

SOUTHEAST ASIA
Physical Geography

CHARTING YOUR COURSE

1. *What body of water separates the Malay Peninsula and the island of Sumatra?*
2. *What Southeast Asian country is landlocked?*
3. *What are three natural resources found in Southeast Asia?*
4. *What major rivers are located in Southeast Asia?*

Laos is the only landlocked country in Southeast Asia. The Mekong River, however, flows through the country, providing Laotians with their chief means of transportation.

Of the more than 7,000 islands in the Philippines, the 11 largest make up 95 percent of the country.

Vietnam is composed of two river deltas. The Mekong River delta is at the southern end of the country, while the Hong (Red) River delta is at the northern end.

Most of Brunei is flat and forest-covered.

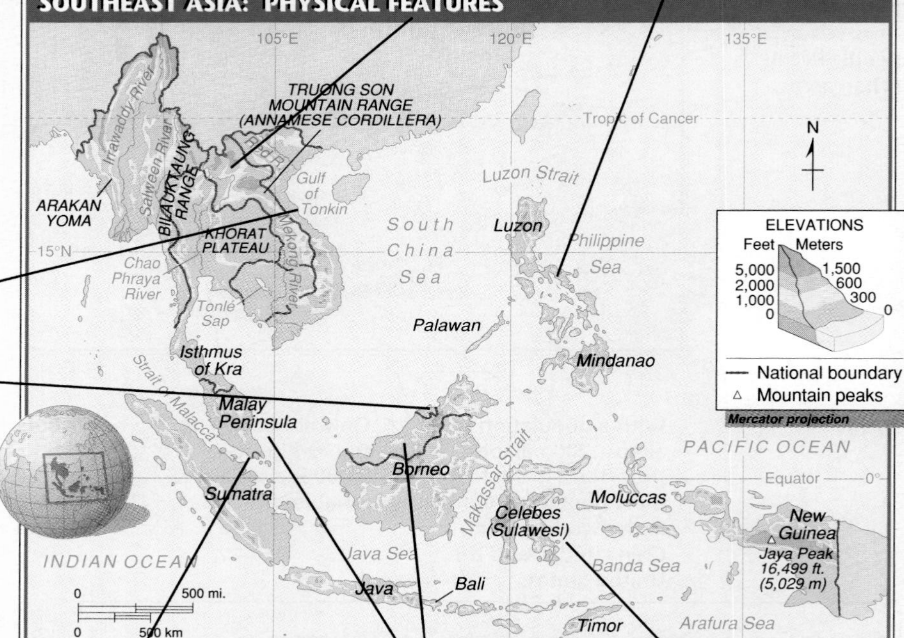

Singapore consists of one main island and more than 50 offshore islets. Most of Singapore lies near sea level.

The country of Malaysia lies partly on the Malay Peninsula and partly on the island of Borneo.

Indonesia consists of more than 13,600 islands. They lie along the Equator and stretch more than 3,000 miles (4,827 km).

Map Activity

Geography/Write Challenge students to recall the five geographic themes. List them on the board as volunteers offer them *(location, place, human/environment interaction, movement, region)*.

Have each student compose three or four incorrect statements about the Southeast Asian countries based on these geographic themes. Ask them to read their statements to classmates and challenge them to find the errors and correct them. Those making the corrections must support them with information from the map. Students may also challenge any question they think is not based on one of the geographic themes.

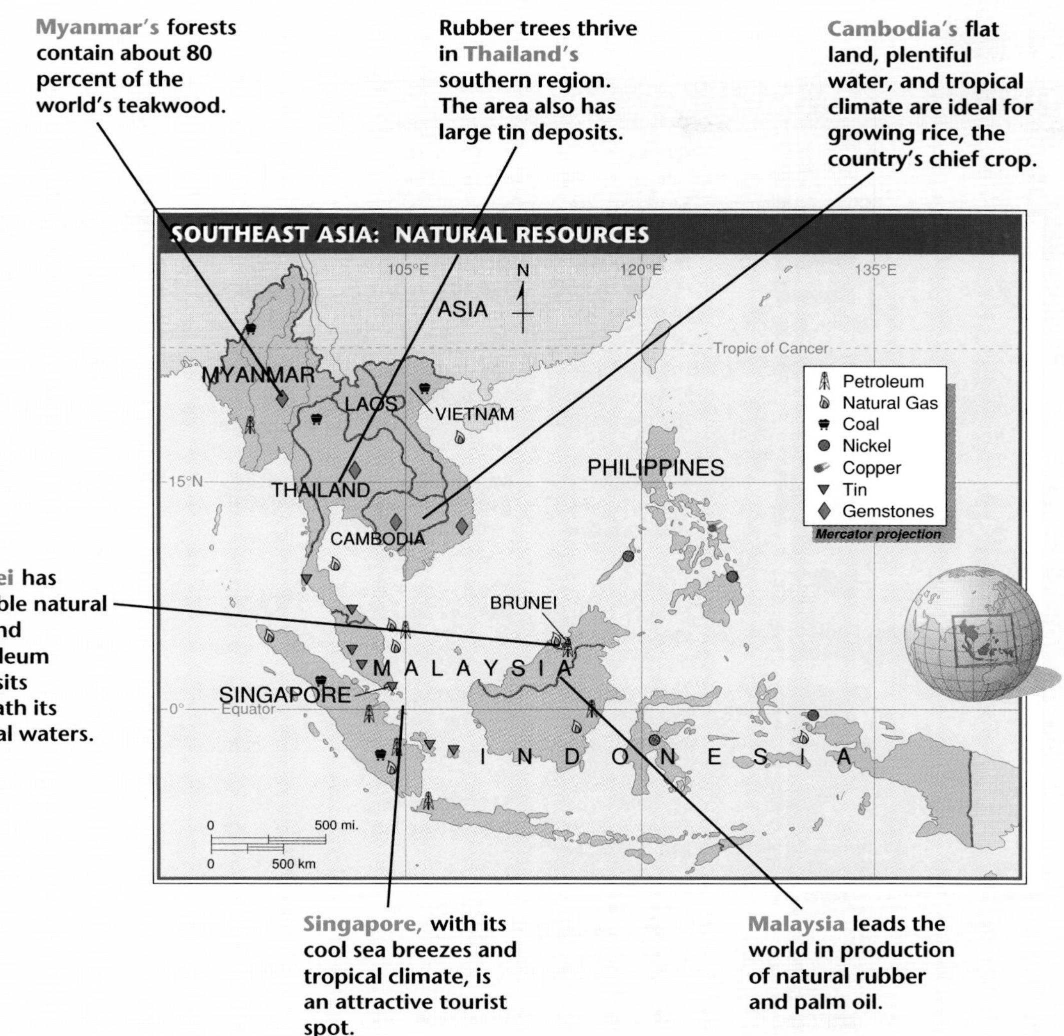

Myanmar's forests contain about 80 percent of the world's teakwood.
Rubber trees thrive in Thailand's southern region. The area also has large tin deposits.
Cambodia's flat land, plentiful water, and tropical climate are ideal for growing rice, the country's chief crop.
SOUTHEAST ASIA: NATURAL RESOURCES
105°E
N
120°E
135°E
ASIA
Tropic of Cancer
MYANMAR
LAOS
VIETNAM
PHILIPPINES
15°N
THAILAND
CAMBODIA
Petroleum
Natural Gas
Coal
Nickel
Copper
Tin
Gemstones
Mercator projection
runei has
aluable natural
as and
etroleum
eposits
eneath its
astal waters.
BRUNEI
MALAYSIA
SINGAPORE
0°
Equator
INDONESIA
0
500 mi.
0
500 km
Singapore, with its cool sea breezes and tropical climate, is an attractive tourist spot.
Malaysia leads the world in production of natural rubber and palm oil.

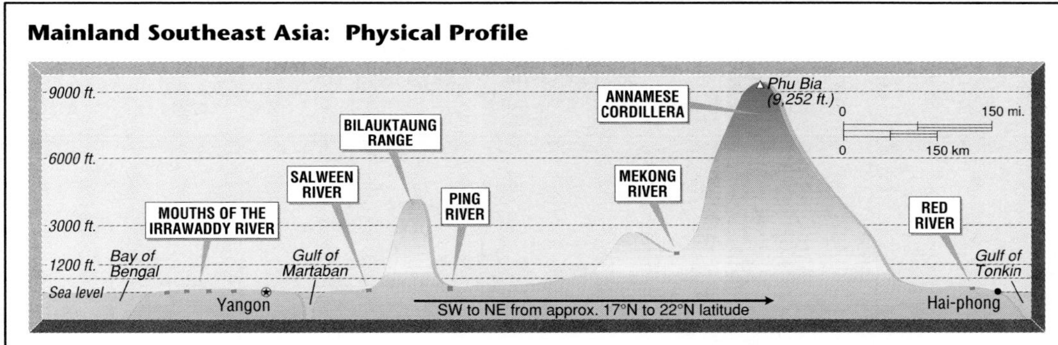

Map Activity

Economics Ask students to study the map on page 593 and speculate about the main economic pursuits in the region. List their speculations on the chalkboard. (Guide them to include farming, logging, and fishing.)

Then have them briefly research each country's agricultural, forestry, and fishing industries. Allow time for students to share their findings; then ask them to create a class chart showing the percentages of the populations of each country that are engaged in the three pursuits.

Have them rank the countries from most agricultural to least. Challenge them to discover the leading economic sectors in the least agricultural countries.

ASSESS

Have students answer the Charting Your Course questions on page 592.

CHARTING YOUR COURSE

This feature may be used to introduce students to the physical geography of Southeast Asia. Use questions to stimulate class discussion and help students become familiar with the region. Accept reasonable answers based on the maps, graph, and captions.

CLOSE

Ask students to predict what the main occupation of the region will be and support their answers with evidence from the maps.

DID YOU KNOW?

An outstanding quality of Southeast Asia is its intermingling of land and water. The region's peninsulas and islands are often compared to those in the Mediterranean. The region is sometimes called "Asian Mediterranean."

IMAGES OF THE WORLD POSTER SET

Display the poster of "Asia." Which of the photos on the poster show countries and people of the Southeast Asia region? *(Harvesting coffee, Indonesia; Girl holding the Quran, Indonesia; Father and son readying their boat, Indonesia)*

LESSON PLAN
Unit 10 Atlas

These features and activities may be used as teaching tools throughout the course of the unit.

DID YOU KNOW?

So many Cambodian men have died in wars that the country has a large number of orphans, widows, and single-parent families. Women who do not remarry often gather in small clans with their children for mutual aid and companionship.

Ways of the World

INDONESIA Indonesians rarely disagree in public, seldom say "No," and generally have time for others. Their personal relationships are very important; embarrassing someone is considered a terrible insult.

Ways of the World

LAOS The Laotian expression *Bo pen nyang*—"never mind"—characterizes their feelings about life. It should be enjoyed at the moment: problems should not be allowed to hinder this enjoyment.

UNIT 10 ATLAS

COUNTRY PROFILE

COUNTRY* AND CAPITAL	FLAG AND LANGUAGES	POPULATION	LANDMASS	PRINCIPAL PRODUCTS EXPORT	PRINCIPAL PRODUCTS IMPORT
Brunei Bandar Seri Begawan	Malay, English, Chinese	300,000 148 per sq. mi. 57 per sq. km	2,030 sq. mi. 5,258 sq. km	Petroleum	Machinery
Cambodia Phnom Penh	Khmer, French	10,300,000 151 per sq. mi. 58 per sq. km	68,150 sq. mi. 176,509 sq. km	Rubber	Machinery
Indonesia Jakarta	Bahasa Indonesia (Malay), Javanese	199,700,000 283 per sq. mi. 109 per sq. km	705,190 sq. mi. 1,826,442 sq. km	Petroleum	Machinery
Laos Vientiane	Lao	4,700,000 52 per sq. mi. 20 per sq. km	89,110 sq. mi. 230,795 sq. km	Wood	Food
Malaysia Kuala Lumpur	Malay, English, Chinese, Indian languages	19,500,000 154 per sq. mi. 59 per sq. km	126,850 sq. mi. 328,542 sq. km	Machinery	Machinery
Myanmar Yangon	Burmese, Karen, Shan	45,400,000 179 per sq. mi. 69 per sq. km	253,880 sq. mi. 657,549 sq. km	Agricultural Products	Machinery
Philippines Manila	Pilipino, English, Cebuano, Bicol	68,700,000 597 per sq. mi. 230 per sq. km	115,120 sq. mi. 298,161 sq. km	Food & Animals	Machinery
Singapore Singapore City	Chinese, English, Malay, Tamil	2,900,000 12,083 per sq. mi. 4,664 per sq. km	240 sq. mi. 622 sq. km	Office Machines	Petroleum
Thailand Bangkok	Thai, Chinese, Malay, regional dialects	59,400,000 301 per sq. mi. 116 per sq. km	197,250 sq. mi. 510,878 sq. km	Machinery	Machinery
Vietnam Hanoi	Vietnamese, Chinese	73,100,000 582 per sq. mi. 225 per sq. km	125,670 sq. mi. 325,485 sq. km	Fuels	Machinery

*Country maps not drawn to scale.

Country Profile Activity

Analyze/Write Organize students into small groups and assign each a country. Direct them to coordinate information about their countries on pages 594–595 with information on pages 589–593. Remind them that maps and graphs are an excellent source of information, along with the text.

Ask the groups to use their gathered data to compose thumbnail sketches of their countries. Then have them examine their sketches and determine any information that may be lacking. Display the sketches and encourage the groups to make additions and changes throughout the unit.

The Akha people are one of many different ethnic groups living in the mountains of northern Thailand and Myanmar (Burma).

Rice is an important crop grown on the Philippine island of Luzon.

This European-style church reflects the influence of Spain and the Roman Catholic Church on the Philippines.

Yangon, the capital of Myanmar, is known for its elaborate Buddhist temples.

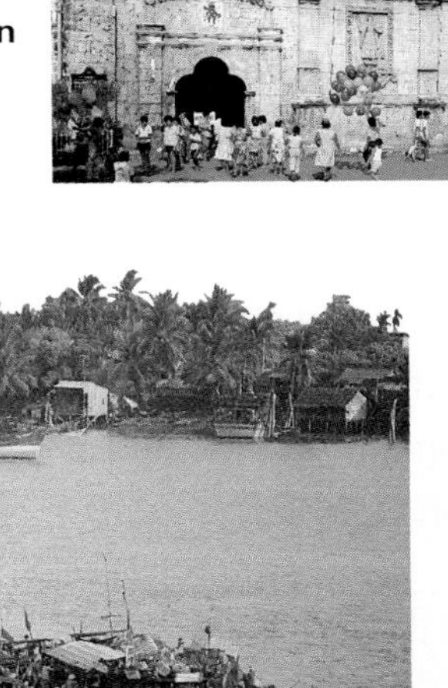

Villages and farms line the banks of the Mekong River in Vietnam.

DID YOU KNOW?

Southeast Asia is often seen as a *shatterbelt:* an area where different ethnic groups have mixed—and occasionally confronted one another—to form complex cultures.

Global Gourmet

In Southeast Asia, *ketchup* describes a variety of sauces made from fish, seafood, or vegetables. Europeans borrowed the word to describe a sauce they make from tomatoes.

DID YOU KNOW?

The Philippines is the world's fourth largest producer of films. People spend much of their leisure time at the movies.

Ways of the World

MALAYSIA Many Malaysians are fatalistic: they believe successes, failures, opportunities, and misfortunes result from fate or the will of a deity.

DID YOU KNOW?

Petroleum deposits make Brunei a wealthy country, and the people have a high standard of living.

Country Profile Activity

Cultural Profiles Assign a country to each student or pair of students. Ask them to use atlases, encyclopedias, and other sources to make a cultural profile of their countries.

Suggest that students list the data on a 3" x 5" index card and include these categories: Ethnic Groups, Languages, Religions, Rural/Urban Percentages, Literacy Rate, Education, Life Expectancy, Age Distribution, Population Trends, Infant Deaths per Thousand, Health System.

Encourage students to make generalizations based on the information they gathered. Allow time for sharing; add the profiles to other materials students have completed during the opening activities. Have students review the profiles for additions or deletions at the end of the unit.

CHAPTER 29

PLANNING GUIDE

The Physical Geography of Southeast Asia

CHAPTER ORGANIZER

Daily Lesson Objectives	Multimedia	Teacher Classroom Resources
SECTION 1 The Land 1. Describe the natural forces that shaped Southeast Asia. 2. Compare mainland and island Southeast Asia. 3. List the kinds of natural resources found in Southeast Asia.	Section Focus Transparency 29-1 Unit Map Overlay Transparencies 10-4, 10-5 Chapter 29 Vocabulary PuzzleMaker Software Geography and the Environment Testmaker STV: World Geography, Volume 1 Physical Geography of the World Transparencies 66, 67, 68, 69	Reproducible Lesson Plan 29-1 Geography Simulation 10 Guided Reading Activity 29-1 Spanish Guided Reading Activity 29-1 Workbook Activity 29-1 Section Quiz 29-1
SECTION 2 The Climate and Vegetation 1. Describe the climate regions of Southeast Asia. 2. Identify the different kinds of vegetation in Southeast Asia.	Section Focus Transparency 29-2 Unit Map Overlay Transparencies 10-2, 10-3 Geography and the Environment Testmaker GTV: Planetary Manager	Reproducible Lesson Plan 29-2 Guided Reading Activity 29-2 Spanish Guided Reading Activity 29-2 Workbook Activity 29-2 Skill Activity 29 Enrichment Activity 29 Section Quiz 29-2
CHAPTER REVIEW AND EVALUATION	Chapter 29 English (or Spanish) Audiocassettes MindJogger Videoquiz Testmaker Student Self-Test and Review Software	Reteaching Activity 29 Spanish Reteaching Activity 29 Chapter 29 Test Form A and Form B

0:00 *If time does not permit teaching the entire chapter, summarize using the Chapter 29 Highlights on page 607, and the Chapter 29 English (or Spanish) Audiocassettes. Review students' knowledge using the Glencoe MindJogger Videoquiz.*

KEY TO ABILITY LEVELS

Teaching strategies have been coded for varying learning styles and abilities.

L1 **BASIC** activities for all students

L2 **AVERAGE** activities for average to above-average students

L3 **CHALLENGING** activities for above-average students

LEP **LIMITED ENGLISH PROFICIENCY** activities

Performance Assessment

Analyzing Points of View The Philippines was once a colony of the United States as a result of the Spanish-American War (1898). In 1946, the United States granted the Philippines independence. Ask groups of students to decide whether the United States should have had an imperial role in Southeast Asia, arguing either "for" or "against" the American colonization of the islands. Groups may work cooperatively in gathering evidence to support their positions.

In their arguments, students should demonstrate knowledge of Southeast Asia's physical geography, hypothesize the impact of these features on American interests in the region, and make convincing arguments. Teachers may limit student assessment to the information found in Chapter 29, or allow students to research American involvement in other parts of the world in order to make analogous arguments.

POSSIBLE RUBRIC FEATURES: Content information, decision-making process steps, persuasive abilities, collaboration skills, relevance of research, viability of relationships found

For additional professional and classroom resources, see Chapter Resources, pages T46–T51.

TEACHER'S CORNER

INDEX TO NATIONAL GEOGRAPHIC MAGAZINE

The following articles may be used for research relating to this chapter:

- "The Mekong: A Haunted River's Season of Peace," by Thomas O'Neill, February 1993.
- "Volcanoes: Crucibles of Creation," by Noel Grove, December 1992.
- "Saving the World's Largest Flower," by Willem Meijer, July 1985.
- "Rain Forests: Nature's Dwindling Treasures," by Peter T. White, January 1983.
- "A Sumatran Journey," by Harvey Arden, March 1981.

NATIONAL GEOGRAPHIC SOCIETY PRODUCTS AVAILABLE FROM GLENCOE

To order the following products for use with this chapter, contact your local Glencoe sales representative or call Glencoe at 1-800-334-7344:

- *Picture Atlas of the World* (CD-ROM)
- *STV: World Geography, Asia and Australia* (Videodisc)
- *ZipZapMap! World* (Software)
- *GeoBee* (Software)
- *Images of the World* (Posters)
- *Eye on the Environment* (Posters)
- *Physical Geography of the World* (Transparencies)
- *Picture Atlas of Our 50 States* (Book)

Introducing
CHAPTER 29

PERFORMANCE ASSESSMENT

Refer to the Planning Guide on page 596B for a Performance Assessment Activity for this chapter. See the *Performance Assessment Activities* booklet for additional suggestions.

CHAPTER OBJECTIVES

1. **Discuss** how the mainland and islands of Southeast Asia differ geographically.
2. **Explain** how Southeast Asian climate patterns affect vegetation throughout the region.

GLENCOE TECHNOLOGY

Videodisc

Use Chapter 29 MindJogger Videoquiz to preview chapter content.

MINDJOGGER VIDEOQUIZ

Chapter 29
Disc 4 Side B

The MindJogger Videoquiz is also available on videocassette.

chapter 29 The Physical Geography of Southeast Asia

CHAPTER FOCUS

Geographic Setting

About half of the nations of Southeast Asia lie on the Indochina and Malay peninsulas, while the others are in the Malay Archipelago. Because Southeast Asia is located astride the Equator, the region's climate is largely tropical.

Geographic Themes

Section 1 The Land
PLACE The mainland and the islands differ geographically in important ways.

Section 2 The Climate and Vegetation
LOCATION The climate and vegetation of Southeast Asia are consistent with their tropical location—the hot, humid, rainy climate gives rise to rain forest vegetation throughout much of the region.

▲ Photograph: *Mountains on the island of Sumatra, Malaysia*

EXTRA CREDIT PROJECT

Diorama Have students work individually or in pairs to create dioramas showing the flora and fauna of Southeast Asia. Some students might include recordings of sounds of the rain forest. Display their completed dioramas.

SECTION 1

The Land

SETTING THE SCENE

Read to Discover . . .

- the natural forces that shaped Southeast Asia.
- how mainland and island Southeast Asia are alike and how they are different.
- the kinds of natural resources found in Southeast Asia.

Key Terms

- cordillera
- archipelago
- flora
- fauna

Identify and Locate

Indochina Peninsula, Malay Peninsula, Ring of Fire, Annamese Cordillera, Makassar Strait, Irrawaddy River, Chao Praya River, Mekong River

Bangkok, Thailand

Swatdee! Right now I'm on vacation on a small island south of Thailand. The island is called Pooket Island, and it has beautiful beaches. Tourists come here to relax and have fun. Wish you were here.

Noy Khunviset

Phuket Island—Noy Khunviset's vacation spot—is one of many scenic coastal areas in the culture region of Southeast Asia. Having mostly a tropical climate, Southeast Asia is mountainous, with fertile river valleys. The region is made up of 10 countries: Thailand, Vietnam, Laos, Cambodia, Myanmar (formerly called Burma), Malaysia, Singapore, the Philippines, Indonesia, and Brunei. The similarities and differences among the cultures of these countries often reflect the influence of other Asian countries and European colonial rule.

Since World War II, the countries of Southeast Asia have seen continual political upheaval and warfare. At the same time, the region has made great advances economically. Southeast Asian countries are also taking steps to cooperate in solving regional problems.

PLACE

Peninsulas and Islands

Southeast Asia was formed by the collision of the Eurasian, Philippine, and Indo-Australian tectonic plates millions of years ago. The clashing of the plates where India joined Asia forced up the mighty Himalayas and created **cordilleras,** or parallel mountain ranges, and river valleys in the Indochina Peninsula. To the east, volcanic and earth-

Classroom Resources for Section 1

BLACKLINE MASTERS:
Guided Reading Activity 29-1
Geography Simulation 10
Workbook Activity 29-1
Section Quiz 29-1

TRANSPARENCIES:
Section Focus Transparency 29-1
Physical Geography of the World Transparencies 66, 67, 68, 69

Unit Map Overlay Transparencies 10-4, 10-5

MULTIMEDIA:

Vocabulary PuzzleMaker Software
Testmaker

Geography and the Environment
STV: World Geography, Volume 1

LESSON PLAN
Chapter 29, Section 1

FOCUS

SECTION OBJECTIVES

1. **Describe** the natural forces that shaped Southeast Asia.
2. **Compare** mainland and island Southeast Asia.
3. **List** the kinds of natural resources found in Southeast Asia.

ABOUT THE POSTCARD

Phuket (Pooket) Island is Noy's favorite place. He enjoys watching the beautiful sunrises and sunsets there.

BELLRINGER MOTIVATIONAL ACTIVITY

Project the Section 1 Focus Transparency and have students answer the questions.

PRETEACHING VOCABULARY

Explain the origins of key terms. *Cordillera* comes from a Spanish word meaning "cord" or "chain"; *archipelago* is a Greek word that means "chief sea"; *flora* is taken from the name of the Roman goddess of flowers and spring; *fauna* comes from the name of the Roman goddess of fields and flocks. **LEP**

Use the Vocabulary PuzzleMaker Software to create a crossword or word search puzzle.

Videodisc

STV: WORLD GEOGRAPHY, VOLUME 1

Side 1, Chapter 1
Frames 27589-42384
Title: *Asia*
Subject: South and Southeast Asia

TEACH

GUIDED PRACTICE

L2 Location Point out the peninsula on which Vietnam, Laos, and Cambodia are located. Have students describe the peninsula's location relative to India and China. Then ask students to infer how the name of the peninsula relates to its location. *(Indochina is a transition zone between India and China.)*

 Implement Geography Simulation 10 as a class activity.

CURRICULUM CONNECTION

VOLCANOLOGY

Most volcanic eruptions cannot be predicted. Some, however, have a built-in warning system. Before erupting, a volcano expands slightly, and many small earthquakes occur. The temperature increases in the surrounding area, and clouds of gas form.

GLENCOE TECHNOLOGY

Videodisc

Use the following to enrich Chapter 29:

GEOGRAPHY AND THE ENVIRONMENT
THE INFINITE VOYAGE
To the Edge of the Earth

Chapter 3
Disc 1 Side B
Title: ***Exploring Volcanoes: To the Center of the Earth***
Subject: A manned submersible is used to study volcanic activity below the surface of the Pacific Ocean

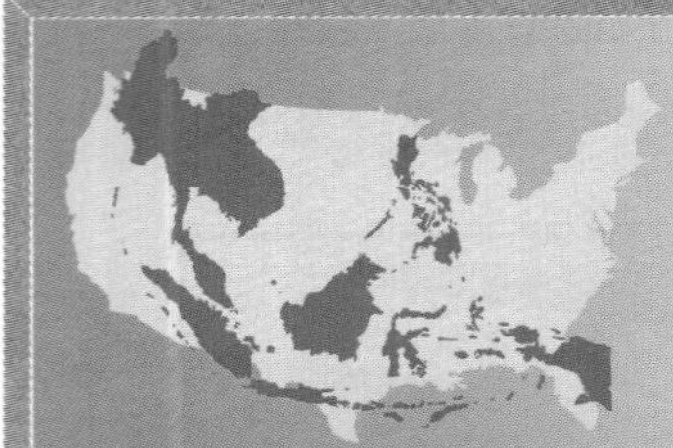

Comparing Lands

The **continental USA** is about one and a half times larger than Southeast Asia.

quake activity gave rise to a number of **archipelagoes**, or island groups.

Until 15,000 years ago, when sea levels were lower, there was a continent that connected what are now the islands of Sumatra, Java, Bali, Borneo, and Palawan (one of the western islands of the Philippines) with the mainland. With the rise in water levels caused by the melting at the end of the last Ice Age, much of the exposed land mass was covered, leaving a series of islands. This development had several important effects. It isolated the **flora**, the plants, and **fauna**, the animals, of the islands. It created a region with a longer coastline than any other comparable area in the world. In addition, it made the region's trade and communication dependent on water routes.

Mainland Southeast Asia

With only one exception, Southeast Asia can be divided into mainland and island countries. Five countries of Southeast Asia lie entirely on the mainland. Vietnam, Laos, Cambodia, and Myanmar lie entirely on the Indochina Peninsula. Thailand lies mainly on the Indochina Peninsula, but also trails southward to the Malay Peninsula.

Malaysia includes the southern end of the Malay Peninsula, as well as the northern part of the island of Borneo.

Island Southeast Asia

Singapore, sometimes referred to as a city-state, lies on an island at the southern tip of the Malay Peninsula. Another island country, Indonesia, is made up of 13,677 islands from the Indian Ocean to Papua New Guinea. Brunei, a small country on the north edge of the island of Borneo, and the Philippines, an archipelago made up of 7,107 islands, are the remaining island countries.

HUMAN/ENVIRONMENT INTERACTION

Mountains

The mountains of mainland Southeast Asia run mainly in north-south ridges. Three of these ridges are the Arakan Range in western Myanmar; the Bilauktaung (bi•LOWK•towng) Range, which runs along the border of Myanmar and Thailand; and the Annamese Cordillera, which separates Vietnam from Laos and Cambodia.

Although few peaks rise above 10,000 feet (about 3,000 m), these ranges are dominant landforms. The highlands in the west and north meet to form a natural barrier between India and China. The ridges also form barriers between and within the Southeast Asian countries.

Mountains on the islands of Southeast Asia are part of the spectacular Pacific Ring of Fire. These volcanoes—many still active—have formed craters on the islands of Indonesia and the Philippines.

Indonesia alone has 327 volcanoes, 200 of which were once active, and 127 that are active today. One of the most famous, Krakatoa, was located in the strait between the islands of Java and Sumatra. In 1883, Krakatoa erupted violently, causing many deaths and great destruction.

Today a staff of volcano watchers in Java regularly checks active sites, prepared to alert the population when there is danger of an eruption.

The 1991 eruption of Mt. Pinatubo some 55 miles (about 90 km) north of Manila, the Philippine capital, was one of the most recent examples of volcanic action in the Ring of Fire. It is said to have been the most powerful volcanic eruption in the 20th century. The lava severely damaged the town of Angeles and destroyed the American-controlled Clark Air Base, covering it with nearly a foot of ash.

Cooperative Learning Activity

Organize students into small groups and assign one or more Southeast Asian countries to each group. Tell students to study the location and physical features of their assigned countries and prepare to teach this information to the class. Suggest that students think of devices to help others remember the physical geography of the region. *(For example, some people think Thailand resembles the head and trunk of an elephant.)*

Display Unit Map Overlay Transparencies 10-4 and 10-5. Have each group teach the class the information that members have prepared.

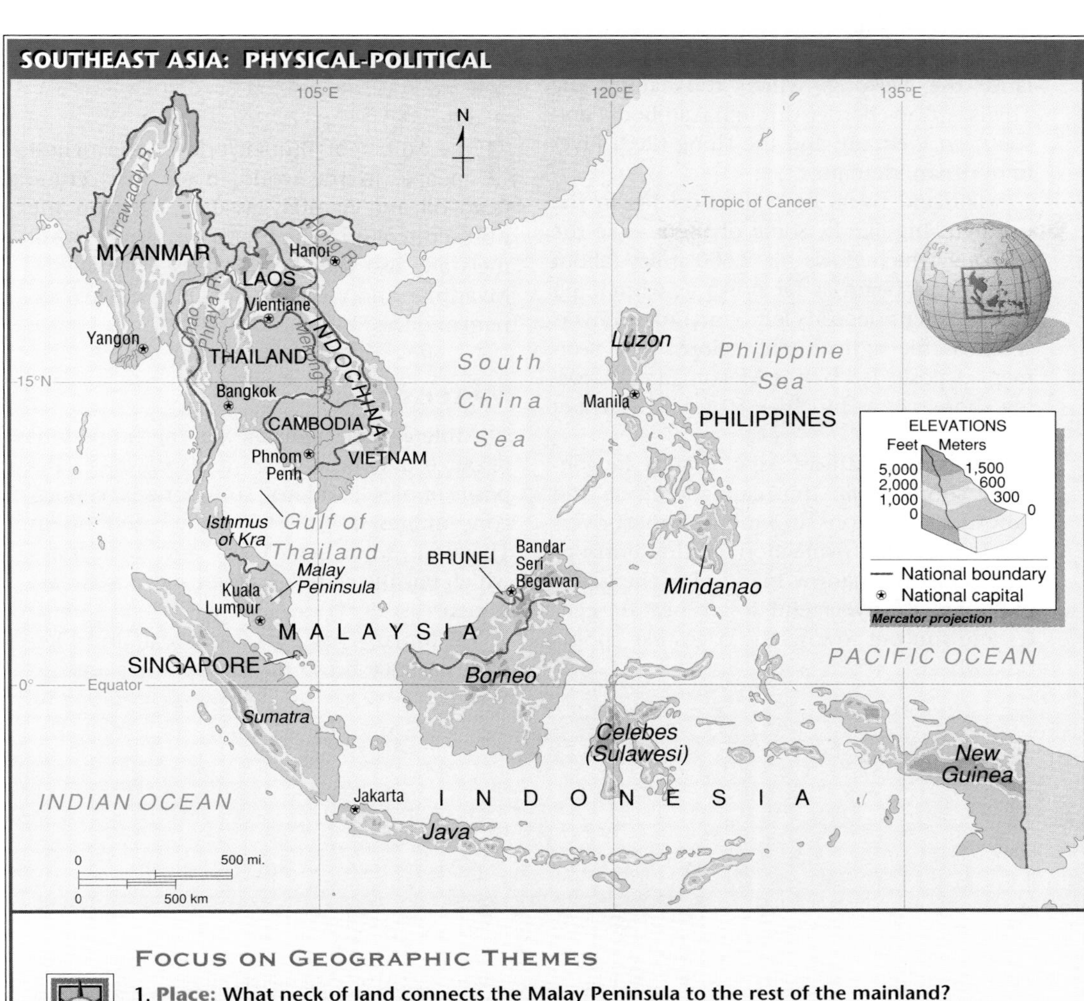

FOCUS ON GEOGRAPHIC THEMES

1. **Place:** **What neck of land connects the Malay Peninsula to the rest of the mainland?**
2. **Region:** **What region includes Vietnam, Laos, and Cambodia?**
3. **Place:** **What city is the capital of Myanmar?**
4. **Location:** **What seas lie to the east and west of the Philippines?**

The volcanoes of the region, however, do not only bring destruction. They are also the source of the fertile soil regions in the islands, which are some of the most productive agricultural areas in the world. Volcanic ash, full of rich nutrients, enriches the soil so much that even wooden fence posts sometimes sprout and grow into dense thickets within a few years.

MOVEMENT

Rivers

The rivers of mainland Southeast Asia flow in the north-south valleys between mountain ranges. The food supply, communication, and transportation throughout the region depend heavily on these waterways. The major rivers include the Irrawaddy in Myan-

L3 Geography: Place Have students identify the Southeast Asian countries whose territory is spread out over a number of islands. *(Malaysia, Philippines, Indonesia)* Discuss difficulties that fragmentation poses to these countries. *(Answers include barriers to political unity and economic development.)*

INDEPENDENT PRACTICE

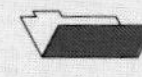

Guided Reading Have students complete Guided Reading Activity 29-1 in the TCR. **LEP**

USING MAPS

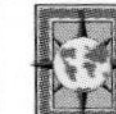

Answers:
1. Isthmus of Kra; **2.** Indochina; **3.** Yangon; **4.** Philippine Sea, South China Sea

Map Skills Practice
Reading a Map What is the only landlocked country in Southeast Asia? *(Laos)*

Meeting Special Needs

Reading Disability The presentation of background knowledge, or "schema," greatly aids reading comprehension. Schema is developed from the reader's current knowledge, then extended with new information from the text and illustrations. Have students with reading comprehension problems read only the postcard and introductory paragraphs on page 597. Compare this information with another region students have studied that has similar geographic characteristics, such as South Asia. After this orientation, have students read the rest of Section 1.

L2 Resources Have students collect illustrations or samples of Southeast Asia's natural resources. Discuss uses of the resources.

DID YOU KNOW?

The rafflesia, which grows in Malaysia, produces the largest flowers of any known plant. They grow up to 3 feet (90 cm) wide.

USING ILLUSTRATIONS

PLACE Luzon is the largest island in the Philippines. Manila lies on its southwest coast.

Answer to Caption: *Mt. Pinatubo*

ASSESS

CHECK FOR UNDERSTANDING

Assign Section 1 Review as homework or an in-class activity.

MEETING LESSON OBJECTIVES

Each objective below is tested by the questions that follow it in parentheses.

1. Describe the natural forces that shaped Southeast Asia. *(1)*

2. Compare mainland and island Southeast Asia. *(3)*

3. List the kinds of natural resources found in Southeast Asia. *(4)*

mar; the Chao Phraya (chau PRY•uh) in Thailand; the Mekong, which runs along the Thailand/Laos border through Cambodia and southern Vietnam; and the Hong (Red) River in northern Vietnam.

Mainland rivers have their origins in the northern highlands. Some of them—like the Mekong which flows for 2,600 miles (about 4,180 km)—begin as far north as China. Silt and sediment deposits left by mainland rivers create fertile agricultural regions. The sediment deposits left by the Mekong are increasing shorelines as much as 50 feet (15 m) per year.

Rivers on Southeast Asian islands are generally shorter than the mainland rivers and flow in all directions. In Indonesia most rivers run in a northerly direction, cutting horizontally across the narrow islands. On the island of Borneo, the rivers tend to start near the center and run out toward the edges like spokes on a wheel.

HUMAN/ENVIRONMENT INTERACTION

Natural Resources

The Sultan of Brunei, one of the richest people in the world, made his fortune from oil and natural gas discovered on the northern coast of the island of Borneo. Fossil fuels are also found in Malaysia, Indonesia, Myanmar, and Vietnam. Coal is found in Vietnam and the Philippines.

Minerals

Minerals and gems are another important resource and product of regional trade. Deposits of nickel and iron in Indonesia, copper-concentrates in the Philippines, and tin in Thailand, Myanmar, Laos, and Malaysia—which has the world's largest tin deposits—are mined.

Myanmar, Thailand, Cambodia, and Vietnam produce breathtaking sapphires and ru-

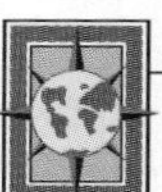

Geographic Themes

Place: Luzon, The Philippines

Volcanic mountains rise on most of the islands of the Philippines. *What recent Philippine volcanic eruption is said to have been the most powerful in this century?*

Critical Thinking

Drawing Conclusions Point out that much of Southeast Asia is surrounded by water. Ask students to list as many ways as possible that the geography of this region might affect the lives of its people. *(Possible answers include isolation of groups of people, problems in transportation and communication, trade and fishing as major economic activities, and a food supply and mineral resources from the sea.)*

bies. Burma rubies, as they are called, are especially prized by gem dealers.

Pearls are found near Sulu and Palawan in the Philippines. In 1934, the largest natural pearl ever found, weighing about 14 pounds (6.4 kg), was discovered in Palawan.

Another product from the earth, natural steam, is also a valuable resource. Trapped in volcanoes the steam has been tapped through wells. It is a source of geothermal energy used to generate electricity.

Flora and Fauna

Mahogany from the Philippines, teak from Myanmar, and rubber from Malaysia are among the trees that are an important resource in Southeast Asia. Because of heavy and unregulated deforestation, several Southeast Asian nations have restricted logging.

The forests also provide important pharmaceuticals. More than 10 percent of prescription drugs are made from products of tropical forests. Thailand has also developed the 1,000-plus species of orchids found there into a valuable trade resource.

The wildlife of Southeast Asia, such as elephants, tigers, several species of rhinoceros, and orangutans, is also considered a resource. Hundreds of animals in the region are found nowhere else in the world. Some of these include the bearded pig of Borneo, the Malayan lacewing butterfly, and Indonesia's Komodo dragon, the largest lizard in the world.

The people of Southeast Asia have an invaluable resource in the 2,500 fish species that thrive in the surrounding tropical waters. Fish are especially found in large quantities in the rivers of mainland Southeast Asia and in the seas near the Philippines, Indonesia, and Myanmar. Seafood, a major source of protein, is eaten in Southeast Asia at almost twice the world average.

Traditionally, local fishers in the region have gone out in sailing boats or canoes to make their catches with lines or traps. In recent decades, the region's small fishers have had to compete with a rapidly growing fleet of trawlers. The result has been an increased yield everywhere in the region. Fish farming is now a major supplement to the economies of Southeast Asian countries. Concerns about the dangers of overfishing, however, have been raised; and the production of seafood for export has started to level off.

Geographic Themes

Place: Malaysia

Malaysia's economy depends heavily on the use of natural resources. Malaysia is the world's leading producer of natural rubber. *What mineral resource is mined in Malaysia?*

SECTION 1 REVIEW

Checking for Understanding

1. **Define** cordillera, archipelago, flora, fauna.
2. **Locating Places** Through which countries does the Mekong River flow?
3. **Region** What are two ways in which the mainland and the islands of Southeast Asia differ? In what two ways are they similar?
4. **Region** What are some of the natural resources found in Southeast Asia?

Critical Thinking

5. **Analyzing Information** Where on the mainland would you expect to find the most densely populated areas?

ANSWERS TO SECTION 1 REVIEW

1. **cordillera:** parallel mountain ranges; **archipelago:** island group; **flora:** plants; **fauna:** animals
2. Thailand, Laos, Cambodia, Vietnam
3. Differences: Volcanoes on the mainland are inactive, while many on the islands are active; fertile soil on the mainland comes from river deltas, while on the islands it comes from volcanoes. Similarities: Both the mainland and islands have mountains and fertile soil.
4. fossil fuels, minerals, gems, fish, mahogany, rubber
5. Possible answers: Densely populated areas are likely to be found along rivers and on river deltas; sparse population is likely in mountain regions.

EVALUATE

Assign the Section 1 Quiz in the TCR.

Use the Testmaker to create a customized quiz for Section 1.

RETEACH

Write the names of mountain ranges and rivers on slips of paper and put them in a box. Call on volunteers to draw a slip and identify a country in which the mountain range or river is found.

USING ILLUSTRATIONS

PLACE Workers collect a white liquid called latex by cutting grooves in the bark of rubber trees.

Answer to Caption: *tin*

ENRICH

Have interested students find out more about rubber production. They might create a booklet showing the process.

CLOSE

Have students write to Noy, describing their favorite vacation spot.

NATIONAL GEOGRAPHIC SOCIETY

PHYSICAL GEOGRAPHY OF THE WORLD TRANSPARENCIES

Display and discuss the physical features of the following transparencies:

66. Monsoon, Malaysia
67. Semeru and Bromo Volcanoes, Indonesia
68. Rain Forest, Malaysia
69. Rice Fields, Philippines

LESSON PLAN
Chapter 29, Section 2

FOCUS

SECTION OBJECTIVES

1. Describe the climate regions of Southeast Asia.
2. Identify the different kinds of vegetation in Southeast Asia.

BELLRINGER MOTIVATIONAL ACTIVITY

Project the Section 2 Focus Transparency and have students answer the questions.

PRETEACHING VOCABULARY

Have students find the meaning of the word *endemic* in the text. *(native to a particular area)* Discuss how climate influences a region's endemic species. *(Climate produces certain vegetation, which provides habitat for certain animals.)* **LEP**

MULTICULTURAL PERSPECTIVE

Culturally Speaking
The name *Singapore* means "lion city" in Sanskrit. It probably referred to the many tigers, mistakenly called lions, that once inhabited the island.

GLENCOE TECHNOLOGY

Videodisc

Use the following to enrich Chapter 29:

GEOGRAPHY AND THE ENVIRONMENT
THE INFINITE VOYAGE
To the Edge of the Earth

Chapter 5
Disc 1 Side B
Title: ***The Tropical Rain Forest***

SECTION 2

The Climate and Vegetation

SETTING THE SCENE

Read to Discover . . .
- the climate regions of Southeast Asia.
- the different kinds of vegetation in Southeast Asia.

Key Terms
- monsoon
- endemic
- deforestation

Identify and Locate
Climate regions: tropical rain forest, tropical savanna

Most of Southeast Asia lies within the tropics and has a tropical climate controlled by the **monsoons**, or seasonal winds. In summer, the moisture-laden monsoons blow from the cooler seas toward the warmer land. In the winter, the dry monsoons blow from the cooling land out to sea.

REGION

Southeast Asia's Climate Regions

Although Southeast Asia largely has a tropical climate, there are exceptions in the region's climate patterns due mainly to latitude, elevation, and local wind patterns. For example, the northernmost parts of Laos and Vietnam are humid subtropical and from November to April are cool and dry with temperatures averaging around 61°F (16°C). The Shan Plateau in Myanmar, called by one traveller a "tropical Scotland," is elevated and cooler than the rest of the country.

Tropical Rain Forest

A tropical rain forest climate—uniformly hot, humid, and rainy throughout the year—is found throughout the islands of Southeast Asia, as well as on the eastern and western coasts of the Indochina Peninsula. The average daily temperature in much of this area hovers around 79°F (26°C). Regional rainfall averages 79 to 188 inches (201 to 478 cm) per year, and the humidity reaches between 80 and 90 percent.

Even within this climate region there is some variation. For example, the farther away an area is from the Equator, the more concentrated the wet season becomes and the more pronounced the dry season becomes. The farther inland, the more rainfall there is likely to be. Other examples of local peculiarity are found in peninsular Malaysia, where most of the rain falls during thunderstorms, and in Singapore, where there are about 180 days with lightning each year.

Tropical Savanna Climate

A tropical savanna climate region extends southeastward across the Indochina Peninsula to the Philippines. It is characterized by alternate wet and dry seasons. In this climate region, monsoon winds bring rain from May or June through October. October to April is the dry season, with the first few months being cooler and the last few being hot. In most of the region monsoon winds blow during the dry months.

An exception is in eastern Indonesia. There, the rainy seasons are reversed, with the South Pacific trade winds bringing the hot, dry season from May to September, and the monsoons bringing the wet season from December to March.

Classroom Resources for Section 2

BLACKLINE MASTERS:
Reproducible Lesson Plan 29-2
Skill Activity 29
Enrichment Activity 29
Section Quiz 29-2

TRANSPARENCIES:
Section Focus Transparency 29-2
Unit Map Overlay Transparencies 10-2, 10-3

MULTIMEDIA:

Testmaker

Geography and the Environment
GTV: Planetary Manager

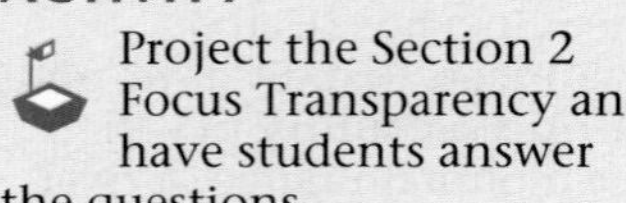

Local peculiarities on the mainland include Sittwe (Akyab) in Myanmar, which gets an average of 204 inches (5,182 mm) of rain each year. Temperatures can drop to freezing in December and January in the Kieng Khoung province of Laos.

Importance of Rains

The heavy rains in Southeast Asia are important in several ways. They cause the flooding of the rivers, which is essential to wet rice cultivation—a crucial element in the agricultural life of the region. The rains also nourish the tropical rain forests that cover most of the area.

Vegetation

The vegetation of Southeast Asia is varied and abundant, characteristic of tropical rain forest and savanna climate regions. Southeast Asia contains 13 different types of tropical rain

SOUTHEAST ASIA: CLIMATE REGIONS

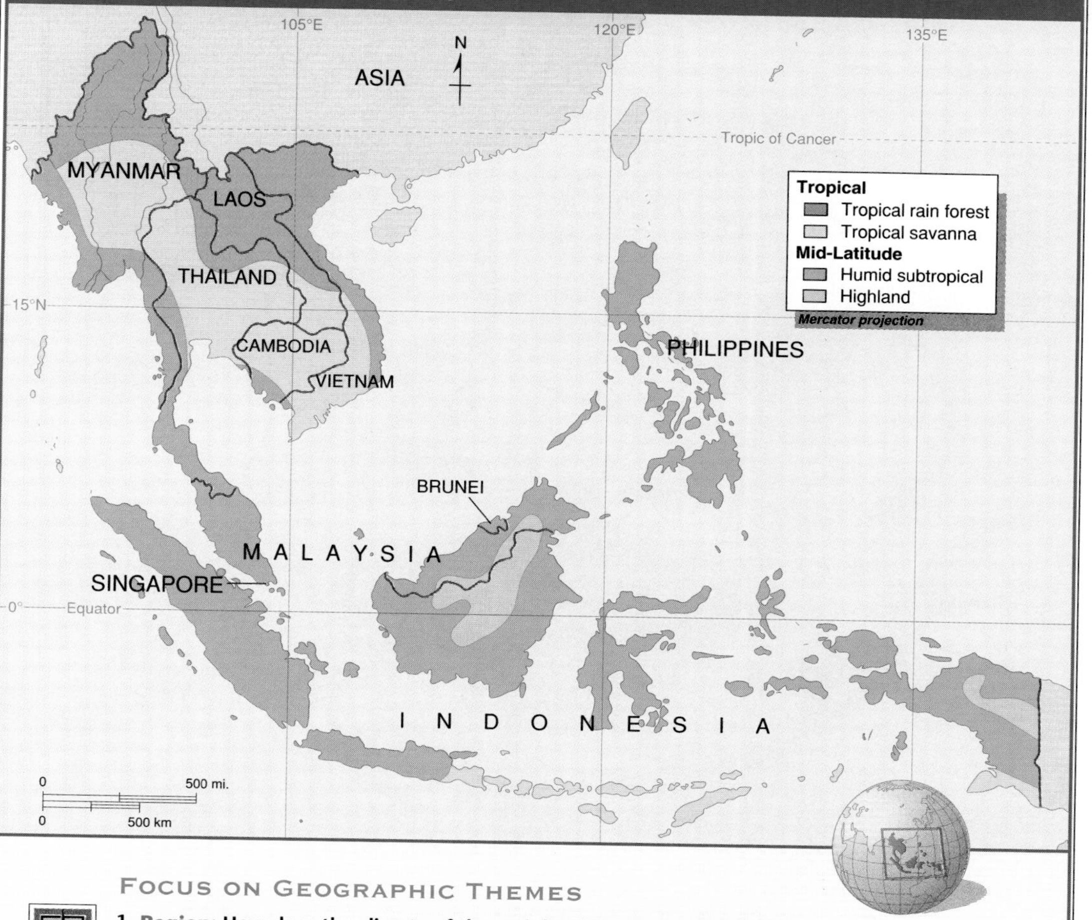

105°E
120°E
135°E
N
ASIA
Tropic of Cancer
MYANMAR
LAOS
THAILAND
15°N
CAMBODIA
VIETNAM
PHILIPPINES
BRUNEI
MALAYSIA
SINGAPORE
0°
Equator
INDONESIA
0 500 mi.
0 500 km

Tropical
Tropical rain forest
Tropical savanna
Mid-Latitude
Humid subtropical
Highland
Mercator projection

FOCUS ON GEOGRAPHIC THEMES

1. **Region:** How does the climate of the mainland countries differ from the climate of the island countries?
2. **Location:** Where are highland climates located in Southeast Asia?
3. **Location:** What part of Southeast Asia has a humid subtropical climate?

TEACH

GUIDED PRACTICE

L2 Compare Have students compare the maps on pages 603 and 604. Display Unit Map Overlay Transparencies 10-2 and 10-3. Ask students to write one or more generalizations about the relationship between climate and vegetation in Southeast Asia.

USING MAPS

Answers:
1. Mainland is mostly humid subtropical and tropical savanna, islands are mostly tropical rain forest; **2.** New Guinea and Borneo; **3.** northern regions of Myanmar, Thailand, Vietnam, and Laos

Map Skills Practice
Reading a Map Which mainland countries have more than two types of climate? *(Myanmar, Thailand, Vietnam)*

L3 Analyze Have students explain reasons for variations within Southeast Asia's tropical climates. Ask students to use maps or other sources to support their conclusions.

INDEPENDENT PRACTICE

Guided Reading
Have students complete Guided Reading Activity 29-2 in the TCR. **LEP**

Cooperative Learning Activity

Organize the class into groups of three or four. Assign one of the following locations to each group: northernmost Laos and Vietnam; Shan Plateau in Myanmar; eastern and western coasts of Indochina Peninsula; Singapore; Philippines. Instruct group members to prepare seasonal weather forecasts for their assigned location. Then have each group present its forecast. Students might create a "television studio," using Unit Map Overlay Transparency 10-3 to illustrate weather patterns.

USING MAPS

Answers:
1. tropical forest; **2.** eastern Myanmar

Map Skills Practice
Comparing Maps What type of climate produces deciduous and mixed forests in northeastern Myanmar? *(humid subtropical)*

ASSESS

CHECK FOR UNDERSTANDING

Assign Section 2 Review as homework or an in-class activity.

MEETING LESSON OBJECTIVES

Each objective below is tested by the questions that follow it in parentheses.
1. Describe the climate regions of Southeast Asia. *(2, 3)*
2. Identify the different kinds of vegetation in Southeast Asia. *(4, 5)*

EVALUATION

Assign the Section 2 Quiz in the TCR.

Use the Testmaker to create a customized quiz for Section 2.

RETEACH

Have students complete Reteaching Activity 29 in the TCR.

forest, and Malaysia alone has more than 145,000 species of flowering plants. The flora of Southeast Asia consists mainly of tropical and subtropical species, but also includes such rarities as cacti in central Myanmar. Tropical-savanna grasslands extend southeastward across the Indochina Peninsula and are also found in some of the easternmost islands, the areas in the region farther from the Equator.

Forests

The forests of Southeast Asia are very old. The Malaysian rain forest is believed to be the oldest in the region, dating back 130 million years. The makeup of Malaysia's forests is an example of the mix of different types of tropical rain forest. Below 2,000 feet (610 m) are the lowland rain forests. Above 2,000 feet (610

SOUTHEAST ASIA: NATURAL VEGETATION

Tropical forest
Deciduous and mixed deciduous-coniferous forest
Temperate grassland
Mercator projection

FOCUS ON GEOGRAPHIC THEMES

1. Region: What is the dominant natural vegetation of Southeast Asia?
2. Place: What part of Southeast Asia has grasslands?

604 UNIT 10

Meeting Special Needs

Reading Disability Students with reading comprehension problems benefit from focused reading exercises. Have students read the material under "Deforestation." Then have them write in their notebooks what they remember. Have them reread the material to answer the following questions:

Why did Southeast Asian nations introduce deforestation programs?

How has the loss of rain forests affected the environment?

How has it affected local groups?

What have Southeast Asian governments done about the problems?

Ask students whether they included this information in their notebooks. Discuss how guided reading questions aid comprehension.

m), highland forest areas are found, while above 4,000 feet (1,220 m) there are mossy forests. In the river valleys, peat swamp forests thrive, while sandy coastal soil supports various shrubs, and the tidal mud flats are covered with mangrove swamp forests.

An Unusual Case

Singapore's vegetation makes it an exception in the region. Although Singapore is a highly developed urban area with one of the highest population densities in the world, it is one of the only two cities in the world to have areas of tropical rain forest within its boundaries (the other is Rio de Janeiro, Brazil). It may be hard to believe that where towering apartment blocks now house 2.7 million people, dense rain forest surrounded by mangroves once covered the island.

Singapore's vegetation is also unusual in that many of the **endemic** species—those native to a particular area—are now gone. Almost 80 percent of the trees and shrubs now growing in Singapore were imported, some from as far away as Central and South America. Along with the loss of its natural habitat, Singapore has lost many of its larger mammals and its variety of exotic animals.

Deforestation

During the 1970s and 1980s, the demand for natural resources, the creation of jobs, and the need for more open land led Southeast Asian nations to introduce deforestation programs. **Deforestation** refers to the removal of large areas of forest by loggers and farmers. Although a useful short-term solution to economic problems, deforestation has had disastrous consequences in the region, often reducing rich forest areas to wastelands. Thailand, for example, has lost half of its forests as a result of logging. Throughout the region, the loss of rain forest has decreased soil quality, created erosion problems, and caused water contamination. Logging has also encroached on lands belonging to local groups, affecting their traditional livelihoods and causing political dissent.

Geographic Themes

Human/Environment Interaction: Northern Thailand

Southeast Asia's forests and plains produce an abundance of flowers that are used for decoration and for festivals. *What human activity poses a threat to Southeast Asia's forests?*

Since the late 1980s, the governments of a number of Southeast Asian countries have tried to reduce logging and the export of timber, but without complete success. Brunei, for example, forbade lumber exports starting in 1989, and Thailand did the same.

Section 2 Review

Checking for Understanding

1. **Define** monsoon, endemic, deforestation.
2. **Locating Places** In which climate region is Southeast Asia mainly located?
3. **Region** What are the variations found in the climates of Southeast Asian countries?
4. **Region** How does the tropical climate affect vegetation in Southeast Asia?

Critical Thinking

5. **Determining Cause and Effect** How does deforestation affect the livelihood of Southeast Asia's people?

USING ILLUSTRATIONS

PLACE Thais celebrate many festivals, such as this flower festival in Chiang Mai.

Answer to Caption: *logging*

ENRICH

Have students complete Enrichment Activity 29 in the TCR.

CLOSE

Ask students to write in their notebooks how they think the physical geography and climates of Southeast Asia affect its people. Ask them to review their statements after studying Chapter 30.

NATIONAL GEOGRAPHIC SOCIETY

Videodisc

GTV: PLANETARY MANAGER

Side 1, Chapter 7
Frames: 32716-37894
Title: ***Vanishing Act***
Subject: Music and graphics contrast the richness of biodiversity with the poverty and danger of its steady decline

GTV: PLANETARY MANAGER

Side 2, Chapter 6
Frames 31907-38777
Title: ***Dust in the Wind***
Subject: Time travel shows the consequences of overgrazing, excessive irrigation, and deforestation

ANSWERS TO SECTION 2 REVIEW

1. **monsoon:** seasonal wind; **endemic:** native to a particular area; **deforestation:** removal of forests
2. tropical rain forest
3. Temperatures can drop to freezing in parts of Laos; the islands are uniformly hot, humid, and rainy throughout the year; some areas have alternate wet and dry seasons.
4. Vegetation is varied and abundant.
5. Deforestation causes soil erosion, water contamination, and loss of wildlife. It endangers agriculture, fishing, and hunting.

TEACH

Have students read the skill on page 606. Ask them to define *cause (an event that makes something occur)* and *effect (the result of another action or event)*. Ask for examples of cause-and-effect relationships, including complex relationships and cause-effect chains. Then ask small groups to develop short skits showing cause-and-effect relationships or chains of events. After each skit, ask the audience to identify and discuss the relationship shown.

Skills Practice
For additional practice, have students complete Skill Activity 29 in the TCR.

CRITICAL THINKING SKILLS

Determining Cause and Effect

Suppose you leave for school one morning and forget to put a carton of milk back into the refrigerator. When you return in the afternoon, the milk has spoiled. What is the connection between these two events?

REVIEWING THE SKILL

Events occur because other events make them happen. An event or person that makes something happen is called a **cause**. In the example above, forgetting to refrigerate the milk caused it to spoil. The **effect**, or result, was the spoilage. The relationship between these two events is called a cause-and-effect relationship. Cause-and-effect relationships explain why things happen and how actions produce other actions.

Cause-and-effect relationships can be simple or complex. Sometimes several different causes produce a single effect. For example, a car accident may have several causes—poor road conditions, a tired or ill driver, bad weather, faulty equipment. On the other hand, one cause can produce several effects. Burning fossil fuels, such as gasoline and coal, may improve productivity and standard of living but also increases air pollution and global warming.

In addition an effect often becomes the cause of yet another event. For example, burning fossil fuels causes more greenhouse gases in the atmosphere; the greenhouse gases increase the global temperature. Global warming may cause ice caps to melt, which would increase the amount of water in the sea, which in turn may cause floods in coastal areas. Strings of causal relationships are called **cause-effect chains.**

When determining cause and effect, apply the following steps:

- Ask questions about why events occur.
- Identify the outcomes of events.
- Look for cause-and-effect relationships among events. Sometimes clue words or phrases, such as *caused, led to, brought about, produced, because, as a result of, so that, thus, as a consequence*, and *therefore*, indicate these relationships.

PRACTICING THE SKILL

A. Identify causes and effects in the following statements. Remember that there may be more than one cause or effect in each statement.

1. The mountain ridges, river valleys, and volcanic islands of Southeast Asia were formed by the collision of the Eurasian and Indo-Australian tectonic plates millions of years ago.
2. The mountain ridges of Southeast Asia produce natural barriers with India and China and also between peoples living within the region.
3. Erupting volcanoes bring destruction but also produce fertile soil and a source of geothermal energy.
4. Water has been the primary method of transportation and trade in Southeast Asia because of its enormous coastline and long rivers.
5. As distance from the Equator increases, wet and dry seasons become more concentrated and defined.
6. Heavy rainfall brings about river flooding, which is essential to rice cultivation.

B. Use the material in Chapter 29 to identify these cause-and-effect relationships.

1. Name three effects produced by the rising water levels after the last Ice Age.
2. Identify two causes and three effects of deforestation in Southeast Asia.

For additional practice in this skill, see Practicing Skills on page 608 of the Chapter 29 Review.

ANSWERS TO PRACTICING THE SKILL

A. 1. cause—tectonic plate collision; effects—mountains, valleys, islands

2. cause—mountains; effects—barriers

3. cause—volcanoes; effects—destruction, fertile soil, geothermal energy

4. causes—coastline, rivers; effects—water transportation, trade

5. cause—increased latitude; effect—more defined wet, dry seasons

6. cause—heavy rainfall; effect/cause—flooding; effect—rice cultivation

B. 1. formed islands, isolated plants/animals, created coastline, water travel, trade

2. causes—logging, farming; effects—secondary forest, soil erosion, water contamination, higher fish prices, disrupted traditions, political dissent

chapter 29

HIGHLIGHTS

Section 1: The Land

Key Terms

cordillera (p. 597)
archipelago (p. 598)
flora (p. 598)
fauna (p. 598)

Summary

- The region of Southeast Asia includes the 2 peninsulas east of India and south of China and the 20,000 islands of the Malay Archipelago.
- Southeast Asia's mountains were formed by the collision of the Indo-Australian plate and the Philippine plate with the Eurasian plate.
- The rivers on the mainland of Southeast Asia are important for agriculture, communication, and transportation.
- Southeast Asia has major reserves of fossil fuels, tropical hardwoods, tin, and gems.

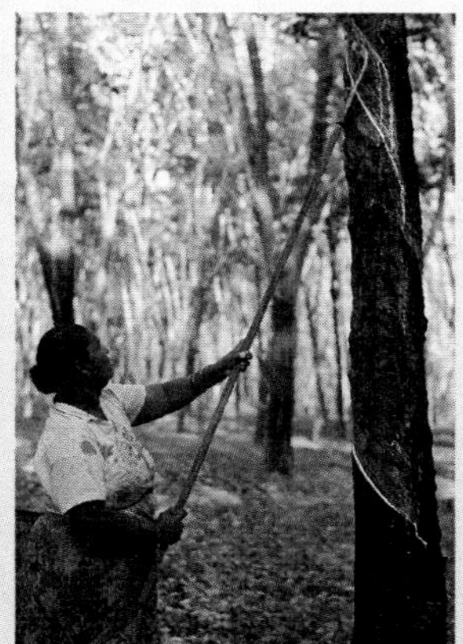

Rubber plantation in Malaysia

Section 2: The Climate and Vegetation

Key Terms

monsoon (p. 602)
endemic (p. 605)
deforestation (p. 605)

Summary

- Most parts of Southeast Asia have a hot and humid climate affected by monsoons.
- A tropical rain forest climate region is found throughout the islands of Southeast Asia, as well as on the eastern and western coasts of the Indochina Peninsula.
- A tropical savanna climate region extends southeastward across the Indochina Peninsula. Some of the southernmost islands in the region also share this climate.
- The vegetation of Southeast Asia consists largely of varieties of tropical rain forest.
- Deforestation in Southeast Asia has affected the ecology, the economy, and the culture of some of the peoples.

Floral festival in Thailand

Map Activity

Identify and Locate Distribute copies of the map on page 34 of the Outline Map Resource Book. Have students label the countries of Southeast Asia. Then have them use their maps to write a card with locator clues (such as latitude and longitude, positions relative to another country, or physical features) for each country. Have students work in small groups to identify the countries based on one another's clues.

CHAPTER 29 HIGHLIGHTS

USING THE CHAPTER 29 HIGHLIGHTS

Use the Chapter 29 Highlights to preview, review, condense, or reteach the chapter.

PREVIEW/REVIEW

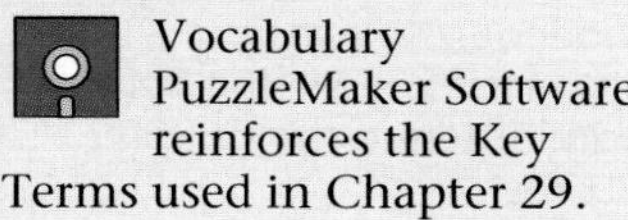

Vocabulary PuzzleMaker Software reinforces the Key Terms used in Chapter 29.

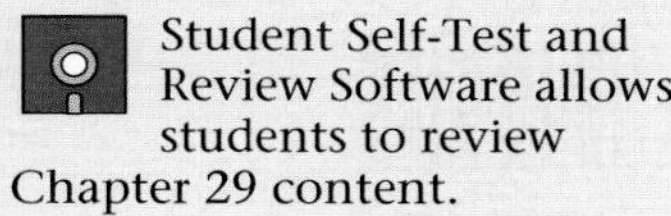

Student Self-Test and Review Software allows students to review Chapter 29 content.

CONDENSE

Have students read the Chapter 29 Highlights.

Have students listen to the Chapter 29 Audiocassettes in the TCR. Spanish Audiocassettes are also available.

Assign the Chapter 29 Audiocassette Activity and give the students the Chapter 29 Audiocassette Quiz.

Have students complete Guided Reading Activities for Chapter 29 in the TCR. Spanish Guided Reading Activities are also available.

RETEACH

Have students complete Reteaching Activity 29 in the TCR. Spanish Reteaching Activities are also available.

Chapter 29 Review

GLENCOE TECHNOLOGY

Videodisc

Use Chapter 29 MindJogger Videoquiz to review students' knowledge before administering the Chapter 29 Test.

MINDJOGGER VIDEOQUIZ

Chapter 29
Disc 4 Side B

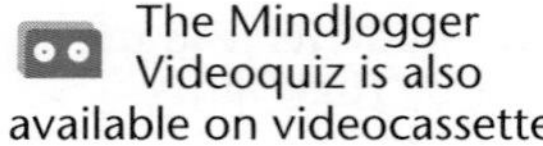

The MindJogger Videoquiz is also available on videocassette.

ANSWERS

Reviewing Key Terms

1. archipelago
2. flora
3. cordillera
4. fauna
5. endemic
6. deforestation
7. monsoons

Reviewing Facts

8. peninsulas, islands, mountains
9. river deltas; volcanoes
10. minerals, gems, volcanic steam, fossil fuels; pearls, shells, fish; rubber, teak, mahogany, orchids
11. tropical rain forest; tropical savanna
12. It decreases soil quality, creates erosion, causes water contamination; it affects the traditional lands and livelihoods of local groups.

chapter 29 REVIEW

Reviewing Key Terms

Choose the vocabulary term that best completes each of the sentences below. Write your answers on a separate sheet of paper.

cordilleras (p. 597)
archipelago (p. 598)
flora (p. 598)
fauna (p. 598)
monsoons (p. 602)
endemic (p. 605)
deforestation (p. 605)

SECTION 1

1. A(n) ____ is a group of islands.
2. ____ refers to the vegetation of a region.
3. Parallel mountain ranges, such as those found on the Indochina Peninsula, are known as ____.
4. ____ refers to the animals of a region.

SECTION 2

5. ____ means native to one particular area.
6. ____ occurs when many trees are logged without regard for the environment.
7. ____ are winds that shift with the seasons.

Reviewing Facts

SECTION 1

8. What are three important landform types in Southeast Asia?
9. What geographic factor is responsible for the most fertile soils on mainland Southeast Asia? On the islands?
10. Name a Southeast Asian resource found underground, underwater, and in a tropical rain forest.

SECTION 2

11. Describe the two dominant climate regions found in Southeast Asia.
12. Why is deforestation a problem for Southeast Asia?

Critical Thinking

13. **Predicting Consequences** What kinds of transportation difficulties might Southeast Asians face on the mainland?
14. **Drawing Conclusions** Southeast Asia has a diversity of peoples and cultures. How might physical geography have shaped this diversity on the mainland? On the islands?

Geographic Themes

15. **Place** Why are the many volcanoes of the Ring of Fire useful as well as dangerous?
16. **Region** What vegetation is found in Southeast Asia's tropical rain forest climate region?

Practicing Skills

Determining Cause and Effect

Refer to the Determining Cause and Effect skill feature on page 606.

Find three cause-and-effect relationships in Chapter 29. For each one, identify the causes and effects.

Using the Unit Atlas

Refer to the physical geography section of the Unit Atlas on pages 592–593.

17. What body of water separates the two major land areas of Malaysia?
18. What landforms make up the nation of Indonesia?

Critical Thinking

13. Possible answers include mountains and rivers that act as barriers to east-west travel; flooding that interrupts navigation and land travel; dense rain forests.
14. Physical barriers, such as mountain ranges and rivers, have kept groups of people separated. Islands also kept people isolated so separate cultures developed.

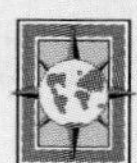

Geographic Themes

15. Volcanoes produce fertile soil and are a source of geothermal energy.
16. different types of rain forests and thousands of species of flowering plants

Projects

Individual Activity

You have learned about some of the resources of Southeast Asia, such as gems, orchids, timber, and minerals. Imagine that you work in an exporting business in a Southeast Asian country. What are some of the problems you might encounter as you try to prepare a particular resource for export? Use your journal record, the text, encyclopedias, and other resources to prepare a brief report about your resource.

Cooperative Learning Activity

Working in a group of four, plan a trip through Southeast Asia. Decide what areas to visit, noting the kinds of landforms to be seen in each place. Determine how to get from one place to another, and work together on a map that shows the route. Finally, prepare a written itinerary and present the travel plans to the class.

Writing About Geography

Description

Use your journal, a film, a book, or a magazine with photographs to investigate a variety of physical features in Southeast Asia. Then write a newspaper story about a volcanic area in the Philippines, a rain forest in Malaysia, or the Mekong Delta in Vietnam.

Locating Places

SOUTHEAST ASIA: PHYSICAL GEOGRAPHY

Match the letters on the map with the places and physical features of Southeast Asia. Write your answers on a separate sheet of paper.

1. Singapore
2. Irrawaddy River
3. Thailand
4. Malay Peninsula
5. Mekong River
6. Vietnam
7. Philippines
8. Java
9. Sumatra
10. Borneo

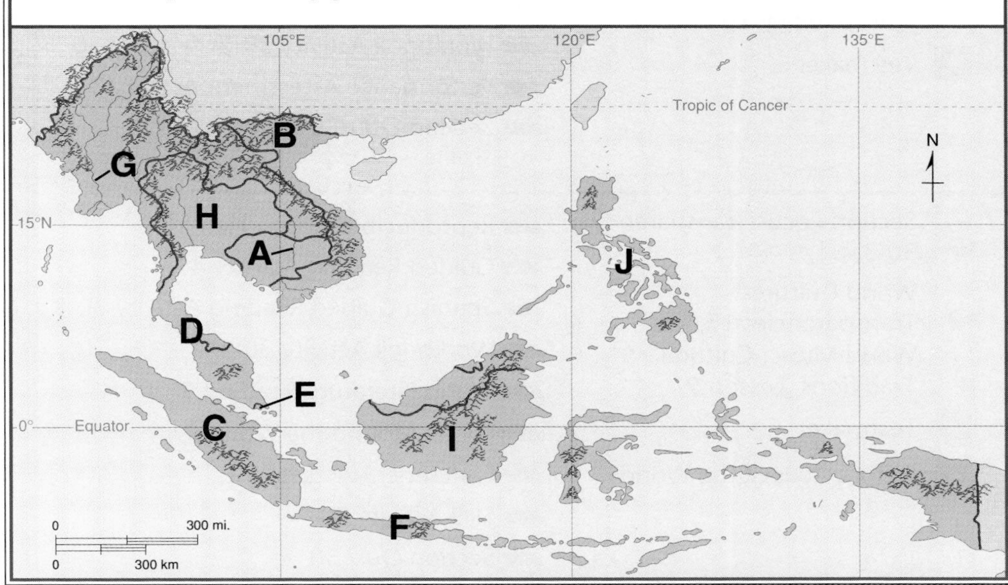

Chapter 29 Review

Practicing Skills

Answers will vary but should follow the steps discussed in the skills feature on page 606.

Using the Unit Atlas

17. South China Sea
18. islands

Locating Places

1. E
2. G
3. H
4. D
5. A
6. B
7. J
8. F
9. C
10. I

Chapter Bonus Test Question

This question may be used for extra credit on the chapter test.

What do you think is the basis for classifying the nations of Southeast Asia as a geographic region?

(Answer: location, similar climate and vegetation, similar landforms)

CHAPTER 30

PLANNING GUIDE

The Cultural Geography of Southeast Asia

CHAPTER ORGANIZER

Daily Lesson Objectives	Multimedia	Teacher Classroom Resources
SECTION 1 Population Patterns 1. Describe the population distribution of Southeast Asia. 2. Compare urban and rural lifestyles in the region. 3. Explain how the population of Southeast Asia is changing.	Section Focus Transparency 30-1 Chapter 30 Vocabulary PuzzleMaker Software Unit Map Overlay Transparency 10-1 Testmaker Reuters Issues in Geography	Reproducible Lesson Plan 30-1 Guided Reading Activity 30-1 Spanish Guided Reading Activity 30-1 Workbook Activity 30-1 Performance Assessment Activity 30 Section Quiz 30-1
SECTION 2 History and Government 1. Discuss the influences that other cultures had on the early people of Southeast Asia. 2. Analyze how the countries of the region gained independence.	Section Focus Transparency 30-2 Unit Map Overlay Transparency 10 Testmaker	Reproducible Lesson Plan 30-2 Guided Reading Activity 30-2 Spanish Guided Reading Activity 30-2 Workbook Activity 30-2 Performance Assessment Activity 30 Section Quiz 30-2
SECTION 3 Cultures and Lifestyles 1. Identify the region's major language families and religions. 2. Describe the variety of arts, literature, and drama found in Southeast Asia. 3. Explain the current lifestyles of Southeast Asians.	Section Focus Transparency 30-3 World Cultures Transparencies 17, 18 World Music: Cultural Traditions, Lesson 9 Testmaker Picture Atlas of the World	Reproducible Lesson Plan 30-3 Guided Reading Activity 30-3 Spanish Guided Reading Activity 30-3 Workbook Activity 30-3 World Literature Reading 9 Foods Around the World 9 Enrichment Activity 30 Skill Activity 30 Section Quiz 30-3
CHAPTER REVIEW AND EVALUATION	Chapter 30 English (or Spanish) Audiocassettes MindJogger Videoquiz Testmaker Student Self-Test and Review Software	Reteaching Activity 30 Spanish Reteaching Activity 30 Chapter 30 Test Form A and Form B

0:00 *If time does not permit teaching the entire chapter, summarize using the Chapter 30 Highlights on page 625, and Chapter 30 English (or Spanish) Audiocassettes. Review students' knowledge using the Glencoe MindJogger Videoquiz.*

KEY TO ABILITY LEVELS

Teaching strategies have been coded for varying learning styles and abilities.

L1 **BASIC** activities for all students

L2 **AVERAGE** activities for average to above-average students

L3 **CHALLENGING** activities for above-average students

LEP **LIMITED ENGLISH PROFICIENCY** activities

Performance Assessment

Hypothesizing The teacher should guide an alternative assessment for the chapter by leading students through a "scientific" research task. Students should provide written evidence of hypotheses, a plan for acquiring information as well as findings/notes, conclusions, and self-assessment of initial hypotheses.

At the beginning of the chapter study, ask groups of students to predict population density and the location of major urban and agricultural areas from the data presented in Chapter 29. Students should write their hypotheses on blank political maps of the area. Students can validate their ideas with information in Section 1 and other relevant sources. Have the groups hypothesize the cultural influences of foreign countries in the region and validate with Sections 2 and 3 and other sources.

POSSIBLE RUBRIC FEATURES: Content information, scientific thinking process steps, predictive and cause/effect skills, collaboration and oral communication skills

For additional professional and classroom resources, see Chapter Resources, pages T46–T51.

TEACHER'S CORNER

INDEX TO NATIONAL GEOGRAPHIC MAGAZINE

The following articles may be used for research relating to this chapter:

- "Hanoi: The Capital Today," by Peter T. White, November 1989.
- "Saigon: Fourteen Years After," by Peter T. White, November 1989.
- "Indonesia: Two Worlds, Time Apart," by Arthur Zich, January 1989.
- "Hope and Danger in the Philippines," by Arthur Zich, July 1986.
- "Time and Again in Burma," by Bryan Hodgson, July 1984.
- "Indonesia Rescues Ancient Borobudur," by W. Brown Morton III, January 1983.
- "Thailand: Luck of the Land in the Middle," by Bart McDowell, October 1982.
- "Singapore: Mini-size Superstate," by Bryan Hodgson, April 1981.
- "Thailand: Refuge from Terror," by W. E. Garrett, May 1980.
- "Bali Celebrates a Festival of Faith," by Peter Miller, March 1980.

NATIONAL GEOGRAPHIC SOCIETY PRODUCTS AVAILABLE FROM GLENCOE

To order the following products for use with this chapter, contact your local Glencoe sales representative or call Glencoe at 1-800-334-7344:

- *Picture Atlas of the World* (CD-ROM)
- *STV: World Geography, Asia and Australia* (Videodisc)
- *ZipZapMap! World* (Software)
- *GeoBee* (Software)
- *Images of the World* (Posters)
- *Eye on the Environment* (Posters)
- *Physical Geography of the World* (Transparencies)
- *Picture Atlas of Our 50 States* (Book)

ADDITIONAL NATIONAL GEOGRAPHIC SOCIETY PRODUCTS

To order the following products for use with this chapter, call National Geographic Society at 1-800-368-2728:

- *The Changing Faces of Communism Series*, "Vietnam." (Video)

Introducing
CHAPTER 30

chapter 30
The Cultural Geography of Southeast Asia

PERFORMANCE ASSESSMENT

Refer to the Planning Guide on page 610B for a Performance Assessment Activity for this chapter. See the *Performance Assessment Activities* booklet for additional suggestions.

CHAPTER OBJECTIVES

1. **Describe** the population patterns of Southeast Asia.
2. **Explain** how cultural influences have affected the history of governments of Southeast Asia.
3. **Gain** an appreciation for the cultural diversity of Southeast Asia.

GLENCOE TECHNOLOGY

Videodisc

Use Chapter 30 MindJogger Videoquiz to preview chapter content.

MINDJOGGER VIDEOQUIZ

Chapter 30
Disc 4 Side B

The MindJogger Videoquiz is also available on videocassette.

CHAPTER FOCUS

Geographic Setting

The culture region of Southeast Asia lies on the trade route from the Western nations to China and the East. As a result, the region has attracted traders and colonizers throughout history.

Geographic Themes

Section 1 Population Patterns
PLACE **Most of Southeast Asia's peoples live in rural areas.**

Section 2 History and Government
MOVEMENT **The region's resources have long attracted foreigners.**

Section 3 Cultures and Lifestyles
REGION **The cultures of Southeast Asia reflect great ethnic diversity.**

▲ Photograph: ***Kuala Lumpur, the capital of Malaysia***

EXTRA CREDIT PROJECT

Population Density Chart Have students research the populations and land areas of the countries of Southeast Asia, then determine each country's population density. Students should present this information in the form of a table.

1 SECTION
Population Patterns

SETTING THE SCENE

Read to Discover . . .
- where people live in Southeast Asia.
- the major factors affecting population distribution in Southeast Asia.

Key Terms
- arable land
- primate city

Identify and Locate
Cambodia, Laos, Myanmar, Thailand, Vietnam, Malaysia, Indonesia, Brunei, Philippines, Singapore

LUANG PRABANG, LAOS

SAYBAYDEE! FROM MY HOME I CAN SEE THE BEAUTIFUL OLD TEMPLE ON TOP OF PHOU SI MOUNTAIN. BELOW THE MOUNTAIN IS THE OLD ROYAL PALACE THAT IS NOW THE NATIONAL MUSEUM. MANY PEOPLE COME TO LOOK AT THE BEAUTIFUL THINGS ON DISPLAY THERE.

BOUN SINGRATHSOMBOUN

Boun Singrathsomboun describes the rich cultural heritage of Laos, a landlocked country in mainland Southeast Asia. About 484 million people, about 9 percent of the world's population, live in the Southeast Asia culture region. The population of the region is growing rapidly and will likely double in about 37 years. This growth will present special challenges for the countries of the region.

PLACE

Population Growth

Southeast Asia's population is divided among 10 countries. Brunei, the country with the smallest population in the region, has about 300,000 people. By contrast more than 199 million people live in Indonesia, one of the most populous countries in the world. Vietnam, the Philippines, Thailand, and Myanmar all have between 45 million and 73 million people. Malaysia has about 20 million people, and the other nations—Cambodia, Laos, and Singapore—have fewer than 10 million.

Population Density

The majority of people in Southeast Asia live either in the river valley lowlands or on the coastal plains. A ready supply of water, fertile land, adequate transportation, and job availability are factors that have contributed to this concentration of people. In general the highlands and mountains have fewer people than the lowlands, and rural areas have fewer people than the cities.

The population density of the region varies widely. The overall density in Indonesia is 283 people per square mile (109 people per sq. km), and the island of Java is one of the most densely populated islands in the world. Singapore, the country with the least area, also has the greatest population density—more than 12,000 people per square mile (4,660 people per sq. km).

LESSON PLAN
Chapter 30, Section 1

FOCUS

SECTION OBJECTIVES
1. **Describe** the population distribution of Southeast Asia.
2. **Compare** urban and rural lifestyles in the region.
3. **Explain** how the population of Southeast Asia is changing.

ABOUT THE POSTCARD
Boun tells us that although there are many things to see in Luang Prabang, those he mentioned in his postcard are his favorites.

BELLRINGER MOTIVATIONAL ACTIVITY

Project the Section 1 Focus Transparency and have students answer the questions.

PRETEACHING VOCABULARY
Explain to students that every capital city in the region is a *primate city*. Have students find the common characteristics of primate cities.

Use the Vocabulary PuzzleMaker Software to create a crossword or word search puzzle.

GLENCOE TECHNOLOGY

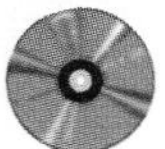
Videodisc

REUTERS ISSUES IN GEOGRAPHY

Chapter 9
Disc 1 Side A

Title: ***Southeast Asia: Patterns of Migration***
Subject: Migration of a family from a rural area of Thailand to the city of Bangkok

Classroom Resources for Section 1

BLACKLINE MASTERS:
- Reproducible Lesson Plan 30-1
- Guided Reading Activity 30-1
- Spanish Guided Reading Activity 30-1
- Workbook Activity 30-1
- Performance Assessment Activity 30
- Section Quiz 30-1

TRANSPARENCIES:
- Section Focus Transparency 30-1
- Unit Map Overlay Transparency 10-1

MULTIMEDIA:

- Vocabulary PuzzleMaker Software
- Testmaker

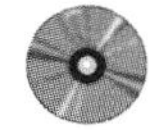
Reuters Issues in Geography

TEACH

GUIDED PRACTICE

Use Unit Map Overlay Transparency 10-1 to help students locate the most densely populated countries of Southeast Asia.

INDEPENDENT PRACTICE

Guided Reading Have students complete Guided Reading Activity 30-1 in the TCR. **LEP**

USING CHARTS

Answers:
Laos (6.1%);
Malaysia (51%)

Skills Practice

Reading a Chart Which two countries have the same percentages of rural and urban populations? *(Thailand and Laos)*

ASSESS

CHECK FOR UNDERSTANDING

Assign Section 1 Review as homework or an in-class activity.

MEETING LESSON OBJECTIVES

Each objective below is tested by the questions that follow it in parentheses.

1. Describe the population distribution of Southeast Asia. *(2)*
2. Compare urban and rural lifestyles in the region. *(2, 3)*
3. Explain how the population of Southeast Asia is changing. *(4, 5)*

SOUTHEAST ASIA: URBAN AND RURAL POPULATION (SELECTED COUNTRIES)

Country	Percent Urban	Percent Rural	Annual Urban Growth %	Annual Rural Growth %
Indonesia	31	69	4.18	0.67
Malaysia	51	49	4.34	0.94
Thailand	19	81	4.70	0.80
Vietnam	20	80	3.75	1.83
Philippines	43	57	3.81	1.56
Myanmar	24	76	2.65	1.91
Cambodia	13	87	3.96	2.29
Laos	19	81	6.10	1.82

Sources: Population Reference Bureau, Inc., 1993; *Encyclopedia of the Third World,* Facts on File

CHART STUDY

Most nations of Southeast Asia are predominantly rural, but are rapidly becoming urban nations as more people move to the region's cities. ***Which nation has the highest annual urban growth rate? Which nation has the highest percentage of urban population?***

Population Growth Rate

For a long time, the population growth rate was lower in Cambodia than in any other nation in the region. Between 1975 and 1979, Cambodia lost 38 percent of its population as a result of starvation, torture, and executions by the Communist Khmer Rouge government that was ruling the country. It has only recently approached its population figure of 10 million. Malaysia, on the other hand, has one of the highest growth rates in the region—2.3 percent, due in part to efforts of the government to increase the population from the current figure of 20 million to 70 million by 2095. The other countries in the region have a growth rate between 1.2 percent and 2.9 percent.

The Indonesian government in recent years has tried to encourage Indonesians in heavily populated areas to limit the size of their families. This effort has met with some success, but Indonesia's population continues to increase by almost 1.5 million people a year. The Singapore government has also carried out a campaign to slow population growth. One measure was to cut government child-care payments to parents having three or more children. By the early 1990s, these efforts had steadily reduced the birthrate.

PLACE

Rural and Urban Populations

The mainland countries of Southeast Asia have a higher percentage of **arable land,** land suitable for growing crops, than the island countries. Therefore, in mainland Southeast Asia, about 75 percent of the population

Cooperative Learning Activity

Organize the class into groups and assign each group one or more of the countries listed in the chart on page 612. Each group should then create a map of their country or countries showing the location of major urban areas, major physical features, and bordering nations or bodies of water. You may wish to use the maps as part of a bulletin-board display.

Geographic Themes

Region: Sumatra, Indonesia

The great majority of Indonesians are farmers who live in small towns or rural villages.
How does Indonesia's population compare with that of other island Southeast Asian countries?

is rural and works in agriculture. On Southeast Asian islands, the rural population ranges from 0 percent in urbanized Singapore to 87 percent in Cambodia.

The populations of several Southeast Asian countries are undergoing a shift from rural to urban areas. This shift has largely been the result of political conflicts and governmental policies, but economic and educational opportunities available in cities have also been factors.

The cities, however, have suffered from this rapid growth. Bangkok, Thailand, for example, had a population of about 1 million people in 1950. By 1992 the city had an estimated population of 10 million. The area of the city has expanded to accommodate the increased population, growing from about 37 square miles (96 sq. km) in 1958 to about 618 square miles (1,601 sq. km) today. Nevertheless it is estimated that more than 1 million residents of Bangkok live in densely populated areas characterized by poverty and poor housing.

In Southeast Asia, there are at least 12 cities with populations of more than 1 million people. The largest cities in the region—except Bangkok, Thailand, and Hanoi, Vietnam—were first developed as colonial ports by European powers. In nearly every country in the region, the largest city is now a **primate city**—a city that serves as the capital of the country as well as the major port and industrial center.

Section 1 Review

Checking for Understanding

1. **Define** arable land, primate city.
2. **Locating Places** Where do most people in Southeast Asia live?
3. **Movement** What geographic characteristic led to the development of most of Southeast Asia's cities?
4. **Movement** What are two ways in which the population of Southeast Asia is changing?

Critical Thinking

5. **Analyzing Information** How have government policies in Southeast Asia affected population characteristics?

Chapter 30, Section 1

EVALUATE

Assign the Section 1 Quiz in the TCR.

Use the Testmaker to create a customized quiz for Section 1.

RETEACH

Work with students to create lists of terms that describe the urban and rural areas.

USING ILLUSTRATIONS

HUMAN/ENVIRONMENT INTERACTION Rice is Indonesia's chief crop. Rubber is the chief agricultural export.

Answer to Caption: *Indonesia is one of the most populated countries in the world.*

ENRICH

Have students find the 12 cities in the region with more than 1 million people.

CLOSE

Have students write a postcard to Boun, telling him what they would take him to see if he came to visit them.

ANSWERS TO SECTION 1 REVIEW

1. **arable land:** land suitable for growing crops; **primate city:** the nation's capital city, as well as the major port and industrial center
2. Most people in Southeast Asia live either in river valley lowlands or on the coastal plain.
3. These cities were first developed as colonial ports.
4. The population is shifting from rural to urban areas, and major cities are becoming overpopulated.
5. Answers may include that some governments are trying to encourage its citizens to limit family size; or that population has been affected by starvation, torture, and executions.

TEACH

Tell students that, in November 1995, an international United Nations conference in Jakarta, Indonesia, released a report titled "Global Biodiversity Assessment." The report stated that nearly 30,000 species are threatened with extinction. The report also gave what was said to be the best estimate of the total number of species in the world—13 to 14 million. Only about 1.75 million species, however, have been formally identified and given scientific names. Can students guess what group includes the most undocumented species? *(insects)*

The report further estimated that the presence of humans has caused 50 to 100 times more extinctions of animals than what would have occurred naturally. Ask students to list reasons for the decline in species. *(increased population and economic development, which depletes biological resources; increased human migration, travel, and international trade; water and air pollution)*

NATIONAL GEOGRAPHIC GEOFACTS

Where are the world's newest mammals?

Few humans have ventured into the Vu Quang Nature Reserve in northern Vietnam. Rocky, rainy, and isolated, its 150,000 acres (60,000 ha) of rain forest have escaped the attention of most of the world. In 1992, biologists found skulls of a long-horned creature that they soon learned was a mammal unknown to science.

The Vu Quang ox is a new large mammal genus—the first to be documented in more than 50 years. But this distant relative of sheep and cattle is not the only new mammal to emerge from the war-ravaged region: Reports of two more large mammals have been made since the Vu Quang ox was assigned its Latin name, *Pseudoryx nghetinhensis.* The giant muntjac, a deer with huge canine teeth, also has been confirmed as a new species; another animal called the slow-running deer is still being studied.

The first live specimen of these mysterious, primitive mammals—a Vu Quang ox calf—was captured recently and taken to a botanical garden in Hanoi for observation.

Vu Quang ox

Hanoi
VIETNAM
LAOS
THAILAND
Vientiane
Vinh
Gulf of Tonkin
Vu Quang Nature Reserve
AREA SHOWN
0 100 km
0 100 mi
India
China
Myanmar (Burma)
Laos
Thailand
Cambodia
Vietnam
Bay of Bengal
South China Sea

Giant muntjac

Mountain rain forest in North Central Vietnam

Designed by BILL PITZER

2 SECTION
History and Government

SETTING THE SCENE

Read to Discover . . .
- how location influenced the development of empires in Southeast Asia.
- the cultural influences that have affected the people of Southeast Asia.
- the changes that resulted from European and American colonization of Southeast Asia.

Key Terms
- maritime
- indigenous
- sphere of influence

Identify and Locate
Strait of Malacca, Sunda Strait, Gulf of Thailand, Indian Ocean, South China Sea, Mekong Delta

Many empires in early Southeast Asia developed around strategic ports. About 2,000 years ago, ports along the Gulf of Thailand were most important.

Sumatra's Srivijaya Empire (A.D. 600 to A.D. 1400) was one of the region's most powerful **maritime**, or seafaring, powers. It controlled shipping along the Strait of Malacca and through the Sunda Strait. Today Singapore, located on the shortest sea route between the Indian Ocean and the South China Sea, is one of the world's most prosperous seaports.

Some Southeast Asian empires were land-based and gained their wealth from the fertile soil. The Khmer Empire of Angkor in present-day Cambodia and the Kingdom of Srivijaya in Java grew three to four crops of rice along with other crops each year.

MOVEMENT

Outside Influences

Countries outside the region wanted involvement in sea routes between China and the West and in the region's resources of rice, forest products, tin, pearls, gold, and spices.

South Asia

In the A.D. 100s Indian traders introduced Hinduism and later Buddhism to the **indigenous**, or local, peoples. By the A.D. 1400s, Buddhism was the primary religion in Myanmar, Thailand, Laos, and Cambodia.

China

The Chinese began maritime trading routes through Southeast Asia early. The Hong (Red) River valley was dominated by the Chinese from the A.D. 100s to the A.D. 900s.

Islam

Islam was brought by Arab and Indian traders in the A.D. 1300s. Melaka (Malacca) on the Malay Peninsula grew into a Muslim center and important seaport by the early 1500s.

The West

Western influence in Southeast Asia lasted until the 1900s. Portugal, Spain, the Netherlands, Great Britain, and France came to trade, spread Christianity, and claim territory. They spread their **spheres of influence**—agreed-

LESSON PLAN
Chapter 30, Section 2

FOCUS

SECTION OBJECTIVES

1. Discuss the influences that other cultures had on the early people of Southeast Asia.

2. Analyze how the countries of the region gained independence.

BELLRINGER MOTIVATIONAL ACTIVITY

Project the Section 2 Focus Transparency and have students answer the questions.

PRETEACHING VOCABULARY

Explain to students that *spheres of influence* are agreed-upon areas of control. Have them skim the section to determine why this term is important to the study of Southeast Asia.

CURRICULUM CONNECTION

SOCIOLOGY
Southeast Asia's lifestyles are affected by climate. Large amounts of rain make rice an ideal crop. The most productive method of growing rice requires the joint effort of an entire village. The outcome of centuries of teamwork are societies in which loyalty to the group is a prime virtue.

Classroom Resources for Section 2

BLACKLINE MASTERS:
Reproducible Lesson Plan 30-2
Guided Reading Activity 30-2
Spanish Guided Reading Activity 30-2
Workbook Activity 30-2
Performance Assessment Activity 30
Section Quiz 30-2

TRANSPARENCIES:
Section Focus Transparency 30-2
Unit Map Overlay Transparency 10

MULTIMEDIA:
Testmaker

TEACH

GUIDED PRACTICE

L1 Demonstrate Using the map on page 617, have students list the countries that had spheres of influence in Southeast Asia.

INDEPENDENT PRACTICE

Guided Reading Have students complete Guided Reading Activity 30-2 in the TCR.

L2 Ask students to create a list of reasons why a country would want a sphere of influence in Southeast Asia.

USING MAPS

Answers:
1. India and China; **2.** Sumatra and Java; **3.** Cambodia; **4.** Penang and Melaka

Map Skills Practice

Reading a Map What strip of land separates the Bay of Bengal from the Gulf of Siam? *(Isthmus of Kra)*

MULTICULTURAL PERSPECTIVE

Culturally Speaking
Invite a Southeast Asian to visit the class and talk about the region's physical features and climate, showing slides, pictures, or a videotape. Encourage students to ask questions of the speaker.

upon areas of control—over all of Southeast Asia except Thailand.

By the mid-1900s the United Kingdom had claimed what is now Brunei, Myanmar, Malaysia, and Singapore. France ruled present-day Cambodia, Vietnam, and Laos. The Netherlands colonized the islands of Indonesia, and Spain ruled the Philippine Islands, which were later acquired by the United States.

Change and Modernization

Westerners expanded tin mining and oil drilling. They also displaced small farms with large rice, rubber, and coffee plantations. They managed these estates using immigrant labor from India and China and imported machinery. Many of the foreign laborers stayed in the region.

The Westerners boosted economic production in the region for their own benefit, not

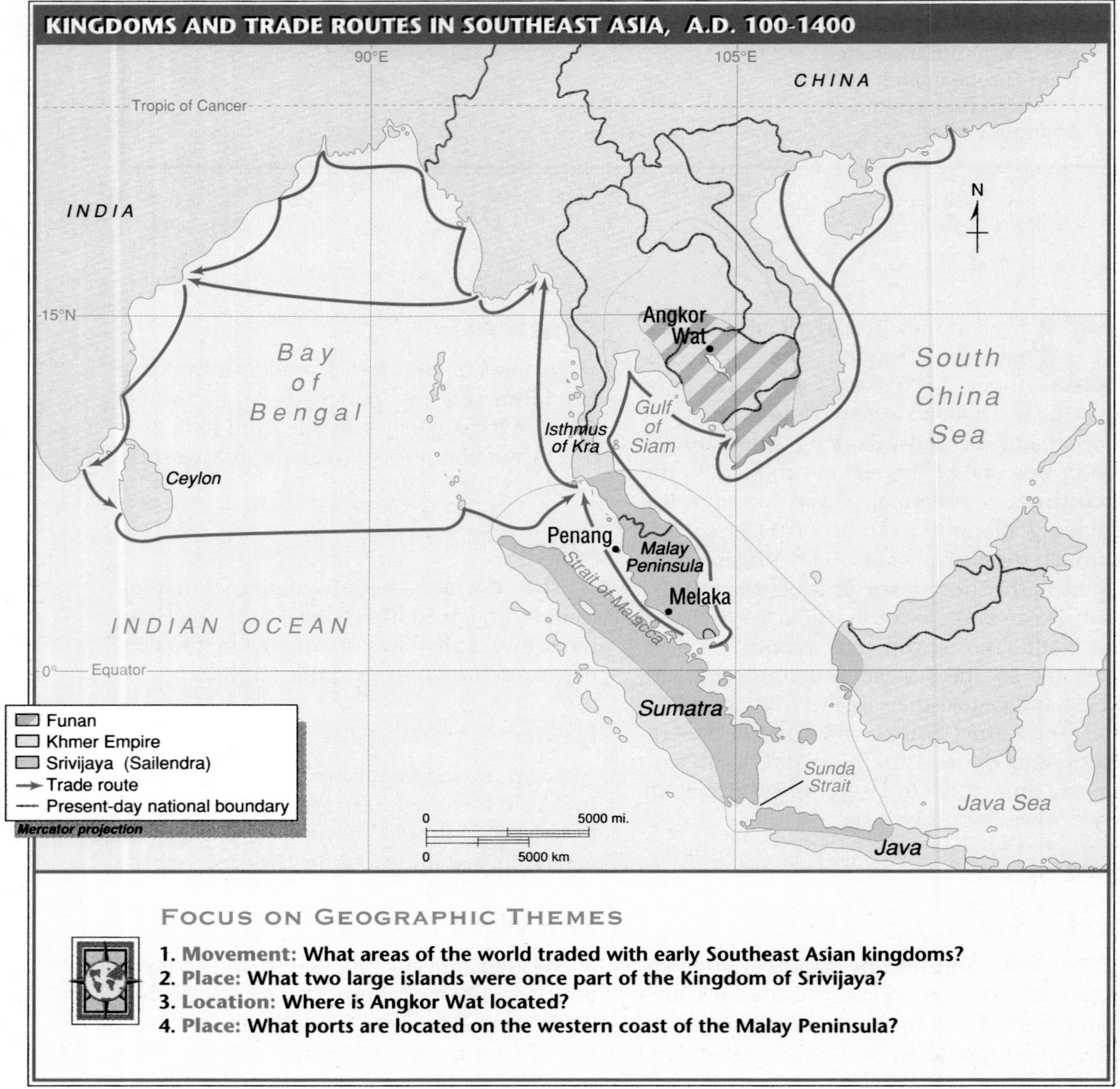

Focus on Geographic Themes

1. **Movement:** What areas of the world traded with early Southeast Asian kingdoms?
2. **Place:** What two large islands were once part of the Kingdom of Srivijaya?
3. **Location:** Where is Angkor Wat located?
4. **Place:** What ports are located on the western coast of the Malay Peninsula?

Cooperative Learning Activity

Organize the class into groups. Assign each group one of the countries that had a sphere of influence in Southeast Asia. Each group should create a map of Southeast Asia showing the extent of their country's sphere of influence. Groups may also wish to make an oral report to the class on spheres of influence that their country had in other parts of the world.

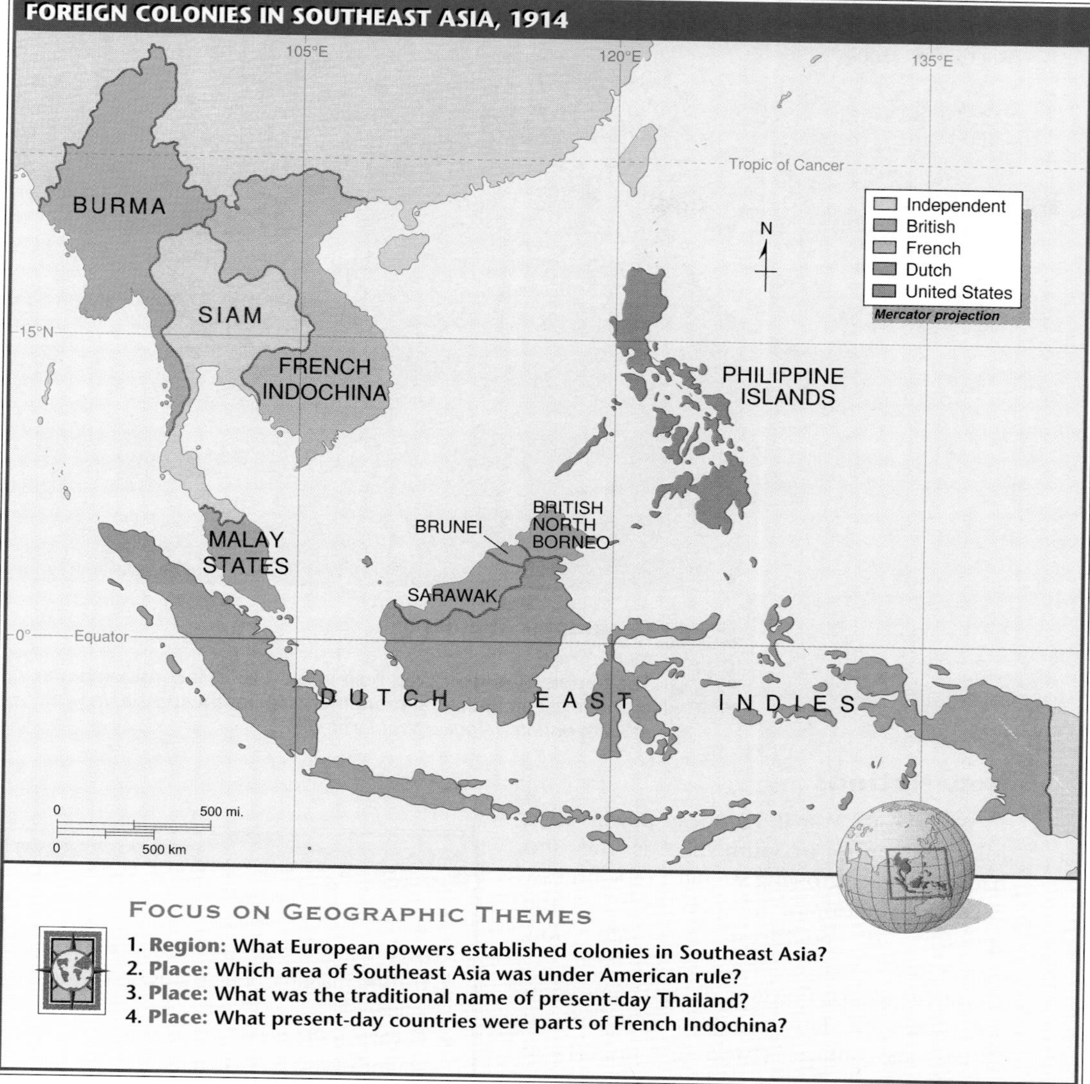

Focus on Geographic Themes

1. **Region:** What European powers established colonies in Southeast Asia?
2. **Place:** Which area of Southeast Asia was under American rule?
3. **Place:** What was the traditional name of present-day Thailand?
4. **Place:** What present-day countries were parts of French Indochina?

for that of Southeast Asians. In Myanmar's Irrawaddy River valley, about 988,400 acres (400,302 ha) of land were cultivated for rice in 1855. By 1930 there were 9,844,000 acres (4 million ha) of rice under cultivation. In Malaysia, rubber trees were introduced by the British in the early 1800s. By 1939 there were about 3.4 million acres (1.4 million ha) of rubber plantations. The Europeans also built networks of roads and railways to link inland production to overseas trade.

REGION

Independence and Conflicts

During World War II, Japan forced Western nations out of Southeast Asia. After Japan's defeat in 1945, the Western powers tried to regain control. They, however, faced growing Southeast Asian demands for freedom. By 1965, all of the region's peoples had won independence.

USING MAPS

Answers: **1.** Britain, France, and the Netherlands; **2.** Philippine Islands; **3.** Siam; **4.** Vietnam, Laos, Cambodia

Map Skills Practice

Reading a Map Which group of islands on the map does the Equator run through? *(the Dutch East Indies)*

ASSESS

CHECK FOR UNDERSTANDING

Assign Section 2 Review as homework or an in-class activity.

MEETING LESSON OBJECTIVES

Each objective below is tested by the questions that follow it in parentheses.

1. Discuss the influences that other cultures had on the early people of Southeast Asia. *(3, 4)*

2. Analyze how the countries of the region gained independence. *(5)*

EVALUATE

Assign the Section 2 Quiz in the TCR.

Use the Testmaker to create a customized quiz for Section 2.

Meeting Special Needs

Categorizing Information Have students use the map on page 617 to create a table listing colonizing powers and colonies in Southeast Asia. At the top of each column of the table write one of the colonizing powers (United Kingdom, France, the Netherlands, United States). Then list each Southeast Asia colony under each appropriate country name. This method will allow students to study the information presented on the map using an alternate modality.

RETEACH

Write the term *sphere of influence* on the board. Ask students to find its definition in the section and to explain its relationship to the study of Southeast Asia.

USING ILLUSTRATIONS

PLACE Angkor Wat was built to honor the Hindu god Vishnu. It later became the tomb of the Cambodian king who ordered its construction.

Answer to Caption: Cambodia

ENRICH

Have students locate and collect photographs of Angkor Wat from various magazines, including NATIONAL GEOGRAPHIC.

CLOSE

Ask students if they think that spheres of influence helped or hindered the development of Southeast Asian nations.

Geographic Themes

Place: Angkor Wat

The temple of Angkor Wat, built in the 1100s, is considered one of the finest architectural monuments in Southeast Asia. *In what modern nation is Angkor Wat located?*

New Nations

After World War II, European powers tried to regain control in Southeast Asia; they too had to face the growing strength of Southeast Asian moves toward independence. All the countries of Southeast Asia are now independent.

Independence, however, did not come without problems. Many countries have suffered ethnic wars, conflicts between Communist and non-Communist groups, and border disputes.

Governments Today

Three types of government are represented in Southeast Asia today. Indonesia, the Philippines, and Singapore are republics. Brunei, Malaysia, and Thailand are constitutional monarchies. Vietnam, Laos, and Myanmar are socialist republics. In May 1993, Cambodia held the first free election in its history. By the end of the year, it had become a constitutional monarchy under King Norodom Sihanouk.

SECTION 2 REVIEW

Checking for Understanding

1. **Define** maritime, indigenous, sphere of influence.
2. **Locating Places** Which parts of Southeast Asia border on the Sunda Strait? The Strait of Malacca?
3. **Movement** What outside influences shaped the historical development of Southeast Asia?
4. **Movement** What major religions were brought to Southeast Asia before World War II?

Critical Thinking

5. **Analyzing Information** Why were European nations interested in colonizing Southeast Asia?

ANSWERS TO SECTION 2 REVIEW

1. **maritime:** seafaring; **indigenous:** local; **sphere of influence:** an agreed-upon area of control
2. Sumatra and Java; Sumatra and the Malay Peninsula
3. The outside influences that shaped the historical development of Southeast Asia were countries outside the region that wanted sea routes. Indian traders brought Hinduism and Buddhism, Arab and Indian traders brought Islam, and Westerners brought Christianity.
4. Hinduism, Buddhism, Islam, and Christianity
5. European nations wanted to establish trade, to spread Christianity, and to claim territory in Southeast Asia.

Geography and History

Singapore: Model of Prosperity

As you read, examine how Singapore became an economic leader.

Trading Center

The city of Singapore surrounds an excellent natural harbor on the southern edge of Singapore Island. Singapore is Southeast Asia's busiest port; in terms of annual tonnage handled, it is also one of the world's largest.

Crowding around the harbor are deep-water facilities for immense oil tankers and cargo ships as well as wharves and docks for local trade. Warehouses stand filled with—or waiting for—thousands of tons of exports and imports. Singapore is a free port: goods can be unloaded, stored, and shipped again without payment of import duties.

Adjoining the docks and port area is the city's commercial and business section. In the towering glass-and-steel skyscrapers are department stores, banks, insurance companies, financial firms—national and international—and Singapore's stock exchange.

To the west of the city, beyond the older shopping and residential areas, is the Jurong industrial park region. Here, more than 800 manufacturing plants produce clothing, textiles, machinery, metals, and electronic, scientific, and transportation equipment.

Singapore is an island nation located off the tip of the Malay Peninsula. Composed of one large island and more than 50 small islands, the country of Singapore has a land area of about 240 square miles (622 sq. km).

Strict Government

Singapore's government plays a major role in the economy. Although the economy is based on free enterprise, the government exercises strict control over economic and social affairs. The government determines what benefits, such as sick leave and vacation time, employers shall provide for their workers.

In 1965, when Singapore became independent, the government embarked on a crash course of industrialization. The People's Action Party, the ruling political party, drove significant opposing parties underground. A government licensing system was established for national newspapers and magazines, and laws were established to keep labor unions politically powerless.

Checking for Understanding

1. What natural feature helped Singapore become an economic center in Southeast Asia?
2. **Place**  What is unusual about the relationship between Singapore's economy and its government?

TEACH

Have students recall other large cities that have been highlighted in the Geography and History selections in previous units *(Buenos Aires, Unit 3; Lagos, Unit 7; Hong Kong, Unit 9)*. Challenge them to compare and contrast the cities.

 **Human/Environment Interaction** How has Singapore taken advantage of its environment? *(has based its economy on business and trading because of the excellence of its natural harbor; agriculture is not possible in any great degree in Singapore because the amount and kind of land available is not suitable for farming)*

Extending the Content

Singapore Until it came under British control, the island of Singapore was a land of rain forests, mangrove swamps, and small fishing villages. Sir Stamford Raffles, British agent for the East India Company, was the first Westerner to realize that, despite the rain forests and swamps, Singapore had a location that was ideal for trade. In 1819, Raffles gained control of the harbor for Britain, and in 1824, all of Singapore came under British control.

DID YOU KNOW?

Singapore's GDP is about $35 billion annually; it has one of the highest per capita incomes in Asia—about $13,000—and very low unemployment.

ANSWERS TO CHECKING FOR UNDERSTANDING

1. Singapore has an excellent natural harbor, which helped the city develop into a leading Southeast Asian port.
2. Singapore has a free enterprise economy, but a strict authoritarian government.

LESSON PLAN
Chapter 30, Section 3

FOCUS

SECTION OBJECTIVES

1. Identify the region's major language families and religions.
2. Describe the variety of arts, literature, and drama found in Southeast Asia.
3. Explain the current lifestyles of Southeast Asians.

BELLRINGER MOTIVATIONAL ACTIVITY

Project the Section 3 Focus Transparency and have students answer the questions.

PRETEACHING VOCABULARY

Explain to students that *wat* is an Indian term for a religious temple. Ask students for words that other cultures use to describe religious buildings.

USING MAPS

Answers:
1. Hinduism, Buddhism, Islam, and Catholicism; **2.** the Philippines

Map Skills Practice
Reading a Map According to the map, what are the dominant religions in Vietnam? *(Chinese religions and Buddhism)*

NATIONAL GEOGRAPHIC SOCIETY

CD-ROM

PICTURE ATLAS OF THE WORLD
Listen to the languages of Southeast Asia by clicking the "Speech" button of selected countries in the region.

SECTION 3 Cultures and Lifestyles

SETTING THE SCENE

Read to Discover . . .
- **how ethnic diversity in Southeast Asia has led to a rich and varied culture.**
- **the effects of religious beliefs on culture in Southeast Asia.**

Key Terms
- **wat**
- **batik**
- **longhouse**

Identify and Locate
Indochina Peninsula, Bangkok, Angkor Wat

The cultures of Southeast Asia reflect migrations by people from other regions. Several major world religions have had a great impact on the region.

The region's artistic development was greatly influenced by the early Indian civilization. Local artists, however, soon adapted the Indian culture to their own needs. Later, Southeast Asian art continued to be influenced by foreign styles but kept its distinctive quality.

SOUTHEAST ASIA: RELIGIONS

Chinese religions
Hinduism
Buddhism
Islam
Catholicism
Traditional religions
Mercator projection

FOCUS ON GEOGRAPHIC THEMES

1. **Place:** What four major religions are found in Southeast Asia?
2. **Place:** Where is Catholicism the major religion?

REGION

Languages and Religions

Hundreds of languages and dialects are spoken in Southeast Asia. These languages stem from three major language families: Malayo-Polynesian, Sino-Tibetan, and Mon-Khmer.

Many of the languages that are spoken in the region are the result of migration and colonization. For example, in the Philippines, Tagalog and English are the official languages. Spanish is also spoken in the Philippines. Chinese, Malay, Tamil, and English are the official languages of Singapore, which reflect the importance of commerce in this tiny island nation. In Malaysia, English is often used in business and daily life. The Malaysian government, however, has taken steps to make Malay the official language, especially in schools and universities. In Vietnamese cities, most people can speak English, French, Chinese, or Russian as well as Vietnamese.

Classroom Resources for Section 3

BLACKLINE MASTERS:
World Literature Reading 9
Foods Around the World 9
Enrichment Activity 30
Skill Activity 30
Section Quiz 30-3

TRANSPARENCIES:
Section Focus Transparency 30-3
World Cultures Transparencies 17, 18

MULTIMEDIA:

Testmaker

***World Music:** Cultural Traditions, Lesson 9*

Picture Atlas of the World

Southeast Asia: Religions	
Muslim	185,700,000
Buddhist	109,600,000
Christian	79,400,000
Confucian	68,300,000
Hindu	5,300,000
Daoist	3,100,000
Other	8,600,000

Source: Population Reference Bureau, Inc., 1993; *World Almanac*, 1995

The people of Southeast Asia practice many different religions. This is the result of the cultural influences of the many peoples who migrated to the region. Buddhism is the major religion of the Indochina Peninsula. Many people who live on the Malay Peninsula and in parts of Indonesia are followers of Islam. Most people who live in the Philippines are Roman Catholics. This religious tradition began when the Philippines came under the control of Spain in the 1500s. A great number of the region's people—mainly those of Chinese ancestry—follow Confucianism or Daoism.

REGION

The Arts

Buddhism and Hinduism have inspired Southeast Asia's art and architecture. Beautiful Indian-style **wats**, or temples, and Chinese-style pagodas are found throughout the region. Some of the greatest ancient structures were built of stone, which was scarce. The temples were often partly coated with a thin, gleaming layer of gold. One of the most famous Hindu temples is Angkor Wat in Cambodia, built by a Khmer king more than 800 years ago. The numerous stone buildings of the temple housed priests as well as libraries. The walls are covered with carvings that described Hindu epics and legends.

Around A.D. 800, a well-known Buddhist shrine called Borobudur was built on the Indonesian island of Java. To build the shrine, 2 million cubic feet (56,000 cu. m) of stone were taken from a riverbed. The stones were carved and decorated with scenes depicting Buddhist beliefs. In the shrine are about 500 smaller shrines, each with a seated Buddha. The hand gestures of each Buddha vary to show different moods. In the city of Pagan, Myanmar, more than 3,000 Buddhist monasteries were built.

Crafts

The rich cultures of Southeast Asia have produced many fine crafts. The people of Myanmar and Vietnam produce fine lacquerware. Boxes, trays, dishes, and furniture are covered with many layers of resin from Asian sumac trees. Colored powders are used to paint the lacquerware.

The Indonesians and Malaysians make beautiful patterns on cloth by a method known as **batik.** Wax or rice paste is placed on cloth to resist dyes. The cloth is then dyed, and a pattern is formed by the dye's reaching only the uncovered parts of the cloth. Finally, the cloth is boiled to remove the wax.

In the Philippines a delicate cloth is made from pineapple fibers. Throughout Southeast Asia the weaving of palm leaves, bamboo, and other plants produce many goods—such as baskets, mats, and hats—for everyday use.

Literature

Early literature in Southeast Asia consisted of oral folktales and legends. Indian literature had a great influence on the development of

TEACH

GUIDED PRACTICE

L1 Demonstrate Using an overhead projector, develop with students a bar graph on religions in Southeast Asia using the information presented on page 621.

INDEPENDENT PRACTICE

Guided Reading Have students complete Guided Reading Activity 30-3 in the TCR. **LEP**

USING GRAPHS

Skills Practice

Reading a Graph Which two religions are practiced by two-thirds of the people in Southeast Asia? *(Buddhism and Islam)*

Have students complete World Music: Cultural Traditions, Lesson 9 Activity in the TCR.

Cooperative Learning Activity

Organize the class into groups. Each group should research and report on a folktale from Southeast Asia. Each group should also create an original folktale on a topic of their choosing. One member of each group should then make an oral presentation of the group's folktale to the class.

USING ILLUSTRATIONS

REGION The dances of Southeast Asia may represent scenes of adventures, battles, or love.

Answer to Caption: *Mostly percussion instruments, such as gongs, drums, and instruments similar to the xylophone, are used.*

ASSESS

CHECK FOR UNDERSTANDING

Assign Section 3 Review as homework or an in-class activity.

MEETING LESSON OBJECTIVES

Each objective below is tested by the questions that follow it in parentheses.

1. Identify the region's major language families and religions. *(2)*

2. Describe the variety of arts, literature, and drama found in Southeast Asia. *(3)*

3. Explain the current lifestyles of Southeast Asians. *(4, 5)*

NATIONAL GEOGRAPHIC SOCIETY

CD-ROM

PICTURE ATLAS OF THE WORLD

Listen to the music of Myanmar, Thailand, Cambodia, Vietnam, Laos, Malaysia, and Indonesia by clicking the "Music" button of each country.

local writings. Today these writings have a distinct character of their own. For example a well-known story from Java, called "Arjunavivaha," tells about the life of a Javanese king. This story comes from a similar tale about an Indian thinker.

In recent times writers of Southeast Asia have been heavily influenced by non-Asian writing. Some writers, however, have worked to translate classic Southeast Asian literature into modern language that can be read and understood by more people.

Music, Dance, and Drama

Traditional folk, religious, and court music remain strong throughout Southeast Asia. Music, dance, and drama are combined to describe legends or historical events. Dancers perform formal traditional dances that often have religious themes. Mostly percussion instruments, such as gongs, drums, and instruments similar to the xylophone are used.

Puppet plays are popular in many parts of Southeast Asia. These plays use local and religious characters to perform tales. Sometimes a human dancer who imitates a puppet's movements performs the play.

Geographic Themes

Place: Bangkok, Thailand

Thai classical dancers wear elaborate costumes as they act out traditional stories and religious themes. *What kinds of musical instruments are played in Southeast Asia?*

REGION

Lifestyles

Despite the recent growth of large urban centers, most Southeast Asians are farmers who live in small villages. A typical village has about 25 or 30 houses made of bamboo or wood. These houses have tiled, corrugated iron, or tin roofs to keep out the heavy rains that are typical of Southeast Asia. In coastal lowlands the houses are often built on raised platforms supported by wooden poles for protection from insects, animals, and flooding. In some rural areas of Indonesia and Malaysia, the people live in **longhouses**—buildings that house up to 100 people who are usually from several related, or extended, families. In general rural homes lack running water, electricity, and other services found in cities.

Most people in the cities live in traditional houses built of brick or wood. Many people still live in poor conditions, but governments are building housing projects to improve this situation. Some people in the cities live in new high-rise apartments or in single-family houses.

Varieties of Food and Clothing

Most people in Southeast Asia live on the food they raise themselves. Rice is the staple, usually served with fish, chicken, or vegetables. Various countries have their own specialties. Some use curry and other spices; some cook in coconut milk and oil. Tea, coffee, and coconut-milk drinks are the region's most popular beverages. Religion also plays an important role in the diet of many Southeast Asians. Buddhists, Muslims, and Hindus must obey the different dietary laws of their religions prescribing specific meat they can eat and periods of fasting.

Rural dwellers wear traditional clothing, which often includes loose-fitting shirts and

Meeting Special Needs

Outlining Students that are having difficulty grasping the main concepts of this section may wish to use an outline form to organize the information. Outlining will enable students to organize information more clearly and precisely.

skirts or pants necessary because of the hot climate. In many of the cities people prefer to dress in Western styles.

Health and Education

Since achieving their independence, many Southeast Asian countries have enjoyed an improved quality of life. Independence has brought industrialization. Per capita incomes in many areas have risen. Life expectancy and infant survival rates have also increased. The general levels of health in Southeast Asia still vary widely, with Singapore having the best overall health conditions. In Laos and Cambodia, life expectancy is only 50 years as compared to 74 years in Singapore.

Since 1945 literacy has increased dramatically in the region although education is still limited. Governments continue efforts to make education available to everyone. The average number of years of schooling range from 2 in Cambodia to 8 in Brunei. Thailand has the highest literacy rate in the region (89 percent), while Cambodia has the lowest (50 percent).

Recreation and Celebration

Southeast Asians enjoy a variety of activities in their leisure time. They sometimes mix their social pleasures with daily chores. In large cities, such as Bangkok, Kuala Lumpur, Jakarta, and Singapore, people visit libraries, museums, theaters, parks, restaurants, and nightclubs. In rural areas, visiting neighbors is enjoyed.

People throughout Southeast Asia enjoy sports, such as soccer, basketball, and badminton. Indonesia has produced some world-class badminton players. Traditional sports and pastimes are also popular. The Indonesians practice a combination of dancing and self-defense known as *silat.* The Thai enjoy a form of boxing in which boxers use both feet and hands.

Many public holidays are celebrated and include Buddhist, Muslim, and Christian religious holidays. New Year's Day is also an important holiday throughout Southeast Asia.

Geographic Themes

Place: Thailand

Rural and urban Southeast Asians alike celebrate festivals that include parades and processions. *What religions influence celebrations and holidays in Southeast Asia?*

SECTION 3 REVIEW

Checking for Understanding

1. **Define** wat, batik, longhouse.
2. **Locating Places** Where is the temple of Borobudur located?
3. **Movement** What country outside Southeast Asia had the most influence on the architecture, literature, dance, and drama in the region?
4. **Region** What are three recreational activities enjoyed by Southeast Asians?

Critical Thinking

5. **Making Comparisons** How does housing and clothing in rural areas of Southeast Asia compare with housing and clothing in urban areas?

USING ILLUSTRATIONS

PLACE Hindu temples hold annual festivals in honor of their gods. These festivals attract huge crowds.

Answer to Caption: *Buddhism, Islam, and Christianity*

EVALUATE

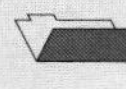
Assign the Section 3 Quiz in the TCR.

Use the Testmaker to create a customized quiz for Section 3.

RETEACH

Have students complete Reteaching Activity 30 in the TCR.

ENRICH

Have students complete Enrichment Activity 30 in the TCR.

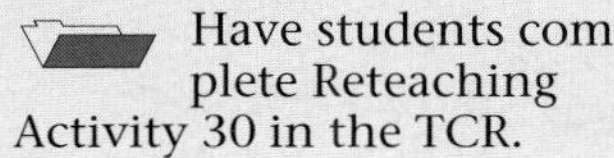

CLOSE

Discuss with students the cultural similarities and differences between Southeast Asia and the United States.

ANSWERS TO SECTION 3 REVIEW

1. **wat:** Indian term for a religious temple; **batik:** method of making patterns on cloth; **longhouses:** buildings that house up to 100 people usually from several related families
2. on the island of Java
3. India
4. basketball, soccer, badminton, and silat
5. The houses in rural areas are typically made of bamboo or wood; most people in cities have houses made of brick or wood. Rural dwellers wear traditional clothing , while in many of the cities people prefer to dress in Western styles.

Teaching Skills

TEACH

Have students find advertisements showing American teenagers. Then say: "Suppose you are using these ads as primary sources to learn about American teens. What information do these ads provide?" *(possible answers: how teens dress, what products they like, what social norms and customs prevail, and so on)* Then discuss the limits of this source of information. What information is missing? Do the ads misrepresent teens and in what ways? Point out: "Primary sources provide valuable information, but we must always identify the limitations, opinions, and biases of each source."

Skills Practice For additional practice, have students complete Skill Activity 30 in the TCR.

STUDY AND WRITING SKILLS

Interpreting Primary Sources

If you witness a fire in your neighborhood and write a letter describing this event, you are a **primary source.**

REVIEWING THE SKILL

Primary sources are firsthand or eyewitness accounts of events. These include letters, journals, oral histories, interviews, autobiographies, and photographs. As primary sources, people recount events in their own words, describing details and personal reactions. By making events seem real, primary sources enable us to feel the impact of events on individuals.

When interpreting primary sources, first identify the speaker and the events being described. Determine when and where these events took place and when the account was actually written. If the account was written years later, the speaker may have forgotten some details. Finally, identify the speaker's emotions, opinions, and biases to determine how they have influenced the account. In interpreting primary sources, use the following steps:

- Identify the speaker and the speaker's relation to the events described.
- Identify when and where the events took place and when the account was written.
- Separate facts from the speaker's emotions, opinions, and biases.
- Determine what kind of information the document provides and what questions are left unanswered.

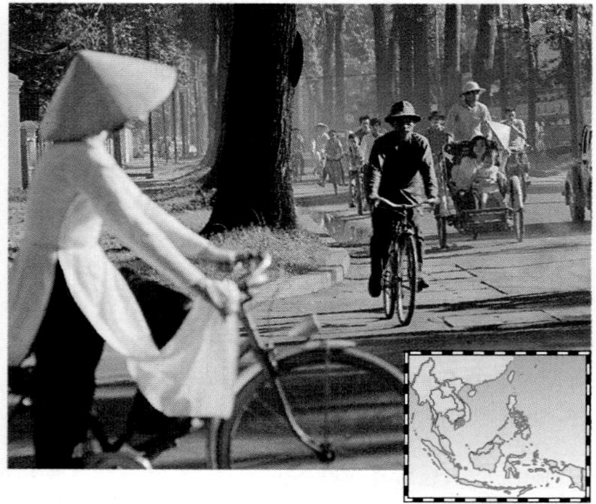

PRACTICING THE SKILL

In the following interview, a Vietnamese student explains why and how he became involved in the resistance movement. After reading the account, answer the questions that follow.

In September 1961 I enrolled in the school of science at Saigon University. . . . I started my studies in Saigon with the same enthusiasm I had before. . . . But even though I was so involved in my studies, I was also learning other things in Saigon. I started to come alive politically. I started with a critical view of Ngo Dinh Diem's government because of the arrests and religious favoritism that I knew about in my home province. Now I saw that Saigon had two faces. In one way it was exactly the rich fairyland I had dreamed about, a city of magnificent buildings, luxurious cars, and wealth. But it was also a place where people lived in the most miserable shanties, or just out on the street. Beggars were all over the place. . . .

The summer of 1963 was when the conflict between Catholics and Buddhists was most intense. . . . One day . . . I went down to Hai Duc [a Buddhist temple] with a friend of mine. . . . I thought maybe there would be some demonstrations or speeches. . . . But when we got there, nothing was going on. . . . We turned around to leave. Just as we did, three men grabbed us and threw us into a car. . . . It took only a couple of minutes to get to the police station. They searched me and took my wallet and ID. Then they shoved me into a cell by myself.[1]

1. When and where did these events take place?
2. How did the speaker's observations of Saigon affect his political views?
3. From this account, what conclusions can you draw about the political system in Vietnam in the early 1960s?

For additional practice in this skill, see Practicing Skills on page 626 of the Chapter 30 Review.

[1] Source: Interview with Nguyen Cong Hoan, *Portrait of the Enemy*, David Chanoff and Doan Van Toai. Random House, New York, 1986, pp. 17–18.

ANSWERS TO PRACTICING THE SKILL

1. Saigon, Vietnam, in 1961-63

2. Seeing the large gap between rich and poor people increased his opposition to Diem's government.

3. The government made little effort to improve economic conditions for the people and maintained control through authoritarian means.

chapter 30

HIGHLIGHTS

Section	Key Terms	Summary
1 Population Patterns	**arable land** (p. 612) **primate city** (p. 613)	• The population of Southeast Asia is growing rapidly. • Although most of Southeast Asia is rural, the number of large, densely populated cities in the region is growing.

Town on the island of Sumatra, Indonesia

Section	Key Terms	Summary
2 History and Government	**maritime** (p. 615) **indigenous** (p. 615) **sphere of influence** (p. 615)	• Early in its history, Southeast Asia became a zone of contact between East Asia and South Asia. • All Southeast Asian countries except Thailand were colonized by foreign powers and are now independent. • The forms of government in Southeast Asia today include constitutional monarchies, republics, and socialist republics.

Ruins of Angkor Wat, Cambodia

Section	Key Terms	Summary
3 Cultures and Lifestyles	**wat** (p. 621) **batik** (p. 621) **longhouse** (p. 622)	• Culture in Southeast Asia reflects earlier migrations by people from other regions as well as regional folk traditions. • Among the major religions, Buddhism and Hinduism have greatly influenced Southeast Asian art, architecture, drama, and celebrations. • In spite of rapid population growth, economic development has led to many improvements and brought many challenges.

Festival procession, Thailand

Map Activity

Identify and Locate Distribute copies of page 34 of the Outline Map Resource Book. Using the Atlas maps at the beginning of the unit and maps from the chapter, have students identify and locate the Strait of Malacca, Sunda Strait, Gulf of Thailand, Indian Ocean, South China Sea, and the Mekong Delta.

CHAPTER 30 HIGHLIGHTS

USING THE CHAPTER 30 HIGHLIGHTS

Use the Chapter 30 Highlights to preview, review, condense, or reteach the chapter.

PREVIEW/REVIEW

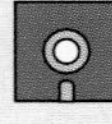

Vocabulary PuzzleMaker Software reinforces the Key Terms used in Chapter 30.

Student Self-Test and Review Software allows students to review Chapter 30 content.

CONDENSE

Have students read the Chapter 30 Highlights.

Have students listen to the Chapter 30 Audiocassettes in the TCR. Spanish Audiocassettes are also available.

Assign the Chapter 30 Audiocassette Activity and give students the Chapter 30 Audiocassette Quiz.

Have students complete the Guided Reading Activities for Chapter 30 in the TCR. Spanish Guided Reading Activities are also available.

RETEACH

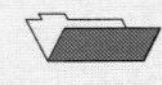

Have students complete Reteaching Activity 30 in the TCR. Spanish Reteaching Activities are also available.

GLENCOE TECHNOLOGY

Videodisc

Use Chapter 30 MindJogger Videoquiz to review students' knowledge before administering the Chapter 30 Test.

MINDJOGGER VIDEOQUIZ

Chapter 30
Disc 4 Side B

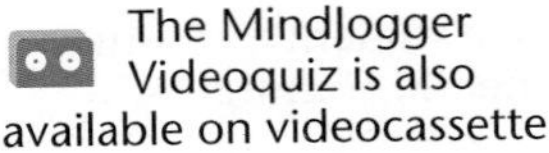

The MindJogger Videoquiz is also available on videocassette.

Reviewing Key Terms

1. primate city
2. arable land
3. spheres of influence
4. indigenous
5. maritime
6. wats
7. longhouses
8. batik

Reviewing Facts

9. the river valley lowlands and the coastal plains
10. Indonesia has the largest population; Brunei has the smallest population.
11. China
12. Thailand
13. Buddhism
14. Some of the distinctive crafts made by Southeast Asians include beautiful clothes using the batik method; and baskets, mats, and hats made of bamboo, palm leaves, and other plants.

chapter 30 REVIEW

Reviewing Key Terms

Choose the vocabulary term that best completes each of the sentences below. Write your answers on a separate sheet of paper.

arable land (p. 612)
primate city (p. 613)
maritime (p. 615)
indigenous (p. 615)
spheres of influence (p. 615)
wats (p. 621)
batik (p. 621)
longhouses (p. 622)

Section 1

1. A _____ is a country's capital as well as its largest city, chief port, and industrial center.
2. An area suitable for the growing of crops is called _____.

Section 2

3. Colonial powers in Southeast Asia established _____ to decide who had power in a certain area.
4. _____ people are native to the place in which they live.
5. When the Chinese lost their land route to trade with the West, they used a _____ route instead.

Section 3

6. _____ are religious temples.
7. In some rural areas of Indonesia and Malaysia, people from several related families often live in _____.
8. Some Southeast Asians make patterns on cloth using a method known as _____.

Reviewing Facts

Section 1

9. What geographic areas in Southeast Asia are the most populous?
10. Which country in Southeast Asia has the largest population? The smallest?

Section 2

11. What was the first foreign influence to reach Southeast Asia?
12. Which Southeast Asian country avoided becoming a colony?

Section 3

13. What is the predominant religion in the Indochina Peninsula?
14. What are some of the distinctive crafts created by the region's peoples?

Critical Thinking

15. **Drawing Conclusions** Why do you think the island of Java has a high population density?
16. **Analyzing Information** Why would huge plantations make it hard for small farms to compete?

Geographic Themes

17. **Movement** What factors have influenced many people in Southeast Asia to move from rural to urban areas?
18. **Movement** How did the early empires of Southeast Asia profit from trade?
19. **Place** In what ways do Southeast Asians have a better quality of life?

Practicing Skills

Interpreting Primary Sources

Refer to the Interpreting Primary Sources skills feature on page 624.

20. How long after these events was this account written?
21. How do you think the speaker's opinions have affected his account of these events?
22. What kind of information is provided in this account? What other information gives you a fuller understanding of the political situation in Vietnam at this time?

Critical Thinking

15. Answers may include that the island is not very large, yet a large number of people live there because of a favorable climate, good farmland, or business opportunities.
16. Answers may include that huge plantations can offer the variety and supply that small farms cannot.

Geographic Themes

17. Political conflicts, governmental policies, and economic and educational opportunities have influenced many people in Southeast Asia to move from rural to urban areas.

Using the Unit Atlas

Refer to the cultural geography section of the Unit Atlas on pages 590–591.

23. In what geographic areas of Vietnam do most people live?
24. What Southeast Asian nation was once under American rule?
25. What ethnic group controls most of Malaysia's businesses?

Projects

Individual Activity

You have learned about elements of the culture of Southeast Asia. Find an example of Southeast Asian culture, such as a painting or a piece of literature from the region, or record someone from Southeast Asia speaking his or her native language. Introduce your find to the rest of your class.

Cooperative Learning Activity

Working in a group of four, think about ways in which other cultures have influenced the cultures of Southeast Asia. Then reread the section in the text as well as other reference books and make a list of the evidence. After completing the list, share your response with other groups and have them share their findings.

Writing About Geography

Narration

Find a book on Borobudur or Angkor Wat. Pretend that you are the first person to "find" one of these "lost" wonders of the world. Write an entry in your journal sharing your first impressions. Your writing should vividly describe the temple you have chosen.

Locating Places

SOUTHEAST ASIA: PHYSICAL GEOGRAPHY

Match the letters on the map with the places and physical features of Southeast Asia. Write your answers on a separate sheet of paper.

1. Cambodia
2. Bangkok
3. Hanoi
4. Strait of Malacca
5. Gulf of Thailand
6. Manila
7. Sumatra
8. Java
9. Indian Ocean
10. South China Sea

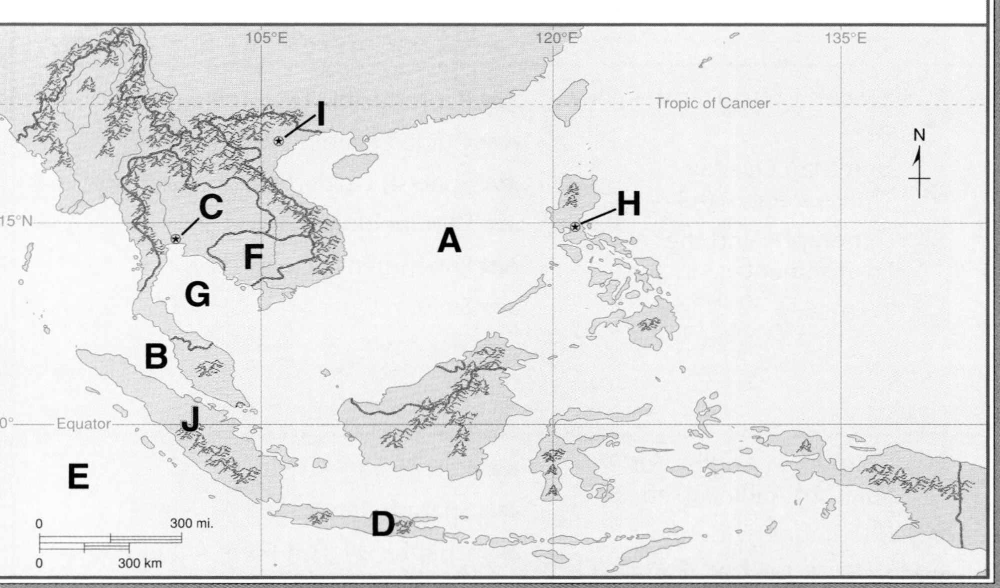

Chapter 30 Review

18. The early empires of Southeast Asia profited from trade because countries outside the region wanted access to sea routes to China, as well as the resources, forest products, gold, and spices found in the region.

19. With independence, increased industrialization has brought higher per capita incomes. Life expectancy and the general levels of health have improved. Literacy has dramatically increased throughout the region.

Practicing Skills

20. 25 years

21. Because the speaker was intensely involved in the resistance movement, his opinions might be considered biased.

22. The information given in this account is from only one person's perspective. To get a fuller understanding of the political situation in Vietnam, one should consult other primary sources, as well as reputable secondary sources.

Using the Unit Atlas

23. Most Vietnamese live along the coast or in the Mekong Delta.
24. Philippines
25. Chinese

Locating Places

1. F
2. C
3. I
4. B
5. G
6. H
7. J
8. D
9. E
10. A

Chapter Bonus Test Question

This question may be used for extra credit on the chapter test.

What cultural impact have the different peoples migrating to Southeast Asia had on the region?

(Answer: Southeast Asia has been greatly influenced by peoples from China, India, and Europe. The Chinese brought much of their own culture, including business skills and style of dress. The Indians brought their culture and religion. The Europeans brought culture, religion, and forms of government.)

CHAPTER 31

PLANNING GUIDE

Southeast Asia Today

CHAPTER ORGANIZER

Daily Lesson Objectives	Multimedia	Teacher Classroom Resources
SECTION 1 Living in Southeast Asia 1. Describe Southeast Asia's key agricultural products. 2. Explain the importance of forestry and mining to the economy of the region. 3. Summarize the commercial and industrial growth in Southeast Asia. 4. Discuss modes of transportation and communication used in Southeast Asia.	Section Focus Transparency 31-1 Chapter 31 Vocabulary PuzzleMaker Software Unit Map Overlay Transparency 10-5 Geography and the Environment Testmaker Picture Atlas of the World	Reproducible Lesson Plan 31-1 Guided Reading Activity 31-1 Spanish Guided Reading Activity 31-1 Geography Simulation 10 Workbook Activity 31-1 Section Quiz 31-1
SECTION 2 People and Their Environment 1. Examine the effects of environmental pollution on Southeast Asia. 2. Explain the variety of natural environmental challenges that the people of the region face.	Section Focus Transparency 31-2 Unit Map Overlay Transparency 10-5 Geography and the Environment Testmaker	Reproducible Lesson Plan 31-2 Guided Reading Activity 31-2 Spanish Guided Reading Activity 31-2 Workbook Activity 31-2 Enrichment Activity 31 Section Quiz 31-2
CHAPTER REVIEW AND EVALUATION	Chapter 31 English (or Spanish) Audiocassettes MindJogger Videoquiz Testmaker Student Self-Test and Review Software	Reteaching Activity 31 Spanish Reteaching Activity 31 Chapter 31 Test Form A and Form B

0:00 *If time does not permit teaching the entire chapter, summarize using the Chapter 31 Highlights on page 641, and the Chapter 31 English (or Spanish) Audiocassettes. Review students' knowledge using the Glencoe MindJogger Videoquiz.*

KEY TO ABILITY LEVELS

Teaching strategies have been coded for varying learning styles and abilities.

L1 **BASIC** activities for all students

L2 **AVERAGE** activities for average to above-average students

L3 **CHALLENGING** activities for above-average students

LEP **LIMITED ENGLISH PROFICIENCY** activities

Performance Assessment

Problem Solving Have student groups work through a problem-solving scenario, each group representing a privately-owned business in Southeast Asia. The groups should proceed through the steps of problem solving: identifying company problems, selecting and researching a particular problem, generating criteria for a solution, brainstorming/evaluating possible solutions, and devising a plan to carry out the chosen solution.

The problems identified by students should reflect data in Chapters 29, 30, and 31. Other problems may be included to preserve the authentic nature of the simulation. Each group should document their work at each step, choose roles reflecting a business format, and present their background information and plans to the class as a proposal to a board of directors. Classmates may question, critique, and offer input that each group may use for revision purposes.

POSSIBLE RUBRIC FEATURES: Content information, problem-solving process steps, cause/effect skills, collaboration skills, relevance of research, fluency and creativity, viability of relationships found

For additional professional and classroom resources, see Chapter Resources, pages T46–T51.

TEACHER'S CORNER

NATIONAL GEOGRAPHIC SOCIETY

INDEX TO NATIONAL GEOGRAPHIC MAGAZINE

The following articles may be used for research relating to this chapter:

- "Return of Java's Wildlife: In the Shadow of Krakatau," by Dieter and Mary Plage, June 1985.
- "Rice: The Essential Harvest," by Peter T. White, May 1994.
- "Volcanoes: Crucibles of Creation," by Noel Grove, December 1992.
- "Monsoons: Life Breath of Half the World," by Priit J. Vesilind, December 1984.
- "Saving the Philippine Eagle," by Robert S. Kennedy, June 1981.

NATIONAL GEOGRAPHIC SOCIETY PRODUCTS AVAILABLE FROM GLENCOE

To order the following products for use with this chapter, contact your local Glencoe sales representative or call Glencoe at 1-800-334-7344:

- *Picture Atlas of the World* (CD-ROM)
- *STV: World Geography, Asia and Australia* (Videodisc)
- *ZipZapMap! World* (Software)
- *GeoBee* (Software)
- *Images of the World* (Posters)
- *Eye on the Environment* (Posters)
- *Physical Geography of the World* (Transparencies)
- *Picture Atlas of Our 50 States* (Book)

Introducing CHAPTER 31

PERFORMANCE ASSESSMENT

Refer to the Planning Guide on page 628B for a Performance Assessment Activity for this chapter. See the *Performance Assessment Activities* booklet for additional suggestions.

CHAPTER OBJECTIVES

1. **Summarize** the importance of agriculture, forestry, and mining to Southeast Asia.
2. **Describe** the region's recent commercial and industrial growth.
3. **Discuss** modes of transportation and communication used throughout the region.
4. **Explain** the environmental challenges that the people face.

GLENCOE TECHNOLOGY

Videodisc

Use Chapter 31 MindJogger Videoquiz to preview chapter content.

MINDJOGGER VIDEOQUIZ

Chapter 31
Disc 4 Side B

The MindJogger Videoquiz is also available on videocassette.

CD-ROM

PICTURE ATLAS OF THE WORLD

Click the "Essay" and "Stats" buttons of selected Southeast Asian countries to learn more about the economies of the region.

chapter 31 Southeast Asia Today

CHAPTER FOCUS

Geographic Setting

Southeast Asia contains a rich variety of natural resources. The people of the region, however, face many environmental challenges as they develop industrialized economies.

▲Photograph: *Floating market in Bangkok, Thailand*

Geographic Themes

Section 1 Living in Southeast Asia

HUMAN/ENVIRONMENT INTERACTION Agriculture is an important part of the economies of Southeast Asia. In addition, about half of the countries depend on expanding industry for economic growth.

Section 2 People and Their Environment

REGION Environmental hazards such as typhoons, volcanoes, earthquakes, and floods often disrupt daily life and economic productivity in Southeast Asia. Air and water pollution are also affecting the quality of urban life in the region.

EXTRA CREDIT PROJECT

Problem Solving As students will learn later in the chapter, environmental pollution is a serious problem in Southeast Asia. Have students research the types of pollution problems that exist in the region and offer suggestions for solving these problems. Students may wish to present their solutions in the form of oral or written reports, posters, bulletin-board displays, or panel discussions.

1 SECTION
Living in Southeast Asia

SETTING THE SCENE

Read to Discover . . .
- the importance of rice cultivation in Southeast Asia.
- how Southeast Asian countries are industrializing their economies.
- the ways in which the countries of Southeast Asia are interdependent.

Key Terms
- sickle
- cash crop
- interdependent
- Association of Southeast Asian Nations (ASEAN)
- free port

Identify and Locate
Strait of Malacca, Manila, Chao Phraya River, Bangkok, Mekong River, Jakarta

Kuala Lumpur, Malaysia

I am helping my father in his business. Due to heavy foreign investment by Americans, Europeans and Japanese, Malaysia has enjoyed an economic boom in the last five years. This surge in the economy has helped my father to be successful in his trading business. Chee Ng

MALAYSIA
15¢
LAPANGAN TERBANG ANTARABANGSA KUALA LUMPUR INTERNATIONAL AIRPORT

Chee Ng lives in Malaysia, one of the most economically successful countries in Southeast Asia today. The economies of the other Southeast Asian countries are developing at varying rates. Almost 65 percent of Southeast Asia's labor force is engaged in agriculture. Manufacturing and commerce, however, are an important factor in the economics of about half of the region's countries.

HUMAN/ENVIRONMENT INTERACTION

Agriculture

Rice farming is the most important agricultural activity in the region. More than 50 percent of the farmland in Southeast Asia is used for growing rice.

Rice Cultivation

Rice grows well in Southeast Asia because most of the region has fertile soil, an abundant water supply, and a warm, wet climate. In addition to providing a major source of food, rice has long been an important export of Myanmar, Cambodia, Thailand, and Vietnam. Rice is also a major crop in Indonesia. For the most part, farmers in Southeast Asia do not use modern machinery. They plant and harvest their crops by hand or with simple hand tools, such as **sickles**—sharp, curved knives. Water buffalo or oxen are used to plow the fields.

Rice needs an abundance of water to grow. Rains provide sufficient water for growing rice in parts of the Philippines and in the Irrawaddy River delta in Myanmar. Seasonal flooding

LESSON PLAN
Chapter 31, Section 1

FOCUS

SECTION OBJECTIVES
1. **Describe** Southeast Asia's key agricultural products.
2. **Explain** the importance of forestry and mining to the economy of the region.
3. **Summarize** the commercial and industrial growth in Southeast Asia.
4. **Discuss** modes of transportation and communication used in Southeast Asia.

ABOUT THE POSTCARD

Chee tells us that his father's trading business is located in Malacca, which was once known as a great trading port, bringing in ships from Portugal and China.

BELLRINGER MOTIVATIONAL ACTIVITY

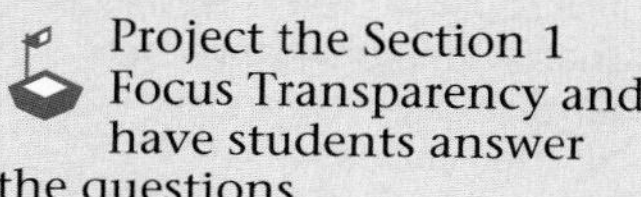
Project the Section 1 Focus Transparency and have students answer the questions.

PRETEACHING VOCABULARY

Discuss the meaning of *cash crop*. Have students name some cash crops in Southeast Asia.

Use the Vocabulary PuzzleMaker Software to create a crossword or word search puzzle.

NATIONAL GEOGRAPHIC SOCIETY

CD-ROM

PICTURE ATLAS OF THE WORLD
You and your students can view rice cultivation in Vietnam by clicking the country's "Video" button.

Classroom Resources for Section 1

BLACKLINE MASTERS:
Reproducible Lesson Plan 31-1
Guided Reading Activity 31-1
Geography Simulation 10
Workbook Activity 31-1
Section Quiz 31-1

TRANSPARENCIES:
Section Focus Transparency 31-1
Unit Map Overlay Transparency 10-5

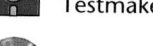

MULTIMEDIA:
Vocabulary PuzzleMaker Software
Testmaker

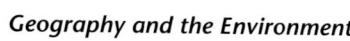

Geography and the Environment

Picture Atlas of the World

TEACH

GUIDED PRACTICE

L1 Discuss Lead a discussion with students on why rice is the most important agricultural product in Southeast Asia. Students should use their texts to find supporting statements.

Project Unit Map Overlay Transparency 10-5. Discuss ways the physical features of the region have impacted the economic development of Southeast Asia.

Implement Geography Simulation 10 as a class activity.

USING ILLUSTRATIONS

PLACE Bali is part of the Lesser Sunda Islands. It has the most people—more than 3 million—and the largest city—Denpasur—of all the islands.

Answer to Caption: *rice*

INDEPENDENT PRACTICE

Guided Reading Have students complete Guided Reading Activity 31-1 in the TCR. **LEP**

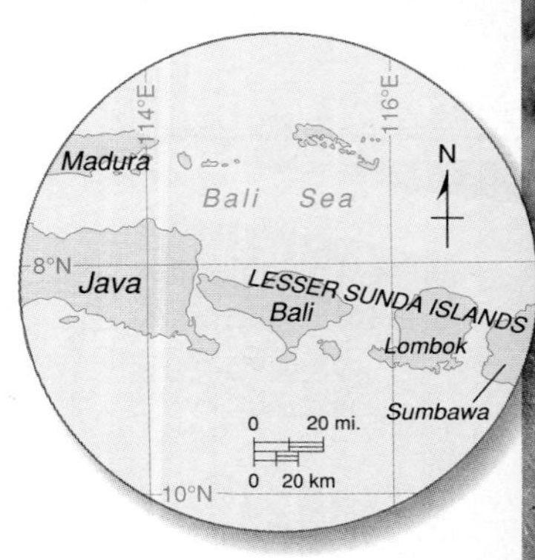

Geographic Themes

Place: Bali, Indonesia
The island of Bali is known for its beautiful scenery, elaborate temples, and fertile soil. *What major crop is grown in Indonesia and other countries of Southeast Asia?*

of the Chao Phraya and Mekong rivers irrigates rice fields in parts of Thailand, Cambodia, and Vietnam. Rice is planted at the beginning of the rainy season in May and is ready for harvest in October. During the dry season, a second rice crop can be grown by irrigating rice fields with water stored from the rains and the flooding river.

Other Crops

Southeast Asian nations also grow edible roots, such as cassavas and yams, and bananas. Many people in Southeast Asia have small garden plots that produce a variety of fruits and vegetables, and they also raise pigs and poultry for food.

Plantations in the coastal lowlands provide many of the region's **cash crops**—crops raised to be sold. Sugar cane is grown on Java and in the Philippines. Rubber, brought to the region from South America less than 100 years ago, is an important cash crop. Malaysia is the world's leading natural-rubber producer. Other regional cash crops are coconuts, coffee, palm oil, and spices.

HUMAN/ENVIRONMENT INTERACTION

Forestry and Mining

Forestry is an important industry in Southeast Asian countries. Myanmar leads the world in teakwood exports. Lumber and products made from teak, ebony, mahogany, and bamboo are important to the economies of Malaysia, the Philippines, Indonesia, and Thailand.

Environmental Protection

Logging, however, has often led to serious deforestation and environmental damage. In recent years, some countries have taken steps to limit the exploitation of the forests. The governments of Thailand, Indonesia, the Philippines, and Malaysia have passed laws to limit certain timber exports, but these restrictions are often not adequately enforced.

Oil and Mining

Oil extraction and mining are important to Southeast Asia's economic growth. Brunei has become rich from its oil industry. Crude oil,

Cooperative Learning Activity

Organize the class into groups. Assign each group one of the following topics: "Forestry and Mining in Southeast Asia," "Agriculture in Southeast Asia," "Commercial and Industrial Growth in Southeast Asia," or "Transportation and Communication in Southeast Asia." Each group should then create a poster on their topic. Posters can include pictures from magazines, student drawings, or a combination of both.

natural gas, and petroleum products account for 95 percent of Brunei's export income. One of the world's largest natural gas plants is found in Brunei.

Indonesia is the largest producer of petroleum in the region and is one of the top 10 producers in the Organization of Petroleum Exporting Countries (OPEC). Economic development has been spurred by the building of pipelines to carry oil from drilling sites to the coasts for shipment. Pipelines have been built on the islands of Sumatra, Java, Borneo, and New Guinea.

Tin mining is a major industry in Southeast Asia. Malaysia, Thailand, and Indonesia are three of the world's leading tin producers. Iron ore is also important in Malaysia and in the Philippines. Manganese, an important mineral for strengthening steel, is found in the Philippines and in Indonesia. Tungsten,

SOUTHEAST ASIA: ECONOMIC ACTIVITY

Commercial farming
Subsistence farming
Manufacturing and trade
Commercial fishing
Mercator projection

MYANMAR
LAOS
THAILAND
CAMBODIA
VIETNAM
PHILIPPINES
MALAYSIA
BRUNEI
SINGAPORE
INDONESIA
ASIA
Yangon
Hanoi
Bangkok
Ho Chi Minh City
Manila
Kuala Lumpur
Palembang
Jakarta
Surabaya
Tropic of Cancer
Equator
105°E
120°E
135°E
15°N
0°
N
0 500 mi.
0 500 km

FOCUS ON GEOGRAPHIC THEMES

1. **Region:** What is the dominant economic activity in Southeast Asia?
2. **Place:** Where is manufacturing and trade an important economic activity? Why?

Meeting Special Needs

Paired Learning You may want to pair a student that has a good grasp of the content with a student that is having difficulty comprehending the information. Students can share and compare class notes with their partners, as well as discuss and summarize what they read in their textbooks.

USING MAPS

Answers:
1. subsistence farming; **2.** mostly in large cities or capitals; because they are located along rivers or seacoasts, which allow for trade

Map Skills Practice
Reading a Map Where is commercial farming dominant? *(on the western coast of mainland Malaysia, on the northeast coast of Sumatra, on the eastern coast of Mindanao)*

Have students complete the Unit Map Overlay Transparency 10 Activity in the TCR.

MULTICULTURAL PERSPECTIVE

Cultural Heritage
Most of Indonesia had converted to Islam by the 1500s. The island of Bali, however, remained a stronghold of the older faith, Hinduism. The people of Bali still celebrate their Hindu holidays with splendid ceremonies.

USING ILLUSTRATIONS

MOVEMENT The chief exports of the Philippines include chemicals, machinery, and petroleum. Its main trading partners are the United States and Japan.

Answer to Caption: *There is a large supply of inexpensive labor, and foreign investments have stimulated the economy.*

CURRICULUM CONNECTION

GOVERNMENT
Thailand has alternated between military rule and democratic government since the 1930s. In spite of constant political changes, the monarchy remains above politics and provides national unity and political stability.

GLENCOE TECHNOLOGY

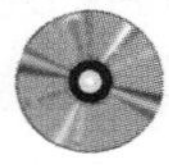

Videodisc

Use the following to enrich Chapter 31:

GEOGRAPHY AND THE ENVIRONMENT
THE INFINITE VOYAGE
To the Edge of the Earth

Chapter 5
Disc 1 Side B

Title: ***The Tropical Rain Forest***

Geographic Themes

Movement: Manila, the Philippines
Manila, the capital of the Philippines, ranks as one of the leading trade centers of Asia. *What two factors have sparked industrial growth in areas of Southeast Asia?*

which is used for electrical purposes and for steel alloys, greatly adds to the economic growth of Myanmar and Thailand.

PLACE

Commercial and Industrial Growth

Newly industrializing countries in Southeast Asia are Malaysia, the Philippines, Singapore, and Thailand. Foreign companies have moved manufacturing and assembly plants to Southeast Asia because of the large supply of inexpensive labor in the region. Foreign investments have stimulated the economies of Southeast Asian nations.

Singapore

Singapore's location and good harbors have led to its development as an important port and manufacturing center. Major industries in Singapore produce chemicals, electronic equipment, transportation equipment, machinery, metals, paper, rubber, textiles, and processed foods. Oil refining and shipbuilding are also important industries in Singapore.

Other Industrialized Countries

Malaysia has used the capital from its mineral and rubber exports to develop many industries. Major manufactured products include cement, chemicals, rubber goods, textiles, and processed foods. Malaysia and the Philippines are developing profitable automobile assembly industries. Textile and clothing industries are important in Thailand and the Philippines. In increasing their exports, Thailand and the Philippines have tried to balance industrial growth with more traditional ventures in agricultural production and fish farming.

Less Industrialized Countries

Other countries of the region, such as Laos, Cambodia, and Vietnam, are developing their industries at a slower rate. Only a small percentage of the people in these countries work in industry. Manufacturing has yet to be developed on a scale larger than small craft industries for a number of reasons.

Wars and political changes in Laos, Cambodia, and Vietnam have affected economic development for many years. A policy of isolationism in Myanmar has long slowed the country's economic growth. Indonesia's economic development is offset somewhat by its rapidly growing population. This means that Indonesia must import many kinds of manufactured goods. Indonesian leaders, however, hope to finance future industrial development and expansion with income from Indonesia's oil exports.

MOVEMENT

Interdependence

Some countries in Southeast Asia have become more **interdependent**, or reliant on

Critical Thinking

Defending a Point of View Organize the class into two groups. One group is traditionalists who want to keep Southeast Asia isolated from foreign cultures. The other group wants to see Southeast Asia expand its exports and have greater participation in the global market. Have each group research their side's opinions. Then hold a class debate in which each side must offer a defense of their position. You may wish to allow each side an opportunity to ask their opponents questions. Allow ample time for responses and rebuttal.

each other, as a result of the formation of two organizations designed to increase regional development and trade. In 1967 Indonesia, Malaysia, the Philippines, Singapore, and Thailand formed the **Association of Southeast Asian Nations (ASEAN).** Brunei joined ASEAN in 1984. One goal of ASEAN is to promote tourism in member countries. ASEAN also works to lower trade barriers in the region. In addition, members of ASEAN share products during shortages.

Although ASEAN is a political and economic alliance, it does not have full political or economic unity as one of its major goals. This is primarily because of Southeast Asia's great diversity. Yet, the association has allowed its members to understand one another through regular meetings of leaders and cultural exchanges of citizens. ASEAN also has provided a sense of security in a region that has long known political instability and conflict.

Another development group is the Asian Development Bank (ADB), based in Manila, the capital of the Philippines. This organization helps the economic development of member countries by lending them money. The ADB helps to finance agricultural, transportation, and industrial-development projects throughout Southeast Asia.

MOVEMENT

Transportation

Water transportation is the most common way to move people and goods in Southeast Asia. In recent years overland transport networks have been developed in many urban areas. Modern and efficient transportation, however, has yet to reach most parts of rural Southeast Asia.

Water Transportation

Because of the long coastlines and many rivers, water transportation is very important in Southeast Asia. Throughout the region's history, boats have carried people and goods to the islands and along rivers and seacoasts. All but one of the countries of the region have at least one harbor for oceangoing vessels. Laos, the only exception, is landlocked.

For centuries Southeast Asia has been the crossroads of major ocean trade routes. Even today most shipping traffic between Europe and East Asia passes through the Strait of Malacca. All the largest cities of Southeast Asia are located near waterways, making these cities trade centers.

The **free port** of Singapore, which lies near the southeastern end of the Strait of Malacca, is one of the world's busiest ports. A free port is a place where goods can be unloaded, stored, and reshipped without the payment of import duties. Thus, Singapore is an important port for Southeast Asia. Other major ports include the Indonesian cities of Palembang, on Sumatra, and Jakarta, on Java. Jakarta is the center for most of Indonesia's trade and is also a leading cultural and manufacturing center.

Manila, in the Philippines, has one of the best natural harbors in the world. Its location makes Manila one of the most important centers for oceangoing trade in Asia. Bangkok, near the mouth of the Chao Phraya, is a port for both Thailand and landlocked Laos.

Overland Transportation

Throughout the region, the quality of transportation varies dramatically. Highways and railroads have been developed on the peninsulas and on some of the larger islands in the region. In general, however, these systems connect only the major cities. Travel outside urban areas is mainly on unpaved roads.

In most countries of the region, bicycles, motor scooters, and oxcarts are common means of transportation. The Philippines, Singapore, and Thailand have better overland transportation systems than the other countries of the region. This has largely been the result of the process of economic development in these countries and their ties with other industrialized countries of the world. The island of Singapore is connected to the Malay Peninsula by a 16-mile (25.6 km) railway. In Jakarta,

Chapter 31, Section 1

ASSESS

CHECK FOR UNDERSTANDING

Assign Section 1 Review as homework or an in-class activity.

MEETING LESSON OBJECTIVES

Each objective below is tested by the questions that follow it in parentheses.

1. Describe Southeast Asia's key agricultural products. *(2, 3)*
2. Explain the importance of forestry and mining to the economy of the region. *(2, 4)*
3. Summarize the commercial and industrial growth in Southeast Asia. *(4, 5)*
4. Discuss modes of transportation and communication used in Southeast Asia. *(5)*

EVALUATE

Assign the Section 1 Quiz in the TCR.

Use the Testmaker to create a customized quiz for Section 1.

RETEACH

Assign each student to write a one-paragraph summary of one of the six major subheads in this section. Ask students to share their summaries with the class.

Meeting Special Needs

Pronouncing Difficult Words Some students may have difficulty pronouncing some of the place-names in this section, such as Thailand, Bali, and Jakarta. You may wish to sound out the correct pronunciation of such places. For example, Jakarta is pronounced juh-KAHRT-uh. You may also direct students to the Gazetteer in the back of their text for these pronunciations.

USING ILLUSTRATIONS

PLACE In the Philippines, *jeepneys*, or taxis, pick up as many passengers as can possibly be crammed into the vehicle. Along with buses, jeepneys provide most of the country's local transportation.

Answer to Caption: *bicycles, motor scooters, oxcarts, trucks, automobiles, buses, and motorcycles*

ENRICH

Have students compare communications in Southeast Asia with the United States by having them research the average number of telephones per person in Indonesia, Cambodia, Vietnam, and the United States. (This information can be found in a world almanac.)

CLOSE

Write a postcard to Chee, telling him about any part-time employment you may have.

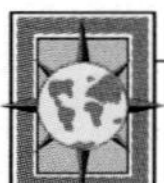

Geographic Themes

Place: Bangkok, Thailand
Small jeep-like vehicles carry people through the busy streets of many Southeast Asian cities. *What are other types of overland transportation in Southeast Asia?*

Indonesia, paved roads are choked with trucks, automobiles, buses, bicycles, and motorcycles. This problem is often made more difficult by peddlers who set up their stalls along major streets.

In rural areas of Southeast Asia, travel is difficult. Heavy rains often wash out unpaved roads. Dense forests, rugged terrain, and the seas that separate the islands of the region also interfere with road and railway development.

In many Southeast Asian countries, governments are working to improve transportation. For example, bridges are being built between the main islands of the Philippines to link major highways. In Vietnam and Cambodia, roads and railroads damaged from recent wars have been repaired.

Air travel links the major cities of the region with the rest of the world. All of Southeast Asia's countries have at least one major airport. In some remote areas, supplies are moved only by air.

MOVEMENT

Communications

Communications services are readily available in the cities of Southeast Asia. These services help to develop the economies of the region by providing rapid communication between businesses. Because of the rugged terrain of Southeast Asia, satellite communication is used to help countries provide telephone service to rural areas. Post offices are found mostly in major urban centers.

Southeast Asia has many daily newspapers and magazine and book publishers. Most publishers are located in cities, such as Bangkok, Jakarta, Yangon, and Singapore. Television networks and radio stations are typically government-owned and controlled. Most people either own or have access to a radio, while television sets are less common. Singapore, Brunei, and the Philippines have the greatest number of television sets per person. Most of the countries of Southeast Asia are making great strides toward the development of modern communication systems. It will take more time, however, for these systems to reach every part of the region.

SECTION 1 REVIEW

Checking for Understanding

1. **Define** sickle, cash crop, interdependent, Association of Southeast Asian Nations (ASEAN), free port.
2. **Locating Places** In what type of areas are many of Southeast Asia's cash crops grown?
3. **Region** Why is rice an important agricultural product in Southeast Asia?
4. **Movement** How have certain industries in the region managed to prosper?

Critical Thinking

5. **Synthesizing Information** In what ways have many Southeast Asian countries become more interdependent?

ANSWERS TO SECTION 1 REVIEW

1. **sickle:** a sharp, curved knife; **cash crops:** crops raised to be sold; **ASEAN:** organization of Southeast Asian states that want to promote tourism in member countries, lower trade barriers in the region, and share products during shortages; **free port:** place where goods can be unloaded, stored, and reshipped without the payment of import duties
2. Most cash crops are grown on plantations.
3. Southeast Asia has the soil conditions, the water supply, and the climate needed for growing rice.
4. Certain industries in the region have prospered due to foreign investments.
5. through the development of international organizations such as ASEAN and ADB

2 SECTION
People and Their Environment

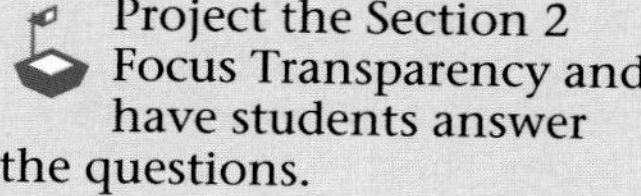

SETTING THE SCENE

Read to Discover . . .
- the causes of air and water pollution in Southeast Asia.
- the dangers posed by typhoons, volcanic activity, and earthquakes in Southeast Asia.

Key Terms
- cyclone
- typhoon

Identify and Locate
Ring of Fire, Philippines, Bali, Bangkok

Southeast Asians face a variety of environmental challenges. Some of these problems stem from human activities. Others are caused by nature, and some by a combination of human and natural factors.

HUMAN/ENVIRONMENT INTERACTION

Environmental Pollution

As Southeast Asian countries become more urbanized and industrialized, air, water, and noise pollution pose increasing dangers to the region's environment. More people living close together means more concerns about housing, water supply, sanitation, and traffic. Increased manufacturing creates industrial waste matter. As societies become wealthier and people purchase more automobiles, toxic emissions are added to the air.

Rapid economic development in Thailand, for example, has brought prosperity to many Thais, but it has also negatively affected their quality of life. Bangkok, Thailand's capital, has become a commercial and industrial center for Southeast Asia. It is a busy city of skyscrapers, factories, noisy expressways, and traffic jams. A rapid increase in population has also brought overcrowding in the city's residential areas. As a result of these changes, the people of Bangkok must deal with air, water, and noise pollution.

Pollution in Southeast Asia even extends beyond the major cities. In the Tai Phi National Park of Thailand, for example, 80 percent of the freshwater wells are contaminated as a result of increased human usage. Other causes of air pollution in rural areas are volcanic eruptions and forest fires. Forest fires in the Indonesian part of Borneo in 1991 created medical problems for people as far away as mainland Malaysia, and disrupted both air traffic and shipping.

HUMAN/ENVIRONMENT INTERACTION

Volcanoes

Because much of Southeast Asia is located on the Ring of Fire, many people in the region have to cope with the threat of volcanic activity. In the Philippines, volcanic mountains rise in most of the country's larger islands, and many of the volcanoes are active. Indonesia also has many volcanoes that have been active in historic times. The Indonesian island of Bali is noted for its 10,308-foot-high (3,142-m) volcano, Gunung Agung. The Balinese people regard the volcano as a sacred centerpiece of their Hindu faith. They continue to

FOCUS

SECTION OBJECTIVES

1. **Examine** the effects of environmental pollution on Southeast Asia.
2. **Explain** the variety of natural environmental challenges that the people of the region face.

BELLRINGER MOTIVATIONAL ACTIVITY

Project the Section 2 Focus Transparency and have students answer the questions.

PRETEACHING VOCABULARY

Ask students if they have ever witnessed a storm such as a *cyclone* or a *typhoon*, or if they have seen pictures of such storms on television. Create a list of adjectives that would describe these types of storms.

GLENCOE TECHNOLOGY

Videodisc

GEOGRAPHY AND THE ENVIRONMENT
THE INFINITE VOYAGE
To the Edge of the Earth

Chapter 3
Disc 1 Side B
Title: ***Exploring Volcanoes: To the Center of the Earth***
Subject: A manned submersible is used to study volcanic activity below the surface of the Pacific Ocean

Classroom Resources for Section 2

BLACKLINE MASTERS:
- Reproducible Lesson Plan 31-2
- Guided Reading Activity 31-2
- Enrichment Activity 31
- Section Quiz 31-2

TRANSPARENCIES:
- Section Focus Transparency 31-2
- Unit Map Overlay Transparency 10-5

MULTIMEDIA:
- Testmaker

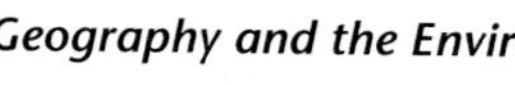

- *Geography and the Environment*

TEACH

GUIDED PRACTICE

Use Unit Map Overlay Transparency 10-5 to help students locate the major mountain ranges and peaks in Southeast Asia.

USING ILLUSTRATIONS

HUMAN/ENVIRONMENT INTERACTION Bangkok was once called the "Venice of the East" because of its many canals. Today, most of the canals have been replaced by streets and highways.
Answer to Caption: *a rapid increase in the city's population*

INDEPENDENT PRACTICE

Guided Reading Have students complete Guided Reading Activity 31-2 in the TCR. **LEP**

ASSESS

CHECK FOR UNDERSTANDING

Assign Section 2 Review as homework or an in-class activity.

MEETING LESSON OBJECTIVES

Each objective below is tested by the questions that follow it in parentheses.

1. **Examine** the effects of environmental pollution on Southeast Asia. *(3, 5)*
2. **Explain** the variety of natural environmental challenges that the people of the region face. *(2, 4)*

live near Gunung Agung, despite a 1963 eruption that took the lives of more than 1,500 people.

In June 1991, after a 600-year period of dormancy, 5,770-foot-high (1,759-m) Mount Pinatubo erupted. Philippine scientists were able to predict the eruption, and government authorities ordered the evacuation of nearby towns. Still, more than 900 people died and about 100,000 homes were destroyed. Pinatubo began erupting again in July 1992. During the next three months, 40,000 more people became homeless. As a result of the eruptions, a cloud of ash and dust spewed into the atmosphere and affected climate and weather thousands of miles away.

PLACE

Floods and Typhoons

Flood conditions are a natural problem in Southeast Asia. The major rivers on the Indochina Peninsula, for example, undergo seasonal flooding every year. Flash floods in Southeast Asia yearly kill hundreds of people and ruin about 10 million acres (about 4 million ha) of crops. The dangers and damage caused by flooding in Southeast Asia, however, have been increased by human activity. In November 1991, for example, a major storm struck the central Philippine islands. Because the land had been cleared of forest, the storm caused extensive damage from runoff and mudslides that would not have occurred otherwise.

Flooding is also a serious problem in Bangkok, which is built on unstable land. Some sections of the city sink as much as 25 inches (about 64 cm) each year. The city's most recent serious flooding occurred in 1983 when one-fourth of its area was submerged.

A **cyclone**—the name means "coil"—is an area of low atmospheric pressure surrounded by circulating winds. Tropical cyclones are among the deadliest storms on the earth. A **typhoon** is a tropical cyclone located in the Pacific area. Typhoons form north of the Equator, usually between July and October, and their winds circulate in a counterclockwise direction.

Geographic Themes

Human/Environment Interaction: Bangkok, Thailand

Bangkok's rapid industrial development has significantly increased air pollution over the city. *What other change has seriously affected Bangkok's quality of life?*

Cooperative Learning Activity

Organize the class into groups. Have each group do research on one natural disaster that has struck Southeast Asia in the last three years. To ensure variety, you may wish to have students tell you the topic of their research before they begin. Students should gather information such as the date(s) the storm hit, where it caused the most damage, the death toll, the extent of destruction, and the rebuilding efforts. Each group should prepare and present an oral report to the class.

Geographic Themes

Human/Environment Interaction: Indonesia
Indonesia has a number of active volcanoes. Some of these volcanoes have erupted, killing people and destroying property. *What other natural disasters occur in Southeast Asia?*

The typhoons that affect Southeast Asia form in the North Pacific Ocean, north of the island of New Guinea. Some travel north to Japan, others go through the northern Philippines and on to the Chinese mainland. Still others pass through the Philippines and across the Indochina Peninsula. Typhoons may have winds from 150 to 180 mph (241 to 290 kmph), and may be accompanied by rain, thunder, and lightning. Typhoons disrupt shipping, and high ocean waves that sometimes accompany typhoons can be devastating.

Asian meteorologists do not participate in the naming system used in the United States to identify tropical storms. Instead, they number storms using the last two digits of the year and a number to designate which storm of the year is being watched—for example, 1:97 would be the first typhoon in 1997.

SECTION 2 REVIEW

Checking for Understanding

1. **Define** cyclone, typhoon.
2. **Locating Places** Name two Southeast Asian countries that are part of the Ring of Fire.
3. **Human/Environment Interaction** What factors account for environmental pollution in Southeast Asia?
4. **Region** How much crop damage does flooding cause in Southeast Asia each year?

Critical Thinking

5. **Predicting Consequences** What effect do you think uncontrolled economic development will have on Bangkok's future?

EVALUATE

Assign the Section 2 Quiz in the TCR.

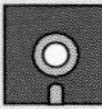

Use the Testmaker to create a customized quiz for Section 2.

RETEACH

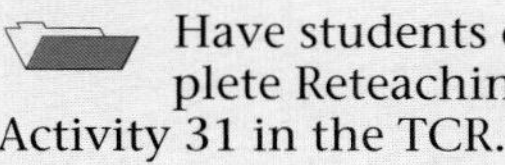

Have students complete Reteaching Activity 31 in the TCR.

USING ILLUSTRATIONS

PLACE Indonesia has about 60 active volcanoes.

Answer to Caption: *storms such as cyclones and typhoons*

ENRICH

Have students complete Enrichment Activity 31 in the TCR.

CLOSE

Discuss the following: *Which has a greater effect on Southeast Asia, environmental pollution or natural disasters?*

ANSWERS TO SECTION 2 REVIEW

1. **cyclone:** an area of low atmospheric pressure surrounded by circulating winds; **typhoon:** a tropical cyclone located in the Pacific area
2. the Philippines and Bali
3. Urbanization, more automobiles, economic development, and a rapidly increasing population all contribute to environmental pollution.
4. About 10 million acres (about 4 million ha) of crops a year are lost due to flooding.
5. Answers may include overcrowding and increased pollution. Steps to remedy this problem might be to limit the number of new businesses and have stricter pollution laws for automobiles and businesses.

FOCUS

Ask students what other world region highlighted loss of forests; encourage them to look back in their books if necessary. *(Costa Rica, Latin America)* Have them share information they remember.

TEACH

Use Unit Map Overlay Transparency 10-4 to familiarize students with the location of Thailand.

L1 Human/Environment Interaction Have students compose a cause-effect chain that explains the present situation in Thailand. Have them begin with the government's decision to allow teak logging.

L2 Examine Suggest students find out more about teak and the products made from it. Students may research books about trees and different kinds of furniture. They may want to visit furniture stores or import-export emporiums to see examples.

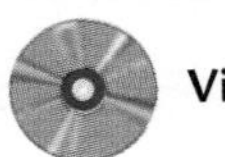

Videodisc

GTV: PLANETARY MANAGER

Side 2, Chapter 6
Frames 31907-38777
Title: ***Dust in the Wind***
Subject: Time travel shows the consequences of overgrazing, excessive irrigation, and deforestation

CASE STUDY

LOGGING IN THAILAND

Some day, I'd like to take my children out to where we were today. . . . I'd like to show them a new forest. . . . I'd like to . . . be able to say, 'Your father helped to make this.'

Nai Mong, Thai forestry official

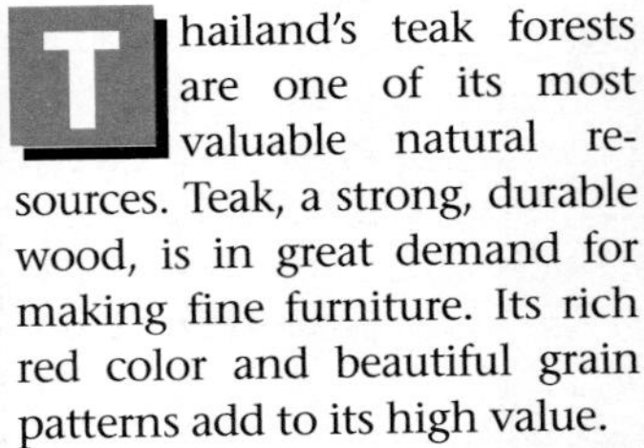

Thailand's teak forests are one of its most valuable natural resources. Teak, a strong, durable wood, is in great demand for making fine furniture. Its rich red color and beautiful grain patterns add to its high value.

In 1961 Thailand introduced a national plan to develop industry. Under the plan, teak exports became a leading source of income for the country.

A truck carries logs of teakwood from a northern Thai forest.

THE ISSUE

Before Thailand's economic program, forests covered 60 percent of the country's land. During the 1960s and 1970s, Thailand's economy prospered: Each year its GDP increased. By the mid-1970s, however, it became obvious that Thailand's forests were diminishing as the forestry sector of the country's economy prospered.

THE BACKGROUND

Like most of the other Southeast Asian countries, Thailand is a newly industrialized nation. To stimulate its economy and provide a better standard of living for its people, Thailand opened its forests to foreign logging companies. The companies established modern logging processes, and provided training, equipment, and jobs for many Thais. The Thai economy benefited from payments by the companies, as well as the additional spending power of the Thai workers.

The companies, however, made little effort to replant as they harvested. Teak trees take about 70 years to produce a full-grown harvestable tree. Logged areas were leveled, then abandoned.

Without the trees' root systems, surface soil was no longer held in place. Topsoil was easily eroded by heavy tropical rains. The soil washed into the streams that crisscross Thailand, clogging them and reducing the amount of water available for irrigation.

THE POINTS OF VIEW

Scientists pointed out that Thailand's forests were a renewable source. With proper management, forests could continue to be a stable part of Thailand's economy.

Extending the Content

Compare/Contrast Have students review the Costa Rican rain forest problem, then the Thailand logging situation. Have them work as a class to compose a comparison/contrast report on the two problems. Encourage them to discuss and choose the most clear, concise way to present their data. When they have completed their analysis, have a volunteer type it up, and make photocopies for each class member. Students can put the analysis in their journals with the other materials they are collecting for this unit.

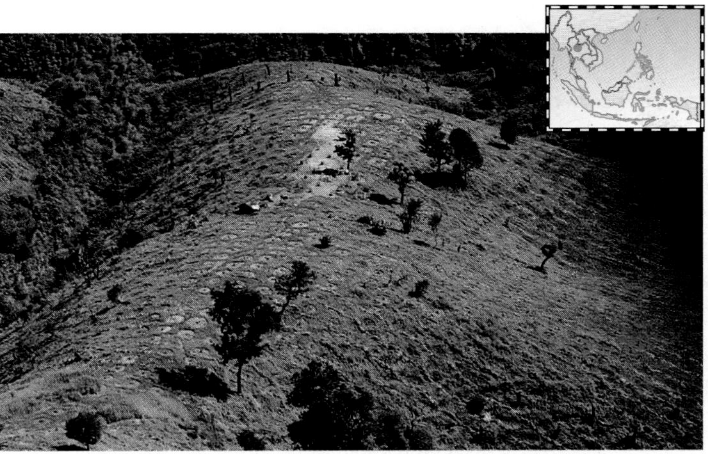

The overcutting of forests has exposed bare hillsides to the effects of violent rainstorms.

By the mid-1970s, however, it became obvious that Thailand's forests were diminishing as the forestry sector of the country's economy prospered.

As it was, not only were the forests being devastated, but other ecological areas—Thailand's rivers and topsoil—were suffering as well.

The Thai government defended its decision to allow the logging companies into Thailand, saying that they provided jobs and income for Thailand.

The logging companies protested that a replanting program would force them to raise their prices and decrease wages to keep returns profitable for their investors.

THE ISSUE TODAY

The Thai government banned the export of teak in 1978, and announced a reforestation program. Illegal logging, however, continued. By the early 1990s, only 20 percent of Thailand's forests remained.

Excessive logging is believed responsible for a major disaster that occurred in Thailand during the late 1980s. A violent thunderstorm that hit one of the deforested regions in November 1988 created flash floods on the bare, muddy hillsides. These floods killed 400 people and left thousands more injured and homeless.

Environmentalists stated that, if the forests had remained to absorb the downpour, floods would not have threatened the valley's residents. They charged, that, by ignoring the consequences of their actions, Thai officials and loggers not only destroyed a vital resource but also created a disaster. Economic experts believed that the destructive floods had set the region's economy back 20 years.

Thailand's reforestation program is moving slowly, under the leadership of the Thai Royal Forestry Department. Although the government is financially prosperous by Southeast Asian standards, it cannot afford a large conservation corps.

Those Thais who work for the corps have begun the tough work of clearing logged land of debris and dead tree stumps. Their work is made doubly hard—as well as dangerous—by illegal loggers who continue to defy the government's ban, and who will kill forestry personnel coming too close to their operations.

Reviewing the Case

1. **Why did Thailand invite foreign logging companies into its teak forests?**
2. **Human/Environment Interaction How did overlogging harm the forests?**

L3 Propose Have students use data about Thailand from the selection, as well as the rest of the unit, to propose methods of increasing industry in Thailand without depleting the teak forests.

DID YOU KNOW?

Thais are proud of their cultural heritage and are often offended by those who equate "developed" with "Westernized."

ASSESS

Have students answer the Reviewing the Case questions on page 639.

CLOSE

Have students discuss ways to halt illegal logging with limited personnel and limited funds.

ANSWERS TO REVIEWING THE CASE

1. Logging was part of a national plan to develop industry, stimulate the economy, and provide a better standard of living for its people.
2. The logging companies did not replant trees as they harvested. Without the trees' root systems, surface soil was easily eroded by Thailand's heavy tropical rains, washing into the streams and clogging them, thus decreasing the water available for irrigation.

TEACH

Have students read the skill on page 640 and define Greenwich Mean Time. Point out that time zone boundaries are irregular because they follow political borders. Then ask: "If you take a five-hour flight from New York to Los Angeles, leaving New York at 10:00 A.M., at what time will you arrive?" *(noon)* "Why?" *(Flying west across three time zones, you lose three hours.)* "If you fly out of Hawaii on Saturday, on what day will you arrive in Japan?" *(Friday)* "Why?" *(You crossed the International Date Line.)* Have students write and solve time zone problems.

Skills Practice For additional practice, have students complete Skill Activity 31 in the TCR.

MAP & GRAPH SKILLS

Understanding Time Zones

The earth revolves 360° in 24 hours; therefore, when it is day on one side, it is night on the other. To clarify time relationships, the earth's surface has been divided into 24 **international time zones.**

REVIEWING THE SKILL

Each zone represents 15° longitude, or the distance the earth rotates in 1 hour. The base time zone, called Greenwich Mean Time (GMT), is set at the Prime Meridian (0°). Traveling west from Greenwich, it becomes 1 hour earlier; traveling east, it becomes 1 hour later. The international date line is set at the 180° meridian. Traveling west across this imaginary line, you add a day; traveling east, you subtract a day. Use the following steps to determine time zones:

- Choose a place for which you already know the time and locate it on the map.
- Locate the place for which you wish to know the time, and determine if it is east or west of the first place.
- Count the time zones between the two places.
- Calculate the time by either adding or subtracting an hour for each time zone.
- Determine whether you have crossed the date line, and identify the day of the week.

PRACTICING THE SKILL

Use the map to answer the following questions.

1. If it is 4 P.M. in Honolulu, what time is it in Rio de Janeiro?
2. If it is 10:00 A.M. in Tokyo on Tuesday, what day and time is it in Moscow? In Washington, D.C.?
3. How many time zones does Southeast Asia have?

For additional practice in this skill, see Practicing Skills on page 642 of the Chapter 31 Review.

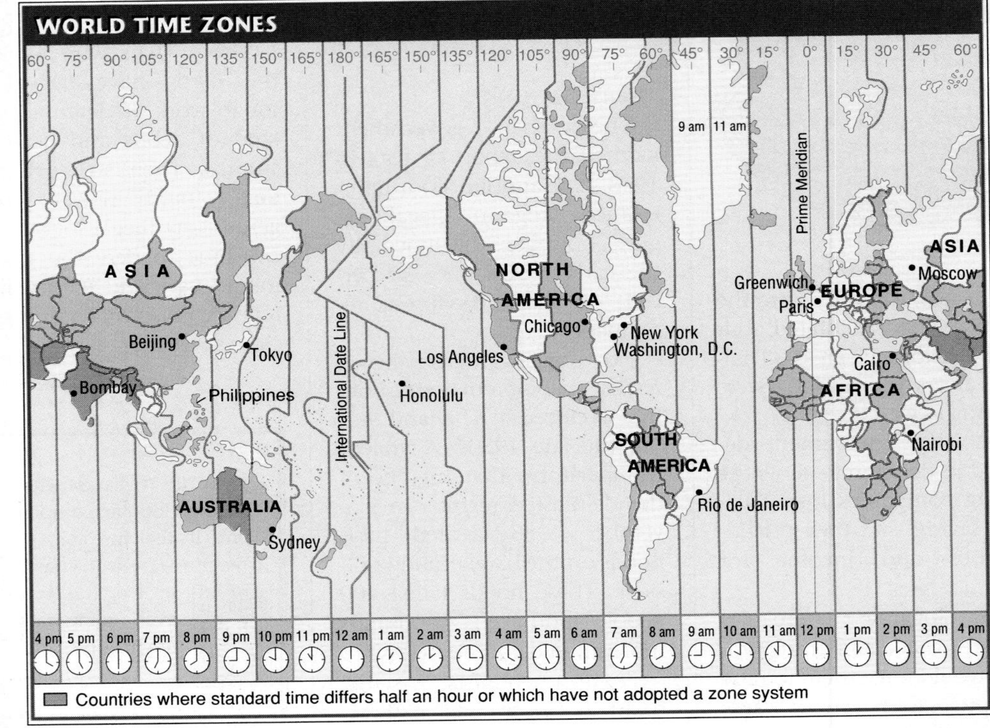

ANSWERS TO PRACTICING THE SKILL

1. 11:00 P.M.
2. Tuesday, 4:00 A.M. in Moscow; Monday, 8:00 P.M.
3. three

chapter 31

HIGHLIGHTS

Section 1: Living in Southeast Asia

Key Terms

- **sickle** (p. 629)
- **cash crop** (p. 630)
- **interdependent** (p. 632)
- **Association of Southeast Asian Nations (ASEAN)** (p. 633)
- **free port** (p. 633)

Summary

- Agriculture is the basis for most of the economies of Southeast Asia. The major crops are rice, sugar cane, rubber, coffee, and coconuts.
- The lush forests of Southeast Asia yield many wood products; mining has also been important to the economies of the region.
- In recent years manufacturing has become increasingly important, and many new industries have developed in Southeast Asia.
- The main form of transportation in Southeast Asia is by water. Land transportation is less developed.

Indonesian farmer with water buffalo

Section 2: People and Their Environment

Key Terms

- **cyclone** (p. 636)
- **typhoon** (p. 636)

Summary

- Industrialization, urbanization, and rapid population increases have brought environmental pollution to many urban and rural areas in Southeast Asia.
- Because they live within the Ring of Fire, large numbers of Southeast Asians are surrounded by volcanoes, many of them active.
- Each year, flash floods destroy lives and crops in Southeast Asia.
- Typhoons are dangerous storms that occur in Southeast Asia between July and October.

Busy expressway in Bangkok, Thailand

CHAPTER 31 HIGHLIGHTS

USING THE CHAPTER 31 HIGHLIGHTS

Use the Chapter 31 Highlights to preview, review, condense, or reteach the chapter.

PREVIEW/REVIEW

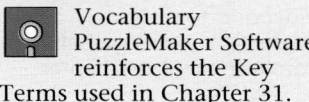

Vocabulary PuzzleMaker Software reinforces the Key Terms used in Chapter 31.

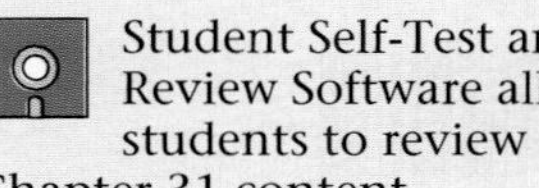

Student Self-Test and Review Software allows students to review Chapter 31 content.

CONDENSE

Have students read the Chapter 31 Highlights.

Have students listen to the Chapter 31 Audiocassettes in the TCR. Spanish Audiocassettes are also available.

Assign the Chapter 31 Audiocassette Activity and give students the Chapter 31 Audiocassette Quiz.

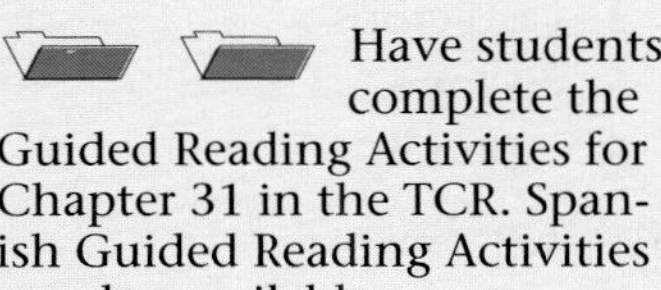

Have students complete the Guided Reading Activities for Chapter 31 in the TCR. Spanish Guided Reading Activities are also available.

RETEACH

Have students complete Reteaching Activity 31 in the TCR. Spanish Reteaching Activities are also available.

Map Activity

Identify and Locate Distribute copies of the map on page 34 of the Outline Map Resource Book. Using the Atlas map on pages A22–A23, have students place and identify the following on their outline maps: Strait of Malacca, Manila, Chao Phraya River, Bangkok, Mekong River, and Jakarta.

GLENCOE TECHNOLOGY

Videodisc

Use Chapter 31 MindJogger Videoquiz to review students' knowledge before administering the Chapter 31 Test.

MINDJOGGER VIDEOQUIZ

Chapter 31
Disc 4 Side B

The MindJogger Videoquiz is also available on videocassette.

ANSWERS

Reviewing Key Terms

1. interdependent
2. sickles
3. free port
4. cash crops
5. cyclone
6. typhoon

Reviewing Facts

7. rice
8. its good location and good harbors
9. to promote tourism in member countries
10. 900 people died, 100,000 homes were destroyed, and in the next three months 40,000 more people became homeless
11. because the city is built on unstable land
12. by using a numbering system that includes the last two digits of the year and a number to designate which storm of the year is being watched

chapter 31 REVIEW

Reviewing Key Terms

Choose the vocabulary term that best completes each of the sentences below. Write your answers on a separate sheet of paper.

sickles (p. 629)
cash crops (p. 630)
interdependent (p. 632)
free port (p. 633)
cyclone (p. 636)
typhoon (p. 636)

SECTION 1

1. Some Southeast Asian countries have become more ____ as a result of regional development and trade organizations.
2. Southeast Asian farmers harvest their crops with simple hand tools, such as ____.
3. The ____ of Singapore is a leading center of trade in Southeast Asia.
4. Rubber, coconuts, palm oil, and spices are ____ exported from Southeast Asia.

SECTION 2

5. The term ____ means "coil."
6. A ____ is a tropical storm located in the Pacific area.

Reviewing Facts

SECTION 1

7. What is the most important agricultural product in Southeast Asia?
8. What factors have led to Singapore's development as an important port and manufacturing center?
9. What is a major goal of the Association of Southeast Asian Nations (ASEAN)?

SECTION 2

10. What impact did the eruption of Mount Pinatubo have on the Philippines?
11. Why is Bangkok's flooding problem getting worse?
12. How do Asian meteorologists designate different typhoons?

Critical Thinking

13. **Predicting Consequences** Brunei reportedly has enough oil reserves to last until 2018. What might happen to other economies in the region if Brunei's oil runs out?
14. **Analyzing Information** How does living within the Ring of Fire affect daily life for many Southeast Asians?

Geographic Themes

15. **Movement** Why have many foreign countries moved their manufacturing and assembly plants to Southeast Asia?
16. **Human/Environment Interaction** What have humans done in Southeast Asia that increases the danger and damages from flooding?

Practicing Skills

Understanding Time Zones

Refer to the Understanding Time Zones skills feature on page 640.

If you take a noon flight from New York to Paris, what time will it be in Paris when you land six hours later?

Using the Unit Atlas

Refer to the physical geography section of the Unit Atlas on pages 592–593.

17. What natural resources have brought wealth to Brunei?
18. What environmental factor accounts for the fertile soil in Indonesia?

Critical Thinking

13. Answers will vary but may include that those economies that relied on Brunei's oil would suffer recession or depression, or that the economies of countries with oil reserves would prosper.
14. The people have to cope with the threat of volcanic activity.

Geographic Themes

15. because of cheap and abundant labor
16. Because some forest land has been cleared, storms cause extensive runoff damage and mud slides that would not have occurred otherwise.

Projects

Individual Activity

You have learned about some environmental hazards in Southeast Asia. Research one type of hazard (such as volcanoes or typhoons) and write a brief report telling what the dangers are and what is being done to safeguard people and property.

Cooperative Learning Activity

Work in groups of four with each student representing one of the following countries: Thailand, Cambodia, Vietnam, and Singapore. Organize a presentation for the United Nations on whether or not Cambodia, Laos, and Vietnam should be allowed to join ASEAN. Think about why it would be advantageous or a problem for your country. Your stand on the issue should be presented to the other group members. In conclusion, each group may present its recommendation to the class as a whole.

Writing About Geography

Classification

Southeast Asians face a number of environmental problems that could be grouped in a variety of ways. Using your journal record as a reference, think about several ways to divide the environmental problems into groups or categories. Then write a short essay explaining and defending your classification system. Tell why the way you have grouped the environmental problems is useful or instructive.

Locating Places

SOUTHEAST ASIA: PHYSICAL GEOGRAPHY

Match the letters on the map with the places and physical features of Southeast Asia. Write your answers on a separate sheet of paper.

1. Bangkok
2. Philippines
3. Singapore
4. Bali
5. Jakarta
6. Strait of Malacca
7. Mekong River
8. Gulf of Thailand
9. Indian Ocean
10. Chao Phraya River

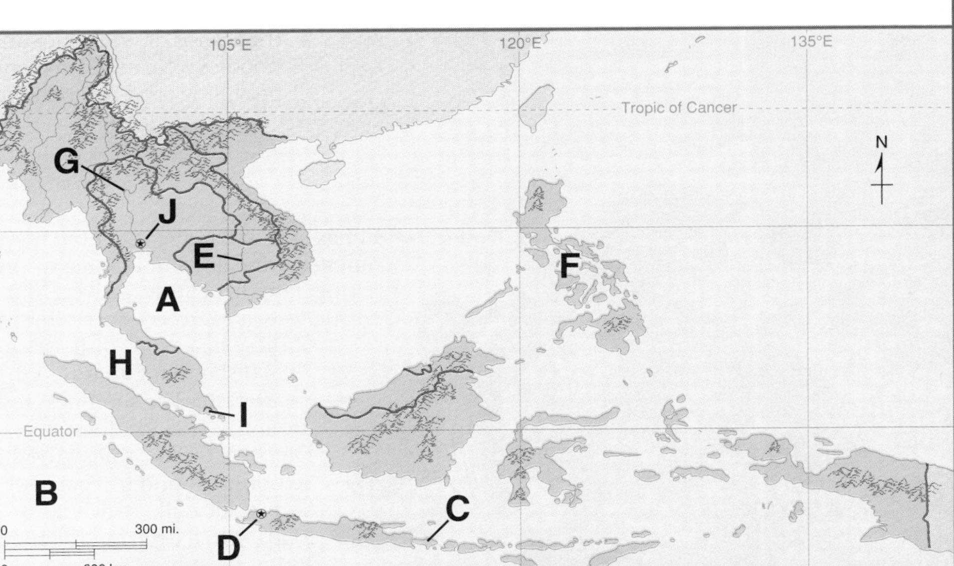

Chapter 31 Review

Practicing Skills

11:00 P.M.

Using the Unit Atlas

17. natural gas, petroleum

18. volcanoes

Locating Places

1. J
2. F
3. I
4. C
5. D
6. H
7. E
8. A
9. B
10. G

Chapter Bonus Test Question

This question may be used for extra credit on the chapter test.

Water has played a major role in the development of Southeast Asia, yet threatens the people who live there. Give examples to support both effects of water.

(Answer: An abundant water supply and wet climate are needed to grow rice. The waterways and harbors are used for international trading and transportation. Heavy rains, flash floods, typhoons, and mud slides are threats people of the region face.)

Geography Connection

FOCUS

Ask students to share any experiences they have had with Thai or Vietnamese cooking. Encourage them to compare the look of their cuisine with the photographs.

TEACH

L1 Location Use Unit Map Overlay Transparency 10-4 to familiarize students with the locations of Vietnam, Thailand, and China.

L2 Analyze Have students analyze the meals shown in the photographs to see if they meet U.S. recommended nutritional standards.

L3 Research Have students find out more about the way Thai and Vietnamese food is served and eaten. Have students compare their information with the way American meals are served.

GEOGRAPHY CONNECTION

Southeast Asia and the United States

SOUTHEAST ASIAN DINING

In the 1840s many Chinese people emigrated to Southeast Asian countries, where Chinese influence was already strong. Other Chinese emigrants went to the United States, taking their unique foods and cooking methods. These have become as popular as New England Yankee pot roast and apple pie.

Since the 1960s immigrants and refugees from Thailand and Vietnam have made the United States their home. They, too, have brought their cuisines, which also reflect the influence of the Chinese.

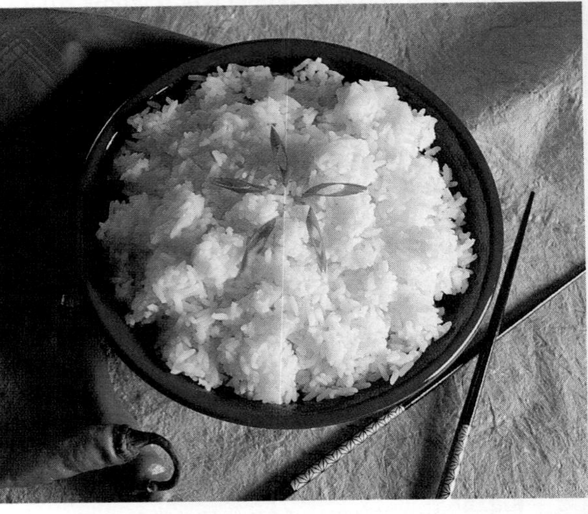

▲ **RICE OR NOODLES** is the most basic ingredient in Chinese, Thai, and Vietnamese cooking. Rice has been a staple food in Southeast Asia and China for thousands of years. Rice and noodles were excellent ways of providing food inexpensively.

◀ **THAI COOKING** has been strongly influenced by Chinese cuisine. It combines flavors in daring, tantalizing ways—sweet and sour, salty and sweet—sometimes all of these in a single dish. Many Thai dishes have an unusual, sharp taste. The sharpness results from the Thai fondness for lemon grass and chilis. Another seasoning found in Thai cooking is coconut milk, which laces foods with a delicate sweetness during steaming.

UNIT 10

Making the Connection

Examine Have students study Southeast Asian and Chinese cookbooks, looking for differences and similarities. Have them make lists of spices, meats, vegetables, and fruits that seem to be characteristic of each cuisine. Encourage students to find out about any foods or spices with which they are unfamiliar by visiting local neighborhood supermarkets. Interested students may wish to prepare a dish or two from each cuisine for the class to sample.

◀ **THE CANTONESE STYLE** of Chinese food is familiar to most Americans, because most of the Chinese who emigrated to the United States came from the southern Chinese city of Canton, now known as Guangzhou. Chinese cooking is also popular in urban centers of Southeast Asia that have large Chinese communities.

VIETNAMESE FOOD ▶ reflects a number of influences, the strongest of which is Chinese. Vietnamese dishes can be spicy, although not so hot as Thai. Also, many dishes often seem like salads to Americans because they are served with large platters of lettuces, fresh herbs, and raw vegetables, such as beans, sprouts, carrots, and cucumbers.

▼ **FISH** is a favorite item on Vietnamese and Thai menus. A standard Vietnamese dish is *nuoc mam,* a clear, salty golden sauce made from fish or shrimp. Thai and Vietnamese dinners may also include other fish dishes, such as eel soup, seafood pancakes, and grilled shrimp balls.

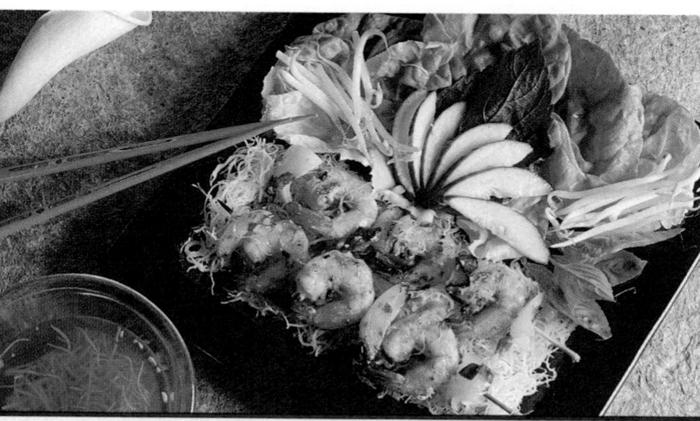

Checking for Understanding

1. Why are Chinese, Thai, and Vietnamese cuisines similar?
2. **Movement** Which Southeast Asian cuisine would best fit into your daily diet? Why?

Geography Connection

ASSESS

Have students answer the Checking for Understanding questions on page 645.

CLOSE

Ask students to discuss how color combination and presentation adds to the appeal of the food.

DID YOU KNOW?

Archaeologists have discovered pots containing grains of rice that date back to 5000 B.C.

ANSWERS TO CHECKING FOR UNDERSTANDING

1. China once ruled the areas that are now Thailand and Vietnam. Large numbers of ethnic Chinese have always lived in Thailand and Vietnam, and have had great influence on the Thai and Vietnamese cultures.
2. Answers will vary.

UNIT OVERVIEW

The three chapters that comprise this unit introduce students to the physical geography and peoples of Australia, Oceania, and Antarctica.

GEOGRAPHY JOURNAL

Activity Besides the sources listed, urge students to read travel guides and magazines in particular. Encourage students to note opinions that are presented as facts as well as any "loaded" words. As students work through the unit, alert them to look for facts that might or might not disprove advertisement claims. Suggest that they also highlight appealing and appropriate descriptive language.

At the unit's close, have students create their own advertisements for the region that are factual as well as strongly appealing.

• This journal activity provides the basis for the "Writing About Geography" exercise in the Chapter Review.

• The Geography Journal may be used as an integral part of Performance Assessment.

GLENCOE TECHNOLOGY

Videodisc

REUTERS ISSUES IN GEOGRAPHY

Chapter 10
Disc 1 Side A

Title: ***Antarctica: The Ozone Hole***

Subject: Physical characteristics and early exploration of Antarctica, as well as current issues affecting Antarctica and the global environment

UNIT 11

Australia, Oceania, and Antarctica

© R. Ian Lloyd

GeoJournal Activity

While studying Australia, Oceania, and Antarctica, check for travel or other kinds of advertisements either on television or in newspapers and magazines. List any that mention the places, people, cultures, and economies of the region. Write your impressions on each advertisement: How does it present the region? Do you agree or disagree with its viewpoints?

646

Where in the World . . . .

Have students look at the map on pages A24–A25 of their texts in which Australia, New Zealand, and Oceania are highlighted. Display Unit Map Overlay Transparency 11-5 and ask students the following questions: What body of water dominates this region? *(Pacific Ocean)* What seas separate Australia from Southeast Asia? *(Timor, Arafura)* From the South Pacific Islands? *(Coral Sea)* From New Zealand? *(Tasman Sea)* What appears to be Australia's outstanding physical feature? *(desert interior)* Antarctica's? *(total isolation from rest of the world)* What geographic feature might give the South Pacific islands warm, tropical climates? *(the islands' location around the Equator)*

Picturing the World

Symbol of the outback and sacred to Aborigines, Uluru, or Ayers Rock, bulges above the plains of Australia's vast Northern Territory. Uluru, the world's largest sandstone monolith, stands 1,142 feet (348 m) high in the middle of two million square miles of flat outback desert. Australia has a wide range of vegetation, from tropical rain forests to desert scrub. Look at the map on page 662.

1. What is the dominant vegetation of Australia?
2. Read to learn about the climate and vegetation of Australia. What geographic factor contributes to this vegetation?

Picture Atlas CD-ROM Enrichment Corner

Many indigenous peoples still live in Oceania. Create a file on these indigenous peoples. (See the *Picture Atlas of the World* User's Guide on how to use the Collector button.) Include the video for Australia and the following photographs: Aboriginal father and daughter in Australia; Huli wigmen and pig hunters in Papua New Guinea; Maori boy in New Zealand getting his face painted; fishers and mother in feathers in Vanuatu; dancers and shoppers in Micronesia; stone dancers and ceremonial drinkers in Fiji. Using these various indigenous groups as topics, create electronic reports and present your reports to the class.

647

interNET CONNECTIONS

The Australia–New Zealand Studies Center at Penn State is an excellent place to start looking for information about the Pacific islands.

World Wide Web
http://www.psu.edu/research/anzsc/areas/Pacifici.html

CD-ROM

PICTURE ATLAS OF THE WORLD
See page T45 for an additional CD-ROM activity to enrich Unit 11.

0:00 OUT OF TIME?

If time does not permit teaching each chapter in the unit, you may use the Chapter Highlights and the Audiocassettes that include a 1-page activity and a 1-page test for each chapter.

ANSWERS TO PICTURING THE WORLD

1. Desert scrub and desert waste are the dominant vegetation of Australia.
2. Subtropical high-pressure air masses above central Australia block moisture-bearing Pacific Ocean winds from reaching large areas of the continent.

These features and activities may be used as an introduction to the unit or as teaching tools throughout the course of the unit.

FOCUS

Ask students to study the maps on pages A24–A25 of their texts for a moment, then formulate generalizations about the region's population and culture.

TEACH

Location/Culture From the information on the map, have students create a chart listing each country and the nation that colonized it. Ask students to suggest challenges that colonization might have presented for both the country or island that was colonized, as well as for the colonizing nation.

Implement Foods Around the World 10 as a class activity.

Have students complete the Political Map Transparency 11 Activity in the TCR.

Have students complete Unit Atlas Activity 11B in the TCR.

Have students complete World Cultures Transparencies 19 and 20 in the TCR.

UNIT 11 ATLAS

AUSTRALIA, OCEANIA,

Cultural Geography

EXPLORING CULTURAL DIVERSITY

1. *What areas of Australia, Oceania, and Antarctica are most heavily populated? Most sparsely populated?*
2. *What countries make up Australia, Oceania, and Antarctica?*

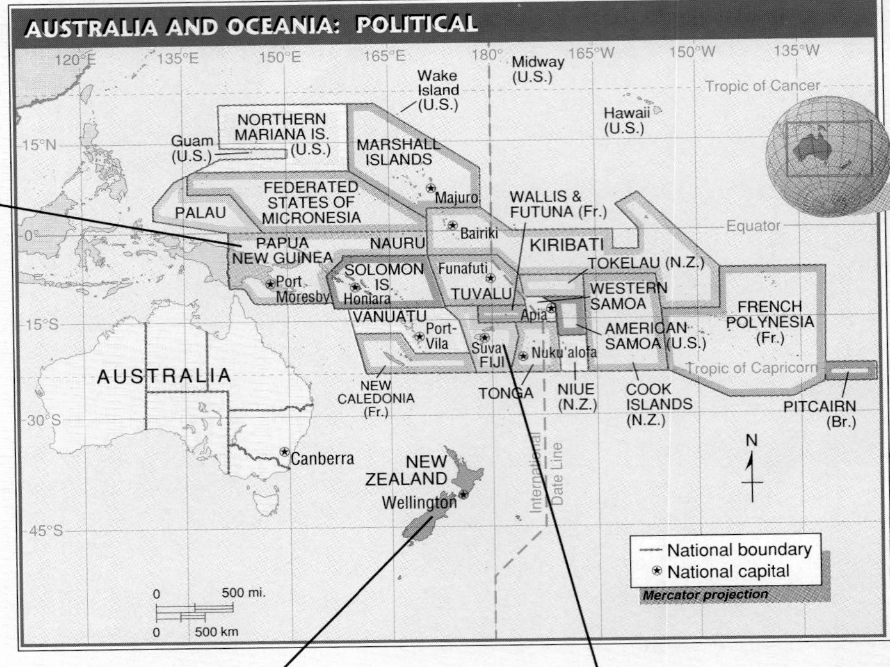

Hundreds of languages are spoken on the Pacific Islands; Papua New Guinea alone has more than 700.

Oceania's population is made up of three main ethnic groups: Melanesian, Micronesian, and Polynesian.

A little more than 90 percent of all New Zealanders are descended from European settlers. The rest are Maori, descendants of New Zealand's first settlers.

Forty-five percent of Fiji's population is of Melanesian descent; 55 percent are descendants of laborers imported from India.

Classroom Resources for Unit 7

BLACKLINE MASTERS:
Geography Simulation 11
Environmental Issue 11
Foods Around the World 10

TRANSPARENCIES:
Unit Map Overlay Transparency 10
Political Map Transparency 11
World Cultures Transparencies 19, 20

MULTIMEDIA:
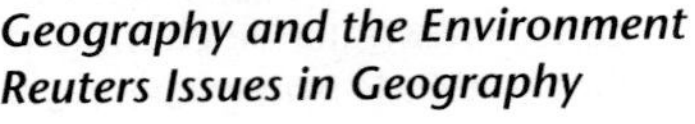
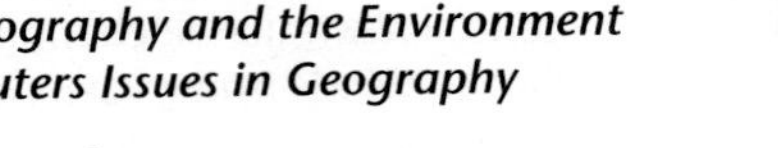
Geography and the Environment
Reuters Issues in Geography

Testmaker

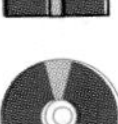
Picture Atlas of the World

Images of the World Poster Set

Australia has about 18 million people. If Australians were evenly spread out across the continent, there would be only 6 persons to every square mile (2 per sq. km). Indeed most of Australia's people crowd into the southeastern corner of the continent.

About three-fourths of all New Zealanders live on **North Island.** About 80 percent of **New Zealand's** population are city dwellers.

Nauru, Tuvalu, and **the Marshall Islands** are the most densely populated island areas of Oceania.

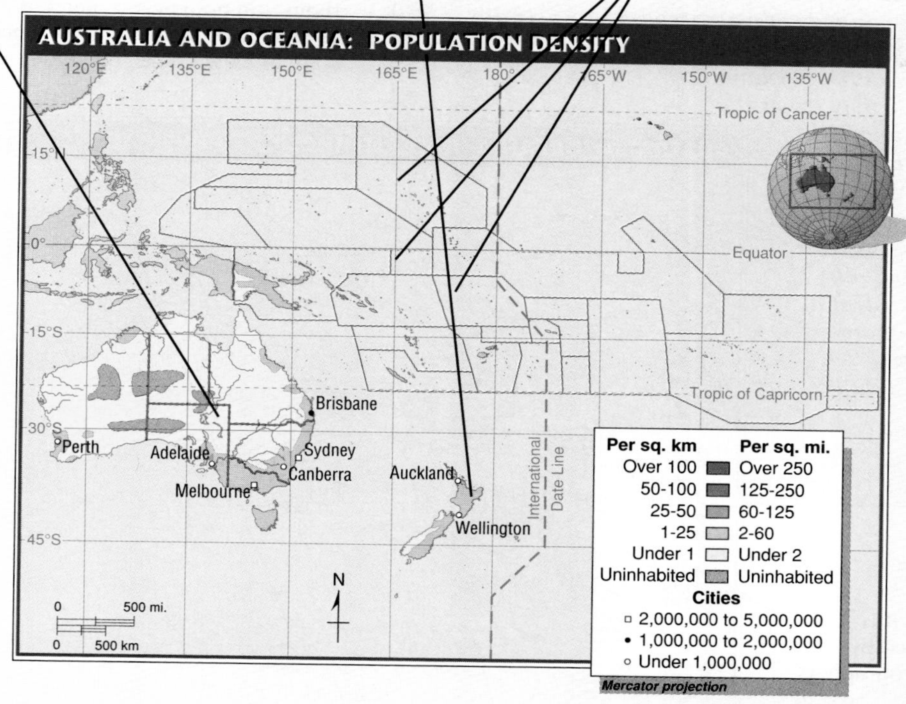

The United States has more than 11 times as many people as Australia, Oceania, and Antarctica.

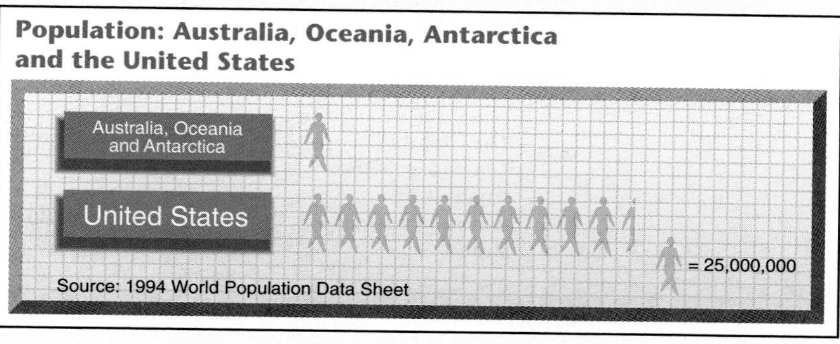

Map and Graph Activity

Regions Using these maps, as well as those on pages A24–A25, have students suggest various countries and routes that early migrants could have taken to settle this region. Have them also speculate what kinds of technology early settlers would have needed to move from the mainland to the islands and from island to island.

Have the class compose an acceptable summary that includes predicted routes and technology. Then have students research to find if their speculations were on target.

LESSON PLAN
Unit 11 Atlas

DID YOU KNOW?

Every piece of land in this world region has been a colony at one time or another. In fact, some remain colonies today.

ASSESS

Have students answer the Exploring Cultural Diversity questions on page 648.

EXPLORING CULTURAL DIVERSITY

This feature may be used to introduce students to the cultural geography of Australia, Oceania, and Antarctica. Use questions to stimulate class discussion and help students become familiar with the region. Accept reasonable answers based on the maps, graph, and captions.

CLOSE

Encourage students to consider cultural challenges presented to the region's ethnic inhabitants by the arrival of Europeans. Ask them also to speculate on what the cultural atmosphere is probably like now.

CD-ROM

PICTURE ATLAS OF THE WORLD

You and your students can learn about the physical features, music, economy, and population of Australia, New Zealand, and Oceania by clicking on these countries.

These features and activities may be used as an introduction to the unit or as teaching tools throughout the course of the unit.

FOCUS

To introduce students to the physical geography of Australia, Oceania, and Antarctica, have students complete Unit Map Overlay Transparency 11 Activity in the TCR.

TEACH

Location The South Pacific islands were one of the last places to be settled by early humankind, and the last places to be discovered during the Great Age of Exploration in the sixteenth and seventeenth centuries. Have students analyze why this was so, using the maps on pages 650–651.

GLENCOE TECHNOLOGY

Videodisc

Use the following to introduce or enrich Unit 11:

GEOGRAPHY AND THE ENVIRONMENT
THE INFINITE VOYAGE
Secrets of a Frozen World

Chapter 1
Disc 2 Side B

Title: ***The Southern Ocean—A Rich Marine Ecosystem***

UNIT 11 ATLAS

AUSTRALIA, OCEANIA, Physical Geography

CHARTING YOUR COURSE

1. ***What body of water separates Australia and New Zealand?***
2. ***What large island lies north of Australia's Cape York Peninsula?***
3. ***What are three natural resources found in Australia, Oceania, and New Zealand?***

All the islands of Oceania—some 20,000 to 30,000 of them—do not cover as much land as the state of Alaska. The islands of New Zealand and New Guinea make up 80 percent of Oceania's total land area.

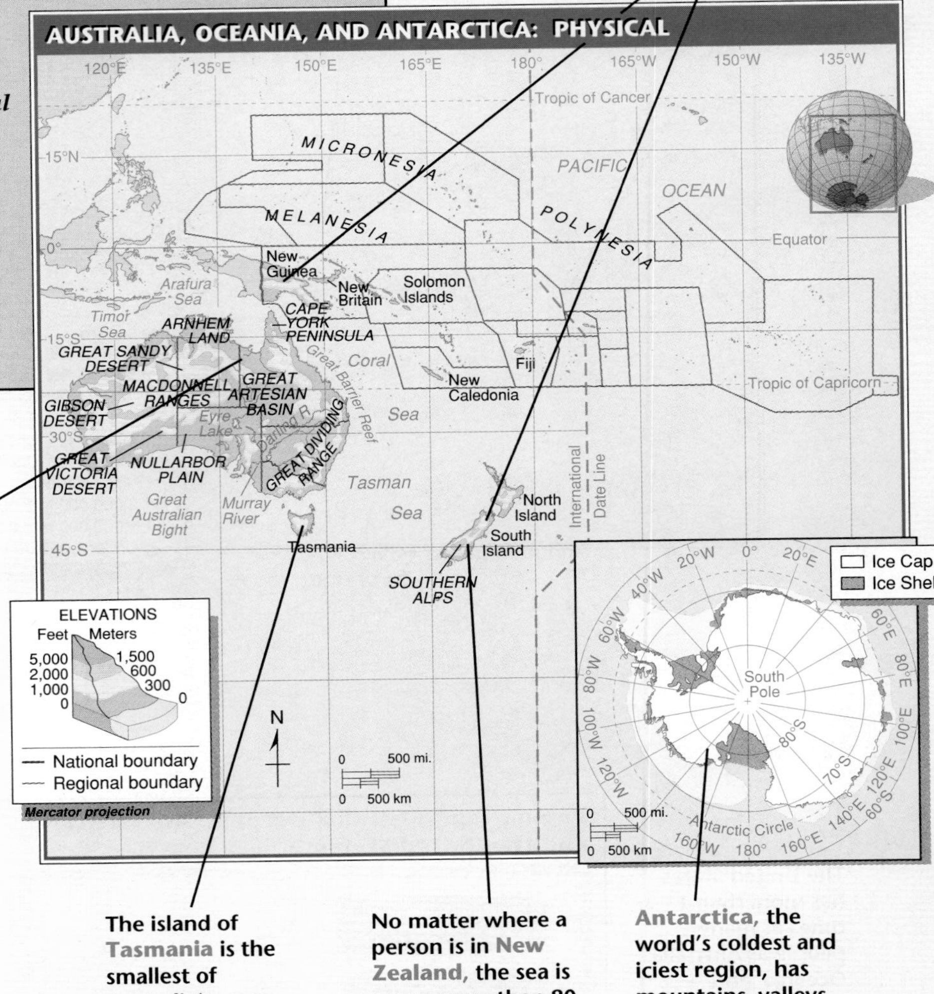

Although it is surrounded by water, geographers classify Australia as a continent rather than an island because of its great size.

The island of Tasmania is the smallest of Australia's seven states.

No matter where a person is in New Zealand, the sea is never more than 80 miles (129 km) away.

Antarctica, the world's coldest and iciest region, has mountains, valleys, and lowlands under its ice cap.

Map Activity

Geography/Economy Have students consider how these geographic characteristics affect the countries in this region: the huge expanse of ocean, the scattered state and small size of the South Pacific islands, the lack of farming land in the region, with the exception of New Zealand. Have students put their speculations in their journals, then research briefly in appropriate sources to find information that supports or contradicts their speculations.

Australia leads the world in the production of lead and bauxite.

About three-fourths of Fiji's exports are sugar, coconut products, and gold.

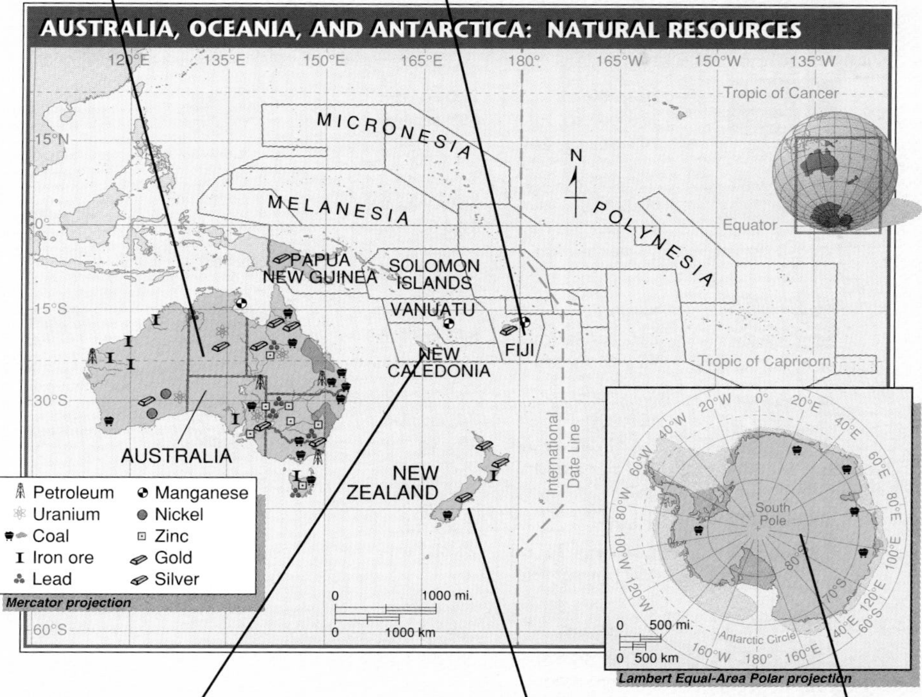

The island of New Caledonia has valuable nickel deposits.

About 55 percent of New Zealand's land—its greatest natural resource—is crop or pastureland. About 25 percent is forests that provide valuable timber.

Scientists hope to find ways to use Antarctica's ice cap as a freshwater source.

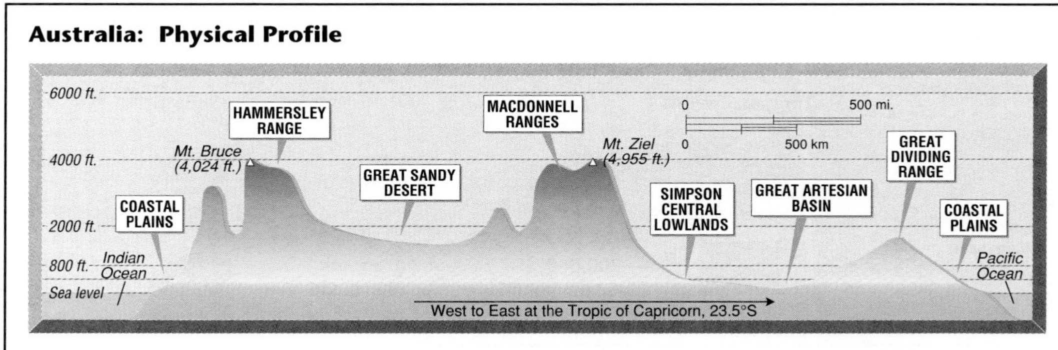

LESSON PLAN Unit 11 Atlas

Have students complete the Unit 11 Geography Simulation found in the TCR.

Have students complete Unit Atlas Activity 11A in the TCR.

ASSESS

Have students answer the Charting Your Course questions on page 650.

CHARTING YOUR COURSE

This feature may be used to introduce students to the physical geography of Australia, Oceania, and Antarctica. Use questions to stimulate class discussion and help students become familiar with the region. Accept reasonable answers based on the maps, graph, and captions.

CLOSE

Ask students to comment on the geographic aspect of the region that strikes them as most interesting. Encourage them to explain their choices.

DID YOU KNOW?

Australia is a major producer of coal, copper, iron ore, nickel, manganese, tin, titanium, tungsten, zinc, and zircon. Its mines bring up large quantities of gold, silver, and diamonds. Australian mines also produce most of the world's high-quality opals.

Map Activity

Place Some people view the South Pacific islands as paradise. Allow students to choose a group of islands and research travel guides, almanacs, and other suitable sources to learn what attracts visitors to the South Pacific islands. Encourage them also to find out what percentage of the islands' economy is based on tourism, as well as the effects of tourism on the islands. Have students note the information in their journals, and/or allow a sharing time. Ask students whether or not they agree with the general opinion of the islands; have them explain their reasons.

LESSON PLAN
Unit 11 Atlas

These features and activities may be used as teaching tools throughout the course of the unit.

DID YOU KNOW?

About 1 percent of Australia's population are Aborigines, descendants of Australia's first settlers. Ancestors of the Aborigines migrated from Asia thousands of years ago.

Ways of the World

FIJI Fijians usually smile and raise an eyebrow upward or nod to greet each other.

Ways of the World

NEW ZEALAND Dinner guests in New Zealand always take a gift: flowers, a potted plant, a box of chocolates. House guests also leave a gift with their host family.

Ways of the World

FIJI A *bure,* the traditional Fiji home, is one large room built of local hardwoods, a tightly-thatched roof, and woven floor coverings. The four doors, one in each wall, are usually kept open for circulation. A bure has little, if any furniture: Fijians don't consider it necessary.

UNIT 11 ATLAS

COUNTRY PROFILE

COUNTRY* AND CAPITAL	FLAG AND LANGUAGES	POPULATION	LANDMASS	PRINCIPAL PRODUCTS EXPORT	IMPORT
Australia Canberra	English, Aboriginal languages	17,800,000 6 per sq. mi. 2 per sq. km	2,941,290 sq. mi. 7,617,941 sq. km	Crude Oil	Machinery
FEDERATED STATES OF Micronesia Kolonia	English	100,000 370 per sq. mi. 143 per sq. km	270 sq. mi. 699 sq. km	Copra	Food
Fiji Suva	English, Fijian, Hindi	800,000 113 per sq. mi. 44 per sq. km	7,050 sq. mi. 18,260 sq. km	Sugar	Machinery
Kiribati Bairiki	English, Gilbertese	76,900 246 per sq. mi. 95 per sq. km	313 sq. mi. 811 sq. km	Copra	Machinery
Marshall Islands Majuro	English, Marshallese, Japanese	100,000 1,429 per sq. mi. 552 per sq. km	70 sq. mi. 181 sq. km	Coconut Oil	Food
Nauru Yaren	Nauruan, English	9,460 1,183 per sq. mi. 450 per sq. km	8 sq. mi. 21 sq. km	Phosphates	Food
New Zealand Wellington	English, Maori	3,500,000 33 per sq. mi. 13 per sq. km	103,470 sq. mi. 267,987 sq. km	Food	Petroleum
Papua New Guinea Port Moresby	English, Melanesian, Papuan languages	4,000,000 22 per sq. mi. 8 per sq. km	174,850 sq. mi. 452,862 sq. km	Gold	Machinery
Solomon Islands Honiara	Melanesian, English, Papuan, Polynesian languages	400,000 37 per sq. mi. 14 per sq. km	10,810 sq. mi. 27,998 sq. km	Fish	Machinery
Tonga Nuku'alofa	Tongan, English	99,100 329 per sq. mi. 127 per sq. km	301 sq. mi. 780 sq. km	Squash	Food
Tuvalu Funafuti	Tuvaluan, English	9,500 1,056 per sq. mi. 396 per sq. km	9 sq. mi. 24 sq. km	Copra	Food
Vanuatu Port Vila	English, French, Bislama	200,000 42 per sq. mi. 16 per sq. km	4,710 sq. mi. 12,199 sq. km	Copra	Machinery

*Country maps not drawn to scale.

Country Profile Activity

Geography Organize students into three groups. Assign each group a set of islands, and have each student in a group choose a particular island to study. Using information from a variety of appropriate sources, have students create political, cultural, and economic profiles for their island in their journals. Then have each group form generalizations—and exceptions—about their set of islands. Have each group present their generalizations, then record and display them in an appropriate place to reread and check as they work through the unit.

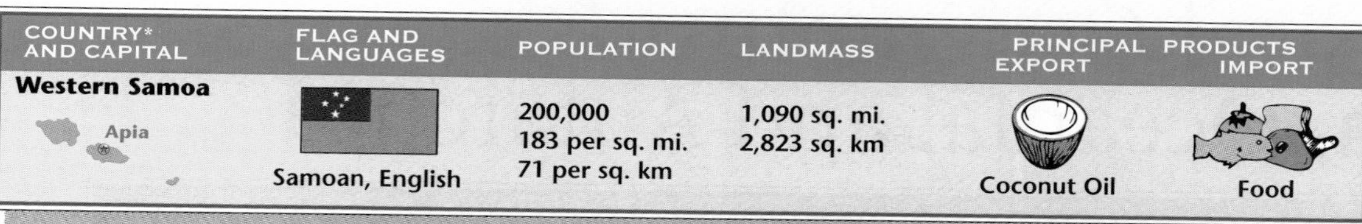

COUNTRY* AND CAPITAL	FLAG AND LANGUAGES	POPULATION	LANDMASS	PRINCIPAL PRODUCTS EXPORT	PRINCIPAL PRODUCTS IMPORT
Western Samoa Apia	Samoan, English	200,000 183 per sq. mi. 71 per sq. km	1,090 sq. mi. 2,823 sq. km	Coconut Oil	Food

*Country maps not drawn to scale.

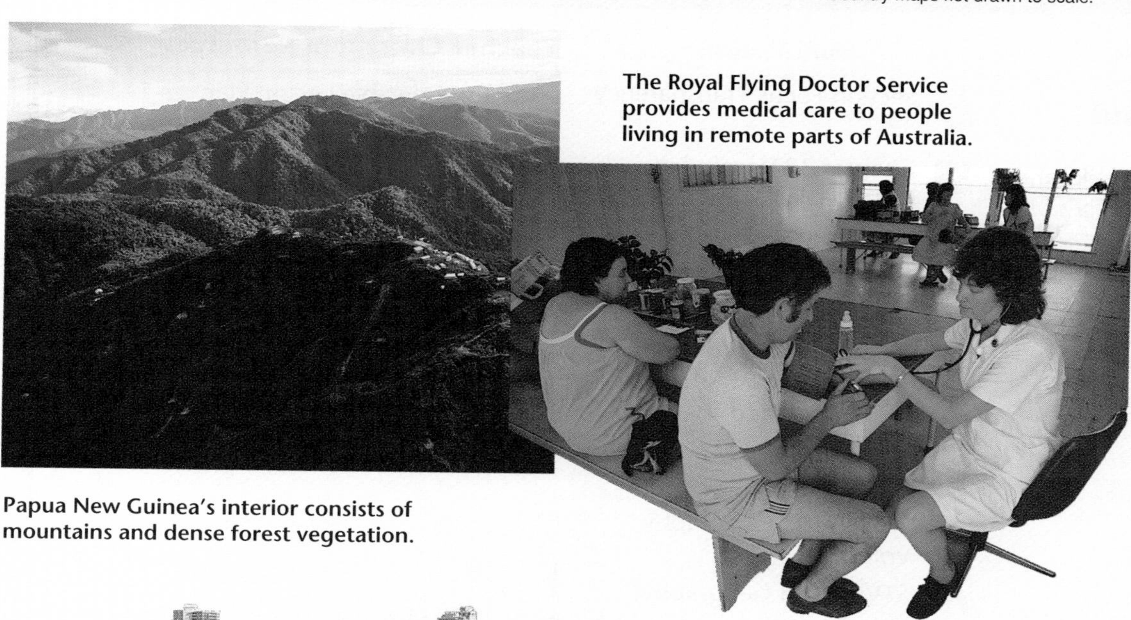

The Royal Flying Doctor Service provides medical care to people living in remote parts of Australia.

Papua New Guinea's interior consists of mountains and dense forest vegetation.

Modern hotels and beaches line the coast of northeast Australia.

DID YOU KNOW?

The island of Tahiti is one of an island group called the Society Islands. The Society Islands, in turn, are part of the island groups that comprise French Polynesia.

Global Gourmet

Australians are famous for their home entertaining. One of their favorite family-and-friends-festivities is the backyard *barby,* or barbecue. Like their American counterparts, Australian barbecuers grill a variety of meats, fish, and vegetables for delectable dining.

Ways of the World

SAMOA In Samoa, it is impolite to speak to someone in a home while standing.

Ways of the World

SOUTH PACIFIC ISLANDS When visiting the homes of any of the islands' ethnic groups, a guest expresses general admiration and appreciation of the host's home or family. Guests avoid admiring a specific item, however: the host will be made to feel duty-bound to offer the item as a gift.

Country Profile Activity

Geography Assign a country to pairs of students. Using the maps and graphs on the previous four pages, have them compose geographic facts using the information presented in the chart or photographs and supported or expanded by information from a map(s) or graph(s) from the previous four pages. Example: Australia's principal export is crude oil. Deposits are located off the continent's southeastern shore, the northeastern coastal region, and the northwestern coast.

CHAPTER 32

PLANNING GUIDE

The Physical Geography of Australia, Oceania, and Antarctica

CHAPTER ORGANIZER

Daily Lesson Objectives	Multimedia	Teacher Classroom Resources
SECTION 1 The Land 1. Locate the mammoth rocks and endless deserts of Australia's interior. 2. Describe the volcanic mountains and coral reefs of the Pacific islands. 3. Explain the icy landscape and ice cap climate of Antarctica.	Section Focus Transparency 32-1 Chapter 32 Vocabulary PuzzleMaker Software Political Map Transparency 11 Unit Map Overlay Transparencies 11, 11-4, 11-5 Geography and the Environment Testmaker STV: World Geography, Volume 1 STV: World Geography, Volume 3 Picture Atlas of the World	Reproducible Lesson Plan 32-1 Geography Simulation 11 Guided Reading Activity 32-1 Spanish Guided Reading Activity 32-1 Workbook Activity 32-1 Performance Assessment Activity 32 Vocabulary Activity 32 Section Quiz 32-1
SECTION 2 The Climate and Vegetation 1. Locate the climate regions of Australia, Oceania, and Antarctica. 2. Identify the vegetation patterns of Australia, Oceania, and Antarctica.	Section Focus Transparency 32-2 Unit Map Overlay Transparencies 11-2 and 11-3 Geography and the Environment Testmaker STV: World Geography, Volume 1 STV: World Geography, Volume 3 Physical Geography of the World Transparencies 71–80	Reproducible Lesson Plan 32-2 Guided Reading Activity 32-2 Spanish Guided Reading Activity 32-2 Workbook Activity 32-2 Enrichment Activity 32-2 Skill Activity 32 Section Quiz 32-2
CHAPTER REVIEW AND EVALUATION	Chapter 32 English (or Spanish) Audiocassettes MindJogger Videoquiz Testmaker Student Self-Test and Review Software	Reteaching Activity 32 Spanish Reteaching Activity 32 Chapter 32 Test Form A and Form B

0:00 *If time does not permit teaching the entire chapter, summarize using the Chapter 32 Highlights on page 665, and the Chapter 32 English (or Spanish) Audiocassettes. Review students' knowledge using the Glencoe MindJogger Videoquiz.*

KEY TO ABILITY LEVELS

Teaching strategies have been coded for varying learning styles and abilities.

L1 **BASIC** activities for all students

L2 **AVERAGE** activities for average to above-average students

L3 **CHALLENGING** activities for above-average students

LEP **LIMITED ENGLISH PROFICIENCY** activities

Performance Assessment

Synthesizing Information Have students complete a creative task using data on the physical geography of Australia, Oceania, and Antarctica. Groups of students should form hypothetical ad agencies. Each agency should put together a campaign to attract both visitors and immigrants to the region. Included in the campaigns may be television commercials, travel brochures, magazine or newspaper ads, and so on. Roles within groups may be assigned to best suit individual talents. The persuasive aspects of the campaign must demonstrate knowledge of both the positive and negative effects of physical features, climate, and vegetation on human activity.

The task should also include the Chapter 32 skills activity "Interpreting Routes on a Map" on page 664. Students should use the transportation data in this activity and other sources to further develop their persuasive cases. Campaigns should be presented to the class as a "client" audience.

POSSIBLE RUBRIC FEATURES: Content information, creativity and persuasive effect of campaigns, collaboration skills

For additional professional and classroom resources, see Chapter Resources, pages T46–T51.

TEACHER'S CORNER

NATIONAL GEOGRAPHIC SOCIETY

INDEX TO NATIONAL GEOGRAPHIC MAGAZINE

The following articles may be used for research relating to this chapter:

- "Wildflowers of Western Australia," by Cary Wolinsky, January 1995.
- "The Simpson Outback," by Jane Vessels, April 1992.
- "Australia's Magnificent Pearls," by David Doubilet, December 1991.
- "New Zealand's Magic Waters," by David Doubilet, October 1989.
- "Australia's Southern Seas: A Cold, Rich World Beneath the Southern Cross," by Richard Ellis, March 1987.
- "The Land Where the Murray Flows," by Louise E. Levathes, August 1985.
- "Monsoons: Life Breath of Half the World," by Priit J. Vesilind, December 1984.
- "A Walk and Ride on the Wild Side," by Carolyn Bennett Patterson, May 1983.

NATIONAL GEOGRAPHIC SOCIETY PRODUCTS AVAILABLE FROM GLENCOE

To order the following products for use with this chapter, contact your local Glencoe sales representative or call Glencoe at 1-800-334-7344:

- *Picture Atlas of the World* (CD-ROM)
- *STV: World Geography, South America and Antarctica* (Videodisc)
- *STV: World Geography, Asia and Australia* (Videodisc)
- *ZipZapMap! World* (Software)
- *GeoBee* (Software)
- *Images of the World* (Posters)
- *Eye on the Environment* (Posters)
- *Physical Geography of the World* (Transparencies)
- *Picture Atlas of Our 50 States* (Book)

ADDITIONAL NATIONAL GEOGRAPHIC SOCIETY PRODUCTS

To order the following products for use with this chapter, call National Geographic Society at 1-800-368-2728:

- *Nations of the World Series*, "Australia." (Video)

Introducing
CHAPTER 32

PERFORMANCE ASSESSMENT

Refer to the Planning Guide on page 654B for a Performance Assessment Activity for this chapter. See the *Performance Assessment Activities* booklet for additional suggestions.

CHAPTER OBJECTIVES

1. **Realize** that Australia and Antarctica are mostly flat plateaus at both high and low elevations.
2. **Describe** how winds from the Pacific Ocean bring the island country of New Zealand moist and warm air in the winter and cool breezes in the summer.

GLENCOE TECHNOLOGY

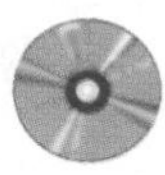

Videodisc

Use Chapter 32 MindJogger Videoquiz to preview chapter content.

MINDJOGGER VIDEOQUIZ

Chapter 32
Disc 4 Side B

The MindJogger Videoquiz is also available on videocassette.

CD-ROM

PICTURE ATLAS OF THE WORLD

Have students click the "Photos" and "Essay" buttons of Australia, New Zealand, and Pacific islands to view and read about the physical features of this region.

chapter 32 The Physical Geography of Australia, Oceania, and Antarctica

CHAPTER FOCUS

Geographic Setting

The culture region of Australia, Oceania, and Antarctica contains the two continents of Antarctica and Australia as well as thousands of islands of varying size in the Pacific Ocean.

Geographic Themes

Section 1 The Land

PLACE Australia and Antarctica are mostly flat plateaus at both high and low elevations.

▲ Photograph: *Harbor in French Polynesia*

Section 2 The Climate and Vegetation

LOCATION Winds from the Pacific Ocean bring the island country of New Zealand moist warm air in the winter and cool breezes in the summer.

EXTRA CREDIT PROJECT

Create a Mural Have interested students re-create a landscape from Australia, Oceania, or Antarctica. Tell them to focus on landforms, vegetation, and animal life. Direct them to the library and issues of NATIONAL GEOGRAPHIC for inspiration. Inform them that they can locate the issues they need by looking for references to Australia, Oceania or the South Pacific, and Antarctica in the *Readers' Guide to Periodical Literature*. After they find a model picture, help them choose a medium that fits the subject: chalk, pastels, watercolors, crayons, or markers. Suggest that they tape together several large sheets of paper to make a wall-sized surface. Display the finished mural on a classroom wall or in the school hallway.

1 SECTION The Land

SETTING THE SCENE

Read to Discover . . .
- the mammoth rocks and endless deserts of Australia's interior.
- the volcanic mountains and coral reefs of the Pacific Islands.
- the icy landscape and ice cap climate of Antarctica.

Key Terms
- artesian water
- coral
- atoll
- lagoon
- continental island
- krill

Identify and Locate
Australia, Oceania, New Zealand, Antarctica, Melanesia, Micronesia, Polynesia, Great Dividing Range, Great Barrier Reef, Western Plateau, Murray River, North Island, South Island, Transantarctic Mountains

ANTARCTICA

GREETINGS FROM ANTARCTICA! WE ARE TRAVELING ON SLEDS AND SNOWMOBILES ON THE POLAR PLATEAU, WHERE THE ICE IS IN PLACES OVER 10,000 FEET THICK! WE ARE ON A SCIENTIFIC EXPEDITION DRILLING ICE CORES FOR INFORMATION ABOUT OUR CHANGING WORLD CLIMATE. SO LONG! DAVID REED

AUSTRALIAN ANTARCTIC TERRITORY
ADÉLIE PENGUIN 7c

David Reed carries out scientific work in Antarctica, one of the coldest areas on the earth. Antarctica, along with Australia and the islands of Oceania, is part of the diverse South Pacific culture region. Covering a huge portion of the world, the South Pacific region contains both polar and tropical landscapes.

REGION

Australia: A Continent and a Country

Australia is unique. It is the only place on the earth that is both a country and a continent.

Great Dividing Range

The major area of hills and mountains in Australia is the Great Dividing Range. The range stretches from the northernmost Cape York Peninsula southward along Australia's eastern coast to the island of Tasmania. Most of Australia's freshwater begins in the Great Dividing Range.

Central Lowlands

West of the Great Dividing Range the land takes on a very different appearance. A thick ribbon of pastureland known as the Central Lowlands runs through the middle of Australia. Underneath the lowlands lies a vast pool of underground water known as the Arte-

LESSON PLAN
Chapter 32, Section 1

FOCUS

SECTION OBJECTIVES

1. **Locate** the mammoth rocks and endless deserts of Australia's interior.
2. **Describe** the volcanic mountains and coral reefs of the Pacific islands.
3. **Explain** the icy landscape and ice cap climate of Antarctica.

ABOUT THE POSTCARD

David also tells us of a storm that kept the expedition members in their tents for five days. The temperature was –20°F (28.9°C) and the wind blew more than 80 miles an hour (128.7 km/hr.).

BELLRINGER MOTIVATIONAL ACTIVITY

Project the Section 1 Focus Transparency and have students answer the questions.

PRETEACHING VOCABULARY

Explain that the word *antarctic* comes from the Greek word *antarkticos,* which means "opposite to the north." Have students find the definition of antarctic in the dictionary and compare it to the Greek meaning.

Use the Vocabulary PuzzleMaker Software to create a crossword or word search puzzle.

Classroom Resources for Section 1

BLACKLINE MASTERS:
Reproducible Lesson Plan 32-1
Geography Simulation 11
Guided Reading Activity 32-1
Section Quiz 32-1

TRANSPARENCIES:
Section Focus Transparency 32-1
Political Map Transparency 11

Unit Map Overlay Transparencies 11, 11-4, 11-5

MULTIMEDIA:
Vocabulary PuzzleMaker Software
Testmaker

Geography and the Environment
STV: World Geography, Volume 1
STV: World Geography, Volume 3

Picture Atlas of the World

TEACH

GUIDED PRACTICE

Implement Geography Simulation 11 as a class activity.

Project Unit Map Overlay Transparency 11-4 onto the chalkboard and have students locate and label the physical features from the section on the map. Project Unit Map Overlay Transparency 11-5 to check the students' accuracy.

INDEPENDENT PRACTICE

Guided Reading Have students complete Guided Reading Activity 32-1 in the TCR. **LEP**

Have students complete Unit Map Overlay Transparency 11 Activity in the TCR.

DID YOU KNOW?

Australia was once part of Antarctica but sailed free long ago when the tectonic plates spread apart.

GLENCOE TECHNOLOGY

Videodisc

Use the following to enrich Chapter 32:

GEOGRAPHY AND THE ENVIRONMENT
THE INFINITE VOYAGE
Living With Disaster

Chapter 4
Disc 3 Side A
Title: ***Save the Beaches: Soil Erosion from Barrier-Reef Islands***
Subject: Ocean City, Maryland, serves as a model for how science has been involved in the prevention of erosion on barrier-reef islands

Comparing Lands

The continental USA is about a third as large as Australia, Oceania, and Antarctica.

sian Basin. **Artesian waters** are pressurized and rise to the surface into ranchers' wells without any pumping.

Western Plateau

A low expanse of flat land called the Western Plateau covers nearly two-thirds of Australia. Australians call this area where few people care to live the outback. Three deserts—the Great Sandy, the Great Victoria, and the Gibson—cover much of the outback. In these deserts are mammoth rock formations—some as much as 6 billion years old. South of the Great Victoria Desert is the Nullarbor Plain. Although the plain borders the Great Australian Bight—a huge arm of the Indian Ocean—the plain receives little rainfall.

Great Barrier Reef

The Great Barrier Reef, one of the world's most famous natural wonders, lies a short distance off Australia's northeastern coast. Made of **coral** formed by the limestone skeletons of tiny sea animals, the reef is a long strip of coral-covered land that is home to a spectacular array of brilliantly colored tropical fish and underwater creatures. A writer described the Great Barrier Reef as follows:

> *. . . A place of beauty, a kaleidoscope of colour and a refuge for a host of strange but interesting animals and plants . . . a major challenge to scientists wishing to unlock the storehouse of new knowledge it contains.*

Natural Resources

Only about 10 percent of Australia's land is arable. Because Australia's farmers use their land and water resources effectively, however, it is one of the world's leading producers of wheat, cattle, and sheep. Australia is one of the world's leading exporters of beef, mutton and lamb, and wool.

Australians are also tapping their country's great wealth of mineral resources. These resources include uranium, bauxite, iron ore, copper, lead, manganese, nickel, zinc, gold, silver, diamonds, and opals.

REGION

Oceania: Island Lands

To understand the very large region of Oceania more easily, geographers identify three major island groups based on location, how the islands were formed, and the culture of the inhabitants. These island groups are Melanesia, Micronesia, and Polynesia. Melanesia lies north and east of Australia, and Micronesia is located north of Melanesia and south of the Japanese islands. Polynesia includes the area from Midway Island on the north to New Zealand on the south.

High Islands

Many of the islands of Oceania were formed millions of years ago as a result of colliding tectonic plates. They are part of the Ring of Fire that is known for its earthquake and volcanic activity. These volcanic islands are the high islands of Oceania. The earth beneath them is still not quiet, and gas can sometimes be seen belching into the sky from volcanic mountains that rise high above sea level.

Low Islands

The low islands of Oceania also began with volcanoes. On these islands, coral has grown along the rim of an underwater volcano, creating a ring-shaped island called an

Cooperative Learning Activity

After the class finishes reading the section, organize students into teams. Have a player on the first team choose one of four areas—Australia, Oceania, New Zealand, or Antarctica. Then ask the player to name one of the following features: a mountain range, a reef, a plateau, a desert, a basin, a plain, a water body, an island group, a continental island, a peninsula, or a rock formation, depending on what features the section mentioned for that area. If the player answers correctly, his or her team earns a point and the first player on the next team chooses an area. If the player answers incorrectly, ask the first player of another team to answer the question. Continue until all the features in the section have been named. The team with the most points wins the game.

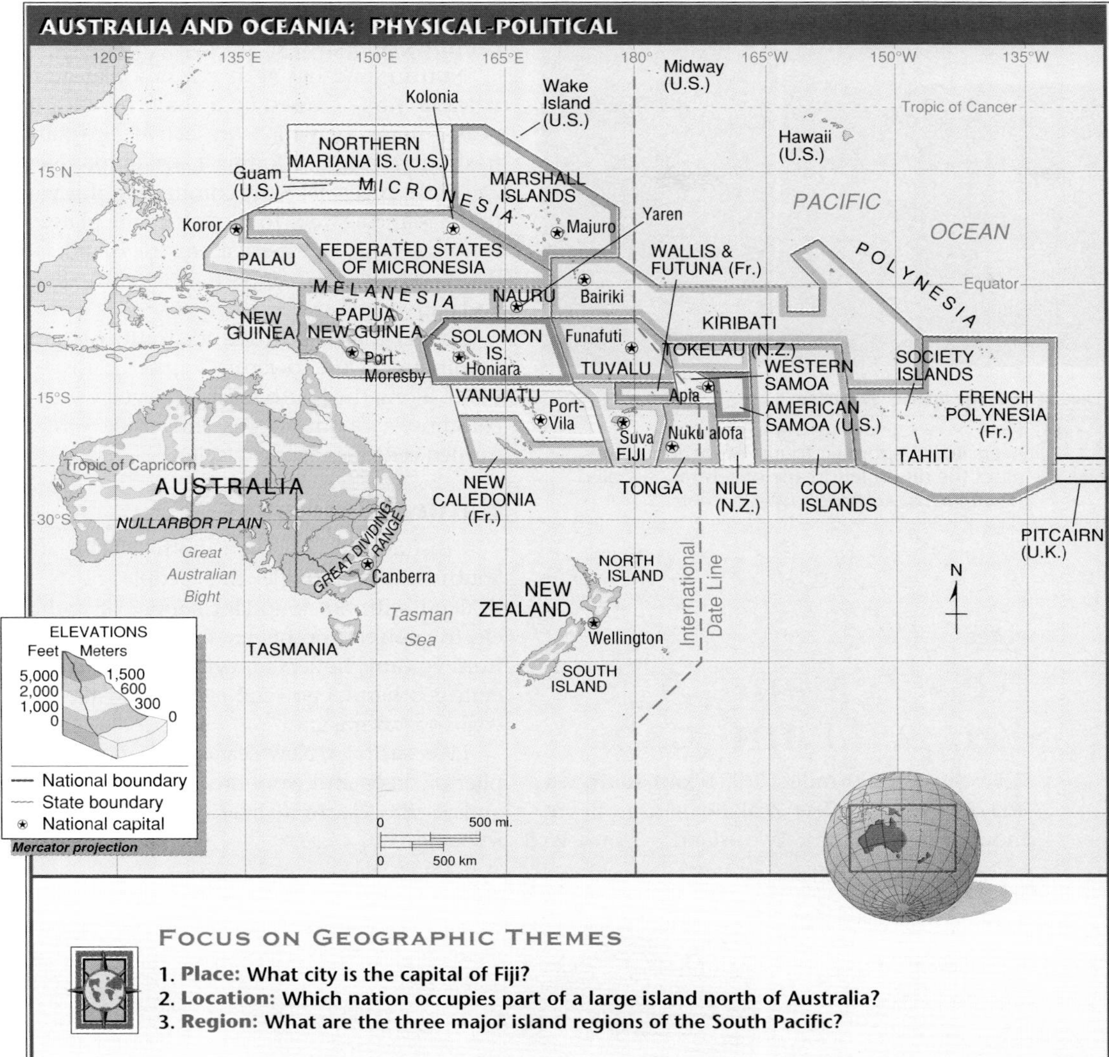

Focus on Geographic Themes

1. **Place:** What city is the capital of Fiji?
2. **Location:** Which nation occupies part of a large island north of Australia?
3. **Region:** What are the three major island regions of the South Pacific?

atoll. At the center of the atoll is shallow, often transparent water called a **lagoon.** Atolls are often so low-lying that waves wash them in and out of view. They have little soil and few natural resources.

Continental Islands

The remaining islands of Oceania, and most of its largest islands, are **continental islands.** They are made of rock that has risen from continental shelves on the ocean floor. Papua New Guinea, New Caledonia, the Bismarck Archipelago, and the Solomon Islands are all continental islands. Although they were not formed by volcanoes, many do have active volcanoes. The continental islands possess the most significant mineral resources in Oceania. These minerals include oil, gold, nickel, and copper.

Meeting Special Needs

Language Delayed Help students with language concept problems categorize information. Direct their attention to headings in this section, "Great Dividing Range," "Central Lowlands," and "Natural Resources." After reading each section, have students think of alternate titles such as "Australian Hills and Mountains," "Pastureland and Artesian Water," and "Soil, Livestock, and Minerals."

USING MAPS

Answers:
1. Suva; **2.** Papua New Guinea;
3. Melanesia, Micronesia, and Polynesia

Map Skills Practice
Reading a Map In what major island region does Tahiti belong? *(Polynesia)*

ASSESS

CHECK FOR UNDERSTANDING

Assign Section 1 Review as homework or an in-class activity.

MEETING LESSON OBJECTIVES

Each objective below is tested by the questions that follow it in parentheses.
1. Locate the mammoth rocks and endless deserts of Australia's interior. *(4)*
2. Describe the volcanic mountains and coral reefs of the Pacific islands. *(1)*
3. Explain the icy landscape and ice cap climate of Antarctica. *(5)*

EVALUATE

Assign the Section 1 Quiz in the TCR.

Use the Testmaker to create a customized quiz for Section 1.

NATIONAL GEOGRAPHIC SOCIETY

Videodisc

STV: WORLD GEOGRAPHY, VOLUME 1

Side 2, Chapter 2
Frames 00002-44834
Title: ***Australia* (in its entirety)**
Subject: Examine the world's smallest and second driest continent, Australia

CURRICULUM CONNECTION

SCIENCE

Geothermal power can pollute the air by releasing hydrogen sulfide, ammonia, and even some radioactivity. It also can pollute water with the dissolved substances it brings to the surface. However, devices are available to control geothermal pollution.

USING ILLUSTRATIONS

PLACE Tourists visit Ayers Rock to see the prehistoric paintings in its caves.

Answer to Caption: *about 10 percent*

USING ILLUSTRATIONS

HUMAN/ENVIRONMENT INTERACTION Generating electricity with geothermal power costs about the same as using coal.

Answer to Caption: *The steam is used to generate geothermal power.*

RETEACH

Have students complete Workbook Activity 32-1 found in the TCR.

ENRICH

Circulate a sample or picture of krill among the students.

Geographic Themes

Place: Ayers Rock, Australia

Ayers Rock, a popular tourist attraction, dominates the desert landscape of central Australia. *How much of Australia's land is arable?*

PLACE

New Zealand: A Rugged Landscape

Located 1,200 miles (1,931 km) southeast of Australia, New Zealand is a group of mountainous islands. Two islands—North Island and South Island—form most of the country's landmass.

North Island has at its center a plateau of volcanic stone crossed by a chain of volcanic peaks, many of which are active. Sparkling freshwater lakes, including Lake Taupo, New Zealand's largest lake, are common in this part of the island as well. To the east of the plateau, running north and south along the island, is a band of hills, their slopes dotted with sheep and dairy cattle.

Longer than North Island, South Island is dominated by the towering Southern Alps. Beyond, along the South Island's jagged western coastline, are numerous finger-like inlets formed centuries ago by glaciers.

Natural Resources

Fast-flowing rivers on both North and South Island provide the people of New Zealand with an abundant supply of hydroelectric power. Another energy source is steam from volcanic hot water, which is used to generate geothermal power. New Zealand also has coal and natural gas.

Like Australia, New Zealand is a global supplier of sheep and wool products. Pine forests and Pacific Ocean fish are other important resources.

Geographic Themes

Human/Environment Interaction: North Island, New Zealand

The central plateau of New Zealand's North Island contains volcanoes, hot springs, and geysers. *How have the hot springs benefited New Zealanders?*

Critical Thinking

Analyzing Information Project Political Map Transparency 11 on the chalkboard and have the students list the resources on each area of Australia, Oceania, and Antarctica as they read the section. Then have them decide which area on the map needs to depend least on imported resources and explain why. *(Australia has more resources than any other area in the South Pacific region and thus would be least dependent on resources imported from other areas.)*

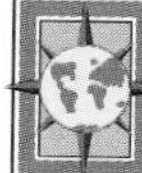

Geographic Themes

Region: Antarctica

Animals, such as penguins, seals, and whales, thrive in Antarctica's coastal waters. *What Antarctic shellfish may one day help feed the world's hungry?*

PLACE

Antarctica: A White Plateau

Nearly twice the size of Australia, Antarctica sits astride the southern end of the globe under an enormous white shield. The ice, which is as much as 2 miles (3.2 km) thick in some places, covers about 95 percent of the continent's landmass.

Landforms

The Transantarctic Mountains cross the continent and extend northward on the Antarctic Peninsula to within 600 miles (965 km) of South America's Cape Horn. The mountains and the peninsula divide the continent into two regions. To the east is a high, flat plateau. To the west of the mountains, the landmass is largely below sea level.

Although significant mineral resources are present in Antarctica, its greatest resources are the scientists who conduct research there. They research weather patterns and observe the sun and stars without obstruction. They also have observed—more clearly in Antarctica than in other parts of the world—the effect of human industrialization on the earth's ozone layer. The waters around Antarctica also contain a wealth of sea resources, such as **krill**, a shrimplike animal that may one day help feed the world's hungry.

SECTION 1 REVIEW

Checking for Understanding

1. **Define** artesian water, coral, atoll, lagoon, continental island, krill.
2. **Locating Places** What continents are located in the South Pacific region?
3. **Human/Environment Interaction** What local resources help to meet New Zealand's energy needs?
4. **Place** Where in the South Pacific are plateaus found?

Critical Thinking

5. **Determining Cause and Effect** Why is most of Antarctica's landmass below sea level?

ANSWERS TO SECTION 1 REVIEW

1. **artesian water:** pressurized water that rises to the surface into ranchers' wells without any pumping; **coral:** limestone skeletons of tiny sea animals; **atoll:** a ring of coral surrounding a sunken volcano; **lagoon:** warm, shallow body of water inside an atoll; **continental island:** made of rock that has risen from continental shelves on the ocean floor; **krill:** small shrimplike animal that lives in Antarctic waters
2. Australia and Antarctica
3. Fast-flowing rivers provide hydroelectricity, and steam from volcanic hot water generates geothermal power.
4. eastern Antarctica; western Australia; and North Island, New Zealand
5. The ice is so heavy it has pushed down the land.

MULTICULTURAL PERSPECTIVE

Cultural Diversity

In 1820 a Russian sea captain was the first person to record seeing Antarctica, and in 1898 Belgian sailors were the first to spend a winter along Antarctica's coast. The sun disappears for months during an Antarctic winter. The ship's log tells how the prolonged darkness affected the sailors: "One seaman had fits. . . . Another went mad. . . . Another died of heart trouble. . . ."

USING ILLUSTRATIONS

PLACE A penguin's wings are like a seal's flippers. Penguins use them to swim, not to fly. A penguin swims as well as a fish.

Answer to Caption: *krill*

CLOSE

Have students list the provisions David and the other members of the expedition probably took with them to help them survive in Antarctica.

Videodisc

STV: WORLD GEOGRAPHY, VOLUME 3

Side 2, Chapter 2
Frames 00001-44754
Title: *Antarctica* **(in its entirety)**
Subject: Visit the coldest, windiest place on Earth, Antarctica, which is also a valuable scientific resource

LESSON PLAN
Chapter 32, Section 2

FOCUS

SECTION OBJECTIVES

1. **Locate** the climate regions of Australia, Oceania, and Antarctica.
2. **Identify** the vegetation patterns of Australia, Oceania, and Antarctica.

BELLRINGER MOTIVATIONAL ACTIVITY

Project the Section 2 Focus Transparency and have students answer the questions.

PRETEACHING VOCABULARY

Distribute copies of a chart with the Key Terms across the top and *animal, mineral, vegetation,* and *other* at the left. Have students check the category in which they think each term belongs. After they read the section, have them reassess their answers.

GLENCOE TECHNOLOGY

Videodisc

Use the following to enrich Chapter 32:

GEOGRAPHY AND THE ENVIRONMENT
THE INFINITE VOYAGE
Secrets From a Frozen World

Chapter 1
Disc 2 Side B
Title: ***The Southern Ocean—A Rich Marine Ecosystem***
Subject: The Southern Ocean around Antarctica is home to one of the world's richest marine ecosystems

SECTION 2 The Climate and Vegetation

SETTING THE SCENE

Read to Discover . . .
- the climate regions of Australia, Oceania, and Antarctica.
- the vegetation patterns of Australia, Oceania, and Antarctica.

Key Terms
- wattle
- doldrums
- typhoon
- manuka
- crevass
- lichens

Identify and Locate
Climate regions: desert, steppe, tropical rain forest, marine west coast, ice cap, tundra

In the South Pacific, water is crucial in creating great contrasts in climate and vegetation. Pacific Ocean currents bring moisture to many islands in Oceania, where lush landscapes prevail. In arid areas, such as Australia's Western Plateau, the land is dry and barren.

REGION

Australia's Climate and Vegetation

Australia is one of the driest continents in the world. The driest area of Australia is the Western Plateau.

Desert

Subtropical high-pressure air masses above central Australia block moisture-bearing Pacific Ocean winds from reaching the Western Plateau. This geographic factor contributes to a desert climate on large areas of the continent.

Steppe

Surrounding Australia's desert region is a ring of steppe climate. Here the landscape changes as more regular rainfall brings vegetation to life. Rains, however, fall only during the wet season. A woman who grew up in southwestern Australia describes the effects of the rains on the steppe landscape:

The transformation of the countryside was magical. As far as the eye could see wild flowers exploded into bloom. Each breeze would waft [the flowers'] pollen round the house, making it seem as though we lived in an enormous garden. . . . Trees sprung up . . . and before long a new clump of . . . saplings was well formed. On walks we would find enormous mushrooms, as large as a dinner plate, but perfectly formed . . . . Stranger still, the whole countryside was green, a color we scarcely knew.

Two native forms of vegetation—acacia and eucalyptus trees—dominate the landscape of the steppe climate region. Early settlers who wattled, or interwove, acacia saplings to create walls and roofs for their homes named the trees **wattles.**

Coasts

Australia's coastal areas have a variety of moister climates. The southern coasts have a Mediterranean climate, while a humid subtropical climate dominates the northeast coast, and a marine west coast climate prevails on the southeastern coast.

Classroom Resources for Section 2

BLACKLINE MASTERS:
Reproducible Lesson Plan 32-2
Skill Activity 32
Section Quiz 32-2

TRANSPARENCIES:
Section Focus Transparency 32-2
Unit Map Overlay Transparencies 11-2, 11-3
Physical Geography of the World Transparencies 71–80

MULTIMEDIA:
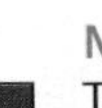
Testmaker

Geography and the Environment
STV: World Geography, Volume 1
STV: World Geography, Volume 3

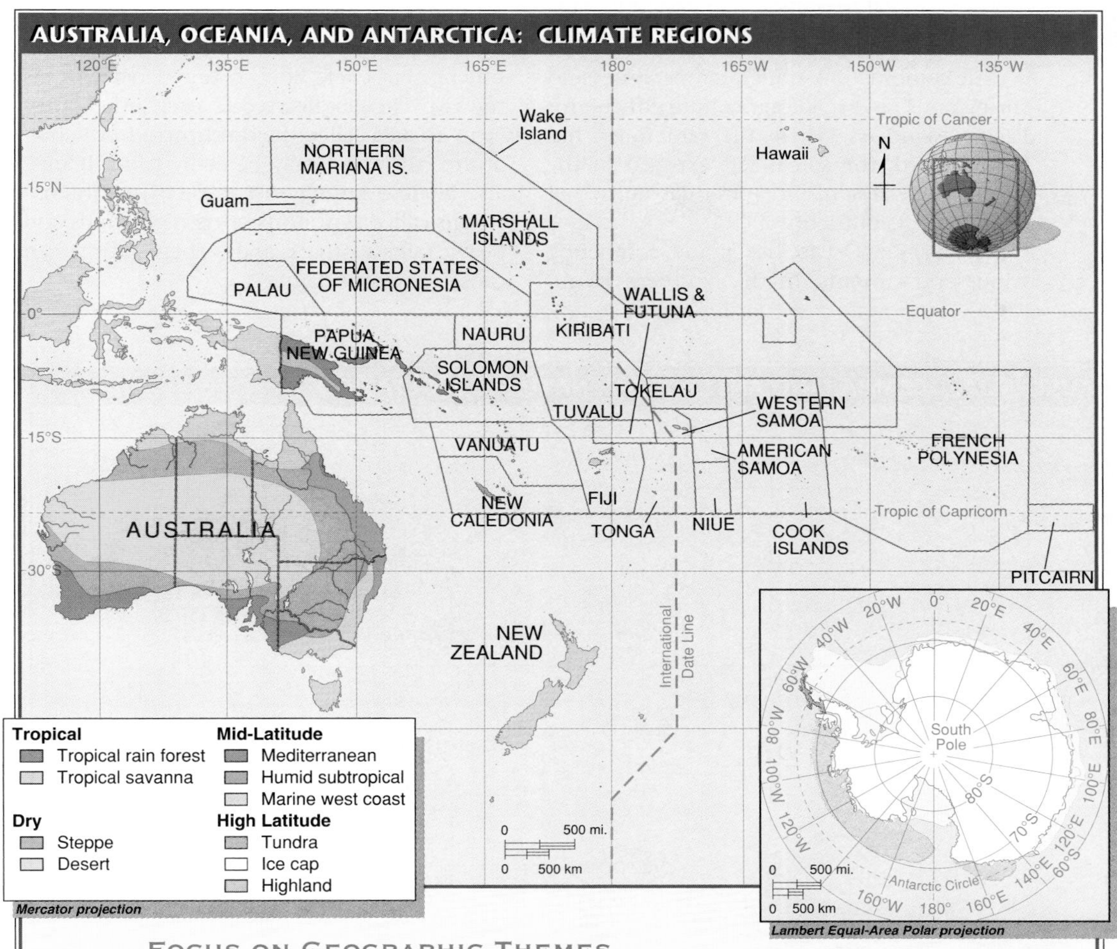

Focus on Geographic Themes

1. **Region: What climate region extends through most of central Australia?**
2. **Location: Where are tropical climate regions located in Australia?**
3. **Place: What is the predominant climate region of Antarctica?**
4. **Place: How might climate affect settlement patterns in Australia?**

REGION

Oceania's Climate and Vegetation

Oceania lies primarily north of the Tropic of Capricorn. It generally has a tropical rain forest climate, in which warm days follow one another in an almost unbroken chain. Most of the region has distinct wet and dry seasons. During the wet season, days are constantly rainy and humid. In the dry season, rainfall decreases, and a brilliant blue sky and ocean blend into one at the endless horizon.

The amount of rain that falls during the wet season varies from island to island. On some of the low coral islands, very little rain falls, and there is little or no vegetation. Tropical plants such as coconut palms cover islands that receive more rain.

The mountainous high islands receive the most rainfall—as much as 150 inches (381

TEACH

GUIDED PRACTICE

L1 Identify Have students identify the vegetation in each climate zone on Unit Transparency 11-3. Project Unit Transparency 11-2 to check students' accuracy.

INDEPENDENT PRACTICE

Guided Reading Have students complete Guided Reading Activity 32-2 in the TCR. **LEP**

Have students complete Workbook Activity 32-2 found in the TCR.

USING MAPS

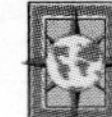

Answers:
1. desert; **2.** along the northern coast; **3.** ice cap; **4.** People probably settle along the coastal areas with moderate climates.

Map Skills Practice

Interpreting a Map Why does Papua New Guinea have a warmer climate than New Zealand? *(Papua New Guinea is closer to the Equator than New Zealand.)*

NATIONAL GEOGRAPHIC SOCIETY

PHYSICAL GEOGRAPHY OF THE WORLD TRANSPARENCIES

Display and discuss the physical features of the following transparencies:

71. Ayers Rock, Australia
72. Australian Alps, Australia
73. Murray River, Australia
74. Great Barrier Reef, Australia
75. Armit Range, Papua New Guinea
76. Bora Bora, French Polynesia
77. Seventy Islands Preserve, Palau
78. Transantarctic Mountains, Antarctica
79. South Pole, Antarctica
80. Dry Valley, Antarctica

Cooperative Learning Activity

Tell students that temperatures on Antarctica are colder than those on some parts of Mars and that a visitor to Antarctica once wrote: "I raised my head to look around and found I couldn't move it back. My clothing had frozen solid as I stood." Allow time for a group of students to research the effects of cold on humans, using encyclopedias or other sources and to report their findings to the class. Then challenge the students to imagine that they are in Antarctica and to describe the effects of the cold in a one-page story. After the students finish writing, invite them to share their stories with the rest of the class.

ASSESS

CHECK FOR UNDERSTANDING

Assign Section 2 Review as homework or an in-class activity.

MEETING LESSON OBJECTIVES

Each objective below is tested by the questions that follow it in parentheses.

1. Locate the climate regions of Australia, Oceania, and Antarctica. *(2, 3, 4, 5)*

2. Identify the vegetation patterns of Australia, Oceania, and Antarctica. *(1)*

EVALUATE

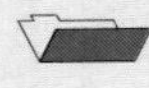

Assign the Section 2 Quiz in the TCR.

Use the Testmaker to create a customized test for Section 2.

USING MAPS

Answers:

1. Antarctica;

2. along the southern coast of Australia;

3. grassland

Map Skills Practice

Reading a Map Where is tundra vegetation found? *(in a small area on the coast of Antarctica)*

NATIONAL GEOGRAPHIC SOCIETY

Videodisc

STV: WORLD GEOGRAPHY, VOLUME 1

Side 2, Chapter 2
Frames 730-5000
Title: ***Australia***
Subject: Overview

cm) a year in western Melanesia. On these islands, steamy rain forests cover the land.

The combination of high temperatures and strong rains have made agriculture difficult for Pacific islanders. Where the rain forest has been cleared, the soil is left exposed to the strong tropical sun and torrential rains that wash away its nutrients.

The Pacific Ocean has many competing winds and currents. In the Northern Hemisphere, the Pacific's currents flow in an enormous clockwise circle. In the Southern Hemisphere, that circle flows counterclockwise. As the two circular flows pass each other, they form an area called the **doldrums.** In the doldrums, the wind may be eerily calm. It may also be devastatingly fierce. Each year intense storms called **typhoons** bring high winds and heavy rains to the islands. These storms can cause enormous damage.

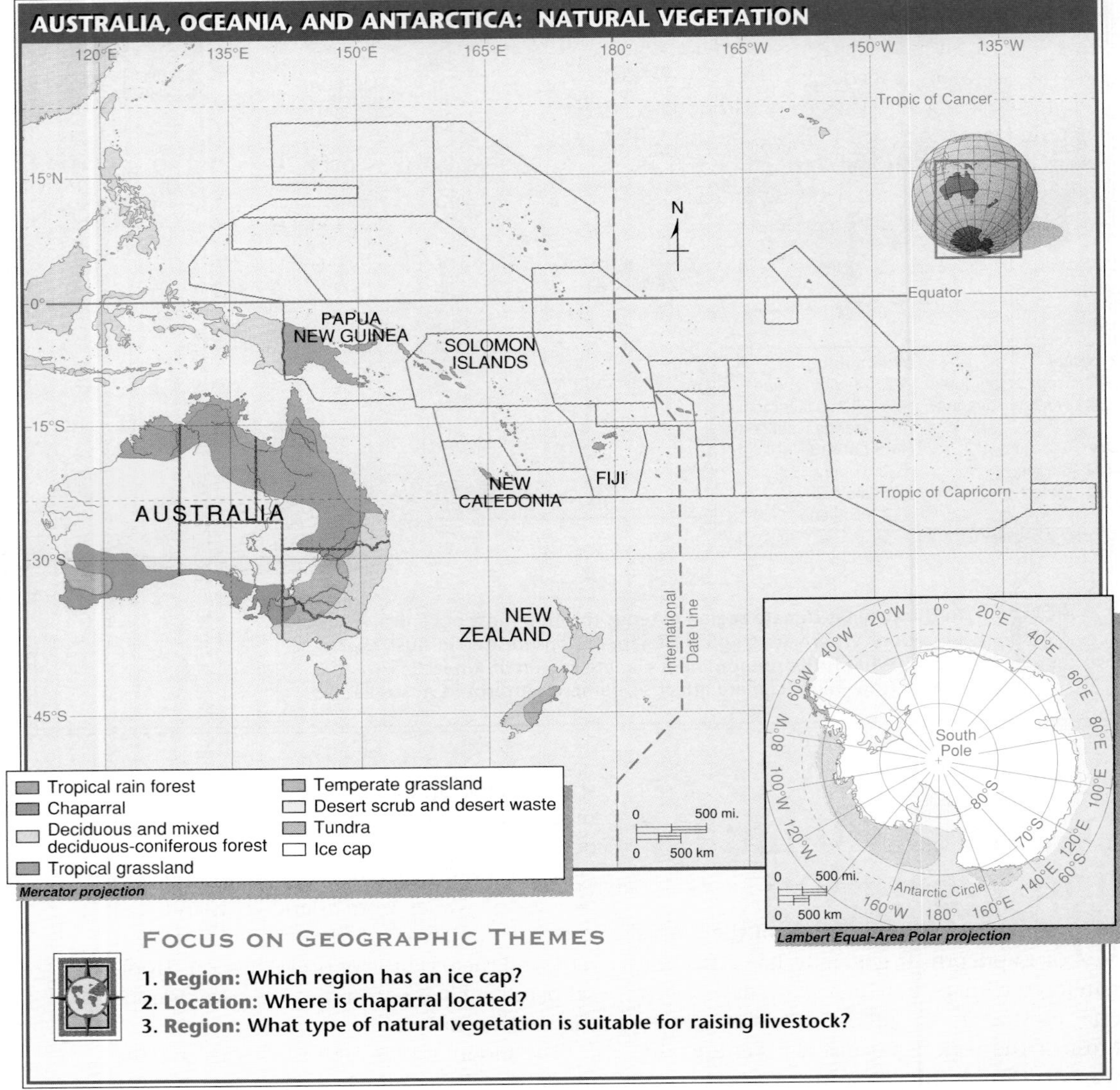

FOCUS ON GEOGRAPHIC THEMES

1. **Region:** Which region has an ice cap?
2. **Location:** Where is chaparral located?
3. **Region:** What type of natural vegetation is suitable for raising livestock?

Meeting Special Needs

Language Delayed Students with difficulty categorizing information will find it helpful to use a framework for comparing climate zones. Have them write *temperature, precipitation,* and *vegetation* across the top of a sheet of paper and list *Australia, Oceania, New Zealand,* and *Antarctica* along the left side of the sheet. Tell the students to look for information to write under the categories at the top of the sheet in the material under each subhead. After students complete their climate comparison chart, suggest that they use it as a study aid.

PLACE

New Zealand's Climate and Vegetation

With the exception of its mountain areas, New Zealand has only one climate region—marine west coast. Rain falls throughout the year and temperatures are mild.

The central volcanic plateau of the North Island and the Southern Alps on the South Island strongly affect New Zealand's climate. Atop the plateau it is warm and sunny in summer. Small shrubs called **manuka** carpet the region, replacing forest that prehistoric eruptions destroyed long ago. Throughout both islands, it is wettest on the western slopes of the mountains. Here, the air coming off the Pacific Ocean drops its moisture.

REGION

Antarctica's Climate and Vegetation

Antarctica is one of the coldest places on the earth. It is also one of the highest and driest of the continents.

Antarctica's plateau, covered year-round by a vast sheet of ice, is drier than Australia's deserts. As the air rises across the plateau, moisture is lost. This dryness in turn makes the air colder. During the long winter, temperatures may fall as low as −100°F (−73°C).

Antarctica's ice is always moving, inching slowly toward the ocean. In the warmer, moister parts of the continent, it moves more quickly, often breaking into pieces. Between the pieces huge cracks called **crevasses** develop.

A small area of Antarctica lies in a tundra climate zone. In this zone, located on the Antarctic Peninsula, summer temperatures may reach almost 60°F (15.6°C). Here, a surprising array of vegetation breaks the endless white of the continent's interior. Mosses dot the rocks, algae tints the ice itself with red, green, or yellow. Sturdy plants called **lichens** flourish.

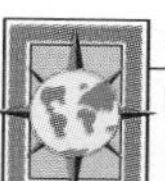

Geographic Themes

Place: Australian Outback

Part of Australia's interior consists of open countryside and has a steppe climate. *What two native forms of vegetation are found in Australia's steppe climate region?*

SECTION 2 REVIEW

Checking for Understanding

1. **Define** wattle, doldrums, typhoon, manuka, crevass, lichens.
2. **Locating Places** What areas in the South Pacific and Antarctica have the wettest climates? The driest climates?
3. **Region** In which climate region is the Antarctic Peninsula located?
4. **Movement** How do Pacific Ocean currents and winds affect the climate of Oceania?

Critical Thinking

5. **Making Comparisons** How does the general climate of New Zealand compare with that of Australia?

ANSWERS TO SECTION 2 REVIEW

1. **wattle:** interweave; **doldrums:** area of unstable winds where northern and southern currents meet; **typhoon:** violent Pacific Ocean storm; **manuka:** shrub found on New Zealand's volcanic plateau; **crevasse:** deep crack formed by the splitting of Antarctic rock; **lichens:** sturdy plants that grow inside Antarctic rocks
2. Papua New Guinea and the northern coast of Australia have the wettest climates; Antarctica and the interior of Australia have the driest climates.
3. tundra
4. They make the climate both eerily calm and intensely stormy.
5. New Zealand's climate is moderate throughout the country while Australia's climate varies from wet to moderate to dry.

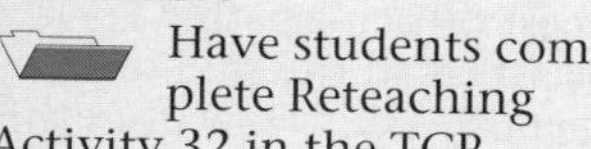

USING ILLUSTRATIONS

PLACE The interior includes occasional "billabongs"—slang for ponds in otherwise dry stream beds.

Answer to Caption: *acacia and eucalyptus*

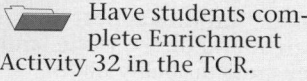

RETEACH

Have students complete Reteaching Activity 32 in the TCR.

ENRICH

Have students complete Enrichment Activity 32 in the TCR.

CLOSE

Have students write slogans that complement aspects of climate and vegetation in Australia, Oceania, or Antarctica.

NATIONAL GEOGRAPHIC SOCIETY

Videodisc

STV: WORLD GEOGRAPHY, VOLUME 3

Side 2, Chapter 2
Frames 00765-3725
Title: ***Antarctica***
Subject: Overview

GLENCOE TECHNOLOGY

Videodisc

GEOGRAPHY AND THE ENVIRONMENT
THE INFINITE VOYAGE
Secrets From a Frozen World

Chapter 1
Disc 2 Side B
Title: ***The Southern Ocean—A Rich Marine Ecosystem***

TEACH

If possible, distribute a map of your neighborhood, town, or county. Have students identify and draw two different routes between the same locations. Have them discuss advantages of each route, such as shortest distance, most scenic, and so on. Explain: "Just as you tried to find the best route, road-builders choose the shortest or least difficult path." Have students read the skill on page 664. Ask: "How does this map show the areas with the most population and commerce?" *(many interlacing routes)* "If routes appear straight and direct, is the land they cross probably flat or mountainous? Why?" *(Straight roads indicate flat land; roads through mountains usually curve through valleys and rivers.)*

Skills Practice For additional practice, have students complete Skill Activity 32 in the TCR.

MAP & GRAPH SKILLS

Interpreting Routes on a Map

Throughout history, merchants have followed trade routes across land and sea. To aid navigation, traders have developed maps of these routes. Since traders usually find the shortest or easiest paths between cities, trade route maps reveal the interaction of human activity with natural landscape.

Reviewing the Skill

Trade routes usually follow the least difficult path between population centers. Because of geography, though, the least difficult route may not be the shortest.

On a trade-route map, some areas have many interlacing routes. These areas generally have much population and commerce. When interpreting routes on a map, apply the following steps:

- Identify the area covered and symbols used in the map.
- Locate major population centers.
- Identify the trade routes on the map and points of connection between routes.
- Use the map to draw conclusions about how the physical geography affects transportation and trade in the region.

Practicing the Skill

Study the map below and then answer the following questions.

1. What modes of transportation does Australia have?
2. What color represents inland waterways on the map?
3. Where are major airports located?
4. How many railroads connect western and eastern Australia?
5. Why do you think there are so many routes in eastern Australia?
6. What are the major seaports of Australia?

For additional practice in this skill, see Practicing Skills on page 666 of the Chapter 32 Review.

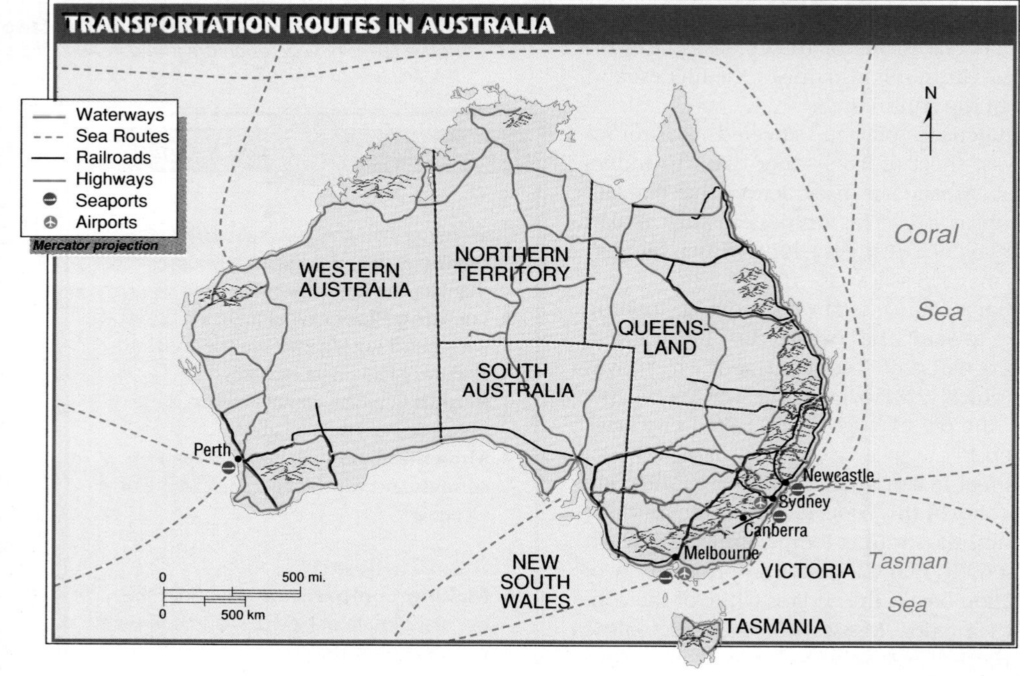

ANSWERS TO PRACTICING THE SKILL

1. highway, railroad, inland waterway, sea, air
2. green
3. Melbourne and Sydney
4. one
5. more population and commerce
6. Perth, Melbourne, Sydney, Newcastle

chapter 32

HIGHLIGHTS

SECTION 1 The Land

KEY TERMS

artesian water (p. 656)
coral (p. 656)
atoll (p. 657)
lagoon (p. 657)
continental island (p. 657)
krill (p. 659)

SUMMARY

- The South Pacific region includes the large continents of Antarctica and Australia, and thousands of islands of varying size that comprise Oceania.
- The islands of Oceania were created either directly or indirectly by volcanic activity.
- New Zealand has a rugged geography with very jagged coastlines, tall mountains, and rapidly flowing rivers.
- While Antarctica may have important mineral resources, its key resource is the information it offers to scientists.

Penguins along the Antarctic coast

SECTION 2 The Climate and Vegetation

KEY TERMS

wattle (p. 660)
doldrums (p. 662)
typhoon (p. 662)
manuka (p. 663)
crevass (p. 663)
lichens (p. 663)

SUMMARY

- Australia generally has a hot, dry climate. Its interior is a vast desert bordered by a wide steppe. Mountains separate the moister coastal areas from the drier interior.
- A tropical rain forest climate is found throughout much of Oceania.
- Because of Pacific Ocean currents and winds that collide with one another, Oceania experiences violent typhoons at certain times of the year.
- New Zealand has a mild, moist marine climate with a moderate range of temperatures throughout the year, especially on North Island.
- An ice cap climate covers nearly all of Antarctica. Except for lichens and mosses in the tundra areas, Antarctica has no vegetation.

The Australian outback, an area of vast expanses

CHAPTER 32 HIGHLIGHTS

USING THE CHAPTER 32 HIGHLIGHTS

Use the Chapter 32 Highlights to preview, review, condense, or reteach the chapter.

PREVIEW/REVIEW

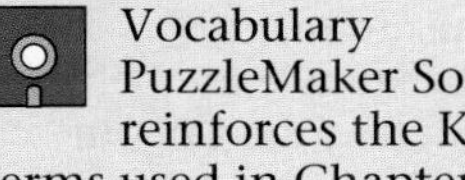

Vocabulary PuzzleMaker Software reinforces the Key Terms used in Chapter 32.

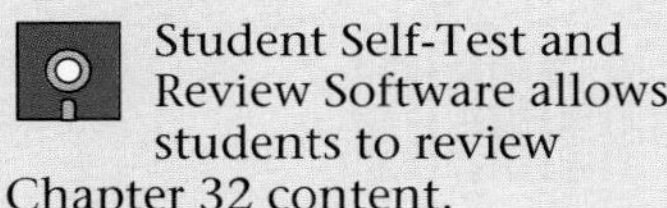

Student Self-Test and Review Software allows students to review Chapter 32 content.

CONDENSE

Have students read the Chapter 32 Highlights.

Have students listen to the Chapter 32 Audiocassettes in the TCR. Spanish Audiocassettes are also available.

Assign the Chapter 32 Audiocassette Activity and give the students the Chapter 32 Audiocassette Quiz.

Have students complete Guided Reading Activities for Chapter 32 in the TCR. Spanish Guided Reading Activities are also available.

RETEACH

Have students complete Reteaching Activity 32 in the TCR. Spanish Reteaching Activities are also available.

Map Activity

Identify and Locate Copy and distribute page 38 of the Outline Map Resource Book. On the map, have students locate and label Australia, Oceania, New Zealand—North Island and South Island, Antarctica, Melanesia, Micronesia, and Polynesia. Also tell them to shade in the climate regions shown on the map on page 661. Remind them to include a key showing the shade for each climate.

GLENCOE TECHNOLOGY

Videodisc

Use Chapter 32 MindJogger Videoquiz to review students' knowledge before administering the Chapter 32 Test.

MINDJOGGER VIDEOQUIZ

Chapter 32
Disc 4 Side B

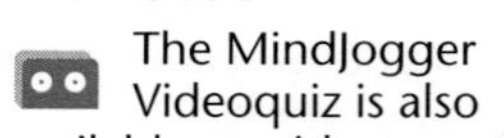

The MindJogger Videoquiz is also available on videocassette.

chapter 32 REVIEW

Reviewing Key Terms

Choose the vocabulary term that best completes each of the sentences below. Write your answers on a separate sheet of paper.

artesian water (p. 656)
atoll (p. 657)
lagoon (p. 657)
continental islands (p. 657)
doldrums (p. 662)
typhoons (p. 662)
manuka (p. 663)
crevasses (p. 663)
lichens (p. 663)

SECTION 1

1. In Australia's Central Lowlands, ____ rises to the ground's surface without pumping.
2. The ring of land that forms around a sunken volcano is called an ____. A ____ of warm water is created inside the ring.
3. ____ form when portions of an ocean shelf are pushed upward.

SECTION 2

4. Unstable winds in the ____ of the Pacific Ocean cause violent storms called ____.
5. Explorers in Antarctica must be careful to avoid ____.
6. Where volcanic activity has destroyed New Zealand's trees, ____ shrubs flourish.
7. Hardy plants called ____ grow inside the rocks of Antarctica's coast.

Reviewing Facts

SECTION 1

8. Why are Australia's highlands called the Great Dividing Range?
9. How were the low islands of Oceania formed?
10. Which mountains cross the continent of Antarctica?

SECTION 2

11. What kind of climate is found on New Zealand's North Island?
12. What is Antarctica's greatest resource?
13. Where in Oceania can you find volcanoes?

Critical Thinking

14. **Drawing Conclusions** Most Australians live along the continent's coast. How might physical geography have determined this pattern of settlement?
15. **Making Generalizations** What geographic factors are responsible for Antarctica's cold, dry climate?

Geographic Themes

16. **Region** What landforms dominate the South Pacific region?
17. **Human/Environment Interaction** How has clearing the rain forests affected agriculture in the Pacific islands?

Practicing Skills

Interpreting Routes on a Map

Refer to the Interpreting Routes on a Map skills feature on page 664.

18. Why do you think there is so little transportation in west central Australia?
19. What kinds of transportation are found in the area around Perth?
20. Which seaport appears to have the most traffic? Why?

Using the Unit Atlas

Refer to the physical geography section of the Unit Atlas on pages 650–651.

21. Why is Australia classified as a continent?
22. What is the world's coldest and iciest region?

ANSWERS

Reviewing Key Terms

1. artesian water
2. atoll, lagoon
3. continental islands
4. doldrums, typhoons
5. crevasses
6. manuka
7. lichens

Reviewing Facts

8. They divide the more humid coastal area from the plateau that covers western Australia.
9. Coral grew along the rims of underwater volcanoes.
10. Transantarctic Mountains
11. marine west coast
12. the scientific information it provides
13. on some high islands

Critical Thinking

14. People prefer the moderate climates on the coast to the desert climate in the interior.
15. high latitude and high altitude of the plateau

Geographic Themes

16. plateaus and mountain ranges such as the Great Dividing Range, the Transantarctic Mountains, and the Southern Alps
17. It has left the soil exposed to sun and heavy rains that wash away the soil's nutrients. This makes agriculture difficult.

Projects

Individual Activity

As discussed in the chapter, volcanic activity played a role in the formation of many islands of Oceania. Choose one island from each of the three types of islands—high, low, and continental. Research the geographic and natural history of each kind of island and summarize your findings in a brief oral report.

Cooperative Learning Activity

Working in pairs, create a visual presentation capturing the climate and vegetation of either Australia, New Zealand, Antarctica, or Oceania. Select visual images—photographs, maps, drawings, paintings. Then exchange the images and write captions to accompany the images you have received. Finally, work together to organize your material in either booklet or bulletin board format for presentation to the class.

Writing About Geography

Proposal

Imagine you live somewhere in Australia, Oceania, or Antarctica. Write a proposal explaining why your area should be used to relieve world overpopulation. Describe the land and climate of your area, and discuss the conditions new residents would find. Use your journal record and text as well as encyclopedias and other reference books.

Locating Places

PHYSICAL GEOGRAPHY: AUSTRALIA AND NEW ZEALAND

Match the letters on the map with the places and physical features of Australia and New Zealand. Write your answers on a separate sheet of paper.

1. Great Barrier Reef
2. Great Victoria Desert
3. Great Dividing Range
4. Tasmania
5. Cape York Peninsula
6. Great Australian Bight
7. Lake Eyre
8. North Island
9. South Island

Chapter 32 Review

Practicing Skills

18. Desert climate has left the area largely unsettled so no major population centers exist there.

19. highways, sea routes, and railways

20. Sydney and Newcastle area; several sea routes come out of these ports.

Using the Unit Atlas

21. because of its large size

22. Antarctica

Locating Places

1. G
2. A
3. F
4. D
5. C
6. E
7. B
8. I
9. H

Chapter Bonus Test Question

This question may be used for extra credit on the chapter test. Choose the number of the correct response.

Which of the following features is *not* found in New Zealand?

(1) Lake Taupo
(2) manuka shrubs
(3) the Southern Alps
(4) a tropical climate

Answer: (4)

CHAPTER 33

PLANNING GUIDE

The Cultural Geography of Australia, Oceania, and Antarctica

CHAPTER ORGANIZER

Daily Lesson Objectives	Multimedia	Teacher Classroom Resources
SECTION 1 Population Patterns 1. Examine the blend of peoples living in the South Pacific. 2. Discuss the sparse and uneven settlement of the region.	Section Focus Transparency 33-1 Chapter 33 Vocabulary PuzzleMaker Software Unit Map Overlay Transparencies 11, 11-3 Testmaker	Reproducible Lesson Plan 33-1 Guided Reading Activity 33-1 Spanish Guided Reading Activity 33-1 Workbook Activity 33-1 Performance Assessment Activity 33 Section Quiz 33-1
SECTION 2 History and Government 1. Name the earliest settlers in the South Pacific. 2. Summarize the impact of European settlement in the region. 3. Examine how the governments in the region have changed over time.	Section Focus Transparency 33-2 Political Map Transparencies 11, 12 Testmaker Picture Atlas of the World	Reproducible Lesson Plan 33-2 Guided Reading Activity 33-2 Spanish Guided Reading Activity 33-2 Vocabulary Activity 33 Performance Assessment Activity 33 Workbook Activity 33-2 Section Quiz 33-2
SECTION 3 Cultures and Lifestyles 1. List factors that have influenced culture in the South Pacific. 2. Appreciate the traditional and Western art forms of the region. 3. Describe the varied South Pacific lifestyles and standards of living.	Section Focus Transparency 33-3 World Cultures Transparencies 19, 20 World Music: Cultural Traditions, Lesson 10 Geography and the Environment Testmaker	Reproducible Lesson Plan 33-3 Guided Reading Activity 33-3 Spanish Guided Reading Activity 33-3 Workbook Activity 33-3 Enrichment Activity 33 Foods Around the World 10 World Literature Reading 10 Section Quiz 33-3
CHAPTER REVIEW AND EVALUATION	Chapter 33 English (or Spanish) Audiocassettes MindJogger Videoquiz Testmaker Student Self-Test and Review Software	Reteaching Activity 33 Spanish Reteaching Activity 33 Chapter 33 Test Form A and Form B

0:00 *If time does not permit teaching the entire chapter, summarize using the Chapter 33 Highlights on page 683, and the Chapter 33 English (or Spanish) Audiocassettes. Review students' knowledge using the Glencoe MindJogger Videoquiz.*

KEY TO ABILITY LEVELS

Teaching strategies have been coded for varying learning styles and abilities.

L1 **BASIC** activities for all students

L2 **AVERAGE** activities for average to above-average students

L3 **CHALLENGING** activities for above-average students

LEP **LIMITED ENGLISH PROFICIENCY** activities

Performance Assessment

Decision Making Conduct a decision-making scenario for assessing cultural factors in the South Pacific. Organize students into groups, and have each group select an American company from the stock exchange list in the paper or from the local area. Each group should determine what its company produces and what the company requires in terms of labor and resources.

Then have each group make a decision on the best place in the South Pacific region to relocate its company. If the company is not suited to the South Pacific, students should give reasons why this is the case. In discussing relocation, the groups should consider what adjustments company workers would have to make if they moved to the South Pacific, considering such cultural factors as homes, education, language, religion, and recreation and the arts.

POSSIBLE RUBRIC FEATURES: Content information, decision-making skills, evaluation and inference skills, collaboration skills

For additional professional and classroom resources, see Chapter Resources, pages T46–T51.

TEACHER'S CORNER

NATIONAL GEOGRAPHIC SOCIETY

INDEX TO NATIONAL GEOGRAPHIC MAGAZINE

The following articles may be used for research relating to this chapter:

- "Reclaiming a Lost Antarctic Base," by Michael Parfit, March 1993.
- "Under the Spell of the Trobriand Islands," by Paul J. Theroux, July 1992.
- "Journey into Dreamtime: The Land of Northwest Australia," by Harvey Arden, January 1991.
- "Australia at 200," by Ross Terrill, February 1988.
- "Children of the First Fleet," by John Everingham, February 1988.
- "The First Australians," by Stanley Breeden, February 1988.
- "New Zealand: The Last Utopia?" by Robert Paul Jordan, August 1982.
- "Maoris: At Home in Two Worlds," by Yva Momaliuk and John Eastcott, October 1984.
- "Papua New Guinea: Nation in the Making," by Robert J. Gordon, August 1982.

NATIONAL GEOGRAPHIC SOCIETY PRODUCTS AVAILABLE FROM GLENCOE

To order the following products for use with this chapter, contact your local Glencoe sales representative or call Glencoe at 1-800-334-7344:

- *Picture Atlas of the World* (CD-ROM)
- *STV: World Geography, South America and Antarctica* (Videodisc)
- *STV: World Geography, Asia and Australia* (Videodisc)
- *ZipZapMap! World* (Software)
- *GeoBee* (Software)
- *Images of the World* (Posters)
- *Eye on the Environment* (Posters)
- *Physical Geography of the World* (Transparencies)
- *Picture Atlas of Our 50 States* (Book)

ADDITIONAL NATIONAL GEOGRAPHIC SOCIETY PRODUCTS

To order the following products for use with this chapter, call National Geographic Society at 1-800-368-2728:

- *Australia's Aborigines* (Video)
- *Nations of the World Series*, "Australia." (Video)

Introducing
CHAPTER 33

PERFORMANCE ASSESSMENT

Refer to the Planning Guide on page 668B for a Performance Assessment Activity for this chapter. See the *Performance Assessment Activities* booklet for additional suggestions.

CHAPTER OBJECTIVES

1. **Explain** how modern travel and communication have decreased the South Pacific's isolation.
2. **Appreciate** that the development of the South Pacific was guided by struggles for control by foreign powers.
3. **Recognize** that ways of life in the South Pacific reflect a vibrant blend of Western and traditional influences.

GLENCOE TECHNOLOGY

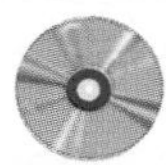

Videodisc

Use Chapter 33 MindJogger Videoquiz to preview chapter content.

MINDJOGGER VIDEOQUIZ

Chapter 33
Disc 5 Side A

The MindJogger Videoquiz is also available on videocassette.

chapter 33

The Cultural Geography of Australia, Oceania, and Antarctica

CHAPTER FOCUS

Geographic Setting

Great distances and landform barriers separate many parts of the South Pacific culture region from one another. Geographic isolation has allowed very distinct cultures to develop.

▲ Photograph: *Sydney Opera House, Sydney, Australia*

Geographic Themes

Section 1 Population Patterns
MOVEMENT Modern travel and communication have decreased the South Pacific's isolation.

Section 2 History and Government
HUMAN/ENVIRONMENT INTERACTION The development of the South Pacific was guided by foreign powers struggling for control.

Section 3 Cultures and Lifestyles
PLACE Ways of life in the South Pacific reflect a vibrant blend of Western and traditional influences.

EXTRA CREDIT PROJECT

Write a Movie Review Suggest that interested students view films set in Australia, such as *A Cry in the Dark, The Day My Voice Broke, Flirting, My Brilliant Career, Crocodile Dundee,* and *Quigley Down Under.* Tell them to look for landscapes and listen for language they have read about in their text. Also have them note how the characters' ways of life reflect Western and traditional influences.

Then have them organize their notes into a review and end the review with a recommendation of three stars (an accurate portrayal of Australian life), two stars (includes local color), or one star (full of stereotypes). Collect the reviews in a binder as a guide to other students in their video viewing.

1 SECTION
Population Patterns

SETTING THE SCENE

Read to Discover . . .
- the blend of peoples living in the South Pacific region.
- how sparsely and unevenly the population is distributed.

Key Term
- primate city

Identify and Locate
Sydney, Melbourne, Auckland, Wellington

Albury, Australia
G'Day! I live in Albury, which is about a three-hour drive from Melbourne. I work after school at a store called "Big W" where I price the stock. I play the electric guitar and hope to be in a heavy metal band one day. I also write poetry and songs.
Your friend,
Bernadine Cook

Bernadine Cook lives in southeastern Australia, one of the most densely populated areas in an otherwise sparsely settled country. Australia, Oceania, and Antarctica together make up the world's most sparsely populated culture region. Its 28 million inhabitants are unevenly distributed across the area.

REGION

Human Characteristics

Most Australians and New Zealanders trace their roots to Great Britain and its settlement of both countries in the late 1700s. In recent years government-sponsored immigration policies, especially in Australia, have encouraged immigration from other parts of the world. Many new Australians have roots in southern and eastern Europe. Others have come from China, Southeast Asia, and various areas of the Pacific.

There are, however, peoples living in the South Pacific that settled in the region long before the arrival of European settlers. In Australia, these native people are called Aborigines from the Latin phrase *ab origine,* which means "from the beginning." During the early period of European settlement, the number of Aborigines declined sharply. Today their population is once again growing.

New Zealand's earliest inhabitants were the Maori (MOWR•ee). Like Australia's Aborigines, the Maori are now a minority in the lands they once dominated.

Over the centuries, as settlers and immigrants have arrived in the South Pacific from different parts of the world, they have added their unique social patterns, languages, and physical characteristics to those already in place. Now the region reflects a wide human

LESSON PLAN
Chapter 33, Section 1

FOCUS

SECTION OBJECTIVES
1. **Examine** the blend of peoples living in the South Pacific.
2. **Discuss** the sparse and uneven settlement of the region.

ABOUT THE POSTCARD
Bernadine is in Year 11 and goes to a Catholic high school. She likes the bush and the wild animals running free, but she would like to visit the United States someday.

BELLRINGER MOTIVATIONAL ACTIVITY

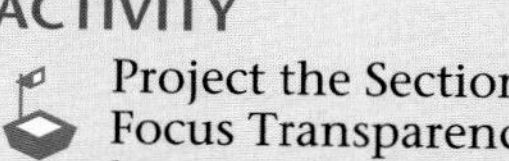
Project the Section 1 Focus Transparency and have students answer the questions.

PRETEACHING VOCABULARY
Ask students to define *prime* in "prime time" and to use this meaning to form a hypothesis about the meaning of *primate city*.

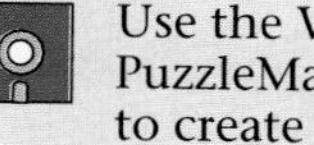
Use the Vocabulary PuzzleMaker Software to create a crossword or word search puzzle.

DID YOU KNOW?
"Kiwis" is a nickname for New Zealanders.

Classroom Resources for Section 1

BLACKLINE MASTERS:
Reproducible Lesson Plan 33-1
Guided Reading Activity 33-1
Spanish Guided Reading Activity 33-1
Performance Assessment Activity 33
Section Quiz 33-1
Workbook Activity 33-1

TRANSPARENCIES:
Section Focus Transparency 33-1
Unit Map Overlay Transparencies 11, 11-3

MULTIMEDIA:

Vocabulary PuzzleMaker Software
Testmaker

TEACH

GUIDED PRACTICE

Project Unit Map Overlay Transparency 11-3. Ask students to predict where population is densest based on the data in the climate map. Have them find support for their predictions as they read.

INDEPENDENT PRACTICE

Guided Reading Have students complete Guided Reading Activity 33-1 in the TCR. **LEP**

ASSESS

CHECK FOR UNDERSTANDING

Assign Section 1 Review as homework or an in-class activity.

MEETING LESSON OBJECTIVES

Each objective below is tested by the questions that follow it in parentheses.

1. Examine the blend of peoples living in the South Pacific. *(5)*

2. Discuss the sparse and uneven settlement of the region. *(2, 3, 4)*

USING ILLUSTRATIONS

REGION Maoris congregate at the community center or *marae.*

Answer to Caption: *Aborigines*

diversity. In Papua New Guinea, for example, more than 700 different languages and dialects are spoken. Throughout the other islands, there are people with Polynesian, Asian, Indonesian, European, and mixed heritages.

Population Distribution

The South Pacific's most heavily populated areas are found in the mild climate regions. The region's most sparsely populated places are its deserts and its polar climate regions. In some parts of the South Pacific, such as Australia's deserts and Antarctica, there is little or no permanent settlement.

Australia is the South Pacific's most heavily populated country, with about 18 million people. Almost all the country's major cities are found in coastal areas. Australian cities of more than 1 million people are all found along the country's coasts, in its mild climate zones. These cities include Sydney and Brisbane on the eastern coast and Melbourne and Adelaide on the southern coast. Perth is the major city along Australia's southwestern coast.

The largest cities in Oceania are the New Zealand ports of Auckland, Wellington, and Christchurch. Most countries in Oceania have a single major city called a **primate city.** These cities generally serve as their countries' capitals and their largest ports.

PLACE

Population Density and Urbanization

Population density in the South Pacific varies greatly throughout the region. The Micronesian island of Nauru, for example, has a population density of more than 1,183 people per square mile (450 per sq. km). Antarctica, on the other hand, does not have a permanently settled population.

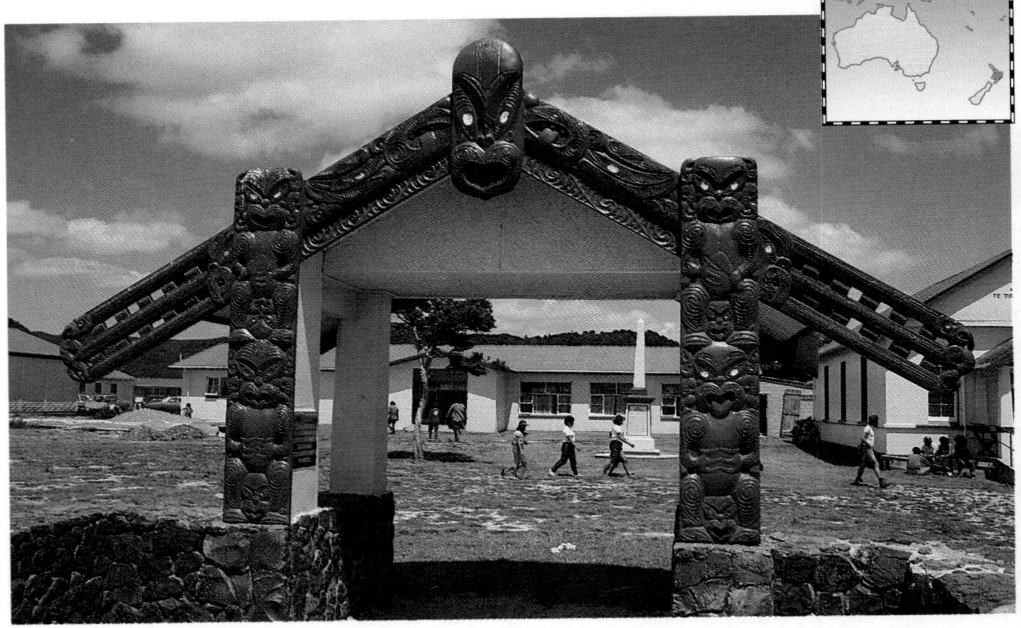

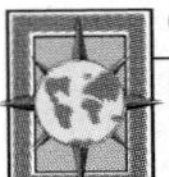

Geographic Themes

Region: New Zealand

The Maori were the first people to live in New Zealand. They came from Polynesian islands northeast of New Zealand. *Which group of people settled Australia before the arrival of Europeans?*

Cooperative Learning Activity

On the chalkboard, copy the following data:

COUNTRY	POPULATION
Australia	18 million
New Zealand	4 million
Papua New Guinea	4 million
Other	4 million

Organize the class into small groups. Have group members work together to draw a circle graph reflecting the population distribution of the region. Remind them to label each part. Ask them to refer to an almanac to find the percentages of ethnic groups in the countries represented. Have the groups draw a circle graph for each country, showing its ethnic makeup.

Geographic Themes

Place: Auckland, New Zealand

Auckland is New Zealand's largest city. Many of its residential areas consist of single-family houses. *What percent of New Zealanders live in urban areas?*

Population density figures for the South Pacific are often misleading because unfavorable climates, terrains, or soil conditions make large parts of the region uninhabitable. The South Pacific's density figures would be much higher if they were based on the amount of living land area only.

Australia and New Zealand are urbanized countries. About 85 percent of Australia's people live in cities or towns. About 80 percent of New Zealand's population is urban. Other South Pacific countries are somewhat less urbanized.

Several factors account for the extensive urbanization in Australia, New Zealand, and other areas of the South Pacific. One factor is that much of the productive land supports grazing but not farming. Sheep need a great deal of land and leave little room for people. Today, as ranchers and farmers replace workers with machines, even fewer people are needed in the rural areas.

Another factor is that Pacific islanders, especially the young, are leaving their homes, where jobs and industry are scarce, and heading to the region's major cities in search of opportunity.

An additional factor is that communication and technology have made the South Pacific area accessible from anywhere in the world. Businesses from around the world have been established in the region's cities—many of which are ports—to tap into its many resources. As the cities of the region have reacted to these different factors, they have blossomed into modern, multicultural urban centers.

Section 1 Review

Checking for Understanding

1. **Define** primate city.
2. **Locating Places** Where are the most sparsely populated parts of the South Pacific culture region?
3. **Place** Why is the South Pacific unevenly populated?
4. **Region** What are two reasons New Zealand and Australia have become highly urbanized?

Critical Thinking

5. **Drawing Conclusions** Improved technology has greatly changed the relative location of Australia and New Zealand, bringing them closer to the world. How do you think this increased interaction might have affected the human diversity of the region?

EVALUATE

Assign the Section 1 Quiz in the TCR.

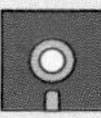

Use the Testmaker to create a customized quiz for Section 1.

RETEACH

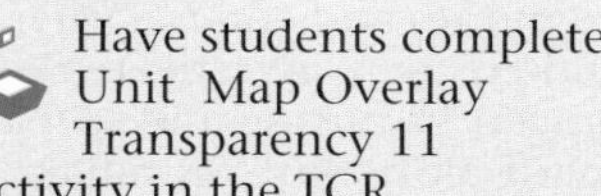

Have students complete Unit Map Overlay Transparency 11 Activity in the TCR.

ENRICH

Share these terms used by Australians: Aussie, an Australian; bloke, the person in charge; cobber, friend; crow eater, a South Australian; Jackeroo, a male ranch hand; and Jilleroo, a female ranch hand.

CLOSE

Have students write a postcard to Bernadine, telling her about their hobbies or part-time jobs.

USING ILLUSTRATIONS

PLACE Even in the cities of New Zealand, crime is rare.

Answer to Caption: *80%*

ANSWERS TO SECTION 1 REVIEW

1. **primate city:** a country's single major city, serving as capital and port
2. Australia's interior and Antarctica
3. Many parts of the region will not support human settlement due to poor climate, soil, or terrain.
4. The land in this region supports grazing but not farming; young people are moving from agricultural areas to cities to find jobs.
5. Technology has made the South Pacific accessible to businesses around the world; increased communication and interaction may reduce the diversity of the region's cultures.

TEACH

Explain that there are about 250 described species of jellyfish. Have students research the various types of jellyfish as well as similar "cousins," such as sea anemones and corals. Other students may investigate the dangers of surfing and scuba diving along the Australian coast.

As a group, students may want to present a documentary outlining the dangers of Australia's waters and precautions one should take when entering them.

NATIONAL GEOGRAPHIC GEOFACTS

What is the most poisonous animal?

Scourge of the coastal waters of Australia, the infamous box jellyfish is the earth's most venomous animal. A single box jelly, also known as a marine stinger or sea wasp, carries enough venom to kill 60 people. Its victims can die in four minutes or less.

Over the past century, these ghostly assassins have killed at least 65 people. The pain of their sting is instantaneous and unbearable. Avoiding these creatures is difficult. Their bodies can be as big as basketballs, but are 95 percent water. Their deadly 15-foot (4.6-m) tails of nearly 60 thin tentacles are almost invisible.

Box jellyfish do not attack their prey. They react when something blunders into them. Not all contacts are fatal. It takes at least 10 feet (3 m) of tentacle to kill a human. Quick treatment with antivenom can save lives. Australian surfers wear "stinger suits"—often made of pantyhose—to protect their skin from lethal punctures.

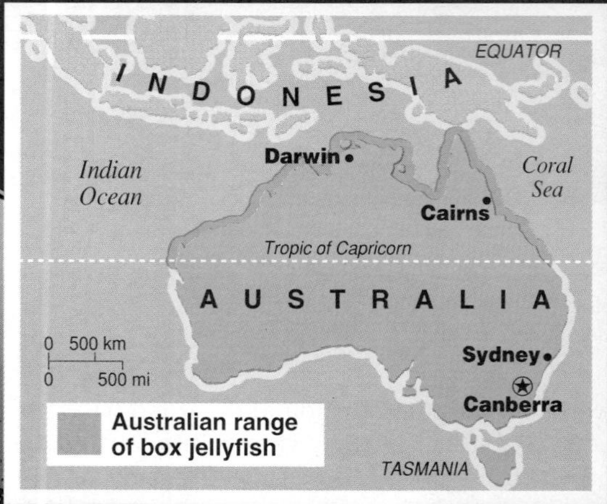

EQUATOR
INDONESIA
Indian Ocean
Darwin
Coral Sea
Cairns
Tropic of Capricorn
AUSTRALIA
0 500 km
0 500 mi
Sydney
Canberra
Australian range of box jellyfish
TASMANIA

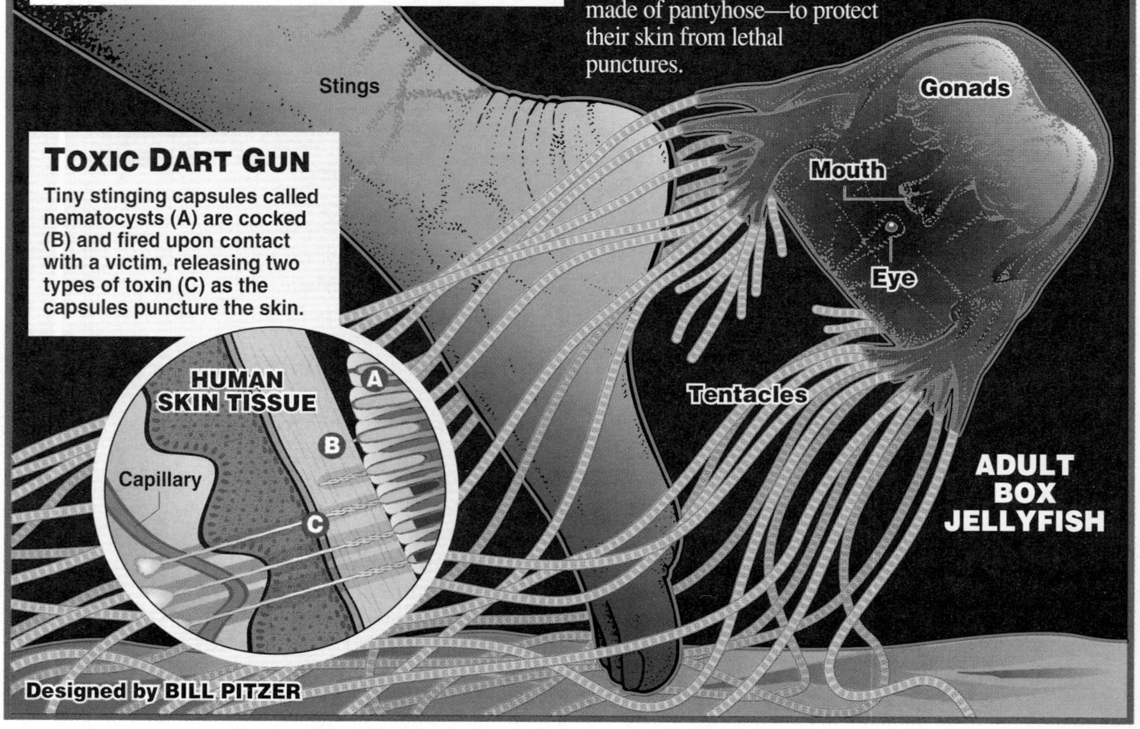

Stings

TOXIC DART GUN

Tiny stinging capsules called nematocysts (A) are cocked (B) and fired upon contact with a victim, releasing two types of toxin (C) as the capsules puncture the skin.

HUMAN SKIN TISSUE
A
B
C
Capillary
Gonads
Mouth
Eye
Tentacles
ADULT BOX JELLYFISH

Designed by BILL PITZER

2 SECTION
History and Government

SETTING THE SCENE

Read to Discover . . .
- the earliest settlers in the South Pacific.
- the impact of European settlement in the region.
- how the governments in the region have changed over time.

Key Terms
- nomadic
- boomerang
- trust territory

Identify and Locate
Southeast Asia, Papua New Guinea, Marquesas Islands, Guam, Iwo Jima, Guadalcanal, Kiribati, Sydney Harbor, Nauru, Vanuatu, Tonga, Western Samoa, Society Islands

Throughout its history, the South Pacific culture region has been greatly affected by its location, its resources, and its climates. The native cultures that developed in the region were influenced very little by outsiders.

MOVEMENT

Early Peoples

Historians today are still uncertain about many aspects of the South Pacific region's earliest history. It is known that people were living in Australia and in parts of Melanesia more than 40,000 years ago.

Migrations

The ancestors of these early people probably reached the South Pacific from East Asia or from Southeast Asia. Some may have migrated over land bridges during the Ice Age, when ocean levels were far lower than they are today. Others probably used canoes and rafts to reach the South Pacific.

Not until about A.D. 300 did advances in shipbuilding and navigation enable people to reach and to settle the far islands of Melanesia and Micronesia. By about A.D. 1000, these excellent seafarers had also discovered and settled almost all of Polynesia. Remote location and harsh climate prevented the discovery of Antarctica until about 1820.

Early Lifestyles

The early peoples who settled the coastal areas of the South Pacific region made their livings mainly by fishing. A fishing lifestyle, however, was not possible in the hot, dry Australian interior. Thus, the Aborigines followed a **nomadic** way of life, traveling from place to place, never establishing permanent settlements. For food, they hunted animals using a slightly curved stick called a **boomerang**, and gathered fruits or seeds. When these foods became scarce, they moved on to a new home.

Unlike the Australian Aborigines, the people who settled the inland parts of Papua New Guinea found much fertile land. These people were able to farm and raise livestock.

The earliest Micronesians developed trade with the distant islands of Melanesia and parts of Asia. The peoples who settled the islands of Polynesia also engaged in overseas trade as well as farming and fishing. The large Polynesian islands of New Zealand were first settled by the Polynesian Maori. They probably arrived as early as A.D. 750 from the Marquesas (mahr•KAY•zuhz) Islands, which lie northeast of New Zealand.

LESSON PLAN
Chapter 33, Section 2

FOCUS

SECTION OBJECTIVES

1. **Name** the earliest settlers in the South Pacific.
2. **Summarize** the impact of European settlement in the region.
3. **Examine** how the governments in the region have changed over time.

BELLRINGER MOTIVATIONAL ACTIVITY

Project the Section 2 Focus Transparency and have students answer the questions.

PRETEACHING VOCABULARY

Tell students that *boomerang* is derived from the Australian words for club—*bumarin* and *womurrang*. Ask a volunteer to draw a boomerang on the chalkboard.

CD-ROM

PICTURE ATLAS OF THE WORLD
Have students click Australia's "Video" button to view the Aborigines.

Classroom Resources for Section 2

BLACKLINE MASTERS:
Reproducible Lesson Plan 33-2
Guided Reading Activity 33-2
Spanish Guided Reading Activity 33-2
Vocabulary Activity 33
Performance Assessment Activity 33
Workbook Activity 33-2
Section Quiz 33-2

TRANSPARENCIES:
Section Focus Transparency 33-2
Political Map Transparencies 11, 12

MULTIMEDIA:

Testmaker

Picture Atlas of the World

TEACH

GUIDED PRACTICE

Project Political Map Transparency 12. As students read the section, have volunteers draw arrows from the early immigrants' homelands to their destinations in the South Pacific.

INDEPENDENT PRACTICE

Guided Reading Have students complete Guided Reading Activity 33-2 in the TCR. **LEP**

Have students complete Political Map Transparency 11 Activity in the TCR.

USING MAPS

Answers:
1. France; **2.** it was divided between Germany and the United Kingdom; **3.** Midway Islands; **4.** the United States

Map Skills Practice
Inferring Information
Why do you think the United States took over Guam? *(to use as a stopover for ships going to and from Asian ports)*

MOVEMENT

Europeans in the South Pacific

During the early 1500s, Spanish and Portuguese explorers became the first Europeans to reach the South Pacific. Within 250 years, Europeans had reached virtually all of the lands in the region.

Early Explorers

During the early and mid-1600s, Dutch navigators discovered Australia and New Zealand. The British sailor Captain James Cook explored and charted many of the more remote stretches of the South Pacific. Between 1768 and 1779, Cook explored the islands of Hawaii, claimed the east coast of Australia for Great Britain, and sailed completely around Antarctica.

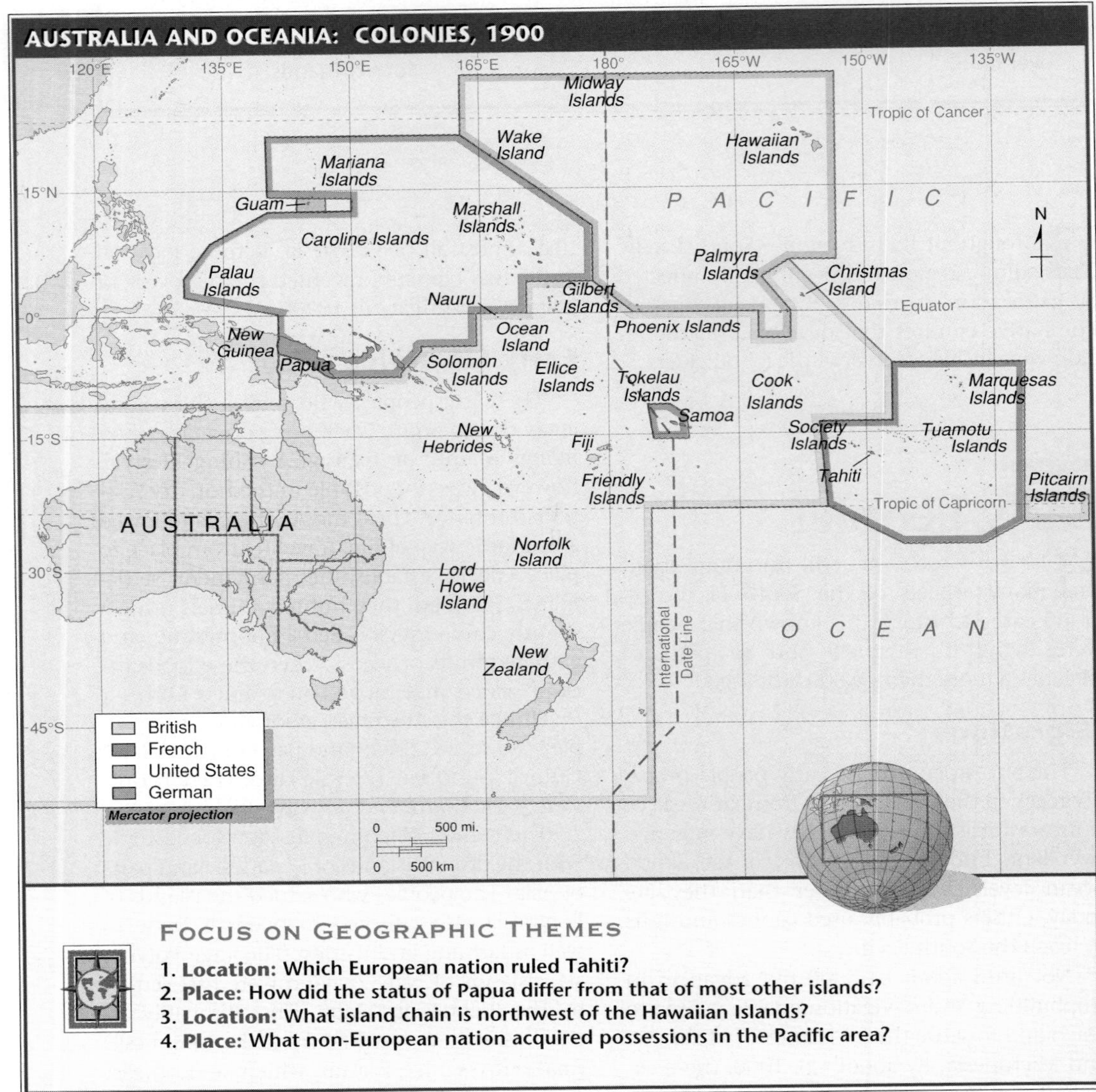

FOCUS ON GEOGRAPHIC THEMES

1. **Location:** Which European nation ruled Tahiti?
2. **Place:** How did the status of Papua differ from that of most other islands?
3. **Location:** What island chain is northwest of the Hawaiian Islands?
4. **Place:** What non-European nation acquired possessions in the Pacific area?

Cooperative Learning Activity

Tell students that Captain James Cook accomplished much. He charted the New Zealand coast, survived a wreck on the Great Barrier Reef, and obtained a wealth of plant and animal specimens unknown to Europeans. He also brought aboard his ships citrus fruits and other foods to prevent scurvy—the sailor's curse. However, just as revisionists now criticize Columbus, some historians call Cook an agent of imperialism.

Ask one group of students to read favorable biographies of Cook, such as *Captain James Cook* by Alan J. Villiers. Assign another group several revisionist essays in *Captain James Cook and His Times,* edited by Robin Fisher and Hugh Johnston. Then have the two groups debate this question: Did Cook cause more harm than good?

Continuing European Interest

During the 1800s the British settled and colonized Australia and New Zealand. Initially the British used Australia as a safe and distant place to set up a colony for convicts. British colonists were attracted to New Zealand's rich soil and fine fishing. The British introduced sheep, cattle, and horses to the region, and raising livestock soon became a profitable business for many British colonists. The discovery of gold in Australia in the 1800s brought thousands of immigrants from the United Kingdom and aided the settlement of the continent.

Antarctica remained largely unexplored during these years. Serious exploration of the continent was not undertaken until the late 1800s. The South Pole was reached first, in 1911, by the Norwegian explorer Roald Amundsen. Large areas of Antarctica's interior remain unexplored today.

Much of Oceania was opened to European settlement by Christian missionaries. Western religious leaders worked to spread their beliefs throughout Oceania during the 1800s. By the end of the century, Christianity had become widespread among the native peoples of Oceania.

REGION

Struggle for Imperial Power

By the early 1900s, Australia and New Zealand had gained independence from the United Kingdom. Even though both nations had won the right to govern themselves, they maintained close ties with the United Kingdom and accepted the British king or queen as their chief of state. This was not the case, however, with many of the island peoples of Oceania.

Throughout the late 1800s and early 1900s, Oceania was the scene of a struggle for imperial control. Many Western countries, including the United Kingdom, France, Germany, and the United States, sought to establish naval bases in the South Pacific. In addition, these countries hoped to extend their overseas trading interests and to find new sources of raw materials to be used in manufacturing.

In 1898, as a result of the American victory in the Spanish-American War, the United States gained control of many of Spain's island possessions in Micronesia. During this same period, Germany, France, and the United Kingdom expanded their holdings in the South Pacific.

The defeat of Germany in World War I led to a new balance of power in the South Pacific. Japan—an increasingly influential Asian and world leader—took over some of Germany's possessions in the region. The struggle for control began anew as the Japanese spread their power throughout the South Pacific. In December 1941, as World War II raged in Europe, the Japanese bombed the United States military bases at Pearl Harbor in Hawaii. Japanese soldiers also captured American, British, and French holdings in the South Pacific.

The region became the scene of some of the bloodiest fighting in World War II as the Allies moved from island to island in an effort to get within striking distance of Japan. Hundreds of thousands of Japanese and Allied soldiers fought savage battles in places such as Iwo Jima and Guadalcanal. By the end of the war in 1945, the Japanese had been driven out of the islands by the United States and its allies.

After World War II, the United Nations placed some parts of Oceania under temporary Western control. Areas of the islands of Micronesia, for example, became a **trust territory** under the United States. While some islands are now self-governing, the United States still helps manage the affairs of some island nations. Many developed nations compete for trade in the Pacific region and try to exert political and economic influence there.

REGION

Governments Today

The European powers that first colonized the South Pacific brought their forms of government to the lands. Some of the countries of the South Pacific region, such as Aus-

Meeting Special Needs

Reading Disability Practice a focused reading exercise with students who experience reading comprehension problems. Have students read the subsection "Struggle for Imperial Power." Have them write in their notebooks what they remember of the subsection.

Then have them reread the subsection to look for the answers to the following questions:

What was the United Kingdom's relationship with Australia and New Zealand after the South Pacific countries won their independence?

What was a result of the American victory in the Spanish-American War?

What happened in the South Pacific during World War II?

ASSESS

CHECK FOR UNDERSTANDING

Assign Section 2 Review as homework or an in-class activity.

MEETING LESSON OBJECTIVES

Each objective below is tested by the questions that follow it in parentheses.

1. **Name** the earliest settlers in the South Pacific. *(2)*
2. **Summarize** the impact of European settlement in the region. *(3, 4)*
3. **Examine** how the governments in the region have changed over time. *(5)*

CURRICULUM CONNECTION

HISTORY

Robert Scott and his British team raced the Amundsen expedition to the South Pole, but they arrived a month after the Norwegians. The British team died there. Scott wrote in his journal: "...feet frozen, no fuel, and a long way from food.... We are very near the end, but have not and will not lose our good cheer."

EVALUATE

 Assign the Section 2 Quiz in the TCR.

 Use the Testmaker to create a customized quiz for Section 2.

RETEACH

Have students complete Workbook Activity 33-2 found in the TCR.

ENRICH

To illustrate how Westerners have changed the Pacific islands, have students study travel posters of Tahiti and Samoa and cross out any signs of European or American influence.

CLOSE

Have students write events and dates from the section in sequence along a line on the chalkboard.

USING ILLUSTRATIONS

PLACE Although independent, Australia belongs to the Commonwealth of Nations, an association of countries formerly under British rule.

Answer to Caption: *parliamentary democracy*

Geographic Themes

Place: Canberra, Australia

Australia's federal parliament building is located in Canberra, a modern capital that serves as an example of successful urban planning. *What type of government does Australia have?*

tralia and New Zealand, adopted these forms of government when they became independent. Thus, Australia and New Zealand, former British colonies, have parliamentary democracies based on the British form of government.

Some of the recently independent countries of the South Pacific region have developed democratic forms of government. Among these are Kiribati, Nauru, and Vanuatu. A few South Pacific nations, such as Tonga and Western Samoa, are monarchies.

Several South Pacific island groups, including American Samoa and the Northern Marianas, are governed by the United States. Other islands are territories of European nations. French claims in Polynesia, for example, include the Society Islands and the Marquesas Islands. Although various countries claim parts of Antarctica, the continent has no official government, because it has no permanent settlement.

SECTION 2 REVIEW

Checking for Understanding

1. **Define** nomadic, boomerang, trust territory.
2. **Locating Places** Where did the ancestors of the earliest Australians and Melanesians originally live?
3. **Movement** How did Christianity reach the South Pacific culture region?
4. **Movement** What event greatly aided the settlement of the Australian continent?

Critical Thinking

5. **Determining Cause and Effect** Why are the governments of Australia and New Zealand parliamentary democracies?

ANSWERS TO SECTION 2 REVIEW

1. **nomadic:** wandering, not creating permanent settlements; **boomerang:** slightly curved wooden stick used by Australian Aborigines for hunting; **trust territory:** parts of Oceania that the United Nations placed under temporary Western control
2. East Asia or Southeast Asia
3. through the efforts of European missionaries
4. the discovery of gold
5. They adopted the government of their colonial ruler, the United Kingdom.

Geography and History

LIVING IN ANTARCTICA

As you read, examine how people are learning to live in Antarctica's hostile environment.

A thick ice cap makes Antarctica the highest continent in terms of average elevation. Towering mountain peaks and glacier-filled valleys are prominent features of the Antarctic coastline. Glaciers and ice sheets often extend out over the ocean to form gigantic ice shelves. Large chunks of ice break off the shelves to form icebergs. Antarctica produces about five thousand large icebergs each year.

Location

Antarctica lies at the "bottom of the world," isolated by stormy seas. It is the highest, coldest, and driest of the continents. Temperatures rarely rise above freezing, and winds sweeping the land often reach hurricane strength.

Because it is so forbidding, Antarctica has had little human settlement. Its harsh environment, however, is also the earth's most unspoiled. This rigorous environment is proving an excellent site for scientific research.

Threatened Environment

Many environmentalists worry that the increasing number of people on the continent will damage the land's ecological systems and pollute its unspoiled environment.

Environmentalists charge scientists living there with dumping untreated sewage into the ocean. Garbage dumps have appeared near some research stations. Fishing fleets from Russia, Poland, Japan, and South Korea seek krill and other fish off the northern Antarctic shores during the continent's short summer. Tourists, mountaineers, boaters, and vacationers in increasing numbers also find Antarctica fascinating.

Many countries also want to open Antarctica for mining. Studies indicate that valuable deposits of oil, gold, and copper could exist in quantities large enough to make the expense of operations worthwhile.

Treaty Signed

In 1991, 26 countries signed the Madrid Protocol Treaty. It included a 50-year ban on mining and oil exploration. Mindful, too, of the habitat erosion already taking place on the fragile continent, the nations set Antarctica aside as a natural reserve dedicated to peace and science.

Environmentalists and scientists alike hope that the treaty will help reverse any adverse effects that human habitation has caused. They also hope that, in 50 years, the world's nations will be sufficiently aware of ecological disaster and that the treaty will be extended, not repealed.

Checking for Understanding

1. **Study the photo on this page. What elements contribute to Antarctica's harsh environment?**
2. **Human/Environment Interaction**  **What are the concerns of ecologists regarding Antarctica?**

ANSWERS TO CHECKING FOR UNDERSTANDING

1. freezing temperatures, snow, ice, winds, dangerous terrain
2. Ecologists worry that human habitation will damage or destroy Antarctica's ecological system.

Geography and History

TEACH

GLENCOE TECHNOLOGY

 **Videodisc**

GEOGRAPHY AND THE ENVIRONMENT
THE INFINITE VOYAGE
Secrets From a Frozen World

Chapter 9
Disc 2 Side B
Title: ***Global Awareness: Preserving the Environment***
Subject: A new treaty signed in June 1991 bans exploitation of Antarctica's mineral resources for 50 years

Location How does Antarctica's location affect its climate? *(At the South Pole, it receives little sun and so is very cold and ice covered.)*

Extending the Content

Living in Antarctica
About 40 research stations house scientists from 25 nations. The buildings are coated with a special blue metal and reinforced with steel and fiberglass to withstand winds of 120 miles (193 km) per hour. Most equipment must be specially designed for temperatures that can dip to −100°F (−73°C). Extra food, tents, and sleeping bags are kept stocked on islands where the scientists work.

DID YOU KNOW?

For eight months of the year, Antarctica receives almost no sunlight.

FOCUS

SECTION OBJECTIVES

1. **List** factors that have influenced culture in the South Pacific.
2. **Appreciate** the traditional and Western art forms of the region.
3. **Describe** the varied South Pacific lifestyles and standards of living.

BELLRINGER MOTIVATIONAL ACTIVITY

Project the Section 3 Focus Transparency and have students answer the questions.

PRETEACHING VOCABULARY

Have students scan the section for Key Terms in bold print and read the paragraphs containing the terms. Then have them use context clues to define the terms.

MULTICULTURAL PERSPECTIVE

Culturally Speaking
Although French is the official language of Tahiti, Tahitians prefer their own language and their own alphabet of only 13 letters.

SECTION 3

Cultures and Lifestyles

SETTING THE SCENE

Read to Discover . . .
- the factors that have influenced culture in the South Pacific.
- the traditional and Western artforms of the region.
- the varied South Pacific lifestyles and standards of living.

Key Terms
- strine
- pidgin English
- subsistence farming
- fale

Identify and Locate
Easter Island, French Polynesia

The cultural traditions of the native peoples of the South Pacific have contributed much to the region's present-day lifestyles. Later immigrants have also had an impact on the region's lifestyles.

MOVEMENT

A Blend of Cultures

The cultural patterns found in the South Pacific today are a result of many different forces. Climate, natural resources, and landforms have strongly influenced life and culture in the region.

Culture and Environment

The movement of different peoples into the South Pacific region has contributed to shaping cultural patterns there. The earliest peoples of the region developed very distinct cultural traditions. In large part, these patterns grew out of lifestyles that were in harmony with the natural environment. Instead of working to change their environment, Aboriginal hunter-gatherers adapted to its demands. For Australia's Aborigines, this meant a lifestyle that worked with, rather than against, the harsh outback. It meant the development of an idea about their relationship to nature that dominates their way of life. This idea, called Dreamtime, is explained by Aboriginal leader Silas Roberts:

> *Aboriginals have a special connection with everything that is natural. . . . We see all things natural as part of us. All the things on earth we see as part human.*

The early fishing peoples of Melanesia also developed cultures and lifestyles that were closely bound to nature. The sea provided for many of their basic needs. Thus, they lived in small villages at the water's edge. The forms of social organization these people followed were generally based on a fishing way of life, and much of their folklore revolved around the sea.

The European Influence

As Europeans began to move into the South Pacific, the region's cultural patterns began to change. By the early 1900s, many parts of the South Pacific, such as Australia and New Zealand, had cultural patterns and lifestyles that were a mixture of traditional and European customs and beliefs.

Classroom Resources for Section 3

BLACKLINE MASTERS:
Reproducible Lesson Plan 33-3
Foods Around the World 10
World Literature Reading 10
Section Quiz 33-3

TRANSPARENCIES:
Section Focus Transparency 33-3
World Cultures Transparencies 19, 20

MULTIMEDIA:

Testmaker

World Music: *Cultural Traditions, Lesson 10*

Geography and the Environment

Today many of the countries in the South Pacific are strongly Western in their lifestyles and forms of cultural expression. For example, a street scene in downtown Sydney, Australia's largest city, easily could be mistaken for a scene in a British city. Nevertheless, large parts of the South Pacific have maintained much of their traditional culture.

Religious Beliefs

The native peoples of the South Pacific followed many different religious beliefs before the Europeans arrived. When Western missionaries and settlers began moving into the region, however, they brought the ideas and values of Christianity. Although traditional religious beliefs continue to be followed in many parts of the area, Christianity is the most widely held religion in the region today.

Geographic Themes

Region: Australia

Rugby, imported from the United Kingdom, is a popular sport in Australia. *How have European influences affected the South Pacific area?*

PLACE

Languages

As the cultures of the South Pacific blended, their peoples faced the challenge of communicating with one another. Mountains, interior deserts, and isolated islands separated one group of people from another. As a result, people speak many different languages.

The most widely spoken languages in the region today are of the Indo-European language family. English is spoken throughout Australia and New Zealand. The English spoken in Australia, known as **strine**, reflects the easygoing Australian culture.

In Oceania, English is also common in areas that the United States and the United Kingdom have influenced. French is widespread in French Polynesia and in other areas of Oceania that remain under French control.

Most of the languages native to Oceania belong to the Malayo-Polynesian language family. The native language of the Australian

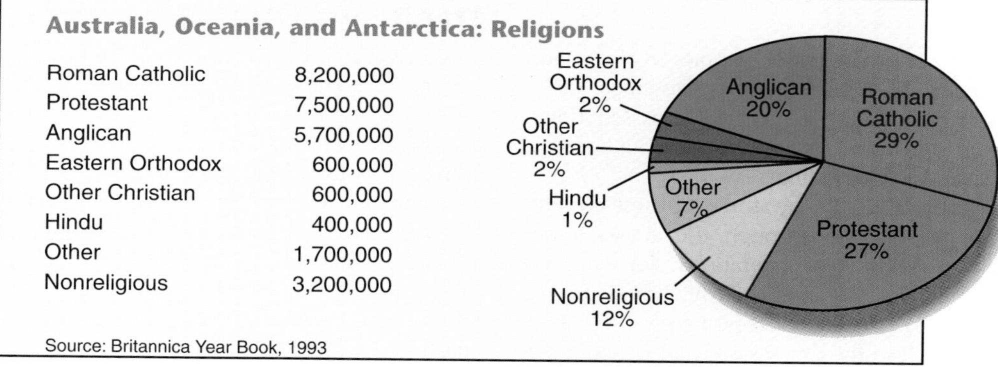

Australia, Oceania, and Antarctica: Religions

Religion	Number
Roman Catholic	8,200,000
Protestant	7,500,000
Anglican	5,700,000
Eastern Orthodox	600,000
Other Christian	600,000
Hindu	400,000
Other	1,700,000
Nonreligious	3,200,000

Source: Britannica Year Book, 1993

Cooperative Learning Activity

Point out that the early peoples of the South Pacific region did not have written languages. Therefore, the origins of these cultures are uncertain.

Organize the class into groups. Have each group choose an early people of the South Pacific and create a plausible history for it. Require the groups to research their chosen people to increase the accuracy of their accounts. Then have the group write and perform a skit about the people's migration to the South Pacific based on their research and hypotheses.

Chapter 33, Section 3

TEACH

GUIDED PRACTICE

Implement Foods Around the World 10 as a class activity.

INDEPENDENT PRACTICE

Guided Reading Have students complete Guided Reading Activity 33-3 in the TCR. **LEP**

Have students complete World Literature Reading 10 in the TCR.

ASSESS

CHECK FOR UNDERSTANDING

Assign Section 3 Review as homework or an in-class activity.

USING ILLUSTRATIONS

REGION Other popular sports in Australia include soccer, cricket, lawn bowling, netball, and fishing.

Answer to Caption: *Europeans brought their lifestyles, religions, and language to the South Pacific.*

GLENCOE TECHNOLOGY

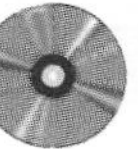

Videodisc

Use the following to enrich Chapter 33:

GEOGRAPHY AND THE ENVIRONMENT
THE INFINITE VOYAGE
Secrets of a Frozen World

Chapter 9
Disc 2 Side B
Title: *Global Awareness: Preserving the Environment*

MEETING LESSON OBJECTIVES

Each objective below is tested by the questions that follow it in parentheses.
1. **List** factors that have influenced culture in the South Pacific. *(3, 5)*
2. **Appreciate** the traditional and Western art forms of the region. *(5)*
3. **Describe** the varied South Pacific lifestyles and standards of living. *(1, 2)*

EVALUATE

 Assign the Section 3 Quiz in the TCR.

 Use the Testmaker to create a customized quiz for Section 3.

RETEACH

 Have students complete Reteaching Activity 33 in the TCR.

USING CHARTS

Answer: 4 percent

Skills Practice

Drawing Conclusions How well do you think the interests of Asians and Aborigines are represented in the Australian government? *(not well; In a democracy, the majority rules.)*

ENRICH

 Have students complete Enrichment Activity 33 in the TCR.

ETHNIC GROUPS OF AUSTRALIA

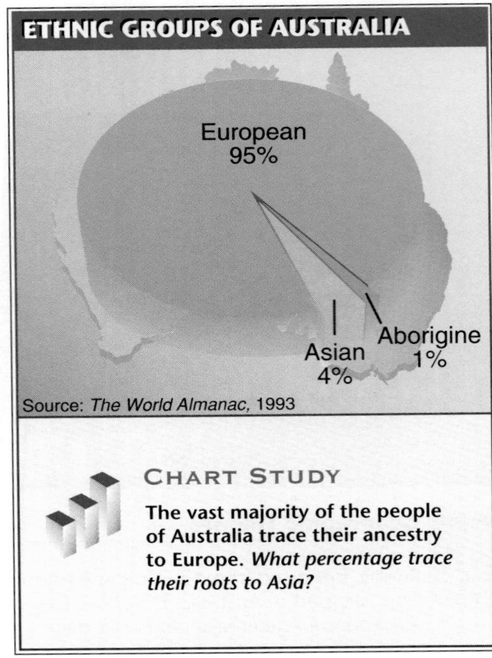

Source: *The World Almanac*, 1993

CHART STUDY

The vast majority of the people of Australia trace their ancestry to Europe. ***What percentage trace their roots to Asia?***

Aborigines, however, belongs to its own separate family.

As trade and contact throughout the South Pacific have increased during recent times, the need for a commonly understood language has become greater. Thus, language forms based upon mixtures of native and European languages have gradually developed. One of these languages is **pidgin English**, a blend of English and native speech.

PLACE

The Arts

Most of the native peoples in the region did not have a written language. History, customs, and beliefs were passed down from generation to generation through music, dance, and storytelling.

Today some of the stories of these cultures can be observed through the art each has passed on to later generations. For example, the people of Easter Island in Polynesia carved huge and mysterious stone figures. While experts believe they may have had religious significance, the stone carvings reflect the artistry of their creators.

In many South Pacific cultures, the arts still derive inspiration from these earlier times. A few Aborigines still paint on the bark of the stringybark tree. Other native artists, in New Zealand for example, are outstanding woodcarvers and woodworkers, creating beautifully carved masks and figurines. By continuing these traditional arts, the region's artists have maintained their heritage of powerful and lively art.

Western forms of art also thrive. In this region described as "a land for the soul to expand into," artists have focused on their individual experiences. Painters such as Arthur Streeton, Charles Conder, and Fred Williams captured their view of the stark Australian outback. In New Zealand, teacher Sylvia Ashton-Warner wrote of her experiences among the Maori people. Australian writer Patrick White received the 1973 Nobel prize in literature for his moving portrayal of life in Australia. The values of native cultures are revealed in the works of Aboriginal poet Kath Walker or Maori novelists such as Patricia Grace.

HUMAN/ENVIRONMENT INTERACTION

Lifestyles

Two general lifestyle patterns are found in the region. One pattern is largely traditional. The other reflects a European background.

Traditional Lifestyles

For many Pacific islanders, daily life is a struggle. Sometimes the soil is too poor to support much agriculture. On these islands, such as Vanuatu or Tonga, native people work at **subsistence farming**, growing only enough food for their own needs. These foods might be bananas, coconuts, or sweet potatoes. Where possible islanders raise chickens and pigs, and fish in the oceans around them. Others work in relatively low-paying jobs for either local or federal governments.

Meeting Special Needs

Reading Disability Students with poor reading skills often learn best by having new procedures, such as restating strategies, modeled for them several times. Explain to students that you are going to model a restating strategy that will help them understand what they read.

Have them turn to the heading "Traditional Lifestyles" and read the third sentence. Then demonstrate restating: "The people on Vanuatu, Tonga, and other Pacific islands are subsistence farmers, growing only enough to live on." Invite volunteers to restate other sentences in the section.

A typical traditional South Pacific home is very simple in design. In Western Samoa for example, the traditional type of home is called a **fale.** Its open sides allow cooling ocean breezes to circulate, and the thatched roof shields dwellers from the hot tropical sun. For privacy, blinds of coconut palm leaves can be lowered.

European Lifestyles

People in Australia and New Zealand, where the strongest European influences exist, live a very different life. Even those living in the Australian outback or working in isolated mining towns enjoy modern conveniences. Some may even commute thousands of miles to and from nearby cities, leading a dual existence that brings current trends and ideas into remote areas.

In the cities, life is typically modern with elegant shopping malls, large sports stadiums, and towering skyscrapers. Ethnic neighborhoods such as the Cabramatta district of Sydney lend an international flavor.

Both in cities and rural areas, Australians and New Zealanders dress in Western styles. Shorts and other casual clothes are popular because of the mild climate.

Health and Education

Many Pacific islanders are in poor health because of the difficulties of life and the remoteness of many islands. Fresh foods and meats are often scarce, and water and electricity are often unavailable. As a result, many of the people have chronic illnesses.

Lack of education may make it difficult for Pacific islanders to improve their lives. In many nations, despite help from wealthier Western countries, most people cannot read or write. Some nations have made great progress. On these islands, children regularly attend government or missionary schools, and literacy rates are much higher.

Geography also poses a challenge to health care and education in Australia. Modern technology, however, allows doctors to consult with patients through the use of 2-way radios or the Royal Flying Doctor Service.

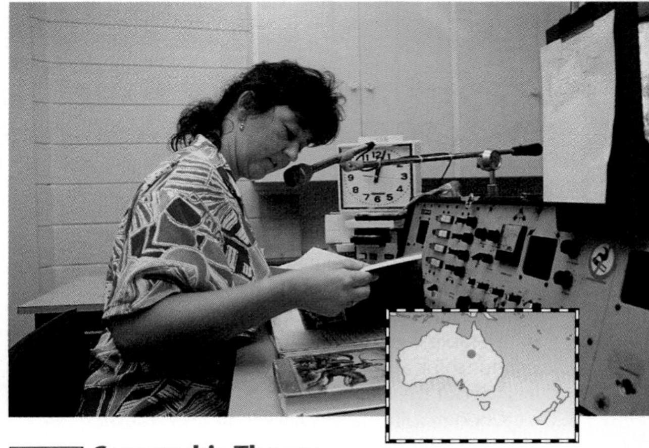

Geographic Themes

Region: Australia

Children in remote areas of Australia receive daily school lessons over "schools of the air." *How does modern technology aid health care in Australia?*

Modern technologies also help Australia's young people in the outback to receive an education. If an area does not have the 8 or 9 children necessary to start a school, students take classes by 2-way radio or through the mail with correspondence courses.

Section 3 Review

Checking for Understanding

1. **Define** strine, pidgin English, subsistence farming, fale.
2. **Locating Places** What is Australia's largest city?
3. **Movement** What communications problems has geography created for the peoples of Australia, New Zealand, and Oceania?
4. **Region** Why is the health of many Pacific Islanders poor?

Critical Thinking

5. **Making Generalizations** In what ways have geographic factors worked to shape cultural development in the South Pacific region?

CLOSE

Have students compare their lifestyles with those described in the section. List the similarities and differences on the chalkboard.

USING ILLUSTRATIONS

REGION Unlike some Pacific islands, Tahiti has a literacy rate almost equal to Australia's: 98.5 percent.

Answer to Caption: *Doctors consult with patients through the use of two-way radios or the Royal Flying Doctor Service.*

ANSWERS TO SECTION 3 REVIEW

1. strine: Australian English; **pidgin English:** simplified English used by Pacific islanders; **subsistence farming:** raising only enough crops for the family's use; **fale:** a Pacific island structure with thatched roof and open sides

2. Sydney

3. In Australia and New Zealand, great distances have made communication, except by radio, difficult. In Oceania, geography has isolated groups, creating so many languages that the peoples cannot communicate.

4. because of the difficulties of daily life and the remoteness of the islands

5. Isolation contributed to the variety of languages and the development of music, dance, and storytelling; natural resources serve as materials for native artists.

TEACH

Help students understand the table by asking: "How is population density measured?" *(total population divided by the area)* "What does annual growth rate measure?" *(how fast a population is increasing)* "What do urbanization rates show?" *(percentage of people living in cities)*

Explain that GDP means gross domestic product, the total value of goods and services produced within a country. Stress that GDP does not show how widely that wealth is distributed. Discuss how life expectancy and the categories listed under it reflect a nation's standard of living.

Skills Practice
For additional practice, have students complete Skill Activity 33 in the TCR.

MAP & GRAPH SKILLS

Reading Tables and Analyzing Statistics

Reading lists of facts and figures can be confusing. Therefore, statistics are often organized into **tables,** which condense numerical information into a compact format.

REVIEWING THE SKILL

In a table, similar kinds of information are organized into columns and rows. Labels across the top and left-hand sides explain what the numbers in the table represent. Identifying patterns and relationships among the figures can reveal a great deal about the topic.

When reading tables and analyzing statistics, apply the following steps:

- Read headings and labels to determine the kinds of information included in the table.
- Look up unfamiliar terms.
- Identify similarities, differences, and other relationships among the data.
- Use the data to draw conclusions.

PRACTICING THE SKILL

Study the table below and answer the following questions.

1. Which countries are compared in the table?
2. How do the countries rank according to total population? Population density?
3. Which country has the highest GDP per capita? The lowest GDP per capita?
4. What is the relationship between infant mortality and life expectancy? Between infant mortality and per capita GDP?
5. What is the relationship between urbanization and electricity consumption?

For additional practice in this skill, see Practicing Skills on page 684 of the Chapter 33 Review.

COMPARATIVE DATA (SELECTED NATIONS)

	Australia	Fiji	New Zealand	Papua New Guinea
Population	17,800,000	800,000	3,500,000	4,000,000
Population density (per square mile)	6/sq. mi.	113/sq. mi.	33/sq. mi.	22/sq. mi.
Annual population growth	0.8%	2.0%	0.9%	2.3%
Urbanization	85%	39%	85%	13%
GDP - US dollars GDP per capita	$311,000,000,000 $18,054	$1,300,000,000 $1,840	$40,000,000,000 $12,200	$2,700,000,000 $725
Life Expectancy	77 years	64.5 years	75.5 years	55.5 years
Infant Mortality Rate (per 1000 births)	7/1000	15/1000	7/1000	72/1000
Population per physician	472	2,745	518	13,827
Literacy Rate	100%	86%	99%	52%
Electricity Consumption per capita (kw hours)	8,258	590	8,235	435

Sources: *The World Almanac,* 1995; The Population Reference Bureau, 1994

ANSWERS TO PRACTICING THE SKILL

1. Australia, Fiji, New Zealand, Papua New Guinea
2. total population: from largest to smallest—Australia, Papua New Guinea, New Zealand, Fiji; from most to least dense—Fiji, New Zealand, Papua New Guinea, Australia
3. highest—Australia; lowest—Papua New Guinea
4. As infant mortality increases, life expectancy rates decrease. Countries with higher per capita GDP have lower infant mortality rates.
5. Countries with higher rates of urbanization also have higher rates of electricity consumption.

chapter 33

HIGHLIGHTS

1 SECTION Population Patterns

KEY TERMS

primate city (p. 670)

SUMMARY

- Many different groups of people have settled in the South Pacific, creating a blend of peoples, cultures, and lifestyles.
- The population of the South Pacific is unevenly distributed because many areas cannot support life.

Auckland, New Zealand

2 SECTION History and Government

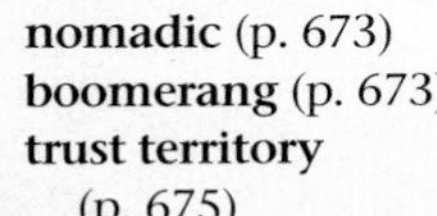

KEY TERMS

nomadic (p. 673)
boomerang (p. 673)
trust territory (p. 675)

SUMMARY

- The first humans to settle the South Pacific probably came from Southeast Asia. Settlement then spread eastward.
- In the late 1700s, the British began settling Australia and then New Zealand.
- European nations and Japan struggled throughout the late 1800s and early 1900s for control of the Pacific islands.

Parliament buildings in Canberra, Australia

3 SECTION Cultures and Lifestyles

KEY TERMS

strine (p. 679)
pidgin English (p. 680)
subsistence farming (p. 680)
fale (p. 681)

SUMMARY

- European culture has become dominant in the South Pacific. Traditional cultural elements, however, continue to shape lifestyles in the region today.
- Settlement patterns in the South Pacific have been largely determined by climates and landforms. Cultural and economic backgrounds have also affected lifestyles and standards of health and education in the South Pacific.

Australian rugby match

CHAPTER 33 HIGHLIGHTS

USING THE CHAPTER 33 HIGHLIGHTS

Use the Chapter 33 Highlights to preview, review, condense, or reteach the chapter.

PREVIEW/REVIEW

Vocabulary PuzzleMaker Software reinforces the Key Terms used in Chapter 33.

Student Self-Test and Review Software allows students to review Chapter 33 content.

CONDENSE

Have students read the Chapter 33 Highlights.

Have students listen to the Chapter 33 Audiocassettes in the TCR. Spanish Audiocassettes are also available.

Assign the Chapter 33 Audiocassette Activity and give students the Chapter 33 Audiocassette Quiz.

Have students complete Guided Reading Activities for Chapter 33 in the TCR. Spanish Guided Reading Activities are also available.

RETEACH

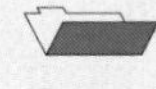

Have students complete Reteaching Activity 33 in the TCR. Spanish Reteaching Activities are also available.

Map Activity

Identify and Locate Distribute copies of page 38 of the Outline Map Resource Book. Have the students use maps from the chapter to identify and label the cities of Sydney, Melbourne, Auckland, and Wellington and the islands of Papua New Guinea, Iwo Jima, Western Samoa, and the Society Islands.

GLENCOE TECHNOLOGY

Videodisc

Use Chapter 33 MindJogger Videoquiz to review students' knowledge before administering the Chapter 33 Test.

MINDJOGGER VIDEOQUIZ

Chapter 33
Disc 5 Side A

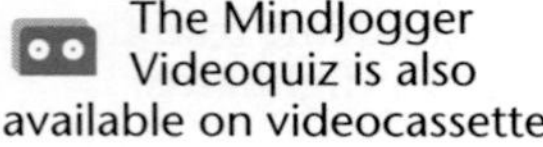

The MindJogger Videoquiz is also available on videocassette.

ANSWERS

Reviewing Key Terms

1. primate city
2. nomadic
3. boomerang
4. subsistence farming
5. strine
6. pidgin English
7. fales

Reviewing Facts

8. Aborigines, Maori
9. the United Kingdom
10. across a land bridge from Southeast Asia
11. to serve time as convicts
12. Christianity
13. through dance, music, and storytelling

chapter 33 REVIEW

Reviewing Key Terms

Choose the vocabulary term that best completes each of the sentences below. Write your answers on a separate sheet of paper.

primate city (p. 670)
nomadic (p. 673)
boomerang (p. 673)
strine (p. 679)
pidgin English (p. 680)
subsistence farming (p. 680)
fales (p. 681)

Section 1

1. A ____ serves as its country's capital, port, and single major urban area.

Section 2

2. ____ people do not establish permanent settlements.
3. A ____ is used for hunting.

Section 3

4. ____ involves growing only enough food for one's own needs.
5. Australians speak ____ .
6. ____ has made it easier for Pacific islanders to understand each other.
7. Many Pacific islanders live in homes called ____ .

Reviewing Facts

Section 1

8. Who were the first settlers in Australia and New Zealand?
9. From what country can most Australians and New Zealanders trace their roots?

Section 2

10. How did the earliest settlers reach Australia?
11. Why were the first British people sent to settle Australia?

Section 3

12. What is the dominant religion in the South Pacific region?
13. In the past how did traditional South Pacific peoples pass their history to the next generation?

Critical Thinking

14. **Analyzing Information** Why are Australia and New Zealand largely urbanized?
15. **Identifying Central Issues** Why did European nations and Japan struggle to control Oceania in the 1800s and 1900s?
16. **Expressing Problems Clearly** How has geography affected health and education in Oceania?

Geographic Themes

17. **Place** Why do most people in Australia live in coastal cities?
18. **Movement** How did the discovery of gold affect the settlement of Australia?
19. **Human/Environment Interaction** How do Australia's Aborigines view their relationship to nature?

Practicing Skills

Reading Tables and Analyzing Statistics

Refer to the statistical table on page 682. Which country has the lowest standard of living? On what figures do you base this conclusion?

Using the Unit Atlas

Refer to the cultural geography section of the Unit Atlas on pages 648–649.

20. Where do most of Australia's people live?
21. What major ethnic groups make up Oceania's population?

Critical Thinking

14. Much of the interior sections, particularly of Australia, support grazing but not farming. As machines replace people in rural areas, these people move to cities. Many young people from Pacific islands move to the cities seeking opportunity. Improved communication and technology attract businesses from around the world.

15. The islands were an important stopping place on Pacific trade routes, and they had natural resources the trading nations wanted.

16. The isolation on the islands has made good health care and education difficult.

Projects

Individual Activity

The work of many writers and artists of the South Pacific culture region reflects their personal view of the region. Study the work of a writer or artist from the region (such as Kath Walker or Sydney Nolan) and explain in a brief oral report how the work captures the spirit of the South Pacific.

Cooperative Learning Activity

Working with a partner, create pairs of sister city locations from throughout the region. One student should choose locations for each pair that are heavily populated while the other student chooses locations with sparse population. List two advantages and disadvantages to human settlement in your areas. Then work together to pair locations with compatible features. If you wish, present the pairs to the rest of the class and invite their input.

Writing About Geography

Cause and Effect

Imagine you are a time traveler who has traveled to the South Pacific islands before European settlement. Write a description of how European settlement has affected your island and its people. Be sure to identify the causes for any changes you discuss. Use your journal, text, and other reference sources to help you gather the necessary information.

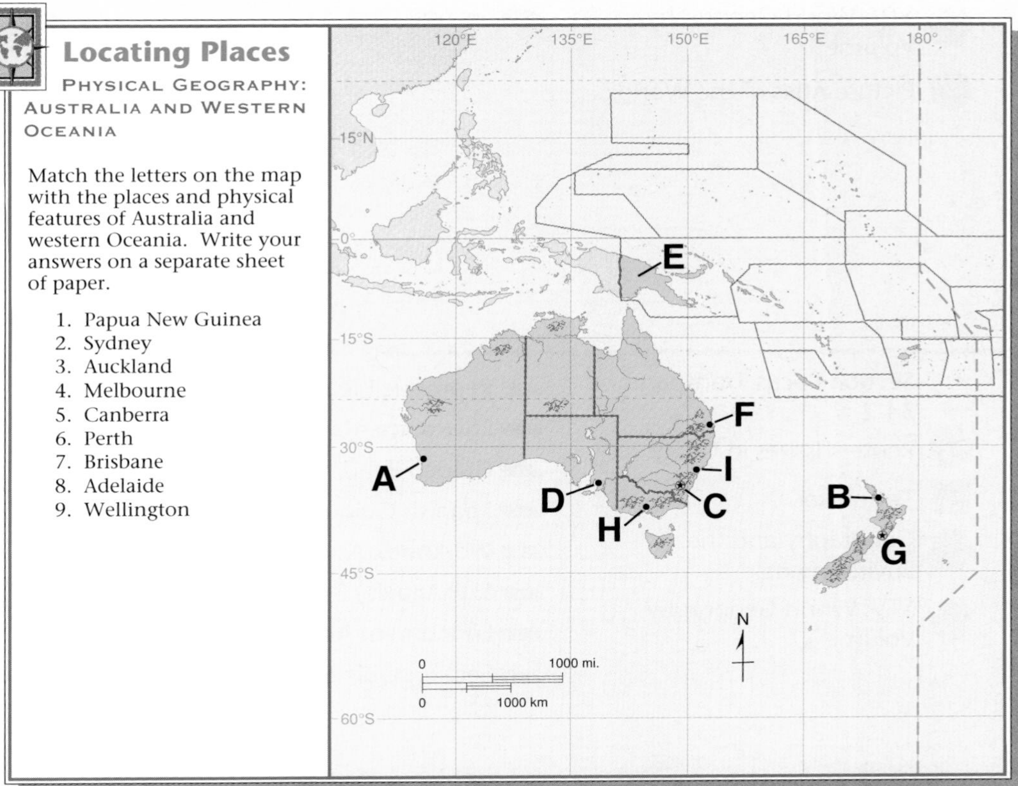

Locating Places

PHYSICAL GEOGRAPHY: AUSTRALIA AND WESTERN OCEANIA

Match the letters on the map with the places and physical features of Australia and western Oceania. Write your answers on a separate sheet of paper.

1. Papua New Guinea
2. Sydney
3. Auckland
4. Melbourne
5. Canberra
6. Perth
7. Brisbane
8. Adelaide
9. Wellington

Chapter 33 Review

Geographic Themes

17. The climate is more moderate on the coast than in the interior; ranches in the outback require few workers.

18. It created a wave of immigration.

19. They see themselves as part of nature and nature as part of them.

Practicing Skills

Papua New Guinea: it has the lowest GDP per capita, the highest infant mortality rate, the most people per physician, and the lowest literacy rate.

Using the Unit Atlas

20. the southeastern part of the country

21. Melanesian, Micronesian, and Polynesian

Locating Places

1. E
2. I
3. B
4. H
5. C
6. A
7. F
8. D
9. G

Chapter Bonus Test Question

This question may be used for extra credit on the chapter test.

How might Australia be different today if gold had never been discovered there?

(Answers will vary but should point out that fewer immigrants would have resulted in a smaller and less varied population.)

CHAPTER 34

PLANNING GUIDE

Australia, Oceania, and Antarctica Today

CHAPTER ORGANIZER

Daily Lesson Objectives	Multimedia	Teacher Classroom Resources
SECTION 1 Living in Australia, Oceania, and Antarctica 1. Compare the kinds of agriculture practiced in the South Pacific region. 2. Examine the reasons for economic interdependence in Australia and Oceania. 3. Identify the transportation and communication challenges facing the Australia, Oceania, and Antarctica regions. 4. Locate the industries that thrive in Australia, Oceania, and Antarctica.	Section Focus Transparency 34-1 Chapter 34 Vocabulary PuzzleMaker Software Unit Map Overlay Transparency 11 Testmaker STV: World Geography, Volume 1 Picture Atlas of the World	Reproducible Lesson Plan 34-1 Outline Map Resource Book, p. 38 Guided Reading Activity 34-1 Spanish Guided Reading Activity 34-1 Performance Assessment Activity 34 Workbook Activity 34-1 Section Quiz 34-1
SECTION 2 People and Their Environment 1. Understand the impact on the environment of new animal species introduced to Australia and Oceania. 2. Illustrate how industrial development has affected the land and climate of South Pacific countries. 3. Explain the impact of human exploration on the environment of Antarctica.	Section Focus Transparency 34-2 Reuters Issues in Geography Testmaker Geography and the Environment STV: World Geography, Volume 3	Reproducible Lesson Plan 34-2 Environmental Issue 11 Guided Reading Activity 34-2 Spanish Guided Reading Activity 34-2 Workbook Activity 34-2 Skill Activity 34 Enrichment Activity 34 Section Quiz 34-2
CHAPTER REVIEW AND EVALUATION	Chapter 34 English (or Spanish) Audiocassettes MindJogger Videoquiz Testmaker Student Self-Test and Review Software	Reteaching Activity 34 Spanish Reteaching Activity 34 Outline Map Resource Book, p. 38 Chapter 34 Test Form A and Form B

0:00 *If time does not permit teaching the entire chapter, summarize using the Chapter 34 Highlights on page 699, and the Chapter 34 English (or Spanish) Audiocassettes. Review students' knowledge using the Glencoe MindJogger Videoquiz.*

KEY TO ABILITY LEVELS

Teaching strategies have been coded for varying learning styles and abilities.

L1 **BASIC** activities for all students

L2 **AVERAGE** activities for average to above-average students

L3 **CHALLENGING** activities for above-average students

LEP **LIMITED ENGLISH PROFICIENCY** activities

Performance Assessment

Analyzing Information Assess student understanding through a scored discussion. Assign students to one of five groups in the classroom. These groups should form study committees to review or expand information on the economies and environmental concerns of Australia, Oceania, and Antarctica. On the day of the discussion, have one group at a time answer a question from the list below:

(1) What is the future of agriculture in the region?
(2) What industries and businesses will prosper in the future? What problems will they have to overcome to do so?
(3) How has human activity affected the environment of the South Pacific? What future trends do you foresee?
(4) What is the most serious environmental problem in the region? What solutions have been tried? What suggestions would you make?
(5) What are some examples of interdependence in the region? What would be the likely effects if any of these links were destroyed?

POSSIBLE RUBRIC FEATURES: Content information, predictive skills, recognizing connections, collaboration skills, communication skills

For additional professional and classroom resources, see Chapter Resources, pages T46–T51.

TEACHER'S CORNER

INDEX TO NATIONAL GEOGRAPHIC MAGAZINE

The following articles may be used for research relating to this chapter:

- "In Bikini Lagoon Life Thrives in a Nuclear Graveyard," by John L. Eliot, June 1992.
- "The Captivating Kiwifruit," by Noel D. Veitmeyer, May 1987.
- "Bikini: A Way of Life Lost," by William S. Ellis, June 1986.
- "Across Australia by Sunpower," by Hans Tholstrup, November 1983.
- "A Marine Park is Born: Australia's Great Barrier Reef," by Soames Summerhays, May 1981.
- "Paradise Beneath the Sea," by Ron and Valerie Taylor, May 1981.

NATIONAL GEOGRAPHIC SOCIETY PRODUCTS AVAILABLE FROM GLENCOE

To order the following products for use with this chapter, contact your local Glencoe sales representative or call Glencoe at 1-800-334-7344:

- *Picture Atlas of the World* (CD-ROM)
- *STV: World Geography, South America and Antarctica* (Videodisc)
- *STV: World Geography, Asia and Australia* (Videodisc)
- *ZipZapMap! World* (Software)
- *GeoBee* (Software)
- *Images of the World* (Posters)
- *Eye on the Environment* (Posters)
- *Physical Geography of the World* (Transparencies)
- *Picture Atlas of Our 50 States* (Book)

Introducing
CHAPTER 34

chapter 34

Australia, Oceania, and Antarctica Today

PERFORMANCE ASSESSMENT

Refer to the Planning Guide on page 686B for a Performance Assessment Activity for this chapter. See the *Performance Assessment Activities* booklet for additional suggestions.

CHAPTER OBJECTIVES

1. **Explain** how modern transportation and communication has brought the Australia, Oceania, and Antarctica culture region closer to the rest of the world.
2. **Discuss** how the unique environment of the South Pacific, no longer protected by distance and isolation, has been damaged by human actions.

GLENCOE TECHNOLOGY

Videodisc

Use Chapter 34 MindJogger Videoquiz to preview chapter content.

MINDJOGGER VIDEOQUIZ

Chapter 34
Disc 5 Side A

The MindJogger Videoquiz is also available on videocassette.

CHAPTER FOCUS

Geographic Setting

Long distances and harsh climates have often posed economic and environmental challenges that Australia, Oceania, and Antarctica have met with varying success.

▲ Photograph: *Sheep farm in New Zealand*

Geographic Themes

Section 1 Living in Australia, Oceania, and Antarctica
MOVEMENT Modern transportation and communication has brought the Australia, Oceania, and Antarctica culture region closer to the rest of the world.

Section 2 People and Their Environment
LOCATION The unique environment of the South Pacific, no longer protected by distance and isolation, has been damaged by human settlement.

EXTRA CREDIT PROJECT

Research Explain that of 102 native mammals in Australia, 28 percent are extinct, and another 40 percent are either endangered, vulnerable, or rare. One of the major threats to native Australian species are competition or predation by introduced species—rabbits, horses, camels, goats, deer, foxes, cats, starlings, pigeons, sparrows, and hundreds of plants. Ask interested students to research several native and introduced species. Then have them use their findings to make a chart with the native species listed across the top and the introduced ones listed down the left side. Ask them to explain on the chart how the introduced species to the left affect the native species at the top. Display the completed charts in the classroom.

1 SECTION
Living in Australia, Oceania, and Antarctica

SETTING THE SCENE

Read to Discover . . .
- the kinds of agriculture practiced in the South Pacific region.
- the reasons for economic interdependence in Australia and Oceania.
- the transportation and communication challenges facing the Australia, Oceania, and Antarctica culture regions.
- the industries that thrive in Australia, Oceania, and Antarctica.

Key Terms
- grazier
- station
- copra
- subsistence farming
- rail gauge

Identify and Locate
St. George Island, Bougainville, Western Australia, Pilbara, Kimberley, Tuvalu, New South Wales, Federated States of Micronesia, the South Island

kahu-huruhuru / Maori feather cloak (detail)
50¢ NEW ZEALAND

Wellington, New Zealand

I live in Wellington, which is a hilly city and the capital of New Zealand. We use trains and buses for transportation, and there is even a cable car. I earn money delivering newspapers, which I do on foot because of the steep hills. My country relies on meat and farm produce for income, so there is always a lot of fresh fruit in the stores, and sheep on the hillsides. Dave Ferguson

As Dave Ferguson's postcard reveals, people who live in the Australia, Oceania, and Antarctica culture region produce a variety of food products. Agriculture is by far the region's most important economic activity.

HUMAN/ENVIRONMENT INTERACTION

Food Production

Farmers in the culture region vary their agriculture according to geographic conditions. Australian farmers, using scientific methods and machinery, adapt their farming methods to the generally dry climate. New Zealand and Australia export large quantities of farm products—especially meat, wool, dairy products, and wheat.

Ranching

Sheep and cattle graze over much of the land in Australia and New Zealand. In Australia livestock, tended by cowhands and sheep **graziers**, or herders, must search a large area to find enough vegetation. As a result some Australian **stations**, or ranches, are

LESSON PLAN
Chapter 34, Section 1

FOCUS

SECTION OBJECTIVES
1. **Compare** the kinds of agriculture practiced in the South Pacific region.
2. **Examine** the reasons for economic interdependence in Australia and Oceania.
3. **Identify** the transportation and communication challenges facing the Australia, Oceania, and Antarctica regions.
4. **Locate** the industries that thrive in Australia, Oceania, and Antarctica.

ABOUT THE POSTCARD
Dave tells us that many people visit his country because of its beautiful and varied landscape.

BELLRINGER MOTIVATIONAL ACTIVITY

Project the Section 1 Focus Transparency and have students answer the questions.

PRETEACHING VOCABULARY
Make and distribute crossword puzzles using the Key Terms and definitions from the section. Tell students to count squares to help them match each Key Term to its definition.

Use the Vocabulary PuzzleMaker Software to create a crossword or word search puzzle.

Classroom Resources for Section 1

BLACKLINE MASTERS:
Reproducible Lesson Plan 34-1
Outline Map Resource Book, p. 38
Guided Reading Activity 34-1
Spanish Guided Reading Activity 34-1
Workbook Activity 34-1
Performance Assessment Activity 34
Section Quiz 34-1

TRANSPARENCIES:
Section Focus Transparency 34-1
Unit Map Overlay Transparency 11

MULTIMEDIA:
Vocabulary PuzzleMaker Software
Testmaker

STV: World Geography, Volume 1

Picture Atlas of the World

TEACH

GUIDED PRACTICE

L1 Product Map Copy and distribute the map of the South Pacific on page 38 of the Outline Map Resource Book. Have students label each region on the map with the names of the products it produces. Refer them to pages 687 and 688 for help. *(New Zealand and Australia: meat, wool, dairy products, and wheat; Oceania: tropical fruits, sugar, coffee, copra, and other coconut products)*

HUMAN/ENVIRONMENT INTERACTION In addition to sugarcane, Fiji produces bananas, rice, cassava, and coconuts.

Answer to Caption: *sheep, cattle, wheat, tropical fruit, coffee, and coconut*

MULTICULTURAL PERSPECTIVE

Cultural Heritage
One coconut product in Tonga is not eaten but worn. Tongans use coconut-fiber ropes to secure *ta'oavalas*—traditional garments made from the leaves of the Pandanus tree—around their waist.

CD-ROM

PICTURE ATLAS OF THE WORLD
You and your students can view a New Zealand sheep ranch by clicking the country's "Video" button.

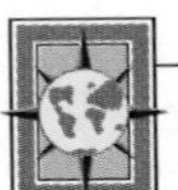

Geographic Themes

Human/Environment Interaction: Fiji
Unlike many other Pacific island countries, Fiji has much commercial farming. Sugar cane is one of Fiji's major agricultural exports. *What agricultural items are raised elsewhere in the Pacific area?*

mammoth—as large as 6,000 square miles (15,540 sq. km). The largest stations are almost self-sufficient economic units, complete with stores and post offices.

Australia and New Zealand have used scientific research and advertising to establish new markets for farm products. Improved machinery and fertilizers and innovative packaging have expanded sales to western Europe and Japan.

Subsistence Farming

In much of Oceania, climate and soil conditions do not support widespread commercial farming. On the low Micronesian islands, **copra,** the dried meat from the coconut palms, is often the only farm product exported. Island farmers generally practice **subsistence farming,** growing only enough food to feed themselves.

Farming is more widespread on the high islands of Oceania, where rich volcanic soil and ample rainfall support a variety of crops. Some people produce cash crops including tropical fruits, sugar, coffee, and copra and other coconut products.

Fishing is also an important source of food, especially on the low islands, and some fish are exported as well.

Because of its harsh climate, Antarctica produces no farm crops. Its icy coastal waters are a rich source of seafood.

HUMAN/ENVIRONMENT INTERACTION

Mining and Manufacturing

Scattered unevenly throughout the region are mineral deposits of copper, iron ore, lead, and coal. Australia has many mines and is a leading exporter of diamonds, gold, bauxite, and iron ore.

Most of the region's ore is exported to Japan to be made into cars and appliances. Australia has a growing economic interdependence with nearby Asia.

The other areas of Oceania have only scattered mining industries. Melanesians, for example, mine copper and in Micronesia, phosphate mining has become important. The possibility of one day reaching the large deposits of valuable minerals believed to lie under the Antarctic ice cap also exists.

Cooperative Learning Activity

On the chalkboard, copy the following outline:

I. AUSTRALIA
  A. Manufactured Products
  B. Transportation and Communication
II. NEW ZEALAND
  A. Manufactured Products
  B. Transportation and Communication
III. OCEANIA
  A. Manufactured Products
  B. Transportation and Communication

Have students complete the outline with details from the section as they read.

Domestic Manufacturing

Geography has limited manufacturing in the South Pacific. Importing equipment and raw materials is too difficult and too expensive. In Oceania a lack of skilled workers, modern transportation, and communications systems are also factors. Almost all manufacturing is done in Australia, near Sydney and Melbourne, and in New Zealand, near Auckland.

Challenges to Growth

Many of Oceania's islands are too small to produce large amounts of goods and are located too far from trading markets.

Modern air travel has increased island tourism. Visitors enjoy the region's scenery and beaches, while boosting island economies. Aid from Western nations also helps many Pacific island countries.

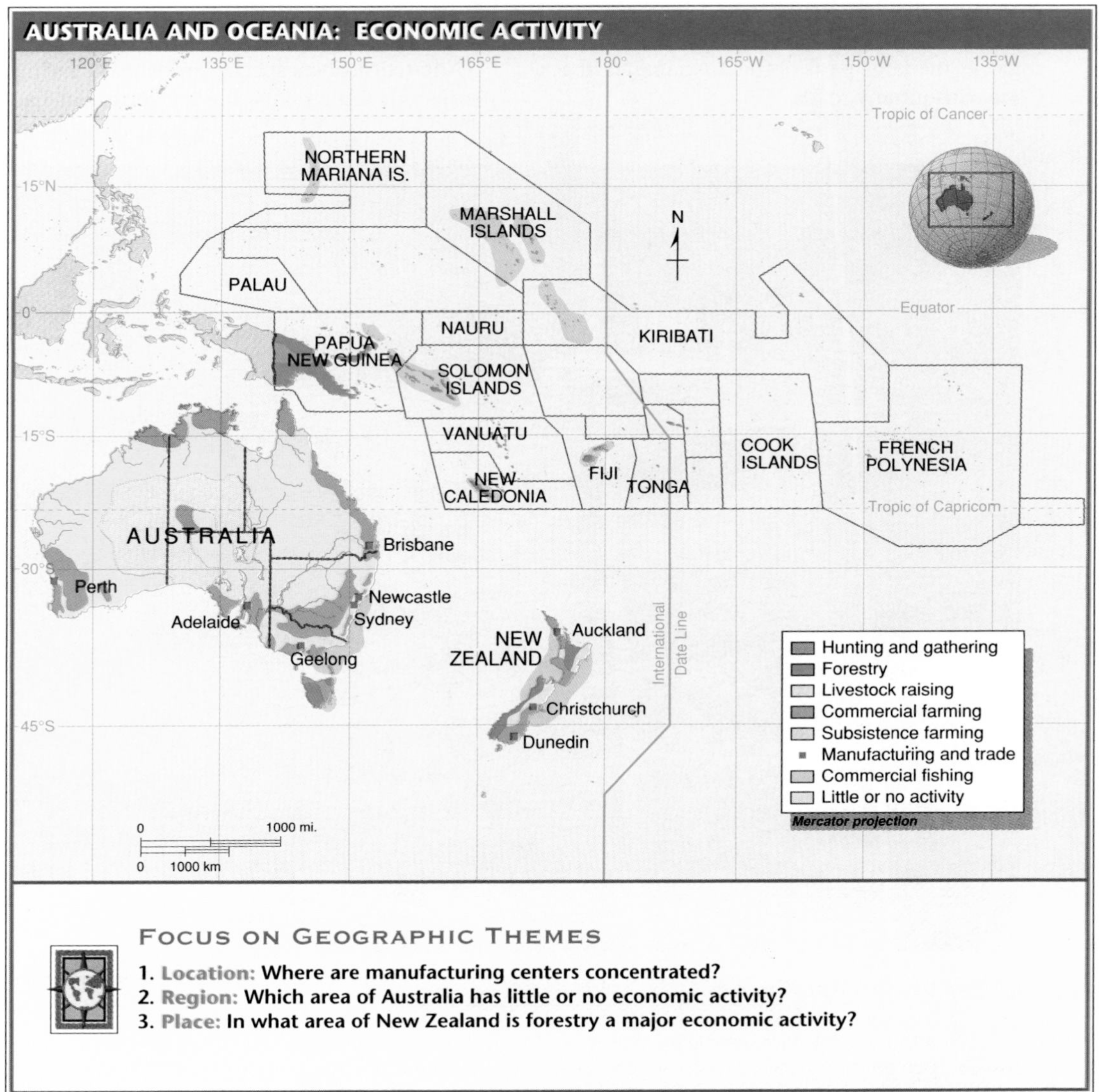

Focus on Geographic Themes

1. **Location:** Where are manufacturing centers concentrated?
2. **Region:** Which area of Australia has little or no economic activity?
3. **Place:** In what area of New Zealand is forestry a major economic activity?

INDEPENDENT PRACTICE

Guided Reading Have students complete Guided Reading Activity 34-1 in the TCR. **LEP**

Have students complete Unit Map Overlay Transparency 11 Activity in the TCR.

CURRICULUM CONNECTION

ZOOLOGY

Captain Cook and his botanists did not find all the new species in the South Pacific. Fiji's crested iguana, one of the rarest reptiles, was not discovered until 1979.

USING MAPS

Answers: **1.** on the southeastern coasts of Australia and New Zealand; **2.** the central part; **3.** the western coast of South Island and the central part of North Island

Map Skills Practice

Drawing Conclusions Why are commercial farming areas near the Australian coast? *(The cities, and thus the major markets for crops, are there.)*

ASSESS

CHECK FOR UNDERSTANDING

Assign Section 1 Review as homework or an in-class activity.

Meeting Special Needs

Language Disability Restating is difficult for students with language problems. They often have trouble finding synonyms for words in the text. Explain that the point of this procedure is for them to use common language and not to make it sound like the textbook.

Under the heading "Domestic Manufacturing," have students look for words that might be somewhat complex and have them replace those words with suitable synonyms. Some changes might be: expensive—costly, import—ship in, and factor—reason.

MEETING LESSON OBJECTIVES

Each objective below is tested by the questions that follow it in parentheses.

1. **Compare** the kinds of agriculture practiced in the South Pacific region. *(5)*
2. **Examine** the reasons for economic interdependence in Australia and Oceania. *(3, 4)*
3. **Identify** the transportation and communication challenges facing the Australia, Oceania, and Antarctica regions. *(2, 4)*
4. **Locate** the industries that thrive in Australia, Oceania, and Antarctica. *(2, 3, 4, 5)*

EVALUATE

Assign the Section 1 Quiz in the TCR.

Use the Testmaker to create a customized quiz for Section 1.

RETEACH

Have students complete Workbook Activity 34-1 found in the TCR.

USING ILLUSTRATIONS

REGION Australia ranks fifth in the world in the number of automobiles per capita.

Answer to Caption: frustrating, because of frequent train changes

Videodisc

STV: WORLD GEOGRAPHY, VOLUME 1

Side 2, Chapter 2
Frames 05001-15553
Title: *Australia*
Subject: Australian outback

MOVEMENT

Transportation and Communication

Australia, Oceania, and Antarctica are partially inaccessible. The region contains thousands of miles of solid ice, endless desert, and vast oceans.

Ground Travel

Australia and New Zealand have the most well-developed road and rail systems in the region. Still, large parts of the Australian outback are without any roads.

Travelers on Australia's rail system are sometimes frustrated. Not all of the country's railroads are built to the same standards. The **rail gauge**—or distance between the rails—from state to state does not match. This results in the use of different rail cars, so traveling across the country means changing trains.

New Zealand's rail and road system is quite good. Even though the terrain is often mountainous, most of New Zealand can be reached.

In Oceania, entire countries do not have well-developed road or rail systems. Countries are working hard to improve the roads and bridges necessary for industrial growth.

Antarctica poses special problems. Lacking permanent settlements, the icy continent has

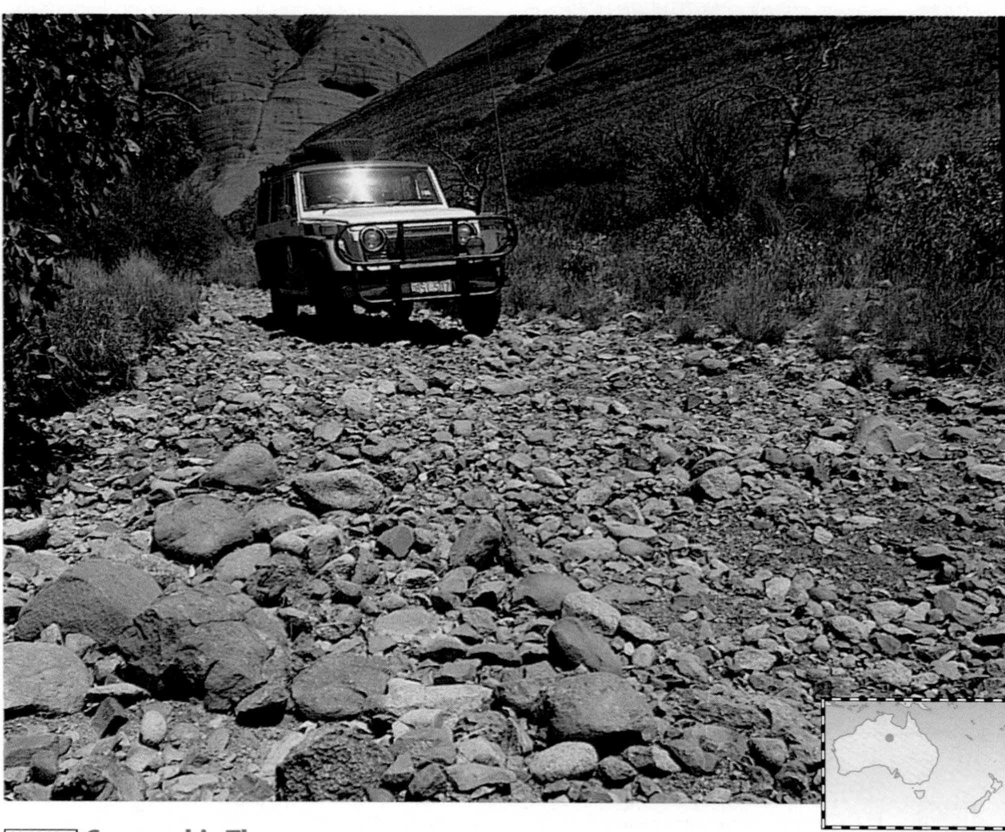

Geographic Themes

Region: Australian Outback

A four-wheel-drive vehicle is ideally suited to Australia's rugged outback. Only about 36 percent of Australia's roads are paved, and few roads exist in the outback region. *What is rail travel like in Australia?*

Critical Thinking

Drawing Conclusions Point out to students that there are advantages and disadvantages to living anywhere, such as a moderate climate or lack of natural resources. Have the students think of factors that would affect people's choices for settling in the South Pacific region. Write their responses on the chalkboard. Then have them decide where in the South Pacific region each of the following people would choose to live: a farmer, a fisher, a millionaire, an actor, a miner, and a scientist. Ask them to list the geographic advantages of each place for that person.

Geographic Themes

Human/Environment Interaction: Antarctica

Air travel is available to Antarctica during the long winter months when ice blocks all forms of water transportation. *Why is air travel an important method of transportation in the Pacific area?*

no need for road or rail systems, and specially designed vehicles are required.

Air and Water Travel

Air and water travel are the most essential to the region. Pacific islanders started traveling by outrigger canoe thousands of years ago. Small wind- or motor-powered boats are still used. New Zealanders ride ferries from the North Island to the South Island.

Scientists in Antarctica's coastal stations depend on cargo ships and airplanes to deliver needed goods. On Australia's large stations, cattle owners use helicopters to reach their cattle. Small airplanes are needed to travel between the islands of Oceania.

The development of modern communication, such as telephones and radios, has had a major effect upon life in Australia, Oceania, and Antarctica. Two-way radios offer people emergency help, education, and social communication.

Section 1 Review

Checking for Understanding

1. **Define** grazier, station, copra, subsistence farming, rail gauge.
2. **Locating Places** Where in New Zealand does most manufacturing take place?
3. **Movement** What country is an important trading partner for Australia's mining industry?
4. **Human/Environment Interaction** Why do many Pacific island countries lack manufacturing centers?

Critical Thinking

5. **Making Comparisons** How is farming in Oceania different from the agriculture practiced in both Australia and New Zealand?

ENRICH

Invite a ham radio operator to show the class how a two-way radio works.

CLOSE

Have students write a postcard to Dave, telling him about the transportation available in their region.

USING ILLUSTRATIONS

REGION In 1774 Captain James Cook reported that even during the summer, sailing through Antarctic waters was "a very dangerous enterprise" because of the huge "Ice Hills [icebergs]."

Answer to Caption: *Scientists depend on airplanes to deliver needed goods; cattle owners own helicopters to reach their cattle; and small airplanes are used to travel between islands.*

NATIONAL GEOGRAPHIC SOCIETY

CD-ROM

PICTURE ATLAS OF THE WORLD

You and your students can view the penguins, sea lions, and seals on the Antarctic Peninsula by clicking the continent's "Video" button.

ANSWERS TO SECTION 1 REVIEW

1. **grazier:** sheep herder; **station:** large livestock ranch in Australia; **copra:** the dried meat of a coconut; **subsistence farming:** growing only enough food to feed themselves; **rail gauge:** the distance between the rails of a rail track
2. near Auckland
3. Japan
4. They are too small to produce trade goods and are located too far from trading markets.
5. In Oceania most farmers grow only enough to support their families. In Australia and New Zealand, farming operates on a large scale, using scientific methods to produce major exports.

FOCUS

Ask students to study the photograph for a moment, then suggest vacation activities that tourists might engage in here.

TEACH

Use Unit Map Overlay Transparency 11-5 to familiarize students with the location of Australia and the Great Barrier Reef.

L2 Debate Have students debate whether tourists should be allowed at all on the Great Barrier Reef.

L2 Research Have students find out more about the marine life that inhabits the Great Barrier Reef.

DID YOU KNOW?

Coral reefs harbor more species of fish than any other marine environment.

STV: BIODIVERSITY

Side 1, Chapter 1
Frames 16738-17995
Title: ***Destroying Diversity***
Subject: Coral reefs

PRESERVING THE GREAT BARRIER REEF

The next ten years will determine whether there is sufficient commitment in the minds and hearts of Australians to ensure that the reef is protected from insidious degradation.

Graeme Kelleher, chairman of the Great Barrier Marine Park Authority, 1992, *Sea Frontiers*

Running along the northeast coast of Australia, the Great Barrier Reef is the largest structure on the earth made by living organisms. Between 500,000 and 1 million years old, the reef is made up of about 2,500 separate coral reefs whose combined length stretches 1,250 miles (about 2,012 km). Most of the reef lies between 10 and 150 miles (16 and 241 km) from the shore of the Australian state of Queensland.

A rich variety of plant life grows in this beautiful underwater garden. The great formation is also home to about 400 species of coral and 1,500 kinds of fish.

THE ISSUE

Because of the richness of its marine environment, the Great Barrier Reef is important to biologists and marine scientists. Its beauty and diverse marine life also attract thousands of tourists and marine enthusiasts each year.

Many kinds of human activities, however, are weakening the Great Barrier Reef. Wide areas appear to be dead. Scientists fear that if overuse continues, the entire reef may break up.

THE BACKGROUND

The surface of the Great Barrier Reef is living, made up of tiny animals called coral polyps. Coral polyps are the reef's builders as well as its foundation. They, however, are only one part in the Great Barrier Reef's delicately balanced environment of plant and animal life. One change, such as a shift in temperature or a change in the amount of sunlight or salt in the water, can damage one part of the reef or interfere with one of the species living on or around the reef.

In recent years the Great Barrier Reef has grown in popularity with tourists. Shell hunting, snorkeling, and spearfishing are among the favorite activities of tourists. Unfortunately, such activities harm the reef.

Shell hunters contribute to the destruction of the reef's coral polyps. Snorkelers bump against or hit the reef with their fins, breaking off pieces or damaging underwater plants. Spearfishers overhunt various species of the reef's fish. Water content is also changing through human activity. Sewage from the resort areas and gasoline from motor boats are polluting the sea. Farmers along the coast use fertilizers that drain into streams and rivers that empty into the Great Barrier Reef's waters. Cities along the coast dump wastes directly into the ocean. Some reefs have been covered with silt and debris from such pollution.

Many kinds of human activities, however, are weakening the Great Barrier Reef. Wide areas appear to be dead.

In the late 1960s, mining companies tried to strip-mine the reef for its limestone content. Oil companies prepared to drill for petroleum they

Extending the Content

Coral Polyps Coral polyps have tube-like bodies about one to 12 inches (2.5 to 30 cm) in diameter. One end of the polyp's body attaches itself to hard surfaces, the other end is the polyp's mouth.

Coral polyps live in colonies and build limestone "skeletons" from calcium they take out of the seawater. As the calcium moves through the polyps, it becomes calcium carbonate—limestone—which is deposited around the lower half of the polyp's body. As new polyps form and grow, they add to the coral reef's limestone foundation. When polyps die, the calcium carbonate in their bodies hardens into "skeletons," which also become part of the coral reef. Between less than half an inch and an inch (0.5 cm and 2.8 cm) of coral rock forms each year.

The Great Barrier Reef lies on the shallow shelf that fringes Australia.

claimed was under the Great Barrier Reef.

THE POINTS OF VIEW

Farmers, city and state governments, and mining and oil companies said that the Australian government should not pass any new laws that would restrict development and growth. Resort owners, shop owners, or other types of tourist-related businesses did not want the Australian government to limit use of the reef. Restrictions, they stated, would decrease the number of people coming to the reef. If the number of tourists dropped off, the area would lose money and jobs.

Environmentalists pointed out that the coral reef could be destroyed easily by tourists. They also warned that sewage and chemicals from farm fields would change the balance of the coastal waters in which the coral reef grows. With human activity and pollution, the Great Barrier Reef could disappear.

THE ISSUE TODAY

In 1981 the Australian government dedicated the Great Barrier Reef as a World Heritage Site. Most of the reef is still open for general use, but the park management is working on a plan to carefully control use of the reef. About 10 percent of the park is open on a "look-but-don't-touch" basis.

Some development is permitted. It is contained, however, in areas traditionally used for that purpose. Oil exploration, mining, and spearfishing are banned. Oil shipping is permitted, though the tankers must be guided by trained reef pilots.

Park rangers have increased efforts to improve their relationships with farm and business owners. Some businesses have hired teams of scientists who monitor changes on the reef, as well as giving tours and talks about the reef. Although the Great Barrier Reef is not entirely safe from business concerns, many more businesses are agreeing that they have as much at stake in the reef's continued existence as scientists and tourists.

Reviewing the Case

1. **What changes in the ecosystem can damage the coral reef?**
2. **Human/Environment Interaction What steps have been taken to protect the Great Barrier Reef?**

ANSWERS TO REVIEWING THE CASE

1. changes in temperature, amount of sunlight, amount of salt, any change in the environment at all
2. oil drilling, mining, and spearfishing banned; stricter tourist rules; businesses beginning cooperative efforts to care for reef

ASSESS

Have students answer the Reviewing the Case questions on page 693.

CLOSE

Have students summarize the case for and against human use of the Great Barrier Reef.

GLENCOE TECHNOLOGY

Videodisc

GEOGRAPHY AND THE ENVIRONMENT
THE INFINITE VOYAGE
Living With Disaster

Chapter 4
Disc 3 Side A
Title: ***Save the Beaches: Soil Erosion from Barrier-Reef Islands***
Subject: Ocean City, Maryland, serves as a model for how science has been involved in the prevention of erosion on barrier-reef islands

EYE ON THE ENVIRONMENT POSTER SERIES

Display the three posters that discuss coral reefs—*Overview, Focus Great Barrier Reef,* and *A Global Look.* Discussion Questions and Activities are presented on page 3 of the Poster Series Teacher's Guide.

LESSON PLAN
Chapter 34, Section 2

FOCUS

SECTION OBJECTIVES

1. **Understand** the impact on the environment of new animal species introduced to Australia and Oceania.
2. **Illustrate** how industrial development has affected the land and climate of South Pacific countries.
3. **Explain** the impact of human exploration on the environment of Antarctica.

BELLRINGER MOTIVATIONAL ACTIVITY

Project the Section 2 Focus Transparency and have students answer the questions.

PRETEACHING VOCABULARY

Compare living on an earth damaged by global warming to living in a greenhouse in summer. Then tell students to look for other effects of global warming as they read the section.

SECTION 2

People and Their Environment

THE ENVIRONMENT

SETTING THE SCENE

Read to Discover . . .
- the impact on the environment of new animal species introduced to Australia and Oceania.
- how industrial development has affected the land and climate of South Pacific countries.
- the impact of human exploration on the environment of Antarctica.

Key Terms
- marsupial
- global warming
- ecosystem

Identify and Locate
Bikini Atoll, Queensland, Banaba, Northern Territory

Distance and isolation make the Australia, Oceania, and Antarctica culture region home to a unique and fragile environment. Separated from the rest of the world by the vast Pacific Ocean, the region abounds with plants and animals not found anywhere else in the world. In many cases the absence of large mammals as predators also helped this special natural world to develop. Now, as modern travel allows humans to visit and settle almost every corner of the region, they have left their footprints on this delicate balance with sometimes devastating effects.

HUMAN/ENVIRONMENT INTERACTION

Animal Life

The Europeans introduced a variety of animals and plants—camels, rabbits, sheep, and sugarcane—to Australia. Some were brought and raised for profit, such as sheep. Others, such as camels, were used as beasts of burden.

The plants and animals already in Australia had never been exposed to these new species. While a few flourished, most suffered. Australia's most well-known native animals include kangaroos, koalas, wallabies, and other **marsupials**, mammals that give birth to offspring that mature in their mothers' pouches. Only a few of these and other native species have been able to survive newly added predators, such as European foxes and rats. Native grasses were also destroyed by the millions of rabbits brought for use in hunting.

Cane Toad

In the 1930s sugarcane farmers in the Australian state of Queensland tried to solve a crop problem by using the system of predator and prey. They introduced a small number of toads into the sugarcane fields to eat the grubs that were destroying their crops. The toads did eat grubs, but they then moved out of the fields, eating native plants, other insects, garbage, and even pet food. Because they were highly poisonous when eaten, the toads had few predators.

In the 1990s the cane toad moved out of Queensland into neighboring New South Wales and the Northern Territory. In the moist, tropical Northern Territory, the toads

Classroom Resources for Section 2

BLACKLINE MASTERS:
- Reproducible Lesson Plan 34-2
- Environmental Issue 11
- Guided Reading Activity 34-2
- Workbook Activity 34-2
- Skill Activity 34
- Enrichment Activity 34
- Section Quiz 34-2

TRANSPARENCIES:
- Section Focus Transparency 34-2

MULTIMEDIA:

- Testmaker

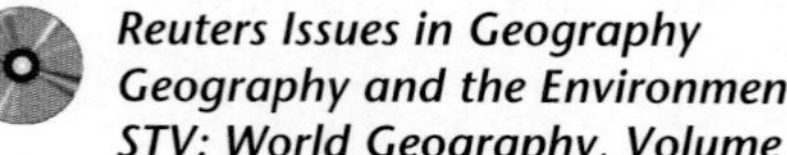

- *Reuters Issues in Geography*
- *Geography and the Environment*
- *STV: World Geography, Volume 3*

are upsetting nature's balance by killing lizards, snakes, birds, and other animals. So far scientists have been unable to solve this problem.

Animal Overpopulation

In 1837 merchants and shippers hoping to start a fur industry brought the brushtail possum to New Zealand. Without natural predators, it quickly spread throughout the country. Until the 1980s some balance was achieved by trapping thousands of possums each year. Then as possums and other animals came under special protection, the world fur market all but disappeared. Now the possums are everywhere. They eat some of New Zealand's most unique and fragile trees. They also carry a highly contagious disease that is deadly to New Zealand's cattle industry.

Geographic Themes

Region: Australia

The koala bear is one of about 150 marsupials that live in every part of Australia. *What impact has human settlement had on Australia's animal life?*

HUMAN/ENVIRONMENT INTERACTION

Industry and Science

The growth of industry has brought great advantages to Australia, Oceania, and Antarctica. It has brought costs as well. Throughout the region, human efforts to improve conditions, boost economic activity, or carry military experiments also have caused problems that must now be solved.

Phosphate Mining

The people of Nauru have lived a comfortable life financed by enormous phosphate deposits, mined and sold for fertilizer. Now the phosphate is running out and the topsoil has long been destroyed. The Naurans must find a way to reclaim this barren land or their economy will fall apart.

Logging

In other parts of Oceania intense logging has caused problems. The land, once thick with rain forest, now lies exposed to the torrential rains and the baking sun. In mountainous Papua New Guinea, landslides have washed away the earth. On other islands the soil has been so stripped of nutrients that crops cannot grow.

Nuclear Testing

In the late 1940s and 1950s, the United States and other nations did not recognize the long-term danger from nuclear testing in the South Pacific. The United States government promised the people of Bikini Atoll, in the Marshall Islands, that they would only be leaving their home for a short time while atomic tests were being conducted.

Almost 50 years later Bikini Atoll is still unsafe for human occupation. Although the land may be recovered one day, its people, relocated and supported by the United States government, have lost their livelihood and the traditional structure of their society.

Cooperative Learning Activity

Have students collect pictures of the kangaroo, the kiwi, the koala, the platypus, the euro, the dingo, the Tasmanian devil, and other animals unique to the South Pacific region. Also have them find a caption for each that gives an interesting fact, such as a newborn joey could fit in a teaspoon. Tell them to mount their pictures and typed captions on sheets of paper. Then make color copies of their work and bind the sheets together to form a book. Suggest that the class donate its book to the library of a nearby elementary school.

TEACH

GUIDED PRACTICE

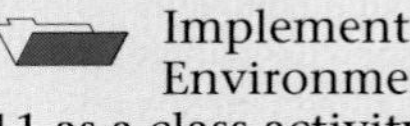

Implement Environmental Issue 11 as a class activity.

INDEPENDENT PRACTICE

Guided Reading Have students complete Guided Reading Activity 34-2 in the TCR. **LEP**

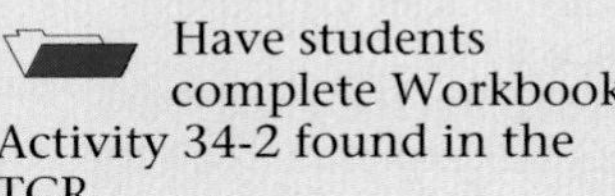

Have students complete Workbook Activity 34-2 found in the TCR.

USING ILLUSTRATIONS

REGION A baby koala rides piggyback on its mother wherever she goes.

Answer to Caption: *While a few species have flourished, most have suffered.*

ASSESS

CHECK FOR UNDERSTANDING

Assign Section 2 Review as homework or an in-class activity.

GLENCOE TECHNOLOGY

Videodisc

REUTERS ISSUES IN GEOGRAPHY

Chapter 10
Disc 1 Side A

Title: *Antarctica: The Ozone Hole*

Subject: Physical characteristics and early exploration of Antarctica, as well as current issues affecting Antarctica and the global environment

MEETING LESSON OBJECTIVES

Each objective below is tested by the questions that follow it in parentheses.

1. **Understand** the impact on the environment of new animal species introduced to Australia and Oceania. *(3)*
2. **Illustrate** how industrial development has affected the land and climate of South Pacific countries. *(4, 5)*
3. **Explain** the impact of human exploration on the environment of Antarctica. *(5)*

EVALUATE

Assign the Section 2 Quiz in the TCR.

Use the Testmaker to create a customized quiz for Section 2.

RETEACH

Have students complete Reteaching Activity 34 in the TCR.

USING ILLUSTRATIONS

PLACE Radioactive material remains dangerous for tens of thousands of years.

Answer to Caption: *Bikini Atoll, a nuclear testing ground, is still unsafe for human habitation.*

GLENCOE TECHNOLOGY

Videodisc

GEOGRAPHY AND THE ENVIRONMENT
THE INFINITE VOYAGE
Secrets From a Frozen World

Chapter 3
Disc 2 Side B
Title: ***Ice Cores: Discovering Causes of the Greenhouse Effect***

Geographic Themes

Place: Uranium Mine, South Australia
Australia has the world's largest undeveloped deposits of uranium, an important element in creating nuclear weapons. *How has the testing of nuclear weapons affected the Pacific area?*

HUMAN/ENVIRONMENT INTERACTION

The Antarctic Wilderness

The British explorer James Cook never reached continental Antarctica in the 1770s; he was defeated by the thick ice. The harsh climate has protected Antarctica. The continent's scientific and economic potential, however, have inspired people to overcome the challenge of reaching it.

What will it mean for Antarctica's environment if people can fly there in a few hours? How will the Antarctic wilderness be protected? These are urgent questions for the nations of the world.

The Scientific Impact

The key to Antarctica's scientific value has always been its isolation. The air and seas are almost untouched by humans, the ice and land almost unchanged for millions of years. This means that experiments about weather patterns, the ozone layer, ancient glaciers, and the living community that are conducted there are not distorted by humans and the environmental changes they make.

Surprisingly the scientists who cherish Antarctica's relatively untouched environment are now causing some of the problems the continent faces. Along with several thousand tourists who visit the continent each summer, an equal number of scientists are leaving garbage and graffiti behind, and disturbing wildlife nesting sites.

Ozone Hole

Perhaps the greatest danger to Antarctica is the change occurring in the ozone layer. Some scientists believe that pollution has made a hole in this protective covering, allowing more of the sun's radiation to reach the earth's surface.

Kiribati and other low atoll islands face the danger of **global warming**, or greenhouse effect, according to some scientists. Experts claim that global warming, created in part by human pollution, will eventually cause the polar regions to melt, raising sea levels more than 8 inches (about 20 cm) thus submerging many Pacific islands.

Scientists also worry that this added radiation will seriously harm the fragile Antarctic **ecosystem**, its community of living things that depend on each other for survival.

Concern is mostly focused on possible damage to the microscopic plants that feed krill, or tiny crustaceans. Like a falling domino, a reduced krill population will, in turn, cause other changes. Without the krill for food, the number of fish will shrink, leaving less food for the penguins and affecting marine life throughout the Antarctic area.

Solving the Problems

Because no one nation controls Antarctica, protecting its environment is an especially difficult challenge. So far, the nations of the world have mostly worked together to gradu-

Meeting Special Needs

Mixed Learners Some students learn best visually. Others are auditory learners. Many are "mixed" learners who use a combination of auditory and visual materials in order to learn. Ask students to look at and then think about the information they get from the map on page 697. Then ask them to read the paragraphs under "The Antarctic Wilderness." Ask students if the map or the paragraphs provide them with more information. Then ask them what the difference is between the kinds of information they can get from a map and from the text.

ANTARCTICA: NATIONAL CLAIMS AND SCIENTIFIC STATIONS

Chile
Argentina
United Kingdom
Norway
Australia
France
New Zealand
Major research station

Lambert Equal-Area Polar projection

120°W 40°W 0° 120°E 40°E 80°S 60°S 40°S
Antarctic Circle
Palmer (U.S.)
Faraday (U.K.)
Rothera (U.K.)
Signy (U.K.)
Orcadas (Argentina)
Arctowski (Poland)
Artigas (Uruguay)
Bellingshausen (Russia)
Com. Ferraz (Brazil)
Great Wall (China)
Jubany (Argentina)
King Sejong (S. Korea)
Machu Picchu (Peru)
Ten. Rodolf Marsh (Chile)
Marambio (Argentina)
Gen. Bernardo O'Higgins (Chile)
San Martin (Argentina)
Siple (U.S.)
Weddell Sea
Halley (U.K.)
Belgrano II (Argentina)
Russkaya (Russia)
Ross Sea
Sanae (S. Africa)
Scott (N.Z.)
McMurdo (U.S.)
Amundsen-Scott (U.S.)
South Pole
Novolazarevskaya (Russia)
Leningradskya (Russia)
Dakshin Gangotri (India)
Asuka (Japan)
Vostok (Russia)
Dumont d'Urville (French)
Syowa (Japan)
Molodeshnaya (Russia)
Progress (Russia)
Casey (Australia)
Mawson (Australia)
Mirnyy (Russia)
Davis (Australia)
0 1000 mi.
0 1000 km

Focus on Geographic Themes

1. **Region:** How many countries maintain research stations in Antarctica?
2. **Place:** Which research stations are owned by the United States?
3. **Region:** Which country claims the most territory in Antarctica?
4. **Place:** Which countries hold conflicting claims?

ally explore Antarctica. The Antarctic Treaty, signed in 1959, defined Antarctica as a "continent for science and peace." There would be no political borders, no military activity, no nuclear waste or explosions and, most importantly, no national claims to ownership.

Without national claims, however, who owns the resources of the continent and will guide its future? In 1989 France and Australia, and Greenpeace and other environmental groups proposed that the continent become a wilderness reserve, owned and protected by all. While the World Park concept remains challenged, 31 nations did agree in the 1991 Madrid Protocol to ban oil and gas exploration in Antarctica for 50 years. As Antarctica moves toward the 21st century, it will test the world's willingness to preserve the earth's last wilderness.

Section 2 Review

Checking for Understanding

1. **Define** marsupial, global warming, ecosystem.
2. **Locating Places** What country claims the Amundsen-Scott research station at the South Pole?
3. **Human/Environment Interaction** What problems has the cane toad caused in Australia?
4. **Region** Why are the plants and animals of the South Pacific region unique?

Critical Thinking

5. **Determining Cause and Effect** How might the hole in the ozone layer threaten Kiribati and Antarctica's marine life?

ANSWERS TO SECTION 2 REVIEW

1. **marsupial:** mammal that gives birth to offspring that mature in the mother's pouch; **global warming:** greenhouse effect created in part by human pollution; **ecosystem:** community of living things that depend on one another for survival
2. the United States
3. It is multiplying without control and upsetting the natural balance by poisoning its own predators and preying on other animals in the food chain.
4. because the region has been isolated by distance and climate
5. Global warming may raise the sea levels above low-lying islands. It may also damage the small plants that feed krill, the tiny crustacean that forms the base of Antarctica's marine life food chain.

ENRICH

Have students complete Enrichment Activity 34 in the TCR.

CLOSE

Have students propose reasons for and against making Antarctica a World Park.

USING MAPS

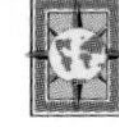
Answers:
1. 17; **2.** McMurdo, Amundsen-Scott, Palmer, and Sipte; **3.** Australia; **4.** Chile, Argentina, and the U.K.

Map Skills Practice

Drawing Conclusions
How does the map show international cooperation in Antarctica? *(Stations of some countries are located on the claims of others.)*

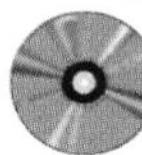
Videodisc

STV: WORLD GEOGRAPHY, VOLUME 3

Side 2, Chapter 2
Frames 15464-24766
Title: ***Antarctica***
Subject: Scientific exploration

STV: WORLD GEOGRAPHY, VOLUME 3

Side 2, Chapter 2
Frames 24767-38800
Title: ***Antarctica***
Subject: Life in Antarctica

STV: WORLD GEOGRAPHY, VOLUME 3

Side 2, Chapter 2
Frames 38802-43570
Title: ***Antarctica***
Subject: The Antarctica Treaty

TEACH

Have each student write a short essay describing an important decision. Essays must address these questions: Did students identify possible actions and predict their consequences? Were students happy with the decision? Why or why not? What information did they need to make a better decision?

Then say: "We use the same process to make decisions about political and social issues." Discuss current issues facing your school or community. For each issue, have students identify possible courses of action and predict consequences. Discuss what information would enable them to make better decisions.

Skills Practice For additional practice, have students complete Skill Activity 34 in the TCR.

CRITICAL THINKING SKILLS

Predicting Consequences

Suppose your teacher has scheduled a test for Monday morning. You plan to study on Sunday evening so the material will be fresh in your mind the next day. Unexpectedly, a friend invites you to go to a movie Sunday night. If you go to the movie, will you perform well on the test the next day?

Reviewing the Skill

To make this decision, you must **predict the consequences** of your actions. We can use information about the situation and our experiences in similar situations to make an intelligent guess about probable outcomes. Predicting consequences can help produce better decisions. The more information and experience you have, the better your predictions will be.

Use the following steps in predicting consequences:

- Gather information about the decision or action.
- Use your knowledge and past experiences to formulate possible consequences of the decision or action.
- Analyze each possible consequence by asking, "How likely is it that this will occur?"
- When considering actions that affect many individuals or groups, predict consequences for the various groups involved.

Practicing the Skill

Read the passage below and answer the questions that follow.

In 1959, 12 nations signed the Antarctic Treaty to preserve the continent for scientific study; to prohibit military activities, nuclear testing, and waste dumping; and to prevent mining for 50 years. As the end of the treaty period approaches, disagreement among nations about mineral use in Antarctica increases. As mineral supplies in other parts of the world decrease, this controversy will grow.

1. What information would help you predict consequences of mining in Antarctica?
2. What are three possible consequences of allowing mining in Antarctica?

For additional practice in this skill, see Practicing Skills on page 700 of the Chapter 34 Review.

ANSWERS TO PRACTICING THE SKILL

1. information on how mining has affected the environments of other areas, and on the environmental value of keeping Antarctica completely undeveloped

2. Possible consequences include: political or military struggle over mining rights; destruction of Antarctica's ecosystem; permanent alteration of the global climate; increased ocean pollution; increased wealth for the countries with mining rights.

chapter 34

HIGHLIGHTS

SECTION 1 Living in Australia, Oceania, and Antarctica

KEY TERMS

grazier (p. 687)
station (p. 687)
copra (p. 688)
subsistence farming (p. 688)
rail gauge (p. 690)

SUMMARY

- Agriculture is the most important economic activity in the South Pacific.
- Farmers in Oceania farm mostly for their own use while those in Australia and New Zealand produce large farm exports, especially livestock and dairy products.
- Antarctica produces no farm crops and has no mining or manufacturing industries. Its waters are a source of seafood.
- Almost all the South Pacific's major manufacturing centers are in Australia and New Zealand.
- Air and water travel has helped to bridge the distances to bring goods and services to remote parts of the South Pacific.

Airplane flying over Antarctica

SECTION 2 People and Their Environment

KEY TERMS

marsupial (p. 694)
global warming (p. 696)
ecosystem (p. 696)

SUMMARY

- Many of the plants and animals in the South Pacific, previously isolated, have suffered from human introduction of new species into the region.
- The efforts of industry and government to pursue political and economic goals in Oceania have caused environmental problems that remain unsolved.
- Antarctica's fragile environment is no longer protected by isolation. Scientists, industry, and tourists alike may be damaging its delicately balanced natural world.

Uranium mine in Australia

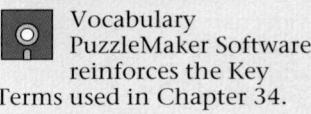

CHAPTER 34 HIGHLIGHTS

USING THE CHAPTER 34 HIGHLIGHTS

Use the Chapter 34 Highlights to preview, review, condense, or reteach the chapter.

PREVIEW/REVIEW

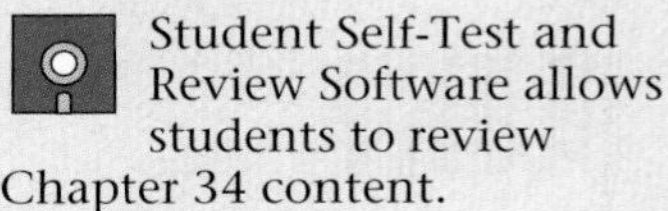

Vocabulary PuzzleMaker Software reinforces the Key Terms used in Chapter 34.

Student Self-Test and Review Software allows students to review Chapter 34 content.

CONDENSE

Have students read the Chapter 34 Highlights.

Have students listen to the Chapter 34 Audiocassettes in the TCR. Spanish Audiocassettes are also available.

Assign the Chapter 34 Audiocassette Activity and give the students the Chapter 34 Audiocassette Quiz.

Have students complete Guided Reading Activities for Chapter 34 in the TCR. Spanish Guided Reading Activities are also available.

RETEACH

Have students complete Reteaching Activity 34 in the TCR. Spanish Reteaching Activities are also available.

Map Activity

Identify and Locate Copy and distribute page 38 of the Outline Map Resource Book. On the map, have students locate and label St. George Island, Western Australia, New South Wales, Federated States of Micronesia, the South Island, Queensland, Bikini Atoll, and Northern Territory. Refer them to the Unit Atlas maps for help.

GLENCOE TECHNOLOGY

Videodisc

Use Chapter 34 MindJogger Videoquiz to review students' knowledge before administering the Chapter 34 Test.

MINDJOGGER VIDEOQUIZ

Chapter 34
Disc 5 Side A

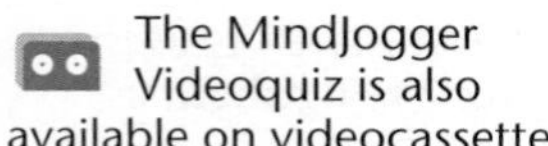

The MindJogger Videoquiz is also available on videocassette.

ANSWERS

Reviewing Key Terms

1. rail gauges
2. graziers
3. stations
4. copra
5. marsupials
6. global warming
7. ecosystem

Reviewing Facts

8. tropical fruits, sugar, coffee, copra, and other coconut products
9. in Australia
10. to reach isolated places in the outback, to travel between small islands, to bring supplies to Antarctica, and to herd cattle
11. trapping
12. Nuclear testing made it unsafe.
13. bans mineral and oil exploration in Antarctica for 50 years

chapter 34 REVIEW

Reviewing Key Terms

Choose the vocabulary term that best completes each of the sentences below. Write your answers on a separate sheet of paper.

graziers (p. 687)
stations (p. 687)
copra (p. 688)
rail gauges (p. 690)
marsupials (p. 694)
global warming (p. 696)
ecosystem (p. 696)

SECTION 1

1. Train travel in Australia can be difficult because the ____ do not match throughout the system.
2. ____ raise sheep in Australia and New Zealand.
3. Livestock ranches in Australia are called ____ .
4. ____ can be found on most Pacific islands.

SECTION 2

5. Many native Australian mammals, called ____, were killed by foxes.
6. Scientists worry that ____ will seriously damage the marine life in Antarctica.
7. Antarctica's fragile ____ may suffer from increased tourism.

Reviewing Facts

SECTION 1

8. What are the main farm products exported from Oceania?
9. Where are most of Australia's manufactured products used?
10. How is air travel used in the South Pacific region?

SECTION 2

11. Until recently, what human activity helped to control New Zealand's possum population?
12. Why is Bikini Atoll now uninhabited?
13. What does the Madrid Protocol do?

Critical Thinking

14. **Determining Cause and Effect** How has the development of modern communication systems affected life in the South Pacific today?
15. **Expressing Problems Clearly** How has industrial activity in Oceania affected the region's environment?

Geographic Themes

16. **Location** Where are the South Pacific's major manufacturing centers?
17. **Human/Environment Interaction** How have tourists and scientists contributed to the problems facing Antarctica's environment?

Practicing Skills

Predicting Consequences

Refer to the skill on page 698.

18. What are two possible consequences of a permanent ban on mining in Antarctica?
19. What are three possible consequences of allowing livestock production in Australia and New Zealand to continue unchecked?

Using the Unit Atlas

Refer to the physical geography section of the Unit Atlas on pages 650–651.

20. What are Fiji's major exports?
21. How do scientists hope to use the Antarctic ice cap?

Critical Thinking

14. They have brought medical care and education to people in remote areas and have created national unity by linking groups together.
15. Logging has exposed the soil, causing landslides and nutrient loss; phosphate mining has destroyed topsoil; and pollution has contributed to global warming.

Geographic Themes

16. Sydney, Melbourne, and Auckland
17. They have left garbage, disturbed nesting sites, and damaged delicate vegetation.

Projects

Individual Activity

Find out more about the economies of two South Pacific countries. In a short written report, compare the countries' economies and the factors that have contributed to the development of each.

Cooperative Learning Activity

In small groups, role-play a meeting of the Antarctic Treaty countries. Each student will focus on a different issue affecting Antarctica. When the group meets, individual members should present their findings, arguing for or against the World Park concept from the viewpoint of their specific issue. If students wish, they may draft a class letter that includes all the arguments.

Writing About Geography

Narration

Imagine you are developing a newspaper or radio station to link remote parts of the South Pacific with one another. Write an article describing the impact that improved communication would have on your community. Use your journal record, text, magazine articles, encyclopedias, and other books. Be sure to consider both positive and negative results of greater interaction between parts of the region—for example, changes to traditional cultures as well as improved economies.

Locating Places

ANTARCTICA: PHYSICAL GEOGRAPHY

Match the letters on the map with the places and physical features of Antarctica. Write your answers on a separate sheet of paper.

1. Weddell Sea
2. Antarctic Circle
3. South Pole
4. Ross Sea
5. Antarctic Peninsula

Chapter 34 Review

Practicing Skills

18. Possible consequences include increased political tension and continued preservation of the Antarctic environment.

19. Possible consequences include gradual destruction of grazing lands that support livestock, leading to increased production costs; increased destruction of forests and wildlife; and increased pace of global warming.

Using the Unit Atlas

20. sugar, coconut products, and gold

21. as a freshwater source

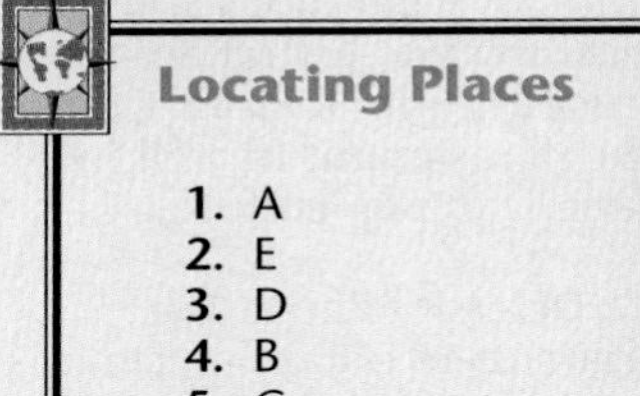

Chapter Bonus Test Question

This question may be used for extra credit on the chapter test. Write each letter in the correct space.

Match each threat from column B with the plant or animal from column A that it threatens.

COLUMN A	COLUMN B
___ 1. native Australian grasses	A. global warming
___ 2. lizards in the Northern Territory	B. cane toad
___ 3. cattle	C. rabbits
___ 4. krill	D. possum

Answers: (1-C, 2-B, 3-D, 4-A)

FOCUS

In their journals, have students list Australian items with which they are familiar.

TEACH

L2 Discussion Have students name items in American pop culture that are similar to the items pictured. For example, the pants mentioned in the Australian clothing caption resemble military fatigues worn by many during their leisure time.

L2 Culture Have students identify local restaurants with Australian fare; stores and/or catalogs that carry Australian clothing. Suggest that they find out what foods and clothing are Australian. Have students offer reasons why the items might fit well into American pop culture.

L2 Diversity Encourage students to obtain music written and/or performed by Australian musicians. Have students analyze the music, looking for similarities and differences to American music.

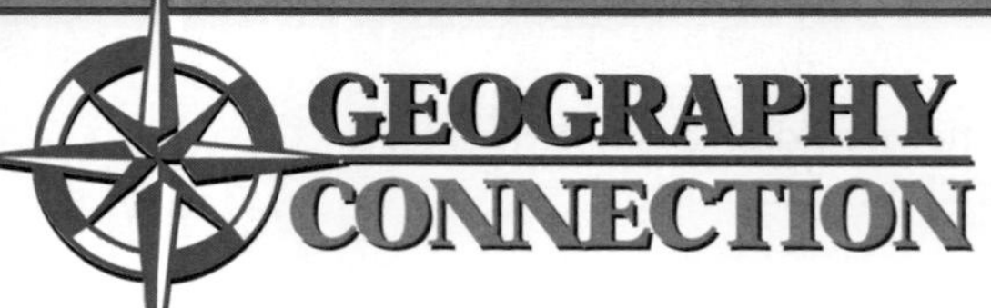

Connections to the United States

AUSTRALIA AND THE UNITED STATES

The American fascination with Australia and its people may stem from the undeniably intriguing animal and plant life, the striking similarity in national character and lifestyle, or the shared parentage with the United Kingdom. Whatever its cause, the fascination is real and has influenced American popular culture in several ways.

PAUL HOGAN ▶ was one of Australia's "favorite sons" in the United States during the 1980s. Americans first met him on television in early 1984, when he appeared in commercials for the Australian Tourist Commission. His relaxed friendliness, from his opening "G'day" to his closing "Slip another shrimp on the barbie" (barbeque), seemed to embody the breezy Australian manner. In the late 1980s, he wrote and starred in several movies about Australian outback hero Crocodile Dundee.

▲ AUSTRALIAN CLOTHING has been popular among Americans interested in hiking and other outdoor activities. Outback shorts or pants have pockets aplenty; some have pockets on pockets, some on the sides of the legs. Like the pockets of a kangaroo or a koala, the pants pockets have a hidden fold, so the pockets can expand to hold objects picked up on a trek.

Making the Connection

Culture/Language Have students find out more about Australian English, its characteristics and practices and some of its vocabulary. Suggest that students list the Australian phrase in their journals with the American equivalent next to it. Provide a time for students to share their findings.

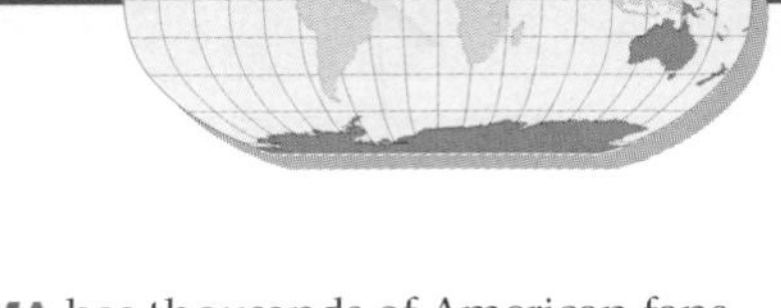

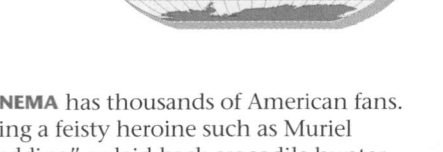

AUSTRALIAN CINEMA has thousands of American fans. Whether meeting a feisty heroine such as Muriel in "Muriel's Wedding" or laid-back crocodile hunter Crocodile Dundee, Americans have come to appreciate Australian films.

AUSTRALIAN MUSICIANS have been great favorites, too, particularly since the mid-1970s and 1980s. During those years, Olivia Newton John and the BeeGees topped American pop charts continuously. In the 1990s, the group Midnight Oil used their musical talents to warn listeners of the consequences of destroying the earth's environment.

THE AUSTRALIAN ARMY "DIGGER" HAT is also a popular item. The brim can be worn down all the way around to shed rain, or flipped up on one side, in the more traditional Australian style.

Checking for Understanding

1. In what areas of American culture has Australian influence made a mark?
2. **Movement** What signs of Australian influence can you find in your community? Why?

ANSWERS TO CHECKING FOR UNDERSTANDING

1. films, music, clothing
2. Answers will vary.

Geography Connection

ASSESS

Have students answer the Checking for Understanding questions on page 703.

CLOSE

Have students share their knowledge and impressions of Australia and Australians.

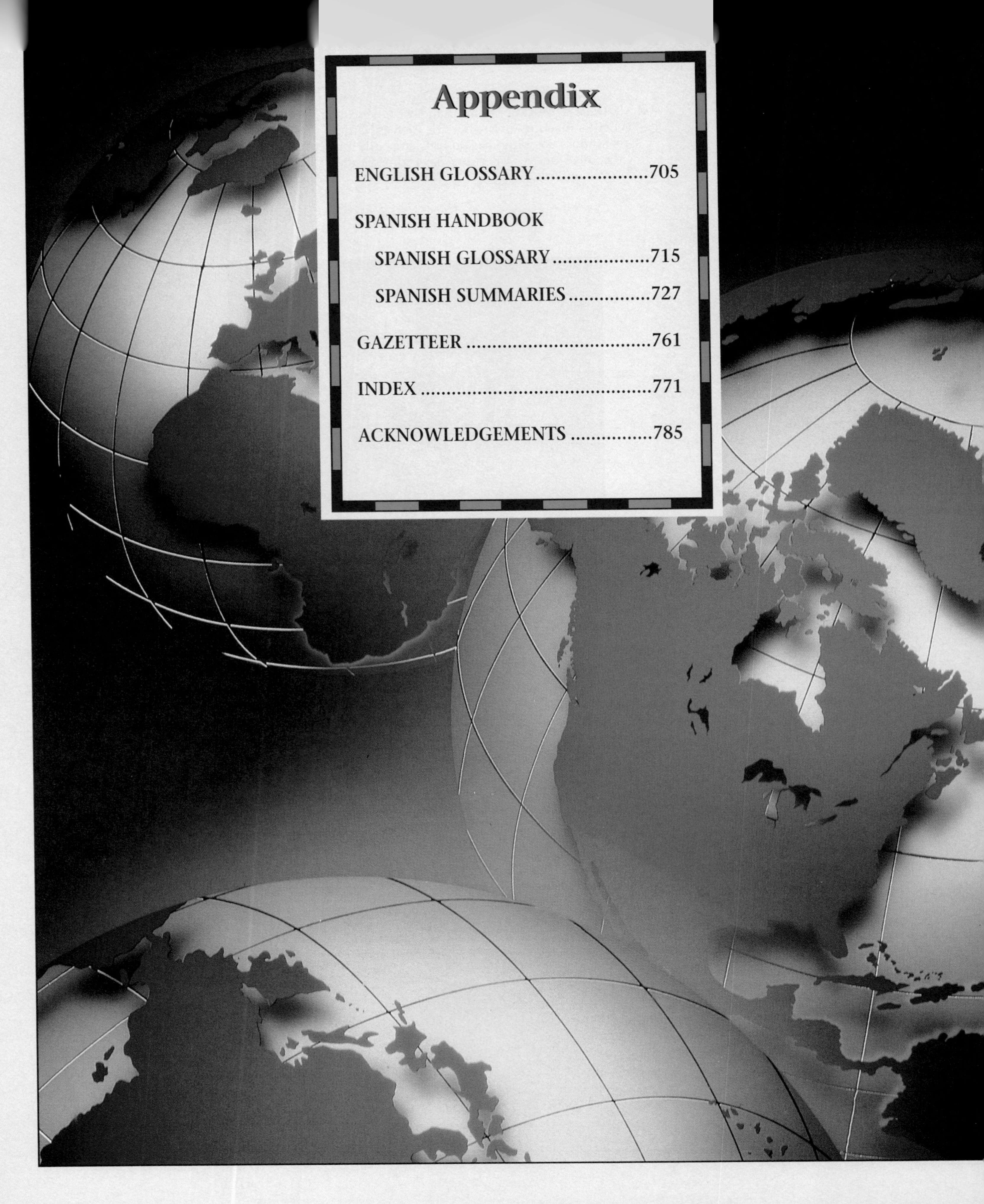

Appendix

Glossary

A

absolute location the position of a place on the earth's surface (p. 5)

abstract art form that expresses the artist's attitudes and emotions (p. 121)

acid deposition wet or dry airborne acids that fall to the earth (p. 271)

acid rain precipitation carrying large amounts of dissolved acids, especially sulfuric acid and nitric acid, which damages buildings, forests, and crops and kills wildlife (pp. 137, 270, 577)

alluvial plain floodplain on which flooding rivers have deposited rich soil, such as the Indo-Gangetic Plain in South Asia (p. 480)

alluvial-soil deposits rich soil made up of sand and mud deposited by running water (p. 359)

amendment in U.S. history, official changes made to the Constitution (p. 117)

apartheid policy of strict separation of the races adopted in South Africa in the 1940s (p. 440)

aquifer underground water-bearing layers of porous rock, sand, or gravel (p. 398)

arable land land suitable for growing crops (p. 612)

archipelago a group or chain of islands (pp. 34, 538, 598)

artesian water underground water supply that is under enough pressure to rise into wells without being pumped (p. 656)

Association of Southeast Asian Nations (ASEAN) organization formed in 1967 to promote regional development and trade in Southeast Asia (p. 633)

atheist person who does not believe in God (p. 317)

atmosphere the air that surrounds the earth (p. 27)

atoll ring-shaped island formed by coral building up along the rim of an underwater volcano (p. 657)

avalanche mass of ice, snow, or rock that slides down a mountainside (p. 232)

axis referring to the earth, an imaginary line that runs through its center between the North Pole and the South Pole (p. 45)

B

batik method of dyeing cloth to produce beautiful patterns, developed in Indonesia and Malaysia (p. 621)

bedouin member of the nomadic desert peoples of North Africa and Southwest Asia (p. 384)

bilingual speaking or using two languages (p. 121)

biologist scientist who studies plant and animal life (p. 274)

biosphere the part of the earth where life—people, plants, and animals—exists (p. 28)

black market any illegal market where scarce or illegal goods are sold, usually at high prices (p. 328)

blizzard a heavy snowstorm with winds of more than 35 miles per hour (p. 100)

boomerang curved throwing stick used for hunting by Aborigines in Australia (p. 673)

bycatch unwanted fish, marine mammals, and birds caught by fishing trawlers and thrown away (p. 141)

C

cabinet heads of departments in the executive branch of the U.S. government who advise the President (p. 118)

calligraphy the art of beautiful and decorative handwriting (p. 565)

campesinos farm workers; generally, people who live and work in rural areas (p. 196)

canopy top layer of a rain forest, where the tops of tall trees come together (p. 167)

capitalism economic system based on free enterprise, in which individuals own and use capital (p. 76)

cash crop farm crop grown to be sold or traded rather than used by the farm family (pp. 113, 195, 452, 512, 630)

caste system in traditional South Asian society, the division of society into rigid groups, based mainly on occupation, that determined social standing, marriage choice, and other actions (p. 496)

cataract a large waterfall (p. 420)

caudillo term for a Latin American political leader from the late 1800s on, often a military dictator (literally, "strong man") (p. 184)

cereal any grain, such as barley, oats, or wheat, grown for food (p. 364)

chaparral type of vegetation made up of dense forests of shrubs and short trees, common in Mediterranean climates (pp. 54, 232)

chart visual presentation of data in rows and columns (p. 22)

chernozem (cher•nuh•ZYAWM) rich black topsoil found in the North European Plain, especially in Russia and Ukraine (p. 291)

chinampas floating artificial farming islands made by the Aztec (p. 181)

chinook seasonal warm wind that blows down the Rocky Mountains in late winter and early spring (p. 100)

Chipko in India, an environmental movement known by the term for "tree-hugger," aimed at saving forests (p. 520)

chlorofluorocarbon chemical substance, found mainly in liquid coolants, that damages the earth's protective ozone layer (p. 578)

city-state in ancient Greece, independent community consisting of a city and the surrounding lands, where democracy first developed (p. 245)

civilization a culture that has organized a social, economic, and political system, built cities, and achieved a certain level of development in the arts and sciences (p. 69)

clan tribal community or large group of people related to one another (pp. 444, 557)

climate weather patterns typical for an area over a long period of time (p. 45)

cold war refers to the power struggle between the Soviet Union and the United States (p. 248)

collective farm under communism, a large, state-owned farm on which farmers received wages plus a share of products and profits; also called a *kholkoz* (p. 264)

command economy economic system in which economic decisions about production and distribution are made by some central authority (p. 328)

commercial farming farming organized as a business (p. 452)

commune in China, a collective farming community whose members were supposed to share work and products (p. 571)

communism social and political movement developed by Marx and Lenin that favored revolution to establish a classless society in which workers would control industrial production (pp. 247, 313)

compass rose directional marker on a map (p. 12)

conquistador Spanish term for "conqueror," referring to soldiers who conquered Native Americans in Latin America (p. 182)

Constitution plan of government made for the new United States in 1787 (p. 117)

consumer goods household goods, shoes, and clothing that individuals buy (pp. 264, 328)

continental divide a line or ridge that separates rivers flowing toward opposite sides of a continent (p. 94)

continental island island formed of rock that has risen from the continental shelf, such as Papua New Guinea (p. 657)

continental shelf shallow ocean area near the coast of a continent (p. 34)

contour lines on a map, lines that connect points of land at the same elevation (p. 14)

contour plowing farming method in which plowed furrows follow the natural curve of the land, lessening erosion (p. 131)

cooperative a voluntary organization whose members work together and share the expenses and profits from their enterprise; also called "co-op" (p. 572)

copra dried meat of a coconut (p. 688)

coral tiny marine animals and the rock-like structures (islands, reefs) formed by the skeletons of coral colonies (p. 656)

cordillera chain or range of mountains (p. 597)

crevass huge, deep crack that forms in thick ice or snow (p. 663)

crop rotation farming method in which different crops are alternated in the same field, preserving soil nutrients (p. 131)

Crusades series of religious wars (c. 1100-1300) in which European Christians tried to retake Palestine from Muslim rule (p. 246)

cultural diffusion the spread of ideas, customs, goods, and people from one culture to another (p. 70)

culture way of life of a group of people who share traditions, interests, beliefs, and ways of making a living (pp. 10, 63)

culture hearth a center where cultures developed and from which ideas and traditions spread outward (pp. 69, 556)

culture region division of the earth based on a variety of factors, including government, social groups, economic systems, language, or religion (p. 74)

cuneiform sumerian writing system using wedge-shaped symbols pressed into clay tablets (p. 377)

current cold or warm "river" of seawater that flows in the oceans, generally in a circular pattern (p. 50)

cyclone storm with heavy rains and high winds that blow in a circular pattern around an area of low atmospheric pressure (pp. 484, 636)

czar in Russian history, the emperor or supreme ruler (p. 312)

D

deciduous describing trees, usually broad-leaved such as oak and maple, that lose their leaves in autumn (p. 54)

deforestation the loss or destruction of forests, due mainly to trees being cleared for logging or farming (pp. 202, 460, 518, 605)

delta triangular section of land built up at a river's mouth that looks like the Greek letter *delta* (Δ) (p. 359)

desalination the removal of salt from sea water to make it usable for drinking and farming (p. 399)

desertification process in which arable land is turned into desert, usually due to destruction of vegetation (p. 458)

developing country country in the process of becoming industrialized (p. 195)

dharma in Hinduism, a person's moral duty, based on class distinctions, which guides his or her life (p. 497)

diagram drawing that shows what something is or how something is done, such as the steps of a process or cycle (p. 22)

dialect local form of a language used in a particular place or by a certain group (pp. 177, 251)

distillation method of desalination in which water is boiled and condensed (p. 399)

doldrums a frequently windless area near the Equator (pp. 50, 662)

domesticate to take plants and animals from the wild and tame them or otherwise make them useful to people (p. 376)

dry farming farming method used in dry regions in which land is plowed and planted deeply to hold water in the soil (p. 116)

dynasty a ruling house or continuing family of rulers, especially in China (p. 556)

E

economic system the way in which the people of a country produce and distribute goods and services (p. 75)

ecosystem the complex community of interdependent living things in a given environment (pp. 202, 696)

ecotourism tourism based on concern for the environment (p. 461)

endemic describing plant or animal species native to a particular area (p. 605)

environmentalist person actively concerned with the quality and protection of the environment (p. 271)

equinox one of two days (about March 21 and September 23) on which the sun is directly above the equator, making day and night equal in length (p. 46)

erosion wearing away of the earth's surface, by wind, flowing water, or glaciers (p. 31)

escarpment steep cliff or slope between a higher and lower land surface (pp. 162, 419)

ethnic diversity differences among groups of people based on their origins, languages, customs, or beliefs (p. 371)

ethnic group group of people who share a common ancestry, language, customs, religion, or combination of such characteristics (pp. 305, 436, 551)

eutrophication process by which the water of a lake or stream becomes too rich in dissolved nutrients, leading to plant growth that depletes oxygen (p. 139)

evaporation the changing of liquid water into water vapor, a gas (p. 36)

exports resources or goods sent from one country to another (pp. 39, 195)

extended family household made up of several generations; for instance, aunts, uncles, and grandparents as well as parents and children (pp. 189, 444)

extinction the disappearance or end of a species of animal or plant (p. 460)

F

fale traditional type of home in Western Samoa, with open sides and thatched roof (p. 681)

farm cooperative organization in which farmers share in growing and selling farm products (p. 264)

fault a crack or break in the earth's crust, usually caused by intense folding (pp. 29, 420)

fauna the animal life of a region (p. 598)

fazenda Portuguese term for huge sugar plantations in Brazil (p. 182)

feudalism in medieval Europe and Japan, system of government in which powerful lords gave land to nobles in return for pledges of loyalty (p. 245)

fishery areas (freshwater or saltwater) where fish or other sea animals are caught (p. 97)

fjord (fee•YORD) long, steep-sided glacial valley now filled by seawater (p. 223)

flora the plant life of a region (p. 598)

foehn (FUHN) warm dry wind that blows from the leeward side of mountains, sometimes melting snow and causing an avalanche; used mainly in Europe (p. 232)

fold a bend in layers of rock, sometimes caused by plate movement (p. 29)

free enterprise an economic system in which private businesses operate with little interference from government (pp. 76, 129)

free port port city, such as Singapore, where goods can be unloaded, stored, and reshipped without the payment of import duties (p. 633)

fútbol Latin American name for soccer (p. 189)

G

general purpose map map showing a wide range of general physical and/or political information about an area (p. 14)

geography the study of the earth and the ways people live and work on it (p. 5)

glacier large bodies of ice that move across the surface of the earth (p. 31)

glasnost Russian term for a new "openness," part of Gorbachev's reform plans (p. 314)

global warming gradual warming of the earth and its atmosphere that may be caused in part by pollution and an increase in the greenhouse effect (p. 696)

government a group or nation's political system (p. 74)

graph way of presenting and comparing information visually, as in a line graph, bar graph, or circle graph (p. 20)

grazier person who raises and herds sheep or cattle (p. 687)

great circle shortest distance between any two places on the earth's surface (p. 16)

green revolution program, begun in the 1960s, to produce higher-yielding, more productive strains of wheat, rice, and other food crops (p. 513)

grid system pattern formed as the lines of latitude and longitude cross one another (p. 6)

gross domestic product (GDP) the value of goods and services created within a country in a year (pp. 393, 434)

groundwater water that lies beneath the surface of the earth, supplied mainly by rain filtering through the soil (p. 35)

H

habitat area with conditions suitable for certain plants or animals to live (p. 460)

haiku form of Japanese poetry consisting of 17 syllables, often about nature (p. 565)

headwaters the sources of river waters (p. 96)

heavy industry the manufacture of machinery and equipment needed for factories and mines (p. 263)

hemisphere half of a sphere or globe, as in the earth's Northern and Southern Hemispheres (p. 5)

hieroglyphics Egyptian writing system using pictures and symbols to represent words or sounds (p. 377)

history the study of written information about events and people in the past (p. 69)

Holocaust term given to the mass killings of 6 million European Jews by Germany's Nazi leaders during World War II (p. 248)

homogeneous describing a group of people or things that are very like one another (p. 552)

hurricane a large, powerful windstorm that forms over warm ocean waters (pp. 66, 100)

hydroelectric power electrical energy generated by falling water (p. 165)

hydrosphere the watery areas of the earth, including oceans, lakes, rivers, and other bodies of water (p. 28)

hypothesis one step in the scientific method, suggesting a scientific explanation for observed events (p. 57)

I

icon religious image, usually including a picture of Jesus, Mary, or a saint, used mainly by Orthodox Christians (p. 317)

ideogram a pictorial character or symbol that has a specific meaning or stands for a syllable (p. 561)

imports resources or goods brought into one country from another (p. 39)

immigrant person who has left his or her home country and settled permanently in another country (p. 107)

impressionism artistic style that developed in Europe in the late 1800s and tried to show the natural appearance of objects with dabs or strokes of color (p. 253)

indigenous native to a place; the original inhabitants—plant, animal, or human (p. 615)

industrialization process of turning to the use of machinery in manufacturing (p. 115)

industrialize to develop industry (p. 336)

interdependent relying on one another for goods, services, and ideas (pp. 8, 133, 632)

isthmus narrow piece of land connecting two large landmasses (p. 33)

J

jai alai (**HY•LY**) traditional handball-type game popular with Mexicans and Cubans (p. 189)

jazz musical form that developed in the United States in the early 1900s, blending African rhythms and European harmonies (p. 122)

jati in traditional Hindu society, a social group that defines a family's occupation and social standing (p. 491)

jute plant fiber used to make string and cloth (p. 512)

K

karma in Hindu belief, the sum of good and bad actions in one's present and past lives, leading to rewards or punishment (p. 497)

key part of a map that explains the symbols used (p. 12)

kolkhoz in the Soviet Union, a large collective farm (p. 329)

krill tiny shrimplike sea animals that live in cold Antarctic oceans (p. 659)

kums regional term for the sandy deserts in the Turan Lowland, as in Kara Kum (p. 292)

L

lagoon shallow pool of water at the center of an atoll (p. 657)

language family group of related languages that have all developed from one earlier language (pp. 76, 251)

latifundia in modern Latin America, large estates owned by families or corporations (p. 196)

latitude imaginary lines running east and west around the globe, used to measure the distance north and south of the Equator in degrees; also called parallels (p. 5)

leach to wash nutrients out of the soil (p. 427)
leeward facing away from the direction from which the wind is blowing (p. 51)
lichens sturdy small plants that grow like a crust on rocks or tree trunks (p. 663)
light industry manufacturing aimed at making consumer goods rather than heavy machinery, such as textiles or food processing (p. 263)
lingua franca a language (such as Swahili) used for communication among people with different native languages (p. 442)
literacy rate the percentage of people in a given place who can read and write (pp. 123, 445)
lithosphere surface land areas of the earth's crust (about 30 percent), including continents and ocean basins (p. 28)
llanos (YAHN•ohz) fertile plains along the Caribbean coast of South America, in Colombia and Venezuela (p. 164)
loess (LES) fine, yellowish-brown topsoil made up of particles of silt and clay, usually carried by the wind (p. 539)
longhouse in rural areas of Indonesia and Malaysia, a large building where people from several related families live (p. 622)
longitude imaginary vertical lines running from pole to pole on the globe, used to measure distance east or west of the Prime Meridian; also called meridians (p. 6)

M

malnutrition poor nutrition due to a badly balanced diet or lack of food (p. 187)
mangrove tree tropical evergreen tree or shrub that usually grows in thick groves near water (p. 518)
mantle thick middle layer of the earth's interior structure, consisting of dense, hot rock made up of silicon, oxygen, aluminum, iron, and magnesium (p. 29)
mantra in Hinduism, a sacred word or phrase repeated in prayers and chants (p. 502)
manuka small shrubs that grow in plateau regions of New Zealand (p. 663)
map projection way of drawing a map to represent the rounded earth on a flat surface (p. 17)
maquiladoras in Mexico, manufacturing plants set up by foreign firms (p. 197)
maritime concerned with travel or shipping by sea (p. 615)
market economy an economic system based on free enterprise, in which businesses are privately owned and production and prices are determined by supply and demand (p. 328)
marsupial type of mammal (such as kangaroos or koalas) that gives birth to offspring that mature in a pouch on the mother's abdomen (p. 694)
mass culture popular culture spread by media such as radio and television (p. 442)
megalopolis a "super-city" that is made up of several large cities and the smaller cities near them, such as the area between Boston and Washington, D.C., or around Tokyo-Yokohama, Japan (pp. 109, 554)
meltwater water formed by melting snow and ice (p. 271)
merchant marine a country's fleet of ships that engage in commerce or trade (p. 576)
mesa flat-topped, elevated landform (from the Spanish term for "table") (p. 94)
mestizo in Latin America, person of mixed Native American and European descent (p. 176)
metropolitan area region that includes a central city and its surrounding suburbs (p. 109)
mica silicate mineral that typically splits into thin, shiny sheets (p. 481)
Middle Passage name given to the route used by slave ships across the Atlantic from West Africa to the Americas (p. 440)
minifundia in Latin America, small farms that produce food chiefly for family use and the local market (p. 196)
mistral strong northerly wind from the Alps that can bring cold air to southern France (p. 231)
mixed farming raising several kinds of crops and livestock on the same farm (p. 264)
mixed forest forestland with both evergreen and deciduous trees (p. 54)
mobile describing things or people that move easily from place to place (p. 122)
modernism Latin American literary move-

ment of the late 1800s, focusing on artistic expression and experimentation (p. 188)

monotheism belief in one God (p. 377)

monsoon in Asia, seasonal wind that brings warm moist air from the oceans in summer, cold dry air from inland in winter (pp. 482, 542, 602)

mosaic picture or design made with small pieces of colored stone, glass, or tile (p. 188)

mosque in Islam, a house of public worship (p. 378)

mulatto person of mixed African and European descent (p. 176)

multicultural having elements that come from more than one culture (pp. 120, 239)

N

nationalism belief in the right of each people to be an independent nation (p. 379)

nationalities large, distinct ethnic groups within a country, used especially in Russia and the Eurasian republics (p. 305)

nationalize to place a company or industry under government control (p. 379)

natural resource element or substance from the earth that is not made by people but can be used by them, such as minerals (p. 37)

natural vegetation plant life that grows in a certain area if people have not changed the natural environment (p. 52)

nirvana in Buddhism, ultimate state of peace and insight toward which people strive (p. 497)

nomadic describing a way of life in which a group travels from place to place rather than establishing a permanent settlement (p. 673)

nonrenewable resource resource that cannot be replaced by natural growth or human action, such as most minerals (p. 38)

North American Free Trade Agreement (NAFTA) trade agreement made in 1993 by Canada, the United States, and Mexico (p. 134)

O

oasis small area in a desert where water and vegetation are found, usually because of underground springs (pp. 53, 362)

oral history legends and stories passed on by word of mouth from generation to generation (p. 444)

organic farming the use of natural substances to enrich the soil and grow crops rather than chemical fertilizers and pesticides (p. 264)

P

Pampas grassy, treeless plains of southern South America, used for growing grain and grazing animals (p. 164)

pastoralism the raising and grazing of livestock (p. 364)

patriarch in church history, an important Christian bishop or leader; today, the head of an independent Eastern Orthodox church or of the Armenian Apostolic Church (p. 318)

peat vegetable matter, mainly mosses, usually found in swamps; sometimes cut and burned as fuel in parts of western Europe (p. 229)

per capita income the total income of a country or region divided by the number of people; income per person (pp. 76, 435)

perestroika (pehr•ehs•TROY•kah) in Russian, "restructuring"; part of Gorbachev's plan for reforming Soviet government (p. 314)

permafrost permanently frozen layer of soil beneath the surface of the ground (pp. 55, 231, 297)

pesticide chemical used to kill insects, rodents, and other pests (p. 341)

petrochemical chemical product derived from petroleum or natural gas (p. 392)

phosphate natural mineral containing chemical compounds often used in fertilizers (p. 361)

pidgin English a dialect mixing English and local languages (p. 680)

plateau flat landmass higher than the surrounding land, with at least one steep side, called a cliff (pp. 34, 94)

poaching illegal hunting of protected animals (p. 460)
pogrom in czarist Russia, an attack on Jews carried out by government troops or officials (p. 318)
polder low-lying area of the Netherlands from which seawater has been drained to create new farmland (p. 228)
polluted contaminated by harmful or impure substances (p. 338)
pollution the existence of impure, unclean, or poisonous substances in the air, water, and land environment (p. 67)
population density average number of people in a square mile or square kilometer (p. 65)
population distribution the pattern of population—where people live—in a country, a continent, or the world (p. 65)
prairie an inland grassland area (p. 54)
precipitation moisture that falls to the earth as rain, sleet, hail, or snow (p. 51)
prehistory the time in a people's past before written records were kept (p. 69)
prevailing wind wind in a region that blows in a fairly constant directional pattern, such as the trade winds that blow toward the Equator in low latitudes (p. 50)
primate city city that dominates a country's economy, culture, and government and in which population is concentrated; usually the capital (pp. 179, 613, 670)
prophet person believed to be a messenger from God (p. 378)

Q

qanat underground canals used in water systems of ancient Persians (p. 377)
quipu (KEE•poo) rope with knotted cords of various lengths and colors used by the Inca to keep records and send messages (p. 182)

R

raga in Indian classical music, a basic melody on which the player improvises or plays variations (p. 503)
rail gauge the distance between the rails on a railroad track, which determines the position of wheels on a railroad car (p. 690)
rain shadow dry area found on the leeward side of a mountain range (p. 51)
realism artistic style portraying everyday life that developed in Europe during the mid-1800s (p. 252)
reforestation replanting young trees or seeds on lands where trees have been cut or destroyed (p. 203)
Reformation religious movement that began in Germany in the 1400s, leading to the establishment of Protestant churches (p. 246)
refugee person who must leave his or her home and flee elsewhere for safety (p. 240)
reincarnated in Hindu belief, being reborn repeatedly in different forms, until one has overcome earthly desires (p. 497)
relative location where a place is located in relation to other places (p. 7)
relief differences in elevation, or height, of land and landforms (p. 14)
religion organized way of worshiping a spiritual being or thinking about life (p. 77)
Renaissance in Europe, a 300-year period of renewed interest in classical learning and the arts, beginning in the 1300s (p. 246)
renewable resource resource that can be grown by people or renewed naturally, such as trees (p. 38)
republic form of government without a monarch, in which people elect their officials, including the head of state (p. 114)
revolution in astronomy, the earth's yearly trip around the sun, taking 365 1/4 days (p. 46)
romanticism artistic style emphasizing individual emotions that developed in Europe in the late 1700s and early 1800s as a reaction to industrialization (p. 252)
russification in 19th-century Russia, a government program that required everyone in the empire to speak Russian and to become a Christian (p. 313)

S

sadhu a Hindu hermit or holy man and teacher (p. 502)
samurai in medieval Japan, a class of pro-

fessional soldiers who lived by a strict code of personal honor and loyalty to a noble (p. 557)

savanna a tropical grassland containing scattered trees (p. 426)

scale on a map, the relationship of measures on the map to actual measurements in feet, miles, meters, or kilometers on the earth's surface (p. 12)

sedentary farming farming carried on at permanent settlements (p. 452)

seismic related to earthquakes (p. 358)

serf laborer owned by a noble and obliged to remain on the land where he or she worked (p. 312)

service industry business that provides a service—such as banking, insurance, or transport—instead of making goods (pp. 132, 196, 393)

shamanism belief in a leader who can communicate with spirits (p. 562)

shifting farming method in which farmers move every few years to find better soil (p. 452)

shogun in medieval Japan, a military ruler of the country (p. 557)

sickle large, curved knife with a handle, used to cut grass or tall grains (p. 629)

sirocco hot desert wind that can blow air and dust from North Africa to western Europe's Mediterranean coast (p. 231)

slash-and-burn farming traditional farming method in which all trees and plants in an area are cut and burned to add nutrients to the soil (p. 202)

smog irritating haze caused by the interaction of ultraviolet solar radiation with chemical fumes from automobile exhausts and other pollution sources (from the words *smoke* and *fog*) (pp. 57, 138)

socialism political philosophy that originally called for ownership of all land and factories by peasants and workers, now refers to government ownership of some or all means of production (pp. 76, 312)

socialist realism in the Soviet Union, realistic style of art and literature that glorified Soviet ideals and goals (p. 320)

solstice one of two days (about June 21 and December 22) on which the sun's rays strike directly at latitude 23 1/2°N (Tropic of Cancer) or 23 1/2°S (Tropic of Capricorn), marking the beginning of summer or winter (p. 47)

sovkhoz in the Soviet Union, a large farm owned and run by the state (p. 329)

special purpose map map emphasizing a special subject matter, such as resources or population (p. 15)

sphere of influence area of a country in which a foreign power has political or economic control (p. 615)

standard of living a measure of people's quality of life, based on access to material goods such as income, food, and housing (p. 75)

state farm under communism, a state-owned farm managed by government officials; also called *sovkhoz* (p. 264)

station Australian term for an outlying ranch or large farm (p. 687)

steppe wide grassy plains of Eurasia, stretching from the Black Sea to the Altai Mountains; also, similar semi-arid climate regions elsewhere (p. 298)

strait narrow waterway connecting two large bodies of water (p. 111)

strine colloquial, informal English spoken in Australia (p. 679)

subcontinent large landmass that is part of a continent but still distinct from it, such as India (p. 477)

subsistence farming traditional agriculture whose goal is to produce just enough to eat for a family or a village to survive (pp. 63, 452, 511, 680, 688)

suburbs outlying communities around a central city (p. 109)

Sunbelt southern part of the United States, so named because of its mild climate (p. 108)

sūq an enclosed marketplace in the region of North Africa and Southwest Asia (p. 385)

T

taiga Russian term for the vast subarctic forest, mainly evergreens, that begins where the tundra ends; also used for subarctic climate regions in general (pp. 55, 297)

tala in Indian classical music, a rhythm pattern, often played on a drum (p. 503)

tariff a tax on imports or exports (p. 265)

temperature a measure of how hot or cold something is, generally measured in degrees on a set scale, such as Fahrenheit or Celsius (p. 45)

tierra caliente Spanish term for "hot country"; the lowest zone (sea level-3,000 feet elevation) of a highland climate near the Equator (p. 167)

tierra fría Spanish term for "cold country"; the highest altitude zone of highland climates in Central and South America (p. 167)

tierra templada Spanish term for "temperate country"; the middle zone (3,000-6,000 ft. elevation) of Latin American highland climates (p. 167)

timberline elevation above which it is too cold for trees to grow (pp. 56, 101)

topography physical features of the earth's surface (p. 14)

tornado a violent windstorm with rotating winds and a funnel-shaped cloud (pp. 66, 100)

trading partner a country that buys from or sells to another country (p. 574)

trekker a mountain hiker; more generally, anyone on a difficult journey (p. 518)

tributary smaller rivers and streams that feed into a larger river (p. 96)

truck farm farm, especially in the northeastern United States, that grows vegetables for markets in nearby cities (p. 131)

trust territory region, such as Micronesia, placed by United Nations under temporary political and economic control of another country after World War II (p. 675)

tsunami Japanese term used for a huge sea wave caused by an undersea earthquake (pp. 67, 538)

tundra vast treeless plains in cold northern climates, characterized by permafrost and small, low plants such as mosses and shrubs (p. 297)

typhoon a hurricane (cyclone), or violent tropical storm, that forms in the Pacific Ocean, usually in late summer (pp. 100, 542, 636, 662)

U

universal suffrage equal voting rights for all adult residents of a nation (p. 440)

urbanization the movement of people from rural areas into cities (p. 436)

V

viceroy representative of the Spanish monarch appointed to enforce laws in American colonies (p. 182)

W

wadi in the desert, a streambed that is dry except during a heavy rain (p. 360)

wat in Southeast Asia, a temple (p. 621)

water cycle regular movement of water from ocean to air to ground and back to the ocean (p. 36)

wattle name given to acacia trees by early Australian settlers who built houses of interwoven (wattled) acacia saplings (p. 660)

weather condition of the atmosphere in one place during a short period of time; for example, a "cold, windy, wet day" (p. 45)

weathering chemical or physical processes, such as freezing, that break down rocks (p. 30)

welfare state nation, such as Great Britain, Norway, or Sweden, in which the government assumes major responsibility for people's welfare in areas such as health and education (p. 253)

windward facing toward the direction from which the wind is blowing (p. 51)

Z

ziggurat large step-like temple of mud brick built in ancient Mesopotamia (p. 383)

Glossary/Glosario

A

absolute location/ubicación absoluta La posición de un lugar en la superficie de la tierra (pág. 5)

abstract/abstracto estilo de arte que expresa las emociones y la actitud del artista. (pág. 121)

acid deposition/deposición ácida Ácidos secos o húmedos que lleva el viento y que caen a la tierra (pág. 271)

acid rain/lluvia ácida Precipitación que lleva grandes cantidades de ácidos disueltos, especialmente ácido sulfúrico y ácido nítrico, los cuales dañan los edificios, los bosques y las cosechas y matan la fauna (págs. 137, 270, 577)

alluvial plain/llanura aluvial Llanura en la que los ríos inundados han depositado tierra rica, como la Llanura Indogangéctica en el Asia del Sur (pág. 480)

alluvial-soil deposits/depósitos de tierra aluvial Tierra rica compuesta de arena y lodo depositados por aguas corrientes (pág. 359)

amendment/enmienda En la historia de los Estados Unidos, cambios oficiales que se le hacen a la Constitución (pág. 118)

apartheid/segregación racial Política de estricta separación de las razas adoptada en Sudáfrica en los años 40 (pág. 440)

aquifer/acuífero/aguas freáticas Capas subterráneas de roca porosa, arena o grava que acumulan agua (pág. 398)

arable land/tierra arable Tierra idónea para cultivar cosechas (pág. 612)

archipelago/archipiélago Un grupo o cadena de islas (pgs. 34, 538, 598)

artesian water/agua artesiana Abastecimiento de agua subterránea que está bajo suficiente presión para subir a los pozos sin tener que ser bombeada (pág. 656)

Association of Southeast Asian Nations (ASEAN)/Asociación de Naciones del Asia del Sudeste (ANSEA) Organización formada en 1967 para promover el desarrollo y el comercio regional en el Asia del Sudeste (pág. 632)

atheist/ateo Persona que no cree en Dios (pág. 317)

atmosphere/atmósfera El aire que rodea la Tierra (pág. 27)

atoll/atolón Isla en forma de aro formada por coral que se acumula por todo el borde de un volcán submarino (pág. 657)

avalanche/avalancha Masa de hielo, nieve o roca que se desliza por el lado de una montaña (pág. 231)

axis/eje Referente a la Tierra, una línea imaginaria que le atraviesa por el centro entre el Polo Norte y el Polo Sur (pág. 45)

B

batik/batik Método de teñir tela para producir bellos estampados, desarrollado en Indonesia y Malasia (pág. 621)

bedouin/beduíno Miembro de los pueblos nómadas del desierto del Africa del Norte y Asia del Sudoeste (pág. 384)

bilingual/bilingüe Que habla o usa dos idiomas (pág. 121)

biologist/biólogo Científico que estudia la vida vegetal y animal (pág. 274)

biosphere/biosfera La parte de la Tierra donde la vida, la gente, las plantas y los animales—existe (pág. 28)

black market/mercado negro Cualquier mercado ilegal donde se vende productos escasos o ilegales, por lo general a precios altos (pág. 328)

blizzard/ventisca Una fuerte tormenta de nieve con vientos de más de 35 millas por hora (pág. 101)

boomerang/bumerang Palo curvo que se tira, lo usan los aborígenes de Australia para cazar (pág. 673)

bycatch/pezca residua los peces, mamiferos marinos y aves que quedan atrapados sin querer en las redes de los pescadores profesionales y luego se desechan (pág. 141)

C

cabinet/gabinete Directores de departamentos en la rama ejecutiva del gobierno de EE.UU. quienes aconsejan al Presidente (pág. 118)

calligraphy/caligrafía El arte de escribir a mano de forma decorativa y bella (pág. 565) *campesinos* Trabajadores agrícolas; generalmente gente que vive y trabaja en áreas rurales (pág. 196)

canopy/follaje o copa Capa superior del bosque de lluvia, donde se juntan las puntas de los árboles altos (pág. 167)

capitalism/capitalismo Sistema económico basado en el libre comercio, en el cual los individuos son dueños del capital que usan (pág. 76)

cash crop/cosecha comercial Cosecha agrícola cultivada para venderse o trocarse en lugar de usarse para la familia del agricultor (págs. 113, 195, 452, 512, 630)

caste system/sistema de casta En la sociedad tradicional del Asia del Sur, la división de la sociedad en rígidos grupos, basada principalmente en la ocupación, que determina la posición social, la selección de conyuge y otras acciones (pág. 496)

cataract/catarata Un gran salto de agua (pág. 420)

caudillo Término para un líder político de Latinoamérica desde los últimos años de los 1800 en adelante, con frecuencia un dictador militar (pág. 184)

cereal/cereal Cualquier grano, como la cebada, la avena o el trigo, que se cultiva para alimento (pág. 364)

chaparral/chaparral Tipo de vegetación compuesta de densos bosques de matorrales y arbustos, común los en climas mediterráneos (págs. 54, 232)

chart/tabla Representación visual de datos en filas y columnas (pág. 22)

chernozem Capa vegetal de tierra negra y rica que se halla en la llanura del norte de Europa, especialmente en Rusia y Ucrania (pág. 291)

chinampas Islas flotantes de agricultura artificial hechas por los aztecas (pág. 181)

chinook/chinuco Viento cálido estacional que sopla por las Montañas Rocosas al final del invierno y al principio de la primavera (pág. 101)

Chipko/chipko En la India, un movimiento ambiental conocido por el término "abraza-árbol," con fines de salvar los bosques (pág. 520)

cholorofluorocarbons/clorofluorocarbonos También llamados CFCs; sustancias químicas que se hallan principalmente en enfriantes líquidos, dañan la capa de ozono que protege la tierra (pág. 578)

city-state/ciudad-estado En la antigua Grecia, comunidad independiente que consistía de una ciudad y las tierras circundantes, donde primero se desarrolló la democracia (pág. 245)

civilization/civilización Una cultura que ha organizado un sistema social, económico y político; que ha construido ciudades y logrado un cierto nivel de desarrollo en las artes y las ciencias (pág. 69)

clan/clan Comunidad tribal o grupo grande de gente relacionas entre sí (pgs. 444, 557)

climate/clima Patrones del tiempo típicos de un área durante un largo período de tiempo (pág. 45)

cold war/querra fría Se refiere a la lucha por el poder entre la Unión Soviética y los Estados Unidos (pág. 248)

collective farm/granja colectiva Bajo el comunismo, una granja enorme, propiedad del estado, en la cual los agricultores recibían sueldos más una parte de los productos y ganancias; también denominada *kholkoz* (pág. 264)

command economy/economía controlada Sistema económico en el que las decisiones económicas acerca de la producción y la distribución las toma alguna autoridad central (pág. 328)

commercial farming/agricultura comercial Agricultura organizada como un negocio (pág. 452)

commune/comuna En la China, una comunidad agrícola colectiva cuyos miembros estaban supuestos a compartir el trabajo y los productos (pág. 571)

communism/comunismo Movimiento sociopolítico desarrollado por Marx y Lenín que favorecía la revolución para establecer una sociedad sin clases en la que los trabajadores controlarían la producción (págs. 247, 313)

compass rose/rosa del compás Marcador direccional en un mapa (pág. 12)

conquistador Término español para referirse a los soldados que conquistaron a los indios de Latinoamérica (pág. 182)

Constitution/Constitución Plan que hizo el gobierno en 1787 para los nuevos Estados Unidos (pág. 118)

consumer goods/bienes de consumidor Enseres domésticos, zapatos y ropas que la gente compra (págs. 264, 328)

continental divide/divisoria continental Una línea o cordillera que separa ríos que fluyen hacia distintos lados de un continente (pág. 96)

continental island/isla continental Isla formada de roca que se ha levantado de la plataforma continental, como Papua Nueva Guinea (pág. 657)

continental shelf/plataforma continental Área no profunda del océano cerca de la costa de un continente (pág. 34)

contour lines/líneas de contorno En un mapa, las líneas que conectan puntos de tierra a la misma elevación (pág. 14)

contour plowing/labranza de contorno Método de labranza en el que los surcos siguen la curva natural de la tierra para reducir la erosión (pág. 131)

cooperative/cooperativa Una organización voluntaria cuyos miembros trabajan juntos y comparten los gastos y ganancias de su empresa (pág. 572)

copra/copra La masa seca del coco (pág. 688)

coral/coral Diminutos animales marinos y estructuras como roca (islas, arecifes) formados por los esqueletos de colonias de coral (pág. 656)

cordillera/cordillera Cadena de montañas (pág. 597)

crevasse/grieta Una brecha enorme y honda que se forma en la nieve o en el hielo grueso (pág. 663)

crop rotation/rotación de cultivo Método de agricultura en el que distintos cultivos se alternan en el mismo terreno para preservar los nutrientes de la tierra (pág. 132)

Crusades/Cruzadas Serie de guerras religiosas (c. 1100-1300) en las que los cristianos europeos trataron de tomar Palestina del control musulmán (pág. 246)

cultural diffusion/difusión cultural La difusión de ideas, costumbres, bienes y personas de una cultura a otra (pág. 70)

culture/cultura Modo de vida de un grupo de gente que comparte tradiciones, intereses, creencias y modos de ganarse la vida (págs. 10, 63)

culture hearth/hogar de la cultura Un centro donde las culturas se desarrollan y desde el cual las ideas y las tradiciones se difunden (págs. 69, 556)

culture region/región cultural División de la Tierra basada en una variedad de factores que incluyen el gobierno, los grupos sociales, los sistemas económicos, el lenguaje o la religión (pág. 74)

cuneiform/cuneiforme Sistema de escritura sumeria que usa símbolos en forma de cuñas hundidas en tabletas de arcilla (pág. 377)

current/corriente "Río" de agua de mar fría o cálida que fluye hacia los océanos, por lo general de forma circular (pág. 50)

cyclone/ciclón Tormenta con lluvias fuertes y vientos altos que sopla en círculo alrededor de un área de baja presión atmosférica (págs. 484, 636)

czar/zar En la historia de Rusia, el emperador o gobernante supremo (pág. 312)

D

deciduous/deciduo Describe árboles, usualmente de hojas anchas como los robles y arces, que pierden las hojas en el otoño (pág. 54)

deforestation/desforestación La pérdida o destrucción de los bosques, debido principalmente a la tala de árboles para el maderero o la agricultura (págs. 202, 460, 518, 605)

delta Sección triangular de tierra que se forma en la boca de un río y que se parece a la letra griega *delta* (Δ) (pág. 359)

desalination/desalación La eliminación de la sal del agua de mar para que se pueda usar para beber y en la agricultura (pág. 399)

desertification/desertificación Proceso en el cual la tierra arable se vuelve desierto, usualmente debido a la destrucción de la vegetación (pág. 458)

developing country/país en vías de desarrollo País en el proceso de industrialización (pág. 195)

dharma En hinduismo, el deber moral que guía la vida de una persona, de acuerdo a las diferencias de clase (pág. 497)

diagram/diagrama Dibujo que muestra lo que algo es o cómo algo se hace, como los pasos de un proceso o ciclo (pág. 22)

dialect/dialecto Variedad local de un lenguaje usado en un lugar en particular o por cierto grupo (págs. 177, 251)

SPANISH HANDBOOK

distillation/destilación Método de desalación en el cual el agua se hierve y se condensa (pág. 400)

doldrums/zona de calmas ecuatoriales Un área cerca del Ecuador frecuentemente sin viento (págs. 50, 662)

domesticate/domesticar El tomar plantas y animales silvestres y domarlos o hacerlos útiles para la gente (pág. 376)

dry farming/agricultura seca Método de agricultura que se usa en regiones secas en que la tierra se ara y se siembra bien hondo para retener el agua en la tierra (pág. 117)

dynasty/dinastía Una casa gobernante o la continuación de una familia de gobernantes, especialmente en la China (pág. 556)

E

economic system/sistema económico La forma en que la gente de un país produce y distribuye los bienes y servicios (pág. 75)

ecosystem/ecosistema La compleja comunidad de seres vivientes que, en cierto medio ambiente, dependen los unos de los otros (págs. 202, 697)

ecotourism/ecoturismo Turismo basado en preocupación por el medio ambiente (pág. 461)

endemic/endémico Que describe especies de plantas o animales nativos de un área particular (pág. 605)

environmentalist/ambientalista Persona activamente preocupada con la calidad y la protección del medio ambiente (pág. 271)

equinox/equinoxio Uno de dos días (entre el del 21 marzo y el 23 de septiembre) cuando cual el Sol está directamente encima del ecuador, haciendo que el día y la noche sean de igual duración (pág. 46)

erosion/erosión El desgaste de la superficie de la Tierra por el viento, el fluir del agua o los glaciares (pág. 31)

escarpment/escarpa Risco o escarpadura entre una superficie de tierra alta y otra más baja (págs. 162, 419)

ethnic diversity/diversidad étnica Diferencias entre grupos o gente basadas en sus orígenes, lenguajes, costumbres o creencias (pág. 371)

ethnic group/grupo étnico Grupo de personas quienes comparten los mismos antepasados, lenguaje, costumbres o una combinación de tales características (págs. 305, 436, 551)

eutrophication/eutroficación Proceso por el cual el agua de un lago o arroyo se hace demasiado rica en nutrientes disueltos, haciendo que la abundancia de plantas agote el oxígeno (pág. 139)

evaporation/evaporación El cambio de agua líquida a vapor de agua, un gas (pág. 36)

exports/exportaciones Recursos o bienes que se envían desde un país a otro (pág. 39)

extended family/parentela Una familia compuesta de varias generaciones de parientes; por ejemplo los tíos y abuelos al igual que los padres y los hijos (pág. 444)

extinction/extinción La desaparición o fin de una especie de animal o planta (pág. 460)

F

fale Tipo de casa tradicional en Samoa occidental, con los lados abiertos y el techo de paja (pág. 681)

farm cooperative/cooperativa agrícola Organización en la que los agricultores comparten en el cultivo y la venta de los productos agrícolas (pág. 264)

fault/falla Una grieta o hendidura en la corteza terrestre, usualmente causada por intensos pliegues (págs. 29, 420)

fauna/fauna La vida animal de una región (pág. 598)

fazenda Término portugués para una enorme plantación azucarera en Brasil (pág. 182)

feudalism/feudalismo Sistema de gobierno durante la época medieval en Europa y el Japón, en que poderosos señores feudales daban tierras a los nobles a cambio de su lealtad (pág. 245)

fishery/pesquería Zonas (de agua fresca o salada) donde se pescan peces u otros animales marinos (pág. 98)

fjord/fiordo Valle glacial con largos acantilados llenos de agua de mar (pág. 223)
flora/flora La vida de las plantas de una región (pág. 598)
foehn/fohn Viento seco y cálido que sopla del lado sotavento de las montañas, a veces derrite la nieve y provoca avalanchas; se usa predominantemente en Europa (pág. 231)
fold/pliegue Una dobladura en las capas de roca, a veces causada por el movimiento de las placas (pág. 29)
free enterprise/libre comercio Un sistema económico en el cual los negocios privados operan con poca interferencia del gobierno (págs. 76, 129)
free port/zona libre Ciudad portuaria, como Singapur, donde los bienes se desembarcan, se almacenan y se vuelven a embarcar sin pago de impuestos portuarios (pág. 633)
fútbol Se conoce en Norteamérica como el "soccer" (pág. 189)

G

general purpose map/mapa de propósito general Mapa que muestra un amplia variedad de información física y/o política acerca de un área (pág. 14)
geography/geografía El estudio de la Tierra y la forma en que la gente vive y trabaja (pág. 5)
glacier/glaciar Grandes cuerpos de hielo que se mueven a través de la superficie de la Tierra (pág. 31)
glasnost/glasnost Término ruso para una nueva "libertad"; parte de los planes de reforma de Gorbachev (pág. 314)
global warming/calentamiento global Calentamiento gradual de la Tierra y su atmósfera que puede ser causado en parte por la contaminación y un aumento del efecto de invernadero (pág. 697)
government/gobierno El grupo o sistema político de una nación (pág. 74)
graph/gráfica Modo de representar y comparar información visualmente, como una gráfica lineal, gráfica de barra o gráfica circular (pág. 20)
graziers/ganaderos Personas que crían y pastorean ganado ovejuno y vacuno (pág. 687)
great circle/gran círculo La distancia más corta entre dos lugares cualquiera en la superficie de la Tierra (pág. 16)
green revolution/revolución verde Programa comenzado en los años 60 para producir cepas de mayor rendimiento de trigo, arroz y otras cosechas de alimento (pág. 513)
grid system/sistema de cuadrícula Patrón formado a medida que las líneas de latitud y longitud se intersectan (pág. 6)
gross domestic product (GDP)/producto interno bruto (PIB) El valor de los bienes y los servicios creados dentro de un país en un año (págs. 393, 435)
groundwater/agua subterránea Agua que yace debajo de la superficie de la Tierra, abastecida mayormente por la filtración de la lluvia a través de la tierra (pág. 35)

H

habitat/hábitat Area con condiciones idóneas para que vivan ciertas plantas y animales (pág. 460)
haiku/haiku Forma de poesía japonesa que consiste de 17 sílabas, con frecuencia trata de la naturaleza (pág. 565)
headwaters/cabeceras Las fuentes de aguas de río (pág. 96)
heavy industry/industria pesada La manufactura de maquinaria y equipo necesario para fábricas y minas (pág. 263)
hemisphere/hemisferio Mitad de una esfera o globo, como en los Hemisferios Norte y Sur de la Tierra (p. 5)
hieroglyphics/jeroglíficos Sistema de escritura egipcia que usa dibujos y símbolos para representar palabras y sonidos (pág. 377)
history/historia El estudio de información escrita acerca de los acontecimientos y personas del pasado (pág. 69)
Holocaust/Holocausto Término designado a la muerte masiva de 6 millones de judíos europeos por los líderes Nazi de Alemania durante la Segunda Guerra Mundial (pág. 248)
homogeneous/homogéneo Describe a un grupo de gente o cosas que son muy parecidas (pág. 552)
hurricane/huracán Una gran tormenta de vientos fuertes que se forma sobre

las aguas cálidas del océano (págs. 66, 101)

hydroelectric power/energía hidroeléctrica Energía eléctrica generada por la caída del agua (pág. 165)

hydrosphere/hidrosfera Las zonas acuosas de la Tierra que incluyen los océanos, lagos, ríos y otros cuerpos de agua (pág. 28)

hypothesis/hipótesis Un paso en el método científico que sugiere una explicación científica para los fenómenos que se observan (pág. 57)

I

icon/icono Imagen religiosa, usualmente incluye un cuadro de Jesús, María o un santo, usado principalmente por los cristianos ortodoxos (pág. 317)

ideogram/ideograma Un caracter pictórico o un símbolo que tiene un significado específico o representa una sílaba (pág. 561)

imports/importaciones Recursos o bienes que vienen de otro país (pág. 39)

immigrant/inmigrante Persona que ha dejado su país y se ha establecido permanentemente en otro país (pág. 107)

impressionism/impresionismo Estilo artístico que se desarrolló en Europa en los últimos años de los 1800 y que trató de mostrar la apariencia natural de los objetos con toques o pinceladas de color ligeros (pág. 253)

indigenous/indígeno Nativo a un lugar; los habitantes originales, ya sean plantas, animales, o seres humanos (pág. 615)

industrialization/industrialización Proceso de usar maquinaria en la manufactura (pág. 116)

industrialize/industrializar Desarrollar industria (pág. 336)

interdependent/interdependiente Depender los unos de los otros para bienes, servicios e ideas (págs. 8, 135, 632)

isthmus/istmo Porción angosta de tierra que conecta a otras dos masas de tierra más grandes (pág. 33)

J

jai alai/jai alai Juego de mano tradicional popular en México y Cuba (pág. 189)

jazz/jazz Forma musical que se desarrolló en los Estados Unidos a principios de siglo, mezcla ritmos africanos con harmonías europeas (pág. 122)

jati/jati En la sociedad tradicional hindú, un grupo social que define la ocupación de una familia y su pocisión social (pág. 491)

jute/yute Fibra vegetal que se usa para hacer cordón y tela (pág. 512)

K

karma/karma En la creencia Hindú, la suma de las acciones buenas y malas en la vida presente y las vidas pasadas de una persona, conduce a premio o castigo (pág. 497)

key/clave Parte de un mapa que explica los símbolos que se usan (pág. 12)

kolkhoz En la Unión Soviética, una enorme granja colectiva (pág. 329)

krill Diminutos animales marinos parecidos a los camarones que viven en los frígidos océanos de la Antártica (pág. 659)

kums Término regional para los desiertos arenosos en las tierras bajas de Turán, como en Kara Kum (pág. 292)

L

lagoon/laguna Estanque de poca profundidad en el centro de un atolón (pág. 657)

language family/familia de lenguajes Grupo de lenguajes relacionados que se desarrollaron de un lenguaje anterior (págs. 76, 251)

latifundia/latifundios En la moderna Latinoamérica, grandes estancias que pertenecen a familias o corporaciones (pág. 196)

latitude/latitud Líneas imaginarias que corren de este a oeste alrededor del globo, se usan para medir la distancia al norte o sur del Ecuador en grados; también se llaman paralelos (págs. 5, 13)

leach/deslave Lavar la tierra para sacarle los nutrientes (pág. 426)

leeward/sotovento Con cara en contra de la dirección de donde sopla el viento (p. 51)

lichens/líquenes Plantas diminutas y fuertes que crecen como una corteza sobre las rocas y los troncos de los árboles (pág. 663)

light industry/industria ligera Manufactura con fines de producir bienes para el consumidor en vez de maquinaria pesada, como textiles o el procesamiento de alimentos (pág. 263)

lingua franca/lengua franca Un lenguaje, como el Swahili, usado para facilitar la comunicación entre personas que hablan diferentes idiomas nativos (pág. 442)

literacy rate/índice de alfabetización El porcentaje de personas en un lugar dado que puede leer y escribir (págs. 123, 445)

lithosphere/litosfera Áreas de superficie terrestre de la corteza de la Tierra (como el 30 por ciento), incluye los continentes y las cuencas de los océanos (pág. 28)

llanos Llanuras fértiles a lo largo de las costas del Caribe de Sudamérica, en Colombia y Venezuela (pág. 164)

loess/loes Capa superficial del suelo, fina, amarillenta y marrón compuesta de partículas de limo y arcilla, usualmente arrastrada por el viento (pág. 539)

longhouse/casa larga En zonas rurales de Indonesia y Malasia, un edificio grande donde vive la gente de varias familias que están relacionadas entre sí (pág. 622)

longitude/longitud Líneas verticales imaginarias que corren de polo a polo del globo, se usan para medir distancias de este u oeste desde el primer meridiano; también se les llama meridianos (págs. 6, 13)

M

malnutrition/malnutrición Nutrición pobre debido a una dieta mal balanceada o a la falta de comida (pág. 187)

mangrove/árbol de Ámanglar Árbol o arbusto tropical perenne que generalmente crece en densas arboledas cerca del agua (pág. 518)

mantletree/manto Gruesa capa mediana de la estructura interior de la Tierra, consiste de densa piedra caliente compuesta de silicio, oxígeno, aluminio, hierro y magnesio (pág. 29)

mantra/mantra En Hinduismo, una palabra o frase sagrada que se repite en los rezos y cantos (pág. 502)

manuka Pequeños arbustos que crecen en las mesetas de Nueva Zelandia (pág. 663)

map projection/proyección de mapa Modo de trazar un mapa para representar en una superficie plana la redondez de la Tierra (pág. 17)

maquiladoras En México, plantas manufactureras montadas por firmas extranjeras (pág. 197)

maritime/marítimo Que concierne los viajes o la transportación por mar (pág. 615)

market economy/economía de mercado Un sistema económico basado en libre comercio, en el que los negocios son de propiedad privada y la producción y los precios se determinan por la oferta y la demanda (pág. 328)

marsupial/marsupio Tipo de mamífero (como canguros o coalas) que dan a luz a crías que maduran en una bolsa en el abdomen de la madre (pág. 694)

mass culture/cultura de las masas Cultura popular extendida por los medios de comunicación como la radio y la televisión (pág. 442)

megalopolis/megalópolis Una "super-ciudad" compuesta por varias grandes ciudades y las pequeñas ciudades cerca de ellas, como el área entre Boston y Washington, D.C. o los alrededores de Tokio-Yokohama, Japón (págs. 109, 554)

meltwater/aguanieve Agua formada al derretirse la nieve y el hielo (pág. 271)

merchant marine/marina mercante La flota de barcos de un país que participa en el intercambio comercial (pág. 576)

mesa/meseta Formación terrestre elevada con la cima plana (pág. 94)

mestizo En Latinoamérica, persona de descendencia mixta de indios y europeos (pág. 176)

metropolitan area/área metropolitana Región que incluye una ciudad central y sus suburbios circundantes (pág. 109)

mica/mica Mineral silicato que típicamente se parte en delgadas láminas brillantes (pág. 481)

Middle Passage/Pasaje Medio Nombre dado a la ruta que usaron los barcos de esclavos para atravesar el Atlántico desde el África Occidental hasta las Américas (pág. 440)

***minifundia*/minifundios** En Latinoamérica, pequeas granjas que producen alimento principalmente para el uso de la familia y el mercado local (pág. 196)

mistral/mistral Viento fuerte del norte desde los Alpes que trae aire frío al sur de Francia (pág. 231)

mixed farming/agricultura mixta Cultivo de varias clases de cosechas y ganado en la misma granja (pág. 264)

mixed forest/bosque mixto Tierras forestales con árboles perennes y deciduos (pág. 54)

mobile/móviles Describe cosas o personas que se mueven fácilmente de lugar en lugar (pág. 122)

modernism/modernismo Movimiento literario latinoamericano de fines de los años 1800, que enfocó la expresión artística y la experimentación (pág. 188)

monotheism/monoteísmo Creencia en un sólo Dios (pág. 377)

monsoon/monzón En Asia, viento veraniego que trae aires cálidos y húmedos desde los océanos, aire seco y frío desde la tierras interiores en el invierno (págs. 482, 542, 602)

mosaic/mosaico Dibujo o diseño hecho con pequeños pedazos de piedra, vidrio o azulejo de colores (pág. 188)

mosque/mezquita En Islam, una casa de oración pública (pág. 379)

mulatto/mulato Persona de descendencia mixta africana y europea (pág. 176)

multicultural/multicultural Que posee elementos que vienen de más de una cultura (págs. 120, 239)

N

nationalism/nacionalismo Creencia en el derecho de cada pueblo a ser una nación independiente (pág. 380)

nationalities/nacionalidades Grandes y diversos grupos étnicos distintis dentro de un país, se usaron especialmente en Rusia y las repúblicas euroasiáticas (pág. 305)

nationalize/nacionalizar Colocar una compañía o industria bajo el control del gobierno (pág. 380)

natural resource/recurso natural Elemento o sustancia de la tierra que no está hecha por la gente pero que ellos la pueden usar, como los minerales (pág. 37)

natural vegetation/vegetación natural Vida vegetal que crece en ciertas zonas si la gente no cambia el medio ambiente (pág. 52)

nirvana En Budismo, el máximo estado de paz y entendimiento que la gente trata de alcanzar (pág. 497)

nomadic/nómada Describe una forma de vida en la cual un grupo viaja de sitio en sitio en vez de establecer un poblado permanente (pág. 673)

nonrenewable resource/recurso no renovable Recurso que no se puede reponer por crecimiento natural o acción humana, como la mayoría de los minerales (pág. 38)

North American Free Trade Agreement (NAFTA)/Tratado de Libre Comercio de Norteamericano (TLCNA) Tratado comercial hecho en 1993 entre Canadá, los Estados unidos y México (pág. 135)

O

oasis Pequeña área en el desierto donde hay agua y vegetación, usualmente debido a manantiales subterráneos (págs. 53, 362)

oral history/historia oral Leyendas y cuentos que se pasan por tradición oral de generación en generación (pág. 444)

organic farming/agricultura orgánica El uso de sustancias naturales en lugar de fertilizantes y pesticidas para enriquecer la tierra y cultivar cosechas (pág. 264)

P

pampas/pampa Llanos herbosos, sin árboles en América del Sur, los cuales, se usan para cultivar cereales y para el pastoreo (pág. 164)

pastoralism/pastoreo críar y pastorear ganado (pág. 364)

patriarch/patriarca En la historia de la iglesia, obispo o líder importante; actualmente, el dirigente de una Iglesia Ortodoxa del Este o de la Iglesia Apostólica Armenia (pág. 318)

peat/turba Materia vegetal, mayormente musgos, se halla usualmente en pantanos; en algunos lugares de Europa occidental, a veces se corta y se quema como combustible (pág. 228)

per capita income/ingresos per cápita Los ingresos totales de un país o región divididos por el número de personas; ingresos por persona (págs. 76, 435)

perestroika En Rusia, "restructuración"; parte del plan de Gorbachev para reformar el gobierno soviético (pág. 314)

permafrost Capa de tierra por debajo de la superficie del suelo que está permanentemente congelada (págs. 55, 231, 297)

pesticide/pesticida Sustancia química que se usa para matar insectos, roedores y otras plagas (págs. 64, 341)

petrochemical/petroquímico Producto químico derivado del petróleo o del gas natural (pág. 392)

phosphate/fosfato Mineral natural que contiene compuestos químicos que a menudo se usan en fertilizantes (pág. 361)

pidgin English/Inglés corrompido Un dialecto que mezcla el inglés con los idiomas locales (pág. 680)

plateau/altiplano Masa de tierra plana más alta que la tierra que le rodea, con al menos un lado escarpado (págs. 34, 94)

poaching/cazar o pescar en vedado La caza o pesca prohibida de animales protegidos (pág. 460)

pogrom En la Rusia zarista, un ataque contra los judíos llevado a cabo por las tropas o los oficiales del gobierno (pág. 318)

polder/pólder Zona en Holanda, bajo el nivel del mar, de la cual se ha drenado el agua del mar para crear nuevas tierras de agricultura (pág. 228)

polluted/contaminado afectado por sustancias dañinas o impuras.

pollution/polución La existencia de sustancias sucias, impuras o venenosas en el aire, el agua y la tierra (pág. 67)

population density/densidad demográfica Número promedio de personas en una milla o kilómetro cuadrado (pág. 65)

population distribution/distribución demográfica La configuración demográfica; donde vive la gente en un país, continente o en el mundo (pág. 65)

prairie/pradera Zona herbosa tierra adentro (pág. 54)

precipitation/precipitación Humedad que cae a la tierra, como lluvia, nevisca, granizo o nieve (pág. 51)

prehistory/prehistoria La época en el pasado de un pueblo antes de que existiera un registro escrito (pág. 69)

prevailing wind/viento dominante Viento en una región que sopla en una dirección casi constantemente, como los alisios que soplan hacia el Ecuador en latitudes bajas (pág. 50)

primate city/ciudad prócer Ciudad que domina la economía, cultura y el gobierno de un país y en la que la población está concentrada; usualmente la capital (págs. 179, 613, 670)

prophet/profeta Persona de quien se cree ser un mensajero de Dios (pág. 379)

Q

qanat Canales subterráneos que se usaban en los sistemas de acueductos en la antigua Persia (pág. 378)

quipu Cuerda con cordones anudados de varios largos y colores que usaban los incas para anotar sus registros y mandar mensajes (pág. 182)

R

raga En la música cálsica de la India, una melodia básica sobre la cual el músico improvisa o toca variaciones (pág. 503)

rail gauge/ancho de vía La distancia entre los rieles en las ferrovías, lo cual determina la posición de las ruedas de los vagones (pág. 691)

rain shadow/sombra de lluvia Zona seca que se halla del lado sotovento de una cordillera (pág. 51)

realism/realismo Estilo artístico que capta la vida cotidiana que se desarrolló en Europa a mediado de los años 1800 (pág. 252)

reáforestation/reforestación La siembra de árboles jóvenes o semillas en terrenos donde los árboles han sido talados o destruídos (pág. 203)

Reformation/Reforma Movimiento religioso que comenzó en Alemania en los

1400 y que condujo al establecimiento de Iglesias Protestantes (pág. 247)

refugee/refugiado Persona que tiene que dejar su hogar y huir a otro lugar para estar a salvo (pág. 240)

reincarnated/reincarnado En la creencia Hindú, el renacer repetidas veces en distintas formas, hasta que uno ha vencido todos los deseos terrenales (pág. 497)

relative location/ubicación relativa La posición de un lugar en relación a otros lugares (pág. 7)

relief/relieve Las diferencias de elevación de la tierra (pág. 14)

religion/religión Forma organizada de alabar a un ser espiritual o de pensar acerca de la vida (pág. 77)

Renaissance/Renacimiento En Europa, un período de renovado interés por las enseñazas y artes clásicas que comenzó cerca del 1300 y duró 300 años (pág. 246)

renewable resource/recurso renovable Recurso que se puede cultivar o que se renueva naturalmente, como los árboles (pág. 38)

republic/república Forma de gobierno sin monarca, en el cual la gente elige a sus oficiales, incluso al jefe de estado (pág. 114)

revolution/revolución En astronomía, el viaje de la Tierra alrededor del Sol que toma 365 1/4 días (pág. 46)

romanticism/romanticismo Estilo artístico que enfatizaba las emociones individuales que se desarrolló en Europa en los últimos años de los 1700 y principios de los 1800 como una reacción a la industrialización (pág. 252)

russification/rusificación En la Rusia del siglo XIX, programa de gobierno que requería que todo el mundo en el imperio hablara ruso y se convirtiera al Cristianismo (pág. 313)

S

sadhu Un hermitaño hindú o un hombre santo y maestro (pág. 502)

samurai/samurai En el Japón medieval, una clase de soldados profesionales quienes se regían por un código estricto de honor personal y lealtad a un noble (pág. 558)

savanna/sabana Un herbazal tropical que contiene árboles dispersos (pág. 425)

scale/escala la relación entre las medidas de un mapa y las verdaderas medidas en pies, millas, metros o kilómetros sobre la superficie de la tierra (pág. 12)

sedentary farming/agricultura sedentaria Agricultura que toma lugar en asentamientos permanentes (pág. 452)

seismic/sísmico Relacionado con los terremotos (pág. 359)

serf/siervo Obrero de la propiedad de un noble y obligado a permanecer en la tierra donde trabajaba (pág. 312)

service industry/industria de servicios Negocios que proveen servicios, como los bancos, las compañías de seguros o transportación, en vez de producir bienes (págs. 134, 196, 393)

shaminism/shamanismo Creencia en un líder que se puede comunicar con los espíritus (pág. 562)

shifting farming/cultivo migratorio Método en el cual los agricultores se mudan cada cuantos años para hallar mejor tierra (pág. 452)

shogun/shogún En el Japón medieval, un gobernante militar del país (pág. 557)

sickle/hoz Cuchillo grande y curvo con un mango, usado para cortar hierba o cereales altos (pág. 629)

sirocco/siroco Viento caliente del desierto que sopla aire y polvo desde el África del Norte hasta la costa mediterránea de Europa (pág. 231)

slash-and-burn farming/agricultura de corte y quema Método tradicional de cultivo en que todos los árboles y plantas en el área se cortan y se queman para añadirles nutrientes al suelo (pág. 202)

smog/smog Calina irritante causada por la interacción de la radiación solar ultravioleta con humos químicos del escape de los automóviles y otras fuentes de contaminación (de las palabras inglesas *smoke*=humo y *fog*=neblina) (págs. 57, 138)

socialism/socialismo Filosofía política que originalmente dictaba que los campesinos y obreros fueran los propietarios de la tierra y de las factorías; ahora se refiere a la propiedad del gobierno de algunos o todos los medios de producción (págs. 76, 312)

socialist realism/realismo socialista En la

Unión Soviética, estilo realista de arte y literatura que glorificaba los ideales y las metas soviéticas (pág. 320)

solstice/solsticio Uno de dos días (aproximadamente entre el 21 de junio y el 22 de diciembre) en que los rayos del Sol dan directamente en la latitud 23 1/2°N (Trópico de Cancer) o 23 1/2°S (Trópico de Capricornio), para marcar el principio del verano o el invierno (pág. 47)

sovkhoz En la Unión Soviética, una enorme granja del estado y que el estado mismo opera (pág. 329)

special purpose map/mapa de propósito especial Mapa que enfatiza un tema especial, como recursos o población (pág. 15)

sphere of influence/esfera de influencia Zona del país en la que una potencia extranjera tiene control político o económico (pág. 615)

standard of living/estándar de vida Una medida de la calidad de vida, basada en el acceso a bienes materiales como ingresos, alimentos y vivienda (pág. 75)

state farm/granja estatal Bajo el comunismo, una granja de propiedad del estado dirigida por oficiales del gobierno; también denominada *sovkhoz* (pág. 264)

station/estación Término australiano para un rancho o granja grande en áreas remotas (pág. 687)

steppe/estepa Vastas llanuras herbosas de Eurasia que se extienden desde el Mar Negro hasta los Montes Altai; también, regiones en otros lugares con climas semiáridos similares (pág. 298)

strait/estrecho Vía fluvial estrecha que conecta dos grandes cuerpos de agua (pág. 111)

strine Inglés coloquial que se habla en Australia (pág. 679)

subcontinent/subcontinente Gran área de tierra que forma parte de un continente pero situada bastante lejos de él, como la India (pág. 477)

subsistence farming/agricultura de subsistencia Agricultura tradicional cuya meta es producir lo suficiente para que una familia o una aldea coma y sobreviva (págs. 63, 452, 511, 681, 688)

suburbs/suburbios Comunidades en las afueras y que circundan una ciudad central (pág. 109)

Sunbelt/franja del Sol Parte sur de los Estados Unidos, denominada así debido a su clima suave (pág. 108)

suq En el África del Norte y el Asia del Sudoeste, plaza de mercado encerrada (pág. 385)

T

taiga Término ruso para un vasto bosque subártico, principalmente de siempreverdes, que comienza donde termina la tundra; también se emplea para regiones climatológicas subárticas en general (págs. 55, 297)

tala En la música clásica de la India, un modelo rítmico, a menudo tocado con tambor (pág. [illegible])

tariff/tarifa [illegible] to s[illegible] bienes importados [illegible] dos (pág. 265)

temperature/temperatura Una medida de cuán caliente o cuán frío está algo, generalmente se mide en grados con una escala fija, como Fahrenheit o Celcio (pág. 45)

tierra caliente La zona más baja (nivel del mar -3,000 pies de elevación) de un clima de montaña cerca del Ecuador (pág. 167)

tierra fría La zona de altitud más alta de los climas de montaña en Centro y Sudamérica (pág. 167)

tierra templada La zona mediana (3,000-6,000 pies de elevación) de los climas de montaña de Latinoamérica (pág. 167)

timberline/límite de la vegetación selvática Elevación por encima de la cual hace demasiado frío para que crezcan los árboles (págs. 56, 101)

topography/topografía Características físicas de la superficie de la Tierra (pág. 14)

tornado Una violenta tormenta de viento con vientos giratorios y una nube en forma de embudo (págs. 66, 101)

trading partner/socios comerciales Países que comercian entre sí (pág. 574)

trekker/excursionista Alguien que escala montañas; generalmente, cualquiera que emprende un viaje difícil (pág. 518)

tributary/tributario Pequeños ríos y arroyos que alimentan los ríos más grandes (pág. 97)

truck farm/granja de hortalizas Granja,

SPANISH HANDBOOK

especialmente en el noreste de los Estados Unidos, que cultiva vegetales para los mercados en las ciudades circundantes (pág. 131)

trust territory/territorio en fideicomiso Región, tal como Micronesia, que después de la Segunda Guerra Mundial fue colocada temporáneamente por las Naciones Unidas bajo el control político y económico de otra nación (pág. 676)

tsunami Término japonés para una ola de mar enorme causada por un maremoto (págs. 67, 538)

tundra Vastas llanuras sin árboles en climas fríos del norte, caracterizadas por la capa del subsuelo congelada y pequeñas plantas como musgos y arbustos (pág. 297)

typhoon/tifón Un huracán, ciclón o tormenta tropical violenta que se forma en el Océano Pacífico, usualmente al final del verano (págs. 101, 542, 636, 663)

U

universal suffrage/sufragio universal Derechos de votación iguales para todos los adultos residentes de una nación (pág. 440)

urbanization/urbanización El movimiento de personas de las áreas rurales a las ciudades (pág. 436)

V

viceroy/virrey Representante del monarca español asignado para hacer cumplir las leyes en las colonias americanas (pág. 182)

W

wadi En el desierto, cauce seco excepto durante la lluvias pesadas (pág. 359)

wat En el Asia del Sudeste, un templo (pág. 620)

water cycle/ciclo de agua Movimiento regular del agua desde el océano hasta el aire y el suelo y de vuelta al océano (pág. 36)

wattle/zarzo Árboles de acacia; los primeros colonos de Australia entretejían los zarzos jóvenes para construir sus casas (pág. 660)

weather/tiempo Condición de la atmósfera en un lugar durante un corto período de tiempo; como la de un día frío, con viento y lluvia (pág. 45)

weathering/desgaste Procesos químicos o físicos, como congelación, que desbaratan las rocas (pág. 30)

welfare state/estado benefactor Nación, como Gran Bretaña, Noruega o Suecia, en la que el gobierno asume la responsabilidad principal por el bienestar de la gente en en cuanto a salud y educación (pág. 253)

windward/barlovento Con la cara hacia la dirección desde donde el viento está soplando (pág. 51)

Z

ziggurat/zigurat En la antigua Mesopotamia, gran templo escalonado hecho de ladrillos de arcilla (pág. 383)

Puntos de interés

Sección 1 Temas de geografía

Los cinco temas: localidad, lugar, interacción humana con el medio ambiente, movimiento y región son importantes para el estudio de la geografía. Los geógrafos usan los temas para comprender las relaciones entre las personas y los lugares. Los geógrafos tambien usan la información de otras disciplinas para ayudarles a entender la interacción de las personas con el medio ambiente.

Sección  Manual de destrezas en geografía

Los geógrafos usan mapas y gráficas para interpretar y analizar datos geográficos. El leer un mapa requiere el conocer sus elementos. Los elementos de un mapa incluyen la clave, la rosa del compás, la escala y la cuadrícula global.

Ya que los mapas son planos, es difícil que representen con precisión la superficie curva de la Tierra. Las diferentes proyecciones de los mapas planos muestran la Tierra redonda aunque con algunas distorciones.

Puntos de interés

Sección  El planeta Tierra

La Tierra consiste de agua, tierra y aire. El agua compone la hidrosfera de la Tierra. La tierra compone parte de la litosfera de la Tierra, mientras que el aire compone la atmósfera.

Secciones de la corteza terrestre flotan y se mueven en el estrato de manto haciendo que algunos continentes se separen y otros se acerquen. También hay fuerzas externas como el agua, el viento y la gravedad que afectan la superficie de la Tierra. Éstas ayudan a configurar la superficie de la Tierra por medio de la erosión, el movimiento y las nuevas formaciones de tierra.

Sección  Características de la Tierra

Las formaciones de tierra son las características que componen la superficie de la Tierra. Los cuatro tipos principales son las montañas, las lomas, las praderas y las mesetas.

El agua es tanto una característica física como un recurso. Los océanos, los ríos, los lagos y los arroyos son características del agua. El agua es un recurso limitado que se circula y se purifica repetidamente por medio del ciclo de agua.

Sección  Recursos de la Tierra

Los muchos recursos naturales de la Tierra no están divididos equitativamente entre los países del mundo. El uso, el abastecimiento y los cambios a través del tiempo son factores para determinar la importancia de los recursos naturales.

Los recursos renovables se reemplazan a sí mismos naturalmente o la gente puede cultivarlos para abastecerse continuamente de ellos. Los recursos no renovables, como los combustibles de fósil, jamás se pueden reponer.

Puntos de interés

Sección 1 Relación de la Tierra y el Sol

La relación entre la Tierra y el Sol afecta el clima de la Tierra. El Sol provee a la Tierra con calor y luz. Las diferentes áreas del planeta, sin embargo, reciben distintas cantidades de luz solar a distintas horas.

Sección 2 Factores que afectan el clima

El sol afecta el clima de la Tierra; sin embargo, el Sol no calienta ni enfría todos los lugares de la Tierra de la misma manera. Otros factores que afectan el clima de la Tierra son la latitud, la elevación, el viento, las corrientes marítimas y las formaciones de tierra.

Sección 3 Modelos del clima mundial

Los geógrafos a menudo dividen la Tierra en cinco importantes regiones climatológicas, basándose por lo general en la latitud. Las regiones son la tropical, la seca, la latitud media, la latitud alta y la montañosa.

Las regiones climatológicas se vuelven a dividir en regiones más pequeñas basado en factores tales como su flora, ubicación, paisaje y temperatura. Los climas cambian con el tiempo debido a causas naturales y humanas.

capítulo 4

Puntos de interés

Sección 1 Límites y oportunidades

Las naciones se pueden clasificar como desarrolladas o en vías de desarrollo. Los países desarrollados están altamente industrializados, mientras que los países en vías de desarrollo son agrícolas.

Tanto las naciones desarrolladas como las que están en vías de desarrollo enfrentan muchos retos. La población del mundo tiene que hacer frente a las tareas de satisfacer las necesidades alimenticias y conservar los recursos. Los peligros del medio ambiente, como los fenómenos relacionados al clima y la contaminación, presentan obstáculos para lograr estas metas.

Sección  Expresión cultural

Las culturas se expresan de distintos modos, como el lenguaje, la religión y las artes. Las primeras culturas altamente desarrolladas, o civilizaciones, se desarrollaron cerca de ríos importantes en áreas donde el clima era templado y los terrenos fértiles. Al evolucionar las culturas a través de los siglos, el comercio aumentó y se hicieron una variedad de contactos culturales.

Sección  Regiones culturales del mundo en la actualidad

Para ayudarles a describir pueblos y culturas, los geógrafos dividen el mundo en regiones culturales. Entre los factores que se usan para determinar las regiones culturales se hallan el medio ambiente, la historia, el lenguaje, la religión, el gobierno, la estructura social y la economía.

Puntos de interés

Sección  Geografía física de los Estados Unidos y Canadá

Los Estados Unidos y Canadá forman una región que compone casi todo el continente de América del Norte. Dos cordilleras dominan las formaciones terrestres del oeste, con altiplanos y depresiones entre ellas. Las cordilleras del oeste y otra importante cordillera en el este bordean los enormes llanos del interior que marcan la porción central de la región. Varios ríos importantes ayudan a arrastrar las aguas de la tierra hacia los océanos que bordean la región. Los Estados Unidos y Canadá son ricos en muchos recursos renovables y no renovables.

Sección  Clima y vegetación

Aunque Canadá y los Estados Unidos comparten algunas regiones climatológicas, otras son peculiares de cada nación. Sin embargo, la mayoría de estas regiones—desde el desierto hasta la tundra—están representadas. Los vientos del Océano Pacífico, el Océano Ártico y el Golfo de México ejercen una tremenda influencia sobre los climas de la región. La diversa vegetación natural de las regiones climatológicas ha sido profundamente afectada por la población humana.

capítulo 6

Puntos de interés

SECCIÓN 1 Configuración demográfica

La mayoría de los inmigrantes que vinieron a los Estados Unidos y Canadá eran de origen europeo. Gran Bretaña aportó el mayor número de ellos. Otros grupos étnicos incluyen franceses, afroamericanos, hispanos y los de origen asiático.

El clima limita la población en dos terceras partes del territorio norte de Canadá. La mayoría de los canadienses viven a lo largo de la frontera con los Estados Unidos. Tanto en los Estados Unidos como en Canadá, la mayoría de las personas viven en áreas urbanas.

SECCIÓN 2 Historia y gobierno

Los científicos creen que los primeros seres humanos que se establecieron en la región cruzaron un puente de tierra entre Asia y América del Norte. Otros inmigrantes siguieron con el tiempo y surgieron dos naciones. En los años 1700, los colonos americanos pelearon la Guerra de Independencia contra los ingleses para establecer los Estados Unidos de América. Casi un siglo después, el Acta Británica Norteamericana (1867) hizo a Canadá una nación autónoma con lazos con Gran Bretaña.

SECCIÓN 3 Culturas y estilos de vida

Las personas de los Estados Unidos y Canadá siempre han valorado su libertad religiosa. Los Estados Unidos tiene una población mayormente angloparlante, aunque muchos americanos hablan español y otros idiomas. Canadá reconoce tanto el inglés como el francés como sus idiomas oficiales. Los ciudadanos de ambos países disfrutan de la variedad de culturas y de un alto estándar de vida.

Puntos de interés

Sección 1 La vida en los Estados Unidos y Canadá

Los suelos ricos, las abundantes aguas y los variados climas de las fincas en los Estados Unidos y Canadá estimulan la producción de una amplia variedad de carnes, cereales, vegetales y frutas. Los adelantos tecnológicos en la agricultura han aumentado el rendimiento de la cosecha y el tamaño de la finca, pero han disminuído el número de trabajadores agrícolas.

La región cultural de los Estados Unidos y Canadá es una de las más adelantadas mundialmente en cuanto a la manufactura de bienes y sus industrias de servicio emplean a la mayor cantidad de personas. La abundancia de productos agrícolas y manufacturados de las dos naciones ponen a la región al mando del comercio mundial. Complejas redes de transporte y de comunicación sostienen a la gente y a la economía de la región.

Sección  La gente y su medio ambiente

La contaminación es un problema ambiental importante en los Estados Unidos y Canadá. Las emisiones de las fábricas y los automóviles producen contaminantes como la lluvia ácida y el smog. El abastecimiento de agua en la región está contaminado por los deshechos industriales, las sustancias químicas de la agricultura y las aguas residuales.

Otros tipos de actividad humana también han tenido un impacto en el medio ambiente de la región. La explotación forestal, especialmente en los terrenos públicos, está poniendo en peligro los bosques de antiguos árboles en el área del noroeste del Pacífico. La pesca excesiva y el desperdicio en la industria marítima han disminuído seriamente el número de peces y, como resultado, ha traído dificultades económicas a las áreas que dependen del mar.

Puntos de interés

Sección 1 El terreno

Latinoamérica consiste de México, Centroamérica, Sudamérica y las Islas del Caribe. Enormes cordilleras, la mayor de las cuales es la de los Andes, dominan la mayor parte de América Latina y a menudo bloquean las comunicaciones. Grandes altiplanos, que se usan para el pastoreo y para la agricultura decoran el paisaje latinoamericano.

A elevaciones más bajas, las áreas llanas de Latinoamérica proveen importantes terrenos para el pastoreo, la agricultura y el terreno boscoso. La mayoría de los sistemas fluviales importantes de Latinoamérica, incluyendo el Amazonas y el Río de la Plata, se hallan en Sudamérica.

Sección 2 Clima y vegetación

Los climas tropicales, como el bosque de lluvia tropical y la sabana tropical, son los climas más comunes en Latinoamérica. Un clima subtropical de inviernos moderados, veranos calientes y una corta temporada seca se halla en las áreas de pradera. Otras partes de la región tienen un clima desértico o un clima de estepa.

La vegetación natural de Latinoamérica varía de acuerdo al clima e incluye desde la llujuriante vegetación perenne del bosque de lluvia tropical hasta los cactus del desierto. Una de las características más significativas del clima y la vegetación de Latinoamérica es las tres zonas montañosas basadas en la elevación. Entre los recursos principales de Latinoamérica están el petróleo, el gas natural, la bauxita, el estaño, el cobre, el oro, la plata y las gemas preciosas.

Puntos de interés

Sección 1 Configuración demográfica

La diversidad étnica de la población de Latinoamérica incluye a indios, europeos, africanos, asiáticos, mestizos y mulatos. La población no está parejamente distribuída por toda la región. La población urbana ha aumentado rápidamente a medida que la gente se ha mudado de las áreas rurales a las urbanas.

Sección 2 Historia y gobierno

Los mayas, los aztecas y los incas desarrollaron civilizaciones altamente avanzadas mucho antes de que los europeos llegaran a las Américas. Los países europeos de España y Portugal controlaron la mayor parte de Latinoamérica por más de 300 años. Hoy, la mayoría de los líderes latinoamericanos desean gobiernos estables y una calidad de vida mejor para sus pueblos.

Sección 3 Culturas y estilos de vida

Los españoles y los portugueses trajeron a Latinoamérica la cultura europea y el Catolicismo Romano, la religión principal de la región. En décadas más recientes, las artes y la literatura se han vuelto menos europeas y más peculiarmente latinoamericanas.

A pesar de las diferencias de clase social, estilos de vida y pasatiempos, los latinoamericanos comparten un fuerte sentido de la familia. Sus familias se han beneficiado de los recientes adelantos en el cuidado de la salud y en la educación.

capítulo 10

Puntos de interés

Sección 1 La vida en Latinoamérica

La economía de muchos países latinoamericanos se basa en la agricultura. Hay dos clases importantes de fincas en la región—*latifundios* y *minifundios*.

La mayoría de los países de Latinoamérica han tardado en industrializarse debido a la falta de fondos, fuerza de trabajo calificada, materias primas y fuentes de energía. El costo y las barreras físicas han retrasado el desarrollo de la transportación y las redes de comunicación en la región. A pesar de estas dificultades, el deseo de Latinoamérica de industrializarse ha hecho que aumente la interdependencia que existe entre la región y algunas naciones del exterior.

Sección  La gente y su medio ambiente

Grandes áreas de la cuenca del río Amazonas están sufriendo la deforestación. La construcción de carreteras, la agricultura a escala menor, la ganadería y la explotación comercial de los árboles ha contribuído a este problema ambiental. Se necesita mejor planificación y regulaciones gubernamentales más fuertes para desarrollar los recursos de la cuenca del río Amazonas sin hacerle daño al medio ambiente.

El rápido crecimiento de las ciudades latinoamericanas también ha causado problemas sociales y del medio ambiente. Los gobiernos de Latinoamérica están cada vez más conscientes de los problemas y están tratando de resolverlos.

Puntos de interés

capítulo 11

Sección 1 El terreno

El continente europeo es una enorme península que se extiende hacia el oeste desde las masas terrestres de Eurasia. Europa tiene una costa larga e irregular con muchas penínsulas e islas rodeadas por distintos mares.

Europa consiste de llanos rodeados de montañas a lo largo de sus bordes sur y norte. Los ríos desempeñan un papel importante de rutas de transporte que unen el interior de Europa con los puertos costeños. Además de estas características físicas, Europa tiene grandes depósitos de carbón, hierro, petróleo y gas natural.

Sección  Clima y vegetación

Debido a las cálidas corrientes marítimas, gran parte de Europa tiene climas más templados que otras partes del mundo que están en las mismas latitudes. La parte noroeste de Europa tiene un clima marino occidental con temperaturas moderadas tanto en verano como en invierno. La mayor parte del sur de Europa tiene un clima mediterráneo con inviernos moderados y lluviosos y veranos secos y calurosos. El interior de Europa experimenta más extremos de temperatura durante las estaciones que las otras partes del continente. Tanto el clima como las personas afectan la vegetación natural de la región.

capítulo 12

Puntos de interés

Sección 1 Configuración demográfica

La diversidad de la población europea refleja una historia de migraciones por todo el continente. La distribución demográfica en Europa ha sido influída por las características físicas, el clima y los recursos. Como resultado de la industrialización, casi tres cuartos de los europeos viven en áreas urbanas.

Sección  Historia y gobierno

La antigua civilización greco romana ha sevido de modelo para el mundo occidental. La admiración europea de sus ideas dió origen al Renacimiento, cuyos logros científicos hizo que los europeos se interesaran y se sintieran capaces de explorar remotos lugares del mundo. La civilización europea se difundió por otros continentes por medio del comercio, la colonización y la inmigración.

Después de la sequnda Guerra Mundial, Europa se convirtió en el centro de la guerra fría, la cual dividió la Europa occidental anticomunista de la oriental, controlada por los comunistas. En años recientes, la Comunidad Europea ha promovido la unidad entre las naciones europeas.

Sección  Culturas y estilos de vida

Las diferencias en los estilos de vida europeos reflejan cultura y tradición, desarrollo económico y sistemas políticos. La industrialización y la urbanización, sin embargo, han reducido muchas de estas diferencias en los últimos años. Otro factor importante de la unificación es el papel que muchos gobiernos europeos ahora desempeñan para proveer bienestar a sus ciudadanos.

Puntos de interés

Sección 1 La vida en Europa

Europa tiene diversas economías basadas en la agricultura, la manufactura y los servicios. Además, sus sistemas de comunicación y de transporte están entre los mejores del mundo. Las ferrovías son un medio importante de transportación de pasajeros y cargas por toda Europa.

En las últimas décadas, las 12 naciones de la Comunidad Europea han colaborado para lograr la unidad económica a pesar de las dificultades que traen los cambios. Mientras tanto, los países del este de Europa han luchado para ajustarse a una economía de libre comercio después de 40 años de control comunista.

Sección  La gente y su medio ambiente

Europa se enfrenta a un número de problemas ambientales. La lluvia ácida ha dañado bosques, fauna y edificios en muchas partes del continente. La contaminación del aire debido a las factorías pone en peligro la salud y contribuye al efecto de invernadero. La contaminación debida a los deshechos industriales, las aguas negras, la basura y el petróleo amenaza el mar Mediterráneo y la fauna que el mar sostiene.

Los europeos, no obstante, comparten una preocupación por el medio ambiente y un sentido de responsabilidad hacia las generaciones futuras. Sus gobiernos han tomado medidas para reducir la contaminación y limpiar el medio ambiente.

capítulo 14

Puntos de interés

Sección 1 El terreno

El terreno que ocupa Rusia y las Repúblicas de Eurasia cubre dos continentes—Europa y Asia. Todas las repúblicas menos Rusia, Georgia y Ucrania carecen de acceso al mar. Áreas de pastoreo cubren la mayor parte de la región. Hay también numerosas cordilleras, mesetas y cuerpos de agua en el interior. La mayoría de los ríos en la región fluyen hacia el norte y están congelados durante gran parte del año. Los minerales, los recursos de energía, los suelos fértiles, la fauna y la pesca abundan en Rusia y las repúblicas de Eurasia.

Sección  Clima y vegetación

Debido a su ubicación al norte, la lejanía de grandes cuerpos de agua y la falta de montañas cerca de las áreas de praderas, la mayoría de las partes de Rusia y de las repúblicas de Eurasia tienen un clima continental o subártico. A través de la región, los veranos son cortos y los inviernos son largos y fríos. Casi la mitad de la tierra rusa y de las repúblicas eurasianas está cubierta de nieve durante casi todo el año. El *permafrost* (subsuelo permanentemente congelado) se halla debajo del 40 porciento del área de la región. En Rusia y las repúblicas de Eurasia, la vegetación natural varía desde la tundra desprovista de árboles en el norte, hasta los densos bosques de la taiga en el centro y los desiertos yermos del sur.

Puntos de interés

capítulo **15**

SECCIÓN 1 Configuración demográfica

Tres grupos étnicos importantes—los eslavos, los turcos y los caucásicos—viven en Rusia y las repúblicas de Eurasia. Cada una de las repúblicas tiene su propio lenguaje principal.

La población no está distribuída parejamente a través de Rusia y las repúblicas eurasiáticas. En los últimos años, también ha habido un cambio en la relación rural/urbana. Mientras que en el pasado la mayoría de la gente de la región vivía en el campo, hoy viven en la ciudad.

SECCIÓN  Historia y gobierno

Los eslavos y varangianos fundaron ciudad-estados a lo largo de los ríos en la parte occidental de la región. Bajo los zares, surgió en Rusia un poderoso estado que creó uno de los imperios más grandes del mundo. A principios de siglo, el imperio ruso se convirtió en una nueva nación llamada la Unión de Repúblicas Socialistas Soviéticas y por más de siete décadas estuvo bajo el poder comunista. Cuando el estado soviético se derrumbó a principios de los 90, las antiguas repúblicas soviéticas se convirtieron en naciones independientes.

SECCIÓN  Culturas y estilos de vida

En la actualidad, las tres religones principales, el Cristianismo, el Islam y el Judaismo, al igual que un número de otras religiones, se practican abiertamente en Rusia como en las repúblicas de Eurasia. Las personas de la región tienen fuertes tradiciones culturales y están dedicados a las artes. Tienen diversos estilos de vidas y gozan de una variedad de celebraciones.

capítulo 16

Puntos de interés

Sección 1 La vida en Rusia y las Repúblicas Eurásicas

Durante muchas décadas, Rusia y las repúblicas eurásicas tenían una sola economía controlada por el gobierno soviético. Al hacerse independiente, cada república tomó control de su propia economía y ahora está tratando de moverse hacia un sistema de libre comercio. Cada una está también tomando medidas para privatizar la agricultura y la industria. Debido al largo período de control central soviético, las repúblicas todavía están dependiendo económicamente las unas de las otras.

La independencia, sin embargo, les ha traído mayor libertad de expresión a los sistemas de comunicaciones y a la mayoría de los medios de información. Aunque las vías fluviales, las carreteras y las ferrovías continúan siendo métodos vitales para la transportación de cargas y pasajeros, las líneas aéreas y los oleoductos están creciendo en importancia.

Sección 2 La gente y su medio ambiente

En su lucha por industrializarse, los soviéticos descuidaron y abusaron el medio ambiente. Comprometidos a la energía nuclear como fuente económica de energía eléctrica, construyeron numerosas estaciones nucleares en varias partes de la nación. El desastre de Chernobyl generó dudas y protestas acerca de la energía nuclear y las armas nucleares. Otros problemas ambientales que se heredan de la era soviética y que aún siguen siendo significativos son la contaminación causada por la industria pesada y el uso de los pesticidas.

capítulo 17

Puntos de interés

Sección 1 El terreno

La región de África del Norte y Asia del Sudoeste se extiende desde Marruecos en el oeste hasta Afganistán en el este. Cubriendo más del 10 por ciento de la superficie total de la tierra, la región de África del Norte y Asia del Suroeste tiene un número de penínsulas y varios mares.

La precipitación en el África del Norte y en el Asia del Sudoeste varía grandemente, yendo desde menos de 4 pulgadas (10cm) en algunas mesetas hasta cantidades mucho más altas en algunas de las áreas montañosas. A pesar de la escasez de lluvia en muchas áreas, el fértil valle del río Nilo y el área cerca de los ríos Tigris y Éufrates provee el terreno donde la agricultura florece. También de gran importancia son el petróleo y el gas natural, dos recursos naturales vitales que proveen ingresos sustanciosos para algunas naciones de la región.

Sección  Clima y vegetación

Las cuatro regiones climatológicas del África del Norte y del Asia del Sudoeste son el desierto, la mediterránea, la estepa y la montañosa. Mucha de la agricultura del África del Norte y del Asia del Sudoeste ocurre a lo largo de zonas costeras que tienen un clima mediterráneo. La precipitación es más prevalente allí que en otras zonas de la región. En zonas donde la precipitación es menos abundante, el desmonte del terreno para la agricultura y el pastoreo excesivo en zonas de estepa han hecho estragos a la vegetación.

capítulo 18

Puntos de interés

Sección 1 Configuración demográfica

La región cultural del África del Norte y del Asia del Sudoeste ha sido la encrucijada donde se encuentran los pueblos y las culturas del Asia, África y Europa. Las concentraciones demográficas más grandes en el África del Norte y en el Asia del Sudoeste están en las zonas costeras y las cuencas de los ríos donde hay agua disponible. El rápido crecimiento demográfico y el aumento de urbanización ha caracterizado la región desde la Segunda Guerra Mundial.

Sección 2 Historia y gobierno

El África del Norte y el Asia del Sudoeste fue el lugar donde se originaron dos de las civilizaciones más antiguas del mundo—Mesopotamia y Egipto. También se originaron allí tres de las religiones más importantes del mundo—el Judaismo, el Cristianismo y el Islam. Tras siglos de influencia europea, fue en este siglo que surgieron los estados independientes de esta región.

Sección 3 Culturas y estilos de vida

La gente del África del Norte y del Asia del Sudoeste que vive en países cuyas economías están basadas en la manufactura y el comercio por lo general disfrutan de un alto estándar de vida. Sin embargo, las personas que viven en países donde las economías se basan en la agricultura, tienen un estándar de vida bajo. El Islam y la lengua árabe han sido las fuerzas unificadoras más importantes de casi todo el África del Norte y el Asia del Sudoeste. Las relaciones familiares también son muy importantes para la gente de esta región. Los pasatiempos más populares incluyen el fútbol, la caza y la pesca.

capítulo 19

Puntos de interés

Sección 1 La vida en África del Norte y Asia del Sudoeste

Aunque la región del África del Norte y el Asia del Sudoeste tiene un terreno arable limitado, un porcentaje relativamente grande de la gente participa en algún tipo de agricultura. La cría de ganado y la pesca son dos fuentes más de alimento para la región.

El nivel de industrialización es disparejo entre las naciones del África del Norte y del Asia del Sudoeste, con más industrialización en muchas de las naciones productoras de petróleo. El gran desarrollo industrial, junto con la necesidad de conectar los centros urbanos y económicos ha producido recientemente un crecimiento en los sistemas de transportación y comunicación. Aunque la dependencia mutua ha aumentado entre las naciones de la región, varios conflictos y guerras han interrumpido la economía de algunos países.

Sección 2 La gente y su medio ambiente

La gente del África del Norte y del Asia del Sudoeste ha tomado medidas para modificar su medio ambiente y para poder tener agua para tomar y para el riego. El agua fluvial necesaria para el regadío extensivo está escasa en la mayoría de las naciones de la región. La desalación se emplea ampliamente para proveer agua, particularmente en la península arábiga.

Recientemente, las actividades humanas en la región han tenido efectos mixtos. La construcción de la Presa del Alto Aswan ha traído beneficios a Egipto, pero también ha tenido efectos negativos sobre el medio ambiente. La Guerra del Golfo Pérsico dañó severamente el medio ambiente natural de esa zona.

capítulo 20

Puntos de interés

Sección 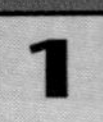 El terreno

El África al sur del Sahara se caracteriza grandemente por una serie de altiplanos escalonados. Altas elevaciones y estrechas praderas costeras han impedido históricamente el viajar al interior del África. Cuatro sistemas fluviales importantes saltan por escarpaduras en dramáticos rápidos y cataratas en su recorrido por el continente. El Valle de la Gran Grieta atraviesa el África oriental, desde Etiopía en el norte, hasta Mozambique en el sur. Muchos de los lagos de agua dulce de la región están situados en el valle.

Sección  Clima y vegetación

Aunque la mayor parte del África yace en el trópico, exhibe diversos climas y vegetaciones. La elevación y la precipitación son los factores principales que influyen en la variedad del clima de África al sur del Sahara. Las principales regiones climatológicas son el desierto, la estepa, la sabana tropical y el bosque de lluvia tropical.

Los desiertos y las estepas cubren más de dos tercios de la superficie de la tierra en África. La región tiene una abundancia de riqueza mineral, pero carece de petróleo para desarrollarla.

Puntos de interés

Sección 1 Configuración demográfica

Con más de 530 millones de personas, el África al sur del Sahara es la tercera región con más habitantes del mundo. Más de 2,000 grupos étnicos, que hablan unos 800 idiomas, componen la población del África al sur del Sahara. La geografía física de la región contribuye a la distribución dispareja de esta diversa población.

El África al sur del Sahara está urbanizándose más rápido que cualquier otra región del mundo. Además de este reto, la gente de la región tiene una expectativa de vida corta debido a la alimentación, el agua y el cuidado médico inadecuado.

Sección  Historia y gobierno

En la antigua África, el movimiento de los Bantú de Niger hacia el sur formó una de las mayores inmigraciones humanas en la historia. En tiempos modernos, la colonización europea cambió las fronteras territoriales que han sido tradicionalmente étnicas. Desde los años 60, la mayoría de las naciones del África ha logrado su independencia. El último baluarte europeo que queda es Sudáfrica, donde en 1990 el sistema de segregación racial fue desmantelado.

Sección  Culturas y estilos de vida

La cantidad de idiomas y la variedad de religiones del África del sur del Sahara contribuyen a la diversidad de la región. Con esta diversidad, los africanos del sur del Sahara han influído en las culturas artísticas del mundo. A pesar de los logros pasados y presentes, el África del sur del Sahara tiene que enfrentarse al reto de reducir su tasa de analfabetismo.

capítulo 22

Puntos de interés

Sección 1 La vida en África al sur del Sahara

La mayoría de la naciones del África del sur del Sahara depende de la exportación de uno o dos cultivos comerciales. La mayoría de las personas de la región, sin embargo, trabajan como agricultores de subsistencia.

Los depósitos de minerales, al igual que las ganancias de su exportación, no están distribuídos parejamente a través del África al sur del Sahara. El desarrollo industrial lo impide la falta de capital y la escasez de mano de obra adiestrada. Para reducir la dependencia extranjera, algunas naciones en la región están desarrollando sistemas regionales de comercio y transporte.

Sección 2 La gente y su medio ambiente

A medida que los africanos del sur del Sahara se dirigen hacia el próximo siglo, esperan obtener la independencia económica. Esta meta está siendo retada por una serie de problemas ambientales. La desertificación, las sequías y la guerra han contribuído al hambre en esta región. En los años 90, dos de las naciones afectadas por estos problemas—Etiopía y Eritárea—han tomado medidas para reparar los daños a su medio ambiente.

La destrucción de los bosques de lluvia no es sólo un problema africano sino mundial. A través del África al sur, el aumento demográfico y la caza han puesto a algunos animales en peligro de extinción. Para ganarse el apoyo rural para preservar las reservas de caza, algunas naciones en la región han compartido las ganacias del ecoturismo.

Puntos de interés

Sección 1 El terreno

Asia del Sur consiste de una enorme península con una isla cerca de la punta sur. La península se conoce como un subcontinente, una masa de tierra grande más pequeña que un continente. La región está limitada por el Himalaya en el norte, el mar Arábigo al oeste, el océano Índico en el sur y el Golfo de Bengala en el este.

La mayoría de la gente de la región vive en las llanuras del norte, una zona agrícola rica. El Asia del Sur tiene tres grandes sistemas fluviales y la llanura aluvial más grande del mundo. La región tiene pocas reservas de petróleo, pero tiene gas natural, carbón y uranio y unos importantes depósitos de hiero y mica.

Sección  Clima y vegetación

El Asia del Sur tiene tierras altas, desierto, estepa y climas tropicales. Un cambio de estación en la dirección del viento conocido como monzón trae lluvias fuertes a la región entre junio y septiembre. La vegetación del Asia del Sur está afectada por la altitud, la lluvia y la actividad humana. En un entonces la región estaba cubierta de bosques, pero en la actualidad tan sólo tiene una pequeña porción de tierras forestales.

capítulo 24

Puntos de interés

SPANISH HANDBOOK

Sección 1 Configuración demográfica

El Asia del Sur es una región étnicamente diversa. Su densidad demográfica es mayor en la llanura Indogangética. Aunque la mayoría de los asiáticos del sur viven en áreas rurales, un número creciente está migrando a las ciudades en busca de trabajo.

Sección 2 Historia y gobierno

El Valle Indio del Asia del Sur fue la cuna de una de las primeras grandes civilizaciones del mundo. Otras civilizaciones que siguieron en la región produjeron dos de las principales religiones del mundo—el Hinduismo y el Budismo.

A través de los siglos, muchos pueblos han conquistado el Asia del Sur, desde los arianos hasta los británicos. Después de la Segunda Guerra Mundial, la región ha logrado independizarse del Imperio Británico. En la actualidad, la mayoría de la gente del Asia del Sur vive en naciones independientes y eligen a sus líderes.

Sección 3 Culturas y estilos de vida

Los asiáticos del sur hablan muchos idiomas diferentes. La India tiene 14 idiomas principales y cientos de dialectos. Las religiones principales del Asia del Sur son el Hinduismo, el Islam y el Budismo. La gente también practica el Cristianismo, el Jainismo y el Sikhismo.

En la mayor parte del Asia del Sur el estándar de vida es bajo y la expectativa de vida es corta. En años recientes, sin embargo, se ha mejorado el cuidado de la salud y la educación.

Puntos de interés

Sección  La vida en el Asia del Sur

Los adelantos agrícolas están ayudando al Asia del Sur a producir suficiente alimento para su creciente población. Las principales cosechas de alimento son el arroz y el trigo; las principales cosechas comerciales son el yute y el té.

Las minas, la pesca y el turismo son también importantes fuentes de ingresos para el Asia del Sur. La industria, tanto ligera como pesada, está creciendo en la región.

Sección  La gente y su medio ambiente

La gente ha deforestado muchas partes del Asia del Sur en busca de madera para combustible, para hacer casas y para la agricultura y el pastoreo. La deforestación trae la amenaza de inundaciones, deslices de tierra, la pérdida de la valiosa capa vegetal y del habitat de los animales además de cambios climatológicos. Los gobiernos e individuos por toda el Asia del Sur están tratando de conservar y volver a sembrar los bosques. A pesar de la pérdida de muchos animales debido a la caza excesiva y la pérdida del hábitat, los surasiáticos están tratando de preservar las especies que todavía existen en las reservas de fauna y en otros lugares.

El uso del agua es controvertido en el Asia del Sur por muchas razones. Las presas se necesitan para controlar las inundaciones y proveer agua para el regadío, pero también causan problemas para el medio ambiente.

capítulo 26

Puntos de interés

Sección 1 El terreno

La región del Asia Oriental consite de la China, Mongolia y Corea en el continente de Asia y dos naciones islas, Japón y Taiwán. La China ocupa el 90 por ciento del área del Asia Oriental. Otras naciones ocupan penínsulas e islas.

El continente de Asia Oriental tiene montañas y en el oeste, mesetas y cuencas en las regiones del centro y el norte y llanos costeros en el este. Debido a que una gran parte del Asia Oriental es montañosa, las ciudades de las llanuras costeras tienen una densa población. Las presiones del exceso de población al igual que las limitadas tierras de agricultura han hecho que los asiáticos del Este consideren el océano una fuente importante de alimento. Respecto a otros recursos, el Asia del Este es rica en minerales, pero no siempre están parejamente distribuídos y a veces son difíciles de encontrar.

Sección  Clima y vegetación

El Asia Oriental tiene una variedad de climas debido a su gran masa de terreno. Mucha de la región está entre latitudes con clima húmedo continental o húmedo subtropical. Los vientos con lluvias de la estación de monzón afectan grandemente el clima del Asia Oriental. Muchas partes de la región, especialmente el Japón, Corea y Taiwán, tienen espesos bosques. Las estepas del interior y las zonas de desiertos, sin embargo, tienen climas secos con temperaturas extremas y escasa vegetación.

capítulo 27

Puntos de interés

Sección  Configuración demográfica

La gente del Asia del Este pertenece a distintos grupos étnicos, el mayor de los cuales es el Han de la China. La población en la región no está distribuída parejamente y está concentrada en las cuencas y en las llanuras costeras. El Japón es la nación más urbanizada del Asia del Este. La China permanece predominantemente rural con cientos de millones de sus ciudadanos viviendo en las afueras de las zonas urbanas.

Sección  Historia y gobierno

La cultura del Asia del Este comenzó en el valle de Huang He en la China y se dispersó a otros lugares de la región. El Confusianismo y Daoismo, dos influyentes escuelas de pensamiento, se desarrollaron en la China cerca del año 500 A.C. El Budismo, una importante religión del Asia del Este, se originó en la India. Durante varios siglos, el Imperio Chino fue la potencia dominante en el Asia del Este. El contacto con el Occidente debilitó a la China pero condujo al Japón a modernizarse.

Sección  Culturas y estilos de vida

El Asia del Este tiene diversos idiomas, culturas y estilos de vida. Los idiomas sinotibetanos son los más hablados de la región, mientras que el coreano y el japonés se hablan en sus respectivos países. En los últimos años, el aumento en el estándar de vida ha traído mejorías en la educación y el cuidado de la salud. La gente del Asia del Este practica las artes y los pasatiempos tradicionales pero también goza de las recreaciones modernas.

capítulo 28

Puntos de interés

SECCIÓN 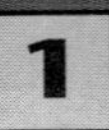 La vida en el Asia del Este

Hubo una época en que el Asia del Este era principalmente agrícola, pero el comercio y la industria han traído prosperidad y crecimiento económico a la mayoría de sus naciones. A pesar del progreso industrial de la China, la mayoría de su gente todavía trabaja en la agricultura, siguiendo las políticas establecidas por el gobierno comunista. Por todas las zonas costeras del Asia del Este, la pesca es importante tanto para la alimentación como para la exportación.

El Japón es la nación industrial principal, pero Taiwán y Corea del Sur también están compitiendo. El comercio y las inversiones comerciales unen a los países capitalistas y comunistas de la región. Las embarcaciones y las ferrovías son vínculos importantes dentro del Asia del Este. La transportación está más desarrollada en la parte oriental de la región.

SECCIÓN  La gente y su medio ambiente

El rápido crecimiento industrial del Asia del Este ha causado contaminación del aire y del agua y ha producido deshechos tóxicos. Pero, durante varias décadas, estos problemas ambientales fueron ignorados. En la actualidad, el Japón se ha convertido en un líder en la protección y en la limpieza del medio ambiente, con leyes estrictas contra la contaminación.

Otros factores impactan el medio ambiente del Asia del Este. La enorme población de la China intensifica el efecto que tiene su desarrollo económico sobre el medio ambiente. El medio ambiente del Asia del Este está propenso a desastres naturales, como las inundaciones, los terremotos, los tsunamis y los tifones.

Puntos de interés

Sección  El terreno

La región del Asia del Sudeste incluye las 2 penínsulas al este de la India y al sur de la China y las 20,000 islas del archipiélago de Malaya. Las montañas del Asia del Sudeste se formaron cuando las placas indoaustralianas y filipinas chocaron contra la placa eurásica. Los ríos del continente del Asia del Sudeste son importantes para la agricultura, la comunicación y la transportación. Otro beneficio vital para el Asia del Sudeste son sus reservas enormes de petróleo, maderas tropicales duras, estaño y gemas.

Sección  Clima y vegetación

Casi todas las partes del Asia del Sureste tienen un clima caliente y húmedo afectado por los monzones. Por todas las islas del Asia del Sureste al igual que en las costas del este y oeste de la península Indochina hay un clima de bosque de lluvia tropical. Un clima de sabana tropical se extiende hacia el sureste y atraviesa la península. Algunas de las islas más al sur en el Asia del Sudeste también comparten este clima.

La vegetación del Asia del Sudeste consiste principalmente de variedades de bosques de lluvia tropical. La desforestación en la región ha afectado la ecología, la economía y la cultura de algunas de sus gentes.

capítulo 30

Puntos de interés

Sección 1 Configuración demográfica

La población del Asia del Sureste está aumentando rápidamente. Aunque gran parte de la región es rural, hay un número creciente de grandes ciudades que están densamente pobladas.

Sección  Historia y gobierno

Temprano en su historia, el Asia del Sudeste se convirtió en una zona de contacto entre el Asia del Este y el Asia del Sur. En siglos posteriores toda la región, con la excepción de Tailanda, fue colonizada por potencias extranjeras. Después de la Segunda Guerra Mundial, los países del Asia del Sudeste se hicieron independientes. Hoy en día, las formas de gobierno en la región son las monarquías constitucionales, las repúblicas democráticas y las repúblicas socialistas.

Sección  Culturas y estilos de vida

Las culturas y los estilos de vida del Asia del Sudeste reflejan las primeras migraciones de los pueblos que vinieron desde otras regiones así como las tradiciones folclóricas regionales. Entre las principales religiones de la región el Budismo, el Hinduismo y el Islam han influído grandemente en el arte, la arquitectura, el drama y las celebraciones del Asia del Sudeste. A pesar del enorme crecimiento demográfico, el desarrollo económico ha traído muchas mejoras y ha presentado muchos retos al Asia del Sudeste.

Puntos de interés

SECCIÓN 1 La vida en Asia del Sudeste

La agricultura es la base de la mayoría de las economías del Asia del Sudeste. Las cosechas principales son el arroz, la caña de azúcar, el caucho, el café y el coco. Los lujuriantes bosques de la región ofrecen muchos productos de madera.

En años recientes, la mina y la manufactura han aumentado en importancia y muchas nuevas industrias se han desarrollado en el Asia del Sudeste. El medio de transporte principal de la región es el agua; la transportación terrestre está menos desarrollada.

SECCIÓN 2 La gente y su medio ambiente

La industrialización, la urbanización y el rápido aumento demográfico han traído la contaminación ambiental a muchas áreas urbanas y rurales del Asia del Sudeste. La gente y el medio ambiente del Asia del Sudeste también están afectados por acontecimientos naturales. Esto se debe a que grandes números de asiáticos del sudeste viven en el Aro de Fuego, o sea rodeados de volcanes, muchos de ellos activos. Además, cada año en la región, las inundaciones repentinas y violentas destruyen vidas y cosechas. Los tifones son tormentas peligrosas que ocurren en el Asia del Sudeste entre julio y octubre.

capítulo 32

Puntos de interés

SPANISH HANDBOOK

Sección  El terreno

La región del Pacífico del Sur incluye los grandes continentes de Antártida, Australia y las miles de islas de variados tamaños que componen Oceanía. Las islas de Oceanía fueron creadas directa o indirectamente por actividad volcánica. Nueva Zelandia, un importante grupo de islas de Oceanía, tiene una geografía accidentada con costas muy irregulares, altas montañas y ríos con fuertes corrientes. Mientras que la Antártida tiene importantes recursos minerales, su recurso principal es la información que ofrece a los científicos.

Sección  Clima y vegetación

La región del Pacífico del Sur tiene una diversidad de clima y vegetación. Casi toda la Antártida tiene un clima polar. A excepción de los líquenes y los musgos en las zonas de la tundra, la Antártida no tiene vegetación. Australia, sin embargo, generalmente tiene un clima caliente y seco. Su interior es un vasto desierto rodeado por una amplia estepa. Las montañas separan las zonas húmedas de las costas de las más secas del interior.

Nueva Zelandia tiene un clima marino templado y húmedo con una variedad de temperaturas moderadas durante el año, especialmente en la Isla Norte. La mayor parte de Oceanía, sin embargo, se caracteriza por un clima de bosque de lluvia tropical. Otra característica del medio ambiente de Oceanía son los violentos tifones durante ciertas épocas del año. Estas tormentas se producen por el choque de las corrientes y los vientos del Océano Pacífico.

capítulo 33

Puntos de interés

Sección 1 Configuración demográfica

Muchos grupos distintos de personas se han establecido en el Pacífico del Sur y han creado una mezcla de gente, culturas y estilos de vida. La población de la región no está distribuída parejamente ya que muchas zonas no pueden sostener vida.

Sección 2 Historia y gobierno

Los primeros seres humanos que se establecieron en el Pacífico del Sur probablemente vinieron del Asia del Sudeste. Los poblados luego se esparcieron hacia el este. A fines de los 1700, Gran Bretaña comenzó a colonizar Australia y luego Nueva Zelandia. Durante el final de los 1800 y a principios de los 1900 las naciones europeas y el Japón lucharon por el control de las islas del Pacífico.

Sección  Culturas y estilos de vida

La cultura europea ha vuelto a dominar en el Pacífico del Sur. Sin embargo, en la actualidad, los elementos culturales tradicionales continúan formando los estilos de vida de la región.

Los patrones de población en el Pacífico del Sur han sido grandemente determinados mayormente por el clima y la configuración de la tierra. Las condiciones geográficas como éstas, al igual que la herencia cultural y económica, han afectado los estilos de vida y los estándares de salud y educación del Pacífico del Sur.

Puntos de interés

Sección  La vida en Australia, Oceanía y Antártida

La agricultura es la actividad económica más importante en el Pacífico del Sur. Los agricultores en las islas del Pacífico cultivan mayormente para su propio consumo mientras que los agricultores de Australia y Nueva Zelandia producen grandes exportaciones agrícolas, especialmente ganado y productos lácteos. La Antártida no tiene minas ni industrias manufactureras. En las últimas décadas, el transporte aéreo y marítimo ha ayudado a reducir las distancias y llevar bienes y servicios a las remotas partes del Pacífico del Sur.

Sección 2 La gente y su medio ambiente

Muchas de las plantas y animales del Pacífico del Sur, que antes se encontraban aislados, han sufrido al introducirse nuevas especies. Además, los esfuerzos de la industria y el gobierno por alcanzar metas políticas y económicas han causado muchos problemas ambientales en la región.

El frágil medio ambiente de Antártica ya no está protegido por el aislamiento. Es posible que tanto los científicos, como la industria y los turistas estén dañando este mundo natural tan delicadamente equilibrado.

Gazetteer

A Gazetteer (GAZ•uh•TIR) is a geographic index or dictionary. It shows latitude and longitude for cities and certain other places. Latitude and longitude are shown in this way: 48°N 2°E, or 48 degrees north latitude and 2 degrees east longitude. This Gazetteer lists most of the world's largest independent countries, their capitals, and several important geographic features. The page numbers tell where each entry can be found on a map in this book. As an aid to pronunciation, many entries are spelled phonetically.

A

Abidjan (A•bih•JAHN) Capital and port of Côte d'Ivoire, Africa. 5°N 4°W (p. 410)

Abu Dhabi (AH•boo DAH•bee) Capital of the United Arab Emirates, on the Persian Gulf. 24°N 54°E (p. 359)

Abuja (ah•BOO•jah) Capital of Nigeria. 8°N 9°E (p. 410)

Accra (uh•KRAH) Port city and capital of Ghana. 6°N 0° longitude (p. 410)

Addis Ababa (A•duhs A•buh•buh) Capital of Ethiopia. 9°N 39°E (p. 410)

Adriatic (AY•dree•AT•ihk) **Sea** Arm of the Mediterranean Sea between the Balkan Peninsula and Italy. 44°N 14°E (p. 225)

Afghanistan (af•GA•nuh•STAN) Country in central Asia, west of Pakistan. 33°N 63°E (p. 359)

Albania (al•BAY•nee•uh) Country on the east coast of the Adriatic Sea, south of Serbia and Montenegro. 42°N 20°E (p. 225)

Algeria (al•JIHR•ee•uh) Country in North Africa. 29°N 1°E (p. 359)

Algiers (al•JIHRZ) Capital of Algeria. 37°N 3°E (p. 359)

Almaty (al•MAH•tee) Capital of Kazakhstan. 43°N 77°E (p. 293)

Alps (ALPS) Mountain system extending east to west through central Europe. 46°N 9°E (p. 225)

Amazon (A•muh•ZAHN) **River** Largest river in the world by volume and second-largest in length. 2°S 53°W (p. 163)

Amman (ah•MAHN) Capital of Jordan. 32°N 36°E (p. 359)

Amsterdam (AM•stuhr•DAM) Capital of the Netherlands. 52°N 5°E (p. 225)

Andes (AN•DEEZ) Mountain system extending north to south along the western side of South America. 13°S 75°W (p. 163)

Andorra (an•DAWR•ah) Small country in southern Europe, between France and Spain. 43°N 20°E (p. 243)

Angola (ang•GOH•luh) Country in Africa, south of Zaire. 14°S 16°E (p. 410)

Ankara (ANG•kuh•ruh) Capital of Turkey. 40°N 33°E (p. 359)

Antananarivo (AN•tuh•NA•nuh•REE•voh) Capital of Madagascar. 19°S 48°E (p. 410)

Argentina (AHR•juhn•TEE•nuh) Country in South America, east of Chile on the Atlantic Ocean. 36°S 67°W (p. 163)

Armenia (ahr•MEE•nee•uh) Southeastern European country between the Black Sea and the Caspian Sea. 40°N 45°E (p. 293)

Ashkhabad (ASH•kuh•BAD) Capital of Turkmenistan. 40°N 58°E (p. 293)

Asunción (uh•SOONT•see•OHN) Capital of Paraguay. 25°S 58°W (p. 163)

Athens (A•thuhnz) Capital and largest city in Greece. 38°N 24°E (p. 225)

Atlas (AT•luhs) **Mountains** Mountain range on the northern edge of the Sahara. 31°N 5°W (p. 359)

Australia (aw•STRAYL•yuh) Country and continent southeast of Asia. 23°S 135°E (p. 648)

Austria (AWS•tree•uh) Country in central Europe, east of Switzerland. 47°N 12°E (p. 225)

Azerbaijan (A•zuhr•BY•JAHN) European-Asian country on the Caspian Sea. 40°N 47°E (p. 293)

B

Baghdad (BAG•DAD) Capital of Iraq. 33°N 44°E (p. 359)

Bahamas (buh•HAH•muhz) Country made up of many islands, between Cuba and the United States. 26°N 76°W (p. 163)

Baku (bah•KOO) Port city and capital of Azerbaijan. 40°N 50°E (p. 293)

Balkan (BAWL•kuhn) **Peninsula** Peninsula in southeastern Europe. 42°N 20°E (p. 225)

Bamako (BAH•muh•KOH) Capital of Mali. 13°N 8°W (p. 410)

Bangkok (BANG•KAHK) Capital of Thailand. 14°N 100°E (p. 599)
Bangladesh (BAHN•gluh•DESH) Country in South Asia, bordered by India and Myanmar. 24°N 90°E (p. 479)
Bangui (BAHN•GEE) Capital of the Central African Republic. 4°N 19°E (p. 410)
Banjul (BAHN•JOOL) Port city and capital of Gambia. 13°N 17°W (p. 410)
Barbados (bahr•BAY•DOHS) Island country between the Atlantic Ocean and the Caribbean Sea. 14°N 59°W (p. 152)
Beijing (BAY•JIHNG) Capital of China. 40°N 116°E (p. 539)
Beirut (bay•ROOT) Capital of Lebanon. 34°N 36°E (p. 359)
Belarus (BEE•luh•ROOS) Eastern European country west of Russia. 54°N 28°E (p. 293)
Belgium (BEL•juhm) Country in northwestern Europe, south of the Netherlands. 51°N 3°E (p. 225)
Belgrade (BEL•GRAYD) Capital of Serbia. 45°N 21°E (p. 225)
Belize (buh•LEEZ) Country in Central America, east of Guatemala. 18°N 89°W (p. 163)
Belmopan (BEL•moh•PAN) Capital of Belize. 17°N 89°W (p. 163)
Benin (buh•NIHN) Country in western Africa. 8°N 2°E (p. 410)
Berlin (BUHR•LIHN) Capital of Germany. 53°N 13°E (p. 225)
Bermuda (BUHR•MYOO•duh) Islands in western Atlantic Ocean, self-governing British colony. 32°N 65°W (p. 199)
Bern (BUHRN) Capital of Switzerland. 47°N 7°E (p. 225)
Bhutan (boo•TAHN) Country in the eastern Himalayas, northeast of India. 27°N 91°E (p. 479)
Bishkek (bihsh•KEK) Largest city and capital of Kyrgyzstan. 43°N 75°E (p. 293)
Bissau (bih•SAU) Capital of Guinea-Bissau. 12°N 16°W (p. 410)
Bogotá (BOH•guh•TAW) Capital of Colombia. 5°N 74°W (p. 163)
Bolivia (buh•LIH•vee•uh) Country in the central part of South America, north of Argentina. 17°S 64°W (p. 163)
Bosnia-Herzegovina (BAHZ•nee•uh HERT•suh•goh•VEE•nuh) Southeastern European country between Yugoslavia and Croatia. 44°N 18°E (p. 225)
Botswana (baht•SWAH•nuh) Country in Africa, north of the Republic of South Africa. 22°S 23°E (p. 410)
Brasília (bruh•ZIHL•yuh) Capital of Brazil. 16°S 48°W (p. 163)
Bratislava (BRA•tuh•SLAH•vuh) Capital and largest city of Slovakia. 48°N 17°E (p. 225)
Brazil (bruh•ZIHL) Largest county in South America. 9°S 53°W (p. 163)
Brazzaville (BRA•zuh•VIHL) Capital of the Congo Republic. 4°S 15°E (p. 410)
Brunei (bru•NY) Country on the northern coast of the island of Borneo. 5°N 114°E (p. 590)
Brussels (BRUH•suhlz) Capital of Belgium. 51°N 4°E (p. 225)
Bucharest (BOO•kuh•REST) Capital of Romania. 44°N 26°E (p. 225)
Budapest (BOO•duh•PEST) Capital of Hungary. 48°N 19°E (p. 225)
Buenos Aires (BWAY•nuhs AR•eez) Capital of Argentina. 34°S 58°W (p. 163)
Bujumbura (BOO•juhm•BUR•uh) Capital of Burundi. 3°S 29°E (p. 410)
Bulgaria (BUHL•GAR•ee•uh) Country in southeastern Europe, south of Romania. 42°N 24°E (p. 225)
Burkina Faso (bur•KEE•nuh FAH•soh) Country in western Africa, south of Mali. 4°N 2°W (p. 410)
Burundi (bu•ROON•dee) Country in central Africa at the northern end of Lake Tanganyika. 3°S 30°E (p. 410)

C

Cairo (KY•ROH) Capital of Egypt, on the Nile River. 31°N 32°E (p. 359)
Cambodia (kam•BOH•dee•uh) Country in Southeast Asia, south of Thailand. 12°N 104°E (p. 599)
Cameroon (KA•muh•ROON) Country in west Africa, on the northeast shore of the Gulf of Guinea. 6°N 11°E (p. 410)
Canada (KA•nuh•duh) Country in North America. 50°N 100°W (p. 95)
Canberra (KAN•buh•ruh) Capital of Australia. 35°S 149°E (p. 657)
Cape Town Legislative capital of the Republic of South Africa. 34°S 18°E (p. 411)
Caracas (kuh•RAH•kuhs) Capital of Venezuela. 11°N 67°W (p. 163)

Caribbean (KAR•uh•BEE•uhn) **Sea** Part of the Atlantic Ocean, bordered by the West Indies, South America, and Central America. 15°N 76°W (p. 163)

Caspian (KAS•pee•uhn) **Sea** Salt lake between Europe and Asia that is the world's largest inland body of water. 40°N 52°E (p. 293)

Central African Republic Country in central Africa, south of Chad. 8°N 21°E (p. 410)

Chad (CHAD) Country in central Africa, west of Sudan. 18°N 19°E (p. 410)

Chang (CHANG) **River** Principal river of China that rises in Tibet and flows into the East China Sea near Shanghai. 31°N 117°E (p. 539)

Chile (CHIH•lee) South American country, west of Argentina. 35°S 72°W (p. 163)

China (CHY•nuh) Country in eastern and central Asia, known officially as the People's Republic of China. 37°N 93°E (p. 539)

Chisinau (KEE•shih•NAU) Largest city and capital of Moldova. 47°N 29°E (p. 293)

Colombia (kuh•LUHM•bee•uh) Country in South America, west of Venezuela. 4°N 73°W (p. 163)

Colombo (kuh•LUHM•BOH) Capital of Sri Lanka. 7°N 80°E (p. 479)

Comoros (KAH•muhr•rohs) **Islands** Small island country in Indian Ocean between the island of Madagascar and the southeast African mainland. 13°S 43°E (p. 421)

Conakry (KAH•nuh•kree) Capital of Guinea. 10°N 14°W (p. 410)

Congo Republic Country in equatorial Africa, south of the Central African Republic. 3°S 14°E (p. 410)

Copenhagen (KOH•puhn•HAY•guhn) Seaport, largest city, and capital of Denmark. 56°N 12°E (p. 225)

Costa Rica (KAHS•tuh REE•kuh) Central American country, south of Nicaragua. 11°N 85°W (p. 163)

Côte d'Ivoire (KOHT dee•VWAHR) West African country, south of Mali. 8°N 7°W (p. 410)

Croatia (kroh•AY•shuh) Southeastern European country on the Adriatic Sea. 46°N 15°E (p. 225)

Cuba (KYOO•buh) Island in the West Indies. 22°N 79°W (p. 163)

Cyprus (SY•pruhs) Island country in the eastern Mediterranean Sea, south of Turkey. 35°N 31°E (p. 359)

Czech (CHEK) **Republic** Central European country south of Germany and Poland. 50°N 15°E (p. 225)

D

Dakar (DA•KAHR) Port city and capital of Senegal. 15°N 17°W (p. 410)

Damascus (duh•MAS•kuhs) Capital of Syria. 34°N 36°E (p. 359)

Dar es Salaam (DAHR•es suh•LAHM) Indian Ocean seaport of Tanzania. 7°S 39°E (p. 411)

Denmark (DEN•MAHRK) Country in northwestern Europe, between the Baltic and North Seas. 56°N 9°E (p. 225)

Dhaka (DA•kuh) Capital of Bangladesh. 24°N 90°E (pp. 479)

Djibouti (juh•BOO•tee) Country in east Africa, on the Gulf of Aden. 12°N 43°E (pp. 410)

Dodoma (DOH•doh•mah) Capital of Tanzania. 7°S 36°E (p. 410)

Doha (DOH•HAH) Capital of Qatar. 25°N 51°E (p. 359)

Dominican (duh•MIH•nih•kuhn) **Republic** Country in the West Indies on the eastern part of Hispaniola Island. 19°N 71°W (p. 163)

Dublin (DUH•bluhn) Port city and capital of Ireland. 53°N 6°W (p. 225)

Dushanbe (doo•SHAM•buh) Largest city and capital of Tajikistan. 39°N 69°E (p. 293)

E

Ecuador (EH•kwuh•DAWR) Country in South America, south of Colombia. 1°S 79°W (p. 163)

Egypt (EE•juhpt) Country in northern Africa on the Mediterranean Sea. 27°N 27°E (p. 359)

El Salvador (el SAL•vuh•DAWR) Country in Central America, southwest of Honduras. 14°N 89°W (p. 163)

Equatorial Guinea (EE•kwuh•TOHR•ee•uhl GIH•nee) Country in western Africa, south of Cameroon. 2°N 17°E (p. 410)

Estonia (e•STOH•nee•uh) Northern European country on the Baltic Sea. 59°N 25°E (p. 225)

Ethiopia (EE•thee•OH•pee•uh) Country in eastern Africa, north of Somalia and Kenya. 8°N 38°E (p. 410)

Euphrates (yu•FRAY•TEEZ) **River** River in southwestern Asia that flows through Syria and Iraq and joins the Tigris River. 36°N 40°E (p. 352)

F

Fiji (FEE•JEE) Country comprised of an island group in the southwest Pacific Ocean. 19°S 175°E (p. 657)

Finland (FIHN•luhnd) Country in northern Europe, east of Sweden. 63°N 26°E (p. 225)

France (FRANTS) Country in western Europe, south of the English Channel. 47°N 1°E (p. 225)

Freetown (FREE•TAUN) Port city and capital of Sierra Leone, in western Africa. 9°N 13°W (p. 410)

G

Gabon (ga•BOHN) Country in western Africa, on the Atlantic Ocean. 0° latitude 12°E (p. 410)

Gaborone (GAH•buh•ROH•NAY) Capital of Botswana, in southern Africa. 24°S 26°E (p. 410)

Gambia (GAM•bee•uh) Country in western Africa, along the Gambia River. 13°N 16°W (p. 410)

Georgetown (JAWRJ•TAUN) Capital of Guyana. 8°N 58°W (p. 163)

Georgia (JAWR•juh) Asian/European country bordering the Black Sea, south of Russia. 42°N 43°E (p. 293)

Germany (JUHR•muh•nee) Country in north central Europe, officially called the Federal Republic of Germany. 52°N 10°E (p. 225)

Ghana (GAH•nuh) Country in western Africa, on the Gulf of Guinea. 8°N 2°W (p. 410)

Greece (GREES) Country in southern Europe, on the Balkan Peninsula. 39°N 22°E (p. 225)

Greenland (GREEN•luhnd) Island in northwestern Atlantic Ocean and the largest island in the world. 74°N 40°W (p. A10)

Guatemala (GWAH•tuh•MAH•luh) Country in Central America, south of Mexico. 16°N 92°W (p. 163)

Guatemala City Capital of Guatemala and the largest city in Central America. 15°N 91°W (p. 163)

Guinea (GIH•nee) West African country, on the Atlantic coast. 11°N 12°W (p. 410)

Guinea-Bissau (GIH•nee bi•SAU) West African country on the Atlantic coast. 12°N 20°W (p. 410)

Gulf of Mexico Gulf on the southeast coast of North America. 25°N 94°W (p. 95)

Guyana (gy•A•nuh) South American country on the Atlantic coast, between Venezuela and Suriname. 8°N 59°W (p. 163)

H

Haiti (HAY•tee) Country on Hispaniola Island in the West Indies. 19°N 72°W (p. 163)

Hanoi (ha•NOY) Capital of Vietnam. 21°N 106°E (p. 599)

Harare (huh•RAH•RAY) Capital of Zimbabwe. 18°S 23°E (p. 410)

Havana (huh•VA•nuh) Seaport, capital city of Cuba, and largest city of the West Indies. 23°N 82°W (p. 163)

Helsinki (HEL•SIHNG•kee) Capital of Finland. 60°N 24°E (p. 225)

Himalayas (HIM•uh•LAY•uhz) Mountain range in South Asia, bordering the Indian subcontinent on the north. 30°N 85°E (p. 479)

Honduras (hahn•DUR•uhs) Central American country, on the Caribbean Sea. 15°N 88°W (p. 163)

Hong Kong (HAHNG KAHNG) British-owned territory and port in southern China. 22°N 115°E (p. 530)

Huang He (HWAHNG HE) **River** in north central and eastern China that is also known as the Yellow River. 35°N 114°E (p. 539)

Hungary (HUHN•guh•ree) Central European country, south of Slovakia. 47°N 18°E (p. 225)

I

Iberian (y•BIR•ee•uhn) **Peninsula** Peninsula in southwest Europe, occupied by Spain and Portugal. 41°N 1°W (p. 225)

Iceland (YS•luhnd) Island country between the North Atlantic and the Arctic oceans. 65°N 20°W (p. 225)

India (IHN•dee•uh) South Asian country, south of China and Nepal. 23°N 78°E (p. 479)

Indonesia (IHN•duh•NEE•zhuh) Group of islands that forms the Southeast Asian country known as the Republic of Indonesia. 5°S 119°E (p. 599)

Indus (IHN•duhs) **River** River in Asia that rises in Tibet and flows through Pakistan to the Arabian Sea. 27°N 68°E (p. 479)

Iran (ih•RAHN) Southwest Asian country that was formerly named Persia. 31°N 54°E (p. 359)

Iraq (ih•RAHK) Southwest Asian country, south of Turkey. 32°N 43°E (p. 359)

Ireland (YR•luhnd) Island west of England, occupied by the Republic of Ireland and by Northern Ireland. 54°N 8°W (p. 225)

Islamabad (is•LAH•muh•BAHD) Capital of Pakistan. 34°N 73°E (p. 479)

Israel (IHZ•ree•uhl) Country in southwest Asia, south of Lebanon. 33°N 34°E (p. 359)

Italy (IH•tuhl•ee) Southern European country, south of Switzerland and east of France. 44°N 11°E (p. 225)

J

Jakarta (juh•KAHR•tuh) Capital of Indonesia. 6°S 107°E (p. 599)

Jamaica (juh•MAY•kuh) Island country in the West Indies. 18°N 78°W (p. 163)

Japan (juh•PAN) Country in East Asia, consisting of the four large islands of Hokkaido, Honshu, Shikoku, and Kyushu, plus thousands of small islands. 37°N 134°E (p. 539)

Jerusalem (juh•ROO•suh•luhm) Capital of Israel and a holy city for Christians, Jews, and Muslims. 32°N 35°E (p. 359)

Jordan (JAWR•duhn) Country in southwest Asia, south of Syria. 30°N 38°E (p. 359)

K

Kabul (kah•BUHL) Capital of Afghanistan. 35°N 69°E (p. 359)

Kampala (kahm•PAH•luh) Capital of Uganda. 0° latitude 32°E (p. 410)

Kathmandu (KAT•MAN•DOO) Capital of Nepal. 28°N 85°E (p. 479)

Kazakhstan (KA•ZAK•STAN) Large Asian country south of Russia, bordering the Caspian Sea. 48°N 65°E (p. 293)

Kenya (KEH•nyuh) Country in eastern Africa, south of Ethiopia. 1°N 37°E (p. 410)

Khartoum (kahr•TOOM) Capital of Sudan. 16°N 33°E (p. 410)

Kiev (KEE•EF) Capital of Ukraine. 50°N 31°E (p. 293)

Kigali (kih•GAH•lee) Capital of Rwanda, in central Africa. 2°S 30°E (p. 410)

Kingston (KIHNG•stuhn) Capital of Jamaica. 18°N 77°W (p. 163)

Kinshasa (kihn•SHAH•suh) Capital of Zaire. 4°S 15°E (p. 410)

Kuala Lumpur (KWAH•luh LUM•PUR) Capital of Malaysia. 3°N 102°E (p. 599)

Kuwait (ku•WAYT) Country between Saudi Arabia and Iraq, on the Persian Gulf. 29°N 48°E (p. 359)

Kyrgyzstan (KIR•giz•STAN) Small central Asian country on China's western border. 41°N 75°E (p. 293)

L

Lagos (LAY•GAHS) Port city of Nigeria. 6°N 3°E (p. 411)

Laos (LOWS) Southeast Asian country, south of China and west of Vietnam. 20°N 102°E (p. 599)

La Paz (luh PAHZ) The administrative capital of Bolivia, and the highest capital in the world. 17°S 68°W (p. 163)

Latvia (LAT•vee•uh) Northeastern European country on the Baltic Sea, west of Russia. 57°N 25°E (p. 225)

Lebanon (LE•buh•nuhn) Country on the Mediterranean Sea, south of Syria. 34°N 34°E (p. 359)

Lesotho (luh•SOH•TOH) Country in south Africa, within the borders of the Republic of South Africa. 30°S 28°E (p. 410)

Liberia (ly•BIR•ee•uh) West African country, south of Guinea. 7°N 10°W (p. 410)

Libreville (LEE•bruh•VIHL) Port city and capital of Gabon. 1°N 9°E (p. 410)
Libya (LIH•bee•uh) North African country on the Mediterranean Sea, west of Egypt. 28°N 15°E (p. 359)
Liechtenstein (LIHK•tuhn•SHTYN) Small country in central Europe, between Switzerland and Austria. 47°N 10°E (p. 243)
Lilongwe (lih•LAWNG•way) Capital of Malawi, in southeastern Africa. 14°S 34°E (p. 410)
Lima (LEE•muh) Capital of Peru. 12°S 77°W (p. 163)
Lisbon (LIHZ•buhn) Port city and capital of Portugal. 39°N 9°W (p. 225)
Lithuania (LIH•thuh•WAY•nee•uh) European country on the Baltic Sea, west of Belarus. 56°N 24°E (p. 225)
Ljubljana (lee•OO•blee•AH•nuh) Capital of Slovenia. 46°N 14°E (p. 225)
Lomé (loh•MAY) Port city and capital of Togo in Africa. 6°N 1°E (p. 410)
London (LUHN•duhn) Capital of the United Kingdom, on the Thames River. 52°N 0° longitude (p. 225)
Luanda (lu•AN•duh) Port city and capital of Angola. 9°S 13°E (p. 410)
Lusaka (loo•SAH•kuh) Capital of Zambia. 15°S 28°E (p. 410)
Luxembourg (LUHK•suhm•BUHRG) Small European country between France, Germany, and Belgium. 50°N 7°E (p. 214)

M

Macedonia (MA•suh•DOH•nee•uh) Southeastern European country north of Greece. 42°N 22°E (p. 225). Macedonia also refers to a geographic region covering northern Greece, the country Macedonia, and part of Bulgaria.
Madagascar (MA•duh•GAS•kuhr) Island in the Indian Ocean off the southeast coast of Africa. 18°S 43°E (p. 410)
Madrid (muh•DRIHD) Capital of Spain. 40°N 4°W (p. 225)
Malabo (mah•LAH•BOH) Capital of Equatorial Guinea. 4°N 9°E (p. 410)
Malawi (muh•LAH•wee) Southeastern African country, south of Tanzania and east of Zambia. 11°S 34°E (p. 410)
Malaysia (muh•LAY•zhuh) Federation of states in Southeast Asia on the Malay Peninsula and the island of Borneo. 4°N 101°E (p. 599)
Maldive (MAHL•DEEV) **Islands** Island country in the Indian Ocean near South Asia. 5°N 42°E (p. 470)
Mali (MAH•lee) Country in western Africa, south of Algeria. 16°N 0° longitude (p. 410)
Managua (muh•NAH•gwuh) Capital of Nicaragua. 12°N 86°W (p. 163)
Manila (muh•NIH•luh) Port city and capital of the Republic of the Philippines. 15°N 121°E (p. 599)
Maseru (MA•suh•ROO) Capital of Lesotho, in southern Africa. 29°S 27°E (p. 410)
Mauritania (MAWR•uh•TAY•nee•uh) Western African country, north of Senegal. 20°N 14°W (p. 410)
Mauritius (maw•RIH•shuhs) Small island country in the Indian Ocean east of Madagascar. 21°S 58°E (p. 410)
Mbabane (EM•bah•BAH•nay) Capital of Swaziland, in southeastern Africa. 26°S 31°E (p. 410)
Mexico (MEK•sih•KOH) Country in North America, south of the United States. 24°N 104°W (p. 163)
Mexico City Capital and most populous city of Mexico. 19°N 99°W (p. 163)
Minsk (MINTSK) Capital of Belarus. 54°N 28°E (p. 293)
Mogadishu (MAH•guh•DIH•SHOO) Major seaport and capital of Somalia, in eastern Africa. 2°N 45°E (p. 410)
Moldova (mahl•DOH•vuh) Small European country between Ukraine and Romania. 47°N 29°E (p. 293)
Monaco (MAH•nuh•KOH) Small country in southern Europe, on the French Mediterranean coast. 44°N 8°E (p. 243)
Mongolia (mahn•GOHL•yuh) Country in Asia between Russia and China 46°N 100°E (p. 539)
Monrovia (MUHN•ROH•vee•uh) Major seaport and capital of Liberia, in western Africa. 6°N 11°W (p. 410)
Montevideo (MAHN•tuh•vuh•DAY•OH) Capital of Uruguay. 35°S 56°W (p. 163)
Morocco (muh•RAH•KOH) Country in northwestern Africa on the Mediterranean Sea and the Atlantic Ocean. 32°N 7°W (p. 359)

Moscow (MAHS•KOH) Capital and largest city of Russia. 56°N 38°E (p. 293)

Mount Everest (EV•ruhst) Highest mountain in the world, in the Himalayas between Nepal and Tibet. 28°N 87°E (p. 472)

Mozambique (MOH•zuhm•BEEK) Country in southeastern Africa, south of Tanzania. 20°S 34°E (p. 410)

Muscat (MUHS•KAT) Seaport and capital of Oman. 23°N 59°E (p. 359)

Myanmar (MYAN•mahr) Country in Southeast Asia, south of China and India, formerly called Burma. 21°N 95°E (p. 599)

N

Nairobi (ny•ROH•bee) Capital of Kenya. 1°S 37°E (p. 410)

Namibia (nuh•MIH•bee•uh) Country in southwestern Africa, south of Angola on the Atlantic Ocean. 20°S 16°E (p. 410)

Nassau (NA•SAW) Capital of the Bahamas. 25°N 77°W (p. 163)

N'Djamena (EN•juh•MAY•nuh) Capital of Chad. 12°N 15°E (p. 410)

Nepal (nuh•PAWL) Mountain country between India and China. 29°N 83°E (p. 479)

Netherlands (NE•thuhr•lundz) Western European country on the North Sea, north of Belgium. 53°N 4°E (p. 225)

New Delhi (NOO DEH•lee) Capital of India. 29°N 77°E (p. 479)

New Zealand (NOO ZEE•luhnd) Major island country in the South Pacific, southeast of Australia. 42°S 175°E (p. 657)

Niamey (nee•AH•may) Capital and commercial center of Niger, in western Africa. 14°N 2°E (p. 410)

Nicaragua (NI•kuh•RAH•gwuh) Country in Central America, south of Honduras. 13°N 86°W (p. 163)

Nicosia (NIH•kuh•SEE•uh) Capital of Cyprus. 35°N 33°E (p. 359)

Niger (NY•juhr) Landlocked country in western Africa, north of Nigeria. 18°N 9°E (p. 410)

Nigeria (ny•JIR•ee•uh) Country in western Africa, south of Niger. 9°N 7°E (p. 410)

Nile (NYL) **River** Longest river in the world, flowing north and east through eastern Africa. 27°N 31°E (pp. 359, 410)

North Korea (kuh•REE•uh) Asian country in the northernmost part of the Korean Peninsula. 39°N 127°E (p. 539)

Norway (NAWR•WAY) Country on the Scandinavian Peninsula. 64°N 11°E (p. 225)

Nouakchott (noo•AHK•SHAHT) Capital of Mauritania. 18°N 16°W (p. 410)

O

Oman (oh•MAHN) Country on the Arabian Sea and the Gulf of Oman. 20°N 58°E (p. 359)

Oslo (AHZ•loh) Capital and largest city of Norway. 60°N 11°E (p. 225)

Ottawa (AH•tuh•wuh) Capital of Canada. 45°N 76°W (p. 95)

Ouagadougou (WAH•guh•DOO•goo) Capital of Burkina Faso, in western Africa. 12°N 2°W (p. 410)

P

Pakistan (PA•ki•STAN) South Asian country on the Arabian Sea, northwest of India. 28°N 68°E (p. 479)

Palau (pah•LOW) Island country in the Pacific Ocean. 7°N 135°E (p. 648)

Panama (PA•nuh•MAH) Country in Central America, on the Isthmus of Panama. 9°N 81°W (p. 163)

Panamá Capital of Panama. 9°N 79°W (p. 163)

Papua New Guinea (PA•pyuh•wuh NOO GIH•nee) Independent island country in the South Pacific Ocean. 7°S 142°E (p. 657)

Paraguay (PAR•uh•GWY) Country in South America, north of Argentina. 24°S 58°W (p. 163)

Paramaribo (PAIR•uh•MAIR•uh•BOH) Port city and capital of Suriname. 6°N 55°W (p. 163)

Paris (PAIR•uhs) River port and capital of France. 49°N 2°E (p. 225)

Persian (PUHR•zhuhn) **Gulf** Arm of the Arabian Sea between Iran and Saudi Arabia. 28°N 51°E (p. 359)

Peru (puh•ROO) Country in South America, south of Ecuador and Colombia. 10°S 75°W (p. 163)

Philippines (FIH•luh•PEENZ) Country in the Pacific Ocean, southeast of Asia. 14°N 125°E (p. 599)

Phnom Penh (NAWM•PEN) Capital of Cambodia. 12°N 106°E (p. 599)

Poland (POH•luhnd) Country on the Baltic Sea in eastern Europe. 52°N 18°E (p. 225)

Port-au-Prince (POHRT•oh•PRINTS) Capital of Haiti. 19°N 72°W (p. 163)

Port Moresby (MOHRZ•bee) Capital of Papua New Guinea. 10°S 147°E (p. 657)

Porto-Novo (POHR•tuh•NOH•voh) Port city and capital of Benin, in western Africa. 7°N 3°E (p. 410)

Portugal (POHR•chih•guhl) Country on the Iberian Peninsula, south and west of Spain. 38°N 8°W (p. 225)

Prague (PRAHG) Capital of the Czech Republic. 50°N 15°E (p. 225)

Pretoria (prih•TOHR•ee•uh) Capital of South Africa. 26°S 28°E (p. 410)

Puerto Rico (PWEHR•tuh•REE•koh) Island in the Caribbean Sea; U.S. commonwealth. 19°N 67°W (p. 163)

Pyongyang (pee•AWNG•YAHNG) Capital of North Korea. 39°N 126°E (p. 539)

Q

Qatar (KAH•tuhr) Country on the southwestern shore of the Persian Gulf. 25°N 53°E (p. 359)

Quito (KEE•toh) Capital of Ecuador. 0° latitude 79°W (p. 163)

R

Rabat (ruh•BAHT) Capital of Morocco. 34°N 7°W (p. 359)

Reykjavík (RAY•kyuh•VIK) Capital of Iceland. 64°N 22°W (p. 225)

Riga (REE•guh) Capital and largest city of Latvia. 57°N 24°E (p. 225)

Riyadh (ree•YAHD) Capital of Saudi Arabia. 25°N 47°E (p. 359)

Romania (ruh•MAY•nee•uh) Country in eastern Europe, south of Ukraine. 46°N 23°E (p. 225)

Rome (ROHM) Capital of Italy, on the Tiber River. 42°N 13°E (p. 225)

Russia (RUH•shuh) Largest country in the world, covering parts of Europe and Asia. 60°N 90°E (p. 293)

Rwanda (roo•AHN•duh) Country in Africa, south of Uganda. 2°S 30°E (p. 410)

S

St. Thomas Island that is part of U.S. Virgin Islands, in the Caribbean Sea 18°N 65°W (p. A9)

San'a (sa•NAH) Capital of Yemen. 15°N 44°E (p. 359)

San José (SAN uh•ZAY) Capital of Costa Rica. 10°N 84°W (p. 163)

San Marino (SAN mah•REE•noh) Small European Country, located in the Italian peninsula. 44°N 13°E (p. 243)

San Salvador (san SAL•vuh•DAWR) Capital of El Salvador. 14°N 89°W (p. 163)

Santiago (SAN•tee•AH•goh) Capital of Chile. 33°S 71°W (p. 163)

Santo Domingo (SANT•uh duh•MIN•goh) Capital of the Dominican Republic. 19°N 70°W (p. 153)

São Tomé and Príncipe (SOWN•tuh•MAY PRIN•suh•pah) Small island country in Gulf of Guinea off the coast of Central Africa. 1°N 7°E (p. 410)

Sarajevo (SAR•uh•YAY•voh) Capital of Bosnia and Herzegovina. 43°N 18°E (p. 225)

Saudi Arabia (SOW•dee uh•RAY•bee•uh) Country on the Arabian Peninsula. 23°N 46°E (p. 359)

Senegal (SEH•nih•GAWL) Country on the coast of western Africa, on the Atlantic Ocean. 15°N 14°W (p. 410)

Seoul (SOHL) Capital of South Korea. 38°N 127°E (p. 539)

Serbia (SUHR•bee•uh) European country south of Hungary. 44°N 22°E (p. 225)

Seychelles (say•SHELZ) Small island country in the Indian Ocean near East Africa. 6°S 56°E (p. 410)

Sierra Leone (see•EHR•uh lee•OHN) Country in western Africa, south of Guinea. 8°N 12°W (p. 410)

Singapore (SIHNG•uh•POHR) Multi-island country in Southeast Asia near tip of Malay Peninsula. 2°N 104°E (p. 590)

Skopje (SKAW•pyah) Capital of the country of Macedonia. 42°N 21°E (p. 225)

Slovakia (sloh•VAH•kee•uh) Central European country south of Poland. 49°N 19°E (p. 225)

Slovenia (sloh•VEE•nee•uh) Small central European country on the Adriatic Sea, south of Austria. 46°N 15°E (p. 225)

Sofia (SOH•fee•uh) Capital of Bulgaria. 43°N 23°E (p. 225)

Somalia (soh•MAH•lee•uh) Country in Africa, on the Gulf of Aden and the Indian Ocean. 3°N 45°E (p. 410)

South Africa Country at the southern tip of Africa. 28°S 25°E (p. 410)

South Korea Country in Asia on the Korean Peninsula between the Yellow Sea and the Sea of Japan. 36°N 128°E (p. 539)

Spain Country on the Iberian Peninsula. 40°N 4°W (p. 225)

Sri Lanka (sree•LAHNG•kuh) Country in the Indian Ocean south of India, formerly called Ceylon. 9°N 83°E (p. 479)

Stockholm (STAHK•HOHLM) Capital of Sweden. 59°N 18°E (p. 225)

Sucre (SOO•kray) Constitutional capital of Bolivia. 19°S 65°W (p. 163)

Sudan (soo•DAN) Northeast African country on the Red Sea. 14°N 28°E (p. 410)

Suriname (SUR•uh•NAH•muh) South American country on the Atlantic Ocean between Guyana and French Guiana. 4°N 56°W (p. 163)

Suva (SOO•vuh) Port city and capital of Fiji. 18°S 177°E (p. 657)

Swaziland (SWAH•zee•LAND) South African country west of Mozambique, almost entirely within the Republic of South Africa. 27°S 32°E (p. 410)

Sweden (SWEE•duhn) Northern European country on the eastern side of the Scandinavian Peninsula. 60°N 14°E (p. 225)

Switzerland (SWIT•suhr•luhnd) European country in the Alps, south of Germany. 47°N 8°E (p. 225)

Syria (SIHR•ee•uh) Country in Asia on the east side of the Mediterranean Sea. 35°N 37°E (p. 359)

T

Taipei (TY•PAY) Capital of Taiwan. 25°N 122°E (p. 539)

Taiwan (TY•WAHN) Island country off the southeast coast of China, and the seat of the Chinese Nationalist government. 24°N 122°E (p. 539)

Tajikistan (tah•JIH•kih•STAN) Central Asian country north of Afghanistan. 39°N 70°E (p. 293)

Tallinn (TA•luhn) Largest city and capital of Estonia. 59°N 25°E (p. 225)

Tanzania (TAN•zuh•NEE•uh) East African country on the coast of the Indian Ocean, south of Uganda and Kenya. 7°S 34°E (p. 410)

Tashkent (tash•KENT) Capital of Uzbekistan and a major industrial center. 41°N 69°E (p. 293)

Tbilisi (tuh•BEE•luh•see) Capital of the Republic of Georgia. 42°N 45°E (p. 293)

Tegucigalpa (tuh•GOO•suh•GAL•puh) Capital of Honduras. 14°N 87°W (p. 163)

Tehran (TAY•RAN) Capital of Iran. 36°N 52°E (p. 359)

Thailand (TY•LAND) Southeast Asian country south of Myanmar. 17°N 101°E (p. 599)

Thimphu (THIHM•boo) Capital of Bhutan. 28°N 90°E (p. 479)

Tiranë (tih•RAH•nuh) Capital of Albania. 42°N 20°E (p. 225)

Togo (TOH•goh) West African country between Benin and Ghana, on the Gulf of Guinea. 8°N 1°E (p. 410)

Tokyo (TOH•kee•OH) Capital of Japan. 36°N 140°E (p. 539)

Trinidad and Tobago (TRIH•nih•DAD tuh•BAY•goh) Island country off the coast of Venezuela. 11°N 61°W (p. 152)

Tripoli (TRIH•puh•lee) Capital of Libya. 33°N 13°E (p. 359)

Tunis (TOO•nuhs) Port city and capital of Tunisia. 37°N 10°E (p. 359)

Tunisia (too•NEE•zhuh) North African country on the Mediterranean Sea between Libya and Algeria. 35°N 10°E (p. 359)

Turkey (TUHR•kee) Country in southeastern Europe and western Asia. 39°N 32°E (p. 359)

Turkmenistan (TUHRK•MEH•nuh•STAN) Central Asian country on the Caspian Sea. 40°N 60°E (p. 293)

U

Uganda (oo•GAN•duh) East African country south of Sudan. 2°N 32°E (p. 410)

Ukraine (yoo•KRAYN) Large eastern European country west of Russia, on the Black Sea. 49°N 30°E (p. 293)

Ulan Bator (OO•LAHN BAH•TAWR) Capital of Mongolia. 48°N 107°E (p. 539)

United Arab Emirates (ih•MIR•uhts) Country made up of seven states on the eastern side of the Arabian Peninsula. 24°N 54°E (p. 359)

United Kingdom Country in Western Europe made up of England, Scotland, Wales, and Northern Ireland. 57°N 2°W (p. 225)

United States of America Country in North America made up of 50 states, mostly between Canada and Mexico. 38°N 110°W (p. 95)

Uruguay (UR•uh•GWY) South American country, south of Brazil on the Atlantic Ocean. 33°S 56°W (p. 163)

Uzbekistan (OOZ•BEH•kih•STAN) Central Asian country south of Kazakhstan, on the Caspian Sea. 41°N 65°E (p. 293)

V

Vanuatu (VAHN•WAH•TOO) Country made up of islands in the Pacific Ocean, east of Australia. 17°S 170°W (p. 657)

Vatican (VA•tih•kuhn) **City** Headquarters of the Roman Catholic Church, located in the city of Rome in Italy. 42°N 13°E (p. 243)

Venezuela (VEH•nuh•ZWAY•luh) South American country on the Caribbean Sea, between Columbia and Guyana. 8°N 65°W (p. 163)

Vienna (vee•EH•nuh) Capital of Austria. 48°N 16°E (p. 225)

Vientiane (VYEHN•TYAHN) Capital of Laos. 18°N 103°E (p. 599)

Vietnam (vee•ET•NAHM) Southeast Asian country, east of Laos and Cambodia. 18°N 107°E (p. 599)

Virgin Islands Island territory of the United States, east of Puerto Rico in the Caribbean Sea. 18°N 65°W (p. 152)

W

Warsaw (WAWR•SAW) Capital of Poland. 52°N 21°E (p. 225)

Washington, D.C. Capital of the United States, in the District of Columbia. 39°N 77°W (p. 95)

Wellington Capital of New Zealand. 41°S 175°E (p. 657)

West Indies (IHN•deez) Islands in the Caribbean Sea, between North America and South America. 19°N 79°W (p. 163)

Windhoek (VIHNT•HOOK) Capital of Namibia, in southwestern Africa. 22°S 17°E (p. 410)

Y

Yamoussoukro (YAH•muh•SOO•kroh) Second capital of Côte d'Ivoire, in western Africa. 7°N 6°W (p. A19)

Yangon (YAHN•GOHN) Capital of Myanmar. 17°N 96°E (p. 599)

Yaoundé (yown•DAY) Capital of Cameroon, in western Africa. 4°N 12°E (p. 410)

Yemen (YEH•muhn) Country on the Arabian Peninsula, south of Saudi Arabia on the Gulf of Aden and the Red Sea. 15°N 46°E (p. 359)

Yerevan (YEHR•uh•VAHN) Largest city and capital of Armenia. 40°N 44°E (p. 293)

Z

Zagreb (ZAH•grehb) Largest city and capital of Croatia. 46°N 16°E (p. 225)

Zaire (zah•IHR) African country on the Equator, north of Zambia and Angola. 1°S 22°E (p. 410)

Zambia (ZAM•bee•uh) Country in south central Africa, south of Zaire and Tanzania. 14°S 24°E (p. 410)

Zimbabwe (zim•BAH•bwee) Country in south central Africa. 18°S 30°E (p. 410)

INDEX

Index

c = chart m = map
d = diagram p = photo
g = graph ptg = painting

A

INDEX

B

C

D

E

F

G

J

K

L

INDEX

N

O

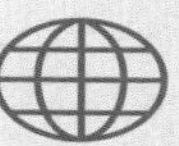

S

INDEX

INDEX

INDEX

V

W

X

Y

Z

Acknowledgments

Cover, ©FBM Photography/Westlight. **iv**, (t) Tony Stone Images, (b) NRSC Ltd./Science Photo Library/Photo Researchers; **v**, (t) ©Craig Aurness/First Light, (b) ©1990 James Randklev/AllStock; **vi**, (l) Frank Wing/Stock Boston, (r) Michael Reagan/FPG International; **vii**, ©1992 G. Cubitt/FPG International; **viii**, (t) ©Stan Way Man/Photo Researchers, (b) ©1990 Travelpix/FPG International; **ix**, (t) ©Ira Kirschenbaum/Stock Boston, (b) ©David R. Austen/Stock Boston; **xvii-A1** © James Westwater; **2-3**, David Doubilet; **4**, ©1992 Jordan Coonrad; **8**, (l) William Johnson/Stock Boston, (r) ©Wolfgang Kaehler; **9**, ©1990 Peter B. Kaplan; **10**, Earth Satellite Corp./Science Photo Library/Photo Researchers; **23**, ©1990 Peter B. Kaplan; **26**, NRSC Ltd./Science Photo Library/Photo Researchers; **32**, (l) ©1991 Chris Noble/AllStock, (r) ©1992 David L. Brown/Tom Stack & Associates; **36**, ©1989 Douglas Faulkner/AllStock; **38**, ©1989 Ray Ellis/Photo Researchers; **39**, ©Tom & Pat Leeson/Photo Researchers; **41**, (t) ©1991 Chris Noble/AllStock, (c) ©1989 Douglas Faulkner/AllStock, (b) ©1989 Ray Ellis/Photo Researchers; **44**, ©Wolfgang Kaehler; **47**, ©Darwin R. Wiggett/First Light; **48**, ©1985 August Upitis/FPG International; **54**, ©Erich Lessing/PhotoEdit; **56**, ©Jim Zuckerman/First Light; **57**, Robert Harding Picture Library; **59**, (t) ©Darwin R. Wiggett/First Light, (c) ©1985 August Upitis/FPG International, (b) ©Eric Lessing/PhotoEdit; **62**, Tony Stone Images; **63**, ©Byron Crader/Ric Ergenbright Photography; **67**, ©Larry Miller/Science Source/Photo Researchers; **68**, ©Peter Boonisar/AllStock; **70**, ©Dallas & John Heaton/Stock Boston; **73**, NASA; **75**, ©1985 Ron Watts/First Light; **79**, (t) ©Byron Crader/Ric Ergenbright Photography, (c) ©Robert Frerck/Odyssey Productions, (b) ©1985 Ron Watts/First Light; **82**, (t) ©Daniel MacDonald/Stock Boston, (c) Aaron Haupt, (b) ©Dallas and John Heaton/Stock Boston; **83**, (tl) ©Stuart Cohen/Comstock, (tr) ©1977 Photoworld/FPG International, (b) ©Ric Ergenbright; **84-85**, ©Annie Griffiths Belt; **90**, (tl) ©Will & Deni McIntyre/AllStock, (tr) ©Dallas & John Heaton/First Light, (b) ©David Barnes/AllStock; **92**, ©1990 James Randklev/AllStock; **96**, ©1993 Dave Gleiter/FPG International; **98**, ©1989 Stacy Pick/Stock Boston; **103**, (t) ©1993 Dave Gleiter/FPG International, (b) ©1989 Stacy Pick/Stock Boston; **106**, ©1993 Rafael Macia/Photo Researchers; **112**, ©1989 Greg Probst/AllStock; **113**, ©Masa Uemura/AllStock; **114**, ©Ken Straiton/First Light; **116**, Culver Pictures, Inc.; **122**, ©1994 The Georgia O'Keeffe Foundation/Artists Rights Society (ARS) NYC, photograph ©1993 Malcolm Varon, NYC; **123**, ©1987 Andy Levin/Photo Researchers; **125**, (t) ©Dallas & John Heaton/First Light, (c) ©Masa Uemura/AllStock, (b) ©1987 Andy Levin/Photo Researchers; **128**, ©Thomas Kitchin/First Light; **131**, ©1992 Inga Spence/Tom Stack & Associates; **133**, ©M. Richards/PhotoEdit; **135**, ©Dorothy Littell Greco/The Image Works; **139**, ©John Shaw/Tom Stack & Associates; **140**, ©1991 Earl Roberge/Photo Researchers; **142**, David Bookstaver/AP/Wide World Photos; **145**, (t) ©1992 Inga Spence/Tom Stack & Associates, (b) ©John Shaw/Tom Stack & Associates; **148**, (t,bl) Hockey Hall of Fame, Toronto, Ontario, (br) ©1980 Paul J. Sutton/Duomo; **149**, (t) ©Bruce Bennett Studios, (b) Steve Reyes/Bruce Bennett Studios; **150-151**, William Franklin; **159**, (tl) ©1991 Travelpix/FPG International, (tr) Telegraph Colour Library/FPG International, (c) Bob Daemmrich/Stock Boston, (b) Luis Villota/Bruce Coleman, Inc.; **160**, ©Manfred Gottschalk/Tom Stack & Associates; **162**, Earth Scenes/Dr. Nigel Smith; **164**, ©Phillip & Karen Smith/Tony Stone Images; **165**, ©Francois Gohier/Photo Researchers; **168**, ©1989 Thomas R. Fletcher/Stock Boston; **171**, (t) ©Phillip and Karen Smith/Tony Stone Images, (b) ©1989 Thomas R. Fletcher/Stock Boston; **174**, Telegraph Colour Library/FPG International; **178**, ©Roland Seitre/Peter Arnold, Inc.; **179**, Earth Scenes/M.P.L. Fogden; **183**, Archive Photos; **184**, Owen Franken/Stock Boston; **185**, ©David R. Frazier Photolibrary; **187**, Bob Thomason/Leo de Wys; **188**, ©Lee Foster/FPG International; **189**, Robert Fried/Stock Boston; **191**, (t) Earth Scenes/M.P.L. Fogden, (c) Archive Photos; (b) Robert Fried/Stock Boston; **194**, ©1988 Dale E. Boyer/Photo Researchers; **196**, ©Carl Frank/Photo Researchers; **198**, Mike Mazzaschi/Stock Boston; **199**, Don Nieman; **201**, ©Wm. Ervin/Comstock; **203**, ©Luiz C. Margio/Peter Arnold, Inc.; **204**, Mike Bacon/Tom Stack & Associates; **205**, Sean Sprague/Lineair; **207**, (t) ©Carl Frank/Photo Researchers, (b) ©Luiz C. Margio/Peter Arnold, Inc.; **210**, (t) ©Bruce Roberts/Photo Researchers, (b) ©Tony Freeman/PhotoEdit; **211**, (tl) ©1992 Marco Corsetti/FPG International, (tr) Chris Brown/Stock Boston, (b) Lois Ellen Frank/Westlight; **212-213**, Christian Sappa, Visa Agence Photographique; **221**, (t) ©Bernard G. Silberstein/FPG International, (b) ©David R. Frazier Photolibrary; **222**, ©1991 David Noble/FPG International; **224**, ©1991 E. Nagele/FPG International; **226**, Frank Wing/Stock Boston; **227**, Earth Scenes/Rocky Jordan; **228**, Telegraph Colour Library/FPG International; **230**, ©1976 Paolo Koch/Photo Researchers; **235**, (t) Frank Wing/Stock Boston, (b) ©1976 Paolo Koch/Photo Researchers; **238**, ©Dallas & John Heaton/Stock Boston; **240**, Boiffin/Photo Researchers; **241**, ©W. Geiersperger/Stock Boston; **246**, (l) Lauros-Giraudon/Art Resource, New York, (r) ©Adam Tanner/Comstock; **247**, ©Vincent J. Modica/Stock Boston; **248**, Margaret Bourke-White, LIFE MAGAZINE ©Time-Warner Inc.; **250**, QA Photos Ltd.; **254**, ©John Eastcott & Yva Momatiuk/The Image Works; **255**, (l) ©Dallas & John Heaton/Stock Boston, (r) Erich Lessing for Art Resource, New York; **256**, ©Wolfgang Kaehler; **257**, (t) Boiffin/Photo Researchers; (c) ©Vincent J. Modica/Stock Boston, (b) ©John Eastcott & Yva Momatiuk/The Image Works; **260**, ©Stuart Cohen/Comstock; **263**, ©David R. Frazier Photolibrary; **266**, ©1985 Karin Reinhard/FPG International; **267**, ©1988 Shinichi Kanno/FPG International; **269**, Lee/Picture Box/Viesti Associates, Inc.; **271**, Earth Scenes/©Richard Packwood, Oxford Scientific Films; **272**, Christopher Pillitz/Matrix; **273**, ©Patrick Walmsley/Envision; **274**, Leo de Wys Inc./J. Tom; **275**, ©1991 Travelpix/FPG International; **276**, ©Ric Ergenbright; **277**, (t) ©David R. Frazier Photolibrary, (b) Earth Scenes/©Richard Packwood, Oxford Scientific Films; **280**, (l) North Wind Picture Archives, ET Archive, London/SuperStock; **281**, (tl) Wide World Photos, (bl) UPI/Bettmann, (r) Rick Weber; **282-283**, Steve Raymer; **289**, (tl) ©Peter Menzel/Stock Boston, (tr) Kaufman Photography/Peter Arnold, Inc., (bl) Galleria Statale Tret'jakov, Moscow/SCALA/Art Resource, New York, (br) ©Dallas & John Heaton/Westlight; **290**, Michael Reagan/FPG International; **292**, L. Sherstenikov, Sovfoto/Eastfoto; **294**, (t) TASS from Sovfoto, (b) Novosti/Sovfoto; **295**, TASS from Sovfoto; **296**, Novosti/Sovfoto; **299**, Ernest Manewal/FPG International; **301**, (t) L. Sherstenikov, Sovfoto/Eastfoto; (b) Ernest Manewal/FPG International; **304**, ©1990 Vadim Sokolov/Sovfoto; **306**, Jeff Greenberg/PhotoEdit; **307**, Rohdan Hrynewych/Stock Boston; **308**, Amanda Merullo/Stock Boston; **309**, Novosti/Sovfoto; **312**, Marcello Bertinelli/Photo Researchers; **313**, Francois Gohier/Photo Researchers; **315**, AP/Wide World Photos; **316**, Musee d'Orsay, Paris/Art Resource, New York; **317**, Jeff Greenberg/Photo Researchers; **319**, Scala/Art Resource; **320**, (t) Helga Lade/Peter Arnold, Inc., (b) Shinichi Kanno/FPG International; **321**, Jim Harrison/Stock Boston; **323**, (t) Amanda Merullo/Stock Boston, (c) Marcello Bertinelli/Photo Researchers; (b) Helga Lade/Peter Arnold, Inc.; **326**, Bruce Gordon/Photo Researchers; **328**, ©Jeff Greenberg/Photo Researchers; **330**, TASS from Sovfoto; **331**, ©Bruno Barbey/Magnum Photos; **332**, Michael Reagan/FPG; **334**, **335**, Novosti/Sovfoto; **337**, **338**, TASS from Sovfoto; **339**, ©1993 Sarah Leeh/Matrix; **340**, J. Mann, Sovfoto/Eastfoto; **341**, Cary Wolinsky/Stock Boston; **342**, Novosti/Sovfoto; **343**, TASS from Sovfoto; **346**, (tl) Shooting Star, (tr) SuperStock, (bl) Archive Photos; **347**, (tl) Movie Still Archives, (bl) ©1993 Steve Gravano, (r) ©Tretiako Gallery/SuperStock; **348-349**, Mehmet Biber/Ajans Biber; **355**, George Holton/Photo Researchers; **356**, Gordon Gahan/Photo Researchers; **360**, Mikr Malyszko/FPG International; **361**, Victor Englebert/Photo Researchers; **365**, Gianni Tortoli/Photo Researchers; **366**, ©Wolfgang Kaehler; **367**, (t) Victor Englebert/Photo Researchers, (b) Gianni Tortoli/Photo Researchers; **370**, Erika Stone/Peter Arnold, Inc.; **372**, (t) AP/Wide World Photos (b) ©David R. Austen/Stock Boston; **374**, Robin Laurance/Photo Researchers; **376**, Richard Nowitz/FPG International; **380**, ©ASAP/Aliza Auerbach/Robert Harding Picture Library; **381**, Geraldo Corsi/Tom Stack & Associates; **383**, Nabeel Turner/Tony Stone Images; **384**, (l) Mark D. Phillips/Photo Researchers, (r) Louis Goldman/FPG International; **387**, (t) Robin Laurance/Photo Researchers, (c) ©ASAP/Aliza Auerbach/Robert Harding Picture Library, (b) Nabeel Turner/Tony Stone Images; **390**, Shinichi Kanno/FPG International; **393**, Ray Ellis/Photo Researchers; **396**, Christine Osborne/Photo Researchers; **401**, ©1991 Peter Jordan/Matrix; **403**, (t) Ray Ellis/Photo Researchers, (b) ©1991 Peter Jordan/Matrix; **406**, (t) Elaine Shay, (bl) Bill Aron/PhotoEdit, (br) Amy C. Etra/PhotoEdit; **407**, (t) Peter Johansky/FPG International, (others) Elaine Shay; **408-409**, Frans Lanting; **418**, ©Hubertus Kanus/Photo Researchers; **422**, (t) ©1992 G. Cubitt/FPG International, (b) ©1976 Tom Pix/Peter Arnold, Inc.;

423, ©Altitude/Peter Arnold, Inc.; **427**, ©Rene Grosjean/The Gamma-Liaison Network; **428**, Pascal Maitre/Matrix; **429**, (t) ©1976 Tom Pix/Peter Arnold, Inc., (b) ©Rene Grosjean/The Gamma Liaison Network; **432**, George Holton/Photo Researchers; **434**, Leo de Wys Inc./Sipa/J. Boutian; **440**, Greg Marinovich/Matrix; **444**, ©1991 Jason Laure; **445**, ©1976 Susan McCartney/Photo Researchers; **447**, (t) Leo de Wys Inc./Sipa/J. Boutian, (c) Greg Marinovich/Matrix; (b) ©1991 Jason Laure; **450**, ©Wolfgang Kaehler; **452**, Earth Scenes/Nigel Cattlin, ©Holt Studios Int.; **454**, Leo de Wys Inc./J. Boutain; **455**, ©Mike Wells/Tony Stone Images; **457**, Robert Harding Picture Library; **461**, ©M. Loup/Photo Researchers; **463**, (t) Earth Scenes/Nigel Cattlin, ©Holt Studios Int., (b) ©M. Loup/Photo Researchers; **466**, (t) courtesy Fisk University, Nashville, TN, (b) Phillip Francis/Black Star; **467**, (t) Movie Still Archives, (c) Fotex/Shooting Star, (b) Fotex/Drechsler/Shooting Star; **468-469**, Nicholas DeVore III, Photographers/Aspen; **475**, (tl) ©Klaus D. Francke/Peter Arnold, Inc., (tr) ©1987 Takeski Takahara/Photo Researchers, (cl) ©Manfred Gottschalk/Tom Stack & Associates, (cr) ©1989 Rudi Herzog/FPG International, (bl) ©1992 Earl Young/FPG International, (br) ©John Elk/Stock Boston; **476**, ©1987 Ted Kerasote/Photo Researchers; **480**, Bill Gillette/Stock Boston; **481**, (l) Vaughn Fleming/Science Photo Library/Photo Researchers, (r) M. Glaye/Jacana/Photo Researchers; **483**, S. Nagenora/Photo Researchers; **486**, ©1989 Galen Rowell/Mountain Light; **487**, (t) Bill Gillette/Stock Boston, (b) S. Nagenora/Photo Researchers; **490**, John Elk; **492**, Travelpix/FPG International; **494**, Jon Hicks/Leo de Wys; **497**, ©Paolo Koch/Photo Researchers; **498**, ©1985 Peter Menzel/Stock Boston; **499**, Margaret Bourke-White, LIFE MAGAZINE ©Time Warner Inc.; **500**, ©Ric Ergenbright; **504**, Telegraph Colour Library/FPG International; **505**, ©DPA/The Image Works; **507**, (t) Jon Hicks/Leo de Wys; (c) ©1985 Peter Menzel/Stock Boston, (b) ©DPA/The Image Works; **510**, Suraj N. Sharma/Dinodia Picture Agency; **512**, Travelpix/FPG International; **515**, ©Hari Mahidhar/Dinodia Picture Agency; **516**, Dinodia Picture Agency; **517**, ©Ric Ergenbright; **519**, ©Gordon Wiltsie/Peter Arnold, Inc.; **521**, ©Stan Way Man/Photo Researchers; **522**, ©Hari Mahidhar/Dinodia Picture Agency; **523**, (t) Travelpix/FPG International, (b) ©Stan Way Man/Photo Researchers; **526**, (l) Adam Woolfitt/Robert Harding Picture Library, (r) IDEAL HOME ©IPC Magazines/Robert Harding Picture Library; **527**, (t) Rick Weber, (c) ©Rudi Von Briel, (b) ©First Image; **528-529**, National Geographic photographer Jodi Cobb; **534**, (l) Malcolm S. Kirk/Peter Arnold, Inc., (r) ©Telegraph Colour Library/FPG International; **535**, (tl) ©Keren Su/Stock Boston, (tr) Dave Bartruff/FPG International, (bl) Werner Forman Archive/Art Resource, New York, (br) ©Jean Kugler/FPG International; **536**, ©1990 Travelpix/FPG International; **540**, **541**, ©Charles Kennard/Stock Boston; **543**, ©Bruno J. Zehnder/Peter Arnold, Inc.; **545**, Ira Kirschenbaum/Stock Boston; **546**, W.H. Hodge/Peter Arnold, Inc.; **547**, (t) ©Charles Kennard/Stock Boston, (b) Ira Kirschenbaum/Stock Boston; **550**, ©1991 Jean Kugler/FPG International; **552**, ©Sylvain Grandadam/Photo Researchers; **553**, ©Bob Daemmrich/Stock Boston; **559**, Leo de Wys Inc./Alon Reininger; **560**, PhotoEdit; **563**, ©Martha Cooper/Peter Arnold, Inc.; **564**, ©Temple G. Matthews III/FPG International; **565**, ©Bruno J. Zehnder/Peter Arnold, Inc.; **567**, (t) ©Sylvain Grandadam/Photo Researchers, (c) Leo de Wys Inc./Alon Reininger, (b) ©Temple G. Matthews III/FPG International; **570**, Robert Harding Picture Library; **572**, ©Ira Kirschenbaum/Stock Boston; **573**, Dave Bartruff/Stock Boston; **576**, ©Bruno J. Zehnder/Peter Arnold, Inc.; **578**, ©David R. Frazier Photolibrary; **579**, SuperStock; **580**, Karen Kasmauski/Matrix; **583**, (t) ©Bruno J. Zehnder/Peter Arnold, Inc., (b) SuperStock; **586**, (l) ©Richard Phelps Frieman/Photo Researchers, (r) ©1988 Steven E. Sutton/Duomo; **587**, (tl) ©G & M Kohler/FPG International, (bl) ©1989 Al Tielemans/Duomo, (r) ©1987 Lawrence Migdale/Stock Boston; **588-589**, Michael S. Yamashita; **595**, (tl) Stock Boston, (tr) ©1991 David Austen/FPG International, (c) ©Travelpix/FPG International, (bl) Owen Franken/Stock Boston, (br) ©1991 Josef Beck/FPG International; **596**, ©1990 G. Cubitt/FPG International; **600**, Leo de Wys Inc./W. Hitte; 601, ©David R. Frazier Photolibrary; **605**, ©1992 Josef Beck/FPG International; **606**, Jean-Claude Lejeune/Stock Boston; **607**, (t) ©David R. Frazier Photolibrary, (b) ©1992 Josef Beck/FPG International; **610**, ©1988 Joachim Messerschmidt/FPG International; **613**, ©1986 D.C. Clegg/FPG International; **618**, Vivian M. Oeevers/Peter Arnold, Inc.; **619**, ©1990 Travelpix/FPG International; **622**, ©Dallas & John Heaton/Stock Boston; **623**, Alain Evrard/Photo Researchers; **624**, Jules Bucher/Photo Researchers; **625**, (t) ©1986 D.C. Clegg/FPG International, (c) Vivian M. Oeevers/Peter Arnold, Inc., (b) Alain Evrard/Photo Researchers; **628**, ©Travelpix/FPG International; **630**, Alan Oddie/PhotoEdit; **632**, Leo de Wys Inc./Steve Vidler; **634**, ©David R. Frazier Photolibrary; **636**, ©1991 David Austen/FPG International; **637**, **638**, ©David R. Austen/Stock Boston; **639**, ©1991 David Austen/FPG International; **641**, (t) Alan Oddie/PhotoEdit, (b) ©1991 David Austen/FPG International; **644**, (t) Elaine Shay, (b) ©1991 Peter Johansky/FPG International; **645**, Elaine Shay; **646-647**, ©R. Ian Lloyd; **653**, (tl) ©David R. Austen/Stock Boston, (tr) ©1991 David Austen/FPG International, (b) ©1992 Ken Ross/FPG International; **654**, ©Dallas & John Heaton/Stock Boston; **658**, (t) ©Manfred Gottschalk/Tom Stack & Associates, (b) ©Travelpix/FPG International; **659**, ©Ira Kirschenbaum/Stock Boston; **663**, ©1991 Terry Qing/FPG International; **665**, (t) ©Ira Kirschenbaum/Stock Boston, (b) ©1991 Terry Qing/FPG International; **668**, ©David R. Austen/Stock Boston; **670**, ©David R. Frazier Photolibrary; **671**, Robin Smith/FPG; **676**, ©Travelpix/FPG International; **677**, ©1992 Galen Rowell/Mountain Light; **679**, ©David R. Austen/Stock Boston; **681**, ©Bill Bachman/Photo Researchers; **683**, (t) Robin Smith/FPG; (c) ©Travelpix/FPG International, (b) ©David R. Austen/Stock Boston; **686**, ©Fritz Prenzel/Peter Arnold, Inc.; **688**, Dave G. Houser; **690**, Carl Wolinsky/Stock Boston; **691**, ©1989 Gordon Wiltsie/Peter Arnold, Inc.; **693**, ©1991 Travelpix/FPG International; **695**, ©Travelpix/FPG International; **696**, ©Manfred Gottschalk/Tom Stack & Associates; **698**, ©1985 Joe Outland/FPG International; **699**, (t) ©1989 Gordon Wiltsie/Peter Arnold, Inc., (b) ©Manfred Gottschalk/Tom Stack & Associates; **702**, (l) Movie Still Archives, (r) ©1991 David Austen/FPG International; **703**, (t) Miramax Films/Archive Newsphotos, (c) Fotex/Mizi/Shooting Star, (b) Rick Weber; **704**, (t) British Museum, London/Bridgeman/Art Resource, New York, (c) Bettmann Archive, (b) The British Library.

Current Events of the United States

Current Events of North America

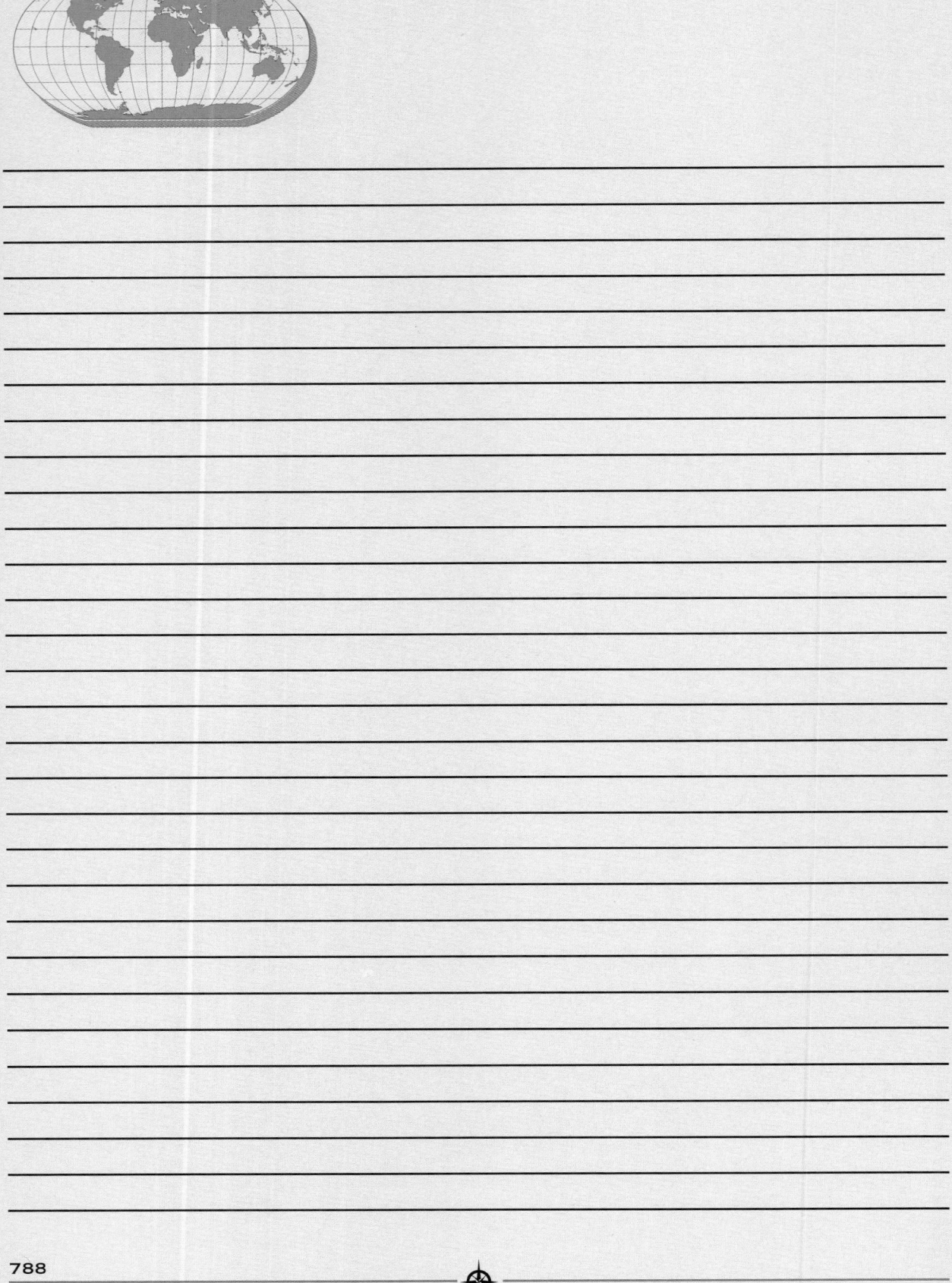

Current Events of South America

Current Events of Europe

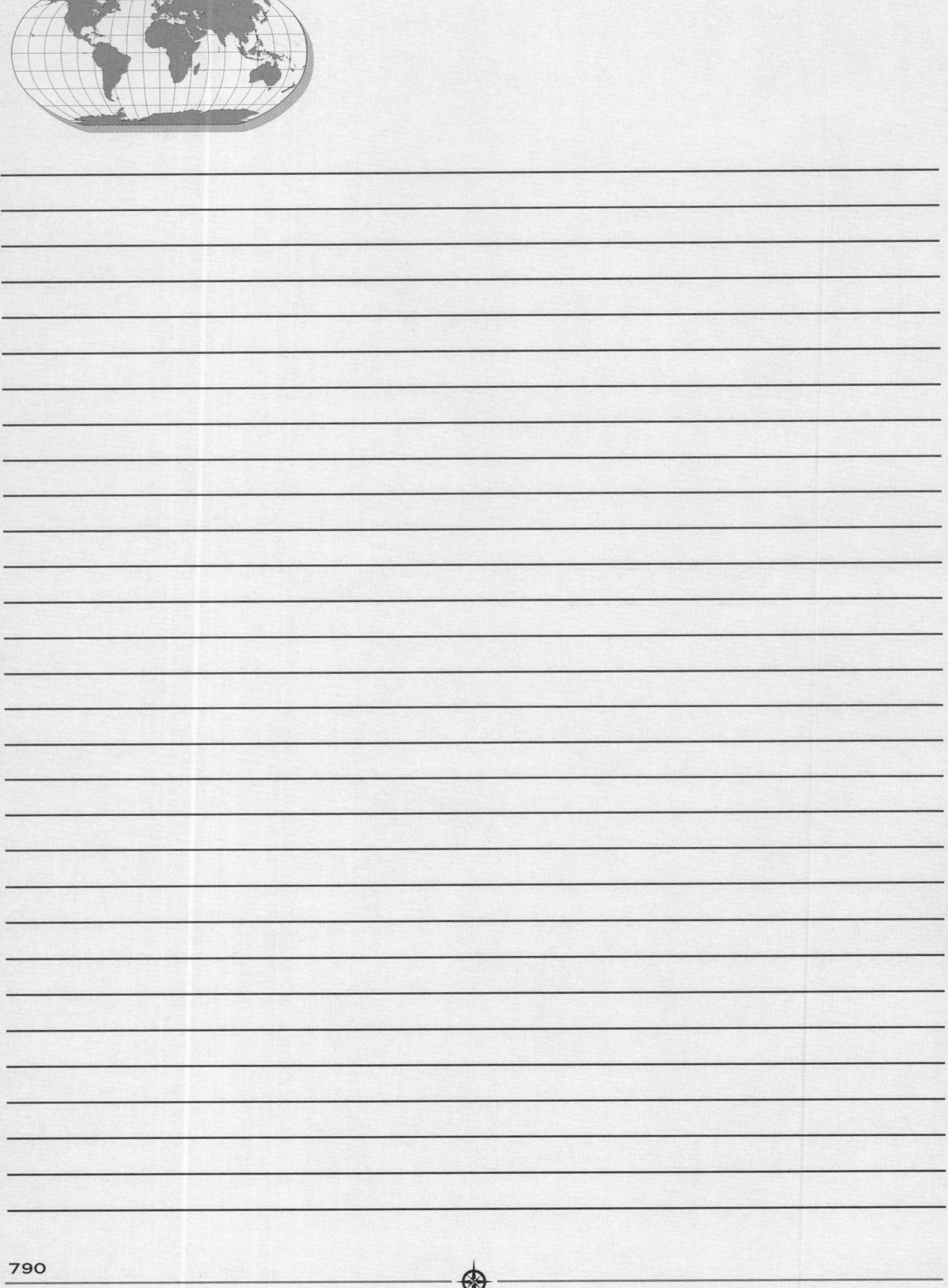

Current Events of Africa

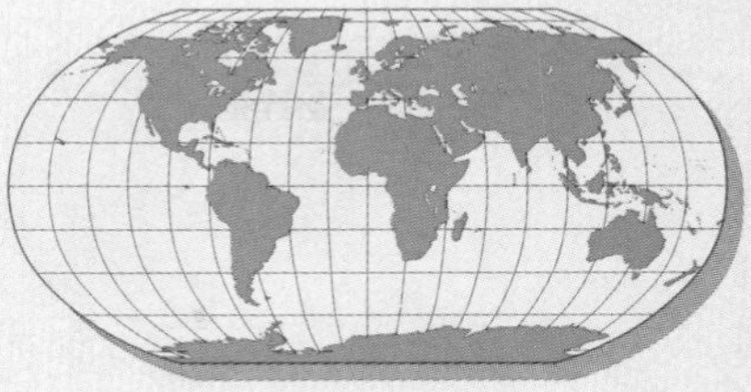

Current Events of Asia

Current Events of Australia

Current Events of Antarctica

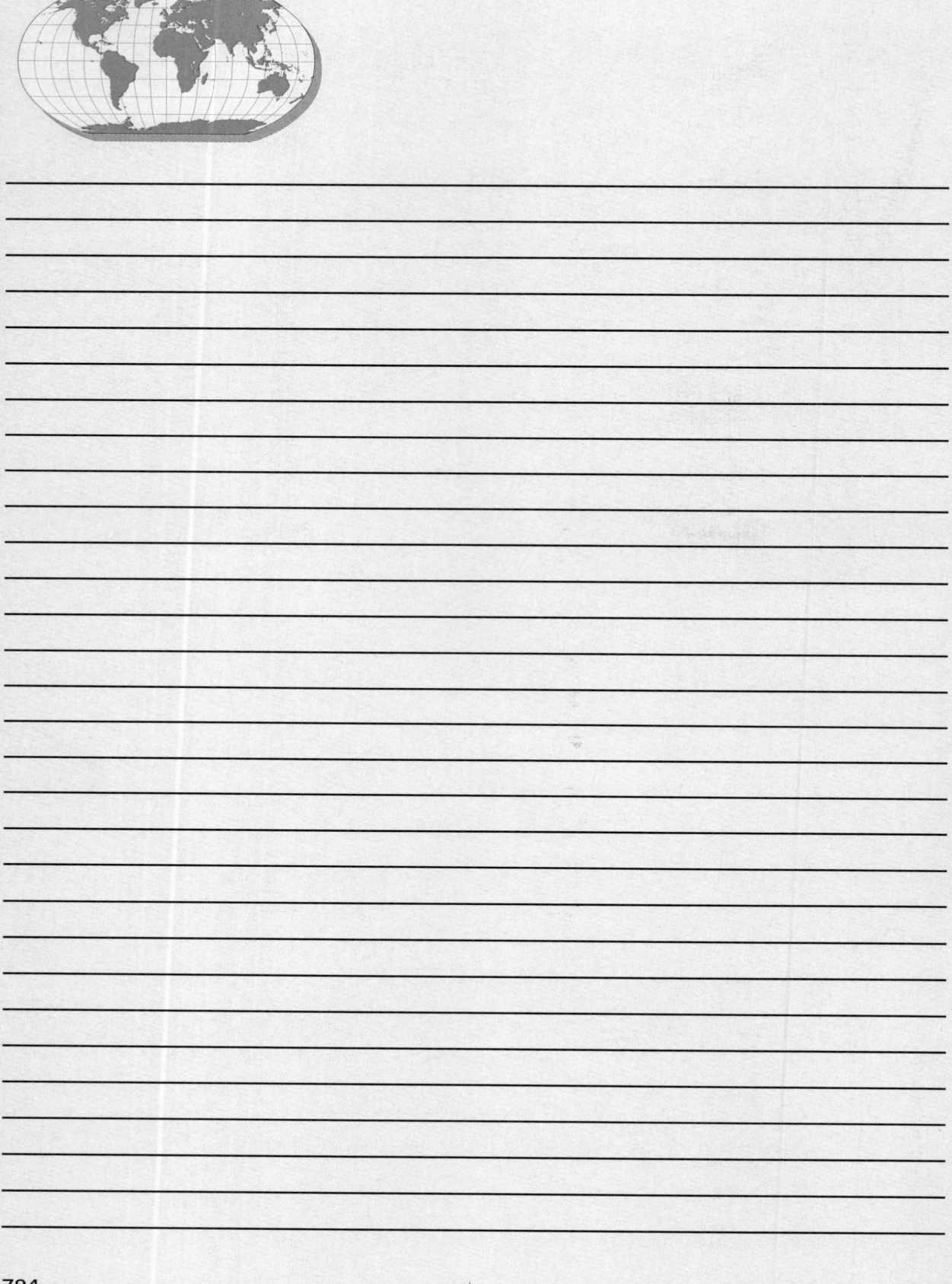